Lecture Notes in Computer Science 13907

Founding Editors

Gerhard Goos
Juris Hartmanis

The series Lecture Notes in Computer Science (LNCS), including its subseries Lecture Notes in Artificial Intelligence (LNAI) and Lecture Notes in Bioinformatics (LNBI), has established itself as a medium for the publication of new developments in computer science and information technology research, teaching, and education.

LNCS enjoys close cooperation with the computer science R & D community, the series counts many renowned academics among its volume editors and paper authors, and collaborates with prestigious societies. Its mission is to serve this international community by providing an invaluable service, mainly focused on the publication of conference and workshop proceedings and postproceedings. LNCS commenced publication in 1973.

Jianying Zhou · Lejla Batina · Zengpeng Li ·
Jingqiang Lin · Eleonora Losiouk ·
Suryadipta Majumdar · Daisuke Mashima ·
Weizhi Meng · Stjepan Picek ·
Mohammad Ashiqur Rahman · Jun Shao ·
Masaki Shimaoka · Ezekiel Soremekun ·
Chunhua Su · Je Sen Teh · Aleksei Udovenko ·
Cong Wang · Leo Zhang · Yury Zhauniarovich
Editors

Applied Cryptography and Network Security Workshops

ACNS 2023 Satellite Workshops
ADSC, AIBlock, AIHWS, AIoTS, CIMSS, Cloud S&P, SCI, SecMT, SiMLA
Kyoto, Japan, June 19–22, 2023
Proceedings

Editors

Jianying Zhou (iD)
Singapore University of Technology and Design
Singapore, Singapore

Zengpeng Li (iD)
Shandong University of Science and Technology
Qingdao, China

Eleonora Losiouk (iD)
University of Padua
Padua, Italy

Daisuke Mashima (iD)
Illinois at Singapore Pte Ltd.
Singapore, Singapore

Stjepan Picek (iD)
Radboud University Nijmegen
Nijmegen, The Netherlands

Jun Shao
Zhejiang Gongshang University
Hangzhou, China

Ezekiel Soremekun (iD)
Royal Holloway University of London
Egham, UK

Je Sen Teh (iD)
Universiti Sains Malaysia
Gelugor, Malaysia

Cong Wang (iD)
City University of Hong Kong
Hong Kong, Hong Kong

Yury Zhauniarovich (iD)
Delft University of Technology
Delft, The Netherlands

Lejla Batina (iD)
Radboud University Nijmegen
Nijmegen, The Netherlands

Jingqiang Lin (iD)
University of Science and Technology of China
Hefei, China

Suryadipta Majumdar (iD)
Concordia University
Montreal, QC, Canada

Weizhi Meng (iD)
Technical University Denmark
Kongens Lyngby, Denmark

Mohammad Ashiqur Rahman (iD)
Florida International University
Miami, FL, USA

Masaki Shimaoka (iD)
SECOM Co., Ltd. and University of Tsukuba
Tokyo / Ibaraki, Japan

Chunhua Su (iD)
University of Aizu
Aizuwakamatsu, Fukushima, Japan

Aleksei Udovenko (iD)
University of Luxembourg
Esch-sur-Alzette, Luxembourg

Leo Zhang (iD)
Griffith University
Southport, QLD, Australia

ISSN 0302-9743   ISSN 1611-3349 (electronic)
Lecture Notes in Computer Science
ISBN 978-3-031-41180-9   ISBN 978-3-031-41181-6 (eBook)
https://doi.org/10.1007/978-3-031-41181-6

This Springer imprint is published by the registered company Springer Nature Switzerland AG
The registered company address is: Gewerbestrasse 11, 6330 Cham, Switzerland

Paper in this product is recyclable.

Preface

These proceedings contain the papers selected for presentation at the ACNS 2023 satellite workshops and the poster session, which were held in parallel with the main conference (the 21st International Conference on Applied Cryptography and Network Security) during 19–22 June 2023. While ACNS 2023 was held as a physical event in Kyoto, Japan, the workshops were organized in a hybrid mode.

In response to this year's call for workshop proposals, there were nine satellite workshops, one of which was a new workshop. Each workshop provided a forum to address a specific topic at the forefront of cybersecurity research.

- 1st ACNS Workshop on Automated Methods and Data-Driven Techniques in Symmetric-Key Cryptanalysis (ADSC 2023), chaired by Je Sen Teh and Aleksei Udovenko
- 5th ACNS Workshop on Application Intelligence and Blockchain Security (AIBlock 2023), chaired by Weizhi Meng and Chunhua Su
- 4th ACNS Workshop on Artificial Intelligence in Hardware Security (AIHWS 2023), chaired by Lejla Batina and Stjepan Picek
- 5th ACNS Workshop on Artificial Intelligence and Industrial IoT Security (AIoTS 2023), chaired by Mohammad Ashiqur Rahman and Daisuke Mashima
- 3rd ACNS Workshop on Critical Infrastructure and Manufacturing System Security (CIMSS 2023), chaired by Leo Zhang and Zengpeng Li
- 5th ACNS Workshop on Cloud Security and Privacy (Cloud S&P 2023), chaired by Suryadipta Majumdar and Cong Wang
- 4th ACNS Workshop on Secure Cryptographic Implementation (SCI 2023), chaired by Jingqiang Lin and Jun Shao
- 4th ACNS Workshop on Security in Mobile Technologies (SecMT 2023), chaired by Eleonora Losiouk and Yury Zhauniarovich
- 5th ACNS Workshop on Security in Machine Learning and its Applications (SiMLA 2023), chaired by Ezekiel Soremekun

This year, we received a total of 76 submissions. Each workshop had its own Program Committee (PC) in charge of the review process. These papers were evaluated on the basis of their significance, novelty, and technical quality. The review process was double-blind. In the end, 34 papers were selected for presentation at the nine workshops, with an acceptance rate of 45%.

ACNS also gave the best workshop paper award. The winning papers were selected among the nominated candidate papers from each workshop. The following two papers shared the ACNS 2023 Best Workshop Paper Award. The authors will also receive the monetary prize sponsored by Springer.

- Linus Backlund, Kalle Ngo, Joel Gartner, and Elena Dubrova. "Secret Key Recovery Attack on Masked and Shuffled Implementations of CRYSTALS-Kyber and Saber" from the AIHWS workshop

– Diana Ghinea, Fabian Kaczmarczyck, Jennifer Pullman, Julien Cretin, Stefan Kölbl, Rafael Misoczki, Jean-Michel Picod, Luca Invernizzi, and Elie Bursztein. "Hybrid Post-Quantum Signatures in Hardware Security Keys" from the SCI workshop

Besides the regular papers presented at the workshops, there were 14 invited talks.

– "Automated Tools for Cryptanalysis: The State of the Arts and Future Directions" by Jian Guo (NTU, Singapore) at the ADSC workshop
– "How to Protect Data Feed to Smart Contracts with Authenticated Zero Knowledge Proof" by Zhiguo Wan (Zhejiang Laboratory, China) at the AIBlock workshop
– "A Look into Side-Channel Vulnerabilities in Lattice-Based Post-Quantum Cryptography" by Shivam Bhasin (NTU, Singapore) and "Side Channel Information Leakage - The Night is Dark and Full of Terrors" by Maria Mushtaq (Télécom Paris, France) at the AIHWS workshop
– "Certifiably Robust Learning via Knowledge-Enabled Logical Reasoning" by Bo Li (UIUC, USA) and "Maritime Cybersecurity: Challenges, Guidelines and Testbeds" by Jianying Zhou (SUTD, Singapore) at the AIoTS workshop
– "Security Evaluation of Modern Industrial Control Systems" by Michail Maniatakos (NYU Abu Dhabi, UAE) and "Trend of Charging Infrastructure Threats: From Mobile Devices to Automotive" by Weizhi Meng (DTU, Denmark) at the CIMSS workshop
– "Controlled Distributed Computations in the Cloud" by Sara Foresti (Università degli Studi di Milano, Italy) and "Toward Privacy-Preserving Aggregate Reverse Skyline Query with Strong Security" by Rongxing Lu (University of New Brunswick, Canada) at the Cloud S&P workshop
– "Measurable and Deployable Security: Gaps, Successes, and Opportunities" by Danfeng (Daphne) Yao (Virginia Tech, USA) at the SCI workshop
– "Towards Quality Assurance of On-device AI Models in Android Apps" by Chunyang Chen (Monash University, Australia) and "How Evidence-based Research Can Enhance Mobile Privacy and Security" by Narseo Vallina Rodriguez (IMDEA Networks Institute Spain) at the SecMT workshop
– "Towards Trustworthy Machine Learning from Weakly Supervised, Noisy, and Biased Data" by Masashi Sugiyama (RIKEN, Japan) at the SiMLA workshop

There was also a poster session chaired by Masaki Shimaoka, and 13 posters were included in the proceedings in the form of extended abstracts. The following two posters shared the ACNS 2023 Best Poster Award, voted on by all participants.

– "Using Verifiable Credentials for Authentication of UAVs in Logistics" by Ken Watanabe and Kazue Sako (Waseda University, Japan)
– "A card-based protocol that lets you know how close two parties are in their opinions (agree/disagree) by using a four-point Likert scale" by Yuji Suga (Internet Initiative Japan Inc., Japan)

The ACNS 2023 workshops were made possible by the joint efforts of many individuals and organizations. We sincerely thank the authors of all submissions. We are grateful to the program chairs and PC members of each workshop for their great effort in providing professional reviews and interesting feedback to authors in a tight time schedule. We thank all the external reviewers for assisting the PC in their particular areas of expertise. We are grateful to Springer for sponsoring the best workshop paper award and the local organizing team for sponsoring the best poster award. We also thank General Chairs Chunhua Su and Kazumasa Omote and the organizing team members of the main conference as well as each workshop for their help in various aspects.

Last but not least, we thank everyone else, speakers, session chairs, and attendees for their contribution to the success of the ACNS 2023 workshops. We are glad to see those workshops have become an important part of ACNS since they were introduced in 2019 and provide a stimulating platform to discuss open problems at the forefront of cybersecurity research.

June 2023   Jianying Zhou
                                                                             ACNS 2023 Workshop Chair

Contents

AIoTS – Artificial Intelligence and Industrial IoT Security

CIMSS – Critical Infrastructure and Manufacturing System Security

Cloud S&P – Cloud Security and Privacy

SCI – Secure Cryptographic Implementation

ADSC – Automated Methods
and Data-Driven Techniques
in Symmetric-Key Cryptanalysis

ADSC 2023

First Workshop on Automated Methods and Data-Driven Techniques in Symmetric-Key Cryptanalysis

21 June 2023

Program Chairs

Je Sen Teh	Universiti Sains Malaysia, Malaysia
Aleksei Udovenko	University of Luxembourg, Luxembourg

Program Committee

Kai Hu	Nanyang Technological University, Singapore
Baptiste Lambin	University of Luxembourg, Luxembourg
Qingju Wang	University of Luxembourg, Luxembourg
Muhammad Reza Z'aba	MIMOS, Malaysia
Wun-She Yap	Universiti Tunku Abdul Rahman, Malaysia
Ryoma Ito	NICT, Japan
Ling Song	Jinan University, China
Jiageng Chen	Central China Normal University, China
Jiqiang Lu	Beihang University, China
David Gerault	Technology Innovation Institute, UAE
Aron Gohr	Independent Researcher, New Zealand

Automatic Search Model for Related-Tweakey Impossible Differential Cryptanalysis

Huiqin Chen[1,4] , Yongqiang Li[1,4(✉)] , Xichao Hu[1,4], Zhengbin Liu[2], Lin Jiao[3], and Mingsheng Wang[1,4]

[1] Institute of Information Engineering, Chinese Academy of Science, Beijing, China
{chenhuiqin,liyongqiang,huxichao,wangmingsheng}@iie.ac.cn
[2] Science and Technology on Communication Security Laboratory, Chengdu, China
[3] State Key Laboratory of Cryptology, Beijing, China
[4] School of Cyber Security, University of Chinese Academy of Sciences, Beijing, China

Abstract. The design and analysis of dedicated tweakable block ciphers constitute a dynamic and relatively recent research field in symmetric cryptanalysis. The assessment of security in the related-tweakey model is of utmost importance owing to the existence of a public tweak. This paper proposes an automatic search model for identifying related-tweakey impossible differentials based on the propagation of states under specific constraints, which is inspired by the research of Hu et al. in ASIACRYPT 2020. Our model is universally applicable to block ciphers, but its search efficiency may be limited in some cases. To address this issue, we introduce the Locality Constraint Analysis (LCA) technique to impossible differential cryptanalysis and propose a generalized automatic search model. Technically, we transform our models into Satisfiability Modulo Theories (SMT) problems and solve them using the STP solver. We have applied our tools to several tweakable block ciphers, such as `Joltik-BC`, `SKINNY`, `QARMA`, and `CRAFT`, to evaluate their effectiveness and practicality. Specifically, we have discovered 7-round related-tweakey impossible differentials for `Joltik-BC-192`, and 12-round related-tweak impossible differentials, as well as 15-round related-tweakey impossible differentials for `CRAFT` for the first time. Based on the search results, we demonstrate that the LCA technique can be effectively performed when searching and determining the contradictory positions for the distinguisher with long trails or ciphers with large sizes in impossible differential cryptanalysis.

Keywords: Tweakable Block Cipher · Related-tweakey · Impossible differential cryptanalysis · LCA technique · SAT method

1 Introduction

Tweakable block ciphers are constructions that have an additional input called tweak compared to traditional block ciphers, which can be defined as a function $C = E(P, K, T)$ from $\mathbb{F}_2^n \times \mathbb{F}_2^\kappa \times \mathbb{F}_2^t \to \mathbb{F}_2^n$ when the tweak length is t bits. The

© The Author(s), under exclusive license to Springer Nature Switzerland AG 2023
J. Zhou et al. (Eds.): ACNS 2023 Workshops, LNCS 13907, pp. 3–22, 2023.
https://doi.org/10.1007/978-3-031-41181-6_1

concept of tweakable block ciphers was first introduced by Schroeppel in the Hasty Pudding Cipher [32], and was later formalized by Liskov et al. [23,24]. They aimed to move the randomization of symmetric primitives by bringing the high-level mode operations, like ΘCB3 [18] or Counter-in-Tweak [29], directly to the design of block ciphers. Unlike the secret key, the tweak is entirely public and offers attackers more flexibility. Designers must therefore handle the tweak more carefully than the key without reducing efficiency. Responding to the high demand, Jean et al. [13] introduced the TWEAKEY framework to bridge the gap between key and tweak inputs by providing a unified framework in ASIACRYPT 2014, which can be viewed as a straightforward generalization of key-alternating ciphers, where the key and tweak basically treated as a whole called *tweakey*. Based on this framework, there are several dedicated tweakable block ciphers, such as Joltik-BC [14], Deoxys-BC [15], SKINNY [3]. Furthermore, with the development of tweakable block cipher, its design also becomes diversified, such as QARMA [1], CRAFT [4], and some other tweakable block ciphers based on Tweak-aNd-Tweak [9] and Elastic-Tweak [6].

Impossible differential cryptanalysis was independently introduced by Biham et al. [5] and Knudsen [17] to evaluate the security of Skipjack and DEAL. In contrast to differential cryptanalysis, impossible differential cryptanalysis aims to identify a differential characteristic that has zero probability. Due to the limitations of manual derivation, various automatic methods have been developed to search for impossible differentials, including the $\mathcal{U}$-method [16], the UID-method [27], and the $\mathcal{WW}$-method [34]. Unfortunately, these methods handle the underlying S-box as ideal and cannot consider its details. However, this problem was soon settled with the Mixed Integer Linear Programming (MILP) application for cryptanalysis. It was first proposed by Mouha et al. [28] to evaluate the lower bound on the number of the differential and linear active S-boxes and then improved by Sun et al. [33] to search for the differential characteristics of bit-oriented block ciphers. Based on this, Cui et al. [7] proposed a MILP-based tool to search the impossible differentials for lightweight block ciphers and an algorithm to verify the impossible differentials. Soon after, Sasaki and Todo [31] presented a MILP-based tool to search the impossible differential for SPN block ciphers by treating the large S-boxes as permutations so that their tool was valid to detect the contradiction in linear components.

However, the above methods are all based on the propagation of the differences and can not evaluate the effect of key schedules in the single-key setting. Hu et al. [12] solved this problem by using the equivalence between the impossible $(s + 1)$-polytopic transitions and impossible differentials. They transformed the differential propagation to the propagation of constraint values. This new approach enables the possibility of handling large state S-boxes or value-dependent operations that are difficult to realize in the traditional sense. Additionally, this approach is applicable to all differential cryptanalysis methods, such as searching for differential trails or differential active S-boxes, which facilitates a more accurate analysis of a block cipher to resist differential cryptanalysis.

Our Contributions. For the majority of current tweakable block ciphers, adversaries have the ability to manipulate tweak values. Drawing inspiration from Hu et al.'s contributions in [12], we present an automatic search model for related-tweakey impossible differentials. Specifically, we transform the problem of identifying an impossible differential into the Satisfiability Modulo Theories (SMT) problem by explicating the propagation of states and the tweakey update function with specific constraints, which can efficiently evaluate the resistance against impossible differential analysis for most of the block ciphers.

Unfortunately, it leads to a significant loss of efficiency with an increase in the state space and number of search rounds if considering all the details of round functions and tweakey update functions. To address this, we propose a generalized search model by introducing the Locality Constraint Analysis (LCA) technique. The optimized model has two significant advantages: improving the search efficiency for long trails and identifying the contradictory positions of impossible differentials.

In terms of practical implementation, we have employed our automatic search model in the evaluation of several tweakable block ciphers. The outcomes of these evaluations are presented below.

- For `Joltik-BC`, we have discovered several 6-round and 7-round related-tweakey impossible differentials for `Joltik-BC-128` and `Joltik-BC-192`, respectively. These differentials were previously unknown.
- For `SKINNY`, we have identified related-tweakey impossible differentials for `SKINNY-64-64`, `SKINNY-64-128`, and `SKINNY-64-192`, with 12-round, 14-round, and 16-round, respectively. Notably, the majority of these differentials had not been previously reported by Sadeghi et al. in [30].
- For `QARMA-64`, we have derived several 7-round asymmetric related-tweak impossible differential distinguishers spanning from the 6th to the 12th round. Particularly, the majority of these distinguishers were not identified using Zong's method in [36].
- For `CRAFT`, we have successfully derived 12-round related-tweak impossible differentials and 15-round related-tweakey impossible differentials, assuming the condition that only one nibble is active in the tweakey differences. It is noteworthy that these differential properties have not been reported before.

Outline. In Sect. 2, we provide a brief overview of the necessary preliminaries utilized in the present paper. Subsequently, in Sect. 3, we introduce an automatic search model for related-tweakey impossible differentials based on the SAT solver. Section 4 is dedicated to the application of our tool in the search for related-tweakey impossible differentials in some tweakable block ciphers, followed by a concise evaluation of our model in Sect. 5. Finally, we conclude this work in Sect. 6. The source codes are publicly available at https://github.com/Rainy1024/ImpossibleDifferentialAnalysis.git.

2 Preliminaries

2.1 Notations

The following notations are used in the present paper. Throughout the paper, we use $\oplus$ to denote the bitwise XOR of two vectors or XOR of two bits.

- $\mathbb{F}_2^n$: the vectors space over the finite field $\mathbb{F}_2$ with dimension n.
- Δ_m^n: the set that $\{(a, a') \in \mathbb{F}_2^n \times \mathbb{F}_2^n | a \oplus a' = m, m \in \mathbb{F}_2^n \setminus \{0\}\}$.
- $BC(n, m, l)$: the set of iterated block ciphers whose block cipher is n-bit, master key size is m-bit, and round key size is l-bit.
- $TBC(n, \kappa, t)$: the set of tweakable block cipher whose cipher size is n-bit, master key size is κ-bit and initial tweak size is t-bit.
- $TK_j^r[i]$: the i-th nibble of the j-th subtweakey of the r-th round. The difference donates as $\triangle TK_j^r[i]$.
- DR: the length of an impossible differential distinguisher.
- ConR: the round index where the contradiction occurs.
- ConPs: The specific location of the contradiction. For instance, S_i means the contradiction is in the S-box with the index i.

2.2 Related-Tweakey Impossible Differential

Related-key impossible differential cryptanalysis is a variant of impossible differential cryptanalysis where an attacker can control the key schedule. In this attack, the attacker can choose two related keys and use them to generate a specific input difference that produces a target output difference with zero probability. Here, we first recall some definitions of impossible 2-polytopic transitions proposed in [12].

For an iterated block cipher $E \in BC(n, m, l)$, the tuple (x, x') with $x, x' \in \mathbb{F}_2^n$ is called a 2-polygon in $\mathbb{F}_2^n$. The 2-polygon (x_{r_b}, x'_{r_b}) propagates through round by round. If there exits an r-round related-key 2-polygonal trail

$$((x_{r_b}, x'_{r_b}), (E^1_{k_{r_b}}(x_{r_b}), E^1_{k'_{r_b}}(x'_{r_b})), \ldots, (E^r_{k_{r_b+r-1}}(x_{r_b+r-1}), E^r_{k'_{r_b+r-1}}(x'_{r_b+r-1})))$$

such that the equations of $(x_{r_e}, x'_{r_e}) = (E^r_{k_{r_b+r-1}}(x_{r_b+r-1}), E^r_{k'_{r_b+r-1}}(x'_{r_b+r-1}))$, are always satisfied, then the triplet $((x_{r_b}, x'_{r_b}), (k_{r_b}, k'_{r_b}), (x_{r_e}, x'_{r_e}))$ is called an r-round dependent-key possible 2-polygons. Otherwise, it is an r-round dependent-key impossible 2-polygons of E. Based on this, we redefine the related-tweakey impossible differential for tweakable block ciphers.

Definition 1 (Related-tweakey Impossible Differential). *For a tweakable block cipher $E \in TBC(n, \kappa, t)$, if $((s_{r_b}, s'_{r_b}), (tk, tk'), (s_{r_e}, s'_{r_e}))$ is an $(r_e - r_b)$-round dependent-tweakey impossible 2-polygons, where tk is the initial tweakey and $\forall(s_{r_b}, s'_{r_b}) \in \Delta_\alpha^n$, $\forall(s_{r_e}, s'_{r_e}) \in \Delta_\beta^n$, $\forall(tk, tk') \in \Delta_\delta^{\kappa+t}$, the triplet (α, β, δ) is called an $(r_e - r_b)$-round related-tweakey impossible differential.*

According to Definition 1, instead of describing the differential propagation, we pay attention to the propagation of values with certain constraints in the present paper. Specifically, referring to the automatic search model proposed in [12], we give an automatic search model for the $(r_e - r_b)$-round related-tweakey impossible differentials by considering the propagation of states from the r_b-th round to the r_e-th round, which is shown in Algorithm 1.

Algorithm 1: The Model for related-tweakey impossible differentials

---

Input: $E \in TBC(n, \kappa, t)$, r_b, r_e
Output: The length of distinguisher and the values of input differentials

1 Generate $\Omega = \{(\alpha, \beta, \delta) | \alpha, \beta \in \mathbb{F}_2^n, \delta \in \mathbb{F}_2^{\kappa+t}, (\alpha, \beta, \delta) \neq (0, 0, 0)\}$;
2 Define: *distinguisher find* = True;
3 **while** *distinguisher find* **do**
4   *distinguisher find* = False;
5   **foreach** $(\alpha, \beta, \delta) \in \Omega$ **do**
      // Step 1: Describe the cipher E in CVC format
6   Declare all variables to be used;
7   Describe the propagation of $(tk_0, tk'_0) \rightarrow \cdots \rightarrow (tk_{r_e}, tk'_{r_e})$;
8   Describe the propagation of $(s_{r_b}, s'_{r_b}) \rightarrow \cdots \rightarrow (s_{r_e}, s'_{r_e})$;
9   Add the constraints: $s_{r_b} \oplus s'_{r_b} = \alpha$, $s_{r_e} \oplus s'_{r_e} = \beta$, $tk \oplus tk = \delta$;
10   Add the statements "QUERY(FALSE);"
      "COUNTEREXAMPLE;";
      // Step 2: Invoke the STP to solve the file
11   Start to solve the file;
12   **if** *solver returns "Valid"* **then**
13   Record the triplets (α, β, δ) and the round number (r_b, r_e);
14   *distinguisher find* = True;
15   Break;
16   **if** *distinguisher find* **then**
17   The distinguisher from r_b to r_e is found in Ω;
18   Let $r_e = r_e + 1$;
19   **else**
20   The distinguisher from r_b to r_e is not found in Ω;

2.3 Boolean Satisfiability Problem

The *Boolean Satisfiability Problem* (SAT) is to find whether a set of variables, which if plugged into a boolean expression, will result in "True". Any boolean expression can be converted to normal form and the conjunctive normal form (CNF) is one of them. The CNF expression is a bunch of clauses consisting of variables, ORs, and NOTs, all of which are then glued together with AND into a full expression. SAT solver is merely a solver of huge boolean equations in CNF form. It just gives the answer, if there is a set of input values that can satisfy CNF expression, and what input values must be. There have been some heuristic SAT solvers. Most support CNF files as the standard input format, such as Cryptominisat [19].

The *Satisfiability Modulo Theories* (SMT) problem is an extension of the SAT problem, in which CNF formulas are enriched by binary-valued functions over a suitable set of binary and (or) non-binary variables. Many works searching for the differential and linear characteristics are based on the SMT problem, where STP[1] is a common solver for SMT problems. STP supports the CVC format and starts from an initial assignment for the literals, then builds a search tree using systematic backtracking until all conflicting clauses are resolved. An SMT problem is unsatisfiable if returning either an assignment of variables for a satisfiable set of clauses or a predicate indicates. However, when invoking STP to solve an SMT problem, the solver first interprets SMT instances in CVC format into SAT instances with CNF and then determines its satisfiability.

3   The Optimized Automatic Search Model

By utilizing Algorithm 1 to investigate related-tweakey impossible differentials, we observe that with an increase in the number of search rounds, the equation system employed to represent the state propagation expands correspondingly. This leads to an exponential escalation in both the runtime and memory requirements caused by the augmented amount of data acquired during the database query process. To overcome these impediments and enhance the efficiency of Algorithm 1, we propose an optimized automatic search model based on the LCA technique in the section.

3.1   Application of LCA in Impossible Differential Cryptanalysis

Locality Constraint Analysis (LCA) is an analytical method that uses the properties of local variables to deduce global features. In the impossible differential analysis, if $E_{r_1}^k(\Delta_\alpha^n) = D_{r_2}^k(\Delta_\beta^n)$ is never satisfied under any k for $E \in BC(n, m, l)$, the differential (α, β) is called an impossible differential. However, according to the security criterion for confusion and diffusion in the design of a block cipher, with the exception of some positions in which contradictions may occur, the value of the other positions almost reaches full diffusion after several rounds of iteration, which means that the values in those positions can traverse the entire space. Therefore, we can use the LCA technique to determine an impossible differential by considering some of the positions instead of the full state.

From the perspective of theoretical analysis, let $x = (x_0, x_1, \cdots, x_{n-1})$, $x_i \in \mathbb{F}_2$ be inactive if $\bigvee_{0 \le i \le n-1} x_i = 0$. Otherwise, x is active. Then we can obtain Theorem 1 according to Definition 1. The proof is omitted in the paper[2].

Theorem 1. *Let $E(x, tk) \in TBC(n, \kappa, t)$ be a tweakable block cipher and $\mathbb{CP}$ be a tuple that includes the sets of possible contradictory positions that need to be constrained in the search model. For any $\alpha, \beta \in \mathbb{F}_2^n$, $\delta \in \mathbb{F}_2^{\kappa+t} \setminus \{0\}$, if there exists a set $\mathbb{P} \subset \mathbb{CP}$, such that*

$$LCA := \bigvee_{i \in \mathbb{P}} C_i(x, y, tk) \oplus C_i(x \oplus \alpha, y \oplus \beta, tk \oplus \delta)$$

---

[1] https://github.com/stp/.

[2] The proof of Theorem 1 can refer to the full version of this paper in https://eprint.iacr.org.

is active for $\forall x, y \in \mathbb{F}_2^n$ *and* $\forall tk \in \mathbb{F}_2^{\kappa+t}$, *where* $C_i(x, y, tk) := E_{r_1}(x, tk)[i] \oplus D_{r_2}(y, tk)[i]$ *and* $D_r(E_r(x, tk), tk) = x$. *Then* (α, β, δ) *is an* $(r_1 + r_2)$-*round related-tweakey impossible differential of* $E(x, tk)$.

The Idea of Our Approach. We use the "miss-in-the-middle" method to find impossible differential distinguishers of block ciphers. In contrast, we weaken the conditions of the intermediate constraints. As shown in Fig. 1, we split an $(r_1 + r_2)$-round impossible differential into an r_1-round encryption and r_2-round decryption and only pay attention to the values of a few bits in the middle with the LCA technique.

In particular, suppose that $\mathbb{P} = \{i_0, i_1, \cdots, i_m\}$ is a set in which contradictions may occur. Then, if the equation

$$\bigvee_{i \in \mathbb{P}} E_{r_1}(x, tk)[i] \oplus E_{r_1}(x', tk')[i] \oplus D_{r_2}(y, tk)[i] \oplus D_{r_2}(y', tk')[i] = 0$$

is never satisfied for $\forall (x, x') \in \Delta_\alpha^n$, $\forall (y, y') \in \Delta_\beta^n$ and $\forall (tk, tk') \in \Delta_\delta^{\kappa+t}$, the triplet (α, β, δ) is an $(r_1 + r_2)$-round related-tweakey impossible differential. However, it is worth noting that a differential triplet (α, β, δ) satisfying Theorem 1 is a related-tweakey impossible differential, not vice versa.

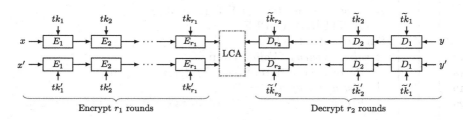

Fig. 1. The Optimization Scheme of Our Automatic Search Model

3.2 The Optimized Automatic Search Model for Related-Tweakey Impossible Differentials

Based on the preceding analysis, we present an optimized automatic search model for related-tweakey impossible differentials, outlined in Algorithm 2.

Specifically, given a tweakable block cipher $E \in TBC(n, \kappa, t)$, the determination of whether a triplet (α, β, δ) is an $(r_e - r_b)$-round related-tweakey impossible differential can be accomplished through three phases: search space determination, statements generation, and STP invocation. Initially, the input parameters are the starting round number r_b, the termination round number r_e, and r_m where the constraints are added. For each triplet (α, β, δ) in the search space Ω, whether (α, β, δ) constitutes an $(r_e - r_b)$-round related-tweakey impossible differential is transformed into the corresponding SMT problem using the CVC language and solved by invocation of the STP solver. Finally, Algorithm

2 outputs the length of distinguishers and the corresponding input and output differentials. Further details of Algorithm 2 are presented below.

Algorithm 2: Optimized automatic search model using LCA technique

---

    Input: $E \in TBC(n, \kappa, t)$, r_b, r_e, r_m
    Output: (α, β, δ), (r_b, r_e, r_m), and $\mathbb{P}$

1 Generate $\Omega = \{(\alpha, \beta, \delta) | \alpha, \beta \in \mathbb{F}_2^n, \delta \in \mathbb{F}_2^{\kappa+t}, (\alpha, \beta, \delta) \neq (0, 0, 0)\}$;

2 Generate a constraint set $\mathbb{CP}$;

3 Define: *distinguisher find* = True;

4 **while** *distinguisher find* **do**

5 | *distinguisher find* = False;

6 | **foreach** $(\alpha, \beta, \delta) \in \Omega$ **do**

7 | | **foreach** $\mathbb{P} \subseteq \mathbb{CP}$ **do**

8 | | | Declare all variables to be used;

9 | | | Describe the propagation of $(tk_0, tk'_0) \rightarrow \cdots \rightarrow (tk_{r_e}, tk'_{r_e})$;

10 | | | Describe the propagation of $(s_{r_b}, s'_{r_b}) \rightarrow \cdots \rightarrow (s_{r_m}, s'_{r_m})$;

11 | | | Describe the propagation of $(\hat{s}_{r_m}, \hat{s}'_{r_m}) \rightarrow \cdots \rightarrow (s_{r_e}, s'_{r_e})$;

12 | | | Add the constraints: $s_{r_b} \oplus s'_{r_b} = \alpha$, $s_{r_e} \oplus s'_{r_e} = \beta$, $tk \oplus tk' = \delta$;
     | | | // Locality Constraint Analysis

13 | | | **foreach** $i \in \mathbb{P}$ **do**

14 | | | | Add the constraints: $s_{r_m}[i] \oplus s'_{r_m}[i] \oplus \hat{s}_{r_m}[i] \oplus \hat{s}'_{r_m}[i] = 0$;

15 | | | Add the statements: "QUERY(FALSE);" "COUNTEREXAMPLE;" ;

16 | | | Start to solve the file;

17 | | | **if** *solver returns "Valid"* **then**

18 | | | | Record the values of (α, β, δ), (r_b, r_e, r_m), and $\mathbb{P}$;

19 | | | | *distinguisher find* = True;

20 | | | | Break ;   // Break out of all *for* loops

21 | **if** *distinguisher find* **then**

22 | | The distinguisher from r_b to r_e is found in Ω;

23 | | Let $r_e = r_e + 1$;

24 | **else**

25 | | The distinguisher from r_b to r_e is not found in Ω;

Specification of the Search Space Determination Phase. The efficacy of our automated search approach hinges predominantly on two factors, as demonstrated in Lines 6 and 7 of Algorithm 2: the duration needed to complete a search and the magnitude of the search space. As the search time is restricted by the size of the cipher and the hardware used, enhancing search efficiency can be challenging under limited resources. Consequently, selecting the search space judiciously so that a minimal number of elements reflect a greater number of differential properties will be pivotal in increasing search efficiency.

The Choice of Ω. The utilization of linear tweak schedules and XOR operations for the purpose of mixing subtweakeys with internal states, as observed in numerous state-of-the-art tweakable block ciphers, can inadvertently benefit potential attackers. Specifically, under the related-tweakey setting, an attacker can manipulate certain state values by XORing the same difference of sub-tweakeys at corresponding positions, thereby nullifying the difference of internal states. This, in turn, enables the attacker to pass one round function without incurring any additional cost, as depicted in Fig. 2.

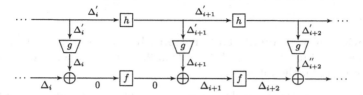

Fig. 2. The differential model under the related-tweakey setting (This is a TWEAKEY framework proposed by Jean et al. [13] to bridge the gap between key and tweak inputs in the design of tweakable block ciphers, which can be viewed as a straightforward generalization of key-alternating ciphers. In the model, f is the round function and h represents the tweakey update function).

Furthermore, Sasaki and Todo [31] have observed that all existing ciphers have the longest impossible differentials with only one active word in both input and output. In light of this, it is common practice to set the input and output difference to zero and only introduce differences to the tweakeys, that is, $\Omega = \{(\alpha, \beta, \delta) | \alpha = 0, \beta = 0, \delta \in \mathbb{F}_2^{\kappa+t} \setminus \{0\}\}$. The specific choice of δ depends on the cipher's structure, with one bit being active for bit-oriented encryption and one cell being active for cell-oriented encryption.

The Choice of r_m and $\mathbb{CP}$. The parameters r_m and $\mathbb{CP}$ jointly determine the locations of the contradictions. Based on empirical observations and experimental tests, we observe that for a distinguisher of odd length, the contradictions typically manifest in the middle round; whereas for even length, they appear in the middle two rounds. As such, we derive the expression $r_m = \lceil \frac{r_b+r_e}{2} \rceil$ if $(r_e - r_b)$ is odd, and $r_m \in \{\frac{r_b+r_e}{2}, \frac{r_b+r_e}{2} + 1\}$ if $(r_e - r_b)$ is even. The selection of the constrained position tuple $\mathbb{CP}$ is also informed by empirical evidence and experimental results.

Especially, for ARX-based block ciphers, we apply a constraint tuple $\mathbb{CP} = \{[i] | 0 \leq i \leq (n-1)\}$, where we constrain one bit of the intermediate state in each search. To verify the effectiveness of this approach, we utilized Algorithm 2 on SIMON and SPECK [2], and the results are presented in Table 1, where only one branch is constrained to define $\mathbb{CP}$ for ciphers based on the Feistel structure. For SPN-based block ciphers, we consider an S-box as a constraint unit in our modified model, i.e., $\mathbb{CP} = \{S_i | 0 \leq i \leq (m-1)\}$, where $S_i = \{i | 0 \leq i \leq (m-1)\}$ for an m-bit S-box. Using this constraint, we applied Algorithm 2 to SKINNY, QARMA, and CRAFT. Notably, we define $\mathbb{CP} = \{\{S_{4i}, S_{4i+1}, S_{4i+2}, S_{4i+3}\} | 0 \leq i \leq 3\}$ when applying Algorithm 2 to Joltik-BC, since the matrix used in its MixNibbles operation is an MDS matrix.

Table 1. The experimental results for SIMON32/64 and SPECK32/64

Ciphers	Input Difference	Output Difference	DR	ConR	ConPs
SIMON32/64	0000 0000 0000 0000 1000 0000 0000 0000	0000 0001 0000 0000 0000 0000 0000 0000	11	6	24
SPECK32/64	0000 0000 0000 1000 0000 0000 0000 0000	1000 0000 0000 0000 1000 0000 0000 0010	6	2	5

Specification of Statements Generation Phase. The statements generation phase is described in lines 8-16 of Algorithm 2. A detailed account of each step is then presented in the following.

- **Line 8.** Declare the variables to describe the propagation of round functions and tweakey schedules, including the variables that represent the input 2-polygon and output 2-polygons, tweakey 2-polygons, and some other intermediate variables.
- **Line 9-11.** According to the propagation rules for Copy, Xor, Modular Addition, Binary Matrix Multiplication and S-box given in [12], construct the propagation from the input 2-polygons (s_{r_b}, s'_{r_b}) to the output 2-polygons (s_{r_m}, s'_{r_m}) with the aid of the tweakey 2-polygons and intermediate variables in CVC format. Especially, the tweakey 2-polygons is constrained according to the tweakey schedule.
- **Line 12.** Generate the statements in CVC format such that the input and output 2-polygons satisfies that $s_{r_b} \oplus s'_{r_b} = \alpha$ and $s_{r_e} \oplus s'_{r_e} = \beta$, while the tweakey 2-polygons satisfies that $tk_{r_b} \oplus tk'_{r_b} = \delta$.
- **Line 13-14.** Generate the statements in CVC format such that the output 2-polygon of the first $(r_m - r_b)$ rounds and the input 2-polygon of the last $(r_e - r_m)$ rounds satisfies that $s_{r_m}[i] \oplus s'_{r_m}[i] \oplus \hat{s}_{r_m}[i] \oplus \hat{s}'_{r_m}[i] = 0$ for $\forall i \in \mathbb{P}$.
- **Line 15.** Add the statements "QUERY(FALSE);" and "COUNTEREXAMPLE" to the statements system, which is a common predicate in STP to determine whether an SMT problem has a solution.

Specification of the STP Invocation Phase. We invoke STP to tackle the file, which comprises a system of statements. If the outcome of STP is "Valid," this implies that no solution exists for the SMT problem. As such, the corresponding triplets (α, β, δ) represent an $(r_e - r_b)$-round related-tweakey impossible differential, where r_m and $\mathbb{P}$ ascertain the contradictory positions. Alternatively, if STP returns "Invalid" along with a collection of solutions, the triplets (α, β, δ) do not denote an $(r_e - r_b)$-round related-tweakey impossible differential, and these solutions constitute the corresponding differential characteristic from round r_b to round r_e for E.

4   Applications from Cryptanalysis Aspect

In this section, we apply our automatic search model to Joltik-BC, SKINNY, QARMA, and CRAFT from the cryptanalysis aspect. Especially, when searching for related-tweakey impossible differentials, only the tweakey is modified while keeping the input and output differences at zero, that is, $\Omega = \{(0, 0, \delta) | \delta \in \mathbb{F}_2^{\kappa+t} \setminus \{0\}\}$, where κ and t are constants. Consequently, by exploiting the relationship between the tweakey and the state of a cipher, an impossible differential can be derived for the $(r+2)$-round if a r-round related-tweakey impossible differential is found within the search space Ω. Furthermore, Δ_{in} and Δ_{out} denote the input and output difference of the operation AddRoundTweakey, respectively.

4.1 Application to Joltik-BC

Joltik-BC is an iterative substitution-permutation network that transforms the initial plaintext through a series of round functions (that depend on the key and the tweak) to a ciphertext. The cipher exists in two variations, namely Joltik-BC-128, with a total key and tweak size of 128 bits, and Joltik-BC-192, with a combined key and tweak size of 192 bits. Additional information regarding Joltik-BC can be found in [14]. Notably, the construction of Joltik-BC is based on the Superposition TWEAKEY design [13], with the tweakey schedule satisfying Proposition 1. This property allows for greater differential properties when assessing differential propagation.

Proposition 1. *(**Cancellation of the Tweak Differences** [14]) Cancellation of differences (in general since the key schedule is linear) in the chosen nibble of TK-p cannot occur more than $(p-1)$ times. For TK-2, this means that the cumulative difference from the subtweakeys can be canceled only once by XOR of the subtweakeys. For TK-3, this can happen twice.*

Previous Cryptanalysis. To the best of our knowledge, the most extensive distinguisher discovered for Joltik-BC-128 is a 6-round related-tweak impossible differential proposed in [36]. This particular impossible differential exhibits two active nibbles for both input and output differences. For Joltik-BC-192, no public impossible differential has been identified, apart from a 7-round meet-in-the-middle distinguisher constructed in [20].

List of 6-Round Related-Tweakey Impossible Differentials for Joltik-BC-128. By introducing the difference to TK_1^r and TK_2^r in a single nibble, we applied Algorithm 1 to Joltik-BC-128 and discovered a 6-round related-tweakey impossible differential with a time of 4.43 s. To confirm the absence of a 7-round impossible differential in the search space, we conducted a verification process by traversing the entire search space, which took approximately 23.4 h. Based on Proposition 1, the search results can be classified into three cases. The corresponding values are presented in Table 2.

List of 7-Round Related-Tweakey Impossible Differentials for Joltik-BC-192. By introducing differences to the same nibble of TK_1^r, TK_2^r, and TK_3^r, respectively, a 7-round related-tweakey impossible differential is obtained

Table 2. The 6-round related-tweakey impossible differentials for `Joltik-BC-128`

Cases	$(\triangle T K_0^r[i], \triangle T K_1^r[i])$	Index
Case 1	$\triangle T K_1^r[i] \oplus KS^1(\triangle T K_2^r[i], 2) = 0$	$i \in \{0, 1, 2, \cdots, 15\}$
Case 2	$\triangle T K_1^{r+6}[i] \oplus KS^5(\triangle T K_2^r[i], 2) = 0$	$i \in \{0, 1, 2, \cdots, 15\}$
Case 3	$(9, 3), (D, 6)$	$i \in \{0, 2, 4, \cdots, 14\}$

with a time of 2403.67 s. It required approximately 25 days[3] to verify the non-existence of an 8-round impossible differential in the search space. As Proposition 1 suggests, the tweakey differences can be canceled twice. The search results can be categorized into the following five cases, as shown in Table 3.

Table 3. The 7-round related-tweakey impossible differentials for `Joltik-BC-192`

Cases	$(\triangle T K_0^r[i], \triangle T K_1^r[i], \triangle T K_2^r[i])$	Index
Case 1	$\triangle T K_r^1[i] \oplus KS^1(\triangle T K_r^2[i], 2) \oplus KS^1(\triangle T K_r^3[i], 4) = 0$ $\triangle T K_r^1[i] \oplus KS^2(\triangle T K_r^2[i], 2) \oplus KS^2(\triangle T K_r^3[i], 4) = 0$	$i \in \{0, 1, 2, \cdots, 15\}$
Case 2	$\triangle T K_r^1[i] \oplus KS^5(\triangle T K_r^2[i], 2) \oplus KS^5(\triangle T K_r^3[i], 4) = 0$ $\triangle T K_r^1[i] \oplus KS^6(\triangle T K_r^2[i], 2) \oplus KS^6(\triangle T K_r^3[i], 4) = 0$	$i \in \{0, 1, 2, \cdots, 15\}$
Case 3	$\triangle T K_r^1[i] \oplus KS^1(\triangle T K_r^2[i], 2) \oplus KS^1(\triangle T K_r^3[i], 4) = 0$ $\triangle T K_r^1[i] \oplus KS^6(\triangle T K_r^2[i], 2) \oplus KS^6(\triangle T K_r^3[i], 4) = 0$	$i \in \{0, 1, 2, \cdots, 15\}$
Case 4	$(1, C, 9), (4, 6, F), (F, 8, E), (F, 6, 8)$	$i \in \{0, 2, 4, \cdots, 14\}$
Case 5	$(3, 6, 7), (4, 9, C), (D, 6, B), (F, A, 2)$	$i \in \{1, 3, 5, \cdots, 15\}$

4.2   Application to `SKINNY`

`SKINNY` is a family of lightweight tweakable block ciphers designed to have the smallest hardware footprint, which was proposed at CRYPTO 2016 by Beierle et al. [3]. It has 6 main variants for `SKINNY`. Particularly, `SKINNY`-n-t is a block cipher that operates on n-bit blocks with t-bit tweakey, where $n = 64$ or 128 and $t = n, 2n$ or $3n$. More details can be found in [3]. This section will apply our model in Algorithm 2 to search the related-tweakey impossible differential for `SKINNY`.

Previous Cryptanalysis. To the best of our knowledge, the longest related-tweakey impossible differentials obtained assuming a single active nibble are 12-, 14-, and 16-round for `SKINNY-64-64`, `SKINNY-64-128`, and `SKINNY-64-192`, respectively, as reported in [25]. Although Sadeghi et al. [30] claimed that they found 13- and 15-round related-tweakey impossible differential for `SKINNY-64-64` and `SKINNY-64-128`, the length of distinguishers in the mode of $(0, 0, \delta)$ was the

---

[3] The size of the search space is about $(16 * 15)^3 \approx 2^{23.7}$.

same as our results. In their results, the extra round was not eligible in our opinion because the input difference of the extra round is not certain.

The 12-Round Related-Tweakey Impossible Differentials for SKINNY-64-64. By introducing the difference to one nibble of TK_1^r, we apply Algorithm 2 to find a 10-round related-tweakey impossible differential (including 10 SubCells operations) with 817.69 s. It took about 1.01 h to prove that there is no 11-round impossible differential in the search space. According to the relationship between the tweakey schedule and the round function, we can further extend the 10-round related-tweakey impossible differentials to the 12-round related-tweakey impossible differentials in the mode of (α, β, δ), which is shown in Table 4.

Table 4. The related-tweakey impossible differentials for SKINNY-64-64

Num.	$\Delta_{in} = \Delta TK_1^r$	Δ_{out}	ConR	ConPs
RTK01	$a000\ 0000\ 0000\ 0000$	$0000\ 000a\ 0000\ 0000$	7	S_8
RTK02	$0a00\ 0000\ 0000\ 0000$	$000a\ 0000\ 0000\ 0000$		$S_{4,10,12}$
RTK03	$00a0\ 0000\ 0000\ 0000$	$0a00\ 0000\ 0000\ 0000$		$S_{8,9}$
RTK04	$000a\ 0000\ 0000\ 0000$	$0000\ 00a0\ 0000\ 0000$		S_7
RTK05	$0000\ 0a00\ 0000\ 0000$	$0000\ a000\ 0000\ 0000$		$S_{9,15}$
RTK06	$0000\ 00a0\ 0000\ 0000$	$00a0\ 0000\ 0000\ 0000$		$S_{9,13}$
RTK07	$0000\ 000a\ 0000\ 0000$	$0000\ 0a00\ 0000\ 0000$		$S_{5,13}$

The 14-Round Related-Tweakey Impossible Differentials for SKINNY-64-128. By introducing differences to the same nibble of TK_1^r and TK_2^r, we have discovered a 12-round related-tweakey impossible differential with a duration of 5.96 h using Algorithm 2. It took approximately 26.89 h to establish the absence of a 13-round impossible differential in the search space. Based on the relationship between the tweakey schedule and the round function, we have extended the 12-round related-tweakey impossible differentials in the $(0, 0, \delta)$ mode to 14-round related-tweakey impossible differentials in the (α, β, δ) mode. Here, $\Delta_{in} = \triangle TK_1^r \oplus \triangle TK_2^r$, $\triangle TK_1^r \oplus L_2(\triangle TK_2^r) = 0$, and $\Delta_{out} = \triangle TK_1^{r+14} \oplus \triangle TK_2^{r+14}$. The values are presented in Table 5.

The 16-Round Related-Tweakey Impossible Differentials for SKINNY-64-192. By introducing the differences to the same nibble of TK_1^r, TK_2^r, and TK_3^r, respectively, we applied our tool to discover the 14-round related-tweakey impossible differential with 6.9 days in the search space. Moreover, we extended the 14-round related-tweakey impossible differentials in the mode of $(0, 0, \delta)$ to the 16-round related-tweakey impossible differentials in the mode of (α, β, δ), where $\Delta_{in} = \triangle TK_1^r \oplus \triangle TK_2^r \oplus \triangle TK_3^r$ and $\Delta_{out} = \triangle TK_1^{r+16} \oplus \triangle TK_2^{r+16} \oplus \triangle TK_2^{r+16}$. Due to the cancellation among the differences between the tweakeys, the search results can be divided into two cases, where L_i^j means the LFSR used in TK_i after j rounds.

Table 5. The related-tweakey impossible differentials for SKINNY-64-128

i	$(\Delta TK_1^r[i], \Delta TK_2^r[i])$	Δ_{in}	Δ_{out}	ConR	ConPs
0	$(1,8), (2,1), (3,9)$	$a000\ 0000\ 0000\ 0000$	$0b00\ 0000\ 0000\ 0000$	8	$S_{4,8,12}$
1	$(4,2), (5,A), (6,3)$	$0a00\ 0000\ 0000\ 0000$	$0000\ 000b\ 0000\ 0000$		$S_{9,12}$
2	$(7,B), (8,C), (9,4)$	$00a0\ 0000\ 0000\ 0000$	$b000\ 0000\ 0000\ 0000$		$S_{14,15}$
3	$(A,D), (B,5), (C,E)$	$000a\ 0000\ 0000\ 0000$	$0000\ 0b00\ 0000\ 0000$		$S_{1,7,14,15}$
4	$(D,6), (E,F), (F,7)$	$0000\ a000\ 0000\ 0000$	$00b0\ 0000\ 0000\ 0000$		$S_{11,13,14}$
5		$0000\ 0a00\ 0000\ 0000$	$0000\ 00b0\ 0000\ 0000$		$S_{3,8,9}$
6		$0000\ 00a0\ 0000\ 0000$	$0000\ b000\ 0000\ 0000$		$S_{5,9,12}$
7		$0000\ 000a\ 0000\ 0000$	$000b\ 0000\ 0000\ 0000$		$S_{0,5,13}$

- **Case 1.** The values of $(\triangle TK_1^r, \triangle TK_2^r, \triangle TK_3^r)$ are subject to the constraint that $\triangle TK_1^r[i] \oplus L_2^1(\triangle TK_2^r[i]) \oplus L_3^1(\triangle TK_3^r[i]) = 0$ and $\triangle TK_1^r[i] \oplus L_2^2(\triangle TK_2^r[i])$ $\oplus L_3^2(\triangle TK_3^r[i]) = 0$ for $i \in \{0, \cdots, 7\}$.
- **Case 2.** The tuple of values $(\triangle TK_1^r, \triangle TK_2^r, \triangle TK_3^r)$ is constrained so that $\triangle TK_1^r[i] \oplus L_2^1(\triangle TK_2^r[i]) \oplus L_3^1(\triangle TK_3^r[i]) = 0$ and $\triangle TK_1^r[i] \oplus L_2^7(\triangle TK_2^r[i]) \oplus L_3^7(\triangle TK_3^r[i]) = 0$ for $i \in \{0, \cdots, 7\}$.

4.3 Application to QARMA

The QARMA block cipher, designed by Avanzi at ToSC'17, is a lightweight tweakable block cipher with three-round Even-Mansour construction. There are two variants of QARMA that support block sizes of $n = 64$ and $n = 128$ bits, denoted by QARMA-64 and QARMA-128, respectively. The tweak is also n bits long and the key is always $2n$ bits long. In the present paper, we pay attention to QARMA-64.

Previous Cryptanalysis. Since the proposal of the tweakable block cipher QARMA, various attacks have been employed to assess its security, such as meet-in-the-middle attacks [22], impossible differential attacks [26,35,36] and statistical saturation attacks [21]. However, the longest related-tweak impossible differential of QARMA is 7-round proposed by Zong et al. [36] by considering the differential relationship between the tweak and a single-tweak impossible differential.

List of 7-Round Related-Tweakey Impossile Differentials for QARMA-64. By modifying a single nibble in the initial tweak, we apply Algorithm 2 to derive several related-tweakey impossible differentials for QARMA-64, ranging from the 7-th to the 11-th round, some of which were not previously discovered. By taking into account the impact of the tweak update function, we further obtain some 7-round related-tweak impossible differentials for QARMA-64, which is covering rounds from the 6-th to the 12-th, as tabulated in Table 6.

4.4 Application to CRAFT

CRAFT is a lightweight tweakable block cipher introduced by Beierle et al. [4] at FSE 2019, which follows the SPN design with 32 rounds. The main goal of

Table 6. The 7-round related-tweak impossible differentials for `QARMA-64`

Num	$\Delta_{in} = \Delta T$	Δ_{out}	ConR	ConPs
RT01	a000 0000 0000 0000	0000 0000 0000 00b0	9	S_1
RT02	000a 0000 0000 0000	0000 c000 0000 0000		S_{13}
RT03	0000 0a00 0000 0000	0c00 0000 0000 0000		S_{14}
RT04	0000 0000 00a0 0000	0000 0000 0000 b000		S_1
RT05	0000 0000 000a 0000	0000 00c0 0000 0000		S_{10}
RT06	0000 0000 0000 0a00	0000 0000 b000 0000		S_5

$a \in \mathbb{F}_{2^4} \setminus \{0\}$, $b = \overline{\omega}(a)$ and $c = \overline{\omega}^2(a)$, where $\overline{\omega} = \omega^{-1}$.

`CRAFT` was to efficiently protect its implementations against Differential Fault Analysis (DFA) attacks. It consists of a 64-bit block, a 128-bit key K and 64-bit tweak T, where the 128-bit key is split into two 64-bit keys K_0 and K_1. Using the permutation Q on the tweak, four 64-bit tweakeys TK_0, TK_1, TK_2 and TK_3 are derived from the tweak T and keys K_0, K_1. Then in each round, without any key update, the tweakey $TK_{i \bmod 4}$ is XORed to the cipher state. More information can be obtained in [4].

Previous Cryptanalysis. In the specification file, Hadipour et al. [4] conducted an extensive analysis of the security of `CRAFT`. Specifically, they identified the 13-round impossible differential under the single-key setting as the longest one in the analysis until now. Subsequently, many studies have been conducted to evaluate the security of round-reduced `CRAFT` under both the single-key mode and related-key mode. However, the majority of research has been centered on differential attacks, as documented in [8,10,11]. Furthermore, Hadipour et al. [11] have reported a 14-round zero-correlation linear distinguisher under the related-tweak setting in previous research, in addition to some probability-type attacks.

List of 12-Round Related-Tweak Impossible Differentials for `CRAFT`. When searching the related-tweak impossible differentials for `CRAFT`, we activate a single nibble of the initial tweak while other differences remain inactive. Specifically, the active set is denoted as $\Omega = \{(0, 0, \delta)|\delta \in \mathbb{F}_2^\kappa \setminus \{0\}\}$ and $\triangle K_0 = \triangle K_1 = 0$. By utilizing Algorithm 2, we discovered several 10-round related-tweak impossible differentials for the first time in a total time of 891.34 s, which also can be extended to 12-round, as shown in Table 7. Additionally, we have proven that there is no 13-round related-tweak impossible differentials in the search space, which required a total time of 4698.06 s.

Table 7. The 12-round related-tweak impossible differentials for `CRAFT`

Num	$\Delta_{in} = \Delta T$	Δ_{out}	ConR	ConPs
RT01	0a00 0000 0000 0000	0a00 0000 0000 0000	7	S_6
RT02	0000 0a00 0000 0000	0000 0a00 0000 0000		S_{10}
RT03	0000 0000 a000 0000	0000 0000 a000 0000		S_{10}

List of 15-Round Related-Tweakey Impossible Differentials for CRAFT.
By setting the input and output differences to zero and modifying only one single nibble of K_0, K_1, and T, i.e., $\Omega = \{(0,0,\delta)|\delta \in \mathbb{F}_2^{64} \setminus \{0\}\}$ and $\triangle K_0 = \triangle K_1 = \triangle T = \delta$, we apply Algorithm 2 to CRAFT and identify the 13-round related-tweakey impossible differentials for the first time within 3263.46 s, which can also be extended to the 15-round with $\delta = (0000\ 0000\ 000a\ 0000)$, $\Delta_{in} = \Delta_{out} = (0000\ 0000\ a00a\ 0000)$. Additionally, we have proven that there are no 16-round related-tweakey impossible differentials within the search space with a total search time of 7040.3 s.

5   Evaluation of the Automatic Search Models

The LCA technique is an analysis method that explicates the complete attributes by way of partial features. Consequently, when juxtaposed with conventional search methods, utilizing the LCA technique can alleviate the interdependence among variables. Subsequently, we will present an assessment of Algorithm 2 compared with Algorithm 1 based on the search results.

Improving the Search Efficiency for Long Trials. The utilization of the LCA technique may enhance search efficiency and significantly reduce time costs, especially when exploring distinguishers with long trails. An illustrative example is provided in Table 8, which presents the computational time required for Algorithm 1 and Algorithm 2 to ascertain the existence of a related-tweakey impossible differential for CRAFT. The experimental evaluation was performed on the platform: Inter(R) Core i7-9700 CPU@3.00 GHz × 8, 8 GB RAM, 64-bit Ubuntu VMware. As evidenced by Table 8, when the number of rounds is limited, Algorithm 2 must sequentially traverse the constraint set and intermediate rounds, resulting in a total time cost comparable to Algorithm 1. However, as the number of rounds increases, the time complexity of Algorithm 1 escalates nearly exponentially, whereas Algorithm 2 maintains a relatively constant and gradual growth trend.

Table 8. The time for the related-tweakey impossible differentials of CRAFT

Scenario	DR	Algorithm 1	Algorithm 2	Results
CRAFT-RT	11	425.18 s	330.06 s	find 11-round RTID.
	12	1752.21 s	1466.48 s	find 12-round RTID
	13	84102.11 s	1998.46 s	find no 13-round RTID
CRAFT-RTK	14	3528.08 s	2902.99 s	find 14-round RTKID
	15	4424.64 s	3263.46 s	find 15-round RTKID
	16	–	7040.30 s	find no 16-round RTKID

RT: Related-tweak impossible differential. RTK: Related-tweakey impossible differential. "–": Terminating the program because it took too long to run.

Additionally, Algorithm 2 exhibits considerably superior performance to Algorithm 1 when applied to the cipher SKINNY, as indicated in Table 9. However, it should be noted that Algorithm 2 does not consistently outperform Algorithm 1. Specifically, in scenarios where the length of the distinguisher is relatively short for QARMA and Joltik-BC, Algorithm 2 provides a lesser advantage over Algorithm 1 when searching for distinguishers. For instance, in the case of QARMA, Algorithm 1 required 1631.37 s to establish the absence of 8-round related-tweak impossible differentials, whereas Algorithm 2 necessitated 1624.66 s. In this particular case, the search efficiency was comparable. However, the discrepancy in efficiency becomes evident for Joltik-BC-128, where Algorithm 1 required 84447.57 s to prove the nonexistence of 7-round related-tweakey impossible differentials, whereas Algorithm 2 demanded 476278.89 s.

Table 9. The time for related-tweakey impossible differentials of SKINNY

(n, t)	DR	Algorithm 1		Algorithm 2		Results
		Single	Total	Single	Total	
$(64, 64)$	12	26950 s	–	6.61 s	817.69 s	find 12-round RTKID
	13	–	–	16.23 s	3643.37 s	find no 13-round RTKID
$(64, 128)$	14	104.17s	–	13.01 s	21439.97 s	find 14-round RTKID
	15	–	–	31.00 s	96791.32 s	find no 15-round RTKID
$(64, 192)$	14	30.71 s	1483.65 s	15.34 s	732.44 s	find 14-round RTKID
	15	32.36 s	1727.89 s	34.00 s†	1744.75 s	find 15-round RTKID
	16	258709s	–	20.24 s†	599280 s	find 16-round RTKID

Single: The time it takes to complete a search, not the average time. Total: The total time it took to find the first distinguisher while traversing the search space. ''†'': In this case, we choose the middle round as r_m for odd-numbered rounds, while the middle two rounds are for even-numbered rounds. So this time is reasonable.

Determining the Contradictory Positions. In cryptanalysis, the "miss-in-the-middle" method has traditionally been employed to manually deduce the contradictory positions of an impossible differential. However, the process becomes challenging if the length of a distinguisher is too long or the cipher with sound diffusions. Therefore, there is a need for automatic tools to assist in determining the locations of contradictions. To this end, similar to the one used for verifying impossible differential distinguishers in [7] and [12], the LCA technique can be also used to derive the contradictory positions. Specifically, if there exists an impossible differential under the constraint set $\mathbb{P}$, then the contradictory occurs in the positions of $\mathbb{P}$. Here, we provide an example of SIMON128, which is obtained by Algorithm 2.

Example 1. The differential $(0x0000000000000000, 0x8000000000000000) \nrightarrow (0x4000000000000000, 0x0000000000000000)$ is a 19-round impossible differential for SIMON128, where the contradictory occurs in the second bit of the 11-th round.

6   Conclusion

This paper evaluates the security of tweakable block ciphers against the related-tweakey impossible differential analysis. The main approach involves constructing a differential propagation system using the SAT method, which describes the propagation of corresponding states under specific constraints and determines whether the transition is invalid. To achieve this goal, an automatic search model is proposed for related-tweakey impossible differentials based on the SMT problem. Subsequently, this method has been employed to identify the related-tweakey impossible differentials for `QARMA-64` and `Joltik-BC`, respectively.

Furthermore, the paper introduces a novel analytical strategy known as Locality Constraint Analysis (LCA), which aims to improve the efficiency of searching the distinguisher with long trails or ciphers with large sizes. A generalized automatic search model is constructed based on LCA, and the proposed method is applied to various ciphers such as `SIMON`, `SPECK`, `QARMA`, `CRAFT`, `Joltik-BC`, and `SKINNY`. Based on the search results, it is demonstrated that introducing the LCA technique to impossible differential cryptanalysis significantly improves the search efficiency and provides much more convenience for deriving the locations of the contradictory positions.

Acknowledgements. We thank the associate editor and the anonymous reviewers for their useful feedback that improved this paper. This research was supported by the National Natural Science Foundation of China (Grant No. 12371525) and the National Key Research and Development Program of China (Grant No. 2022YFF0604702).

References

1. Avanzi, R.: The QARMA block cipher family. Almost MDS matrices over rings with zero divisors, nearly symmetric even-mansour constructions with non-involutory central rounds, and search heuristics for low-latency s-boxes. IACR Trans. Symmetric Cryptol. 4–44 (2017). https://doi.org/10.13154/tosc.v2017.i1.4-44
2. Beaulieu, R., Shors, D., Smith, J., Treatman-Clark, S., Weeks, B., Wingers, L.: The SIMON and SPECK lightweight block ciphers. In: Proceedings of the 52nd Annual Design Automation Conference, pp. 1–6 (2015). https://doi.org/10.1145/2744769.2747946
3. Beierle, C., Jean, J., Kölbl, S., Leander, G., Moradi, A., Peyrin, T., Sasaki, Yu., Sasdrich, P., Sim, S.M.: The SKINNY family of block ciphers and its low-latency variant MANTIS. In: Robshaw, M., Katz, J. (eds.) CRYPTO 2016, Part II. LNCS, vol. 9815, pp. 123–153. Springer, Heidelberg (2016). https://doi.org/10.1007/978-3-662-53008-5_5
4. Beierle, C., Leander, G., Moradi, A., Rasoolzadeh, S.: CRAFT: lightweight tweakable block cipher with efficient protection against DFA attacks. IACR Trans. Symmetric Cryptol. **2019**(1), 5–45 (2019). https://doi.org/10.13154/tosc.v2019.i1.5-45
5. Biham, E., Biryukov, A., Shamir, A.: Cryptanalysis of skipjack reduced to 31 rounds using impossible differentials. In: Stern, J. (ed.) EUROCRYPT 1999. LNCS, vol. 1592, pp. 12–23. Springer, Heidelberg (1999). https://doi.org/10.1007/3-540-48910-X_2

6. Chakraborti, A., Datta, N., Jha, A., Mancillas-López, C., Nandi, M., Sasaki, Yu.: Elastic-Tweak: a framework for short tweak tweakable block cipher. In: Adhikari, A., Küsters, R., Preneel, B. (eds.) INDOCRYPT 2021. LNCS, vol. 13143, pp. 114–137. Springer, Cham (2021). https://doi.org/10.1007/978-3-030-92518-5_6

7. Cui, T., Chen, S., Jia, K., Fu, K., Wang, M.: New automatic search tool for impossible differentials and zero-correlation linear approximations. Sci. China Inf. Sci. **64**(2) (2021). https://doi.org/10.1007/s11432-018-1506-4

8. ElSheikh, M., Youssef, A.M.: Related-key differential cryptanalysis of full round CRAFT. In: Bhasin, S., Mendelson, A., Nandi, M. (eds.) SPACE 2019. LNCS, vol. 11947, pp. 50–66. Springer, Cham (2019). https://doi.org/10.1007/978-3-030-35869-3_6

9. Guo, C., Guo, J., List, E., Song, L.: Towards closing the security gap of tweak-aNd-tweak (TNT). In: Moriai, S., Wang, H. (eds.) ASIACRYPT 2020. LNCS, vol. 12491, pp. 567–597. Springer, Cham (2020). https://doi.org/10.1007/978-3-030-64837-4_19

10. Guo, H., et al.: Differential attacks on craft exploiting the involutory s-boxes and tweak additions. IACR Trans. Symmetric Cryptol. **2020**(3), 119–151 (2020). https://doi.org/10.13154/tosc.v2020.i3.119-151

11. Hadipour, H., Sadeghi, S., Niknam, M.M., Song, L., Bagheri, N.: Comprehensive security analysis of CRAFT. IACR Trans. Symmetric Cryptol. 290–317 (2019). https://doi.org/10.13154/tosc.v2019.i4.290-317

12. Hu, X., Li, Y., Jiao, L., Tian, S., Wang, M.: Mind the propagation of states. In: Moriai, S., Wang, H. (eds.) ASIACRYPT 2020, Part I. LNCS, vol. 12491, pp. 415–445. Springer, Cham (2020). https://doi.org/10.1007/978-3-030-64837-4_14

13. Jean, J., Nikolić, I., Peyrin, T.: Tweaks and keys for block ciphers: the TWEAKEY framework. In: Sarkar, P., Iwata, T. (eds.) ASIACRYPT 2014, Part II. LNCS, vol. 8874, pp. 274–288. Springer, Heidelberg (2014). https://doi.org/10.1007/978-3-662-45608-8_15

14. Jean, J., Nikolic, I., Peyrin, T.: Joltik v1.3. Submission to the CAESAR competition (2015). https://competitions.cr.yp.to/round2/joltikv13.pdf

15. Jean, J., Nikolić, I., Peyrin, T., Seurin, Y.: The Deoxys AEAD family. J. Cryptol. **34**(3), 31 (2021). https://doi.org/10.1007/s00145-021-09397-w

16. Kim, J., Hong, S., Lim, J.: Impossible differential cryptanalysis using matrix method. Discret. Math. **310**(5), 988–1002 (2010). https://doi.org/10.1016/j.disc.2009.10.019

17. Knudsen, L.: Deal - a 128-bit block cipher. NISI AES Proposal (1998)

18. Krovetz, T., Rogaway, P.: The software performance of authenticated-encryption modes. In: Joux, A. (ed.) FSE 2011. LNCS, vol. 6733, pp. 306–327. Springer, Heidelberg (2011). https://doi.org/10.1007/978-3-642-21702-9_18

19. Leventi-Peetz, A.M., Zendel, O., Lennartz, W., Weber, K.: CryptoMiniSat switches-optimization for solving cryptographic instances. arXiv preprint arXiv:2112.11484 (2021)

20. Li, M., Chen, S.: Improved meet-in-the-middle attacks on reduced-round Joltik-BC. IET Inf. Secur. **15**(3), 247–255 (2021)

21. Li, M., Hu, K., Wang, M.: Related-tweak statistical saturation cryptanalysis and its application on QARMA. IACR Trans. Symmetric Cryptol. **2019**(1), 236–263 (2019). https://doi.org/10.13154/tosc.v2019.i1.236-263

22. Li, R., Jin, C.: Meet-in-the-middle attacks on reduced-round QARMA-64/128. Comput. J. **61**(8), 1158–1165 (2018)

23. Liskov, M., Rivest, R.L., Wagner, D.: Tweakable block ciphers. In: Yung, M. (ed.) CRYPTO 2002. LNCS, vol. 2442, pp. 31–46. Springer, Heidelberg (2002). https://doi.org/10.1007/3-540-45708-9_3

24. Liskov, M., Rivest, R.L., Wagner, D.: Tweakable block ciphers. J. Cryptol. **24**, 588–613 (2011). https://doi.org/10.1007/s00145-010-9073-y

25. Liu, G., Ghosh, M., Song, L.: Security analysis of skinny under related-tweakey settings. Cryptology ePrint Archive (2016)

26. Liu, Y., Zang, T., Gu, D., Zhao, F., Li, W., Liu, Z.: Improved cryptanalysis of reduced-version QARMA-64/128. IEEE Access **8**, 8361–8370 (2020). https://doi.org/10.1109/ACCESS.2020.2964259

27. Luo, Y., Lai, X., Wu, Z., Gong, G.: A unified method for finding impossible differentials of block cipher structures. Inf. Sci. **263**, 211–220 (2014). https://doi.org/10.1016/j.ins.2013.08.051

28. Mouha, N., Wang, Q., Gu, D., Preneel, B.: Differential and linear cryptanalysis using mixed-integer linear programming. In: Wu, C.-K., Yung, M., Lin, D. (eds.) Inscrypt 2011. LNCS, vol. 7537, pp. 57–76. Springer, Heidelberg (2012). https://doi.org/10.1007/978-3-642-34704-7_5

29. Peyrin, T., Seurin, Y.: Counter-in-tweak: authenticated encryption modes for tweakable block ciphers. In: Robshaw, M., Katz, J. (eds.) CRYPTO 2016, Part I. LNCS, vol. 9814, pp. 33–63. Springer, Heidelberg (2016). https://doi.org/10.1007/978-3-662-53018-4_2

30. Sadeghi, S., Mohammadi, T., Bagheri, N.: Cryptanalysis of reduced round skinny block cipher. IACR Trans. Symmetric Cryptol. 124–162 (2018). https://doi.org/10.13154/tosc.v2018.i3.124-162

31. Sasaki, Yu., Todo, Y.: New impossible differential search tool from design and cryptanalysis aspects. In: Coron, J.-S., Nielsen, J.B. (eds.) EUROCRYPT 2017, Part III. LNCS, vol. 10212, pp. 185–215. Springer, Cham (2017). https://doi.org/10.1007/978-3-319-56617-7_7

32. Schroeppel, R., Orman, H.: The hasty pudding cipher. AES candidate submitted to NIST, p. M1 (1998)

33. Sun, S., Hu, L., Wang, P., Qiao, K., Ma, X., Song, L.: Automatic security evaluation and (related-key) differential characteristic search: application to SIMON, PRESENT, LBlock, DES(L) and other bit-oriented block ciphers. In: Sarkar, P., Iwata, T. (eds.) ASIACRYPT 2014, Part I. LNCS, vol. 8873, pp. 158–178. Springer, Heidelberg (2014). https://doi.org/10.1007/978-3-662-45611-8_9

34. Wu, S., Wang, M.: Automatic search of truncated impossible differentials for word-oriented block ciphers. In: Galbraith, S., Nandi, M. (eds.) INDOCRYPT 2012. LNCS, vol. 7668, pp. 283–302. Springer, Heidelberg (2012). https://doi.org/10.1007/978-3-642-34931-7_17

35. Yang, D., Qi, W.F., Chen, H.J.: Impossible differential attack on QARMA family of block ciphers. Cryptology ePrint Archive (2018)

36. Zong, R., Dong, X.: MILP-aided related-tweak/key impossible differential attack and its applications to QARMA, Joltik-BC. IEEE Access **7**, 153683–153693 (2019). https://doi.org/10.1109/ACCESS.2019.2946638

Comprehensive Preimage Security Evaluations on Rijndael-Based Hashing

Tianyu Zhang$^{(\boxtimes)}$

School of Physical and Mathematical Sciences, Nanyang Technological University, Singapore, Singapore
tianyu005@e.ntu.edu.sg

Abstract. The Meet-in-the-Middle (MITM) attack is one of the most powerful cryptanalysis techniques, as seen by its use in preimage attacks on MD4, MD5, Tiger, HAVAL, and Haraka-512 v2 hash functions and key recovery for full-round KTANTAN. An efficient approach to constructing MITM attacks is automation, which refers to modeling MITM characteristics and objectives into constraints and using optimizers to search for the best attack configuration. This work focuses on the simplification and renovation of the most advanced superposition framework based on Mixed-Integer Linear Programming (MILP) proposed at CRYPTO 2022. With the refined automation model, this work provides the first comprehensive analysis of the preimage security of hash functions based on all versions of the Rijndael block cipher, the origin of the Advanced Encryption Standard (AES), and improves the best-known results. Specifically, this work has extended the attack rounds of Rijndael 256-192 and 256-256, reduced the attack complexity of Rijndael 256-128 and 128-192 (AES192), and filled the gap of preimage security evaluation on Rijndael versions with a block size of 192 bits.

Keywords: Rijndael · Preimage · Hashing mode · MITM · MILP

1 Introduction

A hash function constructs a fixed-length message digest for an arbitrary-length plaintext. Hash functions have wide applications in cybersecurity infrastructure, including but not limited to, digital signatures, fingerprinting, authentication schemes, commitment schemes, and error correction codes. To be cryptographically secure, a hash function must satisfy the three fundamental security requirements: preimage resistance, second preimage resistance, and collision resistance.

A common strategy for building hash functions follows a two-step approach: first, a compression function is formed by inserting a block cipher into a PGV mode [2]; then, a hash function is constructed by iterating the compression function following the Merkle-Damgård paradigm. It is proven that the resulting hash function enjoys security reduction to the underlying encryption. Typical choices for the PGV mode include Davies-Meyer (DM), Matyas-Meyer-Oseas (MMO), and Miyaguchi-Preneel (MP). The strategy is highly practical since block ciphers

© The Author(s), under exclusive license to Springer Nature Switzerland AG 2023
J. Zhou et al. (Eds.): ACNS 2023 Workshops, LNCS 13907, pp. 23–42, 2023.
https://doi.org/10.1007/978-3-031-41181-6_2

and hash functions often coexist in an information system. The cost of implementing an additional hash function is minimized by applying only an extra mode to the already built-in block cipher.

This work focuses on the preimage security of hash functions built on the Rijndael block cipher. In 2001, NIST selected versions of the Rijndael block cipher with a block size of 128 bits for the Advanced Encryption Standard (AES) [1]. The MMO mode instantiated with AES has been standardized by Zigbee [3] and ISO [29] for building hash functions on block ciphers. The excellent performance and high security of Rijndael motivate dedicated designs built with a similar structure, for instance, Whirlpool [9], Grøstl [30], PHOTON [31] and LED [32].

1.1   The Meet-In-The-Middle (MITM) Technique

MITM is a well-referenced and well-developed cryptanalysis technique for preimage security analysis. The concept of MITM attacks originated from Diffie and Hellman's time-memory trade-off on double encryption [33]. Since its introduction, advanced techniques have been added to the MITM framework to exploit more freedom and structures, for instance, internal state guesses [34], splice-and-cut [4,16], initial structures [19] and indirect partial-matching [18,20].

Pioneered by Aumasson et al. [5] and Sasaki et al. [18,20], MITM has demonstrated its power in the preimage security analysis of hash functions, including but not limited to MD4 [16], MD5 [19], Tiger [16,23], HAVAL [26] and KAN-TAN [10,24]. The intuition of MITM is to divide the compression function into two independent chunks that "meet in the middle" at some matching point. A MITM attack feeds candidate texts into the two chunks independently and filters the preimage space according to the matching conditions.

In 2011, Sasaki et al. [17] mounted the first MITM preimage attack on AES-hashing. The attack circumvented the AES key schedule by fixing round keys to constants and reached 7 rounds for all AES versions. In [6], Bao et al. revisited the attack and retrieved degrees of freedom from the key schedule. The observation led to improvements in the attack rounds of AES-192 and AES-256, from 7 rounds to 8 rounds. In 2021, [7] drove MITM into automation with Mixed-Integer Linear Programming (MILP). The automatic model generalized and incorporated all enhancing tools of MITM attack, and improved 1 attack round for all best-known attacks on AES (8 rounds AES-128, 9 rounds AES-192, and 9 rounds AES-256). The automation model was then renovated in 2022 with a novel superposition framework that parallels linear operations [8]. The paper also presented new technologies to further empower the model and enlarge the search space, including Guess-and-Determine (GnD), Multiple Ways of AddRoundKey (MulAK), and Bi-Directional Attribute-Propagation and Cancellation (BiDir).

1.2   Contributions

While the preimage security of AES-hashing is a widely concerned and repeatedly investigated proposition in symmetric-key cryptanalysis, the resistance of hashing modes built on other versions of Rijndael against preimage attacks is rarely explored. This paper is thus dedicated to initiating the first comprehensive and comparative study of the preimage security of Rijndael-based hashing using MITM attacks, with a refined and enhanced automation model. Contributions include:

Lightweight Model. The automatic search of MITM attacks is extremely time-demanding and can only be partially optimized. Hence, model simplification has been a persistent endeavor for the community to unleash the full potential of automation. In 2022, the superposition structure [8] introduced two virtual states to separate forward and backward propagation for each intermediate state that undergoes linear operators. However, redundancies persist, since the encoding scheme used was originally proposed to address both propagations in one intermediate state. This work provides a dedicated lightweight encoding scheme for the superposition structure that enables simpler modeling of propagation rules, thus laying a solid foundation for the automation model to incorporate more techniques.

Mega-MC Match. In this paper, a new match rule, namely MEGA-MC-MATCH, is proposed to extend the traditional matching through the `MixColumns` operator at intermediate rounds. The MEGA-MC-MATCH further exploits the properties of the diffusion matrix and utilizes information that was previously considered ineligible for matching. The naming of the new match originates from its ability to extend the matching point from a single `MixColumns` operator to a 'mega'-variant that involves 3 rounds.

Accurate Key Schedule. There have been unaddressed dependencies in Rijndael's key schedule that might lead to inaccurate propagation patterns. In this work, such dependencies are identified, and a more accurate model of the Rijndael key schedule is provided. The new model is able to provide adequate treatment to equivalencies and dependencies in the key schedule and prevent repeated consumption of degrees of freedom.

Summary of Application Results. This work has achieved the following accomplishments: extended the maximum attack rounds of Rijndael 256-192 and 256-256 by 1 round, reduced the time complexity of 8-round Rijndael 128-192 (AES192) and 9-round Rijndael 256-128, and filled the gap of preimage security evaluation on Rijndael versions with 192-bit block size. Results are shown in Table 1. Note that due to the page limit, only the figure of a 10-round attack on Rijndael 256-256 is included. For more MITM attack figures, please find the full version uploaded to Cryptology ePrint Archive [43].

2   Preliminaries

2.1   The Rijndael Block Cipher

Versions. Rijndael is a family of iterated block ciphers developed by Belgian cryptographers Joan Daemen and Vincent Rijmen with different key sizes and

Table 1. Updated results on pseudo-preimage and preimage attacks.

Block length length	Key	Rounds	Pseudo-preimage	Preimage	Ref.
128	128	8/10	2^{120}	2^{125}	[7]
	192	8/12	2^{112}	2^{116}	[6]
		8/12	2^{104}	2^{117}	Fig. This work
		9/12	2^{112}	2^{121}	[8]
	256	10/14	2^{120}	2^{125}	[7]
192	128	9/12	2^{184}	2^{189}	This work
	192	9/14	2^{184}	2^{189}	This work
	256	9/14	2^{176}	2^{185}	This work
256	128	9/14	2^{248}	2^{253}	[7]
		9/14	2^{240}	2^{249}	This work
	192	9/14	2^{248}	2^{253}	[7]
		10/14	2^{248}	2^{253}	This work
	256	9/14	2^{248}	2^{253}	[7]
		10/14	2^{248}	2^{253}	Fig. 2

block sizes [1]. Rijndael supports a variety of combinations of block sizes and key sizes, which can be specified independently as 128, 192, or 256 bits. The intermediate result in the encryption is denoted as a *state* and the cipher key as the *key*. Intuitively, a *state* and the *key* can each be pictured as a 4-rowed rectangular array with 1 byte per entry. Conventionally, a column is referred to as a word, and the word size is thus fixed to 32 bits. *Nb* denotes the number of words in a *state* and *Nk* denotes that of the *key*. *Nr* denotes the iterated rounds, which is dependent on *Nb* and *Nk*. In 2001, NIST selected the versions of Rijndael with a 128-bit block length as the new symmetric key encryption standard (AES).

Round Operators. The Rijndael round function consists of 4 different operators:

SubBytes: A non-linear byte-wise substitution taking 1 byte as input and producing 1 byte as output. The input and the output byte are interpreted as polynomials on $GF(2^8)$ in their vector form. The S-Box contains two steps: the input a is first mapped to its multiplicative inverse a^{-1} in $GF(2^8)$. Then, a^{-1} is mapped to the output s by an affine transformation:

$$b = a^{-1} \oplus (a^{-1} \lll 1) \oplus (a^{-1} \lll 2) \oplus (a^{-1} \lll 3) \oplus (a^{-1} \lll 4) \oplus 63_{16}$$

ShiftRows: A linear transformation, visualized as a circular left shift on the rectangular array. The shift offsets for each row are dependent on *Nb*.

MixColumns: A column-wise linear transformation, described as a left multiplication in $GF(2^8)$ with a constant 4-by-4 maximum distance separable (MDS) matrix.

AddRoundKey: The bitwise XOR of the round key and the current state.

Key Schedule. The round keys are derived from the *key* by **KeySchedule** with two steps:

KeyExpansion The *key* is first expanded to an array of bytes w with $|w| = 4 \cdot Nb \cdot (Nr + 1)$. When $i < Nk$, $w[i] = key[i]$. Otherwise, the expansion follows the following equation, where *Rcon* is a constant array, and **Rot** is a permutation on the bytes:

$$w[i] = \begin{cases} w[i - Nk] \oplus \texttt{SubBytes}(\texttt{Rot}(w[i - 1])) \oplus Rcon[i/Nk] & i \bmod Nk \equiv 0 \\ w[i - Nk] \oplus \texttt{SubBytes}(w[i - 1]) & i \bmod Nk \equiv 4 \text{ and } Nk = 8 \\ w[i - Nk] \oplus w[i - 1] & \text{otherwise} \end{cases}$$
$$(1)$$

RoundKeySelection The round keys, each consisting of Nb words, are taken sequentially from w.

Although the round keys are generated one byte at a time, for easier illustration, a **KeySchedule** round is defined as the period when **KeyExpansion** produces an additional Nk words. The key schedule will iterate a total of $Nb*(Nr+1)/Nk$ rounds to generate all round keys. Each byte of a round key is uniquely indexed by (r, i, j) similar to encryption states, where r denotes the key schedule round, and (i, j) denotes the position of the cell on the key grid.

2.2 Preimage and Pseudo-preimage Attacks

A preimage attack finds a preimage of a given digest y for a hash function $\mathcal{H}$:

$$\text{Given } \mathcal{H} : X \to Y, \text{ for } y \in Y, \text{ find } x \in X, \text{ s.t. } \mathcal{H}(x) = y$$

For hash functions built with the Merkel-Damgård construction, a pseudo-preimage attack focuses on the underlying compression function. It finds a pair of messages x and a chaining value H that leads to the target digest y by the compression function $\mathcal{CF}$:

$$\text{Given } \mathcal{CF} : X \to Y, \text{ for } y \in Y, \text{ find } x \in X \text{ and } H \in Y, \text{ s.t. } \mathcal{CF}(H, x) = y$$

2.3 The MITM Pseudo-preimage Attack

The MITM technique is, in essence, used for finding pseudo-preimages. It makes use of the loop structure determined by PGV modes and divides a hash function into two independent functions, forward and backward. In each function, the involved bytes are categorized as:

 – neutral bytes, whose values are only known in the current function and have no influence on the other function.
 – constant bytes, whose values are predefined and globally known in both functions.

The two functions meet structurally in a shared intermediate state called the matching point. Constraints invoked at the matching point for the integrity of the closed loop are called partial-match constraints, which will be exploited as a filter to eliminate ineligible candidates. A full match check is performed only when partial-match constraints are satisfied. The generic MITM attack framework used in multiple references is reiterated as follows [6–8,12]:

1. Assign random values to constant bytes.
2. Determine the candidate values for the neutral bytes N_+ and N_-. Assume that there are 2^{d_1} candidates for N_+ and 2^{d_2} candidates for N_-.
3. For each of the 2^{d_1} candidates of N_+, compute the forward function and store the output at the matching point in a table T_+.
4. For each of the 2^{d_2} candidates of N_-, compute the backward function and store the output at the matching point in a table T_-.
5. Assume that there are 2^m constraints at the matching point. For the indices of T_+ and T_-, select pairs satisfying the 2^m partial-match constraints.
6. For the survived pairs, check for a full match.
7. If there exists a full match, a pseudo-preimage is found. Otherwise, revert to Step 1, change the arbitrary values, and repeat procedures 2 to 6.

The computational complexity of the attack is calculated as follows [6]:

$$2^{n-(d_1+d_2)} \cdot \left(2^{max(d_1,d_2)} + 2^{d_1+d_2-m}\right) \simeq 2^{n-min(d_1,d_2,m)} \tag{2}$$

2.4   Pseudo-preimage to Preimage Conversion

A pseudo-preimage attack with a computational complexity of 2^l ($l < n-2$) can be converted to a preimage attack with a computation complexity of $2^{(n+l)/2+1}$ [40]. To achieve this, $2^{(n-l)/2}$ pseudo-preimages are found. Next, starting from the initialization vector IV, $2^{(n+l)/2+1}$ random values are inserted into the hash function to generate $2^{(n+l)/2+1}$ chaining values. With $2^{(n+l)/2+1}$ chaining values mapped from the real IV and $2^{(n-l)/2}$ pseudo-preimages mapped to the target hash value, a match can be expected thanks to the birthday bound.

In 2008, Leurent improved the general unbalanced meet-in-the-middle method by constructing an unbalanced tree using multi-target pseudo-preimage and using the expandable message technique to overcome the length padding [41]. The overall time complexity is improved to $(n \ln 2 - l \ln 2 + 1) \cdot 2^l$. However, the method assumes a special unbalanced condition where 2^{l-t} computations yield 2^t pseudo-preimages.

3   MILP Modeling for Automated Search

This section describes how the search for MITM preimage attacks on Rijndael is automated with Mixed-Integer Linear Programming (MILP). This paper follows the conventional MITM coloring schemes for visualizing and demonstrating results [6–8,12,17]. A byte or a cell in an intermediate state or a round key is colored as follows:

- A blue cell (■) denotes a neutral byte for the forward function.
- A red cell (■) denotes a neutral byte for the backward function.
- A gray cell (■) denotes a constant byte.
- A white cell (□) denotes an arbitrary byte, incomputable in both functions.

3.1   Automated Search Framework

An overview of the automatic search framework of MITM attacks is provided before digging into the details. The essence of a MITM attack lies in the careful segmentation of the closed computation path. The special states in a MITM attack are identified using the following notations:

- $\overleftrightarrow{S}^{\text{ENC}}$: the starting encryption state for forward and backward functions.
- $\overleftrightarrow{S}^{\text{KSA}}$: the starting key schedule state for forward and backward functions.
- $\overrightarrow{End}$: the terminating state in encryption for the forward function.
- $\overleftarrow{End}$: the terminating state in encryption for the backward function.
- $\overleftrightarrow{M}^{\text{Match}}$: the matching round operator between the two terminating states.

The locations of the special states mentioned above represent different ways of segmenting the closed loop, hence uniquely determining the structure of a MITM attack. The locations are modeled with round-level precision. The attack configuration parameter *config* is defined as the ordered tuple with the following attributes:

- *Total*: the total attacked rounds.
- *EncSt*: the round index of $\overleftrightarrow{S}^{\text{ENC}}$.
- *KeySt*: the round index of $\overleftrightarrow{S}^{\text{KSA}}$.
- *Match*: the round index of $\overleftrightarrow{M}^{\text{Match}}$, $\overrightarrow{End}$ and $\overleftarrow{End}$.

To enable independent computations, the bytes (cells) in $\overleftrightarrow{S}^{\text{ENC}}$ and $\overleftrightarrow{S}^{\text{KSA}}$ are partitioned into subsets with different coloring $\mathcal{B}^{\text{ENC}}$, $\mathcal{R}^{\text{ENC}}$, $\mathcal{G}^{\text{ENC}}$ and $\mathcal{B}^{\text{KSA}}$, $\mathcal{R}^{\text{KSA}}$, $\mathcal{G}^{\text{KSA}}$ satisfying the following relations:

$$\mathcal{B}^{\text{ENC}} \cup \mathcal{R}^{\text{ENC}} \cup \mathcal{G}^{\text{ENC}} = \{0, 1, \ldots, Nb\}$$
$$\mathcal{B}^{\text{ENC}} \cap \mathcal{R}^{\text{ENC}} = \varnothing, \qquad \mathcal{R}^{\text{ENC}} \cap \mathcal{G}^{\text{ENC}} = \varnothing, \qquad \mathcal{G}^{\text{ENC}} \cap \mathcal{B}^{\text{ENC}} = \varnothing \tag{3}$$

$$\mathcal{B}^{\text{KSA}} \cup \mathcal{R}^{\text{KSA}} \cup \mathcal{G}^{\text{KSA}} = \{0, 1, \ldots, Nk\}$$
$$\mathcal{B}^{\text{KSA}} \cap \mathcal{R}^{\text{KSA}} = \varnothing, \qquad \mathcal{R}^{\text{KSA}} \cap \mathcal{G}^{\text{KSA}} = \varnothing, \qquad \mathcal{G}^{\text{KSA}} \cap \mathcal{B}^{\text{KSA}} = \varnothing \tag{4}$$

The initial degrees of freedom of forward and backward computations are denoted by $\overleftarrow{\iota}$ and $\overrightarrow{\iota}$. In the attribute propagation of each function, additional constraints may be imposed to cancel mutual impact and preserve functional independence. The consumed degrees of freedom (DOFs) are denoted as $\overrightarrow{\sigma}$ and $\overleftarrow{\sigma}$. The remaining DOFs at the end of each computation are denoted as $\overrightarrow{d_b}$ and $\overleftarrow{d_r}$. Relations can be formulated intuitively as follows:

$$\overrightarrow{\iota} = |\mathcal{B}^{\text{ENC}}| + |\mathcal{B}^{\text{KSA}}|, \qquad \overleftarrow{\iota} = |\mathcal{R}^{\text{ENC}}| + |\mathcal{R}^{\text{KSA}}| \tag{5}$$

$$\overrightarrow{d_b} = \overrightarrow{\iota} - \overrightarrow{\sigma}, \qquad \overleftarrow{d_r} = \overleftarrow{\iota} - \overleftarrow{\sigma} \tag{6}$$

The distribution of $\overleftrightarrow{M}^{\text{Match}}$, $\overrightarrow{End}$, and $\overleftarrow{End}$ decides the degree of matching $\overrightarrow{m}$. According to Eq. 2, $\min\{\overrightarrow{d_b}, \overleftarrow{d_r}, \overrightarrow{m}\}$ determines the complexity of a MITM attack. Thus, the search for the optimal MITM attack pattern of given *config* is converted to a maximization problem on objective τ_{Obj}:

$$\max_{config} \quad \tau_{\text{Obj}}$$

$$\text{s.t.} \quad \tau_{\text{Obj}} \leq \overrightarrow{d_b}$$
$$\tau_{\text{Obj}} \leq \overleftarrow{d_r} \tag{7}$$
$$\tau_{\text{Obj}} \leq \overrightarrow{m}$$
$$\tau_{\text{Obj}} > 0$$

Given an n-bit target, the pseudo-preimage attack complexity of an attack configuration $(\overrightarrow{d_b}, \overleftarrow{d_r}, \overrightarrow{m})$ will be (in the exponent of 2):

$$n - \min\{\overrightarrow{d_b}, \overleftarrow{d_r}, \overrightarrow{m}\}$$

A preimage attack can be constructed based on a pseudo-preimage attack with time complexity (in the exponent of 2) as follows:

$$\begin{cases} n - \min(\overrightarrow{d_b}, \overleftarrow{d_r}, \overrightarrow{m}) + \log_2(\min(\overrightarrow{d_b}, \overleftarrow{d_r})\ln 2 + 1) & \text{if } \min(\overrightarrow{d_b}, \overleftarrow{d_r}) < \overrightarrow{m} \\ n - \min(\overrightarrow{d_b}, \overleftarrow{d_r}, \overrightarrow{m})/2 + 1 & \text{otherwise} \end{cases} \tag{8}$$

3.2   The Superposition State Structure

For an intermediate state around linear operators, the superposition structure [8] introduces two superposition states, each carrying the propagation of only one function. The rationale behind the separation is due to the linearity of the operators. An intermediate state and its superposition states are denoted as s, s_F, and s_B. If there is a bilinear function λ such that $s = \lambda(s_F, s_B)$, then s propagating through a Rijndael linear operator χ is expressed as $\chi(s) = \chi(\lambda(s_F, s_B))$. For deterministic bilinear function $\lambda' = \chi\lambda(\chi^{-1} \times \chi^{-1})$, $\chi(s)$ can be expressed as $\chi(s) = \lambda'(\chi(s_F), \chi(s_B))$. Hence, the propagation of the intermediate state is equivalent to propagating two superposition states independently if the superposition states are bilinearly associated before. However, such parallel propagation must end when undergoing non-linear operators where the linear relation between two propagation trails will be destroyed.

Specifically, the superposition structure is deployed in Rijndael with the following heuristic:

1. The single state separates into two superposition states after `SubBytes`.
2. The superposition states propagate independently through other operators.
3. The superposition states collapse to a single state.
4. The single state propagates through `SubBytes`.

The superposition technique automatically supports the BiDir technique [8], which generalizes DOF consumptions in forward and backward computations.

3.3 Simplified Encoding Scheme

The conventional encoding scheme [7,8] used two encoders x and y to encode different coloring: $\square = (0,0)$, $\blacksquare = (1,0)$, $\blacksquare = (0,1)$, $\blacksquare = (1,1)$. To uniquely identify $\square$ and $\blacksquare$, two additional encoders are used:

$$g = x \vee y, \qquad w = 1 + g - x - y \qquad (9)$$

The $x-y-g-w$ encoding allows redundancies in the superposition structure. First, the scheme was originally introduced to cover two propagations simultaneously at a single state. However, in superposition states, attribute propagation no longer requires information from both functions. In other words, $\blacksquare$ will never appear in the backward computation and $\blacksquare$ in the forward computation. Second, the identification of $\square$ and $\blacksquare$ (g and w encoders) is complex in implementation and difficult for preprocessing.

In this work, a symmetric and efficient encoding scheme is proposed dedicated to the superposition structure. The scheme involves two variables α and β:

- α: equals 1 if and only if the byte could be calculated in the current function.
- β: equals 1 if and only if the exact value of the byte is known in the current function.

It is easy to observe that $\beta = 1$ is a stronger condition than $\alpha = 1$. Therefore, $\beta \leq \alpha$ is enforced. The propagation is symmetrically encoded as: $\blacksquare$ or $\blacksquare$ $(\alpha, \beta) = (1,0)$, $\blacksquare$ $(\alpha, \beta) = (1,1)$ and $\square$ $(\alpha, \beta) = (0,0)$. In this encoding scheme, $\beta = 1$ uniquely identifies $\blacksquare$, and $\alpha = 0$ uniquely identifies $\square$.

Due to the symmetric nature of the encoding, in subsequent sections, the MILP engraving of propagation rules will only be detailed for the forward computation. The rules for backward computation are autonomous.

Modelling the Start and End of Superposition States. ENTERSUP-RULE describes the separation of a single state $s = (x, y)$ into two superposition states $s_F = (\alpha_F, \beta_F)$ and $s_B = (\alpha_B, \beta_B)$ with the $\alpha - \beta$ encoding. The separation is performed byte-wise: If a byte s is $\square$ or $\blacksquare$, then s_F and s_B are both arbitrary or constant, either way, s_F and s_B share the same coloring as s. Suppose s is $\blacksquare$ or $\blacksquare$, which means that the color of s is preserved in the corresponding computation and the other direction will be compensated with $\blacksquare$ symbolically, indicating a constant influence:

$$(\alpha_F, \beta_F) = (x \vee y, y), \qquad (\alpha_B, \beta_B) = (x \vee y, x) \qquad (10)$$

Before `SubBytes`, the EXITSUP-RULE collapses the two virtual states $s_F = (\alpha_F, \beta_F)$ and $s_B = (\alpha_B, \beta_B)$ into a single state $s = (x, y)$ before `SubBytes`. If the collapsed state is influenced by an arbitrary byte or by both the forward and the backward computations, the state is arbitrary. The rule is formulated as follows:

$$(x, y) = (\alpha_F \wedge \beta_B, \alpha_B \wedge \beta_F) \qquad (11)$$

Modelling `SubBytes` and `ShiftRows`. The `SubBytes` operator itself does not change the attribute of the cells. As long as the superposition states are collapsed properly before `SubBytes`, the operator does an identity transformation on the coloring. The `ShiftRows` operator permutes the state cells according to some predefined constants and thus can be modeled by a set of equalities between dedicated variables or some hardcoded variable substitutions, both of which are intuitive and autonomous.

Modelling `AddRoundKey`. XOR is the basic operator in `AddRoundKey`, which takes two cells as input and outputs one cell. Under the $\alpha - \beta$ encoding, the XOR-RULE could be simplified compared to previous works [7,8]. The rule is described as follows:

- When the inputs contain $\square$, the output is $\square$.
- When the inputs are both $\blacksquare$, the output is $\blacksquare$.
- Otherwise, the output is:
  - $\blacksquare$, with no consumption of DOF.
  - $\blacksquare$, consuming 1 DOF of the forward computation.($\overrightarrow{\sigma} = \overrightarrow{\sigma} + 1$)

The above description is converted to constraints by the convex-hull method [22]. The resulting inequalities should involve the following variables: the (α, β)-encoders of both inputs and the output together with an indicator variable to track DOF consumptions.

Modelling the `KeyExpansion`. KEYXOR-RULE is introduced to identify and address dependencies in the `KeySchedule`. Recall Eq. 1, a node $w[i]$ in `KeyExpansion` has two parents: $w[i-1]$ and $w[i-Nk]$. If the index i satisfies the condition:

$$i \not\equiv \begin{cases} 0 & Nk \leq 6 \\ 0, 4 & Nk > 6 \end{cases}, \quad (\bmod\ Nk) \tag{12}$$

$w[i] = w[i-Nk] \oplus w[i-1]$. If the same condition holds for $i-1$, $w[i]$ can be expressed using only $w[i-2Nk]$ and $w[i-2]$:

$$\begin{aligned} w[i] &= w[i-Nk] \oplus w[i-1] \\ &= w[i-2Nk] \oplus w[i-Nk-1] \oplus w[i-Nk-1] \oplus w[i-2] \\ &= w[i-2Nk] \oplus w[i-2] \end{aligned} \tag{13}$$

Note that the middle term $w[i-Nk-1]$ cancels due to the consecutive XORs without confusion. However, since the basic XOR-RULE sequentially obtains the parents of $w[i]$ and then $w[i]$ itself, the coloring of $w[i-Nk-1]$ will still affect $w[i]$. For instance, if $w[i-Nk-1]$ is $\square$ while $w[i-2Nk]$ and $w[i-2]$ are $\blacksquare$ or $\blacksquare$, then $w[i]$ will be miscolored to $\square$. Moreover, if $w[i-2Nk]$ and $w[i-2]$ are both $\blacksquare$ and $w[i-Nk-1]$ is $\blacksquare$, $w[i]$ will be miscolored as $\blacksquare$ or waste an unnecessary DOF to cancel impact by turning $\blacksquare$. To address such dependencies, two additional encoders α_{eq} and β_{eq} are introduced for KEYXOR-RULE:

$$\begin{aligned} \alpha_{eq} &= \begin{cases} \min(\alpha^{w[i-2Nk]}, \alpha^{w[i-2]}) & i, i-1 \text{ s.t. condition12} \\ 0 & \text{otherwise} \end{cases} \\ \beta_{eq} &= \begin{cases} \min(\beta^{w[i-2Nk]}, \beta^{w[i-2]}) & i, i-1 \text{ s.t. condition12} \\ 0 & \text{otherwise} \end{cases} \end{aligned} \tag{14}$$

Due to the enforced constraint $\beta \leq \alpha$, it follows that $\beta_{eq} \leq \alpha_{eq}$. The KEYXOR-RULE is defined as follows:

- When $\beta_{eq} = 0$, and $\alpha_{eq} = 0$, apply the XOR-RULE with respect to $w[i-1]$ and $w[i-Nk]$
- When $\beta_{eq} = 0$, and $\alpha_{eq} = 1$, apply the XOR-RULE with respect to $w[i-1]$ and $w[i-Nk]$, but override the coloring of the output cell whenever the inputs contain $\square$ as follows:
  - $\blacksquare$, without consumption of DOF.
  - $\blacksquare$, consuming 1 DOF from the forward computations. ($\overrightarrow{\sigma} = \overrightarrow{\sigma} + 1$)
- When $\beta_{eq} = 1$, and $\alpha_{eq} = 1$, the output is $\blacksquare$ without DOF consumption.

The above description is also translated into constraints by the convex-hull method. The inequalities involve the (α, β) encoders of the two inputs and one output, the equivalence encoders α_{eq}, β_{eq}, as well as an indicator variable to track DOF consumption.

Modeling `MixColumns`. A `MixColumns` operator takes a column as input and outputs a column. The propagation rule is described as follows:

- When the inputs contain $\square$, the outputs are all $\square$.
- When the inputs are all $\blacksquare$, the outputs are all $\blacksquare$.
- Otherwise, the output will be (WLOG, in forward computation):
    - 4 blue cells ($\blacksquare$), without consumption of DOF.
    - b blue ($\blacksquare$) cells and g gray ($\blacksquare$) cells, with $b+g=4$ and $g>1$, consuming forward DOF(s) [7].

In [7,8], realizing above rules with $x - y - g - w$ encoding requires three additional columnwise encoders μ, ν, ω. The input column is superscripted I and the output column O. The exact implementation is shown as follows:

$$
\begin{cases}
\sum_{i=0}^{3} x_i^O + 4 \cdot \omega \leq 4 \\
\sum_{i=0}^{3} (x_i^I + x_i^O) - 8 \cdot \mu \geq 0 \\
\sum_{i=0}^{3} (x_i^I + x_i^O) - 5 \cdot \mu \leq NIO - Br \\
\sum_{i=0}^{3} y_i^O + 4 \cdot \omega \leq 4 \\
\sum_{i=0}^{3} (y_i^I + y_i^O) - 8 \cdot \nu \geq 0 \\
\sum_{i=0}^{3} (y_i^I + y_i^O) - 5 \cdot \nu \leq 3 \\
\sum_{i=0}^{3} x_i^O - 4 \cdot \mu = cost_F \\
\sum_{i=0}^{3} y_i^O - 4 \cdot \nu = cost_B
\end{cases}
\tag{15}
$$

The modeling of the `MixColumns` operator can be simplified using the new encoding scheme. Only two additional encoders κ and ψ are introduced to provide quick identification of a column being all $\blacksquare$ or existing $\square$:

$$
\begin{aligned}
\kappa &= \min_i(\alpha_i^I) \\
\psi &= \min_i(\beta_i^I)
\end{aligned}
\tag{16}
$$

By definition, $\kappa = 0$ if and only if there is $\square$ among the input, and $\psi = 1$ if and only if the inputs are all $\blacksquare$. The MC-RULE is thus defined minimally:

$$
\begin{aligned}
\alpha_i^O &= \kappa \\
\beta_i^O &= \psi + \varsigma_i
\end{aligned}
\tag{17}
$$

The binary cost variables ς_i are byte-wise, as an indication of whether a cost of DOF occurs locally for a single cell, instead of integer-valued $cost_F$ and $cost_B$ tracking the total cost for the whole column in previous models [7].

To achieve maximum speedup, the modeling does not provide extra treatment in special scenarios where the actual cost of DOF is less than $\sum_i \varsigma_i$. For example, if the inputs consist of 1 $\blacksquare$ and 3 $\blacksquare$, then the outputs will be all $\blacksquare$ with 1 DOF cost, as the inputs only have 1 DOF. In the above modeling, the total cost will still be 4 since the cost of DOF is counted byte-wise. However, since the MILP model is globally optimized, such a propagation pattern in this model will be equivalent to turning the only ■ in the `MixColumns` inputs to ▨ during the last `AddRoundKey` operator, consuming 1 DOF. By doing so, the input column of `MixColumns` will be all ▨ and the global DOF cost remains the same. Hence, the special scenario is neglected to maintain minimal construction.

Modeling the Matching. There are three types of matching rules used in this work:

- ID-MATCH: identity match in the last round.
- MC-MATCH: match through a single `MixColumns` operator.
- MEGAMC-MATCH: match through a mega-`MixColumns` operator.

Following traditional notations, the cell locates at the i-th row and the j-th column is indexed by $n = 4 \cdot j + i$.

The ID-MATCH happens checks $\overrightarrow{End}$ and $\overleftarrow{End}$ byte by byte in single states, a matching happens when at index n $\overrightarrow{End}[n]$ and $\overleftarrow{End}[n]$ are not □.

The MC-MATCH checks $\overrightarrow{End}$ and $\overleftarrow{End}$ column by column in superposition states: $\overrightarrow{End}_F$, $\overrightarrow{End}_B$, $\overleftarrow{End}_F$, $\overleftarrow{End}_B$. $\zeta_{i,j} = 1$ if and only if at index $n = 4 \cdot j + i$ the forward branch and backward branch are both non-arbitrary $(\overrightarrow{End}_F[n], \overrightarrow{End}_B[n] \in \{■, ▨, ▨\})$. Due to the fact that the `MixColumns` operator has branch number 5, a linear constraint can be constructed when the input and output columns contain 5 eligible bytes, [7]. And one more linear constraint can always be constructed with one more eligible byte than 5. Hence, the rules for MC-MATCH are formulated as follows: a match occurs in column k if: $\sum_{i=1}^{4} \zeta_{i,k} > 4$ with matching degree $m_k = \sum_{i=1}^{4} \zeta_{i,k} - 4$.

The MEGAMC-MATCH is proposed as an extension of MC-MATCH. In the automatic search for long-round MITM attacks, the bottleneck often lies in $\overrightarrow{m}\overleftarrow{}$. The intention of the new match is to exploit □ for matching, which was deemed impossible in previous works, and to increase $\overrightarrow{m}\overleftarrow{}$. $\overrightarrow{End}$ and $\overleftarrow{End}$ are investigated column by column in single states. The input and output columns are denoted X and Y. Then the `MixColumns` operator could be expressed as follows:

$$\mathcal{M}X = Y \tag{18}$$

Equation 18 is equivalent to 19 if X and Y are viewed as inputs:

$$[\mathcal{M} \mid - I_4][X \mid Y] = \mathbf{0} \tag{19}$$

Clearly, the $4 * 8$ matrix $[\mathcal{M} \mid - I_4]$ has a rank 4. Thus, if there exists 4 ■, the exact values of X and Y are known in the forward computation regardless of the coloring. The forward computation can be reverted back from $\overleftarrow{M}^{\texttt{Match}}$ and the matching can be extended to the last superposition states on both sides of $\overleftrightarrow{M}^{\texttt{Match}}$, as illustrated in the diagram below:

$$X'_F, X'_B \xrightarrow{SupP} X' \xrightarrow[\texttt{ShiftRows}]{\texttt{SubBytes}_1} X \overset{match}{\leftrightarrow} Y \xleftarrow[\texttt{AddRoundKey}]{\texttt{SubBytes}_2} Y' \xleftarrow{SupP} Y'_F, Y'_B$$

The matching is equivalently considered as the match between X' and X'_F, X'_B through $\texttt{SubBytes}_1$, and between Y' and $Y'F, Y'B$ through $\texttt{SubBytes}_2$. For instance, in Fig. 1, due to the 4 ■ in $\overrightarrow{End}$ and $\overleftarrow{End}$, all the green circled cells are known in the forward computation. The information in $\overrightarrow{End}[7]$ can be backtracked to $SB^6[3]$, and a partial match constraint can be constructed as: $\texttt{SubBytes}(SB^6_F[3] \oplus SB^6_B[3]) = SB^6[3]$

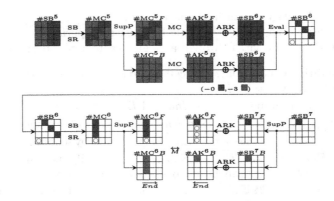

Fig. 1. Example of MegaMC-Match

Using $\zeta_{i,X'}$ and $\zeta_{i,Y'}$ to mark the eligible cells for X' and Y', the degree of match under MegaMC-Match is $m_k = \sum_{i=1}^{4} \zeta_{i,X'} + \zeta_{i,Y'} - 4$, since constructing the relation between X and Y will consume 4 DOFs. Note that to revert the calculations from Y' to Y and produce an eligible byte, the round key at the corresponding position must be ■ or ▨.

4   Application to Rijndael

The preimage security of all versions of Rijndael-based hash functions is assessed with the refined and enhanced automation model. The Rijndael versions are indexed first by block size and then by key size, e.g. Rijndael 128-192 denotes the version of AES192. The results are given in Table 1.

During the automatic search, the BiDir technique and the MegaMC-Match are critical techniques for better attack strategies. The Guess-and-Determine (GnD) strategy [8] and the Multiple AddRoundKey (MulAK) technique [8] are tested in the automatic search, both fail in yielding better results, either in attack rounds or complexity. The observation is in line with the declared Critical Tech. in Table 1 of [8].

In the figures, the intermediate states are indexed according to the type of operator to which they input, and the round index (i.e. SB^8 denotes the intermediate state immediately before the $\texttt{SubBytes}$ operator in round 8). The special state AT denotes the intermediate state before XORing of a known text and the whitening key. Again, following traditional notation, a cell locates at the i-th row and the j-th column is indexed by $n = 4 \cdot j + i$.

4.1 Example: Pseudo-preimage Attack on 10-Round Rijndael 256-256

The MITM attack procedures are demonstrated using Fig. 2, which depicts a pseudo-preimage attack on 10-round Rijndael 256-256. The attack starts with the precomputation of blue and red initial values. Recall that during propagation, certain cells are imposed constraints to preserve propagation trails, represented by the consumption of DOF and the coloring of ■. A MITM attack fixes the value of such ■ beforehand and precomputes the initial values satisfying those constraints.

Precomputation of Red Initial Values. First, KS^4 and MC^3 are equivalently chosen as $\overleftrightarrow{S}^{\text{KSA}}$ and $\overleftrightarrow{S}^{\text{ENC}}$ in backward computation, i.e. $\mathcal{G}^{\text{KSA}} = \{9, 11, 23\}$, $\mathcal{R}^{\text{KSA}} = \{0, 1, \ldots, 31\} \setminus \mathcal{G}^{\text{KSA}}$, $\mathcal{R}^{\text{ENC}} = \{0, 1, 2, 3, 12, 13, 14, 15, 24, 25, 26, 27, 28, 29, 30, 31\}$. All round keys can be expressed with free variables at $\mathcal{R}^{\text{KSA}}$ and predefined constants at $\mathcal{G}^{\text{KSA}} = \{kc_0^r, kc_1^r, kc_2^r\}$. There are two additional constraints imposed by ■ at $KS^7[9] = kc_3^r$ and $KS^9[1] = kc_4^r$. A dependency in the key schedule appears at $KS^9[9]$: when $KS^7[9]$ and $KS^9[1]$ are ■, $KS^9[9] = KS^8[9] \oplus KS^9[5] = KS^7[9] \oplus KS^9[1] = kc_3^r + kc_4^r$ is ■ without DOF consumption. It is clear that the KEYXOR-RULE outperforms basic XOR-RULE since the position ■ is essential for the forward propagation of $SB^9[9]$.

For encryption states, the active inputs on $\mathcal{R}^{\text{ENC}}$ can be constrained according to the predefined constants $c_{0,\ldots 41}^r$ locate at $SB_B^4[4, 5, 17, 18]$, $SB_B^5[5]$, $SB_B^6[0, 1, 2, 3, 17]$, $SB_B^7[2, 12, 17, 20, 22, 29, 31]$, $SB_B^8[13, 22, 27]$, $MC_B^0[1]$, $MC_B^1[0, 19, 22, 29]$, and $MC_B^2[0, 3, 6, 7, 10, 13, 15, 16, 17, 18, 19, 20, 22, 25, 28, 29]$.

To sum up, in backward computations, a total of $\overleftarrow{\sigma} = 47$ constraints have been added for $\overleftarrow{\iota} = 48$ variables according to the chosen values of predefined constants, leaving 2^8 valid candidates.

Precomputation of Blue Initial Values. The precomputation of blue initial values is straightforward. $SB_F^5[5]$ can be selected equivalently to $\overleftrightarrow{S}^{\text{ENC}}$, and since are no constraints on $SB_F^5[5]$, all 2^8 candidates are valid. To simplify the forward propagation trail, the cost of DOF at MC^3 can be equivalently transferred to AK^3. Consequently, all cells in the forward computation can be expressed using the active byte $SB_F^5[5]$ and the predefined constants $c_{0,\ldots 14}^b$ located at $SB_F^5[4, 6, 7]$ and $SB_F^4[5, 6, 7, 8, 10, 11, 16, 17, 19, 20, 21, 22]$.

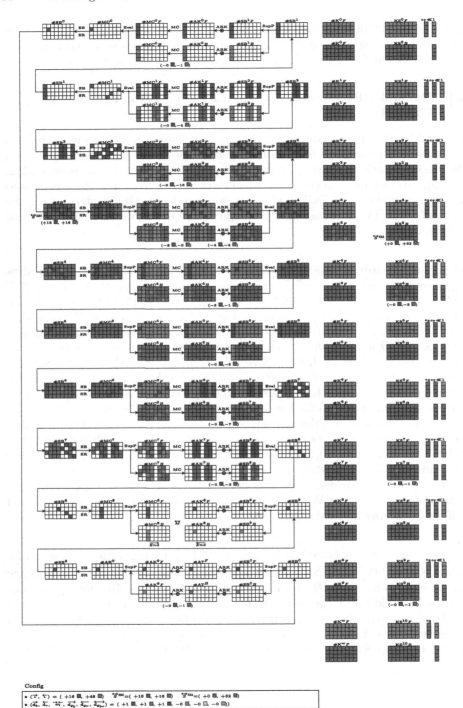

Fig. 2. A 10-round attack on Rijndael 256-256 with search objective 1.

The Pseudo-preimage Attack Procedure. The pseudo-preimage attack is performed as follows:

1. Select an untested set of predefined values for $c^r_{0,\ldots 41}$, $c^b_{0,\ldots 14}$, and $kc^r_{0,\ldots 4}$ from the pool of size 2^x, and initialize forward and backward lists L^f and L^B to empty.
2. Fix the symbolic gray cells $MC^5_F[0, 1, 2, 3, 8, 9, \ldots 31]$ as zeroes.
3. Feed the 2^8 candidates for forward computations into the computation path and compute to the matching point (i.e. $MC^8[9, 10, 11]$ and $AK^8[9]$).
4. With the 4 known blue cells at the matching point, calculate $MC^8[8] = AK^8[9] - 2MC^8[9] - 3MC^8[10] - MC^8[11]$ and subsequently $SB^8[8] = \mathtt{SubBytes}(MC^8[8])$.
5. Store the candidates for forward computations into L^f, index by the value of $SB^8[8]$ and $SB^8_F[8]$.
6. Fix the symbolic gray cells $MC^3_B[4, 5, 6, 7, 8, 9, 10, 11, 16, 17, 18, 19, 20, 21, 22, 23]$ as zeros.
7. Feed the 2^8 candidates for backward computations into the computation path and compute to SB^8_B.
8. Store the candidates for backward computations into L^B, index by the value of $SB^8_B[8]$.
9. Check L^F and L^B for partial-match by testing if $SB^8[8]] = \mathtt{SubBytes}(SB^8_F[8] \oplus SB^8_B[8])$. A total of 2^8 candidates is expected to remain in $L^F \times L^B$ ($2^8 = 2^8 \cdot 2^8 / \overrightarrow{m}$).
10. Check the 2^8 candidates for a full match. If a full match is found, exit with the obtained pseudo-preimage of the given target. Otherwise, repeat procedures from 1 to 9.

Computational Complexity. A remnant of 2^8 candidates (combined forward and backward) that satisfies the 8-bit partial-match can be obtained with one selection from the pool of 2^x potential predefined constant values. The value of x is calculated by $x = 256 - \overrightarrow{d_b} - \overleftarrow{d_r} = 240$. Thus, the time complexity of the above pseudo-preimage attack is $2^{x+8} = 2^{248}$. And by Eq. 8, the time complexity of the converted preimage attack is calculated as $2^{(256+248)/2+1} = 2^{253}$.

5   Conclusions

This work has further refined the MILP modeling of the automatic search of preimage attacks on the Rijndael structure. It has introduced a dedicated and lightweight encoding scheme for the superposition structure [8]. With new matching methods and treatment of dependencies in Rijndael's key schedule incorporated, this work has mounted the first comprehensive study on all versions of Rijndael-based hashing. This work has successfully replicated all referenced attacks and found improvements.

Further studies should focus on exploring and addressing more complex dependencies among neutral bytes to save repeated consumptions of DOFs, as well as discovering equivalence in attack patterns and pruning the search space.

References

1. Daemen, J., Rijmen, V. AES proposal: Rijndael. In: NIST AES Proposal (1999)
2. Preneel, B., Govaerts, R., Vandewalle, J.: Hash functions based on block ciphers: a synthetic approach. In: Stinson, D.R. (ed.) CRYPTO 1993. LNCS, vol. 773, pp. 368–378. Springer, Heidelberg (1994). https://doi.org/10.1007/3-540-48329-2_31
3. ZigBee Alliance. ZigBee Specification. ZigBee Document 053474r17 (2007). http://www.zigbee.org/
4. Aoki, K., Sasaki, Yu.: Preimage attacks on one-block MD4, 63-step MD5 and more. In: Avanzi, R.M., Keliher, L., Sica, F. (eds.) SAC 2008. LNCS, vol. 5381, pp. 103–119. Springer, Heidelberg (2009). https://doi.org/10.1007/978-3-642-04159-4_7
5. Aumasson, J.-P., Meier, W., Mendel, F.: Preimage attacks on 3-pass HAVAL and step-reduced MD5. In: Avanzi, R.M., Keliher, L., Sica, F. (eds.) SAC 2008. LNCS, vol. 5381, pp. 120–135. Springer, Heidelberg (2009). https://doi.org/10.1007/978-3-642-04159-4_8
6. Bao, Z., Ding, L., Guo, J., Wang, H., Zhang, W.: Improved meet-in-the-middle preimage attacks against AES hashing modes. In: ToSC 2019, pp. 318–347 (2019)
7. Bao, Z., et al.: Automatic search of meet-in-the-middle preimage attacks on AES-like hashing. In: Canteaut, A., Standaert, F.-X. (eds.) EUROCRYPT 2021, Part I. LNCS, vol. 12696, pp. 771–804. Springer, Cham (2021). https://doi.org/10.1007/978-3-030-77870-5_27
8. Bao, Z., Guo, J., Shi, D., Tu, Y.: Superposition meet-in-the-middle attacks: updates on fundamental security of AES-like hashing. In: Dodis, Y., Shrimpton, T. (eds.) CRYPTO 2022, Part I. LNCS, vol. 13507, pp. 64–93. Springer, Cham (2022). https://doi.org/10.1007/978-3-031-15802-5_3
9. Barreto, P.S., Rijmen, V.: The Whirlpool hashing function. In: First open NESSIE Workshop, vol. 13, pp. 14. Citeseer (2000)
10. Bogdanov, A., Rechberger, C.: A 3-subset meet-in-the-middle attack: cryptanalysis of the lightweight block cipher KTANTAN. In: Biryukov, A., Gong, G., Stinson, D.R. (eds.) SAC 2010. LNCS, vol. 6544, pp. 229–240. Springer, Heidelberg (2011). https://doi.org/10.1007/978-3-642-19574-7_16
11. Bouillaguet, C., Derbez, P., Fouque, P.-A.: Automatic search of attacks on round-reduced AES and applications. In: Rogaway, P. (ed.) CRYPTO 2011. LNCS, vol. 6841, pp. 169–187. Springer, Heidelberg (2011). https://doi.org/10.1007/978-3-642-22792-9_10
12. Dong, X., Hua, J., Sun, S., Li, Z., Wang, X., Hu, L.: Meet-in-the-middle attacks revisited: key-recovery, collision, and preimage attacks. In: Malkin, T., Peikert, C. (eds.) CRYPTO 2021, Part III. LNCS, vol. 12827, pp. 278–308. Springer, Cham (2021). https://doi.org/10.1007/978-3-030-84252-9_10
13. Fuhr, T., Minaud, B.: Match box meet-in-the-middle attack against KATAN. In: Cid, C., Rechberger, C. (eds.) FSE 2014. LNCS, vol. 8540, pp. 61–81. Springer, Heidelberg (2015). https://doi.org/10.1007/978-3-662-46706-0_4
14. Gauravaram, P., et al. Grøstl a SHA-3 candidate (2009). http://www.groestl.info/Groestl.pdf
15. Gilbert, H., Peyrin, T.: Super-Sbox cryptanalysis: improved attacks for AES-like permutations. In: Hong, S., Iwata, T. (eds.) FSE 2010. LNCS, vol. 6147, pp. 365–383. Springer, Heidelberg (2010). https://doi.org/10.1007/978-3-642-13858-4_21
16. Guo, J., Ling, S., Rechberger, C., Wang, H.: Advanced meet-in-the-middle preimage attacks: first results on full tiger, and improved results on MD4 and SHA-2. In: Abe, M. (ed.) ASIACRYPT 2010. LNCS, vol. 6477, pp. 56–75. Springer, Heidelberg (2010). https://doi.org/10.1007/978-3-642-17373-8_4

17. Sasaki, Yu.: Meet-in-the-middle preimage attacks on AES hashing modes and an application to whirlpool. In: Joux, A. (ed.) FSE 2011. LNCS, vol. 6733, pp. 378–396. Springer, Heidelberg (2011). https://doi.org/10.1007/978-3-642-21702-9_22
18. Sasaki, Yu., Aoki, K.: Preimage attacks on 3, 4, and 5-pass HAVAL. In: Pieprzyk, J. (ed.) ASIACRYPT 2008. LNCS, vol. 5350, pp. 253–271. Springer, Heidelberg (2008). https://doi.org/10.1007/978-3-540-89255-7_16
19. Sasaki, Yu., Aoki, K.: Finding preimages in full MD5 faster than exhaustive search. In: Joux, A. (ed.) EUROCRYPT 2009. LNCS, vol. 5479, pp. 134–152. Springer, Heidelberg (2009). https://doi.org/10.1007/978-3-642-01001-9_8
20. Sasaki, Yu., Aoki, K.: Preimage attacks on step-reduced MD5. In: Mu, Y., Susilo, W., Seberry, J. (eds.) ACISP 2008. LNCS, vol. 5107, pp. 282–296. Springer, Heidelberg (2008). https://doi.org/10.1007/978-3-540-70500-0_21
21. Sasaki, Y., Wang, L., Wu, S., Wu, W.: Investigating fundamental security requirements on whirlpool: improved preimage and collision attacks. In: Wang, X., Sako, K. (eds.) ASIACRYPT 2012. LNCS, vol. 7658, pp. 562–579. Springer, Heidelberg (2012). https://doi.org/10.1007/978-3-642-34961-4_34
22. Sun, S., Hu, L., Wang, P., Qiao, K., Ma, X., Song, L.: Automatic security evaluation and (related-key) differential characteristic search: application to SIMON, PRESENT, LBlock, DES(L) and other bit-oriented block ciphers. In: Sarkar, P., Iwata, T. (eds.) ASIACRYPT 2014. LNCS, vol. 8873, pp. 158–178. Springer, Heidelberg (2014). https://doi.org/10.1007/978-3-662-45611-8_9
23. Wang, L., Sasaki, Yu.: Finding preimages of tiger up to 23 steps. In: Hong, S., Iwata, T. (eds.) FSE 2010. LNCS, vol. 6147, pp. 116–133. Springer, Heidelberg (2010). https://doi.org/10.1007/978-3-642-13858-4_7
24. Wei, L., Rechberger, C., Guo, J., Wu, H., Wang, H., Ling, S.: Improved meet-in-the-middle cryptanalysis of KTANTAN (Poster). In: Parampalli, U., Hawkes, P. (eds.) ACISP 2011. LNCS, vol. 6812, pp. 433–438. Springer, Heidelberg (2011). https://doi.org/10.1007/978-3-642-22497-3_31
25. Wu, S., Feng, D., Wu, W., Guo, J., Dong, L., Zou, J.: (Pseudo) preimage attack on round-reduced Grøstl hash function and others. In: Canteaut, A. (ed.) FSE 2012. LNCS, vol. 7549, pp. 127–145. Springer, Heidelberg (2012). https://doi.org/10.1007/978-3-642-34047-5_8
26. Guo, J., Su, C., Yap, W.: An improved preimage attack against HAVAL-3. Inf. Process. Lett. 115(2), 386–393 (2015)
27. Mouha, N., Wang, Q., Gu, D., Preneel, B.: Differential and linear cryptanalysis using mixed-integer linear programming. In: Wu, C.-K., Yung, M., Lin, D. (eds.) Inscrypt 2011. LNCS, vol. 7537, pp. 57–76. Springer, Heidelberg (2012). https://doi.org/10.1007/978-3-642-34704-7_5
28. Jean, J.: TikZ for cryptographers (2016). https://www.iacr.org/authors/tikz/
29. ISO/IEC. Information technology - Security techniques - Hash-functions - Part 2: Hash-functions using an n-bit block cipher
30. Gauravaram, P., et al.: Grøstl-a SHA-3 candidate. In: Dagstuhl Seminar Proceedings (2009)
31. Guo, J., Peyrin, T., Poschmann, A.: The PHOTON family of lightweight hash functions. In: Rogaway, P. (ed.) CRYPTO 2011. LNCS, vol. 6841, pp. 222–239. Springer, Heidelberg (2011). https://doi.org/10.1007/978-3-642-22792-9_13
32. Guo, J., Peyrin, T., Poschmann, A., Robshaw, M.: The LED block cipher. In: Preneel, B., Takagi, T. (eds.) CHES 2011. LNCS, vol. 6917, pp. 326–341. Springer, Heidelberg (2011). https://doi.org/10.1007/978-3-642-23951-9_22
33. Diffie, W., Hellman, M.E.: Special feature exhaustive cryptanalysis of the NBS data encryption standard. Computer 10(6), 74–84 (1977)

34. Dunkelman, O., Sekar, G., Preneel, B.: Improved meet-in-the-middle attacks on reduced-round DES. In: Srinathan, K., Rangan, C.P., Yung, M. (eds.) INDOCRYPT 2007. LNCS, vol. 4859, pp. 86–100. Springer, Heidelberg (2007). https://doi.org/10.1007/978-3-540-77026-8_8

35. Wagner, D.: The boomerang attack. In: Knudsen, L. (ed.) FSE 1999. LNCS, vol. 1636, pp. 156–170. Springer, Heidelberg (1999). https://doi.org/10.1007/3-540-48519-8_12

36. Mendel, F., Rechberger, C., Schläffer, M., Thomsen, S.S.: The rebound attack: cryptanalysis of reduced whirlpool and Grøstl. In: Dunkelman, O. (ed.) FSE 2009. LNCS, vol. 5665, pp. 260–276. Springer, Heidelberg (2009). https://doi.org/10.1007/978-3-642-03317-9_16

37. Kocher, P.C.: Timing attacks on implementations of Diffie-Hellman, RSA, DSS, and other systems. In: Koblitz, N. (ed.) CRYPTO 1996. LNCS, vol. 1109, pp. 104–113. Springer, Heidelberg (1996). https://doi.org/10.1007/3-540-68697-5_9

38. Biham, E., Shamir, A.: Differential cryptanalysis of DES-like cryptosystems. JOC 4, 3–72 (1991)

39. Matsui, M., Yamagishi, A.: A new method for known plaintext attack of FEAL cipher. In: Rueppel, R.A. (ed.) EUROCRYPT 1992. LNCS, vol. 658, pp. 81–91. Springer, Heidelberg (1993). https://doi.org/10.1007/3-540-47555-9_7

40. Menezes, A.J., VanOorschot, P.C., Vanstone, S.A.: Handbook of Applied Cryptography. CRC Press Series on Discrete Mathematics and its Applications (1997)

41. Leurent, G.: MD4 is not one-way. In: Nyberg, K. (ed.) FSE 2008. LNCS, vol. 5086, pp. 412–428. Springer, Heidelberg (2008). https://doi.org/10.1007/978-3-540-71039-4_26

42. Coron, J.-S., Dodis, Y., Malinaud, C., Puniya, P.: Merkle-Damgård revisited: how to construct a hash function. In: Shoup, V. (ed.) CRYPTO 2005. LNCS, vol. 3621, pp. 430–448. Springer, Heidelberg (2005). https://doi.org/10.1007/11535218_26

43. Zhang, T.: Comprehensive preimage security evaluations on Rijndael-based hashing. Cryptology ePrint Archive (2023). https://eprint.iacr.org/2023/614

Conditional Cube Key Recovery Attack
on Round-Reduced Xoodyak

Mohammad Vaziri$^{(\boxtimes)}$ and Vesselin Velichkov

The University of Edinburgh, Edinburgh, UK
{mohammad.vaziri,vvelichk}@ed.ac.uk

Abstract. Since the announcement of the NIST call for a new
lightweight cryptographic standard, a lot of schemes have been proposed
in response. Xoodyak is one of these schemes and is among the finalists of the NIST competition with a sponge structure very similar to the
Keccak hash function – the winner of the SHA3 NIST competition. In
this paper with conditional cube attack technique, we fully recover the
key of Xoodyak reduced to 6 and 7 rounds with time complexity resp.
$2^{42.58}$ and $2^{76.003}$ in the nonce-reusing scenario. In our attack setting,
we import the cube variables in the absorbing associated data phase,
which has higher degree of freedom in comparison to data absorption
phase. We use MILP tool for finding enough cube variables to perform
the conditional key recovery attack. The 6-round attack is practical and
has been implemented. To the best of our knowledge, this is the first
proposed attack on 7-round Xoodyak.

Keywords: Xoodyak · Symmetric-key · Cryptanalysis · Conditional
Cube Attack · Lightweight Cryptography · MILP

1 Introduction

Due to the importance of lightweight cryptographic algorithms, the US National
Institute of Standards and Technology (NIST) in 2018 [18] announced an open
call for new lightweight cryptographic standards. On March 29, 2021, NIST
announced ten finalists and Xoodyak is one of the finalists. On February 7,
2023, NIST announced Ascon [11] as the winner of the competition [17]. Even
though Xoodyak was not chosen as the winner it still remains of interest as a
secure and efficient lightweight algorithm against which no attack on the full
version has been reported to date. In this paper we improve the best known
attack on Xoodyak reduced to 6 rounds and propose the first 7-round attack.

Xoodyak [6] is a scheme based on the Xoodoo permutation, proposed by the
same research team [5] that designed SHA3/Keccak [10] and has a very similar
structure. Throughout this paper, for the sake of convenience, the expression

Part of this work was done during a research visit of the first author to the Digital
Security (DiS) Group at Radboud University Nijmegen.

J. Zhou et al. (Eds.): ACNS 2023 Workshops, LNCS 13907, pp. 43–62, 2023.
https://doi.org/10.1007/978-3-031-41181-6_3

SHA3-like designs include all of the variants that are derived from the Keccak sponge-based round function or from the Xoodoo permutation.

Cube attacks are a class of symmetric-key attacks, targeting cryptographic primitives with low algebraic degree. In the attack procedure, the cryptographic primitive is interpreted as a polynomial with algebraic degree n. The attack leverages the fact that summing the output of 2^{n-1} inputs composed of all possible values of a set (i.e., a cube) of $n-1$ variables (all other variables being fixed), yields a linear function. If the obtained linear function contains some secret information (e.g. bits from the internal state or the key), the secret information can be recovered by solving a linear system of equations.

To improve the efficiency of the original cube attack, two types of related attacks have been proposed. The first one is called a cube attack-like attack and for the first time was introduced by Dinur et al. [7] at EUROCRYPT 2015. Later in [4,12,19] the authors applied cube attack-like technique to attack different variants of SHA3-like designs. The second semi-cube attack is called the conditional cube attack and for the first time was introduced by Huang et al. ([13]) at EUROCRYPT 2017 and further extended by [15,16,20,22].

Cube attack-like cryptanalysis is similar to the original cube attack and has an offline and an online phase. In the offline phase, a dictionary of all values of some key bits (so-called related keys) and the corresponding value of the output cube sum after certain number of rounds is compiled. In the online phase, by having the real value of the related key bits, the cube sum is computed and one looks for a match in the dictionary. In the conditional cube attack, the value of the cube sum should become zero under certain conditions and by guessing the key bits involved in the conditions, those key bits are recovered.

The proposed attacks in [7], are one of the first works on analyzing the resistance of SHA3-like designs against the cube attack. The authors implemented various types of algebraic attacks on keyed Keccak and Keyak [1][1] variants and broke 6–7 rounds of these variants in practical time. Inspired by [3], with setting up cube variables in the column parity, they bypassed the propagation produced by θ in the first round.

In [13], Huang et al. for the first time, developed a new type of conditional cube tester for SHA3-like designs. Inspired by dynamic cube attack [9], the authors imposed some bit conditions for certain cube variables for controlling the propagation of cube variables caused by the nonlinear operation χ and constructed a cube tester with smaller dimensions. They applied their model to reduced-round Keccak-MAC [3] and Keyak [1] and improved the previous proposed results for recovering the key, in terms of complexity and number of rounds.

Later in [15], by using a MILP tool, the authors improved the key recovery attack in [13] on reduced-round Keccak-MAC-384 and Keccak-MAC-512 by 1 round. For increasing the number of rounds of the attack, the challenge was finding enough ordinary cube variables. For being able to find enough ordinary cube variables, the MILP method proposed by the authors described the relations between ordinary cube variables and conditional cube variables in the first and

---

[1] Keyak is an AE scheme based on Keccak sponge function.

second rounds. In [20], for improving the conditional cube attacks on SHA3-like designs in terms of the complexity and number of rounds, the authors proposed another MILP model, which accurately described the propagations of the cube variables through the two rounds and also proposed a MILP model which was able to linearize first two rounds of SHA3-like designs. The authors applied their technique to attack against KMAC128 and KMAC256 [21].

Some variants of SHA3-like designs such as Ketje Jr [2], Xoodyak, do not have enough degree of freedom to perform the Huang et al.'s technique [13], even with the help of MILP tool. To be more specific, the portion of their state allocated for importing the data is not large enough to put enough cube variables to perform the attack. For dealing with a low degree of freedom in some variants of SHA3-like designs, Li et al. [16] introduced the so-called kernel quadratic term, which was more compatible with such variants.

There exist just 2 works in the area of cube key-recovery attack on Xoodoo structures. The first one is cube attack-like cryptanalysis on 6 rounds of a Xoodoo-based authenticated encryption proposed by [19] with time complexity and memory complexity resp. 2^{89} and 2^{55}. The second one is a conditional cube attack on 6 rounds of Xoodyak proposed by [22] with $2^{43.8}$ time complexity and negligible memory cost.

In this paper by applying Li et al.'s conditional cube attack technique [16], we recover the key of 6 and 7-round reduced Xoodyak. Unlike others [16,22], we import the cube variables in the absorbing associated data phase instead of the absorbing data phase. [2] Table 1 shows related results in comparison to our results.

Table 1. Summary of key recovery attacks on SHA3-like designs

Variant	Capacity	Degree of Freedom	Rounds	Time	Reference
Xoodyak	192	192	6	$2^{43.8}$	[22]
Xoodyak	192	352	6	$2^{42.45}$	Sect. 2
Xoodyak	192	352	7	$2^{76.003}$	Sect. 3

Our Contributions. In this paper, we apply the Li et al.'s conditional cube attack technique [16] on Xoodyak and present the first 7 rounds of attack on Xoodyak, and also 6 rounds with lower complexity in comparison to the proposed attack in [22]. The complexities of our attack are listed in Table 1, and the details are as follows:

- For 6-round Xoodyak in nonce-misuse settings, we recover the 384-bit key with time complexity $2^{42.45}$ and negligible memory cost.
- For 7-round Xoodyak in nonce-misuse settings, we recover the 384-bit key with time complexity $2^{76.003}$ and negligible memory cost.

---

[2] the corresponding source code is available via https://github.com/mohammadvaziri/Conditional-Cube-Attack-on-Xoodyak.

Organization. In Sect. 2 some notations and brief descriptions of Xoodyak are given. Some related works including cube attack and conditional cube attack techniques are introduced in Sect. 3. Section 4 describes the MILP search model for conditional cube attack. Section 5 gives the applications to Xoodyak. Section 6 concludes this paper.

2   Preliminaries

2.1   Notations

Throughout the paper, we will use the following notations for Xoodoo:

S_0 initial state of the Xoodoo permutation,
$S_{i-1,\theta}$ internal state of Xoodoo after θ in the i-th round,
$S_{i-1,\rho_{west}}$ internal state of Xoodoo after ρ_{west} in the i-th round,
$S_{i-1,\chi}$ internal state of Xoodoo after χ in the i-th round,
S_i output state of Xoodoo of the i-th round,
$(i, *, k)$ index of a column,
$(*, j, k)$ index of a row,
$(i, j, *)$ index of a lane,
(i, j, k) index of a bit,
$A[i][j]$ the lane indexed by $(i, j, *)$ of state A,
$A[i][j][k]$ the bit indexed by (i, j, k) of state A.

2.2   Description of Xoodyak

Xoodyak [6] is designed based on Xoodoo [5] permutation which includes an Authenticated Encryption with Additional Data (AEAD) scheme and a hashing scheme. Xoodoo has a 384-bit state A, which is represented as a three-dimensional array of bits, namely $A[4][3][32]$. In the state, the one-dimensional arrays $A[x][*][z]$, $A[*][y][z]$ and $A[x][y][*]$ are called a column, a row, and a lane respectively. The coordinates are computed modulo 4, modulo 3, and modulo 32 for x, y, and z respectively. The round function of Xoodoo is as $R = \rho_{east} \circ \chi \circ \iota \circ \rho_{west} \circ \theta$ and in the following the details of the round function of Xoodoo permutation based on the order are given:

$\theta : A[x][y][z] = A[x][y][z] \bigoplus \sum_{j=0}^{2}(A[x-1][j][z-5] \bigoplus A[x-1][j][z-14])$.
$\rho_{west} : A[x][1][z] = A[x-1][1][z], A[x][2][z] = A[x][2][z-11]$.
$\iota : A[0][0] = A[0][0] \oplus RC_i$.
$\chi : A[x][y][z] = A[x][y][z] \oplus ((A[x][y+1][z] \oplus 1) \wedge A[x][y+2][z])$.
$\rho_{east} : A[x][1][z] = A[x][1][z-1], A[x][2][z] = A[x-2][2][z-8]$.

In Fig. 1, f is the 12-round permutation Xoodoo. As shown in Fig. 1, the structure of the Xoodyak-AEAD is as follows: first, a 128-bit key is absorbed into the 384-bit state, then the Xoodoo permutation is applied to the state;

second, a 128-bit nonce is absorbed then the Xoodoo permutation is applied to the state; third, the 352-bit associated data block is absorbed, then the Xoodoo permutation is applied to the state; then it starts to absorb 192-bit plaintext blocks and output ciphertext blocks in each term; the finalization phase happens at the end. More information on the details of the Xoodyak-AEAD can be found in [6].

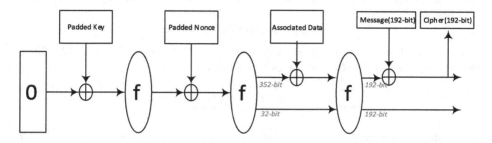

Fig. 1. Xoodyak-AEAD structure

Our attack has two essential characteristics: firstly, we assume that the nonce is reused, as the same assumption used by [16]; secondly, we apply our conditional cube attack in the phase of absorbing associated data, contrary to [16], where the attack is applied in the absorbing data phase. The degree of freedom in the absorbing data phase is 192-bit. Following [6], however, the degree of freedom is 352-bit. To be more specific, according to Sect. 2.3 in [6], the absorb rate R_{kin} is 44 bytes and according to Algorithms 1 and 2 in [6], R_{kin} is used during the absorbing of associated data, which means the degree of freedom in associated data phase is 352-bit. It should be noted that in order to recover the main key, in our attack scenario the full 384-bit state needs to be recovered and the key can be computed inversely, while in the scenario of [16] just half of the state needs to be recovered.

3 Review of Cube Attacks and Related Techniques

In this section, we briefly describe the cube attack and overview 2 types of proposed conditional cube attacks on the structure of the SHA3-like designs. The first type of conditional cube attack is proposed by Huang et al. [13] to attack Keccak keyed mode, and the second type is introduced by Li et al. [16] to attack the schemes that have a lower degree of freedom.

3.1 Cube Attack

Cube attack is a chosen plaintext attack, which can be seen as an extension of higher order differential attacks [14], and was formally introduced by Dinur et al. [8]. In the cube attack, the output of the cipher is regarded as a black box polynomial and by querying the black box polynomial a linear system of equations is created. The linear system of equations contains some (or whole) part of the secret key and by solving this system some (or whole) part of the secret key is recovered. Cube attack is based on the following theorem:

Theorem 1 (Dinur, Shamir [8]). *Given a polynomial $f : X^n \to \{0, 1\}$ of degree d. Suppose that $0 < k < d$ and t is the monomial $x_0...x_{k-1}$. Write the function as*

$$f(x) = t \cdot P_t(x) + Q_t(x)$$

where none of the terms in $Q_t(x)$ is divisible by t. Note that $deg P_t \leq d - k$. Then the sum of f overall values of the cube (defined by t) is

$$\sum_{x'=(x_0,...,x_{k-1}) \in C_t} f(x', x) = P_t(\underbrace{1, ..., 1}_{k}, x_k, ..., x_{n-1})$$

whose degree is at most $d - k$ (or 1 if $k = d - 1$), where the cube C_t contains all binary vectors of the length k.

In Theorem 1, $P_t(x)$ is the "superpoly" of the term t. The original cube attack contains two phases resp. offline and online. In the offline phase, by selecting a random cube set, the superpoly, independent of the secret variables, is obtained and in the online phase, by fixing the secret variables the actual value of the obtained Superpolies is computed, and some linear system of equations is built. As can be seen in [7,8], implementing the original cube attack is very expensive, since the cube variables in the cube set are randomly selected and most of the time the obtained Superpolies do not contain any useful information.

3.2   Conditional Cube Attack

To perform the conditional cube attack on r round of the SHA3-like designs, the attacker looks for a set of cube variables $\{v_0, ..., v_{k-1}\}$, $k \geq 2$ such that the term $v_0...v_{k-1}$ does not appear at the output of the $r - th$ round if some conditions imposed at the first round hold. For doing so, some cube variables are determined as conditional cube variables and for controlling the propagation of the conditional cube variables, the conditions are imposed on the neighboring positions of the conditional cube variables prior to the first χ operation. Therefore, if the imposed conditions hold, the propagation of the conditional cube variables are controlled and the term $v_0...v_{k-1}$ does not appear at the output of the $r - th$ round, otherwise, it does appear. Consequently, the cube sum is zero only if the imposed conditions hold. Since the position of the conditions includes the summation of some secret key bits and constant bits, the conditions with high probability hold, if only the key bits involved in the conditions will be guessed correctly.

Therefore, for performing a conditional cube attack on r rounds of a SHA3-like design, the attacker first tries to find a term that does not appear at the output of the r-th round under certain conditions, then guesses the involved secret key bits in the conditions. If the cube summation is zero, then the guessed key bits with high probability are correct. In the following 2 techniques of conditional cube attack proposed by Huang et al. and Li et al. is presented.

Huang et al.'s Conditional Cube Attack. The first type of conditional cube attack is introduced by Huang et al. [13]. For performing the conditional cube attack, first, they define two types of cube variables as *conditional cube variable* and *ordinary cube variable*. For attacking r rounds of a SHA3-like design, they prove that by having $p(0 \leq p < 2^{n+1})$ conditional cube variable and $q(q = 2^{n+1} - 2p + 1)$ ordinary cube variables, multiplication of conditional and ordinary cube variables will not appear at the output of the r-th round. In the following, the details of the Huang et al.'s conditional cube attack technique are given.

Definition 1 *([13]). Cube variables that have propagation controlled in the first round and are not multiplied with each other after the second round of Keccak are called **conditional cube variables**. Cube variables that are not multiplied with each other after the first round and are not multiplied with any conditional cube variable after the second round are called **ordinary cube variables**.*

Theorem 2 *([13]). For $(n+2)$-round Keccak sponge function $(n > 0)$, if there are p $(0 \leq p < 2^{n+1})$ conditional cube variables $v_0, ..., v_{p-1}$, and $q = 2^{n+1} - 2p + 1$ ordinary cube variables, $u_0, ..., u_{q-1}$ (If $q = 0$, we set $p = 2^{n+1}$), the term $v_0 v_1 ... v_{p-1} u_0 ... u_{q-1}$ will not appear in the output polynomials of $(n+2)$- round Keccak sponge function.*

Theorem 2 indicates that by having a certain amount of conditional cube variables and ordinary cube variables, the multiplication of those does not appear at the output of the certain round of SHA3-like designs.

It is worth mentioning as the number of conditional cube variables is increased the number of conditions is increased, as well, which leads to higher time complexity in recovering the key. Therefore, in most of the works they have used just one conditional cube variable [13,15]. In the case of using one conditional cube variable, the following corollary is used:

Corollary 1. *For $(n+2$ $)$-round Keccak sponge function $(n > 0)$, if there is one conditional cube variable v_0, and $q = 2^{n+1} - 1$ ordinary cube variables, $u_0, ..., u_{q-1}$, the term $v_0 u_0 ... u_{q-1}$ will not appear in the output polynomials of $(n+2$ $)$-round Keccak sponge function.*

The attack procedure of the Huang et al.'s conditional cube attack technique [13], which was later extended with an improved MILP model by Song et al. [20] can be summarized in the following steps:

1. Determine the position of the conditional cube variable(s) at initial state.
2. Use the MILP model proposed by Song et al. [20] to find position of the bit conditions and also the ordinary cube variables satisfying the requirements in Theorem 2.

3. Determine the key bits involved in the bit conditions.
4. Put the value 0 for any constant position at the initial state and for each possible value of the bit conditions compute the cube sum.
5. If the cube sum is zero, then the guessed values of the bit conditions are correct.

Li et al.'s Conditional Cube Attack. Huang et al.'s conditional cube attack [13] becomes invalid for some variants of SHA3-like designs with a lower degree of freedom to find enough ordinary cube variables. To overcome the challenge, Li et al. [16] came up with a new type of conditional cube attack. In their technique instead of using the conditional cube variable, they introduce a degree two term called *kernel quadratic term*. In the following, the definition of the kernel quadratic term and the related corollary for performing the conditional cube attack is presented.

Definition 2 *([16]).* *Suppose all the (q+2) cube variables are $v_0, v_1, u_0, ..., u_{q-1}$, and constraints are as follows:*

– *After the first round, $v_0 v_1$ is the only quadratic term.*
– *In the second round, if the bit conditions are satisfied, $v_0 v_1$ does not multiply with any of $u_0, ..., u_{q-1}$, i.e. no cubic term occurs.*
– *In the second round, if the bit conditions are not satisfied, $v_0 v_1$ multiplies with some of $u_0, ..., u_{q-1}$, i.e. some cubic terms like $v_0 v_1 u_i (i = 0, ..., q-1)$ occur.*

*Then $v_0 v_1$ is called **kernel quadratic term**. The remaining cube variables except v_0 and v_1, i.e. $u_0, ..., u_{q-1}$, are called **ordinary cube variables**.*

From the Definition 2, the following corollary can be deduced.

Corollary 2 *([16]).* *For (n+2)-round Keccak sponge function (n > 0), if there is one kernel quadratic term $v_0 v_1$, and $q = 2^{n+1} - 1$ ordinary cube variables, $u_0, u_1, ..., u_{q-1}$, the term $v_0 v_1 u_0 u_1, ..., u_{q-1}$ will not appear in the output polynomials of (n + 2)-round Keccak sponge function under certain bit conditions. So the distinguisher is approached as follows:*

– *under right bit conditions, the degree of output polynomials of $n + 2$ rounds is no more than 2^{n+1}.*
– *under the wrong bit conditions, the degree of output polynomials of $n + 2$ rounds is $q + 2 = 2^{n+1} + 1$.*

The attack procedure of the Li et al.'s conditional cube attack technique can be summarized in the following steps:

1. Determine the position of the kernel quadratic term at initial state.
2. Use the MILP model proposed by Song et al. [20], customized by Li et al. [16] to find position of the bit conditions and also the ordinary cube variables satisfying the requirements in Corollary 2.
3. Determine the key bits involved in the bit conditions.
4. Put the value 0 for any constant position at the initial state and for each possible value of the bit conditions compute the cube sum.
5. If the cube sum is zero, then the guessed values of the bit conditions are correct.

Comparison of Huang et al.'s and Li et al.'s Technique. In Li et al.'s technique, the kernel quadratic term is set in column parity at the output of the first round. By doing so, the propagation produced by θ at the second round is bypassed on the kernel quadratic term. Therefore, for satisfying the conditions mentioned in Corollary 2, all we need is to avoid having ordinary cube variables in 4 neighboring positions of the kernel quadratic term before the second χ. In Huang et al.'s technique, however, the second θ propagates the conditional cube variable, so the positions that the ordinary cube variables should not appear before the second χ is more than four[3]. This strategy in Li et al.'s technique has made the challenge of finding enough ordinary cube variables easier.

Comparison of Conditional Cube Attack and Original Cube Attack. In the original cube attack, the cube variables are randomly chosen and there is no guarantee on having a superpoly containing some secret key bits. In the conditional cube attack, however, the cube variables are carefully selected and the imposed conditions, always contain secret key bits. Moreover, the original cube attack contains two offline and online phases and consumes a huge memory, while the conditional cube attack is just 1 online phase and memory consumption is negligible.

4   Conditional Cube Attacks on Round-Reduced Xoodyak

As we mentioned, in our attack scenario we insert the cube variables in the associated data phase, and as Fig. 2 shows, the XOR of the associated-data state and unknown-data state is passed through the Xoodoo permutation. Therefore, for recovering the master key, the whole state of the unknown data should be recovered.

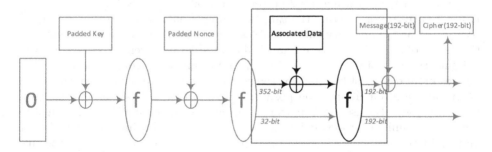

Fig. 2. Cube variables are injected in the associated data state. Our attack is applied at the stage within the red frame. (Color figure online)

For finding a distinguisher, we use Li et al.'s technique. We also applied Huang et al.'s technique but the MILP tool returned "infeasible solution". We

---

[3] By setting up the conditional cube variable in the column parity in the first round, In Keccak sponge function is 22 and in Xoodoo permutation is 14.

suspect that the reason is insufficient degrees of freedom, but further analysis is necessary to confirm this. In the following, the way of finding the positions of the cube variable in the initial state for building the Kernel quadratic term, and the way of constructing the MILP model for having enough ordinary cube variables are explained.

4.1   Finding Kernel Quadratic Term

The best way to control the propagation of the quadratic term is by setting the kernel quadratic term in the column parity at the beginning of the second round. To do this, in [16], they propose a reversing technique in which first they assume the positions of the kernel quadratic term are set in the column parity i.e. two kernel quadratic term $(v_0 v_1)$ exist at the same column at the output of the first round, then they reversely impose the operations of the SHA3-like design.

In order to represent the number of the active bits of a conditional cube variable (kernel quadratic term) in [13] a pattern as x-y-z is introduced, where x, y and z are the number of active bits of a conditional cube variable (kernel quadratic term) in the initial state, the output of first round and the input of second χ operation, respectively. In [16], they propose a 6-2-2 pattern for the propagation of the kernel quadratic term $v_0 v_1$, which acts different than the pattern 2-2-22 proposed by [13], for the propagation of the conditional cube variable v_0. In the 2-2-22 pattern the propagation of the conditional cube variable v_0 is controlled in the first round, but the θ operation in the second round diffuse v_0 in 22 positions, which means the ordinary cube variables should not appear in 44 positions at the input of the second χ operation[4]. However, in the 6-2-2 pattern, the ordinary cube variables should not appear in just 4 positions at the input of the second χ operation.

In [22], instead of using 6-2-2 pattern, they offer to use 8-2-2 pattern. Since in 6-2-2 pattern, for creating the $v_0 v_1$, the cube variable v_0 is not set in column parity, and as the ordinary cube variables are not supposed to multiply with v_0, the degree of freedom for the ordinary cube variables is decreased. However, in 8-2-2 pattern, both of the cube variables v_0 and v_1 are set in column parity, which creates more degree of freedom for the selection of the ordinary cube variables.

In our case, for finding the positions of v_0 and v_1 in the kernel quadratic term $v_0 v_1$, we also use 8-2-2 pattern, and at the same time by following the reversing technique proposed by [16], we try to avoid having the variables v_0 and v_1 in the last lane. The obtained positions for the v_0 and v_1 at the initial state S_0 are as $A[0][1][0] = A[0][2][0] = A[1][0][20] = A[1][2][20] = v_0$ and $A[1][0][21] = A[1][2][21] = A[1][0][31] = A[1][1][31] = v_1$. According to Fig. 3, the kernel quadratic term $v_0 v_1$ appears in the positions $S_1[1][0][0]$ and $S_1[1][1][0]$.

---

[4] To avoid having multiplication, the ordinary cube variables should not appear in the neighboring positions of the conditional cube variable.

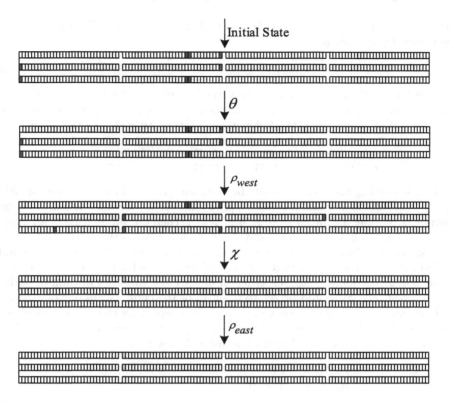

Fig. 3. Forming of the kernel quadratic term in the first round of Xoodyak. Red, blue and yellow squares show the positions of v_0, v_1, and $v_0 v_1$ respectively. (Color figure online)

4.2 MILP Model for Li et al. Technique

In this section, we customize a MILP model for our scenario proposed by Song et al. [20] and also used by [16,22]. This MILP model is meant to find $2^{n+1} - 1$ ordinary cube variables to attack $n + 2$ rounds of Xoodyak, by aiming to minimize the number of bit-conditions. We assume the bit positions of v_0 and v_1 at the kernel quadratic term $v_0 v_1$ in S_0 are the same as we obtained in the previous section. The applied symbols in the model are as follows: $a[x][y][z] = 1, a'[x][y][z] = 1, b[x][y][z] = 1$ means state bit $S_0[x][y][z]$, $S_{0,\rho_{weast}}[x][y][z]$, $S_1[x][y][z]$ contains at least one ordinary cube variable, respectively. The MILP model determines the valid positions for the ordinary cube variables at S_0, $S_{0,\rho_{weast}}$ and $S_{1,\rho_{weast}}$, describes the treatment of θ and χ at the first round, and also determines the total number of the ordinary cube variables, needed to perform the attack.

Modeling the First Round. Due to the absorbing rate of the associated data state, the first set of constraints needs to be added to the MILP model to avoid having any ordinary cube variable in the last lane of the initial state. The constraints 1 are meant for this purpose:

$$a[3][2][z] = 0, \quad 0 \leq z < 32 \tag{1}$$

The bit positions that are already taken by the cube variable v_0 and v_1, at S_0 should not be a potential position for the ordinary cube variables to be taken. To satisfy such constraints, the following equalities are added to the model.

$$
\begin{aligned}
a[0][1][0] = a[0][2][0] = a[1][0][20] = a[1][2][20] = \\
a[1][0][21] = a[1][2][21] = a[1][0][31] = a[1][1][31] = 0
\end{aligned}
\tag{2}
$$

For describing the treatment of the columns $(x, *, z)$ in θ operation in [20], two types of Boolean variables called $f[x][z]$ and $g[x][z]$ are introduced. If at the column $(x, *, z)$ at the initial state A, $g[x][z] = 1$, then the summation of all 3 bits of the column should be nonzero, and if $f[x][z] = 1$, despite the existence of some variable in the column $(x, *, z)$, the summation of all 3 bits of the column should be zero. It should be noted that $f[x][z] = 1$ means a 1-bit degree of freedom is consumed. According to [20], if setting all of the cube variables in column parity is of interest, $g[x][z]$ should be set to 0 for all of the columns. In our case, since we have enough degree of freedom and also for simplifying the MILP model, we set all of the cube variables in column parity. Hence, following [20], the final equations for modeling the θ operation are as follows:

$$
\begin{aligned}
-f[x][z] &\geq -1 \\
-a[x][0][z] + f[x][z] &\geq 0 \\
-a[x][1][z] + f[x][z] &\geq 0 \\
-a[x][2][z] + f[x][z] &\geq 0 \\
a[x][0][z] + a[x][1][z] + a[x][2][z] - 2f[x][z] &\geq 0
\end{aligned}
\tag{3}
$$

As in [16,22] is mentioned, the cube variables v_0 and v_1 should not multiply with any other ordinary cube variable. Since they are supposed to multiply with one another and build the kernel quadratic term. Therefore, for preventing the multiplication of any ordinary cube variables with v_0 and v_1, the neighboring positions of v_0 and v_1 at the state $S_{0,\rho_{weast}}[x][y][z]$ should be 0. According to Sect. 4.1, the cube variables v_0 and v_1 are in 8-bit positions. In total there exists 14 bit-positions in $S_{0,\rho_{weast}}[x][y][z]$ that should be equal to 0:

$$
\begin{aligned}
a[0][0][11] = a[0][1][11] = a[1][1][20] = a[1][2][20] = \\
a[1][1][21] = a[1][2][21] = a[2][0][31] = a[2][2][31] = \\
a[1][0][0] = a[1][1][0] = a[1][2][0] = a[1][0][31] = \\
a[1][1][31] = a[1][2][31] = 0
\end{aligned}
\tag{4}
$$

In [20], for modeling the χ operation, two other Boolean variables so called $v[x][y][z]$ and $h[x][y][z]$ are introduced for describing the bit conditions in which $v[x][y][z] = 1$ indicates the existence of a condition at the state bit $S_{0,\rho_{weast}}[x][y][z]$ that has to be fixed to the amount of $h[x][y][z]$. Following [20], if $a'[x][y][z]$ and $b[x][y][z]$ would represent the existence of the cube variables in the input and output of the χ operation respectively, the constraints 5 describe the treatment of the χ operation:

$$-a'[x][y][z] - a'[x][y+1][z] \geq -1$$
$$-a'[x][y][z] + b[x][y][z] \geq 0$$
$$-a'[x][y+1][z] - v[x][y+1][z] \geq -1$$
$$-a'[x][y+2][z] - v[x][y+2][z] \geq -1$$
$$-a'[x][y][z] - a'[x][y+1][z] - h[x][y+2][z] + b[x][y][z] \geq -1$$
$$-a'[x][y][z] - v[x][y+1][z] - h[x][y+1][z] - b[x][y][z] \geq -2$$
$$a'[x][y][z] - v[x][y+2][z] + h[x][y+2][z] - b[x][y][z] \geq -1$$
$$a'[x][y][z] + a'[x][y+1][z] + a'[x][y+2][z] - b[x][y][z] \geq 0$$
$$-a'[x][y+1][z] - a'[x][y+2][z] + v[x][y+1][z] + v[x][y+2][z] + b[x][y][z] \geq 0$$
$$-a'[x][y+1][z] - a'[x][y+2][z] + v[x][y+2][z] + h[x][y+1][z] + b[x][y][z] \geq 0$$
$$(5)$$

Modeling the Second Round. Preventing the multiplication of any ordinary cube variable with the kernel quadratic term is the only set of constraints that needs to be considered in the second round. Since the kernel quadratic term is set in the column parity, it appears just in two positions before the second χ i.e. $S_{1,\rho_{weast}}$. Therefore, we should avoid having any ordinary cube variable just in 4 neighboring positions of the kernel quadratic term in the same column.

Following the constraints proposed by [20] and used by [16,22], we need to avoid having uncertain propagation in each neighboring bit of the kernel quadratic term. In order to do so, for each neighboring bit position of the kernel quadratic terms, a new dummy variable $e_i, i = 0, 1, 2, 3$ is introduced. $e_i = 1$, if at least one ordinary cube variable exists in the related neighboring position.

To avoid having uncertain propagation at the neighboring positions of the kernel quadratic term, according to the θ operation, each neighboring bit at $S_{1,\rho_{weast}}$ contains a linear expression of 7 bits from S_1, and according to the χ operation in the first round, the existence of ordinary cube variable in each bit at S_1 is dependent on the existence of any ordinary cube variable in two neighboring bits, and corresponded bit at $S_{0,\rho_{weast}}$. As a result, for having certain propagation in the neighboring positions of the kernel quadratic term, for each variable $b[x][y][z]$ that exists in i-th neighboring positions of the kernel quadratic term, the inequalities 6 proposed by [20] is used.

$$-e_i - a'[x][y+1][z] - a'[x][y+2][z] \geq -2$$
$$-e_i - a'[x][y+1][z] + v[x][y+2][z] \geq -1$$
$$-e_i - a'[x][y+2][z] + v[x][y+1][z] \geq -1$$
$$-e_i - a'[x][y+1][z] - v[x][y+1][z] \geq -2$$
$$-e_i - a'[x][y+2][z] - v[x][y+2][z] \geq -2$$
$$-e_i - a'[x][y][z] - a'[x][y+1][z] \geq -2$$
$$(6)$$

The constraints 6 indicate if in the i-th neighboring position of the quadratic term e_i is nonzero, the position contains a linear expression of some certain ordinary cube variable. For canceling the linear expression, a 1-bit degree of freedom is consumed at the initial state. Hence for computing the total number of ordinary cube variables, subtraction of the $\sum_{i=0}^{3} e_i$ is needed to be considered.

Modeling for Finding Ordinary Cube Variables. The steps to build a MILP model to find ordinary cube variables satisfying the conditions in the Definition 2, are as follows:

- The objective is minimizing the number of bit conditions. Since the variables $v[x][y][z]$ indicate the existence of a bit condition in $S_{0,\rho_{west}}[x][y][z]$ the objective function is as follows:

$$\text{Minimize}: \sum_{i=0,j=0,k=0}^{i=3,j=2,k=31} v[x_i][y_j][z_k] \tag{7}$$

- Adding the constraints generated in the Sect. 4.2 for the first round.
- Adding the constraints generated in the Sect. 4.2 for the second round.
- For having $2^{n+1}-1$ ordinary cube variables to attack $n+2$ rounds of Xoodyak, the following constraint should be added to the model:

$$\sum_{i=0,j=0,k=0}^{i=3,j=2,k=31} a[x_i][y_j][z_k] - \sum_{i=0,k=0}^{i=3,k=31} f[x_i][z_k] - \sum_{i=0}^{i=3} e[x_i] = 2^{n+1} - 1 \tag{8}$$

In the above equation, $\sum_{i=0,k=0}^{i=3,k=31} F[x_i][z_k] + \sum_{i=0}^{i=3} e[x_i]$ is the consumed degree of freedom in the initial state S_0.

- In order to avoid not having any bit condition, the following constraint will be added to the model:

$$\sum_{i=0,j=0,k=0}^{i=3,j=2,k=31} v[x_i][y_j][z_k] \geq 1 \tag{9}$$

5   Key Recovery on 6 and 7 Rounds Xoodyak

In this section, we apply the MILP model proposed in Sect. 4.2 for 6 and 7 rounds of Xoodyak respectively. Since the 6-round attack is practical, the full key recovery attack is implemented.

As we mentioned earlier in Sect. 4.1, the bit positions of the kernel quadratic term at the initial state are $A[0][1][0] = A[0][2][0] = A[1][0][20] = A[1][2][20] = v_0$ and $A[1][0][21] = A[1][2][21] = A[1][0][31] = A[1][1][31] = v_1$.

For recovering the key bits involved in the bit-conditions, firstly the key bits are guessed and if the cube sum would be zero, the guessed key bits are expected to be correct with high probability.

5.1   6 Rounds Conditional Cube Attack on Xoodyak

According to Fig. 2, we import the cube variables on the associated-data phase and recover the whole of the unknown state that is XORed with the associated data. The round function of the Xoodoo is reduced to 6 rounds.

Table 2. Parameters set for attack on 6-round Xoodyak

Kernel Quadratic term
$A[0][1][0] = A[0][2][0] = A[1][0][20] = A[1][2][20] = v_0,$ $A[1][0][31] = A[1][1][31] = A[1][0][21] = A[1][2][21] = v_1$
Bit Conditions
$A[0][2][21] = k_{67} + k_{90} + k_{104} + k_{195} + k_{218} + k_{323} + k_{346} + n_{67} + n_{90} + n_{104} +$ $n_{195} + n_{218} + n_{323} + 1$
Ordinary Cube Variables
$A[0][1][3] = u_0, A[0][2][3] = u_0, A[0][0][9] = u_1, A[0][1][9] = u_2,$ $A[0][2][9] = u_1 + u_2, A[0][0][12] = u_3, A[0][1][12] = u_3, A[0][0][23] = u_4,$ $A[0][1][23] = u_5, A[0][2][23] = u_4 + u_5, A[0][0][24] = u_6, A[0][1][24] = u_7,$ $A[0][2][24] = u_6 + u_7, A[0][0][30] = u_8, A[0][1][30] = u_8, A[1][0][2] = u_9,$ $A[1][2][2] = u_9, A[1][0][11] = u_{10}, A[1][1][11] = u_{10}, A[1][0][14] = u_{11},$ $A[1][2][14] = u_{11}, A[1][0][22] = u_{12}, A[1][2][22] = u_{12}, A[2][0][2] = u_{13},$ $A[2][1][2] = u_{14}, A[2][2][2] = u_{13} + u_{14}, A[2][0][5] = u_{15}, A[2][1][5] = u_{16},$ $A[2][2][5] = u_{15} + u_{16}, A[2][1][8] = u_{17}, A[2][2][8] = u_{17}, A[2][0][9] = u_{18},$ $A[2][1][9] = u_{19}, A[2][2][9] = u_{18} + u_{19}, A[2][1][11] = u_{20}, A[2][2][11] = u_{20},$ $A[2][0][12] = u_{21}, A[2][1][12] = u_{22}, A[2][2][12] = u_{21} + u_{22}, A[2][0][14] = u_{23},$ $A[2][1][14] = u_{24}, A[2][2][14] = u_{23} + u_{24}, A[2][1][16] = u_{25}, A[2][2][16] = u_{25},$ $A[2][0][24] = u_{26}, A[2][1][24] = u_{27}, A[2][2][24] = u_{26} + u_{27}, A[2][0][30] = u_{28},$ $A[2][1][30] = u_{28}, A[3][0][1] = u_{29}, A[3][1][1] = u_{29}, A[3][0][25] = u_{30},$ $A[3][1][25] = u_{30}$
Guessed Key Bits
$k_{67} + k_{90} + k_{104} + k_{195} + k_{218} + k_{323} + k_{346}$

By linearizing 1 round of Xoodoo, the degree of the 6th round is 32. Therefore, in total, we need 33 cube variables to mount the attack, 2 of them build the kernel quadratic term and the rest are ordinary cube variables. Table 2 presents kernel quadratic term, ordinary cube variables, and bit conditions obtained by the MILP model.

According to Table 2, the only key bit needs to be recovered is as $k_{12} + k_{21} + k_{58} + k_{140} + k_{149} + k_{268} + k_{277}$. The time complexity to recover a 1-bit key is 2^{34}. Since the Xoodoo permutation is symmetric in z-axis, the key-bit $k_{12+i} + k_{21+i} + k_{58+i} + k_{140+i} + k_{149+i} + k_{268+i} + k_{277+i}$ can be recovered by i-bit $0 \leq i < 32$ rotating all of the parameters in z-axis. We can recover 352 bits by finding a different set of cube variables and also rotating them in z-axis. If we leave 32 remaining key-bit as an exhaustive search, the complexity for recovering 352 key-bit is $2^{8.45}2^{34} = 2^{42.45}$. As a result, the total complexity is $2^{42.45} + 2^{32} \simeq 2^{42.451}$. This complexity is a bit lower than the proposed complexity by [22] i.e. $2^{43.8}$.

In our experiments, we generate 384 random bits as unknown data, which are to be XOR-ed with the associated data state, and in the associated data state we import the cube variables and set the rest of the positions to be zero. We calculate the cube sum on all of the lanes. It is worth mentioning that the probability of having zero cube sum for all of the lanes for a random function is 2^{-384}. Hence, it is safe to declare the guessed key as correct with high probability, once the 33-dimension cube sums become zero.

To test the correctness of the parameters in Table 2, we run experiments, whose steps are summarized in Algorithm 1.

Algorithm 1. Testing the obtained parameters in Table 2
***
input: parameters in Table 2.
output: resulting cube sum for each guess.
Generate 384 random bits as the representation of the unknown data and store the state as Key;
Compute the value of $k_{67} + k_{90} + k_{104} + k_{195} + k_{218} + k_{323} + k_{346}$ and store it as the right key which needs to be recovered;
for each key guess $i, i \in \{0x0, 0x1\}$ **do**
    Initial-State $= Key$
    Final-State $= 0$
    Initial-State[10][26] $= i \oplus 1$
    for each possible value of cube set $j, j \in [0, 2^{34}]$ **do**
        Temp-State $=$ Initial-State
        generate the j-th permutation of cube variables, and store it in Cubes-State
        Temp-State $=$ Temp-state $\oplus$ Cubes-State
        Impose 6-round Xoodoo permutation on Temp-state
        Final-State $=$ Final-state $\oplus$ Temp-State
    end for
    Print Final-State
end for

Next we present the results from experiments for testing the correctness of the parameters given in Table 2.

384-bit key K:
011001101100110100010101011111000   110100011010010000101101010001001
100100011101101100110100001001011   110101110101110110011000100111000
001010101110001001110111101010011   101011000011001000100110001100001
010100010100110110111111110010011   010010101101010010101110101000101010
111100110100010110101100110101101   110111011101001100111100000000001
100000011001010101010001101101101   001001101110101111100001100000010

According to Table 2 and above generated key, the correct value for the guessed key bit is 1.

guessed value: 0, cube sums: 0x10b7a9c8, 0x189ab404, 0x3eeeacfa, 0x3eeeacfa, 0x5c5f184e, 0xd4497ce3, 0xff28ba81, 0xfa3d438c, 0x5155d784, 0x4aca9eb9, 0x748c5ed8, 0x53899c47, 0xad5b47e9

guessed value: 1, cube sums: 0x0, 0x0, 0x0, 0x0, 0x0, 0x0, 0x0, 0x0, 0x0, 0x0, 0x0, 0x0

The program was run in Ubuntu 20.04 operating system with gcc 9.40. Recovery of a 1-bit key needs about 10 h using one CPU core (AMD EPYC 3.3GHz).

Table 3. Parameters set for attack on 7-round Xoodyak

Kernel Quadratic term
$A[0][1][0] = A[0][2][0] = A[1][0][20] = A[1][2][20] = v_0,$ $A[1][0][31] = A[1][1][31] = A[1][0][21] = A[1][2][21] = v_1$

Bit Conditions
$A[0][2][13] = k_4 + k_{13} + k_{50} + k_{132} + k_{141} + k_{260} + k_{269} + n_4 + n_{13} + n_{50} + n_{132} + n_{141} + n_{260}$
$A[0][2][22] = k_{13} + k_{22} + k_{59} + k_{141} + k_{150} + k_{269} + k_{278} + n_{13} + n_{22} + n_{59} + n_{141} + n_{150} + n_{269}$
$A[0][2][27] = k_{18} + k_{27} + k_{146} + k_{155} + k_{160} + k_{274} + k_{283} + n_{18} + n_{27} + n_{146} + n_{155} + n_{160} + n_{274} + 1$
$A[1][2][7] = k_2 + k_{25} + k_{130} + k_{153} + k_{258} + k_{281} + k_{295} + n_2 + n_{25} + n_{130} + n_{153} + n_{258} + n_{281}$
$A[1][2][16] = k_2 + k_{11} + k_{130} + k_{139} + k_{258} + k_{267} + k_{304} + n_2 + n_{11} + n_{130} + n_{139} + n_{258} + n_{267}$

Ordinary Cube Variables
$A[0][0][1] = u_0, A[0][1][1] = u_1, A[0][2][1] = u_0 + u_1, A[0][0][2] = u_2,$
$A[0][1][2] = u_2, A[0][1][9] = u_3, A[0][2][9] = u_3, A[0][0][10] = u_4,$
$A[0][1][10] = u_5, A[0][2][10] = u_4 + u_5, A[0][1][13] = u_6, A[0][2][13] = u_6,$
$A[0][0][14] = u_7, A[0][1][14] = u_8, A[0][2][14] = u_7 + u_8, A[0][0][15] = u_9,$
$A[0][1][15] = u_{10}, A[0][2][15] = u_9 + u_{10}, A[0][0][18] = u_{11}, A[0][1][18] = u_{12},$
$A[0][2][18] = u_{11} + u_{12}, A[0][1][19] = u_{13}, A[0][2][19] = u_{13}, A[0][0][27] = u_{14},$
$A[0][1][27] = u_{15}, A[0][2][27] = u_{14} + u_{15}, A[0][0][28] = u_{16}, A[0][1][28] = u_{16},$
$A[1][0][6] = u_{17}, A[1][2][6] = u_{17}, A[1][0][11] = u_{18}, A[1][2][11] = u_{18},$
$A[1][0][12] = u_{19}, A[1][2][12] = u_{19}, A[1][1][19] = u_{20}, A[1][2][19] = u_{20},$
$A[1][0][24] = u_{21}, A[1][2][24] = u_{21}, A[1][0][25] = u_{22}, A[1][2][25] = u_{22},$
$A[1][0][26] = u_{23}, A[1][2][26] = u_{23}, A[1][0][29] = u_{24}, A[1][2][29] = u_{24},$
$A[2][0][1] = u_{25}, A[2][1][1] = u_{26}, A[2][2][1] = u_{25} + u_{26}, A[2][0][2] = u_{27},$
$A[2][1][2] = u_{28}, A[2][2][2] = u_{27} + u_{28}, A[2][0][6] = u_{29}, A[2][1][6] = u_{30},$
$A[2][2][6] = u_{29} + u_{30}, A[2][1][7] = u_{31}, A[2][2][7] = u_{31}, A[2][0][10] = u_{32},$
$A[2][1][10] = u_{23}, A[2][2][10] = u_{23} + u_{32}, A[2][0][11] = u_{33}, A[2][1][11] = u_{34},$
$A[2][2][11] = u_{33} + u_{34}, A[2][1][12] = u_{35}, A[2][2][12] = u_{35}, A[2][0][14] = u_{36},$
$A[2][1][14] = u_{36}, A[2][0][15] = u_{37}, A[2][1][15] = u_{38}, A[2][2][15] = u_{37} + u_{38},$
$A[2][0][16] = u_{39}, A[2][1][16] = u_{40}, A[2][2][16] = u_{39} + u_{40}, A[2][0][20] = u_{41},$
$A[2][1][20] = u_{41}, A[2][1][21] = u_{42}, A[2][2][21] = u_{42}, A[2][0][24] = u_{43},$
$A[2][1][24] = u_{44}, A[2][2][24] = u_{43} + u_{44}, A[2][0][25] = u_{45}, A[2][1][25] = u_{46},$
$A[2][2][25] = u_{45} + u_{46}, A[2][1][26] = u_{47}, A[2][2][26] = u_{47}, A[2][0][28] = u_{48},$
$A[2][1][28] = u_{49}, A[2][2][28] = u_{48} + u_{49}, A[2][0][29] = u_{50}, A[2][1][29] = u_9 + u_{50},$
$A[2][2][29] = u_9, A[2][0][30] = u_{51}, A[2][1][30] = u_{52}, A[2][2][30] = u_{51} + u_{52},$
$A[3][0][0] = u_{53}, A[3][1][0] = u_{53}, A[3][0][3] = u_{54}, A[3][1][3] = u_{54},$
$A[3][0][4] = u_{55}, A[3][1][4] = u_{55}, A[3][0][5] = u_{56}, A[3][1][5] = u_{56},$
$A[3][0][8] = u_{57}, A[3][1][8] = u_{57}, A[3][0][9] = u_{58}, A[3][1][9] = u_{58},$
$A[3][0][13] = u_{10} + u_{17}, A[3][1][13] = u_{10} + u_{17}, A[3][0][17] = u_{59}, A[3][1][17] = u_{59},$
$A[3][0][19] = u_{60}, A[3][1][19] = u_{60}, A[3][0][22] = u_{61}, A[3][1][22] = u_{61},$
$A[3][0][23] = u_{62}, A[3][1][23] = u_{62}, A[3][0][31] = u_5 + u_{13} + u_{47} + u_{59},$
$A[3][1][31] = u_5 + u_{13} + u_{47} + u_{59},$

Guessed Key Bits
$k_4 + k_{13} + k_{50} + k_{132} + k_{141} + k_{260} + k_{269}, k_{13} + k_{22} + k_{59} + k_{141} + k_{150} + k_{269} + k_{278}$
$k_{18} + k_{27} + k_{146} + k_{155} + k_{160} + k_{274} + k_{283}, k_2 + k_{25} + k_{130} + k_{153} + k_{258} + k_{281} + k_{295}$
$k_2 + k_{11} + k_{130} + k_{139} + k_{258} + k_{267} + k_{304},$

To verify the correctness of our results for 6-round Xoodyak, by parallelism, we have run 76 experiments, which the key was generated randomly, and the correct value of the bit condition was imported at the initial state $A[0][2][21]$. For all of the experiments the zero cube summation was obtained.

5.2   7 Rounds Conditional Cube Attack on Xoodyak

The round function of the Xoodoo is reduced to 7 rounds. By linearizing 1 round of Xoodoo, the degree of the 7-th round is 64. Therefore, we need 65 cube variables to mount the attack, 2 of them build the kernel quadratic term and the rest are ordinary cube variables. Table 3 presents kernel quadratic term, ordinary cube variables, and bit conditions obtained by the MILP model. The process of key recovery is analogous to Algorithm 1.

According to the Table 3, the key-bits need to be recovered are as $k_4 + k_{13} + k_{50} + k_{132} + k_{141} + k_{260} + k_{269}, k_{13} + k_{22} + k_{59} + k_{141} + k_{150} + k_{269} + k_{278}, k_{18} + k_{27} + k_{146} + k_{155} + k_{160} + k_{274} + k_{283}, k_2 + k_{25} + k_{130} + k_{153} + k_{258} + k_{281} + k_{295}, k_2 + k_{11} + k_{130} + k_{139} + k_{258} + k_{267} + k_{304}$. The time complexity to recover a 5-bit key is $2^5 \times 2^{65} = 2^{70}$. By rotating all of the parameters in 64 times, 320 key bits with the complexity of $2^6 \times 2^{70} = 2^{76}$ can be recovered. If we leave the remaining 64 key bits to exhaustive search, the total complexity is $2^{76} + 2^{64} = 2^{76.003}$. This is the first proposed key recovery on 7 rounds of Xoodyak.

6   Conclusion

In this paper, we present a 6-round and 7-round key recovery attack on Xoodyak which is one of the finalists of the lightweight cryptographic algorithm NIST competition with the structure, similar to SHA3 algorithm. As no attack is reported on the full version of Xoodyak, so far, Xoodyak can be regarded as a secure and efficient lightweight algorithm that is still of interest. We use MILP-based tool to find cube variables required to perform the attack and we import our cube variables in the absorbing associated data phase. The complexity of the 6-round attack and 7-round are $2^{42.45}$ and $2^{76.003}$, respectively.

Acknowledgments. The authors would like to thank Prof. Joan Daemen for drawing our attention to the associated data absorption phase of Xoodyak as a suitable target for analysis and for several fruitful discussions. We also thank Dr. Ling Song for explaining and clarifying some of the technical parts of her previous work.

References

1. Bertoni, G., Daemen, J., Peeters, M., Assche, G.V.: Keyak. https://keccak.team/keyak.html
2. Bertoni, G., Daemen, J., Peeters, M., Assche, G.V., Keer, R.V.: The Ketje authenticated encryption scheme. https://keccak.team/ketje.html

3. Bertoni, G., Daemen, J., Peeters, M., Van Assche, G.: Duplexing the sponge: single-pass authenticated encryption and other applications. In: Miri, A., Vaudenay, S. (eds.) SAC 2011. LNCS, vol. 7118, pp. 320–337. Springer, Heidelberg (2012). https://doi.org/10.1007/978-3-642-28496-0_19

4. Bi, W., Dong, X., Li, Z., Zong, R., Wang, X.: MILP-aided cube-attack-like cryptanalysis on Keccak keyed modes. Des. Codes Cryptogr. **87**(6), 1271–1296 (2019). https://doi.org/10.1007/s10623-018-0526-x

5. Daemen, J., Hoffert, S., Assche, G.V., Keer, R.V.: The design of Xoodoo and Xoofff. IACR Trans. Symmetric Cryptol. **2018**(4), 1–38 (2018). https://doi.org/10.13154/tosc.v2018.i4.1-38

6. Daemen, J., Hoffert, S., Peeters, M., Van Assche, G., Van Keer, R.: Xoodyak, a lightweight cryptographic scheme. IACR Trans. Symmetric Cryptol. **2020**(S1), 60–87 (2020). https://doi.org/10.13154/tosc.v2020.iS1.60-87, https://tosc.iacr.org/index.php/ToSC/article/view/8618

7. Dinur, I., Morawiecki, P., Pieprzyk, J., Srebrny, M., Straus, M.: Cube attacks and cube-attack-like cryptanalysis on the round-reduced Keccak sponge function. In: Oswald, E., Fischlin, M. (eds.) EUROCRYPT 2015. LNCS, vol. 9056, pp. 733–761. Springer, Heidelberg (2015). https://doi.org/10.1007/978-3-662-46800-5_28

8. Dinur, I., Shamir, A.: Cube attacks on tweakable black box polynomials. In: Joux, A. (ed.) EUROCRYPT 2009. LNCS, vol. 5479, pp. 278–299. Springer, Heidelberg (2009). https://doi.org/10.1007/978-3-642-01001-9_16

9. Dinur, I., Shamir, A.: Breaking grain-128 with dynamic cube attacks. In: Joux, A. (ed.) FSE 2011. LNCS, vol. 6733, pp. 167–187. Springer, Heidelberg (2011). https://doi.org/10.1007/978-3-642-21702-9_10

10. Division, N.C.S.: SHA-3 standard: permutation-based hash and extendable-output functions. FIPS Publication 202, National Institute of Standards and Technology, U.S. Department of Commerce (2014). http://csrc.nist.gov/publications/drafts/fips-202/fips_202_draft.pdf

11. Dobraunig, C., Eichlseder, M., Mendel, F., Schläffer, M.: Ascon v1.2: lightweight authenticated encryption and hashing. J. Cryptol. **34**(3), 33 (2021). https://doi.org/10.1007/s00145-021-09398-9

12. Dong, X., Li, Z., Wang, X., Qin, L.: Cube-like attack on round-reduced initialization of Ketje Sr. IACR Trans. Symmetric Cryptol. **2017**(1), 259–280 (2017). https://doi.org/10.13154/tosc.v2017.i1.259-280

13. Huang, S., Wang, X., Xu, G., Wang, M., Zhao, J.: Conditional cube attack on reduced-round Keccak sponge function. In: Coron, J.-S., Nielsen, J.B. (eds.) EUROCRYPT 2017, Part II. LNCS, vol. 10211, pp. 259–288. Springer, Cham (2017). https://doi.org/10.1007/978-3-319-56614-6_9

14. Lai, X.: Higher order derivatives and differential cryptanalysis. In: Blahut, R.E., Costello, D.J., Maurer, U., Mittelholzer, T. (eds.) Communications and Cryptography. The Springer International Series in Engineering and Computer Science, vol. 276, pp. 227–233. Springer, Boston (1994). https://doi.org/10.1007/978-1-4615-2694-0_23

15. Li, Z., Bi, W., Dong, X., Wang, X.: Improved conditional cube attacks on Keccak keyed modes with MILP method. In: Takagi, T., Peyrin, T. (eds.) ASIACRYPT 2017. LNCS, vol. 10624, pp. 99–127. Springer, Cham (2017). https://doi.org/10.1007/978-3-319-70694-8_4

16. Li, Z., Dong, X., Bi, W., Jia, K., Wang, X., Meier, W.: New conditional cube attack on Keccak keyed modes. IACR Cryptol. ePrint Arch. 392 (2019). https://eprint.iacr.org/2019/392

17. National Institute of Standards and Technology (NIST): Lightweight Cryptography Standardization Process: NIST Selects Ascon. NIST Website (2023). https://csrc.nist.gov/News/2023/lightweight-cryptography-nist-selects-ascon
18. National Institute of Standards and Technology (NIST): Lightweight Cryptography. NIST Website (2016). https://www.nist.gov/programs-projects/lightweight-cryptography
19. Song, L., Guo, J.: Cube-attack-like cryptanalysis of round-reduced Keccak using MILP. IACR Trans. Symmetric Cryptol. **2018**(3), 182–214 (2018). https://doi.org/10.13154/tosc.v2018.i3.182-214
20. Song, L., Guo, J., Shi, D., Ling, S.: New MILP modeling: improved conditional cube attacks on Keccak-based constructions. In: Peyrin, T., Galbraith, S. (eds.) ASIACRYPT 2018. LNCS, vol. 11273, pp. 65–95. Springer, Cham (2018). https://doi.org/10.1007/978-3-030-03329-3_3
21. The U.S. National Institute of Standards and Technology (NIST): SHA-3 Derived Functions: cSHAKE, KMAC, TupleHash and ParallelHash (2016). http://nvlpubs.nist.gov/nistpubs/SpecialPublications/NIST.SP.800-185.pdf
22. Zhou, H., Li, Z., Dong, X., Jia, K., Meier, W.: Practical key-recovery attacks on round-reduced Ketje Jr. Xoodoo-AE and Xoodyak. Comput. J. **63**(8), 1231–1246 (2020). https://doi.org/10.1093/comjnl/bxz152

AIBlock – Application Intelligence
and Blockchain Security

AIBlock 2023

Fifth Workshop on Application Intelligence and Blockchain Security

22 June 2023

General Chair

Man Ho Au — Hong Kong Polytechnic University, China

Program Chairs

Weizhi Meng — Technical University of Denmark, Denmark

Chunhua Su — University of Aizu, Japan

Program Committee

Mohiuddin Ahmed	Edith Cowan University, Australia
Alessandro Brighente	University of Padova, Italy
Jintai Ding	Tsinghua University, China
Yunguo Guan	University of New Brunswick, Canada
Dieter Gollmann	Hamburg University of Technology, Germany
Jinguang Han	Southeast University, China
Felix Harer	University of Fribourg, Switzerland
Peng Jiang	Beijing Institute of Technology, China
Georgios Kambourakis	University of the Aegean, Greece
William Knottenbelt	Imperial College London, UK
Mario Larangeira	Tokyo Institute of Technology/IOHK, Japan
Wenjuan Li	Hong Kong Polytechnic University, China
Akaki Mamageishvili	ETH Zurich, Switzerland
Zhe Xia	Wuhan University of Technology, China
Peng Xu	Huazhong University of Science and Technology, China
Claudio Juan	University of Zurich, Switzerland
Kouichi Sakurai	Kyushu University, Japan
Jianfeng Wang	Xidian University, China
Hao Wang	Shandong Normal University, China
Ding Wang	Nankai University, China

Qianhong Wu	Beihang University, China
Andreas Veneris	University of Toronto, Canada
Yizhi Ren	Hangzhou Dianzi University, China
Jiale Zhang	Yangzhou University, China
Yongjun Zhao	ByteDance, China

Steering Committee

Robert Deng	Singapore Management University, Singapore
Georgios Kambourakis	University of the Aegean, Greece
Sokratis Katsikas	Norwegian University of Science and Technology, Norway
Man Ho Au	Hong Kong Polytechnic University, China
Weizhi Meng (Chair)	Technical University of Denmark, Denmark
Chunhua Su	University of Aizu, Japan

Additional Reviewer

Fuyang Deng	Beihang University, China

Smart Contract-Based E-Voting System Using Homomorphic Encryption and Zero-Knowledge Proof

Yuxiao Wu and Shoji Kasahara$^{(\boxtimes)}$

Division of Information Science, Nara Institute of Science and Technology,
Nara 6300192, Japan
{wu.yuxiao.ws9,kasahara}@is.naist.jp

Abstract. As an indispensable part of establishing modern representative democratic organizations, election is based on a voting process on site or remotely. With the rapid development of information technology, the application of electronic voting systems in practice is significantly increasing in recent years. Consequently, whether an electronic voting system is secure and reliable enough is the most critical factor of the systems. Whereas, most of the existing proposals neglect to confirm the trustworthiness of the administrator, which may impact the security and availability of the system. For this purpose, we propose an up-to-date electronic voting system based on smart contract using additively homomorphic encryption and non-interactive zero-knowledge proof. In our work, we utilize a concise zero-knowledge proof algorithm and an inbound oracle in combination to allow voters to verify the fidelity of the administrator. We prove the feasibility, efficiency, and scalability of our system can satisfy a majority of application scenarios including large-scale voting. In particular, we evaluate the time performance and cost performance and demonstrate its merits including the low cost in many functions and linear performance when generating zero-knowledge proof.

Keywords: Smart contract · Blockchain · E-voting · Zero-knowledge proof · Homomorphic encryption · Oracle

1 Introduction

With the goal to minimize the expense and maximize the efficiency of executing an election, it is becoming increasingly difficult to ignore the security, privacy and compliance when designing electronic voting systems [11]. For this purpose, in the area of e-voting system, there has been a recent surge in interest and research. However, security, transparency, distributed authority, data integrity,

This research was supported in part by Japan Society for the Promotion of Science under Grant-in-Aid for Scientific Research (A) No. 19H01103, and Grant-in-Aid for Challenging Research (Exploratory) No. 22K19776.

J. Zhou et al. (Eds.): ACNS 2023 Workshops, LNCS 13907, pp. 67–83, 2023.
https://doi.org/10.1007/978-3-031-41181-6_4

privacy and compliance requirements have become the main bottlenecks blocking e-voting systems implemented on a large scale [30].

In order to counter the bottlenecks that mentioned above, a promising data structure known as blockchain is initially introduced to e-voting systems. In essence, blockchain is a distributed ledger that has the property of tamper-resistance. That is, the blockchain's database is maintained by each node on chain rather than single node which leads to blockchain be the immutable ledger with transactions in old blocks preserved and transactions in new blocks irreversibly added [19].

With regard to the e-voting systems proposed for implementation using the blockchain technology, a series of requirements and features are summarized to build proper schemes in [28].

1. **Receipt-freeness** [4]: Any evidence proving the voter's selection for a particular candidate is not allowed to be revealed.
2. **Fairness** [6,9]: Every voter should have the same weight when taking part in the voting.
3. **Data integrity** [12]: Each valid vote is recorded correctly and can't be tampered with by any part, once logged.
4. **Privacy** [33]: The anonymity of voters should be guaranteed.
5. **Eligibility** [22]: The system only accepts the registered voter's ballot.
6. **Reliability** [8]: The system is stable and no vote is missed.
7. **Uniqueness** [24]: Double voting is not allowed.
8. **Verifiability** [16]: Voters have the right to verify whether their ballots are tallied legitimately.

According to the features and requirements that mentioned above, cryptography is considered as one of the most effective technologies that can be utilized to e-voting systems. On one hand, in order to achieve the goal of verifying the trustworthiness of the administrator without information disclosure, zero-knowledge proof is one of the most widely used cryptographic primitives and plays a key role in the field of privacy protection. On the other hand, additively homomorphic encryption has the features that only supports arithmetic for elements of its plaintext space and provides an operation that produces the encryption of the sum of two numbers, given only the encryptions of the numbers [10]. Consequently, it can be effectively applied to e-voting systems that focuses on data confidentiality. In our work, combining these two cryptographic technologies enables us to realize a majority of the above-mentioned requirements relating to information security including receipt-freeness, privacy and verifiability. Whereas, data integrity and reliability relies on the immutability of blockchain and fairness, eligibility and uniqueness is based on the implementation of software system by utilizing solidity and python.

The rest of this paper is organized as follows. Section 2 presents related work and Sect. 3 introduces some fundamental technologies as preliminaries. Section 4 represents our proposed e-voting system, and Sect. 5 shows the performance evaluation of our system from the perspective of time performance and gas fee performance. Finally, Sect. 6 concludes the paper.

2   Related Work

The existing e-voting schemes that blockchain is applied to are classified into two types: blockchain-based e-voting system and e-voting system using blockchain.

2.1   Blockchain-Based E-Voting System

In the blockchain-based e-voting system, the whole system is built upon the blockchain framework. In other words, blockchain is convinced to be the infrastructure that sustains the system. Most of the blockchain-based e-voting system adopt the permissioned blockchain structure instead of permissionless blockchains such as Bitcoin and Ethereum.

In [11], the authors propose a blockchain-based e-voting system based on a permissioned blockchain, and some of the popular blockchain frameworks are evaluated for constructing a blockchain-based e-voting system. Sun et al. propose a simple voting protocol based on the existing Quantum Blockchain [13,25]. It satisfies the most important properties of secure voting protocols by introducing matrix and number theory to the stages of ballot commitment and ballot tallying [24]. In addition, a blockchain-enabled large-scale e-voting system with robustness and universal verifiability is presented in [32]. In this system, a hybrid approach which combines the counting bloom filter and Merkle hash tree is developed in order to break the bottleneck of cost performance.

Generally speaking, this kind of e-voting systems has the merits of cost-friendly performance and high response rate. However, a major problem with this approach is utilizing the permissioned blockchain as the blockchain framework of the system, leading to lower reliability for voters. In particular, most of the nodes in the system are maintained by the administrator, making it more difficult for voters to verify the fidelity of the administrator. This verification by voters is one of our goals.

2.2   E-Voting System Using Blockchain

Referring to the relation between Infrastructure-as-a-service (Iaas) and Platform-as-a-service (Paas) (two kinds of cloud service delivery models) in cloud computing [5], the blockchain in this kind of e-voting system acts as the platform rather than the infrastructure compared with that in blockchain-based e-voting systems. For this reason, this kind of systems mainly focuses on smart contract provided by the blockchain. Consequently, Ethereum is convinced to be one of the most suitable blockchain frameworks for this kind of systems due to its reliability and functionality.

The authors of [31] present a platform-independent secure and verifiable voting system combining with a variety of cryptographic techniques including Paillier cryptosystem that supports the execution of a smart contract. In [18], Lyu et al. propose a trustless e-voting system, which is deployed on Ethereum by smart contract. The authors use linkable ring signature [7,14,15] and threshold encryption without a trusted third party in their system. Except for these e-voting systems focusing on security and privacy by cryptography, some other systems concentrating on the countermeasure for the low efficiency and expensive cost also utilize blockchain as the platform. Based on web3 framework and POA network, Al-Madani et al. make their system to support real-time service without using any cryptosystem [3].

In contrast to blockchain-based e-voting systems, e-voting systems using blockchain are commonly doubted due to the higher expense. However, this kind of systems has great reliability because of introducing the existing famous blockchain framework (e.g. Ethereum). For this reason, we design our system based on the criterion that is similar to e-voting systems using blockchain.

3 Preliminaries

3.1 Smart Contract

In order to minimize contracting cost between transacting parties and to avoid accidental exceptions or malicious actions during contract performance, Nick Szabo suggested translating the clauses of a contract into code and embedding them into software or hardware to make them self-execute, which is known as smart contract [27,34].

As a program running on a blockchain, a smart contract can be correctly executed by a network of mutually distrusting nodes without the need of an external trusted authority. The self-executing nature of smart contracts provides a tremendous opportunity for use in many fields that rely on data to drive transactions [26].

Blockchains can be divided into permissioned blockchains (i.e. non-public) and permissionless blockchains (i.e. public). Permissionless blockchain platforms allow any user to join the network while permissioned blockchain platforms allow only permitted users to join [34]. Different blockchain platforms provide different support for smart contracts. Some (e.g. Bitcoin) may only allow users to use a simple scripting language to develop smart contracts with simple logic; while some platforms, such as Ethereum, support much more advanced programming languages for writing smart contracts [23].

3.2 Homomorphic Encryption

An encryption is homomorphic if from Enc(a) and Enc(b), it is possible to compute Enc(f(a, b)) where Enc(x) represents the encryption of x and f is +, ×, or ⊕ (exclusive OR) and without using the private key for decryption [29].

Homomorphic encryption can be categorized into three types of schemes with respect to the number of allowed operations on the encrypted data; (1) Partially Homomorphic Encryption (PHE), which allows only one type of operation with an unlimited number of times (i.e., no bound on the number of usages), (2) Somewhat Homomorphic Encryption (SWHE), which allows some types of operations a limited number of times, and. (3) Fully Homomorphic Encryption

(FHE), which allows an unlimited number of operations for an unlimited number of times [1].

Paillier encryption is classified as Partially Homomorphic Encryption. In detail, it is an additively homomorphic encryption scheme based on composite degree residuosity classes. Paillier encryption is provably secure under appropriate assumptions in the standard model [20]. Simultaneously, Paillier encryption is proved to have the additive homomorphism so that it can be appropriately applied to e-voting systems because of the massive utilizing of add operation in these systems.

3.3 Zero-Knowledge Proof

Roughly speaking, the zero-knowledge proof realizes a scenario that a prover who wants to convince a verifier that some statement is true without revealing any other information.

As the applications, privacy-preserving systems use zero-knowledge proofs to prove the correctness of outputs without revealing sensitive information about inputs. In online voting systems, voters prove that they correctly encrypted their vote, without revealing any information about the selected candidate [2].

The authors of [17] propose zksk, a well-documented Python library for defining and computing sigma protocols (the most popular class of zero-knowledge proofs). In zksk, smaller proofs can be converted into building blocks that then can be combined into bigger proofs. In addition, compared with the large size of key and proof of traditional zero-knowledge proofs such as zk-SNARKs, zksk is more practical in some areas due to its smaller data size as low as several bytes.

4 Proposed System

This section describes the proposed smart contract-based e-voting system using partially homomorphic encryption and non-interactive zero-knowledge proof. Furthermore, oracle is another crucial technology applied to this system so that data privacy in the Ethereum-based smart contract is feasible to be guaranteed against external homomorphism attackers and internal untrusted entities.

4.1 System Components

The roles of users that participate the voting system are classified into three types: administrator, voter, and observer. The administrator and voter are indispensable for the voting system and have their own nodes, whereas the observer is optional and is not compulsively required to have a node in Ethereum. Moreover, the voter who tries to verify the zero-knowledge proofs associated with other voters is also regarded as an observer. The definitions of the three roles are as follows.

1. **Administrator:** The entity which is set up to manage and maintain the whole process of voting. The administrator's work includes managing voter registration, initializing voter identity, creating smart contracts for the election, verifying ballots from voters, generating zero-knowledge proof, transmitting processed data to the oracle node, and announcing the voting result.
2. **Voter:** The entity which is eligible to act as a participant in the democratic election process. Valid ballots from voters are the essential component that results in formal voting. It is feasible for voters to register in the system using their identifiers such as Ethereum addresses, request the public key published in the blockchain, cast ballots in the smart contract, and verify the corresponding zero-knowledge proof which reveals their own identities.
3. **Observer:** The entity which is an extra part of the system roles to assure the feasibility and availability of the system. Observers are required to verify the zero-knowledge proofs of each voter and publish the verification result individually so that the public can decide whether the result published by the administrator is trusted or not.

We adopt smart contracts for implementing our voting system. The system has three types of smart contracts: Contract Voting, Contract VID, and Contract ZKP. The Contract Voting provides the functions of casting the ballot and processing the original voting data. Contract VID is used for publishing all voter IDs. Contract ZKP provides the functions of zero-knowledge proof for observers and voters. The details of the smart contracts are as follows.

1. **Contract Voting:** The Contract Voting manages the voters' identifiers and announces the administrator's public key to the eligible voters. The voters' identifiers are registered in the address array type named "Alist". The administrator verifies the eligibility of a voter by checking his/her identifier in Alist. If the administrator authenticates the voter as an eligible voter, the administrator announces his/her public key to the voter with a function of "announce_PK". When the voter casts a ballot, the administrator verifies his/her voting data with the function of "verify_ballot".
2. **Contract VID:** The Contract VID manages the identifiers of the voters whose ballots are verified to be valid and publishes them without revealing voters' privacy. All voters' identifiers are stored in a string array type called "VID_list". At the stage of result announcing, any voter and observer can call the function named "return_VID" to acquire all voters' identifiers.
3. **Contract ZKP:** The Contract ZKP manages the zero-knowledge proofs according to ballots that have been verified to be valid and allows the voter to retrieve his/her corresponding proof and verification key. A parameter in the type of string of "ZKP" is utilized to request zero-knowledge proof data downloaded from the server via oracle. When a voter wants to search the corresponding zero-knowledge proof, he/she can get the result with a function known as "search_ZKP" as long as the valid address is provided.

The data format of a vote is the encoding of its ballot. Due to the application of partially homomorphic encryption in this system, the form of voting data is designed to be compatible with it. After generating his/her voting data of which detail will be described in the following part, each voter encrypts the voting data with the public key of the administrator using Paillier encryption.

Let M and N denote the number of candidates and that of voters, respectively. We define the following variables for encoding.

- We define Voted_ballot(j) ($j \in \{1, \ldots, N\}$) as voter j's selection among candidates. If voter j votes for candidate $i \in \{1, \ldots, M\}$, Voted_ballot(j) is set to
$$\text{Voted\_ballot}(j) = (10^8)^{i-1}.$$

For example, consider candidates A and B are indexed with 1 and 2, respectively. If voter j votes for candidate A (resp. B), Voted_ballot(j) is set to 1 (resp. 100,000,000). Here, we set the interval of 10^8 for balancing the data size and the scalability.

- Voter_address(j) is the voter j's address in the blockchain network. For example, in Ethereum, if voter j's address is 0xeC2804Dd9B992C10396b5Af176f06 923d984D90e, this value is substituted to Voter_address(j).

- Each voter has his/her own unique voter ID which is generated by the administrator at the voter registration stage. Let Voter_ID(j) denote the ID of voter j. The administrator randomly generates a number from 1 to 99,999,999 for each voter who passed the identity verification and distributes it to the corresponding voter privately. Consider the case of 100,000,000 voter's participation. Assuming the extreme situation that all of them vote for A, the resulting sum of the Voted_ballot is 100,000,000. Under this condition, we are unable to distinguish the situations that whether there is one voter voting for B or there are 100,000,000 voters voting for A except for additional verification. In order to avoid these matters, we set the maximum capacity of voters to be 99,999,999 and correspondingly make sure that all of voter's ID are in the range from 1 to 99,999,999. Each voter knows his/her own voter ID, and the administrator can check the mapping relation between the voter's address and voter ID.

- At voting, each voter generates his/her own voting data. We define Voting_data(j) as the voting data of voter j, which is given by

$$\text{Voting\_data}(j) =$$
$$\text{Voted\_ballot}(j) + \text{Voter\_address}(j) + \text{Voter\_ID}(j).$$

Each voter calculates his/her Voting_data, encrypts the Voting_data as the ballot and sends it to the Contract Voting for voting.

The voting data processing for the administrator is classified into three task types. The first task type is retrieving the voting data array and address array from Contract Voting, then the administrator will rebuild these two arrays and generate an aggregated list consisting of the voter ID, voting data, and zero-knowledge proof. The second task type is verifying the validity of each ballot and generating the zero-knowledge proof for the voters whose ballots are verified to be valid. Last but not least, the list containing information processed in the former two steps is uploaded to a web page in json type deployed in our server built up for the oracle node to achieve data.

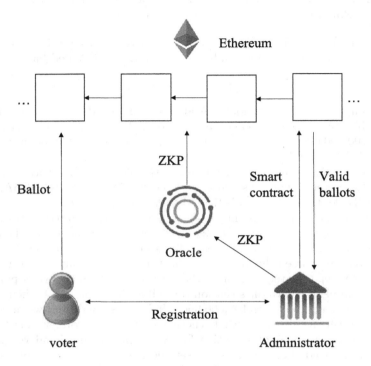

Fig. 1. Overview of the System.

4.2   System Model

Figure 1 illustrates the overview of this system. The procedures included in our system are (1) voter registration, (2) system initialization, (3) contract creation, (4) voting, (5) ballot verification, (6) ballot tallying and result announcing, (7) zero-knowledge proof verification, (8) trustworthiness verification. The functions of each procedure are as follows.

1. **Voter registration:** The registration is held by the administrator and aims to sign up the eligible users and distribute the voter IDs. In detail, the administrator can authenticate the voter identity in two methods in accordance with the authentication site: on-site authentication and online authentication. In on-site authentication, the administrator directly authenticate the valid identity certificate of participants face to face. As soon as authentication finished, the administrator informs the corresponding voter ID to the voter. In the

other case, with the help of technologies including blockchain and encryption, the system assures that the voter's identity is authenticated and the voter ID is distributed in a private channel which is independent of the blockchain.

2. **System initialization:** The administrator processes the information received in voter registration and transforms it into arrays that can be used in the following procedures. On the one hand, the administrator creates an "Alist" containing all voters' addresses and uploads it to contract Voting. On the other hand, the administrator generates a mapping list called "Mlist" that maps the voter's address to the voter ID according to voter registration, and saves it privately and locally.

3. **Contract creation:** In this step, the smart contracts mentioned in Subsect. 4.1 are instantiated and deployed to Ethereum. Except for the instantiation and deployment, the administrator collects the addresses of these contracts from Ethereum and publishes them to voters.

4. **Voting:** Voting is the interactive process between contract Voting and voters, and is considered as a core operation in this system. In advance, voters are required to calculate their voting data in plaintext. Then, without the participation of the administrator, the voter calls the function "announce_PK" to obtain the administrator's public key based on Paillier encryption. Furthermore, voters encrypt the voting data and upload them to contract Voting.

5. **Ballot verification:** Ballot verification is comprised of two stages: verification by contract and verification by the administrator. When contract Voting receives the encrypted voting data, it automatically verifies whether the address that the data come from is registered and whether there is any voter who casts the ballot more than one time. The ballots that do not satisfy the two conditions are discarded. The ballots that are not discarded in the first stage are then verified by the administrator for the correctness of the original voting data. The administrator decrypts the voting data in ciphertext and judges the decrypted voting data using "Mlist". Ballots satisfying the conditions in both two stages are judged as valid.

6. **Ballot tallying and result announcing:** When the process of voting ends, the administrator collects all valid ballots and adds their voting data in ciphertext together to calculate m_{sum}, which is given by

$$m_{sum} = \sum_{j \in \mathcal{N}_{vb}} \text{Voting\_data}(j),$$

where $\mathcal{N}_{vb}$ is the index set of the voters whose ballots are judged as valid. Then, the administrator decrypts m_{sum} and gains the result which can represent the voting result by the following formula

$$\text{Result} = m_{sum} - \sum_{j \in \mathcal{N}_{vb}} \{\text{Voter\_address}(j) + \text{Voter\_ID}(j)\}.$$

Then, the administrator conducts vote counting and announces the winner on the official platform.

7. **Zero-knowledge proof verification:** In this system, we apply a non-interactive zero-knowledge proof proposal called "zksk" [17] as the method of zero-knowledge proof. The proof is generated just after the ballot is verified as valid at both the two stages. Here, each voter's ID is kept secret. The detailed operations of the prover (the administrator) is illustrated in Algorithm 1.

Algorithm 1. Generating Zero-knowledge Proof (operations on the prover's side).

Input: group(G,g), voters' identifiers VID, random values n, r, k
Output: proof π, verification key y
1: $secret = $ VID
2: $y = secret \times g$
3: $stmt = (y, n \times g)$
4: $pre_com = $ None
5: $com = r$
6: $chal = H(y \parallel pre\_com \parallel com)$
7: $resp = k + secret \times chal$
8: $\pi = (pre\_com, chal, resp)$
9: **return** π, y

When the zero-knowledge proof has been generated according to the above algorithm, the administrator uploads it to contract ZKP which is mapped to the voter's address. The voter or any observer can access the proof with the specific address through the calling of contract ZKP. Then, they conduct Algorithm 2 to verify the proof.

Algorithm 2. Verifying Zero-knowledge Proof (operations on the verifier's side).

Input: group(G,g), proof π, verification key y
Output: proving result True/False
1: $new\_com = resp \times g + (-chal) \times y$
2: $new\_chal = H(y \parallel pre\_com \parallel com)$
3: **if** $new\_chal == chal$ **then**
4:     **return** True
5: **else**
6:     **return** False
7: **end if**

If a voter verifies the proof associated with him/her successfully, he/she can trust that his/her ballot is tallied correctly. On the other hand, an observer can verify the proof of any address to check whether there is any extra ballot falsified by the administrator.

8. **Trustworthiness verification:** The procedure of trustworthiness verification is executed to verify the fidelity of the administrator from a different

aspect with zero-knowledge proof verification. The observer utilizes m_{sum} in procedure 6 and does reverse operations to check whether the administrator revised the result. The verification process is shown in Algorithm 3.

Algorithm 3. Trustworthiness Verification.

Input: voting result Result, the sum of voting data m_{sum}, public key (n_1, g_1), voters' addresses Voter_address, voters' identifiers Voter_ID
Output: verification result True/False
1: $m = \text{Result} + \sum_{j \in \mathcal{N}_{vb}} \{\text{Voter\_address}(j) + \text{Voter\_ID}(j)\}$
2: $\exists\, r,\ m_{sum} == g_1{}^m \times r^{n_1} \mod n_1{}^2$
3: $\exists\, r, s,\ m_{sum} + s \times n_1{}^2 == g_1{}^m \times r^{n_1}$
4: **Condition 1:** $\exists\, s, (m_{sum} + s \times n_1{}^2 \mod g_1{}^m) == 0$
5: **Condition 2:** $\exists\, s\ s.t.\ Condition1,\ \sqrt[n_1]{\frac{m_{sum} + s \times n_1{}^2}{g_1{}^m}} \in \mathcal{N}$
6: **if** Condition 1 and Condition 2 are True **then**
7:     **return** True
8: **else**
9:     **return** False
10: **end if**

4.3   System Features

Based on the system components and system model, a slice of features are clarified. In our work, one of the most popular permissionless blockchains known as Ethereum is applied as the blockchain framework of the system so that reliability and robustness of the system is ensured by the stability of Ethereum and smart contract themselves.

As mentioned in Subsect. 4.2, we utilize a succinct zero-knowledge proof known as "zksk". In comparison with other non-interactive zero-knowledge proofs (e.g. zk-SNARK), the size of zksk's proving key and verification key is smaller and can be recorded in a parameter in string type. Thus, zksk is firmly convinced to be extremely compatible with this system rather than many other non-interactive zero-knowledge proofs due to the increasing cost according to data size when using oracle. Consequently, the application of zksk confirms the verifiability ensuring the voter's right to learn that his/her ballot has been correctly tallied.

The voter's privacy is assured by utilizing Paillier encryption, which is also known as an additively homomorphic encryption algorithm. The correctness of the formula that used to check whether the administrator revises the result is based on the additively homomorphism of Paillier cryptosystem.

In addition, receipt-freeness, fairness, data integrity, and uniqueness are ensured by the system structure which has been introduced in Subsect. 4.2. In detail, receipt-freeness and fairness are decided by the procedures including voter registration, voting, and ballot verification whereas data integrity and uniqueness are based on the verification process executed in ballot verification procedure.

5   Performance Evaluation

5.1   Experiment Environment

As explained in Subsect. 4.3, we apply Ethereum to the development of the proposed system, which is a permissionless blockchain as the blockchain infrastructure. Due to the cost saving, we utilize a local Ethereum blockchain known as Ganache to simulate transactions on Ethereum.

In our work, we implement the system in Python and Solidity. The functions described in Subsect. 4.1 are written in solidity. The remaining functions including zero-knowledge generation, server command, the second stage of ballot verification are realized by Python.

In order to enhance the connection between on-chain environment and off-chain environment and to upload zero-knowledge proof to contract ZKP, we select Provable [21] as the oracle in our system. With the merit of low cost and high response speed, Provable is feasible when applied in our system. In Ganache experiment environment, we set up a Ethereum bridge that allows Provable to be utilized to the testnet.

For evaluating the performance of the system, we run voter client, administrator client, and ganache client in the PC with Intel Pentium 4415U CPU, NVIDIA GeForce 940MX GPU, and ADATA DDR4 2666 12G RAM.

5.2   Execution Time Performance

In this subsection, we investigate the component-wise execution-time performance of the proposed voting system in order to figure out the time consumption of the whole system and which function takes over most of the time.

The functions measured in this experiment are: loading ZKP, loading VID, generating ZKP, processing data on administrator side, voting (successful), voting (double voting), voting (not in Alist), encrypting data, and decrypting data. Table 1 illustrates the execution time performance of each function under the condition of one voter's participation.

In Table 1, loading ZKP takes over most of the time, which exceeds 50% of the whole executing time. Following loading ZKP, the execution times of loading VID and generating key are around 2 s. The execution time of voting in case of a valid ballot is over 1 s, while the execution times of voting in cases of double voting and not-in-Alist are smaller than that of valid voting. The reason for this result is that loading operation in smart contract needs to send VIDs and zero-knowledge proofs from the off-chain environment to the on-chain environment using oracle. Therefore, it takes a lot of time for data exchange among different environments. Meanwhile, generating keys and voting also take more time than other operations due to the complicated cryptographic algorithm

Table 1. Execution time performance.

Operation	Time [s]
Generate Key	2.016
Encrypt data	0.054
Decrypt data	0.105
Vote (successful)	1.312
Vote (double voting)	0.516
Vote (not in Alist)	0.797
Process Data on Admin Side	0.787
Generate ZKP	0.003
Load VID	2.224
Load ZKP	9.226

in them. According to the analysis, we have two conclusions. First of all, the whole execution time when casting per ballot is about 1.438 s to 2.243 s, which is better than a majority of existing systems that have been investigated on. What's more, the operations executed by smart contract are the main reasons that result in low efficiency.

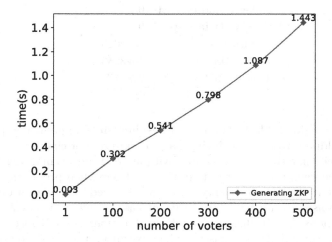

Fig. 2. Generating Zero-knowledge Proof.

Generating zero-knowledge proof is regarded as the most core part of this system. Figure 2 demonstrates the total execution time for generating zero-knowledge proof in cases of the number of voters participating the system equal to 1, 100, 200, 300, 400 and 500. With up to 500 voters' participation, our system has the ability to support zero-knowledge generating within 1.5 s, which is fast enough for a large-scale election at the present stage. Meanwhile, this experiment proves that the proposed voting system exhibits good scalability performance since the time for generating zero-knowledge proof is proportional to the number of voters.

5.3 Gas Fee

In this subsection, we investigate how much gas fee of Ethereum is needed for the proposed voting system. We measure gas fee of the following functions: deploying contract ZKP, deploying contract VID, announcing public key, verifying ballot, achieving address list, achieving data list, returning VID, oracle operation, and receiving ZKP. Table 2 shows the above-mentioned functions' gas fees.

Table 2. Gas Fee Performance.

Operation	Gas Fee (gas)
Deploy voting.sol	151305
Deploy VID.sol	375005
Deploy ZKP.sol	2043210
Announce Public Key	0
Verify Ballot	2796389
Achieve Address List	0
Achieve Data List	0
Return VID	1382626
Utilize Oracle	1623253
Receive ZKP	278617

We observe in Table 2 that operations including announcing public key, achieving address list, and achieving data list are free of charge. The functions designed such that those are executed without revision by marking them with "view" in the definition statements of the functions when programming lead to this result. For this reason, plenty of gas fee is saved. The execution of verifying ballot consumes almost 0.007 Ether of gas fee, which is spent more than other operations. The utilizing of multiply iterations is the cause resulting in the excessive consumption of gas fee when executing the operation of verifying ballot.

Adding all gas fees in Table 2 yields the total cost of the operations under the condition of one voter's participation equal to about 0.027 Ether. From another perspective, by employing qualitative modes of enquiry, we attempt to illuminate that the functions regarding contract deployment and data comparison take over a majority of expense of this system. The strategy on cost saving of the system can be established based on these functions.

6   Conclusion

In this paper, we proposed a smart contract-based e-voting system, which can satisfy most of the requirements, especially verifiability. Through the experiments on the execution-time performance and gas consumption, we showed the feasibility, efficiency, and scalability of our system, that can satisfy a majority of application scenarios including large-scale voting.

In future work, we consider the following aspects.

- We have developed a system that combines multitudinous state-of-the-art techniques to make sure the data integrity and reliability, proving its performance based on qualitative evaluation. However, there is increasing concern that our system is not so stable as our evaluation because of the partial execution of centralized operations in the system. In particular, some of the voter's privacy is possibly disclosed if the administrator has the malicious intention in these operations. According to these factors, we shall focus on how to establish a more decentralized system and to take smart contract as the replacement of the administrator in more functions.
- Through the analysis of the execution-time performance and gas fee, we found that several functions can be modified for building a more cost-saving and efficient system. For this purpose, not only in python, but also in solidity, we shall apply some new strategies to the functions. In one case, as we mentioned, the operation of loading ZKP takes over 50% of the whole execution time, which affects the efficiency of the system. Therefore, our strategy for enhancing the execution time from this perspective is to change the oracle that has a better response performance. Consequently, designing and implementing these strategies are another core points in our future work.

References

1. Acar, A., Aksu, H., Uluagac, A.S., Conti, M.: A survey on homomorphic encryption schemes: theory and implementation. ACM Comput. Surv. **51**(4), 1–35 (2018). https://doi.org/10.1145/3214303
2. Adida, B., De Marneffe, O., Pereira, O., Quisquater, J.J., et al.: Electing a university president using open-audit voting: analysis of real-world use of Helios. EVT/WOTE **9**(10) (2009)
3. Al-madani, A.M., Gaikwad, A.T., Mahale, V., Ahmed, Z.A.: Decentralized E-voting system based on smart contract by using blockchain technology. In: 2020 International Conference on Smart Innovations in Design, Environment, Management, Planning and Computing (ICSIDEMPC), pp. 176–180 (2020). https://doi.org/10.1109/ICSIDEMPC49020.2020.9299581
4. Ali, S.T., Murray, J.: An overview of end-to-end verifiable voting systems. In: Real-World Electronic Voting, pp. 189–234 (2016)
5. Almorsy, M., Grundy, J., Müller, I.: An analysis of the cloud computing security problem (2016). https://doi.org/10.48550/ARXIV.1609.01107, https://arxiv.org/abs/1609.01107

6. Anane, R., Freeland, R., Theodoropoulos, G.: e-voting requirements and implementation. In: The 9th IEEE International Conference on E-Commerce Technology and The 4th IEEE International Conference on Enterprise Computing, E-Commerce and E-Services (CEC-EEE 2007), pp. 382–392 (2007). https://doi.org/10.1109/CEC-EEE.2007.42

7. Au, M.H., Liu, J.K., Yuen, T.H., Wong, D.S.: ID-based ring signature scheme secure in the standard model. In: Yoshiura, H., Sakurai, K., Rannenberg, K., Murayama, Y., Kawamura, S. (eds.) IWSEC 2006. LNCS, vol. 4266, pp. 1–16. Springer, Heidelberg (2006). https://doi.org/10.1007/11908739_1

8. Bokslag, W., de Vries, M.: Evaluating e-voting: theory and practice. CoRR abs/1602.02509 (2016). https://arxiv.org/abs/1602.02509

9. Fujioka, A., Okamoto, T., Ohta, K.: A practical secret voting scheme for large scale elections. In: Seberry, J., Zheng, Y. (eds.) AUSCRYPT 1992. LNCS, vol. 718, pp. 244–251. Springer, Heidelberg (1993). https://doi.org/10.1007/3-540-57220-1_66

10. Hardy, S., et al.: Private federated learning on vertically partitioned data via entity resolution and additively homomorphic encryption. CoRR abs/1711.10677 (2017). https://arxiv.org/abs/1711.10677

11. Hjálmarsson, F.ß., Hreiðarsson, G.K., Hamdaqa, M., Hjálmtýsson, G.: Blockchain-based e-voting system. In: 2018 IEEE 11th International Conference on Cloud Computing (CLOUD), pp. 983–986 (2018). https://doi.org/10.1109/CLOUD.2018.00151

12. Keshk, A.E., Abdul-Kader, H.M.: Development of remotely secure E-voting system. In: 2007 ITI 5th International Conference on Information and Communications Technology, pp. 235–243 (2007). https://doi.org/10.1109/ITICT.2007.4475655

13. Kiktenko, E.O., et al.: Quantum-secured blockchain. Quantum Sci. Technol. 3(3), 035004 (2018). https://doi.org/10.1088/2058-9565/aabc6b, https://dx.doi.org/10.1088/2058-9565/aabc6b

14. Liu, J.K., Wei, V.K., Wong, D.S.: Linkable spontaneous anonymous group signature for ad hoc groups. In: Wang, H., Pieprzyk, J., Varadharajan, V. (eds.) ACISP 2004. LNCS, vol. 3108, pp. 325–335. Springer, Heidelberg (2004). https://doi.org/10.1007/978-3-540-27800-9_28

15. Liu, J.K., Wong, D.S.: Linkable ring signatures: security models and new schemes. In: Gervasi, O., et al. (eds.) ICCSA 2005. LNCS, vol. 3481, pp. 614–623. Springer, Heidelberg (2005). https://doi.org/10.1007/11424826_65

16. Liu, Y., Wang, Q.: An E-voting protocol based on blockchain. Cryptology ePrint Archive, Paper 2017/1043 (2017). https://eprint.iacr.org/2017/1043

17. Lueks, W., Kulynych, B., Fasquelle, J., Bail-Collet, S.L., Troncoso, C.: zksk: a library for composable zero-knowledge proofs. In: Proceedings of the 18th ACM Workshop on Privacy in the Electronic Society (WPES@CCS), pp. 50–54 (2019)

18. Lyu, J., Jiang, Z.L., Wang, X., Nong, Z., Au, M.H., Fang, J.: A secure decentralized trustless E-voting system based on smart contract. In: 2019 18th IEEE International Conference on Trust, Security and Privacy in Computing and Communications/13th IEEE International Conference on Big Data Science and Engineering (TrustCom/BigDataSE), pp. 570–577 (2019). https://doi.org/10.1109/TrustCom/BigDataSE.2019.00082

19. Pahlajani, S., Kshirsagar, A., Pachghare, V.: Survey on private blockchain consensus algorithms. In: 2019 1st International Conference on Innovations in Information and Communication Technology (ICIICT), pp. 1–6 (2019). https://doi.org/10.1109/ICIICT1.2019.8741353

20. Paillier, P.: Public-key cryptosystems based on composite degree residuosity classes. In: Stern, J. (ed.) EUROCRYPT 1999. LNCS, vol. 1592, pp. 223–238. Springer, Heidelberg (1999). https://doi.org/10.1007/3-540-48910-x_16
21. Provable: Provable documentation. https://docs.provable.xyz/
22. Ryan, P.Y.A., Bismark, D., Heather, J., Schneider, S., Xia, Z.: Prêt á voter: a voter-verifiable voting system. IEEE Trans. Inf. Forensics Secur. 4(4), 662–673 (2009). https://doi.org/10.1109/TIFS.2009.2033233
23. Seijas, P.L., Thompson, S., McAdams, D.: Scripting smart contracts for distributed ledger technology. Cryptology ePrint Archive, Paper 2016/1156 (2016). https://eprint.iacr.org/2016/1156
24. Sun, X., Wang, Q., Kulicki, P., Sopek, M.: A simple voting protocol on quantum blockchain. Int. J. Theor. Phys. 58(1), 275–281 (2019)
25. Sun, X., Wang, Q., Kulicki, P., Zhao, X.: Quantum-enhanced logic-based blockchain I: quantum honest-success byzantine agreement and qulogicoin (2018). https://doi.org/10.48550/ARXIV.1805.06768, https://arxiv.org/abs/1805.06768
26. Swan, M.: Blockchain: Blueprint for a New Economy. O'Reilly Media, Inc. (2015)
27. Szabo, N.: Formalizing and securing relationships on public networks. First Monday (1997)
28. Taą, R., Tanrlöver, Ö.Ö: A systematic review of challenges and opportunities of blockchain for E-voting. Symmetry 12(8) (2020). https://doi.org/10.3390/sym12081328, https://www.mdpi.com/2073-8994/12/8/1328
29. Tebaa, M., Hajji, S.E., Ghazi, A.E.: Homomorphic encryption method applied to cloud computing. In: 2012 National Days of Network Security and Systems, pp. 86–89 (2012). https://doi.org/10.1109/JNS2.2012.6249248
30. Vivek, S., Yashank, R., Prashanth, Y., Yashas, N., Namratha, M.: E-voting systems using blockchain: an exploratory literature survey. In: 2020 Second International Conference on Inventive Research in Computing Applications (ICIRCA), pp. 890–895 (2020). https://doi.org/10.1109/ICIRCA48905.2020.9183185
31. Yu, B., Liu, J.K., Sakzad, A., Nepal, S., Steinfeld, R., Rimba, P., Au, M.H.: Platform-independent secure blockchain-based voting system. In: Chen, L., Manulis, M., Schneider, S. (eds.) ISC 2018. LNCS, vol. 11060, pp. 369–386. Springer, Cham (2018). https://doi.org/10.1007/978-3-319-99136-8_20
32. Zhang, S., Wang, L., Xiong, H.: Chaintegrity: blockchain-enabled large-scale E-voting system with robustness and universal verifiability. Int. J. Inf. Secur. 19(3), 323–341 (2020)
33. Zhang, W., et al.: A privacy-preserving voting protocol on blockchain. In: 2018 IEEE 11th International Conference on Cloud Computing (CLOUD), pp. 401–408 (2018). DOI: https://doi.org/10.1109/CLOUD.2018.00057
34. Zou, W., et al.: Smart contract development: challenges and opportunities. IEEE Trans. Softw. Eng. 47(10), 2084–2106 (2021). https://doi.org/10.1109/TSE.2019.2942301

Preventing Content Cloning in NFT Collections

Ivan Visconti[1], Andrea Vitaletti[2], and Marco Zecchini[1(✉)]

[1] Dipartimento di Ingegneria dell'Informazione ed Elettronica e Matematica Applicata, University of Salerno, Fisciano, Italy
{visconti,mzecchini}@unisa.it
[2] Dipartimento di Ingegneria Informatica, Automatica e Gestionale, Sapienza Universitá di Roma, Rome, Italy
vitaletti@diag.uniroma1.it

Abstract. The concept of Non-Fungible Token (NFT) has found many applications with great impact. One of the most appealing uses of NFTs is the possibility of creating and managing an NFT collection where each token regulates the ownership of a digital asset and new tokens can be minted according to some rules.

In this work, we investigate the natural question of whether a digital asset could be duplicated inside a collection of NFTs. Interestingly, while intuitively uniqueness should be enforced by the use of NFTs, we observe that the existence of clones is possible according to the mainstream approaches of Ethereum (i.e., ERC-721 contracts) and Algorand (i.e., ASAs). Moreover, we have scrutinized famous NFT collections that have been built on such decentralized platforms and our findings show that, unfortunately, the uniqueness of a digital asset in a collection (e.g., the guarantee that at most one NFT is generated for the ownership of a specific digital painting) is at risk if the minter (i.e., a single point of failure) is at some point corrupted.

Next, we propose a natural and simple functionality $\mathcal{F}_{CollNFT}$ abstracting the management of NFT collections that, by design, does not allow clones in a collection. While in general, ERC-721 and ASAs do not securely realize $\mathcal{F}_{CollNFT}$, we discuss the design of an NFT collection that is compliant with the ERC-721 standard and at the same time realizes $\mathcal{F}_{CollNFT}$, therefore, guaranteeing by design that even a malicious minter can not introduce clones in the collection.

Keywords: NFT · ERC-721 · ASA · Collection

1 Introduction

A collection is a group of objects of a single type collected in one place, usually by an individual. The elements of a collection are chosen according to some valuable criteria (like historical or artistic or scientific ones) or personal taste (if the collection is a collector's hobby). The pieces of the collections are traded and lent between collectors and galleries, fuelling a relevant business. For example,

Ezra and David Nahmad, two famous art collectors, own one of the most valuable art collections in the world worth \$3 billion[1] and including artwork of worldwide known painters like Picasso and Monet.

In the above example, the collection is composed of collectibles (i.e., elements of a collection) owned by the collectors. In some cases, collectibles owned by a multitude of collectors are grouped together (e.g., in shows, expositions or art galleries).

Considering the natural consequence of the law of supply and demand, the value of a collectible inside a collection depends not only on the content of the collectible but also on the reputation of the collector, on the reputation of the creators of the collectible and on the scarcity or (even uniqueness) of the collectible. Naturally, if one element is duplicated, it is devalued. For instance, a collection composed of unique paintings by very famous painters has significant value. However, if one painter produces multiple versions of the same painting, the value of the one in the collection could significantly decrease.

1.1   New Forms of Digital Collections

The digital era enables a new form of collectibles, such as digital images, recorded audio, and videos. These new types of collectibles can be easily maintained locally on collectors' computers but are easy to copy. Nowadays, there is no technology capable of guaranteeing the uniqueness of a digital file. In other words, it is extremely easy to make multiple indistinguishable copies of an mp3 or a jpeg file. However, there are technologies aiming at guaranteeing the ownership of a digital asset. As an example, even though multiple identical copies of an mp3 file can circulate on the Internet, a certificate of ownership can be associated with a single subject (e.g., using a simple digital certificate released by an authority). There are, indeed, a number of service providers that facilitate the management of digital collectibles and provide solutions to guarantee their ownership.

The ownership of a digital image in a specific collection could, for instance, allow the owner to be the only user that can have a painting with that image inside her digital house in the Metaverse. This feature can, of course, generate a market where users would like to trade the ownership of digital assets belonging to specific collections.

From e-Commerce to NFT Collections. The World Wide Web (Web 2.0) has supported collectors by providing digital certificates to guarantee ownership of collectibles and by providing the technical infrastructure to advertise their collections and trade them (e.g., https://www.blindarte.com/). With the advent of blockchain technologies, we have seen the birth of decentralized applications, enabling Web 3.0, where peers achieve consensus on the system status without relying on trusted third parties. This technology crucially enables a new form of decentralized trading for digital collections and this is achieved by representing collectibles as tokens, where a single token is an on-chain representation of a digital collectible and its ownership. Such tokens are not interchangeable as regular

---

[1] https://www.thecollector.com/8-of-the-worlds-most-valuable-art-collections/.

currency because two distinct tokens represent two distinct collectibles. For this reason, these specific tokens are called NFTs (NFTs). NFTs are unique tokens inside a collection and cannot be replicated, thus guaranteeing the uniqueness of the ownership for a specific asset inside a collection. In other words, even if you have unlimited copies of a digital collectible, the ownership guaranteed by the corresponding NFT inside the collection is unique. The NFTs trading is typically managed by a smart contract, which is a program running on the blockchain. The decentralized nature of smart contracts enhances the security of the trading system because it does not rely anymore on a single entity but on the security of the underlying blockchain technology.

NFT collections gained a lot of attention and their trading market has reached a capitalization of billions of dollars in recent years[2].

Main Approaches for Building NFTs Collections. Given the large amount of money involved in this sector, developer communities started working on standards for creating and trading NFTs avoiding software bugs in smart contracts or in transactions that manage NFTs. To the best of our knowledge, there are two main approaches to build an NFT collection on a blockchain.

The most adopted approach is the de-facto standard on Ethereum [14] for NFTs: ERC-721 [4]. Each instance of an ERC-721 smart contract manages a distinct NFT collection.

An alternative approach has been proposed by Algorand [7] that provides a built-in functionality to securely manage NFTs [1]. To differentiate them from ERC-721 tokens, in the rest of the paper, we refer to this type of token with Algorand Standard Asset (ASA). Every blockchain user (including a smart contract) can be a manager of its own collection of ASAs.

In both approaches, NFTs inside a collection are identified by a numerical index [1, 4] and, usually, only a limited set of users, the minters, are authorized to create a new NFT in the collection, establishing its ownership. An ERC-721 smart contract allows the creation of a new token if and only if its numerical index is not already associated with another token in the collection and the requesting entity is an authorized minter. For ASA management, a global counter in the blockchain identifies every ASA in the ledger and when a new one is created, the counter is incremented by the blockchain validators, and assigned to the new ASA. In any case, the minter plays the role of the manager of the collection, deciding the assets that should be added along with the corresponding original owner. We stress that in the case of ASAs, since all NFTs belong generically all together to the ledger, a collection of NFTs is naturally defined by considering all NFT created by some specific minters.

1.2   The Rise of NFT Clones

A recent article on Cointelegraph [11] discusses a new project named *Mimic My NFT*[3] claimed to be the world's first NFT cloning service.

---

[2] https://mpost.io/top-10-ethereum-nft-collections-listed-by-trading-volume/.
[3] https://www.clonemynft.com/nft/mimic.

The simplest mechanism to clone NFTs is to use the same content in multiple NFTs. Most NFT marketplaces (e.g., OpenSea) remove such content, however, such operation entails trusting the marketplaces, which is in contrast with the main assumption of decentralization. Anyway, the immutable order of the blockchain incontrovertibly shows which asset has been created first and therefore has to be considered the original one.

The main functions implemented in ERC-721 NFTs smart contracts are the management of the ownership and the references to access the asset represented by the token. This latter function is usually provided referencing an external URI, even though the tokenURI function to get such URI is optional.

Since the code of a smart contract is public, anyone can create an NFT with the URI of someone else's NFT. Mimic My NFT exploits this weakness to make NFT cloning extremely simple: the metadata such as name, description, media and other attributes that are provided by the URI can be mimicked.

1.3   Our Contribution

NFT standards foresee the employment of a unique identifier to guarantee the uniqueness of an NFT in a collection. However, this identifier is not necessarily generated in function of the digital content of the collectibles. Indeed, in many smart contracts, the identifier is chosen through a simple counter that increases at the creation of each new NFT. This brings to a number of problems (see the previous discussions and Sect. 2 for further details) and leads to potential cloning attacks to undermine the prestige of a collection and, consequently, the trust on the involved actors. Current solutions to tackle these issues are based on opportunistic approaches that demand an effort by non-necessarily skilled users (i.e., collectors should perform specific checks) and require them to trust the platforms and/or the collectors, thus violating the decentralization assumption. Indeed, the use of decentralized platforms is motivated by the desire to reduce trust in specific actors while enjoying reliable services. We stress that at least in some use cases, the buyer of an NFT should be able to opt for a platform where there will never be a clone of the bought collectible in the same collection regardless of the reputation of the collector.

In this work, we propose mechanisms that better guarantee the link between the unique identifier and the digital asset by design, relying on smart contracts. Our solutions aim at preventing the minting of clones, namely the creation of two NFTs in the same collection pointing exactly to the same digital data.

We have scrutinized the rules allowing to generate NFTs both with ERC-721 and with ASAs in popular NFT collections and we observe that, in general, both approaches allow to mint clones. In several natural applications of NFTs, this is a vulnerability that should be avoided by design.

Our contribution is two-fold:

1. We formally define the concept of NFT collection through a functionality $\mathcal{F}_{CollNFT}$ that guarantees the absence of clones in a collection.

2. We discuss possible approaches to build collections that securely realize $\mathcal{F}_{CollNFT}$. While many popular ERC-721 collections do not avoid cloning by design, our instantiation is fully compliant with the ERC-721 standard and, at the same time, satisfies the requirements enforced by $\mathcal{F}_{CollNFT}$. In our instantiation, the minting process uses a collision-resistant hash function (e.g., sha256) computed on the digital content of a collectible to generate an identifier so that two identical digital assets would produce a collision while instead distinct digital assets will not (except with negligible probability). Then the minting process before completing the generation of a new NFT checks that there is no other NFT in the collection with the same identifier. We discuss the implementation of the above steps by means of key-value maps in ERC-721 and we illustrate other techniques to obtain secure realizations of $\mathcal{F}_{CollNFT}$ using smart contracts with limited capabilities in blockchains offering ad-hoc transactions for the management of NFTs.

Finally, we discuss interesting open questions about relaxing the concept of clones in a collection so that one can be guaranteed that no other *similar* collectible could ever be added to a given collection. We believe that this direction is quite interesting since it corresponds to what is actually desired in some relevant use cases.

1.4 Related Works

Given the many investments in the NFT trading sector of the last few years, an increasing number of security analyses on this topic have emerged. Dipanjan D. et al. [6] present a security analysis on the NFT ecosystem based on a quantitative approach. They start modeling the ecosystem involved in the NFT trading and identify three main actors (content creators, sellers and buyers), each affected by possible security flaws. Among the fraudulent user behaviors penalizing buyers and content creators, they identify the problem of NFT counterfeit creation and the "identical image URLs" as one of the causes of duplicated NFT on-chain. They analyzed around 8 million NFTs on the Ethereum mainnet and they found around 2.5 million duplicates (i.e., NFT with "identical Image URLs"). "Sleepminting" is another attack affecting minting, analyzed in [9], to fake the provenance (i.e., the sequence of transfers) of an NFT. In late March 2021, a person that goes under the pseudonym of Monsieur Personne showed how to mint and transfer tokens on behalf of unaware users[4]. The idea behind the attack is to exploit the notoriety of well-known accounts to increase the value of a token and sell it at a higher price. This attack exploits the fact that all ERC-721 smart contracts actually implement the IERC-721 smart contract interface. Any user can inherit the interface IERC-721 and implements its own version of a compatible ERC-721 smart contract. Blockchain readers (e.g., NFT marketplace) might consider safe ERC-721

---

[4] For instance, this first transaction (0x57f23fde8e4221174cfb1baf68a87858167fec228d9 b32952532e40c367ef04e) mints a token on behalf of another user and this second one (0x57f23fde8e4221174cfb1baf68a87858167fec228d9b32952532e40c367ef04e) transfers it from the user, without its authorization.

compatible NFT, those tokens handled by smart contracts inheriting IERC-721. However, there is no certainty that all the functions in the ERC-721 smart contracts perform all the proper verification for secure minting and transferring (e.g., only the owner of the token can transfer it).

We recall that in our paper, we provide a formal definition of an NFT collection functionality in order to have a rigorous notion that can be useful to evaluate the robustness by design of an NFT collection. To the best of our knowledge, ours is (surprisingly) the first attempt to propose such a definition. There exist literature definitions aiming at modeling a functionality handling the trade of blockchain tokens but their goals deviate from ours. Androulaki et al. [3] describe a functionality realized by a privacy-preserving token management system in permissioned blockchains. A formal definition of an ERC-20 token is proposed in [12] that provides a formal analysis of composable DeFi protocols. The NFT collection functionality defined in our work obviously shares some of the intuitions behind the definition of [12] since there is a natural overlap in the concepts of ERC-721 and ERC-20 tokens.

1.5   Structure of This Work

Section 2 presents the problem related to minting clones in a collection and the dominant approach to tackle this problem. Section 2 also analyzes how relevant collections on Ethereum blockchains take countermeasures to avoid the existence of multiple NFTs representing the same off-chain data. In Sect. 3, we provide a formal definition of a functionality $\mathcal{F}_{CollNFT}$ aiming at abstracting the management of NFT collections. In Sect. 3 we also show how current standards for NFT management are not compliant with $\mathcal{F}_{CollNFT}$. Finally, Sect. 4 concludes the paper and draws future steps for follow-up work.

2   Issues in NFT Collections

In this section, we first discuss the possibility that naturally built NFT collections through ERC-721 and ASA are by design affected by the risk of (undesired) cloned digital assets inside NFT collections.

Then we discuss our findings with respect to well known NFT collections.

2.1   A Single Point of Failure in ERC-721 and Blockchains with Native NFT Designs

As anticipated in Sect. 1, an NFT representing a collectible inside a collection, roughly, is defined as a couple $< id, data\_of\_collectible >$[5] in both ERC-721-based NFTs and ASA-based NFTs.

---

[5] Due to size constraints, usually the digital data of a collectible are stored off-chain and the *data_of_collectible* should be a unique link to the off-chain representation. This is typically enforced through the use of IPFS links.

We notice that such representation still allows two NFTs represented by $< id_1, data\_of\_collectible >$, $< id_2, data\_of\_collectible >$ (i.e., represented by the same data) in the same collection. Essentially these two NFTs correspond to the same digital asset since the only information that makes them distinct could be an artificial identifier generated by the system. Such identifiers are unrelated to the actual content of the asset. As such, the same collectible can appear twice (and even more) in a collection just because it is potentially possible that the minting mechanism of NFTs assigns two different identifiers to the very same asset. Obviously, these two NFTs can be owned by distinct owners, thus introducing a potential vulnerability in uniquely identifying ownership of an asset in a collection and damaging the very first owner. Indeed, the above state-of-the-art setting might allow the minter of a collection to add a collectible associated with an asset that is then transferred at a high price (because of the current uniqueness in the collection). Later on, the minter adds in the same collection many other collectibles referring to the same asset, therefore potentially damaging the buyer who bought the original one.

While such behavior of a minter might look irrational, notice that an adversary might, on purpose, be willing to harm a collection by leveraging some bugs in the infrastructure or exploiting a leakage of the secret key that must be used to generate the minting transactions. Therefore, minters could generate clones also unintentionally without being irrational.

Summing up, minters are a *single point of failure* with respect to guaranteeing uniqueness of assets in NFT collections. Since such collections are commonly implemented in decentralized platforms precisely because they are supposed to mitigate vulnerabilities due to single points of failure, it is somewhat paradoxical that implementations of NFT collections on decentralized platforms expose a so obvious single-point of failure risk.

2.2   Main Approach Mitigating NFT Cloning Attacks

In most platforms, content cloning is not prevented by design. Rather, before buying an NFT, buyers should check whether this is unique in the collection. Clearly, this approach does not stop a malicious minter from creating a second NFT after the sale. A possible way to solve this problem consists of considering valid only the first NFT stored in the ledger. Indeed the total order of the ledger guarantees honest users to identify which NFT has been created first. However, even though this mechanism can resolve the dispute on the owner of the original copy devalues the power of smart contracts and, moreover, is extremely unpractical. Indeed, the buyer must scan the whole blockchain to verify whether an NFT is duplicated and this has a very negative impact on performance. This type of check becomes somewhat impossible if the trader only possesses a light client (i.e., a blockchain node that stores only a portion of the blockchain used to verify information provided by full nodes) because it requires asking a full node to send the entire blockchain which is clearly unmanageable for a light client. Moreover, a light client usually relies on collecting some fresh information about parts of the state of the blockchain from other nodes and the above main approach is completely incompatible with these mechanisms.

2.3 Vulnerability Analysis of Existing NFT Collections

In this subsection, we analyze existing projects in the market with the purpose of identifying the existence of the vulnerability related to the potential existence of cloned assets in a collection. We limit our analyses to projects where the design of the minting process can be clearly understood from the publicly available documentation and/or the smart contract code.

Table 1 reports relevant collections available on Ethereum in terms of ETH capitalization and managed through the ERC-721 standard[6]. The considered collections are part of the following projects/platforms:

- "Bored Ape Yacht Club" is a project where NFTs, representing cartooned apes, grant access to an exclusive club of members. The maximum number of mintable NFTs was fixed to 10 thousand tokens at smart contract deployment (April 2021). All the NFTs were already minted during a sale phase. Part of them (30) were assigned to the deployer to fill its reserve. The remaining ones were minted at the price of 0.008 ETH and at most 20 NFTs could be minted per transaction. Every new NFT was identified with a numerical index assigned with a global counter in the contract. If a new transaction tries to mint a new NFT overcoming the total number of allowed tokens, the smart contract aborts the transaction.
- "Mutant Ape Yacht Club" is a side project of "Bored Ape Yacht Club" with similar goals. At smart contract deployment, the maximum number of mintable NFTs has been fixed to 20 thousand tokens. Unlike the previous project, not all NFTs are minted for sale. Indeed, part of them can be minted if a user possesses an NFT of the "Bored Ape Yacht Club" collection. Therefore, the resilience of this project with respect to the issue of the duplicates is based on the one of the "Bored" project and to the limited number of NFTs mintable by the contract.
- "Art Blocks Curated" is a platform for artists to publish unique editions of generative art. In "Art Blocks Curated", NFTs, representing on-chain these generative artworks, are assigned to different projects. Therefore, the smart contract computes the token index from a counter that combines the project id (identified with another internal counter of projects) with an index keeping count of the number of NFTs in the project.
- "Otherdeed for Otherside" is a project that tokenizes the lands of a parallel digital world, "Otherside". An Otherdeed NFT represents a picture of land and it grants access to participate in further functionality in the Otherside. Tokens are released during a sale phase by authorized users and the NFT index is assigned with a global counter.

---

[6] According to https://mpost.io/top-10-ethereum-nft-collections-listed-by-trading-volume/.

- "Azuki" is a collection of 10 thousand avatars that give to their owners access to a parallel digital universe called "The Garden". Each avatar is represented on-chain through an NFT.
- "Clone X" is another collection of 20 thousand avatars giving access to a parallel digital world. Avatar sale, again modeled as NFT, was split between the pre-sale and a public sale. Also in this case, the NFT index is assigned with a global counter.
- "BEANZ Official" is a side project of "Azuki". Each NFT represents an avatar of a bean that can be used in the "The Garden" universe. Also in this case, the NFT index is assigned with a global counter and a maximum number of tokens is fixed.

Table 1. Relevant NFT Collections on Ethereum and relative mechanisms to assign the index to a new NFT.

Project Name	Contract Address (Ethereum Mainnet)	Control at minting on the index	Maximum supply	Capitalization (ETH)
Bored Ape Yacht Club	0xBC4CA0EdA7647A8aB7C2061c2E118A18a936f13D	Counter	Yes	934M ETH
Mutant Ape Yacht Club	0x60E4d786628Fea6478F785A6d7e704777c86a7c6	Counter or derived from other NFT ids	Yes	727M ETH
Art Blocks Curated	0xa7d8d9ef8d8ce8992df33d8b8cf4aebabd5bd270	Two counters	No	484k ETH
Otherdeed for Otherside	0x34d85c9cdeb23fa97cb08333b511ac86e1c4e258	Counter	Yes	532k ETH
Azuki	0xED5AF388653567Af2F388E6224dC7C4b3241C544	Counter	Yes	434k ETH
Clone X	0x49cf6f5d44e70224e2e23fdcdd2c053f30ada28b	Counter	Yes	356k ETH
BEANZ Official	0x306b1ea3ecdf94ab739f1910bbda052ed4a9f949	Counter	Yes	122k ETH

For all the listed projects, the tokens are created by multiple issuers but their index is assigned incrementally by a smart contract (Counter in the table). For almost all projects, there is a cap on the number of tokens that can be minted and this can limit the problem of duplicates if the cap is reached. However, in some cases, this cap can be really high or might even be missing, like in the case of "Art Blocks Curated".

In contrast to the above works, we propose an approach that is more general and prevents the minting of clones.

"Mutant Ape Yacht Club" is the only project performing further checks at the minting time. Indeed, in some cases of "Mutant Ape Yacht Club", the index of an NFT is derived from the index of an already existing token in another collection, i.e., "Bored Ape Yacht Club". Therefore, for these NFTs, the security of their indexes is based on the ones of the other collection.

All the NFTs of the analyzed projects are associated with images. Since storing high-quality images on-chain is not possible or negatively impacts transaction fees, all the projects store the images off-chain. Some of them host the image on the project servers (like Artblocks, Otherdeed for Otherside and Clone X), while others store them on decentralized platforms, such as IPFS [5] (like Bored Ape

Yacht, Mutant Ape Yacht, Azuki, Beanz project). In all the projects, the images are stored off-chain jointly with some metadata, such as creation timestamp, image description and a list of attributes of items represented in an image.

The vulnerability that allows a compromised minter to generate clones of an asset in an NFT collection also affects NFT collections made of built-in tokens. In 2022, Algorand, in partnership with Federation Internationale de Football Association (FIFA), launched a platform called FIFA+ Collect [2], for collecting and trading NFTs representing short videos of soccer matches. Users buy an initial pack for a few dollars and obtain three NFTs. After that, they can start selling and buying other NFTs to win prizes and other rewards. Also in this case, all NFTs are minted by a specific actor that, if compromised, can potentially create in the future several other NFTs connected to the same short videos of soccer matches[7].

In general, most of the smart contracts of the relevant NFT collections do not seem to take countermeasures to prevent the generation of clones even though their capitalization is consistent.

3   A Robust NFT Collection Functionality

In this section, we provide a definition of the functionality $\mathcal{F}_{CollNFT}$ that an NFT collection should implement in contexts in which we assume the presence of an adversarial minter/collector.

The main goal of this functionality is to enable the trading of NFTs such that each NFT is unique in the collection. NFTs are associated with collectibles. A collectible c is composed of a digital artwork $c.artwork$ (e.g., a jpeg) and some associated metadata $c.meta$, providing additional information on the collectible (e.g., the timestamp of the artwork creation, special attributes of the artwork).

An NFT t represents a collectible c on the ledger. It includes a unique identifier $t.id$ (e.g., usually a counter), information on the owner $t.owner$, and some data $t.data$ including c itself or a pointer to c off-chain. In deployed NFT collections, it is usually inconvenient to store c in-chain, consequently, off-chain storage is by far the most adopted solution and content-based addressing is commonly employed (e.g., IPFS [5]).

In general, the creator of a collection enables a number of issuers $I_1, ..., I_m$ to mint the tokens T in the collections. For the sake of simplicity, we consider a scenario where a creator can generate only a single collection and he/she is also the only issuer I for that collection. In other words, a collection is uniquely identified by the creator/issuer I.

The functionality $\mathcal{F}_{CollNFT}$ can be formalized as in Fig. 1 and manages pairs $< I, T >$ that represent collections.

---

[7] On-chain   tokens   are   issued   by   the   same   entity (X6MNR4AVJQEMJRHAPZ6F404SVDIYN67ZRMD2O3ULPY4QFMANQNZOEYHODE).   See   for example the tokens 952576397 and 961355760.

Functionality $\mathcal{F}_{CollNFT}$ abstracting the management of NFT collections.

The NFT collection functionality $\mathcal{F}_{CollNFT}$ stores pairs $< I, T >$.

- **Create.** Upon input (create, I) from I, if there is already a pair $< I, T >$ then $\mathcal{F}_{CollNFT}$ halts. Otherwise, $\mathcal{F}_{CollNFT}$ initializes an empty set of NFTs $T = \{\}$, and stores $< I, T >$.
- **Mint.** Upon input (mint, c, O) from I, if either there is no collection $< I, T >$ or if c is already in any $t.data$ in T, then $\mathcal{F}_{CollNFT}$ halts. Otherwise, $\mathcal{F}_{CollNFT}$ updates the entry $< I, T >$ adding a new token t in T such that $t.id$ is a value different from all ids of token in T, and setting $t.data = c$ and $t.owner = O$.
- **Transfer.** Upon input^a (transfer, id, I, O) from a party P, if either there is no collection $< I, T >$ or P is not the owner of a token t in $< I, T >$ such that $t.id = id$, then $\mathcal{F}_{CollNFT}$ halts. Otherwise, considering such token t, $\mathcal{F}_{CollNFT}$ updates $t.owner = O$.

^{a} Note that I in input allows us to uniquely identify the collection.

Fig. 1. NFT Collection Functionality $\mathcal{F}_{CollNFT}$

Any party I can initialize its own NFT collection invoking the create function. I can invoke mint to issue a new token uniquely associated with the collectible c. The procedure mint aborts if c is already associated with another token in the collection. Only the owner of a token in a collection can invoke transfer to transfer the ownership to another party.

By inspection, the functionality $\mathcal{F}_{CollNFT}$ forces the following properties:

P1 only the issuer can successfully create new NFTs in its own collection;
P2 only the owner of a token can successfully transfer it;
P3 the collectible c associated with a token is unique in the collection.

We defined $\mathcal{F}_{CollNFT}$ with the primary goal of avoiding clones in the collection and we deliberately neglected to consider relevant details such as the token destruction, modification, etc.

In the following sections, we analyze current standards for NFT, and we discuss how they fail in implementing $\mathcal{F}_{CollNFT}$.

3.1 $\mathcal{F}_{CollNFT}$ and ERC-721 NFTs

On Ethereum-like blockchains, NFTs are created and traded with a smart contract that implements the ERC-721 standard [4]. The main actions performable by the smart contract are mint, which creates a new token in the collection and assigns the token to the issuer, and transfer, which transfers a token from the owner to a new specified Ethereum account. transfer succeeds if and only if the account sending the transaction is the current owner of the NFT or it has been previously "delegated" by its owner. `mint` succeeds if and only the account sending the transaction is the deployer of the smart contract. For these reasons, ERC-721 is compliant with **P1** and **P2**.

An ERC-721 smart contract keeps track of created tokens in a key-value map stored inside the state of an instance of the smart contract. When a token t belongs to the collection, we have that $t.id$ is the key and $(t.owner, t.data)$ is the value in the key-value map. However, the ERC-721 standard does not prevent the presence in the map of two distinct keys $t.id$ and $t'.id$ associated to the same data $t.data = t'.data$. Hence, an ERC-721 smart contract generally does not securely realize the functionality $\mathcal{F}_{CollNFT}$ since **P3** might not be guaranteed. We propose instead to implement ERC-721 smart contracts with the following two steps. First, we require that $t.id = sha256(t.data)$. Then, if the key is not already in the key-value map, the newly created token can be successfully added to the map. With this technique, invoking `mint` for a new token t' that is a clone fails because the key associated with $t'.id$ is already in the map. This guarantees the uniqueness of the data in the collection (**P3**) still remaining inside the requirements of ERC-721 contracts.

3.2 $\mathcal{F}_{CollNFT}$ and Blockchains with Native Support of NFTs

To facilitate the development of NFT collections, some blockchain technologies, like Algorand [1], allow the trading of NFTs through layer-0 functionalities. Differently from the Ethereum-based blockchain, where only two types of transactions are present in the ledger (i.e., those issued by users and those issued by smart contracts), Algorand provides by design more types of transactions, among which the ones for creating a token, transferring a token and modifying a token. Every blockchain user can be an issuer of its own NFT collection or a set of users can join in issuing a common NFT collection arbitrated by a smart contract. One can program the smart contract so that minting transactions from users that are not part of the allowed list of issuers (respecting **P1**) are refused.

By design, **P2** is guaranteed because the transferring token transaction succeeds if and only if the blockchain user that produces the transaction owns the token. However, token management (in contrast to the case of ERC-721) is not designed to be controlled by a smart contract logic but by the blockchain consensus, checking the validity of the various types of transactions. Therefore, tokens (e.g., ASAs in Algorand) are uniquely identified in the system through a numerical index assigned at creation time by the consensus. This index is a counter handled by the validators of the blockchain. Hence, there is no guarantee that two tokens with different ids represent different data. Therefore, such an approach is not compliant by design with $\mathcal{F}_{CollNFT}$ since it does not satisfy **P3**.

A Potential fix Using Pruned Merkle Trees. Depending on the capabilities of smart contracts in the considered blockchain, a potential approach to securely realize $\mathcal{F}_{CollNFT}$ is the following. The tokens of a collection are created by a smart contract keeping track of the already created tokens (in the same collection) and minting new tokens only upon request of legitimate issuers. In some blockchains, the smart contract has constraints on the size of the storage. For this reason, the smart contract handling the NFT collection should maintain in its state a succinct representation of all the tokens issued over time. A typical succinct representation consists of a root of a Merkle tree [10].

Tokens can be assigned to leaves of the Merkle tree as follows. We can identify leaves in the Merkle tree by a string obtained considering the path from the root to a leaf and assigning a 0 when crossing a link towards a left child and 1 vice-versa. This simple procedure allows us to find a leaf on the tree, given in input the corresponding string.

We simply represent the token t through the string $sha256(t.data)$, and with the above-described procedure, we can check whether a token is already in the Merle tree or not. Initially, the root of the tree is set to nil. This represents the fact that there is no token yet and thus, the tree is empty.

To add a new token t, the issuer has first to prove that t does not already exist in the collection. This is achieved by providing a Merkle proof that the corresponding leaf, namely the one in a position identified by $sha256(t.data)$, has not been inserted yet. This is easy to achieve, showing that starting from the root, the path induced by the value of the identifier of the token at some point prematurely ends with a nil that refers to a missing child. In other words, the issuer provides a proof that there is a nil in the path from the root to $sha256(t.data)$. If the token can be added, the smart contract adds it and updates the Merkle root correspondingly.

Notice that this is not a pure Merkle tree since entire subtrees are pruned. This is necessary for efficiency reasons, indeed, the entire, complete binary tree can not be computed since the number of leaves is 2^{256}. For some blockchains like Algorand, the expected workload to implement such a procedure might be unpractical. Indeed, seemingly, a smart contract can manage a Merkle tree with a height of at most 15 [13].

Preventing Clones at the Consensus Layer. While preventing cloning in NFTs collections through a logic encoded in smart contracts (in particular when the underlying blockchain imposes restrictions on the capabilities of smart contacts) can be challenging, we notice a connection with the mere validity of a blockchain transaction. Indeed, preventing cloning is strictly related to logically defining as invalid a transaction violating some rules according to the state of the blockchain. Consequently, an alternative approach that is viable for those blockchains that provide NFT management transactions (e.g., ASAs in Algorand) consists of requiring at the consensus layer to discard those transactions trying to mint NFTs that are clones of existing NFTs in the same collections. To this purpose, data structures similar to the ones used in Ethereum to store the state of a collection (e.g., a key-value map) can also be used by the blockchain validators.

3.3   Discussion on the Implementation of $\mathcal{F}_{CollNFT}$

This subsection investigates how to concretely realize a collection of images compatible with $\mathcal{F}_{CollNFT}$.

Images can be represented according to various encoding schemes. One of the most adopted schemes is the RGB color model, an additive color model in which the red, green and blue primary colors of light are added together in various ways to reproduce a broad array of colors. In detail, each pixel of the image is represented with a tuple of three values representing the red, the yellow and the blue components. Hence, an RGB image is a matrix of M pixels of width and N pixels of height and 3 values for each cell.

As a toy example, we consider a collection of images of 16 pixels of width, 9 pixels of height and where the value of each color component can be set between 0 and 255. Therefore, every image is an array of bytes of dimension $16 \times 9 \times 3 = 432$. Every image is associated with metadata information on the creation time measured with a UNIX timestamp representable with an unsigned integer of 4 bytes. Altogether, a collectible c of this collection comprises an image $c.artwork$ of 432 bytes and 4 bytes as $c.meta$.

To obtain a collection compliant with $\mathcal{F}_{CollNFT}$, we directly upload c on the smart contract that forces the image to respect the RGB format (i.e., verify that for each cell of the $M \times N$ matrix, there are three values in the interval $[0, 255]$) with specified dimension. Then, the smart contract sets $t.data = c$, computes $hash(c)$ and sets it as the value of $t.id$.

The limitation of this approach is that it requires to fully upload c. In our example, $c.artwork$ is small, but we need 432 bytes to represent it. Note that tiny NFTs exist, and even single-bit NFTs have been proposed (see https:// foundation.app/@aaa/foundation/42796). However, images usually have bigger dimensions that are in the magnitude of thousands of pixels for width and height. Hence, these images can not be uploaded on-chain on many technologies (e.g., Algorand [1], Ethereum [14]) and, even if that would be possible, big files would impact transaction fees.

To overcome this problem, there are some possible solutions:

- A common approach relies on uploading the collectible c on IPFS [5], a peer-to-peer network to share files accessible via a piece of information computed on their content (i.e., the sha256 of the file). On the token t, we set $t.id = t.data = addr_{ipfs}$ where $addr_{ipfs} = sha256(c)$. However, there is no simple mechanism to prevent a malicious minter to mint a new token t' where $t'.id = addr'_{ipfs} = sha256(c')$ and $c'.artwork = c.artwork$, while $c'.meta$ differs. In other words, the digital contents $c.artwork$ and $c'.artwork$ are the same, while their descriptions $c.meta$ and $c'.meta$ differ. In contexts in which $c.meta$ is not necessary, it can be dropped by design and thus, this attack can not be performed.
- It is reasonable to assume that digital assets are signed by their creators (e.g., the artists) upon generation to guarantee their genesis. The creator (e.g., the artist) of c cryptographically and deterministically signs it producing σ. We can set $t.id = \sigma$ to maintain the uniqueness of the token because trying to add the same $t.data$ of the same author would produce the same σ. However, the creator can always be compromised (e.g., an attacker steals the secret

key to produce σ), as it happens in the case of the minters. In this way, the attacker would be able to produce clones changing *c.meta* and signing again.
- Alternatively, the minting transaction could carry a proof of knowledge that the succinct value stored as id of the token in the smart contract is the cryptographic hash of a value *c.artwork*. This could be implemented through succinct non-interactive arguments of knowledge (SNARKs). In our case, the minter uploads a cryptographic hash s (that will be the id) and a SNARK π proving knowledge of *c.artwork* such that $s = sha256(c.artwork)$ and that *c.artwork* is a picture encoded with RGB color model (i.e., for each cell of the $M \times N$ matrix representing the image, there are three values in the interval $[0, 255]$). The last constraint avoids that a malicious minter computes a valid π for $hash' = sha256(c)$ arbitrary setting *c.meta*, as in the case of IPFS. The smart contract verifies that π is correct and then sets $t.id = t.data = sha256(c.artwork)$ guaranteeing the unicity of $t.data$ in the collection. SNARKs proving knowledge of an anti-image of $sha256$ are too inefficient but one might actually use other cryptographic hash functions, such as Poseidon [8], that have been designed with the goal of allowing more efficient instantiations of SNARKs proving such claims.

4   Conclusions and Future Work

Minting clones in NFT collections can represent an issue for the trading of digital collectibles represented as NFT. Current standards do not prevent the existence of clones by design and, consequently, many existing projects of a market worth billions of dollars might suffer from such vulnerability.

This state of affairs, therefore, shows the paradoxical use of a decentralized platform to reduce risks of single points of failure along with the use of an application of such platforms that (avoidably, at least in some scenarios) is affected by risks of single points of failure.

In this work, we have formally described the functionality $\mathcal{F}_{CollNFT}$ that can be used to evaluate if an NFT collection is secure by design with respect to the above potential vulnerability. In addition, we have shown that current standards and existing projects for NFT collections seemingly do not securely realize $\mathcal{F}_{CollNFT}$. We have also discussed how to properly design an NFT collection remaining compatible with standards[8], but at the same time making sure to realize $\mathcal{F}_{CollNFT}$. However, the discussed approach, proposed in Sect. 3.3, has some limitations because it requires uploading on-chain the collectible entirely. We have proposed alternative solutions and we leave as future work a deeper analysis of these approaches in terms of performance and security.

Our approach relies on cryptographic hash functions. This implies that two digital contents that have a single different bit are identified by two completely different ids, even if, from the point of view of a human, they might appear identical (e.g., two high-resolution images with a single different bit). However,

---

[8] This is extremely important since several web3 dapps (e.g., wallets) can be used only on standard mechanisms.

according to our definition of $\mathcal{F}_{CollNFT}$, these two objects are indeed different. This opens a new interesting research direction where two objects are indistinguishable if they are sufficiently similar according to a given metric. Notice that this would also help in fighting against plagiarism.

References

1. Algorand Developer Docs - Algorand Developer Portal (2023). https://developer. algorand.org/docs. Accessed 13 Feb 2023
2. FIFA+ Collect (2023). https://collect.fifa.com. Accessed 7 Mar 2023
3. Androulaki, E., Camenisch, J., De Caro, A., Dubovitskaya, M., Elkhiyaoui, K., Tackmann, B.: Privacy-preserving auditable token payments in a permissioned blockchain system, p. 255–267. AFT 2020, Association for Computing Machinery, New York, USA (2020)
4. Bauer, D.P.: ERC-721 nonfungible tokens. In: Getting Started with Ethereum: A Step-by-Step Guide to Becoming a Blockchain Developer, pp. 55–74. Springer (2022). https://doi.org/10.1007/978-1-4842-8045-4_5
5. Benet, J.: Ipfs-content addressed, versioned, p2p file system. arXiv preprint arXiv:1407.3561 (2014)
6. Das, D., Bose, P., Ruaro, N., Kruegel, C., Vigna, G.: Understanding security issues in the NFT ecosystem. In: Proceedings of the 2022 ACM SIGSAC Conference on Computer and Communications Security, pp. 667–681. CCS 2022, Association for Computing Machinery, New York, NY, USA (2022)
7. Gilad, Y., Hemo, R., Micali, S., Vlachos, G., Zeldovich, N.: Algorand: scaling byzantine agreements for cryptocurrencies. In: Proceedings of the 26th Symposium on Operating Systems Principles, pp. 51–68 (2017)
8. Grassi, L., Khovratovich, D., Rechberger, C., Roy, A., Schofnegger, M.: Poseidon: a new hash function for Zero-Knowledge proof systems. In: 30th USENIX Security Symposium (USENIX Security 21), pp. 519–535. USENIX Association (2021). https://www.usenix.org/conference/usenixsecurity21/presentation/grassi
9. Guidi, B., Michienzi, A.: Sleepminting, the brand new frontier of non fungible tokens fraud. In: Proceedings of the 2022 ACM Conference on Information Technology for Social Good, pp. 75–81. GoodIT 2022, Association for Computing Machinery, New York, NY, USA (2022)
10. Merkle, R.C.: A digital signature based on a conventional encryption function. In: Pomerance, C. (ed.) CRYPTO 1987. LNCS, vol. 293, pp. 369–378. Springer, Heidelberg (1988). https://doi.org/10.1007/3-540-48184-2_32
11. Nabben, K.: You can now clone NFTs as 'Mimics': Here's what that means."I think I just broke the NFT market." (2023). https://cointelegraph.com/magazine/you-can-now-clone-nfts-as-mimics-heres-what-that-means/. Accessed 24 Mar 2023
12. Tolmach, P., Li, Y., Lin, S.-W., Liu, Y.: Formal analysis of composable DeFi protocols. In: Bernhard, M., et al. (eds.) FC 2021. LNCS, vol. 12676, pp. 149–161. Springer, Heidelberg (2021). https://doi.org/10.1007/978-3-662-63958-0_13
13. Vitaletti, A., Zecchini, M.: A tale on decentralizing an app: the case of copyright management. In: Submission to the 5th Distributed Ledger Technology Workshop (DLT 2023). CEUR-WS (2023)
14. Wood, G.: Ethereum: A secure decentralised generalised transaction ledger. Ethereum project yellow paper (2014)

NFT Trades in Bitcoin with Off-Chain Receipts

Mehmet Sabir Kiraz[1], Enrique Larraia[2(✉)], and Owen Vaughan[2]

[1] De Montfort University, Leicester, UK
mehmet.kiraz@dmu.ac.uk
[2] nChain, London, UK
{e.larraia,o.vaughan}@nchain.com

Abstract. Non-fungible tokens (NFTs) are digital representations of assets stored on a blockchain. It allows content creators to certify authenticity of their digital assets and transfer ownership in a transparent and decentralized way. Popular choices of NFT marketplaces infrastructure include blockchains with smart contract functionality or layer-2 solutions. Surprisingly, researchers have largely avoided building NFT schemes over Bitcoin-like blockchains, most likely due to high transaction fees in the BTC network and the belief that Bitcoin lacks enough programmability to implement fair exchanges. In this work we fill this gap. We propose an NFT scheme where trades are settled in a single Bitcoin transaction as opposed to executing complex smart contracts. We use zero-knowledge proofs (concretely, recursive SNARKs) to prove that two Bitcoin transactions, the issuance transaction tx_0 and the current trade transaction tx_n, are linked through a unique chain of transactions. Indeed, these proofs function as "off-chain receipts" of ownership that can be transferred from the current owner to the new owner using an insecure channel. The size of the proof receipt is short, independent of the total current number of trades n, and can be updated incrementally by anyone at anytime. Marketplaces typically require some degree of token ownership delegation, e.g., escrow accounts, to execute the trade between sellers and buyers that are not online concurrently, and to alleviate transaction fees they resort to off-chain trades. This raises concerns on the transparency and purportedly honest behaviour of marketplaces. We achieve *fair* and *non-custodial* trades by leveraging our off-chain receipts and letting the involved parties carefully sign the trade transaction with appropriate combinations of `sighash` flags.

Keywords: Blockchain · Bitcoin · Zero-knowledge proofs · NFT tokens

1 Introduction

Non-fungible Tokens (NFTs) are digital representations of assets providing ownership records stored on a blockchain. They are cryptographic assets on a blockchain with unique identification codes and pointers to associated metadata,

J. Zhou et al. (Eds.): ACNS 2023 Workshops, LNCS 13907, pp. 100–117, 2023.
https://doi.org/10.1007/978-3-031-41181-6_6

possibly stored off-chain. They can be seen as digital passports or a conventional proof-of-purchase of a digital asset, functioning in the same manner than paper invoices. Blockchains allow two mutually distrustful parties to exchange token ownership for cryptocurrency without a trusted intermediary. The exchange is usually atomic in the sense that it happens in the same transaction or is controlled by a smart contract. NFTs have received huge interest due to their transparency in transaction details, public verifiability and trustless transfer [32]. Unlike conventional systems, public verifiability and transfer of ownership can be tracked continuously [3,27,31,33]. Despite the fact that the complete capabilities of NFTs have not yet been fully realized, they are already being utilized in various business models, including decentralized gaming [18] or e-commerce [7].

NFTs cannot be traded or exchanged in the same way as fungible tokens. Their size can be dynamically large and they cannot be replicated due to its non-fungibility. In Ethereum, the ERC-721 standard [16] defines a minimal interface to exchange NFTs. It specifies ownership details, security, and metadata. The ERC-1155 standard [29] builds on top improving several aspects, such as reducing transaction and storage costs by up to 90%, and batching multiple types of NFTs into a single contract. On a separate note, platforms that incorporate off-chain infrastructure enable the listing of tokens, the creation of new tokens (minting), the connection of sellers with buyers, and on-chain settlement of the exchange. NFT marketplaces (NFTM) like OpenSea, Rarible, SuperRare, Foundation, or Nifty, fill this gap and sit between the end users and the blockchain.

NFT Security. Token authenticity is the main concern with NFTs. After all, digital assets can easily be copied in fraudulent tokens. In all existing solutions, the burden of verifying the authenticity of the purchased token lies on the buyer. However, as blockchain technology evolves, it becomes harder for regular users (without specialized hardware) to access the network and check by themselves the on-chain state. NFTMs facilitate the trades, but they can impose his view of the blockchain, unilaterally remove tokens from their listings, and tend to rely on off-chain centralized databases that can serve arbitrary content [23]. This questions the purported decentralization and transparency of such platforms. In a recent study [15] a large number of potential vulnerabilities related to NFTMs were identified. We highlight some of the identified issues.

- *Buggy token contracts.* Code of custom contracts deployed by users are not properly audited. They may not pay the seller after the trade, or do not transfer the ownership at all (non-atomicity).
- *Lack of transparency in trading.* For example, Nifty uses escrow accounts and off-chain trades to reduce the transaction fees.
- *Control delegation.* The NFTM takes control of the token and funds to execute the trade without interaction between sellers and buyers. If the NFTM is given full control, it introduces a single point of failure in the security of all its users. Nifty, Foundation and SuperRare follow this approach via escrow accounts. OpenSea has a somewhat safer delegation mechanism, requiring authorization from the seller.

- *Royalty evasion.* If enforcement of royalties fees is delegated to NFTMs, buyers can avoid paying the fee by trading in plattforms that do not set royalties. Also, on-chain standards like ERC-721 do not capture royalties neither. Hence, payments can be settled off-chain, and transfer ownership on-chain (assuming the parties are willing to conduct non-atomic exchanges).
- *Wash trading.* Sales volume is artificially inflated to create an illusion of demand or to inflate financial metrics of their interests. For example, in Rarible, the more a user spends, the more $RARI tokens it receives. It is suspected that high-value NFTs such as CryptoKitties are example of wash trading.

Related Work. The authors in [28] proposed a solution called zero-knowledge Address Abstraction (zkAA) to eliminate the need for mapping and enables the direct use of web2 identity in the blockchain. In this way, users can utilize their web2 identities on blockchain through smart contracts leveraging zero-knowledge proofs without disclosing their identity.

In [20], the authors presented an auction protocol for NFTs with supports in multi-chain platforms. The design uses hash time lock transactions and additional strategies to control users malicious behaviour. However, without supporting trustless bridges the multichain platform (i.e., the cross-chain asset exchange process) could be secured. The authors in [12] presented a multi-stage NFT transaction protocol, called LiftChain, which builds a NFT transaction protocol performing a batch of NFT transactions off-chain and then propagates them on-chain. Although it aims to optimize the cost, the existing interfaces as a whole are still very expensive and not scalable.

More related to our work, Ordinal Inscriptions [17,26] is a numbering system that allows individual satoshis (the smallest Bitcoin denomination), referred to as sequence numbers, to be tracked and transferred in ownership. In short, Ordinals can be considered digital assets inscribed in satoshis. More concretely, satoshis are numbered in the order they are mined and transferred based on the first-in, first-out principle of transaction inputs and outputs. Proofs can be created to show that a specific satoshi is indeed present in a specific output. However, these proofs are large, consisting of the block headers and the Merkle path to the coinbase transaction that creates the satoshi, and every transaction that spends the satoshi. Note that the proof size is linear in the number of total current spends, and it increases with each spend. Unlike NFTs that can be purchased through platforms like OpenSea and Nifty Gateway, there are currently no marketplaces or wallets dedicated to Ordinals. They can be traded through Telegram and Discord channels, and the order book is currently maintained as a Google sheet.

Our Contributions and Techniques. Researchers generally refrained from creating and sending NFTs over the BTC network due to its expensive transaction fees and purported lack of programmability. In this paper, we fill this gap by explaining how to achieve fair exchanges without control delegation on Bitcoin-like blockchains with few transaction fees. More specifically, our main contributions are as follows.

- We design, implement, and benchmark, a proof system to prove and verify that an issuance transaction tx_0 (with an embedded representation of the token), and the current trade transaction tx_n are linked through a unique transaction chain. Our proof system is a recursive SNARK [2,5,10,11,14,22]. This means that if an additional transaction tx_{n+1} is added to the chain, then the proof π_n can be updated into π_{n+1} incrementally, without requiring all previous transactions. The proof receipt π_n functions as an '*off-chain receipt*' handed by the current owner to the new owner of the token. Since we use SNARKs, the size of π_n is constant or just logarithmic in the number n of total current trades.
- We present a new scheme NFT $=$ (mint, list, sell, buy) to trade NFTs on Bitcoin-like blockchains in the presence of untrusted marketplaces. A trade is settled in just one transaction tx_n and hence it is atomic: the payment and the ownership transfer cannot be decoupled. We guarantee token authenticity leveraging the off-chain proof receipt π_n to dispense access to the blockchain or the need of trusted intermediaries. To provide fairness for sellers and buyers without delegating control of tokens or funds to intermediaries, we employ appropriate combinations of sighash flags when signing (unlocking) inputs of tx_n.

In our NFT scheme, all trades appear on-chain, therefore it is transparent by design. As mentioned, the trade is settled by publishing a single transaction on-chain, as opposed to deploying complex smart contracts. The off-chain mechanism for token authenticity is also very flexible and can be enhanced in a number of ways. For example, the issuer can enforce royalty fees, or wash trading can be mitigated. Last, it is worth mentioning that although we describe our NFT scheme for Bitcoin, our techniques are fundamentally independent of the underlying blockchain technology. This does not come as a surprise as the main bulk of work happens off-chain, as we shall see. For example, it could be adapted to Ethereum's smart contract logic.

Paper Organisation. Section 2 gives some background needed. Section 3 introduces transaction chains and discuss their properties. Section 4 explains how to prove existence of transaction chains in Bitcoin using SNARKs. Finally, Sect. 5 presents our non-fungible token scheme NFT and analyses its security.

2 Preliminaries

2.1 Bitcoin Transactions

A transaction tx in the Bitcoin network has a unique identifier txid which is defined as the double SHA256 of the serialized transaction data. The txid is not part of the transaction itself. A transaction input tx.in contains several fields. Including a reference to previous transaction ID prevtxid, an output index vout, (this pair is known as the *outpoint*), and the unlocking script scriptSig. A transaction output tx.out contains the index vout of the output, a locking script scriptPubKey, and the amount of satoshis value locked.

Embedding Data in Transactions. Data can be inserted into transactions at several positions. Data payloads do not play a role in script validation as they can be embedded between OP_PUSH and OP_DROP codes or positioned often an OP_RETURN opcode. For example, it is possible to have a pay-to-public-key script P2PK with embedded data. During the transaction validation, the unlocking script of the spending transaction tx, and the locking script of the parent transaction prevtx are combined:

$$\langle \texttt{scriptSig} \rangle \parallel \texttt{scriptPubKey} := \langle \sigma\ \texttt{sighash} \rangle \parallel [\texttt{P2PK pk}]\ \texttt{OP\_RETURN}\ \langle \texttt{data} \rangle \quad (1)$$

The unlocking script contains the signature σ, and the locking script is the P2PK script (with public key pk) and the embedded data. Note that we are not writing out explicitly the set of opcodes comprising [P2PK pk]. The script is evaluated in reverse polish notation in the stack of the Bitcoin engine starting by pushing the data of scriptSig to the stack. Once the P2PK script has been executed successfully, which includes the signature check, the script becomes OP_RETURN ⟨data⟩ The script execution terminates when opcode OP_RETURN is reached. Hence the appended data is never pushed to the stack, but stored in the Bitcoin network as part of tx.

Choosing Which Inputs and Outputs are Signed. The result of the P2PK script evaluation above is either true or false. It depends on the signature check, which involves verifying the signature σ using public key pk. The message that is verified against σ is essentially a portion of the spending transaction tx. The parts of tx that are signed is controlled with the flag sighash. For example, if set to sighash_all||anyonecanpay in the unlocking script of the i-th input tx.in$_i$, the signature verification discards all other inputs but uses all outputs of tx. This allows different parties to add inputs to partially signed Bitcoin transactions (PSBT) while fixing the outputs (destination addresses). We will make use of different sighash flags in our NFT scheme of Sect. 5. See Table 1 for all possible flag values.

Table 1. Values of sighash flag in Bitcoin. Taken from [6].

Flag value	Meaning
sighash_all	Sign all inputs and all outputs
sighash_none	Sign all inputs and no output
sighash_single	Sign all inputs and the output with the same index
sighash_all||anyonecanpay	Sign its own input and all outputs
sighash_none||anyonecanpay	Sign its own input and no output
sighash_single||anyonecanpay	Sign its own input and the output with the same index

2.2 Recursive SNARKs – Proof Carrying Data

Proof-carrying data (PCD) [14] allows to prove correct execution of distributed computations run in mutually distrustful nodes. It is a generalization of incrementally verifiable computation (IVC) [30]. It allows to prove that a value z_n is the result of applying a function F iteratively n times

$$z_n = F(z_{n-1}), \ldots, z_1 = F(z_0) \tag{2}$$

In short, $z_n = F^n(z_0)$. In blockchains, PCDs have already found applications, most notably Mina [25] and others [9,13,21].

PCD Scheme and Properties. One can see (2) as the transcript T of a computation between n nodes where the i-th nodes applies F to its incoming message z_{i-1} to produce an outgoing message z_i. If this is the case, the whole transcript is said to be *compliant* with F. Likewise, z_n is compliant with F, if it is the output of a transcript T compliant with F. A PCD scheme is a triplet of algorithms $\mathsf{PCD} = (\mathbb{G}, \mathbb{P}, \mathbb{V})$ with the following interface:

- $\mathbb{G}(1^\lambda, F) \to (\mathsf{pk}, \mathsf{vk})$. It takes as input a security parameter λ, and a function F seen as an arithmetic circuit C_F. It produces a pair of verification and proving keys.
- $\mathbb{P}(\mathsf{pk}, z_n, (z_{n-1}, \pi_{n-1})) \to \pi_n$. It takes as public input the outgoing message z_n, and as private input the incoming message z_{n-1} and a proof π_{n-1}. It outputs a proof π_n for the F-compliance of z_n. Namely, a proof for the existence of messages $z_0, \ldots, z_{n-1}$ as in (2).
- $\mathbb{V}(\mathsf{vk}, z_n, \pi_n) \to \{\mathsf{accept}, \mathsf{reject}\}$. It takes the public input z_n and a proof π_n. It either accepts or rejects the proof for the F-compliance of z_n.

We informally state the properties of a PCD scheme, and refer to [2,5,14] for formal definitions. The scheme is *complete* if $\mathbb{V}$ always accepts proofs π_n generated by the honest prover $\mathbb{P}$. It is *succinct* if the size of π_n is $\mathrm{poly}(\lambda, |C_F|)$. In particular the proof does not grow at each iteration, it only depends on the complexity of the arithmetic circuit for F. The scheme is *knowledge sound* if, given access to the random coins of any cheating prover $\mathbb{P}^*$ that produces a pair (z_n, π_n) accepted by the verifier $\mathbb{V}$, it is possible to extract a compliant transcript T as in (2) with overwhelming probability in the security parameter λ.

Constructing PCDs from SNARKs. PCDs can be constructed in two ways. It was first realized in [2] from preprocessing succinct non-interactive arguments of knowledge (SNARKs) [4] with sublinear verification time (also known as *succinct* verification) over a cycle of elliptic curves. Given a preprocessing $\mathsf{SNARK} = (\mathbf{G}, \mathbf{P}, \mathbf{V})$, the statement $z_n = F^n(z_0)$ is split in two parts. The first part proves existence of z_{n-1} such that $z_n = F(z_{n-1})$; this is done by expressing F as an arithmetic circuit C_F, that is satisfied on public input z_n and private input z_{n-1} only if $z_n = F(z_{n-1})$. The second part proves existence of a valid proof π_{n-1} attesting to the correctness of the $n-1$ previous iterations. This is done expressing the verifier $\mathbf{V}$ as a circuit $C_{\mathbf{V}}$, satisfied on public input vk and private inputs z_{n-1}, π_{n-1}, only if $\mathbf{V}(\mathsf{vk}, z_{n-1}, \pi_{n-1}) = \mathsf{accept}$, where vk is the preprocessed verification key generated by $\mathbf{G}$. The PCD prover proves satisfiability of both circuits C_F and $C_{\mathbf{V}}$ on public input z_n and private inputs z_{n-1}, π_{n-1} using vk as part of its proving key. Another way of constructing PCDs, initiated in Halo [10], is using a SNARK without succinct verification, but with an accumulation scheme that allows to accumulate the proofs at each step, and postpone the verification of the proofs. The requirement is that the accumulator must be succinctly verifiable [8,10,11]. Recently, PCDs have been constructed from folding schemes, without using SNARKs at all, in Nova [22].

3   Transaction Chains

In this section, we introduce our notion of *transaction chains*. In the next section, we show how to prove the existence of a chain succinctly. The inputs and outputs of a Bitcoin transaction form ordered sets. We write $\mathsf{tx.in}_s$ and $\mathsf{tx.out}_r$ to respectively denote the s-th input and r-th output.

Definition 1 (*Transaction Chain*). *Let* T *be a set of transactions. The sequence* $\mathbf{c}_{\mathsf{tx}_0 \to \mathsf{tx}_n} := (\mathsf{tx}_0, \mathsf{tx}_1, \dots, \mathsf{tx}_{n-1}, \mathsf{tx}_n)$ *with* $\mathsf{tx}_i \in \mathsf{T}$, *is a* transaction chain *of length* n *if for each* $1 \le i \le n$ *some of the inputs of* tx_i *references an output of* tx_{i-1}.

As mentioned in Sect. 2.1, in Bitcoin, a transaction tx_i references a parent transaction tx_{i-1} in its inputs using the identifier txid_{i-1}. We can rely on the collision resistance of the hash function to ensure distinct identifiers for all Bitcoin transactions. This ensures that any chain $\mathbf{c}_{\mathsf{tx}_1 \to \mathsf{tx}_n}$ has no repeated transactions. Also, note that transaction chain is a transitive relation, therefore we can concatenate two chains $\mathbf{c}_{\mathsf{tx}_0 \to \mathsf{tx}_n}$, $\mathbf{c}_{\mathsf{tx}_n \to \mathsf{tx}_m}$ to obtain a longer transaction chain $\mathbf{c}_{\mathsf{tx}_0 \to \mathsf{tx}_m}$ (i.e., by removing the first transaction of the second chain $\mathbf{c}_{\mathsf{tx}_n \to \mathsf{tx}_m}$).

We note that there could be more than one chain linking two transactions. For example, consider the set $\mathsf{T} = \{\mathsf{tx}_0, \mathsf{tx}_1, \mathsf{tx}_2, \mathsf{tx}_3\}$, where tx_0 has two outputs, the first output is spent by tx_1, and the second output by tx_2. If tx_3 spends both tx_1 and tx_2, then we have two chains $\mathbf{c}_1 = (\mathsf{tx}_0, \mathsf{tx}_1, \mathsf{tx}_3)$, and $\mathbf{c}_2 = (\mathsf{tx}_0, \mathsf{tx}_2, \mathsf{tx}_3)$ linking tx_0 with tx_3.

We are also interested in chains that are unique. That is, given two transactions there exists only one possible way to link them. We address this issue fixing the inputs and outputs through which the link is established.

Definition 2 (*(r, s)-Primary Chain*). *Let a set of transactions* T *and a sequence* $\mathbf{c}_{\mathsf{tx}_0 \to \mathsf{tx}_n} = (\mathsf{tx}_0, \dots, \mathsf{tx}_n)$ *with* $\mathsf{tx}_i \in \mathsf{T}$. *We say* $\mathbf{c}_{\mathsf{tx}_0 \to \mathsf{tx}_n}$ *is a* (r, s)-*primary chain if it is a transaction chain and the input r-th input of* tx_i *references the s-th output of* tx_{i-1}.

Fig. 1. A $(1, 2)$-primary chain. The first input of tx_i spends the second output of tx_{i-1}.

In the lemma below we characterize the set of all possible (r, s)-primary chains starting at tx_0. Namely, there can only be chains that are subsequences of the largest chain in the set $C^{(T_B)}_{\mathsf{tx}_0\to}$, where:

$$C^{(T_B)}_{\mathsf{tx}_0\to} := \left\{ \mathbf{c} = (\mathsf{tx}_0, \ldots, \mathsf{tx}_n) \;\middle|\; \begin{array}{l} \mathbf{c} \text{ is a } (r, s)\text{-primary chain (Defn. 2)} \\ \mathsf{tx}_i \in T_B \; \forall 0 \le i \le n \end{array} \right\} \quad (3)$$

Lemma 1 (Non-Diverging Primary Chains). *Let T_B be the set of all transactions in the Bitcoin network. Let any transaction tx_0 in T_B, and let $\mathbf{c}^{max}_{\mathsf{tx}_0\to\mathsf{tx}_n}$ be an (r, s)-primary chain of maximal length. Then, the set $C^{(T_B)}_{\mathsf{tx}_0\to}$ of all (r, s)-primary transactions starting at tx_0 are subsequences of $\mathbf{c}^{max}_{\mathsf{tx}_0\to\mathsf{tx}_n}$. That is:*

$$C^{(T_B)}_{\mathsf{tx}_0\to} = \{(\mathsf{tx}_0, \ldots, \mathsf{tx}_i) \mid \mathsf{tx}_i \in \mathbf{c}^{max}_{\mathsf{tx}_0\to\mathsf{tx}_n}\}$$

Proof. This is a direct consequence of the double-spending resistance property of a blockchain. First observe that $\mathbf{c}^{max}_{\mathsf{tx}_0\to\mathsf{tx}_n}$ is of maximal length, so it cannot be a subsequence of any other primary chain. Now, if there exists an (r, s)-primary chain $\mathbf{c}_{\mathsf{tx}_0\to\mathsf{tx}_m}$ that is not a proper subsequence of $\mathbf{c}^{max}_{\mathsf{tx}_0\to\mathsf{tx}_n}$, then, since both chains share the same origin tx_0, at some point they must diverge. Say they are equal up to the i-th transaction tx_i. This means that the s-th output tx_i has been spent twice, which is not possible. □

The lemma above also proves that there is only one primary chain of maximal length. Not surprisingly, the largest (r, s)-primary chain $\mathbf{c}_{\mathsf{tx}_0\to\mathsf{tx}_n}$ in Bitcoin is that whose end transaction tx_n has the s-th output unspent.

Lemma 2 (Largest Primary Chain). *Let T_B be the set of all transactions in the Bitcoin network. Let any tx_0 in T_B, and let $\mathbf{c}_{\mathsf{tx}_0\to\mathsf{tx}_n}$ be an (r, s)-primary chain such that the s-th output of tx_n is unspent. Then, $\mathbf{c}_{\mathsf{tx}_0\to\mathsf{tx}_n}$ is the largest (r, s)-primary chain starting at tx_0.*

Proof. Lemma 1 shows that all (r, s)-primary chains must be subsequences of the largest (r, s)-primary chain. Now, $\mathbf{c}_{\mathsf{tx}_0\to\mathsf{tx}_n}$ cannot be a subsequence of any other primary chain because the s-th output of tx_n is unspent. We conclude that $\mathbf{c}_{\mathsf{tx}_0\to\mathsf{tx}_n}$ is the largest chain starting at tx_0. □

4   Succinct Proofs for Transaction Chains

Consider the following scenario with a prover Alice and a verifier Bob. The first transaction tx_0 is already in the blockchain $\mathcal{B}$ and is known to both Alice and Bob. Alice submits a transaction tx_n to $\mathcal{B}$ and also sends it to Bob. Both parties now have two transactions (tx_0, tx_n). Alice wants to prove to Bob the statement:

$$\text{"}tx_n \text{ is linked to } tx_0 \text{ through a primary chain } \mathbf{c}_{tx_0 \rightarrow tx_n}\text{"} \tag{4}$$

Alice generates a proof π_n that attest to the veracity of her statement. If Bob accepts π_n as valid, he has the triplet (tx_0, tx_n, π_n). Now consider a third actor Charlie. Bob creates a new transaction tx_{n+1} such that (tx_n, tx_{n+1}) is a primary chain. He amends Alice's proof π_n to create a new proof π_{n+1} to also show that tx_{n+1} is linked to tx_0 through a primary transaction chain. He sends (tx_{n+1}, π_{n+1}) to Charlie. The information flow can be visualised in Fig. 2. The point we are trying to make is that proof generation is incremental; new parties can come in, augment an existing chain in $\mathcal{B}$, and prove correctness of the augmentation based on older proofs.

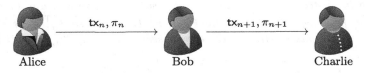

$$tx_n, \pi_n \qquad\qquad tx_{n+1}, \pi_{n+1}$$

Alice   Bob   Charlie

Fig. 2. Incremental chain augmentation. tx_0 is known to all parties. π_i proves existence of chain $\mathbf{c}_{tx_0 \rightarrow tx_i}$.

Trivial Solution: Send the Primary Transaction Chain. Alice simply sends the entire chain $\mathbf{c}_{tx_0 \rightarrow tx_n} = (tx_0, \ldots, tx_n)$ as her proof π_n. Bob can explicitly check that $\mathbf{c}_{tx_0 \rightarrow tx_n}$ is a primary chain appearing in the blockchain $\mathcal{B}$. This solution requires communication and verification cost linear in the size of the chain $\mathcal{O}(n)$. It also incurs in repetition cost: Charlie has to check the entire chain again, even though Bob checked it already up to the n-th link.

Efficient Solution: Use SNARKs. Alice sends to Bob the last transaction tx_n, and a short SNARK proof π_n attesting to the existence of $\mathbf{c}_{tx_0 \rightarrow tx_n}$. Bob verifies π_n and checks that tx_n is in $\mathcal{B}$. The size of the transmitted proof is now $|\pi_n| = \mathcal{O}(\log(n))$, a significant improvement compared with the trivial solution above. See Table 2 for a comparison summary.

4.1   Proving Existence of Primary Chains Recursively

Recall from Sect. 3 that for a set of transactions $\mathsf{T}_\mathcal{B}$ in blockchain $\mathcal{B}$, and $tx_0 \in \mathsf{T}_\mathcal{B}$, the set $\mathsf{C}_{tx_0 \rightarrow}^{(\mathsf{T}_\mathcal{B})}$ denotes all the (r, s)-primary chains starting at tx_0. Thus, we can formalize the informal statement (4) in the following NP relation:

Table 2. Comparison of solutions to check primary chains $\mathbf{c}_{\mathsf{tx}_0 \to \mathsf{tx}_n}$.

Method	Communication	Verification
Send chain	$\mathcal{O}(n)$: send $n-1$ transactions	$\mathcal{O}(n)$: check $n-1$ transactions
SNARK-based	$\mathcal{O}(\log(n))$: send tx_n and π_n	$\mathcal{O}(\log(n))$: verify π_n

$$\mathcal{R}_{\mathsf{T}_\mathcal{B}, \mathsf{tx}_0} := \left\{ (\mathsf{tx}_n ; \mathbf{c}) \;\middle|\; \begin{array}{l} \mathbf{c} = (\mathsf{tx}_0, \mathsf{tx}_1, \ldots, \mathsf{tx}_{n-1}, \mathsf{tx}_n) \\ \mathbf{c} \in C_{\mathsf{tx}_0 \to}^{(\mathsf{T}_\mathcal{B})} \end{array} \right\} \tag{5}$$

In principle the prover needs the entire chain $\mathbf{c}$ linking tx_n to tx_0 as private information to prove statement (4). He would somehow need to get the chain $\mathbf{c}$ either from the previous prover or from $\mathcal{B}$. This poses a problem because the chain may be large and we would like to avoid sending it between parties. The observation is that *provided* the chain from tx_0 up to the parent tx_{n-1} is a primary chain, we just need to ensure the last link holds. We ensure the chain $\mathbf{c}_{\mathsf{tx}_0 \to \mathsf{tx}_{n-1}}$ is a primary chain validating a proof π_{n-1} for the parent transaction tx_{n-1} using a recursive SNARK.

Description of the Circuit. The recursive circuit $\mathsf{C}_{\mathsf{ptc}}$ for primary transaction chains is described in Fig. 3. Note that the circuit has hard-coded in its description the transaction identifier txid_0 of the first transaction tx_0 of the chain. Also, as described, the circuit uses a SNARK with succinct verification.

$\mathsf{C}_{\mathsf{ptc}}((\mathsf{tx}_n, b_{\mathsf{base}}); (\mathsf{tx}_{n-1}, \pi_{n-1}))$:

Public input $\mathsf{tx}_n, b_{\mathsf{base}}$. The last transaction in the chain, and a 'base case' flag
Private input $\mathsf{tx}_{n-1}, \pi_{n-1}$. The parent transaction and (an optional) proof π_{n-1} for satisfiability of $\mathsf{C}_{\mathsf{ptc}}$ on public input tx_{n-1}.

1. Parse $\mathsf{tx}_n.\mathsf{in}_r = \mathsf{txid} \| \mathsf{vout}$
2. Check $\mathsf{vout} = s$
3. If $b_{\mathsf{base}} = \mathsf{true}$ (base case), check $\mathsf{txid} = \mathsf{txid}_0$ // txid_0 hard-coded
4. If $b_{\mathsf{base}} = \mathsf{false}$ (recursive case):
   (a) Check $\mathsf{txid} = \mathsf{SHA256d}(\mathsf{tx}_{n-1})$
   (b) Check π_{n-1} is valid for public input $(\mathsf{tx}_{n-1}, b_{\mathsf{base}})$

Fig. 3. Circuit to prove existence of a (r, s)-primary chain $\mathbf{c}_{\mathsf{tx}_0 \to \mathsf{tx}_n}$.

The Recursive SNARK (PCD) for Primary Transaction Chains. Having described the circuit $\mathsf{C}_{\mathsf{ptc}}$, the preprocessing PCD to prove satisfiability of $\mathsf{C}_{\mathsf{ptc}}$ is the triplet of algorithms $\mathsf{PCD}_{\mathsf{ptc}} = (\mathbb{G}_{\mathsf{ptc}}, \mathbb{P}_{\mathsf{ptc}}, \mathbb{V}_{\mathsf{ptc}})$ with the following interface.

- $\mathbb{G}_{\text{ptc}}(1^\lambda, \text{txid}_0) \rightarrow (\text{pk}, \text{vk})$. On input a security parameter λ and the identifier of the first transaction txid_0 it outputs a pair of proving and verification keys pk, vk.
- $\mathbb{P}_{\text{ptc}}(\text{pk}, (\text{tx}_n, b_{\text{case}}); (\text{tx}_{n-1}, \pi_{n-1})) \rightarrow \pi_n$. On input a proving key, the public input $(\text{tx}_n, b_{\text{case}})$, and the private input $(\text{tx}_{n-1}, \pi_{n-1})$ it generates a proof π_n attesting to the existence of a chain $\mathbf{c}_{\text{tx}_0 \rightarrow \text{tx}_n}$. Thus $(\text{tx}_n, \mathbf{c}_{\text{tx}_0 \rightarrow \text{tx}_n}) \in \mathcal{R}_{T_\mathcal{B}, \text{tx}_0}$.
- $\mathbb{V}_{\text{ptc}}(\text{vk}, (\text{tx}_n, b_{\text{case}}), \pi_n) \rightarrow \{\text{accept}, \text{reject}\}$. On input a verification key vk and the public input $(\text{tx}_n, b_{\text{case}})$ it either accepts or rejects.

We emphasize that txid_0 needs to be known in advance to use it in step (3) of C_{ptc}. The later means that PCD_{ptc} can be used only for the chain that starts at tx_0.

Theorem 1. *Let $T_\mathcal{B}$ be the set of transactions in the Bitcoin network. If the verifier $\mathbb{V}_{\text{ptc}}$ accepts a proof π_n for $\text{tx}_n \in T_\mathcal{B}$, then there exists a chain $\mathbf{c}_{\text{tx}_0 \rightarrow \text{tx}_n}$ in $T_\mathcal{B}$ with overwhelming probability.*

Proof. Using the soundness of PCD_{ptc}, it is enough to show that if the circuit C_{ptc} accepts tx_n then it exists a chain $\mathbf{c}_{\text{tx}_0 \rightarrow \text{tx}_n}$ with overwhelming probability. We will use the following claim that holds true in Bitcoin.

Claim. All coinbase transactions in the Bitcoin network have one unique outpoint whose parent ID reference is the zero-byte array.

The proof of the theorem is concluded proving the following lemma.

Lemma 3. *Let $T_\mathcal{B}$ be the set of Bitcoin transactions at a given time. If $\text{tx}_0 \in T_\mathcal{B}$ is not an ancestor of $\text{tx}_n \in T_\mathcal{B}$, then C_{ptc} rejects on public input tx_n. Thus, $\forall \text{tx}_{n-1}, \pi, b_{\text{base}}$ it holds $\text{false} = C_{\text{ptc}}((\text{tx}_n, b_{\text{base}}), (\text{tx}_{n-1}, \pi_{n-1}))$ with overwhelming probability.*

Proof. All transactions in Bitcoin originate from a coinbase transaction. Let $\mathbf{c} = (\text{tx}_{\text{cb}}, \text{tx}_1 \ldots, \text{tx}_n)$ be an (r, s)-primary chain connecting a coinbase transaction tx_{cb} with tx_n. Now, assume by contradiction that C_{ptc} accepts tx_n. By hypothesis tx_0 is not an ancestor of tx_n, and we assume all transactions in $T_\mathcal{B}$ have different identifiers. Therefore the base case of C_{ptc} is not triggered, and there must be a valid proof π_{n-1} for the parent tx_{n-1}. Repeating this argument backwards, there must exist a valid proof $\pi_{\text{cb}-1}$ for the parent of the coinbase transaction tx_{cb}. In other words, the prover used a 'parent' transaction $\text{tx}_{\text{cb}-1}$ for tx_{cb} whose identifier is the zero-byte array—see the claim above. The later cannot occur in practice due to the collision resistance of SHA256. This concludes the proof of the lemma and the theorem. $\qquad \square$

4.2   Implementation Details and Benchmarks

Circuit Logic. We have implemented several circuit gadgets to construct C_{ptc} from Fig. 3. For simplicity we set $r = s = 0$.

- first_outpoint_OK(tx, txid). Evaluates to true iff $\text{tx.in}_0 = \text{txid}\|0$
- txid_OK(tx, txid). Evaluates to true iff $\text{txid} = \text{SHA256d}(\text{tx})$
- proof_OK(tx, π). Evaluates to true iff $\mathbf{V}(\text{vk}, (\text{tx}, \text{false}), \pi) = \text{accept}$. Here recall from Sect. 2.2 that $\mathbf{V}$ is the verification logic of the underlying SNARK used in the construction of the PCD, and vk the verification key.

Using the above gadgets, we can construct the following circuits for the base case and recursive case, respectively:

$$\text{parent\_is\_txid}_0(\text{tx}_n) := \text{first\_outpoint\_OK}(\text{tx}_n, \text{txid}_0)$$

$$\text{primary\_chain\_OK}(\text{tx}_n, \text{tx}_{n-1}, \pi_{n-1}) :=$$
$$\text{txid\_OK}(\text{tx}_{n-1}, \text{txid}_{n-1}) \wedge \text{first\_outpoint\_OK}(\text{tx}_n, \text{txid}_{n-1}) \wedge \text{proof\_OK}(\text{tx}_{n-1}, \pi_{n-1})$$

The circuit C_{ptc} is then set to:

$$\mathsf{C}_{\text{ptc}}((\text{tx}, b_{\text{base}}); (\text{tx}_{n-1}, \pi_{n-1})) :=$$
$$(b_{\text{base}} = \text{true} \wedge \text{parent\_is\_txid}_0(\text{tx}_n))$$
$$\vee$$
$$(b_{\text{base}} = \text{false} \wedge \text{primary\_chain\_OK}(\text{tx}_n, \text{tx}_{n-1}, \pi_{n-1}))$$

PCD Scheme. We have implemented the SNARK scheme PCD_{ptc} defined in the previous section following the approach of [2]. Namely, using cycles of elliptic curves to implement the verification logic as part of the circuit in step (4b) of C_{ptc}. The underlying SNARK is Groth16 [19]. Our implementation is written in Rust and uses arkworks library [1]. The cycle of curves is MNT4-MNT6. These are MNT curves [24] of embedding degrees 4 and 6, respectively. For production code, the size of the fields should be large, i.e. of size ≈ 750 bits.

In Table 3 we report benchmarks for the time it takes to prove and verify a proof. The tests have run in a laptop, 2019 MacBook Pro 2.6 GHz 6 Cores i7, 12 Threads, 32 GB Memory, and in an embedded processor (SoC) Raspberry Pi ARM BCM2835 1.80 GHz 1 Processor, 4 Cores, 4 Threads, 3.71 GB Memory. The most expensive gadgets are txid_OK and proof_OK. The former needs to generate constraints for two evaluations of the hash function SHA256, which is not zero-knowledge friendly. The later contains the logic of the Groth16 verifier $\mathbf{V}$. We have fixed the transaction size to 226 bytes – the minimum size of a Bitcoin transaction. This means the compression function of SHA256 is applied twice to generate txid from tx.

5 An Application: NFTs with Atomic and Fully-Fair Swaps

We define a non-fungible token scheme (NFT) as a tuple of algorithms NFT = (mint, list, sell, buy). In our scheme, minting a token tk essentially embeds tk in a transaction tx_0. A user with public key pk_U is the owner of tk, if there exist a (r, s)-primary transaction chain $\mathbf{c}_{\text{tx}_0 \to \text{tx}_n}$, with the s-th output of tx_n unspent and controlled by pk_U. Owners can list their tokens for trading, and listed tokens can be exchanged placing sell or buy trade orders.

Table 3. Times for proving and verifying satisfiability of circuit C_{ptc} recursing Groth16 over MNT-753 cycle.

	Standard laptop (MacBook Pro)	Smartphone (Raspberry Pi)
Proving time	171 s ($\approx$ 3 min)	970 secs ($\approx$ 16 min)
Verification time	3 s	5 s
Proof size	270 bytes	

5.1 Description of the Scheme

Mint Tokens. The issuer embeds the digital token tk in an *issuance* transaction tx_0. He then creates the SNARK proving key and verification key, and generates the *mint* transaction tx_1 as the first link of an (r, s)-primary chain $c_{tx_0 \to tx_1}$ along with a proof π_1. Both transactions tx_0, tx_1 are uploaded to the blockchain and the mint process is finished. See Fig. 4 for the algorithm mint.

Note that only the issuer can unlock the s-th output of tx_0 using his secret signing key sk_I. Hence, the issuer owns freshly minted tokens.

$\mathsf{mint}(1^\lambda, \mathsf{tk}, \mathsf{pk}_I, \mathsf{sk}_I)$:

1. Create the **issuance transaction** tx_0 with token tk embedded in some of the outputs. (See equation (1) for OP_RETURN data). The s-th output locks no funds with a P2PK script using a public key pk_I controlled by the issuer.
2. Run the setup of the NFT program using the identifier $txid_0$ of tx_0:

$$(\mathsf{pk}, \mathsf{vk}) \leftarrow \mathbb{G}_{ptc}(1^\lambda, \mathsf{txid}_0)$$

3. Create the **mint transaction** tx_1 whose r-th input spends the s-th output of tx_0. Unlock the r-th input using the signing key sk_I.
4. Create a proof for the (r, s)-primary chain $\vec{c}_{tx_0 \to tx_1} = (tx_0, tx_1)$, running:

$$\pi_1 \leftarrow \mathbb{P}_{ptc}(\mathsf{pk}, (\mathsf{tx}_1, b_{case}); (\mathsf{tx}_0, \pi_0)),$$

the boolean flag is set to $b_{case} = \mathsf{true}$, and since this is the first link of the chain, the previous proof is empty $\pi_0 = \emptyset$.
5. Upload both transactions tx_0, tx_1 to the blockchain, and publish pk, vk.

Fig. 4. Minting tokens in Bitcoin.

List Tokens (with Off-Chain Receipts). Before a token tk can be traded, the keys pk, vk, and the first proof π_1 generated by the issuer are publicly announced. This can be done via embedding the keys in the mint transaction tx_1. Additionally, the data can stored off-chain such as a list maintained by a marketplace. We emphasize that the keys and the mint transaction tx_1 can be also published by the issuer. Ultimately, the issuer is responsible for authenticating this data, not the marketplace.

To mark a token ready for trading, the marketplace receives the transaction tx_n from the current owner (if $n = 1$, from the issuer), checks it is linked with the previous transaction tx_{n-1}, and if so generates the proof π_n (the off-chain receipt). The algorithm for listing is given in Fig. 5.

$list(L_{nft}, tk, n, tx_n)$:

1. If $n = 1$, add entry $(tk, pk, vk, tx_1, \pi_1)$ to list L_{nft}. // tx_1 is the mint transaction
2. Else $(n > 1)$ do:
   (a) Retrieve entry $e_{tk} = (tk, pk, vk, tx_{n-1}, \pi_{n-1})$ from L_{nft}
   (b) Check r-th input of tx_n spends s-th output of tx_{n-1}. If not, abort and halt.
   (c) $\pi_n \leftarrow \mathbb{P}_{ptc}(pk, (tx_n, false); (tx_0, \pi_{n-1}))$ // generate proof (off-chain receipt)
   (d) Update entry $e_{tk} = (tk, pk, vk, tx_n, \pi_n)$ in L_{nft}

Fig. 5. Listing tokens in an marketplace with off-chain receipts.

Transfer Tokens. We explain how to transfer tokens via an (r, s)-primary chain with $r \neq s$. For simplicity we use a $(1, 2)$-primary chain as in Fig. 1. The trade is a non-interactive process that is fair for both parties, the seller and the buyer. The outcome of the process is a single transaction tx_{n+1} with two inputs and two outputs. The first output pays the seller, and the second output transfers token ownership to the buyer. If tx_{n+1} is accepted in the blockchain, the seller gets paid and the buyer is the new owner of the token (via the $(1, 2)$-primary chain). Otherwise, none of them gets anything.

We detail two flavours of transfers (trading orders). In sell orders, the seller initiates the trade and sets the offer price sats. In buy orders, the buyer initiates, and sets the bid price. In either case, the initiator of the trade creates a partially-signed bitcoin transaction (PSBT) tx_{n+1}, and sends it to the other party, who finalizes it filling the remaining inputs and outputs. The inputs of the transaction are unlocked signing with an appropriate combination of sighash flags for security. The exchanged information flows in one direction (one round), which means the parties do not need to be online at the same time. See Fig. 6 for the algorithms sell, buy.

5.2 Fairness for the Buyer and Seller

We deem an NFT scheme *correct* if there cannot be multiple legitimate owners of the same token tk at a given time. We say the exchange is *fair* if, provided a sell or buy trade transaction tx_{n+1} is accepted in the blockchain, then the buyer is the new owner of the token tk, and the seller is rewarded in sats.

sell($\mathsf{sats}, \mathsf{pk}_S, \mathsf{pk}_B, \mathsf{tx}_n, \pi_n, \mathsf{vk}$):	buy($\mathsf{sats}, \mathsf{pk}_S, \mathsf{pk}_B, \mathsf{tx}_n, \pi_n, \mathsf{vk}$):
– Seller inputs: $\mathsf{sats}, \mathsf{pk}_S, \mathsf{tx}_n$ – Buyer inputs: $\mathsf{pk}_B, \mathsf{tx}_n, \pi_n, \mathsf{vk}$	– Seller inputs: $\mathsf{pk}_S, \mathsf{tx}_n$ – Buyer inputs: $\mathsf{sats}, \mathsf{pk}_B, \mathsf{tx}_n, \pi_n, \mathsf{vk}$
Offer: The seller initiates the trade.	**Bid:** The buyer initiates the trade.
1. Create a PSBT tx_{n+1} with the first input spending the second output of tx_n. The first output of tx_{n+1} locks sats (the offer price) with his public key pk_S. 2. Unlock the first input of tx_{n+1} signing with `sighash_single‖anyonecanpay`. From now on, the first output of tx_{n+1} cannot be changed, but more inputs and outputs can be added. 3. Publicly announce the PSBT tx_{n+1}.	1. Check accept $\stackrel{?}{=}$ $\mathbb{V}_{\mathsf{ptc}}(\mathsf{vk}, (\mathsf{tx}_n, \mathsf{false}), \pi_n)$. If the proof is not valid, reject and halt. 2. Create a PSBT tx_{n+1} with the first input spending the second output of tx_n. The first output of tx_{n+1} is left unspecified. 3. Add a second input funding tx_{n+1} with sats (the bid price). Add a second output locked with his public key pk_B. 4. Unlock the second input signing with `sighash_single`. From this point on, neither the second output nor the two inputs can be changed, but more outputs can be added. 5. Publicly announce the PSBT tx_{n+1}.
Finalize: The buyer settles the trade.	**Finalize:** The seller settles the trade.
1. Check accept $\stackrel{?}{=}$ $\mathbb{V}_{\mathsf{ptc}}(\mathsf{vk}, (\mathsf{tx}_n, \mathsf{false}), \pi_n)$. If the proof is not valid, reject and halt. 2. Add a a second input to tx_{n+1} with funds sats, and a second output to tx_{n+1} locked with his public key pk_B. 3. The second input is unlocked signing with `sighash_all` or with `sighash_single`. From now on, no input, in particular the first one, nor the second output can be changed. 4. The transaction tx_{n+1} is ready	1. Add the first output of tx_{n+1} locking sats with his public key pk_S. 2. Unlocks the first input of tx_{n+1} signing with `sighash_all` (or any other flag that signs its own output). 3. The transaction tx_{n+1} is ready

Fig. 6. Selling and buying tokens without control delegation in Bitcoin.

Correctness. The correctness of our scheme $\mathsf{NFT} = (\mathsf{mint}, \mathsf{list}, \mathsf{sell}, \mathsf{buy})$ is due to the non-diverging property of primary chains (cf. lemma 1). Primary chains originating at a given transaction tx_0 can only be subsequences of the largest primary chain. Put differently, there cannot be 'forked' chains.

Fairness for the Buyer. This is achieved due to two observations. First, since the buyer successfully verifies the proof π_n of the seller, then there exists a primary chain $\mathbf{c}_{\mathsf{tx}_0 \to \mathsf{tx}_n}$; this follows from the soundness of $\mathsf{PCD}_{\mathsf{ptc}}$ and theorem 1. Therefore, there also exists a $(1, 2)$-primary chain $\mathbf{c}_{\mathsf{tx}_0 \to \mathsf{tx}_{n+1}}$ because the buyer explicitly adds the second output of tx_{n+1} (in both, sell and buy orders). Second, at the time tx_{n+1} is accepted in the blockchain, since its first output is unspent, it is guaranteed that $\mathbf{c}_{\mathsf{tx}_0 \to \mathsf{tx}_{n+1}}$ is the largest primary chain (cf. Lemma 2); note the second output of tx_{n+1} is controlled by the public key pk_B of the buyer, and the first input is always signed by the buyer when he funds tx_n (signing with either `sighash_all` or `sighash_single`). If the seller sends the token to someone else in between, the first input of tx_{n+1} is a double spend, so it will not be accepted in the blockchain. If someone else changes the second output (so the buyer would not acquire ownership), his payment will not go through neither.

Fairness for the Seller. This trivially holds because the seller always locks the payment sats in the first output of tx_{n+1}, which is always signed (using either `sighash_single||anyonecanpay` in sell orders, or any other flag that signs the first output in buy orders); if the buyer does not fund tx_{n+1} properly, it will never be accepted on-chain, and the seller still owns the token because the second output of tx_n remains unspent.

5.3   Further Remarks

Identifying Corrupted Users. The seller can prove knowledge of the signing key needed to unlock the first input of the last traded transaction tx_n to the NFTM when he engages in the list algorithm (e.g., by signing a challenge message). The buyer can also prove the knowledge of the signing keys that unlocks the sats funding the trade transaction tx_{n+1} when she initiates a buy order or finalises a sell order.

Trade Latency. The main overhead of our NFT scheme is when listing tokens. Therein, the off-chain proof receipt π_n for the previous transaction trade tx_n is generated. We report roughly three minutes runtime for the prover $\mathbb{P}_{ptc}$ to generate π_n for the previous trade transaction tx_n (see Table 3). However, since π_n is *independent* of tx_{n+1}, the algorithm list can be executed well ahead of time. Due to the full fairness of our NFT scheme, the buyer only needs to check π_n in a sell or buy order. This means that from users perspective, the trade is done almost instantaneous, which is the time to verify the proof π_n with $\mathbb{V}_{ptc}$.

Royalties and Wash Trading. Each transaction in a chain can have a distinguished output with a specific amount locked by a fixed public key pk_I controlled by the NFT issuer. Similarly, wash trading can be mitigated by putting a cap in the number of trades for which a proof receipt can be generated. Both features can be encoded in the primary chain circuit C_{ptc} of Fig. 3. If the fee is not paid, or the trade counter reaches the upper bound, users will not be able to generate the off-chain proof receipt.

References

1. **Arkworks** zksnark ecosystem (2023). https://arkworks.rs
2. Ben-Sasson, E., Chiesa, A., Tromer, E., Virza, M.: Scalable zero knowledge via cycles of elliptic curves. In: Garay, J.A., Gennaro, R. (eds.) CRYPTO 2014. LNCS, vol. 8617, pp. 276–294. Springer, Heidelberg (2014). https://doi.org/10.1007/978-3-662-44381-1_16

3. Besançon, L., Da Silva, C.F., Ghodous, P., Gelas, J.P.: A blockchain ontology for DApps development. IEEE Access **10**, 49905–49933 (2022)
4. Bitansky, N., Canetti, R., Chiesa, A., Goldwasser, S., Lin, H., Rubinstein, A., Tromer, E.: The hunting of the SNARK. IACR Cryptol. ePrint Arch. (2014)
5. Bitansky, N., Canetti, R., Chiesa, A., Tromer, E.: Recursive composition and bootstrapping for SNARKS and proof-carrying data. In: STOC. ACM (2013)
6. Bitcoin SV Wiki. https://wiki.bitcoinsv.io/index.php/SIGHASH_flags
7. Blancaflor, E., Aladin, K.: Analysis of the NFT's potential impact in an e-commerce platform: a systematic review. In: Proceedings of the 10th International Conference on Computer and Communications Management. ACM (2022)
8. Boneh, D., Drake, J., Fisch, B., Gabizon, A.: Halo Infinite: proof-carrying data from additive polynomial commitments. In: Malkin, T., Peikert, C. (eds.) CRYPTO 2021. LNCS, vol. 12825, pp. 649–680. Springer, Cham (2021). https://doi.org/10.1007/978-3-030-84242-0_23
9. Bonneau, J., Meckler, I., Rao, V., Shapiro, E.: Coda: decentralized cryptocurrency at scale. IACR Cryptology ePrint Archive (2020)
10. Bowe, S., Grigg, J., Hopwood, D.: Halo: recursive proof composition without a trusted setup. IACR Cryptology ePrint Archive (2019)
11. Bünz, B., Chiesa, A., Mishra, P., Spooner, N.: Proof-carrying data from accumulation schemes. IACR Cryptol. ePrint Arch. (2020)
12. Chaparala, H.K., Doddala, S.V., Showail, A., Singh, A., Gazzaz, S., Nawab, F.: Liftchain: a scalable multi-stage NFT transaction protocol. In: 2022 IEEE International Conference on Blockchain (Blockchain) (2022)
13. Chen, W., Chiesa, A., Dauterman, E., Ward, N.P.: Reducing participation costs via incremental verification for ledger systems. IACR Cryptology ePrint Archive (2020)
14. Chiesa, A., Tromer, E.: Proof-carrying data and hearsay arguments from signature cards. In: Innovations in Computer Science - ICS. Proceedings. Tsinghua University Press (2010)
15. Das, D., Bose, P., Ruaro, N., Kruegel, C., Vigna, G.: Understanding security issues in the NFT ecosystem. CoRR (2021)
16. Entriken, W., Shirley, D., Evans, J., Sachs, N.: ERC-721: non-fungible token standard. EIP (2018). https://eips.ethereum.org/EIPS/eip-721
17. Ordinal inscription (2023). https://ordinals.com/
18. Fowler, A., Pirker, J.: Tokenfication - the potential of non-fungible tokens (NFT) for game development. In: Annual Symposium on Computer-Human Interaction in Play. ACM (2021)
19. Groth, J.: On the size of pairing-based non-interactive arguments. In: Fischlin, M., Coron, J.-S. (eds.) EUROCRYPT 2016. LNCS, vol. 9666, pp. 305–326. Springer, Heidelberg (2016). https://doi.org/10.1007/978-3-662-49896-5_11
20. Guo, H., Chen, M., Ou, W.: A lightweight NFT auction protocol for cross-chain environment. In: Xu, Y., Yan, H., Teng, H., Cai, J., Li, J. (eds.) ML4CS 2022. LNCS, vol. 13655, pp. 133–146. Springer, Cham (2023). https://doi.org/10.1007/978-3-031-20096-0_11
21. Kattis, A., Bonneau, J.: Proof of necessary work: succinct state verification with fairness guarantees. IACR Cryptology ePrint Archive (2020)
22. Kothapalli, A., Setty, S., Tzialla, I.: Nova: recursive zero-knowledge arguments from folding schemes. In: Dodis, Y., Shrimpton, T. (eds.) CRYPTO 2022. LNCS, vol. 13510, pp. 359–389. Springer, Cham (2022). https://doi.org/10.1007/978-3-031-15985-5_13

23. Marlinspike, M.: My first impressions of web3 (2022). https://moxie.org/2022/01/07/web3-first-impressions.html
24. Miyaji, A., Nakabayashi, M., Nonmembers, S.: New explicit conditions of elliptic curve traces for FR- reduction. IEICE Trans. Fundam. Electron. Commun. Comput. Sci. **84**, 1234–1243 (2001)
25. O(1) Labs: Mina cryptocurrency (2017). https://minaprotocol.com
26. Ordinal theory handobbok (2023). https://docs.ordinals.com/
27. Park, A., Kietzmann, J., Pitt, L., Dabirian, A.: The evolution of nonfungible tokens: complexity and novelty of NFT use-cases. IT Prof. **24**, 9–14 (2022)
28. Park, S., et al.: Beyond the blockchain address: zero-knowledge address abstraction. Cryptology ePrint Archive (2023)
29. Radomski, W., Cooke, A., Castonguay, P., Therien, J., Binet, E., Sandford, R.: ERC-1155: multi token standard. EIP (2018). https://eips.ethereum.org/EIPS/eip-1155
30. Valiant, P.: Incrementally verifiable computation or proofs of knowledge imply time/space efficiency. In: Canetti, R. (ed.) TCC 2008. LNCS, vol. 4948, pp. 1–18. Springer, Heidelberg (2008). https://doi.org/10.1007/978-3-540-78524-8_1
31. Vasan, K., Janosov, M., Barabási, A.L.: Quantifying NFT-driven networks in crypto art. Sci. Rep. **12**, 2769 (2022)
32. Wang, Q., Li, R., Wang, Q., Chen, S.: Non-fungible token (NFT): overview, evaluation, opportunities and challenges. CoRR (2021)
33. Wu, B., Wu, B.: NFT: Crypto As Collectibles. Apress (2023)

AIHWS – Artificial Intelligence
in Hardware Security

AIHWS 2023

Fourth Workshop on Artificial Intelligence in Hardware Security

19 June 2023

Program Chairs

Lejla Batina	Radboud University, The Netherlands
Stjepan Picek	Radboud University, The Netherlands

Program Committee

Shivam Bhasin	Nanyang Technological University, Singapore
Ileana Buhan	Radboud University, The Netherlands
Lukasz Chmielewski	Masaryk University, Czech Republic
Elena Dubrova	KTH Royal Institute of Technology, Sweden
Fatemeh Ganji	Worcester Polytechnic Institute, USA
Naofumi Homma	Tohoku University, Japan
Dirmanto Jap	Nanyang Technological University, Singapore
Alan Jovic	University of Zagreb, Croatia
Liran Lerman	SWIFT, Belgium
Luca Mariot	University of Twente, The Netherlands
Kostas Papagiannopoulos	University of Amsterdam, The Netherlands
Guilherme Perin	Leiden University, The Netherlands
Vincent Verneuil	NXP Semiconductors, Germany
Lichao Wu	Radboud University, The Netherlands

Web Chair

Marina Krcek	Delft University of Technology, The Netherlands

A Comparison of Multi-task Learning and Single-Task Learning Approaches

Thomas Marquet[1(✉)] and Elisabeth Oswald[1,2]

[1] Digital Age Research Center (D!ARC), University of Klagenfurt,
Klagenfurt, Austria
{thomas.marquet,elisabeth.oswald}@aau.at
[2] University of Birmingham, Birmingham, UK

Abstract. In this paper, we provide experimental evidence for the benefits of multi-task learning in the context of masked AES implementations (via the ASCADv1-r and ASCADv2 databases). We develop an approach for comparing single-task and multi-task approaches rather than comparing specific resulting models: we do this by training many models with random hyperparameters (instead of comparing a few highly tuned models). We find that multi-task learning has significant practical advantages that make it an attractive option in the context of device evaluations: the multi-task approach leads to performant networks quickly in particular in situations where knowledge of internal randomness is not available during training.

Keywords: Side Channel Attacks · Masking · Deep Learning · Multi-Task Learning

1 Introduction

The rapid adoption of deep learning methods as an alternative to classical statistics in profiled side-channel attacks is due to their superior capability to efficiently utilize information from multiple tracepoints. However, many deep learning architectures still rely on the conventional thinking of statistics-based attacks, where a single intermediate target is learned at a time, resulting in a single learning task being executed.

Multi-task learning is a technique where multiple optimisation functions and their respective ground truths are combined in order to improve the learning of a deep network model. As is so often the case, the idea for multi-task learning is inspired by how humans often learn: in order to perform a new task, humans often try to combine the knowledge gained from (many) related tasks. And maybe to learn a new task that is difficult, humans might first try to learn a related easier task and then move on to the harder problem. These ideas are the key to multi-task learning.

Most fields connected to pattern recognition are investing heavily in the multi-task paradigm with a clear trend to move towards it. The learning goals in side channel analysis can be linked to goals within the field of pattern recognition.

J. Zhou et al. (Eds.): ACNS 2023 Workshops, LNCS 13907, pp. 121–138, 2023.
https://doi.org/10.1007/978-3-031-41181-6_7

However, so far multi-task learning has not shown significant promise in the side channel setting.

We believe that this is mostly because the architectures introduced in the initial works are not leveraging what multi-task learning is good at. In the first two works by Maghrebi [5] and Masure and Strullu [8], a classical multi-task architecture as summarised in [14] has been used. However, our previous work [6], showed that this kind of architecture is typically inferior to single-task training. However, better ways of defining multi-task architectures are available, and the goal of this paper is to convince readers that such approaches have strong benefits over single-task learning.

1.1   Summary of Contributions and Outline

Using the public databases ASCADv1-r and ASCADv2, we study the application of multi-task learning in the context of masked AES-128 implementations. Using different masking schemes allows us to explore very different scenarios and highlight the benefits of multi-task learning approaches. The work of our paper is done assuming no knowledge about the Boolean mask during profiling and attack. With masking countermeasures, the trace complexity of the problem increases exponentially with the number of masks/shares. Therefore even one unknown mask decreases greatly the chances of finding a successful model. After providing some notation and background in Sect. 2, we provide empirical evidence for the improvement of the single-task approach [7] in Sect. 3; we introduce the methodology and present our first experiment on the ASCADv1-r dataset in Sect. 4. We continue with experiments on the ASCADv2 dataset in Sect. 5 and summarise our findings in Sect. 6.

- We propose a methodology for comparing deep learning approaches rather than resulting trained models.
- We demonstrate that the adoption of an "expert" based approach is not only beneficial for multi-task learning but also for single-task architectures.
- We provide evidence that multi-task architectures benefit from shared variables, like masks, even if they are not provided as labels during training.
- We show that multi-task learning enables us to find more working models than single-task learning at a fraction of the training time.

We provide the code and our extracted datasets used in this paper at:

- https://github.com/sca-research/multi-vs-single-experiments/
- https://zenodo.org/record/7885814

1.2   Relevant Related Works

Mahgrebi [5] introduces the multi-task learning paradigm to the side channel community. The model defined in this paper, is a model that learns bit per bit the masked intermediate values, and the related mask. It provides attacks on the ASCADv1 database but with extracted samples.

The paper Perin et al. [10] continues and improves the work done by the community on the ASCADv1-r dataset. Their main discussion evolves around the point of interest selection, which is a critical step in profiled attacks. They set a new state of the art in the scenario where no knowledge about the randomness is assumed during training, and where the training is based on the raw traces (i.e. no points of interest must be extracted).

The introduction and characterisation of the ASCADv2 dataset are done in Masure and Strullu [8]. They provide an extracted version of the dataset and then propose a first utilisation of multi-task learning in a scenario where the knowledge of randomness is assumed during profiling, but also in two cases when a part of the randomness isn't assumed (permutations, and then the multiplicative mask). They set the first state-of-the-art for this dataset, with 60 traces with a single multi-task learning model. However, they use an architecture that doesn't fully take advantage of the benefits of multi-task learning, as the model possesses a branch for each task and then does not connect those branches again.

The paper by Masure et al. [7] explores the idea of training two models simultaneously. In their architecture, they apply a loss function on the predicted combined probabilities of their respective softmax outputs. This approach relaxes the difficulty of the problem, as the network doesn't have to learn how to combine the leakages. The authors solely focus on the PI metric and don't present any attack outcomes.

A further study of multi-task learning is provided in [6]. They propose a new best attack on the ASCADv2 dataset in the scenario where randomness is fully assumed. The authors introduce several novel multi-task architectures and they also utilise custom layers to combine knowledge from multiple branches.

2 Preliminaries

To perform side-channel attacks with deep learning, the attacker typically operates over two stages. The first stage consists of exploring the device leakage, building a dataset, and then training a model. In the second stage, the attacker performs the attack. Such side-channel attacks are often called profiled attacks.

Deep nets aim to learn the leakage distribution of intermediate values. A specific intermediate x corresponds to the chosen points of interest from a leakage trace l and we refer to these points by l_x.

An approach to deep learning consists of the choice of an architecture and a training regime; we focus on single-task vs multi-task architectures specifically. An architecture is a set of layers (of different types) and their connections. Training an architecture results in a deep net model which we call m_θ, whereby θ is the set of hyperparameters corresponding to the model. The output layers of those models are by default unactivated. We call $\sigma(x)$ the activation of the layer x by a softmax function.

2.1 Profiling Based on Deep Learning

To perform attacks on newly observed traces, an attacker must first train one or multiple models to build a distinguisher. To build a training dataset, one must obtain a clone of the device to capture training traces. Once the dataset is built, it is possible to train and then utilise the models. Since it is unlikely that the model will recover the target key in only one trace, one must combine the predictions from multiple traces. We note $S_{i,j}$ the scores related to the target byte i of the key, obtained on the trace j picked randomly from the set of attack traces N_a. The recovery of the key will be done using the sum of the logarithm of $S_{i,j}$ in the following way $d[k_i] = \sum_{j=1}^{N_a} log(S_{i,j})$

2.2 Training Methodology

To enable meaningful comparisons, we use the same learning rate, optimizer, and number of epochs across all training regimes. The only difference is that we train all bytes together in the multi-task models instead of byte by byte training in the single-task models (the multi-task models consist of multiple identical copies of the respective single-task models; we explain them in more detail later in this paper).

Our datasets are split into three different sets: training (size N_T), validation (size N_V), and attack (size N_A) dataset. All results reported in this paper are made on the attack dataset. Training and validation sets are labeled with intermediates derived from random keys. In the ASCADv1-r dataset, fixed keys are provided and therefore our attack dataset is labeled with a fixed key. However, in the ASCADv2 dataset, only random keys are provided. A simple re-labeling of the keys and plaintexts allow us to artificially fix the key. We use a callback to save the best model from the training phase. This callback will either monitor the validation accuracy in the case of single-task models, or the minimum validation accuracy over all bytes, in the case of multi-task learning. Even though accuracy is a problematic metric in side-channel analysis as demonstrated first in Cagli et al. [1] and then in Picek et al. [11], it is difficult to find a better way to judge the quality of the model during the training phase.

2.3 Comparison Methodology

We wish to compare different approaches to deep learning in the context of masked AES implementations. We consider an approach as "better" if desirable qualities (accuracy, time to find a model, time for training) are favorable compared to other approaches. Comparing approaches cannot be done by picking just one or two models because individual models are not necessarily representative of an approach. To compare approaches we need to compare a lot of models (of each approach), and then check how many models of one approach outperform the models from another approach.

This type of comparison also ties in with the reality of side channel evaluations: a model that works well on one device, might not perform well on another device. However, if an approach performs well, then this means that it is likely that we can find a good model for any device. Thus a good approach is beneficial in the long run for an evaluator.

Summarising, we consider the quality of an approach as the reliability with which the approach is going to yield performing models. It might be hard to estimate the best model possible with an approach, however, the average performance on many hyperparameter sets is a reliable metric. Therefore, to compare approaches, we instantiate many models with random hyperparameters.

2.4   Computing Resources

We are using two GPUs: one Nvidia A30 with 24 GB of dedicated memory, and one Nvidia A4000 with 16 GB of dedicated memory. In addition to the GPUs, we're using 4 cores of an AMD EPYC at 2.6 GHz with 128 GB of RAM. As OS we use an Ubuntu 22.04.1 kernel, with TensorFlow 2.10.1.

2.5   ASCADv1-r

The paper of Prouff et al. [13] introduces the dataset in 2018, along with a characterization of the leakage characteristics. the ASCADv1-r dataset possesses a total of 300k traces of a Boolean masking implementation of an AES. The device on which the dataset has been acquired through electromagnetic emissions is a simple 8-bit microcontroller and therefore is very leaky. About two third of the traces are based on using random keys, intended for training and validation purposes, and the rest is based on a fixed key to perform attacks. Because 50k traces are more than enough for the training dataset, we decided to only include 60k traces from the random key split and 10k traces from the fixed key traces.

The dataset contains the encryption up to the beginning of the second round of the AES. The masking scheme is a simple Boolean masking with two shares. Before encryption, a masked SubBytes table $SubBytes^*$ is precomputed using the randomness r_{in} and r_{out}, and during the computation of a masked encryption round, all state bytes are masked by a state mask r_i. The input to the masked SubBytes step is protected by r_{in}, and the corresponding output is protected by r_{out}, as defined by $SubBytes^*$. The output is then remasked with r_i.

The usual target on this dataset is the Subbytes outputs s_i along with the state byte share $(s_i \oplus r_i, r_i)$. However, to investigate the power of multi-task learning, we need a shared mask for all learning tasks, and consequently, we target the less leaky intermediate $(t_i \oplus r_{in}, r_{in})$.

2.6   ASCADv2

Introduced in 2020, the ASCADv2 dataset is less researched in the literature perhaps because it is based on a better protected implementation of AES. The dataset has been generated using the EM waves from an STM32 microcontroller with an ARM Cortex M4. It has in total of 800k traces with a million points per trace. This is because it has been purposely over-sampled and should be resampled for better use. All traces are created based on random keys and therefore it is necessary to artificially fix the key in the attack time. Also, it is very important to shuffle the files, as during acquisition, physical perturbations impacted on the leakage from the device. Therefore, one might observe different attack results when attacking different files if, initially, the training dataset doesn't contain traces from all files. After shuffling the traces, we pick 300k traces at random to build our dataset.

The masking scheme is a shuffled affine masking as defined in [3]. It possesses a non-zero multiplicative mask (note: a few zeros are present in the dataset), and an additive mask. Those masks are respectively noted α and β. Those masks are common for all bytes of the state, implying that the representation of the state bytes around the Subbytes operation is $\alpha \otimes x \oplus \beta$. On the other operations, the masking is done with α and a state mask. We do not use the state mask in this paper. Permutations over all 16 state bytes are present over the whole encryption except MixColumns, in which only the column elements are permuted.

We kept the original notation from the ASCAD database. The subkey of the byte i, is denoted by k_i, along with the Subbytes input and outputs, respectively t_i, s_i. The multiplicative mask is noted r_m, the additive mask for the Subbytes inputs is r_{in}, and the additive mask from the Subbytes outputs is r_{out}. The permuted state bytes are noted respectively k_j, t_j, s_j.

2.7   Custom Layers

To fit our design needs, we use several custom layers that were defined in [6], and we include the basic principle to combine outputs of layers for ease of reading. The custom layers compute the joint probability distribution of two variables x, y given the probability distributions of two layers (that we understand to be statistically independent) that depend on x and a function of x, y:

$$
\begin{cases}
f_\oplus(x,y)[i] = \sum_{j=0}^{255} x[j] \times y[i \oplus j] \quad \forall\, i \,\in\, [0, 255] & (1) \\[4mm]
f_\otimes(x,y)[i] = x[0] + \sum_{j=1}^{255} x[j] \times y[i \otimes j] \quad \forall\, i \,\in\, [0, 255] & (2)
\end{cases}
$$

The function $f_\otimes$ has to discriminate the first case where $j = 0$, being a null element. We decided that in this case, the probabilities of x should be unchanged. The use of these functions will become clear from the architecture.

2.8   Multi-task Learning

Multi-task learning is a very natural concept introduced in Caruana [2]. It can be defined as a network architecture that has multiple outputs and is trained with multiple labels. During training, multi-task models try to optimise multiple objective functions. Across all domains where deep learning is the state-of-the-art, multi-task learning approaches are among the most used, see [14].

The main potential benefits according to Caruana [2], are the following: data amplification, attribute selection, eavesdropping, and representation bias. **Data**

amplification can also be understood as data augmentation. The idea is that the samples from different tasks sharing features might share the signal but not the noise as the noise is independent of the signals. By training both tasks together, the noise is effectively reduced. The concept of **attribute selection**, is subsequent to the concept of data amplification. As the noise is reduced and the signal clearer for a shared feature, the relevant inputs will be easier to find. **Eavesdropping** is a very interesting case where two tasks share a feature. But this feature is hard to understand for one task and easy to learn for the other. Then, the first task is going to benefit from collaborating with the second task since the knowledge of the feature will be shared. And finally, **representation bias** is the idea that a model trained with multiple labels is going to yield more consistent results. Since the training of deep networks is a stochastic process, the "path" taken by the gradient depends on the initialisation. However, since there are multiple objectives to learn, the gradient will take the path that is best for all objectives instead of just one. This will lead the model weights to prefer a reduced set of representations.

However, those strengths might also be the drawbacks of this technique. Some potential benefits listed above assume that tasks share features. If there is no feature shared between the different objectives, this technique can yield sub-optimal models as the gradient will struggle to find a common "path". Even though, some results [9,15] have shown that including unrelated tasks in the training procedure can lead to improvements, it is very hard to infer from previous literature if one set of tasks will perform better trained jointly. One reason is the lack of a cross-domain formalism that would explain when tasks collaborate or compete.

3 Utilising Experts to Improve Single-Task Architectures

Only in very recent work [6], multi-task learning appears to show any real benefit over single-task learning. In this section, we show that a seemingly small "tweak" in combining learned distributions within a network can significantly benefit its performance. We do this by referring back to a recent single-task architecture that combines information that is learned about a mask and the corresponding masked value and modify it by borrowing inspiration from [6], and then show that our tweak improves the network's performance in a single task setting. We will use this tweak then in our multi-task architectures as well.

The initial single-task architecture proposed in [7] produces probabilities from the activated outputs of two "models", trained with one loss function. One model that we denote m_{θ_r} is expected to learn the mask r, and the other model denoted $m_{\theta_{x \oplus r}}$ is supposed to learn the masked intermediate $x \oplus r$. This technique feels natural in the sense that the probability distribution of x can be derived by the learned distributions of the two branches. We provide a visual representation of this architecture in Fig. 1a.

In [6] the idea of "weighing" up learning results was introduced in the context of multi-task learning. This way of combining the learning from related branches can be understood as a "multi-gate mixture of experts model", see [4]. In a multi-gate mixture of experts model the idea is that one branch acts as an "expert" for one or more other branches, by contributing its learning to update the learning of the other branch(es). We find that this idea is appealing when different parts of a network learn intermediate values that are related to the same internal randomness (aka mask) and thus use this to further improve the recent results of [7].

We suggest that the idea of using experts can also be applied to single learning tasks. For instance, we can view the related learning tasks for $x \oplus r$, and r as training two experts who can influence each other. Their outputs are combined via a custom layer and only thereafter a softmax layer is applied to produce a distribution for x. This is in line with the design of [6], but simplified, and adapted to the single-task approach from [7]. We provide a visual representation of this architecture in Fig. 1b.

To evaluate if there is merit in this idea, we run a set of experiments on the ASCADv2 dataset. The setup of this experiment is the same as the extracted scenario in Fig. 5 and therefore the final architectures used in the experiment are based on Fig. 6. We are targeting the unmasked values of the subbytes inputs t_j to compare the better positioning of the softmax activation σ. Knowledge of the multiplicative mask r_m and the permutations j_i is being assumed. Therefore we have in this experiment $x_i = r_m \otimes t_j$ and $r = r_{in}$.

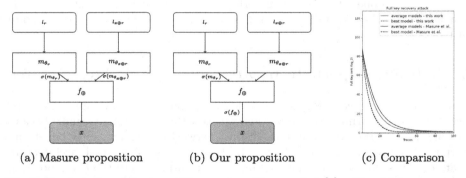

(a) Masure proposition   (b) Our proposition   (c) Comparison

Fig. 1. Single-task architecture difference from Masure et al. [7], with a full key recovery comparison

We can see in Fig. 1c that the architecture where we use the learning of one share as an expert for the other share increases the average performance of the models while keeping the same best performances.

4   ASCADv1-r: Comparing Multi-task and Single-Task Architectures

In this section, we will use the idea of experts for all architectures alike.

4.1 Assumptions, Contributions and State of the Art

ASCADv1-r has been extensively researched by the community in all sorts of scenarios and it has come to light that this dataset leaks many intermediate values, giving many opportunities for attacks. In this paper, we use only the raw traces, without access to any randomness. The state of the art in this scenario is an attack using **1** trace, in [10], while targeting the SubBytes outputs. We choose another target and therefore a straightforward comparison is difficult. We choose to attack the SubBytes inputs t_i because they all share the same mask across all state bytes, and thereby enable this multi-task learning approach. Recall that the shared mask is r_{in}. Therefore we note in this section $x_i = t_i$ and $r = r_{in}$

4.2 Architectures

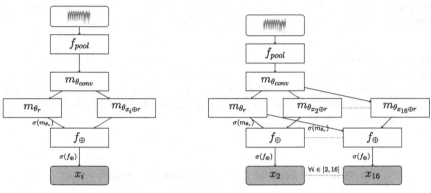

(a) Single-task-xor model for one byte   (b) Multi-task model for all bytes

Fig. 2. Architectures used in the Ascadv1 experiment

We provide a visual representation of network architectures that we use in the context of the ASCADv1-r dataset in Fig. 2. In addition to those two architectures, we also define **single-task-twin-xor**, which is an architecture similar to Fig. 2a but with two separate convolutions m_{conv}. All architectures take as input the raw traces from the ASCADv1-r dataset. Those raw traces are 250k samples long and include the full execution of the masking scheme up to the end of the first round. Inspired by the work in [10] in relation to the NOPOI scenario, we give each model a weighted average pooling of the traces. This pooling takes place in the f_{pool} layer. After this layer, which in the multi-task architecture is provided to all tasks, the model is going to split into multiple branches supposed to learn each one a piece of the puzzle t_i.

We have two models in the single-task learning approach. This is because we were interested in comparing the impact of shared convolutions in a single-task scenario. Even though it is not given multiple labels, each branch is supposed to learn a different part of the problem. This might cause an increase in the difficulty of learning.

4.3   Training Many Models

We train 50 CNNs for each approach. We do not train all bytes for the single-task scenarios because of the significant overhead. Instead, we only compare byte 6. The attacks are therefore also only on this byte. All bytes are trained for the multi-task model and reach similar accuracies.

Training Time. On our A30 GPU, each epoch for both single-task models takes about 17–25 s while each epoch from the multi-task model takes 20–27 s depending on the hyperparameters. This is relatively close since the input is huge and the "processing" layers are the bottleneck of the model. Therefore the difference in training time between the two approaches is almost irrelevant, except that in the case of the multi-task model, all bytes are trained.

Hyperparameter Choices. The choice of hyperparameter is done fully randomly. Both models start with a layer that reduces the size of the input using weighted average pooling, followed by convolutions. Those convolutions are shared for both models, however, the architecture splits with different fully connected layers (Table 1).

Table 1. Table of the architectural hyperparameters

Set	Hyperparameter	Interval
θ_{conv}	convolution block	$[1, 3]$
	kernel of block i	$[16, 64] \; \forall \; i$
	filters	$[3, 16]$
	strides	$[2, 30]$
	pooling size	$[2, 5]$
$\theta_r, \theta_{x \oplus r}$	dense blocks	$[1, 5]$
	dense units	$[64, 512]$

Fixed Hyperparameters. The number of epochs is 100 for all models with a batch size of 250. We're using an Adam optimiser with 0.001 learning rate.

4.4   Results of the Experiments

For every model trained, we perform 1000 key recovery attacks using 1000 randomly picked traces from the attack dataset. In this section, a model is deemed successful if on average, the subkey rank reaches 1 under 1000 traces.

The main metric used to compare the approaches is the number of successful models n_{win}. Additionally, we compare the best models and the average performance of successful models. Those key metrics are given in Fig. 3; and Table 2. Note that **unsuccessful approaches do not appear** in Fig. 3.

Table 2. Successful models

Model type	n_{win}
single-task-xor	0
single-task-twin-xor	2
multi-task	8

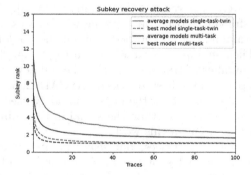

Fig. 3. 7-th subkey recovery attack results for the successful models

Single-task-xor vs Single-Task-xor-twin. In the case of single-task models, we see that the model that does not share the convolutions outperforms the one with shared convolutions. The extra hyperparameters help the model converge twice, while the single-task-xor architecture struggles to even find one model.

Single-Task vs Multi-task Models. In this experiment, which is based on traces that are very long, we hypothesise that the main difficulty for any network is to find the leaking trace points; the amount of leakage in "the right trace points" is known to be strong. Our results suggest that multi-task learning seems to be better in finding working models. The average model performance for both successful approaches is low because only very few models managed to converge according to the results in Tab. . In the case of the single-task-twin-xor model, the best model reached rank one on average at trace 5, while the second model converged, after 444 traces. For the multi-task approach, while 6/8 models managed to reach on average rank 1 using fewer than 20 traces, the two other models were significantly less performant. This make-or-break success is highlighting the fact that the difficulty for the networks is to make sense of the samples. Another reason for this disparity is the problematic relationship between accuracy and key ranking [1]. On this dataset, the networks are often likely to overfit and be over confident. Because they do not learn the leakage distributions, their first "bad" predictions are hard to fix. In this case, multi-task learning brings a much better approach than single-task learning. While it requires almost as much time to train all bytes with this approach than training a single byte with single-task learning, it yields more often successful models, with a better overall performance.

5   ASCADv2

5.1   Assumptions and State of the Art

The first best results were achieved by Masure and Strullu [8]. They required only **60** traces for successful key recovery in a setting where access to all randomness is assumed during training, but no knowledge about the randomness is assumed during the attack. Then an improvement of the state of the art has been achieved in [6], reducing the number of traces to recover the full key at **24** traces. Their results show that to perform the best attacks on ASCADv2, one has to target the input of the AES Sboxes t instead of the more commonly used output s because the signal in the inputs is stronger than the signal in the SubBytes output. We also select the SubBytes input in this work.

We do not work with raw traces, but select points of interest to contain only the leakages from all bytes of the SubBytes inputs of the first round, and their mask r_{in} (we thus assume knowledge about these locations for this purpose). However, we do not include knowledge about additive randomness, and the choice to extract "windows of interest" is to speed up experiments (we already considered a scenario with long traces in the previous section). Extracting points does not impact the comparison between single-task and multi-task models, because the selection is helping both approaches (and perhaps slightly more the single-task models).

In addition to the assumption needed to extract the samples from the raw traces, we give to both approaches the knowledge of the multiplicative mask r_m and the permutations. Therefore the only randomness not assumed during profiling and attack is the additive mask r_{in}. Since the multiplicative mask and the permutations are assumed, $x_i = r_m \otimes t_j$ and $r = r_{in}$ are in the following section for clarity purposes.

5.2   Input Scenarios

We recombine the selected points of interest of different intermediate values into three different "extraction levels": fully-extracted, separated, and concatenated.

- "Fully-extracted" is a scenario where the samples from the mask but also the individual bytes of the targeted intermediate, are given as inputs independently.
- "Separated" is a scenario where the samples related to the mask are given independently from the samples related to all bytes of the intermediate. However, the latter is fed to the network in a concatenated manner.
- "Concatenated" is a scenario where all extracted samples are concatenated in a single input.

In both fully-extracted and separated scenarios, the leakage related to the mask r_{in} is given to the "mask" branch of the network. This will make it easier for the network as this branch will only see helpful samples. In the concatenated strategy, all extracted samples are concatenated to recreate a large trace. This will allow us to further investigates the attribute selection benefit of the multi-task approach.

In the "fully-extracted" scenario, each byte's samples are kept away from the others. This means that each model branch will have only the samples from which it should learn the distribution. This represents the best-case scenario.

5.3   Architectures

We define three architecture types : single-task, single-task-xor, and multi-task. We give a visualisation of the considered single-task-xor architectures in Fig. 4.

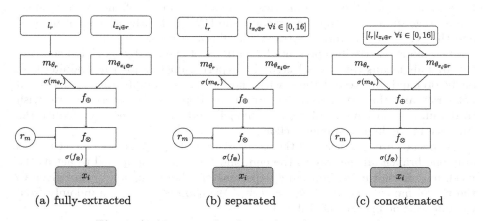

(a) fully-extracted   (b) separated   (c) concatenated

Fig. 4. Architectures for the single-task-xor approach

In the case of the single-task type, the architectures are provided in Fig. 4a, 4b. They are the same as before with the exception that the custom layer $f_\oplus$ is the multiplication layer. However, in the concatenated scenario, the architecture differs as can be seen in Fig. 5.

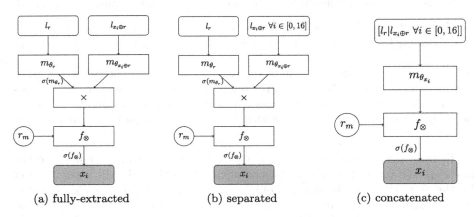

(a) fully-extracted   (b) separated   (c) concatenated

Fig. 5. Architectures for the single-task approach

The multi-task models are extensions of the architectures in Fig. 4 in the same manner as Fig. 2b. The branching is the same but the model is extended to all x_i.

5.4   Training Many Models

To better compare the approaches, we train many models with random sets of hyperparameters and observe metrics such as the number of successful models, the average number of traces to recover the full key for the successful models, and the best model in terms of traces for all approaches.

The model that will represent the learning of the mask, m_{θ_r} has been pre-tuned. This means that we selected the hyperparameters for this training task on beforehand and tested them with the labels. We supply this model to all networks, and the only reason for pre-tuning is performance because we wish to obtain a good amount of working models and therefore need to reduce the variance in the hyperparameter choices.

A special case is the case of the architecture in Fig. 5c. This architecture has only one branch all the way to the end, and the branch supposed to act as the mask m_{θ_r} doesn't exist. So the hyperparameters chosen for $m_{\theta_{x_i \oplus r}}$ are given to the model named $m_{\theta_{x_i}}$ with $\theta_{x_i} = \theta_{x_i \oplus r}$. We choose the $\theta_{x_i \oplus r}$ randomly from the intervals defined in the Table 3.

Fixed Training Hyperparameter. We train all our models with 25 epochs and a batch size of 500. The chosen optimizer is Adam, with a learning rate of 0.0001. No search of any kind has been done for those hyperparameters.

Table 3. Table of the architectural hyperparameters

Hyperparameter	m_{θ_r}	$m_{\theta_{x_i \oplus r}}$
convolution block	1	$[1, 3]$
kernel of block i	32	$[4, 32]\ \forall i \in [1, cb]$
filters	16	$[3, 16]$
strides	10	1
pooling size	2	$[2, 5]$
dense blocks	2	$[1, 5]$
dense units	256	$[64, 512]$
batch norm	yes	yes

Training Time. One epoch of a multi-task model in the fully-extracted scenario takes between 80–85 s on our A30 GPU. This can be compared to the 10–15 s it takes for one epoch of a single-task-xor model with the same input scenario. Training all bytes at once takes 2 times less than the single-task-xor approach.

5.5 Results of the Experiments

To test the attack performances of our models in a full key recovery attack. We perform an attack with all models over 1000 experiments. In each experiment, we pick at random 1000 traces from the attack set and we try to recover the full key. A model is deemed successful if it recovers the key in all experiments. We note the number of successful models for each approach and each scenario in Table 4. The Figs. 6, 7, 8 present the average performance over all successful models, along with the best model found for each input scenario.

Single-Task vs Single-Task-xor. First, it appears clear that the single-task-xor is a better approach than the classical idea (i.e. single-task [10,12,13]) that a deep net can learn to find the leakage from the sample, but also how to combine it. Doing a conditional probability between the output of a "mask" branch and the output of an "intermediate" branch, give significantly better results than the naive approach. This result confirms the results from [7], on actual attacks. On the 25 sets of hyperparameters chosen, the single-task didn't get a single one successful in all scenarios.

Single-Task-xor vs Multi-task. Secondly, we see that the "mask expert" (i.e. m_{θ_r}) has a better understanding of the mask distribution and therefore helps the networks trained with this approach to outperform the lone single-task-xor models. In this experiment, the difficulty isn't in finding the tracepoints, as in the first experiment, but in how to not overfit. The regularisation effect of multi-task learning yields more performant models on average. In addition to that, the shared expert is forced to learn a distribution fitting all bytes instead of one. This will help yield more successful models.

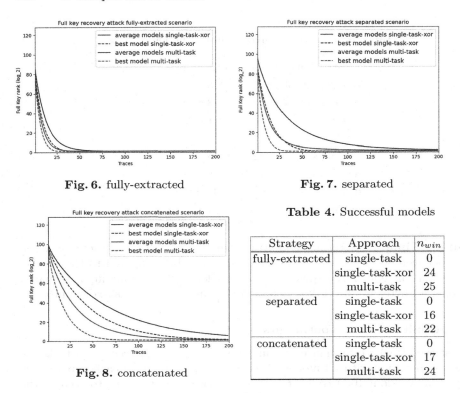

Fig. 6. fully-extracted

Fig. 7. separated

Fig. 8. concatenated

Table 4. Successful models

Strategy	Approach	n_{win}
fully-extracted	single-task	0
	single-task-xor	24
	multi-task	25
separated	single-task	0
	single-task-xor	16
	multi-task	22
concatenated	single-task	0
	single-task-xor	17
	multi-task	24

ASCADv2: Results of the experiments

Fully Extracted. In the fully extracted scenario, the average performance is close to the best model which itself is catching up with the best attack in a white box scenario reported in [6]. Even though there are obvious differences because here r_m and the permutations are assumed. This means that most of the leakage has been captured by the model. The difference between the single-task-xor isn't yet significant. Still, one model didn't succeed to recover the key and the best model from the single-task-xor approach is inferior to the average performance of the multi-task approach.

Separated. The most significant difference happens in the separated scenario. Where the samples related to each byte aren't extracted. The multi-task learning scenario is doing much better at identifying the good samples since it knows a little bit more about the problem. The multi-task best model is close to the fully extracted scenario. In a single-task-xor approach, only 64% of the hyperparameter sets yield a successful model against 88% from its multi-task counterpart.

Concatenated. Finally, in the concatenated, where the inputs are given altogether. We see a significant difference in performance between the two approaches. Even the best model from the single-task-xor models is a lot less trace efficient than the average multi-task model. Only 68% of the single-task-xor models recover the key, while 96% of their multi-task counterparts succeed to do so.

6 Conclusion

Throughout our two examples, we showcase the strengths of multi-task learning over multiple input sizes when the access of the randomness is not possible, or limited. From our point of view, the key takeaway points are the following:

- Single-task-xor learning, as introduced in [7] and [6], is improving significantly the previous single-task learning paradigm.
- Training in a multi-task learning scenario will yield more models that can perform an attack.
- Training in a multi-task learning scenario improves the performance of successful models thanks to its regularisation effect.
- In addition to performance gains, the training time can be radically improved.

The results presented in this paper contribute to the community by showcasing the strength of multi-task learning against single-task approaches. We propose a methodology to compare approaches through the training of many models with random hyperparameters. Using this methodology, we highlight the difficulty in the previous single-task learning paradigm, to find models able to perform attacks without the knowledge of randomness thereby confirming [7]. We show evidence that multi-task learning has huge advantages over single-task learning methods at a minimal cost, especially in the case of large traces.

Acknowledgment. Thomas Marquet has been supported by the KWF under grant number KWF-3520-31870-45842. Elisabeth Oswald has been supported in part by the European Research Council (ERC) under the European Union's Horizon 2020 research and innovation program (grant agreement No 725042).

References

1. Cagli, E., Dumas, C., Prouff, E.: Convolutional neural networks with data augmentation against jitter-based countermeasures. In: Fischer, W., Homma, N. (eds.) Cryptographic Hardware and Embedded Systems - CHES 2017. LNCS, vol. 10529, pp. 45–68. Springer, Cham (2017). https://doi.org/10.1007/978-3-319-66787-4_3
2. Caruana, R.: Multitask learning. In: Thrun, S., Pratt, L.Y. (eds.) Learning to Learn, pp. 95–133. Springer, Boston (1998). https://doi.org/10.1007/978-1-4615-5529-2_5
3. Fumaroli, G., Martinelli, A., Prouff, E., Rivain, M.: Affine masking against higher-order side channel analysis. In: Biryukov, A., Gong, G., Stinson, D.R. (eds.) Selected Areas in Cryptography. LNCS, vol. 6544, pp. 262–280. Springer, Heidelberg (2011). https://doi.org/10.1007/978-3-642-19574-7_18

4. Ma, J., Zhao, Z., Yi, X., Chen, J., Hong, L., Chi, E.H.: Modeling task relationships in multi-task learning with multi-gate mixture-of-experts. In: Proceedings of the 24th ACM SIGKDD International Conference on Knowledge Discovery and Data Mining. p. 1930–1939. KDD 2018, Association for Computing Machinery, New York, NY, USA (2018). https://doi.org/10.1145/3219819.3220007

5. Maghrebi, H.: Deep learning based side-channel attack: a new profiling methodology based on multi-label classification. Cryptology ePrint Archive, Report 2020/436 (2020). https://eprint.iacr.org/2020/436

6. Marquet, T., Oswald, E.: Exploring multi-task learning in the context of two masked AES implementations. IACR Cryptol. ePrint Arch, p. 6 (2023). https://eprint.iacr.org/2023/006

7. Masure, L., Cristiani, V., Lecomte, M., Standaert, F.X.: Don't learn what you already know: scheme-aware modeling for profiling side-channel analysis against masking. IACR Trans. Cryptographic Hardware Embedded Syst. **2023**(1), 32–59 (2022). https://doi.org/10.46586/tches.v2023.i1.32-59, https://tches.iacr.org/index.php/TCHES/article/view/9946

8. Masure, L., Strullu, R.: Side channel analysis against the ANSSI's protected AES implementation on ARM. Cryptology ePrint Archive, Report 2021/592 (2021). https://eprint.iacr.org/2021/592

9. Paredes, B.R., Argyriou, A., Berthouze, N., Pontil, M.: Exploiting unrelated tasks in multi-task learning. In: Lawrence, N.D., Girolami, M. (eds.) Proceedings of the Fifteenth International Conference on Artificial Intelligence and Statistics. Proceedings of Machine Learning Research, vol. 22, pp. 951–959. PMLR, La Palma, Canary Islands (2012). https://proceedings.mlr.press/v22/romera12.html

10. Perin, G., Wu, L., Picek, S.: Exploring feature selection scenarios for deep learning-based side-channel analysis. IACR Trans. Cryptographic Hardware Embedded Syst. **2022**(4), 828–861 (2022). https://doi.org/10.46586/tches.v2022.i4.828-861, https://tches.iacr.org/index.php/TCHES/article/view/9842

11. Picek, S., Heuser, A., Jovic, A., Bhasin, S., Regazzoni, F.: The curse of class imbalance and conflicting metrics with machine learning for side-channel evaluations. IACR Trans. Cryptographic Hardware Embedded Syst. **2019**(1), 209–237 (2018). https://doi.org/10.13154/tches.v2019.i1.209-237, https://tches.iacr.org/index.php/TCHES/article/view/7339

12. Picek, S., Perin, G., Mariot, L., Wu, L., Batina, L.: Sok: deep learning-based physical side-channel analysis. ACM Comput. Surv. **55**(11), 1–35 (2023). https://doi.org/10.1145/3569577

13. Prouff, E., Strullu, R., Benadjila, R., Cagli, E., Dumas, C.: Study of deep learning techniques for side-channel analysis and introduction to ascad database. Cryptology ePrint Archive, Paper 2018/053 (2018). https://doi.org/10.1007/s13389-019-00220-8. https://eprint.iacr.org/2018/053

14. Ruder, S.: An overview of multi-task learning in deep neural networks. CoRR abs/1706.05098 (2017)

15. Zheng, Y., Fan, J., Zhang, J., Gao, X.: Exploiting related and unrelated tasks for hierarchical metric learning and image classification. IEEE Trans. Image Process. **29**, 883–896 (2020). https://doi.org/10.1109/TIP.2019.2938321

Hide and Seek: Using Occlusion Techniques for Side-Channel Leakage Attribution in CNNs
An Evaluation of the ASCAD Databases

Thomas Schamberger[1]([✉]), Maximilian Egger[2], and Lars Tebelmann[1]

[1] Chair of Security in Information Technology, TUM School of Computation, Information and Technology, Technical University of Munich, Munich, Germany
{t.schamberger,lars.tebelmann}@tum.de
[2] Institute for Communications Engineering, TUM School of Computation, Information and Technology, Technical University of Munich, Munich, Germany
maximilian.egger@tum.de

Abstract. Deep learning-based side-channel analysis has gained popularity due to its relaxed feature engineering effort in contrast to classical profiled side-channel analysis approaches. This however comes at the cost of a reduced explainability of attack results. In this work we propose occlusion techniques for neural network attribution that allow the identification of points-of-interest related to side-channel leakage used by the networks to defeat masking countermeasures. We evaluate results for both ASCAD databases and are able to identify occlusion parameters that are suitable in the side-channel context. We reason that due to side-channel measurement characteristics multiple adjacent samples have to be occluded at once, which has not been considered in related work. In addition, with our higher-order occlusion we are able to identify leakage combinations that are exploited by a network in order to mount a higher-order attack. Using our methods we are able to show that networks actually utilize varying leakage characteristics observable for different key bytes of the ASCAD databases. This work shows that occlusion is a viable addition to established gradient-based attribution methods.

1 Introduction

The publication of the ANSSI SCA Database (ASCAD) database [5] marked the starting point of a large amount of research in the domain of deep learning (DL) approaches for side-channel analysis (SCA). These forms of profiled side-channel attacks have several advantages in comparison with classical profiled attacks like template attacks [6]: a) the points-of-interest (POIs) identification in the measurements traces is performed internally and therefore countermeasures can be defeated; b) the effort on preprocessing the measurements is reduced. For a detailed discussion we refer the reader to [16].

Research in the domain of DL-based SCA is manifold. One main research direction is the development of novel network architectures that improve attack results [18,22,27]. Other works improve on the network training by either data augmentation [10,11] or a favorable feature selection [23]. With this work we are going into a third direction, namely neural network *attribution*, which tries to solve the problem of understanding which features/samples of a measurement trace are learned by a network during its training process. This knowledge provides valuable insights for designers of masked implementations on how to fix weaknesses in their implementations by comparison with known leakage of intermediates. Additionally, it can also be used to reason about performance differences between classical attacks and DL-based approaches. In essence attribution methods are a valuable tool to increase the confidence in the usage of DL-based SCA.

Related Work: When looking at the explainability of neural networks in the side-channel context, there are two different directions. First the question of *"What is the influence of the different elements, e.g., a single node in a specific layer, on the training outcome?"* can be answered. Wu et al. [24] use a method called ablation, where they successively remove parts of the network, in order to identify which parts of the network are needed to defeat common hiding countermeasures. A second work in this direction is shown by Perin et al. [15]. Their approach uses an information-theoretic metric to reason about which layer learns a specific intermediate of a masked implementation.

The second explainability direction is the question of neural network *attribution*, i.e., which input features are learned by the network and therefore are significant for the inference process and hence the classification result. In this category the majority of techniques are gradient-based visualization approaches that utilize a single forward and backward pass through the network. The basic method is a so-called *saliency map* [20] that performs attribution by computing the absolute partial derivative of an output class with respect to the input features. An improvement of this method, which takes the signed derivative and multiplies it with the input feature, is called *Gradient * Input* [19]. A more advanced method called *Layer-wise Relevance Propagation (ϵ-LRP)* is proposed by Bach et al. [3]. It is computed with a backward pass on the network by using a propagation rule that maps the found class relevance of a given layer onto the previous one until the input layer is reached. Ancona et al. [2] provide an in-depth discussion about these gradient-based methods leading to their attribution framework called *DeepExplain*[1], which can be readily integrated in common machine learning frameworks. In the side-channel context several of the presented methods or variants of them have been discussed. Masure et al. [12] propose a method similar to Gradient * Input, while others deviate from the general ML literature like Timon [21] who uses partial derivatives of the first layer network weights and Zaid et al. [25] who propose a method based on weight visualization. Perin et al. [14] use a variant of ϵ-LRP. Hettwer et al. [9] extensively

---

[1] The implementation is publicly available at https://github.com/marcoancona/DeepExplain, accessed 20.02.2023.

use the DeepExplain framework to analyze different publicly available datasets, including ASCAD, and conclude that ϵ-LRP is the most appropriate method.

A second class of attribution methods can be grouped as *perturbation methods*. These methods work by altering or removing (occluding) some parts of the input with the goal of comparing the results after running a second forward pass on the network. The first occlusion method has been proposed by Zeiler and Fergus [26] in the context of image classification with Convolutional Neural Networks (CNNs) where they use a gray patch occluding parts of the image. Prediction Difference Analysis [28] improves this method and identifies that a multivariate analysis, e.g., modifying multiple pixels at once, has significant influence on explainability. Regarding DL-based SCA, occlusion methods have only been studied by Hettwer et al. [9] who additionally evaluate the integrated 1-occlusion method of DeepExplain on their datasets. Occlusion methods allow for straightforward interpretation and are applicable to any model architecture. However, for large input feature sizes these methods suffer from large or even infeasible computation times. Additionally, the number of simultaneously occluded features as well as the occlusion method significantly influences the results [2].

Contribution: The current work investigates advanced occlusion techniques used for leakage attribution in CNNs[2] for SCA. In particular, the contributions are as follows:

- We introduce *n-occlusion*, which allows for identifying POIs based on a trained CNN. By adapting the number n of occluded samples, the relevant samples are narrowed down. Compared to 1-occlusion from prior work [9], our approach reliably identifies leakage that is spread across multiple samples, which is usually observed in side-channel measurements.
- We investigate the influence of the occlusion method, i.e., how samples are exchanged, and show that the *gray box method* [26] widely used in image recognition is not the best choice for time series signals like side-channel measurements.
- We propose *higher-order occlusion* methods that occlude multiple parts of a trace and thus enable the identification of POI combinations for higher-order SCA attacks.
- Finally, we employ our occlusion methods to analyze two different network architectures trained on both ASCAD datasets. A comparison with a leakage analysis allows to foster a better understanding of what CNNs actually deem relevant in these side-channel measurements. Our results show that, especially for other key bytes of the ASCAD databases than the proposed third key byte of the ASCAD authors, the networks infer information from leakage not considered in prior work.

---

[2] Occlusion methods are inherently model-agnostic [2] and therefore our methods should in theory be applicable to other network architectures frequently used in SCA, e.g., Multi Layer Perceptrons (MLPs).

2   Preliminaries

In this section we provide the preliminaries for our work. We define the notation in Sect. 2.1, followed by an introduction to DL-based SCA in Sect. 2.2. Finally, in Sect. 2.3 we describe the evaluated datasets in combination with selected network architectures.

2.1   Notation

We define the number of side-channel measurement traces as N_t, each consisting of N_s samples. The i-th trace of the whole set is defined as t_i and individual samples of this trace are defined as $t_{i,j}$ with j being the sample index. When referring to a range of samples we use $t_i[j_{start}, j_{end}]$ with $t_i[0, 99]$ indicating samples 0 to 99 of the i-th trace.

2.2   Deep Learning-Based SCA

Utilizing deep learning for SCA represents a conventional classification task. An attack on Advanced Encryption Standard (AES) [1] encryption provides probabilities $p_{l,t}$ for each class l at the output of the softmax layer, and each trace t that is provided to the network. The classes are usually chosen as the S-box output of byte i after the first round $y = \mathrm{S}(ptxt_i \oplus k_i)$ (ID model) or its Hamming weight $y = \mathrm{HW}\left(\mathrm{S}(ptxt_i \oplus k_i)\right)$ (HW model), according to the label from training. Thus, to get the probabilities $p_{c,t}$ for the $N_c = 256$ different key byte candidates $\hat{k}_c$ with $c \in \{0, \ldots, 255\}$, a transformation is required. In case of the identity (ID) model simply inverting the S-box maps to the respective key byte, while for HW labels, the $N_l = 9$ softmax output probabilities $p_{l,t}$ are assigned to $N_c > N_l$ different $\hat{k}_c$, i.e., several $\hat{k}_c$ share the same $p_{l,t}$. In the following, the $N_c \times N_t$ matrix $\mathbf{P}$ contains the $p_{c,t}$ as its entries, i.e., the probabilities for the candidate $\hat{k}_c$ and trace t, for all N_c key byte candidates and N_t traces available. Usually a single prediction does not suffice to reliably predict the correct secret and therefore several predictions have to be combined. This combination is done as product of the probabilities $p_{c,t}$ for a given subset of traces with cardinality $N \le N_t$, which is usually determined by the sum of logarithmic probabilities

$$p_c(N) = \prod_{t=0}^{N-1} p_{c,t} = \sum_{t=0}^{N-1} \log(p_{c,t}) \tag{1}$$

to avoid numerical underflows or overflows.

Ultimately, as an attacker we are interested in the capability of the network to retrieve the correct value of the attacked secret key byte denoted as $k^\star$. We use the *key rank* [13] as a measure for the remaining uncertainty about the correct key value given the predictions of the network. Taking the probabilities p_c for all N_c key candidates, a rank vector $rank = [r_0, r_1, \cdots, r_{N_c-1}]$ can be computed by sorting all p_c in decreasing order with r_0 presenting the most likely candidate.

Now the key rank, which we define as $KR(N)$, represents the position of $k^\star$ in *rank*, where a key rank of zero indicates that the correct key is found. Note that other works frequently use guessing entropy as an attack metric which is defined as the mean key rank of several attacks (not to be confused with several traces used for a single attack). We additionally express the key rank in terms of entropy in bits as

$$H_{KR}(N) = \log_2 \left(KR(N) + 1 \right), \tag{2}$$

ranging from 0 to $\log_2 (N_c)$. An entropy of 0 corresponds to a successful attack.

In order to evaluate our proposed occlusion techniques we define an additional metric N'. It defines the number of traces for which the final key rank after N_t traces occurs for the first time, i.e.,

$$N' := \min_N (N \mid KR(N) \leq KR(N_t)). \tag{3}$$

The implicit assumption of the metric is that the key rank decreases with an increasing number of traces and reaches an optimum after a certain amount. The number of traces for which the key rank reaches zero is denoted N_0. The metric provides an insight whether additional traces would potentially further decrease the key rank. If $N' = N_t$, the network requires all available traces for its best performance and might still be improving with more traces. Similarly, if $N' << N_t$ most likely additional traces do not add information and the network reaches its optimal performance.

2.3   Datasets and Used Architectures

We provide experimental results for our occlusion methods with two publicly available datasets, called ASCAD fixed key (ASCAD fix) and ASCAD variable key (ASCAD variable), with measurements of a masked AES implementation. Both datasets [5] are frequently used and serve as the standard datasets for research on DL-based SCA. An overview of their characteristics is given in Table 1.

Table 1. Overview of the ASCAD datasets.

	N_{train}	N_{attack}	N_s	N_s/clock cycle
ASCAD fix	50 000	10 000	700	50
ASCAD variable	200 000	100 000	1400	125

The datasets contain measurements of a first-order boolean masked implementation of AES [4] running on an 8-bit ATmega8515 microcontroller. The datasets contain the entire first round of the AES encryption, but usually an excerpt of N_s samples is used as a target corresponding to the SubBytes operation processing the third key byte k_2 as proposed by Benadjila et al. [5]. The implementation masks each key byte k_i using a mask byte r_i. In order to protect the S-box look-up, a masked S-box is computed by determining for all possible entries $x \in \{0, \ldots, 255\}$ the masked S-box output values according to $S_m(x) = S(x \oplus r_{in}) \oplus r_{out}$, where r_{in} and r_{out} refer to the S-box input and output masks that are used for all bytes. A block diagram of the whole masked SubBytes operation is shown in Fig. 1. For an in-depth discussion of the databases including a leakage analysis for all key bytes as well as their measurement characteristics we refer the reader to [8].

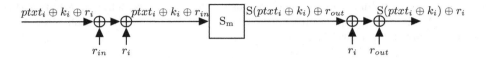

Fig. 1. Block diagram of the masked SubBytes implementation of the first AES round used in the ASCAD databases. Adapted from [8].

In this work we focus on attribution for CNNs and evaluate two different architectures published in the literature. To compare to related work, we evaluate the VGG16-based architecture published by the ASCAD authors [5], which we refer to as CNN_{best}. We stick to the convention, also used in the evaluation scripts by the ASCAD authors, of adapting the input layer of the architecture to account for the different N_s of both datasets. The second architecture CNN_{small} is published by Rijsdijk et al. [18] and was found by automating the hyperparameter search through reinforcement learning. This architecture is tailored for the specific datasets, and additionally is a much smaller network in terms of trainable parameters. We chose the network corresponding to the correct leakage model and dataset given in Appendix B of [18]. An overview of both networks can be found in Table 2.

Table 2. Overview of the used architectures.

	N_{train}	epochs	trainable parameters (ID)	trainable parameters (HW)
ASCAD fix				
CNN_{best} [5]	48 000	100	43 583 872	42 571 913
CNN_{small} [18]	48 000	100	79 439	8 480
ASCAD variable				
CNN_{best} [5]	100 000	100	66 652 544	65 640 585
CNN_{small} [18]	100 000	100	70 492	15 241

3   Revisiting Gradient-Based Attribution Methods

In this section we revisit gradient-based attribution methods for our chosen datasets and network architectures. We use the DeepExplain framework to generate the so-called attribution maps using saliency maps, Gradient*Input, and the ϵ-LRP method after each training epoch. We chose these attribution methods since they correspond to methods used in related work, while saliency maps and the more general Gradient*Input are similar to self-made gradient-based methods that are not established ML-based approaches as, e.g., published by Masure et al. [12]. Attribution maps generate an attribution value for each sample point of the used attack traces averaged over the amount of used traces, which we denote as N_{attr}. We additionally normalize the attribution values for each method individually by scaling them relative to their absolute maximum. The resulting attributions are shown in Fig. 2 given a training of 100 epochs using the ID model and $N_{attr} = 1000$ traces.

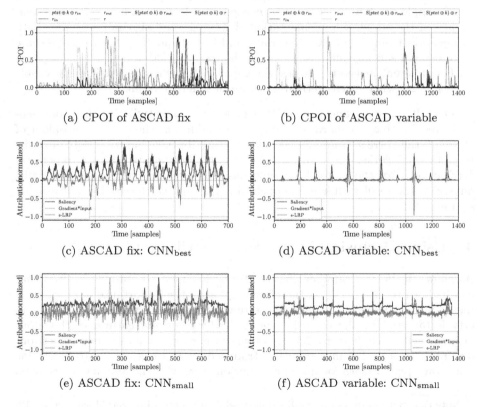

(a) CPOI of ASCAD fix

(b) CPOI of ASCAD variable

(c) ASCAD fix: CNN$_{best}$

(d) ASCAD variable: CNN$_{best}$

(e) ASCAD fix: CNN$_{small}$

(f) ASCAD variable: CNN$_{small}$

Fig. 2. Gradient-based attribution results in comparison with a leakage evaluation of intermediates from [8]. The attribution is performed after 100 training epochs.

A comparison with a leakage evaluation of intermediates as shown in Figs. 2a and 2b allows for interpreting the attribution results. The shown leakage evaluation is performed using the CPOI method [7] with all identified intermediates for the chosen trace segments of the database. For a detailed evaluation including a discussion about included intermediates as well as results for all key bytes of the datasets we refer the reader to [8]. A direct comparison leads to the following observations:

- Gradient-based attribution does not reliably identify POIs in the setting of related works [9,12], which evaluate their methods on ASCAD fix[3] corresponding to Fig. 2c. The resulting attribution indicates several peaks that can hardly be distinguished. In [9, Fig. 1] a similar behavior is shown while in [12] the authors only achieve reliable results for an evaluation at a specific training epoch found with early stopping.
- The methods indicate multiple POIs, which makes it difficult to identity single leakages, in combination with their respective samples, that are essential for the attack success. This ambiguity additionally prevents the identification of sample combinations that are needed to defeat the masking countermeasure of the attacked implementation. This characteristic can be seen for both networks trained on ASCAD variable in Figs. 2d and 2f with the extreme case of using a saliency map for CNN_{best} shown in Fig. 2d.
- The different methods indicate divergent POIs, which is particularly visible in Fig. 2e, where each method generates a different result.

Overall, our experiments show that gradient-based attribution methods generate results that are hard to interpret. In addition, there is the problem of choosing the correct training epoch for the attribution due to possible overfitting of the networks, as also discussed in [12]. For our results we chose to perform attribution after the network training has finished (100 epochs). Additionally, analyzing the results after each epoch did not improve the attribution insights significantly.

4   Using Occlusion for Leakage Attribution

As shown in Sect. 3, gradient-based attribution methods provide results that can be hard to interpret. We therefore emphasize the importance of attribution methods that allow for a direct and straightforward interpretation. This property is targeted by the occlusion method where certain features of the input are removed (occluded), to directly observe their impact on the neural network output. The occlusion method was introduced by Zeiler et al. [26] to determine important pixel ranges for image recognition. However, the amount of occluded

---

[3] Note that both authors use modified networks for their evaluation. Masure et al. [12] use a network close to CNN_{best} with fewer neurons in the fully connected layers and an additional global pooling layer. Hettwer et al. [9] use their own architecture in order to facilitate an evaluation of multiple datasets.

features as well as the occlusion method have a significant influence on the attribution results [2]. This limitation has not been investigated in the SCA context. Related work by Hettwer et al. [9] only shows occlusion results by replacing a single measurement sample with the value zero. As side-channel leakage is usually not limited to a single sample, we provide an in-depth evaluation of several occlusion methods in this work.

In Sect. 4.1, we introduce n -*occlusion* that hides several samples at once. We show that the occlusion technique can leverage the accumulated probabilities for multiple predictions, which closely reflects the underlying SCA problem, where single observations usually do not provide sufficient attack results. In a second step, we explore different occlusion techniques and the impact of the occlusion window size in Sect. 4.2. In Sect. 4.3, we provide attribution results for selected datasets and architectures. Finally, in Sect. 4.4 we extend the method to higher-order occlusion where multiple non-consecutive parts of a trace are occluded, reflecting the nature of SCA attacks on masked implementations which requires the combined leakage of multiple samples.

4.1 n-Occlusion: Hide and Seek

The n-occlusion attribution technique requires a trained network able to recover the correct key. In a first step, the key rank for different numbers of traces $N \in [1, N_{attr}]$ is calculated from an attack set of N_{attr} traces. The number of traces N_0 required for the successful attack, i.e., such that $\mathrm{KR}(N_0) = 0$, determines a reference for the occlusion results. In a second step, n samples around a center sample $\dot{n}$ are occluded in all traces of the attack set[4]. The modified inputs are provided to the trained network and the performance is evaluated similar to the reference evaluation. If the network is not able to reach key rank 0 anymore, the occluded samples can be considered important to the network. An increase in the number of traces to reach key rank 0 indicates that the occluded samples are important, but can be compensated with other parts of the measurements – in Sect. 4.4 we introduce higher-order occlusion to detect combinations of important samples. Finally, the center $\dot{n}$ is shifted by $n \geq \Delta_n \geq 1$ samples and the procedure is repeated until the different parts of the traces have gradually been hidden from the network. This results in $M = \lfloor \frac{N_s - n}{\Delta_n} + 1 \rfloor$[5] different input ranges that can be occluded. A visualization of the method is shown in Fig. 3.

---

[4] Note that a perfect centering around $\dot{n}$ is only possible for odd values of n, and for even n we define the occlusion area left of $\dot{n}$ to include the additional sample.

[5] Note that for $\Delta_n > 1$ we ignore the remaining samples at the end of the trace that do not fit in a complete occlusion window of size n anymore.

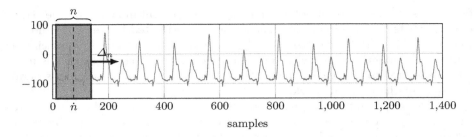

Fig. 3. Visualization of the n-occlusion method.

4.2 Exploring Different Occlusion Methods

With n-occlusion as defined in Sect. 4.1 there are two degrees of freedom[6]: the occlusion technique, i.e., how to replace occluded samples, and the occlusion window size n. We evaluate both parameters in this section and give recommendations suitable for the ASCAD databases. The occlusion technique requires a method to replace input samples that are hidden from the network, as for an attribution of the pretrained network we can not change its architecture, e.g., the input layer. In image processing it is common to use gray squares [26], since they represent the center of the RGB value range. An analogy to SCA measurements would be a substitution by zeros, since these measurements are usually represented by signed integers. However, this is only one possible method, which is why we additionally investigate three other approaches for an occlusion interval $x = [x_0, \ldots, x_{n-1}]$ of size n:

1. Substitute by a constant value, either zeros $x_0 = [0 \ldots 0]$ or the mean over all N_s samples of the N_p profiling traces t_i as $x_{const.} = [\bar{t} \ldots \bar{t}]$ with $\bar{t} := 1/(N_s N_p) \cdot \sum_{i=0}^{N_p-1} \sum_{j=0}^{N_s-1} t_i[j]$.

2. Draw for each sample a new realization $\tilde{X}$ of a normal Gaussian distribution parametrized by the mean $\bar{t}$ and standard deviation σ of all samples in the N_p profiling/training traces resulting in $x_{gauss} = [\tilde{X}_0 \ldots \tilde{X}_{n-1}]$ with $\tilde{X}_i \sim \mathcal{N}(\bar{t}, \sigma)$.

3. Preserve the approximate shape of the input traces by a substitution with the sample-wise mean over all profiling traces $\hat{t}[j] := 1/N_p \cdot \sum_{i=0}^{N_p-1} t_i[j]$ resulting in $x_{avg} = \left[\hat{t}\left[\dot{n} - \frac{n-1}{2}\right] \ldots \hat{t}\left[\dot{n} + \frac{n-1}{2}\right]\right]$ for odd values of n and $x_{avg} = \left[\hat{t}\left[\dot{n} - \frac{n}{2}\right] \ldots \hat{t}\left[\dot{n} + \frac{n}{2} - 1\right]\right]$ for even values of n.

To select an appropriate occlusion method, we first define some desired properties by which we can evaluate the occlusion results afterwards. First, a good occlusion method should not significantly change attack results when occluding a region without necessary information for the network. Second, it should also induce the opposite, i.e., the key rank increases when a sample region with necessary information is occluded. Finally, the key rank should also increase the more

---

[6] Δ_n does not impact the occlusion itself but only affects the accuracy of visualization.

information is occluded, i.e., with an increasing size of the occlusion window. We show the resulting key rank evolution for different occlusion methods for both ASCAD databases using CNN_{best} trained with the HW model[7] in Fig. 4. We use two different occlusion centers for comparison: The range around occlusion center $\dot{n} = 150$ (ASCAD fix) and $\dot{n} = 175$ (ASCAD variable) contains several leakages according to the analysis in Figs. 2a and 2b, while the region around $\dot{n} = 380$ (ASCAD fix) and $\dot{n} = 600$ (ASCAD variable) does not show any significant leakage[8]. Furthermore, we gradually increase the occlusion width n up to a full clock cycle (c.f. Table 1).

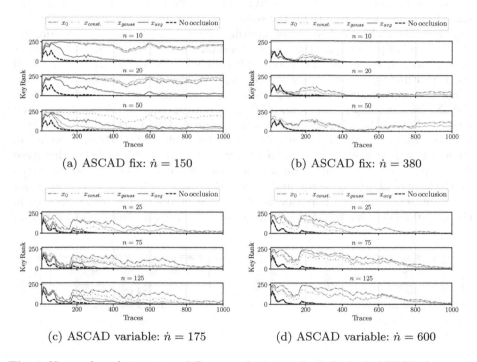

(a) ASCAD fix: $\dot{n} = 150$ (b) ASCAD fix: $\dot{n} = 380$

(c) ASCAD variable: $\dot{n} = 175$ (d) ASCAD variable: $\dot{n} = 600$

Fig. 4. Key rank evolution using different occlusion methods for both ASCAD datasets.

---

[7] We show evaluation results for the HW model for which the best combination function for a second-order attack is proven to be a combination of both the mask and the masked value [17]. This reduces the possibility of additional leakage that the networks are able to learn, and therefore the attribution results are easier to interpret. However, we also evaluated training with the ID model, which shows the same characteristic but not as pronounced.

[8] Note that the evaluation in Figs. 2a and 2b uses the ID model and with the HW model the leakage of $ptxt \oplus k \oplus r_{in}$ is reduced significantly.

Influence of the Occlusion Technique. Figure 4 shows that the chosen occlusion method has a significant impact on the attack results. For the occlusion of important leakage in Figs. 4a and 4c we expect the resulting key rank to increase with an increasing occlusion width since additional leakage is removed. This is only observable for the sample-wise mean occlusion method (x_{avg}). The other occlusion techniques do not show deterministic and comprehensible changes while being very sensitive to the starting and ending point of the occlusion rather than the window size. For a region without important leakage as shown in Figs. 4b and 4d the occlusion should not significantly influence the attack result. A consistent behavior for both datasets is again only observable for the sample-wise mean occlusion method (x_{avg}).

In order to emphasize the sensitivity of the different occlusion methods we show the n-occlusion results for the sample-wise mean (x_{avg}) and zero occlusion (x_0) method in Fig. 5. Instead of limiting the analysis to particular samples, these waterfall plots depict the occlusion center $\dot{n}$ on the x-axis and the number of used attack traces on the y-axis. This allows to visualize the evolution of the logarithmic key rank, according to Eq. 2 as remaining entropy, for a fixed window n shifted by a chosen Δ_n with an increasing number of attack traces. For $\Delta_n = 1$ each pixel in a waterfall plot corresponds to the final key rank after occluding the n measurement samples around $\dot{n}$. Dark colors indicate a high key rank, i.e., the information required for a successful attack is occluded, while white represents a successful attack with a key rank of 0 for the given N_{attr} traces. For the comparison we chose the zero occlusion method evaluated by Hettwer et al. [9]. Since the underlying AES implementation is equivalent for both datasets, a similar behavior would be expected - except for differences in the measurement characteristics. This is only the case for the sample-wise mean

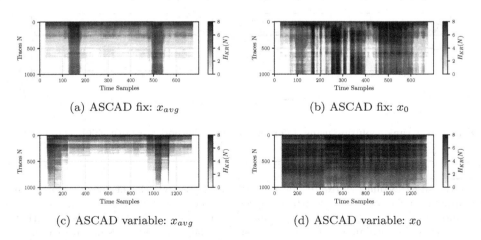

(a) ASCAD fix: x_{avg} (b) ASCAD fix: x_0

(c) ASCAD variable: x_{avg} (d) ASCAD variable: x_0

Fig. 5. Occlusion results for the different methods with $\Delta_n = 1$, $N_{attr} = 1000$, and an occlusion width of a whole clock cycle with $n = 50$ (ASCAD fix) and $n = 125$ (ASCAD variable).

occlusion, which highlights two regions of interest corresponding to the leakage of the masked S-box and the mask itself (c.f. Figs. 2a and 2b) as expected for a training with the HW model. Note that the ranges for the datasets differ slightly as explained in [8], which is why the regions are not exactly aligned between both datasets. The results of the zero occlusion method differ between both datasets and do not lead to valuable attribution results.

We conclude from our analysis that the sample-wise mean occlusion method meets all criteria for an interpretable attribution technique and is therefore used in the remainder of this work.

Influence of the Occlusion Width n. After establishing a suitable occlusion method we investigate the width n of the occlusion window. Intuitively, the larger n, the more samples are occluded, which increases the chance of removing leakage that is important for the model's inference. On the other hand, decreasing n allows to narrow down the sample ranges where the main leakage occurs, allowing for a more precise attribution of POIs. We analyze the impact of the window size for both ASCAD datasets for a training with HW labels and $\Delta_n = 1$ in Fig. 6.

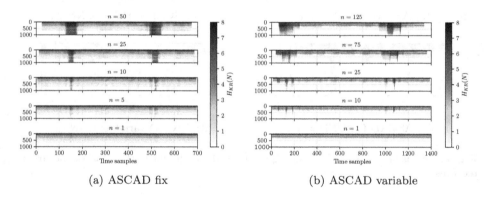

(a) ASCAD fix   (b) ASCAD variable

Fig. 6. Occlusion results for different widths n of the occlusion window for both ASCAD databases.

The results show that the occlusion window can be decreased up to a minimum width for which the occlusion does not have an influence on the attack result anymore, i.e., the remaining leakage is sufficient to reach a key rank of zero. For ASCAD fix (Fig. 6a) and ASCAD variable (Fig. 6b) a width of $n < 10$ does not change attack results significantly. The occlusion width in relation to the clock cycle is smaller for ASCAD variable, since in this dataset the leakage is much more confined on a few samples, as it can be seen with the leakage analysis in Fig. 2b.

Our findings stress that the occlusion width n has to be adapted to fit the underlying data, and an approach like 1-occlusion [9] is not suited to find relevant

POIs in deep learning-based SCA. This is because leakage in side-channel measurements is usually spread over multiple samples of a clock cycle as a result of the low pass characteristics of side-channel measurement setups. For the remainder of this paper we show results for an occlusion width corresponding to the sample range of one clock cycle. The main leakage samples then correspond to the center of highlighted occlusion regions, as it can be seen in Fig. 6.

4.3   Experimental Results

Using the established parameters for the occlusion method in the previous sections, we provide occlusion results for both databases and networks additionally using the ID model in Fig. 7.

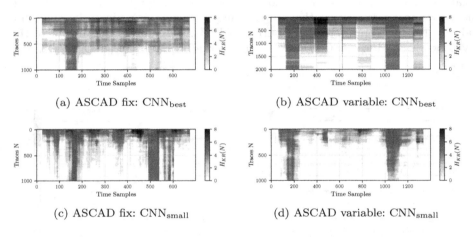

(a) ASCAD fix: CNN$_{\text{best}}$ (b) ASCAD variable: CNN$_{\text{best}}$

(c) ASCAD fix: CNN$_{\text{small}}$ (d) ASCAD variable: CNN$_{\text{small}}$

Fig. 7. Occlusion results for a training with the ID model for both datasets and architectures.

The method reliably identifies POI regions with leakage required by the CNNs for a successful attack. In comparison to gradient-based methods in Fig. 2, the attribution enables an easier interpretation of results compared to the actual leakage regions shown in Figs. 2a and 2b. All networks require the leakage of the masks, around sample 150 (ASCAD fix) and 200 (ASCAD variable), and the masked value, around sample 525 (ASCAD fix) and 1050 (ASCAD variable) for a successful attack. For ASCAD fix and CNN$_{\text{small}}$ the network additionally deems the leakage around 100 and 580 as relevant, which corresponds to the additional leakage of these intermediates. Note that occlusion results for ASCAD variable and CNN$_{\text{best}}$ in Fig. 7b are shown with an increased amount of $N_{attr} = 2000$ traces. In this scenario the method identifies additional POIs around sample ranges 300 and 450 for which the network is able to compensate with other leakage given the additional traces. An explanation is that the network has a significantly higher amount of trainable parameters then CNN$_{\text{small}}$, and therefore it is able to learn additional combinations of leakages that are required for a successful attack. This could be an indicator of network overfitting to these additional leakages.

4.4   Higher-Order Occlusion: Hiding Multiple Parts at once

We have shown in the previous sections that the n-occlusion method is able to identify sample ranges that have an impact on the attack results. Nevertheless, for higher-order attacks against a masked implementation leakage of multiple samples, corresponding to both shares of the masked intermediate, has to be combined for a successful attack [17]. These shares are usually processed in different clock cycles for masked software implementations (c.f. Figs. 2a and 2b). We therefore introduce higher-order occlusion that hides multiple parts of the traces simultaneously to identify important sample range combinations. This also enables the identification of POIs in the presence of learned redundant leakage where the network is able to compensate occluded information with leakage from other samples. For a d-th order occlusion, d sample ranges around $\dot{n}_0, \ldots, \dot{n}_{d-1}$ are occluded and the impact on the resulting key rank is evaluated. We use the same size $n < N_s$ and a shift $\Delta_n \leq n$ for all occlusion windows. A visualization of the method for $d = 2$ is shown in Fig. 8.

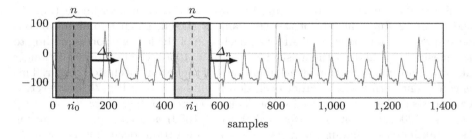

Fig. 8. Visualization of the higher-order occlusion method with order $d = 2$.

In the following, we focus on second-order occlusion ($d = 2$), as it fits the first-order masked AES implementation of the ASCAD databases. In Fig. 9 we show second-order occlusion results for ASCAD variable and CNN_{best} trained with the ID model, corresponding to the first-order occlusion shown in Fig. 7b. Note that the graphs are symmetric regarding its diagonal, i.e., only unique inputs ranges are displayed. For clarity, we show the entropy of the key rank after a fixed number of traces $N_{attr} = 2000$ in Fig. 9a instead of the waterfall visualization. Figure 9b depicts the first occurrence N' of the final key rank according to Eq. 3, and provides additional insights into the evolution of the key rank. While Fig. 9a could also be analyzed on its own to determine important input ranges and combinations thereof, Fig. 9b visualizes whether the result reaches a stable point ($N' \ll N_{attr}$, light colors) or the attack is still improving (N' close to N_{attr}, dark colors). Due to the computational complexity of higher-order occlusion we present results for shifting $\dot{n}$ by $\Delta_n = 20$. This implies that for the visualization in Fig. 9 we show the same key rank for these 20 samples centered around the gradually shifted $\dot{n}$.

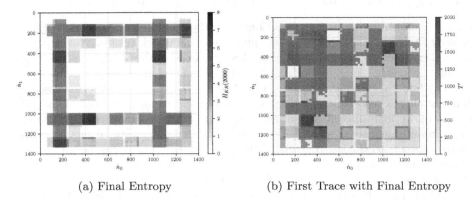

(a) Final Entropy   (b) First Trace with Final Entropy

Fig. 9. Second-order occlusion for ASCAD variable and CNN$_{\text{best}}$ using the ID model for $N_{attr} = 2000$ and $\Delta_n = 20$.

Figure 9a can be interpreted in the way that for each coordinate $(\dot{n}_0, \dot{n}_1)$ the resulting final entropy of the key rank is shown, given two simultaneous occlusions at the respective $\dot{n}$. After an occlusion of the leakage corresponding to the masks ($\dot{n}_0 = 200$) or the masked S-box ($\dot{n}_0 = 1050$), the network is no longer able to perform a successful attack regardless of the second occlusion center. This is consistent with the first-order occlusion results shown in Fig. 7b. However, it can be seen that if additionally the leakage corresponding to $ptxt \oplus k \oplus r_{in}$ at ($\dot{n}_0 = 200$, $\dot{n}_1 = 400$) or ($\dot{n}_0 = 400$, $\dot{n}_1 = 1050$) is occluded, the resulting key rank increases significantly. As a second observation, occluding the leakage corresponding to r_{in} ($\dot{n}_0 = 1300$) significantly increases the key rank. In this case, if the leakage of the mask is occluded in combination ($\dot{n}_0 = 1300$, $\dot{n}_1 = 200$), the network is not able to retrieve the correct secret key anymore. We conclude that in addition to a combination of both shares of the masked S-box, the network infers information from a combination of $ptxt \oplus k \oplus r_{in}$ with r_{in}. If one leakage part of both combinations is not available to the networks, the resulting key rank is increased significantly.

We conclude that higher-order occlusion can be a viable tool for leakage attribution in deep learning-based SCA to identify sample combinations for masked implementations.

5   Occlusion Results of Other ASCAD Key Bytes

Having established the n-occlusion method and its higher-order variant we use both methods to show that networks trained on other key bytes of the

ASCAD variable database focus on different leakages than for the usually targeted byte two (k_2). For a detailed explanation about the leakage ranges of additional key bytes in the databases we refer the reader to [8]. Due to space restrictions we only show results using ASCAD variable and a training with CNN_{best}. We start with an evaluation of a training on key byte k_3 for which the occlusion results are shown in Fig. 10.

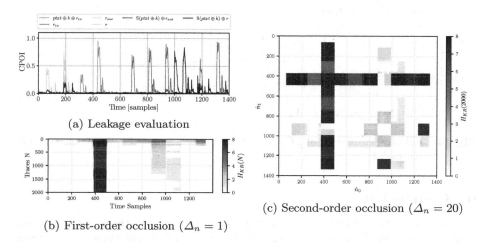

(a) Leakage evaluation

(b) First-order occlusion ($\Delta_n = 1$)

(c) Second-order occlusion ($\Delta_n = 20$)

Fig. 10. Occlusion evaluation of a CNN_{best} training for key byte k_3 of ASCAD variable using the ID model.

When comparing the first-order occlusion results for k_3 in Fig. 10b with the leakage evaluation, we find that the network requires the leakage of $ptxt \oplus k \oplus r_{in}$ ($\dot{n} = 450$) for a successful attack. Hence, it is able to combine this leakage with r_{in} to infer the correct class label. Occluding the masked S-box ($\dot{n} = 1050$) can mostly be compensated after 1500 traces. In the second-order occlusion Fig. 10c it can be seen that the network has learned redundant leakage of r_{in}, since only if ($\dot{n}_0 = 1300$, $\dot{n}_1 = 950$) is occluded together the network is not able to reach key rank zero anymore. Please note that in contrast to k_2 (c.f. Fig. 2b) the leakage of r_{in} is increased significantly.

We additionally show occlusion results for a training on key byte k_5 in Fig. 11, which demonstrates the case of the network having learned enough redundant leakage such that a first-order occlusion is not sufficient to find important samples. The cause for this phenomenon is the additional and redundant leakage of the state mask r for k_5 as indicated in the leakage evaluation (Fig. 11a). This leads to the fact that first-order occlusion, shown in Fig. 11b, is not able to indicate important sample ranges. Only second-order occlusion, shown in Fig. 11c, reveals that a complete occlusion of both clock cycles containing leakage of the corresponding masked S-box value ($\dot{n}_0 = 1050$, $\dot{n}_1 = 1200$) decreases the attack performance. This indicates that the network has learned to use leakage of r from more than two clock cycles.

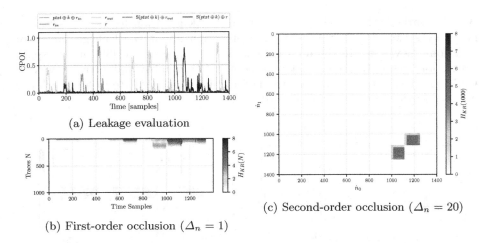

(a) Leakage evaluation

(b) First-order occlusion ($\Delta_n = 1$)

(c) Second-order occlusion ($\Delta_n = 20$)

Fig. 11. Occlusion evaluation of a CNN_{best} training for key byte k_5 of ASCAD variable using the ID model.

6   Conclusion

In this paper, we studied leakage attribution techniques in the context of deep learning-based side-channel analysis. We introduced different types of occlusion methods, which provide a valuable addition to gradient-based approaches, whose results are often hard to interpret and subject to the exact epoch after which they are generated. While related work, performing attribution for image classification, indicates that the number of features being simultaneously occluded and the replacement technique is important, this fact has not been considered in the context of side-channel analysis. We therefore introduced n-occlusion, where we occlude multiple samples at once and additionally analyze the evolution of the resulting key rank for an increasing number of attack traces. Our results show that replacing an entire clock cycle by each samples' mean across all profiling traces is a promising approach. In order to identify leakage combinations required for an attack on masked implementations, we developed higher-order occlusion. Our reasoning is based on the analysis of two different network architectures for the established ASCAD databases. With our methods we showed that the networks are able to actually exploit varying leakage characteristics observable for different key bytes of the targeted AES implementation.

A future interesting research direction is to investigate retraining a model with omitted features and analyzing the resulting behavior. Future work might also explore inverted occlusions, i.e., only feeding small windows of actual data to the model instead of occluding certain regions. Finally, the applicability of our methods to other network architectures, e.g., MLPs could be investigated.

Acknowledgment. This work was supported by the German Research Foundation (Deutsche Forschungsgemeinschaft, DFG) under Grant No. SE2989/1-1 and by the Federal Ministry of Education and Research of Germany in the joint project 6G-life, project identification number, 16KISK002.

References

1. Advanced encryption standard (AES). Technical report (2001). https://doi.org/ 10.6028/nist.fips.197
2. Ancona, M., Ceolini, E., Öztireli, C., Gross, M.: Gradient-based attribution methods. In: Samek, W., Montavon, G., Vedaldi, A., Hansen, L.K., Müller, K.-R. (eds.) Explainable AI: Interpreting, Explaining and Visualizing Deep Learning. LNCS (LNAI), vol. 11700, pp. 169–191. Springer, Cham (2019). https://doi.org/10.1007/ 978-3-030-28954-6_9
3. Bach, S., Binder, A., Montavon, G., Klauschen, F., Müller, K.R., Samek, W.: On pixel-wise explanations for non-linear classifier decisions by layer-wise relevance propagation. PLOS ONE **10**, e0130140 (2015)
4. Benadjila, R., Lomné, V., Prouff, E., Roche, T.: Secure aes128 encryption implementation for atmega8515. https://github.com/ANSSI-FR/secAES-ATmega8515
5. Benadjila, R., Prouff, E., Strullu, R., Cagli, E., Dumas, C.: Deep learning for side-channel analysis and introduction to ASCAD database. J. Cryptographic Eng. **10**, 163–188 (2019)
6. Choudary, M.O., Kuhn, M.G.: Efficient, portable template attacks. IEEE Trans. Inf. Forensics Secur. **13**(2), 490–501 (2018)
7. Durvaux, F., Standaert, F.-X.: From improved leakage detection to the detection of points of interests in leakage traces. In: Fischlin, M., Coron, J.-S. (eds.) EUROCRYPT 2016. LNCS, vol. 9665, pp. 240–262. Springer, Heidelberg (2016). https:// doi.org/10.1007/978-3-662-49890-3_10
8. Egger, M., Schamberger, T., Tebelmann, L., Lippert, F., Sigl, G.: A second look at the ASCAD databases. In: Balasch, J., O'Flynn, C. (eds.) COSADE 2022. LNCS, vol. 13211, pp. 75–99. Springer, Cham (2022). https://doi.org/10.1007/978-3-030-99766-3_4
9. Hettwer, B., Gehrer, S., Güneysu, T.: Deep neural network attribution methods for leakage analysis and symmetric key recovery. In: Paterson, K.G., Stebila, D. (eds.) SAC 2019. LNCS, vol. 11959, pp. 645–666. Springer, Cham (2020). https:// doi.org/10.1007/978-3-030-38471-5_26
10. Kim, J., Picek, S., Heuser, A., Bhasin, S., Hanjalic, A.: Make some noise. unleashing the power of convolutional neural networks for profiled side-channel analysis. IACR Trans. Cryptographic Hardware Embedded Syst. **2019**, 148–179 (2019)
11. Luo, Z., Zheng, M., Wang, P., Jin, M., Zhang, J., Hu, H.: Towards strengthening deep learning-based side channel attacks with mixup (2021). https://ia.cr/2021/ 312
12. Masure, L., Dumas, C., Prouff, E.: Gradient visualization for general characterization in profiling attacks. In: Polian, I., Stöttinger, M. (eds.) COSADE 2019. LNCS, vol. 11421, pp. 145–167. Springer, Cham (2019). https://doi.org/10.1007/ 978-3-030-16350-1_9
13. Papagiannopoulos, K., Glamocanin, O., Azouaoui, M., Ros, D., Regazzoni, F., Stojilovic, M.: The side-channel metric cheat sheet (2022). https://ia.cr/2022/253
14. Perin, G., Ege, B., Chmielewski, L.: Neural network model assessment for side-channel analysis (2019). https://ia.cr/2019/722

15. Perin, G., Wu, L., Picek, S.: I know what your layers did: Layer-wise explainability of deep learning side-channel analysis (2022). https://ia.cr/2022/1087
16. Picek, S., Perin, G., Mariot, L., Wu, L., Batina, L.: SoK: deep learning-based physical side-channel analysis. ACM Comput. Surv. **55**, 1–35 (2022)
17. Prouff, E., Rivain, M., Bevan, R.: Statistical analysis of second order differential power analysis. IEEE Trans. Comput. **58**(6), 799–811 (2009)
18. Rijsdijk, J., Wu, L., Perin, G., Picek, S.: Reinforcement learning for hyperparameter tuning in deep learning-based side-channel analysis. IACR Trans. Cryptographic Hardware Embed. Syst. **2021**(3), 677–707 (2021)
19. Shrikumar, A., Greenside, P., Shcherbina, A., Kundaje, A.: Not just a black box: learning important features through propagating activation differences. CoRR (2016)
20. Simonyan, K., Vedaldi, A., Zisserman, A.: Deep inside convolutional networks: visualising image classification models and saliency maps. In: ICLR (2014)
21. Timon, B.: Non-profiled deep learning-based side-channel attacks with sensitivity analysis. IACR Trans. Cryptographic Hardware Embed. Syst. **2**, 107–131 (2019)
22. Wouters, L., Arribas, V., Gierlichs, B., Preneel, B.: Revisiting a methodology for efficient CNN architectures in profiling attacks. IACR Trans. Cryptographic Hardware Embed. Syst. **2020**(3), 147–168 (2020)
23. Wu, L., Picek, S.: Remove some noise: on pre-processing of side-channel measurements with autoencoders. IACR Trans. Cryptographic Hardware Embed. Syst. **2020**(4), 389–415 (2020)
24. Wu, L., Won, Y.S., Jap, D., Perin, G., Bhasin, S., Picek, S.: Explain some noise: ablation analysis for deep learning-based physical side-channel analysis. Cryptology ePrint Archive, Report 2021/717 (2021). https://ia.cr/2021/717
25. Zaid, G., Bossuet, L., Habrard, A., Venelli, A.: Methodology for efficient CNN architectures in profiling attacks. IACR Trans. Cryptographic Hardware Embed. Syst. 1–36 (2020)
26. Zeiler, M.D., Fergus, R.: Visualizing and understanding convolutional networks. In: Fleet, D., Pajdla, T., Schiele, B., Tuytelaars, T. (eds.) ECCV 2014. LNCS, vol. 8689, pp. 818–833. Springer, Cham (2014). https://doi.org/10.1007/978-3-319-10590-1_53
27. Zhou, Y., Standaert, F.X.: Deep learning mitigates but does not annihilate the need of aligned traces and a generalized ResNet model for side-channel attacks. J. Cryptographic Eng. **10**, 85–95 (2019)
28. Zintgraf, L.M., Cohen, T.S., Adel, T., Welling, M.: Visualizing deep neural network decisions: prediction difference analysis. In: International Conference on Learning Representations (2017)

Secret Key Recovery Attack on Masked and Shuffled Implementations of CRYSTALS-Kyber and Saber

Linus Backlund[✉], Kalle Ngo[✉], Joel Gärtner[✉], and Elena Dubrova[✉]

KTH Royal Institute of Technology, Stockholm, Sweden
{lbackl,kngo,jgartner,dubrova}@kth.se

Abstract. Shuffling is a well-known countermeasure against side-channel attacks. It typically uses the Fisher-Yates (FY) algorithm to generate a random permutation which is then utilized as the loop iterator to index the processing of the variables inside the loop. The processing order is scrambled as a result, making side-channel attacks more difficult. Recently, a side-channel attack on a masked and shuffled implementation of Saber requiring 61,680 power traces to extract the long-term secret key was reported. In this paper, we present an attack that can recover the long-term secret key of Saber from 4,608 traces. The key idea behind the 13-fold improvement is to recover FY indexes directly, rather than by extracting the message Hamming weight and bit flipping, as in the previous attack. We capture a power trace during the execution of the decryption algorithm for a given ciphertext, recover FY indexes 0 and 255, and extract the corresponding two message bits. Then, we modify the ciphertext to cyclically rotate the message, capture a power trace, and extract the next two message bits with FY indexes 0 and 255. In this way, all message bits can be extracted. By recovering messages contained in $k * l$ chosen ciphertexts constructed using a new method based on error-correcting codes of length l, where k is the module rank, we recover the long-term secret key. To demonstrate the generality of the presented approach, we also recover the secret key from a masked and shuffled implementation of CRYSTALS-Kyber, which NIST recently selected as a new public-key encryption and key-establishment algorithm to be standardized.

Keywords: Public-key cryptography · Post-quantum cryptography · CRYSTALS-Kyber · Saber · Side-channel attack · Power analysis

1 Introduction

The National Institute of Standards and Technology (NIST) has recently selected one of the third round finalists in the Post-Quantum Cryptography (PQC) project, a Learning With Errors (LWE)-based scheme CRYSTALS-Kyber [25], as a Public-Key Encryption (PKE) and Key Encapsulation Mechanism (KEM)

J. Zhou et al. (Eds.): ACNS 2023 Workshops, LNCS 13907, pp. 159–177, 2023.
https://doi.org/10.1007/978-3-031-41181-6_9

to be standardized [19]. The other two lattice-based finalists, an NTRU-based scheme NTRU [8] and a Learning With Rounding (LWR)-based scheme Saber [11], were dropped from the competition.

The motivation behind the PQC process is to choose new cryptographic primitives that will remain secure after the potential construction of a large-scale quantum computer. The first two rounds of the NIST PQC selection process mainly focused on the theoretical security of the candidate designs and their implementation efficiency. The third round, however, put the spotlight on the security of the actual implementations. The resistance to side-channel attacks, which are considered one of the main security threats to implementations of cryptosystems at present, has received particular attention. This topic is the focus of this paper.

An attack on a cryptosystem is usually either a Chosen Plaintext Attack (CPA) or a Chosen Ciphertext Attack (CCA). Indistinguishability under CPA (IND-CPA) means that one cannot distinguish two ciphertexts based on the messages they encrypt. This property is a basic requirement for most provably secure PKE schemes. Indistinguishability under adaptive CCA (IND-CCA2) extends this requirement further. By allowing the use of a decryption oracle that can decrypt any ciphertexts except the given ones, one cannot improve the guess. The respective PKEs of the CRYSTALS-Kyber and Saber KEMs are IND-CPA secure. Utilizing a variation of the Fujisaki-Okamoto (FO) transform, they achieve IND-CCA2 security [15].

By re-encrypting the decrypted message and comparing the resulting cipher-text with the one received (yielding the true decrypted message only if they match) the IND-CCA2 schemes are protected against CCAs in theory. However, this may not hold for the implementations of the schemes. By recovering the decrypted message during KEM execution via side-channels, the theoretical security provided by the FO transform can be bypassed. All cryptosystems run on physical devices that leak information through non-primary channels such as timing [17], power consumption [16], or electromagnetic (EM) emanations [2]. No physical device free of side-channels has yet been constructed. Instead countermeasures such as masking [7], shuffling [29], random delays insertion [9], etc. are used to combat side-channel leakage.

Masking [7] attempts to eliminate the leakage by partitioning a secret variable into two or more shares and executing all operations separately on them. Since the shares are randomized at each execution, none of them is expected to contain any exploitable information about the secret variable they mask. There are two main types of masking: Boolean and arithmetic. Boolean masking uses the XOR to combine the shares into the original secret. Arithmetic masking uses the arithmetic addition.

Shuffling [29] is another well-known countermeasure applicable to operations on secret variables that are not dependent on each other. It typically uses the Fisher-Yates (FY) algorithm to create a random permutation which is then utilized as the loop iterator to index the processing of the variables inside the loop. By shuffling the order of the operations, the correlation between executed instructions and time can be hidden. Combined with masking, shuffling was previously believed to provide sufficient protection against side-channel attacks. However, in [21] an attack defeating the combined protection was shown, which uses the bit flipping ciphertext malleability of LWE/LWR PKEs discovered in [24]. The attack requires 61,680 power traces to extract the secret key from a first-order masked and shuffled implementation of Saber on an ARM Cortex-M4.

A ciphertext malleability is a means of modifying the unknown message contained in a given ciphertext without re-encrypting it. The work of [24] presents two ways to accomplish this utilizing the fact that ciphertexts of ring-based LWE/LWR PKE/KEM schemes like e.g. CRYSTALS-Kyber and Saber correspond to polynomials in negacyclic polynomial rings. The first one is a method of flipping an individual message bit by adding a fixed value to the corresponding polynomial coefficient. The second one is a method of cyclically rotating the message by rotating the ciphertext polynomials.

In a KEM, the recovery of a message encapsulated in a properly generated ciphertext trivially leads to a recovery of the shared (session) key (because it is derived from the message using hash functions). Furthermore, since the security of the FO-transform can be bypassed using side-channels, a set of Chosen Ciphertexts (CCTs) can be used to recover the long-term secret key from the decrypted messages. A method for constructing CCTs assuming a perfect message recovery was presented in [24]. In [20], an Error-Correcting Code (ECC)-based CCT construction method was presented, which waives the requirement for a perfect message recovery.

Our contributions: In this paper, we demonstrate a side-channel attack on a first-order masked and shuffled implementation of Saber on an ARM Cortex-M4 which requires 4,608 power traces to extract the secret key. The key ideas behind the 13-fold improvement over the attack of [21] are:

- *A message recovery method using 0 and 255 FY indexes and rotations.* Rather than extracting the message Hamming Weight (HW) and bit flipping, as in [21], we recover "corner" FY indexes 0 and 255, extract the corresponding two bits of the message, and then cyclically rotate the message by modifying the ciphertext. In this way, all message bits can be extracted.
- *An incremental CCT construction method.* We construct CCTs iteratively so that CCTs based on an ECC with code distance $d + 1$ are a superset of the CCTs based on an ECC with code distance d. For a given implementation, there is an optimal code that minimizes the number of traces required for the attack. However, the optimal code is not known in advance. The presented CCT construction method reduces the total capture time for CCTs based on different codes.
- *A method for error-free cyclic rotation of CCTs.* It has previously been discussed how to cyclically rotate a message by modifying the corresponding ciphertext [24,35]. However, for arbitrary ciphertexts, the rotation may flip a wrapped-around message bit. We offer a solution tailored to the specifics of the presented CCT construction method.

To demonstrate the generality of the presented approach, we also extract the secret key from a first-order masked and shuffled implementation of CRYSTALS-Kyber, which has been recently selected for standardization by NIST [19]. Given that the National Security Agency (NSA) has included CRYSTALS-Kyber in the suite of cryptographic algorithms recommended for national security systems [1], it is important to thoroughly assess the security of CRYSTALS-Kyber implementations in order to improve the future versions.

In this paper, we focus on the parametrizations of Saber and CRYSTALS-Kyber that use module rank $k = 3$ and target NIST security level 3. The other security levels with $k = 2$ and 4 can be treated similarly.

2   Previous Work

This section describes previous work on protected implementations of Saber and CRYSTALS-Kyber and related side-channel attacks.

2.1   Implementations

Several implementations of Saber [4,18] and CRYSTALS-Kyber [6,12,13] protected by masking have been presented.

Masking brings a significant execution time overhead to software implementations. Linear operations are repeated twice. Non-linear operations require even more complex solutions that decrease the speed substantially. For Saber, the most lightweight implementation, presented by Van Beirendonck et al. [4], has an overhead factor of 2.5 on an ARM Cortex-M4 compared to an unmasked one. This implementation employs first-order masking of the Saber CCA-secure decapsulation algorithm. It is based on masked logical shifting on arithmetic shares and a masked binomial sampler.

The vulnerabilities discovered in the early version of the Saber implementation of Van Beirendonck et al. [4] helped improve the subsequently released versions of the implementation, as well as the higher-order masked implementation of Saber by Kundu et al. [18]. Some procedures with the bit-dependent leakage (easiest to exploit) were patched by re-implementing them to accumulate the message bits into a packed byte array in memory. This results in a byte-dependent leakage, making side-channel analysis more difficult. Additionally, in the implementation [18], the procedure performing arithmetic to Boolean conversion of shares was re-implemented to work in a bitsliced fashion. Stronger mitigation techniques against side-channel attacks, such as those presented in [3,14,28], were proposed to strengthen side-channel resistance of the NIST PQC candidates.

To the best of our knowledge, the implementation of Saber presented in [21] is the only available masked and shuffled implementation of a module-LWE/LWR PKE/KEM scheme.

2.2   Attacks

Since both CRYSTALS-Kyber and Saber are based on module lattices, they have many similarities. Side-channel attacks on one are typically applicable to the other [24, 26, 30].

In [24], the authors discussed how to attack a masked implementation of LWE/LWR PKE/KEMs in two steps by recovering each share separately using templates created on traces with known masks, and then combining the shares.

The first attack on a first-order masked implementation of Saber KEM was presented in [20]. It recovers a message from a single trace with a high probability using a neural network trained at the profiling stage. The key idea is to recover messages in one step, without explicitly extracting random masks at each execution. It was also shown in [20] how to recover the secret key from 24 power traces captured during the execution of the decryption procedure for CCTs. The ciphertexts are constructed using an ECC-based method which can correct some errors in the recovered messages. In [23] the attack was extended to the implementation of Saber from [18].

An attack applying the method of [20] to a first-order masked implementation of CRYSTALS-Kyber was presented in [30], targeting the message encoding vulnerability found in [27]. In [22], it was demonstrated that the method of [20] can also be used to break a higher-order masked implementation of Saber. It was shown that the neural networks are capable to recover more than two shares and then XOR them to get the message. In [5], side-channel attacks on two implementations of masked polynomial comparison were demonstrated on CRYSTALS-Kyber.

The closest related work to the presented one is [21] where a side-channel attack on a first-order masked and shuffled implementation of Saber is described. The attack requires $257 \times N$ power traces to recover a message m and $24 \times 257 \times N$ power traces to recover the secret key, where N is the number of repetitions of the same measurement. In [21], $N = 10$ is used. Similarly to the method of [20], a neural network trained at the profiling stage is used to recover each bit of m. However, since the bits are shuffled, their order is unknown. Thus, only the HW of m, $HW(m)$, can be deduced in this way. To find the values of individual bits of m, 256 additional traces are captured for a ciphertext created using the bit flipping method of [24]. This ciphertext encrypts a message m', in which one bit of m is flipped, and recovering $HW(m')$ allows determining the flipped bit of m by comparing $HW(m)$ and $HW(m')$.

3   Saber and CRYSTALS-Kyber Algorithms

In this section, we briefly describe CRYSTALS-Kyber and Saber algorithms. For more details, the reader is referred to [25] and [11].

Figure 1 shows pseudocode of the CPA-PKE algorithms, upon which the respective KEMs are built. The pseudocode is applicable to both CRYSTALS-Kyber and Saber [31]. CPA-PKE contains three algorithms: key genera-

CPA-PKE.KeyGen()
1: $seed_\mathbf{A} \leftarrow \mathcal{U}(\{0,1\}^{256})$
2: $\mathbf{A} \leftarrow \mathcal{U}(R_q^{k \times k}; seed_\mathbf{A})$
3: $\mathbf{s} \leftarrow \chi_1(R_q^{k \times 1})$
4: $\mathbf{e} \leftarrow \chi_2(R_q^{k \times 1})$
5: $\mathbf{b} = \lfloor \mathbf{As} + \mathbf{e} \rceil_{p_1}$
6: $pk = (seed_\mathbf{A}, \mathbf{b}), sk = \mathbf{s}$
7: **return** (pk, sk)

CPA-PKE.Dec($\mathbf{s}, c = (\mathbf{u}, v)$)
1: $x = \lfloor v \cdot q/p_3 \rceil - \mathbf{s} \lfloor \mathbf{u} \cdot q/p_2 \rceil$
2: $m' = \mathsf{decode}(x)$
3: **return** m'

CPA-PKE.Enc($pk = (seed_\mathbf{A}, \mathbf{b}), m, r$)
1: $\mathbf{A} \leftarrow \mathcal{U}(R_q^{k \times k}; seed_\mathbf{A})$
2: $\mathbf{s}' \leftarrow \chi_1(R_q^{k \times 1}; r)$
3: $\mathbf{e}' \leftarrow \chi_3(R_q^{k \times 1}; r)$
4: $e'' \leftarrow \chi_3(R_q^{1 \times 1}; r)$
5: $\mathbf{u} = \lfloor \mathbf{s}'\mathbf{A} + \mathbf{e}' \rceil_{p_2}$
6: $v' = \mathbf{s}' \lfloor \mathbf{b} \cdot q/p_1 \rceil + e''$
7: $v = \lfloor v' + \mathsf{encode}(m) \rceil_{p_3}$
8: **return** $c = (\mathbf{u}, v)$

Fig. 1. Pseudocode of CPA-PKE algorithms.

tion, CPA-PKE.KeyGen; encryption, CPA-PKE.Enc; and decryption, CPA-PKE.Dec.

The ring R_q in CPA-PKE is the quotient ring $\mathbb{Z}_q[X]/(X^{256} + 1)$, where $\mathbb{Z}_q$ is the ring of integers modulo a positive integer q. Sampling v from a distribution χ_i over a set S is denoted by $v \leftarrow \chi_i(S)$ while $v \leftarrow \chi_i(S; r)$ denotes deterministic sampling from χ_i using seed r. The uniform distribution is denoted by $\mathcal{U}$ and $\lfloor v \rceil_p$ stands for $\lfloor v \rceil_p = \lfloor v \cdot (p/q) \rceil$, where $\lfloor x \rceil$ means rounding of x to the closest integer with ties being rounded up.

The encode function in CPA-PKE encodes a message to a polynomial by letting each coefficient of the polynomial be equal to the corresponding bit of the message times $\lfloor p_3/2 \rceil$. Similarly, the decode function decodes a polynomial to a message by letting each bit of the message be determined by the corresponding polynomial coefficient. If the coefficient is closer to $\lfloor q/2 \rceil$ than to 0, the message bit is 1. Otherwise, the message bit is 0.

The PKEs of both CRYSTALS-Kyber and Saber can be seen as different parametrizations of CPA-PKE, with the security levels of the schemes mainly differ by the rank k of the module that they use. For the parametrizations considered in this paper, both CRYSTALS-Kyber and Saber use $k = 3$.

The most significant difference between CRYSTALS-Kyber and Saber is in the type of distributions χ_i that the schemes use and in rounding parameters p_1, p_2, p_3. In CRYSTALS-Kyber, all distributions χ_i are centered binomial distributions with $p_1 = 1$, $p_2 > 1$ and $p_3 > 1$. In Saber, only χ_1 is a centered binomial distribution while samples from the other distributions χ_i are always equal to 0. This is compensated by using larger rounding, with $p_1 = p_2$ greater than 1 and p_3 significantly greater than 1.

4 Attack Scenario

We assume a scenario in which the attacker has physical access to the target device to acquire side-channel information and has the ability to query the device with chosen ciphertexts. In addition, we assume that the keys (pk, sk) are static and that the attacker has a fully controllable profiling device similar to the device under attack.

```
void masked_poly_tomsg(uint8 msg[2][32],      void FY_Gen(uint8* permutation, int max)
uint16 poly[2][256])                          1: for (i = 0; i < max; i++) do
uint16 c[2];                                  2:    permutation[i] = i;
uint8 permutation[256];                       3: end for
1: FY_Gen(permutation, 256);                  4: for (i = max - 1; i > 0; i=i-1) do
2: for (x = 0; x < 256; x++) do               5:    int index = rand() % (i+1);
3:    x_rand = permutation[x];                6:    uint8 temp = permutation[index];
4:    i = x_rand / 8;                          7:    permutation[index] = permutation[i];
5:    j = x_rand % 8;                          8:    permutation[i] = temp;
6:    ... Processing ...                       9: end for
7:    msg[0][i] += ((c[0] >> 15) & 1)<<j;
8:    msg[1][i] += ((c[1] >> 15) & 1)<<j;
9: end for
```

Fig. 2. Modified C code of the masked_poly_tomsg() procedure of masked CRYSTALS-Kyber with shuffling added.

5 Experimental Setup

This section presents the equipment which we use for trace acquisition and the target implementations of Saber and CRYSTALS-Kyber.

5.1 Equipment

For trace acquisition, we use a ChipWhisperer-Pro, a CW308 UFO board, and two CW308T-STM32F4 target boards, one for profiling, D_P, and another for the attack, D_A. To verify that the negative effect of intra-device/board variations, which would be expected in a real attack scenario, is not preventing the presented attack, we selected D_P and D_A as a pair of boards acquired from different chip vendors with different ages and wear-out.

Similar equipment is used in the attack on Saber from [21] except that in [21] ChipWhisperer-Lite is used instead of ChipWhisperer-Pro. ChipWhisperer-Pro has a larger buffer size of 98K samples compared to that of ChipWhisperer-Lite, which is 24K samples.

The target board CW308T-STM32F4 contains an ARM Cortex-M4 with an STM32F415-RGT6 chip. It runs at 24 MHz. The traces are sampled at 24 MHz for CRYSTALS-Kyber and 72 MHz for Saber. The choice of sampling rate is limited by the size of ChipWhisperer-Pro buffer[1]. For CRYSTALS-Kyber, all points of interest do not fit into the buffer if a higher sampling rate is used.

---

[1] ChipWhisperer-Pro has an option of streaming, however, streaming can be used only at a maximum of 10 MHz sampling frequency.

5.2 Target Implementations

To the best of our knowledge, there are no publicly available implementations of CRYSTALS-Kyber protected by both masking and shuffling. The experiments presented in this paper are performed using the C implementation which we built on top of the first-order masked implementations of CRYSTALS-Kyber from [13].

The attack point of the presented side-channel attack is the procedure masked_poly_tomsg(). It is called by CPA-PKE.Dec() during the decode operation at line 2 in Fig. 1. The modified code of masked_poly_tomsg(), with shuffling added, is shown in Fig. 2. The lines marked in blue and red indicate vulnerabilities exploited in the presented attack. The blue lines of FY_Gen() are where the index is being loaded and stored in its randomized position during generation. The blue line in masked_poly_tomsg() shows where the random index is loaded for use in the inner loop. In red color are the lines representing the processing of indexed message bits. The side-channel leakage from this part is used for recovering the message.

For Saber, we used the same C implementation as in the attack of [21] upgraded to the latest release. The attack point is the procedure poly_A2A().

The C implementations of Saber and CRYSTALS-Kyber were compiled using **arm-none-eabi-gcc** with the optimization level -O3 (recommended default).

Table 1. The MLP layer widths.

Width	Saber		CRYSTALS-Kyber	
	N_Y	N_M	N_Y	N_M
Input	215	35	820	225
Layer 1	512	256	1024	512
Layer 2	256	128	512	128
Layer 3	128	64	256	64
Output	256	2	256	2

6 Profiling Stage

Our profiling strategy is similar to [21] except that we train two types of neural networks: one for FY index recovery, N_{FY}, and another for message bit recovery, N_m. We use the same three dense layer Multilayer Perceptron (MLP) architecture as in [21], but with different layer widths (see Table 1). For CRYSTALS-Kyber two separate models N_m are trained for the first and the last bits of a byte (because their leakages differ).

We train on 15K traces for Saber and 50K traces for CRYSTALS-Kyber, captured from the profiling device D_P. As in [21], we cut-and-join traces across bits to increase the training set without having to capture more traces. Unlike in [21], we do not use traces captured from the device under attack D_A for profiling. In addition, we use standardization of the traces. The implementation of the index generation function FY_Gen() which we use is not constant-time due to entropy sourcing in the random number generator. Thus, the traces have to be synchronized before training. We perform this by cutting the segments corresponding to each FY index at points identified through correlation.

For FY index recovery, the input to the neural networks is a concatenation of two intervals covering the FY index generation and the FY index usage in the inner loop. Each of those intervals covers the target index and both of its neighbors. For message bit recovery, the input trace to neural networks is an interval covering the processing of both shares for the targeted message bit.

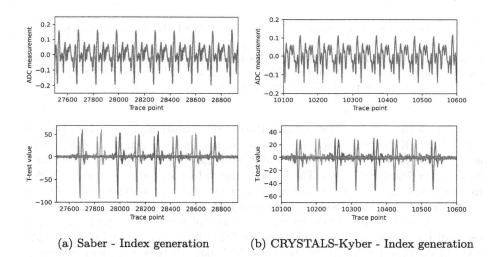

(a) Saber - Index generation   (b) CRYSTALS-Kyber - Index generation

Fig. 3. An average trace representing the generation of the FY indexes 64–72 (top) and its t-test (bottom) for Saber (a) and CRYSTALS-Kyber (b), respectively. Both t-tests are performed on 5K traces with known FY indexes.

To find where the FY indexes are generated, we apply Welch's t-test [33] to a set of 5K traces T with known FY indexes captured from D_P during the execution of CPA-PKE.Dec(). For each $i \in \{0, 1, \ldots, 255\}$, we partition T into two subsets such as:

$$T_0 = \{T_j \in T \mid HW(FY_j[i]) < 4\},$$
$$T_1 = \{T_j \in T \mid HW(FY_j[i]) > 4\},$$

where $HW(FY_j[i])$ is the HW of the FY index of ith processed bit of message m_j in trace T_j, for all $j \in \{0, 1, \ldots, |T|\}$. The Welch's t-test determines if there is a noticeable difference in the means of T_0 and T_1.

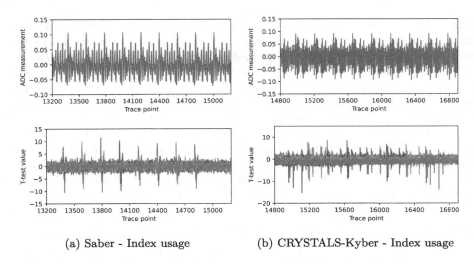

(a) Saber - Index usage   (b) CRYSTALS-Kyber - Index usage

Fig. 4. An average trace representing the usage of FY indexes during message processing (top) and its t-test (bottom) for Saber (a) and CRYSTALS-Kyber (b), respectively. Both t-tests are performed on 5K traces with known FY indexes.

Figure 3 show the t-test results for the index generation part of Saber (a) and CRYSTALS-Kyber (b), respectively. We can see that in both cases the leakage is of similar type. This is because Saber and CRYSTALS-Kyber use the same implementation of FY_Gen(). The higher t-test values for Saber are probably due to oversampling. With more samples taken per clock cycle, the probability to catch a point with the strongest leakage is higher.

In a similar way, one can locate a segment of traces corresponding to the usage of FY indexes in the inner loop, see Fig. 4 for Saber (a) and CRYSTALS-Kyber (b), respectively. We can see that the leakage here is considerably weaker than the one in the index generation part. Still, making use of both segments helps maximize the prediction accuracy of the neural networks.

The message bits are recovered from the same trace segments where FY indexes are used. Saber and CRYSTALS-Kyber implementations have different types of leakage during message processing. In Saber, the leakage is stronger because poly_A2A() procedure decodes the message bits one-by-one and stores them in a memory in an unpacked fashion. Thus, the leakage patterns of all message bits are similar. Contrary, in CRYSTALS-Kyber, the message bits are accumulated into a packed byte array in memory during their processing by masked_poly_tomsg() procedure. As a result, within each byte, the bit accumulated first leaks stronger than the bit accumulated last. This makes message recovery more difficult. The order in which the bits are set is randomized for each execution due to shuffling. This makes incremental recovery with regard to previously set bits unfeasible.

For CRYSTALS-Kyber, we train N_{FY} and N_m models on standardized trace segments covering FY index generation and usage, and message processing, respectively, without any modifications. For Saber, however, we trim some redundant input data points which we identify using the stuck-at-0 fault method of [32] and retrain to improve the accuracy. We remove all points whose assignment to 0 decreases the prediction accuracy of N_{FY} and N_m less than 0.5% and 0.01%, respectively. We also applied trimming to CRYSTALS-Kyber, but the attack results got worse. A higher effect of trimming on Saber is likely due to oversampling.

For each case, N_{FY} and N_m, we train ten models. At the attack stage, these models are used in an ensemble. For the index prediction, the output of the ensemble is determined by multiplying the probabilities of score vectors of all ten models N_{FY}. For the message bit prediction, the output of the ensemble is obtained by majority voting, considering only the votes by models N_m with prediction confidence higher than 0.9.

Due to the 3-stage pipelining of ARM Cortex M4, the first and last processed indexes and message bits look different. Therefore, additional model ensembles are trained specifically for each of them.

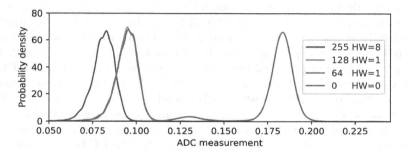

Fig. 5. Distribution of power consumption during the generation of FY indexes 0, 64, 128 and 255 at the trace point with the maximum absolute t-test value in Saber. Index 0 to the left, 64 and 128 in the middle, and 255 to the right.

7   Attack Stage

7.1   Message Recovery Using 0 and 255 FY Indexes and Rotation

If it was possible to recover all FY indexes from power traces during their generation or inner loop usage, one could recover a message by first extracting its bits in the unknown order, then recovering the FY indexes of the bits, and finally re-ordering the bits accordingly. However, we found that neural networks cannot classify all possible FY indexes with a high probability from a single power trace. This is due to the high overlap in the distributions of power consumption of some indexes, see Fig. 5. Bytes that have the same HW are almost completely overlapping. Only the "corner" indexes 0 and 255, whose HW is unique, can be distinguished with a high probability because their distributions are nearly disjoint. For this reason, we use the following method for message recovery.

To recover the message m encrypted in a given ciphertext c, we capture a power trace during the decryption of c, recover FY indexes 0 and 255 using neural networks for index recovery, N_{FY}, and extract the corresponding two bits of m using neural networks for message recovery, N_m. Then, we modify c to c' which encrypts m rotated by two bit positions, capture a power trace during the decryption of c', and extract the next two message bits with FY indexes 0 and 255. This way, by rotating m by two bit positions 128 times, all message bits are extracted.

7.2   Cyclic Rotation of CCTs

It is known [24,35] that a message m of a ring-based LWE/LWR can be cyclically rotated by manipulating a ciphertext c encrypting it. However, an aspect not covered earlier is that the output values computed by decode($-x$) and decode(x) can be different, where x is defined in line 1 of CPA-PKE.Dec() in Fig. 1. The function decode(x) essentially decodes a bit of the message by deciding if x is closer to 0 or $q/2$, but for neither CRYSTALS-Kyber nor Saber this function is completely symmetric, meaning that x is decoded to 0 because its value is closer to 0, while $-x = q - x$ is decoded to 1 as if its value is closer to $q/2$. This introduces a source of potential errors during negacyclic rotation of the CCTs. We fix this by rotating CCTs in a way adopted to their specific construction.

A ciphertext $c = (\mathbf{u}, v)$ consists of polynomials in the ring $\mathbb{Z}_q[X]/(X^{256} + 1)$. Cyclic rotation of the message m encrypted in a properly generated c is performed by multiplying both $\mathbf{u}$ and v by indeterminant X, corresponding to a negacyclic rotation of the polynomial coefficients. For the CCTs, we instead only multiply $\mathbf{u}$ by X. In general, this is not equivalent to a cyclic rotation of m. However, in this way we can control which coefficient of the secret key $\mathbf{s}$ affects a given bit of m in the CCTs. Since we construct the CCTs so that a specific message bit $m[i]$ is determined by a specific key coefficient $\mathbf{s}[i]$, this is sufficient for the full secret key recovery. Care should be taken to keep track of whether $\mathbf{s}[i]$ has wrapped around modulo n or not. In the former case, the message bit is determined by $-\mathbf{s}[i]$ and not $\mathbf{s}[i]$.

7.3   Incremental CCT Construction Method

In the ECC-based CCT construction method of [20], the secret key coefficients are mapped into the codewords of an $[8, 4, 4]$ extended Hamming code[2]. We found that the total number of traces required for secret key recovery can be reduced if more powerful codes are used. We use $[l, w, d]$ linear codes with code distances up to 6 for Saber and up to 8 for CRYSTALS-Kyber. We designed incremental

---

[2] In the notation $[l, w, d]$, l is the codeword length, w is the dataword length, and d is the code distance. A code distance is the minimum Hamming distance between any two codewords of the code.

mapping tables in which CCTs based on an ECC with code distance $d+1$ are a superset of the CCTs based on an ECC with distance d. Our experimental results show that, for a given implementation, there is an optimal code minimizing the number of attack traces. However, the optimal code is not known in advance. The incremental CCT construction method helps reduce the total capture time for CCTs based on different codes. An attacker can capture as many CCT traces as the access time to the device under attack allows, and then try different codes.

Table 2. CCT construction table for Saber.

Order of codeword bits for a code with distance d				CCT constants	Mapping of message bits into secret key coefficients								
6	5	4	3	(k_1, k_0)	-4	-3	-2	-1	0	1	2	3	4
0	0	6	5	(240,10)	1	1	0	0	1	1	0	0	1
1	4			(377,10)	0	0	1	0	1	1	0	1	0
2	6	0	3	(613,4)	1	0	1	0	1	1	0	1	0
3	1	2	0	(373,15)	1	0	1	1	0	1	0	0	1
4	9	5	2	(913,15)	1	1	1	0	0	0	0	1	1
5	10	7	6	(12,3)	1	0	0	0	0	0	0	0	0
6	2	3	1	(793,10)	1	0	0	1	1	0	0	1	1
7				(755,4)	0	1	0	0	1	1	0	0	1
8	8			(917,10)	0	1	1	1	1	0	0	0	0
9	5			(806,10)	0	0	0	1	1	0	0	1	1
10	7	4		(456,15)	1	1	0	1	0	1	0	1	0
11	3	1	4	(68,4)	1	1	1	1	1	0	0	0	0

The presented method uses $3l$ ciphertexts to recover the secret key coefficients $\mathbf{s}[256r+i]$, for all $i \in \{0, 1, \ldots, 255\}$ and $r \in \{0, 1, 2\}$. The coefficient $\mathbf{s}[256r+i]$ is derived from the codeword $(m_{rl}[i], \ldots, m_{(r+1)l-1}[i])$ of an $[l, w, d]$ linear code using the mapping defined by Tables 2 and 3 for Saber and CRYSTALS-Kyber, respectively.

For all $j \in \{0, 1, \ldots, l-1\}$, the message m_{rl+j} is recovered from the CCT $c_{rl+j} = (\mathbf{u}, v)$ which is constructed as

$$\mathbf{u} = \begin{cases} (k_1, 0, 0) \in R_q^{3 \times 1} & \text{for } r = 0 \\ (0, k_1, 0) \in R_q^{3 \times 1} & \text{for } r = 1 \\ (0, 0, k_1) \in R_q^{3 \times 1} & \text{for } r = 2 \end{cases}$$

and

$$v = \begin{cases} k_0 \sum_{i=0}^{255} X^i & \text{for Saber} \\ k_0 + (k_2 \sum_{i=1}^{254} X^i) + k_0 X^{255} & \text{for CRYSTALS-Kyber} \end{cases}$$

for all $r \in \{0, 1, 2\}$, where the constants (k_2, k_1, k_0) are defined in Tables 2 and 3.

Table 3. CCT construction table for CRYSTALS-Kyber.

Order of codeword bits for a code with distance d							CCT constants	Mapping of message bits into secret key coefficients				
8	7	6	5	4	3	2	(k_2, k_1, k_0)	-2	-1	0	1	2
0	0	1	8	5	0		(1,153,8)	0	1	1	1	0
1	9	7	0	6	4	1	(0,77,5)	1	1	1	0	0
2	4	0	5	4	1	0	(2,335,15)	1	1	0	1	1
3	6	10	1	1	5		(3,432,3)	0	1	0	0	1
4	1	2	2	3	2	3	(3,606,3)	1	0	0	1	0
5	7	5	9				(1,864,8)	0	1	1	1	0
6	2	3	4	2			(0,915,5)	0	0	1	1	1
7	3	4					(0,898,5)	0	0	1	1	1
8	10	8	3	0	3	2	(3,432,8)	1	0	1	0	1
9	11						(0,105,5)	1	1	1	0	0
10	8	6	7				(3,632,3)	1	0	0	1	0
11							(3,386,3)	0	1	0	0	1
12	12						(3,606,8)	1	0	1	0	1
13	5	9	6				(2,321,15)	1	1	0	1	1

The non-empty entries in the first multi-column of Tables 2 and 3 define indexes j of the CCTs c_{rl+j}, i.e. the order of codeword bits. Each column contains l non-empty entries, where l is the codeword length. For example, in Table 3, for $d = 2$, the codeword length is 4, so there are 4 non-empty entries, $j \in \{1, 0, 3, 2\}$, in the column.

For each non-empty entry j, the constants (k_2, k_1, k_0) listed in the second column at the same line as j define **u** and v parts of c_{rl+j}. In the previous example, CCTs $c_{4r}, c_{4r+1}, c_{4r+2}, c_{4r+3}$, are constructed using the constants $(2, 335, 15)$, $(0, 77, 5)$, $(3, 432, 8)$, $(3, 606, 3)$, respectively.

Similarly, the message bits listed in the third multi-column at the same line as non-empty entries j compose a codeword that determines the secret key coefficient. In the previous example, if the codeword is $(0, 1, 1, 0)$, then the secret key coefficient is 0. If the codeword is $(1, 0, 1, 0)$, then the key coefficient is 2.

As in [20], we select the constants k_1 and k_0 so that each secret key coefficient is uniquely mapped into some codeword composed from the l decrypted message bits. For CRYSTALS-Kyber, in which the leakage of different bits within a byte is non-uniform and affected by previously set bits, we also use one more constant, k_2, which allows us to minimize the HW of messages. This helps reduce the interference of previously accumulated bits on the success rate of the bit recovery.

We found that, in the masked implementation of CRYSTALS-Kyber from [13], the decoding does not perfectly match the decoding in the unprotected reference implementation [25]. To handle this, we select the constants (k_2, k_1, k_0) for CRYSTALS-Kyber so that $\mathsf{decode}(x \pm \varepsilon) = \mathsf{decode}(x)$ for small ε, results in equivalent ciphertexts in both implementations.

8 Experimental Results

For both Saber and CRYSTALS-Kyber, we performed 10 secret key recovery attacks on the implementation programmed into the device D_A for 10 different secret keys selected at random. For Saber, we used CCTs based on ECCs with code distances 4 and 6. For CRYSTALS-Kyber, we used ECCs with code distances 2, 4, 6 and 8. So, in total, we carried out 60 secret key recovery attacks.

Table 4. Success rate of CRYSTALS-Kyber secret key recovery using an ECC with code distance d and N repetitions for 10 attacks.

N	d	# Incorrect key coeff. (mean)		Success	Attack time (the worst case)		
		Undetected	Detected	rate	Capture	Message rec.	Enum.
30	8	0	0	100%	19.5 h	20.1 h	0 s
	6	0	0.2	100%	15.3 h	15.8 h	0.01 s
	4	0	2.1	100%	9.8 h	10.0 h	0.08 s
	2	17.3	0.9	0%	5.6 h	5.8 h	0.02 s
20	8	0	0	100%	13.0 h	13.4 h	0 s
	6	0	0.4	100%	10.2 h	10.5 h	0.01 s
	4	0.1	5.4	90%	6.5 h	6.7 h	15 s
	2	29.1	3.0	0%	3.7 h	3.9 h	0.4 s
10	8	0	1.8	100%	6.5 h	6.7 h	0.05 s
	6	0.1	9.1	90%	5.1 h	5.3 h	96 min
	4	0.4	27.8	0%	3.3 h	3.4 h	–
	2	73.1	15.8	0%	1.9 h	2.0 h	–

The results are summarized in Tables 4 and 5. The most important part is column 3; if there are undetected incorrect key coefficients, the attack fails. We count incorrect coefficients by comparing the recovered key to the true key, excluding the detected incorrect coefficient.

Next in importance is column 4; if the number of detected incorrect key coefficients is small, the coefficients can be recovered by enumerating all their possible values. With i detected incorrect coefficients, at most 9^i and 5^i enumerations are required to find the true secret key for Saber and CRYSTALS-Kyber, respectively. If the number of detected incorrect coefficients is large, one can instead consider the LWE problem given by these coefficients only. Such an LWE problem has a smaller dimension than the original problem, potentially

Table 5. Success rate of Saber secret key recovery using an ECC with code distance d and N repetitions for 10 attacks.

N	d	# Incorrect key coeff. (mean)		Success rate	Attack time (the worst case)		
		Undetected	Detected		Capture	Message rec.	Enum.
3	6	0	0	100%	4.0 h	26.0 min	0 s
	4	0	0.3	100%	2.7 h	17.3 min	0.01 s
2	6	0	1.7	100%	3.3 h	17.3 min	10.5 s
	4	0.4	5.7	80%	2.2 h	11.6 min	12 min
1	6	0	4.9	100%	3.0 h	8.7 min	2 min
	4	0.7	13.2	0%	2.0 h	5.8 min	–

allowing typical lattice-based attacks against LWE [10] to succeed in recovering the remaining coefficients.

Column 5 states the success rate, i.e. the percentage of experiments in which the secret key was successfully extracted.

The last three columns show the time required for capturing traces for CCTs, recovering the corresponding messages, and enumerating the detected incorrect key coefficients (in the worst-case) using a simple single-threaded implementation on a PC with a processor running at 2.2 GHz. The sign "–" means that enumeration is not feasible. Note that only the CCT trace capture requires physical access to the device under attack D_A. Other computations are done offline, so their time is not as crucial.

Table 6. Number of traces required for successful key recovery in all 10 attacks.

Algorithm	Code distance			
	8	6	4	2
Saber		4608	9216	
CRYSTALS-Kyber	48384	38016	59136	–

Finally, in Table 6 we compare the number of traces required for secret key recovery using different ECCs. For both Saber and CRYSTALS-Kyber, the ECC with code distance 6 seems the best choice. We believe that two main reasons for the higher number of attack traces required for CRYSTALS-Kyber are:

- Non-uniform leakage of masked message bits in CRYSTALS-Kyber implementation [13].
- The traces were sampled at a third of the rate used to acquire Saber traces.

9 Countermeasures

The following techniques could make the presented attack more difficult:

1. Protecting the shuffling index generation procedure using masking or other countermeasures.
2. Bitslicing the implementations.

The following techniques would make the presented attack impossible:

1. Prevent decryption of sparse or low-entropy ciphertexts by introducing a check for minimal entropy as suggested by [34].
2. Prevent decryption of chosen ciphertexts by using e.g. Encrypt-then-Sign method suggested by [3].
3. Re-generating the keys (pk, sk) for each new shared key establishment.

10 Conclusion

We demonstrated a secret key recovery attack on first-order masked and shuffled implementations of Saber and CRYSTALS-Kyber by deep learning power SCA.

Note that the ChipWhisperer platform is essentially noise free. Therefore, the conditions in the experiments can be considered the best-case. Yet, the presented attack shows a 13-fold improvement over previous work (also performed on the ChipWhisperer platform), requires no profiling traces from the target device, and is more robust to inter-device/board variations.

The new message recovery method might have significance beyond the scope of the presented work. The idea of classifying all-0 and all-1 binary tuples only (instead of all possible) and rotating the message, may be useful in side-channel attacks on other software and hardware implementations of ring-based LWE/LWR PKE/KEMs.

We are currently working on developing deep learning-resistant countermeasures for LWE/LWR PKE/KEM implementations.

Our code is available at https://github.com/lbacklund/SCA-Masked-Shuffled-Saber-Kyber.

Acknowledgments. This work was supported in part by the Swedish Civil Contingencies Agency (Grant No. 2020-11632) and the Swedish Research Council (Grant No. 2018-04482).

References

1. Announcing the commercial national security algorithm suite 2.0. National Security Agency, U.S Department of Defense (2022). https://media.defense.gov/2022/Sep/07/2003071834/-1/-1/0/CSA_CNSA_2.0_ALGORITHMS_.PDF
2. Agrawal, Dakshi, Archambeault, Bruce, Rao, Josyula R.., Rohatgi, Pankaj: The EM side—channel(s). In: Kaliski, Burton S.., Koç, çetin K.., Paar, Christof (eds.) CHES 2002. LNCS, vol. 2523, pp. 29–45. Springer, Heidelberg (2003). https://doi.org/10.1007/3-540-36400-5_4

3. Azouaoui, M., et al.: Post-quantum authenticated encryption against chosen-ciphertext side-channel attacks. IACR Trans. Cryptogr. Hardw. Embed. Syst. 372–396 (2022). https://doi.org/10.46586/tches.v2022.i4.372-396

4. Beirendonck, M.V., et al.: A side-channel-resistant implementation of saber. J. Emerg. Technol. Comput. Syst. **17**(2) (2021). https://doi.org/10.1145/3429983

5. Bhasin, S., et al.: Attacking and defending masked polynomial comparison for lattice-based cryptography. IACR Trans. Cryptogr. Hardw. Embed. Syst. 334–359 (2021). https://doi.org/10.46586/tches.v2021.i3.334-359

6. Bos, J.W., et al.: Masking kyber: first-and higher-order implementations. IACR Trans. Cryptogr. Hardw. Embed. Syst **2021**(4), 173–214 (2021). https://doi.org/10.46586/tches.v2021.i4.173-214

7. Chari, Suresh, Jutla, Charanjit S.., Rao, Josyula R.., Rohatgi, Pankaj: Towards sound approaches to counteract power-analysis attacks. In: Wiener, Michael (ed.) CRYPTO 1999. LNCS, vol. 1666, pp. 398–412. Springer, Heidelberg (1999). https://doi.org/10.1007/3-540-48405-1_26

8. Chen, C., et al.: NTRU algorithm specifications and supporting documentation (2020). https://csrc.nist.gov/projects/postquantum-cryptography/round-3-submissions

9. Coron, Jean-Sébastien., Kizhvatov, Ilya: An efficient method for random delay generation in embedded software. In: Clavier, Christophe, Gaj, Kris (eds.) CHES 2009. LNCS, vol. 5747, pp. 156–170. Springer, Heidelberg (2009). https://doi.org/10.1007/978-3-642-04138-9_12

10. Dachman-Soled, Dana, Ducas, Léo., Gong, Huijing, Rossi, Mélissa.: LWE with side information: attacks and concrete security estimation. In: Micciancio, Daniele, Ristenpart, Thomas (eds.) CRYPTO 2020. LNCS, vol. 12171, pp. 329–358. Springer, Cham (2020). https://doi.org/10.1007/978-3-030-56880-1_12

11. D'Anvers, J., et al.: Saber algorithm specifications and supporting documentation (2020). https://www.esat.kuleuven.be/cosic/pqcrypto/saber/files/saberspecround3.pdf

12. D'Anvers, J.P., et al.: Revisiting higher-order masked comparison for lattice-based cryptography: algorithms and bit-sliced implementations. Cryptology ePrint Archive, 2022/110 (2022). https://eprint.iacr.org/2022/110

13. Heinz, D., et al.: First-order masked Kyber on ARM Cortex-M4. Cryptology ePrint Archive, Report 2022/058 (2022). https://eprint.iacr.org/2022/058

14. Hoffmann, C., et al.: Towards leakage-resistant post-quantum CCA-secure public key encryption. Cryptology ePrint Archive, Report 2022/873 (2022). https://eprint.iacr.org/2022/873

15. Hofheinz, Dennis, Hövelmanns, Kathrin, Kiltz, Eike: A modular analysis of the Fujisaki-Okamoto transformation. In: Kalai, Yael, Reyzin, Leonid (eds.) TCC 2017. LNCS, vol. 10677, pp. 341–371. Springer, Cham (2017). https://doi.org/10.1007/978-3-319-70500-2_12

16. Kocher, Paul, Jaffe, Joshua, Jun, Benjamin: Differential power analysis. In: Wiener, Michael (ed.) CRYPTO 1999. LNCS, vol. 1666, pp. 388–397. Springer, Heidelberg (1999). https://doi.org/10.1007/3-540-48405-1_25

17. Kocher, Paul C..: Timing attacks on implementations of Diffie-Hellman, RSA, DSS, and other systems. In: Koblitz, Neal (ed.) CRYPTO 1996. LNCS, vol. 1109, pp. 104–113. Springer, Heidelberg (1996). https://doi.org/10.1007/3-540-68697-5_9

18. Kundu, S., et al.: Higher-order masked Saber. Cryptology ePrint Archive, Report 2022/389 (2022). https://eprint.iacr.org/2022/389

19. Moody, D.: Status Report on the Third Round of the NIST Post-Quantum Cryptography Standardization Process. Nistir 8309, pp. 1–27 (2022). https://nvlpubs. nist.gov/nistpubs/ir/2022/NIST.IR.8413.pdf

20. Ngo, K., Dubrova, E., Guo, Q., Johansson, T.: A side-channel attack on a masked IND-CCA secure saber KEM implementation. IACR Trans. Cryptogr. Hardw. Embed. Syst. **2021**(4), 676–707 (2021). https://doi.org/10.46586/tches.v2021.i4. 676-707

21. Ngo, K., Dubrova, E., Johansson, T.: Breaking masked and shuffled CCA secure saber KEM by power analysis. In: Proceedings of the 5th Workshop on Attacks and Solutions in Hardware Security, pp. 51–61. ACM (2021)

22. Ngo, K., Wang, R., Dubrova, E., Paulsrud, N.: Side-channel attacks on lattice-based KEMs are not prevented by higher-order masking. Cryptology ePrint Archive, Report 2022/919 (2022). https://eprint.iacr.org/2022/919

23. Paulsrud, N.: A side channel attack on a higher-order masked software implementation of saber. Master's thesis, KTH (2022)

24. Ravi, P., et al.: On exploiting message leakage in (few) NIST PQC candidates for practical message recovery and key recovery attacks. Crypt. ePrint Arch., 2020/1559 (2020). https://eprint.iacr.org/2020/1559

25. Schwabe, P., et al.: CRYSTALS-Kyber algorithm specifications and supporting documentation (2020). https://csrc.nist.gov/projects/postquantum-cryptography/round-3-submissions

26. Shen, M., et al.: Find the bad apples: an efficient method for perfect key recovery under imperfect SCA oracles - a case study of Kyber. Cryptology ePrint Archive, Report 2022/563 (2022). https://eprint.iacr.org/2022/563

27. Sim, B.Y., et al.: Single-trace attacks on the message encoding of lattice-based kems. Cryptology ePrint Archive, Report 2020/992 (2020). https://eprint.iacr.org/ 2020/992

28. Tsai, T.T., et al.: Leakage-resilient certificate-based authenticated key exchange protocol. IEEE Open J. Comput. Soc. **3**, 137–148 (2022). https://doi.org/10.1109/ OJCS.2022.3198073

29. Veyrat-Charvillon, Nicolas, Medwed, Marcel, Kerckhof, Stéphanie., Standaert, François-Xavier.: Shuffling against side-channel attacks: a comprehensive study with cautionary note. In: Wang, Xiaoyun, Sako, Kazue (eds.) ASIACRYPT 2012. LNCS, vol. 7658, pp. 740–757. Springer, Heidelberg (2012). https://doi.org/10. 1007/978-3-642-34961-4_44

30. Wang, J., et al.: Practical side-channel attack on masked message encoding in latticed-based KEM. Cryptology ePrint Archive, Report 2022/859 (2022). https:// eprint.iacr.org/2022/859

31. Wang, R., Ngo, K., Dubrova, E.: A message recovery attack on LWE/LWR-based PKE/KEMs using amplitude-modulated EM emanations. In: International Conference on Information Security and Cryptology (2022). https://eprint.iacr.org/ 2022/852

32. Wang, R., Ngo, K., Dubrova, E.: Side-channel analysis of Saber KEM using amplitude-modulated EM emanations. In: Proceedings of the 25th Euromicro Conference on Digital System Design (2022). https://eprint.iacr.org/2022/807

33. Welch, B.L.: The generalization of 'Student's' problem when several different population variances are involved. Biometrika **34**(1/2), 28–35 (1947)

34. Xu, Z., et al.: Magnifying side-channel leakage of lattice-based cryptosystems with chosen ciphertexts: the case study of Kyber. Cryptology ePrint Archive, Paper 2020/912 (2020). https://doi.org/10.1109/TC.2021.3122997

35. Yajing, C., et al.: Template attack of LWE/LWR-based schemes with cyclic message rotation. Entropy **24**(10), 15 (2022). https://doi.org/10.3390/e24101489

SoK: Assisted Fault Simulation
Existing Challenges and Opportunities Offered by AI

Asmita Adhikary$^{(\boxtimes)}$ and Ileana Buhan$^{(\boxtimes)}$

Radboud University, Nijmegen, The Netherlands
{asmita.adhikary,ileana.buhan}@ru.nl

Abstract. Fault injection attacks have caused implementations to behave unexpectedly, resulting in a spectacular bypass of security features and even the extraction of cryptographic keys. Clearly, developers want to ensure the robustness of the software against faults and eliminate production weaknesses that could lead to exploitation. Several fault simulators have been released that promise cost-effective evaluations against fault attacks. In this paper, we set out to discover how suitable such tools are, for a developer who wishes to create robust software against fault attacks. We found four *open-source* fault simulators that employ different techniques to navigate faults, which we objectively compare and discuss their benefits and drawbacks. Unfortunately, none of the four open-source fault simulators employ artificial intelligence (AI) techniques. However, AI was successfully applied to improve the fault simulation of cryptographic algorithms, though none of these tools is open source. We suggest improvements to open-source fault simulators inspired by the AI techniques used by cryptographic fault simulators.

Keywords: Fault simulation · Open-source · Software · AI

1 Introduction

An adversary with physical access to a device can induce unforeseen effects in a software program by subjecting the device to extreme operating conditions. Faults can be introduced in several ways [22], for example, through clock glitches, where short glitches are inserted into the clock signal, which may cause timing violations or voltage glitches, where the device is supplied with power outside the range of values specified in the datasheet. *Fault injection* is the deliberate action of modifying or skipping the intended flow of operations that could result in the software acting unexpectedly. A successful fault injection attack may allow unauthorized individuals to access off-limits memory locations or bypass necessary authorization conditions that could crash the system or cause it to behave unexpectedly, leading to dire consequences.

Fault injection attacks in vehicle immobilizer systems [37], or key recovery of Playstation Vita AES-256 [20] provide enough incentive to prevent further attacks by injection of faults. Unauthorized access to a Linux operating system

J. Zhou et al. (Eds.): ACNS 2023 Workshops, LNCS 13907, pp. 178–195, 2023.
https://doi.org/10.1007/978-3-031-41181-6_10

[34] or exploring embedded systems [35, 36] by exploiting faults further proves the disastrous effects of fault injection attacks.

Assisted fault simulation automates detecting and testing vulnerabilities in a given program's control flow or due to data modification. A *fault simulator* is a software tool that simulates the effects of faults or errors in digital circuits or software programs. When targeting software, a fault simulator will replicate (either by simulating or emulating[1]) the underlying architecture on which the program will run. A user-specified *fault model* specifies the parameters for the fault simulator to look for exploitable locations. The target of the fault simulator can be any part of the implementation, hardware, or software. To determine whether the target is vulnerable to faults, a *test case* modifies the target according to one instance of the fault model and executes the target. If the target behaves as expected, the tested location is not vulnerable. Alternatively, the target is vulnerable, and the user can determine what caused the fault.

One of the benefits of using a fault simulator is the possibility of performing a root cause analysis. When performing fault injection on targets, it is impossible to determine what caused the fault. A fault simulator allows users to determine the cause of a successful fault and harden the implementation without needing a physical target and expensive tools. Additionally, using fault simulators may be less complex and expensive than testing for faults using real fault injection tooling on an actual target. Given the appeal of fault simulators, we sought to investigate state-of-the-art open-source fault simulators. The target audience for this paper is developers of *general-purpose software* and not specifically cryptographic implementations. Although many fault simulators [1, 5, 6, 14, 16–18, 24, 26–29, 31, 33] can verify the implementations of cryptographic algorithms, we exclude them in this work because there is already an overview of such tools [4]. We found four fault simulators in the public domain suitable for such a developer, namely FiSim [25], ZOFI [23], ARMORY [13] and ARCHIE [12].

In this paper, we discuss what features existing tools offer, which use cases they cover, and how easy it is to adapt them to different examples. AI was successfully applied to improve the fault simulation of cryptographic algorithms [4]. Hence, we explore the use cases where AI was successfully applied and discuss the opportunities to apply the techniques employed by the latter to optimize the former. A fault simulator must satisfy the following conditions to provide a significant advantage over performing fault injection on an actual target:

1. It must be fast enough to cover as many test cases as possible in a reasonable amount of time.
2. It needs to be scalable, as it should handle smaller code snippets and full-fledged implementations of real-world applications.
3. It should offer interpretability so that a developer can use the results to harden the implementation.

Not all *vulnerable locations* are *exploitable* as attacking a vulnerable location may or may not result in an exploitable fault. For example, the fifth-round byte

---

[1] The terms, simulation, and emulation, have been used interchangeably.

fault in AES is not exploitable, whereas the eighth- or ninth-round byte fault in AES is exploitable [31]. Therefore, there might be innumerable vulnerable locations, but not all of them will be exploitable. The goal of a fault simulator is to find exploitable locations.

Contribution. In this paper, we offer the following contributions:

1. We propose a grammar to express fault models that can be used to compare the capabilities of each tool at a glance in Sect. 3.
2. We define a set of parameters to compare the tools to help a prospective user quickly decide which tools best suit his use case in Sect. 4.
3. We objectively compare existing open-source fault simulators designed for general-purpose software while discussing their operation and features in Sect. 5.
4. We present challenges of existing fault simulators in Sect. 6.
5. We suggest optimizations to improve existing fault simulators with AI techniques in Sect. 7.

Paper Organization. The remainder of the paper is organized as follows. Section 2 presents the development of fault simulator over the years. Section 3 outlines our proposed grammar to express fault models. Section 4 describes the criteria we chose to evaluate the four fault simulators. Section 5 details the experimental setup along with the fault simulators and their functioning and features. Section 6 identifies the challenges of using the existing fault simulators, followed by suggestions for improvements using AI techniques in Sect. 7. Finally, we conclude in Sect. 8.

2   Background

There are surprisingly many tools available to perform fault simulations. We first divide existing tools according to the type of implementations, *hardware circuits* vs. *software programs*. The intended application for the verified target can be divided into *cryptographic implementations* vs. *general-purpose software*. Lastly, we consider whether the tools are open source. When discussing related work, we mention fault simulators that we could not execute. Due to the large number of tools available [2, 3, 8, 10–13, 15, 21, 23, 25, 32], we make a representative selection of simulators available for general-purpose software.

Fault Simulation on Hardware Circuits. The first general-purpose tool published to test circuit fault resistance is MEFISTO (Multilevel Error/Fault Injection Simulation TOol) [15], a proprietary tool. Using VHDL as the simulation language, MEFISTO validates the dependability of fault-tolerant systems by applying fault injection to different levels of abstraction, which in turn is used to create an abstraction hierarchy of fault models. It also estimates the possible coverage with the given fault-tolerance mechanisms. LIFTING (LIRMM Fault Simulator) [3] is an open source, object-oriented tool designed in Verilog on an event-driven logic simulation engine that focuses on both logic and fault simulations for stuck-at faults and single-event upsets (SEU). The simulator checks if the design meets the expectations of the functional specifications and introduces fault injections for stuck-at and SEU fault models. [32] has proposed an automated integration of fault injection into the ASIC design flow.

Fault Simulation on Software Programs. All fault simulators in this category use QEMU as the underlying emulator. QEFI [8] focused on the ARM architecture, executes a system-wide and kernel-based fault simulation to check its susceptibility to faults. The next framework is XEMU [2], a language and compiler-independent tool that performs efficient mutation-based testing of software binaries by injecting mutations at run-time using dynamic code translation. It uses QEMU in user mode, which emulates a single program on a Linux OS. Without access to the source code, the control flow graph (CFG) analysis of the disassembled code (before the execution of the software binary) is used to create a mutation table to facilitate injection. XEMU approaches 100% accuracy for test quality metrics compared to source code instrumentation. The CFG offers a speed-up of up to 100–1000 times with a GDB/ARMulator. EQEFI [10] is automatic and non-intrusive, minimizing the effect of fault simulation on emulator performance by simulating the presence of permanent, intermittent, and transient faults in the CPU registers of both RISC and CISC architectures.

AI-based Fault Simulators. Cryptographic fault simulators turned to AI to help cover as many test cases as possible. Techniques vary from data mining to machine learning and deep learning. The first of its kind, ExpFault [31], used data mining to detect exploitable locations (for differential fault analysis) in block-cipher implementations. ExpFault mines distinguishers from fault simulation data using association rule mining to group frequent items. For the recovery of the key after the implementation of the cipher, DL-FALAT [27] uses the deep learning-based leakage detection test based on the principle of non-interference [9] as an improvement to the t-test used in ALAFA [29]. To construct a dataset for the machine learning algorithm, [28] uses a SAT solver to retrieve the key from a few instances of the cipher implementation. The dataset is used to train the machine learning algorithm to predict if there exist any other fault instances in the same cipher implementation. Different algorithms will use different datasets and models. Carpi et al. [7] were the first to use genetic algorithms to improve parameter selection for fault injection. Their solution to narrow down the space of exploitable locations from the vulnerable locations could be beneficial. Krcek et al. [19] utilizes genetic algorithms and machine learning to develop a solution that allows them to find more exploitable faults compared to using either of the approaches.

3   A Taxonomy of Fault Models

Due to the lack of a taxonomy regarding fault models, different fault simulators use different terminologies to refer to the supported fault models. For example,

Table 1. Fault Models with Abbreviations

How	Who	Resolution	Action
Permanent(P)	Instruction(I)	Bit(b)	Clear(C)
Transient(T)	Data(D)	Byte(B)	Fill(F)
Until-	Address(A)	Register(R)	Set(S)
overwrite(U)			Flip/Toggle(G)
			Skip/NOP(instruction)(N)

ZOFI supports a single-event upset fault model in which it attempts to perform a bit-flip in a register whereas ARMORY supports 24 fault models. ARCHIE supports four fault models. The set 0 and set 1 fault models replace the bits to 0 and 1, respectively, while the toggle fault model switches the bits represented by the fault mask. The overwrite fault model ensures that instructions can be skipped. However, the description of the fault model lacks clarity and it remains unspecified whether the fault is to affect an instruction (I), data (D) or address (A). Having a taxonomy helps the fault simulators present the supported fault models in a concise manner. As seen from the Table 1, set 0, set 1, toggle and overwrite fault models correspond to the actions, clear (C), set (S), flip/toggle (G) and skip/NOP (instruction) (N) respectively. However, different fault simulators using different terminologies to refer to the same fault model adds ambiguity. Moreover, the duration of the fault manifestation and its effects remain undefined.

We found no unified view to describe fault models when comparing existing tools, so we proposed a solution that allows us to describe the fault models for the tools we compared.

Table 1 shows our solution to describe the characteristics of a fault. The first parameter, *how*, describes the duration during which the faults manifest. Unlike *transient faults*, which affect only the current run of the target program, *permanent faults* affect the current and all future executions. *Until-overwrite* refers to the faulting of a register or any other memory location, the effects of which become nullified once its value is overwritten. The parameters *who* and *resolution* describe which implementation fragment is affected. Finally, each fault model is described by an *action* with the help of which the fault is injected.

For example, FiSim [25] supports two fault models: *transient instruction skipping* ([T][I][N]) and *transient instruction bit flips*([[T][I][b][G]]). While the former fault model skips the subsequent instruction, the latter flips the value of a bit corresponding to an instruction for a particular execution of the program. The combination in *fault models* does not imply that the tools support all possible combinations of fault models.

4   Criteria for Evaluating the Fault Simulators

This section discusses our criteria for evaluating the four open-source fault simulators. From a developer's perspective, these criteria aim to provide quick insight into the working of each tool to help decide which tool to use. Figure 1 illustrates the various parameters that we use to evaluate the fault simulators.

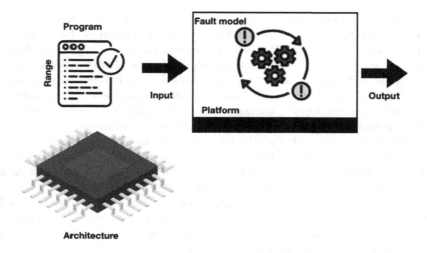

Fig. 1. Illustration of our criteria for evaluating fault simulators

Table 2. Evaluation Criteria: E=Exhaustive, U=User-defined, D=Deterministic, R=Random, Refer to Table 1 for fault model's grammar

Tool	Platform	OS	Architecture	Range	Coverage	Fault Models	Memory Consumption
FiSim	Unicorn	Windows (Pre-built) Linux & Mac	ARM	E	D	[T][I][b][G,N]	≈50%
ZOFI	Native hardware	Linux	x86_64	E	R	[T][A][b,R][G]	≈50%
ARMORY	M-ulator	Linux	ARMv6M, ARMv7M, ARMv7EM	U	D	[*][I][*][*]	>50%
ARCHIE	QEMU	Linux	Depends on QEMU	U	D	[P,T][I,D][b,R] [C,S,G,F]	≈100%

Figure 1 portrays the inputs needed to run the target program on the fault simulators. Foremost is the implementation itself, which can be cross-compiled, as suggested by the OS and the architecture. Depending on the fault simulator, the developer can specify the range of the implementation to be considered when the fault simulator attempts to induce faults into it. The "program" is supposed to run on the "architecture". Hence architecture can also be looked at as an input. Depending on the inherent design of the fault simulator, certain fault models will be executed either deterministically or randomly. The "platform" helps users decide on the host system to run the fault simulator.

Table 2 is a concise overview of the parameters we selected for comparison. *Platform* informs us about the underlying simulation or emulation engines. The *OS* informs us about the operating system for which the fault simulator will run and compatible cross-compilers. *Architecture* describes the supported hardware device on which the execution of the software can be replicated. *Range* specifies whether a tool is *exhaustive*(E) and will consider the entire implementation or is *user-defined*(U), and the user can specify the range of instructions. At first glance, tools that support an exhaustive search for vulnerable locations might seem tempting, but could hinder handling an implementation that consumes substantial resources. On the contrary, the tools supporting user-defined range help us fine-tune as per requirements and might prove beneficial.

Coverage determines whether the injected faults are *deterministic* (D), where multiple runs of the fault simulation experiments will always produce the same results, or *random*(R), where multiple runs of the fault simulation experiments will produce different results. Deterministic faults do not capture the essence of fault injections. Still, they are readily reproducible, whereas random faults function exactly as fault injections in an actual setup. However, the results may not be so easily reproducible. One of the most important features of a fault simulator is the supported *fault models* (Sect. 3).

The parameter *memory consumption* tells us how much memory the simulator occupies while working. Using significant memory resources could cause the system to terminate the simulation forcibly.

5   Experimental Setup

We installed ZOFI (version 0.9.7)[2] [23], ARMORY[3] [13] and ARCHIE[4] [12] on a VirtualBox running Ubuntu 22.04.1 LTS with one core, one thread, and 10.44 GB of RAM. The VirtualBox was running on a PC with Ubuntu 20.04.4 LTS, with Intel(R) Xeon(R) CPU ES-2620 v4 @ 2.10 GHz, 1 physical processor, 8 cores, and 16 threads with 50.43 GB of RAM. We installed the ARM GNU toolchain and the Meson build system as prerequisites to run ARMORY. We ran FiSim[5] [25] on Windows 11 Pro, AMD Ryzen 5 PRO 5650U @ 2.30 GHz, and 16 GB of RAM to facilitate the use of its GUI.

To compare, we first run each tool with the default example. Initially, our goal was to run the same code on all tools, but this was impossible due to differences in the platforms. So, we ran each tool with a different example. In the next section, we describe each tool in detail.

5.1   FiSim

Description. FiSim [25], based on the Unicorn emulator and Capstone disassembler, is a prototype of a deterministic fault attack simulator. It supports cross-platform simulation of ARM32/ARM64 architectures. Its GUI is pre-built

---

[2] https://github.com/vporpo/zofi.

[3] https://github.com/emsec/arm-fault-simulator.

[4] https://github.com/Fraunhofer-AISEC/archie.

[5] https://github.com/Riscure/FiSim/releases.

for Windows but supports Linux and Mac OSX systems. FiSim implements two fault models, as shown in Table 2.

Operation. FiSim comes preloaded with a secure bootloader implementation. The first boot stage takes as input the implementation of the bootloader. The tool provides console output for debugging and visualizing the execution trace. In the second boot stage, the execution trace is used as input to provide the good and bad signatures, giving two different execution traces. Once the traces start to differ, the logic of the boot stage decides whether authentication succeeded. Then the execution trace is placed in the fault simulator. The number of test cases depends on the size of the code. For every instruction and the two supported fault models, FiSim will modify the target program according to the fault model, run the program, and compare the result of the execution with the expected output. If and when the code is vulnerable, the authentication will succeed, and the next boot stage will be executed, which signifies that the glitch bypassed the authentication. The target source code of the secure bootloader is compiled, and the resulting binary code is used for simulation. When the implementation is run, FiSim shows a list of assembly instructions.

Features. FiSim provides ways to harden the bootloader by pointing out its weaknesses and testing the effectiveness of its countermeasures. FiSim aims to find the balance between accuracy and speed. However, loading other than the default programs for simulation is not straightforward.

5.2   Zero Overhead Fault Injector

Description. ZOFI [23] is a timing-based fault simulator based on the Capstone library. Unlike the other tools, it uses native hardware (x86_64 Linux systems), to run the target program. ZOFI implements a register single-bit flip fault model.

Operation. ZOFI does not have a default example, but takes as input any x86_64 Linux binary. During the golden run, ZOFI executes the unmodified binary at native speed to measure its execution time and collect its original output. The execution time of the golden run serves as an upper bound for the fault simulation time. It helps to approximate whether the binary needs to be terminated. The results of the golden run help ZOFI compare the results of the subsequent test cases to categorize instructions as corrupted, masked[6], detected, stuck in an infinite loop, or throwing an exception. For each test case, ZOFI forks and launches a new process to run the binary, pausing the binary for a random period (between zero and the execution time of the golden run) to simulate faults, after which the execution of the binary is resumed. For the fault simulation, the execution of the binary is interrupted by a signal emitted by ZOFI. Then ZOFI modifies the state of the binary by injecting a register bit-flip. Depending on whether the registers are read or written by an instruction, ZOFI behaves differently. In the case of the registers written to, ZOFI steps into

---

[6] By masked instructions, the authors mean instructions that are not vulnerable to fault effects.

the next instruction to modify the register bit so that it doesn't get overwritten. Either the execution leads to completion or is interrupted by a signal. In case of infinite loops, ZOFI sets up an alarm to receive a signal if the binary gets stuck.

Features. ZOFI offers a variety of optional arguments to fine-tune a fault simulation experiment. Its main feature is the speed with which it can analyze a given workload. The user can specify a fault model by choosing the specific registers and the particular bits affected by a fault. It provides users with different arguments, making the tool customizable, handles binaries protected by error detection techniques, and can run multiple concurrent test runs depending upon the number of CPU threads. It has a built-in tracking system for workload executions, output checking, and statistics collection. ZOFI provides ample optional arguments for users to fine-tune their search for exploitable faults. ZOFI allows the user to determine the number of test cases and faults injected per test run. Depending upon the user's choice, outputs can be obtained in CSV file and Moufoplot format apart from having it on the console. The user can also decide the maximum number of fault simulation attempts and the degree of parallelization.

5.3 ARMORY

Description. ARMORY [13] is an efficient, instruction-accurate emulator for ARM-M binaries. It uses M-ulator which can work with ARMv6-M, ARMv7-M, and ARMv7-EM instruction set architectures and can handle faulty assembly instructions. ARMORY considers a total of 24 fault models (Table 2), both instruction-level (permanent, transient) and register-level (permanent, transient, active until overwrite). It determines all exploitable arbitrary (and customizable) fault combinations while automatically utilizing all available CPU cores.

Operation. ARMORY uses an optimized fault simulation strategy by executing a dry run first. For the next run, once ARMORY encounters exploitable locations, it adds it to a list of exploitable locations and instead of starting afresh, starts from the unmodified version of the implementation which was stored as a state in M-ulator, thus saving emulation time. M-ulator runs a fault-free simulation at first until the execution of the binary is completed or the supplied timeout is reached, thus providing the sequence of executed instructions and used registers. This sequence gives all injection points in order. After doing so, the M-ulator continues until the next injection point, and the current state is stored as a backup. This approach saves emulation time by eliminating the need to start from the beginning for each fault. Then the fault model is applied. On reaching one of the halting points, ARMORY checks the exploitability model to determine whether the fault encountered is to be added to the list of exploitable faults. If no such halting point is reached or an invalid instruction is met, then the M-ulator's state is restored. However, this might not be enough when dealing with multivariate fault simulation. So, in the case of higher-order fault simulation, even if the current fault combination isn't exploitable, the tool recursively runs the current state with the next fault model. Hence, the following fault model starts with M-ulator where a specific fault combination has already been applied. Also, for multivariate faults, the order of faults holds significance.

Features. As advantages, we can enumerate that it offers fault simulation for multivariate faults and is highly customizable. ARMORY provides outputs both on the console and as a log file which helps in future referencing. ARMORY attempts to optimize using M-ulator backups and efficient multicore support. It automatically utilizes all the available CPU cores. M-ulator, explicitly designed for fault simulation, outperforms the Unicorn emulator and harbors the ability to handle incorrect assembly code, unlike other emulators. It focuses on lower abstraction levels for fault simulation binaries of ARM-M since applying isolated fault models on higher abstraction levels overlooks exploitable faults.

5.4   ARCHitecture-Independent Evaluation

Description. ARCHIE [12] is a fault simulator for analyzing any binary files which can run on a QEMU-supported architecture. ARCHIE can be used for different white-, gray-, and black-box architecture testing. The tool supports specialized microcontrollers. ARCHIE executes a user-defined fault campaign. It natively supports four fault models. ARCHIE needs the developer to input the parameters of each test case. The tool does not perform fault exploration, but tests if a fault is exploitable. Instead of requiring the developer to specify the exploitable locations, it would be helpful if ARCHIE could independently predict the possible fault locations.

Operation. The ARCHIE controller script takes inputs, compiled binary, QEMU configuration, and fault configuration to launch several parallel processes. Each of these parallel processes handles one QEMU instance and one of the fault models from the fault configuration to run their experiment independently. Once these processes have completed their task, they collect and store all the results in an HDF5 file. The user can set the number of parallel processes. Each worker launches their QEMU instance along with their unique fault configuration. In effect, ARCHIE does not exhaustively or randomly simulate the entire space. It checks whether our hypothesis regarding the faults turns out to be correct or not. It uses terminal and log files to record its findings. It uses up the entire memory and uses various percentages of the CPU. Since it takes up the whole RAM, it causes the kernel to kill or terminate the execution of the tool. For a few executions of these mentioned binaries, the process was killed by the kernel.

Features. ARCHIE is equipped with debugging functionality.

5.5   Experimental Results

To compare the tools available, we recorded their execution times with different implementations. For FiSim, we considered the implementation of a password authenticator. Similarly, as with the secure bootloader implementation, the password authentication procedure would compare the input password with the stored password. For ZOFI and ARMORY, we chose a simple implementation of a counter-loop. We executed ARCHIE on an implementation that led to the blinking of LEDs on a STM32VLDISCOVERY board.

Table 3 shows the results of the experiments for each tool[7] that highlight the implementation size, the time required, and the number of successful faults. We noticed that memory requirement heavily influences performance. Therefore, we monitor it (in Table 2) to guide us toward selecting a host machine.

6   Limitations of Existing Fault Simulators

The Fault Exploration Problem. The fault simulators we explored employ *exhaustive search* to find exploitable faults. From a security perspective, exhaustive exploration might seem tempting. The more test cases a fault simulator executes, the more successful the tool becomes in ruling out possible fault attacks and the more trust we have in a negative outcome. However, when dealing with real-world implementations, exhaustive search falls short of expectations because the required resources depend on the implementation size, the fault models supported (see Table 1), and the time it takes to run each test case. The results reported in Table 3 only consider the single fault model, while attacks involving multiple faults are known. When multiple fault instances are considered, the space for exhaustive search will increase further. Therefore, the exhaustive search might not be the goal to aim for, but having a smart selection of test cases might be a better alternative.

FiSim and ARMORY exhaustively simulate all possible faults. The examples we run in our tests are fairly small (a few KB), and testing took up to 24 h for

Table 3. Experimental results. The *default examples* are depicted in italic font.

Tool	Implementation	Binary Size	Execution Time	#Successful Faults
FiSim	*Secure bootloader*	5KB	1:49.17 min	364
	Password Checker	1KB	40.85 s	139
ZOFI	System file	48KB	55.015 s	74 (for 100 runs)
	Counter	16KB	26.566 s	82 (for 100 runs)
ARMORY	*Fault insertion*	711B	0.979 s	24
	AES	6.1KB	24:38.730 min	823192
	Secure bootloader	3.5KB	24:46:39.962 h	1124
	Counter	227B	1.746 s	2
ARCHIE	*Blinking LED on STM32F0DISCOVERY*	500B	6:16.714 min	4
	AES	7.1KB	2:06:58.019 h	4
	Blinking LED on STM32VLDISCOVERY	148KB	1:1.414 min	1

---

[7] 24:46:39.962 h implies 24 h, 46 min and 39.962 s.

some examples. When adding more complex fault models, the simulation time will increase further.

Cryptographic fault simulators such as [5,14,14,28] have an advantage in this respect, since cryptographic implementations follow a structure that can be analyzed using cryptanalysis. The structured nature of a cryptographic implementation helps narrow the search space, as not all parts of the implementation are equally susceptible to faults. Therefore, approaches that use SAT solvers [28], or SMT solvers [14], or data flow graphs (DFGs) (DATAC [5], TADA [14]) are suitable for this purpose. DFGs tend to grow exponentially with the size of implementation, so targeting the entire implementation space when expressed as a DFG is not feasible. When considering general-purpose software implementations, we are left with the option of exhaustively searching for faults throughout the implementation. This quickly becomes infeasible with the increased implementation size, supported fault models, and time required to run each test case.

The Need for Speed. Although the fault simulators might perform satisfactorily for relatively small implementations, as seen in Table 3, how these tools will scale for real-world applications is unclear. Several optimizations have been proposed in the literature to reduce testing time. Table 3 does not serve as a benchmark for comparing the speed of the fault simulators. The same binary can not be executed on all the fault simulators due to platform differences. The binary size, execution time, and the number of successful faults, as depicted in Table 3, are inconclusive. The reason is the differences in platforms and fault simulators. For example, implementing a simple counter-loop for ZOFI and ARMORY differs. The loop in the case of ZOFI has to be made large enough so that its runtime was more than 0.05 s. However, ARMORY can execute smaller loops. The implementation of the secure bootloader for FiSim and ARMORY is different as the example codes came embedded with the fault simulators. ARMORY requires the developer to define the starting and halting points, and ARCHIE requires the developer to define the fault locations. The AES implementations for ARMORY and ARCHIE differ, too, since the former performs a one-byte fault attack after the MixColumns operation of round 7 and before the final SubBytes operation to reduce the key-search space while the latter performs a tenth round skip attack and a diagonal fault attack on AES.

Based on the platform used by the fault simulators, we can expect the fault simulators to behave as described henceforth. ZOFI might be the fastest tool. As it runs on the native architecture, its execution does not depend on any emulator. ZOFI pauses the binary for a random duration (with the maximum duration recorded from the golden run) to induce a fault that randomizes the fault simulation. We expect its performance to be closely followed by FiSim, which uses Unicorn, a lightweight and stripped-down variant of QEMU that offers smaller size and memory consumption as it emulates just the CPU. Since M-ulator, which underlies ARMORY, emulates only ARMv6-M, ARMv7-M, and ARMv7-EM architectures while leaving out some features, its speed is faster than QEMU. Furthermore, the M-ulator stores an intermediate unmodified state of a binary so that ARMORY can resume testing the saved state after encountering an exploitable location instead of having to execute the binary from the very beginning. This reduces emulation time considerably. Depending on the fault specifications, ARCHIE might take the most time to complete its executions. QEMU, the platform ARCHIE uses, emulates the full system, taking up more time and memory. The time consumed by ARCHIE also depends on the fault specifications provided by the developer. The fewer the test cases, the less time is required for the simulation.

ZOFI, ARMORY and ARCHIE employ parallelization to engage in optimum usage of the system's resources and reduce the time required to run the fault simulations. ZOFI lets the developer decide or, depending on the number of available cores, decides the number of parallel threads to deploy on the fault simulations. ARMORY automatically utilizes all the available CPU cores, while ARCHIE launches independent worker threads, each of which pertains to a single QEMU instance. Finally, all the worker threads report to the main controller script, consolidating the results in a user-readable format.

Interpretability. Learning the exact instruction or data register responsible for the fault and the exact fault model is an important feature of a fault simulator. Knowing the cause will help a developer harden the implementation. For a security evaluation, the availability of debugging functionality that describes the operations of the simulator could also prove helpful. While reporting the number of successful faults is common, information on the most successful fault models is not readily available in the tools we tested. However, the lack of clarity of the results provided by simulators such as ZOFI poses a problem to the developer since it fails to provide any details of the exploitable locations. ZOFI refrains from pointing to faulted instructions and provides just the number of faults. ARMORY provides the faulted instructions along with the fault model that caused it. ARCHIE provides a debugging functionality that takes us step-by-step through its working. The lack of information on the number of test cases is another drawback of the aforementioned fault simulators. All but ARMORY are not transparent with their success percentage, i.e., number of injected faults vs. successful faults. The number of injected vs. successful faults informs us of the success percentage of the fault simulator. Due to the timing-based design, ZOFI fails to function correctly if the workload runs for a variable or a short time, as it attempts to inject faults after the binary has completed its execution, thus affecting its *accuracy*.

Realistic Fault Models. FiSim supports two fault models that it exhaustively applies over all possible fault locations (instructions). However, all potential faults are not equally realistic or probable in the real world. Although ARMORY supports 24 fault models, it is unclear which ones are the most probable. Although many fault models are known in the literature, no study indicates which are more *likely*. We would like to note that this is not a failure of existing simulators, but a gap of knowledge in the state of the art.

7   Opportunities of Using AI Techniques

Artificial intelligence (AI) techniques and overlapping disciplines like data mining provide us with ideas to optimize the operations of fault simulators. AI models learn from a training dataset to develop and hone their search space rather than exhaustively trying all combinations. Tools such as XFC [18], SAFARI [26], FEDS [17], SOLOMON [33] and ALAFA [29] use the concept of non-interference to their advantage, while tools such as DL-FALAT [27], or ExpFault [31], or the ones presented in [30] and [28] employ deep learning and data mining, respectively, to counter the limitations outlined in Sect. 6. ALAFA [29] and DL-FALAT [27] attempts to detect leakage in protected block cipher implementations using the principle of non-interference to improve upon the t-test methodology without the knowledge of the cipher or the countermeasure implementation. Both of them function by observing the distributions of the faulty ciphertexts. However, unlike ALAFA [29], DL-FALAT [27] employs deep learning to enhance the leakage assessment t-test used by the former with respect to data complexity. Saha et al. [27] show that the leakage detection test needed five times less ciphertexts when employing the deep learning aproach. Unlike the t-test based leakage assessment, the deep learning based leakage detection ensures the coverage of all the necessary points in the trace for leakage detection without having the user define the order of the statistical test as well as covers the fault space reasonably better as compared to conventional approaches. This could help fault simulators in their operations. Of course, creating a representative training dataset comes with its set of challenges.

Informed Fault Exploration. Inspired by [27] we could integrate AI into the design of fault simulators by simulating simpler but structurally similar implementations. In this way, the fault simulator could exhaustively search vulnerable locations to identify exploitable locations. Executing fault simulations on numerous simplified implementations could train the model to predict faulty locations in the original target implementation. Since the original target implementation is much larger, this could be a significant improvement.

FiSim and ARMORY could apply this method to prevent solving each fault instance exhaustively and deterministically. Fault simulators attract developers because manual identification of exploitable locations is cumbersome and error-prone. However, ARCHIE requires the developer to specify the fault configurations explicitly. Hence, it could benefit from an AI model which could predict the test case for target implementations instead of the developer. This would enhance their scalability and help them closely replicate real-world scenarios by preventing deterministic exploration of faults.

Prioritizing Fault Models. FiSim and ARMORY simulate all the fault models described individually to arrive at a result. ARCHIE depends on the developer to specify the fault model along with the locations. So, in essence, the simulators consider all models indiscriminately or the developer is left to decide. AI models could be used to inform the choice of the parameters for the test cases as done by [7] and [19] which showed that a certain combination of parameters leads to an increase in the number of exploitable faults. A successful AI model would be able to eliminate (to an extent) less probable fault models from the ones which occur more frequently.

Cryptographic fault simulators use SAT solvers to solve a few instances. These solutions are fed to the machine learning algorithm during its training phase. However, fault simulators pertaining to any programs could not employ similar techniques. Our suggestion would be to use exhaustive search on a few instances comprising smaller implementations of similar structure. The resulting exploitable locations could be used to build the dataset for the training phase of the AI model. The AI model could be trained to differentiate between exploitable and non-exploitable locations. It is expected that the model would predict exploitable locations for target implementations.

8   Conclusion

To evaluate fault simulators, we compared FiSim, ZOFI, ARMORY and ARCHIE objectively. They employ different techniques to navigate faults and present varying difficulty levels to a developer not used to performing fault injection attacks.

FiSim is the most intuitive to use if only its engine were written in a way to incorporate different kinds of implementations. ZOFI is the simplest tool to set up because it just takes as input the binary file and the number of test runs. Though there are several arguments to fine-tune the search for faults, defining them is optional. As long as the golden run takes more than 0.05 s to execute, ZOFI will return valid results. Unfortunately, it provides little information to its user. The output records the number of faulted instructions sans any details. So, the tool doesn't provide any address pointing to the fault. It could be tedious to make an implementation fault attack resistant since one would need to run it through ZOFI numerous times. Furthermore, the lack of addresses where faults are injected could make it relatively hard to rectify the faulty locations.

If the developer is interested in an ARMv6-M, ARMv7-M, or ARM7-EM implementation, then ARMORY would be the fault simulator to pick. However, unlike other tools based upon an existing emulator, ARMORY comes with an emulator of its own, the M-ulator. Naturally, there are pros and cons to both sides. Built upon a current emulator gives the tool's user more confidence, acceptance, and access to all the architectures that the platform can emulate. Building one's platform could be advantageous in designing per target, making it more compatible with the fault simulator.

Unlike the other fault simulators, which actively search for faulty locations, ARCHIE only confirms if the user's test case is exploitable. The tool offers support for all the architectures that QEMU emulates. Though if that architecture is not ARM, the user needs to build it before executing ARCHIE. Also, it uses an older version of QEMU, and it is unclear if the tool is forward-compatible with newer QEMU versions.

The choice of fault simulator depends on one's purpose. If the implementation follows the program structure of a bootloader, and one cares about first-order faults, FiSim works best. If it is an x86_64 Linux binary and the user doesn't require the fault locations, then ZOFI might be a better choice. If it is an ARM-M binary, ARMORY is the tool of choice. If the user is experienced enough to estimate fault configurations and has ample memory resources, then going for ARCHIE is preferable since it provides detailed working for debugging purposes.

To conclude, applying the optimizations with the help of AI techniques could enhance the fault simulators' speed and efficiency. While the deterministic nature of fault simulations might seem appealing as the results could be readily reproduced, it fails to capture the essence of fault injections. AI techniques could help in introducing a non-deterministic or probabilistic approach, which would be closer to real-life use cases. It can also help rule out fault models which aren't as equally probable as other fault models, thus, further fine-tuning the probabilistic approach of inducing faults. Conserving memory could be another incentive for employing AI in the design and development of fault simulators.

Acknowledgment. This work received funding in the framework of the NWA Cybersecurity Call with project name PROACT with project number NWA.1215.18.014, which is (partly) financed by the Netherlands Organisation for Scientific Research (NWO).

References

1. Arribas, V., Wegener, F., Moradi, A., Nikova, S.: Cryptographic fault diagnosis using VerFI. In: 2020 IEEE International Symposium on Hardware Oriented Security and Trust, HOST 2020, San Jose, CA, USA, 7–11 December 2020, pp. 229–240. IEEE (2020)
2. Becker, M., Baldin, D., Kuznik, C., Joy, M.M., Xie, T., Müller, W.: XEMU: an efficient QEMU based binary mutation testing framework for embedded software. In: Jerraya, A., Carloni, L.P., Maraninchi, F., Regehr, J. (eds.) Proceedings of the 12th International Conference on Embedded Software, EMSOFT 2012, part of the Eighth Embedded Systems Week, ESWeek 2012, Tampere, Finland, 7–12 October 2012, pp. 33–42. ACM (2012)
3. Bosio, A., Natale, G.D.: LIFTING: a flexible open-source fault simulator. In: 17th IEEE Asian Test Symposium, ATS 2008, Sapporo, Japan, 24–27 November 2008, pp. 35–40. IEEE Computer Society (2008)
4. Breier, J., Hou, X., Bhasin, S.: Automated Methods in Cryptographic Fault Analysis. Springer, Cham (2019). https://doi.org/10.1007/978-3-030-11333-9
5. Breier, J., Hou, X., Liu, Y.: Fault attacks made easy: differential fault analysis automation on assembly code. IACR Trans. Cryptogr. Hardw. Embed. Syst. **2018**(2), 96–122 (2018)
6. Burchard, J., et al.: AutoFault: towards automatic construction of algebraic fault attacks. In: 2017 Workshop on Fault Diagnosis and Tolerance in Cryptography, FDTC 2017, Taipei, Taiwan, 25 September 2017, pp. 65–72. IEEE Computer Society (2017)
7. Carpi, R.B., Picek, S., Batina, L., Menarini, F., Jakobovic, D., Golub, M.: Glitch it if you can: parameter search strategies for successful fault injection. In: Francillon, A., Rohatgi, P. (eds.) CARDIS 2013. LNCS, vol. 8419, pp. 236–252. Springer, Cham (2014). https://doi.org/10.1007/978-3-319-08302-5_16

8. Chyłek, S., Goliszewski, M.: Qemu-based fault injection framework. Stud. Inform. **33**, 25–42 (2012)

9. Clark, D., Hunt, S., Malacaria, P.: Quantified interference: information theory and information flow. In: Workshop on Issues in the Theory of Security (WITS'04) (2004)

10. Ferraretto, D., Pravadelli, G.: Efficient fault injection in QEMU. In: 16th Latin-American Test Symposium, LATS 2015, Puerto Vallarta, Mexico, 25–27 March 2015, pp. 1–6. IEEE Computer Society (2015)

11. Grycel, J.T., Schaumont, P.: Simplifi: hardware simulation of embedded software fault attacks. Cryptogr. **5**(2), 15 (2021)

12. Hauschild, F., Garb, K., Auer, L., Selmke, B., Obermaier, J.: ARCHIE: a QEMU-based framework for architecture-independent evaluation of faults. In: 18th Workshop on Fault Detection and Tolerance in Cryptography, FDTC 2021, Milan, Italy, 17 September 2021, pp. 20–30. IEEE (2021)

13. Hoffmann, M., Schellenberg, F., Paar, C.: ARMORY: fully automated and exhaustive fault simulation on ARM-M binaries. IEEE Trans. Inf. Forensics Secur. **16**, 1058–1073 (2021)

14. Hou, X., Breier, J., Zhang, F., Liu, Y.: Fully automated differential fault analysis on software implementations of block ciphers. IACR Trans. Cryptogr. Hardw. Embed. Syst. **2019**(3), 1–29 (2019)

15. Jenn, E., Arlat, J., Rimén, M., Ohlsson, J., Karlsson, J.: Fault injection into VHDL models: the MEFISTO tool. In: Digest of Papers: FTCS/24, The Twenty-Fourth Annual International Symposium on Fault-Tolerant Computing, Austin, Texas, USA, 15–17 June 1994, pp. 66–75. IEEE Computer Society (1994)

16. Keerthi, K., Rebeiro, C.: FaultMeter: quantitative fault attack assessment of block cipher software. IACR Trans. Cryptogr. Hardw. Embed. Syst. **2023**(2), 212–240 (2023)

17. Keerthi, K., Roy, I., Rebeiro, C., Hazra, A., Bhunia, S.: FEDS: comprehensive fault attack exploitability detection for software implementations of block ciphers. IACR Trans. Cryptogr. Hardw. Embed. Syst. **2020**(2), 272–299 (2020)

18. Khanna, P., Rebeiro, C., Hazra, A.: XFC: a framework for exploitable fault characterization in block ciphers. In: Proceedings of the 54th Annual Design Automation Conference, DAC 2017, Austin, TX, USA, 18–22 June 2017, pp. 8:1–8:6. ACM (2017)

19. Krcek, M., Ordas, T., Fronte, D., Picek, S.: The more you know: improving laser fault injection with prior knowledge. In: Workshop on Fault Detection and Tolerance in Cryptography, FDTC 2022, Virtual Event/Italy, 16 September 2022, pp. 18–29. IEEE (2022)

20. Lu, Y.: Attacking hardware AES with DFA. CoRR abs/1902.08693 (2019)

21. Nasahl, P., et al.: SYNFI: pre-silicon fault analysis of an open-source secure element. IACR Trans. Cryptogr. Hardw. Embed. Syst. **2022**(4), 56–87 (2022)

22. Piscitelli, R., Bhasin, S., Regazzoni, F.: Fault attacks, injection techniques and tools for simulation. In: 10th International Conference on Design & Technology of Integrated Systems in Nanoscale Era, DTIS 2015, Napoli, Italy, 21–23 April 2015, pp. 1–6. IEEE (2015)

23. Porpodas, V.: ZOFI: zero-overhead fault injection tool for fast transient fault coverage analysis. CoRR abs/1906.09390 (2019)

24. Richter-Brockmann, J., Shahmirzadi, A.R., Sasdrich, P., Moradi, A., Güneysu, T.: FIVER - robust verification of countermeasures against fault injections. IACR Trans. Cryptogr. Hardw. Embed. Syst. **2021**(4), 447–473 (2021)

25. Riscure: Riscure/fisim: An open-source deterministic fault attack simulator proto-type. https://github.com/Riscure/FiSim
26. Roy, I., Rebeiro, C., Hazra, A., Bhunia, S.: SAFARI: automatic synthesis of fault-attack resistant block cipher implementations. IEEE Trans. Comput. Aided Des. Integr. Circuits Syst. **39**(4), 752–765 (2020)
27. Saha, S., Alam, M., Bag, A., Mukhopadhyay, D., Dasgupta, P.: Leakage assessment in fault attacks: a deep learning perspective. IACR Cryptology ePrint Archive, p. 306 (2020)
28. Saha, S., Jap, D., Patranabis, S., Mukhopadhyay, D., Bhasin, S., Dasgupta, P.: Automatic characterization of exploitable faults: a machine learning approach. IEEE Trans. Inf. Forensics Secur. **14**(4), 954–968 (2019)
29. Saha, S., Kumar, S.N., Patranabis, S., Mukhopadhyay, D., Dasgupta, P.: ALAFA: automatic leakage assessment for fault attack countermeasures. In: Proceedings of the 56th Annual Design Automation Conference 2019, DAC 2019, Las Vegas, NV, USA, 02–06 June 2019, p. 136. ACM (2019)
30. Saha, S., Kumar, U., Mukhopadhyay, D., Dasgupta, P.: An automated framework for exploitable fault identification in block ciphers - a data mining approach. In: Kühne, U., Danger, J., Guilley, S. (eds.) PROOFS 2017, 6th International Workshop on Security Proofs for Embedded Systems, Taipei, Taiwan, 29th September 2017. EPiC Series in Computing, vol. 49, pp. 50–67. EasyChair (2017)
31. Saha, S., Mukhopadhyay, D., Dasgupta, P.: ExpFault: an automated framework for exploitable fault characterization in block ciphers. IACR Trans. Cryptogr. Hardw. Embed. Syst. **2018**(2), 242–276 (2018)
32. Simevski, A., Kraemer, R., Krstic, M.: Automated integration of fault injection into the ASIC design flow. In: 2013 IEEE International Symposium on Defect and Fault Tolerance in VLSI and Nanotechnology Systems, DFTS 2013, New York City, NY, USA, 2–4 October 2013, pp. 255–260. IEEE Computer Society (2013)
33. Srivastava, M., Slpsk, P., Roy, I., Rebeiro, C., Hazra, A., Bhunia, S.: SOLOMON: an automated framework for detecting fault attack vulnerabilities in hardware. In: 2020 Design, Automation & Test in Europe Conference & Exhibition, DATE 2020, Grenoble, France, 9–13 March 2020, pp. 310–313. IEEE (2020)
34. Timmers, N., Mune, C.: Escalating privileges in Linux using voltage fault injection. In: 2017 Workshop on Fault Diagnosis and Tolerance in Cryptography, FDTC 2017, Taipei, Taiwan, 25 September 2017, pp. 1–8. IEEE Computer Society (2017)
35. Timmers, N., Spruyt, A., Witteman, M.: Controlling PC on ARM using fault injection. In: 2016 Workshop on Fault Diagnosis and Tolerance in Cryptography, FDTC 2016, Santa Barbara, CA, USA, 16 August 2016, pp. 25–35. IEEE Computer Society (2016)
36. Wiersma, N., Pareja, R.: Safety != security: on the resilience of ASIL-D certified microcontrollers against fault injection attacks. In: 2017 Workshop on Fault Diagnosis and Tolerance in Cryptography, FDTC 2017, Taipei, Taiwan, 25 September 2017, pp. 9–16. IEEE Computer Society (2017)
37. Wouters, L., den Herrewegen, J.V., Garcia, F.D., Oswald, D.F., Gierlichs, B., Preneel, B.: Dismantling DST80-based immobiliser systems. IACR Trans. Cryptogr. Hardw. Embed. Syst. **2020**(2), 99–127 (2020)

Using Model Optimization as Countermeasure against Model Recovery Attacks

Dirmanto Jap[✉] and Shivam Bhasin

Nanyang Technological University, Singapore, Singapore
{djap,sbhasin}@ntu.edu.sg

Abstract. Machine learning (ML) and Deep learning (DL) have been widely studied and adopted for different applications across various fields. There is a growing demand for ML implementations as well as ML accelerators for small devices for Internet-of-Things (IoT) applications. Often, these accelerators allow efficient edge-based inference based on pre-trained deep neural network models for IoT setting. First, the model will be trained separately on a more powerful machine and then deployed on the edge device for inference. However, there are several attacks reported that could recover and steal the pre-trained model. For example, recently an attack was reported on edge-based machine learning accelerator demonstrated recovery of target neural network models (architecture and weights) using cold-boot attack. Using this information, the adversary can reconstruct the model, albeit with certain errors due to the corruption of the data during the recovery process. Hence, this indicate potential vulnerability of implementation of ML/DL model on edge devices for IoT applications. In this work, we investigate generic countermeasures for model recovery attacks, based on neural network (NN) model optimization technique, such as quantization, binarization, pruning, *etc*. We first study and investigate the performance improvement offered and how these transformations could help in mitigating the model recovery process. Our experimental results show that model optimization methods, in addition to achieving better performance, can result in accuracy degradation which help to mitigate model recovery attacks.

Keywords: deep learning · model recovery attacks · physical attacks

1 Introduction

Deep learning (DL) has been growing in popularity over the past decades. It has been widely applied in various fields with great success. At the same time, with the growth of Internet-of-Things (IoT), there is also a growing demand to perform efficient computation on edge devices employed at the network edge. As such, the deployment of DL has now focused on smaller devices, which typically

J. Zhou et al. (Eds.): ACNS 2023 Workshops, LNCS 13907, pp. 196–209, 2023.
https://doi.org/10.1007/978-3-031-41181-6_11

have lower processing power, while still being expected to have similar performance. In the past few years, various edge DL accelerators have been developed to accommodate DL implementations for IoT applications.

On the other hand, based on the field of information theory and cryptography, it has been widely reported that any physical implementation could possess potential vulnerabilities. By simply having access to the physical device, an adversary could have the capability to perform several attacks, such as side-channel attacks (SCA), fault injection attacks (FIA), *etc*, to retrieve secret information being processed or corrupt its computation [1]. This issue can also be extended to DL implementations, namely it raises the possibility of an adversary performing several attacks that could compromise the privacy and integrity of DL implementations, such as intellectual property (IP) theft [2,3] or adversarial attack [4].

Most of the reported attacks on DL have focused on creating adversarial examples that could fool the DL algorithm to cause errors or misclassifications during the inference process. One of the more critical attacks that could be performed is the recovery of the model, such as IP theft. Often, due to the use of confidential training data or the resources spent on collecting them alongside training/tuning the models, trained DL models have become valuable IPs, which attract the attention of the adversaries. There are some critical parameters to protect after the lengthy training of the target model such as the secret architecture or weight parameters.

With regards to the attack on edge AI accelerators, in one of the more recent work [5], it was demonstrated that it is possible to retrieve and reconstruct such model parameters using memory content recovered in a cold-boot attack, targeting Intel Neural Compute Stick (NCS) 2 [6]. *While countermeasures to these practical attacks, such as cold-boot attacks, are known from a hardware perspective [7], we investigate countermeasures from the model training perspective as hardware updates are not always possible.* We attempt to protect the model itself, by making it harder to perform model recovery. This approach can also be used together and integrated with standard cold boot countermeasures.

In this work, our aim is to investigate the model optimization techniques and analyze if these methods could provide inherent resistance against the model recovery attacks. Since our target implementation is on a resource constrained edge device, the optimizations provide additional benefit, namely a more efficient implementation. From the experimental results, we show that classical model optimization approaches like quantization, could reduce the recovery success rate of model recovery attacks, making it harder to recover DL model close to original model.

2   Background

In this section we provide some background on different aspects which are relevant to our work, and will be used throughout the rest of the paper. We first provide the basic overview of model extraction attack, and then the overview of the toolkit used for the attack. We then introduce the previous work and introduce our proposed approach of using model optimization as countermeasure.

2.1 Model Extraction Attack

With the increase in processing power of Graphics Processing Unit (GPU), more research have been conducted in developing complex ML and DL models. Among these models, Deep Neural Network (DNN) has been widely adopted to deal with many different classification problems. DNN can also be categorized into several classes, such as Convolutional Neural Networks (CNN), Multi Layer Perceptron (MLP), *etc.* However, training such complex models will usually require a lot of resources, such as the knowledge and expertise for tuning the model as well as time and resources spent for the data collection. Sometimes, it also has to deal with the confidential training data, which might be worked back from the ML algorithm [8]. As such, a trained model can be of the utmost importance and theft of such model has become the primary target for different adversaries.

Model recovery or model extraction is considered one of commonly studied attack in ML and has been widely investigated. The general idea is to recover and reconstruct the trained model. The first model extraction attack was proposed by Tramer *et al.* [2]. In the paper, they assumed a black box model, with no prior knowledge of the model parameter and training data. The aim of the attack is then to reconstruct a new model with the functionality of the target model, simply by observing the output of the model. There are different level of model recovery or extraction attacks. In [9], the authors proposed a taxonomy for the model extraction attacks on ML. Basically, the attacks can be classified into several categories.

- *Exact Extraction:* the extracted model is an exact duplicate of the target model, with same parameters (up to certain degree of precision),
- *Functionally Equivalent Extraction:* the outputs of the extracted and target models only have to agree for all the elements within the intended data domain or distribution,
- *Fidelity Extraction:* the extracted model maximises the similarity function or agrees with the original model for most of the data within the target distribution, and
- *Task Accuracy Extraction:* the extracted model only has to match (or exceed) the accuracy of the target model.

Most of the reported model extraction attacks so far which utilize physical means can be considered as either exact extraction (recovering the architecture and weights up to certain degree of precision) or task accuracy extraction (achieve similar or better performance than the original model).

Related Works: Several model recovery attacks exploiting the physical access have been reported in literature. Most of the reported attacks are exploiting direct physical access on the edge devices, using different physical channels, such as power or electromagnetic side-channel attacks [3], fault injection attacks [10] *etc.* However, to our knowledge, only one work reported exact model extraction with high success rate, using cold-boot attacks [5]. In this work, the adversary tried to recover the files corresponding to the architecture and weights for DNN model. The main principle for the cold-boot attacks [7] is to steal sensitive information stored in the SRAM, by forcing memory to extreme low temperatures, where the data persists in SRAM even after the device is powered off. Won et al [5] showed that the files recovered after a cold boot attack on DL accelerator can then be used to reconstruct the target model. The reconstructed model will contain some errors for which they propose heuristic based error correction procedures. More details on this work are in the next section.

2.2   OpenVINO ToolKit

OpenVINO is a Python framework provided by Intel. One can design and train a DL model on a more powerful system, load the trained model into smaller edge device, which then performs inference and receives the results [11]. The trained model usually has to be first converted into OpenVINO's IR format. It supports the models trained in popular frameworks, such as PyTorch, TensorFlow, Keras *etc.*

The model, after the conversion to IR format, is stored as two separate files: one containing the model architecture in XML format as `.xml` file and the other containing the weights of the model in a binary `.bin` file. Upon inspection, the weights are typically stored in sequential order in `.bin` file. The first byte/word usually corresponds to the weight value of the first neuron (or first filter in the case of convolutional layer) stored in `int8` ('I8') or `float32` ('FP32') format, and so on. Often, to lower the storage space, multiple weights, if they all have the same value, can be stored as single entry in the `.bin` file. To run an inference the target device is first paired with a host device, in this case, it could be a host PC or a Raspberry Pi. The host device will then load the model to the target device, send the data to be classified and finally receive the inference output.

2.3   Previous Work: Cold-Boot Model Recovery Attack on Intel NCS 2

In cold-boot attacks [7], the adversary exploits the fact that even though the SRAM usually loses data after power-off, when forcing the memory to extreme cold temperature, it would cause the data in the memory to decay at lower rate, thus it maintains the (sensitive) content for a longer period of time. Hence, an adversary can exploit this behavior to read and recover the data if sensitive or private data are stored in the memory. This attack was used in recent work [5], where the authors exploited the vulnerability of Raspberry Pi against cold-boot attack, in order to retrieve the model being loaded to Intel NCS 2.

The summary of the attack is as follow: the adversary tries to recover a replica model M', which is comparable in performance to the target model M from the victim device. Through physical access to the host device, the adversary performs the cold-boot attacks, to recover the .xml and .bin file. Using the information from these two files, the adversary can then rebuild the model M'. Due to the nature of the cold-boot attacks, the model M' might contain some errors and might need to be corrected. They then proposed some heuristic approach for the correction. With regards to model recovery, there are two things to be recovered by the adversary:

Model Architecture Recovery. The data corruption due to cold-boot attacks are incurred on both .xml file and .bin file. Regarding model correction, the data from the .xml file can be corrected much easier, since the data in .xml file has a better-defined structure. Every part of the model will be properly tagged, and hence, one can simply fix errors in the form of typos.

For other parameters such as input/output dimension, *etc*, one can observe the mapping from one layer to the next and correct accordingly. In short, the adversary can perform a fix on the data through manual inspection of the .xml file. In addition, the adversary could also employ other means for correction, such as performing visual inspection using side-channel attacks to identify the general architecture [12] of the model.

Model Weight Recovery. The weight parameters can be reconstructed from the .bin file. Following the reconstruction, a heuristic approach is adopted for weight correction. We follow the correction approach as described in Algorithm 1 [5].

The weights are stored sequentially from input to output layer. The algorithm will try to recover the model weight parameters, which are stored not as valid UTF-8 characters. The algorithm first checks for every 2 floating point values or 8 potential UTF-8 characters to see if those form a valid UTF-8 sequence. If not, those are considered as weight parameters, which the adversaries then store as part of the model. Then, it checks if the number of weights recovered matches the expected number based on the reconstructed architecture. If they agree, the adversaries consider that they have obtained the necessary information regarding the model weight parameters. In the next step, the algorithm tries to identify whether the weights have been corrupted to become out of range, such as Inf or NaN, and if yes, these values will be set to 0 value.

Since most of the implementations are done using the IEEE-754 floating point standard, a heuristic approach is then used for correction. The algorithm considers weights that are not in the range of –5 to +5 as incorrect, since in most implementation, the weights are usually to fall within this range. In addition, it also considers weights with an absolute value less than 10^{-5} to also be incorrect. Once these erroneous weights are identified, large weight values are divided by 2 until its value is within the range of $[-5, +5]$ and small weights are multiplied by 2 until their absolute value is more than 10^{-5}.

Algorithm 1: Weight correction algorithm as described in [5]

Input: RAM Dump(D), Total Weights(T);
Initialization: *count = 0, weight_array=[]*;
while *bit in D* **do**
    while *count ≤ T* **do**
        bits = Read next 64 bits from D;
        if *not valid_UTF8(bits)* **then**
            count=count+2;
            weight_array.append(*bits*);
        else
            count=0;
            weight_array=[];
        end
    end
    range_count=Count(*weight_array* in Range(-5, 5));
    range_percent=range_count/Length(*range_count*);
    if *range_percent ≥ 0.9* **then**
        break;
    else
        count = 0;
        weight_array=[];
    end
end

2.4 Model Optimization

For practical application, the trained model will often need to be optimized to achieve better and faster performance. In OpenVINO framework, there are several tools for optimization that has been offered. One of the approach is to convert the model to a lower precision one, while maintaining the accuracy. In this work, we use Neural Network Compression Framework (NNCF) [13], which is incorporated into OpenVINO. NNCF supports different compression algorithms, such as quantization, sparsity, filter pruning, binarization *etc.* These optimizations can be applied during a model fine-tuning process to achieve a better performance and accuracy trade-off. NNCF is designed to work with models generated from both PyTorch and TensorFlow. The details for each optimization method are provided and elaborated further in [13].

Quantization: It converts data from the high-precision format, such as 32-bit floating point value, into a lower-precision format, such as 8-bit integer. By converting the data into lower precision, the quantization allows the network to have a lower overhead. In NNCF, the quantization is performed by using *FakeQuantize* modules. Using this approach, the high-precision parameters are stored in quantized form (often in the mix of 'FP16' and 'I8'), which will be dequantized before the operations, such as convolution or fully connected layers (see Fig. 1 for illustration). Often, *FakeQuantize* is preferred as compared to full integer quantization when the problems are more towards bandwidth rather than computation limitation [14]. Also, *FakeQuantize* can make the network more immune to precision loss due to quantization.

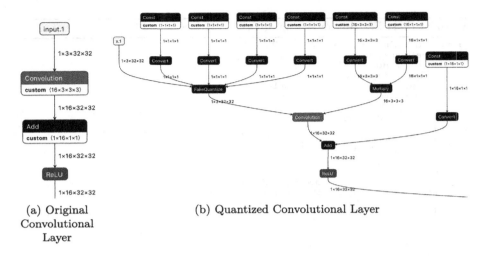

(a) Original
Convolutional
Layer

(b) Quantized Convolutional Layer

Fig. 1. Comparison between convolutional layers for original model and 8-bit quantized model. This is based on the model generated from OpenVINO Toolkit

Binarization: It allows binarizing the weights and activations of NN model, though currently it is only supported for PyTorch 2D convolutional layers. The binarization can be done through either XNOR binarization [15] or DoReFa binarization [16].

Pruning: It sets some of the output filters in the convolutional layers to 0. The filters chosen are determined using filter importance criterion [17,18]. It basically evaluates the filters and those with lower importance will be pruned. There is also sparsity, which typically zeroes the weights in convolutional and fully connected layers. It is mostly done by setting the less important weights to zero.

3   Experiments

For the experiments, we first implement a target model, ResNet-18 [19] which is pre-trained on TinyImage dataset with 200 output classes. We implement the target model using PyTorch framework (the procedure should also work for TensorFlow, since the weights are usually stored using the same number representation).

We then perform several model optimization techniques using NNCF on the target model. We conduct the preliminary investigations to identify the parameters for the optimization algorithms that result in better performance or accuracy. After identifying the optimal parameters, we then obtain 3 optimized models, based on the quantization, pruning, and binarization algorithms. Upon the generation of the models, we convert them to the corresponding IR formats (generation of .xml files and .bin files).

To investigate the effect of the corruption after the cold-boot attacks, we simulate the behavior using similar error rates as reported in [5]. We use simulation to demonstrate the effect of error rate, since the practical setting might not be capable to do this. Also, the simulation could offer the option to control the error rate, which can be used to evaluate our proposed countermeasures.

Based on [5], there are 2 error rates to be considered, ρ_0, the probability of an original bit value 1 flipping to 0, and ρ_1, the probability of a original bit value 0 flipping to 1. The ρ_0 and ρ_1 are reported to be 0.00027% and 0.000009% respectively, which we will use as basis for this work.

For comparison and evaluation metric, we adopt Relative Accuracy Drop (RAD [20]) to quantify the drop in performance of the model:

$$RAD = \frac{Acc_M - Acc_{M'}}{Acc_M}, \tag{1}$$

where M and M' are the original and recovered models respectively. Lower RAD indicates that the accuracy of the recovered model is closer to the original model.

In the first step, by using manual inspection, we are able to reconstruct the architecture of the model through the .xml file. Next, for weight recovery, after obtaining the data from the .bin file, we use the approach as described in Algorithm 1. Note that in original model, the data for the weights are typically stored in 'FP32', 32-bit floating point format. However, after model optimization, some parameters are stored in other format with lower precision, such as 8-bit or 16-bit integer format. For floating point values, it is easier to check and identify if the value is faulted, since it can results in very large values (if the exponent bits are affected) or out of range (Inf or NaN), which can then be corrected. However, there is no such issue for integer values, and hence, the error is harder to spot (all the possible corruption will result in valid range). As such, we keep the integer values as read from the .bin files.

For comparison purposes, OpenVINO provides a benchmarking tool to compare the performance of the trained models. We run the benchmarking tool and reported the results in Table 1 Based on the benchmark results run in Open-VINO, we observed that the accuracy for different models seems to be quite consistent. However, based on the latency and throughput, quantization seems to perform better than the other models. It shows an improvement in performance around 2.5×, whereas for rest of the model, they are quite similar in performance.

For the RAD, we observe that for quantization, the RAD is higher, roughly 3× the original model, which indicates that it is harder to correct the recovered quantized model. On the other hand, we also observe that the RAD for pruning and binarization are actually lower than the original model, indicating better recovery of the model. This is not ideal if we want to design the countermeasure based on these results. As such, we decide to investigate further only on quantization since it shows more a promising result in the preliminary phase.

Table 1. Comparison of theoriginal and optimized models after recovery using Open-VINO benchmark. The comparison is done on basic Intel CPU i5, which emulates a small, less powerful edge device. We also report the changes in performance accuracy of the optimized models in the bracket when compared to the original model.

	Original	Quantization	Pruning	Binarization
Accuracy (change)	55.52% (–)	**57.08% (–1.56)**	57.03% (–1.51)	56.59% (–1.07)
Latency	12.76 ms	**4.78 ms**	10.53 ms	11.64 ms
Throughput	311.74 FPS	**828.86 FPS**	377.95 FPS	341.96 FPS
RAD	0.00234192	**0.00689813**	0.00125809	0.0027973

Overall, we use the simulation setting and assume that the error from the cold-boot attack is only on the `.bin` file, and the `.xml` file is assumed to be corrected with 100% accuracy. As such, we assume a stronger attacker model and show that the quantization still provides harder recovery compared to original model. Moreover, as shown in [13], and based on our experiment so far, the compressed model mostly retains its performance, and the accuracy change is quite low. Also, in the case of severe accuracy loss after quantization, several methods, such as quantization aware training [21] could be used, where the model is re-trained after quantization to improve its performance. We are not doing it here, since for our case, the changes in the accuracy loss is minimal and it even improves when compared to original model's accuracy.

3.1 Investigation on Different Models

We generate several CNN models, which are then trained on MNIST and CIFAR-10 dataset. For MNIST dataset, we consider 3 relatively smaller models, namely:

- Model_1 (2 C and 1 FC layers),
- Model_2 (3 C and 2 FC layers). and
- Model_3 (5 C and 2 FC layers),

where C and FC denotes number of convolutional and fully connected layers. We repeat the experiment 10×, each with different number of parameters, such as number of neurons in a layer, size of the kernel and stride, *etc.* All of the reported networks achieve accuracy around 97–98% on MNIST dataset.

In addition, we also consider training on CIFAR-10 dataset. We design and train a network with 6 C and 3 FC layers. Similar to previous setting, we also consider different parameters, and in general, the accuracy of the models are around 78–81%.

We then use NNCF to convert these models into the quantized versions. We refer these quantized models with "q" (MNIST_1q, MNIST_2q, MNIST_3q, CIFARq). After the optimization, we convert the models into their IR representation and corrupt the `.xml` and `.bin` files.

For the recovery experiments, we repeat the process 50×. In addition to the previously stated noise level earlier (which we will refer to as low noise level),

Table 2. RAD for recovery of original and optimized models after recovery

Model/Noise	Low	High
MNIST1	0.0000	0.2671
MNIST1q	0.0001	0.6644
Improvement (%):	*43.33*	*148.75*
MNIST2	0.0000	0.3623
MNIST2q	0.0003	0.7080
Improvement (%):	*2924.33*	*95.42*
MNIST3	0.0000	0.4351
MNIST3q	0.0002	0.5326
Improvement (%):	*1711.23*	*22.41*
CIFAR	0.0003	0.7950
CIFARq	0.0007	0.8523
Improvement (%):	*133.33*	*7.21*

we also consider a scenario for higher error rate, where ρ_0 and ρ_1 are observed to be 1% and 0.1% respectively, as reported in [5].

We then record the average of the RAD over 50 independent trials. The results are then shown in Table 2. For the RAD distribution, it is highlighted in Fig. 2. In general, we could see that even in low noise setting, the RAD for recovered quantized model is higher than the recovered original model. In general, these experimental results indicate that there is higher difficulty in recovering the model and as such, the extracted models usually perform worse, as indicated by higher RAD.

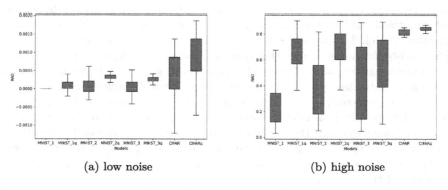

(a) low noise   (b) high noise

Fig. 2. RAD for different noise level

To get a better generalization, we trained some well known models on CIFAR-10, namely: DenseNet-121 [22], ResNet-18 [23] and GoogleNet [24]. The recorded

Table 3. RAD for recovery of original and optimized pre-trained models for CIFAR-10 after recovery

Model/Noise	Low	High
DenseNet	0.0002127	0.0617757
DenseNet_q	0.0013934	0.0988211
Improvement (%):	*555.101*	*59.968*
ResNet	0.0001074	0.0109595
ResNet_q	0.0047624	0.0126637
Improvement (%):	*4334.264*	*15.555*
GoogleNet	0.0001077	0.0071541
GoogleNet_q	0.0106371	0.0103738
Improvement (%):	*9776.602*	*45.005*

accuracy for the trained models (as well as for the quantized models) are 94.05%, 93.07% and 92.85% (93.33%, 92.39% and 92.13%) respectively. The results are reported in Table 3. It can be observed from the table that the RAD is worse for quantized models. In general, the worse degradation can be observed on low noise setting. With the increase of error rates, the differences are getting smaller, however in general, for higher noise scenario, the model extraction already results in higher RAD or worse performance. In this case, it is beneficial for us and works to our advantage, as in overall scenario, it makes the model recovery harder in both cases.

4   Discussions

After the experiments, we observed that through quantization, the recovered quantized models will have higher RAD in comparison to recovered non-quantized model. This indicates lower accuracy for the reconstructed model. As such, this observation indicates that quantization could be a promising candidate for countermeasure against the model recovery attack. As standalone model optimization, quantization provide better and more efficient implementation, suited for target implementation on edge devices. One of the issue that might arise with model optimization is that there could be performance or accuracy loss. In general, one can check the accuracy of the quantized model and verify if the accuracy loss is within acceptable limits. If the accuracy drop is too much, several approach can be adopted, such as quantization aware training. However, this is out of the scope of this paper.

In addition, quantization also results in worse recovery for the case of model recovery attack. One of possible justification is that in conversion to lower precision or integer format, the format pattern is not as regular as for floating point format. In floating point format, some corruptions can results in very large or out of range value, for example, changes in the exponent bits. This in turn makes it easier to detect and correct. However, in integer format, the changes still result in valid value, which make the correction harder.

However, in the case of pruning and binarization, they are performing quite similar to original model. We have checked the models and observe that for these models, the weights are mostly 0 s. Based on the error rates, $\rho_1 < \rho_0$, the corruption affects these model less, and thus basic recovery method is sufficient to recover the models with high accuracy.

For the quantized model, the resulting network is smaller in size with regards to the weights, since the weights are usually stored in lower precision value. However, there are other constant values which are also stored. These constant are most likely the constant offset used for quantizing and dequantizing the parameters. This might make the recovery harder, since unlike weight parameters, these are harder to fix during the recovery, and in some experiments, this sometimes results in the recovered model always returning the same label no matter the input given. This can also be observed on the more complex models (DenseNet, etc).

In higher noise scenario, it requires several attempts to recover the model with decent accuracy, since the error might causes issue that even when average values recovered have small error ($1e - 4$), the recovered model only return the same class prediction for any given input, the same with the quantized model. As such, when the error rate is high, it is basically spreading the influence of multiple errors, so the network is rendered useless.

In general, for low noise scenario, the quantized models demonstrate worse recovery rate and in higher noise scenario, with the additional effect from the noise, the recovery rate is also worse. As such, in general, the quantized models help in both scenarios to make the model recovery attack harder.

5   Conclusion

We have investigated the use of model optimization as possible countermeasures against model recovery attack. Through the experiments, it can be observed that among model optimization techniques, quantization is shown to achieve better performance as well as reducing the effectiveness of the model recovery after the model recovery attacks. We then conducted the experiments to recover the corrupted model using heuristic recovery algorithm. We observed that quantized model results in higher RAD than the original model, which indicates worse recovery of the models.

Acknowledgment. This research is supported by the National Research Foundation, Singapore, and Cyber Security Agency of Singapore under its National Cybersecurity Research & Development Programme (Cyber-Hardware Forensic & Assurance Evaluation R&D Programme). Any opinions, findings and conclusions or recommendations expressed in this material are those of the author(s) and do not reflect the view of National Research Foundation, Singapore and Cyber Security Agency of Singapore.

References

1. Kocher, P., Jaffe, J., Jun, B.: Differential power analysis. In: Wiener, M. (ed.) CRYPTO 1999. LNCS, vol. 1666, pp. 388–397. Springer, Heidelberg (1999). https://doi.org/10.1007/3-540-48405-1_25
2. Tramèr, F., Zhang, F., Juels, A., Reiter, M.K., Ristenpart, T.: Stealing machine learning models via prediction APIs. In: 25th {USENIX} Security Symposium ({USENIX} Security 16), pp. 601–618 (2016)
3. Batina, L., Bhasin, S., Jap, D., Picek, S.: {CSI}{NN}: reverse engineering of neural network architectures through electromagnetic side channel. In: 28th USENIX Security Symposium (USENIX Security 19), pp. 515–532 (2019)
4. Chakraborty, A., Alam, M., Dey, V., Chattopadhyay, A., Mukhopadhyay, D.: Adversarial attacks and defences: a survey. CoRR abs/1810.00069 (2018). http://arxiv.org/abs/1810.00069
5. Won, Y.S., Chatterjee, S., Jap, D., Basu, A., Bhasin, S.: DeepFreeze: cold boot attacks and high fidelity model recovery on commercial EdgeML device. In: 2021 IEEE/ACM International Conference On Computer Aided Design (ICCAD), pp. 1–9. IEEE (2021)
6. Neural Compute Stick 2. https://software.intel.com/content/www/us/en/develop/hardware/neural-compute-stick.html
7. Halderman, J.A., et al.: Lest we remember: cold-boot attacks on encryption keys. Commun. ACM **52**(5), 91–98 (2009)
8. Shokri, R., Stronati, M., Song, C., Shmatikov, V.: Membership inference attacks against machine learning models. In: 2017 IEEE Symposium on Security and Privacy (SP), pp. 3–18. IEEE (2017)
9. Jagielski, M., Carlini, N., Berthelot, D., Kurakin, A., Papernot, N.: High accuracy and high fidelity extraction of neural networks. In: 29th {USENIX} Security Symposium ({USENIX} Security 20), pp. 1345–1362 (2020)
10. Liu, W., Chang, C.H., Zhang, F., Lou, X.: Imperceptible misclassification attack on deep learning accelerator by glitch injection. In: 2020 57th ACM/IEEE Design Automation Conference (DAC), pp. 1–6. IEEE (2020)
11. Intel OpenVINO Toolkit. https://software.intel.com/content/www/us/en/develop/tools/openvino-toolkit.html
12. Won, Y.S., Chatterjee, S., Jap, D., Bhasin, S., Basu, A.: Time to leak: cross-device timing attack on edge deep learning accelerator. In: 2021 International Conference on Electronics, Information, and Communication (ICEIC), pp. 1–4. IEEE (2021)
13. Kozlov, A., Lazarevich, I., Shamporov, V., Lyalyushkin, N., Gorbachev, Y.: Neural network compression framework for fast model inference. arXiv preprint arXiv:2002.08679 (2020)
14. Naumov, M., et al.: Deep learning recommendation model for personalization and recommendation systems. arXiv preprint arXiv:1906.00091 (2019)
15. Rastegari, M., Ordonez, V., Redmon, J., Farhadi, A.: XNOR-Net: ImageNet classification using binary convolutional neural networks. In: Leibe, B., Matas, J., Sebe, N., Welling, M. (eds.) ECCV 2016. LNCS, vol. 9908, pp. 525–542. Springer, Cham (2016). https://doi.org/10.1007/978-3-319-46493-0_32
16. Zhou, S., Wu, Y., Ni, Z., Zhou, X., Wen, H., Zou, Y.: DoReFa-Net: training low bitwidth convolutional neural networks with low bitwidth gradients. arXiv preprint arXiv:1606.06160 (2016)
17. He, Y., Liu, P., Wang, Z., Hu, Z., Yang, Y.: Filter pruning via geometric median for deep convolutional neural networks acceleration. In: IEEE Conference on

Computer Vision and Pattern Recognition, CVPR 2019, Long Beach, CA, USA, 16–20 June 2019, pp. 4340–4349. Computer Vision Foundation/IEEE (2019). https://doi.org/10.1109/CVPR.2019.00447. http://openaccess.thecvf. com/content_CVPR_2019/html/He_Filter_Pruning_via_Geometric_Median_for_ Deep_Convolutional_Neural_Networks_CVPR_2019_paper.html

18. He, Y., Ding, Y., Liu, P., Zhu, L., Zhang, H., Yang, Y.: Learning filter pruning criteria for deep convolutional neural networks acceleration. In: 2020 IEEE/CVF Conference on Computer Vision and Pattern Recognition, CVPR 2020, Seattle, WA, USA, 13–19 June 2020, pp. 2006–2015. Computer Vision Foundation/IEEE (2020). https://doi.org/10.1109/CVPR42600.2020.00208. https://openaccess. thecvf.com/content_CVPR_2020/html/He_Learning_Filter_Pruning_Criteria_for_ Deep_Convolutional_Neural_Networks_Acceleration_CVPR_2020_paper.html

19. He, K., Zhang, X., Ren, S., Sun, J.: Deep residual learning for image recognition. In: Proceedings of the IEEE Conference on Computer Vision and Pattern Recognition, pp. 770–778 (2016)

20. Hong, S., Frigo, P., Kaya, Y., Giuffrida, C., Dumitraş, T.: Terminal brain damage: exposing the graceless degradation in deep neural networks under hardware fault attacks. In: 28th {USENIX} Security Symposium ({USENIX} Security 19), pp. 497–514 (2019)

21. Wang, K., Liu, Z., Lin, Y., Lin, J., Han, S.: HAQ: hardware-aware automated quantization with mixed precision. In: IEEE Conference on Computer Vision and Pattern Recognition, CVPR 2019, Long Beach, CA, USA, 16–20 June 2019, pp. 8612–8620. Computer Vision Foundation/IEEE (2019). https://doi.org/10.1109/ CVPR.2019.00881. http://openaccess.thecvf.com/content_CVPR_2019/html/ Wang_HAQ_Hardware-Aware_Automated_Quantization_With_Mixed_Precision_ CVPR_2019_paper.html

22. Huang, G., Liu, Z., van der Maaten, L., Weinberger, K.Q.: Densely connected convolutional networks (2016). https://doi.org/10.48550/ARXIV.1608.06993, https:// arxiv.org/abs/1608.06993

23. He, K., Zhang, X., Ren, S., Sun, J.: Deep residual learning for image recognition (2015). https://doi.org/10.48550/ARXIV.1512.03385, https://arxiv.org/abs/1512. 03385

24. Szegedy, C., et al.: Going deeper with convolutions (2014). https://doi.org/10. 48550/ARXIV.1409.4842, https://arxiv.org/abs/1409.4842

AIoTS – Artificial Intelligence
and Industrial IoT Security

AIoTS 2023

Fifth Workshop on Artificial Intelligence and Industrial IoT Security

21 June 2023

Program Chairs

Mohammad Ashiqur Rahman   Florida International University, USA
Daisuke Mashima   Illinois at Singapore Pte Ltd & National University of Singapore, Singapore

Web Chair

Chuadhry Mujeeb Ahmed   Newcastle University, UK

Publicity Chairs

Sridhar Adepu   University of Bristol, UK
Kazuhiro Minami   Institute of Statistical Mathematics, Japan
Nur Imtiazul Haque   Florida International University, USA

Program Committee

Magnus Almgren   Chalmers University, Sweden
John Castellanos   CISPA Helmholtz Center for Information Security, Germany
Luca Davoli   University of Parma, Italy
Carl Dickinson   Newcastle University, UK
Amrita Ghosal   University of Limerick, Ireland
Joseph Gardiner   University of Bristol, UK
Luis Garcia   University of Southern California, USA
Vasileios Gkioulos   Norwegian University of Science and Technology, Norway
Sheikh Rabiul Islam   University of Hartford, UK
Jorjeta Jetcheva   San José State University, USA
Charalambos Konstantinou   KAUST, Saudi Arabia
Marina Krotofil   Maersk, UK
Xin Lou   Singapore Institute of Technology, Singapore

Subhash Lakshminarayana	University of Warwick, UK
Rajib Ranjan Maiti	Birla Institute of Technology, India
Weizhi Meng	Technical University of Denmark, Denmark
Venkata Reddy Palleti	Indian Institute of Petroleum and Energy, India
Neetesh Saxena	Cardiff University, UK
Biplab Sikdar	National University of Singapore, Singapore
Giedre Sabaliauskaite	Swansea University, UK
Utku Tefek	Advanced Digital Sciences Center, Singapore
Alma Oracevic	University of Bristol, UK
Zheng Yang	Southwest University, China
Katsunari Yoshioka	Yokohama National University, Japan
Pengfei Zhou	University of Pittsburgh, USA

Blockchain-Enabled Data Sharing in Connected Autonomous Vehicles for Heterogeneous Networks

Ali Hussain Khan[1], Naveed UL Hassan[1(✉)], Chuadhry Mujeeb Ahmed[2], Zartash Afzal Uzmi[1], and Chau Yuen[3]

[1] Lahore University of Management Sciences (LUMS), Lahore, Pakistan
{ali_k,naveed.hassan,zartash}@lums.edu.pk
[2] University of Newcastle, Newcastle, UK
mujeeb.ahmed@newcastle.ac.uk
[3] Nanyang Technological University (NTU), Singapore, Singapore
chau.yuen@ntu.edu.sg

Abstract. In this paper, we consider the use of blockchain for a challenging Connected Autonomous Vehicles (CAV) application scenario of data sharing that has stringent security requirements. We discuss enhanced delegated Proof-of-Stake (dPoS) consensus and combine it with three different reputation schemes, which are Multi-Weight-Subjective-Logic (MWSL), beta, and sigmoid-based reputation schemes. To determine malicious miners in the system, we first compute the overall latency of block generation as the sum of communication, computational, information propagation and queuing latency. We then evaluate the performance of this scheme under simple and orchestrated adversary attack models. We do the same analysis for a heterogeneous network, where we validate our results with a 5G/6G hybrid network. Our results indicate that in large scale networks, MWSL reputation based enhanced dPoS scheme can detect orchestrated attacks in few seconds for 6G networks. Heterogeneous deployment schemes also perform relatively well. In comparison, 4G and 5G perform poorly, and might not be suitable for blockchain implementations.

Keywords: Blockchain · Simple and orchestrated adversary · Heterogeneous network

1 Introduction

Completely autonomous vehicles (AVs) are embedded with multiple sensors and electronic control units (ECUs) [9] which communicate with each other to facilitate the intra-vehicle decisions. AVs communicate with other AVs as well as the infrastructure to share their data for streamlined traffic flow. AVs also communicate with remote cloud and servers for storage and computation requirements. Given the complexity of the application, the large amount of data being shared and the millions of lines of code, the attack surface is huge [10]. There are privacy,

J. Zhou et al. (Eds.): ACNS 2023 Workshops, LNCS 13907, pp. 215–230, 2023.
https://doi.org/10.1007/978-3-031-41181-6_12

data integrity, auditability and non-repudiation concerns originating from compromised data. Recent proposals about Connected AVs (CAVs) communication frameworks depend on centralized architecture [4] which have single point-of-failure along with privacy and security concerns.

Recently, blockchain has emerged as an all-in-one solution to all the security and privacy related needs of many applications [2]. In a blockchain, cryptography and hash functions are used together to form a chain of blocks where each block is added to the chain after achieving consensus within the network in a decentralized way. These consensus mechanisms ensure the trustless nature of blockchain by making all the entities verify the state of the network themselves. Popular consensus mechanisms in blockchain are Proof-of-Work (PoW), Proof-of-Stake (PoS), Delegated Proof-of-Stake (dPoS) and Practical Byzantine Fault Tolerance (PBFT) [11].

Previously, blockchain has been utilized in data sharing among AVs. In [12], the authors presented vehicles as blockchain nodes which brought limitations. In [7], the authors presented a framework where road side units (RSUs) were blockchain nodes and vehicles utilized RSUs for mobile edge computing and the high convergence latency of public network is mitigated by using a consortium network. The recurring limitation in these blockchain-based data-sharing schemes is that although all of them highlighted the long convergence times, none of them quantified the latency of their scheme.

The data shared between AVs and network has to pass through multiple RSUs which may be operating on different cellular technologies with backward and forward compatibility. Currently, the commercial deployment of 5G is observed to be in phases. Therefore, 5G is expected to coexist with 4G for a long period of time. Recently, many works have studied the coexistence and interworking of 4G and 5G network. In [14], the authors claim that the network shift will be from 4G to 5G Non-Standalone (NSA), and then to 5G Standalone (SA), where, first the Radio Access Network (RAN) infrastructure will move from 4G to 5G followed by the control infrastructure. In [15], the authors state that 4G and 5G will coexist initially. This is because 4G has more coverage than 5G. In that case, specific applications that prefer coverage over data rates and latency can use 4G in the same frequency band as 5G. These works also suggest that there is backward compatibility between 4G and 5G i.e., depending on available resources, the same infrastructure may provide 4G or 5G connectivity.

The security measures vary across networks, which may pose significant challenges in data sharing among CAV applications [8]. Blockchain can be added as an over-the-top solution on wireless networks. Because of the recent large-scale move towards wireless networks, research community has started to focus its interest towards blockchain in wireless networks. Blockchain provides an elegant solution to these data sharing challenges. However, the difference in the network speeds might still impact the overall security of the application. Therefore, in this paper, we perform an end-to-end latency analysis of an enhanced dPoS scheme [6] with the objective of analyzing the security of CAV applications. This dPoS scheme is selected because it has several safeguards to detect malicious activities and it can also be deployed on several types of networks. It is also not computationally intensive like PoW and PoS, and therefore, convergence latency can be tamed by the choice of network.

In this work, we consider a CAV application scenario for studying and providing a solution to its security requirements. The employment of blockchain in CAV is discussed in great detail in [9]. The application is highly dynamic and some decisions require extremely strict deadlines. We consider a data sharing scenario where the data shared between the AVs and RSUs is stored in a blockchain, which employs reputation-based enhanced dPoS consensus scheme [6]. The major contributions of this work are as follows:

1. We study the data sharing among CAVs in a heterogeneous network with different coexisting networks. This is a particularly important problem, because the shift from one generation to another is incremental (as discussed before for the case of 5G deployment), which has not been studied in the literature.
2. We present an end-to-end latency of the considered enhanced dPoS scheme. This is done by presenting analytical expressions and performing numerical simulations.
3. Reputation management is a robust way to characterize an entity as malicious or honest based on their behavior. Therefore, it is a vital component of blockchain consensus. For CAV application, it is especially important because data integrity is a critical requirement. We present a security analysis of this scheme where we evaluate three different reputation models i.e., Multi-Weight Subjective Logic (MWSL) [6], beta [5], and sigmoid-based [1] reputation models, and show their performance in terms of aggressiveness towards malicious behavior in a simple and orchestrated adversary model.
4. Based on aggresiveness towards malicious miner detection, we derive the time required to detect and ultimately remove malicious miners in both homogeneous and heterogeneous networks for these reputation schemes.

The rest of the paper is organized as follows. In Sect. 2, we discuss the blockchain-enabled data sharing scenario. In Sect. 3, we present an end-to-end latency analysis for both homogeneous and heterogeneous networks. In Sect. 4, we discuss our simulation setup and present the results based on that. Finally, in Sect. 5, we conclude the paper.

2 Blockchain Based CAV Application Scenario

In this section, we describe a blockchain based CAV application scenario.

2.1 System Model

The data sharing system consists of a Trusted Authority (TA), RSUs and CAVs.

TA: The TA is responsible for registering the CAVs and RSUs in the system. CAVs and RSUs submit their registration information and get their public/private key pairs and the digital certificates. The TA also registers RSUs as miner candidates based on their reputation values stored on the blockchain.

RSUs: The infrastructure elements in the system are RSUs, which are deployed on the sides of the roads to assist in data sharing and storing. RSUs have high computational and storage resources that enable them to act as blockchain nodes. They are responsible for carrying out consensus in the system and updating the blockchain after every cycle along with storing the blockchain and the reputation matrix. We consider a heterogeneous network, where some RSUs are connected with 5G while others are connected with 6G.

CAVs: CAVs share data with each other and share the data sharing as a transaction to the nearest RSU. After the consensus, when the block is added to the blockchain, the CAVs download the block. Based on the correctness of the uploaded data, they update the reputation values of the RSUs.

2.2   Trust Model

Trust is a very important parameter in a blockchain network which entails the credibility of an entity in the network. In the CAV application, the network is dynamic and it is necessary to choose a robust trust model. The trust model used in this work is based on the reputations of the consensus nodes. Reputation depends on the extent of positive and negative interactions of vehicles with different RSUs. Positive interactions increase the reputation and negative interactions decrease the reputation. Positive and negative interactions are compiled using reputation models. Higher reputation translates into more trustworthiness and vice versa. Reputation plays an integral role when it comes to miner voting as it is an indicator that can be used by the stakeholders to prefer specific miners over the others.

2.3   Blockchain-Based Data Sharing CAV Scenario

Here we describe the blockchain-based data sharing scenario based on the enhanced dPoS [6] as summarized in Fig. 1.

Step 1: The CAVs having high stakes in the network act as stakeholders and RSUs as delegates. Stakeholders vote for their choice of miners. Out of the elected miners, a predefined number is selected as active miners, which act as block managers for the next few time instants, and the rest as standby miners. Block managers are the same as leaders in PBFT and its derivatives. Standby miners improve the security of the system by increasing the number of miners that verify the data. Verifiers are divided into different types based on their reputations. The CAVs share data with each other via Vehicle-to-Vehicle (V2V) communication. This data sharing record is sent to the nearest RSU via Vehicle-to-Infrastructure (V2I) communication. In a heterogeneous network, RSUs may be connected to different networks. Then this data is routed to the block manager.

Step 2: The block manager forms an unverified block out of this data and encodes smart contracts based on the number of verifier types in the system. Then this block is broadcasted to the whole network of verifiers. The verifiers work on the smart contracts based on their type, as doing so maximizes their utility. After verification, the results are sent to their local neighborhood, where these results are audited by verifiers in their one hop vicinity. After verification, this block is sent back to the block manager.

Step 3: Block manager receives the verified block from all the miners and verify whether 2/3 of the miners agree on the block creation or not. If the consensus is achieved, the block manager broadcasts this block to all the RSUs in the system to add to their local blockchains.

Step 4: After the block is added to the blockchain, AVs download the latest data block and check whether their transaction is added correctly. Based on that, they calculate the reputation of the respective miner.

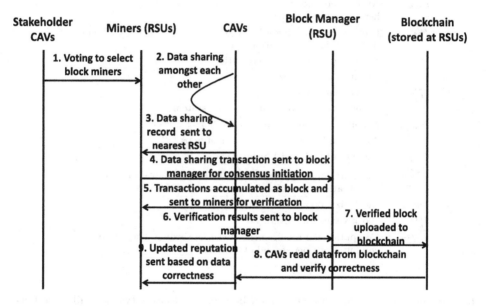

Fig. 1. Information flow of enhanced dPoS algorithm for data sharing

In the next section, we provide a latency and security analysis of this blockchain scheme for homogeneous and heterogeneous network conditions. It is important to understand how quickly malicious activities can be detected in CAV applications and this analysis provides a basis for that.

3 Latency and Security Analysis for CAV Data Sharing

In this section, we present latency and security analysis of blockchain-based CAV data sharing scenario. We present the analysis for both homogeneous and

Table 1. Description of Relevant Notations.

Notation	Description
M	Total active and standby miners in the system
k	Number of active miners in the system
N_{veh}	Number of AVs in the system
I_{vote}	Vote Size
r_v	Download and upload data rates of vehicles
r_m	Download and upload data rates of miners
r_l	Download and upload data rates of miners connected to lower generation network in heterogeneous network
r_h	Download and upload data rates of miners connected to higher generation network in heterogeneous network
r_{avg}	Average download and upload data rates of miners in heterogeneous network
P_{hl}	Probability of having a lower genration node at the outbound link of a higher generation node
I_k^d	Data block size before verification
I_k^r	Reputation block size
I_k^{SC}	Smart contract size
β	Number of types of verifiers in the system
N_{hops}	Maximum end-to-end number of hops
α	Averaging factor for the number of hops
N_{vd}	Number of RSUs with vehicular data
$\frac{Task_m^k}{c_m^k}$	Computational requirement of the smart contract relative to computations per second of a miner
O_k	Block size after verification
I_k^{ver}	Block verification overhead
$\frac{C_{inst}^k}{c_m^k}$	Computational requirement of the forwarding flow relative to computations per second of a miner

heterogeneous networks. As mentioned before, practical networks will have heterogeneous network nodes. Therefore, an end-to-end latency analysis in such networks is an important problem which has not been discussed previously in the literature. The description of different notations used in this paper are given in Table 1.

In this section, we compute the overall latency of block generation i.e., one round of consensus and block update for both homogeneous and heterogeneous networks, which is the sum of transmission, computational, and information diffusion latency. The computational latency comes from the computations required for parsing the IP headers and relaying the block. The information diffusion latency comes from broadcasting the block in the complete network. For heterogeneous networks, we also consider queuing latency as when we move from higher generation to lower generation nodes, packets are buffered at the lower generation node due to differences in data rates, and there is queuing latency. The data sharing scenario as described above is further split into sub-steps and the latency for each sub-step is analyzed as follows.

3.1 Latency Analysis for Homogeneous Networks

Step 1a: CAVs participate in a decentralized voting process to determine the miners. Voting results are broadcast. There is vote broadcast and vote tallying in this sub-step. The transmission latency (averaged over k rounds) for that is

$$\frac{M \times I_{vote}}{r_v \times k}$$

The computation latency (averaged over k rounds) is

$$\frac{C_{inst}}{c_m^k} \times N_{hops} + \frac{M^2}{k \times c_m^k}$$

and the diffusion latency (averaged over k rounds) is

$$\frac{(M \times I_{vote}) \times N_{hops}}{r_m \times k}$$

Step 1b: CAVs exchange data and share transactions (data and latest reputation scores) with the nearest RSU. The transmission latency of this process is

$$\frac{\frac{I_k^d + I_k^r}{N_{veh}}}{r_v}$$

The computation latency associated with this substep is

$$\frac{C_{inst}}{c_m^k}$$

The information propagation latency associated with this sub-step is zero because there is no broadcast of information.

Step 1c: RSUs route these transactions to the block manager of current round. There is no transmission latency. The computation latency is given as

$$\frac{C_{inst}}{c_m^k} \times N_{hops} \times \alpha$$

and the information propagation latency is given as

$$\frac{\frac{(I_k^d + I_k^r)}{N_{vd}} \times N_{hops} \times \alpha}{r_m}$$

Step 2a: Block manager forms an unverified block and encodes smart contracts based on number of verifier groups. The unverified block and the smart contracts are broadcast to the miners. The transmission latency of this process is

$$\frac{I_k^d + I_k^r + \beta I_k^{SC}}{r_m}$$

The computation latency is

$$\frac{C_{inst}}{c_m^k} \times N_{hops} \times \alpha$$

and the information propagation latency is

$$\frac{I_k^d + I_k^r + \beta I_k^{SC}}{r_m} \times N_{hops} \times \alpha$$

Step 2b: Miners work on the smart contract and get the block verified in their local neighborhood. There is no transmission latency of this process. The computational latency is given as

$$\frac{Task_m^k}{c_m^k}$$

and the information propagation latency associated with relaying the verification result to one hop neighborhood is

$$\frac{I_k^{ver}}{r_m}$$

Step 2c: Verified block is sent back to the block manager. There is no transmission latency associated with this sub-step. The computation latency is given as

$$\frac{C_{inst}}{c_m^k} \times N_{hops} \times \alpha$$

and the information propagation latency is given as

$$\frac{(I_k^d + I_k^r + I_k^{ver} + I_k^{SC})}{r_m} \times N_{hops} \times \alpha$$

Step 3: Block manager broadcasts the verified block to the network to be added to the local blockchain copies. The transmission latency of this process is

$$\frac{O_k}{r_m}$$

The computation latency of this process is

$$\frac{C_{inst}}{c_m^k} \times N_{hops} \times \alpha$$

and the information propagation latency is

$$\frac{O_k}{r_m} \times N_{hops} \times \alpha$$

Step 4a: Finally, CAVs download the latest data block and reputation opinions of the RSUs. This incurs only a transmission latency of

$$\frac{O_k}{r_v}$$

and no computation or information propagation latency.

Step 4b: Based on the correctness of the uploaded data, new reputation values are calculated for the relevant RSUs, which requires minimal computational latency and zero transmission, and information diffusion latency.

3.2 Latency Analysis for Heterogeneous Network

For heterogeneous network, the computational latency is the same as that in homogeneous networks. The transmission and propagation latency change based on the average data rate based on the number of nodes from different networks. The queuing latency comes from buffering of packets when we a higher generation RSU has a lower generation RSU on its outbound. The latencies for heterogeneous network are as follows.

Step 1a: The transmission latency of this sub-step is the same as that for homogeneous networks and the diffusion latency is

$$\frac{(M \times I_{vote}) \times N_{hops}}{r_{avg} \times k}$$

The queuing latency of this sub-step is

$$P_{hl} \times \frac{(M \times I_{vote}) \times N_{hops}}{r_h \times k} \times (\frac{r_h}{r_l} - 1)$$

Step 1b: The transmission latency of this process is the same as that for homogeneous networks. The information propagation latency and the queuing latency associated with this sub-step is zero because there is no broadcast of information.

Step 1c: There is no transmission latency. The information propagation latency is given as

$$\frac{\frac{(I_k^d + I_k^r)}{N_{vd}} \times N_{hops} \times \alpha}{r_{avg}}$$

and the queuing latency is given as

$$P_{hl} \times \frac{\frac{(I_k^d + I_k^r)}{N_{vd}} \times N_{hops} \times \alpha}{r_h} \times (\frac{r_h}{r_l} - 1)$$

Step 2a: The transmission latency of this process is

$$\frac{I_k^d + I_k^r + \beta I_k^{SC}}{r_{avg}}$$

The information propagation latency is

$$\frac{I_k^d + I_k^r + \beta I_k^{SC}}{r_m} \times N_{hops} \times \alpha$$

and the queuing latency is

$$P_{hl} \times \frac{I_k^d + I_k^r + \beta I_k^{SC}}{r_h} \times N_{hops} \times \alpha \times (\frac{r_h}{r_l} - 1)$$

Step 2b: There are no transmission and queuing latencies for this process. The information latency for this process is

$$\frac{I_k^{ver}}{r_{avg}}$$

Step 2c: There is no transmission latency of this process and the information propagation latency is given as

$$\frac{(I_k^d + I_k^r + I_k^{ver} + I_k^{SC})}{r_{avg}} \times N_{hops} \times \alpha$$

and the queuing latency is given as

$$P_{hl} \times \frac{\frac{(I_k^d + I_k^r)}{N_{vd}} \times N_{hops} \times \alpha}{r_h} \times (\frac{r_h}{r_l} - 1)$$

Step 3: The transmission latency of this process is

$$\frac{O_k}{r_{avg}}$$

and the information propagation latency is

$$\frac{O_k}{r_{avg}} \times N_{hops} \times \alpha$$

The queuing latency of this process is

$$P_{hl} \times \frac{O_k}{r_h} \times N_{hops} \times \alpha \times (\frac{r_h}{r_l} - 1)$$

Step 4: The latency of this step is the same for both homogeneous and heterogeneous networks as there is no role of RSUs in this step. The queuing latency is also zero (Table 2).

Table 2. Latency of One Complete Cycle

Steps	Description	Transmission Latency	Computation Latency	Information Propagation Latency	Queuing Latency (for heterogeneous networks)
Step 1	CAVs participate in a voting process to determine the miners. Voting results are broadcast	$\frac{M \times I_{vote}}{r_v \times k}$	$\frac{C_{inst}}{c_m^k} \times N_{hops} + \frac{M^2}{k \times c_m^k}$	$\frac{(M \times I_{vote}) \times N_{hops}}{r_m(r_{avg}\ for\ het) \times k}$	$L_{21} \times \frac{(M \times I_{vote}) \times N_{hops}}{r_2 \times k} \times \left(\frac{r_2}{r_1} - 1\right)$
	CAVs exchange data and share transactions (data and latest reputation scores) with the nearest RSU	$\frac{\frac{I_k^d + I_k^r}{N_{veh}}}{r_v}$	$\frac{C_{inst}}{c_m^k}$	0	0
	RSUs route transactions to the block manager of current round	0	$\frac{C_{inst}}{c_m^k} \times N_{hops} \times \alpha$	$\frac{\frac{(I_k^d + I_k^r)}{N_{vd}} \times N_{hops} \times \alpha}{r_m(r_{avg}\ for\ het)}$	$L_{21} \times \frac{\frac{(I_k^d + I_k^r)}{N_{vd}} \times N_{hops} \times \alpha}{r_2} \times \left(\frac{r_2}{r_1} - 1\right)$
Step 2	The unverified block and the smart contracts (SC) are broadcast to the miners	$\frac{I_k^d + I_k^r + \beta I_k^{SC}}{r_m}$	$\frac{C_{inst}}{c_m^k} \times N_{hops} \times \alpha$	$\frac{I_k^d + I_k^r + \beta I_k^{SC}}{r_m(r_{avg}\ for\ het)} \times N_{hops} \times \alpha$	$L_{21} \times \frac{I_k^d + I_k^r + \beta I_k^{SC}}{r_2} \times N_{hops} \times \alpha \times \left(\frac{r_2}{r_1} - 1\right)$
	Miners work on the SC and get the block verified in their local neighborhood	0	$\frac{Task_m^k}{c_m^k}$	$\frac{I_k^{ver}}{r_m}$	0
	Verified block is sent back to the block manager	0	$\frac{C_{inst}}{c_m^k} \times N_{hops} \times \alpha$	$\frac{(I_k^d + I_k^r + I_k^{ver} + I_k^{SC})}{r_m(r_{avg}\ for\ het)} \times N_{hops} \times \alpha$	$L_{21} \times \frac{(I_k^d + I_k^r + I_k^{ver} + I_k^{SC})}{r_2} \times N_{hops} \times \alpha \times \left(\frac{r_2}{r_1} - 1\right)$
Step 3	Block manager broadcasts the verified block to the network to be added to the local blockchain copies	$\frac{O_k}{r_m}$	$\frac{C_{inst}}{c_m^k} \times N_{hops} \times \alpha$	$\frac{O_k}{r_m(r_{avg}\ for\ het)} \times N_{hops} \times \alpha$	$L_{21} \times \frac{O_k}{r_2} \times N_{hops} \times \alpha \times \left(\frac{r_2}{r_1} - 1\right)$
Step 4	CAVs download the latest data block and reputation opinions	$\frac{O_k}{r_v}$	0	0	0
	CAVs calculate reputation updates	0	simple arithmetic computations	0	0

3.3   Threat Model and Security Analysis

In the described blockchain model, there are multiple threat dimensions. We are assuming that the only trustworthy party is the TA while the RSUs and CAVs can be compromised.

Malicious RSUs: Malicious RSUs can add incorrect verifications of the data to sabotage the data to be added to the blockchain. Malicious RSUs can also collude with the malicious vehicles to maintain a high reputation and have higher chances to stay in the system.

Malicious CAVs: Malicious high stake stakeholder CAVs can vote for their choice of malicious RSUs to serve as block managers or verifiers in the upcoming block verifications. CAVs can also collude with malicious RSUs to make them stay in the system longer by giving positive reputation opinions.

Based on the above threat model, we analyze the security of the system. Legitimate transactions, when reported incorrectly will be audited by the CAVs when they are added to the blockchain. They can report them as an incorrect transaction which will decrease the miner reputation. Since the data represents sensor readings which are very important for driving decisions, the data is very sensitive. Whenever data is uploaded to blockchain, the credibility of data is verified. Based on that, invalid data is identified and ignored.

The reputation value varies from 0 to 1 and the reputation threshold for honest and malicious miners is set to be 0.5. Different reputation models have different update sensitivities. In this analysis, we show that a malicious RSU will be eventually eliminated by the system as its reputation falls below the threshold. We consider three different reputation models i.e., MWSL reputation model [6], beta reputation model [5], and sigmoid-based reputation model [1] with the blockchain based dPoS scheme, to observe the number of rounds in which malicious activities can be detected which impacts system security. The upload and download speeds are different in 4G, 5G, and 6G networks, which impacts the transmission, information propagation and queuing latency of various steps. Therefore, through this analysis we can easily determine the overall time required to generate a single block in different networks. Based on the above analysis, we compare the time required to detect malicious miners in the system for all three networks. This will impact the network and security performance of the system.

4   Numerical Case Study

In this section, we design a numerical case study to apply our framework to determine end-to-end latency and security of blockchain-based CAV application in 4G, 5G, and 6G networks as well as a heterogeneous 5G/6G network.

4.1   Simulation Setup

We consider a large-scale CAV system with 10000 AVs and 10000 RSUs uniformly distributed in a $150\,km^2$ area. The download and upload data rates of

CAVs as well as RSUs are 10 Mbps for 4G, 500 Mbps for 5G and 100 Gbps for 6G. We consider an unverified block size, vote size, reputation block size, and the smart contract size to be 5MB, 100KB, 150KB and 150KB respectively. We consider 10 types of verifiers. There are 199 active miners and the number of RSUs with vehicular data in each round is a uniformly distributed random variable between [1000, 4000]. Task computational latency is assumed to be a constant value of 0.5 s in each case. The computational latency of each forwarding flow is assumed to be 10 μs [13]. The values of α and β are respectively set as 0.75 and 10. The maximum end-to-end number of hops are calculated assuming a coverage range of 250 m using [3], which comes out to be 97.

In heterogeneous networks, we assume that the nodes have different data rates. We assume that there are 50% 6G RSUs with overall 10% network nodes where there is a 5G node present at the outbound of 6G node. The rest of the nodes are 5G nodes. We call this case as Het1 in simulations. We also consider 25% 6G RSUs and because the probability of 5G node at the outbound of 6G node increases as overall 6G nodes in the system decrease, we consider that 15% 6G nodes have 5G nodes at their outbound. We call this case Het2. The remaining nodes are 5G nodes. Using these parameters, we calculate the time required for detecting malicious miners under different reputation models in different networks under simple and orchestrated attacks with different percentages of colluding AVs ranging between 0% to 50%.

In the simple attack, a malicious miner remains honest for first 20 rounds and then switches to bad behavior. In the orchestrated adversary model, the miner also acts honestly for the first 20 interactions to gain reputation. However, it then behaves maliciously and honestly for 15 and 5 interactions interchangeably. We determine the number of cycles required to detect malicious miners under different reputation schemes and multiply it with one cycle latency to calculate the minimum latency required to detect malicious miners.

4.2   Simulation Results

In Fig. 2, we compare the total time required for malicious miner detection in 4G, 5G, 6G, Het1 and Het2 networks for MWSL (M1), beta (M2) and sigmoid (M3) reputation models at different collusion rates (between malicious RSUs and CAVs) for simple adversary model. We simulated the three reputation models for both adversary models and calculated the number of interactions it will take to fall under the reputation threshold. In Fig. 3, we repeated the same results for the orchestrated adversary model. In both figures, due to the extremely large time needed by 4G network, we plot the y-axis on a logarithmic scale. This is a stacked bar graph, where the total height of the bar indicates the total latency in 4G network, the sum of first four, three and two segments indicate the latency in 5G network, Het2 network and Het1 network respectively, while the bottom portion indicates the latency in 6G network.

6G network can detect malicious miners in few seconds, as compared to 4G and 5G. It is clear that 4G and 5G are not feasible for such a system. However, the Het1 and Het2 networks show significant improvement over 5G performance. If we compare the reputation models, we observe that for lower collusion rates, in a simple attack scenario, all the reputation models combined with dPoS blockchain consensus have similar detection performance. For large collusion rates, there is a significant difference between the detection latency and M1 performs much better as compared to M2 and M3. At 40% collusion, M1 detects malicious miner in 48.7 s in 6G system. In Het1 and Het2, M1 detects malicious miners in 150.8 s and 200.3 s respectively. M2 and M3 reputation models combined with dPoS blockchain take 78.58 s and 79.23 s respectively for 6G. Het1 and Het2 perform the detection in 243.25 s & 323.1 s and 245.26 s & 325.78 s respectively. For 50% collusion rate, M1 takes 69.49 s, 215.1 s and 285.72 s for 6G, Het1 and Het2 respectively. M2 converges after an extremely large number of interactions, while M3 fails to detect the malicious miner. The results for 50% collusion are not plotted on the graph.

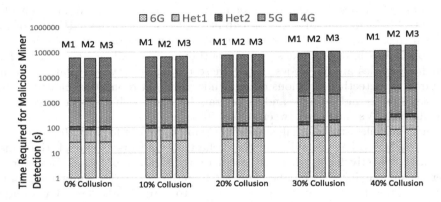

Fig. 2. Simple Adversary Model: Time required to detect malicious miner

For the orchestrated adversary attack shown in Fig. 3, at lower collusion rates, the three models show very similar behavior. However, even at 20% collusion rates, the time required for M1 becomes 43.5 s, 134.69 s and 178.91 s for 6G, Het1 and Het2 respectively. On the other hand, for M2 and M3, detection time is much larger at 61 s, 188.97 s & 251 s and 61.7 s, 190.98 s & 253.68 s respectively. At 30% collusion, M1 detects a malicious miner in 56.5 s, 174.9 s & 232.6 s whereas M2 detects it at more than triple the time i.e., 201.3 s, 623.2 s & 827.8 s. M3 has much higher latency than the upper limit of 400 interactions, which was set as a failure limit (the limit assumed in the simulations for 4G, 5G, and 6G and the heterogeneous networks are shown as dotted lines on the figure). For 40% collusion rate, M1 detects a malicious miner in 83.12 s, 257.3 s & 341.8 s whereas M2's latency is higher than the failure limit. M3 doesn't converge at all at this collusion rate. Based on these results we can see that when 6G is combined with blockchain in a large-scale CAV application scenario, M1 based dPoS consensus can detect malicious activity in few seconds (less than a minute in most cases). Heterogeneous deployment scheme also has very promising results and can be particularly useful for such timely detection.

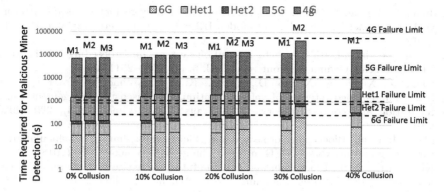

Fig. 3. Orchestrated Adversary Model: Time required to detect malicious miner

5   Conclusion

In this paper, we considered the use of blockchain for a challenging CAV application scenario that has stringent security requirements. We discussed enhanced dPoS consensus and combined it with three different reputation schemes, which are MWSL reputation, beta reputation, and sigmoid-based reputation schemes. To determine malicious miners in the system, we first computed the overall latency of block generation as the sum of communication, computational, information propagation and queuing latency. We then evaluated the performance of this scheme under simple and orchestrated adversary attack models. We did the same analysis for a heterogeneous network, where we validated our results with a 5G/6G hybrid network. Our results indicated that in large scale networks, MWSL reputation based enhanced dPoS scheme can detect orchestrated attacks in few seconds for 6G networks. Heterogeneous deployment schemes also perform relatively well. In comparison, 4G and 5G perform poorly, and might not be suitable for blockchain implementations. Further reduction in detection times may be achieved through less resource intensive consensus algorithms at the expense of some reduction in security performance.

References

1. Gai, F., Wang, B., Deng, W., Peng, W.: Proof of reputation: a reputation-based consensus protocol for peer-to-peer network. In: Pei, J., Manolopoulos, Y., Sadiq, S., Li, J. (eds.) DASFAA 2018. LNCS, vol. 10828, pp. 666–681. Springer, Cham (2018). https://doi.org/10.1007/978-3-319-91458-9_41
2. Hassan, N.U., Yuen, C., Niyato, D.: Blockchain technologies for smart energy systems: fundamentals, challenges, and solutions. IEEE Ind. Electron. Mag. **13**(4), 106–118 (2019). https://doi.org/10.1109/MIE.2019.2940335
3. Jerew, O., Blackmore, K.: Estimation of hop count in multi-hop wireless sensor networks with arbitrary node density. Int. J. Wirel. Mob. Comput. **7**(3), 207–216 (2014)

4. Jiang, H., Zhang, Z., Wu, L., Dang, J.: A non-stationary geometry-based scattering vehicle-to-vehicle MIMO channel model. IEEE Commun. Lett. **22**(7), 1510–1513 (2018)
5. Josang, A., Ismail, R.: The beta reputation system. In: Proceedings of the 15th Bled Electronic Commerce Conference, vol. 5, pp. 2502–2511 (2002)
6. Kang, J., Xiong, Z., Niyato, D., Ye, D., Kim, D.I., Zhao, J.: Toward secure blockchain-enabled internet of vehicles: optimizing consensus management using reputation and contract theory. IEEE Trans. Veh. Technol. **68**(3), 2906–2920 (2019)
7. Kang, J., et al.: Blockchain for secure and efficient data sharing in vehicular edge computing and networks. IEEE Internet Things J. **6**(3), 4660–4670 (2018)
8. Khan, A.H., et al.: Blockchain and 6G: the future of secure and ubiquitous communication. IEEE Wirel. Commun. 1–8 (2021). https://doi.org/10.1109/MWC. 001.2100255
9. Mollah, M.B., et al.: Blockchain for the internet of vehicles towards intelligent transportation systems: a survey. IEEE Internet Things J. **8**(6), 4157–4185 (2021). https://doi.org/10.1109/JIOT.2020.3028368
10. Parkinson, S., Ward, P., Wilson, K., Miller, J.: Cyber threats facing autonomous and connected vehicles: future challenges. IEEE Trans. Intell. Transp. Syst. **18**(11), 2898–2915 (2017)
11. Ferdous, M.S., Chowdhury, M.J.M., Hoque, M.A., Colman, A.: Blockchain consensus algorithms: a survey. arXiv preprint arXiv:2001.07091 (2020)
12. Singh, M., Kim, S.: Blockchain based intelligent vehicle data sharing framework. arXiv preprint arXiv:1708.09721 (2017)
13. Song, H.: Protocol-oblivious forwarding: unleash the power of SDN through a future-proof forwarding plane. In: Proceedings of the second ACM SIGCOMM Workshop on Hot Topics in Software Defined Networking, pp. 127–132 (2013)
14. Suthar, P., Agarwal, V., Shetty, R.S., Jangam, A.: Migration and interworking between 4G and 5G. In: 2020 IEEE 3rd 5G World Forum (5GWF), pp. 401–406. IEEE (2020)
15. Wan, L., Guo, Z., Chen, X.: Enabling efficient 5G NR and 4G LTE coexistence. IEEE Wirel. Commun. **26**(1), 6–8 (2019)

A Security Policy Engine for Building Energy Management Systems

Jiahui Lim, Wenshei Ong, Utku Tefek, and Ertem Esiner(✉)

Advanced Digital Sciences Center, Singapore, Singapore
{jiahui.lim,wenshei.ong,u.tefek,e.esiner}@adsc-create.edu.sg

Abstract. This paper presents a Policy Engine for securing building energy management systems (BEMSs), a class of industrial control systems (ICSs) requiring additional protection due to their complex and interconnected nature. The Policy Engine supports multiple deployment modes for legacy compliance and features seamless integration of new security policies. We have implemented a provenance verification solution and integrated it into the Policy Engine. To evaluate the effectiveness of the proposed solution, we have established a testbed that utilizes real BEMS equipment. We compared the security features and performance of the Policy Engine with a state-of-the-art security solution in BEMS, i.e., MQTT using TLS. Results indicate that the Policy Engine with provenance verification policy can secure BEMSs against signal injection, duplication, and remote attacks, with minimal operational impact.

Keywords: Authentication · Cyberphysical system · Cybersecurity · BEMS · Integrity · Policy · Provenance

1 Introduction

With the increasing automation and reliance on digital technologies in industrial control systems (ICS), the vulnerability to cyberattacks is a growing concern. To mitigate the risk of such attacks, various standards and protocols, such as IEC 62351 [11] and Transport Layer Security (TLS), have been developed to provide authentication and encryption, thereby ensuring data integrity and confidentiality. However, despite the availability of such measures, many critical infrastructure systems remain largely unprotected and vulnerable to cyberattacks, as evidenced by recent incidents [2,5].

Protection of building energy management systems (BEMSs) as a class of ICS comes with additional challenges. As with ICS, protecting BEMSs is critical for the safe and reliable operation of buildings and related infrastructure. BEMSs are traditionally designed as an isolated system utilized for controlling and monitoring a single building. However, BEMSs have been evolving into complex sub-systems that are intertwined physically and digitally with potentially unprotected connections. Measurements and control commands travel through

© The Author(s), under exclusive license to Springer Nature Switzerland AG 2023
J. Zhou et al. (Eds.): ACNS 2023 Workshops, LNCS 13907, pp. 231–244, 2023.
https://doi.org/10.1007/978-3-031-41181-6_13

multiple devices, often crossing the boundaries of multiple organizations including BEMS providers, building operators and cloud service providers for data storage and analytics. Even a minor security breach in one sector can cascade and escalate to the whole system. This poses the challenge of securing all components, as the attackers can gain access to BEMS via its weakest link. As BEMSs typically manage geographically dispersed assets, maintenance and upkeeping of security solutions can be challenging as well. Another major challenge is implementing security with minimal operational impact since high availability and timeliness of messages are of great importance in energy systems. Moreover, similar to other ICSs, it is often difficult to upgrade or replace the deployed devices to add security features. Therefore, legacy-compliant solutions with transparent plug-and-play hardware or application programming interface (API) with virtual segregation are desirable, rather than implementing security checks and validations within system components and the software itself.

This paper proposes a Policy Engine capable of running security policies tailored to the security requirements of the system to be protected. The Policy Engine can be configured to validate compliance with user-defined security rules by checking who is performing an action, who authorizes it, and whether the action aligns with the system's expected operation. The Policy Engine goes beyond basic policy verification and provides tools to comply with security rules. We equipped the Policy Engine with a provenance verification technology [6], which authenticates not only the source of a packet but also the entire path of nodes traversed by the packet. We also present our testbed that simulates a BEMS with real components, namely, sensors, industrial PCs running the gateway, publisher, broker, and subscriber software. We tested our Policy Engine and the provenance verification solution on the testbed. We compared the security features and performance against a state-of-the-art security solution in BEMS, i.e., MQTT using TLS.

The rest of this paper is organized as follows. In Sect. 2, we discuss examples of past attacks that underscore the importance of adequate security measures. We propose our Policy Engine as a solution in Sect. 3 with a provenance verification technology that we have implemented as a policy in our Policy Engine and introduce the BEMS testbed we set up to provide a realistic environment for evaluation purposes in Sect. 4. The evaluation results are shared in Sect. 5, followed by a comparison of our solution with other existing security measures in Sect. 6, and finally conclusions in Sect. 7.

2   Background and Known Attacks

There have been several cyberattacks on energy systems and ICS resulting in data loss and even physical damage. In this section, we discuss high-profile real-world cybersecurity incidents in ICS and relevant domains to define the attacker model in our scope.

The cyberattacks on ICS include command/data injection, denial-of-service (DoS), phishing and man-in-the-middle (MITM) attacks. One example is the attack on the Ukraine power grid in 2015, where the attackers used a combination of attacks [5]. The initiation of the attack was via spear-phishing which enabled the attackers to plant a malware in the system. Once they had access to the system, the attackers modified the configuration to keep the Uninterruptible Power Supply switched off during a power outage, resulting in a city-wide blackout lasting several hours. On top of that, the disks were wiped out, and a DoS attack on the call center disrupted the phone system, delaying the restoration of power significantly.

An IT software supplier company SolarWinds fell victim to a sophisticated supply-chain attack that resulted in hackers accessing confidential information from numerous US companies and government agencies. The attack was initiated by injecting malicious software into SolarWinds' software updating system, which created a backdoor to the IT systems of its customers. The attack remained undetected for several months until the damage became evident [3].

The VPN interface of a system can be a point of vulnerability, as it can be remotely accessed by attackers. For example, attackers can exploit a vulnerability such as Shellshock [16] to gain virtual access to a BEMS local area network. Once inside, they can execute shell commands on the VPN server, which would allow them to inject malicious commands into the system. Similarly, a malicious insider with knowledge of VPN credentials can remotely manipulate the system.

Attackers and malware can target devices that are less protected to gain access to a BEMS. The CrashOverride malware, for instance, demonstrated how advanced malware can be used to publish malicious control commands, execute features beyond its intended scope, and launch MITM attacks [4].

Based on the anecdotal evidence of attacks against ICS, we categorize most serious attacks under three broad categories:

- Malicious command/data injection: An attacker can replay, forge, or tamper with messages by mounting a MITM attack through a LAN or WAN.
- Injection via compromised or duplicated devices: Legitimate devices can be duplicated or compromised via malware to send or execute harmful commands using valid credentials.
- Remote attacks: Through the VPN interface, an attacker can virtually become a part of the system network, execute commands, and inject false data using the credentials of a legitimate device. A device under the control of malware can be exploited to mount a similar attack.

The above examples demonstrate the need for strong security guarantees, verification of the sources and intermediaries of commands, and the validation of actions in a system. To prevent command/data injection, it is essential to verify the source and integrity of messages. This protection is commonly achieved through message authentication. However, message source verification is insufficient for devices compromised via malware, as the source here is already a legitimate source in the system and possesses valid credentials.

To address the risk of injection through compromised rogue field devices, it's imperative to verify the message delivery path. If an attacker gains access to authorized source credentials and inserts a message through an alternate entry point (e.g., through VPN), verifying the delivery path enables the destination to check whether the message has indeed gone through the expected set of nodes.

3   Policy Engine

This section introduces the Policy Engine, and discusses its capabilities and deployment modes.

The Policy Engine is a tool to secure components and communications of a networked system. Given a set of policies selected by the user based on their needs, the Policy Engine enforces the policies on all incoming and outgoing packets. The Policy Engine also provides the tools at the source and intermediaries to comply with the enforced policies. Integration of new policies into the Policy Engine is straightforward and only requires the user to select the code files of the policies to be implemented.

Upon receiving a network packet, the Policy Engine runs all of its policies on the received packet, as shown in Fig. 1. The overall result of the Policy Engine operation is determined based on the result of each policy, and it will be used to determine the action that will be taken for that packet.

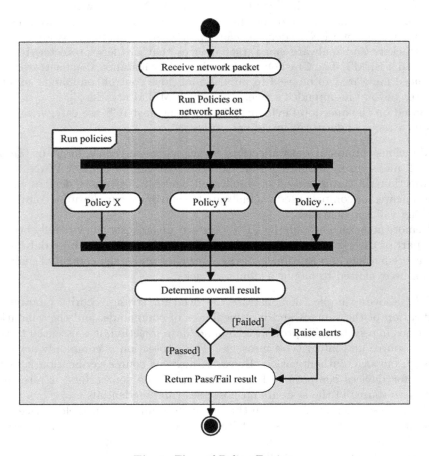

Fig. 1. Flow of Policy Engine

Depending on the deployment mode, the execution of the Policy Engine can be called either within the network communication module of the user's program or before and after the network system calls in the kernel, as further explained below. The devices on which Policy Engine can be deployed and where to equip Policy Engine are outside the scope of this work.

3.1 Deployment Modes

There are three deployment modes for the Policy Engine: API Mode, Bump-In-The-Wire (BITW) Mode and Sidebar Mode. For new systems or systems which have easily modifiable code, the API mode is suitable as the Policy Engine can be directly integrated into the user's system. However, for legacy systems which may be unfeasible to modify, the BITW and Sidebar modes could be the better options as the Policy Engine would run as a separate process. Alternatively, the Policy Engine may also be deployed in BITW or Sidebar Modes on a separate device if the user devices do not have the hardware capability to run it.

3.1.1 API Mode We provide a Policy Engine API that can interface with the existing device software. For this deployment mode, the functions to execute Policy Engine have to be called within the network communication module of the user's program – upon receiving a packet and just before sending out a packet.

3.1.2 Bump-In-The-Wire (BITW) Mode For the BITW deployment, the Policy Engine runs as a separate process alongside the user's program. Thus, the user's program does not require any modifications. The Policy Engine has to be executed before and after the kernel network calls for outgoing and incoming packets respectively, either in the same device or in a separate device that is connected between the user's device and the network. For this deployment mode, packets get intercepted by the Policy Engine to enforce the policies before continuing to the user device. Any packet that fails the checks will be dropped and thus will not reach the user device.

3.1.3 Sidebar Mode The Sidebar deployment of the Policy Engine is similar to the BITW mode in that the Policy Engine runs as a separate process and gets executed before and after the network system calls in the kernel. The main difference is that the packets do not get intercepted in the Sidebar mode; instead, copies of the packets get sent to the Policy Engine for checking. This allows the continuous flow of the user program as the Policy Engine acts as a warning system instead of completely rejecting failed packets.

3.2 Example Policies

This section presents example policies, some of which are integrated with the Policy Engine to demonstrate its capabilities. The Policy Engine can virtualize most network security functions typically implemented via firewalls, access control, intrusion detection, and monitoring systems. It can also provide virtual network segmentation with appropriate data egress policies if implemented in API or BITW modes. Implementing a security policy is as simple as selecting the policy code files from the user interface of the Policy Engine.

Besides enforcing network access control and traffic monitoring, filtering, and segregation, the Policy Engine can also execute cryptographic security functions to protect the data transmitted over the network. These functions include encryption, decryption, signing with digital signatures, Message Authentication Code generation, and verifications to guarantee confidentiality, integrity, and authentication [7,17]. The Policy Engine can adapt to different security requirements and scenarios by using different policy codes that specify the appropriate cryptographic algorithms and parameters.

The use of cryptographic security functions such as encryption and integrity verification is insufficient unless the destination device also ensures that the messages indeed go through the right network paths and hence undergo the necessary security checks implemented via the Policy Engine or other tools. For instance, a remote attacker in possession of the credentials of a device or user can bypass the firewalls and intrusion detection systems in sending a harmful command, unless the integrity of the command's delivery path (i.e., provenance) is verified. This motivates the implementation of a provenance verification policy at the Policy Engine.

We implemented a message authentication and provenance verification technology [6] as a policy in the Policy Engine. At a high level, the policy adds verifiable provenance information to the messages for the destination to check if the message followed an expected path. When equipped with the provenance verification policy, the Policy Engine at the source node wraps the message for additional security. The Policy Engine at each intermediate node wraps another layer around the message as a form of endorsement that they did, in fact, see the message. Finally, at the destination node, the Policy Engine unwraps the message to verify the source and path taken by the message before passing the message to the protected node.

3.3 Provenance Verification Policy

The provenance verification policy consists of five main algorithms: Setup, Initiate, Witness, Extend, and Verify. Setup is part of the configuration stage, while Initiate, Witness, Extend, and Verify are algorithms carried out on the fly when messages arrive and depart from each node. From this point onwards in this section, when we refer to "policy", we specifically mean the provenance verification policy implemented in the Policy Engine. Moving forward, we will provide a brief summary of each algorithm in the policy.

3.3.1 Setup In order to meet the stringent latency requirements for smart grids [1], the provenance verification policy uses pre-shared symmetric keys instead of public keys. Every device has its own master key and shares a derived

key with every destination node. These derived keys are referred to as Authentication Tokens (ATs). Setup creates the keys and authentication tokens and distributes them to all devices in the system.

3.3.2 Initiate At the source node, the policy generates a piece of cryptographic evidence h_0 from the AT between the source and destination nodes (AT_{SD}), the timestamp (ts) of the message being sent and the message itself (msg).

$$h_0 = hash(AT_{SD}, ts, msg)$$

The policy then forms a signature as follows, with sig_len being the length of the signature, ts the timestamp, h_0 the cryptographic evidence, op_I the Initiate operation indicator done by the policy, ID_S the unique identification of the source node and msg_len the length of the message being sent.

sig_len	ts	h_0	op_I	ID_S	msg_len

3.3.3 Witness When the packet passes through an intermediate node without getting modified, the policy generates a cryptographic digest h_1 from the previous digest h_0, the AT between that node and the destination node AT_{WD}, the timestamp of origin and the message:

$$h_1 = hash(h_0, AT_{WD}, ts, msg)$$

The policy then alters the signature that is already attached to the message to endorse that it witnessed the packet by adding an identification of itself ID_W with the indication of the Witness operation it performed op_W as well.

sig_len	ts	h_1	op_S	ID_S	op_W	ID_W	msg_len

3.3.4 Extend When the packet passes through an intermediate node which modifies the message, e.g., a protocol translation, the policy also alters the cryptographic evidence accordingly to include the AT between itself and the destination node (AT_{ED}) as well as the modified message (msg2).

$$h_2 = hash(h_1, AT_{ED}, ts, msg, msg2)$$

It then updates the signature to endorse that the packet did pass through and that the message was modified by the user device. The previous message is included in the new signature that is attached to the modified message, and the length of the modified message, msg2_len is added to the end of the signature as well.

sig_len	ts	h_2	op_S	ID_S	op_W	ID_W	msg	msg_len	op_E	ID_E	msg2_len

3.3.5 Verify At the destination node, the message has its final signature, which comprises the signature length, the timestamp of the origin of the message, the cryptographic evidence which is a chain of keyed cryptographic digests derived from all versions of the message and the nodes' ATs and the IDs of all nodes the message has passed through in order. The policy checks the authenticity of the cryptographic evidence and either accepts or rejects the message.

4   Testbed

In this section, we describe a typical BEMS, followed by our in-house testbed.

A typical BEMS comprises many components, such as sensors, actuators, a controller, and a user interface. These components are interconnected via a local area network (LAN) for sharing sensor data and transmitting control commands. Modern BEMSs also feature an external data collection server and an analytics service at a remote location, such as in public or private cloud servers. These remote servers are connected through standard wide area network (WAN) technologies.

The meters collect measurements such as voltage, temperature, airflow, and power consumption and send such data to the controller over the LAN. The controller then processes the data to determine if any action has to be carried out through the actuators. The motive of external data collection and analytics is to aggregate and monitor energy assets up to the component level in real-time. These data collection services provide a user interface enabling service providers to study the BEMS and incorporate/suggest actions for energy efficiency and better cost-to-performance ratio.

4.1   Testbed Implementation

We have sourced industrial PCs (IPCs) as well as energy meters from our industry partner, who specializes in providing building energy management systems and analytics. There are two types of IPCs used in the testbed, one type used for the broker and the other for the publishers and subscribers. The IPC type for the broker uses Intel(R) Core(R) i5-5200U @ 2.20 GHz, while the IPC type used for the publishers and subscribers employs Intel(R) Celeron(R) J1900 @ 1.99 GHz. Both IPC types have 4 GB of RAM and run Ubuntu 18.04 operating system. The energy meter used in the testbed is the Janitza UMG 96RM which comes with three current transformer inputs and is capable of measuring voltage, current, power, and frequency.

The meters and IPCs communicate using Modbus and MQTT (a standard for IoT messaging) protocols. MQTT is a lightweight messaging protocol that follows a publisher/subscriber model, where publishers publish messages under a "topic", and the subscribers subscribe to the "topic" to receive those messages.

Publishing and subscribing are facilitated by a broker, which acts as the middleman between publishers and subscribers and forwards messages of relevant topics to subscribers.

The testbed provides a testing environment for network security solutions, including our Policy Engine. Thus, in building the testbed, we had to account for realistic network behavior in the sense that the sensors measure real loads and send them to data analytics services, as in a modern BEMS product. We eliminated detailed controller functions in pursuit of creating an easy-to-grasp test environment focused on data collection. The testbed allows straightforward extensions for actuators, other sensors, as well as security appliances.

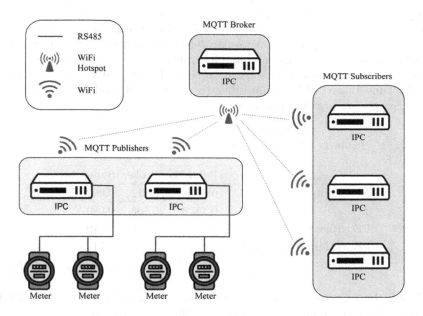

Fig. 2. High-Level Diagram of our testbed

As shown in Fig. 2, our testbed consists of energy meters on real electrical loads in an office, a set of IPCs for publishing energy meter data and relaying such data to the subscribers, and a user interface at the subscriber IPCs for displaying the collected data. Upon collecting the data from the meters via Modbus over RS485 serial communication, the publisher IPCs translate it to the MQTT protocol. The publishers send the collected data to the MQTT broker IPC via Wi-Fi. This link represents the Internet connection in a real implementation where the broker typically resides on a cloud server. The MQTT broker then forwards the messages to the subscribed (MQTT) IPCs (representing the service providers), depending on their interests. For ease of use, we implemented a user interface for the subscribers to visualize the collected energy meter data.

5 Evaluation

We briefly describe the implementation of the Policy Engine that we have used for the evaluation. The Policy Engine is developed in C++, and it employs OpenSSL, SQLite, and spdlog open-source libraries. The Policy Engine is deployed on the Industrial PCs described in the testbed explained in Sect. 4. The testbed has been designed to showcase the effectiveness of security solutions, including the one being tested in this instance, in preventing the attacks described in Sect. 2 and to evaluate their delay overhead.

To conduct a more precise evaluation of the Policy Engine's overhead, we deployed it in API Mode. This mode has lower "non-Policy Engine" overheads than other modes, ensuring greater accuracy in our assessment.

For the overhead assessment, the average time taken for a single packet is measured across 500 packets. We separately measured the time taken for the publisher to send a message successfully, the total time taken for the broker to receive the message and forward it to the subscriber of the relevant topics, and the time taken for the subscriber to receive and read the message. The measurements are presented in Table 1.

Table 1. Measurements of time taken per packet (in ms)

	Publisher	Broker	Subscriber
No security	0.384	0.112	0.062
TLS	0.427	0.163	0.080
PE without policies	0.387	0.172	0.110
PE with provenance policy	0.973	1.25	0.712

As can be seen from Table 1, there is no noticeable delay in the publisher and minimal delay in the broker and subscriber (approximately 0.05 ms) when running the Policy Engine as compared to no security setting. The delay values of the Policy Engine are comparable with that of the TLS. As for the Policy Engine equipped with the provenance verification technology, the delay increases by about 0.6 and 0.65 ms for the publisher and subscriber, respectively. The delay increase for the broker is considerably larger at 1.1 ms. These delay overheads are broken down and explained below.

The code of the provenance verification technology was analyzed to identify the main causes of delay, including database queries, hashing, reading the signature from the socket, and for the broker, map operations. The publisher, broker, and subscriber all perform multiple calls to query the database and at least one hash operation. The subscriber and broker have an additional step of reading the received signature from the socket, further contributing to the delay increase.

The main cause of the larger delay in the broker compared to the publisher and subscriber is that the broker performs several map operations for every message it receives. The time taken for a single map insertion where both the message and signature have to be stored together was measured to be about 0.15 ms.

Table 2. Protection against attacks ($\checkmark$ = Yes, $\times$ = Depends on deployment mode)

	Signal Injection	Duplication (of broker)	Remote Attacks
No Security			
TLS	$\checkmark$	$\times$	
Provenance policy	$\checkmark$	$\checkmark$	$\checkmark$

We also compare the Policy Engine against TLS on whether it provides protection against several attacks that were described in Sect. 2. Table 2 compares the security features of Policy Engine equipped with the provenance verification technology against TLS.

Both TLS and Policy Engine protect against signal/command injection attacks where the attacker attempts to inject malicious commands into the payload of messages in transit, as they perform message integrity and authenticity checks.

When equipped with provenance verification technology, the Policy Engine prevents duplication attacks, where the attacker uses a duplicated device to send valid messages. Assuming that the attacker is able to duplicate the entire device (including keys used for authentication/encryption), an attacker will be able to disguise as a valid source. As the Policy Engine can be deployed in a separate BITW device, the keys/tokens used are separated from the device. While the same applies to the BITW implementation of TLS, it is rarely used. Therefore, we indicated the protection of TLS against duplication attacks with "depends on deployment mode". The Policy Engine also checks if the message followed the expected path. Therefore, the message from a duplicated device fails the provenance check unless the attacker follows the same expected path for the messages from the duplicated device.

TLS fails to protect against attacks where the attacker remotely gains control over a valid device in the network, as malicious commands and messages will originate from a source with valid credentials. The Policy Engine, with the provenance verification technology, performs provenance and end-to-end path verification. Hence, even if the message source is valid, the message will be blocked if its path is not expected, which could prevent attacks via a compromised device.

Policy Engine can be loaded with other policies that perform automated verification of device configurations, firmware and updates, the contents of messages/commands generated by the devices and users, and the expected changes each action will cause in the system. The Policy Engine can thus virtualize most security functions, including those of firewalls, intrusion detection and deep packet inspection tools, boundary protection devices, and VPN gateways. While most of these security functions would otherwise require their own dedicated hardware or network function virtualization, Policy Engine potentially aggregates all such security functions into a plug-and-play security appliance.

The implementation represents a prototype solution that demonstrates the feasibility of our approach. Despite the promising results, we acknowledge that further optimizations are possible and desirable in future work.

6   Related Work

A commonly adopted security solution in the ICS industry is TLS and the datagram-based TLS, i.e., DTLS. TLS uses asymmetric cryptography and digital certificates that are issued by a trusted certificate authority to establish secure sessions with other hosts. The communication between the hosts throughout the session is both encrypted and protected for integrity. Certain network protocols used in ICS/BEMSs have already been extended to support TLS, such as Modbus, DNP3, MQTT and BACnet. However, while TLS provides source authentication, the encryption of application data in TLS may hinder additional protection measures, such as security middle-boxes like intrusion detection systems which need to analyze application data to detect anomalies in network traffic [8]. Middlebox-Enhanced TLS (ME-TLS) proposed by [13] and other proposed TLS variants for middle-boxes can solve this problem, but as evaluated above, TLS alone could not prevent duplication and remote attacks. Additionally, since TLS operates on top of the transport layer, it may require significant software and/or hardware updates or replacements, as well as network downtime, to deploy a TLS-enabled network.

Similar to our Policy Engine, commercial-off-the-shelf (COTS) hardware solutions are proposed to reduce downtime during deployment. Securosys' Centurion Network Encryptor [15] is such a COTS solution that offers point-to-point authenticated encryption using AES-256 GCM. Thales has a similar offering with their Network Encryptor series [19]. However, these solutions are fixed in their capabilities as they focus on providing security through authenticated encryption, which alone cannot prevent all attacks, as can be inferred from past attacks.

Various techniques have been proposed and researched for ensuring the integrity of data in ICSs, including digital signatures ECDSA [12], RSA [14], Message Authentication Codes [9], and other proprietary solutions tailored for ICS [10,18]. While these methods offer message authentication and enable intrusion detection systems to analyze application data, they lack a holistic approach to security, therefore, may fail to prevent the attacks discussed in this paper.

7   Conclusion

This paper presented a Policy Engine tool to enable BEMS operators and suppliers to enhance the cybersecurity of their systems. The tool allows easy integration with existing infrastructure with multiple deployment options and can be configured to run different checks based on security needs. The key feature of the

Policy Engine is that it is essentially a shell that can incorporate various security policies. In this work, we have demonstrated this by deploying a provenance verification security policy in the Policy Engine that performs provenance verification and end-to-end path verification without encryption. This ability to deploy customized policies to fulfill the security needs of ICS/BEMS operations differentiates it from other solutions. We also introduced a realistic BEMS testbed which has proven useful for testing out cybersecurity solutions for BEMS. Using the testbed, we evaluated the provenance verification technology running on the Policy Engine and compared its performance with state-of-the-art solutions. We would like to extend an invitation to other researchers to use our testbed for their own investigations.

Acknowledgements. This research is supported in part by the National Research Foundation, Prime Minister's Office, Singapore under its Campus for Research Excellence and Technological Enterprise (CREATE) programme, and in part by National Research Foundation, Singapore, Singapore University of Technology and Design under its National Satellite of Excellence in Design Science and Technology for Secure Critical Infrastructure Grant (NSoE_DeST-SCI2021TG-0002).

References

1. IEEE standard communication delivery time performance requirements for electric power substation automation. IEEE Std 1646–2004, pp. 1–36 (2005). https://doi.org/10.1109/IEEESTD.2005.95748
2. Alexander, O., Belisle, M., Steele, J.: Mitre att&ck for industrial control systems: design and philosophy. The MITRE Corporation: Bedford, MA, USA, p. 29 (2020)
3. Cassottana, B., Roomi, M.M., Mashima, D., Sansavini, G.: Resilience analysis of cyber-physical systems: a review of models and methods. Risk Anal. (2023)
4. Cybersecurity and Infrastructure Security Agency: Crashoverride malware (2017). www.us-cert.gov/ncas/alerts/TA17-163A. Accessed 17 Mar 2023
5. Case, D.U.: Analysis of the cyber attack on the Ukrainian power grid. Electr. Inf. Sharing Anal. Center (E-ISAC) **388**, 1–29 (2016)
6. Esiner, E., Mashima, D., Chen, B., Kalbarczyk, Z., Nicol, D.: F-pro: a fast and flexible provenance-aware message authentication scheme for smart grid. In: 2019 IEEE International Conference on Communications, Control, and Computing Technologies for Smart Grids (SmartGridComm), pp. 1–7. IEEE (2019)
7. Esiner, E., et al.: LoMoS: less-online/more-offline signatures for extremely time-critical systems. IEEE Trans. Smart Grid **13**(4), 3214–3226 (2022)
8. Fauri, D., de Wijs, B., den Hartog, J., Costante, E., Zambon, E., Etalle, S.: Encryption in ICS networks: a blessing or a curse? In: 2017 IEEE International Conference on Smart Grid Communications (SmartGridComm) (2017)
9. Hayes, G., El-Khatib, K.: Securing modbus transactions using hash-based message authentication codes and stream transmission control protocol. In: 2013 Third International Conference on Communications and Information Technology (ICCIT), pp. 179–184. IEEE (2013)
10. Hussain, S.S., Farooq, S.M., Ustun, T.S.: Analysis and implementation of message authentication code (MAC) algorithms for goose message security. IEEE Access **7**, 80980–80984 (2019)

11. IEC 62351–6:2020: Power systems management and associated information exchange-data and communications security-part 6: Security for IEC 61850 (2020)
12. Johnson, D., Menezes, A., Vanstone, S.: The elliptic curve digital signature algorithm (ECDSA). Int. J. Inf. Secur. **1**(1), 36–63 (2001)
13. Li, J., Chen, R., Su, J., Huang, X., Wang, X.: ME-TLS: middlebox-enhanced TLS for internet-of-things devices. IEEE Internet Things J. **7**(2), 1216–1229 (2020)
14. Rivest, R.L., Shamir, A., Adleman, L.: A method for obtaining digital signatures and public-key cryptosystems. Commun. ACM **21**(2), 120–126 (1978). https://doi.org/10.1145/359340.359342
15. Securosys SA: Centurion network encryptor securosys (2020). www.securosys.com/en/product/network-encryptor
16. Symantec Security Response: Shellshock: All you need to know about the bash bug vulnerability (2014). www.symantec.com/connect/blogs/shellshock-all-you-need-know-about-bash-bug-vulnerability. Accessed 17 Mar 2023
17. Tefek, U., Esiner, E., Mashima, D., Chen, B., Hu, Y.C.: Caching-based multicast message authentication in time-critical industrial control systems. In: IEEE INFOCOM 2022-IEEE Conference on Computer Communications, pp. 1039–1048. IEEE (2022)
18. Tefek, U., Esiner, E., Mashima, D., Hu, Y.C.: Analysis of message authentication solutions for IEC 61850 in substation automation systems. In: 2022 IEEE International Conference on Communications, Control, and Computing Technologies for Smart Grids (SmartGridComm), pp. 224–230. IEEE (2022)
19. Thales: High speed encryption network encryptor thales (2020). www.cpl.thalesgroup.com/encryption/network-encryption

EARIC: Exploiting ADC Registers in IoT and Control Systems

Eyasu Getahun Chekole$^{(\boxtimes)}$, Rajaram Thulasiraman, and Jianying Zhou

Singapore University of Technology and Design, Singapore, Singapore
{eyasu_chekole,jianying_zhou}@sutd.edu.sg,
thulasiraman_rajaram@alumni.sutd.edu.sg

Abstract. An analog-to-digital converter (ADC) is a critical part of most computing systems as it converts analog signals into quantifiable digital values. Since most digital devices operate only on digital values, the ADC acts as an interface between the digital and analog worlds. Hence, ADCs are commonly used in a wide-range of application areas, such as internet of things (IoT), industrial control systems (ICS), cyber-physical systems (CPS), audio/video devices, medical imaging, digital oscilloscopes, and cell phones, among others. For example, programmable logic controllers (PLCs) in ICS/CPS often make control decisions based on digital values that are converted from analog signals by ADCs. Due to its crucial role in various applications, ADCs are often targeted by a wide-range of physical and cyber attacks. Attackers may exploit vulnerabilities that could be found in the software/hardware of ADCs. In this work, we first conduct a deeper study on the ADC conversion logic to scrutinize relevant vulnerabilities that were not well explored by prior works. Hence, we manage to identify exploitable vulnerabilities on certain ADC registers that are used in the ADC conversion process. These vulnerabilities can allow attackers to launch dangerous attacks that can disrupt the behaviour of the targeted system (e.g., an IoT or control system) in a stealthy way. As a proof of concept, we design three such attacks by exploiting the vulnerabilities identified. Finally, we test the attacks on a mini-CPS testbed we designed using IoT devices, analog sensors and actuators. Our experimental results reveal high effectiveness of the proposed attack techniques in misleading PLCs to make incorrect control decisions in CPS. We also analyze the impact of such attacks when launched in realistic CPS testbeds.

Keywords: ADC Security · ADC Vulnerabilities · ADC Attacks · CPS Security · ICS Security · PLC Attacks · IoT Security

1 Introduction

A signal that represents a continuous range of values that varies over time is referred to as an analog signal [30]. Such signals can also be characterized by natural phenomena, such as lightning, earthquake, wind speed, volcano, sound

© The Author(s), under exclusive license to Springer Nature Switzerland AG 2023
J. Zhou et al. (Eds.): ACNS 2023 Workshops, LNCS 13907, pp. 245–265, 2023.
https://doi.org/10.1007/978-3-031-41181-6_14

waves, weight measurements, etc. Analog signals are often in the form of electrical energy, such as voltage, current or electromagnetic power. These signals typically come from sound, light, temperature or motion sensors. However, analog signals, which have more than 2 distinct readings, are not compatible in digital computation. This is because, digital devices, such as computers and microcontrollers (MCUs)[1], operate only on binary or digital values, i.e., 0 s and 1 s. As such, it is required to convert analog signals to digital values (i.e., discrete-time values) in order to process them using digital devices. This is where the analog-to-digital converter (ADC) [23] comes in handy. As the name implies, ADC is a system that converts an analog signal (i.e., continuous voltage values) to digital values, which can be understood by most computers and MCUs for digital computation. Most state-of-the-art MCUs have an inbuilt ADC. Therefore, such binary encoding of analog signals facilitates the interface between digital circuits and the real world. The analog-to-digital conversion logic of ADC typically involves three steps: sampling and holding (S/H), quantization and encoding [33].

ADCs are widely used in most digital systems that involve analog signals in its computations. These includes IoT, control systems (e.g., ICS/CPS), image processing, digital multimeters, cell phones, and medical imaging, to name a few. For example, PLCs [2] in ICS [34]/CPS [24,39] often make control decisions based on the inputs obtained from analog sensors (e.g., temperature, pressure and force sensors). However, they cannot directly use analog inputs as they cannot understand analog signals. Hence, they have inbuilt ADCs that serve to convert the analog signals into digital values. The PLCs will then use these digital values to make control decisions [21].

Since ADC is an integral and critical part of most computing systems, such as IoT and ICS/CPS, it has been targeted by various types of cyber criminals. The attackers may exploit vulnerabilities that could be found in the hardware or software of ADCs. For example, Bolshev et al. [5] has exploited vulnerabilities in the sampling frequency and dynamic range of the ADC conversion logic. There are also attacks that exploited the strong correlation between the ADC digital output codes and the ADC supply current waveforms [17]. Other attacks exploited fast attack automatic gain control (AGC) vulnerability in ADC [3,16,19]. Other class of attacks exploited the DAC-to-DAC crosstalk vulnerability in the ADC conversion logic [22,31,36]. Numerous side-channel attacks have also exploited various types of vulnerabilities in ADC [4,11,13,26,27,29]. Hardware trojan attacks were also launched on the analog circuits of ADCs [12]. Other researchers have conducted a security analysis on the output signals of the ADC datapath and its control unit [35] and ADC power noise measurement attacks [37]. However, we are not aware of existing attack techniques in the literature that specifically exploit vulnerabilities related to ADC registers (the smallest and fastest memory locations that are built into the processor). Hence, this work aims to bridge this gap in ADC security.

---

[1] https://www.arrow.com/en/research-and-events/articles/engineering-basics-what-is-a-microcontroller.

In this work, we first conduct a deeper analysis and study on ADCs to explore exploitable vulnerabilities in the analog-to-digital conversion logic. In particular, we study the various types of ADC registers involved in the analog-to-digital conversion process. After systematically analyzing the nature of these registers, we find out that most of them are vulnerable to a manipulation attack. This is because, registers for low-end MCUs are often controllable by user code and have no or little protections built in against unauthorized manipulations. Consequently, an attacker may modify or clear certain values or flags of the registers to deceive the output of the ADC conversion logic. Moreover, the attacks can be performed in a stealthy way so that it will be very hard to be detected using conventional techniques. The attacks can also be carried out physically or remotely through malicious code injection or malevolent system configuration. In control systems, such as ICS/CPS, systematically manipulated ADC outputs can mislead PLCs to make wrong control decisions. This may, in return, result in a disaster to the physical plant of the ICS/CPS. To the best of our knowledge, there are no prior attacks presented in the literature that specifically targeted ADC registers to deceit the ADC conversion process.

To scrutinize the actual exploitability of the registers, we design EARIC (Exploiting ADC Registers in IoT and Control systems) – a scheme comprising the three types of attacks we designed to manipulate the ADC conversion logic. In EARIC, we particularly target three critical ADC registers that are commonly used in the ADC conversion logic. This includes, ADC multiplexer selection register (ADMUX), analog comparator control and status register (ACSR), and two ADC data registers (i.e., ADC High register (ADCH) and ADC Low register (ADCL)). By systematically manipulating the values or flags of these registers, we manage to deceive or interrupt outputs of the ADC. That means, we force the ADC to return undesirable digital values from analog signals. To this end, we design and perform three types of attacks on the ADC conversion logic: (1) Deceiving the ADC conversion process - changing the expected ADC output into a totally different value; (2) Creating denial of service (DoS) in the ADC process - hanging the ADC conversion process and causing system unavailability; (3) Resetting the ADC conversion process - making the ADC to always return an empty output. Finally, we assess and evaluate the effectiveness of the proposed attacks using a minimalist CPS (mini-CPS) testbed we designed using IoT devices, such as Arduino (as a soft PLC), analog sensors and actuators.

In general, the main motivation of this work is to show that dangerous stealthy attacks can be launched into critical systems by exploiting certain ADC registers. In this work, we make the following technical contributions.

1. We conduct a deeper study in the ADC conversion logic and identify vulnerabilities on the ADC registers used in the analog-to-digital conversion process.
2. We design and perform three types of attacks by exploiting the vulnerabilities we identified.
3. We assess and evaluate the effectiveness (in terms of accuracy, efficiency and impact) of the proposed attacks using an IoT-based mini-CPS testbed we designed.

2   Background

In this section, we provide relevant background information to this work. Specifically, we provide a high-level information on the ADC conversion logic and cyber-physical systems (CPS). For easy reference, Table 1 lists out all the relevant acronyms and notations used in this paper.

Table 1. Description of acronyms and notations

Notation	Description	Notation	Description
ACBG	Analog comparator band gap	DAC	Digital-to-analog converter
ACD	Analog comparator disable	DoS	Denial of service
ACIC	Analog comparator input capture enable	FS	Full scale
ACI	Analog comparator interrupt	GND	Ground
ACIE	Analog comparator interrupt enable	GUI	Graphical user interface
ACIS	Analog comparator interrupt mode select	HMI	Human machine interface
ACME	Analog comparator multiplexer enable	ICS	Industrial control systems
ACO	Analog comparator output	IF	Intermediate frequency
ACSR	Analog comparator control and status register	IoT	Internet of things
ADC	Analog-to-digital converter	LM35	An analog temperature sensor
ADMUX	ADC multiplexer selection register	LSB	Least significant bit
ADCH	ADC high register	MCU	Microcontroller
ADCL	ADC low register	MSB	Most significant bit
ADEN	ADC enable	MUX	Multiplexer selection register
ADFR	ADC free running	PCM	Pulse code modulation
ADIE	ADC interrupt enable	PLC	Programmable logic controller
ADIF	ADC interrupt flag	PSA	Power side-channel attack
ADPS	ADC pre-scaler selection	R/W	Read/Write
ADSC	ADC start conversion	REFS	Reference selection
AREF	Analog reference	S/H	Sampling and holding
ADLAR	ADC left adjust result	SAR	Successive approximation register
ADMUX	ADC multiplexer selection register	SCADA	Supervisory control and data acquisition
AIN	Analog input pin	SoC	System-on-Chip
AVCC	Analog voltage common collector	SRAM	Static random-access memory
CPS	Cyber-physical systems	VREF	reference voltage

2.1   Overview of ADC

Analog and Digital Signals. As highlighted in the introduction, analog signals are electromagnetic signals that are characterized by a series of continuous values that varies with time. These signals are illustrated in Fig. 1. Such signals can be obtained from sound, temperature, light, and motion phenomena using analog sensors.

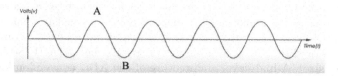

Fig. 1. Analog signals

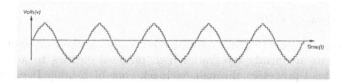

Fig. 2. Digital signals

Analog signals can be used as an input to solve various real-world problems. For example, IoT services and control systems can use them to automate or control processes. However, these signals cannot be directly used since digital devices, such as computers and microcontrollers, can read only digital values. Hence, the analog signals need to be first converted to digital signals before it is used by digital devices further computations. Unlike analog signals, which are represented by a sequence of continuous values, digital signals are broken down into a set of discrete values with time series or sampling rates. It usually have only two values – high (1) and low (0). Consequently, all values in digital signal transmissions are in the form of 0's and 1's. Digital signals are illustrated in Fig. 2.

Analog to Digital Conversion. The conversion of analog signals to digital signals is carried out by an analog-to-digital converter (ADC). In other words, ADCs serve to convert continuous-time analog signals to discrete-time digital signals, which will be consumed by digital devices for digital computations. Hence, most digital devices have builtin ADC, integrated with their processors. They can also be connected to an external ADC.

ADCs convert analog signals to digital signals using pulse code modulation (PCM)[2] method, which involves three main steps – sampling, quantizing and encoding [15,32]. ADCs on most microcontrollers, e.g., PIC32[3], typically have a 10-bit wide resolution, i.e., with 1024 quantization levels. Most microcontrollers also have multiple analog input channels due to their multiplexed ADC. For example, the PIC32MX460F512L[4] microcontroller has 16 10-bit wide ADC channels. The ADC analog comparator [25] is an essential building block in ADC

---

[2] https://www.tutorialspoint.com/digital_communication/
digital_communication_pulse_code_modulation.htm.

[3] https://www.microchip.com/en-us/products/microcontrollers-and-
microprocessors/32-bit-mcus/pic32-32-bit-mcus.

[4] https://www.microchip.com/en-us/product/PIC32MX460F512L.

that compares two input voltages and produces an output. ADCs also involve a wide-range of memory registers that play various roles in the analog-to-digital conversion process. For example, the ADC's output data, i.e., the converted digital value, is stored in a 16-bit double data registers, i.e., ADCH (8-bit size) and ADCL (8-bit size). A high-level architecture of the ADC conversion logic involving the main memory registers is illustrated in Fig. 3. A detailed discussion of some of the registers is also provided in Sect. 4.

2.2   Overview of CPS

Cyber-physical systems (CPS) are engineering systems where computations and communications are firmly integrated with physical entities to automate and control industrial processes through feedback control [24,39]. It comprises the following main entities [6]: physical plant (the physical system where actual processes take place), sensors (devices that read state information of physical processes), PLCs (embedded devices that issue control commands based on sensor inputs), actuators (physical entities that implement control commands issued by PLCs), SCADA [38] (a software designed for process monitoring and controlling), HMI (a system to display the state information of physical processes), and historian server (a server used to store operational and historical data). A typical CPS is also constrained by stringent real-time and availability requirements [9].

As discussed above, the PLC is at the heart of the CPS. It issues control commands based on the inputs obtained from sensors. However, the sensors could be digital or analog. In the latter case, the PLC cannot read analog signals like many other digital devices (see the discussion in Sect. 2.1). Hence, the ADC is required to convert the analog signals to digital values before the PLC uses them to make control decisions. To facilitate the conversion process, most PLCs nowadays come with inbuilt ADCs.

3   Threat Model

In our threat model, we consider adversaries that target digital systems, such as IoT and control systems, by exploiting vulnerabilities of the ADC registers that are used in the analog-to-digital conversion logic. The goal of the assumed adversary is manipulating outputs of the ADC in a stealthy manner so that it cannot be easily detected using conventional techniques. In fact, detecting the assumed attack is even more difficult since it is to be performed on the interface between the physical and digital worlds.

In reality, no attack would be successfully performed without creating a connection with the targeted device. Therefore, in our threat model, we assume that a connection can be established with the targeted digital devices (e.g., PLCs in CPS) either physically (e.g., via a serial connection) or remotely (e.g., via the Internet). Hence, we consider both physical attacks (e.g., insider attacks) and remote attacks (i.e., cyberattacks) in our threat model. In the former case, the attack can be performed by injecting malicious code to the targeted device through a serial connection. In the latter case, the attack can be launched by uploading malicious code to the targeted device over Internet. Note that most digital devices (including IoT and control devices) nowadays are connected to the Internet to facilitate over-the-air OS/firmware update or remote code upload to the devices. For example, the Arduino board has an Ethernet bootloader[5] that allows users to upload code remotely. Such facilities may allow the adversary to remotely upload malicious code to the devices.

In either physical or remote attack, the adversary is required to systematically tailor malicious code that allows him to control the registers of low-end MCUs. Note that the ADC registers can be controlled by user code and have no or little underlying protections against manipulation attacks. Hence, the adversary can manipulate the default values of the registers using his tailored malicious code. The designed malicious code can be injected to the device's firmware. In some cases, the attacks might be performed through malevolent system configurations. In our case, we perform the attacks by injecting our malicious code into the Arduino firmware (details are provided in Sect. 4).

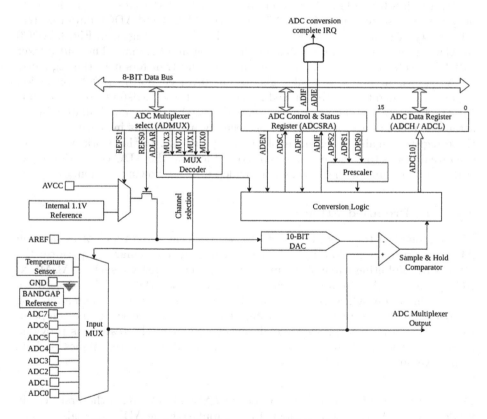

Fig. 3. A high-level architecture of ADC with registers

---

[5] https://github.com/loathingKernel/ariadne-bootloader.

4   EARIC: The Proposed Attacks

4.1   Overview

In this section, we introduce EARIC – a scheme comprising the three attack techniques we designed. As discussed in the preceding sections, we propose and develop new ADC attack techniques by exploiting the registers used in the analog-to-digital conversion logic. To simplify the presentation of our proposed attacks, it is essential to highlight how the ADC conversion logic works and the relevant registers involved in the process. As discussed in Sect. 2.1, ADC converts the voltage value on the analog input pin and returns a digital value from 0 to 1023 (for a 10-bit wide ADC), relative to the reference value. The analog input channel is selected using an analog multiplexer [18], and the input value is processed in ADC with a reference voltage for certain clock timings. When the analog-to-digital conversion is completed, the output result (often called the "ADC output data") is stored in the two ADC data registers, i.e., ADCH and ADCL (each 8-bit wide). More precisely, for a 10-bit ADC resolution, the ADC output will be stored in the 9th to 0th bits of the ADCH and ADCL data registers (cf. Fig. 4). A typical schematic of ADC is illustrated in Fig. 3. In Fig. 3, ADC0 to ADC7 represents the input pins for the analog input signals. The multiplexer (MUX) selects the input voltage from the pins and transfers it to the registers.

As shown in Fig. 3, several registers are involved in the ADC conversion logic. As highlighted in the preceding sections, these registers are vulnerable to attacks since its default values (data or flags) can be manipulated by an attacker. This is because, there are no security mechanisms in place to protect these registers against such malevolent manipulations. In this work, we exploit such weaknesses to perform three types of attacks on the ADC conversion logic. A detailed account of the attacks is provided in the following section.

4.2   The Proposed Attacks

As mentioned in the preceding sections, we perform three types of attacks on ADC to scrutinize exploitability of its registers. In particular, we perform the attacks by exploiting three of the most critical ADC registers, such as ADMUX, ACSR, and the ADC data registers (i.e., ADCH and ADCL). The attacks are tested using a mini-CPS testbed simulating an alarm system based on an analog temperature sensor. In brief, the system triggers an alarm when the temperature read is beyond a threshold. A detailed account of the testbed is provided in Sect. 5. Below, we discuss each of the proposed attack techniques and its respective outcomes.

Deceiving the ADC Conversion Logic (Attack 1). With the first attack, we deceive the ADC conversion logic by manipulating the ADMUX register. The ADMUX register is used to select the reference voltage as well as to determine which analog input channel is to be chosen. Furthermore, this register is used to determine whether the ADC output data should be left-justified (i.e., the output data is to be read from the left-most bits) or right-justified (i.e., the output data is to be read from right-most bits) with respect to the 16-bit ADC data registers (i.e., ADCH + ADCL). As shown in Table 2, the ADMUX register comprises 8 bits. A high-level discussion of the bits is provided as follows.

- *REFS (Reference Selection Bits)*: REFS1 (Bit 7) and REFS0 (Bit 6) are reference selection bits in ADMUX that are used to select the voltage reference for the ADC. The internal voltage reference options may not be used if an external reference voltage is applied to the AREF pin.

- *ADLAR (ADC Left Adjust Result)*: ADLAR (Bit 5) affects the presentation of the ADC output data in the ADC data registers (refer Sect. 4.2). Depending on the value set to the ADLAR bit, the ADC output data can be either right-justified (i.e., ADLAR = 0) or left-justified (i.e., ADLAR = 1) in the ADCH and ADCL data registers. The default mode is right-justified. The left-justified mode is not supported by most microcontrollers, including the Arduino board we used in our experimental setup (cf. Sect. 5).

- *MUX3 (Multiplexer)*: MUX3 (Bit 0 to 3) are the analog channel selection bits that are used to select the analog input channel (refer ADC0 to ADC7 in Fig. 3). A detailed account of how the analog channel selection bits work in ADC can be found in [28].

Attack Synopsis: The default values of the ADMUX register bits are shown in Table 2. That is, REFS1 is '1', REFS0 is '1', ADLAR is '0', and MUX0 to MUX3 is '0'. As discussed above, the value of ADLAR affects the presentation of the ADC output data in the ADCH and ADCL data registers. By default, the ADC output data is right-justified (i.e., ADLAR = 0). That means, the output data will be read from the 9th to 0th bits of the ADCH and ADCL data registers (for a 10-bit ADC resolution). The ADCH and ADCL data presentation with respect to the ADLAR value (i.e., '0' or '1') is illustrated in Fig. 4. However, as shown in Table 3, the ADLAR bit of the ADMUX register can be set to '1' to reverse the ADC output data presentation (i.e., left-justified). Meaning, the ADC output data will be read from the 15th to 6th bits, where the 15th to 10th bits contain garbage (junk) data as shown in Fig. 4. When the digital device (e.g., the PLC in CPS) tries to read the ADC output data, it will be referred to the

Table 2. ADMUX register bits with its default values

ADMUX Bits	REFS1 (Bit 7)	REFS0 (Bit 6)	ADLAR (Bit 5)	- (Bit 4)	MUX3 (Bit 3)	MUX2 (Bit 2)	MUX1 (Bit 1)	MUX0 (Bit 0)
Read/ Write	R/W	R/W	R/W	R	R/W	R/W	R/W	R/W
Default Values	1	1	0	0	0	0	0	0

Table 3. ADMUX register bits after manipulating the ADLAR bit

ADMUX Bits	REFS1 (Bit 7)	REFS0 (Bit 6)	ADLAR (Bit 5)	- (Bit 4)	MUX3 (Bit 3)	MUX2 (Bit 2)	MUX1 (Bit 1)	MUX0 (Bit 0)
Read/ Write	R/W	R/W	R/W	R	R/W	R/W	R/W	R/W
Bit Values (ADLAR = 1)	1	1	1	0	0	0	0	0

garbage location, which returns an undesirable value (often a very high value). In practice, this attack might be achieved in different ways. For example, it could be launched by sending a malicious ADC command to the PLC at runtime or by systematically synthesising and injecting a malicious code to the PLC firmware. In our case, we follow the latter. We inject the following code into the Arduino firmware, which sets the ADLAR bit to '1'.

$$ADMUX \mathrel{|}= (1 << 5);$$

After performing the above attack on our experimental setup, the ADC was forced to return a temperature of 1588.13°C from the analog temperature sensor even though the actual temperature reading was 24.49°C. The output of this attack is depicted in Fig. 5. This misleads the PLC to issue and send a wrong control command (i.e., "ON" command) to the actuator, i.e., a siren alarm set in our experimental setup (refer Sect. 5). As a result, the siren alarm was triggered even though the actual temperature was below the threshold. That means, the wrong ADC read from the garbage location misleads the PLC to make a wrong control decision, which in turn could cause a disaster or damage to the CPS plant.

In sum, the main aim of this attack is deceiving the ADC output data presentation on the ADC data registers (i.e., ADCH and ADCL) by manipulating the ADLAR value on the ADMUX register. Consequently, PLCs will be forced to read undesirable ADC output data, hence misleading them to make wrong control decisions. A high-level architectural illustration of this attack is provided in Fig. 6. As shown in Fig. 6, the attack is performed on the ADLAR flag of the ADMUX register and, consequently, the ADCH and ADCL data registers are impacted.

Creating a DoS Attack on the ADC Process (Attack 2). In this attack, we create a denial of service (DoS) attack on the ADC conversion process by manipulating the ADC analog comparator control and status register (ACSR). As highlighted in Sect. 2, the ADC analog comparator [25] is an essential part of the ADC conversion process. It is managed and controlled by the ACSR register. As depicted in Table 5, the ACSR register is represented by 8 bits comprising Analog Comparator Interrupt Mode Select (ACIS0 and ACIS1), Analog Comparator Input Capture Enable (ACIC), Analog Comparator Interrupt

ADLAR = 0

ADCH								ADCL							
15	14	13	12	11	10	9	8	7	6	5	4	3	2	1	0
G	G	G	G	G	G	x	x	x	x	x	x	x	x	x	x

ADLAR = 1

Fig. 4. ADC output data presentation in ADCH and ADCL registers with respect to the ADLAR value *Note: "G" is for garbage data, "x" (from bit 9 to 0) represents the ADC output data values in binary format, i.e., 0's and 1's. For example, Table 4 shows how a temperature reading of 24.49°C is stored in the ADCH and ADCL data registers.*

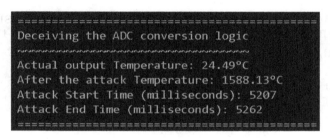

Fig. 5. Output of Attack 1

Enable (ACIE), Analog Comparator Interrupt (ACI), Analog Comparator Output (ACO), Analog Comparator Band Gap (ACBG) and Analog Comparator Disable (ACD). All the ACSR bits except bit 5 (which is read-only) are readable and writable (R/W). The default value of these bits is '0' except ACO, which is not applicable (NA).

Attack Synopsis: Each logical bit in the ACSR register plays different roles and functionalities in the ADC conversion logic, depending on the logical value (i.e., 0' or 1') set to it. For example, the analog comparator will be disabled if the logical bit ACD is set to 1', the analog comparator interruption will be enabled if the logical bit ACIE is set to 1', etc. A detailed information regarding the roles and functionalities of the ACSR bits in the ADC conversion logic can be found in [28]. When we simultaneously set the ACD and ACIE bits to 1' in the ACSR register, the ADC conversion process will hang, hence leading to DoS attack. This will render system unavailability, which is a critical concern in time-sensitive systems, such as CPS. Our construction of *Attack 2* (i.e., DoS attack) in the ADC conversion logic is formally captured as follows:

$$DoS\_Attack := (ACD == 1) \wedge (ACIE == 1)$$

In our experimental setup, we perform this attack by injecting the code "*ACSR — = 0b10001000;*" into the Arduino firmware. Here, the 4th bit (i.e., ACIE) and 8th bit (i.e., ACD) of the ACSR register are set to 1', which causes the system to hang (the output is shown in Fig. 7).

Table 4. The ADC output data presentation in data registers

ADCH								ADCL							
15	14	13	12	11	10	9	8	7	6	5	4	3	2	1	0
G	G	G	G	G	G	0	0	0	1	0	0	1	1	0	0

Table 5. ACSR register bits

ACSR Bits	ACD (Bit 7)	ACBG (Bit 6)	ACO (Bit 5)	ACI (Bit 4)	ACIE (Bit 3)	ACIC (Bit 2)	ACIS1 (Bit 1)	ACIS0 (Bit 0)
Read/ Write	R/W	R/W	R	R/W	R/W	R/W	R/W	R/W
Initial Values	0	0	NA	0	0	0	0	0

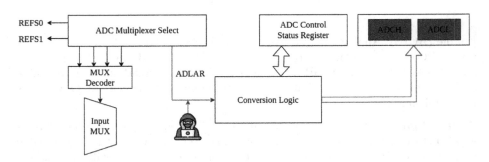

Fig. 6. Attacking the ADMUX register

Resetting the ADC Process (Attack 3) In this attack, we reset the ADC process by manipulating the ADC data registers, such as ADCH and ADCL. As discussed in the preceding sections, ADC has two 16-bit wide data registers, i.e., ADCH and ADCL. These registers are used to store the ADC digital output obtained from the analog conversion. For example, Table 4 shows how our

```
> Executing task: C:\Users\rtram\.platformio\penv\Scripts\platformio.exe device monitor <

--- Available filters and text transformations: colorize, debug, default, direct, hexlify,
--- More details at https://bit.ly/pio-monitor-filters
--- Miniterm on COM6  9600,8,N,1 ---
--- Quit: Ctrl+C | Menu: Ctrl+T | Help: Ctrl+T followed by Ctrl+H ---
```

Fig. 7. The output of *Attack 2*

temperature sensor reading of 24.49°C is stored in the ADC data registers. The equation to translate the sensor reading temperature value to binary format and vice versa can be referred in [1].

Attack Synopsis: Like the other ADC registers, the ADC data registers (i.e., ADCH and ADCL) can also be manipulated by an attacker. One way to manipulate these registers would be by clearing the ADC outcome data stored in them. However, we cannot directly do that since these registers are read-only. Meaning, we can only read the data stored in these registers, but not modifying it. So, how can we achieve the attack on the ADC data registers? We discuss details of our proposed attack technique as follows.

The ADC output data is read by the the "analogRead()" function – a function (often used in Arduino) that reads the digital value from a specified analog pin. However, there are some implicit tasks to be performed before reading the digital value. First, the analog value (e.g., the voltage between 0 and 5V) from the analog pin will be converted to a digital value between 0 to 1023 (for a 10-bit long ADC). As discussed in the preceding sections, this digital value (i.e., the ADC output) will be then stored in the ADCH and ADCL registers. Then, the "analogRead()" function defines two variables, say "low" and "high", to read the ADC output from the ADCL and ADCH data registers, respectively. That means, the "low" variable reads values from the ADCL register and the "high" variable reads values from the ADCH register. The final ADC output will be a combination of the two variables, i.e., $low = ADCL \&\& high = ADCH$. However, we can attack this logic by including a malicious script in the device's (the Arduino in our case) firmware, and particularly in the "analogRead()" function. Instead of assigning the ADCL and ADCH register values to the "low" and "high" variables mentioned above, we can maliciously assign 0' to both. That means, we inject the "$low = 0;$" and "$high = 0;$" codes to the source-code of the "analogRead()" function in the Arduino firmware. This might also be done through system configuration. This leads the ADC output to be always 0' instead of the actual result. We tested this attack on our temperature reading setup. Even though the actual temperature was 24.17°C, the temperature reading after launching the attack was always 0°C. The outcome of this attack is shown in Fig. 8. Therefore, this attack can also mislead the control decision of PLCs in CPS. In a similar way, more critical and complex attacks can also be performed on the ADC data registers.

Fig. 8. Output of Attack 3

5   Experimental Design

In this section, we present details of our experimental setup designed to test the proposed attack techniques. Our experimental setup simulates a temperature-based alarm control system. In brief, the system periodically reads the surrounding temperature, and it triggers an alarm when the temperature value is above a threshold, e.g., 30°C.

To simulate the above process, we design a mini-CPS testbed using IoT devices, sensors and actuators. Specifically, we use Arduino MEGA[6] as a soft PLC, which makes control decisions based on the temperature readings of the sensor. We use an analog temperature sensor LM35[7] to read the surrounding temperature and feed it to the PLC. We use an 8Ω siren alarm[8] as an actuator, which activates the alarm when it receives an "ON" command from the PLC. A high-level schemata of the experimental setup is depicted in Fig. 9.

As shown in Fig. 9, the analog temperature sensor (LM35) is connected to the Arduino board (via the analog input A0) to read the surrounding temperature. The sensor is also connected to the internal voltage reference 3.3V. The Arduino board has 16 analog input pins and 54 digital input/output pins. It also contains an inbuilt ADC and MCU. The inbuilt ADC (integrated in the same electrical circuit board with the MCU) converts the analog temperature values to a discrete-time digital values. The MCU acts as a PLC and makes control decisions, such as triggering the alarm, based on the digital temperature value obtained from the ADC. More specifically, it issues an "ON" or "OFF" control command depending on the the temperature value and the threshold set. The "ON" control command triggers the alarm while the "OFF" control command turns off the alarm. An 8Ω mini speaker (a siren alarm) is connected to the Arduino board to act as an actuator. It activates the alarm when it receives an "ON" command from the PLC, and it turns off the alarm otherwise.

Due to lack of access, we did not conduct our experiments on real-world CPS testbeds with vendor-supplied PLCs. Yet, we believe that our experimental setup described above is substantially sufficient to evaluate the effectiveness of

---

[6] https://store.arduino.cc/products/arduino-mega-2560-rev3.

[7] https://www.electronicwings.com/sensors-modules/lm35-temperature-sensor.

[8] https://circuit.rocks/mini-metal-speaker-w-wires-8-ohm-0-5w.html.

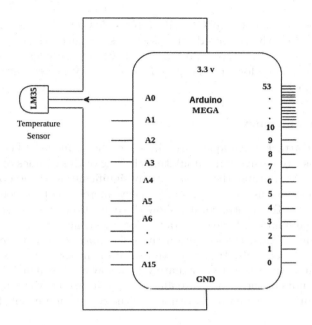

Fig. 9. Schematic diagram of the experimental setup

the proposed attach techniques. This is because, Arduino boards are widely used both in experimental and production settings. For example, it is widely used in various IIoT, ICS and CPS systems. Hence, protecting such systems against ADC-based attacks is also desirable. Moreover, the analog-to-digital conversion logic and software/hardware design of most ADCs are very similar. Hence, the ADC architecture (including its memory registers) of Arduino-based PLCs is highly likely to be similar with that of real-world PLCs. Therefore, we expect that the presented ADC attacks will also be effective when applied to real-world PLCs, which is left as a future work.

6   Evaluation and Discussion

In this section, we discuss a detailed evaluation of our proposed attacks. In brief, we evaluate the proposed attack techniques along three dimensions: 1) Accuracy 2) Efficiency and 3) Impact. Furthermore, we discuss possible countermeasures to prevent such types of ADC attacks.

6.1   Attack Accuracy

There were no much significant internal or external factors that could influence our experimental results. The only sensible factor or variable is the temperature environment. Hence, we conduct the experiments in different temperature conditions, such as cold ($< 16°C$), mild ($16°C$–$25°C$) and hot ($> 25°C$). In all such circumstances, the proposed attacks always produced the expected results. Meaning, we have not observed any false positive or false negative results in all our experiments. Therefore, the proposed attacks are very accurate in achieving the intended goal.

6.2 Attack Efficiency

The proposed attack techniques are simple to be launched. The attacks are performed by systematically manipulating the flag or data values of the targeted ADC registers. At runtime, there was not any significant overhead observed, both in CPU and memory usage. It takes only a few microseconds to conduct each of the three attacks. To experimentally show the execution time of each attack, we performed 50 simulations for each attack. The experimental results are depicted in Table 6. That means, the execution time of *Attack 1* and *Attack 3* are 60.2 μ and 60.3 μ, respectively. However, we could not measure the execution time of *Attack 2* since the system immediately hangs after this attack is performed. Therefore, outputs of the attacks are almost instantaneous. Meaning, impacts of the attacks can be reflected in real-time – without any significant delay.

6.3 Attack Impact

ADCs are commonly used in a wide-range of critical systems, such as ICS, CPS, and IoT, among others. Hence, manipulating the ADC conversion logic may result in a catastrophic impact to the systems. For example, the ADC outcome (i.e., the converted digital value) is a crucial input to the PLC to make control decisions in CPS. If the ADC outcome is manipulated, it will mislead the PLC to make wrong control decisions. This will result in incorrectly controlling the physical process in CPS. Hence, the entire CPS system could be severely impacted, including destruction of the physical plant. Although the proposed attacks are tested on an Arduino-based soft PLC, we believe that it can also be applied and tested on real-word CPS systems (refer the discussion in Sect. 5).

Table 6. The average execution time of the attacks for 50 simulations

Attack 1	*Attack 2*	*Attack 3*
60.2 μs	Not applicable since the system hangs after the attack	60.3 μs

6.4 Proposed Countermeasures

As discussed in the preceding sections, attacking the ADC logic can result a catastrophic impact on various systems and infrastructures. In particular, manipulating values of the ADC registers is a critical stealthy attack that might not even be easily detected. Therefore, it is essential to design appropriate counter-measures against these attacks. In this work, we highlight possible countermeasures and research directions to overcome such security concerns.

Enforcing write-protected policy to ADC registers As discussed, the register manipulation attacks are carried out by overwriting the exiting data or flags of certain critical registers in ADC, such as ADMUX, ACSR and the ADC data registers. One possible direction to address such attacks is by systematically enforcing a stringent"write-protected" policy to critical ADC registers and other memory locations. Such measures may help to prohibit an unauthorized overwriting of ADC registers, hence preventing manipulation attacks in ADC registers.

Authorizing and tracking firmware updates Properly authenticating and authorizing PLCs would be another approach to prevent ADC-based attacks. To minimize attacks that inject malicious ADC commands to the PLC firmware, only authorized users should be allowed to make such changes. A logging system should also be in place that tracks and traces all authorized and unauthorized software/firmware changes made or inputs provided to the system.

7   Related Work

In this section, we discuss prior works that are closely related to the security of ADC. In particular, we discuss prior attacks performed on the ADC logic.

As discussed in the introduction, ADCs have been targeted by various types of attackers. Attackers often target certain vulnerabilities that can be discovered in the hardware or software of ADCs. Bolshev et al. [5] has conducted an extensive study both on the hardware and software based vulnerabilities of ADCs. They then developed an attack technique by exploiting vulnerabilities in the sampling frequency and dynamic range of the ADC conversion logic. There are also side-channel attacks that exploited the strong correlation between the ADC digital output codes and the ADC supply current waveforms [17]. If the power side-channel attack (PSA) of the ADC is exploited, it can expose the private signal change data [16]. When applied to a successive approximation register (SAR) without PSA protection, the power supply current waveforms of the SAR are attacked. Other side-channel attacks have been also developed by exploiting various vulnerabilities in ADC [4,11,13,20,26,27,29].

Other class of attacks have exploited fast attack automatic gain control (AGC) vulnerability in ADC to deceive the outcome of the analog to digital conversion [3,16,19]. Some other attacks exploited the DAC-to-DAC crosstalk vulnerability in the ADC logic [22,31,36]. However, we are not aware of any existing attack techniques that exploit vulnerabilities related to ADC registers.

In CPS, an attacker who has access to the PLCs can generate a signal with a frequency that is interpreted as being valid by the ADC, when in reality it can cause serious damage to the physical process [19]. In spite of ADCs having anti-aliasing filter that restricts the bandwidth of a signal, these filters do not prevent frequency attacks. Another ADC-related CPS attack involves manipulating the device's input and output (I/O) at a low level, which allows the attacker to control the PLC without triggering any alarms [20].

System-on-Chip (SoC) integrators may design a Hardware Trojan with the intention of perturbing the ADC from malfunctioning by manipulating input or output signals or by affecting the modulator's output bit [36]. Another stealthy hardware trojan attack was also recently launched on the analog integrated circuits (ICs) of ADCs [12]. However, all these attacks did not specifically target the ADC registers.

Memory corruption attacks are another common threats against IoT devices or PLCs in ICS/CPS. They typically exploit memory-safety vulnerabilities, such as buffer overflows and dangling pointers, that could be found in the software or firmware of the devices to corrupt the process memory or execution flow of programs at runtime [7,8,10,14]. However, these attacks target the runtime process memory of the devices, not specifically the ADC memory registers.

In summary, there are several types of ADC-related attacks presented in the literature. To the best of our knowledge, none of them specifically target ADC registers. In this work, we identify and exploit certain ADC registers used in the analog-to-digital conversion process, which appear to be the unexplored attack surfaces in ADC.

8   Conclusion

ADCs are integral components in most critical systems, such as IoT and control systems. However, ADCs have been targeted by a wide range of physical or cyber attacks. The attackers may exploit various types of vulnerabilities that could be found in the software or hardware of ADCs. In this work, we first conducted a more in-depth study of the ADC conversion logic to discover relevant ADC vulnerabilities that were not well explored by previous work. Consequently, we managed to find relevant vulnerabilities on ADC registers. To demonstrate its exploitability, we developed three types of ADC attacks and tested it in an IoT-based mini-CPS environment.

By manipulating the ADC registers, we showed that it is possible to deceive the ADC outcome or maliciously halt the analog-to-digital conversion process. The ADC process can be forced to return an output that is much different from the expected result. This is carried out by changing the flag in the ADC multiplexer selection register, called ADMUX. An attack can also be carried out by manipulating the analog comparator control and status registers, called ACSR. We managed to maliciously hang the ADC conversion process by simultaneously enabling the ACD (analog comparator disable) and ACIE (analog comparator input enable) bits of the ACSR register, which resulted in system unavailability. We also showed that the ADC conversion process can be rendered useless by setting its output values to zero. This is achieved by resetting the data reader when it reads the ADC output from the ADCH and ADCL data registers. This was an attempt to show that ADC registers can most definitely be manipulated if no underlying protection mechanism is set for the ADC conversion process.

In the future, we plan to extend our experiments on real-world CPS testbeds using vendor-supplied PLCs. We also intend to conduct additional research to further explore key ADC vulnerabilities. Proposing and developing appropriate countermeasures for register-based ADC attacks is also left as a future work.

Acknowledgment. The work is partially supported by A*STAR under its RIE2020 Advanced Manufacturing and Engineering (AME) Industry Alignment Fund - Pre Positioning (IAF-PP) Award A19D6a0053. Any opinions, findings and conclusions or recommendations expressed in this material are those of the author(s) and do not reflect the views of A*STAR.

References

1. adafruit.com/: Using a temp sensor (2022). https://learn.adafruit.com/tmp36-temperature-sensor/using-a-temp-sensor
2. Alphonsus, E.R., Abdullah, M.O.: A review on the applications of programmable logic controllers (plcs). Renew. Sustain. Energy Rev. **60** (2016)
3. analog.com: Ad9364 register map reference manual (2021). https://www.analog.com/media/cn/technical-documentation/user-guides/ad9364_register_map_reference_manual_ug-672.pdf
4. Ashok, M., Levine, E.V., Chandrakasan, A.P.: Randomized switching SAR (RS-SAR) ADC protections for power and electromagnetic side channel security. In: 2022 IEEE Custom Integrated Circuits Conference (CICC), pp. 1–2 (2022)
5. Bolshev, A., Larsen, J., Krotofil, M., Wightman, R.: A rising tide: design exploits in industrial control systems. In: 10th USENIX Workshop on Offensive Technologies (WOOT 16). USENIX Association, Austin, TX (2016)
6. Chekole, E.G., Castellanos, J.H., Ochoa, M., Yau, D.K.Y.: Enforcing memory safety in cyber-physical systems. In: Katsikas S. et al. (eds.) Computer Security. SECPRE 2017, CyberICPS 2017 (2017)
7. Chekole, E.G., Chattopadhyay, S., Ochoa, M., Huaqun, G.: Enforcing full-stack memory safety in cyber-physical systems. In: Proceedings of the International Symposium on Engineering Secure Software and Systems (ESSoS 2018) (2018)
8. Chekole, E.G., Chattopadhyay, S., Ochoa, M., Guo, H., Cheramangalath, U.: CIMA: compiler-enforced resilience against memory safety attacks in cyber-physical systems. Comput. Secur. **94**, 101832 (2020)
9. Chekole, E.G., Huaqun, G.: ICS-SEA: formally modeling the conflicting design constraints in ICS. In: Proceedings of the Fifth Annual Industrial Control System Security (ICSS) Workshop, pp. 60–69. ICSS, Association for Computing Machinery, New York, NY, USA (2019). https://doi.org/10.1145/3372318.3372325
10. Chekole, E.G., Ochoa, M., Chattopadhyay, S.: SCOPE: secure compiling of PLCs in cyber-physical systems. Int. J. Crit. Infrastruct. Prot. **33**, 100431 (2021). https://doi.org/10.1016/j.ijcip.2021.100431
11. Chen, R., Wang, H., Chandrakasan, A., Lee, H.S.: RaM-SAR: a low energy and area overhead, 11.3fj/conv.-step 12b 25ms/s secure random-mapping SAR ADC with power and EM side-channel attack resilience. In: 2022 IEEE Symposium on VLSI Technology and Circuits (VLSI Technology and Circuits), pp. 94–95 (2022)
12. Elshamy, M., Di Natale, G., Pavlidis, A., Louërat, M.M., Stratigopoulos, H.G.: Hardware trojan attacks in analog/mixed-signal ICS via the test access mechanism. In: 2020 IEEE European Test Symposium (ETS), pp. 1–6 (2020)

13. Gattu, N., Imtiaz Khan, M.N., De, A., Ghosh, S.: Power side channel attack analysis and detection. In: 2020 IEEE/ACM International Conference on Computer Aided Design (ICCAD), pp. 1–7 (2020)
14. Geng, Y., et al.: Defending cyber-physical systems through reverse engineering based memory sanity check. IEEE Internet Things J., 1–1 (2022)
15. Grami, A.: Chapter 5 - analog-to-digital conversion. In: Grami, A. (ed.) Introduction to Digital Communications, pp. 217–264. Academic Press, Boston (2016)
16. Jeong, T.: Secure analog-to-digital conversion against power side-channel attack (2020). https://dspace.mit.edu/handle/1721.1/127018
17. Jeong, T., Chandrakasan, A.P., Lee, H.S.: S2adc: A 12-bit, 1.25ms/s secure SAR ADC with power side-channel attack resistance. In: 2020 IEEE Custom Integrated Circuits Conference (CICC), pp. 1–4 (2020)
18. Jogdand, R.R., Dakhole, P.K., Palsodkar, P.: Low power flash ADC using multiplexer based encoder. In: 2017 International Conference on Innovations in Information, Embedded and Communication Systems (ICIIECS), pp. 1–5 (2017)
19. Kovacs, E.: ADC attacks can cause damage in industrial environments (2016). https://www.securityweek.com/adc-attacks-can-cause-damage-industrial-environments
20. Kovacs, E.: PLCs vulnerable to stealthy pin control attacks (2016). https://www.securityweek.com/plcs-vulnerable-stealthy-pin-control-attacks
21. Lab, M.: Analog to digital converter - how ADC works and types? (2017). https://microcontrollerslab.com/analog-to-digital-adc-converter-working/
22. Langmann, R., Stiller, M.: The PLC as a smart service in industry 4.0 production systems. Appl. Sci. 9(18), 3815 (2019)
23. Le, B., Rondeau, T., Reed, J., Bostian, C.: Analog-to-digital converters. IEEE Signal Process. Mag. 22(6), 69–77 (2005)
24. Lee, E.A.: Cyber physical systems: design challenges. In: 2008 11th IEEE International Symposium on Object and Component-Oriented Real-Time Distributed Computing (ISORC), pp. 363–369 (2008). https://doi.org/10.1109/ISORC.2008.25
25. Li, P., Yi, X., Liu, X., Zhao, D., Zhao, Y., Wang, Y.: All-optical analog comparator. Sci. Rep. 6 (2016). https://doi.org/10.1038/srep31903
26. Miki, T., Miura, N., Sonoda, H., Mizuta, K., Nagata, M.: A random interrupt dithering SAR technique for secure ADC against reference-charge side-channel attack. IEEE Trans. Circ. Syst. II: Express Briefs 67(1), 14–18 (2020)
27. Miki, T., Nagata, M.: Countermeasures against physical security attacks on ICs utilizing on-chip wideband ADCs. Japan. J. Appl. Phys. 61(SC), SC0803 (2022)
28. Mitescu, M., Susnea, I.: Interfacing to analog signals. Microcontrollers Pract., 93–106 (2005)
29. Munny, R., Hu, J.: Power side-channel attack detection through battery impedance monitoring. In: 2021 IEEE International Symposium on Circuits and Systems (ISCAS), pp. 1–5 (2021). https://doi.org/10.1109/ISCAS51556.2021.9401542
30. Mynbaev, D.K., Scheiner, L.L.: Analog signals and analog transmission, pp. 103–201 (2020). https://doi.org/10.1002/9781119521501.ch2
31. docs.rs online.com: 8-channel, 12-bit, configurable ADC/DAC with on-chip reference, i2c interface (2014). https://docs.rs-online.com/1e6a/0900766b813daba4.pdf
32. Prathiba, G., Santhi, M., Ahilan, A.: Design and implementation of reliable flash ADC for microwave applications. Microelectron. Reliab. 88, 91–97 (2018). 29th European Symposium on Reliability of Electron Devices, Failure Physics and Analysis (ESREF 2018)

33. Satoh, T., Takahashi, K., Matsui, H., Itoh, K., Konishi, T.: 10-GS/s 5-bit real-time optical quantization for photonic analog-to-digital conversion. IEEE Photonics Technol. Lett. **24**(10), 830–832 (2012)

34. Stouffer, K., Falco, J., Scarfone, K., et al.: Guide to industrial control systems (ICS) security. NIST Spec. Publ. **800**(82), 16–16 (2011)

35. Taheri, S., Lin, J., Yuan, J.S.: Security interrogation and defense for SAR analog to digital converter. Electronics **6**(2), 48 (2017)

36. Taheri, S., Yuan, J.S.: Mixed-signal hardware security: attacks and countermeasures for $\delta \sum$ ADC. Electronics **6**(3), 60 (2017)

37. Wadatsumi, T., Miki, T., Nagata, M.: A dual-mode successive approximation register analog to digital converter to detect malicious off-chip power noise measurement attacks. Japan. J. Appl. Phys. **60**(SB), SBBL03 (2021)

38. Yadav, G., Paul, K.: Architecture and security of scada systems: a review. Int. J. Crit. Infrastruct. Prot. **34**, 100433 (2021)

39. Zanero, S.: Cyber-physical systems. Computer **50**(4), 14–16 (2017)

CIMSS – Critical Infrastructure and Manufacturing System Security

CIMSS 2023

Third Workshop on Critical Infrastructure and Manufacturing System Security

20 June 2023

Program Chairs

Leo Zhang · Griffith University, Australia
Zengpeng Li · Shandong University, China

Publicity Chair

Chenglu Jin · CWI Amsterdam, The Netherlands

Program Committee

Irfan Ahmed · Virginia Commonwealth University, USA
Cristina Alcaraz · University of Malaga, Spain
Binbin Chen · Singapore University of Technology and Design, Singapore
Chao Chen · RMIT University, Australia
Long Cheng · Clemson University, USA
Jairo Giraldo · University of Utah, USA
Charalambos Konstantinou · King Abdullah University of Science and Technology, Saudi Arabia
Andres Murillo · Singapore University of Technology and Design, Singapore
Marco Rocchetto · V-Research, Italy
Carlos Rubio-Medrano · Texas A&M University - Corpus Christi, USA
Alexandru Stefanov · Delft University of Technology, The Netherlands
Nan Sun · University of New South Wales, Australia
Richard J. Thomas · University of Birmingham, UK
Mark Yampolskiy · Auburn University, USA
Zheng Yang · Southwest University, China
Yanjun Zhang · University of Technology Sydney, Australia

Round-Efficient Security Authentication Protocol for 5G Network

Guining Geng[1], Junfeng Miao[2(✉)], and Nan Xiao[2]

[1] 360 Digital Security Technology Group Co. Ltd, No 2 Building, No 6 Yard, Jiuxianqiao Road, Chaoyang District, Beijing 100015, China
Gengguining@360.cn
[2] University of Science and Technology Beijing, Beijing 100089, China
miaojunfengwu@gmail.com, nan.xiao@ucdconnect.ie
http://www.springer.com/gp/computer-science/lncs

Abstract. The security access problem of Fifth Generation Mobile communication (5G) system has become a research hotspot. The 3GPP defines 5G authentication and key agreement (5G AKA) protocol, which is used to protect the access security of mobile devices in 5G network. But it is found that there are still some security loopholes and some unrealistic system assumptions which play a decisive role in security, such as user tracking, pre-shared key K disclosure, security between service network and home network, which makes 5G vulnerable to various attacks. Therefore, we propose a security authentication protocol for 5G network based on Schnorr signature and bilinear algorithm to solve the above problems. Then the security of the protocol is proved by using Scyther. Finally, the theoretical analysis verifies the security of the protocol, and the security comparison and efficiency analysis further verify that the protocol has good resistance performance.

Keywords: 5G · security · bilinear pairing · Schnorr Signature · protocol

1 Introduction

The proliferation of mobile smart communication devices and the continuous growth of multimedia communications have led to a substantial increase in the amount of mobile traffic, and may soon exceed the capacity of the fourth-generation (4G) mobile communication system. Therefore, the 5G [1] came into being and has become a current research hotspot. Compared with the 4G network, the 5G network supports more application scenarios on the original basis, and penetrates into the Internet of Things fields such as smart home, car networking, and drones. These high-quality services not only bring convenience and quick experience for users, but also ensure the safety of users' access to the network. Concurrently it ensures that the network connects with legitimate

J. Zhou et al. (Eds.): ACNS 2023 Workshops, LNCS 13907, pp. 269–283, 2023.
https://doi.org/10.1007/978-3-031-41181-6_15

users, and constructs a safe and legal mobile communication network environment, which has become an indispensable requirement and challenge in modern communication technology.

5G network protocol security is a key area of 5G network security research [2]. When a mobile device supporting 5G network needs to access 5G network, it first needs mutual authentication with 5G network. No matter user access through 3GPP or non-3GPP, they will choose one of the two authentication protocols 5G AKA and EAP-AKA supported by 5G network [3]. Because of the openness of air interface, the above authentication protocol must have strong security. When the user completes the authentication, he can safely access the network and use the services provided by the network, and the user can move the location of the device at any time, and can keep the network connection and service uninterrupted, which requires the support of non-access layer protocol. Because the protocol involves the mobility management and connectivity management of user devices, it is necessary to prevent attackers from using the protocol to launch DOS or MITM attacks on users or networks [4]. In addition, some scholars have made formal analysis of 5G AKA protocol, but they have not fully considered the security of service network and home network channel and the leakage of pre-shared key. In this case, whether the security of 5G AKA protocol can be guaranteed.

Other parts of this paper are as follows. Section 2 introduces the related work of this paper. Section 3 introduces the preliminary research work of this paper. We introduce Schnorr Signature and bilinear algorithm and propose a new scheme in Sect. 4. We analyze the security of the new scheme in Sect. 5. Finally, we summarize the full paper in Sect. 6.

2   Relation Work

At present, many literatures have studied and analyzed the 5G AKA protocol security, pointed out the security loopholes of the protocol, and put forward many improvement suggestions. On this basis, some new protocols have been proposed.

In [5–10], the author points out that some unrealistic system assumptions that are important to 5G network security have been identified, which makes 5G system vulnerable to user activity leakage, active attack, malicious network and other attacks. In [4], the authors propose a new, formal and comprehensive 5G aka protocol model. They gave the precise requirements of 5G network and gave a new security goal. Tamarin, a security protocol verification tool, is used to comprehensively and systematically evaluate the security of the model. It is found that due to the lack of additional assumptions, some key security goals are not satisfied, such as the security between SN and HN, the disclosure of pre-shared key K, and so on. In [11], the author instantiates 5GReasoner with two model checkers and one cryptographic protocol checker, and combines them lazily by using the abstraction refinement principle, and identifies 11 design weaknesses that lead to security and privacy attacks. In addition, their analysis also found five previous design defects inherited from 4G, which may be used to violate its security and privacy. Attacks in [12] - [14] can track specific users by obtaining synchronization failure or MAC failure information. The authors in [15] found a new attack that can reveal the complete activity pattern of users. This new attack is also called active surveillance attack. It collects data by skillfully selecting multiple timestamps, breaking the confidentiality of serial number. In [16], the authors proposed a new version of 5G AKA protocol, which overcome all the weaknesses in the protocol by replacing the sequence number with a random number, and reduce the number of communication stages and steps required in the protocol. But the leakage of long-term key K and the security between service network (SN) and home network (HN) are not considered. Ikram et al. [17] proposed a secure, efficient and lightweight authentication and key protocol SEL-AKA for 5G cellular networks. The protocol takes into account the different constraints in 5G AKA, and does not rely on the global public key infrastructure. However, this is based on the assumption of long-term key K security and SN and HN line security. In [18], this paper proposes a 5G AKA protocol based on symmetric key. The protocol can resist all known attacks and provide the security features required by the protocol. However, the author also does not consider the security between SN and HN. In [19], the author proposed the security of SN and HN, and ensured the communication security between SN and HN by generating public and private key pairs.

In this paper, in view of the security defects of 5G AKA mentioned above, especially the security between SN and HN, and the disclosure of pre-shared key K, we propose a secure and efficient 5G authentication protocol. Through ECDH and bilinear pairing, the protocol negotiates session key, encrypts messages with session key, and authenticates protocol entity through Schnorr Signature Algorithm. All of the above security vulnerabilities are solved. The integrity and confidentiality of message are guaranteed.

3   Preliminary

3.1   5G AKA Authentication Protocol

The 5G network is mainly composed of user equipment, access network and core network. Core network includes service domain network and home domain network. The user authentication function is mainly completed by terminal equipment, service network and home network. There are many kinds of terminal devices in 5G network, which are no longer limited to traditional personal communication terminals, but also include many Internet of things terminals, vertical industry user terminals, etc.; the service network mainly realizes user access management, session management and other functions, including AMF, SEAF, SMF and other network elements. Home network is mainly responsible for user identity authentication and identity information management. 5G network is shown in Fig. 1 [19].

According to the 5G security standard [20], The implementation of the agreement is as follows:

(1) In the beginning, the user equipment UE sends SUCI to the service network SN, and SN sends SN_{name} and SUCI to the ownership network HN after receiving SUCI.

(2) The ownership network HN generates an authentication vector $AV(RAND, AUTN, HXRES^*, K_{AUSF})$ and sends it to the service network SN.

(3) The service network combines the parameters RAND,AUTN and other parameters ngKSI and ABBA to the authentication request and sent to UE.

(4) UE checks the message authentication code MAC and synchronization sequence number SQN. If the both are verified successfully, the generated response message RES^* is sent to SN, and transmitted by SN to HN for verification.

(5) If HN and SN are checked successfully, the authentication is successful, and UE and the network can carry out normal business afterwards.

(6) If the SQN checks fail, UE explicitly returns the synchronization failure message and attaches AUTS.

(7) If the MAC check fails, the UE returns the MAC check failure in plaintext.

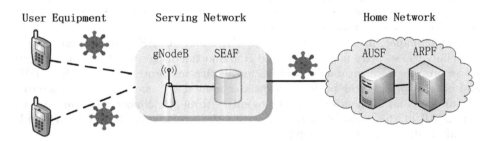

Fig. 1. 5G network.

Since the design of 5G network, the security function has been enhanced. The most typical one is to enhance the security of user identity subscription permanent identifier (SUPI) in the air interface. In the scenario where SUPI needs to be transmitted in the air interface, the terminal uses asymmetric encryption mechanism to encrypt SUPI, A subscription accepted identifier (SUCI) is generated, and SUCI is used to replace SUPI to transmit in the air interface to prevent the leakage of user identity information in the air interface. The relevant encryption mechanism of the details can be referred to [20].

3.2   Assumed Attack Models and Security Requirements

According to the previous analysis, the attack model is not only limited to UE and SN, but also to SN and HN [4]. Attackers can wiretap and monitor the data transmitted by these channels to attack passively. Of course, assuming that they are active attackers, they can intercept, manipulate, replay and destroy the data sent through the channel. In general, passive attackers only attack through listening channels, while active attackers need to establish a fake base station to attack. Therefore, it is necessary to consider the existence of active attackers. In addition, we assume that there are malicious UE and malicious SN for the aggrieved party. Here, the attacker can establish and access an authenticated channel through HN to authenticate some UE [17]. For example, this attack occurs when roaming. Here, we summarize the important safety features of 5G AKA from the formal evaluation of Scheme [3], and refer to the safety objectives of 5G standard [20].

1) Mutual authentication. The most important security requirement of the protocol is to ensure mutual authentication between communication entities.
2) Confidentiality on K_{SEAF} Ensure that the session key will not be leaked, and ensure its forward security and backward security.
3) Confidentiality of SUPI. Ensure the security of SUPI under attack, otherwise user information and location information will be exposed.
4) Confidentiality of SQN. Ensure the security of the attacked Sqn, or else the attacker will get the activity mode of the target user.

3.3 5G-AKA Weaknesses

Although the security of 5G protocol has been enhanced, there are still some security flaws and some unrealistic system assumptions [4]. Some system assumptions are very important to the security of the protocol. If an attack occurs in this case, the security of the protocol cannot be guaranteed. This situation makes 5G system vulnerable to a variety of attacks [5], as follows:

- Security between SN and HN channels. First, the attacker can destroy the SN and access the channel between SN and HN, and eavesdrop and inject messages through the channel. In this case, the attacker may have a real USIM and access all the secret values stored in it. The attacker can obtain the pre-shared key K and SUPI. Therefore, it is necessary to solve the security between SN and HN, and ensure that the leakage of the pre-shared key K will not affect the security of K_{SEAF}.
- In order to provide privacy protection and prevent user identity disclosure SUPI, 5G uses the Elliptic Curve Integrated Encryption Scheme (ECIES) profiles to protect SUPI. However, this leads to computational overhead and PKI problems [16].
- By taking advantage of different failure causes (MAC failure or synchronization failure), the target user may be tracked [13].
- The SQN hiding mechanism is not fully protected, resulting in SQN leakage, which leads to active monitoring attacks [15].
- As described in [4], a successful key confirmation round is required after the protocol is executed. The standard does not specify this additional key

validation round, nor does it specify that the UE must wait for it, which creates a serious vulnerability. A malicious SN may impersonate a legitimate SN, initiate key change dynamically, and switch security context, including key and parameters.

- The UE's weak agreement with its SN is violated. This is due to the fact that K_{SEAF} and a corresponding SUPI (identifies the UE) that the SN receives are not bonded, because it receives K_{SEAF} prior to SUPI. If a pair of SN and HN are running concurrently, the SUPI that SN receives at the end might not correspond to the correct K_{SEAF}.

3.4   Weil Pairing

Suppose G_1 and G_2 are additive subgroups and multiplicative subgroups of elliptic curve rational point group on finite field R, and the order q is large prime number. In G_1 and G_2, the discrete logarithm problem is difficult to solve. P (x, y) is the generator of G, called the base point, satisfying qP=O(O represents the infinite far point on the elliptic curve) [25].

G_1 and G_2 are respectively additive cyclic groups and multiplicative cyclic groups of order q. q is a large prime. Bilinear mapping refers to the mapping of G_1 and G_2 from the pair of Weil on the elliptic curve to the following propertiese : $G_1 \times G_1 \to G_2$.

a) Bilinear: $e(aP, bQ) = e(P, Q)^{ab}, P, Q \in G_1$ and $a, b \in Z_q^*$.
b) Alternative:$e(P, Q) \neq 1, P, Q \in G_1$.
c) non-degeneracy: This mapping does not map all the points in $G_1 \times G_1$ to G_2.
d) Computability: For all $P, Q \in G_1$, we can calculate e(P,Q).

Bilinear Diffie-Hellman Assumption (BDHA). Let G_1 and G_2 be two cyclic groups of prime order q. $e : G_1 \times G_1 \to G_2$ is a bilinear mapping and P is the generator of G_1. BDH assumption: for $a, b, c \in Z_q^*$, given (P,aP,bP,cP), it is difficult to calculate $e(P, P)^{abc}$.

Discrete Logarithm Assumption (DLA). G_1 is a cyclic group of prime q and P is the generator of G_1. Given P, Q=yP, $y \in Z_q^*$,it is difficult to calculate y.

3.5   ECDH Key Agreement

ECDH key agreement is the implementation of Diffie-Hellman key agreement protocol on ECC [21]. Assuming that the communication parties are X and Y, the ECDH key agreement protocol is described as follows.

X randomly selects a private key $k_X \in Z_q^*$, and calculates the public key $Q_X = k_X P$ and sends it to Y.

Y randomly selects a private key $k_Y \in Z_q^*$, and calculates the public key $Q_Y = k_Y P$ and sends it to X.

After receiving Q_Y from Y, X calculates $K_X = k_X Q_Y = k_X k_Y P$. Similarly, after receiving Q_X from X, Y calculates $K_Y = k_Y Q_X = k_Y k_X P$. In this way, X and Y complete the key which is agreed by both parties is $K = k_X k_Y P$.

3.6 Schnorr Signature Algorithm

Schnorr signature algorithm [22] has the characteristics of small computation and fast speed, and has been widely used. It is as follows:

Let G be an elliptic curve, M be the data to be signed, usually a 32-byte hash value, x be the signer's private key, P $=$xG, and P be the signer's public key corresponding to x. $H : \{0,1\}^* \rightarrow Z_q$ is a hash function. The signer selects a random number $k \in Z_q^*$, calculates R=kG, $s = k + H(M \parallel R \parallel P)x$;Then, the signature of public key P to message M is: (R, s) is Schnorr Signature. What the verifier knows is: G is an elliptic curve; $H : \{0,1\}^* \rightarrow Z_q$ is a hash function; M is a message; P is a signer's public key; (R, s) is the signer's Schnorr Signature; It verifies the following equation: $sG = R + H(M \parallel R \parallel P)P$; If the equality holds, the signature can be proved to be legal.

Schnorr group signature refers to a group of N public keys, and then N signatures are obtained. The N signatures can be added to get a signature. If the signature is verified, it means that n has verified all the public key signatures [23].

4 Protocol Proposition

In order to solve the above-mentioned security vulnerabilities and prevent other possible attacks, we propose a security authentication scheme based on Schnorr signature and bilinear algorithm to ensure the security of the protocol.

4.1 Assumptions

We define the assumptions of the proposed scheme:

- Each user device has a user identity (Subscription Permanent Identifier, SUPI), which can be registered in 3GPP network.
- Each user equipment and service network has a pre-shared key K.

4.2 Preparation Phase

Suppose G_1 and G_2 are additive subgroups and multiplicative subgroups of elliptic curve rational point group on finite field R, and the order q is large prime number. In G_1 and G_2, the discrete logarithm problem is difficult to solve. P is the generator of G, called the base point, The Weil pair on the elliptic curve obtains a mapping that satisfies the following properties $e : G_1 \times G_1 \rightarrow G_2$. $H_i : \{0,1\}^* \rightarrow Z_q^*, i = 1, 2, 3$ is used the three hash functions. Then, the HN randomly chooses $s \in Z_q^*$, and calculates $P_{pub} = sP.\{G_1, G_2, q, e, P, P_{pub}, H_1, H_2, H_3\}$ are published and s is secretly used as the master key.

4.3 Authentication Procedure

An authentication procedure of the proposed protocol shown in Fig. 2 is as follows:

(1) UE selects the random number $a_1 \in Z_q^*$ and generates $P_{UE}^1 = a_1P$. By using the public key P_{pub} of HN, it calculated the key $SK_{UE}^1 = a_1P_{pub} = a_1sP$; UE selects a random value R_{UE}, uses the shared key K to compute $AT = SUPI \oplus E_K(R_{UE})$, and encrypts SUPI and $E_K(R_{UE})$ with the key SK_{UE}^1 to obtain $SUCI = E_{SK_{UE}^1}(AT)$; UE selects new random $a_2 \in Z_q^*$ and calculates $P_{UE}^2 = a_2P$, hash value $H_{UE} = H_1((P_{UE}^1 + P_{pub}) \parallel P_{UE}^2 \parallel SUCI)$ and calculates $S_{UE} = a_2 + a_1H_{UE}$. It generates signature information $\sigma_{UE} = (P_{UE}^2, S_{UE})$. Finally, it outputs the message $Mes_{UE} = (SUCI, P_{UE}^1, \sigma_{UE}, R_{UE})$ and sents Mes_{UE} to SN.

(2) After receiving the message Mes_{UE}, SN first calculates $H_{UE}' = H_1((P_{UE}^1 + P_{pub}) \parallel P_{UE}^2 \parallel SUCI)$, $S_{UE}' = P_{UE}^2 + P_{UE}^1H_{UE}'$, and verifies $S_{UE}P = S_{UE}'$. SN verified the identity of UE. SN selects the random number $b_1 \in Z_q^*$ and generates $P_{SN}^1 = b_1P$. By using the public key P_{pub} of HN, it calculates the key $SK_{SN}^1 = b_1P_{pub} = b_1sP$; SN selects a random value R_{SN}, calculates hash value $RH_{SN} = H_2(R_{SN})$ and encrypts SN_{name} with the key SK_{SN}^1 to obtain $ASN = RH_{SN} \oplus E_{SK_{SN}^1}(SN_{name})$; SN selects new random $b_2 \in Z_q^*$ and calculates $P_{SN}^2 = b_2P$, hash value $H_{SN} = H_1((P_{pub} + P_{SN}^1) \parallel P_{SN}^2 \parallel SUCI)$ and calculates $S_{SN} = b_2 + b_1H_{SN}$. It generates signature information $\sigma_{SN} = (P_{SN}^2, S_{SN})$. Finally, it outputs the message $Mes_{SN} = (SUCI, P_{UE}^1, R_{UE}, \sigma_{UE}, \sigma_{SN}, R_{SN}, P_{SN}^1, P_{UE}^2, P_{SN}^2, ASN)$ and sents Mes_{UE} to HN.

(3) HN receives the message and first calculates $H_{UE}' = H_1((P_{UE}^1 + P_{pub}) \parallel P_{UE}^2 \parallel SUCI)$, $H_{SN}' = H_1((P_{pub} + P_{SN}^1) \parallel P_{SN}^2 \parallel SUCI)$, $S_{UE}' = P_{UE}^2 + P_{UE}^1H_{UE}'$, $S_{SN}' = P_{SN}^2 + P_{SN}^1H_{SN}'$, and verifies $S_{UE}P = S_{UE}'$, $S_{SN}P = S_{SN}'$. HN authenticates the identity of UE and Sn. By using the public key P_{SN}^1 of SN, it calculates the key $SK_{SN}^1 = sP_{SN}^1 = sb_1P$; It gets the value $E_{SK_{SN}^1}(SN_{name})$ by calculating $ASN \oplus H_2(R_{SN})$ and decrypts $E_{SK_{SN}^1}(SN_{name})$ to get SN_{name}; HN judges whether SN_{name} is authorized or not. If it is authorized, HN will continue; By using the public key P_{UE}^1 of UE, it calculates the key $SK_{UE}^1 = sP_{UE}^1 = sa_1P$; It decrypts SUCI to get AT,and calculating $AT \oplus E_K(R_{UE})$ to get SUPI; HN verifies that SUPI is correct, and selects the random number $c_2 \in Z_q^*$, generates $P_{HN}^2 = c_2P$ and calculates the session key $MK_{HN} = e(P_{UE}^1 + P_{UE}^2, P_{SN}^1 + P_{SN}^2)^{(s+c_2)} = e(P,P)^{((a_1+a_2)(b_1+b_2)(s+c_2))}$; K_{SEAF} is derived as follows: $K_{SEAF} = KDF(K, MK_{HN}, R_{UE}, SN_{name})$; HN selects a random value R_{SN} and calculates hash value $RH_{HN} = H_2(R_{UE} \parallel R_{SN} \parallel R_{HN} \parallel SN_{name})$, $H_{HN} = H_1((P_{pub} + P_{SN}^1 + P_{UE}^1) \parallel (P_{UE}^2 + P_{SN}^2 + P_{HN}^2) \parallel RH_{HN})$ and calculates $S_{HN} = c_2 + sH_{HN}$; It generates signature information $\sigma_{HN} = (P_{HN}^2, S_{HN})$,and calculates $XRES = f_4(SN_{name}, K_{SEAF}, R_{UE}, R_{SN}, R_{HN}, SUCI, K)$, $AR = H_3(MK_{HN} \parallel SN_{name})$, $KSN = K_{SEAF} \oplus AR$, $M_{HN} = E_{MK_{HN}}(KSN, XRES)$; Then, it sends the message $Mes_{HN} = (M_{HN}, P_{HN}^2, R_{HN}, \sigma_{HN})$ to SN.

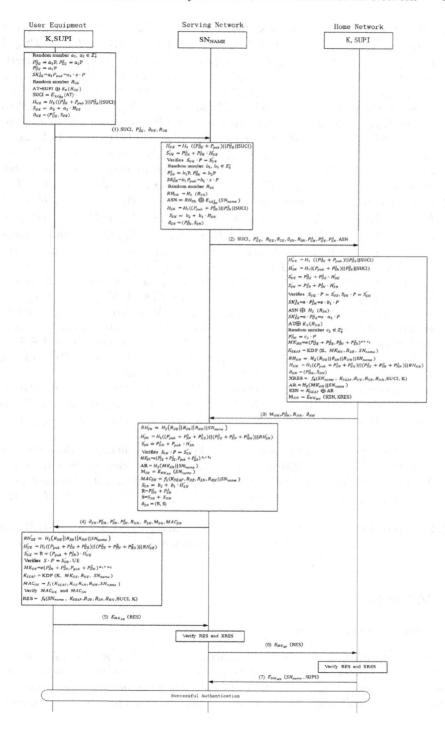

Fig. 2. The proposed protocol.

(4) Upon SN receives the message, SN calculates $RH'_{SN} = H_2(R_{UE} \parallel R_{SN} \parallel R_{HN} \parallel SN_{name})$, $H'_{SN} = H_1((P_{pub} + P^1_{SN} + P^1_{UE}) \parallel P^2_{UE} + P^2_{SN} + P^2_{HN} \parallel RH'_{SN})$, $S'_{SN} = P^2_{HN} + P_{pub}H'_{SN}$, and verifies $S_{SN}P = S'_{SN}$. SN authenticate the identity of HN, and calculates the session key $MK_{SN} = e(P^1_{UE} + P^2_{UE}, P_{pub} + P^2_{HN})^{(b_1+b_2)} = e(P, P)^{((a_1+a_2)(b_1+b_2)(s+c_2))}$;It decrypts M_{HN} to get KSN, and calculates $AR = H_3(MK_{SN} \parallel SN_{name})$, $KSN \oplus AR$ to obtain K_{SEAF}; XRES and K_{SEAF} are stored.HN uses the key MK_{SN} to encrypt SN_{name} to get $M_{SN} = E_{MK_{SN}}(SN_{name})$ and calculates $MAC_{SN} = f_1(K_{SEAF}, R_{UE}, R_{SN}, R_{HN}, SN_{name})$, $S_{SN} = b_2 + b_1H'_{SN}$, $R = P^2_{HN} + P^2_{SN}$, $S = S_{SN} + S_{HN}$ and generates group signature $\sigma_{SN} = (R, S)$;It transmits $Mes_{SN} = (\sigma_{SN}, P^2_{HN}, P^1_{SN}, P^2_{SN}, R_{HN}, R_{SN}, M_{SN}, MAC_{SN})$ to UE.

(5) After receiving the message, UE calculates $RH'_{UE} = H_2(R_{UE} \parallel R_{SN} \parallel R_{HN} \parallel SN_{name})$, $H'_{UE} = H_1((P_{pub} + P^1_{SN} + P^1_{UE}) \parallel (P^2_{UE} + P^2_{SN} + P^2_{HN}) \parallel RH'_{UE})$, $S'_{UE} = R + (P_{pub} + P^1_{SN})H'_{UE}$, and verifies $SP = S'_{UE}$. UE to authenticate the identity of HN,SN and calculates the session key $MK_{UE} = e(P^1_{SN} + P^2_{SN}, P_{pub} + P^2_{HN})^{(a_1+a_2)} = e(P, P)^{((a_1+a_2)(b_1+b_2)(s+c_2))}$; It decrypts M_{SN} to get SN_{name}.It calculates K_{SEAF} as follows: $K_{SEAF} = KDF(K, MK_{UE}, R_{UE}, SN_{name})$ and calculates $MAC_{UE} = f_1(K_{SEAF}, R_{UE}, R_{SN}, R_{HN}, SN_{name})$, verify whether MAC_{UE} and MAC_{SN} are equal. If they are equal, it means that K_{SEAF} generated by SN and UE is equal. It calculates $RES = f_4(SN_{name}, K_{SEAF}, R_{UE}, R_{SN}, R_{HN}, SUCI, K)$ and encrypt RES to get $M_{UE} = E_{MK_{UE}}(RES)$;Then it sends M_{UE} to the SN.

(6) After receiving the M_{UE}, SN decrypts M_{UE} to get RES by using MK_{SN} and verify whether RES and XRES are equal. By comparison, the UE is successfully authenticated by SN, and SN sends the $M_{SN} = E_{MK_{SN}}(RES)$ to HN.

(7) Upon the receipt of the message M_{SN}, For mutual authentication, the HN decrypts M_{SN} to get RES by using MK_{HN} and verifies whether RES and XRES are equal. If the comparison is equal, HN transmits the encrypted successful authentication message $M_{HN} = E_{MK_{HN}}(SN_{name}, SUPI)$ to the SN.

(8) SN receives the message M_{HN}, and decrypts M_{HN} to get SN_{name}, SUPI and a confirmation message. After the SN verifies SN_{name}, if SN_{name} matches, the authentication is complete.

5   Validation

5.1   Formal Verification

The development of formal protocol analysis methods has led to the development of formal protocol analysis tools. Scyther has comprehensive advantages in security protocol analysis. Scyther not only has a simple and understandable formal language and graphical interface, but also has the characteristics of clear termination, multi software parallel analysis, graphical interaction interface, and providing concise description of traces. Excellent performance in large-scale protocol analysis, discovery of protocol attacks, and verification of protocol security. Another advantage of the Scyther tool is that the adversary model can be manually selected and parameter set, such as adding long-term private key leakage, session key leakage, state leakage, and other adversary models under strong security models.

This article uses the formal verification tool Scyther [24] to conduct security simulation analysis on the proposed scheme. In the proposed scheme, there are three main roles: UE, SN, and HN, and this process only involves mutual authentication of devices. For the implementation scenario proposed in this scheme, the Dolev Yao model is chosen to check the security of the scheme. In this model, attackers can fully control the network and carry out a series of attacks. Finally, we use Security Protocol Description Language (SPDL) to model the proposed scheme in this paper. From Fig. 3, it can be seen that our scheme successfully meets all Scyther confidentiality and authentication requirements, and no attacks are found under the testing of Scyther tools.

5.2   Security Analysis

Here, we informally analyze the security of the proposed protocol.

- Because of the insecure channel between UE, SN and HN, they authenticate each other and encrypt the message for transmission, which can avoid the data leakage and impersonation attack caused by the insecurity of the channel. At the beginning, UE negotiate encryption key with HN to encrypt SUPI through ECDH, and generate signature through SSH (Schnorr Signature Algorithm). The SN receives message, verifies signature and UE. At the same time, SN also generates encryption key with HN through ECDH to encrypt SN_{name}, and generate signature through SSA. After receiving the message, HN verifies UE and SN respectively. After successful verification, it generates decryption key, and generates shared key of UE, SN and HN through bilinear pairing. The later messages are sent through the shared key encryption, and SSH signature is generated and sent to SN for verification, And SN generate a group signature and send it to UE. UE verifies the signature and verifies both UE and SN.
- For the freshness of data, we no longer rely on SQN, we guarantee the freshness of messages by generating random numbers and verifying them.
- In the whole process of the protocol, SUPI is encrypted transmission, and the SUPI which is sent to SN after authentication is also encrypted transmission, which can effectively prevent anonymity and unlinkability. As long as the decryption key is possessed, the correct SUPI can be obtained.
- The session key is generated through ECDH and bilinear pairing, which ensures the confidentiality of the message and reduces the public key infrastructure and computing cost.
- The proposed protocol uses session key encryption in the process of transmitting information. Whether it is a fault or the final key confirmation, it must

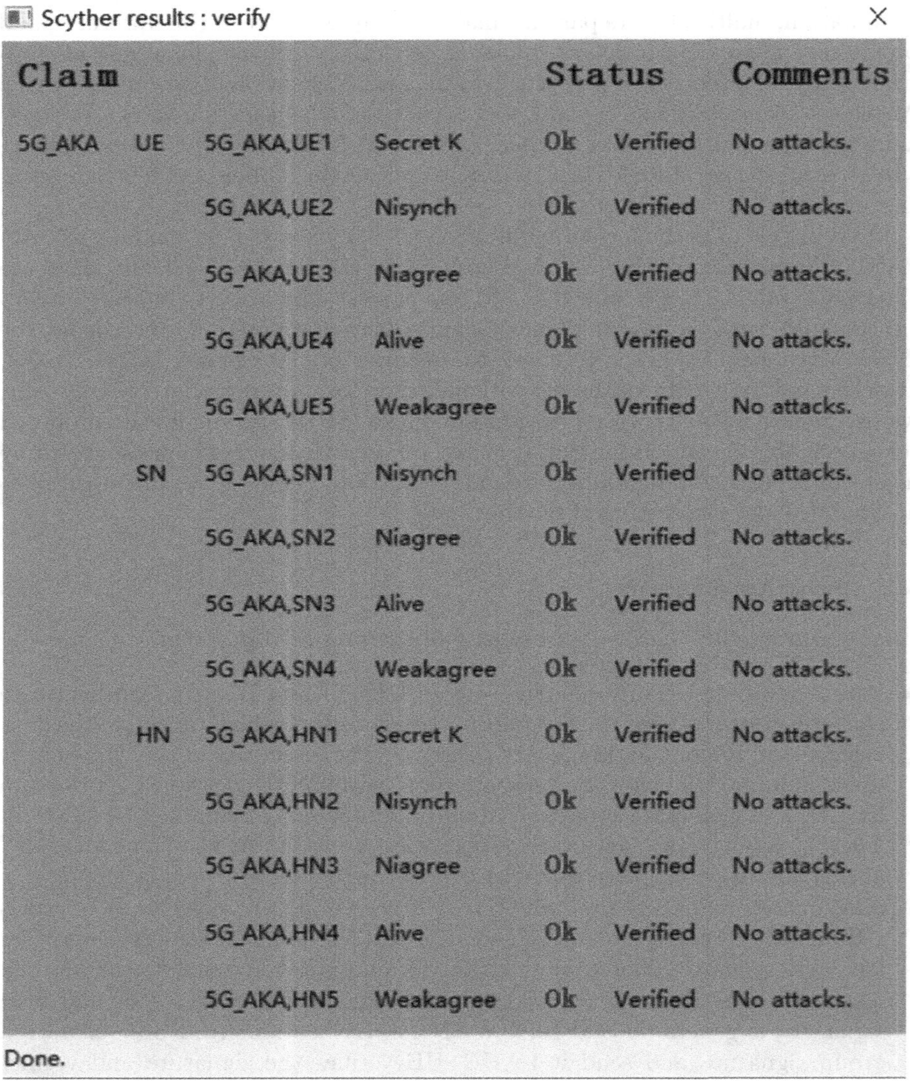

Scyther results : verify

Claim				Status		Comments
5G_AKA	UE	5G_AKA,UE1	Secret K	Ok	Verified	No attacks.
		5G_AKA,UE2	Nisynch	Ok	Verified	No attacks.
		5G_AKA,UE3	Niagree	Ok	Verified	No attacks.
		5G_AKA,UE4	Alive	Ok	Verified	No attacks.
		5G_AKA,UE5	Weakagree	Ok	Verified	No attacks.
	SN	5G_AKA,SN1	Nisynch	Ok	Verified	No attacks.
		5G_AKA,SN2	Niagree	Ok	Verified	No attacks.
		5G_AKA,SN3	Alive	Ok	Verified	No attacks.
		5G_AKA,SN4	Weakagree	Ok	Verified	No attacks.
	HN	5G_AKA,HN1	Secret K	Ok	Verified	No attacks.
		5G_AKA,HN2	Nisynch	Ok	Verified	No attacks.
		5G_AKA,HN3	Niagree	Ok	Verified	No attacks.
		5G_AKA,HN4	Alive	Ok	Verified	No attacks.
		5G_AKA,HN5	Weakagree	Ok	Verified	No attacks.

Done.

Fig. 3. Scyther result.

use session key encryption transmission. In this way, only the correct entity can decrypt the received information, which effectively prevents counterfeiting attacks and tracing users through fault messages.

- K_{SEAF} is generated by the session key K and the random number. It is encrypted and sent to SN to ensure the confidentiality of K_{SEAF}. Only the correct session key can be decrypted to obtain K_{SEAF}. Moreover, the session key and random number are not the same each time. In this way, if the pre-shared key K is revealed, the security of K_{SEAF} is not affected, and the perfect forward/backward secrecy of K_{SEAF} is ensured. Moreover, K_{SEAF} is transmitted by session key encryption and will not be disclosed. In addition, after receiving key K_{SEAF} sent by HN, SN uses K_{SEAF} to generate MAC_{SN}. After UE receives the message, it generates the key K_{SEAF}, and verifies the MAC_{SN}, which proves that the key K_{SEAF} of UE and SN are equal. At this point, UE and SN mutually verify the key K_{SEAF}. UE no longer needs the final key confirmation, only needs HN to send encrypted SUPI to SN, that is to complete the protocol.

- Because the random number is bound to the signature process, the entity gets the uniqueness of the session in time during the verification process.
- When generating MAC, the parameters used include random number and SN_{name}, which can link authentication to the original session.
- The SSH is used to ensure mutual authentication between entities at the beginning stage, which effectively avoids DoS attacks. Moreover, messages are transmitted through encryption between entities. Even if the attacker collects authentication information and sends it to HN, HN also sends information through encrypted transmission. The information cannot be decrypted and authenticated without the correct decryption key.

5.3   Security Comparison

Through security analysis, we have summarized the security attributes of our proposed protocol. Then it compares with other existing 5G authentication schemes, as shown in Table 1. It can be seen from the table that our proposed protocol has better security performance than other schemes.

Table 1. Security Comparison.

Functionality	Gharsallah [16]	Braeken [17]	XinxinHU [19]	our
Forgery Attack	Yes	Yes	Yes	Yes
Man-In-The-Middle Attack	Yes	Yes	Yes	Yes
Replay Attack	Yes	Yes	Yes	Yes
DoS Attack	Yes	Yes	Yes	Yes
Disclosure of pre-shared key K	No	No	No	Yes
The security between SN and HN	No	No	Yes	Yes
Mutual Authentication	Yes	Yes	Yes	Yes
Data Integrity	Yes	Yes	Yes	Yes
Forward Secrecy	Yes	Yes	Yes	Yes
Backward Secrecy	Yes	Yes	Yes	Yes

5.4   Efficiency Analysis

In this section, we analyze the computational complexity of the algorithm and compare it with the scheme in reference [19]. In reference [19], the main time consumption of the scheme is five times of public and private key encryption. In our scheme, bilinear pairing is time-consuming, so we only use this algorithm in key agreement. In terms of time consumption, our proposed scheme consumes more time than reference [19], but the reference [19] requires the third-party key distribution and escrow overhead. Compared with these, our scheme has better advantages.

6   Conclusion

In this article, we analyze the vulnerability of the standard 5G AKA, especially the disclosure of pre-shared key K, the security between SN and HN, and so on. Then we propose a secure and efficient authentication protocol, which uses bilinear pairing to negotiate session key, Schnorr Signature Algorithm to authenticate entities. The proposed protocol solves the vulnerability of 5G AKA protocol. Then the proposed protocol is verified by Scyther and its security is analyzed, which shows that our protocol has high authentication security and confidentiality.

References

1. Next Generation Mobile Networks, white paper: Alliance N. 5Gwhitepaper, pp. 1–125 (2015)
2. Bargh, M.S., et al.: UMTS-AKA and EAP-AKA inter-working for fast handovers in All-IP networks. In: IEEE Globecom Workshops, pp. 1–6 (2008). https://doi.org/10.1109/GLOCOMW.2007.4437814
3. Security Architecture and Procedures for 5G System, document 3GPP, TS33.501 (2019). www.3gpp.org/DynaReport/33501.htm. Accessed 26 Jan 2019
4. Basin, D., et al.: A formal analysis of 5g authentication. In: 2018 ACM SIGSAC, pp. 1383–1396 (2018). https://doi.org/10.1145/3243734.3243846
5. Jover, R.P., et al.: Security and protocol exploit analysis of the 5G specifications. IEEE Access, 1–1 (2019). https://doi.org/10.1109/ACCESS.2019.2899254
6. Behrad, S., et al.: Securing authentication for mobile networks, a survey on 4G issues and 5G answers. In: Conference on Innovation in Clouds, pp. 1–8 (2018). https://doi.org/10.1109/ICIN.2018.8401619
7. Rupprecht, D., et al.: On security research towards future mobile network generations. IEEE Communications Surveys and Tutorials, pp. 2518–2542 (2017). https://doi.org/10.1109/COMST.2018.2820728
8. Ahmad, I., et al.: Overview of 5G security challenges and solutions. IEEE Commun. Stan. Mag. **2**, 36–43 (2018). https://doi.org/10.1109/MCOMSTD.2018.1700063
9. Mantas, G., et al.: Security for 5G Communications.in Fundamentals of 5G Mobile Networks. Wiley, London, U.K. (2015)
10. Ahmad, I., et al.: 5G security: analysis of threats and solutions. In: IEEE Conference on Standards for Communications and Networking (CSCN), pp. 193–199 (2017). https://doi.org/10.1109/CSCN.2017.8088621

11. Hussain, S.R., et al.: 5GReasoner: a property-directed security and privacy analysis framework for 5G cellular network protocol. In: 2019 ACM SIGSAC Conference, pp. 669–684 (2019). https://doi.org/10.1145/3319535.3354263
12. Arapinis, M., et al.: New privacy issues in mobile telephony: fix and verification. In: 2012 ACM Conference on Computer and Communications Security, pp. 205–216 (2012). https://doi.org/10.1145/2382196.2382221
13. Hahn, C., et al.: A privacy threat in 4th generation mobile telephony and its countermeasure. In: WASA 2014: Wireless Algorithms, Systems, and Applications, pp. 624–635 (2014). https://doi.org/10.1007/978-3-319-07782-656
14. Fouque, P.A., et al.: Achieving better privacy for the 3GPP AKA protocol. In: Proceedings on Privacy Enhancing Technologies, pp. 255–275 (2016). https://doi.org/10.1515/popets-2016-0039
15. Borgaonkar, R., et al.: New privacy threat on 3G, 4G, and upcoming 5G AKA protocols (2019). www.eprint.iacr.org/2018/1175.pdf. Accessed 26 Jan 2019
16. Gharsallah, I., et al.: A secure efficient and lightweight authentication protocol for 5G cellular networks: SEL-AKA. In: 2019 15th International Wireless Communications and Mobile Computing Conference (IWCMC) (2019). https://doi.org/10.1109/IWCMC.2019.8766448
17. Braeken, A., et al.: Novel 5G authentication protocol to improve the resistance against active attacks and malicious serving networks. IEEE Access (2019). https://doi.org/10.1109/ACCESS.2019.2914941
18. Braeken, A.: Symmetric key based 5G AKA authentication protocol satisfying anonymity and unlinkability. Comput. Netw. **181**, 107424 (2020). https://doi.org/10.1016/j.comnet.2020.107424
19. Xinxin, H.U., et al.: A security enhanced 5G authentication scheme for insecure channel. IEICE Trans. Inf. Syst. **103**, 711–713 (2020). https://doi.org/10.1587/transinf.2019EDL8190
20. 3GPP TS33. 501 Security Architecture and Procedures for 5G System (2019)
21. Diffie, W., Hellman, M.: New directions in cryptography. IEEE Trans. Inf. Theory **22**(6), 644–654 (1976). https://doi.org/10.1587/transinf.2019EDL8190
22. Schnorr, C.P.: Efficient signature generation by smart cards. J. Cryptol. **4**(3), 161–174 (1991). https://doi.org/10.1007/BF00196725
23. Maxwell, G., et al.: Simple Schnorr multi-signatures with applications to Bitcoin. Designs Codes Cryptogr. **87**(4) (2019). https://doi.org/10.1007/s10623-019-00608-x
24. Cremers, C.: Scyther tool. University of Oxford, Department of Computer Science. www.cs.ox.ac.uk/people/cas.cremers/scyther
25. Boneh, D., et al.: Identity-based encryption from the Weil pairing. SIAM J. Comput. **32**(3), 586–615 (2003). https://doi.org/10.1137/S0097539701398521

A Framework for TLS Implementation Vulnerability Testing in 5G

Yong Wang[1]([✉]), Rui Wang[2,3], Xin Liu[2], Donglan Liu[2], Hao Zhang[2], Lei Ma[2], Fangzhe Zhang[2], Lili Sun[2], and Zhenghao Li[1]

[1] State Grid Shandong Electric Power Company, Jinan, China
earthol@126.com
[2] State Grid Shandong Electric Power Research Institute, Jinan, China
[3] Shandong Smart Grid Technology Innovation Center, Jinan, China

Abstract. A 5G TLS implementation vulnerability testing framework is proposed. By constructing a TLS vulnerability database using the public TLS security vulnerabilities, the framework can estimate vulnerabilities for the TLS implementation deployed in 5G core network and entity devices, based on the TLS version and TLS implementation library information obtained during the scanning. Multi-dimensional features of the interactive information of the TLS implementation and online machine-learning methods are used to build a model, thus being used to obtain the TLS implementation library information. The vulnerabilities are also tested by simulating the handshake process and sending customized interactive information.

Keywords: 5G · TLS · vulnerability testing · framework

1 Introduction

Mobile communication technology has been developing in the past few years, and the latest version of 5G has appeared. Today, 5G technology has spread to the market. In order to meet such high-quality requirements, not only the wireless access network needs to be changed and upgraded, but also the core part of 5G needs to be changed and upgraded. The advantages of 5G are enhanced mobile broadband, being suitable for large-scale Internet of Things and reliability with low latency. The 5G core network mainly guarantees the continuity of calls, completes the mobility management function of user equipment access, provides the management of user and group subscription data, and provides encryption and authentication functions. The control plane is mainly used to process the user's data. It is used to transfer information between multiple nodes. Unlike 4G, 5G network slice architecture is based on network virtualization technology. 5G technology adopts the concept of virtualization, and divides its physical infrastructure into several virtual logical networks called network slices. Each network slice is composed of several virtual network functions, which together create an environment to serve various services with different characteristics. 3GPP

J. Zhou et al. (Eds.): ACNS 2023 Workshops, LNCS 13907, pp. 284–298, 2023.
https://doi.org/10.1007/978-3-031-41181-6_16

recommends that 5G service providers use TLS to protect the communication between different network functions (NFs) in the 5G core network. However, the incorrect implementation of TLS protocol and some incorrect configurations in use will be used by attackers to decrypt and tamper with the encrypted data, which will cause serious security incidents.

2 Preliminaries and Related Work

2.1 5G Slicing and Security

Network Slicing refers to the use of Software Defined Network (SDN) and Network Function Virtualization (NFV) technology by 5G operators to establish multiple isolated virtual networks on limited physical network devices [1]. Different network slices achieve different network performance indicators and provide different communication methods and security policies. The 5G core network slice [2] consists of virtual network elements such as Access and Mobility Management Function (AMF), Session Management Function (SMF), Network Slice Selection Function (NSSF), and Authentication Server Function (AUSF), and is divided into a control layer and a user data layer. Different core network slices can independently own a group of virtual network elements or share a group of virtual network elements.

The core network slices need to establish secure channels between network elements, and mutual authentication is even more necessary to resist malicious behaviors such as man-in-the-middle attacks and eavesdropping attacks. In [3], the authors enumerated a list of technologies that ensure the slicing security, including technologies based on VPN-based network slice isolation. These technologies employs special security protocols such as IPSec, SSL/TLS, DTLS. In order to ensure secure communication between network elements at the control layer, HU et al. [4] and others proposed using the HTTP/2 protocol to complete authentication, authorization, and accounting between network element nodes at the control layer and background nodes at the user data layer. Compared to the Diameter protocol in 4G networks, the HTTP/2 protocol is simpler to operate and has lower latency, making it suitable for mobile animal networking scenarios such as the Internet of Vehicles. However, the HTTP/2 protocol has the characteristics of traffic control and trust dependency, resulting in its vulnerability to replay attacks and dependency consumption attacks. In addition, because the authentication scheme using the HTTP/2 protocol uses TLS certificates, attackers can forge legitimate network element nodes by forging TLS certificates, thereby implementing man-in-the-middle attacks on truly legitimate network element nodes. Sathi et al. [5] proposed a secure communication protocol for GroupB core network slicing. The protocol is embedded with a bilinear proxy re encryption algorithm based on elliptic curves, which supports mutual authentication between network elements within core network slices to resist man in the middle attacks.

2.2 Transport Layer Security

The core communication protocols of Internet, such as TCP, UDP and IP are inherently insecure. In order to solve the problem of secure transmission in TCP layer, Netscape company proposed secure socket layer protocol in 1994, known as socket security protocol. SSL 1.0, SSL 2.0, SSL 3.0 are designed and maintained by Netscape. IETF designed TLS 1.0, TLS 1.1 and TLS 1.2. SSL/TLS protocol can provide the following security objectives: using digital certificate to authenticate the identity of server and client to prevent identity forgery, confidentiality, preventing third party eavesdropping with encryption, protecting data integrity and preventing message tampered with MAC, using implicit serial numbers to prevent replay attacks. SSL/TLS protocol is designed as a two-phase protocol: in handshake phase, the client and server authenticate each other's identity and negotiate security parameters, cipher suite and the master secret used in communication; in application phase, the communication parties use negotiated key for secure communication.

There are many known TLS vulnerabilities such as BEAST [6], CBC padding oracle [7], Lucky 13 [8], POODLE [9], CRIME [10], BREACH [11], Bleichenbacher's attack [12], Heartbleed [13], Weak Algorithms, etc., and can be roughly divided into following categories:

1. TLS protocol design is insufficient. For example, a series of encryption methods based on CBC mode and weak encryption algorithms such as RC4 have a serious impact.
2. The implementation of the TLS protocol is insufficient. Because many TLS developers do not implement the protocol strictly in accordance with the standard and some programs themselves have implementation problems, the implementation of TLS protocol has many flaws.
3. Issues related to the digital certificates used by TLS. The complexity of certificate management and verification causes a series of attacks related to certificates.

Table 1 shows the TLS/SSL vulnerabilities.

2.3 Port Scanning Technology

Scanning the network requires first discovering the surviving IP addresses and ports open on the surviving IP addresses. Port scanning mainly uses four methods to determine whether the target port is open, using the characteristics of TCP or UDP protocols. The four methods are as follows:

1. TCP SYN scanning. It is a semi open scan that sends SYN packets to the target port. If the target port is open, it will receive SYN-ACK packets, otherwise it will receive RST packets. If there is no response, there is a possibility that the target port will be blocked by a firewall.
2. TCP connect scanning. It establishes a TCP connection with the target port. If the connection is successfully established, it indicates that the port is open.

Table 1. TLS/SSL vulnerabilities

Incorrect use of algorithm	BEAST	Attackers can exploit vulnerabilities in CBC mode
	Lucky13	The attack allows a man in the middle attacker to intercept TLS packets and modify packets from TLS connections when CBC mode encryption is enabled
	POODLE	An attacker can downgrade the protocol to SSLv3 and utilize the SSLv3 protocol to verify only the padding byte length in CBC mode
	Robot	When the session key is encrypted using the RSA algorithm and the system is populated using PKCS 1.5, a Robot vulnerability can occur
	Drown	Using outdated SSLv2 protocols to decrypt traffic protected by TLS protocols that use the same key
Security caused by compression	Crime	Use information disclosure in compression algorithms in earlier versions of TLS and SPDY to obtain sensitive information such as session cookies and passwords. An attacker can guess sensitive information based on the length of the ciphertext
	Breach	Utilize the data compression algorithm provided by HTTP. This will compress duplicate text, which will only appear once. Duplicate text appearing in clear text affects the length of ciphertext. Attackers can guess sensitive information based on the length of the ciphertext
Insufficient strength	FREAK	Use the RSA cipher suite when the maximum encryption strength is 40 bits and the maximum key exchange strength is 512 bits
	LOGJAM	Using weak DH Keys in Diffie-Hellman key exchange algorithms
	RC4	Single byte deviations and double byte deviations
	SWEET32	For encryption algorithms using 3DES and Blowfish
	SLOTH	Attackers force clients or servers to use weak hashes
Vulnerability in implementation	HeartBleed	Openssl 1.0.2-beta and Openssl 1.0.1 have a vulnerability in processing TLS heartbeat extension boundaries, which can be exploited by an attacker to read the contents of the client or server's memory
	TicketBleed	A software vulnerability exists in the TLS/SSL stack of F5 BIG-IP that allows attackers to obtain up to 31 bytes of data from uninitialized memory
	CVE-2016-2107	AES-NI is enabled for Openssl, there is a vulnerability in the detection of padding in the CBC encryption mode, and the server reports an error message in clear text when the TLS handshake is not completed
Backdoor	InvalidCurve	Using a vulnerability that may exist during key negotiation in ECDHE, when establishing a TLS connection using ECDHE, determine whether the server accepts points on an invalid curve to generate a shared key
	WeakCurve	Use weak curves such as SECP160K1 to negotiate shared keys
	DH Backdoor	Check whether p and q are large enough, and check whether p and q are both prime numbers

When a TCP connection is established with the target device, the target device will record connection logs, so the scanning of TCP connect scanning is not covert enough.

3. TCP ACK scanning. It sends ACK packets to the target device, and determines whether the target port is shielded by a firewall based on whether the RST packet is received.
4. UDP scanning. It determines whether the target port supports the UDP protocol. This method will send UDP protocol detection packets to the target port, and determine the opening status of the UDP port based on whether the "ICMP port unreachable" message is received. If received, it indicates that the port is closed.

2.4 Related Work

As one of the most widely used security protocols, the security of TLS protocol has attracted a great deal of attention, and has been carefully and thoroughly analyzed by various researchers and attackers. There are a range of security threats from cryptographic attacks [14–16] to protocol implementation vulnerabilities [8,17,18].

Durumeric et al. [19] used ZMap to scan the IPv4 address space to quantify the impact of the Heartbleed vulnerability [13]. Heninger et al. scanned TLS and SSH for weak keys generated using insufficient entropy [20]. Attacks on authentication are presented in [21] and [22]. Adrian et al. introduced the Logjam vulnerability [23]. Aviram et al. introduced the DROWN vulnerability and scanned it Internet-wide and quantified its impact [17]. In paper [24], several critical vulnerabilities were detected in commonly used TLS implementations. Systematic testing of TLS implementations with tools based on such state machine errors is presented in [25] and provides the user with the possibility to create custom TLS message flows and arbitrarily modify the message content. The work in [26] followed the model-based approach [25] to test TLS implementations. The cryptographic analysis of the TLS 1.3 is discussed in [27]. Bóck et al. performed a large-scale scan of the Bleichenbacher vulnerability [28] and also observed the side-channel information such as TCP connection state changes. Valenta et al. scanned for known vulnerabilities in elliptic curve implementations [29].

To analyze the impact of SSL libraries on the security of the TLS protocol, Nemec et al. counted the deployment of SSL libraries by scanning the entire Internet and using the distribution characteristics of the RSA public keys generated by different SSL libraries [30]. Kotzias et al. analyzed the changes in the Internet-wide TLS security ecosystem since 2012 [31], showing that although various TLS libraries have been upgraded, there are still a large number of servers that cannot resist the existing vulnerabilities. For the first time, the authors in [32] applied a deep reinforcement learning framework to test the certificate validation part of the SSL/TLS implementation. Samarasinghe et al. [33] used data from Censys [34] to make a comprehensive analysis of TLS deployments on the Internet and found serious problems in the cryptographic protection of IoT devices. Calzavara et al. [35] proposed an evaluation criterion to assess the vulnerability of HTTPS in the Web ecosystem in conjunction with data from Shodan [36]. In [37], a modular framework extensible with new features was proposed, which can detect TLS vulnerabilities and provide the mitigation.

Our Contribution. In order to evaluate the implementation of the TLS protocol deployed in 5G scenario including 5G core network and 5G entity devices, we propose a 5G TLS vulnerability testing framework, which can effectively detect the vulnerabilities of the TLS implementation in 5G core network and entity devices. As shown in Fig. 1, the framework mainly consists of five modules, including TLS version identification, SSL library identification, TLS vulnerability database construction, vulnerability matching, and vulnerability testing. The framework crawls the public vulnerability information of the TLS protocol specifications and the TLS implementations using TLS vulnerability database construction module, as well as the public research results of the TLS vulnerabilities. Then use this information to build a TLS vulnerability database. During a specific testing, TLS version identification module and SSL library identification module are used to quickly obtain the protocol version and SSL library information, which are used to match the corresponding vulnerabilities from the TLS vulnerability database. At last, vulnerability testing module is used to test the matched vulnerabilities, and the results are stored into the statistical information database.

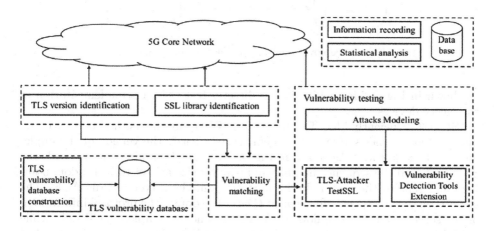

Fig. 1. The framework.

3   The Framework

The framework can evaluate the implementation of the TLS protocol deployed in 5G core network following the steps:

Step 1. Establish the scanning entity. In a selected core network slice, scanning entity can be deployed in the selected core network slice for detection, as shown in Fig. 2. If the scanning entity is deployed outside the core network slice, it cannot directly connect to the 5G network and the registration phase is needed

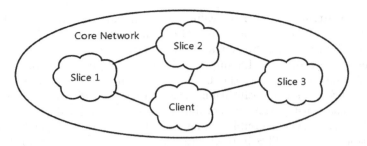

Fig. 2. Deploying entity in core network.

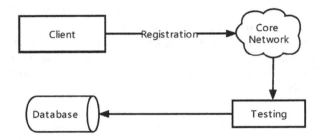

Fig. 3. Deploying entity outside the core network.

as shown in Fig. 3. Meanwhile, it can directly test the TLS implementation in the entity devices.

Step 2. Efficiently identify TLS version. We apply the method of identifying unexpected internet services [38] to efficiently identify the version of the implemented TLS protocol. As shown in Fig. 4, the client (scanning entity) sends the SYN first, and the sequence number and window size are set to be random numbers and sent to the server. If the port is open, the server returns ACK. The client then sends a specific fingerprint (Data1) to obtain the protocol information of the server (Data2). The flow in the Fig. 4 is not a complete TCP link, while a TLS fingerprint is sent during the third handshake. If the service is identified as a TLS service, the version information of TLS is identified by sending all the versions of TLS protocol (Data3) to the server and checking the responses (Data4). This method starts to exchange data in the third handshake in the TCP handshake process, and sends the TLS fingerprint to the server to obtain the protocol information to reduce the number of interactions. If the server provides TLS service on the port, the client continues to send fingerprints to identify the TLS version of the TLS implementation in the core network slice. Otherwise, the client sends RST instead of performing four normal breakup, which reduces the time required to perform scanning the ports providing non-TLS services. Algorithm 1 shows the details of the TLS version identification process.

Step 3. Make the following tests based on the TLS version information:

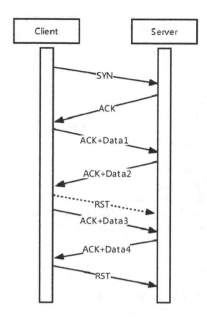

Fig. 4. Flow of identifying TLS version.

Step 3.1. Identify the SSL library information used to implement the TLS protocol. By obtaining the specific SSL library information used in implementing the TLS services, we can better analyze the defects of the TLS protocol implementation. For example, TLS services built using the same SSL library may have the same vulnerabilities. We use the multi-dimensional features of the responses of TLS services, and apply the machine-learning model to identify the SSL library. Furthermore, the result feedback mechanism is used, and the online learning method is applied to the model training process, so that we can improve the recognition accuracy according the real-time result feedbacks of recognition. Figure 5 shows a framework for identifying the SSL library information. Specifically, we first collect the features of the SSL libraries. These features include: supported TLS versions, supported cryptographic suites, resistance to known attacks, distribution characteristics of the generated RSA keys [19], distribution characteristics of the generated ECC keys, etc. It is necessary to collect the mainstream TLS implementations, such as openssl, boringssl, libressl, s2n, polarssl, gnutls, cyassl, and the cryptographic libraries such as libcrypto, libcrypt, cryptlib, libgcrypt, wolfcrypt, LibTomCrypt, Nettle and other open source libraries. Then we use these SSL libraries to repeatedly generate RSA keys and ECC keys, and analyze the distribution features of the RSA keys and ECC keys, and get their deviations from the uniform random distribution. Using these features, the model is trained using the deep learning method. Finally, the model is used for identifying the SSL library information.

Algorithm 1. Identifing TLS version

Input: IP.
Output: IP,Port,TLS version.

```
 1: allportscan_res← ∅
 2: for all ports do
 3:     send(ip,port,SYN)
 4:     if resv(ACK) then
 5:         if ACK.window and ACK.port=port then
 6:             send(ip,port,ACK1)
 7:         end if
 8:         if resv(ACK2) then
 9:             if ACK2.DATA then
10:                 for all fingerprint do
11:                     if match(ACK2.DATA.fingerprint,fingerprint)==True then
12:                         allportscan_res←(ip,port,TLS version)
13:                     end if
14:                     break
15:                 end for
16:             end if
17:             if !ACK2.DATA and RST then
18:                 send(ip,port,SYN)
19:             end if
20:             if !ACK2.DATA and !RST and FIN then
21:                 send(ip,port,RST)
22:                 continue
23:             end if
24:         end if
25:     end if
26: end for
27: return allportscan_res
```

Step 3.2. Estimate vulnerabilities depending on the TLS version, implementation and the SSL library information. There are some known vulnerabilities in different versions of TLS specification, TLS implementations and SSL libraries. Therefore, we can estimate security vulnerabilities based on this information. To this end, we firstly use the crawler to collect the public vulnerability information of the TLS specifications, implementations and SSL libraries mentioned in **Step 3.1.** on the Internet. The collected vulnerability information includes the library name, the version, and the vulnerability description. Secondly, we collect the public research results of TLS protocol vulnerabilities in academic papers. Then, we use the information to build a vulnerability database, which stores the vulnerabilities corresponding to different versions of TLS specification, implementation and SSL library. Table 2 shows the example contents of the built vulnerability database.

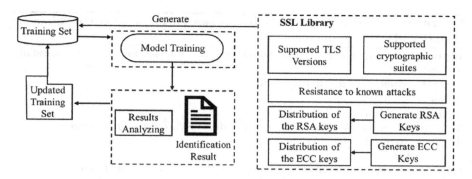

Fig. 5. A framework for identifying the SSL library information.

Table 2. Example of the contents of the vulnerability database

Library name	TLS/SSL Version	Vulnerability
OpenSSL 1.0.1	\	SWEET32
OpenSSL 1.0.2	\	SWEET32
\	SSLv2	Drown
\	SSLv3	POODLE
OpenSSL1.0.1*	\	Heartbleed
. . .	. . .	. . .

Finally, we use the obtained TLS version and the version information of the SSL implementation library to get the corresponding vulnerabilities from the vulnerability database. Algorithm 2 shows details of matching the corresponding vulnerabilities.

Step 4. Vulnerability verifying.

For all the TLS vulnerabilities mentioned above, we firstly integrate TestSSL [39] and TLS-Attacker [40] for vulnerability verification. For the vulnerabilities that TestSSL and TLS-Attacker cannot detect [29,41], we build specific tools to detect them. TestSSL is a command-line tool that can detect SSL/TLS flaw on any port. TLS-Attacker is a Java-based framework for analyzing TLS libraries by sending arbitrary (modified) protocol messages in an arbitrary order to the TLS server. This makes the developer easier to define a custom TLS protocol flow and test it against the TLS library. In the following, we give specific descriptions about how to test two vulnerabilities in TLS key agreement process [29,41], which cannot be detected by TestSSL and TLS-Attacker. The testing processes are shown Fig. 6.

Algorithm 2. Matching the vulnerabilities base on TLS version and SSL implementation library information

---

Input: TLS version and SSL implementation library information (vinfo), vulnerability database (vdb).
Output: Vulnerabilities (matched_vul).

1: matched_vul← ∅
2: **for** each VulInfo ∈ vdb **do**
3:     **if** fuzzymatch(VulInfo.TLSVersion,vinfo.TLSVersion)==True **then**
4:         matched_vul+={VulInfo.vul}
5:     **end if**
6:     **if** fuzzymatch(VulInfo.SSLlibInfo,vinfo.SSLlibInfo)==True **then**
7:         matched_vul+={VulInfo.vul}
8:     **end if**
9: **end for**
10: **return** matched_vul

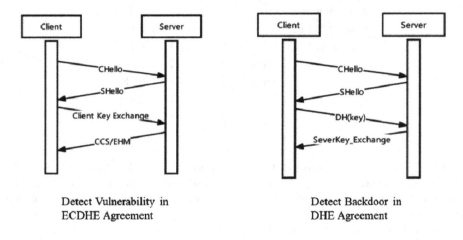

Detect Vulnerability in
ECDHE Agreement

Detect Backdoor in
DHE Agreement

Fig. 6. Vulnerability testing processes.

a) The interactive information in the ECDHE key agreement process of the TLS protocol includes points on the selected elliptic curve. However, in the specific implementation, both parties may not verify whether the points sent by the other party are on the selected elliptic curve. Attackers can use this vulnerability to perform man-in-the-middle attacks [29], by intercepting the information sent by the client, and then instead of the client sending negotiation request to the server using some weak curves. As the order of the weak curve is small, by calculating the discrete logarithm, the attacker can obtain the secret information which is used by the server to calculate the points on the curve. Therefore, the attacker can obtain the session key negotiated by both parties.

The vulnerability can be detected by simulating the TLS handshake process. Firstly, a specific elliptic curve called *Invalid Curve* is generated for each type of curve supported in the TLS protocol, which will not be used for ECDHE key agreement. Figure 7 gives an example of *Invalid Curve*. Then an ECDHE key agreement process is started with the server. When the scanning entity establishes a handshake with the server, it selects the point on the *Invalid Curve*, encapsulates the point on the Client_ Key_ Exchange message and sends the message to the server. If the server returns Change_Cipher_Spec and Encrypted_Handshake_Message messages, then the vulnerability exists in the server TLS implementation.

Invalidcurve={"p":0xffffffff00000001000000000000000000000000ffffffff

ffffffffffffffff,"a":0xffffffff00000001000000000000000000000000ffffffff

fffffffffffffffc,"b":0x5ac635d8aa3a93e7b3ebbd55769886bc651d06b0cc53b

0f63bce3c3e27d2604a,"g":(0xbfd35739ed4b4d938c91e8357c7ec4c41de9

fdfc166988ebd1dfa09c79596661,0x89492141e9e81674979862d9fc6221c

4a672b89033e07b86da40d67d5c0f53e3),"n":0x5,"h":0x1}

Fig. 7. Example of *Invalid Curve*.

b) In the DHE key agreement process of the TLS protocol, if the modulus used by one party is with short length or is a composite number that is hard to factorize, then there is a back door to obtain the private key of the other party with a large probability [41]. The scanning entity can start the DHE key agreement process with the server, and get the modulus parameters of the server in the Sever_Key_Exchange message. By checking the length of the parameters and whether the parameter is prime, it can determine whether there is a back door.

4 Conclusion

To evaluate the implementation of the TLS protocol deployed in 5G scenario, in this paper, we propose a 5G TLS vulnerability testing framework, which can effectively detect the vulnerabilities of the TLS implementation in 5G core network and entity devices. It can efficiently identify TLS services provided on any port and extract TLS version information. Further, utilizing the multi-dimensional features of the interactive information of the TLS implementation, it can apply online machine-learning methods to build a model to identify the TLS implementation information. Then, most of the known security vulnerabilities can be estimated according to the extracted TLS protocol version information and the TLS implementation information. By simulating the handshake process and sending customized interactive information, special vulnerabilities in the key agreement process can be detected.

Acknowledgment. This research is sponsored by the project of State Grid Shandong Electric Power Company Science and Technology Program, Project Name: Research on Key Technologies of Smart Grid 5G Secure Access and Trusted Data Sharing - Topic 1: Research on Key Technologies of Smart Grid 5G Terminals and Network Security Detection and Risk Assessment, ERP Number: 520626220016.

References

1. Barakabitze, A.A., Ahmad, A., Mijumbi, R., Hines, A.: 5G network slicing using SDN and NFV: a survey of taxonomy, architectures and future challenges. Comput. Netw. **167**, 106984 (2020)
2. 3GPP TS 23.501. System Architecture for the 5G System [EB/OL]. https://www.3gpp.org/ftp/Specs/archive/23_series/23.501/. Accessed 19 July 2019
3. Del Piccolo, V., Amamou, A., Haddadou, K., Pujolle, G.: A survey of network isolation solutions for multi-tenant data centers. IEEE Commun. Surv. Tutor. **18**(4), 2787–2821 (2016)
4. Hu, X., Liu, C., Liu, S., You, W., Zhao, Y.: Signalling security analysis: is HTTP/2 secure in 5G core network? In: Proceedings on IEEE 10th International Conference on Wireless Communications and Signal Processing, Hangzhou, China, pp. 1–6. IEEE (2018)
5. Sathi, V.N., Srinivasan, M., Thiruvasagam, P.K., Chebiyyam, S.R.M.: A novel protocol for securing network slice component association and slice isolation in 5G networks. In: Proceedings on the 21st ACM International Conference on Modeling. Analysis and Simulation of Wireless and Mobile Systems, Montreal, QC, Canada, pp. 249–253. ACM (2018)
6. AlFardan, N.J., Bernstein, D.J., Paterson, K.G., Poettering, B., Schuldt, J.C.N.: On the security of RC4 in TLS. In: Proceedings on the 22nd USENIX Conference on Security, USA, pp. 305–320. USENIX Association (2013)
7. Yau, A.K.L., Paterson, K.G., Mitchell, C.J.: Padding oracle attacks on CBC-mode encryption with secret and random IVs. In: Gilbert, H., Handschuh, H. (eds.) FSE 2005. LNCS, vol. 3557, pp. 299–319. Springer, Heidelberg (2005). https://doi.org/10.1007/11502760_20
8. Al Fardan, N.J., Paterson, K.G.: Lucky thirteen: breaking the TLS and DTLS record protocols. In: Proceedings on IEEE Symposium on Security and Privacy, San Francisco, CA, USA, pp. 526–540. IEEE Computer Society (2013)
9. Moller, B., Duong, T., Kotowicz, K.: This POODLE bites: exploiting the SSL 3.0 fallback (2014)
10. Alawatugoda, J., Stebila, D., Boyd, C.: Protecting encrypted cookies from compression side-channel attacks. In: Böhme, R., Okamoto, T. (eds.) FC 2015. LNCS, vol. 8975, pp. 86–106. Springer, Heidelberg (2015). https://doi.org/10.1007/978-3-662-47854-7_6
11. Kelsey, J.: Compression and information leakage of plaintext. In: Daemen, J., Rijmen, V. (eds.) FSE 2002. LNCS, vol. 2365, pp. 263–276. Springer, Heidelberg (2002). https://doi.org/10.1007/3-540-45661-9_21
12. Bleichenbacher, D.: Chosen ciphertext attacks against protocols based on the RSA encryption standard PKCS #1. In: Krawczyk, H. (ed.) CRYPTO 1998. LNCS, vol. 1462, pp. 1–12. Springer, Heidelberg (1998). https://doi.org/10.1007/BFb0055716
13. Heartbleed, CVE-2014-0160 (2015). http://heartbleed.com/

14. Garman, C., Paterson, K.G., Van der Merwe, T.: Attacks only get better: password recovery attacks against RC4 in TLS. In: Proceedings on USENIX Security Symposium, Washington, D.C., USA, pp. 113–128. USENIX Association (2015)
15. Vanhoef, M., Piessens, F.: All your biases belong to us: breaking RC4 in WPA-TKIP and TLS. In: Proceedings on USENIX Security Symposium, Washington, D.C., USA, pp. 97–112. USENIX Association (2015)
16. Alfardan, N., Bernstein, D.J., Paterson, K.G., Poettering, B., Schuldt, J.C.N.: On the security of RC4 in TLS. In: Proceedings on USENIX Security Symposium, Washington, D.C., USA, pp. 305–320. USENIX Association (2013)
17. Aviram, N., et al.: DROWN: breaking TLS using SSLv2. In: Proceedings on USENIX Security Symposium, Austin, TX, USA, pp. 689–706. USENIX Association (2016)
18. Karthikeyan, B., Leurent, G.: Transcript collision attacks: breaking authentication in TLS, IKE, and SSH. Br. J. Psychiatry J. Ment. Sci. 41(7), 8–13 (2016)
19. Durumeric, Z., et al.: The matter of heartbleed. In: Proceedings on ACM Internet Measurement Conference, Vancouver, BC, Canada, pp. 475–488. ACM (2014)
20. Heninger, N., Durumeric, Z., Wustrow, E., Halderman, J.A.: Mining your Ps and Qs: detection of widespread weak keys in network devices. In: Proceedings on USENIX Security Symposium, Bellevue, WA, USA, pp. 205–220. USENIX Association (2012)
21. Bhargavan, K., Lavaud, A.D., Fournet, C., Pironti, A., Strub, P.Y.: Triple handshakes and cookie cutters: breaking and fixing authentication over TLS. In: Proceedings on IEEE Symposium on Security and Privacy (SP), San Francisco, CA, USA, pp. 98–113. IEEE Computer Society (2014)
22. Bhargavan, K., Leurent, G.: Transcript collision attacks: breaking authentication in TLS, IKE, and SSH. In: Proceedings on Network and Distributed System Security Symposium (NDSS), San Diego, CA, USA (2016)
23. Adrian, D., et al.: Imperfect forward secrecy: how Diffie-Hellman fails in practice. In: Proceedings on ACM SIGSAC Conference on Computer and Communications Security, Denver, Colorado, USA, pp. 5–17. ACM (2015)
24. Beurdouche, B., et al.: A messy state of the union: taming the composite state machines of TLS. In: Proceedings on IEEE Symposium on Security and Privacy, San Francisco, CA, USA. IEEE Computer Society (2015)
25. Somorovsky, J.: Systematic fuzzing and testing of TLS libraries. In: Proceedings on ACM SIGSAC Conference on Computer and Communications Security (CCS), Vienna, Austria, pp. 1492–1504. ACM (2016)
26. de Ruiter, J., Poll, E.: Protocol state fuzzing of TLS implementations. In: Proceedings on USENIX Security Symposium, Washington, D.C., USA, pp. 193–206. USENIX Association (2015)
27. Dowling, B., Fischlin, M., Gunther, F., Stebila, D.: A cryptographic analysis of the TLS 1.3 handshake protocol candidates. In: Proceedings on ACM SIGSAC Conference on Computer and Communications Security, Denver, Colorado, USA, pp. 1197–1210. ACM (2015)
28. Bock, H., Somorovsky, J., Young, C.: Return of Bleichenbacher's Oracle Threat (ROBOT). In: Proceedings on USENIX Security Symposium, Baltimore, MD, USA, pp. 817–849. USENIX Association (2018)
29. Valenta, L., Sullivan, N., Sanso, A., Heninger, N.: Search of CurveSwap: measuring elliptic curve implementations in the wild. In: Proceedings on IEEE European Symposium on Security and Privacy, San Francisco, CA, USA, pp. 384–398. IEEE Computer Society (2018)

30. Nemec, M., Klinec, D., Svenda, P., Sekan, P., Matyas, V.: Measuring popularity of cryptographic libraries in internet-wide scans. In: Proceedings on Annual Computer Security Applications Conference, Dallas, Texas, USA, pp. 162–175. ACM (2017)
31. Kotzias, P., Razaghpanah, A., Amann, J.: Coming of age: a longitudinal study of TLS deployment. In: Proceedings on ACM Internet Measurement Conference, Boston, MA, USA, pp. 415–428. ACM (2018)
32. Chen, C., Diao, W., Zeng, Y., Guo, S., Hu, C.: DRLgencert: deep learning-based automated testing of certificate verification in SSL/TLS implementations. In: Proceedings on IEEE International Conference on Software Maintenance and Evolution, Madrid, Spain, pp. 48–58. IEEE (2018)
33. Samarasinghe, N., Mannan, M.: Short paper: TLS ecosystems in networked devices vs. web servers. In: Kiayias, A. (ed.) FC 2017. LNCS, vol. 10322, pp. 533–541. Springer, Cham (2017). https://doi.org/10.1007/978-3-319-70972-7_30
34. Censys. https://censys.io/
35. Calzavara, S., Focardi, R., Nemec, M., et al.: Postcards from the post-HTTP world: amplification of HTTPS vulnerabilities in the web ecosystem. In: Proceedings on IEEE Symposium on Security and Privacy, San Francisco, CA, USA, pp. 281–298. IEEE Computer Society (2019)
36. Shodan. https://www.shodan.io/
37. Rizzi, M., Manfredi, S., Sciarretta, G., Ranise, S.: A modular and extensible framework for securing TLS. In: Proceedings on ACM Conference on Data and Application Security and Privacy, Washington, D.C., USA, pp. 119–124. ACM (2022)
38. Izhikevich, L., Teixeira, R., Durumeric, Z.: LZR: identifying unexpected internet services. In: Proceedings on USENIX Security Symposium, pp. 3111–3128. USENIX Association (2021)
39. TestSSL (2022). https://testssl.sh
40. TLS-attacker 3.8.1 (2022). https://github.com/RUB-NDS/TLS-Attacker
41. Wong, D.: How to backdoor Diffie-Hellman. Cryptology ePrint Archive, Paper 2016/644 (2016)

Safety Watermark: A Defense Tool for Real-Time Digital Forensic Incident Response in Industrial Control Systems

Sim Siang Tze Victor[1] (ID), Chuadhry Mujeeb Ahmed[2] (ID), Koh Yoong Keat Kelvin[3] (ID), and Jianying Zhou[1](✉) (ID)

[1] Singapore University of Technology and Design, Singapore, Singapore
victor_sim@mymail.sutd.edu.sg, jianying_zhou@sutd.edu.sg
[2] Newcastle University, Newcastle Upon Tyne, UK
mujeeb.ahmed@newcastle.ac.uk
[3] Public Utilities Board, Singapore, Singapore
kelvin_koh@pub.gov.sg

Abstract. Industrial Control Systems (ICSs) including those executing process safety controls, alarms, and interlocks are becoming more interconnected with other systems. Traditional process hazard analysis (PHA) rarely considered the possibility of cyber-attacks causing safety incidents in the process. Practitioners have viewed safety and security traditionally as systems with different properties. Both communities worked separately using their respective terminologies and frameworks. With the view of limited resources especially in the protection of security, it is important to be able to prioritize. A strategy is to take a top-down approach by identifying system losses that needed protection. This results in a more manageable set of potential losses. Rather than starting from the angle on how best to protect the network against the myriad of threats, a strategic approach would be to know what services and functions require protection. The novelty of this work is to use a subset of the invariants derived using a top-down approach by focusing on hazards manifestations that require protection from being comprisable digitally. This approach is called the safety watermark concept in this paper. In its most basic form, it is successfully shown to alert operators of potential safety risk manifestations with varying importance. In certain situations where the likelihood of the safety risk manifestations increases towards a cyber-attack, the safety watermark raises the alert level to potential cyber incidents. The safety watermark has been effectively utilized to demonstrate the ability in real-time to identify potential indicators of compromises in terms of system components, a yet to be commercially available capability for industrial control systems. The safety watermark possesses the ability to scale, and an example is illustrated for a consequence driven methodology like the Consequence-Based Cyber-Informed Engineering (CCE) by Idaho National Laboratory.

Keywords: Industrial Control System · Cyber-Physical System Security · Process Hazard Analysis · Safety Watermark · Invariants · Consequence-based Cyber-Informed Engineering

J. Zhou et al. (Eds.): ACNS 2023 Workshops, LNCS 13907, pp. 299–320, 2023.
https://doi.org/10.1007/978-3-031-41181-6_17

1 Introduction

Successful attacks on industrial control systems can have catastrophic consequences for life and severe economic damage to entire supply chains [1]. Before the 1970s, safety systems were easily understood and had well-defined failure modes. Since the 1970s, electronic and programmable electronic systems were introduced to safety system. The move away from proprietary protocols towards more economical and efficient fully integrated process and safety systems meant safety systems can integrate with other networked systems such as industrial control systems. There are many hazards in process industries that can result in loss of containment and the manifestation of a hazard to impact health, safety, environment, and plant assets. The best way to secure process safety is the use of inherently safe processes. When this is not practical or possible, protective systems are introduced to mitigate the risk to an acceptable level [2].

Practitioners have viewed safety and security traditionally as systems with different properties. Both communities work separately using their respective terminologies and frameworks. Safety is concerned with the prevention of losses caused unintentionally by benevolent actors. On the other hand, security is concerned with the prevention of losses caused intentionally by malevolent actors [3]. With the view of limited resources, especially in the protection of security, it is important to be able to prioritize. A strategy is to do a top-down approach by identifying system losses that deems protection. This results in a more manageable set of potential losses. Rather than starting to know how best to protect the network against the myriad of threats, a strategic approach is to know what services and functions requires protection. The "whats" becomes the basis for further deliberation on the "hows" that can lead to specific undesirable outcomes [3].

Undesirable outcomes in the physical world are the real manifestations of the physics or chemistry controlled in the CPS. This is based on state related conditions that must hold operationally when system components are in a given state and are termed invariants [4]. These are the classic invariants and like a bottom-up approach, the original approach attempts to classify all types of state related conditions that depends on how it is deployed, can be computationally intensive and occupy significant network bandwidth through the all-encompassing approach.

In this work, a subset of the invariants is derived using a top-down approach by focusing on hazards manifestations that requires protection from being comprisable digitally. This methodology is called the safety watermark concept. In its most basic form, it alerts operators of potential safety risk manifestations with varying importance. At certain situations where the likelihood of the safety risk manifestations increases towards a cyber-attack, the safety watermark can raise the alert level to potential cyber incidents. The identification of "whats" services and functions to protect occurs through the employment of HAZOP (Hazard and Operability) methodology, a type of PHA to identify worst-case health, safety, security, and environment (HSSE) consequences for the asset. In consideration for the practical implementation in an operational theatre on the "hows", the safety watermark views false positive seriously using rule-based decisions. To be utilized effectively, the safety watermark has demonstrated the ability to identify potential indicators of compromises in terms of system components and its capability to scale in a consequence driven methodology like the Consequence-Based Cyber-Informed Engineering (CCE) by Idaho National Laboratory.

Organization: Section 2 introduces the ICS as a form of cyber-physical system to appreciate its boundaries transcending from the digital to the real world. Section 3 introduces the safety watermark concept and its active defense philosophy. Sections 4 illustrates how the safety watermark concept is implemented and Sect. 5 shows the results of the implementation. Section 6 shares the scalability of the safety watermark to be applied in other risk assessments such as the consequence-based method. Section 7 provides the conclusion.

2 ICS – A Cyber-Physical System

Industrial control systems are a form of cyber-physical system (CPS) and can be classified as an operational technology system that monitors and controls the physical world. It is the boundary where interactions between the cyber and physical worlds occur. It comprises of three main components: communication, computation and control, and monitoring and manipulation [5]. To accomplish this, the CPS is usually made up of sensors to measure the physical process state and uses actuators to execute the control commands. A Programmable Logic Controller (PLC) is a microprocessor then enables the CPS to connect to the physical world through the sensors and actuators, with the enabling of wireless and/or wired communication. Supervisory Control and Data Acquisition (SCADA) is software installed on a normal computer and connected to the PLC that acts as the human-machine interface for display and control [5].

The CPS boundaries can be further described by the cyber, cyber-physical and physical aspects. The cyber aspects of a CPS are the cyber interactions with the PLC (communications with HMI, control center). The cyber-physical aspects are those that connect cyber and physical aspects (PLC, the actuator, and the sensor). The physical aspects are the physical objects that need monitoring and control (the pumps, valves and various field devices). A successful cyber-attack on the CPS typically occurs by compromising the cyber aspect and then manifests its intention through the cyber-physical aspect and results in a physical consequence to inflict damage to safety, environment, or equipment. Figure 1 shows the illustration of the CPS boundaries and how a cyber-attack on the CPS can manifest itself. From the cyber-physical aspect, PLC is the final boundary that converts the cyber manifestations into the physical world.

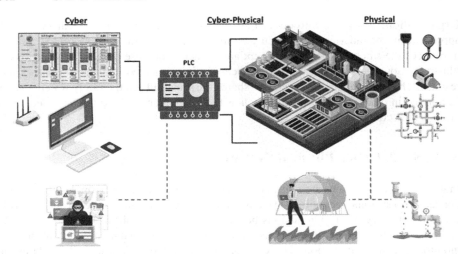

Fig. 1. CPS boundaries [5] and the manifestation of a CPS cyber-attack from the cyber aspect to the physical aspect (red dotted lines) (Color figure online)

3 Safety Watermark Concept

Operational technology (OT) and information technology (IT) systems value the Confidentiality, Integrity, and Availability (CIA) triads differently. OT prioritizes availability whereas IT prioritize confidentiality. OT system requires strong process safety risk and safety integrity awareness. This requires the assessment of the potential hazards associated with industrial processes through the identification of worst-case health, safety, and environment consequences to the OT environment, and any hazard scenarios arising from the cyber risks to the OT system [6]. With reference to ISA-TR84.00.09–2017, Table 1 illustrates the main differences between IT and OT systems.

Table 1. Differences between IT and CPS – OT System [6]

Criteria for Comparison	IT	OT
Response Time Performance	Limited Knowledge of Process Response Time Requirements	Real Time Relative to Process Dynamics, milliseconds to seconds
Availability	Occasional Outages Tolerated	Outages Not Tolerated
Data Confidentiality	Data Privacy is critical	Data Privacy generally less critical
Data Integrity and/or Software Integrity	Critical	Critical
Technology Lifecycle	3 – 5 years	20 years
Outsourcing	Common	Less Common
Patching	Timely	Less Frequent / As Required
Anti-Virus	Common	Legacy systems may not be supported. Potential side-effects with real-time process software
Cybersecurity Awareness	Good	Poor / Improving
Process Safety Risk Awareness	Poor	Good
Safety Integrity Awareness	Poor	Good
Changes	Easy to Implement	Difficult to Implement

Invariants are known as conditions among "physical" and/or "chemical" properties of the process that must hold whenever an CPS system is in a given state [4]. It is referred to a unified knowledge model for CPS and are also "attack symptoms" to detect attacks in an intrusion detection system [7]. At any given time instant, measurements of a suitable set of these properties make up the observable state of the CPS. An invariant-based intrusion detection system has a few advantages, namely in the context of implementation, physical boundaries, and detection method [4]. An invariant-based detection can be implemented as a procedure and integrated directly as part of the CPS. The invariants are real manifestations of the physics or chemistry controlled in the CPS. Detection is attack agonistic since it is done without reference to attacks and is based on state related conditions that must hold operationally when system components are in a given state [4].

Inspired by digital watermarking, physical watermarking is a control theoretic model to authenticate the correct operation of a control system [8]. The idea of physical watermarking has been applied to detect replay attacks by using a physical nonce through the addition of a known noisy signal and observing its impact on the system outputs. The concept can be considered as a form of challenge-response protocol commonly found in the information security literature where the watermark signal acts as a challenge and sensor measurements being a response [9].

Combining the ingenuity of the physical watermark and the invariant-based detection, a safety watermark concept is proposed. The watermark signal takes cue from the process safety risk manifestations that act as the challenge and invariants being the response that are conditions among "physical" and/or "chemical" properties of the process that must hold whenever a CPS is experiencing a specific hazardous event. Process safety risk manifestations can be potentially used as potential indicator of compromises like a detection tool in real time to derive the procedures of an adversary in an OT system like the MITRE ATT&CK® Industrial Control Systems Framework's tactics on impair control process and impact [10].

Unlike IT cyber-attacks that involve around data breach or financial loss, OT cyber-attacks on process systems can cause physical damage to equipment, environment, and personnel [11]. This is due to the risk realization when a hazardous condition is allowed sufficient time to manifest itself as a consequence and cause an impact. IEC 61511 and IEC 61508 define Safety Instrumented Functions (SIF) as part of the Safety Function that is instrumented, has an associated Safety Integrity Level (SIL) and is carried out by a Safety Instrumented System (SIS) to prevent a hazard or mitigate its consequences [12]. SIS is only a type of Instrumented Protection System (IPS) to reduce risk in the process industry. The basic process control system (BPCS) also serves as another IPS performing alarms, interlocks, permissive functions, or controls [13]. Both SIS and BPCS operate similarly. They contain a sensory subsystem, a logic solver subsystem and a final element subsystem. An IPS contains the sensor subsystem that senses an abnormal process condition and represent a potential hazard, the logic solver subsystem that activates a defined executive response to a hazardous event, and a final element that activates to prevent the hazardous event or mitigate the event consequences. Intuitively, the three functions of IPS serve as indicator of compromises for process safety risk manifestations to understand the tactics on impair control process and impact.

Two important concepts arise when the behavior of the IPS can be predicted if the logic code and sensor measurements are known and collaborated as ground truths. In the safety watermark concept, the logic solver subsystem and the sensor subsystem are collaborated as Ground Truth #1 (GT #1), and Ground Truth #2 (GT #2), respectively.

- Concept 1: As the logic code executes based on the input measured by the sensor subsystem collaborated as GT #2, the output executed by the logic solver and manifested by the actuator subsystem can be predicted.
- Concept 2: The output cannot be used to predict the input but if GT #2 is true, logic solver subsystem (GT #1) can be checked for integrity based on the output.

For GT #2 in an OT environment, the sensor subsystem can be physical measurement field devices known as level 0 devices under the hierarchy approach [14] that are usually states of pumps, states of valves or states of other measurements. The logic solver will only execute the logic based on GT #2 as the input and output the expected behavior. It is important to note while the states of pumps and valves can be manipulated in a cyber-attack, they still represent the actual state of the pumps and valves send as input to the logic solver. Provided integrity of PLC tags (variables) are intact, these states can be truthfully obtained via PLC active query.

On the other hand, physical sensory measurements such as level transmitters and other meters (e.g. pH, ORP, conductivity etc.) can have its digital signals bypassed to a deliberate static manner using the PLC's engineering or maintenance mode under normal circumstances. These engineering or maintenance modes under normal circumstances are meant for plant operators to legitimately bypass faulty sensors or field devices so that the automated process can continue its normal functions in a calibrated scenario. In a cyber-attack, the PLC can be misled deliberately to accept such cyber inputs. This attack can be performed using the PLC's engineering or maintenance mode under normal circumstances even though digital signals from functional field devices are continuously transmitted to the PLC via the I/O card. Interestingly, the I/O card connected to the physical sensors inherently has an ultra-high refresh rate of milliseconds to the PLC due to the requirement of high reliability. Therefore, this inherent ultra-high refresh rate can be utilized to validate GT #2 even during an active cyber-attack [15]. Active querying to the PLC in the form of switching off this engineering or maintenance mode even momentarily can re-establish GT #2 even when the adversary is continuously instructions for engineering or maintenance mode [15].

Figure 2 shows the components for a CPS system for an instrumented protection system with GT #1 and GT #2 labelled. In summary,

- Ground Truth (GT) #1 – Logic solver in the PLC executes based on input and logic code.
- Ground Truth (GT) #2 – Physical sensory measurement digitally measuring the physical world.

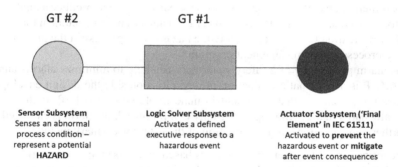

Fig. 2. Components of an Instrumented Protection System [12]

3.1 SWaT Testbed

A HAZOP study is performed on iTrust[1] Secure Water Treatment (SWaT) system that is delivering drinking water to the subsequent Water Distribution (WADI) system to form a complete and realistic water treatment, storage and distribution network. Secure Water Treatment (SWaT) system is a six-stage water purification plant capable of producing five gallons of safe drinking water per minute through processes such as ultra-filtration, de-chlorination, and reverse osmosis. It contains 68 sensors and actuators. Its sensors variously read the level of tanks, pressure, and flow across the system, whereas its actuators include motorised valves and pumps. Sensor readings are typically continuous values, whereas actuators are typically discrete (e.g. 'open'/'closed'; 'on'/'o') [4].

SWaT provides the only source of potable water to the WADI. If the SWaT is taken down because of an attack, WADI will not be able to have sufficient water storage and distribution. Functional disruption at SWaT resulting in a reduction of WADI's capability to store and distribute potable water in accordance with the Singapore Environmental Public Health (Water Suitable for Drinking) (No. 2) Regulations 2019 for drinking water quality.

3.2 Safety Watermark Active Defense Philosophy

Safeguards are determined using the HAZOP (Hazard & Operability Studies) study that is a type of Process Hazard Analysis (PHA). The HAZOP study is limited to only the automation operability as it is the cyber-attacks that can affect the cyber aspects of a CPS. The study requires multi-disciplinary team members (mechanical, electrical, process, and instrumentation and control automation) for participation to produce a quality study in the form of a risk register. The risk register is meant as a living document that requires periodic revalidation to reflect accurately the hazards of a process in the presence of an effective process safety management program.

The alarm philosophy of a safety watermark can help to minimize alarms annunciate. HAZOP is a systematic evaluation of deviations outside the design envelope and identifies unique causes that can result in undesirable situations [16]. If there are no safety safeguards malfunctioning or digitally compromised, no alarm is expected.

Further considerations in the derivation of the safety watermark includes:

i. Categorization of the safety watermark is based on the principle of invariants where it is the condition of "physical" and/or "chemical" properties of the process that must hold when the industrial control system is in a given state. Using Chosen Scenario – Deliberate Dosing of Sodium Hypochlorite in Sect. 4 as an example,
   a. Safeguards Category Group 1: AIT203 (ORP) and AIT302 (ORP) are measuring the oxidation-reduction potential of the same water source that has not been affected by any treatment process.

---

[1] iTrust is a multidisciplinary research center located at the Singapore University of Technology and Design (SUTD), established collaboratively by SUTD and the Singapore Ministry of Defence in 2012.

b. Safeguards Category Group 2: UV401, AIT402 (ORP) & NaHSO3 dosing system, AIT502 (ORP) are measuring the destruction of chlorine through the proxy of the oxidation-reduction potential of the same water source.

c. Safeguards Category Group 3: FIT502, AIT504 (Conductivity), MV501 and MV 503 are measuring the failure of the RO membrane integrity to desalt the water and prevent contamination of downstream process post RO membranes by dumping water into the drain through controlling of the valves.

ii. For alarm prioritization, the categories of safeguards are prioritized in accordance with the hierarchy of controls as shown in Fig. 3, i.e. elimination controls are allocated the highest priority whereas administrative controls such as requiring operators for intervention are allocated lower priority. As personal protection equipment (PPE) does not constitute an alarm, it is not included. Using the same scenario in Sect. 4 as an example,

a) Safeguards Category Group 1: AIT203 (ORP) and AIT302 (ORP), is an administrative control group and is allocated Level 1 Severity. The safeguards are predominantly measurement alarms that indicate the water quality and require operators to make an assessment before addressing the hazard.

b) Safeguards Category Group 2: UV401, AIT402 (ORP) & NaHSO3 dosing system, AIT502 (ORP), is an elimination control group and is allocated Level 4 Severity. The safeguards are predominantly meant to eliminate the chlorine through measurement alarms that indicate the oxidation-reduction potential of the water. Without operators to make an assessment, the safeguards automate the elimination of the hazard.

c) Safeguards Category Group 3: FIT502, AIT504 (Conductivity), MV501 and MV 503, is an engineering control group and is allocated Level 2 Severity. The safeguards predominantly remove the out-of-spec water before coming into contact with downstream process through measurement alarms that measure the water quality and integrity of RO membranes.

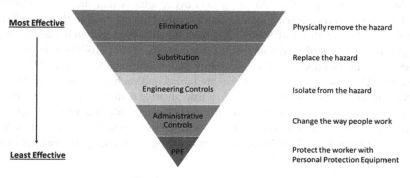

Fig. 3. Hierarchy of Controls

iii. In the event more than 1 category of safety watermark alerts occur, the possibility of cyber-attack can be considered since double jeopardy concept is not practiced during the identification of safeguards in the HAZOP study. Double jeopardy refers to the occurrence of two deviations or two initiating events at the same time.

iv. Safeguards in the risk register form the corresponding invariants in the safety watermark. The identification of these safeguards is adapted from the Security-Process Hazard Analysis (Security-PHA) [18]. The invariants response for the safety watermark concept further assumes two things:

    a. Safety watermark equates the only possible condition for the occurrence of the invariant state under normal design envelope, i.e. UV401 On when P401/P402 On and FIT401 Normal.

    b. Only normal and maintenance mode are considered for this project. Start-up and shutdown sequences are specific operating modes not commonly encountered. However, it can have a secondary set of advanced alarms using the same safety watermark and HAZOP methodology. When utilised for start-up and shutdown, the safety watermark is a separate set of invariants and activated specifically.

3.3 Related Work

The original approach of the classic invariants [4] attempts to classify all types of state related conditions while this work is to derive a sub-set of invariants to form the safety watermark by focusing on hazards manifestations. The safety watermark is customized for operators by considering international standard (IEC 62682:2014) for the management of alarms systems for the process industries [19]. To the best of the authors, no existing signature- and host-based detection system has ever used PHA as an approach.

4 Chosen Scenario – Deliberate Overdosing of Sodium Hypochlorite

The chosen scenario is subjected to various cyber-attacks and the safety watermark code. Pycomm python 2 is used to deliberately read/write tags within the Allen Bradley ControlLogix L5571 PLCs of SWaT [20]. Results are tabled and analyzed. Each category group of safeguards are compromised separately. This is followed by a multiple categories group of attacks chosen randomly and a final attack scenario of all digital safeguards. The results for each scenario are tabled and each red cross indicates detection with the invariant state that will give a true positive using the safety watermark. A false negative indicates the inability for the safety watermark to detect the appropriate invariant state for the attack and is labelled with a black triangle. As the safety watermark is a signature-based host-based detection system, it does not generate false positive alerts. These are the general observations:

i. Results are expected in real-time with the real-time constraint of the PLC respective cycle time of SWaT is in the order of tens of milliseconds [20] and analyzed to illustrate the success of the safety watermark alarms. If the alarm is due to a specific safety watermark category group, it raises a safety risk manifestation. If the alarm is due by two or more different specific safety watermark category groups, it raises an additional alert for potential cyber incident.

ii. An analysis is further conducted on the compromised safeguards in each attack scenario to see if the resultant worst-case consequences could have been averted with or without an operator intervention.

   a. If the safeguards for elimination or engineering controls are not compromised, the worst-case consequences would usually be averted automatically by the remaining safeguards.

   b. If the safeguards for elimination or engineering are affected, the operator's intervention is the remaining safeguard that can prevent or mitigate the hazard(s) from an eventual realization to a worst-case consequence.

iii. The analysis identified unique guaranteed disruptions in the elimination control category for consequence-based targets. Consequence-based targeting is the path taken by the adversary to achieve the highest impact effects, where the attack needs to be conducted, and the information required to achieve these goals [17]. This applies especially for scenarios when all safeguards are 'hackable' as analyzed by Security-PHA [18]. These present specific scenarios that can benefit when non-digital engineering controls such as analogue interlocks are introduced, the final consequence can be prevented even when all digital safeguards are compromised. A primary reason for this observation is that all interlocks in SWaT are currently digital that can be compromised.

- Safety Watermark Category Group 1: AIT203(ORP) High & AIT302(ORP) High – Administrative Control. Measure oxidant concentration with little degradation.
- Safety Watermark Category Group 2: UV401 On, AIT402(ORP) High & NaHSO3 dosing system On, AIT502 (ORP) High – Elimination Control. Remove oxidant PRESENT and ensure water to RO is not overly oxidizing.
- Safety Watermark Category Group 3: FIT502 High, AIT504 (Conductivity) High, MV501 Close and MV503 Open – Engineering Control. RO membrane integrity is based on TMP (low TMP, integrity compromised) and RO high salt rejection.

Figure 4 shows the various safety watermark category groups with the various cyber-attack scenarios. All safeguards' categories can pick up all the attacks. There is an observation of a unique non-digital safeguard highlighted in yellow which if implemented will have guaranteed aversion of consequence without operator intervention.

Safeguards		Attack Case 1	Attack Case 2	Attack Case 3	Attack Case 4 (Multiple Controls)	Attack Case 5 (All Controls)
Administrative Control	AIT203 (ORP) High†	Δ			X (AIT302 High)	Δ
	AIT302 (ORP) High	X (AIT203 High)				X (AIT203 High)
Elimination Control	UV401 On		X (P401/P402 On)		X (P401/P402 On)	X (P401/P402 On)
	AIT402 (ORP) High† & $NaHSO_3$ dosing system		X (AIT402 High)		X (AIT402 High)	X (AIT402 High)
	AIT502 (ORP) High		X (AIT402 High)			Δ
Engineering Control	FIT502 High			X (PIT501 Low)		X (PIT501 Low)
	AIT504 (Conductivity) High†			X (AIT503 Normal)	X (AIT503 Normal)	X (AIT503 Normal)
	MV501 Open and MV503 Close			X (AIT504 High)	X (AIT504 High)	X (AIT504 High)

† Ground Truth #1 check as sensor subsystem is used to control final elements. Bypassing this sensor subsystem for engineering or maintenance mode is highly undesirable due to potential hazardous outcome caused by uncontrolled final elements. Recommends active query and strict oversight.

Legend:

Δ – Digitally compromised (cyber-attack)

X (AIT203 High) – Safety watermark detection with the identified invariant state causing a true positive

AIT402 (ORP) High† & NaHSO3 dosing system – Unique elimination controls where non-digital mitigation (i.e. analogue interlocks, pressure relief, overflow devices etc) will have guaranteed aversion of consequence without operator intervention.

Fig. 4. Attacks versus Safety Watermark Categories

Figure 5 shows the various cyber-attack scenarios against the safety water alert detections and consequences aversion. The attacks that compromise both the elimination and engineering control categories will not be able to avert the consequence without the operation intervention. However, a non-digital engineering control implemented at one of the identified compromised safeguards [AIT402 (ORP) High & NaHSO3 dosing system] will have guaranteed aversion of consequence without operator intervention. Otherwise, the consequence will only be averted if the operator has intervened in time.

	Attack Case 1 (Admin Control)	Attack Case 2 (Elimination Control)	Attack Case 3 (Engineering Control)	Attack Case 4 (Multiple Controls)	Attack Case 5 (All Controls)
Safety Watermark Alert *	Successful Detection (Safety)	Successful Detection (Safety)	Successful Detection (Safety)	Successful Detection (Safety/ Cyber)	Successful Detection (Safety/ Cyber)
Consequence Averted w/o operator	Y	Y	Y	N	N
Consequence Averted with operator				Y	Y

* Safety refers to any 1 safety watermark category detected and cyber refers to 2 or more concurrently safety watermark category alerts.

N – Consequence averted without operator if any elimination controls had been equipped with non-digital engineering controls.

Fig. 5. Consequences for Attacks versus Safety Watermark Alerts

5 Safety Watermark Detection

Safety Watermark Code was deployed for the Chosen Scenario – Deliberate Overdosing of Sodium Hypochlorite in Sect. 4. The various attack cases except Attack Case 5 were performed, and the safety watermark successfully detected with the results exhibiting similar observations in Fig. 5 and Fig. 6. Attack Case 4 is expected to perform like Attack Case 5 that have similar types of safety watermark categories compromised.

5.1 SWaT HMI and Safety Watermark (Normal Operation)

Figures 6 and 7 show the normal operation of SWaT for HMI and the safety watermark. During normal operation of SWaT, the safety watermark performs as expected and is not supposed to display any alert since there are no safety or cyber incidents.

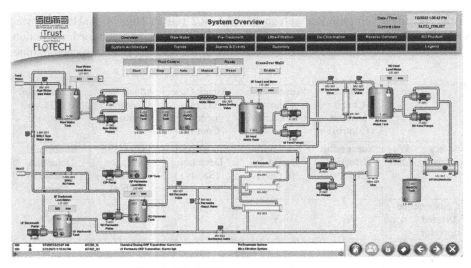

Fig. 6. SWaT HMI under normal operation

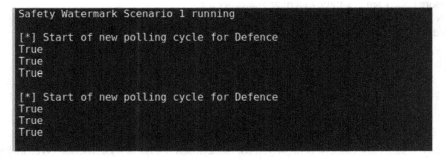

Fig. 7. Safety Watermark under normal operation with no alerts

5.2 Attack Case 1 (Administrative Control)

AIT 203 (ORP), AIT 302 (ORP) successfully spoofed to other values, and P205 turned on. Safety watermark successfully detected this as a Safety Watermark Category Group 1 – Administrative Controls alert (Level 1 Severity), (Figs. 8 and 9).

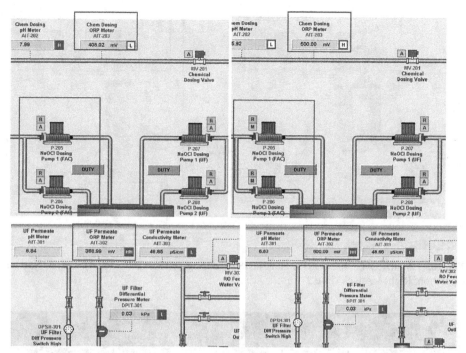

Fig. 8. AIT 203 (ORP), AIT 302 (ORP) and P205 values. Left – Normal Operation, Right – Attack Case 1

```
Safety Watermark Scenario 1 running

[*] Start of new polling cycle for Defence
True
True
True
ID 18 compromise for AIT 203/AIT 302 - Level 1 Severity Safety Watermark Category

[*] Start of new polling cycle for Defence
True
True
True
ID 18 compromise for AIT 203/AIT 302 - Level 1 Severity Safety Watermark Category
```

Fig. 9. Safety Watermark Category – Level 1 Severity Alert

5.3 Attack Case 2 (Elimination Control)

AIT 402 (ORP) successfully spoofed to other values while UV 401 and NaHSO3 dosing system (P403/P404) turned off. Safety watermark successfully detected this as a Safety Watermark Category Group 2 – Elimination Controls alert (Level 4 Severity), (Figs. 10 and 11).

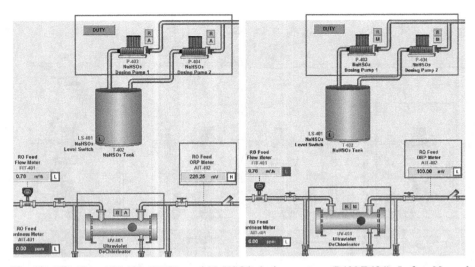

Fig. 10. UV 401, AIT 402 (ORP), and NaHSO3 dosing system (P403/P404). Left – Normal Operation, Right – Attack Case 2

```
[*] Start of new polling cycle for Defence
True
True
True
ID 18 compromise for UV 401 / P205 or P206 - Level 4 Severity Safety Watermark Category
ID 18 compromise for NaHSO3 Dosing System / P403 or P404 - Level 4 Severity Safety Watermark Category
ID 18 compromise for AIT 502 / AIT 402 - Level 4 Severity Safety Watermark Category

[*] Start of new polling cycle for Defence
True
True
True
ID 18 compromise for NaHSO3 Dosing System / P403 or P404 - Level 4 Severity Safety Watermark Category
ID 18 compromise for AIT 502 / AIT 402 - Level 4 Severity Safety Watermark Category
```

Fig. 11. Safety Watermark Category – Level 4 Severity Alert

5.4 Attack Case 3 (Engineering Control)

FIT 502, AIT 504 (Conductivity) successfully spoofed to other values, and MV 501 opened and MV 503 closed. Safety watermark successfully detected this as a Safety Watermark Category Group 3 – Engineering Controls alert (Level 2 Severity), (Figs. 12 and 13).

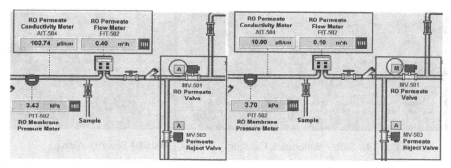

Fig. 12. FIT 502, AIT 504 (Conductivity), and MV 501 and MV 503. Left – Normal Operation, Right – Attack Case 3

```
[*] Start of new polling cycle for Defence
True
True
ID 18 compromise for FIT 502 / delta TMP - Level 2 Severity Safety Watermark Category
ID 18 compromise for AIT 504 / AIT 503 - Level 2 Severity Safety Watermark Category
ID 18 compromise for MV 501 and MV 503 / AIT 504 - Level 2 Severity Safety Watermark Category

[*] Start of new polling cycle for Defence
True
True
ID 18 compromise for FIT 502 / delta TMP - Level 2 Severity Safety Watermark Category
ID 18 compromise for AIT 504 / AIT 503 - Level 2 Severity Safety Watermark Category
ID 18 compromise for MV 501 and MV 503 / AIT 504 - Level 2 Severity Safety Watermark Category
```

Fig. 13. Safety Watermark Category – Level 2 Severity Alert

5.5 Attack Case 4 (Multiple Controls)

AIT 203 (ORP), UV 401, AIT 402 (ORP), AIT 504 (Conductivity) successfully spoofed to other values, and MV 501 opened and MV 503 closed. Safety watermark successfully detected this as multiple Safety Watermark Categories – Administrative, Elimination and Engineering Controls alert (Level 1, 2 and 4 severity). Since multiple Safety Watermark Categories are compromised, potential and likely cyber-attack alerts are also triggered. Potential cyber-attack is when two safety watermark categories alerts consecutively met while likely cyber-attack is when more than two safety watermark categories alerts consecutively met. The likelihood of a failure of digital safeguards due to safeguards naturally failing on demand diminishes greatly when more safety watermark categories alerts are met (Fig. 14).

Fig. 14. Safety Watermark Category – Levels 1, 2 and 4 Severity Alerts

6   Consequence-Driven Cyber-Informed Engineering (CCE)

Information technology (IT) cybersecurity focuses on data security that is known as information assurance to maintain the CIA triad, confidentiality, integrity, and availability of information. On the other hand, cyber-informed engineering (CIE) is an engineering discipline for operational technology (OT) environments where the primary goal is not protecting security for security's sake but to maintain the reliability and resiliency of the OT environment. CIE aligns well with asset-intensive, critical infrastructure industries such as water, power and other similar critical infrastructure environments. CIE is best implemented at the design and construction stage of a project or program. In brownfield activities that have existing operational assets, a similar approach is known as consequence-driven cyber-informed engineering (CCE) to prevent cyber sabotage. In summary, CIE is for greenfield sites whereas CCE is for brownfield activities [21].

As infrastructure increases its digitalization push, it becomes costly to apply cybersecurity protocols and controls afterwards. Most OT environments employ a small cybersecurity team without enough bandwidth to manage the magnitude of vulnerabilities present in the OT environment. Beyond the labor shortage, it's also diverting the institution's focus from performing its primary capability of essential services. There exists a need for a change of focus in how OT industry protect itself. Typically for a utility to provide safe and reliable services, the recommendation is to focus on a much smaller set of assets that is usually 5% - 20% of the total assets to secure and operate its primary functions [21]. For CCE, operators must think of the impact when cyber-attacks happen whereas CIE improves by encouraging teams to notice patterns or bad instances that is a recurring occurrence that requires constant remediation [21].

Idaho National Laboratory (INL) developed the CCE methodology to protect critical infrastructure assets in a collaborative approach. It is an iterative and considerable process like a company's culture. CCE comes with 3 main baseline assumptions [22].

1. Adversary has necessary access to the system, logically and physically through access to all credentials, IP addresses, and firewall and application configurations etc.
2. Adversary is knowledgeable where they understand the system inside out and have the necessary knowledge to impact the system.
3. Adversary has sufficient resources by having the required equipment, tools and engineering expertise.

In summary, cyber-adversaries are drawing upon different disciplines and skills sets. Outcome is goal-oriented, and they will do all necessary gathering of information, planning, specialized tools and benchmark their attacks against frontline security solutions. The most sophisticated network defenses can be defeated by considering all types of man-made and supply-chain compromises. For a threat that is co-adaptive like a human adversary, technology becomes the field of contest and can be used to defeat the underlying engineering design. Given enough freedom to cause damage and leveraging on resources, the adversaries' success becomes a direct function of the knowledge, thoughtful provision, and planning of system designers and operators [23].

6.1 CCE Methodology

In the heart of CCE, engineering is used to remove the assumption of trust and attempts with a series of processes and procedures to fill the existing cyber security gaps. It accommodates the co-adaptive nature of the hazard and comes up with potential mitigation strategies for safe and secure operations. It consists of four phases namely [23]:

- Phase 1: Consequence Prioritization
  Parameters for catastrophic events (cyber and physical) to the organization are developed. These are prioritized to determine the High Consequence Events (HCEs). HCEs are disruptive physical events caused by cyber that significantly hinders the provision of the services deemed critical to the organization's function, i.e. essential services for a critical infrastructure.
- Phase 2: System-of-Systems Analysis
  HCEs identified in Phase 1 map out the systems and processes. The dependencies and "unverified trust" of enablers are investigated.
- Phase 3: Consequence-based Targeting
  The requirements for an adversary to fully understand and execute the attack are further refined by the team.
- Phase 4: Mitigations and Protections

Priority is given to engineering or process changes to remove the physical effect of the cyber-attack. If this is not possible, the identification of requirements in Phase 3 is used for detection of malicious activity and implement other types of mitigations.

The safety watermarks categories group 1 to 3 in Sect. 4 cover the mitigations as it enables active defense, allowing operators to detect, respond and recover accordingly. The safety watermark responds by verifying the subsequent output independently based on the input and the logic solver. It takes the PLC as the final boundary between cyber and physical manifestation of the cyber-physical aspect. Through active querying of the PLC, it reads off the input and predicts the output based on an assumed integrity of the logic code. This identifies the invariant(s) under attack and resolved by the operator intervention through a differentiated alarm annunciation. In the event operator fails to respond in-time, non-digital engineering controls for the elimination controls category serve to break the kill chain. For example, analogue hard-wired interlock of the sodium bisulphite dosing system will enable the last dechlorination safeguard to hold no matter how the cyber-attack. This is analogous in the usage of pressure relief valve to prevent overpressure and overflow pipe for the tanks in SWaT.

This safety watermark can be used as an input to the cybersecurity management system (CSMS) [13] to identify the severity level (SL) target of the zones and conduits. The category of controls can give an indication on the SL of the areas. In SWaT case, elimination control categories are found in all PLCs and can be assigned the same SL. The usage of process hazard analysis like HAZOP with safety watermark concept and network analysis in Phase 4 can achieve disruption to the consequence-based targets.

7 Conclusions

The safety watermark has utilized the digital safeguards of the HAZOP output, a type of PHA to identify worst-case HSSE consequences for the asset. The safety watermark has considered a suite of practical recommendations for implementation in an operational theater and rule-based decisions to declare a safety incident and potentially identify a cyber incident. It has taken into consideration both aspects of safety and cybersecurity. It reflects the possible consequences of a failure to provide adequate cybersecurity countermeasures as well as non-digital engineering layers of protection where appropriate for a given facility with a specific design such as a water treatment plant, SWaT in iTrust or other automated facility of reference.

The safety watermark has been demonstrated to minimize alarm annunciation during normal operations and detect the attack in accordance with the hierarchy of safety controls. Upon attacks on multiple categories of safety controls, the safety watermark raises the alert to indicate potential cyber incidences. Taking reference from the requirements of Functional Safety – Safety Instrumented Systems for the Process Industry [12], Security for Industrial Automation and Control Systems [13], and Cybersecurity related to the Functional Safety Lifecycle [6], the safety watermark embraces process safety risk manifestations as indicator of compromises like a piece of digital forensics to derive the procedure on how the adversary is to impair control process and impact [10].

In a final evaluation of the usefulness of the safety watermark, it can be effectively utilized in Phase 4 – Mitigations and Prevention covered by the Consequence-Based Cyber-Informed Engineering (CCE) methodology developed by Idaho National Laboratory. The safety watermark covers the mitigations through detection and gives operators the capability to respond and recover for normal operations.

Acknowledgements. This research is supported by the National Research Foundation, Singapore, and Cyber Security Agency of Singapore under its National Cybersecurity R&D Programme (NCRP20-S01-CiMS). Chuadhry Mujeeb Ahmed is supported by the PETRAS National Center of Excellence for IoT Systems Cybersecurity through Roast-IoT project. Jianying Zhou is supported in part by the National Research Foundation, Singapore, under its Maritime Transformation Programme (SMI-2022-MTP-05). Any opinions, findings and conclusions or recommendations expressed in this material are those of the author(s) and do not reflect the views of National Research Foundation, Singapore and Cyber Security Agency of Singapore.

References

1. Reinecke, P., Saxena, N.: Cyber-Physical Systems Security. Centre for Cyber Security Research, Cardiff University Homepage (2023). https://www.cardiff.ac.uk/__data/assets/pdf_file/0008/2508182/Centre-for-Cyber-Security-Research-204x204-leaflets-English-final.pdf. Accessed 03 Feb 2023
2. Bochman, A.A., Freeman, S.: Countering Cyber Sabotage: Introducing Consequence-driven, Cyber-informed Engineering (CCE). CRC Press, Informa UK Limited, Boca Raton (2021)
3. Young, W., Leveson, N.G.: Inside risks: an integrated approach to safety and security based on systems theory. Commun. ACM **57**(2), 31–35 (2014)
4. Adepu, S., Mathur, A.: Distributed attack detection in a water treatment plant: method & case study. IEEE Trans. Dependable Sec. Comput. **18**, 86–99 (2021)
5. Humayed, A., Lin, J., Li, F., Luo, B.: Cyber-physical systems security – a survey. IEEE Internet Things J. **4**(6), 1802–1831 (2017)
6. ISA-TR84.00.09–2017, "Cybersecurity Related to the Functional Safety Lifecycle", International Society of Automation
7. Hsiao, S.-W., Sun, Y., Chen, M.C., Zhang, H.: Cross-level behavioral analysis for robust early intrusion detection. In: IEEE International Conference on Intelligence and Security Informatics, pp. 95–100 (2010)
8. Mo, Y., Weerakkody, S., Sinopoli, B.: Physical authentication of control systems. IEEE Control Syst. Magaz. **35**, 93–109 (2015)
9. Chuadhry, M.A., Venkata, R.P., Vishrut, K.M.: A practical physical watermarking approach to detect replay attacks in a CPS. J. Process Control **116**, 136–146 (2022)
10. Alexander, O., Belisle, M., Steele, J.: MITRE ATT&CK® for Industrial Control Systems: Design and Philosophy. The MITRE Corporation Homepage, https://attack.mitre.org/docs/ATTACK_for_ICS_Philosophy_March_2020.pdf. Accessed 15 Jan 2023
11. O'Brien, P.: Five Things to Know About Cybersecurity in Process Safety. Chemical Engineering Process, American Institute of Chemical Engineers, 22–28 December 2022
12. Timms, C., Kirkwood, D.: The Principles of IEC 61508 and IEC 61511 – Functional Safety Instrumented Systems for the Process Industry Sector (Ed 2.0 of IEC 61511)", TüV Rheinland Functional Safety Engineer Program, C&C Technical Support Services (2022)
13. ANSI/ISA 62443-3-2-2020. Security for industrial automation and control systems, Part 3–2: Security risk assessment for system design. International Society of Automation
14. ANSI/ISA-95.00.01-2010. (IEC 62264-1 Mod), Enterprise-Control System Integration - Part 1: Models and Terminology. International Society of Automation
15. Shin, H., Son, Y., Park, Y., Kwon, Y., Kim, Y.: Sampling race: bypassing time-based analog active sensor spoofing detection on analog-digital systems. In: WOOT '16 – Proceedings of the 10th USENIX Conference on Offensive Technology, pp. 200–210 (2016)
16. Thia, C.M.: Applied HAZOP for Engineers. Centre for Professional and Continuing Education, Nanyang Technological University (2022)
17. Cook, S., Freeman, S.G.: CCE Phase 3: consequence-based targeting – consequence-driven cyber-informed engineering. Cybercore Integration Center, Idaho National Laboratory (2020)
18. Marszal, E., McGlone, J.: Security PHA Review for Consequence-Based Cybersecurity. International Society of Automation (2019)
19. IEC 62682:2014. Management of alarms systems for the process industries. European Committee for Electrotechnical Standardization
20. Chekole, E.G., Castellanos, J.H., Ochoa, M., Yau, D.K.Y.: Enforcing Memory Safety in Cyber-Physical Systems. Computer Security: SECPRE CyberICPS (2017)

21. Morris, M.: How Cyber-Informed Engineering Can Be The Way Forward For Critical Infrastructure. Forbes Technology Council, Forbes (2022). https://www.forbes.com/sites/for bestechcouncil/2022/11/09/how-cyber-informed-engineering-can-be-the-way-forward-for-critical-infrastructure. Accessed 02 Feb 2023

22. Freeman, S.G., Johnson, N.H., St. Michel, C.P.: CCE Phase 1: Consequence Prioritization – Consequence-driven Cyber-informed Engineering. Cybercore Integration Center, Idaho National Laboratory (2020)

23. Idaho National Laboratory. Consequence-driven Cyber-Informed Engineering (CCE). Mission Support Center Support Paper, National & Homeland Security Directorate, Idaho National Laboratory (2016)

Leveraging Semantic Relationships to Prioritise Indicators of Compromise in Additive Manufacturing Systems

Mahender Kumar[✉], Gregory Epiphaniou, and Carsten Maple

Cyber Security Research Group, WMG, University of Warwick, Coventry, UK
{Mahender.kumar,Gregory.epiphaniou,CM}@warwick.ac.uk

Abstract. Additive manufacturing (AM) offers numerous benefits, such as manufacturing complex and customised designs quickly and cost-effectively, reducing material waste, and enabling on-demand production. However, several security challenges are associated with AM, making it increasingly attractive to attackers ranging from individual hackers to organised criminal gangs and nation-state actors. This paper addresses the cyber risk in AM to attackers by proposing a novel semantic-based threat prioritisation system for identifying, extracting and ranking indicators of compromise (IOC). The system leverages the heterogeneous information networks (HINs) that automatically extract high-level IOCs from multi-source threat text and identifies semantic relations among the IOCs. It models IOCs with a HIN comprising different meta-paths and meta-graphs to depict semantic relations among diverse IOCs. We introduce a domain-specific recogniser that identifies IOCs in three domains: *organisation_specific*, *regional_source-specific*, and *regional_target-specific*. A threat assessment uses similarity measures based on meta-paths and meta-graphs to assess semantic relations among IOCs. It prioritises IOCs by measuring their severity based on the frequency of attacks, IOC lifetime, and exploited vulnerabilities in each domain.

Keywords: Indicators of Compromise · Cyber-Physical Systems · Threat Intelligence · Threat Prioritisation · Heterogeneous Information Networks

1 Introduction

Industry 4.0, the fourth industrial revolution, refers to integrating advanced digital technologies and manufacturing systems to automate and optimize industrial processes. Additive manufacturing (AM) is a key enabler of Industry 4.0, as it allows for the rapid and flexible production of customized parts and products [1]. AM is a process that enables the production of complex devices by applying successive layers of materials. AM offers many advantages, such as on-demand customisation, enhanced logistics, reduced labour and production lead times,

J. Zhou et al. (Eds.): ACNS 2023 Workshops, LNCS 13907, pp. 321–335, 2023.
https://doi.org/10.1007/978-3-031-41181-6_18

streamlined production, reduced waste, reduced inventory, and reduced transportation costs. However, cyber and physical attacks in AM pose severe concerns and formidable challenges [2], making AM supply chains susceptible to various attack vectors. As a result, protecting the security of AM has become increasingly important, and developing robust security mechanisms that protect against a range of potential attacks has become a significant challenge for researchers and industry practitioners alike.

Modern attacks on AM are often sophisticated and can exploit hidden vulnerabilities that go undetected for long periods [3–7]. A prime example is Advanced Persistent Threats (APTs), which have been used to target AM industries for espionage, economic gain, and intellectual property theft. APTs are commonly described as an extended attack campaign in which one or more intruders execute a long-term plan to take control of a network or system. In 2020, more than 1000 data breaches were reported in the United States alone, affecting more than 155.8 million individuals through data exposure [3]. Perhaps the most famous kinetic cyber attack of all time was aimed at Iran's nuclear program, considered unprecedented in the industry [4]. The Stuxnet attack involved a complexly targeted worm that executed zero-day exploits on operating systems and software for managing programmable logic controllers (PLCs). The attack resulted in tens of billions of dollars in damage. Another famous example of a cyberattack is the sewage attack in Maroochy Shire, which caused a system failure and millions of litres of untreated sewage to leak into the water supply [5]. Belikovetsky et al. [6] conducted a study on the vulnerability of additive manufacturing to cyber attacks. He demonstrated the sabotage attack on a propeller blueprint that can be 3D printed at home. The findings of their study emphasized the vulnerability of additive constructs to cyber attacks, which was also confirmed by another recent paper [7]. The authors of the latter paper identified AM as the second most vulnerable industry to cyberattacks, second only to the financial sector. With AM's growing national and industrial importance, cyberattacks have become more attractive and induced threat actors are increasingly involved in cybercrime-as-a-service, commoditising cyberattacks. As a result, APTs are now employing common attack patterns to compromise targets. Therefore, early identification of threat exposure and breaches is critical to preventing significant damage to an organization and providing reliable evidence during prosecution trials.

Cyber Threat Intelligence (CTI) can be a valuable tool for assessing the threat landscape in AM and developing effective strategies for mitigating cyber risks. Threat intelligence feeds can help organizations stay informed about emerging threats and new attack techniques. This can be especially useful in the fast-paced world of AM, where new technologies and processes are constantly being developed. CTI involves the extraction of threat intelligence from threat-related information from multiple sources, utilising several attributes, including Indicators of Compromise (IOCs), Tactic, Technique, and Procedure (TTP) and the skills and motive of the threat actor [8]. Some example of CTI feeds are Structured Threat Information Expression (STIX), OpenDef, Cybox, and OpenIOC, but a massive amount of information remain unstructured. IBM X-force [9], Facebook ThreatExchange [10], OpenCTI [11] and MISP [12] are a few vendors who provide threat intelligence feeds by extracting threat intelligence from multiple open sources using IOC extraction methods such as PhishTank, and IOCFinder.

These structured threat information feeds have several disadvantages, including a limited scope, delayed information, high cost, inflexibility and false positives, making it very challenging for AM industry to rely on them. On the other hand, unstructured threat feeds can provide a more comprehensive and flexible approach to threat intelligence that can be more effective for many organizations. However, unstructured reports may not be well-organized, making it hard to identify the relationships between different pieces of information. Other challenges include errors, inaccuracies, and missing information. As a result, it requires advanced natural language processing (NLP) techniques and machine learning algorithms to extract meaningful and relevant threat information from unstructured reports.

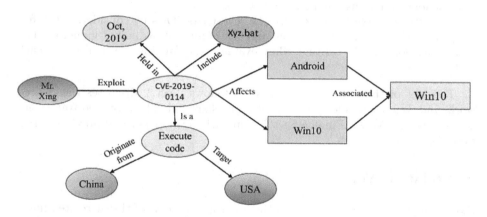

Fig. 1. An annotated example of CTI includes IOCs such as attack actor, vulnerability, time, region, file, attack type, device and platform, and their relationship.

Consider the following instance of a security-related post: *"In October 2019, Mr Xing from China exploited the CVE-2019-0114 vulnerability, which affected multiple Android and Win10 devices in the United States. CVE-2019-0114 is a remote code execution vulnerability that contains the malicious file abc.bat"*. Figure 1 displays a graphical representation of CTI, including eight IOCs such as attack actor, vulnerability, time, region, file, attack type, device and platform, and the relationship between them. Existing methods only consider IOCs but avoid the relationship between them, and as a result, they cannot grasp a comprehensive picture of the threat landscape. To overcome the limitations of existing structured threat feed tools, this paper aims to automate IOC extraction by exploiting Heterogeneous Information Network (HIN) that provides insight into the interdependencies between heterogeneous IOCs.

This paper presents a novel semantic-based threat prioritisation framework for identifying, extracting and ranking IOCs. The summary of the paper is as follows:

- *Recogniser.* We propose a recogniser that automatically extracts threat-related information from multi-source threat text. It also identifies the domains to which IOCs belong and integrates IOCs with their domain, forming three domain-specific IOCs such as *organisation_domain-specific*, *regional_source-specific*, and *regional_target-specific* threat intelligence.
- *Threat modelling.* We model the range of IOCs with a Heterogeneous Information Network (HIN), which comprises different meta-paths and meta-graphs that depicts the semantic relations among diverse IOCs to capture a more comprehensive landscape of threat events.
- *Threat assessment.* We present a CTI assessment framework that uses similarity measures based on meta-paths and meta-graphs and assesses the interdependent relations among diverse IOCs.
- *Prioritisation.* We then measure the severity of IOCs by considering the frequency of attacks, IOC lifetime, and the number of exploited vulnerabilities in each domain. As a result, they evaluate the ranking mechanism for each IOC.

The rest of the paper is organized as follows: Sect. 2 discusses the related work, and Sect. 3 provides the conceptual background. The proposed framework is presented in Sect. 4. Finally, Sect. 5 summarizes the paper and provides directions for future research.

2 Related Work

Extracting threat intelligence from the unstructured text of threat-related information has become an exciting research topic in cyber security. This section briefly describes key methodologies for identifying cyber threats by extracting IOCs from multiple sources.

Noor et al. [13] have proposed a model to automate cyber threat attribution by considering high-level IOCs to determine threat actors. Their technique extracts high-level IOCs from unstructured CTI reports and then semantically profiles threat actors with the high-level IOCs taken from MITRE's ATT&CK. Zhao et al. [14] present TIMiner, a method to extract and assess domain-specific CTIs that automatically classify the domains associated with related CTIs. Gao et al. [15] proposed a cyber threat intelligence method based on the Hierarchical Information Network (HINCTI) system to identify threat types. HINCTI provides a threat intelligence-based meta-schema to capture the semantic relationship between threat nodes leveraging a meta-path and meta-graph-based similarity method. Zhao et al. [16] proposed a CTI framework, HINTI, based on HIN that proposed a multi-granular-based IOC recogniser to enhance the accuracy of the IOC extraction method. HINTI defines different types of IOCs using meta-paths to identify the relationship between IOCs, profile the threat events and rank the significance of IOCs to understand the threat landscape.

Liao et al. [17] proposed a novel automated threat-related information collection and extraction (iACE) technique from unstructured text that uses a natural language processing method to extract IOC data from text documents and then analyse the IOC data using graph mining methods. iACE aims to identify the grammatical semantic relationships between token threat patterns associated with IOC in text documents. The method integrates name entity recognition and relation extraction methods. Gao et al. [18] proposed a threat-hunting system (THREATRAPTOR) that extracts threat behavioural information from unstructured CTI reports to facilitate threat hunting. THREATRAPTOR provides an accurate NLP-based auditing framework to extract structured threat information from unstructured CTI text and defines a domain-specific query language to detect malicious system activities. Wang et al. [19] develop an efficient automated process that recognises and extracts entities and their relationship from text reports.

3   Conceptual Background

3.1   Cyber Threat Intelligence

Modern cybercriminals have developed sophisticated tactics, techniques, and procedures (TTP) to realise their aim of compromising their targets quickly and efficiently. Thus, traditional defence mechanisms, such as anti-virus software, firewalls and intrusion detection methods, struggle to effectively detect cyber attacks such as advance persistent threats (APTs) and zero-day attacks. Cyber attacks have successfully compromised systems in a wide range of sectors. For example, the WannaCry ransomware attack extorted money to unlock sensitive information and designs across various industries [20]. Security experts have increasingly turned to sharing cyber threat intelligence (CTI) to combat such emerging cyber threats. CTI is any relevant information that helps detect, monitor, assess, and respond to cyber threats. CTI facilitates a comprehensive and significant threat warning and includes information such as IOCs [21].

Nowadays, a rich source of commercial and free CTI feeds are available, making it difficult for network defenders to evaluate the quality of information and select the optimal set of data feeds to pay attention to. Acting on results from low-quality feeds can give rise to many false alerts while concentrating on only a few data feeds increases the risk of missing relevant threats. However, it is challenging to extract IOCs from unstructured form sources. Several automated methods for extracting IOCs (such as malicious IP addresses, malware, and file hashes of malicious payloads) are based on the OpenIOC standard, including PhishTank, IOCFinder, and CleanMX [14]. To facilitate efficient threat intelligence sharing among organisations, CybOX [22], STIX [23], and TAXII [24] have emerged as de-facto standards for describing threat intelligence and are widely consumed by the threat intelligence sharing platforms, including MISP [12] and AT&T Open Threat eXchange (OTX).

3.2 Indicators of Compromise

Cyber Threat Intelligence (CTI) includes IOCs, which organisations can use to identify possible threats and protect themselves and their customers. Specifically, IOCs are artefacts observed about an attacker or their behaviour, such as tactics, techniques and procedures [25]. IOCs can be kept at a network or host level and help network defenders block malicious traffic and identity actions or determine if a cyber intrusion has occurred. Security and forensic analysts prepare reports of in-depth analysis of cyber attacks, including the IOCs, to be shared with communities, often through public data sources. Examples of IOC found in reports from data sources include actor identity behind cyber attacks, the malware used in threat attacks and their typical behaviour, communication and control server list, and other types of information. The information used in creating these reports is gathered from multiple sources, such as host logs, proxy logs and alerts. The reports may be widely distributed through various channels, including blogs, forums and social media.

The pyramid of pain (PoP) classifies the common types of IOCs. The PoP identifies the types of indicators that a system defender might use to detect an adversary's activities. The pyramid organises the pain an adversary will cause when the defender can deny those indicators. At the bottom end, if a defender identifies hash values of malicious files and then blocks these, it causes the attacker little pain since making an insignificant change to the file to produce the same outcome with a different hash is trivial. TTP sit at the top of the pyramid. When a defender detects and responds at this level, this disrupts behaviours much more complicated for an adversary to change; defining new behaviours is a significant challenge for adversaries.

3.3 Heterogeneous Information Network

Heterogeneous Information Network (HIN) is a simple way of modelling a problem as a graph compromising different types of nodes and one or more correlations between nodes (edges) [26]. The set of node and edge types correspond to the network scheme. HIN delivers a high conceptualisation of modelling for a complex collection of data. From the graphical representation of the dataset, feature vectors can be extracted by defining meta-paths and meta-graphs corresponding to the graph and implementing a guided random walk over defined meta-paths and meta-graphs. A meta-path is a path defined within the graph of network schema, covering a specific sequence of relation types. A meta-graph [27] can handle the in-depth relationship between nodes by employing a direct acyclic graph of nodes defined over the HIN from a single source node to a single target node. The guided random walk generates a sequence of nodes processed in an embedding model such as word2vec, skip-gram or Continuous Bag-of-Words

(CBOW). Once the nodes are represented numerically, it is possible to determine a set of nodes and resolve many problems (classification, clustering, and similarity search).

3.4 Overview

We introduce a novel system designed to automatically extract and prioritise high-level IOCs (Indicators of Compromise) from multiple sources of threat text. Our system addresses the limitations of existing IOC extraction methods by considering the semantic relationships among different IOCs. We present a novel approach to extracting threat-related information and identifying the domains IOCs belong to. This information is then integrated with their respective domains to form three domain-specific threat intelligence categories: the organisational domain, regional-source domain, and regional-target domain. We also present a threat modelling that utilizes a Heterogeneous Information Network (HIN) comprising different meta-paths and meta-graphs. The proposed system captures the interdependent relationships among diverse IOCs and provides a more comprehensive view of the landscape of threat events. Our system then utilizes similarity measures based on these meta-paths and meta-graphs to assess the interdependent relationships among different IOCs.

To prioritize IOCs, we measure their severity by considering various factors, including the frequency of attacks, the lifetime of the IOC, and the number of exploited vulnerabilities in each domain. Our system then evaluates the ranking mechanism for each IOC, providing a more comprehensive and accurate view of the threat landscape. Our system significantly contributes to cybersecurity, providing a more effective and efficient method for automatically extracting, assessing, and prioritizing high-level IOCs. With the increasing frequency and complexity of cyber threats, the need for such a system has become more critical.

4 Methodology

The architecture of the proposed method, as shown in Fig. 2, comprises of following phases: Data collection and Preprocessing, Relation Extraction and Threat Modelling, Domain Recognition and Tag Generation, Domain-specific threat identification and Tagging, and Severity measure and Threat Prioritisation. Table 1 summarises the list of notations and abbreviations used throughout the paper.

4.1 Data Collection and Preprocessing

The system automatically collects threat information identifying IOCs from multiple resources, including forums, blogs, security news, and bulletins. We use a breadth-first search to capture the HTML course code and Xpath for data extraction. We then reduce the dimension of each text report and remove noisy features by pre-processing. This pre-processing includes the removal of stopwords, punctuations, and markup characters.

Table 1. List of Abbreviations and Notations

Notations	Description
IOC	Indicators of Compromise
AM	Additive manufacturing
HIN	Heterogeneous Information Network
APT	Advanced Persistent Threats
CTI	Cyber Threat Intelligence
TTP	Tactic, technique and procedure
PoP	Pyramid of pain
STIX	Structured threat information exchange
TAXII	Trusted Automated eXchange of Indicator Information

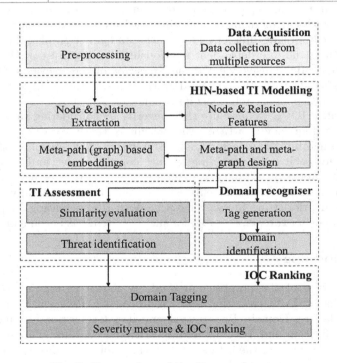

Fig. 2. Process flow of the Proposed system

4.2   Relation Extraction and Threat Intelligence Modelling

Using a heterogeneous information network (HIN) for threat intelligence, we first build a graph that shows the interdependent (semantic) relationships between the different IOCs involved in the attack. By denoting nodes (IOCs) and relationships, we can identify patterns and anomalies that may indicate the presence of a threat. For example, we can use HINs to identify groups of attackers that share common attack vectors or targets or to track the evolution of an attack over time as new entities become involved. To better understand, we can characterise the nodes and relations as follows.

Node Features. In the context of risk in Additive Manufacturing, it is essential to consider the domain-specific threat information. For instance, a threat post discussing the Stuxnet virus and its impact on industrial control systems is more relevant to manufacturing organisations than those in the finance or healthcare sectors. This highlights the need for threat intelligence tailored to an organisation's domain.

Additionally, geographical location plays a significant role in cyber attacks. Over 500 geopolitical cyber attacks have been reported worldwide in the past decade, with 30% originating from China or Russia and 26.3% targeting the USA. In 2018 alone, 27% of attacks occurred in the USA [28]. Therefore, when developing threat models for Additive Manufacturing, it is crucial to consider the regional source and target source of cyber attacks.

To account for these domain-specific and regional factors in our threat intelligence model for Additive Manufacturing, we define nodes as organisation-specific, regional_source-specific, and regional_target-specific. This enables us to capture the complex relationships between entities involved in cyber attacks, such as attackers, attack vectors, and targets. Moreover, we consider time-related node features such as attack frequency and IOC lifecycle, which can provide valuable insight into the TTPs of attackers and help defenders calculate the level of risk posed by a particular threat.

Semantic Relation Features. The node features in the HIN represent a specific action, but actions can be employed multiple times in conjunction with other activities in a campaign. These complex relationships among nodes can provide more valuable intelligence for threat identification; therefore, we consider relation-based and node features. This allows us to analyse highly sophisticated malicious cyber attacks. To model the interdependent relationship between eight IOCs, we define the following semantic relationships:

- **R1**: The relation **actor-exploit-vulnerability** matrix A represents the link between the threat actor and vulnerability. For each element, $A_{i,j} \in \{0,1\}$, where $A_{i,j} = 1$ means actor i exploits vulnerability j.
- **R2**: The relation **actor-invade-device** matrix B represents the link between the threat actor and device. For each element, $B_{i,j} \in \{0,1\}$, where $B_{i,j} = 1$ means actor i invades device j.
- **R3**: The link between two actors is represented by the relation **actor-assist-actor** matrix C. For each element, $C_{i,j} \in \{0,1\}$, where $C_{i,j} = 1$ means actor i assists actor j.
- **R4**: The relation **attack_type-originate_from-region** matrix D represents the link between the attack type and location. For each element, $D_{i,j} \in \{0,1\}$, where $D_{i,j} = 1$ means attack type i originate from region j.

- **R5**: The relation **attack_type-target-region** matrix E represents the link between the attack type and location. For each element, $E_{i,j} \in \{0,1\}$, where $F_{i,j} = 1$ means attack type i target to region j.
- **R6**: The relation **vulnerability-affect-device** matrix F represents the link between the vulnerability and the device. For each element, $F_{i,j} \in \{0,1\}$, where $F_{i,j} = 1$ means vulnerability i affects device j.
- **R7**: The relation **attack_type-associate-vulnerability** matrix G represents the link between the attack type and vulnerability. For each element, $G_{i,j} \in \{0,1\}$, where $G_{i,j} = 1$ means attack type i carry vulnerability j.
- **R8**: The relation **vulnerability-held-time** matrix H represents the link between the vulnerability and time. For each element, $H_{i,j} \in \{0,1\}$, where $H_{i,j} = 1$ means vulnerability i held in time j.
- **R9**: The relation **vulnerability-include -file** matrix B represents the link between the vulnerability and malicious file. For each element, $I_{i,j} \in \{0,1\}$, where $I_{i,j} = 1$ means vulnerability i include malicious file j.

R10: The relation **vulnerability-evolve-vulnerability** matrix B represents the link between the vulnerabilities. For each element, $J_{i,j} \in \{0,1\}$, where $J_{i,j} = 1$ means vulnerability i evolve to vulnerability j.

We initiate dependency parsing to leverage the semantic relationships among the eight IOCs and extract them in a structured format. Using this approach, we can represent the IOCs as triplets, each consisting of two IOCs and a relation between them. For instance, if IOC1 is dependent on IOC2, we would define the relationship as (IOC1-relation-IOC2), where 'relation' denotes the nature of the relationship between the two IOCs.

Meta-Path and Meta-Graph. Figure 3 presents 12 distinct types of meta-paths and meta-graphs denoted by χ_i that capture interdependent relationships among seven different IOCs. While the meta-path illustrates the connections between the IOCs, it falls short in capturing intricate relationships. To address this limitation, the proposed HIN-based Threat Intelligence (TI) model utilizes a directed acyclic graph of nodes to handle more complex structures in the HIN architecture. By learning and analyzing these 12 different meta-paths and meta-graphs, the model can convey the context of a threat event and offer threat insights across heterogeneous IOCs. For instance, the χ_1 meta-path is a length-2 meta-path that represents the relatedness of "threat actors (A) exploiting the same vulnerability (V)."

Similarly, χ_8 is a meta-path that describes the relationships between IOCs that "two attack types who leverage the same vulnerability held at the same time". Likewise, χ_{10} is a meta-graph that portrays the relationship over threat infrastructure with more comprehensive insight that integrates both external and intrinsic relationships. Meta-graph χ_{10} depicts the relationship among IOCs: "two attack types originated from the same region, and their associated vulnerabilities affect the same device occur at the same time".

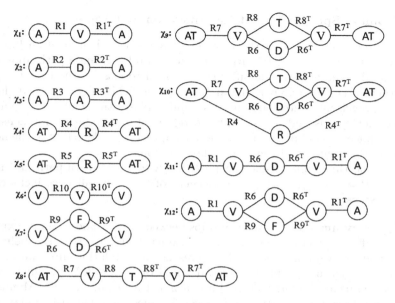

Fig. 3. Proposed meta-path and meta-graph for threat type identification, where A denotes threat actor, V denotes vulnerability, D denotes device, R denotes a region, AT denotes attack type, F denotes file, and T denotes time.

4.3   Domain Recognition and Tag Generation

To extract domain-specific IOCs, it is essential first to identify the domain of threat information. This initial step helps to ensure that IOCs are tailored to the specific context of the threat landscape, enabling more effective threat detection and response. Here, we consider three domains, *organisation_domain-specific*, *regional_source-specific*, and *regional_target-specific*. *Organisational_domain-specific* threat information includes financial, health, manufacturing, government, and IoT information. *Regional_source-specific* and *Regional_target-specific* threat information originated and targeted the geographic region, such as China, Russia, India, Korea, USA, UK, and Europe. We first trained the word2vec model specific to a threat description embedding that inputs a large corpus (threat description) and generates a low-dimension vector. Each unique word in the corpus is allocated an assigned vector in latent space. The convolution function sets a filter for each word vector to generate a feature called local_feature. Our model captures the most significant features by leveraging the max-pooling operation that takes the maximum values of local-feature and runs over a local feature set. This will generate tags for three domains, i.e., OD_t, SD_t, and TD_t denotes the tags corresponding to organisation_domain-specific, regional_source-specific, and regional_target-specific threat, respectively.

4.4   Domain-Specific Threat Identification and Tagging

After successfully extracting the features of IOCs and their relationships and identifying the relevant meta-paths and meta-graphs, a meta-path and meta-graph-based heterogeneous classifier is developed to classify the threat type of infrastructure nodes in Cyber Threat Intelligence (CTI). The proposed classification approach integrates node features and explores the semantic similarities between meta-paths and meta-graphs to represent the nodes comprehensively. These advanced techniques enable a more comprehensive depiction of the nodes, enhancing the accuracy of the threat classification.

Given the threat intelligence graph $G = (N, R)$, and meta-path and meta-graph set $P = \{\chi_1, \chi_2, ..\chi_n\}$, the assessment of threat intelligence includes the following steps:

- **Adjacency matrix.** The relationships between threat nodes can be explored using different meta-paths and meta-graphs, which capture the behaviour of threats in various aspects. To represent these relationships, we propose using an adjacent weighted matrix, denoted by $Adj_i \in R^{N \times N}$, which can be generated using similarity algorithms such as Euclidean distance, Manhattan distance, Cosine similarity, word mover distance, and Jaccard similarity. To assess the similarity between IOCs, we generate a corresponding weighted adjacency matrix, Adj_i, based on the meta-path and meta-graph path set, P. The use of weighted adjacency matrices Adj_i enables the identification of the most significant relationships between the different nodes, which can be used to prioritise threat mitigation efforts.
- **Feature matrix.** By incorporating attributed information of nodes, we can construct an attributed feature matrix F_i of size $N \times d$, where N denotes the number of IOCs in Adj_i, and d is the dimension of the node feature. This allows us to integrate the attribute information of IOCs and create a node feature matrix $F_i \in R^{N \times d}$. To recognize previously unnoticed IOCs, we employ the word2vec method to develop a threat intelligence embedding, which transforms words into a latent vector space. To achieve this, threat-related texts are pre-processed, accumulated into a word set, and converted into a latent vector space using word2vec. This approach enables us to represent threat-related information in a low-dimensional vector space, facilitating the detection and analysis of potential threats.
- **Quantify threat intelligence.** After designing an adjacent weighted and attributed feature matrix, we assess the threat intelligence. Different types of assessment methods to quantify the proposed HIN-based threat intelligence. For example, graph convolution network (GCN) and Bidirectional Encoder Representations from Transformers (BERT). Given the adjacency matrix Adj_i, and its corresponding feature matrix F_i (low-dimensional space), we utilise the graph convolution network (GCN) method to quantify the relationship between IOCs. This will fuse the adjacency matrix Adj_i, and feature matrix F_i as $Z = (F, Adj)$ and output the predicted labels of IOCs. Then, the model integrates the domain-specific tags OD_t, SD_t and TD_t to the predicted

IOC, representing that the IOCi belongs to the organisation OD_t, originates from the country SD_t and is targeted to the country TD_t and are considered as the domain-specific IOCs.

4.5   Severity Measure and Threat Prioritisation

Utilizing the learned domain-specific IOCs, we can evaluate the severity of potential threats of various attack vectors within each domain. This motivates us to develop a quantitative measure to assess threat risks corresponding to each domain. The proposed severity measure is based on several key assumptions.

1. Firstly, we assume that the frequency of attacks may significantly influence the severity and scope of the threats manifested.
2. Secondly, we postulate that chain exploits, where multiple vulnerabilities use an attack, can cause considerably more damage.
3. Finally, we recognize that the severity of a threat may decrease over time, particularly during the zero-day risk period.

Consequently, the severity of a threat can be measured by examining the frequency of attacks, the lifetime of the IOC, and the number of exploited vulnerabilities in each domain. This approach allows us to develop a more nuanced and comprehensive understanding of the potential threats facing a domain, enabling us to take appropriate measures to mitigate risk and enhance security.

5   Conclusion and Future Scope

This paper presented a novel semantic-based threat prioritisation system for AM that intends to expose the comprehensive behaviour of threat events in the relationships among different IOCs with high accuracy. We proposed an intelligent IOC acquisition and ranking system based on a Heterogeneous Information Network (HIN). The proposed system collects threat-related from multiple sources that automatically extract threat-related information, measure the severity of IOCs, and quantify them based on the severity. We considered individual IOCs and one or more relationships among semantically similar IOCs. We proposed an efficient recogniser to identify domain-specific IOCs focusing on three domains: *organisational_domain-specific, regional_source-specific,* and *regional_target-specific* threat intelligence. Further, we evaluated the severity of IOC by exploring the frequency of attacks, IOC lifetime, and the number of exploited vulnerabilities in each domain.

The proposed semantic-based threat prioritisation system for AM has potential future scopes that can be explored, such as:

- *Integrating with existing security tools*: The proposed system can be combined with existing security tools to provide real-time threat intelligence and prioritisation of threats. The integration can help security teams to automate the detection, investigation, and response to threats and reduce the time to mitigate them.

- *Exploring additional domains*: The proposed system focuses on three domains: *organisational_domain-specific*, *regional_source-specific*, and *regional_target-specific*. However, other domains, such as *industry-specific* or *technology-specific*, can be explored to provide a more comprehensive view of the threat landscape.
- *Improving the ranking system*: The proposed system ranks the IOCs based on severity. However, the ranking system can be improved to consider the evolving threat landscape and real-time threat intelligence data to enhance the accuracy of the prioritisation system.

References

1. Haleem, A., Javaid, M.: Additive manufacturing applications in industry 4.0: a review. J. Ind. Integr. Manage. **4**(04), 1930001 (2019)
2. Dietz, M., Pernul, G.: Unleashing the digital twin's potential for ICS security. IEEE Secur. Priv. **18**(4), 20–27 (2020)
3. Sobers, R.: Data breach response times: trends and tips—Varonis. Varonis (2020). https://www.varonis.com/blog/data-breach-response-times/. Accessed 17 June 2020
4. Langner, R.: Stuxnet: dissecting a cyberwarfare weapon. IEEE Secur. Priv. **9**(3), 49–51 (2011)
5. Slay, J., Miller, M.: Lessons learned from the Maroochy water breach. In: Goetz, E., Shenoi, S. (eds.) ICCIP 2007. IIFIP, vol. 253, pp. 73–82. Springer, Boston, MA (2008). https://doi.org/10.1007/978-0-387-75462-8_6
6. Belikovetsky, S., Yampolskiy, M., Toh, J., Gatlin, J., Elovici, Y.: dr0wned-cyber-physical attack with additive manufacturing. In: 11th USENIX Workshop on Offensive Technologies (WOOT) (2017)
7. Kumar, M., Chand, S.: A provable secure and lightweight smart healthcare cyber-physical system with public verifiability. IEEE Syst. J. **16**(4), 5501–5508 (2021)
8. Wagner, T.D., Mahbub, K., Palomar, E., Abdallah, A.E.: Cyber threat intelligence sharing: survey and research directions. Comput. Secur. **87**, 101589 (2019)
9. IBM X-Force: IBM X-force threat intelligence report 2016 (2016)
10. Github: Facebook ThreatExchange Report. https://github.com/facebook/ThreatExchange. Accessed 22 July 2021
11. OpenCTI. https://www.opencti.io/en/. Accessed 22 July 2021
12. Wagner, C., Dulaunoy, A., Wagener, G., Iklody, A.: MISP: the design and implementation of a collaborative threat intelligence sharing platform. In: Proceedings of the 2016 ACM on Workshop on Information Sharing and Collaborative Security, pp. 49–56 (2016)
13. Noor, U., Anwar, Z., Amjad, T., Choo, K.-K.R.: A machine learning-based Fin-Tech cyber threat attribution framework using high-level indicators of compromise. Futur. Gener. Comput. Syst. **96**, 227–242 (2019)
14. Zhao, J., Yan, Q., Li, J., Shao, M., He, Z., Li, B.: TIMiner: automatically extracting and analysing categorised cyber threat intelligence from social data. Comput. Secur. **95**, 101867 (2020)
15. Gao, Y., Li, X., Peng, H., Fang, B., Philip, S.Y.: HinCTI: a cyber threat intelligence modeling and identification system based on heterogeneous information network. IEEE Trans. Knowl. Data Eng. **34**, 708–722 (2020)

16. Zhao, J., Yan, Q., Liu, X., Li, B., Zuo, G.: Cyber threat intelligence modeling based on heterogeneous graph convolutional network. In: 23rd International Symposium on Research in Attacks, Intrusions and Defenses (RAID 2020), pp. 241–256 (2020)
17. Liao, X., Yuan, K., Wang, X., Li, Z., Xing, L., Beyah, R.: Acing the IOC game: toward automatic discovery and analysis of open-source cyber threat intelligence. In: Proceedings of the 2016 ACM SIGSAC Conference on Computer and Communications Security, pp. 755–766 (2016)
18. Gao, P., et al.: Enabling efficient cyber threat hunting with cyber threat intelligence. In: 2021 IEEE 37th International Conference on Data Engineering (ICDE), pp. 193–204 (2021)
19. Wang, X., et al.: A method for extracting unstructured threat intelligence based on dictionary template and reinforcement learning. In: 2021 IEEE 24th International Conference on Computer Supported Cooperative Work in Design (CSCWD), pp. 262–267 (2021)
20. Ehrenfeld, J.M.: Wannacry, cybersecurity and health information technology: a time to act. J. Med. Syst. **41**(7), 104 (2017)
21. Akram, B., Ogi, D.: The making of indicator of compromise using malware reverse engineering techniques. In: International Conference on ICT for Smart Society (ICISS), pp. 1–6 (2020)
22. Barnum, S., Martin, R., Worrell, B., Kirillov, I.: The cybox language specification. MITRE Corp. (2012)
23. Barnum, S.: Standardising cyber threat intelligence information with the structured threat information expression (STIX). Mitre Corp. **11**, 1–22 (2012)
24. Connolly, J., Davidson, M., Schmidt, C.: The trusted automated exchange of indicator information (TAXII). MITRE Corp., pp. 1–20 (2014)
25. Iklody, A., Wagener, G., Dulaunoy, A., Mokaddem, S., Wagner, C.: Decaying indicators of compromise. arXiv Prepr. arXiv1803.11052 (2018)
26. Fu, T., Lee, W.-C., Lei, Z.: HIN2Vec: explore meta-paths in heterogeneous information networks for representation learning. In: Proceedings of the 2017 ACM on Conference on Information and Knowledge Management, pp. 1797–1806 (2017)
27. Zhao, H., Yao, Q., Li, J., Song, Y., Lee, D.L.: Meta-graph based recommendation fusion over heterogeneous information networks. In: Proceedings of the 23rd ACM SIGKDD International Conference on Knowledge Discovery and Data Mining, pp. 635–644 (2017)
28. Robinson, J.: Cyberwarfare statistics: a decade of geopolitical attacks. Privacy Affairs (2019). https://www.privacyaffairs.com/geopolitical-attacks/. Accessed 5 Sept 2021

WiP: Towards Zero Trust Authentication in Critical Industrial Infrastructures with PRISM

Fuyi Wang[1], Yanping Wang[2(✉)], Leo Yu Zhang[3], Yuval Hertzog[4],
Michael Loewy[4], Dominique Valladolid[4], Julio Medeiros[4],
Muna Al-Hawawreh[1], and Robin Doss[1]

[1] Deakin University, School of Information Technology,
Waurn Ponds, VIC 3216, Australia
[2] University of Electronic Science and Technology of China, Chengdu 69121, China
wangyp1108@gmail.com
[3] Griffith University, School of Information and Communication Technology,
Gold Coast, QLD 4215, Australia
[4] TIDE Foundation, 65-71 Belmore Road, Randwick, NSW 2031, Australia

Abstract. With the increasing threat of cyber attacks on critical infrastructures, the need for robust security measures has become more pressing. In response, decentralized secure computation has gained traction as an effective approach to minimizing the risks associated with such threats. We introduce this computation into the decentralized registration and authentication applications, and present the PRISM scheme. To ensure the security of the registration phase, the threshold secret sharing (TSS) technique is used to protect the credential against single-point failures. The threshold oblivious pseudorandom function (TOPRF) technique further enhance the security of PRISM scheme in the password-based authentication phase, by allowing the user to reconstruct the authentication messages from any subset of t parties and pass the verification. This study is a work in progress, and we are currently analyzing the detailed scheme and its security to better understand the practicality of our PRISM scheme. The theoretical security analysis demonstrates that our PRISM scheme achieves the properties of privacy preservation, unpredictability, and obliviousness. Experimental evaluation of the performance and practicability of our scheme will be presented in the full version.

Keywords: Decentralized systems · Privacy-preserving authentication · Secure registration · Threshold secret sharing · Threshold oblivious pseudorandom function

1 Introduction

As cyber attacks on critical infrastructures continue to pose a growing threat, the need for strong security measures has become paramount. In this context,

J. Zhou et al. (Eds.): ACNS 2023 Workshops, LNCS 13907, pp. 336–354, 2023.
https://doi.org/10.1007/978-3-031-41181-6_19

zero trust architecture (ZTA) has emerged as an effective approach to mitigating the risks associated with such attacks [1]. By implementing ZTA, critical infrastructure systems can significantly reduce the risk of successful cyber attacks through continuous verification of the user's identity and authorization, safeguarding against potentially devastating consequences. Therefore, it is widely used in security-oriented application scenarios, such as multi-factor authentication (MFA) [2–4], access control and permission management [5–8], and cloud and mobile device security [9–12].

Presently, some enterprises and organizations have begun to practice the ZTA and implement measurements in their registration and login authentication applications. For example, the Department of Homeland Security (DHS) in the United States released the Zero Trust Architecture Guide in 2018 [13]. Cisco also launched Zero Trust-related products and solutions, such as Cisco Zero Trust Secure Access [14]. However, due to diverse practitioners and application scenarios, the ZTA still faces many challenges and issues in practical registration and login authentication applications.

In practical ZTA applications, authentication is one of the core mechanisms for achieving security [9,15], since it can guarantee that only authorized users have access to the system and private data, and can limit the activities of malicious users. The password-based authenticated key-exchange (PAKE) protocols [16–19] are designed to provide both authentication and key exchange functionalities in a scenario where users authenticate themselves by means of a password. In some ZTA schemes, the use of PAKE provides a more secure authentication method for users, preventing man-in-the-middle attacks and password sniffing during transmission [20].

In the era of mobile interconnection, users' registration and authentication are outsourced to third-party cloud servers in many PAKE protocols [21]. However, these centralized management practices make the cloud a single point of trust and can cause single-point collapses. For example, due to a serious collapse of a third-party service provider, Optus, an Australian telecommunications company, experienced a customer secret information leak in May 2019. Additionally, centralized PAKE protocols are vulnerable to offline dictionary attacks, where an attacker/adversary can try all possible passwords offline until the correct one is found.

A new and emerging strategy, distributed PAKE protocols, has become a hot topic in information security recently for making a zero-trust model more robust and fault-tolerant [19]. Threshold secret sharing (TSS) [22] is the key technology that has contributed to the development of such protocols. TSS technology splits secret information into multiple shares, and these shares can be reconstructed into a complete secret only when certain conditions are met. Compared with traditional centralized encryption and authentication technologies, the TSS-based approaches have high security, flexibility, scalability, and increasing resilience of access validation, which can provide reliable encryption and login authentication for enterprises and organizations, thereby protecting the security of their confidential information and data.

Based on the above discussion, we present an ongoing decentralized zero-trust registration and authentication scheme, PRISM, consisting of a registration phase and an authentication phase. The registration is secured by nested TSS, and authentication is built upon threshold oblivious pseudorandom function (TOPRF) [23]. The TSS technique guarantee that an adversary must compromise a certain number of parties (i.e., servers) to obtain an authentication key (called credential). The TOPRF technique further enhances the security of the PRISM scheme by ensuring that the password is not revealed to the servers during the whole process. The combination of these two techniques continuously strengthens the protection of credentials and user passwords to achieve greater security and reliability. In a nutshell, our contributions are threefold.

- We propose PRISM, a decentralized authentication system consisting of a secure registration phase and a secure authentication phase. Our PRISM combined with TSS and TOPRF techniques and can enhance security by ensuring that no single party possesses the entire credential and the password. This can help prevent attacks where an adversary compromises a single party (server) and uses its secret to impersonate the user in the authentication process.
- We pay attention to the safeguard for the registration phase and propose a distributed threshold key generation scheme by introducing nested TSS, which splits the user's credential among the servers without secure channels. Meanwhile, the TOPRF technique aims to guarantee the secrecy requirement during the login phase, thus realizing the full coverage of authentication protection.
- We analyze and perform an extensive security proof of PRISM. The result shows that the registration and authentication phases of PRISM scheme are provably secure under the Elliptic Curve Discrete Logarithm (ECDL) and the Gap Threshold One-More Diffie-Hellman (Gap T-OMDH) intractability assumption.

The rest of this work is structured as follows. We introduce the preliminary in Sect. 2. Sect. 3 presents the detailed decentralized registration and authentication scheme, and its security properties. We provide the security proof in Sect. 4. Sect. 5 concludes this paper.

2 Preliminaries

In this section, we introduce the preliminaries underlying PRISM's construction. The key notations involved throughout the PRISM are summarized in Table 1.

2.1 Threshold Secret Sharing

The (t, n)-threshold secret sharing ((t, n)-TSS) protocol, first presented by Shamir [22], is a fundamental supporting block for many cryptographic primitives like distributed key generation and multiparty computation. The (t, n)-TSS

Table 1. The summary of notations.

Notions	Description
λ	The security parameter
n	The total number of servers
pp	The public group parameter set
p	The user's password
S_i	The server i, where $i \in [n]$
$\mathcal{C}$	The client/user
$\mathcal{U}$	The corrupted servers set
f	The key of OPRF (also called the credential)
f_i	The share of f for S_i
G_j	A random element in the Elliptic Curve Cryptography group
t, t'	The threshold and the number of corrupted users, respectively
$F(\cdot)$	The polynomial function with the degree $t - 1$
$l_{x,i}$	The Lagrange interpolation coefficient corresponding to the share f_i, which is used to recover the value $F(x)$
PPT	Probabilistic Polynomial-Time
negl	A negligible function
non $-$ negl	A non-negligible function

protocol is typically composed of *sharing* and *reconstruction* process [24]. In the *sharing* process, a dealer divides a secret s into n shares, with each share assigned to a separate party. The shares are generated using a random polynomial $F(x)$ of degree $(t-1)$ with the secret s as its constant term. In the *reconstruction* process, any subset of at the minimum t parties (i.e., servers) can congregate their shares to reassemble the original secret s. The reconstruction process involves using Lagrange interpolation to evaluate the polynomial $F(x)$ at $x = 0$ to recover the secret s.

Let m be a prime number and let $1 \leq t \leq n \neq m$, the (t, n)-TSS protocol [22] can be formulated as follows:

- **Sharing**: The dealer, who owns a secret $s \in \mathbb{Z}_m$, generates a random polynomial $F(x)$ of degree $t - 1$ with coefficients $a_0, a_1, \cdots, a_{t-1}$, i.e., $F(x) = a_0 + a_1 x + \cdots + a_{t-1} x^{t-1}$. The constant element a_0 is set to be equal to the secret value s, i.e., $a_0 = s$. For $1 \leq i \leq n$, the dealer evaluates the polynomial $F(x)$ at the value i, i.e., $s_i = F(i)$. The dealer then sends the value s_i to the corresponding secret shareholder S_i, without revealing the values of the polynomial coefficients $a_0, a_1, \cdots, a_{t-1}$ or the secret value s to anyone else.
- **Reconstruction**: A group honest shareholders S with $|S| \geq t$ can reconstruct s by using interpolation. More precisely, for any $x \in \mathbb{Z}_m$ and any $j \in [|S|]$, we first calculate the Lagrange basis polynomial $l_{x,j} = \prod_{k \neq j} \frac{x - x_k}{x_j - x_k}$. Then we have $F(x) = \sum_{j \in [|S|]} l_{x,j} \cdot s_j$. Therefore, we can express s as follows:

$$s = a_0 = F(0) = \sum_{j \in [|S|]} l_{0,j} \cdot s_j.$$

Hence, given the values x_j with $j \in [|S|]$, we can compute the basis polynomial $l_{x,j}$ for any $x \in \mathbb{Z}_m$, and use them to reconstruct the secret value s as described above.

The Shamir's (t, n)-TSS protocol, which is provably secure against an efficient adversary that corrupts at most $(t-1)$ parties, can satisfy the *secrecy* and *reconstruction* properties [24]. *For the secrecy*, if the dealer is uncorrupted, any adversary learns no information about the original secret s. *For the reconstruction*, a set of t or more honest parties can reconstruct the s.

2.2 Oblivious Pseudorandom Function

A two-party protocol between a client and a server is a strongly private Oblivious Pseudo-Random Function (OPRF) if it satisfies: given the input x from the client and the input k from the server, after the protocol is executed, the server never learns anything about the client's input x, while the client can only learn the output $\mathcal{F}_k(x)$ [23], where $\mathcal{F}_k(\cdot)$ is a pseudo-random function (PRF) (k is the private key).

Let H be a hash function that produces uniformly random elements from an Elliptic Curve Cryptography (ECC) group $\mathbb{G}$ that with order m and generator G, the PRF $\mathcal{F}_k(x) = k \cdot H(x)$ can be used to generate a Diffie-Hellman (DH) instance $(H(x), \mathcal{F}_k(x))$, where $H(x) = a \cdot G$ and $\mathcal{F}_k(x) = a \cdot k \cdot G$. Thus, this PRF is called *HashDH*. Additionally, since $a \cdot G$ is uniformly random, the *HashDH* is strongly private, and will be used to construct our PRISM to support the secure login authentication.

The *HashDH* can be evaluated with a simple protocol, which is depicted below:

- **Encode:** The client encodes the input x, hiding it against the server, by randomly selecting an exponent $r \leftarrow \mathbb{Z}_m$ and computing $r \cdot H(x)$. The client sends $r \cdot H(x)$ to the server.
- **Evaluation:** The server embeds the secret k into the $r \cdot H(x)$, by computing $k \cdot (r \cdot H(x))$, and sends $k \cdot r \cdot H(x)$ to the client.
- **Recover:** The client recover the function $\mathcal{F}_k = k \cdot H(x)$ by computing $r^{-1} \cdot k \cdot r \cdot H(x)$.

3 PRISM Scheme and Its Properties

The personal password (key) market is projected to increase significantly due to the growing demand for client personal passwords and the emergence of new data sources, such as the Internet of Things. This reality introduces an urgent need for a new framework to facilitate regulatory compliance for password management and data storage. Here we present our ZTA-based decentralized registration and authentication scheme, PRISM.

3.1   Construct Overview

The PRISM scheme is a cryptographic construction that consists of four probabilistic polynomial-time (PPT) algorithms: Init, Encode, Eval, and Recover. They satisfy the consistency property, described below.

- **Init** $(1^\lambda, n, t) \to (\llbracket f \rrbracket, \text{pp})$. It yields n secret key shares $f_1, f_2, \cdots, f_n$ and distributes share f_i $(i \in [n])$ to the corresponding server i. pp is an assumed parameter set for the algorithms below, involving the ECC group $\mathbb{G}$, the order m, and the hash functions H and H_1, where $H : \mathbb{G} \to \{0,1\}^l$ and $H_1 : \{0,1\}^* \to \mathbb{G}$.
- **Encode** $(p, pp) \to B$. It computes $A = H_1(p)$ and outputs an encoded value $B = r \cdot A$ for password $p \in \mathcal{X}$ using randomness $r \in \mathbb{Z}_m$, where $\mathcal{X}$ is the password space.
- **Eval** $(f_i, B) \to C_i$. It outputs fragment C_i of PRISM. Server i computes the i-th value $C_i = f_i \cdot B$.
- **Recover** $(\{(i, C_i)\}_{i \in S}, r, pp) \to k$. It aggregates the shares of the response server set S $(|S| \geq t)$, using randomness r to recover a $K = \sum_{i=1}^{|S|} (l_{0,i} \cdot C_i) \cdot r^{-1}$, and returns a value $k = H(K)$.

3.2   Registration Safeguard

Init $(1^\lambda, n, t)$ mentioned in Sect. 3.1 is the registration phase. The nested threshold secret sharing technique protects the user's credential against the servers, splitting the credential into random numbers within a given range. The distributed PRISM key generation protocol involves three components: sharing, reconstruction, and verification. To further explain the registration scenario, each component is elaborated in Algorithm 1.

3.3   Password Authentication

The combination of the three algorithms, **Encode** (p, pp), **Eval** (f_i, B), and **Recover** $(\{(i, C_i)\}_{i \in S}, r, pp)$ mentioned in Sect. 3.1, is the password authentication phase. The threshold oblivious pseudorandom function (TOPRF) is introduced to recover the possible key for decrypting the encrypted authentication information, so that the user can be authenticated. Algorithm 2 elaborately explains the authentication scenario.

3.4   Security Properties

Following the security hypothesis of [25], the PRISM is required to fulfill two security properties, *Unpredictability* and *Obliviousness*. *Unpredictability* implies that predicting the correct PRISM output, namely k, must be incredibly challenging, even though there are t' $(t' < t)$ servers compromised. *Obliviousness* mandates that the correct password, namely p, is exceptionally tricky to speculate regardless of whether the PRISM output k is accessible or not and there are t' servers compromised.

Algorithm 1. The registration phase of PRISM: distributed threshold key generation.

Input: $\mathbb{G}$: the ECC group with generator G and prime order m; (sk_i, vk_i): the private/public key pairs of S_i ($i \in [n]$); aesEnc: AES encryption function; aesDec: AES decryption function;

Output: the shares of the credential $\{f_1, f_2, ..., f_n\}$ and the public verification key Y, or $\perp$.

1:    Client $\mathcal{C}$ selects n servers $\{S_1, \cdots, S_n\}$.
2:    Client $\mathcal{C}$ prepare $x_1, \cdots, x_n$ for n servers $\{S_1, \cdots, S_n\}$ and sends them to all servers.

   # **Sharing**

3:    Each selected S_i chooses a random polynomial $F_i(z)$ over $\mathbb{Z}_m$ of degree $t - 1$: $F_i(z) = a_{i,0} + a_{i,1} \cdot z + \cdots + a_{i,t-1} \cdot z^{t-1}$.
4:    Each S_i computes the shares $s_{i,j} = F_i(x_j) \bmod m$ for $j \in [n]$.
5:    Each S_i encrypts $s_{i,j}$ by computing $Y_{i,j} = \text{aesEnc}_{H_{i,j}}\{a_{i,0} \cdot G, s_{i,j}\}$ for $j \in [n]$, where the symmetric key $H_{i,j} = sk_i \cdot vk_j$.
6:    Each S_i sends $\{a_{i,0} \cdot G, Y_{i,j}\}$ to client $\mathcal{C}$.
7:    Client $\mathcal{C}$ computes $Y = \sum_{i=1}^{n} a_{i,0} \cdot G = f \cdot G$.
8:    Client $\mathcal{C}$ sends the $Y_{i,j}$ to S_j for $i \in [n]$.

   # **Reconstruction**

9:    For $i \in [n]$, each S_j reveals the share $s_{i,j}$ by computing $H_{i,j} = sk_i \cdot vk_j$ and $\{a_{i,0} \cdot G, s_{i,j}\} = \text{aesDec}_{H_{i,j}}(Y_{i,j})$.
10:    Each S_j computes $Y = \sum_{i=1}^{n} a_{i,0} \cdot G$.
11:    Each S_j computes $f_j = \sum_{i=1}^{n} s_{i,j}$.

   # **Verification**

12:    Each S_j randomly chooses a $r_j \in \mathbb{Z}_m$ and computes $R_j = r_j \cdot G$.
13:    Each S_j computes a test value $TY_j = f_j \cdot G$ and sends the $\{R_j, TY_j\}$ to client $\mathcal{C}$.
14:    Client $\mathcal{C}$ aggregates all the R_j by computing $R = \sum_{j=1}^{n} R_j$.
15:    Client $\mathcal{C}$ aggregates all the TY_j by computing $Y' = \sum_{j=1}^{t} TY_j \cdot l_{0,j}$, where $l_{0,j}$ is the lagrange coefficients introduced in Sect. 2.1.
16:    Client $\mathcal{C}$ sends $\{R, M\}$ to S_j for $j \in [n]$, where M is the message needed to be signed.
17:    Each S_j computes $T_j = r_j + f_j \cdot l_{0,j} \cdot H(R||Y||M)$ and sends the T_j to client $\mathcal{C}$.
18:    Client $\mathcal{C}$ aggregates all the T_j by computing $T = \sum_{j=1}^{n} T_j$ for $j \in [n]$.
19:    Client $\mathcal{C}$ tests whether $T \cdot G == R + Y' \cdot H(R||Y||M)$. If it holds, it sends T ($\{T, R\}$ is equivalent to the signature of M) to S_j for $j \in [n]$, otherwise outputs $\perp$.
20:    Each S_j tests whether $T \cdot G == R + Y' \cdot H(R||Y||M)$ holds. If yes, it means that the verification is successful and each S_j stores the $\{Y, f_j\}$, otherwise outputs $\perp$.

We define the *Unpredictability* of the PRISM via an experiment executed between an adversary $\mathcal{A}$ and a challenger, and the security experiment makes use of the following oracles:

- $\mathcal{O}_{\text{encode\& eval}}()$: This oracle computes a value $B = \text{Encode}(\tilde{p}, r)$ for $r \xleftarrow{R} \mathbb{Z}_m$ and password $\tilde{p}$. It computes $C_i \leftarrow \text{Eval}(f_i, A)$ for $i \in [n] \backslash \mathcal{U}$, where $\mathcal{U}$ is the set of corrupted server. It then returns $B, \{C_i\}_{i \in [n] \backslash \mathcal{U}}$.

Algorithm 2. The password authentication phase of PRISM.

Input: $\mathcal{C}$: password p; $\mathcal{S}_i$: the share f_i and the encrypted message $EMasg$.

Output: $\mathcal{C}$ obtains the decrypted message $Prize$. // $Prize$ is the plain-text of the cipher $EMasg$ under a symmetry key.

    # $\mathcal{C}$: **Encode**

1:     Compute $A \leftarrow H_1(p)$, where $H_1(\cdot)$ stands for the map-to-point hash function in Elliptic Curve.

2:     Select $r \in \mathbb{Z}_m$ randomly.

3:     Mask A with the assistance of the random number $r \in \mathbb{Z}_p$ and learn $B = r \cdot A$.

4:     Send B to $\mathcal{S}_i$.

    # $\mathcal{S}_1, \mathcal{S}_2, \cdots, \mathcal{S}_n$: **Eval**

5:     Compute $C_i = f_i \cdot B$ to insert its share f_i to the value B.

6:     Send C_i to $\mathcal{C}$.

    # $\mathcal{C}$: **Recover**

7:     Compute $K = (\sum_{i=1}^{t} C_i) \cdot r^{-1} = f \cdot A$.

8:     Compute $k = H(K)$, where $H(\cdot)$ stands for the hash function.

9:     Using k to decrypt the encrypted message $EMasg$ derived from $\mathcal{S}_i$ to obtain the $Prize$.

- $\mathcal{O}_{eval}(i, X)$: On the input of (i, X), where $i \in [n]$ and $X \in \mathbb{G}$, this oracle increments q_i by 1, and returns $\text{Eval}(f_i, X)$, where f_i is the share hold by server $\mathcal{S}_i$.
- $\mathcal{O}_H(Y)$: On the input of any value $Y \in \mathbb{G}$, this oracle returns a value $k \in \{0,1\}^l$.
- $\mathcal{O}_{H_1}(K)$: On the input of any value $p \in \mathcal{X}$, this oracle returns a point $A \in \mathbb{G}$.

Definition 1 (Unpredictability). *The PRISM is Unpredictable if for all $n, t, t' \in \mathbb{N}, t' < t \leq n$, and PPT adversary $\mathcal{A}$, there exists a negligible function* negl *satisfies:*

$$Pr\left[Unpredictability_{PRISM,\mathcal{A}}\left(1^\lambda, n, t, t'\right) = 1\right] \leq \frac{C_{t-t'}^{Unpre}(q_1, \cdots, q_n)}{|\mathcal{X}|} + \text{negl}(\lambda),$$

where the maximum number of DH pairs of type $(X, f \cdot X)$ can be obtained in the $\mathcal{O}_{eval}(\cdot)$ oracle is $C_{t-t'}^{Unpre}(q_1, \cdots, q_n)$. And the Unpredictability experiment is defined below.

EXP$_{\mathcal{A}}^{\text{Unpredictability}_{PRISM}}(1^\lambda, n, t, t')$:

1. $([\![f]\!], \text{pp}) \overset{R}{\leftarrow} \text{Init}\left(1^\lambda, n, t, t'\right)$
2. $\mathcal{U} \leftarrow \mathcal{A}(\text{pp})$, where $|\mathcal{U}| = t'$
3. $\tilde{p} \overset{R}{\leftarrow} \mathcal{X}, q_1, \cdots, q_n = 0$
4. $k^\star \leftarrow \mathcal{A}^{(\mathcal{O}_{\text{encode\& eval}}(), \mathcal{O}_{\text{eval}}(i,X), \mathcal{O}_H(Y), \mathcal{O}_{H_1}(p))}\left(\{f_i\}_{i \in \mathcal{U}}\right)$
5. output 1 if $H(f \cdot H_1(\tilde{p})) = k^\star$

We define the *Obliviousness* of the PRISM also via an experiment executed between an adversary $\mathcal{A}$ and a challenger, and the experiment makes use of the following oracles:

- $\mathcal{O}_{\text{encode\& eval}}()$: This oracle computes a value $B = \text{Encode}(\tilde{p}, r)$ for $r \overset{R}{\leftarrow}$ $\mathbb{Z}_m$ and password $\tilde{p}$. The oracle also computes $C_i \leftarrow \text{Eval}(f_i, A)$ for $i \in [n] \backslash \mathcal{U}$, where $\mathcal{U}$ is the set of corrupted server. It computes $k = \text{Recover}(p, \{(i, C_i)\}_{i \in [n]}, r)$ and then returns $B, k, \{C_i\}_{i \in [n] \backslash \mathcal{U}}$.
- $\mathcal{O}_{\text{eval}}(i, X)$: This oracle performs as the $\mathcal{O}_{\text{eval}}(i, X)$ oracle of Unpredictability experiment.
- $\mathcal{O}_H(Y)$: This oracle performs as the $\mathcal{O}_H(Y)$ oracle of Unpredictability experiment.
- $\mathcal{O}_{H_1}(K)$: This oracle performs as the $\mathcal{O}_{H_1}(K)$ oracle of Unpredictability experiment.

Definition 2 (Obliviousness). *The PRISM is oblivious if for all $n, t, t' \in \mathbb{N}, t' \le t \le n$, and PPT adversary $\mathcal{A}$, there exists a negligible function negl satisfies*

$$Pr\left[Obliviousness_{PRISM, \mathcal{A}}\left(1^\lambda, n, t, t'\right) = 1\right] \le \frac{C_{t-t'}^{Obliv}(q_1, \cdots, q_n) + 1}{|\mathcal{X}|} + \text{negl}(\lambda),$$

where the maximum number of DH pairs of type $(X, f \cdot X)$ can be obtained in the $\mathcal{O}_{\text{eval}}(\cdot)$ oracle is $C_{t-t'}^{Obliv}(q_1, \cdots, q_n)$. And the Obliviousness experiment is defined below.

$\text{EXP}_{\mathcal{A}}^{\text{Obliviousness}_{\text{PRISM}}}\left(1^\lambda, n, t, t'\right)$:

1. $([\![f]\!], \text{pp}) \overset{R}{\leftarrow} \text{Init}\left(1^\lambda, n, t, t'\right)$
2. $\mathcal{U} \leftarrow \mathcal{A}(\text{pp})$, where $|\mathcal{U}| = t'$
3. $\tilde{p} \overset{R}{\leftarrow} \mathcal{X}$
4. $p^\star \leftarrow \mathcal{A}^{(\mathcal{O}_{\text{encode\& eval}}(), \mathcal{O}_{\text{eval}}(i, X), \mathcal{O}_H(Y), \mathcal{O}_{H_1}(p))}\left(\{f_i\}_{i \in \mathcal{U}}\right)$
5. output 1 if $\tilde{p} = p^\star$

4   Security Proof of PRISM Scheme

4.1   Hard Problems

The security of our PRISM scheme is reduced almost tightly to the Elliptic Curve Discrete Logarithm (ECDL) problem and the Gap Threshold One-More Diffie-Hellman (Gap T-OMDH) problem. Before we prove that the PRISM satisfies the security properties we mentioned above, we introduce the hard problems of the ECDL problem and the Gap T-OMDH problem.

Definition 3 (Elliptic Curve and ECDL assumption). *An elliptic curve E over a prime finite field $\mathbb{F}_m$ with order m is defined as: $y^2 = x^3 + \alpha x + \beta \bmod m$, where $\alpha, \beta \in \mathbb{F}_m, 4\alpha^3 + 27\beta^2 \neq 0$. The corresponding elliptic curve group $\mathbb{G}$ consists of all solutions (x, y) of the above equation and $\mathcal{P}$ which is the point at infinity. We have $\mathbb{G} = \{(x, y) | x, y \in \mathbb{F}_m, (x, y) \in E\} \cup \{\mathcal{P}\}$. The ECDL assumption on $\mathbb{G}$ states that, for any unknown scalar $a \overset{R}{\leftarrow} \mathbb{Z}_m$, given two points $\{G, Q\}$ such that $Q = a \cdot G$, the probability of outputting a is negligible for any polynomial time algorithm.*

T-OMDH: The T-OMDH assumption pertains to the scenario where a random number $f \in \mathbb{Z}_m$ is shared using a random polynomial $F(\cdot)$ of degree $t-1$, and the shares $f_1 = F(1), \cdots, f_n = F(n)$ are held by n servers. An oracle $\text{TOMDH}_F(\cdot, \cdot)$ is defined as: take inputs $(i, G) \in [n] \times \mathbb{G}$, it outputs $F(i) \cdot G$. To compute $f \cdot G$ for a given $G \in \mathbb{G}$ and $f = F(0)$, a set I is chosen such that $I \subseteq [n]$ and $|I| = t$. The value $B = f \cdot G$ is derived as $\sum_{i \in I} l_{0,i} \cdot C_i$ using Lagrange interpolation coefficients $l_{0,i}$, where $C_i = \text{TOMDH}_F(i, G) = f_i \cdot G$, and $f = \sum_{i \in I} l_{0,i} \cdot f_i$.

The T-OMDH assumption states that to compute $F(0) \cdot G$ for a given random challenge point G, it is necessary to query the $\text{TOMDH}_F(\cdot, G)$ oracle on at least t different $i \in [n]$. More conceptually, T-OMDH describes a scenario where an adversary has access to the $\text{TOMDH}_F(\cdot, \cdot)$ oracle for random chosen polynomial $F(\cdot)$ with $t - 1$ degree and is presented with a challenge set $R = \{G_1, \cdots, G_N\}$ consisting of random elements from the group $\mathbb{G}$. T-OMDH also states that the adversary can compute $f \cdot G_j$ for $f = F(0)$ for no more than $C_t(q_1, \cdots, q_n)$ elements G_j in set R, where q_i is the number of queries made by the adversary $\mathcal{A}$ to $\text{TOMDH}_F(i, \cdot)$. We take the following example to explain how to compute the bound $C_t(q_1, \cdots, q_n)$.

Example. Suppose we have a vector $q = [3, 3, 4]$. To compute $C_2(q)$, we need to find the largest value of ℓ such that there exist binary vectors $\mathbf{u}_1, \cdots, \mathbf{u}_\ell \in \{0, 1\}^n$ (not necessarily distinct), where each $\mathbf{u}_i$ has $t = 2$ number of 1 (the weight of each $\mathbf{u}_i$ is t) and $(q_1, \cdots, q_n) \geq \sum_{i \in [\ell]} \mathbf{u}_i$. To solve this, we can try to express q as a linear combination of binary vectors with weight $t = 2$. In this case, we can write $q = 2 \cdot [1, 0, 1] + [1, 1, 0] + 2 \cdot [0, 1, 1]$. Notice that each of these vectors has weight $t = 2$, and their sum gives q. Therefore, $\ell = 5$ and $C_2(q) = \ell = 5$.

Definition 4 *((t', t, n, N, Q)-**T-OMDH** assumption). Let $\mathcal{U}$ be a subset of $[n]$ with $|\mathcal{U}| = t' < t$. This assumption means the probability that any polynomial-time adversary $\mathcal{A}$ wins the following game is negligible.*
Game: *Adversary $\mathcal{A}$ receives a challenge set $R = \{G_1, \cdots, G_N\}$ where $G_i \in \mathbb{G}$ for $i \in [N]$, and specifies a set of t' values $\{f_j\}_{j \in \mathcal{U}}$ in $\mathbb{Z}_m$. A random polynomial $F(\cdot)$ with $t - 1$ degree over $\mathbb{Z}_m$ is then chosen such that $F(j) = f_j$ for $j \in \mathcal{U}$. The adversary $\mathcal{A}$ is then given access to the oracle $\text{TOMDH}_F(\cdot, \cdot)$. We say that $\mathcal{A}$ wins if it outputs $f \cdot G_j$ where $f = F(0)$ for $Q + 1$ different elements G_j in set R, and if $C_{t-t'}^{tomdh}(q_1, \cdots, q_n) \leq Q$, where q_i for $i \notin \mathcal{U}$ is the number of $\mathcal{A}$'s queries to $\text{TOMDH}_F(i, \cdot)$, and $q_i = 0$ for $i \in \mathcal{U}$.*

Definition 5 *(**Gap** (t', t, n, N, Q)-**T-OMDH** assumption). It is a variant of the T-OMDH assumption in Definition 4 except that $\mathcal{A}$ has access to the Decisional Diffie-Hellman DDH oracle in group $\mathbb{G}$. This oracle takes as input four ECC group elements (a, b, c, d) and outputs 1 if (a, b) and (c, d) are the DH pair of the same private key (assuming k), i.e., $a = k \cdot b$ and $c = k \cdot d$, and outputs 0 otherwise.*

4.2 Security Proof for Registration

The *secrecy* requirement is a crucial property in cryptographic schemes that involve the generation of secret values or keys. In the case of a distributed threshold key generation scheme in Algorithm 1, the secrecy requirement ensures that the secret value f (shared among n servers) is kept confidential and cannot be learned by an adversary beyond what follows from equality $Y = f \cdot G \bmod m$.

Simulatability is a more formal expression for proving the security of cryptographic protocols [26], in which the output of a real protocol execution is indistinguishable from the output of a simulated (ideal world) protocol execution, even for an adversary $\mathcal{A}$ with arbitrary computational power. The simulator sim, which holds no information about the actual secret value f, is designed to mimic the behavior of the honest parties in the expected polynomial time while providing no information about the actual secret value. If the adversary $\mathcal{A}$ cannot distinguish between the real and simulated outputs, then the protocol is considered secure.

More precisely, in the context of a distributed threshold key generation scheme, the simulatability proof shows that even if the adversary $\mathcal{A}$ has some knowledge of the $t - 1$ corrupted servers and the public value $Y = f \cdot G$, it cannot use this information to learn anything about the secret information on f beyond what can be learned from Y. This provides a strong guarantee that the secret value remains confidential and secure.

Theorem 1. *Under the ECDL assumption and in the random oracle model, the registration scheme is secure against static adversaries.*

Proof. Assuming an adversary $\mathcal{A}$ who knows Y and corrupts $t - 1$ servers at the beginning of the protocol. $\mathcal{A}$ learns all the corrupted servers' secrets and actively controls their behaviors, while the simulator Sim plays the role of client and all good servers. Additionally, the Sim has full control of the values returned by the hash function $H(\cdot)$. Without loss of generality, we denote $\mathcal{U} = \{1, \cdots, t'\}$ the set of servers controlled by the adversary $\mathcal{A}$ and $\mathcal{G} = \{t' + 1, \cdots, n\}$, $t' < t$ the set of honest servers (run by Sim). The description of the simulation is as follows:

- In the **Sharing** process, for each honest server S_i ($i \in \mathcal{G}$), except one honest server(assuming S_n^*), Sim chooses at random $a_{i,0}$ and $(t - 1)$ other values $a_{i,k}$ for $k \in [t - 1]$. Sets $F_i(z) = \sum_{k=0}^{t-1} a_{i,k} \cdot z^k \in \mathbb{Z}_m[z]$, computes $s_{i,j} = F_i(x_j) \bmod m$ for $j \in [n]$ and computes $Y_i = a_{i,0} \cdot G$. Performs the share distribution (Step 5–8 of Algorithm 1) as real run.
  For server S_n^*, Sim chooses at random a function $f_n^*(z) = \sum_{k=0}^{t-1} a_{n^*,k} \cdot z^k \in \mathbb{Z}_m[z]$. Instead of setting Y_n^* equal to $a_{n^*,0} \cdot G$, Sim sets $Y_n^* = Y + (\sum Y_i)^{-1}$ to ensure the ending value to be Y. Sim then generates n values $s_{n^*,j} = f_n^*(j)$ for $j \in [n]$ and sends the encrypted shares to all servers.
- In the **Reconstruction** process, performs Step 9–11 of Algorithm 1 on behalf of the uncorrupted servers, i.e., recovers s_i and Y_i in the clear for every S_i ($i \in \mathcal{G}$ and $i \in [n]$) and computes the aggregation Y.
- In the **Verification** process, for each server S_i ($i \in \mathcal{G} \backslash n^*$), performs steps 12–15 of Algorithm 1 as real run. For server S_n^*, computes $TY_n^* = l_{0,n^*}^{-1} \cdot (Y + (\sum TY_i \cdot l_{0,i})^{-1})$ for $i \in [n] \backslash n^*$ and computes R_n^* as real run. Generally, if $Y = \sum_1^{t-1} TY_i + a_{n^*,0} \cdot G$ for $i \in \mathcal{G} \backslash n^*$, it means the chose corrupted servers

perform correctly, and Sim then randomly picks $c, T \in \mathbb{Z}_m, M \in \{0,1\}^*$, computes $R = T \cdot G - c \cdot Y$, and sends $\{R, Y, M\}$ to each S_i, where $i \in [n]$, and continues.

After receiving a set of responses T_j in step 18, Sim sends the pre-chosen T to each server as the aggregated signature in Step 19. In the random oracle model, where the simulator has a full control of the values returned by the hash function, it can define the value of $H(\cdot)$ at $(R||Y||M)$ to be c. It is oblivious that the equation $T \cdot G == R + Y \cdot H(R||Y||M)$ holds. Therefore, the signature can pass the verification algorithm.

We now show that the view of the adversary $\mathcal{A}$ that interacts with Sim is the same as that interacts with the honest server and client in a regular run.

- First note that all the honest servers' (except for S_n^*) outputs are identical since the actions of these honest servers interacting with $\mathcal{A}$ are as the real run of Algorithm 1.
- For the output of server S_n^*, all the shares are generated from a randomly chosen polynomial with the same distribution as the real run, and the adversary $\mathcal{A}$ cannot recover the real $a_{n^*,0} \cdot G$ due to the reconstruction property of the threshold secret sharing, so the output distribution of S_n^* is also identical with the real execution from the view of $\mathcal{A}$.
- In the verification process, since Sim fully control of the values returned by the hash function $H(\cdot)$, the distributions of c and $H(R||Y||M)$ are equivalent.

From the above, we can see that only the good server S_i^* has an inconsistent internal state because she/he does not know the discrete logarithm of Y_n^*. However, this server will not be attacked because in this static model all corrupted servers are chosen at the beginning of the game. Additionally, the distribution produced by the simulator Sim is statistically close to perfect, which means the adversary $\mathcal{A}$ cannot learn whether the distribution comes from a simulator or from a real run. Thus, we can conclude that the adversary $\mathcal{A}$ cannot learn knowledge from the secret shares of the uncorrupted servers, and if the adversary $\mathcal{A}$ obtains the secret f, it must learn from the public value Y, which means the ECDL assumption is broken.

4.3 Security Proof for Authentication

We here prove the security properties: unpredictability and obliviousness, of the password authentication phase.

Theorem 2. *No such a PPT adversary $\mathcal{A}$ that can make the probability*

$$Pr\left[Unpredictability_{PRISM,\mathcal{A}}\left(1^\lambda, n, t, t'\right) = 1 \right] \geq \frac{C_{t-t'}^{Unpre}(q_1, \cdots, q_n)}{|\mathcal{X}|} + \text{non} - \text{negl}(\lambda),$$

where $\text{non} - \text{negl}$ *is a non-negligible function.*

Proof. We prove Theorem 2 by analyzing whether a PPT adversary $\mathcal{A}$ can win the unpredictability game of PRISM scheme with a non-negligible advantage. If $\mathcal{A}$ can can win, then there is an adversary $\mathcal{B}$ that can break the Gap T-OMDH assumption or the predicting game (defined in Fig. 1).

Let $e \in \mathbb{N}$ be the number of valid DH pair (G, Y) satisfies $Y = f \cdot G$ in the hash oracles, where Y is the input the H oracle and G is the output of H_1 oracle (see below for more details). There are two cases of e, case 1: $e > C_{t-t'}^{Unpre}(q_1, \cdots, q_n)$; and case 2: $e \leq C_{t-t'}^{Unpre}(q_1, \cdots, q_n)$. In the next, we will prove that in case 1, if there is an adversary $\mathcal{A}$ shattering the unpredictability game, then the adversary $\mathcal{B}$ can break the Gap T-OMDH assumption; and in case 2, $\mathcal{A}$ can break the predicting game.

Case 1. In this case, $e > C_{t-t'}^{Unpre}(q_1, \cdots, q_n)$. We construct $\mathcal{B}$ as follows.

Init: It first obtains $(p, \mathbb{G}, G_1, \cdots, G_N)$ from the Gap TOMDH game, sends $pp = (p, \mathbb{G}, n, t)$ to $\mathcal{A}$ and retrieves the corrupted server set $\mathcal{U}$ from $\mathcal{A}$. Then, it randomly selects $\{f_i\}_{i \in \mathcal{U}}$, sends $\{(i, f_i)\}_{i \in \mathcal{U}}$ and the set $\{f_i\}_{i \in \mathcal{U}}$ to the Gap TOMDH game and $\mathcal{A}$, respectively. It initializes the following variables: $\mathcal{LIST} := []$, $\mathcal{L} := []$, sets $e, q, q_1, q_2, ..., q_n = 0$.

Query: $\mathcal{B}$ handles $\mathcal{A}$'s oracle queries as follows:

- **Query $\mathcal{O}_{encode\& eval}()$:** Randomly select G_j and set $B = G_j$, compute $C_i \leftarrow$ **Eval**(f_i, B) for $i \in \mathcal{U}$. It calls $\mathcal{O}(i, B)$ of the Gap TOMDH game to get the other $(t - t')$ C_i, where $i \in [n] \backslash \mathcal{U}$. Find the Lagrange coefficients $\{l_{0,i}\}_{i \in [n]}$ and computes $\tilde{K} = \sum_{i \in [n]}(l_{0,i} \cdot C_i)$. Increment q by 1 and add $(G_j, \tilde{K})$ into $\mathcal{LIST}$. Returns $\left(B, \{C_i\}_{i \in [n] \backslash \mathcal{U}}\right)$ to $\mathcal{A}$.
- **Query $\mathcal{O}_{eval}(i, X)$:** Call $\mathcal{O}(i, X)$ of the Gap TOMDH game to get C_i. Increment q_i by 1 and return C_i to $\mathcal{A}$.
- **Query $\mathcal{O}_{H_1}(p)$:** If $p \in \mathcal{L}$, return $\mathcal{L}[p]$; otherwise, pick an unused G_i, set $\mathcal{L}[p] = G_i$ and return G_i to $\mathcal{A}$.
- **Query $\mathcal{O}_H(K)$:** If there is a $G_i \in \mathcal{L}$ satisfied $DH(G_i, K) = DH(G_j, \tilde{K})$ and the new valid pair $(G_i, K) \notin \mathcal{LIST}$, $e = e + 1$ and (G_i, K) is appended to $\mathcal{LIST}$. When $C_{t-t'}^{Unpre}(q_1, \cdots, q_n) < e$, output $\mathcal{LIST}$. Compute $H(K)$ honestly and return it to $\mathcal{A}$.

Analysis: From the construction of $\mathcal{B}$, we deduce that $|\mathcal{LIST}| = q + e$, and the $C_{t-t'}^{tomdh}(q_1, \cdots, q_n)$ of the gap TOMDH game is equal to $C_{t-t'}^{Unpre}(q_1, \cdots, q_n) + q$. Since $e > C_{t-t'}^{Unpre}(q_1, \cdots, q_n)$, thus we have:

$$|\mathcal{LIST}| = q + e > q + C_{t-t'}^{Unpre}(q_1, \cdots, q_n). \tag{1}$$

The above equation can be transformed as

$$|\mathcal{LIST}| > C_{t-t'}^{tomdh}(q_1, \cdots, q_n). \tag{2}$$

Thus, more DH tuples are found and the adversary breaks the T-OMDH assumption.

Predicting$_{\mathcal{A}}\left(1^{\lambda}\right)$:

1. for every $p \in \mathcal{X}, \mathcal{M}[p] := k$, where $k \xleftarrow{R} \{0,1\}^{\lambda}$
2. $\tilde{p} \xleftarrow{R} \mathcal{X}, \tilde{k} := \mathcal{M}[\tilde{p}]$
3. set $e = 0$
4. $k^{\star} \leftarrow \mathcal{A}^{(\mathcal{O}_{\text{compute}}(p))}\left(1^{\lambda}\right)$
5. output 1 iff $k^{\star} = \tilde{k}$

$\mathcal{O}_{\text{compute}}(p)$:

1. increment e by 1
2. return $\mathcal{M}[p]$

Fig. 1. The predicting game.

Case 2. In this case, $e \leq C_{t-t'}^{Unpre}(q_1, \cdots, q_n)$, and if this case happens, we can prove that the adversary $\mathcal{A}$ cannot win the predictability game.

The predicting game is depicted in Fig. 1. Theoretically, we have information that for any PPT adversary $\mathcal{A}$, there exists a function negl [21]:

$$\Pr\left[\text{Predicting}_{\mathcal{A}}\left(1^{\lambda}\right) = 1 \right] \leq \frac{e}{|\mathcal{X}|} + \text{negl}(\lambda).$$

If $e \leq C_{t-t'}^{Unpre}(q_1, \cdots, q_n)$, we can use $\mathcal{A}$ to construct an adversary $\mathcal{B}$ to break the predicting game.

The construction of $\mathcal{B}$ is the following. It first runs Init $\left(1^{\lambda}, n, t, t'\right)$ to generate $([\![f]\!], pp)$, sends pp to $\mathcal{A}$ and gets back $\mathcal{U}$. It then gives $\{f_i\}_{i \in \mathcal{U}}$ to $\mathcal{A}$. It sets $\mathcal{LIST} := [], \mathcal{L} := []$, and then handles $\mathcal{A}$'s oracle queries as follows:

- On $\mathcal{A}$'s call to $\mathcal{O}_{\text{encode\& eval}}()$: Sample $B \xleftarrow{R} \mathbb{G}$, compute $C_i \leftarrow \text{Eval}(f_i, B)$ for $i \in [n]$, and return $\left(B, \{C_i\}_{i \in [n] \backslash \mathcal{U}}\right)$ to $\mathcal{A}$.
- On $\mathcal{A}$'s call to $\mathcal{O}_{\text{eval}}(i, X)$: Return $\text{Eval}(f_i, X)$.
- On $\mathcal{A}$'s call to $\mathcal{O}_{H_1}(p)$: If $p \in \mathcal{L}$, return $\mathcal{L}[p]$; otherwise, choose an used $G_i \xleftarrow{R} \mathbb{G}$, set $\mathcal{L}[p] = G_i$ and return it to $\mathcal{A}$.
- On $\mathcal{A}$'s call to $\mathcal{O}_H(K)$:
  - If $K \in \mathcal{LIST}$, let $k := \mathcal{LIST}[K]$.
  - If $K \notin \mathcal{LIST}$ and for all $A \in \mathcal{L}$, $K \neq f \cdot A$, then sample $k \xleftarrow{R} \{0,1\}^{\lambda}$ and set $\mathcal{LIST}[K] := k$.
  - If $K \notin \mathcal{LIST}$ and there is a $A \in \mathcal{L}$ satisfies $K = f \cdot A$ (i.e., (A, K) is a valid DH pair), retrieve p according to A in $\mathcal{L}$ and call $\mathcal{O}_{\text{compute}}(p)$ to get a k. Set $\mathcal{LIST}[K] := k$. Return k to $\mathcal{A}$.

Output: $\mathcal{A}$ outputs the challenge value $k^{\star}$.

Finally, $\mathcal{A}$ outputs its guess $k^{\star}$ and $\mathcal{B}$ relays $k^{\star}$ as the outputs of predicting game. The challenge $k^{\star}$ of the predicting game has been combined with the challenge of the unpredictability game. If $\mathcal{A}$ guess correctly with probability as least $\frac{C_{t-t'}^{Unpre}(q_1,\cdots,q_n)}{|\mathcal{X}|} + \text{non} - \text{negl}(\lambda)$, then $\mathcal{B}$ shatters the guessing game with

$$\Pr\left[\text{Predicting}_{\mathcal{B}}\left(1^\lambda\right) = 1\right] \geq \frac{C_{t-t'}^{Unpre}(q_1,\cdots,q_n)}{|\mathcal{X}|} + \text{non} - \text{negl}(\lambda)$$

$$\geq \frac{e}{|\mathcal{X}|} + \text{non} - \text{negl}(\lambda)$$

It is information-theoretically impossible for the adversary $\mathcal{B}$ to win the predicting game with a non-negligible advantage. However, if $e \leq C_{t-t'}^{Unpre}(q_1,\cdots,q_n)$ and $\mathcal{A}$ can win the predictability game with a non-negligible advantage, then $\mathcal{B}$ can utilize $\mathcal{A}$ to win the predicting game with a non-negligible advantage. This leads to a contradiction. Thus, we can conclude that $\mathcal{A}$ cannot win the predictability game in this case with a non-negligible advantage.

$\text{Guessing}_{\mathcal{A}}\left(1^\lambda\right)$:

1. $\tilde{p} \xleftarrow{R} \mathcal{X}$
2. set $e = 0$
3. $p^\star \leftarrow \mathcal{A}^{(\mathcal{O}_{\text{guess}}\,(p))}\left(1^\lambda\right)$
4. output 1 iff $p^\star = \tilde{p}$

$\mathcal{O}_{\text{guess}}\,(p)$:

1. increment e by 1
2. return 1 if $p = \tilde{p}$; otherwise return 0

Fig. 2. The guessing game.

Theorem 3. *No such a PPT adversary $\mathcal{A}$ that can make the probability*

$$Pr\left[\text{Obliviousness}_{PRISM,\mathcal{A}}\left(1^\lambda, n, t, t'\right) = 1\right] \geq \frac{C_{t-t'}^{Obliv}(q_1,\cdots,q_n)+1}{|\mathcal{X}|} + \text{non} - \text{negl}(\lambda),$$

where $\text{non} - \text{negl}$ *is a non-negligible function.*

Proof. We prove this by proving if a PPT adversary $\mathcal{A}$ can win the obliviousness game of PRISM with a non-negligible advantage, then there is an adversary $\mathcal{B}$ that can break the Gap T-OMDH assumption or the guessing game (defined in Fig. 2).

Similar to the proof of the unpredictability property, we define $e \in \mathbb{N}$ to be the number of valid DH pairs in the H oracle (see below for more details) and prove the obliviousness property from, case 1: $e > C_{t-t'}^{Obliv}(q_1,\cdots,q_n)$; and case 2: $e \leq C_{t-t'}^{Obliv}(q_1,\cdots,q_n)$.

In the **case 1**, We construct $\mathcal{B}$ as follows.

Init: It first obtains $(p, \mathbb{G}, G_1, \cdots, G_N)$ from the Gap TOMDH game, sends $pp = (p, \mathbb{G}, n, t)$ to $\mathcal{A}$ and retrieves the corrupted server set $\mathcal{U}$. Then, it randomly selects $\{f_i\}_{i \in \mathcal{U}}$, sends $\{(i, f_i)\}_{i \in \mathcal{U}}$ and the set $\{f_i\}_{i \in \mathcal{U}}$ to the Gap TOMDH game and $\mathcal{A}$, respectively. It initializes the following variables: $\mathcal{LIST}=[]$, $\mathcal{L}=[]$, sets $e, q, q_1, q_2, ..., q_n = 0$.

Query: $\mathcal{B}$ handles $\mathcal{A}$'s oracle queries as follows:

- **Query$\mathcal{O}$_{encode&eval}():** Choose an unused G_j, set $B = G_j$, compute $C_i \leftarrow$ **Eval**(f_i, B) for $i \in \mathcal{U}$. It calls $\mathcal{O}(i, B)$ of the Gap TOMDH game to get the other $(t - t')$ C_i, where $i \in [n] \backslash \mathcal{U}$. Find the Lagrange coefficients $\{l_{0,i}\}_{i \in [n]}$ and computes $\tilde{K} = \sum_{i \in [n]} (l_{0,i} \cdot C_i)$. Increment q by 1 and add $(G_j, \tilde{K})$ into $\mathcal{LIST}$. Returns $\left(B, \{C_i\}_{i \in [n] \backslash \mathcal{U}}\right)$ to $\mathcal{A}$.

- **Query$\mathcal{O}$_{eval}(i, X):** Call $\mathcal{O}(i, X)$ of the gap TOMDH game to get C_i. Increment q_i by 1 and return C_i to $\mathcal{A}$.

- **Query $\mathcal{O}_{H_1}(p)$:** If $p \in \mathcal{L}$, return $\mathcal{L}[p]$; otherwise, pick an unused G_i, set $\mathcal{L}[p] = G_i$ and return G_i to $\mathcal{A}$.

- **Query $\mathcal{O}_H(K)$:** If there is a $G_i \in \mathcal{L}$ satisfied $DH(G_i, K) = DH(G_j, \tilde{K})$ and the new valid pair $(G_i, K) \notin \mathcal{LIST}$, $e = e + 1$ and (G_i, K) is appended to $\mathcal{LIST}$. When $C_{t-t'}^{Obliv}(q_1, \cdots, q_n) < e$, the $\mathcal{LIST}$ is output. Compute $H(K)$ honestly and return to $\mathcal{A}$.

Analysis: From the construction of $\mathcal{B}$, we know that $|\mathcal{LIST}| = q + e$, and the the $C_{t-t'}^{tomdh}(q_1, \cdots, q_n)$ is equal to $C_{t-t'}^{Obliv}(q_1, \cdots, q_n) + q$.

In this case, $e > C_{t-t'}^{Obliv}(q_1, \cdots, q_n)$, thus

$$|\mathcal{LIST}| = q + e > q + C_{t-t'}^{Obliv}(q_1, \cdots, q_n). \tag{3}$$

The above equation can be transformed as

$$|\mathcal{LIST}| > C_{t-t'}^{tomdh}(q_1, \cdots, q_n). \tag{4}$$

Thus, more DH tuple is found and the adversary breaks the T-OMDH assumption.

Case 2. In this case, $e \leq C_{t-t'}^{Obliv}(q_1, \cdots, q_n)$. Similar to research [21], we define a guessing game in Fig. 2. Information theoretically, we have that for any PPT adversary $\mathcal{A}$, there exists a negligible function negl:

$$\Pr\left[\text{Guessing}_{\mathcal{A}}\left(1^\lambda\right) = 1\right] \leq \frac{e+1}{|\mathcal{X}|} + \text{negl}(\lambda).$$

If $e \leq C_{t-t'}^{Obliv}(q_1, \cdots, q_n)$, we use $\mathcal{A}$ to construct an adversary $\mathcal{B}$ that breaks the guessing game.

The construction of $\mathcal{B}$ is the following. It first runs Init $\left(1^\lambda, n, t, t'\right)$ to generate $([\![f]\!], pp)$, presents pp to $\mathcal{A}$ and gets back $\mathcal{U}$. It then gives $\{f_i\}_{i \in \mathcal{U}}$ to $\mathcal{A}$. It samples $\tilde{k} \leftarrow \{0,1\}^\lambda$, sets $\mathcal{LIST} := []$, $\mathcal{L} := []$, and then handles $\mathcal{A}$'s oracle queries as follows:

- On $\mathcal{A}$'s call to $\mathcal{O}_{\text{enc\& eval}}()$: Sample $B \xleftarrow{R} \mathbb{G}$, represent $B = H_1(\tilde{p})^r$ for some unknown $\tilde{p}$ and r. Compute $C_i \leftarrow \text{Eval}(f_i, c)$ for $i \in [n]$, and return $\left(B, \{C_i\}_{i\in[n]\setminus\mathcal{U}}\right)$ to $\mathcal{A}$.
- On $\mathcal{A}$'s call to $\mathcal{O}_{\text{eval}}(i, X)$: Return $\text{Eval}(f_i, B)$.
- On $\mathcal{A}$'s call to $\mathcal{O}_{H_1}(p)$: If $p \in \mathcal{L}$, return $\mathcal{L}[p]$; Else choose $A \xleftarrow{R} \mathbb{G}$, set $A := \mathcal{L}[p]$ and return A.
- On $\mathcal{A}$'s call to $\mathcal{O}_H(K)$
   • If $K \in \mathcal{LIST}$, let $k := \mathcal{LIST}[K]$.
   • If $K \notin \mathcal{LIST}$ and for all $A \in \mathcal{L}$, $K \neq f \cdot A$, then sample $k \xleftarrow{R} \{0,1\}^\lambda$ and set $\mathcal{LIST}[K] := k$.
   • If $K \notin \mathcal{LIST}$ and there is a point $A \in \mathcal{L}$ satisfies $K = f \cdot A$ (i.e., (A, K) is a new valid DH pair), retrieve p according to A in $\mathcal{L}$ and call $\mathcal{O}_{\text{guess}}(p)$. If the output if 1, then set $k := \tilde{k}$, and output 1 in the final obliviousness game; otherwise sample $k \xleftarrow{R} \{0,1\}^*$. Set $\mathcal{L}[K] := k$. Return k to $\mathcal{A}$.

Output: $\mathcal{A}$ outputs the challenge value $p^\star$.

When $\mathcal{A}$ outputs $p^\star$ of the obliviousness game. If all the $\mathcal{O}_{\text{guess}}(\cdot)$ in the H query phase returns 0, then $\mathcal{B}$ relays $p^\star$ as its challenge to obliviousness game. If $\mathcal{A}$ breaks the obliviousness game with probability at least $\frac{C_{t-t'}^{Obliv}(q_1,\cdots,q_n)+1}{|\mathcal{X}|} +$ non $-$ negl(λ), then $\mathcal{B}$ shatters the guessing game with probability

$$\Pr\left[\text{Guessing}_{\mathcal{B}}\left(1^\lambda\right) = 1\right] \geq \frac{C_{t-t'}^{Obliv}(q_1,\cdots,q_n)+1}{|\mathcal{X}|} + \text{non} - \text{negl}(\lambda)$$

$$\geq \frac{e+1}{|\mathcal{X}|} + \text{non} - \text{negl}(\lambda)$$

It is information-theoretically impossible for the adversary $\mathcal{B}$ to win the guessing game with a non-negligible advantage. However, if $e \leq C_{t-t'}^{Obliv}(q_1,\cdots,q_n)$ and $\mathcal{A}$ can win the obliviousness game with a non-negligible advantage, then $\mathcal{B}$ can utilize $\mathcal{A}$ to win the guessing game with a non-negligible advantage. This leads to a contradiction, and therefore, we can conclude the proof that $\mathcal{A}$ cannot win the obliviousness game with a non-negligible advantage.

5   Conclusion

In this paper, we have presented a novel PRISM scheme that utilizes decentralized secure computation to ensure the privacy and security of registration and authentication processes. Our scheme leverages threshold secret sharing and threshold oblivious pseudorandom function techniques to protect credentials against single-point failures and enhance the security of passwords. Our theoretical security analysis has shown that our scheme meets the desired properties of privacy preservation, unpredictability, and obliviousness. While our study is still a work in progress, we aim to conduct extensive simulations to demonstrate the performance and practicability of our scheme in the future. We believe that our promising scheme can be extended to many scenarios that require identity verification and authorization.

Acknowledgements. We would like to acknowledge that PRISM was conceived of and tested by TIDE Foundation as part of a broader decentralized identity and access management framework. PRISM in this context is intended to allow typical web users high-level security authentication in the form of the simplest, most ubiquitous experience.

References

1. Gilman, E., Barth, D.: Zero Trust Networks. O'Reilly Media, Sebastopol (2017)
2. Ali, B., Hijjawi, S., Campbell, L.H., Gregory, M.A., Li, S.: A maturity framework for zero-trust security in multiaccess edge computing. Secur. Commun. Netw. **2022** (2022)
3. He, Y., Huang, D., Chen, L., Ni, Y., Ma, X.: A survey on zero trust architecture: challenges and future trends. Wirel. Commun. Mob. Comput. **2022** (2022)
4. Jarecki, S., Kiayias, A., Krawczyk, H., Xu, J.: TOPPSS: cost-minimal password-protected secret sharing based on threshold OPRF. In: Gollmann, D., Miyaji, A., Kikuchi, H. (eds.) ACNS 2017. LNCS, vol. 10355, pp. 39–58. Springer, Cham (2017). https://doi.org/10.1007/978-3-319-61204-1_3
5. Liu, Y., et al.: A blockchain-based decentralized, fair and authenticated information sharing scheme in zero trust internet-of-things. IEEE Trans. Comput. **72**, 501–512 (2022)
6. Mehraj, S., Banday, M.T.: Establishing a zero trust strategy in cloud computing environment. In 2020 International Conference on Computer Communication and Informatics (ICCCI), pp. 1–6. IEEE (2020)
7. Tang, F., Ma, C., Cheng, K.: Privacy-preserving authentication scheme based on zero trust architecture. Digital Commun. Netw. (2023)
8. Sonnino, A., Al-Bassam, M., Bano, S., Meiklejohn, S., Danezis, G.: Coconut: threshold issuance selective disclosure credentials with applications to distributed ledgers. arXiv preprint arXiv:1802.07344 (2018)
9. Xiaojian, Z., Liandong, C., Jie, F., Xiangqun, W., Qi, W.: Power IoT security protection architecture based on zero trust framework. In: 2021 IEEE 5th International Conference on Cryptography, Security and Privacy (CSP), pp. 166–170. IEEE (2021)
10. Li, S., Iqbal, M., Saxena, N.: Future industry internet of things with zero-trust security. Inf. Syst. Front. pp. 1–14 (2022)
11. Dhar, S., Bose, I.: Securing Iot devices using zero trust and blockchain. J. Organ. Comput. Electron. Commer. **31**(1), 18–34 (2021)
12. García-Teodoro, P., Camacho, J., Maciá-Fernández, G., Gómez-Hernández, J.A., López-Marín, V.J.: A novel zero-trust network access control scheme based on the security profile of devices and users. Comput. Netw. **212**, 109068 (2022)
13. DHS. Zero trust architecture guide, published by the U.S. department of homeland security in 2018. https://www.cisa.gov/news-events/news/cisa-releases-cloud-security-technical-reference-architecture-and-zero-trust. Accessed 18 Feb 2023

14. Cisco. Zero trust secure access. https://www.cisco.com/c/en/us/products/security/zero-trust.html. Accessed 18 Feb 2023
15. Hao, F., van Oorschot, P.C.: SoK: password-authenticated key exchange-theory, practice, standardization and real-world lessons. In Proceedings of the 2022 ACM on Asia Conference on Computer and Communications Security, pp. 697–711 (2022)
16. Lamport, L.: Password authentication with insecure communication. Commun. ACM **24**(11), 770–772 (1981)
17. Bresson, E., Chevassut, O., Pointcheval, D.: Security proofs for an efficient password-based key exchange. In Proceedings of the 10th ACM conference on Computer and Communications Security, pp. 241–250 (2003)
18. Gennaro, R., Lindell, Y.: A framework for password-based authenticated key exchange. In: Biham, E. (ed.) EUROCRYPT 2003. LNCS, vol. 2656, pp. 524–543. Springer, Heidelberg (2003). https://doi.org/10.1007/3-540-39200-9_33
19. Jarecki, S., Krawczyk, H., Xu, J.: OPAQUE: an asymmetric PAKE protocol secure against pre-computation attacks. In: Nielsen, J.B., Rijmen, V. (eds.) EURO-CRYPT 2018. LNCS, vol. 10822, pp. 456–486. Springer, Cham (2018). https://doi.org/10.1007/978-3-319-78372-7_15
20. Chen, C.-M., Wang, K.-H., Yeh, K.-H., Xiang, B., Tsu-Yang, W.: Attacks and solutions on a three-party password-based authenticated key exchange protocol for wireless communications. J. Ambient Intell. Humanized Comput. **10**, 3133–3142 (2019)
21. Miao, P.: Towards Secure Computation with Optimal Complexity. University of California, Berkeley (2019)
22. Shamir, A.: How to share a secret. Commun. ACM **22**(11), 612–613 (1979)
23. Freedman, M.J., Ishai, Y., Pinkas, B., Reingold, O.: Keyword search and oblivious pseudorandom functions. In: Kilian, J. (ed.) TCC 2005. LNCS, vol. 3378, pp. 303–324. Springer, Heidelberg (2005). https://doi.org/10.1007/978-3-540-30576-7_17
24. Erwig, A., Faust, S., Riahi, S.: Large-scale non-interactive threshold cryptosystems through anonymity. IACR Cryptol. ePrint Arch. **2021**, 1290 (2021)
25. Agrawal, S., Miao, P., Mohassel, P., Mukherjee, P.: PASTA: password-based threshold authentication. In: Proceedings of the 2018 ACM SIGSAC Conference on Computer and Communications Security, pp. 2042–2059 (2018)
26. Gennaro, R., Jarecki, S., Krawczyk, H., Rabin, T.: Secure distributed key generation for discrete-log based cryptosystems. J. Cryptology **20**, 51–83 (2007)

Cloud S&P – Cloud Security and Privacy

Cloud S&P 2023

Fifth Workshop on Cloud Security and Privacy

20 June 2023

Program Chairs

Suryadipta Majumdar	Concordia University, Canada
Cong Wang	City University of Hong Kong, China

Program Committee

Irfan Ahmed	Virginia Commonwealth University, USA
Chadi Assi	Concordia University, Canada
Elias Bou-Harb	University of Texas at San Antonio, USA
Mauro Conti	University of Padua, Italy
Helei Cui	Northwestern Polytechnical University, China
Nora Cuppens	École Polytechnique de Montréal, Canada
Sabrina De Capitani di Vimercati	Universitá degli studi di Milano, Italy
Sara Foresti	Università degli Studi di Milano, Italy
Yosr Jarraya	Ericsson Security, Sweden
Kallol Krishna Karmakar	University of Newcastle, UK
Rongxing Lu	University of New Brunswick, Canada
Taous Madi	King Abdullah University of Science and Technology, Saudi Arabia
Makan Pourzandi	Ericsson Security, Sweden
Pierangela Samarati	Università degli studi di Milano, Italy
Paria Shirani	Ryerson University, Canada
Lingyu Wang	Concordia University, Canada
Xingliang Yuan	Monash University, Australia
Mengyuan Zhang	Hong Kong Polytechnic University, China

Web Chair

Ehsan Khodayarseresht	Concordia University, Canada

Steering Committee

Cong Wang	City University of Hong Kong, China
Kim-Kwang Raymond Choo	University of Texas at San Antonio, USA
Lingyu Wang	Concordia University, Canada
Mauro Conti	University of Padua, Italy
Xingliang Yuan	Monash University, Australia
Suryadipta Majumdar	Concordia University, Canada

Additional Reviewers

Harsha Vasudev	University of Padua, Italy
Mark Karanfil	Concordia University, Canada
Kurt Friday	University of Texas at San Antonio, USA

slytHErin: An Agile Framework for Encrypted Deep Neural Network Inference

Francesco Intoci[1]([✉]), Sinem Sav[1], Apostolos Pyrgelis[1], Jean-Philippe Bossuat[2], Juan Ramón Troncoso-Pastoriza[2], and Jean-Pierre Hubaux[1,2]

[1] EPFL, 1015 Lausanne, Switzerland
{francesco.intoci,sinem.sav,apostolos.pyrgelis}@epfl.ch
[2] Tune Insight SA, 1015 Lausanne, Switzerland
{jean-philippe.bossuat,juanramon.troncoso-pastoriza,
jean-pierre.hubaux}@tuneinsight.com

Abstract. Homomorphic encryption (HE), which allows computations on encrypted data, is an enabling technology for confidential cloud computing. One notable example is privacy-preserving Prediction-as-a-Service (PaaS), where machine-learning predictions are computed on encrypted data. However, developing HE-based solutions for encrypted PaaS is a tedious task which requires a careful design that predominantly depends on the deployment scenario and on leveraging the characteristics of modern HE schemes. Prior works on privacy-preserving PaaS focus solely on protecting the confidentiality of the client data uploaded to a remote model provider, e.g., a cloud offering a prediction API, and assume (or take advantage of the fact) that the model is held in plaintext. Furthermore, their aim is to either minimize the latency of the service by processing one sample at a time, or to maximize the number of samples processed per second, while processing a fixed (large) number of samples. In this work, we present slytHErin, an agile framework that enables privacy-preserving PaaS beyond the application scenarios considered in prior works. Thanks to its hybrid design leveraging HE and its multiparty variant (MHE), slytHErin enables novel PaaS scenarios by encrypting the data, the model or both. Moreover, slytHErin features a flexible input data packing approach that allows processing a batch of an arbitrary number of samples, and several computation optimizations that are model-and-setting-agnostic. slytHErin is implemented in Go and it allows end-users to perform encrypted PaaS on custom deep learning models comprising fully-connected, convolutional, and pooling layers, in a few lines of code and without having to worry about the cumbersome implementation and optimization concerns inherent to HE.

Keywords: Confidential Cloud Computing · Cryptography · Homomorphic Encryption · Multiparty Computation · Prediction-as-a-Service · Privacy-Preserving Machine Learning

F. Intoci and S. Sav—These authors contributed equally to this work.

J. Zhou et al. (Eds.): ACNS 2023 Workshops, LNCS 13907, pp. 359–377, 2023.
https://doi.org/10.1007/978-3-031-41181-6_20

1   Introduction

With recent advances in deep learning, cloud service providers expose trained deep neural networks (DNNs) to end-users for prediction-as-a-service (PaaS) through their application programming interfaces (APIs) [4,5,7,25,56]. For instance, Amazon Forecast enables business analytics by performing forecasting on client time-series data [3] and Azure's Cognitive summarizes and classifies financial documents [6]. However, PaaS applications raise privacy concerns as both the user data (e.g., client time-series, text, or health data) and the machine learning model (due to intellectual property concerns), can be sensitive information, and cloud service providers must comply with privacy regulations such as CCPA [12], GDPR [20], and HIPAA [30]. Thus, it is now needed more than ever to protect the privacy of the data used in PaaS applications.

To enable privacy-preserving PaaS, various works propose performing encrypted DNN inference by employing homomorphic encryption (HE) schemes which allow computations directly on ciphertexts [8,10,11,16,17,22,29,31,33, 37,38,41,42,49]. However, to cope with the computational overhead introduced by HE operations and to account for the characteristics of modern HE schemes, e.g., their support of Single Instruction, Multiple Data (SIMD) operations, these works rely on various optimizations which are tailored to specific PaaS scenarios, the most common of which comprises a cleartext DNN model and encrypted data. As a result, existing HE-based works cannot support emerging scenarios, e.g., edge machine learning [2,44,55], that require outsourcing the prediction to the client (while protecting the model's intellectual property), or privacy-preserving federated learning where inference is performed on a model that is trained in encrypted form by multiple data providers [52,53,57]. Moreover, these works rely on data packing schemes adapted to specific DNN architectures and application requirements, aiming either to minimize prediction latency (typically by processing one sample at a time, e.g., for real-time analytics), or to maximize the number of samples processed per second (usually by collecting and then processing in parallel a large number of samples leveraging on SIMD capabilities).

In this work, we design slytHErin, an agile framework for encrypted DNN inference. Built on HE and its multiparty variant, our framework can be adapted to various and novel PaaS scenarios where: (i) the client's data is encrypted while the model is in cleartext, (ii) the client's data is in cleartext and the model is encrypted, and (iii) both the client's data and the model are encrypted. Moreover, slytHErin features application- and model-agnostic optimizations which make it suitable for various settings. For instance, slytHErin implements an intuitive and flexible packing scheme that efficiently enables SIMD operations for *arbitrary* batch sizes, and generic optimizations for encrypted matrix operations. We implement slytHErin in Go and provide the building blocks that enable the encrypted execution of any DNN model composed of fully-connected, convolutional, and pooling layers. Contrary to prior works, our implementation is not centered around a system model, specific assumptions, or DNN architectures, making it a versatile tool for securing different PaaS pipelines. Our evaluation shows that slytHErin achieves accuracy similar to performing inference on cleartext data and/or models. Moreover, it yields an interesting trade-off between latency and throughput, and its overall performance is on par with that of the state-of-the-art HE-based inference solutions, while being more flexible than specialized solutions. Our implementation can be found on https://github.com/ldsec/slytHErin.

2 Related Work

Given the potential privacy issues that might arise in PaaS, a number of works that build encrypted PaaS frameworks have been proposed. These works rely on homomorphic encryption (HE) and/or multiparty computation (MPC) to protect the confidentiality of both the ML model and the client's evaluation data during prediction [8,10,11,15,16,22,29,31,33,37,38,41,42,46,48,49].

HE-Based Solutions. Cryptonets was the first work in this research direction that enabled DNN evaluation on encrypted data using an HE scheme [22]. Its overhead, in terms of latency, was later improved by Brutzkus et al. which proposed novel approaches to represent the input data [11]. Other works focus on improving the efficiency of encrypted matrix operations [32,39] or on designing novel techniques for the encrypted evaluation of more complex ML models such as graph convolutional networks [47]. The latter has been used in downstream tasks such as human action recognition [34] achieving better latency than [11]. Other works develop compilers that ease the deployment of trained ML models with HE libraries, e.g., SEAL [54], HElib [27], or Palisade [50], for encrypted inference. Boemer et al. [8,9] build a graph compiler for SEAL that simplifies the use of a model trained with Tensorflow [1] or PyTorch [45] for encrypted PaaS. CHET, on the other hand, is a domain-specific optimizing compiler that allows the specification of tensor circuits suitable for HE-based DNN inference [18]. All of these works propose specific input data representations (packing) and optimizations for either latency or throughput for specific scenarios (e.g., featuring a cleartext model vs. encrypted data) and DNN architectures. Moreover, to cope with DNN non-linear operations that are not supported by HE schemes, e.g., activations, they either use interactions with the client [8], modify their functionality to low-degree polynomial functions [11,18,22,34], or use polynomial approximations [13,47].

Hybrid Approaches. To ease the encrypted execution of non-linear functions, some works rely on hybrid approaches combining two-party computation with HE [31,33,37,48], or secret sharing with garbled circuits [42,46,49]. For instance, Liu et al. [37] utilize HE for matrix multiplications and garbled circuits for the non-linear activations. Juvekar et al. [33] employ HE for matrix-vector multiplication and convolution operations and garbled circuits for comparisons which are widely used in activation functions. Similarly, we provide a hybrid framework for privacy-preserving PaaS that supports a wide range of applications by relying on a multiparty variant of HE. Moreover, thanks to our generic data representation scheme and optimizations, our framework is agnostic of the DNN architecture and parameters such as batch size, while achieving on par performance with the state-of-the-art.

3 Background

3.1 Homomorphic Encryption

Homomorphic encryption (HE) schemes enable the execution of arithmetic operations directly on ciphertexts, i.e., without requiring decryption; this makes them ideal candidates for privacy-preserving machine learning inference applications. In this work, we employ the Cheon-Kim-Kim-Song (CKKS) scheme [14], which is suitable for machine learning tasks as it enables approximate arithmetic over $\mathbb{C}^{\mathcal{N}/2}$ (hence, over real values as well). The ring $R_{Q_L} = \mathbb{Z}_{Q_L}[X]/(X^{\mathcal{N}} + 1)$ of dimension $\mathcal{N}$ with coefficients modulo $Q_L = \prod_{i=0}^{L} q_i$ defines the plaintext and ciphertext spaces, hence both plaintexts/ciphertexts are represented by polynomials of degree $\mathcal{N} - 1$ whose coefficients encode a vector of $\mathcal{N}/2$ values. The security of CKKS is based on the ring learning with errors problem [40]. CKKS supports the homomorphic evaluation of operations such as additions, multiplications, and rotations, and any operation is simultaneously performed on all encoded values, hence offering Single Instruction, Multiple Data (SIMD). Non-linear operations, e.g., comparisons, are supported via polynomial approximations, introducing a computation overhead versus accuracy tradeoff. CKKS is a leveled HE scheme, i.e., an L-depth circuit can be evaluated before the ciphertext is exhausted. Then, a costly procedure, called bootstrapping [21], is required to refresh the exhausted ciphertext and enable more operations on it. We refer to the traditional bootstrapping operation (performed by a single party) as *centralized bootstrapping*.

Multiparty Homomorphic Encryption (MHE). To make our framework adaptable to various PaaS scenarios (see Sect. 4), we also rely on a multiparty variant of the CKKS scheme [43]. In the multiparty homomorphic encryption (MHE) scheme, a set of parties (e.g., model-providers) collectively generate a public key while the corresponding secret key is secret-shared among them. This setting enables secure collaboration between N parties, as parties use the collective public key to encrypt their inputs and perform joint operations on them using the MHE scheme. The result decryption by the client, however, requires the participation of all parties. Hence, this scheme ensures confidentiality under a passive adversary model with up to $N - 1$ collusions. Moreover, the multiparty CKKS scheme offers efficient multiparty computation protocols. For instance, it enables a collective bootstrapping operation, where the costly centralized bootstrapping which homomorphically evaluates the decryption and consumes many levels, is substituted by a lightweight one-round interactive protocol ($\mathsf{CBootstrap}(\cdot)$) which does not consume levels. Moreover, the scheme supports ($\mathsf{CKeySwitch}(\cdot)$), a collective key-switch operation which can change the encryption key of a ciphertext.

3.2 Deep Neural Networks

Deep neural networks (DNNs) are able to model complex non-linear relationships and find applicability in various domains such as computer vision. A DNN consists of multiple hidden layers between the input and output layers. Our framework enables the encrypted evaluation of DNNs comprising fully connected (FC), convolutional (CONV), and pooling (POOL) layers. We succinctly present the functionalities of these layer types:

Fully Connected layer: Given an input vector $\mathbf{x}$, a weight matrix $\mathbf{W}$ and a bias vector $\mathbf{b}$, a FC-layer computes $\mathbf{x}\mathbf{W}^{\mathbf{T}} + \mathbf{b}$.

Convolutional layer: Given an input tensor (e.g., an image) $\mathbf{X}$ with c_i channels of dimensions $w \cdot h$ and a set of c_o kernels $\mathbf{K}$ each made up of c_i filters of size $f_w \cdot f_h$, a CONV-layer computes a tensor $\mathbf{O}$ with c_o channels. Each channel $\mathbf{O}_i$ is computed as $\sum_{n=0}^{c_i} \mathbf{X}_n * \mathbf{K}_{i,n}$, with $\mathbf{X}_n$ the n-th channel of the input image, $\mathbf{K}_{i,n}$ the n-th filter of the i-th kernel, and $*$ the cross-correlation operator.

Pooling layer: It performs dimensionality reduction on the input. The most common types are SumPooling, AveragePooling, and MaxPooling, where the feature-map is the sum, average, and the maximum of the features in a region of the input, respectively. Max-Pooling requires non-linear operations, i.e., comparisons, which are non-trivial to implement under encryption, thus we only consider the first two types.

Each layer can be paired with an activation function which is evaluated on its output. The output of the DNN's last layer is the prediction result (output).

4 slytHErin Overview

Building on the CKKS HE scheme and its multiparty variant (see Sect. 3), we design a framework that is flexible for various encrypted PaaS scenarios (Fig. 1). We first describe the involved entities before detailing slytHErin's objectives and workflow for each PaaS scenario.

- **Model-provider(s):** This entity (one or more) has trained an ML model and exposes it to end-users for queries (PaaS) through a prediction API hosted on a cloud service provider.
- **Client:** This entity is a user of the PaaS that inputs its own sensitive data which is evaluated on the model exposed by the model-provider. The client obtains the output of the PaaS process, i.e., the prediction.

We consider that the client and the model-provider are *honest-but-curious*, i.e., they follow the protocol specification, but they might try to infer information about each other's data. slytHErin's objective is to protect both the confidentiality of the client's and the model-provider's data. In particular, the model-provider should not learn any information about the client's evaluation data and the prediction result, whereas the client should not obtain any knowledge about the model beyond what can be inferred from the PaaS output.

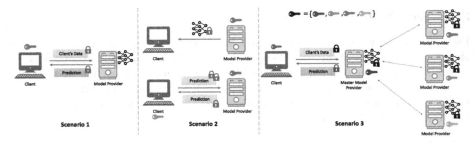

Fig. 1. Encrypted PaaS scenarios enabled by `slytHErin`. Encryption is depicted with a lock whose color is the same as the corresponding secret key. The black key (rightmost figure) corresponds to the model-providers' collective key. **Scenario 1:** The client sends its encrypted data to the model-provider that evaluates it on the plaintext model. **Scenario 2:** The encrypted model is sent to the client for evaluation on its cleartext data. **Scenario 3:** The client sends encrypted data to a cohort of model-providers that retain an encrypted model.

4.1   Scenario 1: Encrypted Client Data - Cleartext Model

This is the traditional HE-based PaaS setting, where a client encrypts its data with its own public key and sends the ciphertext to the model-provider that stores its ML model in plaintext form. The model-provider evaluates its model on the client's encrypted data – without interacting with the client – and returns the encrypted prediction to the client. The client decrypts the ciphertext with its secret key and obtains the prediction result. In this scenario, the client's data confidentiality is ensured as its inputs are encrypted throughout the DNN evaluation and the model-provider does not learn the prediction result. The model confidentiality is protected as the model remains on the model-provider's side. Scenario 1 represents a typical PaaS setting, where a model-holder exposes a prediction service that receives sensitive data as inputs [11,16,22,33]. For instance, imagine a health-care insurance provider that uses its customer data and trains a DNN that predicts the probability of patient re-admission to a hospital. The model is exposed through an API to clients (e.g., hospitals) who wish to obtain predictions about their own cohorts of patients. However, hospitals cannot share their patient data with third-parties due to ethical and data privacy requirements, hence, `slytHErin` could be an enabler for such a service as it ensures data confidentiality.

4.2   Scenario 2: Cleartext Client Data - Encrypted Model

In this scenario, the model-provider outsources the computation of the prediction to the client. However, the model is an intellectual property that needs to be protected. Thus, the model-provider encrypts its model with its own public key and sends it to the client in encrypted form. The client evaluates the encrypted model on its own (plaintext) data and obtains an encrypted prediction. Finally, the client sends the prediction ciphertext to the model provider, which obliviously decrypts the result and communicates it back to the client (Sect. 5.6). The client's data confidentiality is ensured as its evaluation data is never transferred and the model-provider does not learn the prediction result due to the oblivious decryption phase. The model confidentiality is protected as the model is encrypted with the model-provider's public key. Scenario 2 is suitable for applications that require outsourcing a trained model to the client side for predictions. For instance, this could be the case for model trading platforms that offer a *try-before-you-buy* option, where customers locally test the performance of an ML model on their data before purchasing it. Another relevant application is model outsourcing to edge devices [2,44], e.g., mobile phones or smartwatches, that monitor their owners' activity and provide feedback to them through predictions, e.g., health recommendations or activity tracking [55]. We note that this is a novel PaaS scenario enabled by slytHErin.

4.3   Scenario 3: Encrypted Client Data - Encrypted Model

In this scenario, we assume that the model-provider is represented by a cohort of N nodes that have collectively trained a DNN on their joint data with a state-of-the-art encrypted collaborative learning framework [52,53,57]. For this, we rely on a multiparty variant of homomorphic encryption (MHE). In particular, the nodes (model-providers) generate a collective public key (black key in Fig. 1, **Scenario 3**) whose corresponding secret key is secret-shared among them (colored keys in Fig. 1, **Scenario 3**). We assume that the nodes collectively train a DNN on their data and retain it under encryption for PaaS to mitigate model-targeting attacks and protect its intellectual property. For this scenario, the client encrypts its evaluation data with the collective public key and a master node from the cohort performs the prediction (with both the model and the data encrypted) with the assistance of the other nodes for collective interactive operations (e.g., ciphertext refresh – CBootstrap($\cdot$), Sects. 3.1 and 5.6). Finally, the ciphertext storing the prediction result is re-encrypted (i.e., CKeySwitch($\cdot$), Sects. 3.1 and 5.6) under the public key of the client which decrypts it to obtain the prediction. In this case, both the model and the client data are encrypted with the cohort's collective public key, hence, their confidentiality is ensured as long as one of the cohort nodes is honest and does not participate in decryption. The confidentiality of the prediction output is protected, as only the client can decrypt it. Scenario 3 is suitable for PaaS applications after a model-provider outsources the model training procedure to a cohort of N nodes that leverage on distributed learning techniques for improved efficiency or after a federation of N model-providers, each with their own data, uses a state-of-the-art framework to train a collective ML model *under encryption* [19,52,53]. We note that previous works that focused on encrypted DNN inference do not support (or implement) inference on encrypted models or collaborative functionalities such as bootstrapping or re-encryption.

5   Cryptographic Building Blocks

We describe slytHErin's underlying cryptographic building blocks that make it flexible and efficient for different encrypted PaaS scenarios (Sect. 4) and various DNN architectures. We first introduce the data packing approach adopted to encode/encrypt the input data (Sect. 5.1). Then, we describe the algorithms used to evaluate fully-connected, convolutional, and pooling layers under encryption in Sects. 5.2 and 5.3, respectively. We also present several optimizations that slytHErin implements (Sect. 5.4) and how non-linear activation functions are evaluated (Sect. 5.5). Finally, we present the multiparty computation protocols which allow slytHErin to support novel PaaS scenarios (Sect. 5.6).

5.1   Input Data Packing

Modern homomorphic encryption schemes can encode (pack) a vector of values into one ciphertext, thus enabling SIMD operations via the parallel computation of a function on all ciphertext slots. Designing an efficient packing scheme is crucial, yet challenging, due to the costs of re-arranging the ciphertext slots via rotations. Prior work on encrypted DNN inference [11,22,31,33,34,37,48] designed efficient packing schemes but these are tailored to specific system models and assumptions (e.g., the client's availability for the evaluation of certain operations). slytHErin employs a simple yet generic data packing scheme that is agnostic of the encrypted PaaS scenario and also flexible in terms of batch size that results in optimized latency and throughput. Given a batch consisting of n input samples each with d features, a naive approach is to encrypt/encode each feature of an input sample separately, yielding an inefficient execution due to the high number of ciphertexts/plaintexts. To leverage on SIMD operations and enable efficient encrypted inference, we flatten the batch and encrypt/encode all values in a single ciphertext/plaintext. For an input sample represented by a tensor of size $h \times r \times c$ (where, e.g., for an image, h is the number of channels, while r and c represent the size of the pixel matrix of each channel), we encrypt/encode a batch of size n in a tensor of size $n \times h \times r \times c$ as follows: First, we row-flatten (RowFlatten($\cdot$)) each of the n tensors, such that the batch-tensor is transformed into a matrix of size $n \times d$, with $d = h \times r \times c$. This is done by iterating through all the channels of the input, by row-flattening the corresponding 2D matrix, and by horizontally stacking their flattened representation. The $n \times d$ matrix is then transposed and row-flattened (TensorFlatten($\cdot$)), thus yielding a vector of size $m = d \times n$. Our packing scheme requires that $m \leq s$, where s is the ciphertext capacity (i.e., $s = \mathcal{N}/2$ for CKKS) and if that is not possible, we employ block matrix arithmetic optimizations (see Sect. 5.4).

5.2   Matrix Multiplication

To support the evaluation of fully-connected layers under encryption, slytHErin relies on the following matrix multiplication algorithm. Given two encrypted matrices, $\mathbf{A}$ and $\mathbf{W}$, where $\mathbf{A}$ is of size $n \times d$ and $\mathbf{W}$ of size $d \times h$, slytHErin

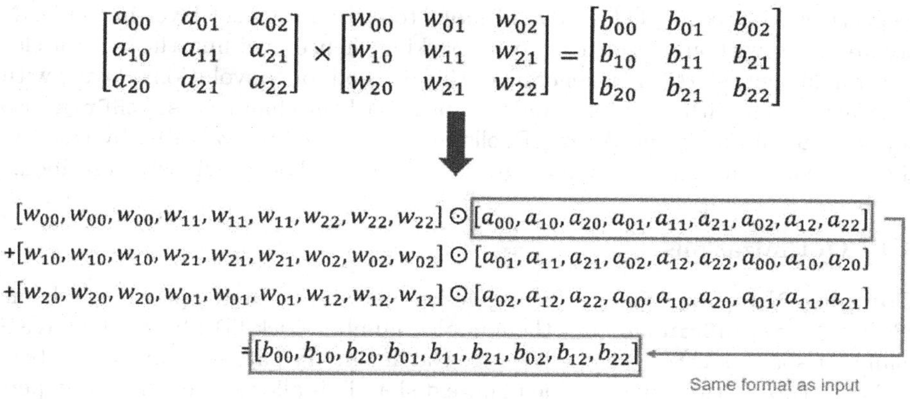

$$\begin{bmatrix} a_{00} & a_{01} & a_{02} \\ a_{10} & a_{11} & a_{21} \\ a_{20} & a_{21} & a_{22} \end{bmatrix} \times \begin{bmatrix} w_{00} & w_{01} & w_{02} \\ w_{10} & w_{11} & w_{21} \\ w_{20} & w_{21} & w_{22} \end{bmatrix} = \begin{bmatrix} b_{00} & b_{01} & b_{02} \\ b_{10} & b_{11} & b_{21} \\ b_{20} & b_{21} & b_{22} \end{bmatrix}$$

$$[w_{00}, w_{00}, w_{00}, w_{11}, w_{11}, w_{11}, w_{22}, w_{22}, w_{22}] \odot [a_{00}, a_{10}, a_{20}, a_{01}, a_{11}, a_{21}, a_{02}, a_{12}, a_{22}]$$
$$+[w_{10}, w_{10}, w_{10}, w_{21}, w_{21}, w_{21}, w_{02}, w_{02}, w_{02}] \odot [a_{01}, a_{11}, a_{21}, a_{02}, a_{12}, a_{22}, a_{00}, a_{10}, a_{20}]$$
$$+[w_{20}, w_{20}, w_{20}, w_{01}, w_{01}, w_{01}, w_{12}, w_{12}, w_{12}] \odot [a_{02}, a_{12}, a_{22}, a_{00}, a_{10}, a_{20}, a_{01}, a_{11}, a_{21}]$$
$$= [b_{00}, b_{10}, b_{20}, b_{01}, b_{11}, b_{21}, b_{02}, b_{12}, b_{22}]$$

Same format as input

Fig. 2. Multiplication of two matrices $\mathbf{A}$ and $\mathbf{W}$ of size 3×3.

implements their multiplication following the diagonal approach of [28]. First, $\mathbf{W}$ is represented by its *generalized diagonals* [28], where the element i,j of the diagonal is: $d_{i,j} = \mathbf{W}_{(i+j) \bmod d, j}$. Additionally, we replicate n times the element $d_{i,j}$. The matrix multiplication, then, can be evaluated as follows:

$$\mathbf{A} \times \mathbf{W} = \sum_{i=1}^{d} \mathbf{d_i} \odot \mathsf{RotateCyclic}_{d \times i}(\mathsf{RowFlatten}(\mathbf{A}^T))$$

where $\mathsf{RotateCyclic}_k(\mathbf{v})$ represents a cyclic rotation of the values in $\mathbf{v}$ by k positions to the left and $\odot$ represents the Hadamard product. Figure 2 represents a multiplication of two 3×3 matrices with this algorithm.

5.3 Convolutional and Pooling Layers

To evaluate convolutional layers under encryption, slytHErin represents the convolution operation as a matrix multiplication by expressing the filter as a *Toeplitz* matrix [23,26]. For ease of presentation, consider a toy-example with a convolution between a single-channel input $\mathbf{I} \in R^{3 \times 3}$ and a filter $\mathbf{h} \in R^{2 \times 2}$ operating on the input with unitary stride and no padding. We can compute the convolution as: $\mathbf{O} = \mathsf{TensorFlatten}(\mathbf{h} * \mathbf{I})^T = \mathbf{h}' \times \mathbf{I}'$ where $\mathbf{I}' = \mathsf{TensorFlatten}(\mathbf{I})^T$ and $\mathbf{h}' = \mathcal{T}(\mathbf{h})$ for a function $\mathcal{T}$ that returns a Toeplitz matrix [23] as follows:

$$\mathbf{h}' = \begin{pmatrix} h_{1,1} & h_{1,2} & 0 & h_{2,1} & h_{2,4} & 0 & 0 & 0 & 0 \\ 0 & h_{1,1} & h_{1,2} & 0 & h_{2,1} & h_{2,4} & 0 & 0 & 0 \\ 0 & 0 & 0 & h_{1,1} & h_{1,2} & 0 & h_{2,1} & h_{2,4} & 0 \\ 0 & 0 & 0 & 0 & h_{1,1} & h_{1,2} & 0 & h_{2,1} & h_{2,4} \end{pmatrix}$$

Note that computing $\mathbf{O}^T = \mathbf{I}'^T \times \mathbf{h}'^T$ allows us to utilize the matrix multiplication algorithm and the input data packing protocol of Sects. 5.2 and 5.1, respectively. Moreover, $\mathbf{O^T}$ is a valid input to any subsequent layer in the DNN architecture, without requiring any re-packing, hence avoiding the cost of slot re-arrangement. slytHErin generalizes this method for convolutional layers with k kernels, each with m filters, and n inputs with m channels. slytHErin also supports SumPooling and AveragePooling layers: these are evaluated by treating them as convolutional layers, and employing the method previously described.

5.4 Optimizations

Complex-Number Trick. To optimize the input data packing scheme (Sect. 5.1), slytHErin employs the complex-number trick [51]: Since the CKKS plaintext space is $\mathbb{C}^{\mathcal{N}/2}$, we can leverage the imaginary part of complex numbers and pack (up to) two values in one plaintext slot. This allows us to effectively perform the multiplication and sum of two values with just one multiplication. As a toy example, let us consider the vectors: $\mathbf{a} = (a_1, \dots), \mathbf{b} = (b_1, \dots), \mathbf{c} = (c_1, \dots)$, and $\mathbf{d} = (d_1, \dots)$. To compute $\mathbf{a} \odot \mathbf{c} + \mathbf{b} \odot \mathbf{d} = (a_1 c_1 + b_1 d_1, \dots)$, we compress the first two and the two last vectors each into one vector with the following complex representation: $\mathbf{g} = (a_1 + i b_1, \dots), \mathbf{h} = (c_1 - i d_1, \dots)$. Then, $\mathbf{g} \odot \mathbf{h} = (a_1 c_1 + b_1 d_1 + i.e., \dots)$ for some value e, and the real part of the result can be extracted with complex conjugation, addition and constant multiplication. We apply this technique to the input matrix $\mathbf{A}$ and to the weight matrix $\mathbf{W}$. In particular, we embed pairs of adjacent columns of $\mathbf{A}$ into one column, i.e., column k is paired with column $k + 1 \mod d$, where d is the number of columns, hence the entry $\mathbf{A}_{(k,j)}$ becomes $\mathbf{A}_{(k,j)} + i\mathbf{A}_{(k,j+1)}$. For $\mathbf{W}$, we compress the pairs of adjacent *diagonals* into one, padding with an extra 0-diagonal if the number of diagonals is odd. The newly packed matrix $\tilde{\mathbf{W}}$ has $\lceil \frac{d}{2} \rceil$ diagonals instead of d, reducing the complexity of the matrix multiplication algorithm by a factor of 2.

Block Matrix Arithmetic. When the size of the input batch exceeds the ciphertext capacity, slytHErin employs block-matrix arithmetic [52]. The input matrix $\mathbf{A}$ of size $n \times d$, is represented as a block-matrix $\bar{\mathbf{A}}$ of size $q \times p$, i.e., a matrix consisting of *blocks* (or sub-matrices) of size $\frac{n}{q} \times \frac{d}{p}$ for some divisors q and p of n and d, respectively. Similarly, the weight matrix $\mathbf{W}$ of size $d \times h$ is partitioned to enable the multiplication $\bar{\mathbf{O}} = \bar{\mathbf{A}} \times \bar{\mathbf{W}}$ under two constraints: (i) $\bar{\mathbf{W}}$ must have p row partitions, and (ii) every inner block $\mathbf{W}_{k,j}$ must be compatible for matrix multiplication with the inner blocks $\mathbf{A}_{i,k}$. $\bar{\mathbf{O}}$ is a block-matrix of size $n \times h$ with q row partitions and m column partitions (and m the number of column partitions of $\bar{\mathbf{W}}$). Each block $\mathbf{O}_{i,j}$ is computed as: $\mathbf{O}_{i,j} = \sum_{k=1}^{p} \mathbf{A}_{i,k} \mathbf{W}_{k,j}$. Hence, by choosing suitable partitions, each matrix inner block is small enough to be encrypted/encoded independently following the input data packing and the generalized-diagonals approach described earlier (Sects. 5.1 and 5.2). Figure 3 represents the encryption of matrix $\mathbf{A}$ with 2×2 partitioning. Then, the matrix multiplication between two large matrices is evaluated as a series of sums and multiplications between these smaller blocks. Given a model to evaluate (i.e., the dimensions of its layers), the number of input features, and a set of CKKS parameters, slytHErin follows a heuristic-based approach to automatically find

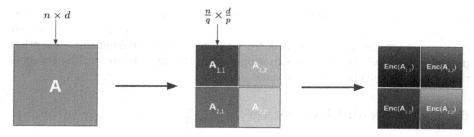

Fig. 3. Partitioning of an input matrix **A** in a 2 × 2 block matrix.

the best batch size and partition strategy. In more detail, slytHErin explores the space of possible splits, starting from divisors of the number of samples (if provided by the user) or divisors of the features dimension, and picks the split sequence and batch size that minimize the overall complexity of the pipeline in terms of homomorphic operations (i.e., it minimizes the number of homomorphic multiplications required to evaluate the model), thus optimizing throughput. In any case, the user can also declare a customized batch size which overrides the optimized batch size, and let slytHErin operate with a sub-optimal block matrix representation. An advantage of the block matrix arithmetic approach is that it is amenable to parallelization: Given $q \times p \times m$ threads, the matrix multiplication between two blocks $\mathbf{A}_{i,k}$ and $\mathbf{W}_{k,j}$ can be delegated to each thread, while using $q \times m$ of them to combine the individual results. Moreover, for a given set of cryptographic parameters and the corresponding evaluation keys, the client does not need to regenerate the keys for the evaluation of arbitrary size matrices, which is a computationally intensive task.

5.5   Non-Linear Operations

As non-polynomial functions, e.g., comparisons, are not computable under HE, some works modify common activation functions (e.g., ReLU) with simple polynomial functions [22] (e.g., x^2), or use polynomial approximations [53]. slytHErin employs the second approach and relies on *Chebychev interpolants* to approximate any Lipschitz continuous function on any finite real interval.

5.6   Multiparty Computation Protocols

We remind that slytHErin relies on CKKS and its multiparty variant (MHE) which enables interactive functionalities such as CBootstrap(·) for collective bootstrapping and CKeySwitch(·) for collective key-switching. The latter enables changing the encryption key of a ciphertext. In **Scenario 3**, the model-providers rely on these functionalities to refresh the ciphertexts noise and to change the encryption key of the prediction result, so that only the client can decrypt it.

We also design and implement an oblivious decryption protocol ObvDec(·), for **Scenario 2** (Sect. 4.2). In this protocol, the client masks its prediction result (encrypted under the model provider secret key) with an encryption of 0 under an ephemeral secret key, and sends the result to the model provider, which can remove one layer of encryption from the result (by invoking the decryption procedure of CKKS), without exposing the underlying plaintext. The result is finally sent to the client that unmasks it.

6 Experimental Evaluation

6.1 Implementation and Experimental Setup

We implemented `slytHErin` in Go [24], using Lattigo as the cryptographic library [35]. Our implementation is modular, reusable, and easy to adapt to several PaaS applications. Detailed documentation can be found along with our source code on https://github.com/ldsec/slytHErin. We evaluate `slytHErin` using the following DNN architectures:

- **NN5**: A 5-layer convolutional neural network described in [22] for which we replace the square activation function with a degree 2 Chebyshev approximation of Softplus.
- **NN20**: A 20-layer DNN composed of convolutional and fully connected layers described in [16] ($\sim$754K model parameters) for which we replace the activation functions with a degree-63 approximation of SiLU and train it with the MSE loss function.
- **NN50**: Similar to **NN20** but comprising 50 layers ($\sim$1M model parameters [16]).

We use the **MNIST** dataset [36] for encrypted image classification, as it is the de-facto benchmark dataset used in prior work for privacy-preserving inference tasks [8,9,11,16,17,22,33]. All models were trained from scratch, achieving similar accuracy to the original works (and with minimal accuracy loss in the encrypted inference, none for **NN5**, approximately $\sim$0.13% for **NN20**, and $\sim$2% for **NN50**). The CKKS parameters are configured to achieve 128-bit security. For the multiparty interactive protocols, we deploy `slytHErin` on a local cluster with an average network delay of 20ms and 1Gbps bandwidth. All experiments were executed on machines running Ubuntu 22.04, with 12-core Intel Xeon E5-2680 2.5 GHz CPUs and 256GB RAM DDR4. The results are averaged over 3–5 runs.

6.2 Empirical Results

We first demonstrate how `slytHErin` supports different batch sizes by evaluating **NN5** on **Scenario 1** (Sect. 6.2.1). We also compare `slytHErin` with prior work on private PaaS as **NN5** is the predominantly used benchmark. Then, in Sect. 6.2.2, we evaluate **NN20** on **Scenario 3** to discuss `slytHErin`'s scalability aspects with the number of model-providers. Finally, we demonstrate `slytHErin`'s application and model agility by evaluating the more complex model **NN50** in all scenarios of Sect. 4 (Sect. 6.2.3).

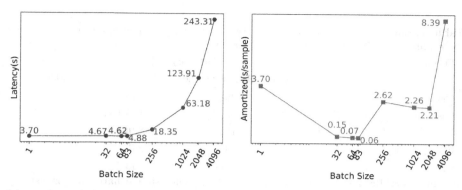

(a) slytHErin's latency for **NN5** and different batch sizes.

(b) slytHErin's amortized runtime for **NN5** and different batch sizes.

Fig. 4. slytHErin's amortized runtime with different batch sizes.

6.2.1 Elastic Data Packing

We demonstrate the benefits of our packing approach (Sect. 5.1), by benchmarking **NN5** [22] in the traditional PaaS setting (**Scenario 1**) for various batch sizes. For this experiment, slytHErin heuristically estimates the optimal batch size for throughput at 83, as described in Sect. 5.4; this is experimentally confirmed by observing Figs. 4a and 4b. In particular, Fig. 4a shows slytHErin's latency for varying batch sizes up to 4,096 in semi-log scale. We observe a linear increase in latency after the optimal size. This is expected, as slytHErin automatically splits batch sizes larger than the optimal size into sub-batches of optimal size, and processes them sequentially. Figure 4b shows the amortized runtime of slytHErin for variable batch sizes: We observe that a batch of size 83 is indeed the optimal point which minimizes the amortized runtime (or maximizes the throughput). Finally, we compare slytHErin's performance with related works that evaluate **NN5** in the same application scenario with polynomial activation functions (thus, we exclude Gazelle [33] which relies on Garbled Circuits). Table 1 shows that slytHErin's performance is on par with or better than previous works, while providing enhanced flexibility in terms of batch size. The approach followed by CryptoNets and inspired works [8,17,22] allows them to achieve a good throughput by processing large batches of data items (up to $\mathcal{N}/2$), but their runtime is independent of the batch size (hence, it will not decrease for smaller batches as per Table 1). Conversely, the approach followed by LoLa [11] achieves low latency for a single sample, but cannot amortize the runtime when processing multiple samples. With slytHErin, the end-user can define its custom batch size without a major impact on performance.

Table 1. Latency comparison between slytHErin and prior encrypted frameworks for the evaluation of **NN5** and various batch sizes.

Framework	Latency (s)		
	Batch size = 1	Batch size = 83	Batch size = 4,096
CryptoNets [22]	250	250	250
Faster CryptoNets [17]	39.1	3,245	160,153
LoLa [11]	2.2	182.6	8,951
nGraph-HE2 [8][a]	2.05	2.05	2.05
slytHErin	3.7	4.08	243.4

[a] While slytHErin and related works [11,17,22] employ similar hardware for testing, we note that nGraph-HE2 [8] employs compiler optimizations and a more performant hardware with 376GB of RAM and 112 cores

Table 2. slytHErin's performance for **NN20** on **Scenario 3** (Sect. 4.3) with increasing number of parties (model-providers).

# of Parties	Latency (s)	Throughput (samples/s)
3	245.58 (±0.50)	1.19
5	238.15 (±4.12)	1.22
10	278.19 (±9.11)	1.05
20	354.17 (±10.66)	0.82

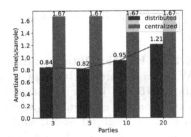

Fig. 5. Benchmarking decentralized vs. centralized bootstrapping on encrypted **NN20** for variable number of parties (model-providers).

6.2.2 Interactive MPC Protocols

We evaluate **NN20** in **Scenario 3** where the model is trained and retained under encryption by multiple parties using a privacy-preserving collaborative training framework [19,52,53] (Sect. 4.3). Note that this scenario requires the use of the collective bootstrapping protocol CBootstrap(·), thus, it is not supported by prior encrypted inference frameworks. Table 2 shows slytHErin's latency and throughput for increasing number of parties, while in Fig. 5 we compare slytHErin's amortized runtime when employing CBootstrap(·) versus the centralized bootstrapping. Overall, we observe a linear increase (decrease) in slytHErin's latency (throughput) as the number of parties increases. We note that the CBootstrap(·) operation is executed in an asynchronous fashion by the master model provider, i.e., the protocol is initiated concurrently with all the model providers and the output is generated as soon as the last party provides its share. For this reason, we can even experience lower latency when increasing the number of parties by a limited amount (3 vs. 5), as the protocol becomes particularly sensible to the network conditions. In any case, the benefits of employing

Table 3. slytHErin's performance for **NN50** in **Scenarios 1, 2,** and **3** (Sect. 4). For **Scenario 3**, the number of model-providers is $N=3$.

	Latency(s)	Amortized (s/sample)	Throughput (samples/s)	Avg. latency/layer (s)
Plaintext model Encrypted data (Scenario 1)	2,496.83	4.26	0.234	48.95
Encrypted model Plaintext data (Scenario 2)	2,699.75	4.62	0.216	52.93
Encrypted model Encrypted data (Scenario 3)	613.52	2.09	0.476	12.02

CBootstrap($\cdot$) over the centralized version (when possible) are evident, as the former enables refreshing the ciphertext noise with an efficient interactive protocol, rather than with a computationally expensive homomorphic circuit.

6.2.3 Application and Model Agility

Finally, we demonstrate the high degree of flexibility offered by slytHErin, both in terms of variety of enabled use-cases and supported architectures, by evaluating a more complex model on all the scenarios described in Sect. 4. In particular, we benchmark slytHErin with **NN50** and a batch of 585 samples on: (i) **Scenario 1** with encrypted data and a plaintext model (Sect. 4.1), (ii) **Scenario 2** with an encrypted model and plaintext data (Sect. 4.2), and (iii) **Scenario 3** where the encrypted model is kept by $N=3$ model-providers and encrypted data. Note that evaluating **NN50** in **Scenarios 1** and **2** requires the invocation of the centralized bootstrapping operation, that is not supported by most of the related works [8, 11, 22, 33].

Table 3 shows the performance results for all scenarios. First, we note that by leveraging on our data packing approach and processing multiple samples in a SIMD fashion, slytHErin achieves reasonable runtime given the complexity of the **NN50** model (**Scenario 1**). For reference, the original work by Chillotti et al. achieves at best an amortized time of 37.69s/sample and a throughput of 0.02samples/s. Then, we also observe that slytHErin's generic optimizations enable the efficient evaluation of encrypted models: Evaluating **NN50** under encryption on **Scenario 2**, which involves a matrix multiplication, addition, polynomial activation, and centralized bootstrapping operations, is only ~7% slower than evaluating a plaintext model evaluation (c.f. **Scenario 1**). slytHErin achieves the best performance results on **Scenario 3** thanks to its support for interactive multiparty protocols such as collective bootstrapping (Sect. 6.2.2). Overall, we remark that `slytHErin` is the first framework for encrypted inference that can support all these application scenarios.

7   Conclusion

In this work, we presented `slytHErin`, an agile framework for privacy-preserving deep neural network inference using homomorphic encryption. Thanks to our hybrid design that leverages on HE and its multiparty variant, and generic setting-agnostic optimizations, `slytHErin` can support various and novel scenarios for encrypted inference featuring untrusted model providers and clients. These scenarios include: (i) the client sending encrypted data to an untrusted model-provider for inference, (ii) the model-provider sending an encrypted model to a client for local inference (without the need of mutual trust between them), and (iii) the client sending the encrypted data to a cohort of model-providers holding an encrypted model. Thus, `slytHErin` extends the applicability of privacy-preserving PaaS beyond previous works. Moreover, with our intuitive and flexible input data packing scheme, `slytHErin` can be adapted to various deep neural network architectures and can accommodate diverse application requirements, being able to process an arbitrary number of samples without incurring major performance loss. Our experimental results show that the simplicity of our packing approach and the agility of our framework does not harm its performance as it is on par with, and occasionally better than, state-of-the-art related works, while introducing an increased degree of flexibility over previous works.

References

1. Abadi, M., et al.: TensorFlow: large-scale machine learning on heterogeneous systems (2015). http://tensorflow.org/
2. Almeida, M., Laskaridis, S., Venieris, S.I., Leontiadis, I., Lane, N.D.: DynO: dynamic onloading of deep neural networks from cloud to device. ACM Trans. Embed. Comput. Syst. 21(6), 1–24 (2022). https://doi.org/10.1145/3510831
3. Amazon Forecast (2023). https://aws.amazon.com/forecast/. Accessed 01 Jan 2023
4. Machine Learning on AWS (2023). https://aws.amazon.com/machine-learning/. Accessed 01 Jan 2023
5. Azure Machine Learning (2023). https://azure.microsoft.com/en-us/products/machine-learning/. Accessed 01 Jan 2023
6. Microsoft Azure Cognitive Service (2023). https://learn.microsoft.com/en-us/azure/cognitive-services/language-service/. Accessed 01 Jan 2023
7. Machine Learning made beautifully simple for everyone (2023). https://bigml.com/. Accessed 01 Jan 2023
8. Boemer, F., Costache, A., Cammarota, R., Wierzynski, C.: nGraph-HE2: a high-throughput framework for neural network inference on encrypted data. In: ACM WAHC (2019)
9. Boemer, F., Lao, Y., Wierzynski, C.: nGraph-HE: a graph compiler for deep learning on homomorphically encrypted data. CoRR abs/1810.10121 (2018). http://arxiv.org/abs/1810.10121

10. Boura, C., Gama, N., Georgieva, M.: Chimera: a unified framework for B/FV, TFHE and HEAAN fully homomorphic encryption and predictions for deep learning. IACR Cryptol. ePrint Arch. **2018**, 758 (2018)

11. Brutzkus, A., Gilad-Bachrach, R., Elisha, O.: Low latency privacy preserving inference. In: International Conference on Machine Learning, pp. 812–821. PMLR (2019)

12. California Consumer Privacy Act (CCPA) (2023). https://www.oag.ca.gov/privacy/ccpa. Accessed 01 Jan 2023

13. Chabanne, H., de Wargny, A., Milgram, J., Morel, C., Prouff, E.: Privacy-preserving classification on deep neural network. IACR Cryptol. ePrint Arch. **2017**, 35 (2017)

14. Cheon, J.H., Kim, A., Kim, M., Song, Y.: Homomorphic encryption for arithmetic of approximate numbers. In: Takagi, T., Peyrin, T. (eds.) ASIACRYPT 2017. LNCS, vol. 10624, pp. 409–437. Springer, Cham (2017). https://doi.org/10.1007/978-3-319-70694-8_15

15. Chillotti, I., Gama, N., Georgieva, M., Izabachène, M.: TFHE: fast fully homomorphic encryption over the torus. J. Cryptology **33**(1), 34–91 (2020). https://doi.org/10.1007/s00145-019-09319-x

16. Chillotti, I., Joye, M., Paillier, P.: Programmable bootstrapping enables efficient homomorphic inference of deep neural networks. Cryptology ePrint Archive, Paper 2021/091 (2021)

17. Chou, E., Beal, J., Levy, D., Yeung, S., Haque, A., Fei-Fei, L.: Faster cryptoNets: leveraging sparsity for real-world encrypted inference. CoRR abs/1811.09953 (2018). http://arxiv.org/abs/1811.09953

18. Dathathri, R., et al.: CHET: an optimizing compiler for fully-homomorphic neural-network inferencing. In: Proceedings of the 40th ACM SIGPLAN Conference on Programming Language Design and Implementation, pp. 142–156. PLDI 2019, Association for Computing Machinery, New York, NY, USA (2019). https://doi.org/10.1145/3314221.3314628

19. Froelicher, D., et al.: Scalable privacy-preserving distributed learning. In: PETS (2021)

20. The EU General Data Protection Regulation (2023). https://gdpr-info.eu/. Accessed 01 Jan 2023

21. Gentry, C.: Fully homomorphic encryption using ideal lattices. In: Proceedings of the Forty-First Annual ACM Symposium on Theory of Computing, pp. 169–178. STOC 2009, Association for Computing Machinery, New York, NY, USA (2009). https://doi.org/10.1145/1536414.1536440

22. Gilad-Bachrach, R., Dowlin, N., Laine, K., Lauter, K., Naehrig, M., Wernsing, J.: CryptoNets: applying neural networks to encrypted data with high throughput and accuracy. In: ICML (2016)

23. Gnacik, M., Lapa, K.: Using Toeplitz matrices to obtain 2D convolution (2022). https://doi.org/10.21203/rs.3.rs-2195496/v1

24. Go Programming Language (2023). https://golang.org. Accessed 01 Jan 2023

25. AI and machine learning products (2023). https://cloud.google.com/products/ai. Accessed 01 Jan 2023

26. Gray, R.M.: Toeplitz and circulant matrices: a review. Found. Trends® Commun. Inf. Theory **2**(3), 155–239 (2006). https://doi.org/10.1561/0100000006

27. Halevi, S., Shoup, V.: HElib - an implementation of homomorphic encryption (2014). https://github.com/shaih/HElib/. Accessed 01 Jan 2023

28. Halevi, S., Shoup, V.: Algorithms in HElib. In: Garay, J.A., Gennaro, R. (eds.) CRYPTO 2014. LNCS, vol. 8616, pp. 554–571. Springer, Heidelberg (2014). https://doi.org/10.1007/978-3-662-44371-2_31
29. Hesamifard, E., Takabi, H., Ghasemi, M., Wright, R.: Privacy-preserving machine learning as a service. PETS **2018**, 123–142 (2018)
30. Centers for Medicare & Medicaid Services. The Health Insurance Portability and Accountability Act of 1996 (HIPAA) (2023). https://www.cms.gov/Regulations-and-Guidance/Administrative-Simplification/HIPAA-ACA/PrivacyandSecurityInformation. Accessed 01 Jan 2023
31. Huang, Z., Lu, W.J., Hong, C., Ding, J.: Cheetah: lean and fast secure two-party deep neural network inference. In: 31st USENIX Security Symposium (2022)
32. Jiang, X., Kim, M., Lauter, K., Song, Y.: Secure outsourced matrix computation and application to neural networks. In: Proceedings of the 2018 ACM SIGSAC Conference on Computer and Communications Security, pp. 1209–1222. CCS 2018, Association for Computing Machinery, New York, NY, USA (2018). https://doi.org/10.1145/3243734.3243837
33. Juvekar, C., Vaikuntanathan, V., Chandrakasan, A.: GAZELLE: a low latency framework for secure neural network inference. In: USENIX Security (2018)
34. Kim, M., Jiang, X., Lauter, K., Ismayilzada, E., Shams, S.: Secure human action recognition by encrypted neural network inference. Nat. Commun. **13**(1), 4799 (2022). https://doi.org/10.1038/s41467-022-32168-5
35. Lattigo: a library for lattice-based homomorphic encryption in go (2023). https://github.com/ldsec/lattigo. Accessed 01 Jan 2023
36. LeCun, Y., Cortes, C.: MNIST handwritten digit database (2010)
37. Liu, J., Juuti, M., Lu, Y., Asokan, N.: Oblivious neural network predictions via MiniONN transformations. In: ACM CCS (2017)
38. Lloret-Talavera, G., et al.: Enabling homomorphically encrypted inference for large DNN models. IEEE Trans. Comput. **7**, 1145–1155 (2021). https://doi.org/10.1109/TC.2021.3076123
39. Lu, W.J., Sakuma, J.: More practical privacy-preserving machine learning as a service via efficient secure matrix multiplication. In: Proceedings of the 6th Workshop on Encrypted Computing & Applied Homomorphic Cryptography, pp. 25–36. WAHC 2018, Association for Computing Machinery, New York, NY, USA (2018)
40. Lyubashevsky, V., Peikert, C., Regev, O.: On ideal lattices and learning with errors over rings. J. ACM (JACM) **60**(6), 1–35 (2013)
41. Meftah, S., Tan, B.H.M., Mun, C.F., Aung, K.M.M., Veeravalli, B., Chandrasekhar, V.: DOReN: toward efficient deep convolutional neural networks with fully homomorphic encryption. IEEE Trans. Inf. Forensics Secur. **16**, 3740–3752 (2021). https://doi.org/10.1109/TIFS.2021.3090959
42. Mishra, P., Lehmkuhl, R., Srinivasan, A., Zheng, W., Popa, R.A.: Delphi: A cryptographic inference service for neural networks. In: USENIX Security (2020)
43. Mouchet, C., Troncoso-Pastoriza, J.R., Bossuat, J.P., Hubaux, J.P.: Multiparty homomorphic encryption from ring-learning-with-errors. PETS **2021**, 291–311 (2021)
44. Murshed, M.G.S., Murphy, C., Hou, D., Khan, N., Ananthanarayanan, G., Hussain, F.: Machine learning at the network edge: a survey. ACM Comput. Surv. **54**(8), 1–37 (2021). https://doi.org/10.1145/3469029
45. Paszke, A., et al.: Automatic differentiation in PyTorch. In: 31st Conference on Neural Information Processing Systems (NIPS 2017) (2017)
46. Patra, A., Suresh, A.: BLAZE: blazing fast privacy-preserving machine learning. In: NDSS (2020)

47. Ran, R., Wang, W., Gang, Q., Yin, J., Xu, N., Wen, W.: CryptoGCN: fast and scalable homomorphically encrypted graph convolutional network inference. In: Oh, A.H., Agarwal, A., Belgrave, D., Cho, K. (eds.) Advances in Neural Information Processing Systems (2022). https://openreview.net/forum?id=VeQBBm1MmTZ
48. Rathee, D., et al.: CrypTFlow2: practical 2-party secure inference. In: ACM CCS, pp. 325–342 (2020)
49. Riazi, M.S., Samragh, M., Chen, H., Laine, K., Lauter, K.E., Koushanfar, F.: XONN: XNOR-based oblivious deep neural network inference. In: USENIX Security (2019)
50. Rohloff, K.: The PALISADE lattice cryptography library (2018). https://git.njit.edu/palisade/PALISADE
51. Sav, S., Bossuat, J.P., Troncoso-Pastoriza, J.R., Claassen, M., Hubaux, J.P.: Privacy-preserving federated neural network learning for disease-associated cell classification. Patterns 3(5) (2022). https://doi.org/10.1016/j.patter.2022.100487
52. Sav, S., Diaa, A., Pyrgelis, A., Bossuat, J.P., Hubaux, J.P.: Privacy-preserving federated recurrent neural networks. CoRR abs/2207.13947 (2022). https://arxiv.org/abs/2207.13947
53. Sav, S., et al.: POSEIDON: privacy-preserving federated neural network learning. In: Network and Distributed System Security Symposium (NDSS) (2021)
54. Microsoft SEAL (release 3.3) (2023). https://github.com/Microsoft/SEAL. Accessed 01 Jan 2023
55. Sim, S.H., Paranjpe, T., Roberts, N., Zhao, M.: Exploring edge machine learning-based stress prediction using wearable devices. In: 2022 21st IEEE International Conference on Machine Learning and Applications (ICMLA), pp. 1266–1273 (2022). https://doi.org/10.1109/ICMLA55696.2022.00203
56. Watson Machine Learning (2023). https://cloud.ibm.com/catalog/services/watson-machine-learning. Accessed 01 Jan 2023
57. Xu, G., et al.: Hercules: boosting the performance of privacy-preserving federated learning. IEEE Trans. Dependable Secure Comput. 1–18 (2022). https://doi.org/10.1109/TDSC.2022.3218793

Trust Management Framework for Containerized Workloads Applications to 5G Networks

Aicha Miloudi[1], Luis Suárez[2(✉)], Nora Boulahia Cuppens[1], Frédéric Cuppens[1], and Stere Preda[2]

[1] Polythecnique Montréal, 2500 Chem. de Polytechnique, Montreal, QC, Canada
{aicha.miloudi,nora.boulahia-cuppens,frederic.cuppens}@polymtl.ca
[2] Ericsson Canada, 8275 Rte Transcanadienne, Saint-Laurent, QC, Canada
{luis.suarez,stere.preda}@ericsson.com

Abstract. As mobile networks grow, managing the security of communication between all its internal components becomes more challenging because of the increasing number of services, network functions, and stakeholders involved. Among the different dimensions of security, trust is one that 5G communication service providers (CSP) must prioritize to provide secure services for their users. This requires a strategy for assessing trust between network assets at scale, considering the complexity of interactions, service layers, and deployment options. To address this problem, we propose a trust management framework that deals with requests to perform operations on a Kubernetes® cluster based on trust labels. The context of the assets is one of the attributes used in the framework, used to describe the environment in which the assets operate. In addition, we consider past interactions between the assets. Since trust is dynamic through time, it needs to be evaluated continuously. This paper focuses on defining parameters for trust that are tailored to the unique properties of the various assets involved in the operations to be secured. The proposed model is implemented in Kubernetes® using its admission control module. Finally, an adversary model and a threat assessment are defined to evaluate the security of the trust framework.

Keywords: Trust Management · 5G · Kubernetes® · Security · Access Control

1 Introduction

5G networks are characterized by their many stakeholders and interconnected devices. Securing the interactions in such complex networks may seem challenging given the many facets to attain this goal. Among them, there is detection and prevention of attacks coming from malicious nodes to counter attempts to abuse and cause harm in the rest of the network.

Evaluating the trust level associated with each asset (something of value that we want to protect [1]) in the network is critical for guaranteeing high level of assurance in such an environment. The intricacy of such networks requires a

J. Zhou et al. (Eds.): ACNS 2023 Workshops, LNCS 13907, pp. 378–393, 2023.
https://doi.org/10.1007/978-3-031-41181-6_21

method that considers the context of every asset and all interactions between these assets. In addition, we must consider the dynamic nature of trust, as it changes and evolves over time. Mechanisms to assess and maintain trust's validity need to be put in place. These requirements become more important thanks to paradigms such as Zero Trust Architecture [2], that considers constant insider threat and continuous verification of the security of the assets.

To fulfill these requirements, we propose a new trust life cycle management framework for containerized workloads applicable to 5G networks, using a widely used orchestrator such as Kubernetes®. Our solution determines the different parameters that define trust. These parameters are evaluated to give a verdict on whether or not the communication between two assets is authorized according to a security policy.

The contributions of this paper are threefold:

- We propose a novel approach to incorporate more attributes to assess trust and manage it according to policy requirements.
- We provide an implementation of the trust management framework to verify its applicability in Kubernetes®.
- We propose an evaluation of the trust model via a threat assessment model when facing a malicious actor that we defined through an adversary model. The added value the proposed framework provides will be proved in this way.

This paper is organized as follows. First, we review the relevant literature and state of the art in Sect. 2. Then, in Sect. 3, we describe the proposed trust model framework. In Sect. 4, we present the adversary model. In Sect. 5 we show how the trust model is implemented. The evaluation of the trust model is analyzed in Sect. 6 where a risk assessment with the DREAD model is conducted. We discuss the results of the risk assessment in Sect. 7. Finally, in Sect. 8 we draw conclusions on this research topic.

2   Related Work

In this section, we describe recent approaches and strategies to manage trust in telecommunication environments. Mainly, the approaches to assess trust in 5G environments are via blockchain technology, artificial intelligence (AI), reputation based on previous interactions, and context-based trust.

Several new studies in trust management in 5G networks use blockchain technology [3–6]. This approach is mainly prevalent for vehicular networks. Baktayan and Albaltah [3] propose a model based on blockchain in 5G networks to guarantee the trust for a new device connecting to a Cloud Radio Access Network (C-RAN). This is done by authenticating through a public blockchain, so a new trust value is calculated and assigned to the device. Blockchain restrains communications with this device if it behaves maliciously. Zhang et al. [4] present another blockchain-based trust management model for the internet of vehicles. They rely on a reputation metric to manage the trust. Blockchain is used to implement a data storage system to protect reputation values. Blockchain technology consumes too many resources, generates significant latency, and is unsuitable for complex systems with many services. Wang et al. [7] attempted to resolve this problem by developing a lightweight blockchain solution for access control in IoT. This is done by establishing a decentralized application that serves as an alternative for resources with lower security requirements to lower overhead.

Artificial intelligence is recurrent in many papers on the subject of trust in 5G networks [8–10]. Usually, it is used as a way to support the trust calculation. In [8], the authors use a Generative Adversarial Network (GAN) to jointly address privacy preservation and trust management for computation in modern IoT networks (e.g. vehicular networks and smart healthcare systems).

Other research relies on the concept of reputation to ensure trust. In Fang et al. [11], in order to evaluate the trust between two nodes i and j, node j calculates a trust value based on the direct interaction with node i and another indirect one based on the history of interactions between i and its neighbors. Zhang et al. [4] calculate the reputation of a vehicle with cross-validation of the evaluations assigned by other vehicles. The notion of reputation allows us to define trust in multi-tenant networks where multiple assets communicate with each other. Therefore, reputation should be a factor to consider in the trust evaluation of mobile networks. However, this metric needs a history of past interactions. Building this history is not always possible to do at system initialization or when a new asset joins the system. Another method is required to calculate the trust at these stages.

One crucial property that trust depends on is the context. Context is defined as the environment in which the enterprise (or network) operates and how this environment is influenced by the risks involved [12]. This property can be incorporated to infrastructure, virtualization, services or any other scope. The context of assets, like their location in a data center, influences the trust decision between these assets. The assignment of trust to an asset relies on the conditions linked to the context [13]. Rehman et al. [14] focus on this property in their development of a trust management framework. This framework is composed of four modules: the parameter module, the context module, the trust evaluation module, and malicious node detection.

Since trust is a dynamic metric, it needs to be continuously managed [13]. Nonetheless, the upkeep of trust in case of deterioration is not considered in most papers above-mentioned. If a mission critical service's trust level decreases for an unexpected reason, it would be relevant to establish a negotiation mechanism to mitigate such a situation.

Based on the findings of this literature review, we argue that to assess trustworthiness, an important feature to consider is the context of the state of each asset. Context is key for trust calculation at boot time, knowing that there are not enough interactions to build a history for that asset. However, attestation procedures or seed context values can help to set an initial value for this feature. Other important feature is the reputation of the assets which is built based on the history of interactions with other assets. Leaving aside the feature and attribute selection, there are operational contracts that must be met for critical services even if trust is not guaranteed. The management of this special case can be addressed in future research through predefined playbooks [15] and later incorporate machine learning aspects to cover other types of scenarios.

3 Trust Model Framework

The objective of the proposed trust model is to bridge the gaps from the aforementioned literature review. The creation of the trust model framework requires the consideration of the context of the assets and the different hierarchies of the assets for the target system. With the objective to illustrate the usage of the model, a simplified use case scenario will be provided. This use case will be used as a base to be generalized (e.g., communication between assets of two different service providers -two different nodes) as a mean to offer more flexibility of implementation.

3.1 Context

In order to create the proposed trust management framework, we determine the different parameters that define trust in a particular context. As previously stated, context is a property tied to trust. Context needs to be considered to determine if an asset A should trust an asset B.

The context definition is inspired by the Organization Based Access Control (OrBAC) model [16]. We will be mainly focused on three types of context variables: temporal context, spatial context, and other contexts that characterize the role and the type of the asset. The *temporal* context determines when it is authorized to perform an action on a given asset. The *spatial* context restricts where a request targeting an asset is coming from. Lastly, the context related to the *type of service* the asset plays is used to make sure only the needed services are allowed to communicate together. These context parameters are borrowed into our model and distributed in three different vectors to better classify the context parameters of each asset. The proposed vectors are: current context, context requirements and a global vector.

Current Context Vector. This vector contains the different parameters of the current context of an asset. The way to get this information is asset and implementation dependent. The vector is specified as $< ti, cpl, cll, ce, dt, st >$ and contains the following attributes:

- Trust Index (ti): pre-calculated trust value assigned to the asset at its creation. This index gives us an evaluation of the trust level initially assigned to the asset based on software properties and other information we have on the functions deployed in the asset. These properties depend on the type of function or service the asset provides. The content of the functions is out of the scope of the current model. However, for the purpose of this work, we assume that an asset such as a Security Manager or Security Agent fulfills this task and provides this value, as suggested by ETSI in [17].

- Current Physical Location (*cpl*): expresses the current geographical location of the asset. For example, the city, data center, rack number.
- Current Logical Location (*cll*): expresses the current logical location of the asset. For example, subnet mask, VLAN ID.
- Domain Type (*dt*): the domain type specifies the nature of the traffic that the asset processes according to the purpose of the domain, e.g., control plane, user plane, management plane, service plane [18].
- Service Type (*st*): the type of service that the asset offers such as enhanced mobile broadband (eMBB), ultra-reliable and low-latency communications (URLLC), and massive machine-type communications (mMTC). These services are defined by 3GPP in [19].

Context Requirements Vector. This vector contains the different context parameters that an asset requires from other assets to accept a request. The vector is specified as $< tii, rpl, rll, tr, pe, rdt, rst >$ and contains the following attributes:

- Trust Index Interval (*tii*): interval to delimit the trust index of other assets that want to communicate with the one in question. If the index value of an asset falls outside of the interval, its communication attempt is denied.
- Required Physical Locations (*rpl*): the geographical locations permitted to interact with the asset.
- Required Logical Locations (*rll*): the logical locations permitted to interact with the asset.
- Temporal Requirements (*tr*): the times during which a given asset allows communication attempts.
- Permitted Events (*pe*): List of authorized events the asset can trigger.
- Required Domain Types (*rdt*): list of types of domains authorized to communicate with the asset.
- Required Service Types (*rst*): list of services that are authorized to communicate with the asset.

Global Vector. The last vector is composed of variables that define the global context. These variables are not specific to an asset but to the system in general. The vector is described as $< cdt, ce >$ and has the following attributes:

- Current Date and Time (*cdt*): We need to be able to define the current time and date globally for the system in order to have traceability of the freshness of requests and the state of the asset.
- Current Event (*ce*): the event we want to allow or deny when validating the trust (request, action or operation).

3.2   Hierarchies for the Target System

The variables presented at the beginning of this section need to be combined and relations need to be made in order to validate that trust is fulfilled. In particular, we consider a Kubernetes deployment scenario to illustrate the different types of interactions between assets. The assets are the containers that deploy different network functions. In the case of Kubernetes, the container is instantiated in a Pod and the Pod is placed inside a node. Programs and applications operate within containers, with Pods serving as the smallest computational unit of software in Kubernetes. It can be easily deduced that these Kubernetes objects (denominated in a generic form as assets) are arranged into hierarchies.

The use case described in the next subsection will leverage on the hierarchies between assets to fashion the management of trust within the architecture.

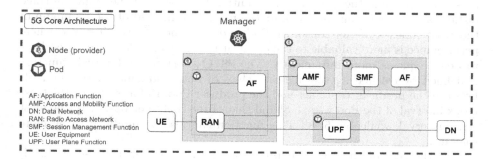

Fig. 1. Proof-of-concept of a deployment of a simplified 5G Core architecture.

3.3   Use-Case: Communication Between Two Containers in the Same Node

To prove the feasibility of our approach, we deployed a Kubernetes cluster as illustrated in Fig. 1. While this does not correspond to a real 5G deployment, we identify the various Kubernetes objects using 5G terminology to facilitate a deeper understanding of our proposed solution and the frameworks it can apply.

In this scenario, two virtual network functions in the same node, such as a Session Management Function (SMF) and a User Plane Function (UPF), need to communicate with each other to direct traffic to the internet (towards the data network) as illustrated in Fig. 1 in the node on the right.

If a network function consumer demands a service from a network function producer, we request that the consumer proves its level of trust to access the service. The conditions to prove this trust level are written as logical expressions, based on relations between parameters of their vectors specified at the beginning of this section. In the following logical expressions, p is the producer container, c is the container that consumes the service, cp is the consumer Pod and pp is the producer Pod. The logical expressions are:

$$Min(ti_c, ti_{cp}) \in \texttt{MSI}(tii_p, tii_{pp}) \tag{1}$$

$$cpl_c \in rpl_p \tag{2}$$

$$cll_c \in rll_p \tag{3}$$

$$cdt \in tr_p \wedge cdt \in tr_c \tag{4}$$

$$ce \in pe_c \wedge ce \in pe_p \tag{5}$$

Logical expression 1 validates the consumer's trust index value. We take the weakest level of trust from the consumer side and the most strict index interval formed by the producer and its Pod which would guarantee the highest level of trust. It is possible the modify this condition to allow more flexibility in some instances by calculating the mean or the maximum instead of the minimum of the trust indexes of the consumer Pod and container. In the instance where performance is more valuable to the client, it is pertinent to lower the trust level to deny requests more infrequently. The $\texttt{MSI}()$(Most Strict Interval) function is defined by calculating the highest values of both endpoints of the intervals between the producer container and the producer Pod. If, for example, the trust index interval of the Pod was [4, 8] and that of the container was [5, 7], the most strict interval would be [5, 8]. This function can also be modified to be more tolerant.

For the rest of the logical expressions (2 to 5), we do not use the Pods parameters as they are either similar to that of their respective containers or non-applicable. Specifically, logical expressions 2 and 3 confirm that the consumer's request is coming from the expected physical and logical locations. If there are any temporal requirements, logical expression 4 will enforce them. Logical expression 5 ensures that each asset authorizes the current event.

Next, we have logical expressions 6 and 7, which rely on lists of services and domains allowed by the producer to validate the type of domain and type of service of the consumer.

$$dt_c \in rdt_p \tag{6}$$

$$st_c \in rst_p \tag{7}$$

With these logical expressions, it is possible to handle the different attributes needed to manage trust of the assets that are involved in the use case. Trust management in dynamic environments (e.g., containerized workloads) is addressed since the logical expressions are evaluated for each request that is received. In addition, it is flexible enough to be generalized to other use cases, as we show in the following subsection.

3.4   Generalization of the Use Case to n-Layer Variants

The trust model presented in this section has a fixed number of layers of encapsulation (the container or workload, the Pod, and the node). Different environments will require different configurations and our model should be adaptable according to them. For the model to work, there must be a minimum of two layers. Adding a layer on top requires the new layer's trust index parameters in the first logical expression. Scaling down from three to two layers is more complex because we need to determine what to do if the lower layer is compromised. The lower layer holds all the important parameters because the interactions are going to be between the assets in that layer. In this case, we combine the lower layer with the one just on top. To do so, we take the lowest trust index between the Pod and the containers inside it. We use the most strict interval from the two layers. The required locations, permitted events, domain types, and service types will become the union of all lists of the assets in the lower layer. The same happens for the temporal requirements. We combine all the time and date requirements of the containers and assign them to the parent Pod. This way, the logical expressions are adapted accordingly.

4 Adversary Model

In this section, we present an adversary model that defines the adversary's capabilities that can be used against our model. We will only focus on the trust model and not the 5G architecture or Kubernetes security issues, as these are outside this paper's scope.

To define a complete adversary model, we need to determine the adversary's assumptions, goals, and capabilities. These three items are described in Table 1 according to the proposed use case scenario [20]. In one situation, we assume that the adversary is inside the network and has low privileges. The adversary is connected through a regular account and does not have visibility over the whole network, and only has access to the assets created by the compromised user. Role restrictions are put in place to define better the actions a user makes. To influence the trust model, a malicious actor can create a Pod with the correct labels to try and get it scheduled in a trusted node. Because the user does not have visibility over node labels and other information, it is difficult or almost impossible for the adversary to take advantage of the trust management model this way. The adversary would have to use brute force to try and guess the right combination of labels.

Another interesting situation is when an adversary with low privileges wants to retrieve information about other assets that the compromised user does not own. To do so, the adversary could establish communication with other assets in the network to try and perform privilege escalation. With the implementation of the trust model, most communication attempts will be blocked due to the limited visibility and low privileges the attacker has on the system. To communicate with another Pod created by another user, the adversary needs to know the exact requirement context vector of the target.

In the case that the adversary has a credential with higher privileges, the attacker could read and modify the labels at the node level. If trust index labels are changed to arbitrary values, legitimate service requests could be rejected, leading to a denial of service. The trust model will perform well it prevents the attacker to modify node labels.

Table 1. Adversary model for the use case scenario.

Assumptions	Goals	Capabilities
Local Attack	Gain more trust inside the network	Create a Pod with modified trust vector labels
Low privilege credentials	Retrieve information about networks and gain	Communicate with other assets via new
Limited network visibility	access to workloads	services or network
Restricted role impact	from other users	policies
Local Attack High privilege credentials	Denial of Service	Modify the trust index label
Wide network visibility		
Role with more impact		

Via these previous examples, we show that the proposed trust model is able to circumvent the attempts of an attacker to reach the proposed goals.

5   Implementation

The implementation helps to demonstrate that the model we defined is general and can be deployed in any cloud environment. The model explained in Sect. 3 was deployed in Kubernetes which includes an admission control module to manage the trust in the system. This module allows the semantic validation of Kubernetes objects during create, update, and delete operations. Integrating the Open Policy Agent[TM] (OPA) as a controller allows the definition of constraints and the application of policies to authorize or deny the communication between the different containers according to their respective trust value.

To test different node configurations without requiring multiple machines, a MiniKube cluster was deployed to create multiple nodes on a single machine. Since Pods are the smallest deployable unit in Kubernetes, we cannot manage containers as objects directly. Instead of calculating the trust of a container, we work directly with Pods in a two-layer approach as detailed in Sect. 3.4.

The different parameters we defined in Sect. 3 are implemented using labels that we attach to Kubernetes objects. Each Pod and node will have its own labels. For example, the labels for the trust index are the following: `TI`, `TI_interval_max`, and `TI_interval_min`. For the current and required logical and physical localization, we have these labels: `Current_logic_loc`, `Current_phys_loc`, `Req_logic_loc`, `Req_phys_loc`. An assumption in this implementation is that the value of the labels is pre-calculated beforehand, being this process out of scope for this paper.

For the proposed use case scenario, we relied on OPA Gatekeeper [21] to write policies that allow or deny the creation or update of a NetworkPolicy object based on the condition we established in Sect. 3. A network policy is a Kubernetes object that controls traffic flow at the IP address or port level. Network policies specify who is allowed to communicate with a certain Pod. If, for example, we want Pod A to send requests to Pod B, we can define a NetworkPolicy that allows ingress traffic to reach Pod B only if it is from Pod A's IP address. OPA Gatekeeper will then decide if the creation of this Kubernetes object is allowed by evaluating the seven expressions defined in Sect. 3. To do so, we need to create a constraint template containing the definition of violations to the different conditions written in Rego, OPA's policy language. Rego is a declarative language inspired by Datalog [22]. The condition for a two-layer architecture is described in logical expression 8:

$$ti_{cp} \in tii_{pp} \tag{8}$$

The pseudo-code of the violation of the first condition is the following.

```
violationContidition_2_1(PodA, PodB) {
    return PodA.TI < PodB.TI_interval_min or
           PodA.TI > PodB.TI_interval_max
}
```

The pseudo-code of the violation of a condition that considers nodes and Pods is as follows:

```
violationContidition_3_1(PodA, nodeA, PodB, nodeB) {
    minimum_TI = Min(PodA.TI, nodeA.TI)
    highest_start = Max(PodB.TI_interval_min, nodeB.TI_interval_min)
    highest_end = Max(PodB.TI_interval_max, nodeB.TI_interval_max)
    return minimum_TI < highest_start or minimum_TI > highest_end
}
```

This proves that OPA Gatekeeper has the capability to manage operation request on Kubernetes objects according to trust requirements specified by rules.

6 Evaluation

To evaluate the proposed trust management model, we have to prove that the trust model is able to secure the environments where it will be deployed against the adversary we defined in Sect. 4. We also need to formalize the evaluation of the level of security that the trust model provides for communications between different assets, which is one of the main goals of this paper.

6.1 Threat Assessment

DREAD is a threat modeling program developed by Microsoft [23]. It is composed of 5 categories:

- **Damage Potential:** The level of damage caused by the attack

- **Reproducibility:** How easy is it to reproduce the attack
- **Exploitability:** How much effort and knowledge is required to launch the attack
- **Affected users:** How many users will be affected by the attack
- **Discoverability:** How easily can the vulnerability be discovered

The categories that this model covers makes it suitable to be used for our purpose. The next step is to define the potential threats the model can face and how the model prevents the vulnerabilities from being exploited. Threat modeling helps us establish a quantitative evaluation of the security of our model. For our DREAD model [24], first we assigned numerical values to the level of security, as shown in Table 2. Then, the trust rating is calculated by summing the scores of the five categories. The resulting score is interpreted following the notation in Table 3.

Table 2. Definition of the DREAD Model.

Damage Potential		Reproducibility		Exploitability		Affected users		Discoverability	
Level	Item	Level	Item	Level	Item	Level	Item	Level	Item
0	No damage	0	Difficult or impossible	2.5	Advanced programming, networking skills	0	No users	0	Hard to discover the vulnerability
5	Information disclosure	5	Complex	5	Available attack tools	2.5	Individual user	5	HTTP requests can uncover the vulnerability
8	Non-sensitive user data is compromised	7.5	Easy	9	Web application proxies	6	Few users	8	Vulnerability found in the public domain
9	Non-sensitive admin data is compromised	10	Very easy	10	Web browser	8	Admin users	10	Vulnerability found in web address bar or form
10	Destruction of information system: application unavailability	-	-	-	-	10	All users	-	-

Table 3. Trust rating score and interpretation.

Score	Description
Critical (40–50)	Critical vulnerability; address immediately
High (25–39)	Severe vulnerability; consider for review and resolution soon
Medium (11–24)	Moderate risk; review after addressing severe and critical risk
Low (1–10)	Low risk to infrastructure and data

Table 4. Results from risk assessment.

Threat	Damage	Reproducibility	Exploitbility	Affected users	Discoverability	Threatrating
1. Set labels manually to schedule Pod in a trusted node	0	0	2.5	0	5	7.5
2. Privilege escalation by sending unauthorized requests to other workloads	8	0	2.5	2.5	5	18
3. Denial of service	0	0	2.5	0	5	7.5

6.2 Analysis of the Threat Assessment Results

The results of the risk assessment are shown in Table 4. For the described threats, the desired risk severity levels are medium or low. Each threat is described as follows.

For the first threat, a malicious actor can try to influence the trust model by manually setting a Pod's context parameters seen in Sect. 3. As discussed in the adversary model, the attack will be difficult to reproduce if made from a low-privileged user account because the user only has visibility over its own assets. The attacker needs advanced skills in, e.g., 5G networking, to launch this attack. Due to the complexity of the attack, even if it succeeds, no users will be affected, and no damage will be done.

For the second threat, an attacker can send malicious requests to the other assets by establishing communication with other users' assets. As such, the attacker can try to exploit their vulnerabilities and gain more privilege and trust in the network. This threat is harder to exploit because it requires visibility over other users' workloads and their context labels. In addition, the attacker needs advanced knowledge of 5G networking to be able to launch and reproduce the attack. This time, individual users are affected simultaneously because of the difficulty of reproducing the attack. The potential damage goes up to non-sensitive users and application data if the target is the containers running inside the compromised Pod.

The third threat, the denial of service attack, as explained in Sect. 4, can be achieved by changing the trust index of a node to lower it or raise it to an extreme level so that it causes the API server to deny all scheduling requests of Pods. This vulnerability is impossible to exploit and therefore not possible to reproduce if we put in place a policy that prohibits a user from modifying the trust index of a node when the existing Pods inside no longer fit the requirements. Furthermore, if the node is empty, its trust index should not be allowed to change drastically from one modification to the other. This way, no user is impacted and the attack attempt causes no damage.

Finally, all these vulnerabilities are not found in the public domain but can be discovered by sending and observing prior requests made to the API server.

6.3 Verification of the Threat Assessment

To prove that our model can face the different threats as shown in Sect. 6.2, we calculate the complexity to the system the trust framework adds. We can interpret the problem as the adversary attempting to manipulate the trust model to obtain greater privileges within the network. The attacker is trying to guess the requirement of its target asset. If an attacker wants to, for example, target the Pod8 in Fig. 2 and was able to access a user account, the attacker could take advantage of the existing assets created by the compromised user and send requests to others. The Pods with an evil red logo are the ones compromised by the attacker. The attacker can use them to send malicious requests to the target P8. Normally, the unique constraint put in place would be based on logical localization. The minimum that could be done to secure Pod P8 would be to restrict the ingress traffic. To successfully send a request to P8, the attacker needs to try different sources. If P8 only accepts requests from nodes N1 and N3, he has a 2/5 chance of succeeding, which is very high. With our proposed model, there are other requirements the adversary does not have visibility over. The attacker needs to guess, in addition to the logical location, the precise values of the other six attributes of the context requirement for P8. For this demonstration, let us assume that the trust index values vary from zero to ten, there are two physical locations, data centers 1 and 2, and 5 subnets (one for each node). There are four domains and three services. The Pod context requirements are as follows:

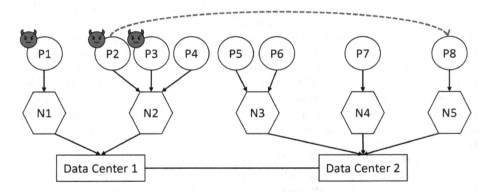

Fig. 2. Example topology to verify the threat assessment.

$tii = [6, 8]$
$rpl = [\text{datacenter1, datacenter2}]$
$rll = [\text{subnet1,subnet3}]$
$tr = \text{Monday 8 am - 5 pm}$
$rdt = [\text{user-plane, control-plane}]$
$rst = [\text{eMBB}]$

We assume that the current event is accepted by the target Pod. The adversary has a chance of 3/10 to guess the right trust index, a 2/2 chance to guess the right physical location (the target accepts requests from both locations), and a 2/5 chance for the right logical location. Because the temporal requirement is Monday from 9 am to 5 pm there are only 8 h in the week when the attack is possible. There is a chance of $8/(24 * 7) = 8/168$ of sending a request at the right time if the adversary tries every hour. If we calculate the chance of success, we have:

$$3/10 * 2/2 * 2/5 * 2/4 * 1/3 * 8/168 = 1/1050$$

The attacker has one chance on 1050 different combinations of labels to succeed on the attack. Furthermore, meeting the time and date requirements may prolong the duration of the attack to as many as 7 days before it can be successful. This is an improvement from a 2/5 chance of success in normal circumstances.

In a more realistic scenario, with additional nodes and network functions deployed, the complexity of realizing the attack increases. If Pod1 did not exist, the user would have to create a Pod in that node N1 to succeed in the attack. This would take another attempt at guessing the context vector needed to create a Pod in node N1.

For the last threat, the denial of service, the attacker will only need to modify one parameter: the trust index interval of each node. This would be simple for the attacker to achieve. However, the mechanisms put in place to restrict the changes made to the value of the trust index interval are sufficient to claim that the model will be robust against the malicious attacks described in the DREAD model.

7 Discussion

In the previous section, a few scenarios were introduced to represent situations threatening the security of interactions between assets. These scenarios are limited to the adversary model's assumptions. These conditions could be extended to consider more possibilities making the trust framework more dynamic. Adding a reputation metric could make attacks more difficult to be performed by blocking requests from assets with lower reputations. A misbehaved, compromised asset will have its reputation rating diminished based on previous actions and interactions.

As the level of complexity of the target network increases and as the adversary model becomes richer in assumed capabilities and disruption power, the proposed trust management framework is scalable and flexible to include additional layers and additional attributes for the trust evaluation. The API server has the logical capabilities to enforce a policy that can stop, or at least make it more difficult for an attacker to succeed in compromising the target network. Replay attacks, privilege abuse and lateral movement can be stopped via our framework.

As future work, reputation and negotiation capabilities will be added, for an extra layer of increased dynamicity. These added capabilities permit to handle unusual cases where context parameters are insufficient to provide trust. Likewise, adhering to Zero Trust principles requires to perform mutual trustworthiness verification. Next steps in this research seek to prove that the network function producer is also trusted to the network function consumer.

8   Conclusion

Trust management is a crucial aspect of 5G network security. The literature review shows that it is a metric used to have confidence about the secure nature of an interaction between the different devices and network functions in complex 5G systems. This paper presented our approach for trust management, aiming to control the communication between two virtual network functions in a 5G core scenario. Context variables were defined, and several logical expressions were formulated to perform operations on the trust value of each asset. These operations allow to know whether to approve or deny an interaction. A key use case scenario has been used to represent the situation where the trust needs to be evaluated. The implementation of the model has been realized in a Kubernetes® environment, leveraging on the OPA™ framework to configure the policy rules and implement the logic in order to reach a decision. The evaluation through an adversary model and a threat model proved that the proposed framework was resilient to threats under certain circumstances. Different threat scenarios have been described to help better define the trust framework capacity to provide security between the different interactions in a cloud setting. Overall, our proposal represents a guideline to implement a trust life cycle management framework for containerized workloads that is needed and is relevant to 5G networks.

References

1. Ross, R., Pillitteri, V., Graubart, R., Bodeau, D., McQuaid, R.: Developing cyber-resilient systems: a systems security engineering approach. No. NIST SP 800–160v2r1 (2021)
2. Rose, S., Borchert, O., Mitchell, S., Connelly, S.: Zero trust architecture (2020)
3. Baktayan, A., Albaltah, I.A.: A blockchain-based trust management system for 5G network slicing enabled C-RAN. Sustain. Eng. Innov. 4(1), 8–21 (2022)
4. Zhang, H., Liu, J., Zhao, H., Wang, P., Kato, N.: Blockchain-based trust management for internet of vehicles. IEEE Trans. Emerg. Top. Comput. 9(3), 1397–1409 (2021)
5. Li, B., Liang, R., Zhu, D., Chen, W., Lin, Q.: Blockchain-based trust management model for location privacy preserving in VANET. IEEE Trans. Intell. Transp. Syst. 22(6), 3765–3775 (2021)
6. Liu, Y., Zhang, C., Yan, Y., Zhou, X., Tian, Z., Zhang, J.: A semi-centralized trust management model based on blockchain for data exchange in IoT system. IEEE Trans. Serv. Comput. 16, 858–871 (2022)
7. Wang, P., Xu, N., Zhang, H., Sun, W., Benslimane, A.: Dynamic access control and trust management for blockchain-empowered IoT. IEEE Internet Things J. 9(15), 12997–13009 (2022)
8. Le, T., Shetty, S.: Artificial intelligence-aided privacy preserving trustworthy computation and communication in 5G-based IoT networks. Ad Hoc Netw. 126, 102752 (2022)
9. G. Carrozzo, et al.: AI-driven zero-touch operations, security and trust in multi-operator 5G networks: a conceptual architecture. In: 2020 European Conference on Networks and Communications (EuCNC), pp. 254–258. IEEE (2020)

10. Awan, K.A., Din, I.U., Almogren, A., Almajed, H., Mohiuddin, I., Guizani, M.: NeuroTrust-artificial-neural-network-based intelligent trust management mechanism for large-scale internet of medical things. IEEE Internet Things J. **8**(21), 15672–15682 (2021)

11. Fang, W., Zhang, W., Chen, W., Liu, Y., Tang, C.: TMSRS: trust management-based secure routing scheme in industrial wireless sensor network with fog computing. Wirel. Netw. J. Mob. Commun. Comput. Inf. **26**(5), 3169–3182 (2020)

12. Stine, K., Quinn, S., Witte, G., Gardner, R.K.: Integrating Cybersecurity and Enterprise Risk Management (ERM) (2020)

13. ETSI. GR NFV-SEC 003 v1.1.1, NFV Security; Security and Trust Guidance (2014). https://www.etsi.org/deliver/etsi_gs/nfv-sec/001_099/003/01.01.01_60/gs_nfv-sec003v010101p.pdf

14. Rehman, A., et al.: CTMF: context-aware trust management framework for internet of vehicles. IEEE Access **10**, 73685–73701 (2022)

15. Mavroeidis, V., Eis, P., Zadnik, M., Caselli, M., Jordan, B.: On the integration of course of action playbooks into shareable cyber threat intelligence. In: 2021 IEEE International Conference on Big Data (Big Data), pp. 2104–2108 (2021)

16. Cuppens, F., Cuppens-Boulahia, N.: Modeling contextual security policies. Int. J. Inf. Secur. **7**, 285–305 (2008)

17. ETSI: GS NFV-SEC 024 v0.0.6 Security Management Specification (2022)

18. 5G-PPP: View on 5G architecture v4 (2021). https://5g-ppp.eu/wp-content/uploads/2021/08/Architecture-WP-v4.0_forPublicConsultation.pdf

19. 3GPP: Specification 28.530, management and orchestration; concepts, use cases and requirements (2021). https://portal.3gpp.org/desktopmodules/Specifications/SpecificationDetails.aspx?specificationId=3273

20. Do, Q., Martini, B., Choo, K.-K.R.: The role of the adversary model in applied security research. Comput. Secur. **81**, 156–181 (2019)

21. Gatekeeper introduction. https://open-policy-agent.github.io/gatekeeper/website/docs/

22. Policy Language. https://openpolicyagent.org/docs/latest/policy-language/

23. Threat Modeling with Microsoft DREAD. https://satoricyber.com/glossary/threat-modeling-with-microsoft-dread/

24. Threat Modeling with DREAD. https://cyral.com/glossary/threat-modeling-with-dread/

SCI – Secure Cryptographic Implementation

SCI 2023

Fourth Workshop on Secure Cryptographic Implementation

22 June 2023

Program Chairs

Jingqiang Lin	University of Science and Technology of China, China
Jun Shao	Zhejiang Gongshang University, China

Publication Chair

Bo Luo	University of Kansas, USA

Publicity Chairs

Hao Peng	Zhejiang Normal University, China
Fangyu Zheng	Chinese Academy of Sciences, China

Program Committee

Sebastian Berndt	University of Lübeck, Germany
Florian Caullery	HENSOLDT Cyber GmbH, Germany
Bo Chen	Michigan Technological University, USA
Jiankuo Dong	Nanjing University of Posts and Telecommunications, China
Haixin Duan	Tsinghua University, China
Niall Emmart	NVIDIA Corporation, USA
Johann Großschädl	University of Luxembourg, Luxembourg
Shanqing Guo	Shandong University, China
Bingyu Li	Beihang University, China
Fengjun Li	University of Kansas, USA
Ximeng Liu	Fuzhou University, China
Rongxing Lu	University of New Brunswick, Canada
Chunli Lv	China Agricultural University, China
Di Ma	ZDNS, China
Yuan Ma	Chinese Academy of Sciences, China
Kui Ren	Zhejiang University, China

Ruisheng Shi

Ding Wang
Juan Wang
Danfeng (Daphne) Yao

Fangyu Zheng
Cong Zuo

Beijing University of Posts and
  Telecommunications, China
Nankai University, China
Wuhan University, China
Virginia Polytechnic Institute and State
  University, USA
Chinese Academy of Sciences, China
Nanyang Technological University,
  Singapore

cPSIR: Circuit-Based Private Stateful Information Retrieval for Private Media Consumption

Wenyuan Li[1,2], Wei Wang[1(✉)], Fan Lang[1,2], Linli Lu[1], and Heqing Huang[1]

[1] State Key Laboratory of Information Security, Institute of Information Engineering, Chinese Academy of Sciences, Beijing 100089, China
liwenyuan@iie.ac.cn
[2] School of Cyber Security, University of Chinese Academy of Sciences, Beijing 100089, China

Abstract. Private information retrieval (PIR) is a fundamental cryptographic primitive to protect client privacy. Preprocessing techniques are extensively employed for PIR schemes to minimize online computation. A single-server PIR with preprocessing, namely PSIR, has sublinear computation complexity and prevents collusion attacks in multi-server schemes. Unfortunately, functional limitations exists in state-of-the-art PSIR schemes for real-world applications, such as private media consumption.

Our work cPSIR extends the recent PSIR framework to provide two application features of private media consumption: keyword search and variable-sized file retrieval, for the identifier and payload of database entries, respectively. In cPSIR, a binary search tree structure is utilised to implement mapping from keyword to index and incremental database update. And a logic circuit is designed to characterize file retrieval procedure with current homomorphic schemes BFV and TFHE, considering various database properties. The BFV-based solution outperforms on the computation of a given circuit, without bootstrapping, and has small ciphertext expansion. And the TFHE-based solution is more flexible due to the design of logic gates, while has great potential to improve in bootstrapping with hardware backends. We finally apply cPSIR to private audio consumption with low startup delay (less than 1 s) and high playback rate (320 kbps).

Keywords: Private information retrieval · Private media consumption · Homomorphic Encryption

1 Introduction

Private information retrieval (PIR) [12] is a protocol that allows a client to retrieve an object from a database without revealing the desired object. As

This work was supported by the National Key R&D Program of China (Award No. 2020YFB1005800).

a valuable privacy-preserving mechanism, PIR has many applicable scenarios, including password checkup [3], contact discovery [13], etc. There are two types of PIR (ITPIR involves lightweight operations but demands non-colluding servers; CPIR asks for a single server, avoids making non-collusion assumptions, but is more computationally expensive).

As a major PIR application, private media consumption [19] is beneficial for image, audio, and video content providers supported by paid subscription, like Amazon, Spotify, and Netflix. Though PIR is promising, several challenges of applying it to private media consumption exist: the linear overhead of PIR (It necessitates a linear computation of the database to prevent the scope of the client's query from leaking out); strict deadlines of online media delivery; prescient object index (PIR assumes that clients are aware of the index of objects queried); variable object sizes (PIR assumes objects of identical size).

Popcorn [19], a Netflix-like media delivery system, combined both types of PIR, building on non-collusion assumptions. To handle variable object sizes, Popcorn chooses a representative object, then pads smaller objects and compresses longer objects to the same size which is hard to ensure the quality of content dissemination. This paper explicitly targets image and audio content protection, and avoids making non-collusion assumptions for servers while ensuring media quality.

Recent CPIR works [23,25], named *Private Stateful Information Retrieval* (PSIR), applied preprocessing techniques for the computational overload reduction, without making non-collusion assumptions. The idea of preprocessing is to preprocess the database to generate auxiliary information or hints (which could be stored at the server or clients depending on the proposal) during an offline phase, and then use the hints during an online phase to answer one or more queries with sublinear computation and communication. In PSIR, the public-key operations are performed almost in the offline phase, and plaintext operations involved in the online phase ensure low response latency, addressing the contradiction between PIR linear cost and strict deadlines of media delivery. Compared to video content, PSIR is more applicable to image and audio content protection which asks for smaller cache for hints.

PSIR seems to be an ideal scheme for private media consumption, but it still has some functional limitations, confined to databases with dense object indexes and fixed object sizes).

- PSIR is inapplicable when requiring keyword search (i.e., clients can fetch an object by using a meaningful label or "keyword" rather than an index). Meanwhile, keyword search with search data structures [11] cannot support incremental preprocessing with the database updates which would impact the structure.
- PSIR uses Paillier [24] or BFV [15] scheme for homomorphic integer addition with a fixed object size in the offline phase. *Fully homomorphic encryption* (FHE) [18] schemes like BFV are parameterized so that the circuit representing a given function can be evaluated homomorphically without resorting to the bootstrap operation.

In this paper, we propose a novel PSIR protocol named cPSIR, mainly focusing on its implementation for real-world applications. Our adaptation to private media consumption is embodied in both online and offline phases of PSIR. For keyword search when the database is generally sparse (i.e., the amount of empty objects is significantly larger than that of non-empty objects), we apply a lightweight encoding approach named *Minimal Binary Tree* (MBT) [28]. MBT supports mapping from keyword to index by compressing the distribution of non-empty objects into a binary tree. As a persistent data structure, MBT can also be incrementally updated. For file retrieval, we modify the offline sub-protocol *Private Batched Sum Protocol* (PBSR) of PSIR to *Private Batched File Protocol* (PBFR) by replacing integer addition with bit-wise exclusive OR. We innovatively represent PBFR by a logic circuit, and design PBFR protocols based on FHE schemes aiming at database properties. Based on state-of-the-art PIR schemes, we design a BFV-based file retrieval scheme, oPBFR, for databases with constant length and number of objects. While schemes like TFHE [10] are devised with the primary purpose of minimizing the computation overhead induced by the bootstrapping, supporting logic gate operations. Then we apply TFHE to PSIR for the first time to implement a more flexible PBFR named tPBFR. Moreover, we apply existing optimizations including packing ciphertexts [9] and hardware-accelerated bootstrapping [2] to enhance the availability of our protocol.

We give analysis and evaluation for cPSIR. Compared with other solutions, cPSIR with MBT not only realizes keyword search and incremental update, but also makes the computation cost linearly related to the number of non-empty objects. We also compare MBT with other sparse data compression schemes supporting keyword-index mapping, and the results show that the encoding size of MBT is about 50% smaller than that of other compression schemes. In addition, we test the costs of FHE operations, including integer computation in BFV and logic gates in TFHE as well as bootstrapping. The results show that oPBFR has advantages on the computation of a given circuit, without bootstrapping. For tPBFR, due to the design of the gates with low noise and computation overhead, the flexibility and feasibility of tPBFR is better than oPBFR, but the number of bootstrapping needs to be further optimized. We finally apply cPSIR for private media consumption when the file is an audio, and design an online PIR for strict startup delay and delivery deadline. Due to the expansion of ciphertext and bootstrapping, offline communication and computation overheads are expensive. But the costs of tPBFR can be optimized by more than 100× with GPU acceleration and LUT packing techniques. The online computation has a small startup delay (less than 1 s) and satisfies the highest playback rate 320 kbps of Spotify.

In summary, the contributions of this work are:

- We propose a novel PSIR protocol, namely cPSIR, satisfying the properties of private media consumption, including strict online deadline, keyword search, and variable-sized file retrieval.

1) We utilise a lightweight binary search tree structure to implement both keyword-index mapping and incremental update.

2) We represent the offline sub-protocol of cPSIR as a logic circuit innovatively for file retrieval. Two concrete solutions are introduced and optimized based on FHE schemes.

- We give performance analysis and evaluation for our cPSIR protocol to prove the usability on private media consumption.

We organize this paper as follows: Sect. 2 provides background of binary search tree and fully homomorphic encryption. In Sect. 3, we give a technical overview and definitions of our protocol. Then we introduce our PSIR with two construction for applications in Sect. 4 and give optimization methods in Sect. 5. Analysis and evaluation of our scheme are given in Sect. 6 and a conclusion is given in Sect. 7.

2 Background and Preliminary

2.1 Minimal Binary Tree

k-d tree [4] is a space-partitioning data structure for organizing points in a multi-dimensional space, which can be used for the compression of sparse data such as a sparse matrix. The ratio of n non-zero elements in a sparse matrix is always less than or equal to 0.05, denoted as the density ds of the matrix. 2-dimensional matrices whose size is s_m are taken as examples in this paper, and ds is equal to n/s_m.

Based on k-d tree, MBT performs an evenly decomposition to a sparse matrix in alternating directions: first *horizontally*, then *vertically*, and so on. Each node in the MBT represents a submatrix, and is stored in one array (or stream) in a breadth-first way. Since the size of the input matrix is given, the locations of all child nodes can be computed. In addition, all nodes of an MBT contain only two bits. Each of them is set to 1 if the corresponding half of the submatrix (upper/lower or left/right) contains at least one non-zero element, otherwise it is set to 0. Depending on the distribution of non-zero elements, Eq. 1 and Eq. 2 are the lower bound and the upper bound of MBT space complexity. We give an example of MBT format of a matrix in Fig. 1.

$$S_{MBT_l} = 2 \cdot (n - 1 + log_2(s_m/n)) = 2 \cdot (n - 1 - log_2 d) \tag{1}$$

$$S_{MBT_u} \approx 2 \cdot n(1 + log_2(s_m/n)) = 2 \cdot n(1 - log_2 d) \tag{2}$$

2.2 Fully Homomorphic Encryption

The security of lattice-based FHE is based on the hardness of *Learning With Ring* (LWE) or its variant on the polynomial ring (RLWE).

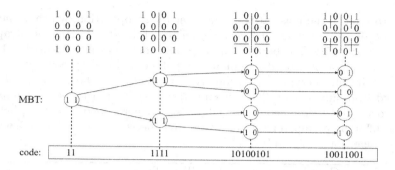

Fig. 1. MBT format of a matrix.

BFV. In the BFV scheme, plaintexts are polynomials of degree at most N with integer coefficients modulo t from the quotient ring $\mathbb{Z}_t[x]/(x^N + 1)$. The *polynomial modulus degree*, N, is a power of 2, and t is the *plaintext modulus* that determines how much data can be packed into a single BFV plaintext. Ciphertexts in BFV consist of two polynomials, each of which is in $\mathbb{Z}_q[x]/(x^N+1)$. Here q is the *coefficient modulus* that affects how much noise a ciphertext can contain, as well as the security of the cryptosystem. In addition to the standard operations of a cryptosystem (key generation, encryption, decryption), BFV also supports homomorphic addition, plaintext multiplication, and multiplication.

TFHE. TFHE is a fully homomorphic cryptosystem with security based on a torus variant of Learning With Error (LWE) named TLWE. We denote the real Torus as $\mathbb{T} = \mathbb{R}/\mathbb{Z} = \mathbb{R} \bmod 1$. $\mathbb{T}_N[X]$ is the module $\mathbb{R}[X]/(X^N + 1) \bmod 1$ of torus polynomials, where N is a power of 2 and the set 0, 1 is written as $\mathbb{B}$. A TLWE sample is a pair $(b, \mathbf{a}) \in \mathbb{T}^{n+1}$, where $\mathbf{a}$ is sampled uniformly over $\mathbb{T}^n$ and $b = \langle \mathbf{a}, \mathbf{s} \rangle + e$. The secret key $\mathbf{s}$ and error e are sampled from a key distribution χ on $\mathbb{Z}^n$ and a Gaussian with standard deviation $\alpha > 0$. TFHE has two variants of TLWE sample. TLWE is extended to polynomial Torus to obtain a TRLWE sample. A TGSW sample is the matrix extension of TLWE, and each row is a TLWE sample.

External Product. An external product $\boxdot$ that maps $\boxdot$: TLWE $\times$ TGSW $\longrightarrow$ TLWE can be defined by TFHE. The product of the TGSW ciphertext of a polynomial message and the TLWE ciphertext of a polynomial message becomes a TLWE ciphertext of a polynomial message. External product can also be computed between a RGSW [7] ciphertext and a RLWE ciphertext can outputs a RLWE ciphertext. External product is used in Controlled MUX, called CMux (Eq. 3).

$$\text{CMux}(c, a, b) = b + c \boxdot (a - b) \tag{3}$$

Bootstrapping. Each TFHE logic operation inevitably introduces a certain amount of noise into the resulting ciphertext. A bootstrapping has to be performed to remove the noise at the end of each logic operation, which is the bottleneck of all proposals for FHE schemes. The details of a TFHE bootstrapping can be viewed in [10]. The bootstrapping procedure is shown in Algorithm 1. The *BlindRotate* algorithm rotates a plaintext polynomial encrypted as a TRLWE ciphertext by an encrypted position. And messages can be homomorphically unpacked from any slot of TRLWE ciphertext using the (noiseless) *SampleExtract* procedure. A *KeySwitch* procedure is also performed to switch between keys in different parameter sets and to switch between the scalar and polynomial message spaces $\mathbb{T}$ and $\mathbb{T}_N[X]$.

Algorithm 1. Gate bootstrapping TLWE-to-TLWE

    Input: A TLWE sample $(b, \mathbf{a})$ whose plaintext is $x \in \mathbb{B}$, a constent $\mu_1 \in \mathbb{T}$, a bootstrapping key $\mathbf{BK} = (BK_i)_{i \in [1,n]}$.
    Output: A TLWE sample $(b, \mathbf{a})$ encrypting $x \cdot \mu_1$.
1: $\mu = \frac{1}{2}\mu_1 \in \mathbb{T}$
2: $\bar{b} = \lfloor 2Nb \rceil$ and $\bar{a}_i = \lfloor 2Na_i \rceil$ for each $i \in [1, n]$
3: $v := (1 + X + \ldots + X^{N/2}) \cdot X^{N/2} \cdot \mu$
4: ACC $\leftarrow$ *BlindRotate*$((0, v), (a_1, \ldots, a_n, b), \mathbf{BK})$
    return: $(0, \mu) + SampleExtract(\text{ACC})$

---

3   Technical Overview and Definitions

We assume that the client holds a keyword of queried object, and the server holds a database containing n objects. We denote the domain of queried keywords by D $(|D| \gg n)$, and the density of the database by $ds = n/|D|$ which is always no more than 5% in practice.

3.1   Setting

Our protocol follows the original PSIR protocol introduced by Patel et al. [25] which performs an offline phase and an online phase. We make improvements for both phases, and propose two sub-protocol to realize private file retrieval and keyword search.

Offline Phase. In the protocol of Patel et al., the client privately retrieves some hints from the server, which is defined as *Private batched sum retrieval* (PBSR). In PBSR step, given c subsets $S_1, \ldots, S_c$, each consisting of k random indices, the client privately retrieves the sum $s_1, \ldots, s_c$ of all objects in each subset. Generally, PBSR can encode databases with batch code [20] to support multiple queries, called BatchCodePBSR [25]. A (n, m, k, b)-batch code takes n objects as input, and produces a set of m codewords, distributed among b buckets. Thus any k objects can be retrieved from b buckets by performing a normal CPIR to fetch at most one codeword from each bucket. Mughees et al. [23] proposed an efficient PBSR construction OnionPBSR with Beneš copy networks [14]. For simplicity of exposition, BatchCodePBSR with (n, m, k, k)-batch code is used as a template throughout this paper.

Private Batched File Retrieval. For private media consumption, we modify PBSR to *Private Batched File Retrieval* (PBFR), when the object type is converted from fixed-length integer to variable-length file. Padding, compressing, and splitting objects have to be performed to ensure computational efficiency in BFV, sacrificing the quality of services. Thus bit-wise exclusive OR (XOR) can be adopted, and the client privately retrieves the results of XOR $r_1, ..., r_c$ for each subset. We design two circuits of PBFR consisting of Boolean gates in Sect. 4.2 for fixed-length and variable-length files.

Online Phase. Based on offline PBFR, the client uses the subset XOR results obtained to retrieve objects. Suppose the client wants to retrieve an object i, he will find an unused subset S' in the local storage that does not contain i and the XOR is r'. Then the client splits the database into random ordered partitions, each of size $k+1$ and finds the partition P' equal to $S' \cup i$. Given a succinct description of the partition by the client, the server can XOR the contained objects for each partition which is a plaintext operation. The client then performs a stateless PIR to retrieve the XOR result of P', and recovers the i-th object by XOR it with r'. We suppose that the client can obtain the length of i-th object with the original PSIR. Once the client runs out of subset XOR results to use, it will perform the offline phase again.

PSIR by Keywords. The client is supposed to be aware of the indices of objects in original protocol. In private media consumption, the client queries with keywords of media files, rather than the indices which cannot be obtained. And simply partition the domain of keywords with PRF is quite expensive. Thus our protocol needs to support keyword-index mapping for the client, and each subset contains k keywords randomly picked from all keywords of n non-empty objects. For updates in the database, incremental preprocessing for non-empty objects when implementing keyword search can avoid re-execution of the offline phase, and no effective method has been proposed. In Sect. 4.1, we realize PSIR by keywords and design an incremental update algorithm which can help refresh hints.

3.2   Baseline CPIR

As the objects in the database are media files, we choose OnionPIR [23] as the baseline CPIR to decrease communication cost. As shown in Fig. 2 for example, OnionPIR represents a bucket as a 3-dimensional hypercube. The first dimension's query vector consists of BFV ciphertexts, and plaintext multiplication is operated between the query vector and plaintexts. The remaining dimensions are RGSW ciphertexts of 2-bit query vectors, and external product that introduces noise additively is operated between the query vector and the result of the previous dimension. We assume the size of first dimension is N_1 and the rest dimension size is $N_2 = 2$.

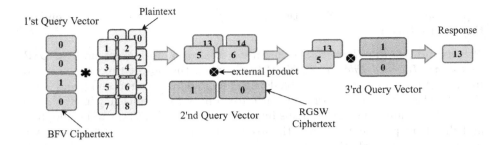

Fig. 2. OnionPIR.

4 Our Protocol: *c*PSIR

We propose a novel PSIR named *c*PSIR consisting of two constructions: 1) a lightweight binary search tree supporting keyword search and incremental update; 2) efficient circuits for diverse database properties with homomorphic operations.

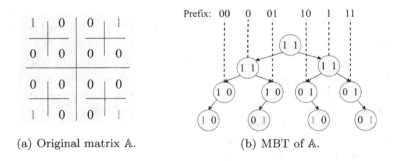

(a) Original matrix $\mathbb{A}$.   (b) MBT of $\mathbb{A}$.

Fig. 3. Matrix in MBT.

4.1 PSIR by Keywords

For applications supporting keyword search, the construction of MBT code can be used for keyword-index mapping. Figure 3a and 3b show an example of matrix $\mathbb{A}$ and its representation in the MBT format. We also give the prefix of matched keywords in each node which represents a submatrix of $\mathbb{A}$. In the initial stage of PSIR, the server represents the query domain D as a sparse matrix, where the value of a bit in the position of a non-empty object is set to 1. Then the server encodes the matrix containing the distribution of non-empty objects, and sends the MBT code (e.g., 11111110100101110011001 for $\mathbb{A}$) to the client. Given the MBT code, the client can index all non-empty objects with keywords, and randomly generate subsets with an equal size for them. In addition, the code can also assist with the filtration of the queries that are empty in the database.

Incremental Update. Relying on the fixed decomposition method, MBT is a persistent data structure which supports incremental update. Addition and deletion operations[1] will not alter the structure of MBT but will only influence the corresponding nodes. The update information $u_i = \{t_i, p_i\}$ consists of the operation type t_i (i.e., add or delete) and the position p_i of changed bit in the bottom layer of MBT. Given the update information, the client will perform incremental update algorithm in Algorithm 2 to bottom-up refresh the MBT. Based on the updated MBT, the client can request updated objects privately from the database to refresh the local hints which should be sampled uniformly from all keywords of non-empty objects in the updated database.

Algorithm 2. Incremental update

Input: An MBT M representing the database, the update information $U = u_1, u_2, ..., u_t$.
Output: The updated MBT M'
Notation: M_p: the bit value in postion p, $parent(u_i)$: the information of parent bit of u_i, $neighbor(u_i)$: the neighbor bit in the same node as u_i.
1: $ulist = U, M' = M$
2: **while** $ulist$ **do**
3:     **for** $u_i \in ulist$ **do**
4:         **if** $t_i ==$ "add" **then** $M'_{p_i} = 1$
5:             **if** $!neighbor(u_i)$ **then**
6:                 $ulist.push(parent(u_i))$
7:                 $M'_{p_i\%2?p_i-1:p_i+1} = 0$
8:         **else**
9:             **if** $neighbor(u_i) = 0$ **then**
10:                $ulist.push(parent(u_i))$
11:                $M'_{p_i} = M'_{p_i\%2?p_i-1:p_i+1} = null$
12:         $ulist.pop(u_i)$

4.2 Private Batched File Retrieval

To support private file retrieval, we replace homomorphic addition between numbers by homomorphic XOR between files in PBFR, and design the retrieval procedure as a logic circuit consisting of gate operations. We compare the FHE schemes which support gate operations, and design appropriate circuits for various applications. According to specific features of applications, we propose two PBFR schemes, based on BFV and TFHE respectively. We first construct a circuit of PBFR with BFV for constant file lengths and static databases, and then a novel circuit with TFHE for various file lengths and dynamic databases.

---

[1] Modification of objects is ignored since payloads are not encoded in MBT.

Homomorphic Schemes Supporting Gate Operations. For BFV, it is possible to emulate Boolean circuits in integer schemes by setting a non-power-of-two polynomial ring degree, which causes addition to behave as XOR and multiplication to behave as AND. While in Microsoft SEAL library [21] which implements BFV, bit-wise computation is not supported since it hurts the performance of either homomorphic evaluation or encryption, or both. Appropriate parameters are chosen to avoid decryption failure caused by noise exceeding the threshold, so bootstrapping is not needed. Thus, BFV is not realistic for circuits of arbitrary depth and operations without prior knowledge of the circuit.

TFHE supports the homomorphic evaluation of the 10 binary gates (e.g., XOR, OR, AND, NOT, etc.), as well as MUX and CMux gates. Distinguished from the other schemes, TFHE can evaluate an arbitrary binary gate on encrypted bits followed by a bootstrapping which is very fast and able to evaluate a function at the same time as it reduces the noise. Despite of additional bootstrapping overhead, TFHE can be computed for arbitrary circuits, especially for a wide range of file lengths.

*o***PBFR.** For applications with a constant file length and database size, we apply OnionPIR with BFV to PBFR, named *o*PBFR, as shown in Fig. 4. We represent *o*PBFR as an arithmetical circuit which has two phases: File Selection and File XOR. Plaintext multiplication is regarded as N_1:1 MUX gate. And external product is regarded as CMux gates with the query vector turning into control bits of CMux gates (i.e., if the query vector is $\{0, 1\}$, the control bit is 1, otherwise it is 0).

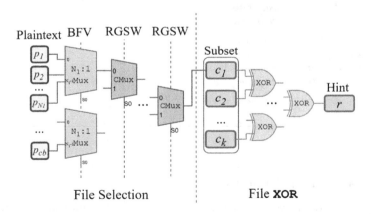

Fig. 4. *o*PBFR.

<u>*Phase 1*</u>: File Selection. For the indices in a subset, the corresponding bucket is known to the client, which contains about cb objects. The inputs of the circuit are plaintexts $p_{1,i}, ..., p_{cb,i}$ of all files in the bucket, and query vectors in BFV and RGSW ciphertexts. After N_1:1 MUX gate and CMux gate operations, the output of

selection is a BFV ciphertext of the queried file. The circuit depth of file selection depends on the number of dimensions.

Phase 2: File XOR. The files whose indices are in the subset go through addition operations of BFV to output encrypted hint r of the subset. And the circuit depth of file XOR depends on the subset size.

tPBFR. For applications with various file lengths and a dynamic database, considering the computational efficiency, BFV may sacrifice the quality of service when compressing or splitting objects. Thus, imitating the circuit of *o*PBFR, we propose *t*PBFR as a Boolean circuit in Fig. 5, using the TFHE scheme. The inputs of the circuit consist of i-th non-null bit of plaintexts $p_{1,i}, ..., p_{cb',i}$ ($cb' \leq cb$), and query vectors in TLWE and TGSW ciphertexts. The output is a TLWE ciphertext, one bit of the hint r.

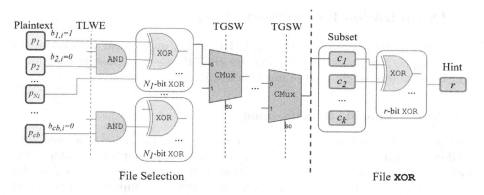

Fig. 5. *t*PBFR.

Phase 1: File Selection. TLWE and TGSW take the place of BFV and RGSW in *o*PBFR. The first dimension's query vector consists of TLWE ciphertexts, and N_1:1 MUX in this paper is decomposed into AND (between a plaintext and a ciphertext, equivalent to the ciphertext XOR with itself) and XOR. If the input bit is 0, the relevant TLWE ciphertext has to perform AND before XOR, otherwise the input bit in plaintext can be directly involved in XOR. The remaining dimensions are TGSW ciphertexts, and CMux gate is operated, similar to *o*PBFR.

Phase 2: File XOR. XOR gate in TFHE replaces the addition operation in BFV. We will discuss the XOR operations for various object sizes in Sect. 6.1.

The steps of *t*PBFR for one bit of a hint are summarized in Algorithm 3. XOR of multiple bits *multbit_*XOR can be simply performed as pairwise recursive XOR, and the number of XOR operations is related to the shorter ciphertext.

Algorithm 3. tPBFR for one bit of a hint

Input: query vectors $v_1, ..., v_d$ for each database dimension, the size N_1 of first dimension, the subset size k, the bits $b_1, ..., b_{cb}$ of cb files in each bucket.

Output: The encrypted bit b of hint.

1: $g = \lceil cb/N_1 \rceil, temp[g] = \{0\}$
2: $b_i \leftarrow (b_i == 1) \ ? \ v_1[i]; \ \texttt{XOR}(b_i, b_i)$ for each $i \in range(cb)$
3: $temp[i] \leftarrow multbit\_\texttt{XOR}(N_1, b_{iN_1}, .., b_{(i+1)N_1})$ for each $i \in range(g)$
4: **for** $k' = 1 \rightarrow k$ **do**
5:     **for** $d' = 2 \rightarrow d$ **do**
6:         $temp[i] \leftarrow \quad \texttt{CMux}(v_{d'}[1], temp[i], temp[i \ + \ 1])$ for each $i \ \in$ $range(0, \lceil g/2^{d'-1} \rceil, 2)$
7:     $C_{k'} \leftarrow temp[0]$
8: $b \leftarrow multbit\_\texttt{XOR}(k, C_1, ..., C_k)$

---

5 Optimization for Bootstrapping

Since the computational overhead of TFHE is still impractical with each-gate bootstrapping, we apply optimizations for tPBFR based on existing techniques which have been widely used in machine learning.

5.1 Programmable Bootstrapping

The programmable bootstrapping [8] allows resetting the noise to a fixed level while at the same time evaluating a function on the input ciphertext. Our arithmetic function of recursive CMux operations can be expressed with a *Look-Up Table* (LUT) containing a list of input values (each one composed by l bits) and corresponding LUT values for the sub-functions.

The evaluation of an LUT can be accelerated by horizontal and vertical packing bits in a TLWE ciphertext into a TRLWE ciphertext. In *horizontal packing*, the inputs can be computed file-wise rather than bit-wise. In *vertical packing*, as shown in Fig. 6b, a TLWE ciphertext of a single bit is taken from each file and packed into a TRLWE ciphertext. Horizontal packing can be mixed with vertical packing to speed up the evaluation. A compressed CMux tree is used to select the desired TRLWE. Then *BlindRotate* (similar to Gate Bootstrapping in Algorithm 1) rotates the desired result to the first one (the 0 position), which is extracted using *SampleExtract*.

For various object sizes, it is consuming to find an uniform split criterion for all objects for horizonal packing, thus we adopt vertical packing in our scheme whose split criterion depends on the bucket size. In the File Selection phase after the first dimension, the input values are the result of the first dimension shown in Fig. 6a when $n' = \lceil cb/N_1 \rceil$ and corresponding LUT values for the sub-functions are controlled by the TGSW query vectors.

5.2 Hardware-Accelerated Bootstrapping

The most promising efforts to make bootstrapping in FHE practical are focused on acceleration via hardware platforms. FHE workloads exhibit a high level of task and data parallelism that can be exploited by parallel processors. A low-cost but computationally efficient and highly optimized hardware co-processor is an ideal platform for accelerating the execution of bootstrapping. The achieved and projected speedup from hardware acceleration of FHE uses hardware backends, including CPU-AVX-512 [5], FPGA [26], GPU [22], and ASIC [16]. The bootstrapping procedure requires expensive Fast Fourier Transform (FFT) operations ($O(nlogn)$). The existing implementation uses the Fastest Fourier Transform in the West (FFTW) [17] which inherently uses AVX. GPU-accelerated TFHE libraries like cuFHE [1] (26× speedup) and NuFHE [2] (100× speedup) port the TFHE to GPU and device novel optimizations for boolean and arithmetic circuits employing the multitude of cores. Among them, [22] achieves a speedup of 20× for any 32-bit boolean operation.

	Inputs			TGSW ciphertexts		
I_1	$b_{1,1}$	$b_{1,2}$ ⋅⋅	$b_{1,l}$	$C_{1,1}$	$C_{1,2}$ ⋯	$C_{1,l}$
I_2	$b_{2,1}$	$b_{2,2}$ ⋯	$b_{2,l}$	$C_{2,1}$	$C_{2,2}$ ⋯	$C_{2,l}$
⋮	⋮	⋮	⋮	⋮	⋮	⋮
$I_{n'}$	$b_{n',1}$	$b_{n',2}$ ⋯	$b_{n',l}$	$C_{n',1}$	$C_{n',2}$ ⋯	$C_{n',l}$

(a) LUT

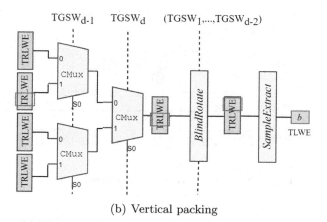

(b) Vertical packing

Fig. 6. Horizontal packing and vertical packing with LUT.

6   Analysis and Evaluation

We give an analysis on the performance of MBT, and PBFR with BFV and TFHE. We also evaluate the coding size of MBT and the operation costs of oPBFR and tPBFR. Then we apply cPSIR with oPBFR and tPBFR to private media consumption.

6.1   Performance Analysis

We analyze our constructions for PSIR respectively, and present the performance overhead through complexity analysis. For keyword search with MBT, Table 1 compares the asymptotic complexity of our proposed PBSR with the PBSR schemes given by Patel et al. [25] and Mughees et al. [23]. Since $|D| \gg n$, our PBSR with MBT has the request and computation overloads than existing PBSR schemes, proportional to the database size other than the query domain size.

Table 1. Comparison of response, request and computation of our MBT-based PBSR with existing PBSR for keyword search.

	BatchCodePBSR [25]	OnionPBSR [23]	Our PBSR
Response	$O(k)$	$O(k)$	$O(k)$
Request	$O(k)$	$O(|D| \cdot log(|D|) + |D|)$	$O(n \cdot log(n) + n)$
Computation	$O(k \cdot |D| + |D|)$	$O(|D| \cdot log(|D|) + |D|)$	$O(n \cdot log(n) + n)$

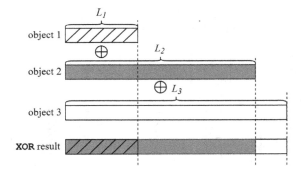

Fig. 7. XOR operations of variable-sized objects.

We first demonstrate XOR operations for variable-sized objects. As a result shown in Fig. 7, with the exception of the longest object, the sum of the object lengths represents the total number of XOR operations. And the length of the longest object determines the size of the final XOR result of multiple objects. For private media retrieval, we assume that l' bits of TLWE can be packed into a TRLWE sample, and the operations can be accelerated w times after hardware acceleration. As shown in Table 2, the operations in oPBFR include plaintext multiplication, external product, and addition. And the operations in tPBFR consist of AND (between plaintexts and TLWE ciphertexts), CMux and XOR gates. In addition, We give the number of optimization operations in tPBFR after horizonal packing and hardware acceleration. oPBFR has advantages on the computation of a given circuit without bootstrapping when the file length is constant. In tPBFR, the operation number of a file is linearly related to the file length. While in oPBFR, the operation number depends on the preset BFV parameters. Moreover, due to the design of two optimization methods, tPBFR can be feasible and has better flexibility for variable circuits.

Table 2. The number of bit-wise gate operations in oPBFR and tPBFR for one subset. k, l and cb are the sizes of subset, object, and bucket. For tPBFR, l is the size of the object lengths except the longest object.

PBFR	AND (plain mult)	XOR (add)	CMux (extern)	bootstrapping
oPBFR	$lk \cdot cb$	$add_t = lk - l + lk \cdot cb(N_1 - 1)/N_1$	$lk \cdot (cb/N_1 - 1)$	N/A
tPBFR	N/A	$add_t + lk \cdot cb/2$	$lk \cdot (cb/N_1 - 1)$	$add_t + lk \cdot cb/2$
programmable tPBFR	N/A	$add_t/w + lk \cdot cb/2w$	$lk/l' \cdot (cb/N_1 - 1)/w$	$add_t/w + lk \cdot cb/2w$

6.2 Evaluation

Experimental Setting. We run our experiments on 4-core Intel Skylake i7-6700 3.4 GHz, NVIDIA Corporation GM107GLM [Quadro M1000M] (CUDA Version 11.7), 16 GB DRAM, Ubuntu 18.04. And we implement our scheme using gcc 8.4.0, Microsoft SEAL (version 4.0.0) [21], TFHE (version 1.1) [29] and NuFHE [2] libraries.

Parameters. For BFV, we use degree polynomials $N = 4096$, coefficient modulus $q = 124$ bits and plaintext modulus $t = 60$ bits, thus the expansion factor is $F = 2log(q)/log(t) \approx 4.2$ and 30 KB plaintext can be packed into one ciphertext. For TFHE, we choose the parameters to guarantee 128-bit security when the expansion factor is constant and equal to $F = 2 \times 10^3$. A TRLWE sample whose size is 8 KBytes can pack 1024 TLWE samples to reduce the ciphertext expansion to 62.5×, encrypting 1024 bits.

For keyword search, we give the coding size of MBT in Table 3, compared with common sparse storage formats including Coordinate (COO) [27] and Compressed Sparse Row (CSR) [6]. We set the domain size $|D| = 2^{12}, 2^{16}, 2^{20}$ and the density $ds = 0.75\%, 1.25\%, 1.25\%, 5\%$. MBT code size is less than 60 kB when $|D|$ is 2^{20} and the number of non-empty entries is about 10k. The results show that the MBT encoding size is acceptable for both the offline traffic and the client-side storage.

Table 3. Coding size (KB) of Sparse Storage Formats.

$|D|$	COO [27]			CSR [6]			MBT [28]		
	2^{12}	2^{16}	2^{20}	2^{12}	2^{16}	2^{20}	2^{12}	2^{16}	2^{20}
$ds = 0.75\%$	0.09	1.97	39.32	0.009	1.30	21.45	0.05	0.88	14.15
$ds = 1.25\%$	0.15	3.28	65.54	0.13	1.99	34.69	0.08	1.32	21.25
$ds = 2.5\%$	0.31	6.55	131.07	0.22	3.66	67.58	0.14	2.28	36.12
$ds = 5\%$	0.61	13.11	262.14	0.38	6.97	133.25	0.23	3.74	59.80

For private media retrieval, we test the costs of operations required in oPBFR and tPBFR as shown in Table 4. The costs of gates in TFHE exclude the cost of a bootstrapping. The cost of MUX mainly includes two AND which requires a bootstrapping without *KeySwitch*. For a given circuit, BFV outperforms by integer operations, without bootstrapping. Once a bootstrapping is required, the computation overhead of BFV increases significantly. While ignoring the cost of bootstrapping, tPBFR has a better performance than oPBFR based on gate operations. And compared with external product in oPBFR, the cost of external product in TFHE is cheaper than that in BFV, which reduces the computation overload in the File Selection phase of tPBFR. Moreover, CMux gate in TFHE with LUT is more suitable for large scale circuits. However, the overhead of tPBFR with bootstrapping, even if the number of bootstrapping is optimized, is much higher than oPBFR and requires further optimization.

Table 4. Operation costs (ms) in BFV and TFHE.

library	Boots.	AND (mult)	XOR (add)	plain mult	CMux (extern)	NOR	MUX
SEAL [15]	$>10^6$	3.82	0.07	0.61	2.67	N/A	N/A
TFHE [10]	13	0.0045	0.0057	N/A	1.10	0.0045	26
NuFHE [2]	0.13	–	–	N/A	–	–	0.22

6.3   Application: Private Media Consumption

We take private audio consumption as an example for audio files which have an extra dimension, time, and thus are larger than static image files. In our experiments for applying cPSIR, we set a music library of $n = 4096$ songs with average playing time of $T = 4$ minutes, playback rate $\mu = 320$ kbps. We set the parameters $k = \sqrt{n} = 64$, $N_1 = 32$, and $cb = 192$ when $m = 3n$. We evaluate cPSIR with tPBFR, and report the offline/online computational cost, request size, and response size.

Table 5. Costs of oPBFR and tPBFR for one hint.

	oPBFR	tPBFR (optimized)
Request size (KB)	9.4	97.02
Response size (MB)	39.5	585.94
Computation cost (sec/bit)	9.32	2.70

Offline PBFR. The per-hint costs for oPBFR and tPBFR after optimization are shown in Table 5. There is no storage problem after decryption for offline hints. The results show that the communication cost of oPBFR is 90% lower than tPBFR. And the bit-wise computation cost of tPBFR has about 60% lower than oPBFR. While in practice, oPBFR still has its advantages due to the small expansion factor and SIMD packing technique of BFV, especially for large object sizes. For private media consumption, the offline computation will not influence the online query, and only needs to be performed once since the hints can be incremental refreshed. Thus, it is feasible to implement PBFR using TFHE in our scheme.

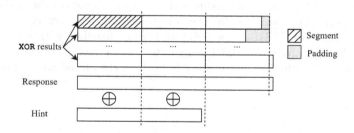

Fig. 8. Private online media retrieval.

Private Online Media Retrieval. We design an online solution for strict deadline and various object sizes for media retrieval, as shown in Fig. 8. After XOR the contained objects for each partition, the length of XOR result is equal to the length of the largest object in the partition. All the results are with high probability in an order of magnitude. Thus, after splitting the result into segments, the server pads the shorter objects slightly and does not need to

Table 6. Costs of private online media retrieval for various segment sizes.

segment size (KB)	private online media retrieval			
	30	120	480	1960
Request size (KB)	1.05	1.05	1.05	1.05
Response size (KB)	137.5	512.1	2100.3	8450.5
Computation cost/delay (ms)	21.69	95.98	391.4	1573.2

compress the longer objects. Then, in the stateless CPIR, the server successively adds the segments of each partition with addition operations in BFV, and returns the sum to the client. The client recovers the target file by XOR the binary representation of the sum and the corresponding hint. We set the segment size to a multiple of 30 KB so each segment can be packed into BFV plaintexts. The startup delay (including server's computation and client's decryption) should be unobservable (i.e., less than 1 s). The results show that the segment size should be less than 1200 KB and then the playback rate is larger than 320 kbps Table 6.

7   Conclusion

Our work cPSIR extends recent PSIR framework to satisfy two crucial application features: keyword search and variable-sized file retrieval. We implement keyword-index mapping and incremental update through a lightweight encoding, and implement circuit-design-based file retrieval through FHE schemes for various database characteristics. The experimental results show that the encoding hint has an acceptable size and reduces the computational overhead. Moreover, BFV-based solution is suitable for the computation for a given circuit, without bootstrapping, while TFHE-based solution is more feasible, with room for optimization. We also apply our PSIR scheme to private media consumption when the file is an audio file and find it feasible both in the offline and online phases.

References

1. CUDA-accelerated fully homomorphic encryption library (2019). https://github. com/vernamlab/cuFHE
2. NuFHE, a GPU-powered torus FHE implementation (2019). https://github.com/ nucypher/nufhe
3. Ali, A., et al.: Communication-computation trade-offs in PIR. In: 30th USENIX Security Symposium (USENIX Security 2021), pp. 1811–1828. USENIX Association (2021). https://www.usenix.org/conference/usenixsecurity21/presentation/ ali
4. Bentley, J.L.: Multidimensional binary search trees used for associative searching. Commun. ACM **18**(9), 509–517 (1975). https://doi.org/10.1145/361002.361007

5. Boemer, F., Kim, S., Seifu, G., de Souza, F.D.M., Gopal, V.: Intel HEXL: accelerating homomorphic encryption with Intel AVX512-IFMA52. In: Proceedings of the 9th on Workshop on Encrypted Computing & Applied Homomorphic Cryptography, pp. 57–62 (2021)

6. Buluç, A., Fineman, J.T., Frigo, M., Gilbert, J.R., Leiserson, C.E.: Parallel sparse matrix-vector and matrix-transpose-vector multiplication using compressed sparse blocks. In: Proceedings of the Twenty-First Annual Symposium on Parallelism in Algorithms and Architectures, pp. 233–244 (2009)

7. Chen, H., Chillotti, I., Ren, L.: Onion ring ORAM: efficient constant bandwidth oblivious RAM from (leveled) TFHE. Cryptology ePrint Archive, Paper 2019/736 (2019). https://eprint.iacr.org/2019/736

8. Chillotti, I., Gama, N., Georgieva, M., Izabachène, M.: Faster packed homomorphic operations and efficient circuit bootstrapping for TFHE. In: Takagi, T., Peyrin, T. (eds.) ASIACRYPT 2017. LNCS, vol. 10624, pp. 377–408. Springer, Cham (2017). https://doi.org/10.1007/978-3-319-70694-8_14

9. Chillotti, I., Gama, N., Georgieva, M., Izabachene, M.: Improving TFHE: faster packed homomorphic operations and efficient circuit bootstrapping (2017)

10. Chillotti, I., Gama, N., Georgieva, M., Izabachène, M.: TFHE: fast fully homomorphic encryption over the torus. J. Cryptol. 33(1), 34–91 (2020). https://doi.org/10.1007/s00145-019-09319-x

11. Chor, B., Gilboa, N., Naor, M.: Private information retrieval by keywords. Citeseer (1997)

12. Chor, B., Kushilevitz, E., Goldreich, O., Sudan, M.: Private information retrieval. J. ACM 45(6), 965–981 (1998). https://doi.org/10.1145/293347.293350

13. Danezis, G., Borisov, N., Goldberg, I.: DP5: a private presence service. Proc. Priv. Enhancing Technol. 2015(2), 4–24 (2015)

14. Deng, Y., Lee: Crosstalk-free conjugate networks for optical multicast switching. J. Lightwave Technol. 24(10), 3635–3645 (2006). https://doi.org/10.1109/jlt.2006.882249

15. Fan, J., Vercauteren, F.: Somewhat practical fully homomorphic encryption. Cryptology ePrint Archive, Paper 2012/144 (2012). https://eprint.iacr.org/2012/144

16. Feldmann, A., et al.: F1: a fast and programmable accelerator for fully homomorphic encryption (extended version). CoRR abs/2109.05371 (2021). https://arxiv.org/abs/2109.05371

17. Frigo, M., Johnson, S.G.: FFTW: an adaptive software architecture for the FFT. In: Proceedings of the 1998 IEEE International Conference on Acoustics, Speech and Signal Processing, ICASSP 1998 (Cat. No. 98CH36181), vol. 3, pp. 1381–1384. IEEE (1998)

18. Gentry, C.: A fully homomorphic encryption scheme. Stanford University (2009)

19. Gupta, T., Crooks, N., Mulhern, W., Setty, S., Alvisi, L., Walfish, M.: Scalable and private media consumption with popcorn. In: Proceedings of the 13th USENIX Conference on Networked Systems Design and Implementation, NSDI 2016, USA, pp. 91–107. USENIX Association (2016)

20. Ishai, Y., Kushilevitz, E., Ostrovsky, R., Sahai, A.: Batch codes and their applications. In: Proceedings of the Thirty-Sixth Annual ACM Symposium on Theory of Computing, pp. 262–271 (2004)

21. Microsoft SEAL (2022). https://github.com/microsoft/SEAL/tree/4.0.0

22. Morshed, T., Aziz, M.M.A., Mohammed, N.: CPU and GPU accelerated fully homomorphic encryption. CoRR abs/2005.01945 (2020). https://arxiv.org/abs/2005.01945

23. Mughees, M.H., Chen, H., Ren, L.: OnionPIR: response efficient single-server PIR. In: Proceedings of the 2021 ACM SIGSAC Conference on Computer and Communications Security, pp. 2292–2306 (2021)

24. Paillier, P.: Public-key cryptosystems based on composite degree residuosity classes. In: Stern, J. (ed.) EUROCRYPT 1999. LNCS, vol. 1592, pp. 223–238. Springer, Heidelberg (1999). https://doi.org/10.1007/3-540-48910-X_16

25. Patel, S., Persiano, G., Yeo, K.: Private stateful information retrieval. In: Proceedings of the 2018 ACM SIGSAC Conference on Computer and Communications Security, pp. 1002–1019 (2018)

26. Pedrosa, A.R.: Implementing fully homomorphic encryption schemes in FPGA-based systems. Technical report, ETS de Ingenieros Informáticos (UPM), Madrid, Spain (2016)

27. Scipy.sparse.coo_matrix (2022). https://docs.scipy.org/doc/scipy/reference/generated/scipy.sparse.coo_matrix.html

28. Simecek, I., Langr, D.: Tree-based space efficient formats for storing the structure of sparse matrices. Scalable Comput. Pract. Exp. **15**(1), 1–20 (2014)

29. TFHE (2020). https://github.com/tfhe/tfhe

A Deep-Learning Approach for Predicting Round Obfuscation in White-Box Block Ciphers

Tongxia Deng[1], Ping Li[1(✉)], Shunzhi Yang[1,4], Yupeng Zhang[1], Zheng Gong[1], Ming Duan[2], and Yiyuan Luo[3]

[1] School of Computer Science, South China Normal University, Guangzhou, China
`liping26@mail2.sysu.edu.cn`
[2] State Key Laboratory of Mathematical Engineering and Advanced Computing, Information Engineering University, Zhengzhou, China
[3] School of Computer Science and Engineering, Huizhou University, Huizhou, China
[4] Institute of Applied Artificial Intelligence of the Guangdong-HongKong-Macao Greater Bay Area, Shenzhen Polytechnic, Shenzhen, China

Abstract. It has been proven that side-channel analysis such as differential computation/fault analysis can break white-box implementations without reverse engineering efforts. In 2020, Sun *et al.* proposed noisy rounds as a countermeasure to mitigate the side-channel attacks on white-box block ciphers. The principle is to desynchronize the computation traces of cryptographic implementations by introducing several redundant round functions. In this paper, we propose a multi-label classification method and three deep-learning models (CNN, RNN, and CRNN) to predict the locations of the obfuscated rounds. The experimental results show that the obfuscation of noisy rounds also could not be identified by the deep-learning model. However, the RNN is more effective than the CNN and CRNN with fewer time costs. Subsequently, we investigate the influence of specific components such as the key, affine masking, and transformation matrix on round obfuscation recognition. The extended experiments demonstrate that without the transformation matrix, the deep learning models can successfully distinguish the noisy rounds.

Keywords: White-box block cipher · Side-channel analysis · Noisy rounds · Deep learning

1 Introduction

In the black-box attack context, it is typically assumed that the environment in which the cryptographic algorithms are executed is secure. Attackers only have access to the input and output of the algorithm, and not the computational details. However, side-channel information is often leaked during the execution process, particularly for hardware implementations. In this grey-box

© The Author(s), under exclusive license to Springer Nature Switzerland AG 2023
J. Zhou et al. (Eds.): ACNS 2023 Workshops, LNCS 13907, pp. 419–438, 2023.
https://doi.org/10.1007/978-3-031-41181-6_23

attack context, an attacker can use this side-channel information to build a model to recover the key. As environments in which cryptographic algorithms are used become more varied, such models will be unable to fully evaluate the capability of attackers in real-world applications. The white-box attack context refers to a scenario in which an attacker has full access to the internal data and implementation details of a system or application. In such an environment, the attacker has complete knowledge of the system's structure, code, and data, as well as the ability to manipulate and control all aspects of the system. Chow et al. introduced the seminal white-box implementations of DES [6] and AES (CEJO_WBAES) [7], which fall under the CEJO framework. This framework aims to convert full-round operations into a series of look-up tables (LUTs) with embedded keys. Billet et al. [3] later used a structural approach, called BGE analysis, to deduce the key and encodings from CEJO_WBAES. Subsequently, a number of white-box AES (WBAES) approaches were presented based on the CEJO framework [5,9,26]. However, these solutions were later broken using BGE-like analysis [12,16,17]. Following the CEJO framework, Xiao and Lai [27] proposed the first white-box SM4 (XL_WBSM4) implementation with LUTs and affine transformation. However, Lin and Lai [24] used the BGE analysis principle and differential analysis to recover the key of XL_WBSM4. These BGE-like approaches require the knowledge of implementation details, which implies that the attacker needs reverse engineering efforts. To avoid these time-consuming processes, an alternative is to use side-channel analysis (SCA) techniques to evaluate the security of white-box implementations.

At CHES 2016, Bos et al. [4] presented SCA for white-box implementations, and defined it as differential computation analysis (DCA) and differential fault analysis (DFA). During the execution of the white-box implementation, DCA converts the read and write data of the memory into the computation traces. It then combines the differential power analysis model with statistical analysis to recover key information. DCA poses a significant threat to all white-box AES (WBAES) algorithms because it does not require the knowledge of internal encoding details and reverse engineering processes. Bock et al. [1] analyzed the ineffectiveness of 8-bit linear coding and 4-bit nonlinear coding for DCA protection. Multiple DCA-like attacks were subsequently proposed [2,19,30], to increase the correlation between the sensitive variables and the computation traces. Zhang et al. modified the source code [28,31] and used the computed intermediate value as the computation traces to exploit the key correlation of the white-box SM4 (WBSM4).

Dummy rounds [8] and noisy rounds [22] are two countermeasures proposed to enhance the security of white-box block ciphers against DFA. The main idea of these countermeasures is to randomly insert redundant round functions between the normal round functions. The operation steps and LUTs used by the redundant round functions are the same as those used by normal round functions. Therefore, the only difference between the functions is the normal/redundant key. During an attack, the collected computation traces collected contain redundant intermediate values. These introduce "noise" into the traces, which makes it difficult to discern the original logical structure of the cryptographic algorithm. Additionally, the use of noisy rounds results in misaligned traces. As the locations of these rounds depend on the internal random function, the attackers are unable to distinguish the traces that correspond to normal rounds and noisy rounds. Consequently, identifying the location of noisy rounds is crucial for successful attacks on white-box block ciphers that use these techniques.

As artificial intelligence has been developed, many researchers have explored the application of machine learning methods to practical attacks. Using the black-box model, some researchers have improved attack effectiveness by automatically establishing a link between the power traces and the sensitive variables through model training. Lerman et al. compared their approach with template attacks and demonstrated that support vector machines (SVMs) could attack the masked AES encryption algorithm [13]. At SPACE 2016, Maghrebi et al. proposed a multilayer perceptron (MLP) to enhance template attacks in SCA [14]. Subsequently, convolutional neural networks (CNNs) have been shown to be superior to MLP and SVM. Picek et al. analyzed the role of convolutional neurons and other machine learning techniques from multiple perspectives using SCA and explored the best use cases for the CNN [18]. In 2020, Zaid et al. [29] proposed a strategy for designing a CNN architecture that performs well in side-channel attacks. Wu et al. [25] developed an autoencoder to process the noise in side-channel measurements. Lee and Han [11] applied deep learning to identify dummy operations in block ciphers, which was previously impossible on IC cards. In their experiments, the round boundary was visible in the trace because of the normal repetition, which allowed for successful deep-learning recognition.

However, the trace of a white-box implementation consists of at least 17696-bit binary values. Thus, it is difficult to directly identify the round boundary. Inspired by the experimental method of Lee and Han, we adopted multi-label classification to predict the round obfuscations. Additionally, in this case, the white-box block ciphers are protected by additional countermeasures that result in random traces. Therefore, we constructed three training models based on the characteristics of the data. However, the experimental results showed that it was difficult to distinguish the normal rounds and noisy rounds in the computation traces. To counteract the noisy rounds, we further investigated the factors that affect model learning and demonstrated that the transformation matrix significantly affected the recognition ability of the model.

Our Contribution. In this study, our contribution can be described as follows:

1. **We select the model for predicting round obfuscation.** We propose to overcome the problem of detecting round obfuscation through a multi-label classification approach using appropriate models. Specifically, we built three models based on the CRNN, CNN, and RNN to address this problem. The RNN model captures the relationship between data, the CNN extracts the local features, and the CRNN combines the advantages of both models.

2. **We prove that noisy rounds are applicable to white-box implementations to resist (deep learning aided) SCA.** According to our experimental results, the recognition rates for distinguishing the noisy rounds and

normal rounds were almost the same as the random expectation. The experimental results demonstrated that it is difficult for deep learning methods to distinguish the normal rounds and noisy rounds.

3. **We prove that the extra countermeasures in the white-box block cipher affect the deep learning prediction.** To investigate the factors that affect the recognition of deep learning models, we modified the key, affine masking, and transformation matrix in the algorithm implementation, and generated new traces for model training. Our experimental results demonstrated that affine masking and random keys had little effect on deep learning recognition. Conversely, the transformation matrix had a considerable impact on the recognition accuracy of the algorithm.

2   Preliminaries

2.1   White-Box AES/SM4 with the CEJO Framework

White-Box AES. Chow *et al.* proposed CEJO_WBAES [7]. Figure 1 illustrates the flow of four bytes of the state through Round 1 the data flow for the other bytes is similar. The input state is at the top of the diagram, whereas the output state is at the bottom. The T-box is represented as follows for a byte of input x:

$$T_i^r(x) = S(x \oplus \hat{k}_{r-1}[i]),$$

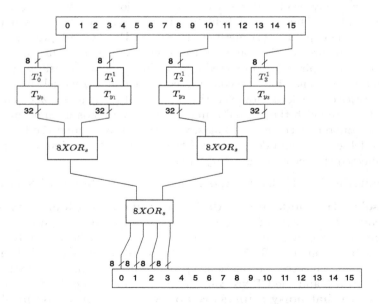

Fig. 1. Data flow for one round of CEJO_WBAES with respect to bytes 0, 5, 10 and 15 of the input state (i.e., plaintext) [15].

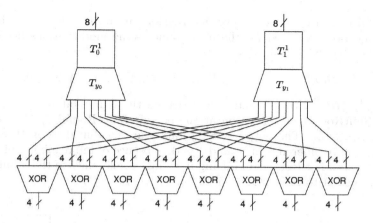

Fig. 2. Computing an XOR of two 32-bit values uses eight XOR tables. The inputs enter at the top of the diagram and the outputs appear at the bottom [15].

where S represents the WBAES S-box, where $i = 0, ..., 15$ and $r = 1, ..., 9$. k_r represents the subkey of the rth round, whereas k_0 represents the key of AddRoundKey before the first round. Let $\hat{k}_{r-1}[i]$ denote the CEJO_WBAES subkey byte in position i, j in Round r.

The Round 10 T-boxes are as follows:

$$T_i^{10}(x) = S(x \oplus \hat{k}_9[i]) \oplus k_{10}[i].$$

MixColumns can be implemented by multiplying a 4×4 matrix over $GF(2^8)$ and a 4×1 vector. Here T_{y_i} is the LUT, where $i = 0, 1, 2, 3$:

$$T_{y0}(x) = x \cdot [2\ 1\ 1\ 3]^T,\ T_{y1}(x) = x \cdot [3\ 2\ 1\ 1]^T,$$
$$T_{y2}(x) = x \cdot [1\ 3\ 2\ 1]^T,\ T_{y3}(x) = x \cdot [1\ 1\ 3\ 2]^T.$$

We define an XOR operation that takes two nibbles as input and maps them to their exclusive-or:

$$XOR(x, y) = x \oplus y.$$

In each of Rounds 1 to 9, 12 32-bit XOR operations are required to determine the result of MixColumns. Figure 2 shows the XOR computation.

Table Composition and Encodings. Wherever a T-box feeds directly into a T_{y_i} table (i.e., in Rounds 1 to 9), we can replace the two separate tables with their composition. The $T\text{-}boxes/T_{y_i}$ are defined as

$$T\text{-}boxes/T_{y_i}^1(x) = MB \cdot T_{y_i}(T_i^r(x)), i = 0, 1, 2, 3.$$
$$T\text{-}boxes/T_{y_i}^r(x) = MB \cdot T_{y_i}(T_i^r((L_i^r) \cdot x)), i = 0, 1, 2, 3, r = 2, 3, ..., 9.$$

As the output of each table, a 32-bit to 32-bit mixing bijection MB is composed. Additionally, four 8-bit to 8-bit mixing bijections L_0^2, L_1^2, L_2^2, and L_3^2 are selected for these tables. To remove the transformation MB, and apply the 8-bit mixing bijections required for the next round, some modifications need to be made. The $BijBox$ is defined as

$$BijBox_i^r(x) = L^{r+1} \circ MB_i^{-1} \cdot x, i = 0, 1, 2, 3, r = 1, 2, ..., 9.$$

Let MB_0^{-1}, MB_1^{-1}, MB_2^{-1}, and MB_3^{-1} denote the four 8-bit to 32-bit tables. For the ShiftRows transformation at the beginning of Round 3, L^r is defined as $L_0^r || L_{13}^r || L_{10}^r || L_7^r$. The outputs of the tables are combined using three XOR tables. The only difference in Round 1 is the absence of input mixing bijections on the T-boxes. For Round 10, mixing bijections are applied to the input of the T-boxes, but not to the output [15].

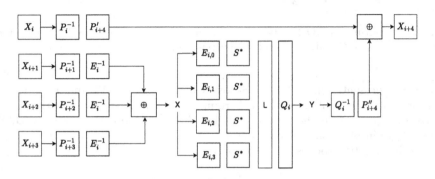

Fig. 3. XL_WBSM4 algorithm scheme.

White-Box SM4. To confound the LUT input and output, XL_WBSM4 uses linear coding. Furthermore, the input part of the subsequent transformation compensates for the confusion caused by the previous output section. The calculation process of a round of the XL_WBSM4 scheme is shown in Fig. 3. Let X_i, X_{i+1}, X_{i+2} and X_{i+3} be the four 32-bit inputs of the ith round, X_{i+4} be a round of 32-bit output. The encoding in this round is $P_{i+j}^{-1} \circ E_i^{-1}(X_{i+j}), (j = 1, 2, 3)$. The $X \rightarrow Y$ transformation process is implemented in the form of LUTs. After the $E_{i,0}, E_{i,1}, E_{i,2}$ and $E_{i,3}$ encoding, the value resulting from the S^* operation is $(x_{i,0}, x_{i,1}, x_{i,2}, x_{i,3})$. Function L denotes the linear transformation of the SM4 algorithm. As the output confusion of this part, Q_i is a reversible affine transformation. Functions P_{i+4}' and P_{i+4}'' are the encoding.

2.2   Dummy/Noisy Rounds Obfuscation Techniques

Dummy Rounds. Gierlichs *et al.* [8] proposed the dummy countermeasure to defend against fault attacks. The basic principle of the dummy round is to prevent attackers from obtaining any information about the secret key by analyzing faulty ciphertext.

Algorithm 1. Feistel cipher with smart dummy rounds. [8]

Input: $P, k_i \ for \ i \in \{1, ..., n\}$ $(n \ subkeys \ from \ key \ K)$ (β, α, k_0)
Output: $C = BlockCipher(P, K)$
1: *State* $R_0 \leftarrow P_r$; *Dummy state* $R_1 \leftarrow \beta$; $i \leftarrow 1$;
2: *State* $T_0 \leftarrow P_i$; $T_i \leftarrow \alpha$;
3: **while** $i \leq n$ **do**
4:    $\lambda \leftarrow RamdomBit()$; $//\lambda = 0$ implies a dummy round
5:    $k \leftarrow i\lambda$;
6:    $R_{\neg\lambda} \leftarrow RoundFunction(R_{\neg\lambda}, k_k) \oplus T_{\neg\lambda}$; $//$infection of the dummy state
7:    $R_0 \leftarrow R_0 \oplus R_1 \oplus \beta$; $//$infection of the cipher state
8:    $T_0 \leftarrow T_0 \oplus R_1 \oplus \beta$; $//$infection of the cipher state
9:    $i \leftarrow i + \lambda$;
10: **end while**
11: **return** $T_0 \parallel R_0$

The plaintext consists of P_r and P_l, respectively. Let α be an arbitrary constant such that $RoundFunction(\beta, \ k_0) \oplus \alpha = \beta$, where β is the intermediate value during encryption. Algorithm 1 illustrates the application of the countermeasure to a simple block cipher of the Feistel structure. The dummy round involves taking a secret input value β that produces the result of β after a round when combined with the secret dummy round-key k_0. The output of the dummy round is then XORed into the cipher state and then XORed with β, which ensures that any fault is propagated into the block cipher. This approach makes it difficult for an attacker to derive information about the secret key used by analyzing the faulty ciphertext.

Algorithm 2. CEJO-WBAES with an F-Noisy round [22].

Input: P, k_i , $\hat{k}_i \ for \ i \in \{0, 1, ..., 10\}$, $rk_i \ for \ i \in \{0, 1, ..., n\}$
Output: $C = AES(P, \ K)$

1: $R \leftarrow P$;
2: $r \leftarrow 1$;
3: **while** $r \leq n$ **do**
4:    $R = F_1^r(R, rk_i)$
5:    $R = F_2^r(R, rk_i)$
6: **end while**
7: $r \leftarrow 1$;
8: **while** $r \leq n$ **do**
9:    $R = ShiftRows(R)$;
10:    $R = T_i^r(R, \hat{k}_{r-1})$
11:    $R = Ty_i(R)$
12:    $R = XOR(R)$;
13: **end while**
14: $R = ShiftRows(R)$;
15: $R = T_i^r(R)$
16: **return** R

Noisy Rounds. Based on dummy rounds and CEJO_WBAES, Sun *et al.* [22] proposed noisy round white-box protection technology. This technology interferes with DCA and DFA by randomly adding noisy rounds. The basic principle

Algorithm 3. CEJO-WBAES with an L-Noisy round [22].

Input: P, k_i , $\hat{k}_i$ $for\,i \in \{0, 1, ..., 10\}$, rk_i $for\,i \in \{0, 1, ..., n\}$
Output: $C = AES(P,\ K)$

1: $R \leftarrow P$;
2: $r \leftarrow 1$;
3: **while** $i \leq 9$ **do**
4:    $R = ShiftRows(R)$;
5:    $R = T_i^r(R,\ \hat{rk_i})$;
6:    $R = Ty_i(R)$;
7: **end while**
8: $R = ShiftRows(R)$;
9: $R = T_i^r(R,\ \hat{k_9})$;

10: $R = T_i^r(R,\ k_{10})$;
11: $r \leftarrow 1$;
12: **while** $i \leq n$ **do**
13:    $R = L_0^r(R,\ rk_{r-1},\ rk_r)$;
14:    $R = L_1^r(R)$;
15:    $R = L_2^r(R)$;
16:    $R = L_3^r(R,\ rk_{r-1},\ rk_r)$;
17: **end while**
18: **return** R

of the noisy round is that random round keys are used to participate in the calculation of the block cipher.

A noisy round is mainly divided into F-Noisy rounds (see Algorithm 2) and L-Noisy rounds (see Algorithm 3). F-Noisy rounds are used to interfere with DCA, whereas L-Noisy rounds are used to interfere with DFA. In Algorithms 2 and 3, variable P denotes plaintext. The number of L-Noisy rounds or F-Noisy rounds is denoted by n, and K_i is the subkey of the master key. The result after ShiftRows is denoted by $\hat{k}_i$, and rk_i indicates that the round key is generated randomly. F_1^j is formed by combining AddRoundKey and SubBytes. InvSubBytes and AddRoundKey are combined in a round as F_2^j to cancel out SubBytes and AddRoundKey in F_1^j. The structure of L_3^j is identical to the 10th round of the original CEJO_WBAES algorithm. Let L_0^j be the AddRoundKey, invSubBytes, and L_3^{j-1}. L_1^j contains invShiftRows and invMixColumns. MixColumns must generate a separate round because it acts on the column, which is L_2^j.

2.3   Deep Neural Networks

CNN. Used widely in computer vision, a CNN [10] usually consists of convolutional layers, nonlinear layers, pooling layers, and fully connected layers (see Fig. 4). According to the dimensions of the feature maps, CNN can be divided into x-dimensional convolutional networks (xD-CNN, $x \in \{1, 2, 3\}$).

RNN. To allow output from some nodes to affect subsequent input to the same nodes, the RNN [20] is a class of feedforward neural network. It is designed to recognize the sequential characteristics of data using the ability to remember the information calculated as shown in Fig. 5. During the training process, the architecture of RNN commonly triggers gradient vanishing and exploding problems.

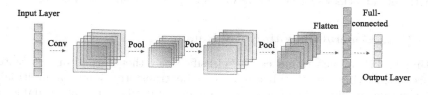

Fig. 4. CNN architecture.

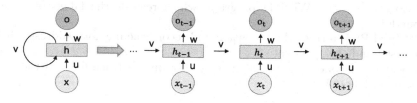

Fig. 5. RNN architecture. x: input layer, o: output layer, h: hidden layer, u, w, and v: network parameters. At any given time t, the current input is a combination of the output of h_{t-1} and x_t.

CRNN. The CRNN [21] is shown in Fig. 6. It is composed of a convolutional layer, a recurrent layer, and a transcription layer. The CRNN integrates the advantages of CNN and RNN, which are widely used in image-based sequence recognition tasks.

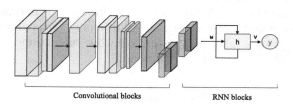

Fig. 6. CRNN architecture.

3   Detection of Noisy Rounds

Before an attack, feature engineering is a common stage in classical machine learning. Deep learning uses basic characteristics. In this section, we create differentiating attacks using neural networks to predict round obfuscation.

3.1   Data Generation with Noisy Rounds

Within WBSM4, each round can be classified as either normal or obfuscated. Hence, identifying round obfuscation can be transformed into a multi-label classification problem. As open-source implementations were not available, we developed CEJO_WBAES_Noisy and XL_WBSM4_Noisy using the WBMatrix library [23]. Our data collection process is described as follows:

1. Create a modified WBSM4 program, which records the labels of running rounds.
2. Use Intel PIN to trace the execution and record the memory addresses being accessed and their content.
3. Repeat the second step 10,000 times to obtain the trace file and the corresponding label file.

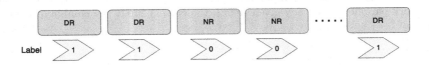

Fig. 7. Generate labels for distinguishing noisy rounds. DR denotes the noisy rounds, and NR denotes the normal rounds.

Label. The location of noisy rounds in each encryption algorithm is determined by a random sequence of 0/1 values, where 0 indicates a normal round and 1 indicates a noisy round (refer to Fig. 7). Additionally, we compute the random sequence of labels in a label file. In the following subsections, we provide the details of the CNN, RNN, and CRNN models.

3.2   CNN for Predicting Noisy Rounds

In our application scenario, the trace consists of a significant amount of noise-free memory-logged data that is regularly collected. A CNN model is effective for identifying interesting features. For the time-series analysis of sensor data such as gyroscope or accelerometer data, a one-dimensional CNN (1D-CNN) can be advantageous. It is also useful for analyzing period-fixed signal data, such as audio signals. Furthermore, in the deep learning of SCA, CNN models have been shown to achieve remarkable key recovery performance with very small

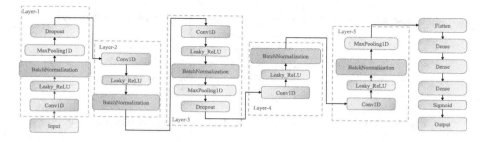

Fig. 8. Construction of the CNN model for predicting noisy rounds.

architectures on previously evaluated public datasets. Therefore, in this scenario, the model is constructed using a CNN, with the main components illustrated in Fig. 8.

Overall CNN Structure. The model is constructed using five convolutional neural layers and three dense layers. Every convolutional layer uses small kernels, typically two or three. The leaky ReLU activation function is used to prevent neuronal cell death caused by the specificity of the data. The filter size ranges from 16 to 64, and dropout layers are used to prevent overfitting. The final sigmoid activation function performs the binary classification.

Convolutional Blocks. The input layer is connected in channel-first mode to one layer of bit-sliced convolutions with a width of 1 and 32 output channels. Batch normalization is applied to the output of the convolution. In layer 1 and layer 3, max-pooling and dropout are applied to the outputs of batch normalization. Max-pooling is a pooling operation that selects the maximum element from the region of the feature map covered by the filter. Dropout is a technique in which randomly selected neurons are ignored during training to prevent overfitting.

Prediction Head. The prediction head consists of four hidden layers and one output unit. The flattened layer, which is commonly used in the transition from the convolution layer to the fully connected layer, is the first layer that flattens the multidimensional input to 1D. Following that, three densely connected layers are used, and the output units in the final layer are activated using a sigmoid function.

3.3   RNN for Predicting Noisy Rounds

In a physical side-channel trace, analogue values are sampled at a fixed rate, and the time axis represents time linearly. In software execution traces, information is recorded only when it is relevant. Because of serialization and on-demand sampling, the time axis of DCA does not represent an actual time scale. However, the data still exhibit correlations with each other. The RNN is a type of neural

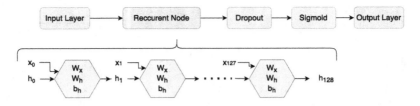

Fig. 9. Construction of the RNN model for predicting noisy rounds.

network that is designed to process sequential data. It is derived from feedforward neural networks and can use its internal state to process variable-length sequences of inputs. RNNs are used in a wide range of applications, including natural language processing, speech recognition, image captioning, and time series prediction. They are particularly well-suited for tasks in which the current output depends on previous inputs, such as traces.

RNN Blocks. Essentially, the RNN layer was consists of a single rolled RNN cell that unrolls according to the "number of steps" value (as shown in Fig. 9). For multi-label classification problems, the activation function is still the sigmoid function.

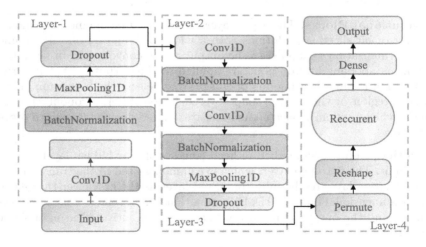

Fig. 10. Construction of the CRNN model for predicting noisy rounds.

3.4 CRNN for Predicting Noisy Rounds

The CNN and RNN were used to predict noisy rounds in Sects. 3.2 and 3.3. The CNN is typically a feed-forward architecture. The CRNN combines two of the most prominent neural networks: CNN and RNN (see Fig. 10).

Convolutional Blocks. The network starts with the traditional 1D-CNN followed by batch normalization, ELU activation, max-pooling, and dropout with a dropout rate of 50%. Compared with ReLU and its variants, using ELU can shorten the training time in the neural network and improve accuracy.

RNN Blocks. The convolutional layers are developed on two-dimensional feature vectors, whereas the RNNs are developed on 1D feature vectors. The convolutional layers are followed by the permute and the reshape layer, which was necessary for the CRNN because the shape of the feature vector differs from the CNN to the RNN. The RNN is compatible with 1D feature vectors.

3.5 Evaluation Methodology

To enhance the resistance against DCA attacks, we add a certain number of noisy rounds at the beginning and end of the algorithm.

Definition 1 (ORP-Exp). *ORP-Exp is a representation of a random guess by the attacker regarding the position of the noisy rounds. Let m denote the number of noisy rounds, and n denote the number of real rounds. The calculation formula for the expectation is as follows:*

$$ORP\text{-}Exp = \sum_{i=0}^{m} \frac{iC_m^i C_n^{m-i}}{mC_{m+n}^m}.$$

Definition 2 (ORP-Acc). *ORP-Acc calculates the percentage probability of correctly predicted "1" tags in Y'_{ij} relative to the total number of "1" tags in Y_{ij}. Y'_{ij} represents the set of labels predicted by the classifier, and Y_{ij} represents the true set of labels corresponding to the sample. Let $\delta = 1$ where $Y'_{ij} = Y_{ij} = 1$ and $\delta = 0$ where $Y'_{ij} \neq Y_{ij} = 1$. The total number of noisy samples is n, and the number of labels with 1 is m. The calculation formula for accuracy is as follows:*

$$ORP\text{-}Acc = \frac{1}{n} \sum_{i=1}^{n} \left(\frac{1}{m} \sum_{j=1}^{m} \delta(Y'_{ij}, Y_{ij}) \right).$$

Note that the effect of fixed rounds is removed by default when calculating accuracy and expectation.

4 Experimental Results

In this section, we provide the experimental results for various models. Moreover, we analyze security and the performance have been analyzed with the round obfuscation techniques. Table 1 provides the details of the hardware setup and software version used in the experiments.

Table 1. Hardware and software environment used in the experiment.

Hardware	configuration	Software	Version
CPU	AMD Ryzen 7 5800H @3.2 GHz	CUDA	10.0
GPU	NVIDIA GeForce RTX 2080 Ti	Python	3.9.7
RAM	64G	GCC	8.2.0

4.1   The Comparison of Various Neural Networks

Experimental Process. In practice, the noisy round is typically added to the first and last rounds of a cryptographic algorithm, and inserting a fixed number of noisy rounds is inserted at random positions in the middle. We generated the trace and label files based on the method proposed in Sect. 3.1. Therefore, we constructed a test set with 1000 cases and a training set with 10000 cases have been constructed. We trained the models (CNN, RNN, and CRNN) in the experiment. The model structures were described in Sect. 3. The approach in Definition 2 calculates the ORP-Acc values, and the approach in Definition 1 calculates the ORP-Exp values. Table 2 displays the training accuracy (ORP-Acc) with various noisy rounds for the three models (CNN, RNN, and CRNN).

Optimizer Selection and Hyperparameter Settings. In the experimental test, the SGD optimizer demonstrated better convergence than the Adam optimizer. Therefore, in this experiment, we used the SGD optimizer. We chose the weight initialization method He_normal, which is suitable for the RELU activation function. We selected the hyperparameters based on the best outcome from the experiments. We performed training for 50 epochs with a batch size of 64 and applied a single learning rate drop from 0.0005 to 0.00001 was applied at epoch 40.

Table 2. Comparison of the models for predicting noisy rounds.

Ciphers	Round	Trace_length (bit)	ORP-Exp	Model		
				CNN	RNN	CRNN
				ORP-Acc	ORP-Acc	ORP-Acc
CEJO_WBAES_Noisy	19	42496	23.07%	27.17%	25.93%	27.23%
	22	49408	37.50%	39.76%	42.81%	44.03%
	25	56320	47.36%	48.81%	51.54%	51.06%
	31	70144	60.00%	62.40%	63.66%	62.66%
XL_WBSM4_Noisy	40	17696	11.11%	12.82%	12.30%	12.73%
	64	27680	46.67%	49.24%	49.67%	49.75%
	96	40992	65.22%	67.59%	67.97%	67.74%
	160	67616	79.49%	81.19%	81.27%	81.30%

Comparison of the Three Neural Networks. Figure 11 shows the bias between ORP-Acc and ORP-Exp, computed from the data in Table 2.

For CEJO_WBAES_Noisy, the bias was higher compared with other rounds when the CNN model had 19 rounds. The trace length was relatively short when the number of additional rounds was small. The CNN model was better suited to this algorithm because it aided in the extraction of relevant features. For RNN models with 25 or more noisy rounds, their bias was higher than those of the CNN and CRNN. The RNN had a better capacity to learn and perform sophisticated data conversion over an extended period, which allowed more content to be learned from the data. Therefore, for CEJO_WBAES_Noisy, the RNN was more suitable for a long trace length. For XL_WBSM4_Noisy, the change curves for the CNN, RNN, and CRNN were similar. Overall, all biases were positive, with the bias peaking when the number of noisy rounds is equal to or slightly higher than the number of normal rounds of the algorithm. For instance, when the total round number of XL_WBSM4_Noisy was 64, and the total round number of CEJO_WBAES_Noisy was 22, the deep learning approach learned more information to distinguish noisy rounds.

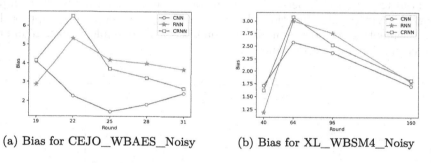

(a) Bias for CEJO_WBAES_Noisy   (b) Bias for XL_WBSM4_Noisy

Fig. 11. Bias variations for three models (CNN, RNN, and CRNN).

4.2 Analysis of the Security and Performance with the Round Obfuscation Techniques

On examining the relationship between the number of redundant rounds and deviations, we found no clear correlation between the two. We conducted experimental analyses on the effects of the key, affine masking, and transformation matrix on deep learning recognition.

Analysis of the Influence of Key and Affine Maskings on Model Learning. We chose the CNN model for analysis. In the XL_WBSM4_Noisy implementation, we explored the following four situations (Table 3). We set the number of noisy rounds to 32. The experimental results showed that affine masking and

Table 3. Influences of various keys and countermeasures on model accuracy.

Serial number	Keys	Countermeasures	ORP_Acc	Cost (s)
1	1 fixed key	None	49.35%	601
2	1 fixed key	Affine masking	49.42%	598
3	Random keys	None	49.88%	604
4	Random keys	Affine masking	49.21%	594

random keys did not impact deep learning recognition. We also conducted experiments on CEJO_WBAES_Noisy, and the conclusion was the same as that for XL_WBSM4_Noisy.

Analysis of the Influence of the Round-type Array and Transformation Matrix on Model Learning. The ShiftRow operation is not included in the noisy operation of the CEJO_WBAES_Noisy implementation. This ensures consistency between the ciphertext state before and after the noisy round. However, the ShiftRow operation is included in the normal encryption round. It is essential to distinguish between normal rounds and noisy rounds when implementing cryptographic functions. In our experiment, we adopted two approaches to implementing the noisy rounds: the round-type array implementation and the transformation matrix implementation.

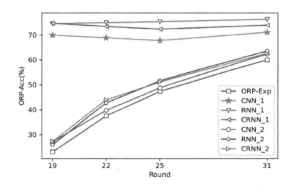

Fig. 12. For CEJO_WBAES_Noisy, the accuracy of the round-type array (CNN_1, RNN_1 and CRNN_1) and transformation matrix (CNN_2, RNN_2 and CRNN_2) on model learning.

In the first scheme, we recorded each round type (noisy round or normal round) in an array and included it as a part of the encryption round key table. Before starting each round of encryption, we would read the round type from the array and use an IF statement to determine whether the ShiftRow operation should be executed before that round. The second scheme eliminated the need for IF statements by storing the transformation matrix before each round of encryption. The transformation matrix was a 128×128 square matrix. Before each encryption round, we left-half multiplied the ciphertext state by the transformation matrix from the previous round to obtain the new ciphertext state. We generated the relevant transformation matrix by shifting each byte in the ciphertext state according to the ShiftRow operation. Alternatively, we could use an identity matrix without ShiftRow operations.

We constructed two implementations of CEJO_WBAES_Noisy based on two schemes and trained the data using three models (CNN, RNN, and CRNN). The results of our experiments are presented in Fig. 12, where the suffix 1 represents the first scheme, and the suffix 2 represents the second scheme. Figure 12 shows that, for various models, the recognition accuracy of the second scheme was lower than that of the first scheme. We attribute this result to the IF statement in the round-type array. During the execution process, different code segments were accessed based on different round types, which resulted in differences in the trace obtained during the execution of normal and noisy rounds. However, for the second scheme, the transformation matrix was located in a contiguous address space, which made the difference between the traces of normal and noisy rounds less apparent.

Table 4. Training/Testing cost of models for predicting noisy rounds.

Cipher	Round	Model					
		CNN		RNN		CRNN	
		Training/Testing cost (s)					
CEJO_WBAES_Noisy	19	1102.59	5.83	317.21	3.12	1470.37	11.04
	22	1281.47	6.41	322.88	3.14	1652.31	11.24
	25	1465.59	7.02	335.75	3.21	1889.59	12.39
	31	1842.43	7.65	369.18	3.32	2263.56	12.92
XL_WBSM4_Noisy	40	380.50	4.14	269.78	3.15	720.12	9.28
	64	590.86	4.91	275.88	3.22	1018.12	10.08
	96	877.08	5.89	330.48	3.45	1420.73	11.02
	160	1593.93	6.76	360.53	3.75	2216.92	13.36

Training/Testing Cost. Table 4 shows the costs of model training and testing. Among the three models, the RNN took the least training time. The most intricate and time-consuming model to train was the CRNN, which combines the CNN and RNN models. The RNN was better suited for longer trace lengths, and its training costs were substantially lower than those of the other two models (CNN and CRNN). Considering the results for ORP_ACC and the training cost, the RNN appeared to be more effective than the CNN and CRNN.

5 Conclusion

In this study, we explored deep-learning methods for predicting redundant rounds. After analyzing the features of software traces, we constructed deep learning models: CNN, RNN, and CRNN. Our experiments demonstrated that deep learning methods could effectively attack noisy rounds without a transformation matrix. In future research, it will be a challenging task to develop a deep-learning model that could be better suited for attacking noisy rounds with a transformation matrix. Additionally, it would be interesting to further explore constructing models for white-box implementations to defeat masking/shuffling.

Acknowledgments. This work was supported by the National Natural Science Foundation of China (62072192), National Defense Technology 173 Basic Improvement Project (2121-JCJQ-JJ-0931), National Cryptography Development Fund (MMJJ20180206), Guangdong Basic and Applied Basic Research Foundation (2022A1515140090), the Research Project of Science and Technology Plan of Guangzhou (No. 2023B 03J0172).

References

1. Alpirez Bock, E., Brzuska, C., Michiels, W., Treff, A.: On the ineffectiveness of internal encodings - revisiting the DCA attack on white-box cryptography. In: Preneel, B., Vercauteren, F. (eds.) ACNS 2018. LNCS, vol. 10892, pp. 103–120. Springer, Cham (2018). https://doi.org/10.1007/978-3-319-93387-0_6
2. Banik, S., Bogdanov, A., Isobe, T., Jepsen, M.B.: Analysis of software countermeasures for whitebox encryption. Cryptology ePrint Archive (2017)
3. Billet, O., Gilbert, H., Ech-Chatbi, C.: Cryptanalysis of a white box AES implementation. In: Handschuh, H., Hasan, M.A. (eds.) SAC 2004. LNCS, vol. 3357, pp. 227–240. Springer, Heidelberg (2004). https://doi.org/10.1007/978-3-540-30564-4_16
4. Bos, J.W., Hubain, C., Michiels, W., Teuwen, P.: Differential computation analysis: hiding your white-box designs is not enough. In: Gierlichs, B., Poschmann, A.Y. (eds.) CHES 2016. LNCS, vol. 9813, pp. 215–236. Springer, Heidelberg (2016). https://doi.org/10.1007/978-3-662-53140-2_11
5. Bringer, J., Chabanne, H., Dottax, E.: White box cryptography: another attempt. Cryptology ePrint Archive (2006)
6. Chow, S., Eisen, P., Johnson, H., van Oorschot, P.C.: A white-box DES implementation for DRM applications. In: Feigenbaum, J. (ed.) DRM 2002. LNCS, vol. 2696, pp. 1–15. Springer, Heidelberg (2003). https://doi.org/10.1007/978-3-540-44993-5_1
7. Chow, S., Eisen, P., Johnson, H., Van Oorschot, P.C.: White-box cryptography and an AES implementation. In: Nyberg, K., Heys, H. (eds.) SAC 2002. LNCS, vol. 2595, pp. 250–270. Springer, Heidelberg (2003). https://doi.org/10.1007/3-540-36492-7_17
8. Gierlichs, B., Schmidt, J.-M., Tunstall, M.: Infective computation and dummy rounds: fault protection for block ciphers without check-before-output. In: Hevia, A., Neven, G. (eds.) LATINCRYPT 2012. LNCS, vol. 7533, pp. 305–321. Springer, Heidelberg (2012). https://doi.org/10.1007/978-3-642-33481-8_17

9. Karroumi, M.: Protecting white-box AES with dual ciphers. In: Rhee, K.-H., Nyang, D.H. (eds.) ICISC 2010. LNCS, vol. 6829, pp. 278–291. Springer, Heidelberg (2011). https://doi.org/10.1007/978-3-642-24209-0_19

10. Krizhevsky, A., Sutskever, I., Hinton, G.E.: ImageNet classification with deep convolutional neural networks. In: Proceedings of the 25th International Conference on Neural Information Processing Systems, NIPS 2012, Red Hook, NY, USA, vol. 1, pp. 1097–1105. Curran Associates Inc. (2012)

11. Lee, J.H., Han, D.-G.: DLDDO: deep learning to detect dummy operations. In: You, I. (ed.) WISA 2020. LNCS, vol. 12583, pp. 73–85. Springer, Cham (2020). https://doi.org/10.1007/978-3-030-65299-9_6

12. Lepoint, T., Rivain, M., De Mulder, Y., Roelse, P., Preneel, B.: Two attacks on a white-box AES implementation. In: Lange, T., Lauter, K., Lisoněk, P. (eds.) SAC 2013. LNCS, vol. 8282, pp. 265–285. Springer, Heidelberg (2014). https://doi.org/10.1007/978-3-662-43414-7_14

13. Lerman, L., Bontempi, G., Markowitch, O.: A machine learning approach against a masked AES. J. Cryptogr. Eng. 5(2), 123–139 (2015). https://doi.org/10.1007/s13389-014-0089-3

14. Maghrebi, H., Portigliatti, T., Prouff, E.: Breaking cryptographic implementations using deep learning techniques. In: Carlet, C., Hasan, M.A., Saraswat, V. (eds.) SPACE 2016. LNCS, vol. 10076, pp. 3–26. Springer, Cham (2016). https://doi.org/10.1007/978-3-319-49445-6_1

15. Muir, J.A.: A tutorial on white-box AES. In: Kranakis, E. (ed.) Advances in Network Analysis and Its Applications. MATHINDUSTRY, vol. 18, pp. 209–229. Springer, Heidelberg (2013). https://doi.org/10.1007/978-3-642-30904-5_9

16. De Mulder, Y., Roelse, P., Preneel, B.: Cryptanalysis of the Xiao – Lai white-box AES implementation. In: Knudsen, L.R., Wu, H. (eds.) SAC 2012. LNCS, vol. 7707, pp. 34–49. Springer, Heidelberg (2013). https://doi.org/10.1007/978-3-642-35999-6_3

17. De Mulder, Y., Wyseur, B., Preneel, B.: Cryptanalysis of a perturbated white-box AES implementation. In: Gong, G., Gupta, K.C. (eds.) INDOCRYPT 2010. LNCS, vol. 6498, pp. 292–310. Springer, Heidelberg (2010). https://doi.org/10.1007/978-3-642-17401-8_21

18. Picek, S., Samiotis, I.P., Kim, J., Heuser, A., Bhasin, S., Legay, A.: On the performance of convolutional neural networks for side-channel analysis. In: Chattopadhyay, A., Rebeiro, C., Yarom, Y. (eds.) SPACE 2018. LNCS, vol. 11348, pp. 157–176. Springer, Cham (2018). https://doi.org/10.1007/978-3-030-05072-6_10

19. Rivain, M., Wang, J.: Analysis and improvement of differential computation attacks against internally-encoded white-box implementations. IACR Trans. Cryptogr. Hardw. Embed. Syst. 2019(2), 225–255 (2019)

20. Rumelhart, D.E., Hinton, G.E., Williams, R.J.: Learning internal representations by error propagation, pp. 318–362. MIT Press, Cambridge (1986)

21. Shi, B., Bai, X., Yao, C.: An end-to-end trainable neural network for image-based sequence recognition and its application to scene text recognition. CoRR abs/1507.05717 (2015). http://arxiv.org/abs/1507.05717

22. Sun, T., Tang, G., Wu, X., Mao, Z., Gong, Z.: A noisyrounds-based white-box AES implementation and corresponding differential fault analysis. J. Cryptol. Res. 7(3), 342–57 (2020)

23. Tang, Y., Gong, Z., Sun, T., Chen, J., Liu, Z.: WBMatrix: an optimized matrix library for white-box block cipher implementations. IEEE Trans. Comput. 71(12), 3375–88 (2022)

24. Tingting, L., Xuejia, L.: Efficient attack to white-box SMS4 implementation. J. Softw. **24**(9), 2238–2249 (2013)
25. Wu, L., Picek, S.: Remove some noise: on pre-processing of side-channel measurements with autoencoders. IACR Trans. Cryptogr. Hardw. Embed. Syst. **2020**(4), 389–415 (2020)
26. Xiao, Y., Lai, X.: A secure implementation of white-box AES. In: 2009 2nd International Conference on Computer Science and Its Applications, pp. 1–6. IEEE (2009)
27. Xiao, Y., Lai, X.: White-box cryptography and implementations of SMS4. In: Proceedings of the 2009 CACR Annual Meeting, Guangzhou, China, pp. 24–34 (2009)
28. Yueyu, Z., Dong, X., Jie, C.: Analysis and improvement of white box SM4. J. Electron. Inf. Technol. **43**, 1–11 (2021)
29. Zaid, G., Bossuet, L., Habrard, A., Venelli, A.: Methodology for efficient CNN architectures in profiling attacks. IACR Trans. Cryptogr. Hardw. Embed. Syst. **2020**(1), 1–36 (2020)
30. Zeyad, M., Maghrebi, H., Alessio, D., Batteux, B.: Another look on bucketing attack to defeat white-box implementations. In: Polian, I., Stöttinger, M. (eds.) COSADE 2019. LNCS, vol. 11421, pp. 99–117. Springer, Cham (2019). https://doi.org/10.1007/978-3-030-16350-1_7
31. Zhang, Y., Xu, D., Cai, Z., Chen, J.: Analysis of the mean difference of intermediate-values in a white box SM4. J. Xidian Univ. **49**(1), 111–120 (2022)

Efficient Arithmetic for Polynomial Multiplication in Post-quantum Lattice-Based Cryptosystem on RISC-V Platform

Haosong Zhao[1], Rui Su[1], Rui Lin[1], Jiankuo Dong[2], and Donglong Chen[1(✉)]

[1] Guangdong Provincial Key Laboratory of Interdisciplinary Research and Application for Data Science, BNU-HKBU United International College, Zhuhai, China
{haosongzhao,ruisu,ruilin,donglongchen}@uic.edu.cn
[2] School of Computer Science, Nanjing University of Posts and Telecommunications, Nanjing, China
djiankuo@njupt.edu.cn

Abstract. With the development of quantum computers, NIST started post-quantum cryptography standardization to design post-quantum-secure cryptographic algorithms. Saber is a cryptosystem in third-round public-key encryption and key-establishment algorithm finalists. Because of its power of 2 number theoretic transform (NTT)-unfriendly ring, originally, Karatsuba polynomial multiplication algorithm (KPMA) and Toom-Cook polynomial multiplication algorithm (TCPMA) are used to speed up its computation-intensive matrix-vector multiplications. In later studies, NTT-based methods are applied to Saber on ARM platforms and result in a 61% speed-up. This work aims at adapting Saber with existing polynomial multiplication algorithms (PMAs), including non-NTT-based and NTT-based PMAs, to two energy-efficient RISC-V development boards, SiFive HiFive1 Rev B as well as Terasic T-Core. A 32-bit multiplier adapting Barrett reduction is designed to solve the overflow problem caused by RISC-V platform limitation. Experiment results show that the computation complexity depends on the algorithm choice and the underlying platform. NTT-based algorithms analytically have obvious advantages compared with non-NTT-based PMAs. However, the on-board cycle count on T-Core shows that NTT-based algorithms may have no comparability with non-NTT-based algorithms due to the high complexity overflow solutions. In addition, using the newly designed 32-bit multiplier can result in a 36.4% speed-up in practice. These results suggest several criteria for selecting algorithms on different platforms. This project can serve as a reference for future exploratory studies.

Keywords: Polynomial multiplication · Barrett reduction · Number theoretic transform · RISC-V · Saber · Post quantum cryptography (PQC)

© The Author(s), under exclusive license to Springer Nature Switzerland AG 2023
J. Zhou et al. (Eds.): ACNS 2023 Workshops, LNCS 13907, pp. 439–458, 2023.
https://doi.org/10.1007/978-3-031-41181-6_24

1   Introduction

Nowadays, the public key cryptosystems are all built upon the hardness of mathematical problems. For example, the basis of RSA algorithm is the factorization of large integers while elliptic curve cryptography (ECC) is based on the discrete logarithm problem. However, never as today, with the invention and development of quantum computer prototypes, the computational force has already reached another level and people can solve considerably tough computational problems mentioned above substantially faster than they used to with classical computers. In other words, the quantum computer breakthrough is a risk for all communication systems because it may break essentially all public key schemes currently in use.

Therefore, new cryptographic algorithms, also called post-quantum cryptography (PQC), which are built upon new types of harder problems are required so that communications are still secure even against an attack by a quantum computer. As a result, the National Institute of Standards and Technology (NIST) starts the PQC standardization process in order to stay ahead and get the new PQC ready before 2023. There were 69 candidates for its first-round, 26 of them for the second round, and only 15 algorithms which include 7 considered finalists and 8 alternate schemes remained in the third round.

Among all candidate algorithms, Saber [5], a lattice-based cryptography that built upon module-learning with rounding (M-LWR) problem, can be regarded as the most different public-key encryption and key-establishment algorithm. Based on the M-LWR problems and moduli of power of two, Saber has several advantages such as the elimination of modular reductions and rejection sampling, extraordinary flexibility and ease of implementation. But based on NTT-unfriendly rings, Saber are designed to use TCPMA and KPMA [9] to solve its most time-consuming matrix-vector multiplication process instead of NTT-based PMA even though NTT PMA is considerably more efficient than TCPMA in general. This is mainly because the original implementation pays more attention to keep the smallness of the polynomial elements as well as to reach low bandwidths. The special design of Saber underlying moduli provides significant differences between other cryptosystems as well as large research potential in algorithm efficiency improvement.

As a result, the study of adapting NTT on NTT-unfriendly ring as well as its efficient arithmetic has become an important aspect of PQC related research. Several later literatures [1,4,6–8] claimed that a significant improvement in speed can be achieved by applying a special version of NTT PMA for general moduli to various PQC schemes on platforms such as ARM Cortex M4 processor. According to the results displayed by literature [4], using NTT PMA is 61% faster than using TCPMA and KPMA to solve matrix-vector multiplications and lead to a 22% speed-up of Saber encapsulation process. It seems that even Saber is not designed for NTT PMA but it can gain a lot of benefits after adapting it. At the same time, it is a fact that an algorithm designed for embedded area can't be regarded as useful unless it can be reproduced on different platforms and has no dependency as well as other limitation.

According to the current knowledge, Saber has multiple PMA choices based on different platforms. It then creates large research potential from 2 perspectives which are the efficient implementation on other platforms as well as the efficiency comparison between different PMAs. First, there are three settings that may contain potential improvement possibility for non-NTT-based PMAs. They are stopping point selections, algorithm choices and algorithm application orders. Besides, the efficiency of NTT-based PMA will be influenced after the adaptation on RISC-V. New multipliers or algorithms may be required to achieve the same performance.

This project aims at further adapting Saber cryptosystem with NTT-based PMAs and non-NTT-based PMAs to 2 energy-efficient RISC-V development boards, SiFive HiFive 1 Rev B as well as Terasic T-Core, and making comparison between existing PMAs according to the run time benchmark. In this project, 6 PMAs are designed and tested, including 5 non-NTT-based hybrid PMAs adapted from TCPMA and KPMA, and a NTT-based algorithm using negacyclic convolution. To overcome the unexpected overflow occurred in 32-bit RISC-V platform implementation and further accelerate the computation, a 32-bit multiplier adapting Barrett reduction is designed and deployed.

According to practical cycle count obtained during on-board experiments, the computation efficiency not only depends on the algorithm choice itself but also the underlying platform. At the analytical level, NTT-based algorithms have obvious advantages compared with current Saber PMA which uses TCPMA at first and then two times of KPMAs [9]. However, the on-board cycle count on T-Core shows that NTT-based algorithms are much worse than non-NTT-based algorithms due to the high complexity overflow solutions. In addition, a 36.4% speed-up can be achieved with the self-designed 32-bit multiplier. The whole experiment can provide several important observations which can be regarded as the reference for follow-up study.

Major Contribution. Three major contributions have been made in this paper:

- Five hybrid non-NTT-based PMAs, which are derived from TCPMA/KPMA through varied algorithmic selections and sequence of application, have been tailored for Saber parameter configuration. Furthermore, a 32-bit multiplier that utilizes Barrett reduction has been devised to address the issue of overflow encountered in NTT-based PMA implementation for RISC-V platforms.
- This project adapts all classical as well as latest PMAs to the RISC-V platforms with Saber parameter settings. Some of adapted PMAs are only verified on ARM and CPU currently. Specifically, in the case of non-NTT-based PMAs, we have developed three variations of the base case solution to attain optimal performance. Additionally, for NTT-based PMAs, we provide a specific parameter configuration which effectively avoids computational overflow on 32-bit RISC-V platforms.
- This project serves as a preliminary analysis of the on-board performance of six distinct PMAs on two energy-efficient RISC-V development boards,

SiFive HiFive 1 Rev B and Terasic T-Core. In particular, all aforementioned PMAs have been implemented on both SiFive HiFive 1 Rev B and Terasic T-Core development board. The resulting cycle counts demonstrate that the underlying platform wields a significant influence on PMA efficiency. This benchmarking can be considered a valuable reference point for future studies.

Paper Organization. Section 2 introduces Saber, non-NTT-based PMAs, and the theoretical basis about NTT-based PMAs. Section 3 presents methodology of different NTT-based and non-NTT-based PMAs, containing the NTT parameter settings, hybrid PMA design, and overflow handling on RISC-V platforms. Section 4 lists the implementation and benchmark details of previously mentioned PMAs. Section 5 displays the run-time benchmark on T-Core and HiFive1 Rev B. Section 6 makes conclusions about all of the work on hand.

2   Preliminaries

2.1   Saber

In a word, Saber is a lattice-based cryptography scheme built upon M-LWR problem. It is built on polynomial ring $R_q = \mathbb{Z}_q[x]/(X^n+1)$ with underlying modulus $q = 2^{13}$ and polynomial degree $n = 256$. In Saber encryption and decryption processes, the matrix-vector multiplication is the most time-consuming process. It is worth mentioning that the multiplication between elements contained in the matrix-vector multiplication process is polynomial multiplication indeed.

There are three versions of Saber: LightSaber (level I), Saber (level III), and FireSaber (Level V). These three versions have different security levels which differentiate by lattice size l, rounding parameter T, and binomial distribution parameter μ. In this project, all of the theoretical analysis as well as the practical implementation is based on Saber version. So, the secret polynomial s is a 3×1 vector and public polynomial A is a 3×3 matrix. As mentioned before, the degree of the polynomial multiplicands is $n = 256$. $q = 2^{13}$ means the multiplicand sampled form the uniform distribution $\mathcal{U}$ is in range $[0, q - 1]$. And $p = 2^{10}$ indicates that the final result after rounding will fall into the range $[0, p - 1]$. Finally, $\mu = 8$ is related to the centered binomial distribution $\mathcal{B}$. To facilitate understanding, the other polynomial multiplicand can be regard as being in range $[0, \mu - 1]$.

2.2   Polynomial and Polynomial Multiplication

It is necessary to introduce polynomial and polynomial multiplication problem before talking about detailed PMAs. In general, there are mainly 2 ways to represent a polynomial, the coefficient representation and the point-value representation. Under the context of Saber, two polynomials, $A(x)$ and $B(x)$, both have n degree and are in coefficient representation. The polynomial multiplication of $A(x)$ and $B(x)$ takes $O(n^2)$ times by using schoolbook multiplication algorithm, which is the way that people solve polynomial multiplication problem by hand, following the definition, which is:

$$C(x) = A(x) \times B(x) = \sum_{k=0}^{2n-2} c_k x^k \qquad (1)$$

$$\text{where } c_k = \sum_{0 \le i,j < n, k=i+j} a_i b_j, \text{ for all } 0 \le k < 2n-1.$$

Schoolbook multiplication algorithm is a benchmark for other PMAs to compare with. But it is unacceptable for cryptosystem implementation because the computational cost would be extremely high when the degree n gets bigger and bigger (for example, $n = 256$ in Saber).

Polynomial multiplication for point-value representation is quite different. When $A(x)$ and $B(x)$ are represented in extended point-value form which has $2n$ points and corresponding values, the polynomial multiplication problem can be written as: given $2n$ points $X = (x_0, x_1, ..., x_{2n-2}, x_{2n-1})$ and 2 extended point-value represented polynomials $A = \{(x_0, y_0^a), (x_1, y_1^a), ..., (x_{2n-1}, y_{2n-1}^a)\}$ and $B = \{(x_0, y_0^b), (x_1, y_1^b), ..., (x_{2n-1}, y_{2n-1}^b)\}$, compute $C(x) = A(x) \times B(x)$, where

$$C = \{(x_0, y_0^a y_0^b), (x_1, y_1^a y_1^b), (x_2, y_2^a y_2^b), ..., (x_{2n-1}, y_{2n-1}^a y_{2n-1}^b)\}$$

In this way, the multiplication only takes $O(n)$ times. Based on this observation, it is feasible to convert coefficient representation into point-value representation before multiplication and then restore the result back to coefficient representation. The process converting coefficient representation to point-value representation is called evaluation. The inverse process is called interpolation. With low-complexity evaluation and interpolation, polynomial multiplication process can be accelerated. Most PMAs are designed based on this idea.

2.3   Karatsuba and Toom-Cook Multiplication

KPMA and TCPMA are two classical and popular non-NTT-based PMAs which are originally used in Saber matrix-vector multiplication process [2].

Karatsuba Polynomial Multiplication Algorithm. KPMA is a divide-and-conquer approach that improves the time complexity of polynomial multiplication problem from $O(n^2)$ to $O(n^{\log_2 3})$. In detail, it splits two input polynomials into half-sized A_0, A_1 and B_0, B_1 where $A(x) = A_0 + A_1 \cdot x^{n/2}$ and $B(x) = B_0 + B_1 \cdot x^{n/2}$ respectively, where n is the degree of $A(x)$ and $B(x)$ (Under the context of this paper, $A(x)$ and $B(x)$ have the same degree n). And then, the multiplication of these two polynomial can be calculated as:

$$A(x) \times B(x) = A_0 B_0 + ((A_0 + A_1)(B_0 + B_1) - A_0 B_0 - A_1 B_1) x^{n/2} + A_1 B_1 \cdot x^n \quad (2)$$

This algorithm will be applied recursively until the degree of sub-polynomials is small enough to solve directly or equal to 1.

Toom-Cook n-Way Polynomial Multiplication Algorithm. TCPMA, or more specifically, the Toom-Cook k-way polynomial multiplication, is a generalization of KPMA. It means each multiplicand polynomial is divided into k smaller polynomials and each of them has n/k coefficients. Specifically, Toom-Cook 4-way is commonly used and it is the standard implementation of polynomial multiplication in Saber due to its binary essence. In detail, there are four main steps in Toom-Cook 4-way: splitting, evaluation, interpolation and recombination. In the evaluation step, it needs to choose different x_p values which are from points $\{0, \pm 1 \pm 1/2, 2, \infty\}$ and put them into the polynomials as $A(x_p)$ and $B(x_p)$. The evaluation point choices can be modified but these choices of points can simplify the hardware evaluation process because multiplying a number which is the power of two with positive or negative sign can be simply implemented by shifting the bits toward left or right [3].

For the time complexity, using Toom-Cook 4-way to solve size n problem takes $O(n^{\log_4 7})$ time. Thus, Toom-Cook 4-way has a slight improvement over KPM. But it's necessary to be careful of the loss in precision due to the division operations in algorithm. However, the divisors such as 3 and 5 can be replaced by multiplying their modulo inverses.

2.4   Number Theoretic Transform and Its Variants

In a word, NTT is a specialized version of the Discrete Fourier Transform (DFT) on a well-selected finite ring. To understand the application of NTT, there are several concepts need to be interpreted.

Discrete Fourier Transform. DFT is a way to evaluate a polynomial. Suppose we wish to evaluate a degree n polynomial $A(x)$ at points $\{\omega_n^0, \omega_n^1, \omega_n^2, ..., \omega_n^{n-1}\}$ which are the complex n^{th} roots of unity). The evaluation result $y_k = A(\omega_n^k)$, for $k = 0, 1, ..., n-1$, can be computed as:

$$y_k = A(\omega_n^k) = \sum_{i=0}^{n-1} a_i \omega_n^{ik} \qquad (3)$$

Then, the vector $Y = (y_0, y_1, \cdots, y_{n-1})$ is the DFT of the coefficient vector $A = (a_0, a_1, \cdots, a_{n-1})$, which is usually written as $Y = DFT_n(A)$.

The inverse process of DFT is called inversed discrete Fourier transform (IDFT). IDFT can transform a DFT representation back to its original form. Under the same assumption, A, the IDFT of Y, denoted as $DFT_n^{-1}(Y)$, is given by:

$$a_k = 1/n \sum_{i=0}^{n-1} y_i \omega_n^{-ik} \text{ for } k = 0, 1, ..., n-1 \qquad (4)$$

Number Theoretic Transform. DFT is not widely used in efficient arithmetic design because of introducing complex numbers into equation. Instead, the number theoretic transform (NTT) is more popular, especially in cryptography area. NTT is a specialized version of DFT. For NTT, the ω_n is an element of a finite ring, which is called primitive n^{th} root of unity modulus q. Here, q is a prime. It has similar property as complex n^{th} root of unity under certain finite ring. As DFT, NTT also has inverse process, INTT. Its computational formula is same as IDFT while original ω_n, n^{th} root of unity, is changed into primitive n^{th} root of unity modulus q.

Polynomial Multiplication Algorithm Based on NTT. The general steps of NTT-based PMA are: First, NTT is applied to transform the input polynomials which are in time domain to frequency domain. This process can be regarded as evaluation. Then, two polynomials in frequency domain will do the point-wise multiplications. At this time, INTT is used to transform the results back to time domain. This inverse operation can be regarded as interpolation. The NTT and INTT can be implemented in a divide-and-conquer way called Fast Fourier Transform (FFT). The time complexity of FFT is $O(nlogn)$. The point-wise multiplications are $O(n)$ complexity operation. So, the overall time complexity is only $O(nlogn)$. FFT (NTT) is the best PMA when it is applicable.

2.5 Low Complexity NTT

NTT-based PMAs take advantage of low complexity while multiplying two polynomials in point-value representation. Two methods can further speed up the NTT and INTT process.

NTT-Based Negacyclic Convolutions. As NTT process is indeed the evaluation process, NTT-based PMAs are inevitable to inherit the disadvantage of point-value multiplication, which needs extended point-value form input. Specifically, the zero-padding is required to make the n-degree input become $2n$-degree. As the result, the problem size of NTT process doubles. In addition, the degree of polynomial multiplication result also doubles. Under the cryptography context, a reduction process is required to keep the multiplication result size same as the input size.

Negacyclic convolution is a trick for NTT-based PMAs to omit the zero padding process so that it can halve the NTT problem size and directly get the reduced results. Its main idea shows that $C = A \times B \mod (x^n + 1)$ can be regarded as a length-n negacyclic convolution of A and B. The computation follows that

$$C \mod (x^n + 1) \equiv \sum_{k=0}^{n-1} (\sum_{i+j=k} a_i b_j - \sum_{i+j=k+n} a_i b_j) x^k$$

In this way, there is no need to zero-pad the two input coefficients and do the reduction before output the final results.

Low Complexity Negacyclic NTT. As mentioned above, we can compute the polynomial multiplication problem as $C = \text{INTT}_n(\text{NTT}_n(A) \cdot \text{NTT}_n(B))$ if negacyclic convolution is applied. Specifically, if ω_n, primitive n^{th} root of unity modulus q has square root γ_{2n}, suppose $\hat{a}_i = a_i \gamma_{2n}^i$, $\hat{b}_i = b_i \gamma_{2n}^i$, $\hat{c}_i = c_i \gamma_{2n}^i$, $C = A \times B \mod (x^n + 1)$ can be computed as: $\hat{C} = \text{INTT}_n(\text{NTT}_n(\hat{A}) \cdot \text{NTT}_n(\hat{B}))$ In this way, we avoid doubling the size of NTT as well as INTT, and the explicit reduction. However, the pre-processing that scales the A, B with γ_{2n}^i before NTT, and post-processing that scales the $\hat{C}$ with γ_{2n}^{-i} after INTT are required. According to literature [11], the low complexity negacyclic NTT method can eliminate the pre-processing and post-processing. The Algorithm 1 shows the low complexity NTT algorithm without pre-processing while the Algorithm 2 shows the low complexity INTT without post-processing. All NTT and INTT in this paper are implemented according to these two algorithms.

Algorithm 1: NTT Algorithm without Pre-processing

Input: $a, n, q, \gamma_{2n} = \sqrt{\omega_n}$
Output: $A = \text{NTT}(a)$

1   $A \leftarrow \text{BITREVERSAL}(a)$
2   **for** $s = 1$ to $\log_2 n$ **do**
3      $m = 2^s$
4   **for** $j = 0$ to $m/2 - 1$ **do**
5         $\hat{\omega} = \gamma_{2n}^{(2j+1)n/m}$
6   **for** $k = 0$ to $n/m - 1$ **do**
7            $u = A_{km+j}$
8            $t = \hat{\omega} \cdot A_{km+j+m/2} \mod q$
9            $A_{km+j} = u + t \mod q$
10            $A_{km+j+m/2} = u - t \mod q$

11 **return** A

Algorithm 2: INTT Algorithm without Post-processing

Input: A, n, q, γ_{2n}
Output: $A = \text{INTT}(A)$

1   **for** $s = \log_2 n$ to 1 **do**
2      $m = 2^s$
3   **for** $j = 0$ to $m/2 - 1$ **do**
4         $\hat{\omega} = \gamma_{2n}^{-(2j+1)n/m}$
5   **for** $k = 0$ to $n/m - 1$ **do**
6            $u = A_{km+j}$
7            $t = A_{km+j+m/2} \mod q$
8            $A_{km+j} = (u+t)/2 \mod q$
9            $A_{km+j+m/2} = (u-t)/2 \cdot \hat{\omega} \mod q$

10 $A \leftarrow \text{BITREVERSAL}(A)$
11 **return** A

2.6 Barrett Modular Multiplication

Barrett modular multiplication is an efficient way to compute $c = a \times b \mod q$ when q is fixed. It use multiplication, subtractions, and shifts to replace the slow long division operation to speed up the modular reduction process. The Barrett modular multiplication has mainly two steps: precomputation and reduction. The detailed operations are listed below.

1. Precomputation
   (a) Select $k \in \mathbb{N}$ where $2^k > q$. Usually, $k = \lceil \log_2 q \rceil$ which is the smallest choice and it is the bit length of q.
   (b) Calculate the precomputed factor $r = \lfloor \frac{4^k}{q} \rfloor$.
2. Reduction
   (a) Compute the multiplication result $x = a \times b$, such that $x \in \mathbb{N}$ and $0 \leq x < q^2$.
   (b) Calculate $t = x - \lfloor \frac{xr}{4^k} \rfloor q$. Now, $0 \leq t < 2q$ and $t \mod q \equiv c = a \times b \mod q$.
   (c) Return $c = t - q$ when $t \leq q$. Otherwise, return $c = t$.

In order to benefit fixed-size implementation, it is useful to conduct bit width analysis. First, it is known that the modulus q has k bits, so $r = \lfloor \frac{4^k}{q} \rfloor$ has $k+1$ bits. Then, because $x = a \times b$ fits in $2k$ bits and $xr = x \lfloor \frac{4^k}{q} \rfloor < x \frac{4^k}{q} < q^2 \frac{4^k}{q} = 4^k q$, xr fits in $3k$ bits. Next, it is clear that $\lfloor \frac{xr}{4^k} \rfloor$ fits in k bits, and $\lfloor \frac{xr}{4^k} \rfloor q$ fits in $2k$ bits. In addition, $t \in [0, 2q)$. So, t fits in $k+1$ bits.

Based on these observations, further optimization can be made if bit manipulation is applicable. For the multiplication $\lfloor \frac{xr}{4^k} \rfloor q$, only $k+1$ low-order bits are required. Because it is used in $t = x - \lfloor \frac{xr}{4^k} \rfloor q$ where the result t has $k+1$ bits at most. There is no need to clearly know the upper bits due to the elimination.

3   NTT-Based and Non-NTT-Based Polynomial Multiplication Algorithm on RISC-V

In this section, the detailed methodology about the design and adaptation of different PMAs for Saber on RISC-V platforms will be introduced. First, the parameter settings and their rationality for NTT-based PMA are discussed in Sect. 3.1. Then, 5 hybrid non-NTT-based PMAs adapted from KPMA and TCPMA are purposed in Sect. 3.2. Next, in Sect. 3.3, we present our solution to the overflow on resource-constrained RISC-V platforms with RV32I instruction set architecture(ISA).

3.1   NTT in Saber

In this paper, a low complexity NTT using negacyclic convolution (LCNTT) is adopted as the NTT-based PMA. To start with, it is important to talk about how to use NTT on NTT-unfriendly ring.

NTT on NTT-Unfriendly Ring. For NTT computation, the coefficient ring should be a prime and contain primitive roots of unity. As mentioned above, this restriction prevents Saber with power of 2 ring from adapting NTT. But in fact, NTT can be calculated with any prime $\hat{q} > nq^2$, where n is the polynomial degree and q is the original modulus [4]. The idea is that NTT can be applied to any modulus when a larger modulus that never truncates any result during the modular reduction is found.

NTT PMA Parameter Choice. For this project, the NTT PMA is designed to solve a 256° polynomial multiplication problem. According to the modulus selection criteria mentioned above, the minimum value of the modulus should satisfy the following inequality:

$$\hat{q} > \text{MinMod} = Max(a_i) \times Max(b_i) \times 2n + 1, \text{where } i = 1, 2, ..., n.$$

In `Saber`, $Max(a_i) = p = 2^{10}$ and $Max(b_i) = \mu = 8$. Polynomials are represented as extended point-value forms whose length are $2n$. So,

$$\text{MinMod} = 1024 \times 8 \times 512 + 1 = 4194305$$

Starting with the number 4194305, many prime numbers have primitive 256th roots of unity (It should also have 512th roots of unity while applying negacyclic convolution tricks) and are considered as potential modulus during the parameter selection process. The smallest modulus that satisfies all restrictions is 4205569 and it was once used as the underlying modulus for NTT PMA implementation but on-board adaptation has serious overflow risk. After modifying the selection criteria talking the overflow issue into consideration, another modulus 4206593 is selected. For the details about additional requirements respect to overflow and corresponding rationality, further explanations are given in Sect. 3.3.

3.2 Non-NTT-Based Polynomial Multiplication Algorithm in Saber

Based on observations of PMAs used in original Saber implementation submitted to NIST, we design five hybrid PMAs which are combinations of KPMA and TCPMA with different application orders and algorithm choices. To begin with, it is necessary to recall the polynomial multiplication solution provided in Saber design.

Original Solution to Polynomial Multiplication in Saber. According to the Saber reference C codes provided by [5], the polynomial multiplication algorithm used in Saber design is a combination of TCPMA, KPMA and schoolbook multiplication. Its computation procedure can be briefly illustrated as follows: First, TCPMA will be applied to the original input polynomials and create 7 sub-problems with problem size $n_1 = 64$. Then, KPMA will be invoked twice. Each time of using KPMA will generate 3 sub-problems. So, after these operations, there will be $7 \times 3 \times 3 = 63$ problems with size $n_{sp} = 16$. At this time, they will be directly solved by schoolbook multiplication. When the partial results are all available, they are merged into final result through interpolation processes of previous PMAs in reverse order.

Observations of Polynomial Multiplication in Saber. KPMA and TCPMA in previous computation procedure have three functions: dividing the original polynomials into several sub-problems, invoking PMAs to solve sub-problems, and merging the sub-results into the global result. Also, there are two kinds of operations to solve the sub-problems: invoking other PMAs or recursively invoking itself. Based on these facts, three settings may contain potential improvement. They are:

- Stopping point choice: Schoolbook multiplication is applied to sub-problems whose size is 16. Is size $n_{sp} = 16$ a good stopping point? What if it stops at a larger size or even a smaller size, such as $n_{sp} = 32$ or $n_{sp} = 8$?
- Algorithm choice: Polynomial multiplication in Saber is solved by a combination of different PMA. What if it only recursively uses KPMA or TCPMA?
- Order of the application of different algorithms: Current PMA is executed in "TC-K-K" order. What if the application order is "K-K-TC" or "K-TC-K"?

Based on these observations, we design five hybrid PMAs which are different combinations of KPMA and TCPMA adapted for Saber. All of these adaptations and corresponding rationality will be discussed in the following paragraphs.

Stopping Point Selection. Both KPMA and TCPMA will recursively invoke PMAs until the degree of sub-problems is small enough to solve directly. A sub-problem of polynomial multiplication is called a base case if its size is small enough to be directly solved using schoolbook multiplication. The current base case size for Saber is 16. What if base case is set to be 32 or 8? Before the discussion of this question, three observations need to be mentioned:

- First, neither TCPMA nor KPMA will solve the problem, they just use some "tricks" to reduce the total number of computation remaining in sub-problems.
- Second, TCPMA is more "complex" than KPMA.
- Third, the use of any PMA is to reduce the computational complexity. If the "trick" itself is more complex, nothing should be applied but schoolbook multiplication should be used to solve the problem directly.

Follow these three observations, an analytical boundary should exist and indicate the best stopping point choice. To compute this boundary, it is a good idea to use the number of integer addition and multiplication as the measurement of complexity. For a polynomial multiplication problem with size n, solving it directly with schoolbook multiplication contains $(n - 1)^2$ times of addition and n^2 times of multiplication. When KPMA is applied, KPMA itself contains $10n$ times of addition and 3 half-size sub-problems need to be solved using schoolbook multiplication. Then $3 \times (n/2 - 1)^2$ times of addition and $3 \times (n/2)^2$ times of multiplication are needed. In total, using KPMA for one more step have a complexity of $10n + 3(n/2 - 1)^2$ additions and $\frac{3}{4}n^2$ multiplications. Here, we assume that the execution time of addition and multiplication are the same. Then, the boundary is the solution of the following inequality:

$$(n - 1)^2 + n^2 > 10n + 3(\frac{n}{2} - 1)^2 + \frac{3n^2}{4}$$

After computation, the solution is $n > 18$. It means that KPMA and TCPMA can reduce the computation complexity if and only if the problem size is larger than 18. Based on current application scenario, the stopping point should be 16.

Hybrid Polynomial Multiplication Algorithm Design. With base case size $n_{sp} = 16$, PMAs used between $n = 256$ and $n_{sp} = 16$ as well as the order of them need to be discussed. In this project, we design and implement five hybrid PMAs. The general information of them is listed in Table 1.

Table 1. Five Hybrid Polynomial Multiplication Algorithms.

Algorithm Name	$256 \rightarrow 128$	$128 \rightarrow 64$	$64 \rightarrow 32$	$32 \rightarrow 16$	$16 \rightarrow solved$
TC-TC	TC256TC		TC64		Schoolbook
TC-K-K	TC256KK		K64	K32	Schoolbook
K-TC-K	K256TC	TC128		K32	Schoolbook
K-K-TC	K256KTC	K128TC	TC64		Schoolbook
K-K-K-K	K256KK	K128K	K64	K32	Schoolbook

There are 5 different combinations of KPMA and TCPMA, which start from $256°$ input and end at $16°$ base case. Indicated by the PMA names and application order, these five hybrid PMAs are "TC-TC", "TC-K-K", "K-TC-K", "K-K-TC" and "K-K-K-K". To construct these hybrid PMAs, 11 PMA functions have been implemented. Their names are shown in Table 1. For the naming schema, function names follow the format "FUN1 + LENGTH + FUN2". Here, "FUN1" means the method used in this function. "LENGTH" defines the input size. FUN2" indicates the sub-problem solutions invoked. Besides, schoolbook multiplication is implemented as the base case solution invoked by every hybrid PMA. So, "FUN2" will be omitted when it is schoolbook multiplication. Also, a function may have multiple sub-problem solution choices. For example, sub-problem with degree $n_1 = 128$ can be solve with both "K128TC" and "K128K". To avoid confusion, "FUN3" will be added after "FUN2" to point out the sub-problem solution. So, "K256KTC" indicates that it will use "K128TC" as its sub-problem solution while "K128K" will be used by "K256KK".

Base Case Solution Implementation. Based on the observations, the base cases that invoke high-complexity schoolbook multiplication contribute the majority of integer addition and multiplication operations. As a result, small modification made on base case solution may gain a big improvement. During the implementation process, we adapt three versions of base case solution. A brief introduction of them is given below:

- Original version: Original version follows the procedure that human computes the multiplication of two polynomials. Within a nested loop, the product of each pair of coefficients will be computed one by one and products with same degree will be added together.
- Loop-free version: Loop-free version uses fixed and tiled statements to directly compute the result at each degree to reduce the extra computation, such as controller updating, comparison, and jumps, contained in loop structure. In practical on-board experiments, loop-free version saves a non-negligible proportion of time and provides the best performance.
- Assembly version: Assembly version follows the same algorithm but is implemented in RISC-V assembly language.

These 3 versions of base case solution are combined with all hybrid PMAs. The on-board performance of them are given in Sect. 5.

3.3   Modular Multiplication on RISC-V

Until now, most contents mentioned above are based on theoretical analysis. However, during the adaptation of different PMAs on RISC-V development boards, T-Core as well as HiFive 1 Rev B, the overflow problem has serious influence on algorithm applicability and computational complexity, especially for the NTT-based PMAs. In this section, we will talk about the overflow encountered in RISC-V platform implementation and the 32-bit restricted multiplier we proposed as the corresponding solution.

Overflow on RISC-V RV32I Implementation. As the name suggests, platforms based on RV32I ISA are only good at dealing with 32-bit operations. Even though T-Core and HiFive1 Rev B support 64-bit operation of "long long" type, all operations related to "long long" type are inefficient. So, the overflow may influence the efficiency of PMAs. For non-NTT-based PMAs, the overflow is relatively rare to happen and has no negative effects on algorithm correctness since the modular reduction can be implemented by keeping least significant 13 bits. However, with enlarged NTT modulus $\hat{q} > nq^2$ (for Saber, $\hat{q} > 4194305$), every integer multiplication under NTT-based PMA has the risk of overflow and Barrett reduction should be used to avoid using "long long" type mod operation. Besides, the multiplication results which are longer than 32 bits but shorter than 64 bits will be split and stored in half using RISC-V instructions mul and $mulh$. So, modular reduction operation is compulsory after each time of multiplication. As a result, the 32-bit restricted multiplier that conducts the multiplication and modular reduction at the same time is required. Under this circumstance, we designed a 32-bit restricted multiplier with modified Barrett reduction [10] for 32-bit RISC-V platforms.

32-Bits Restricted Multiplier. The min modulus we selected in Sect. 3.1, 4194305 has 23 bits. So, direct multiplications under current modulus will have the risk of overflow. However, the multiplications in NTT are $a \times b \mod \hat{q} = c$. It means that even though $a \times b$ will produce a number which is possibly larger than 32 bits, it would not be longer than modulus's bit length after modular reduction. This observation provides a possible solution: discard the high bits in advance to reduce the problem size. Based on this idea, a restricted 32-bit multiplier with modified Barrett reduction [10] is designed. Algorithm 3 shows the general steps of it. In Algorithm 3, $[a]^k$ means the most significant k bits of a while $[a]_k$ means the least significant k bits of a. All multiplication results are split and stored in half.

The main improvement is about the bit shift operation after multiplication. Suppose the $\hat{q}$ has k bits and a modular multiplication $c = a \times b \mod \hat{q}$ is required, while using Barrett reduction, an important step is to compute the $(a \times b \gg k) \times r$, where $r = \lfloor 4^k/q \rfloor$. The general idea of the improved bit shift operation after multiplication can be divided into three steps. The first step is to divide the 32-bit a, b into 16-bit a_0, a_1, b_0, b_1, where $a = a_0 + a_1 2^{16}$, $b = b_0 + b_1 2^{16}$. Then, the second step is to compute the result components c_0, c_1, c_2, where $c_0 = a_0 b_0$, $c_1 = a_0 b_1 + a_1 b_0 = (a_0 + a_1) \times (b_0 + b_1) - c_0 - c_2$, and $c_2 = a_1 b_1$. The last step is the bit shift and recovery. The bit shift is implemented as following:

$$a \times b \gg k = (c_0 + c_1 2^{16} + c_2 2^{32}) \gg k$$
$$= (c_1 + c_0 \gg 16) \gg (k - 16) + c_2 \ll (32 - k)$$

Specifically, $c_2 = a_1 b_1$, so the bit size of c_2, l_{c_2} is at most $l_{a_1} + l_{b_1}$, which means $l_{c_2} \leq 2(k - 16)$. In addition, $(c_1 + c_0 \gg 16) \gg (k - 16)$ is definitely less than 32 bits. So, if $c_2 \ll (32 - k)$ and $r = \lfloor 4^k/q \rfloor$ have bits less than 64, then the whole modified Barrett reduction will have no overflow risk. So, if $R_{32} = 2^{32} \mod \hat{q}$, we have new requirement for the parameter choice, which is $2k + l_{R_{32}} \leq 64$. Also, as mentioned in Sect. 3.1, the modulus 4206593 is selected instead of the original 4205569 according to this criteria.

4   Implementation and Experiment

In this section, the implementation and benchmark details of previously mentioned PMAs will be introduced and discussed. For the content organization, basic information of two development boards, T-Core as well as HiFive 1 Rev B, and the experiment environment settings will be provided in Sect. 4.1. In Sect. 4.2, implementation techniques used in algorithm adaptation will be described. Besides, the measurements contained in the benchmark will be listed.

Algorithm 3: 32-Bit Restricted Multiplication with Modified Barrett Reduction

Input: Two integer a,b, modular q, constant $k = \lceil \log_2 q \rceil$, $r = \lfloor 4^k/q \rfloor$, $cons = 2^{k+1}$

Output: $c = a \times b \mod q$

1   $x_0 = [a \times b]_{32}$
2   $x_1 = [a \times b]^{32}$
3   $X = [x_0]_{k+1}$
4   $V_1 = [x_0]_{k-1} + [x_1] << 32 - k + 1$
5   $Y_0 = [V_1 \times r]_{32}$
6   $Y_1 = [V_1 \times r]^{32}$
7   $W = [Y_0]_{k+1} + [Y_1] << 32 - k - 1$

8   $Y = [W \times q]_{k+1}$
9   **if** $X \geq Y$ **then**
10 | $c = X - Y$
11   **else**
12 | $c = X - Y + cons$
13   **if** $c \geq 2q$ **then** **return** $c = c - 2q$;
14   **if** $c \geq q$ **then**
15 | **return** $c = c - q$
16   **else**
17 | **return** c

4.1 Experiment Platform and Environment Setting

To provide comparison between different PMAs based on run-time performance, it is necessary to select good underlying platforms. SiFive HiFive1 B Rev is one of the most popular RISC-V-supportive system-on-chips (SoC) all over the world. Besides, Hummingbird E203 is also a good RISC-V SoC made by China. To provide better application generalization as well as result significance, T-Core which uses Hummingbird E203 as its micro-controller unit and HiFive1 B Rev are used as the underlying experiment platforms.

Terasic T-Core & SiFive HiFive 1 Rev B. To start with, brief introductions to these two SoCs will be given respectively.

T-Core is designed and produced by Terasic Incorporation. It is based on Intel MAX10 FPGA with 64 MB QSPI Flash, which provides more hardware resources compared to SiFive HiFive1 Rev B though it utilizes Hummingbird E203 SoC, which is similar to the SoC of HiFive1 Rev B. It has a JTAG USB-Blaster II supporting users to develop RISC-V projects on it. Its main frequency is about 50–100 MHz. For on-chip memory system, T-Core has flexible-size ITCM for instruction and 4 KB ROM. It also has 64 MB off-chip QSPI flash read, flexible size on-chip DTCM-SRAM for data storage, and ITCM-SRAM for instruction, which means it uses ITCM instead of instruction cache.

SiFive HiFive1 Rev B is the first commercial development board based on RISC-V. It has been used as a benchmarking platform for cryptographic algorithms on RISC-V. It uses FE310 core with RV32IMAC as the ISA and uses JTAG as the debugger. Its main frequency is 320 MHz. It has 16 KB L1 instruction cache for on-chip memory system, 32 MB off-chip flash, 16 KB data RAM for SRAM, and 16 KB instruction cache.

Experiment Environment Setting. To compare the time complexity of various PMAs meaningfully, configurations on both two platforms for each test project keep identical during the whole benchmark process. The configuration information for T-Core and HiFive1 Rev B is listed below.

T-Core Environment Specification. Terasic has provided a mirror of Ubuntu 16.04 in which some development tools and requited environment including Quartus Prime Lite v19.1 for creating RISC-V core, USB Blaster II driver, T-Core RISC-V E203 SDK and Open On-Chip Debugger (OpenOCD), the GNU MCU Eclipse IDE for development of RISC-V on embedded hardware have been installed. The programs implemented on the board will be run in this Ubuntu system. RISC-V GCC is used as the C compiler of T-Core C implementation. Its version is riscv-none-embed-gcc8.3.0-1-1. The ISA contains RV32I and its extensions of RVM, RVA and RVC. For each project, the integer ABI is set to ILP32, and the code model is medium low. The C library used in this project is set as newlib-nano. For run configuration, OpenOCD is used for debugging and generating an *.elf* file. The debugger configuration is referred in an openocd_tcore.cfg file provided by BSP.

HiFive1 Rev B Environment Specification. The toolchain for RISC-V development on HiFive1 Rev B has been included in Freedom Studio, the official IDE for this board. Freedom Studio as an IDE contains the development kit, Freedom E SDK, for compiling RISC-V on the board. This choice of IDE enables development on Windows. The default configurations support for normal running. For this project, the development on HiFive1 Rev B is done on Windows. The bundled toolchains have been installed with the Freedom studio IDE itself, so no more configuration is needed.

4.2   Algorithm Implementation and Benchmark

To get the most representative results, some extra techniques are applied to further accelerate the computation. At the same time, the run-time benchmark on two RISC-V platforms have different purposes. The techniques and benchmark settings are briefly introduced below.

Algorithm Implementation Tricks. Besides adapting the most efficient algorithms mentioned in current literature, two kinds of optimization techniques are used.

- Precomputation: For NTT and INTT process, when modulus is fixed, many variables will never change such as twiddle factors, inverse of n, n-th root of unity, and positions in bit reversal process. All of the following data are precomputed and stored as constant.
- General Efficient Arithmetic: Bit shifting is used instead of multiplication when possible. Karatsuba trick is used to compute $c_1 = (a_0b_1 + a_1b_0) = ((a_0 + a_1) \times (b_0 + b_1) - c_0 - c_2)$ in restricted 32-bit multiplier.

Benchmark Setting. In general, the on-board experiments of all NTT-based and non-NTT-based PMAs on their computational efficiency are mainly conducted on T-Core because of the convenience provided by Tarsic technical support. After preliminary experiment on T-Core, superior PMAs will be tested on HiFive1 Rev B to provide more generalized efficiency measurement.

The run-time benchmark is designed to conduct three groups of contrast test. The first contrast test is to compare the efficiency of 5 non-NTT-based hybrid PMAs with 3 different base case solutions. The second one aims at making a comparison between non-NTT-based PMAs and NTT-based PMA. The third goal is to explore the performance of the same PMA adapted on different platforms.

For the run-time benchmark measurement, considering the non-negligible differences between two development boards, we choose the cycle count instead of time to measure the run-time complexity.

5   Experiment Result

There are 17 versions of PMAs which are tested on T-Core, including 15 combinations of 5 hybrid PMAs and 3 base case solutions and 2 NTT-based PMAs which are LCNTT and LCNTT using 32-Bit restricted multiplier with modified Barrett reduction (namely, LCNTT(BR)). After the on-board experiment on T-Core, 7 versions of PMAs are tested on HiFive1 Rev B, which includes the 5 hybrid PMAs combined with the most efficient base case solution (loop-free version) and 2 NTT-based PMAs. The corresponding experiment results are shown in Table 2 and Table 3.

5.1   Non-NTT-Based PMAs on T-Core

Table 2. Cycle count Comparison Between Hybrid Polynomial Multiplication Algorithms with Different Base Case Solutions on T-Core.

	TC-TC	TC-K-K	K-TC-K	K-K-TC	K-K-K-K
Original Version	410716	523347	521639	524801	666455
Assembly Version	441046	580320	560243	584622	719593
Loop-free Version	327366	417769	414326	421436	531840

As shown in Table 2, there are several discoveries about the run-time performance of non-NTT-based hybrid PMAs on T-Core.

First, compared with the performance while using different hybrid PMAs and different base case solutions, the relationships between them are stable. It means that the influence of changing the base case solution is stable for all hybrid PMAs. While changing the base case solution from original C implementation into loop-free version, PMA performance will always improve. Besides, the relative complexity ranks among hybrid PMAs are stable no matter what kind of base case solution is used. While using the same base case solution, Hybrid PMAs' complexity always follows the rank: TC-TC < K-TC-K < TC-K-K < K-K-TC < K-K-K-K.

Second, the performance of a PMA highly depends on the base case solution complexity. For example, when changing K-K-TC's base case solution from original C implementation into loop-free version by simply removing the loop structure, it will have a 28% speedup. It shows that the small modification made in base case solution may result in a big speed-up. Besides, the complexity rank follows the rank of base case numbers. The fact is that "TC-TC" who has only 49 base case solutions invoked becomes the most efficient hybrid PMA and its superiority is significant. At the same time, with the most base case solution invocation, "K-K-K-K" is unsurprisingly the worst one. "TC-K-K", "K-TC-K", and "K-K-TC" have the same base case numbers, so their differences in cycle count are not that significant.

Last, self-implemented assembly base case function performed worst among 3 versions. It demonstrates that it is hard to make improvement by simply change the codes into assembly versions without algorithm level modification in nature.

5.2 Non-NTT-Based and NTT-Based PMAs on T-Core and HiFive1 Rev B

Table 3. Cycle Count Comparison Between Different Polynomial Multiplication Algorithms on T-Core and HiFive1 Rev B.

	TC-TC	TC-K-K	K-TC-K	K-K-TC	K-K-K-K	LCNTT	LCNTT (BR)
T-Core	327366	417769	414326	421436	531840	1263541	795448
HiFive1 Rev B	724924	794719	763813	771071	859156	688288	551771

Based on the first line of Table 3, neither LCNTT nor LCNTT(BR) has comparability with other hybrid PMAs. A conclusion can be made that the modular reductions required in NTT-based PMAs are too complex that increase the complexity in a large scale on T-Core. At the same time, due to the overflow handing, modular reductions take place almost every time an operation is carried out. On the contrary, built upon powers of two moduli, TCPMA and KPMA can directly ignore the modular reduction operations, which save a lot of computational forces.

However, the second line of Table 3 shows the excellence given by LCNTT. It shows that by adapting LCNTT on HiFive1 Rev B, the efficiency of NTT-based PMA overcomes the extra complexity required in overflow handling and result in a 5% speedup compared with the most efficient hybrid PMA, "TC-TC". In addition, the cycle count on HiFive1 Rev B is significantly larger than the one on T-Core. This may because the basic computation operations on HiFive1 Rev B need more cycles, so the influence of high-complexity modular reduction has been attenuated.

It is worth mentioning that the 32-bit restricted multiplier with modified Barrett reduction designed by us speeds up the LCNTT PMA on both two platforms. It decrease 37% of cycle count on T-core and 20% on HiFive1 Rev B. It shows that our multiplier is efficient on modular multiplication implemented on RISC-V platforms using RV32I ISA.

5.3 Discussion on the Gap Between Theory and Practice

As shown in Table 2 and Table 3, the hybrid PMA with the best performance is "TC-TC" while the current implementation uses the third performance "TC-K-K". The reason may be that in literature [9], it can use Advanced Vector Extensions (AVX) and compute 16 16-degree polynomial multiplication problems using single extension instruction. While using "TC-K-K", its 63 base cases can be perfectly solved using 4 times of extension instruction mentioned above. However, "TC-TC" will generate 49 base case problems. It is really awkward to have an extra one and prevent it from using only 3 times.

6 Conclusion

In this paper, five non-NTT-based hybrid PMAs adapted from TCPMA and KPMA have been designed based on the Saber parameter settings. LCNTT for Saber on RISC-V platforms has been adapted with new parameter selection criteria. Besides, a 32-bit restricted multiplier with modified Barrett reduction is designed to solve the overflow problem and speed up the modular reduction operation. In practice, a 36.4% speed-up is achieved compared with original Barrett modular multiplication. Next, a benchmark analyzing the on-board performance of different PMAs has been conducted on two RISC-V development boards, SiFive HiFive 1 Rev B and Terasic T-Core. The experiment results show that PMA's on-board performance not only depends on the algorithm itself, but also the platform features. So, large research potential remains in the adaptation of PMAs on RISC-V platforms. This paper can be regarded as a reference for future studies which focus on efficient arithmetic of energy-efficient platforms.

Acknowledgments. The authors would like to thank the anonymous reviewers for their constructive suggestions and comments on our paper. This work is partially supported by the National Natural Science Foundation of China (No. 62002023), Guangdong Provincial Key Laboratory of Interdisciplinary Research and Application for Data Science, BNU-HKBU United International College (2022B1212010006), and UIC research grant (R0400001-22).

References

1. Abdulrahman, A., Chen, J., Chen, Y., Hwang, V., Kannwischer, M.J., Yang, B.: Multi-moduli NTTs for saber on Cortex-M3 and Cortex-M4. IACR Trans. Cryptogr. Hardw. Embed. Syst. **2022**(1), 127–151 (2022). https://doi.org/10.46586/tches.v2022.i1.127-151

2. Bernstein, D.J.: Batch binary Edwards. In: Halevi, S. (ed.) CRYPTO 2009. LNCS, vol. 5677, pp. 317–336. Springer, Heidelberg (2009). https://doi.org/10.1007/978-3-642-03356-8_19

3. Bodrato, M., Zanoni, A.: Integer and polynomial multiplication: towards optimal Toom-Cook matrices. In: Wang, D. (ed.) Proceedings of the 2007 International Symposium on Symbolic and Algebraic Computation, ISSAC 2007, Waterloo, Ontario, Canada, 28 July–1 August 2007, pp. 17–24. ACM (2007). https://doi.org/10.1145/1277548.1277552

4. Chung, C.M., Hwang, V., Kannwischer, M.J., Seiler, G., Shih, C., Yang, B.: NTT multiplication for NTT-unfriendly rings new speed records for Saber and NTRU on Cortex-M4 and AVX2. IACR Trans. Cryptogr. Hardw. Embed. Syst. **2021**(2), 159–188 (2021). https://doi.org/10.46586/tches.v2021.i2.159-188

5. D'Anvers, J.-P., Karmakar, A., Sinha Roy, S., Vercauteren, F.: Saber: module-LWR based key exchange, CPA-secure encryption and CCA-secure KEM. In: Joux, A., Nitaj, A., Rachidi, T. (eds.) AFRICACRYPT 2018. LNCS, vol. 10831, pp. 282–305. Springer, Cham (2018). https://doi.org/10.1007/978-3-319-89339-6_16

6. Fritzmann, T., et al.: Masked accelerators and instruction set extensions for post-quantum cryptography. IACR Trans. Cryptogr. Hardw. Embed. Syst. **2022**(1), 414–460 (2022). https://doi.org/10.46586/tches.v2022.i1.414-460

7. Fritzmann, T., Sigl, G., Sepúlveda, J.: RISQ-V: tightly coupled RISC-V accelerators for post-quantum cryptography. IACR Trans. Cryptogr. Hardw. Embed. Syst. **2020**(4), 239–280 (2020). https://doi.org/10.13154/tches.v2020.i4.239-280

8. Hwang, V., et al.: Verified NTT multiplications for NISTPQC KEM lattice finalists: Kyber, SABER, and NTRU. IACR Trans. Cryptogr. Hardw. Embed. Syst. **2022**(4), 718–750 (2022). https://doi.org/10.46586/tches.v2022.i4.718-750

9. Mera, J.M.B., Karmakar, A., Verbauwhede, I.: Time-memory trade-off in Toom-Cook multiplication: an application to module-lattice based cryptography. IACR Trans. Cryptogr. Hardw. Embed. Syst. **2020**(2), 222–244 (2020). https://doi.org/10.13154/tches.v2020.i2.222-244

10. Ye, Z., Cheung, R.C.C., Huang, K.: PipeNTT: a pipelined number theoretic transform architecture. IEEE Trans. Circ. Syst. II Express Briefs **69**(10), 4068–4072 (2022). https://doi.org/10.1109/TCSII.2022.3184703

11. Zhang, N., Yang, B., Chen, C., Yin, S., Wei, S., Liu, L.: Highly efficient architecture of NewHope-NIST on FPGA using low-complexity NTT/INTT. IACR Trans. Cryptogr. Hardw. Embed. Syst. **2020**(2), 49–72 (2020). https://doi.org/10.13154/tches.v2020.i2.49-72

Generic Constructions of Server-Aided Revocable ABE with Verifiable Transformation

Feng Yang[1]([✉]), Hui Cui[2], and Jiwu Jing[3]

[1] School of Computer Science and Technology, University of Chinese Academy of Sciences, Beijing, China
yangfeng181@mails.ucas.edu.cn
[2] Department of Software Systems & Cybersecurity, Monash University, Melbourne, Australia
[3] School of Cryptology, University of Chinese Academy of Sciences, Beijing, China

Abstract. Attribute-based encryption (ABE) is a promising approach in cloud computing services to enable scalable access control on encrypted data. Server-aided revocable attribute-based encryption (SR-ABE) was proposed to realize user revocation and optimize the workloads of data users in ABE. In this paper, we revisit the notion of SR-ABE and present a generic construction of verifiable SR-ABE, which can not only transform a revocable attribute-based encryption (RABE) scheme into an SR-ABE scheme but also provide verifiability to check whether the server behaves as expected. We additionally give an instantiation of verifiable SR-ABE by applying the generic construction on a concrete revocable ABE scheme, and evaluate the performance of the instantiation in terms of functionality, storage overhead, computational cost, and security.

Keywords: Cloud computing · Access control · Server-aided revocable attribute-based encryption · Verifiable transformation

1 Introduction

As the rise of vehicle-networking, smart-home, collaborative-office etc., there is an increasing trend in accessing data across multiple platforms. In these scenarios, cloud computing services have been widely used to facilitate data sharing [6]. However, since cloud computing services often deal with massive amounts of valuable data, they become attractive to (insider) attackers.

A natural solution to this problem is to share data in encrypted form. Traditional "one-to-one" encryption techniques may be inefficient in cloud environments, as they lack the scalability of sharing the data among a group of recipients. A secure and flexible fine-grained access control mechanism over encrypted data is desirable.

J. Zhou et al. (Eds.): ACNS 2023 Workshops, LNCS 13907, pp. 459–479, 2023.
https://doi.org/10.1007/978-3-031-41181-6_25

Sahai and Waters [18] firstly consider this issue by introducing attribute-based encryption (ABE). In such a cryptosystem, each user is described by a set of attributes and holds a decryption key corresponding to these personal attributes. A data owner can share encrypted data with multiple recipients whose attributes meet the access conditions of the ciphertext.

Despite of the advantages, ABE fails to address the challenge that a legitimate user's access may expire over time. The notion of revocable ABE [17] was proposed to address this issue, in which a key generation center (KGC) periodically distributes key update information that only allows non-revoked users to update their decryption keys (by combining their private keys with the key update information). But it requires each user to store a private key of the logarithmic size, and asks each non-revoked user to periodically update his/her decryption key.

To further optimize user revocation in ABE, a server-aided revocable ABE (SR-ABE) scheme [7] has been proposed, in which almost all workloads of users incurred by the user revocation are outsourced to an untrusted server, and each user only needs to keep a private key of the constant size. In addition, a user only needs to perform a small amount of calculations to decrypt a ciphertext.

1.1 Motivation

In an SR-ABE-based system, data users will benefit from outsourcing most of the workloads of decryption to a server by adding a new transformation algorithm into traditional attribute-based encryption. In a secure SR-ABE [8,14], data confidentiality is guaranteed since a server cannot make final decryption by itself or colluding with revoked users. The server can be operated by any third proxy, and any external proxy can be considered as untrusted. However, when considering employing an untrusted server, users may naturally doubt whether this server will always work as expected. What if a server returns a wrong transformation result? Strictly speaking, the above notion is indeed a "half" untrusted server whereas it satisfies the data confidentiality required by data owners but fails to meet the correctness assurance argued by data users. A straightforward way that can be used by data users is re-running the transformation algorithm and comparing the result with that received from a server. But this manner shall conflict with our original intention to reduce the computational overhead through transformation. A more efficient way to verify the transformation in SR-ABE-based cloud computing services is required.

1.2 Our Contribution

We revisit the notion of the untrusted server in SR-ABE, and consider it one step further by tolerating an untrusted server that may behave in transformation in an unpredictable manner. That is, an untrusted server may transform the ciphertext as expected or even in a disordered way. We start by providing a generic way to build a verifiable SR-ABE, and after proving the security of the proposed generic construction under the defined security model, we additionally give an instantiation on verifiable SR-ABE. The detailed contributions of the paper can be summarized as:

- We shall present a generic construction for building server-aided revocable attribute-based encryption with verifiable transformation. At a high level, we can transform a revocable ABE scheme into a verifiable SR-ABE scheme, by assuming that there exists a secure revocable ABE scheme [19, 21], a secure public-key encryption (PKE) scheme and a secure non-interactive commitment scheme. The general construction has the following merits:
  - A data user only needs to keep a private user-key, the size of which is independent of the attribute set, the access structure, or the revocation structure.
  - A data user generates a private user-key by himself/herself, and forwards the corresponding public user-key to the key generation center to apply the public attribute-keys. A key generation center only distributes attribute-keys and transformation-key updating information that all can disclose to the public.
  - Attribute-related decryption operations are all outsourced to a third server. A data user only performs final decryption on a partially decrypted ciphertext.
  - Our construction reduces the restriction for a third server in SR-ABE to be untrusted. On the one hand, a data user can utilize an untrusted server to help transform a ciphertext to a partially decrypted one without revealing the underlying encrypted message. On the other hand, our proposal provides verifiability for a data user to check whether an untrusted server behaves as expected. Therefore, an untrusted server could be operated by anyone including the cloud. We should note that a data user can check the behavior of a server by re-running the whole transformation and decryption algorithm by himself/herself, straightforwardly. However, the verification is much more efficient within our construction.
- By instantiating our generic construction based on Cui et al.'s revocable ciphertext-policy attribute-based encryption (CP-ABE) scheme [19] which is indistinguishable under chosen plaintext attacks (IND-CPA secure), Boneh et al.'s linear encryption scheme [4], and Pedersen commitment [12], we present a concrete server-aided revocable CP-ABE scheme that has the advantages declared by the generic construction.

1.3 Related Work

To realize efficient user revocation in identity-based encryption (IBE), Qin et al. [13] proposed the notion of server-aided revocable identity-based encryption (SR-IBE). In the framework of SR-IBE, a server is introduced to partially decrypt a ciphertext using a time-based short-term transformation key. Later, Cui et al. [7] extended SR-IBE in attribute-based setting and proposed the notion of server-aided revocable attribute-based encryption (SR-ABE). Qin et al. [14, 15] enhanced the results in [7] by capturing the decryption key exposure attacks.

However, in the existing SR-ABE schemes, a data user cannot efficiently verify whether the transformation process is correctly proceeded by the untrusted server or not.

Organization. We briefly give an organizational outline to the paper. In Sect. 2, we review the necessary preliminaries used in our scheme. The framework and security model are described in Sect. 3. Section 4 presents our generic construction of the verifiable SR-ABE along with its security proofs. In Sect. 5, we give an instantiation scheme based on our generic construction and make comparisons of the proposal with several related works. Section 6 offers a conclusion.

2   Preliminaries and Definitions

2.1   Bilinear Groups

An asymmetric prime-order (Type-III) pairing group generator $\mathcal{G}$ is defined as an algorithm that takes a security parameter κ as input and outputs $(p, \mathbb{G}, \mathbb{H}, \mathbb{G}_T, e, g, h)$, where $\mathbb{G}$, $\mathbb{H}$ and $\mathbb{G}_T$ are cyclic groups of the same order p, g generates $\mathbb{G}$, h generates $\mathbb{H}$, and $e : \mathbb{G} \times \mathbb{H} \to \mathbb{G}_T$ is an efficiently polynomial time computable bilinear map with following properties:

- $\forall u \in \mathbb{G}, v \in \mathbb{H}, a, b \in \mathbb{Z}_p, e(u^a, v^b) = e(u, v)^{ab}$.
- $\forall u \in \mathbb{G}, v \in \mathbb{H}, a, b \in \mathbb{Z}_p, e(u^{a+b}, v) = e(u^a, v)e(u^b, v)$.

2.2   Access Structures and Linear Secret Sharing

Definition 1 *(Access Structure [16]). Let $P = \{P_1, P_2, ..., P_n\}$ be a set of parties. A collection $\mathbb{A} \subseteq 2^P$ is monotone for $\forall B, C$: if $B \in \mathbb{A}$ and $B \subseteq C$, then $C \in \mathbb{A}$. The (monotone) access structure is a (monotone) collection $\mathbb{A}$ of nonempty subsets of P, i.e., $\mathbb{A} \subseteq 2^P \backslash \{\emptyset\}$. The sets in $\mathbb{A}$ are called authorized sets, or else the sets are called the unauthorized sets.*

In attribute-based encryption, since the role of the parties is taken by the attributes, the access structure contains the authorized sets of attributes.

Definition 2 *(Linear Secret Sharing Schemes (LSSS) [20]). A secret sharing scheme Π over a set of parties P is called linear over $\mathbb{Z}_p$ if*

- *The shares for each party form a vector over $\mathbb{Z}_p$.*
- *There exists a matrix M with ℓ rows and n columns called the share-generating matrix for Π. For $x = 1, 2, ..., \ell$, the x'th row M_x of M is labeled by a party $\rho(x)$, where ρ is a function that maps a row of M into a party $\in P$. Consider the column vector $\vec{v} = (s, t_2, t_3, ..., t_n)$, where $s \in \mathbb{Z}_p$ is the secret to be shared and $t_2, t_3, ..., t_n \in \mathbb{Z}_p$ are randomly selected. Then $M\vec{v}$ is the vector of l shares of the secret s; here the share $\lambda_x = (M\vec{v})_x = M_x \cdot \vec{v}$ belongs to the corresponding party $\rho(x)$.*

It is shown in [2] that according to the above definition, each secret sharing scheme also enjoys the linear reconstruction property. Assuming that Π is an LSSS for the access structure $\mathbb{M}$. Suppose $S \in \mathbb{M}$ is an authorized set, and define $I \in \{1, 2, ..., \ell\}$ as $I = \{x : \rho(x) \in S\}$. There exists a set of constants $\{w_x \in \mathbb{Z}_p\}_{x \in I}$ satisfying that $\sum_{x \in I} w_x M_x = (1, 0, ..., 0)$, such that, if $\{\lambda_x\}$ are valid shares of the secret s according to Π, we have $\sum_{x \in I} w_x \lambda_x = s$. In addition, those constants $\{w_x\}$ can be found in polynomial time in the size of the share-generating matrix M [2].

2.3 Public-Key Encryption

A PKE scheme is composed of the following algorithms:

- Setup(1^κ) $\rightarrow$ *par*. Taking a security parameter 1^κ as input, this algorithm outputs the public parameters *par*.
- KeyGen(par) $\rightarrow$ (pk, sk). Taking the public parameters *par* as input, it outputs a public and private key pair (pk, sk).
- Encrypt(par, pk, m) $\rightarrow$ ct. Taking the public parameters *par*, the public key pk and a message $m \in \mathcal{M}$ (here $\mathcal{M}$ is the message space) as input, it outputs a ciphertext ct.
- Decrypt(par, sk, ct) $\rightarrow$ m or $\perp$. Taking the public parameters *par*, the private key sk as input, it outputs a message m or a failure symbol $\perp$.

The correctness of a PKE scheme requires that for any security parameter κ and any message $m \in \mathcal{M}$, we have Decrypt(par, sk, ct) $= m$.

A PKE scheme is indistinguishable under chosen plaintext attacks (IND-CPA secure) if: for any probabilistic polynomial time (PPT) adversary $\mathcal{A}$ and a challenger $\mathcal{C}$, let $(m_0, m_1) \leftarrow \mathcal{A}$, $ct_b = \mathcal{PKE}$.Encrypt($\cdot, \cdot, m_b$) $\leftarrow \mathcal{C}$(where b is uniformly selected in $\{0, 1\}$), the advantage $Adv = |\Pr[b = b'] - \frac{1}{2}|$ is negligible in the security parameter κ.

2.4 Revocable Attribute-Based Encryption

Take the revocable CP-ABE as an instance, which consists of seven algorithms. Let $\mathcal{M}$ denote the message space, and $\mathcal{T}$ be the space of time periods.

- Setup($1^\kappa, N$) $\rightarrow$ (par, msk, rl, st). Taking a security parameter κ and the maximal number of system users N as input, the key generation center (KGC) runs this algorithm. The algorithm outputs the public parameter *par*, the master secret key msk, an initially empty revocation list rl and a state st.
- KeyGen(par, id, S) $\rightarrow$ (sk_{id}^S, st). Taking the public parameter *par*, an identity id and a set of attributes S as input, it outputs a secret key sk_{id}^S and an updated state st.
- KeyUp(par, msk, t, rl, st) $\rightarrow$ ku_t. Taking the public parameter *par*, the master secret key msk, a time period t, a revocation list rl and a state st as input, this algorithm outputs a key update message ku_t.

- DecKeyGen$(par, sk_{id}^S, ku_t) \rightarrow dk_{id,t}^S$. Taking the public parameter par, the secret key sk_{id}^S of an identity id, a key update message ku_t, it outputs a decryption key $dk_{id,t}^S$ for identity id. This algorithm is run by the data user id.
- Encrypt$(par, (\mathbb{M}, \rho), t, m) \rightarrow ct$. Taking the public parameter par, an access structure $(\mathbb{M}, \rho)$, a time period t and a message m as input, a data owner runs this algorithm to generate the ciphertext ct.
- Decrypt$(par, ct, dk_{id,t}) \rightarrow m$ or $\perp$. Taking the public parameter par, the ciphertext ct and a decryption key $dk_{id,t}^S$, the data user id runs this algorithm and retrieves the underlying message m or a failure symbol $\perp$.
- Revoke$(id, t, rl) \rightarrow (rl', st')$. Taking an identity id to be revoked, a time period t and a revocation list st, this algorithm outputs the updated revocation list rl' and the updated state st'.

Due to space limitation, some basic cryptographic notions are omitted here, including the correctness and the security definition of a revocable ABE. They can be found in [8].

2.5 Non-interactive Commitment

A commitment scheme is a two-phase protocol between two participants, a sender and a receiver. Here we only consider the so-called non-interactive commitment scheme, in which all the communication goes from the sender to the receiver. A non-interactive commitment scheme $\mathcal{COM}.(\mathsf{Init}, \mathsf{Commit}, \mathsf{Reveal})$ with message space $\mathcal{M}$, random space $\mathcal{V}$ and commitment space $\mathcal{D}$ is composed of the following algorithms [11]:

- Init$(1^\kappa) \rightarrow par$. Taking a security parameter 1^κ as input, the initialization algorithm outputs the public commitment parameters par.
- Commit$(par, m, r) \rightarrow cm$. Taking the public commitment parameters par, a message $m \in \mathcal{M}$ and the auxiliary information $r \in \mathcal{V}$ as input, the committing algorithm outputs a commitment $cm \in \mathcal{D}$.
- Reveal$(par, m, r, cm) \rightarrow b \in \{0, 1\}$. Taking the public commitment parameters par, a message m, the auxiliary information r and a commitment cm as input, the revealing algorithm outputs $b = 1$ to indicate that cm is a commitment to m; otherwise, it outputs $b = 0$.

The correctness of a commitment scheme requires that for all public commitment parameters par output by $\mathsf{Init}(1^\kappa)$ and for any message $m \in \mathcal{M}$ and any auxiliary information $r \in \mathcal{V}$, we have $\mathsf{Reveal}(par, m, r, \mathsf{Commit}(par, m, r)) = 1$.

A commitment scheme is secure if it satisfies two security properties, namely the hiding and binding properties. Informally, the hiding property indicates that a commitment cm to m does not reveal any information about m, whereas the binding property guarantees that a commitment cm to m cannot be opened to another value m'.

3   Framework and Security Model

In this section, we describe the framework and security model of the verifiable SR-ABE (with ABE being CP-ABE). Note that it also works for key-policy attribute-based encryption (KP-ABE) except that the attribute set S in the PubKeyGen algorithm will be replaced by the access structure $(\mathbb{M}, \rho)$, and the relevant access structure $(\mathbb{M}, \rho)$ in the Encrypt algorithm will be replaced by the attribute set S.

3.1   Framework

There are four entities in the system architecture: the KGC, data users, data suers and an untrusted server.

- Key generation center(KGC). The KGC keeps the master private key and publishes the public parameters. The KGC is responsible for distributing public attribute-keys for non-revoked users. It also periodically generates key updating information for non-revoked users and publicly transmits them to the untrusted server.
- Data owner. Before uploading a message to the cloud, the data owner specifies an access structure and encrypts the message under this access structure and a valid time period.
- Untrusted server. An untrusted server is responsible for transforming the original ciphertext into a partially decrypted one by using a data user's public transformation key. An untrusted server can generate such a transformation key from a data user's public attribute-key and the public key updating information distributed by the KGC. The server involves in our scheme is untrusted so that it could be operated by anyone including the cloud.
- Data user. A data user intends to decrypt the encrypted data. To do this, a data user generates a public and private user-key pair by himself/herself and forwards the public user-key to KGC to require the corresponding public attribute-keys. Then a public transformation key can be generated by the public attribute-key and the public updating information. The data user forwards the ciphertext to an untrusted server and obtains the partially decrypted ciphertext. When a data user receives the partial decrypted ciphertext from an untrusted server, he/she can make the final decryption using his/her private user-key. He/She can also verify whether the transformation process is correctly proceeded or not. A data user can eventually obtain the underlying message if and only if his/her attributes satisfy the access structure and he/she is not revoked at (or before) the valid time.

A generic server-aided revocable ABE (with ABE being CP-ABE) with verifiable transformation consists of ten PPT algorithms given below:

- Setup($1^{\kappa}, N$) $\rightarrow$ (par, msk, rl, st). Taking a security parameter κ and the maximal number of system users N as input, the key generation center (KGC) runs this algorithm. The algorithm outputs the public parameter par, the master secret key msk, an initially empty revocation list rl and a state st.

- UserKeyGen$(par, id) \rightarrow (pk_{id}, sk_{id})$. Taking the public parameter par, an identity id as input, this algorithm outputs a public and private user-key pair (pk_{id}, sk_{id}).
- PubKeyGen$(par, msk, st, pk_{id}, \mathcal{S}) \rightarrow (pk_{id}^{\mathcal{S}}, st')$. Taking the public parameter par, the master secret key msk, a state st, the public user-key pk_{id}, and a set of attributes $\mathcal{S}$, this algorithm outputs a public attribute-key $pk_{id}^{\mathcal{S}}$ for the identity id and a state st. The KGC runs this algorithm and sends $(pk_{id}^{\mathcal{S}}, st)$ to the untrusted server, and update the state $st' \leftarrow st$.
- TKeyUp$(par, msk, t, rl, st) \rightarrow tku_t$. Taking the public parameter par, the master secret key msk, a time period t, a revocation list rl and a state st as input, this algorithm outputs a transformation key update information tku_t. The KGC runs this algorithm and sends tku_t to the untrusted server.
- TranKeyGen$(par, pk_{id}^{\mathcal{S}}, t, tku_t, rl, st) \rightarrow tk_{id,t}^{\mathcal{S}}$. Taking the public parameter par, the public attribute-key $pk_{id}^{\mathcal{S}}$ of an identity id, a time period t, a key update message tku_t, a revocation list rl and a state st, the server runs this algorithm and outputs a transformation key $tk_{id,t}^{\mathcal{S}}$ for identity id.
- Encrypt$(par, (\mathbb{M}, \rho), t, m) \rightarrow ct$. Taking the public parameter par, an access structure $(\mathbb{M}, \rho)$, a time period t and a message m as input, a data owner runs this algorithm to generate the ciphertext ct.
- Transform$(par, tk_{id,t}^{\mathcal{S}}, ct) \rightarrow tct\ or \perp$. Taking the public parameter par, a transformation key $tk_{id,t}^{\mathcal{S}}$ of identity id, and a ciphertext ct as input, this algorithm outputs a transformed (partially decrypted) ciphertext tct if the attribute set $\mathcal{S}$ associated with $tk_{id,t}^{\mathcal{S}}$ satisfies the access structure of ct; otherwise, it output $\perp$ to indicate the failure of the transformation. The server runs this algorithm and returns the transformed ciphertext tct to the data user id.
- Decrypt$(par, tct, sk_{id}) \rightarrow m'$. Taking the public parameter par, the transformed ciphertext tct and a private user-key sk_{id}, the data user id runs this algorithm and obtains the decrypted message m'.
- Verify$(par, m') \rightarrow m$ or $\perp$. This algorithm verifies the decrypted message m', and outputs m to indicate that the transformation is processed correctly; otherwise, it outputs a failure symbol $\perp$.
- Revoke$(id, t, rl, st) \rightarrow (rl', st')$. Taking an identity id to be revoked, a time period t and a revocation list st, this algorithm outputs the updated revocation list rl' and the updated state st'.

3.2   Security Model

Below we describe the security definition of indistinguishability under chosen plaintext attacks (IND-CPA secure) for verifiable SR-ABE between an adversary algorithm $\mathcal{A}$ and a challenger algorithm $\mathcal{B}$.

- Setup. Algorithm $\mathcal{B}$ runs the Setup algorithm, and gives the public parameter par to algorithm $\mathcal{A}$, and keeps the master private key msk, an initially empty revocation list rl and a state st.
- Phase 1. Algorithm $\mathcal{A}$ adaptively issues a sequence of following queries to algorithm $\mathcal{B}$.

- Private-User-Key oracle. Algorithm $\mathcal{A}$ issues a private user-key query on an identity id. Algorithm $\mathcal{B}$ returns sk_{id} by running UserKeyGen(par, id). Note that once algorithm $\mathcal{B}$ runs UserKeyGen(par, id), it adds (id, pk_{id}, sk_{id}) to a list so that the same (pk_{id}, sk_{id}) is used for all queries on id.
- Public-Attribute-Key oracle. Algorithm $\mathcal{A}$ issues a public attribute-key query on an identity id and an attribute set $\mathcal{S}$. Algorithm $\mathcal{B}$ returns $pk_{id}^{\mathcal{S}}$ by running UserKeyGen(par, id) (if id has not been issued to the Private-User-Key oracle) and PubKeyGen($par, msk, st, pk_{id}, \mathcal{S}$).
- Transformation-Key-Update oracle. Algorithm $\mathcal{A}$ issues a key update query on a time period t. Algorithm $\mathcal{B}$ runs TKeyUp(par, msk, t, rl, st) and returns tku_t.
- Transformation-Key oracle. Algorithm $\mathcal{A}$ issues a transformation key query on a time period t and an identity id with an attribute set $\mathcal{S}$. Algorithm $\mathcal{B}$ returns $tk_{id,t}^{\mathcal{S}}$ by running UserKeyGen (par, id) (if id has not been issued to the Private-User-Key oracle), PubKeyGen($par, msk, st, pk_{id}, \mathcal{S}$), TKeyUp($par, msk, t, rl, st$),   TranKeyGen ($par, pk_{id}^{\mathcal{S}}, t, tku_t, rl, st$).   Note that this oracle cannot be queried on a time period t before a transformation key update oracle has been queried on t.
- Revocation oracle. Algorithm $\mathcal{A}$ issues a revocation query on an identity id and a time period t. Algorithm $\mathcal{B}$ runs Revoke(id, t, rl, st) and outputs an updated revocation list rl'. Note that a time period t on which a transformation key update query has been issued cannot be issued to this oracle.

- Challenge. Algorithm $\mathcal{A}$ outputs two messages m_0^*, m_1^* of the same size, an access structure $(\mathbb{M}^*, \rho^*)$ and a time period t^* satisfying the following constraints.
  - Case 1: if (1) an identity id^* has been queried to the Private-User-Key oracle, and (2) $(\mathbb{M}^*, \rho^*)$ can be satisfied by a query on $(id^*, \mathcal{S}^*)$ issued to the Public-Attribute-Key oracle, then (1) the revocation oracle must be queried on (id^*, t) on $t = t^*$ or any t occurs before t^*, and (2) the Transformation-Key oracle cannot be queried on (id^*, t^*).
  - Case 2: if an identity id^* whose attribute set $\mathcal{S}^*$ can be satisfied by the challenge access structure $(\mathbb{M}^*, \rho^*)$ is not revoked at or before t^*, then id^* should not be previously queried to the Private-User-Key oracle.
  Algorithm $\mathcal{B}$ randomly chooses $b \in \{0, 1\}$, and forwards the challenge ciphertext ct^* to algorithm $\mathcal{A}$ by running Encrypt($par, (\mathbb{M}^*, \rho^*), t^*, m_b^*$).
- Phase 2. Algorithm $\mathcal{A}$ continues issuing queries to algorithm $\mathcal{B}$ as in Phase 1, following the restrictions defined in the Challenge phase.
- Guess. Algorithm $\mathcal{A}$ makes a guess b' for b, and it wins the game if $b' = b$.

The advantage of algorithm $\mathcal{A}$ in this game is defined as $|\Pr[b = b'] - 1/2|$. A verifiable SR-ABE scheme is IND-CPA secure if any probabilistic polynomial time (PPT) adversary has at most a negligible advantage in the security parameter κ. In addition, a verifiable SR-ABE scheme is said to be selectively IND-CPA secure if an Init stage is added before the Setup phase where algorithm $\mathcal{A}$ commits to the challenge access structure $(\mathbb{M}^*, \rho^*)$ (and the challenge time period t^*) which it attempts to attack.

4 Generic Construction

Let $\mathcal{PKE}.$(Setup, KeyGen, Enc, Dec) be a PKE scheme. Let $\mathcal{RABE}.$(Setup, KeyGen, KeyUp, DecKeyGen, Encrypt, Decrypt, Revoke) be a RABE scheme. Let $\mathcal{COM}.$(Init, Commit, Reveal) be a commitment scheme. We describe the proposed generic construction as follows:

- Setup($1^\kappa, N$) $\rightarrow$ (par, msk, rl, st). It runs the $\mathcal{PKE}.$Setup, $\mathcal{RABE}.$Setup and $\mathcal{COM}.$Init, and outputs the public parameter $par = (par_{\mathcal{PKE}}, par_{\mathcal{RABE}}, par_{\mathcal{COM}})$, the master secret key $msk = msk_{\mathcal{RABE}}$, a revocation list rl and a state st.
- UserKeyGen(par, id) $\rightarrow$ (pk_{id}, sk_{id}). This algorithm runs the $\mathcal{PKE}.$KeyGen to obtain pk, sk, and outputs pk, sk as the public and private user-key pair (pk_{id}, sk_{id}) for a user id.
- PubKeyGen($par, msk, st, pk_{id}, \mathcal{S}$) $\rightarrow$ $(pk_{id}^{\mathcal{S}}, st')$. This algorithm first runs the $\mathcal{RABE}.$KeyGen to obtain $((sk_{id}^{\mathcal{S}})_{\mathcal{RABE}}, st)$, and then it runs the $\mathcal{PKE}.$Encrypt to encrypt $(sk_{id}^{\mathcal{S}})_{\mathcal{RABE}}$ to generate a ciphertext $ct_{\mathcal{PKE}}$, and outputs $(ct_{\mathcal{PKE}}, st')$ as the public attribute-key $pk_{id}^{\mathcal{S}}$ and a state st'.
- TKeyUp(par, msk, t, rl, st) $\rightarrow$ tku_t. This algorithm runs $\mathcal{RABE}.$KeyUp to obtain ku_t, and outputs ku_t as the transformation key update information tku_t.
- TranKeyGen($par, pk_{id}^{\mathcal{S}}, t, tku_t, rl, st$) $\rightarrow$ $tk_{id,t}^{\mathcal{S}}$. This algorithm runs algorithm $\mathcal{RABE}.$DecKeyGen on $pk_{id}^{\mathcal{S}}$ and tku_t to obtain $dk_{id,t}^{\mathcal{S}}$, and outputs $dk_{id,t}^{\mathcal{S}}$ as the transformation key $tk_{id,t}^{\mathcal{S}}$ for user id who possesses a set of attributes $\mathcal{S}$ during a time period t.
- Encrypt($par, (\mathbb{M}, \rho), t, m$) $\rightarrow$ ct. This algorithm chooses a random element r, and then it runs $\mathcal{RABE}.$Encrypt to encrypt $m||r$ to obtain a ciphertext $ct_{\mathcal{RABE}}$. Additionally, this algorithm runs $\mathcal{COM}.$commit to obtain a commitment $cm_{\mathcal{COM}}$ of m using the element r. Finally, this algorithm outputs $(ct_{\mathcal{RABE}}, cm_{\mathcal{COM}})$ as a final ciphertext ct.
- Transform($par, tk_{id,t}^{\mathcal{S}}, ct$) $\rightarrow$ tct or $\perp$. This algorithm runs the $\mathcal{RABE}.$Decrypt on $tk_{id,t}^{\mathcal{S}}$ and ct, and outputs a transformed ciphertext tct or a failure symbol $\perp$.
- Decrypt(par, tct, sk_{id}) $\rightarrow$ $m||r$. This algorithm runs the $\mathcal{PKE}.$Decrypt on sk_{id} and tct, and outputs a message $m||r$.
- Verify($par, m||r, cm$) $\rightarrow$ m or $\perp$. This algorithm runs the $\mathcal{COM}.$Reveal on $m||r$ and cm. $\mathcal{COM}.$Reveal outputs 1 to indicate that cm is a commitment to m; otherwise, it outputs $b = 0$ to indicate a failure $\perp$.
- Revoke(id, t, rl, st) $\rightarrow$ (rl', st'). This algorithm runs the $\mathcal{RABE}.$Revoke, and outputs an updated revocation list rl' and an updated state st'.

4.1 Security Proofs for Generic Construction

In this subsection, we analysis the security of the generic construction presented above.

Theorem 1. *Assuming that the underlying RABE scheme is (selectively) IND-CPA secure, the underlying PKE scheme is IND-CPA secure and the underlying commitment scheme is computationally hiding, then the above generic construction on revocable SR-ABE is (selectively) IND-CPA secure.*

Proof. Assuming that there exists an adversary algorithm $\mathcal{A}$ that breaks the IND-CPA security of the proposed generic construction, then we can build an algorithm $\mathcal{B}$ that breaks the IND-CPA security of the underlying RABE scheme, or the IND-CPA security of the underlying PKE scheme, or the hiding property of the underlying commitment scheme. Denote $\mathcal{C}_0$ by the challenger algorithm in the IND-CPA security game of the underlying RABE scheme, and $\mathcal{C}_1$ by the challenger algorithm in the IND-CPA security game of the underlying PKE scheme, and $\mathcal{C}_2$ by the challenger algorithm in the hiding property game of the underlying commitment game.

Note that for the selective IND-CPA security, there will be an Init stage before the Setup phase where algorithm $\mathcal{A}$ outputs a challenge access structure $(\mathbb{M}^*, \rho^*)$ (and a challenge time period t^*), which algorithm $\mathcal{B}$ sets as its own output in the Init stage for the IND-CPA security game of the underlying RABE scheme.

Assuming that the equal-length challenge messages submitted by the adversary during the challenge phase have length l_1. We additionally assume that the random element r generated during Encrypt has fixed length l_2. A series of hybrid games are defined for proving the IND-CPA security of the proposed structure:

- $Game_0$: This game is the original IND-CPA security game of RABE. In the challenge phase, the adversary algorithm $\mathcal{A}$ submits two equal-length challenge messages m_0, m_1, an access structure $(\mathbb{M}^*, \rho^*)$ and a time period t^*. The algorithm $\mathcal{B}$ flips a random coin $b \in \{0, 1\}$, chooses a random element r^*. The ciphertext component ct^* will be obtained by running $\mathcal{RABE}.\mathsf{Encrypt}(par, (\mathbb{M}^*, \rho^*), t^*, m_b || r^*)$, and the commitment is generated by running $\mathcal{COM}.\mathsf{Commit}(par, m_b, r^*)$. Note that the simulator $\mathcal{B}$ turns to $\mathcal{C}_0$ for the ciphertext components ct^*.
- $Game_1$: This Game is the same as $Game_0$ except that in the challenge phase, the ciphertext component ct^* is generated by running $\mathcal{RABE}.\mathsf{Encrypt}(par, (\mathbb{M}^*, \rho^*), t^*, 0^{l_1+l_2} || r^*)$.
- $Game_2$: This game is the same as $Game_1$ except that in the challenge phase, the ciphertext component cm^* is generated by running $\mathcal{COM}.\mathsf{Commit}(par, 0^{l_1}, r^*)$.

Lemma 1. *If the underlying RABE scheme is IND-CPA secure, then no PPT adversary can attain a non-negligible difference in advantage between $Game_0$ and $Game_1$.*

Proof. Suppose that there exists a PPT adversary $\mathcal{A}$ that exhibits a non-negligible difference in advantage between $Game_0$ and $Game_1$, then we can build a simulator $\mathcal{B}$ that breaks the IND-CPA security of the underlying RABE scheme with a non-negligible advantage.

Recall that $\mathcal{C}_0$ denotes the challenger of $\mathcal{B}$ in the IND-CPA security game of the underlying RABE scheme, and $\mathcal{C}_1$ is the challenger in the IND-CPA security game of the underlying PKE scheme. The Games are proceeded as follows.

- Setup. Algorithm $\mathcal{B}$ is given only the $par_{\mathcal{RABE}}$ from $\mathcal{C}_0$, $par_{\mathcal{PKE}}$ from $\mathcal{C}_1$. Then algorithm $\mathcal{B}$ generates $par_{\mathcal{COM}}$ by running $\mathcal{COM}.\mathsf{Init}$. Algorithm $\mathcal{B}$ sends $par = (par_{\mathcal{RABE}}, par_{\mathcal{PKE}}, par_{\mathcal{COM}})$ to adversary algorithm $\mathcal{A}$.
- Phase 1. Algorithm $\mathcal{A}$ adaptively issues the following sequence of queries to Algorithm $\mathcal{B}$.
    - Private-User-Key oracle on an identity id. Algorithm $\mathcal{B}$ returns sk_{id} by running $(pk_{id}, sk_{id}) \leftarrow \mathsf{UserKeyGen}(par, id)$. Algorithm $\mathcal{B}$ records (id, pk_{id}, sk_{id}) in a list L for consistence to future queries on id.
    - Public-Attribute-Key oracle on identity id and a set of attributes $\mathcal{S}$. Algorithm $\mathcal{B}$ issues the secret key generation query on $(id, \mathcal{S})$ to algorithm $\mathcal{C}_0$, and algorithm $\mathcal{C}_0$ returns $(sk_{id}^{\mathcal{S}})_{\mathcal{RABE}}$ to algorithm $\mathcal{B}$.
        * If (id, pk_{id}, sk_{id}) already exists in the list L, algorithm $\mathcal{B}$ returns $pk_{id}^{\mathcal{S}}$ by running $pk_{id}^{\mathcal{S}} \leftarrow \mathcal{PKE}.\mathsf{Encrypt}(par, pk_{id}, (sk_{id}^{\mathcal{S}})_{\mathcal{RABE}})$.
        * Otherwise, algorithm $\mathcal{B}$ runs $(pk_{id}, sk_{id}) \leftarrow \mathsf{UserKeyGen}(par, id)$ to generate pk_{id}, and then returns $pk_{id}^{\mathcal{S}} \leftarrow \mathcal{PKE}.\mathsf{Encrypt}(par, pk_{id}, (sk_{id}^{\mathcal{S}})_{\mathcal{RABE}})$.
        At some point, $\mathcal{B}$ randomly selects $(sk_{id*}^{\mathcal{S}})_{\mathcal{RABE}}$, and returns $pk_{id*}^{\mathcal{S}}$ by running $pk_{id*}^{\mathcal{S}} \leftarrow \mathcal{PKE}.\mathsf{Encrypt}(par, pk, (sk_{id*}^{\mathcal{S}})_{\mathcal{RABE}})$. That is to say, algorithm $\mathcal{B}$ implicitly sets the public key pk as the public key for $id*$, and puts $(id^*, pk, \bot)$ to the list L. Based on the IND-CPA security of the PKE scheme, algorithm $\mathcal{A}$ cannot distinguish whether $(sk_{id*}^{\mathcal{S}})_{\mathcal{RABE}}$ is randomly selected or not; otherwise, $\mathcal{B}$ can utilize $\mathcal{A}$ to break the IND-CPA security of the underlying PKE scheme.
    - Transformation-Key-Update oracle on a time period t. Algorithm $\mathcal{B}$ issues the key update query on t to algorithm $\mathcal{C}_0$ and takes the result as the transformation update information tku_t and sends to algorithm $\mathcal{A}$.
    - Transformation-Key oracle on a time period t and an identity id with an attribute set $\mathcal{S}$. Algorithm $\mathcal{B}$ issues the decryption key query on $(id, \mathcal{S}, t)$ to algorithm $\mathcal{C}_0$, and returns the result as the transformation key $tk_{id,t}^{\mathcal{S}}$ to algorithm $\mathcal{A}$.
    - Revoke oracle on an identity id and a time period t. Algorithm $\mathcal{B}$ issues the revoke query on (id, t) to algorithm $\mathcal{C}_0$.
- Challenge. Algorithm $\mathcal{A}$ submits two equal-length messages m_0, m_1 of length l_1, an access structure $(\mathbb{M}^*, \rho^*)$ and a time period t^*. Algorithm $\mathcal{B}$ randomly chooses an element r^*, flips a random coin $b \in \{0, 1\}$ and generates $cm^* \leftarrow \mathcal{COM}.\mathsf{Commit}(par, m_b, r^*)$. It then forwards $(M_0, M_1) = (m_b||r^*, 0^{l_1+l_2})$ and $(\mathbb{M}^*, \rho^*)$ along with t^* to algorithm $\mathcal{C}_0$ to query the challenge ciphertext component ct^*. The algorithm $\mathcal{C}_0$ flips a random coin $\beta \in \{0, 1\}$, and generates ct^* by running $\mathcal{RABE}.\mathsf{Encrypt}(par, (\mathbb{M}^*, \rho^*), t^*, M_\beta)$. Algorithm $\mathcal{B}$ obtains ct^* from $\mathcal{C}_0$, and returns (ct^*, cm^*) to algorithm $\mathcal{A}$.
- Phase 2. Algorithm $\mathcal{A}$ continues issuing queries to algorithm $\mathcal{B}$ as in Phase 1, following the restrictions defined in the security model.

– Guess. Algorithm $\mathcal{A}$ makes a guess b' for b. If $b' = b$, algorithm $\mathcal{B}$ outputs 0; otherwise, it outputs 1.

When algorithm $\mathcal{B}$ makes encryption query to $\mathcal{C}_0$, if $\mathcal{B}$ obtains an encryption of $m_b||r^*$, then adversary algorithm $\mathcal{A}$ is exactly in Game$_0$; otherwise, $\mathcal{A}$ is exactly in Game$_1$. If $\mathcal{A}$ can distinguish Game$_0$ and Game$_1$ with a non-negligible advantage, we can build an algorithm $\mathcal{B}$ to break the IND-CPA security of the underlying RABE with a non-negligible advantage. This completes the proof of Lemma 1.

Lemma 2. *If the underlying commitment scheme is computationally hiding, then no PPT adversary can attain a non-negligible difference in advantage between Game$_1$ and Game$_2$.*

Proof. Suppose that there exists a PPT adversary $\mathcal{A}$ that exhibits a non-negligible difference in advantage between Game$_1$ and Game$_2$, then we can build a simulator $\mathcal{B}$ that breaks the hiding property of the underlying commitment scheme with a non-negligible advantage.

Recall that $\mathcal{C}_2$ denotes the challenger of $\mathcal{B}$ in the hiding property game of the underlying commitment scheme. The Games are proceeded as follows.

– Setup. Algorithm $\mathcal{B}$ queries the $par_{\mathcal{COM}}$ from $\mathcal{C}_2$. Algorithm $\mathcal{B}$ generates $par_{\mathcal{RABE}}$ by running $\mathcal{RABE}$.Setup, and creates $par_{\mathcal{PKE}}$ by running $\mathcal{PKE}$.Setup. Algorithm $\mathcal{B}$ sends $par = (par_{\mathcal{RABE}}, par_{\mathcal{PKE}}, par_{\mathcal{COM}})$ to adversary algorithm $\mathcal{A}$.
– Phase 1. Algorithm $\mathcal{A}$ adaptively issues sequence of queries to Algorithm $\mathcal{B}$. Since the simulator algorithm $\mathcal{B}$ knows the master secret key msk of RABE scheme and the secret key sk of PKE scheme, $\mathcal{B}$ can respond to queries of algorithm $\mathcal{A}$ in a natural way.
– Challenge. Algorithm $\mathcal{A}$ submits two equal-length messages m_0, m_1 of length l_1, an access structure $(\mathbb{M}^*, \rho^*)$ and a time period t^*. Algorithm $\mathcal{B}$ generates $ct^* \leftarrow \mathcal{RABE}$.Encrypt$(par, (\mathbb{M}^*, \rho^*), t^*, 0^{l_1+l_2})$. $\mathcal{B}$ flips a random coin $b \in \{0,1\}$, and forwards $(M_0, M_1) = (m_b, 0^{l_1})$ to algorithm $\mathcal{C}_2$. $\mathcal{C}_2$ flips a random coin $\beta \in \{0,1\}$ and generates $cm^* \leftarrow \mathcal{COM}$.Commit$(par, M_\beta, r^*)$, where r^* is chosen by $\mathcal{C}_2$. Algorithm $\mathcal{B}$ obtains cm^* from $\mathcal{C}_2$, and then forwards (ct^*, cm^*) to $\mathcal{A}$ as the challenge ciphertext.
– Phase 2. Algorithm $\mathcal{A}$ continues issuing queries to algorithm $\mathcal{B}$ as in Phase 1, following the restrictions defined in the security model.
– Guess. Algorithm $\mathcal{A}$ makes a guess b' for b. If $b' = b$, algorithm $\mathcal{B}$ outputs 0; otherwise, it outputs 1.

When algorithm $\mathcal{B}$ makes encryption query to $\mathcal{C}_0$, if $\beta = 0$, then adversary algorithm $\mathcal{A}$ is exactly in Game$_1$; otherwise, $\mathcal{A}$ is exactly in Game$_2$. If $\mathcal{A}$ can distinguish Game$_1$ and Game$_2$ with a non-negligible advantage, we can build an algorithm $\mathcal{B}$ to break the hiding property of the underlying commitment scheme with a non-negligible advantage. This completes the proof of Lemma 2.

Finally, we give the proof of the verifiability of transformation for the proposed construction.

Theorem 2. *If the underlying commitment scheme is computationally binding, then the proposed construction with server-aided transformation is verifiable.*

Proof. Suppose that there exists an algorithm $\mathcal{A}$ that breaks the above construction in the verifiability game with a non-negligible advantage, than we can build a simulator $\mathcal{B}$ which breaks the binding property of the underlying commitment scheme with a non-negligible advantage. $\mathcal{B}$ executes as follows.

$\mathcal{B}$ makes initialization query to algorithm $\mathcal{C}_2$ and obtains the public commitment parameters $par_{\mathcal{COM}}$. Algorithm $\mathcal{B}$ generates $par_{\mathcal{RABE}}$ by running algorithm $\mathcal{RABE}$.Setup, and creates $par_{\mathcal{PKE}}$ by running $\mathcal{PKE}$.Setup. Algorithm $\mathcal{B}$ sends $par = (par_{\mathcal{RABE}}, par_{\mathcal{PKE}}, par_{\mathcal{COM}})$ to adversary algorithm $\mathcal{A}$. Since the simulator algorithm $\mathcal{B}$ knows the master secret key msk of RABE scheme and the secret key sk of PKE scheme, $\mathcal{B}$ can respond to queries of algorithm $\mathcal{A}$ in a natural way. When algorithm $\mathcal{A}$ submits a message m^* and an access structure $(\mathbb{M}^*, \rho^*)$ along with a time period t^*, $\mathcal{B}$ returns the challenge ciphertext (ct^*, cm^*) in the expected way. Algorithm $\mathcal{A}$ continues issuing queries to algorithm $\mathcal{B}$, and $\mathcal{B}$ will answer in the same way as described above. Finally, algorithm $\mathcal{A}$ outputs $tk_{id^*,t^*}^{S^*}$ and a transformed ciphertext tct^*. Note that it is a reasonable assumption that algorithm $\mathcal{A}$ has issued a transformation-key query on (id^*, S^*, t^*), since $\mathcal{B}$ can issue such a query by itself. $\mathcal{B}$ knows $(sk_{id^*}, tk_{id^*,t^*}^{S})$, so that $\mathcal{B}$ can make decryption. Algorithm $\mathcal{A}$ wins the game if $\mathcal{COM}$.Verify$(par, \mathcal{RABE}$.Decrypt$(par, tct^*, sk_{id^*}), cm^*) \notin \{m^*, \bot\}$.

If algorithm $\mathcal{A}$ wins in the above game, we have $m'||r' \leftarrow \mathcal{RABE}$.Decrypt$(par, tct^*, sk_{id^*})$ and $\mathcal{COM}$.Reveal$(par, m', r', cm^*) = 1$, where $m' \notin \{m^*, \bot\}$. Algorithm $\mathcal{B}$ then reveals two different messages m' and m^* from a single commitment cm^*. This exactly violates the binding property of the underlying commitment scheme. This completes the proof of Theorem 2.

5   Instantiation

In this section, we present a concrete server-aided revocable CP-ABE with verifiable transformation, and analyze its performance.

5.1   Proposed SR-ABE with Verifiable Transformation

Below we give a concrete server-aided revocable CP-ABE with verifiable transformation based on Cui et al.'s adaptively IND-CPA secure revocable CP-ABE scheme [19], Pedersen commitment [12] (which is computationally binding and perfectly hiding), and Boneh et al.'s linear encryption scheme [4] (which is secure in the generic groups under the Linear assumption). Note that [19] is constructed based on a fully secure CP-ABE called FAME [1]. FAME is a fast CP-ABE based on a standard assumption on Type III pairing groups and does not put any restriction on policy type or attributes. Our instantiation inherits these advantages. The proposed scheme consists of the following algorithms.

- **Setup.** Obtain $(p, \mathbb{G}, \mathbb{H}, \mathbb{G}_T, e, g, h) \leftarrow \mathcal{G}(1^\kappa)$. Let $\mathcal{R} : \mathbb{G}_T \rightarrow \{0,1\}^*$ be a pseudo-random generator. Choose two collusion resistant cryptographic hash functions $\mathcal{H} : \{0,1\}^* \rightarrow \mathbb{G}$ and $\mathcal{F} : \{0,1\}^* \rightarrow \mathbb{Z}_p$. In the following algorithms, we assume that the inputs to hash functions are appropriately encoded so that no two different tuples collide [1]. Randomly choose $a_1, a_2, b_1, b_2 \in \mathbb{Z}_p^*$, $d_1, d_2, d_3 \in \mathbb{Z}_p$ and $h_1, h_2 \in \mathbb{H}$. Compute $T_1 = e(g,h)^{d_1 a_1 + d_3}$, $T_2 = e(g,h)^{d_2 a_2 + d_3}$, and output

$$par = (h, h_1, h_2, H_1 = h^{a_1}, H_2 = h^{a_2}, T_1, T_2, \mathcal{H}, \mathcal{F}, \mathcal{R})$$

  as the public parameter. Set

$$msk = (g, a_1, a_2, b_1, b_2, g^{d_1}, g^{d_2}, g^{d_3})$$

  as the master secret key. Also, let $rl \leftarrow \emptyset$ be an empty list recording revoked users and BT be a binary tree with at least N leaf nodes, where N is the maximal number of system users. Let $st \leftarrow$ BT be the initial state.

- **UserKeyGen.** Randomly pick $\beta_1, \beta_2 \in \mathbb{Z}_p$, $g_3 \in \mathbb{G}$, compute $g_1 = g_3^{\frac{1}{\beta_1}}$, $g_2 = g_3^{\frac{1}{\beta_2}}$. It outputs a public and private key pair $(pk_{id}, sk_{id}) = ((g_1, g_2, g_3), (\beta_1, \beta_2))$ for user id.

- **PubKeyGen.** Choose an undefined leaf node θ from the binary tree BT, and stores id in this node. Randomly choose $r_1, r_2 \in \mathbb{Z}_p$ and set

$$pk_{id,0} = (h^{b_1 r_1}, h^{b_2 r_2}, h^{r_1 + r_2}).$$

  For all $y \in \mathcal{S}$ and $z = 1, 2$, set

$$pk_{id,y,z} = \mathcal{H}(y1z)^{\frac{b_1 r_1}{a_z}} \cdot \mathcal{H}(y2z)^{\frac{b_2 r_2}{a_z}} \cdot \mathcal{H}(y3z)^{\frac{r_1 + r_2}{a_z}} \cdot g^{\frac{\sigma_y}{a_z}},$$

$$pk'_{id,z} = g^{d_z} \cdot \mathcal{H}(011z)^{\frac{b_1 r_1}{a_z}} \cdot \mathcal{H}(012z)^{\frac{b_2 r_2}{a_z}} \cdot \mathcal{H}(013z)^{\frac{r_1 + r_2}{a_z}} \cdot g^{\frac{\sigma'}{a_z}},$$

  where $\sigma_y, \sigma' \in \mathbb{Z}_p$ is randomly picked.
  Set $pk_{id,y} = (pk_{id,y,1}, pk_{id,y,2}, g^{-\sigma_y})$ and $pk'_{id} = (pk'_{id,1}, pk'_{id,2})$. Then the algorithm randomly chooses $r_3, r_4 \in \mathbb{Z}_p$, and computes $pk_{id,1} = (g_1^{r_3}, g_2^{r_4})$. For each node $x \in \text{Path}(\theta)$ it runs as follows:
  - Fetch g_x from the node x. If x has not been defined, it randomly picks $g_x \in \mathbb{G}$ and stores g_x in the node x.
  - Set $pk_{id,x} = g_3^{r_3 + r_4} \cdot g^{d_3} \cdot g^{-\sigma'}/g_x$.

  Finally, output $pk_{id}^{\mathcal{S}} = (\mathcal{S}, pk_{id,0}, pk_{id,1}, \{pk_{id,y}\}_{y \in \mathcal{S}}, pk'_{id}, \{x, pk_{id,x}\}_{x \in \text{Path}(\theta)})$.

- **TKeyUp.** For all $x \in \text{KUNodes}(st, rl, t)$, fetch g_x from the node x. Note that g_x is predefined in the PubKeyGen algorithm. Randomly pick $r_x \in \mathbb{Z}_p$, and set $tku_{t,x} = (g_x \cdot \mathcal{H}(1t)^{r_x}, h^{r_x})$.
  Output $tku_t = (t, \{x, tku_{t,x}\}_{x \in \text{KUNodes}(st, rl, t)})$ as the transformation key update information.

- TranKeyGen. Denote I as $\mathrm{Path}(\theta)$, J as $\mathrm{KUNodes}(st, rl, t)$. If $I \cap J = \emptyset$, return $\perp$. Otherwise, for any node $x \in I \cap J$, pick $r'_x \in \mathbb{Z}_p$ and set

$$pk'_{id,3} = pk_{id,x} \cdot tku_{t,x,1} \cdot \mathcal{H}(1t)^{r'_x} = g_3^{r_3+r_4} \cdot g^{d_3} \cdot g^{-\sigma'} \cdot \mathcal{H}(1t)^{r_x+r'_x},$$

$$pk_{id,0,4} = tku_{t,x,2} \cdot h^{r'_x} = h^{r_x+r'_x}.$$

Note that $tku_{t,x,1}$ and $tku_{t,x,2}$ denote the first and the second elements of $tku_{t,x}$, respectively.

Set
$pk''_{id} = (pk'_{id,1}, pk'_{id,2}, pk'_{id,3})$ and $pk'_{id,0} = (pk_{id,0,1}, pk_{id,0,2}, pk_{id,0,3}, pk_{id,0,4})$. Similarly, $(pk_{id,0,1}, pk_{id,0,2}, pk_{id,0,3})$ denote the first, second and third elements of $pk_{id,0}$.
Set the transformation key for id as $tk^{\mathcal{S}}_{id,t} = (\mathcal{S}, t, pk'_{id,0}, pk_{id,1}, \{pk_{id,y}\}_{y \in \mathcal{S}}, pk''_{id})$.

- Encrypt. Randomly choose $s_1, s_2 \in \mathbb{Z}_p$, set $ct_0 = (H_1^{s_1}, H_2^{s_2}, h^{s_1+s_2}, \mathcal{H}(1t)^{s_1+s_2})$. Suppose $\mathbb{M}$ has n_1 rows and n_2 columns. For $i = 1, \ldots, n_1$ and $\ell = 1, 2, 3$, set

$$ct_{i,\ell} = \mathcal{H}(\rho(i)\ell 1)^{s_1} \cdot \mathcal{H}(\rho(i)\ell 2)^{s_2} \cdot \prod_{j=1}^{n_2} [\mathcal{H}(0j\ell 1)^{s_1} \cdot \mathcal{H}(0j\ell 2)^{s_2}]^{\mathbb{M}_{i,j}}.$$

Here, $\mathbb{M}_{i,j}$ denotes the $(i,j)_{th}$ element of $\mathbb{M}$. Randomly chooses $r \in \{0,1\}^*$. Set $ct_i = (ct_{i,1}, ct_{i,2}, ct_{i,3})$ and $ct' = (m||r) \oplus \mathcal{R}(T_1^{s_1} \cdot T_2^{s_2})$. Compute the commitment $cm = h_1^{\mathcal{F}(m)} h_2^{\mathcal{F}(r)}$. Output $ct = (ct_0, ct_1, \ldots, ct_{n_1}, ct', (\mathbb{M}, \rho), t, cm)$ as the ciphertext.

- Transform. Parse the transformation key for id as $tk^{\mathcal{S}}_{id,t} = (\mathcal{S}, t, pk'_{id,0}, pk_{id,1}, \{pk_{id,y}\}_{y \in \mathcal{S}}, pk''_{id})$. Suppose that $\mathcal{S}$ in $tk^{\mathcal{S}}_{id,t}$ satisfies the access structure $(\mathbb{M}, \rho)$ in ct. Let I be defined as $I = \{i : \rho(i) \in \mathcal{S}\}$. Then there exist constants $\{\gamma_i\}_{i \in I}$ that satisfy $\sum_{i \in I} \gamma_i \mathbb{M}_i = (1, 0, \ldots, 0)$. Output the transformed ciphertext $tct = (\frac{num}{den}, ct', ct_{0,3}, cm, pk_{id,1})$, where

$$den = e\left(\prod_{i \in I} ct_{i,1}^{\gamma_i}, pk_{id,0,1}\right) \cdot e\left(\prod_{i \in I} ct_{i,2}^{\gamma_i}, pk_{id,0,2}\right) \cdot e\left(\prod_{i \in I} ct_{i,3}^{\gamma_i}, pk_{id,0,3}\right)$$
$$\cdot \, e\left(ct_{0,4}, pk_{id,0,4}\right),$$

$$num = e\left(pk'_{id,1} \cdot \prod_{i \in I} pk_{id,\rho(i),1}^{\gamma_i}, ct_{0,1}\right) \cdot e\left(pk'_{id,2} \cdot \prod_{i \in I} pk_{id,\rho(i),2}^{\gamma_i}, ct_{0,2}\right)$$
$$\cdot \, e\left(pk'_{id,3} \cdot \prod_{i \in I} pk_{id,\rho(i),3}^{\gamma_i}, ct_{0,3}\right).$$

- Decrypt. Parse the transformed ciphertext tct as $(\frac{num}{den}, ct', ct_{0,3}, cm, pk_{id,1})$, and parse the private key sk_{id} as (β_1, β_2). Retrieve $m||r$ by computing $ct' \oplus \mathcal{R}(\frac{num}{den} \cdot \frac{1}{e(pk_{id,1,0}^{\beta_1} \cdot pk_{id,1,1}^{\beta_2}, ct_{0,3})})$, where $(pk_{id,1,1}, pk_{id,1,2})$ denote the first and the second elements of $pk_{id,1}$.

- Verify. If $h_1^{\mathcal{F}(m)} h_2^{\mathcal{F}(r)} = cm$ holds, this algorithm outputs m which indicates that the transformation process is correctly proceeded; otherwise, this algorithm outputs a failure symbol $\perp$.
- Revoke. Output $rl' \leftarrow rl \cup \{(id, t)\}$ and an updated state st'.

5.2 Security Analysis

We analysis the security of the above instantiation as follows.

Theorem 3. *Assuming that the underlying revocable CP-ABE is IND-CPA secure, and the underlying PKE scheme is IND-CPA secure, and the underlying commitment scheme is computationally hiding, then the above server-aided revocable CP-ABE with verifiable transformation is IND-CPA secure.*

Theorem 4. *Assuming that and the underlying commitment scheme is computationally binding, and the underlying revocable CP-ABE is IND-CPA secure, and the underlying PKE scheme is IND-CPA secure, then the above server-aided revocable CP-ABE with verifiable transformation is verifiable.*

Proof. The underlying revocable CP-ABE is proved IND-CPA secure. The underlying linear encryption scheme is also known to be IND-CPA scheme, and the Pedersen commitment is computationally binding and perfectly hiding. It is clear that the proposed instantiation is IND-CPA secure and verifiable according to Theorem 1 and 2.

5.3 Performance Analysis

In this subsection, we give detailed comparisons between the proposed server-aided revocable CP-ABE (with verifiable transformation) and the existing revocable CP-ABE schemes, in terms of functionality, storage overhead, computational cost and security.

Table 1 compares the recently revocable CP-ABE schemes [14, 17, 19, 21, 22] and ours. Let N denote the number of all users, R denote the number of revoked users. Also let k denote the size of the attribute set associated with an attribute-key, m denote the size of rows utilized during transformation or decryption, respectively.

The previous schemes, as described in Table 1, realize revocation on prime-order groups except Sahai et al. [17], where [17] chooses composite-order pairing groups to allow adaptively secure under Subgroup Decision Problem (SDP). Our scheme is adaptively secure under standard assumptions on asymmetric prime-order (Type-III) pairing groups. It is reported in [10] that bilinear pairings are 254 times slower in composite-order than in prime-order groups for the same 128-bit security. Type-III pairings is the recommended choice [9] to build pairing-based cryptographic schemes, since there are no efficiently computable homomorphisms between $\mathbb{H}$ and $\mathbb{G}$, and there exist assumptions available only in the asymmetric setting.

Sahai et al. [17] provides a generic way to support dynamic credentials for ABE, where the key generation center (KGC) realizes the revocation by stopping updating the keys for revoked users. Xu et al. [22] proposes a generic revocable ABE with decryption key exposure resistance and ciphertext delegation. Among these ABE schemes that make use of a server, [17] and [22] need a type of semi-trusted server since it is assumed that the server will not collude with revoked users. Qin et al. [14] introduces a server-aided revocable ABE scheme resilient to decryption key exposure. The server involves in [14] is untrusted. That is, in [14], revoked users cannot obtain more advantage in revealing the encrypted message even if they can collude with the third server. Our scheme also does not need any trusted server, and we take a step forward to verify whether the server behaves as expected.

Table 1. The comparison between verifiable SR-ABE and the existing revocable ABE.

	[22]	[17]	[21]	[19]	[14]	Ours
Group-order	Prime	Composite	Prime	Prime	Prime	Prime
Asymmetric Pairing	No	No	Yes	Yes	No	Yes
Revocation	Yes	Yes	Yes	Yes	Yes	Yes
Verifiable Transform	No	No	No	No	No	Yes
Require Secure Channel	Yes	Yes	Yes	Yes	Yes	No
Server-aided	Semi-trusted	Semi-trusted	–	–	Untrusted	Untrusted
Security	Selective	Adaptive	Adaptive	Adaptive	Selective	Adaptive
Size of Key for Updating	$O(R \cdot \log \frac{N}{R})$	$O(R \cdot \log \frac{N}{R})$	$O(R \cdot \log \frac{N}{R})$	$O(R \cdot \log \frac{N}{R})$	$O(R \cdot \log \frac{N}{R})$	$O(R \cdot \log \frac{N}{R})$
Size of Key Stored by Data Users	$O(k \cdot \log N)$	$O(k \cdot \log N)$	$O(k + \log N)$	$O(k + \log N)$	$O(1)$	$O(1)$
Computation Cost in Transformation	–	–	–	–	$O(m)$	$O(m)$
Computation Cost in Decryption	$O(m)$	$O(m)$	$O(m)$	$O(m)$	$O(1)$	$O(1)$

It is straightforward to see from Table 1 that both [14] and ours have constant size of key stored by data users. Meanwhile, ours does not require any secure channel during the key distribution, as data users create their private keys by themselves and send their public keys for the attribute keys (which are also publicly known). Among these schemes, the same technology named Tree-Based Structure [3] is adopted for revocation. As a result, the size of key for updating (e.g., the transformation key update information in ours) is at the same level.

In the final decryption, [14] and ours only needs constant size of bilinear group operations which is independent of the size of access structure (M, ρ). Specifically, a data user will calculate two pairing operations in [14] and will undertake one pairing operations in ours. The workloads are delegated to an untrusted server during the transformation. Note that even if there are some users who do not need the assistant of a server (this scenario is realistic, since users may have enough computing power or may not accept the potential charging conditions), they can also accomplish the transformation by themselves. The total computation cost is $O(m)$ as well. That is to say, we provide data users the opportunity to enjoy a significant transformation along with verifiability without bringing much overhead.

6   Conclusion

Considering that existing server-aided revocable attribute-based encryption (SR-ABE) does not support user verification on the behavior of the untrusted server, we proposed a generic construction for building a verifiable SR-ABE based on a basic revocable attribute-based encryption (RABE) scheme. After proving that the proposed generic verifiable SR-ABE construction is secure under the defined security model, we presented an instantiation that transformed an IND-CPA secure RABE scheme into an IND-CPA secure verifiable SR-ABE scheme using the proposed generic construction. Compared with the previous solutions on SR-ABE, our scheme tolerated a more realistic notion of the untrusted server. That was, an untrusted server cannot learn the underlying encrypted message, and the correctness of the transformation proceeded by the untrusted server can be efficiently verified.

Acknowledgment. This work is supported by the National Key Research and Development Program of China under Grant No. 2022YFB3103303.

References

1. Agrawal, S., Chase, M.: FAME: fast attribute-based message encryption. In: CCS, pp. 665–682. ACM (2017)
2. Beimel, A.: Secure schemes for secret sharing and key distribution. Ph.D. thesis, Israel Institute of technology, Technion (1996)
3. Boldyreva, A., Goyal, V., Kumar, V.: Identity-based encryption with efficient revocation. In: CCS, pp. 417–426. ACM (2008)
4. Boneh, D., Boyen, X., Shacham, H.: Short group signatures. In: Franklin, M. (ed.) CRYPTO 2004. LNCS, vol. 3152, pp. 41–55. Springer, Heidelberg (2004). https://doi.org/10.1007/978-3-540-28628-8_3
5. Cheng, L., Meng, F.: Server-aided revocable attribute-based encryption revised: multi-user setting and fully secure. In: Bertino, E., Shulman, H., Waidner, M. (eds.) ESORICS 2021. LNCS, vol. 12973, pp. 192–212. Springer, Cham (2021). https://doi.org/10.1007/978-3-030-88428-4_10

6. Costello, K.: Gartner forecasts worldwide public cloud revenue to grow 17.5 percent in 2019 (2019). https://www.gartner.com/en/newsroom/press-releases/2019-04-02-gartner-forecasts-worldwide-public-cloud-revenue-to-g
7. Cui, H., Deng, R.H., Li, Y., Qin, B.: Server-aided revocable attribute-based encryption. In: Askoxylakis, I., Ioannidis, S., Katsikas, S., Meadows, C. (eds.) ESORICS 2016. LNCS, vol. 9879, pp. 570–587. Springer, Cham (2016). https://doi.org/10.1007/978-3-319-45741-3_29
8. Cui, H., Yuen, T.H., Deng, R.H., Wang, G.: Server-aided revocable attribute-based encryption for cloud computing services. Concurr. Comput. Pract. Exp. **32**(14), e5680 (2020)
9. Galbraith, S.D., Paterson, K.G., Smart, N.P.: Pairings for cryptographers. Discrete Appl. Math. **156**(16), 3113–3121 (2008)
10. Guillevic, A.: Comparing the pairing efficiency over composite-order and prime-order elliptic curves. In: Jacobson, M., Locasto, M., Mohassel, P., Safavi-Naini, R. (eds.) ACNS 2013. LNCS, vol. 7954, pp. 357–372. Springer, Heidelberg (2013). https://doi.org/10.1007/978-3-642-38980-1_22
11. Mao, X., Lai, J., Mei, Q., Chen, K., Weng, J.: Generic and efficient constructions of attribute-based encryption with verifiable outsourced decryption. IEEE Trans. Dependable Secur. Comput. **13**(5), 533–546 (2016)
12. Pedersen, T.P.: Non-interactive and information-theoretic secure verifiable secret sharing. In: Feigenbaum, J. (ed.) CRYPTO 1991. LNCS, vol. 576, pp. 129–140. Springer, Heidelberg (1992). https://doi.org/10.1007/3-540-46766-1_9
13. Qin, B., Deng, R.H., Li, Y., Liu, S.: Server-aided revocable identity-based encryption. In: Pernul, G., Ryan, P.Y.A., Weippl, E. (eds.) ESORICS 2015. LNCS, vol. 9326, pp. 286–304. Springer, Cham (2015). https://doi.org/10.1007/978-3-319-24174-6_15
14. Qin, B., Zhao, Q., Zheng, D., Cui, H.: Server-aided revocable attribute-based encryption resilient to decryption key exposure. In: Capkun, S., Chow, S.S.M. (eds.) CANS 2017. LNCS, vol. 11261, pp. 504–514. Springer, Cham (2018). https://doi.org/10.1007/978-3-030-02641-7_25
15. Qin, B., Zhao, Q., Zheng, D., Cui, H.: (Dual) server-aided revocable attribute-based encryption with decryption key exposure resistance. Inf. Sci. **490**, 74–92 (2019)
16. Rouselakis, Y., Waters, B.: Practical constructions and new proof methods for large universe attribute-based encryption. In: CCS, pp. 463–474. ACM (2013)
17. Sahai, A., Seyalioglu, H., Waters, B.: Dynamic credentials and ciphertext delegation for attribute-based encryption. In: Safavi-Naini, R., Canetti, R. (eds.) CRYPTO 2012. LNCS, vol. 7417, pp. 199–217. Springer, Heidelberg (2012). https://doi.org/10.1007/978-3-642-32009-5_13
18. Sahai, A., Waters, B.: Fuzzy identity-based encryption. In: Cramer, R. (ed.) EURO-CRYPT 2005. LNCS, vol. 3494, pp. 457–473. Springer, Heidelberg (2005). https://doi.org/10.1007/11426639_27
19. Tian, Y., Miyaji, A., Matsubara, K., Cui, H., Li, N.: Revocable policy-based chameleon hash for blockchain rewriting. Comput. J. (2022)
20. Waters, B.: Ciphertext-policy attribute-based encryption: an expressive, efficient, and provably secure realization. In: Catalano, D., Fazio, N., Gennaro, R., Nicolosi, A. (eds.) PKC 2011. LNCS, vol. 6571, pp. 53–70. Springer, Heidelberg (2011). https://doi.org/10.1007/978-3-642-19379-8_4
21. Xu, S., Ning, J., Ma, J., Xu, G., Yuan, J., Deng, R.H.: Revocable policy-based chameleon hash. In: Bertino, E., Shulman, H., Waidner, M. (eds.) ESORICS 2021.

LNCS, vol. 12972, pp. 327–347. Springer, Cham (2021). https://doi.org/10.1007/978-3-030-88418-5_16

22. Xu, S., Yang, G., Mu, Y.: Revocable attribute-based encryption with decryption key exposure resistance and ciphertext delegation. Inf. Sci. **479**, 116–134 (2019)

Hybrid Post-quantum Signatures in Hardware Security Keys

Diana Ghinea[1,2], Fabian Kaczmarczyck[2(✉)], Jennifer Pullman[2], Julien Cretin[2], Stefan Kölbl[2], Rafael Misoczki[2], Jean-Michel Picod[2], Luca Invernizzi[2], and Elie Bursztein[2]

[1] ETH, Zürich, Switzerland
ghinead@ethz.ch
[2] Google, Zürich, Switzerland
{dianamin,kaczmarczyck,jpullman,cretin,kste,
jmichel,invernizzi,elieb}@google.com

Abstract. Recent advances in quantum computing are increasingly jeopardizing the security of cryptosystems currently in widespread use, such as RSA or elliptic-curve signatures. To address this threat, researchers and standardization institutes have accelerated the transition to quantum-resistant cryptosystems, collectively known as Post-Quantum Cryptography (PQC). These PQC schemes present new challenges due to their larger memory and computational footprints and their higher chance of latent vulnerabilities.

In this work, we address these challenges by introducing a scheme to upgrade the digital signatures used by security keys to PQC. We introduce a hybrid digital signature scheme based on two building blocks: a classically-secure scheme, ECDSA, and a post-quantum secure one, Dilithium. Our hybrid scheme maintains the guarantees of each underlying building block even if the other one is broken, thus being resistant to classical and quantum attacks. We experimentally show that our hybrid signature scheme can successfully execute on current security keys, even though secure PQC schemes are known to require substantial resources.

We publish an open-source implementation of our scheme at https://github.com/google/OpenSK/releases/tag/hybrid-pqc so that other researchers can reproduce our results on a nRF52840 development kit.

Keywords: PQC · FIDO · Dilithium · Embedded

1 Introduction

Recent advances in quantum computing are increasingly jeopardizing the security of cryptosystems currently in widespread use, such as RSA [34] and DSA [21]. For example, even the comparatively-newer ECDSA, based on elliptic curve cryptography [20], is vulnerable to quantum attacks (i.e., attacks that leverage quantum computers).

To address this threat, researchers and standardization institutes have accelerated the transition to quantum-attack-resistant cryptosystems, collectively

© The Author(s), under exclusive license to Springer Nature Switzerland AG 2023
J. Zhou et al. (Eds.): ACNS 2023 Workshops, LNCS 13907, pp. 480–499, 2023.
https://doi.org/10.1007/978-3-031-41181-6_26

known as Post-Quantum Cryptography (PQC). These PQC schemes rely on a new set of underlying hard problems, that researchers believe to be impervious to quantum attacks. However, these schemes present new challenges due to their substantial memory and computational footprints and their higher chance of latent vulnerabilities due to the schemes' novelty, such as the one recently discovered by Castryck and Decru [9] against SIKE. To mitigate the potential damage, researchers are pursuing hybrid signature schemes [6], which maintain the classical scheme's security against classical attackers.

One class of protocols that needs upgrading to PQC is security-key-based authentication protocols, such as FIDO's CTAP and WebAuthn [15,22]. Through these protocols, a user can prove their identity with a hardware token (commonly called a *security key*), either as a first-factor or second-factor authentication.

In this work, we address this challenge by introducing a PQC digital signature scheme for hardware security keys, focusing on both the theoretical and practical aspects of this scheme. Specifically, we introduce a hybrid scheme based on two building blocks: a classically-secure scheme, ECDSA, and a post-quantum secure one, Dilithium. We picked Dilithium [13] as it is one of the schemes recently selected by United States National Institute of Science and Technology (NIST) [28] as the PQC standard for digital signature schemes and because of the fast speed of its signing—the most frequent operation in our use case.

On the practical aspect, we show that our hybrid signature scheme can be executed by current security keys, even though secure PQC schemes require substantial resources. Specifically, we implement our hybrid scheme in OpenSK [31], an open-source firmware for security keys written in Rust. We provide our implementation as open-source software with an Apache2 license at https://github.com/google/OpenSK/releases/tag/hybrid-pqc.

Our contributions are as follows:

- We prove the strong unforgeability of a previously proposed hybrid signature scheme [6] in the context of security key authentication. Our hybrid scheme maintains the guarantees of each underlying scheme even if the other one is broken, thus being resistant to classical and quantum attacks.
- We release an implementation of our hybrid scheme with ECDSA and Dilithium as underlying components. We have implemented this scheme in Rust on top of the security-key firmware OpenSK. To allow deployment on diverse hardware, we do not take advantage of any hardware-specific acceleration and we ensure that the memory footprint of our hybrid scheme fits in 64 kB of RAM. This requirement leads us to reduce Dilithium's memory footprint.

1.1 Related Work

Hybrid Cryptosystems. For the transition period to prevalent quantum computers, hybrid cryptosystems provide security against future quantum attackers, while mitigating potential design or implementation bugs in the face of classical attackers. Hybrid solutions exist for e.g., authenticated key exchange [2,12], public-key encryption [25], and digital signatures [6].

The hybrid scheme we are implementing in this work follows one of the designs presented in [6]. The difference is that we investigate the feasibility of achieving post-quantum security under the constraints of embedded hardware. Furthermore, we show that this design actually achieves stronger security definitions than shown in [6] (i.e., strong existential unforgeability versus existential unforgeability). In addition, we show a natural extension to a larger class of hybrid signature schemes of the non-separability property introduced by Bindel et al., and we show how it can be applied in the context of passwordless authentication.

PQC for FIDO. In a concurrent work, Bindel et al. [5] have analyzed whether FIDO can provide PQC guarantees from a theoretical point of view and formally verify parts of the FIDO protocols. They argue how PQC can be integrated to maintain theoretical guarantees. Our work complements theirs in the following aspects:

- They focus on the PIN protocol, and mostly omit registration and authentication. We propose a signing scheme for this use case.
- They formally prove parts of the FIDO protocols. We prove the security guarantees of a hybrid signing primitive.
- They propose changes to the FIDO protocols, leaving the cryptographic primitives as an open choice. We implement a PQC primitive that works on embedded hardware, and open-source fully-working firmware.

Dilithium vs Other PQC. Dilithium [13] and Falcon [24] both won NIST's post-quantum signature algorithm standardization challenge. We compare the two schemes in Fig. 1. As will be discussed in Sect. 5, for security keys, we are mainly interested in the signing speed and the private key size, whereas verification is not performed on embedded hardware. The private key size affects how many credentials can be stored on the security key.

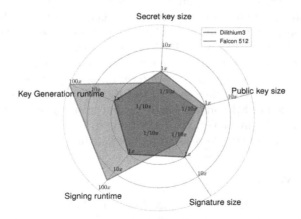

Fig. 1. Relative performance of Falcon 512 compared to the reference implementation of Dilithium3 as the baseline for the security key use case, as reported by Raavi et al. [33] in Figure 6.

We optimize Dilithium in Sect. 5 to get closer to Falcon in key sizes. Our implementation maintains competitive signing speeds, while having favorable properties overall. We use some of the optimization techniques in Bos et al. [7], and implement them in Rust for added memory safety.

- *Private key size:* We store the 256-bit secret that we use to regenerate the private key on the fly. Given the amount of entropy we need, this is near-optimal in terms of required storage.
- *Public key and signature size:* Public keys and signatures have to be small enough for transmission over USB and NFC. Falcon has 2× smaller public keys and 3× smaller signatures than Dilithium for comparable security levels. Dilithium is still compatible with the CTAP protocol's constraints.
- *Key generation speed:* Dilithium is 100x faster for key generation [18] than Falcon. That is why we can regenerate private keys on the fly from the stored random seed.
- *Memory:* Falcon has smaller requirements, but Dilithium can be optimized to fit embedded devices.

Outside of lattice-based signatures, there are stateless hash-based signature schemes like SPHINCS+ [3] which has been selected as a standard by NIST. However, their much larger signature size is infeasible for our use case, and the performance cost of signing compared to lattice schemes is significantly worse.

Improvements to Dilithium's Performance. Multiple works have focused on improving Dilithium's reference implementation [32] in terms of speed and memory footprint. Another direction is vulnerability against side-channel attacks, Migliore et al. [27] analyze Dilithium on an ARM Cortex-M3 microcontroller, and remove unexpected leakages through masking. Greconici et al. [17] obtain a constant-time Dilithium implementation on the Cortex-M3, which is necessary for limiting potential side-channel attacks. In addition, they present different strategies for the signing procedure that allow trading between the stack and flash memory usage and speed, which can be applied for Cortex-M3 and Cortex-M4. Abdulrahman et al. [1] focused on further improvements of Dilithium's speed on the ARM Cortex-M4.

Concurrently to our work, Bos et al. [7] have focused on reducing Dilithium's memory footprint to less than 9 kB. While our implementation requires less than 22 kB, one can choose to compile different optimizations according to the use case. Minimizing for binary size shrinks it to 9.3 kB compared to 9.8 kB for Bos et al. Letting the compiler optimize for speed makes our code 6% to 18% faster than them instead. Other advantages are: it ensures memory safety as it is written in Rust, it is open-source and ready to use for security keys, even in the hybrid setting.

2   Background

In this section, we introduce the relevant cryptography, describe our use case of security keys and explain our hardware and firmware stack for embedded development.

2.1 Digital Signatures

We first recall the definition of a digital signature scheme. For our scope, we only consider signature schemes deployed on classical computers.

Definition 1 *(Digital signature scheme). A digital signature scheme Σ is a triple of polynomial time algorithms (Σ.KeyGen, Σ.Sign, Σ.Verify) such that:*

- Σ.KeyGen(1^κ) *is a probabilistic algorithm that takes the security parameter 1^κ as input and outputs a public verification key* pk *and a secret signing key* sk.
- Σ.Sign(m, sk) *is a probabilistic algorithm that takes a message m and a secret key* sk *as inputs and outputs a signature σ.*
- Σ.Verify(m, σ, pk) *is a deterministic algorithm that takes a message m, a signature σ and a public key* pk *as inputs. It outputs* true *or* false, *where* true *means that σ is accepted as a signature for the message m and public key* pk, *and* false *means that the signature is not accepted.*

Digital signature schemes must achieve two properties: *correctness* and *security*. Correctness requires that for every key pair (sk, pk) $\leftarrow\!\!\$ $ Σ.KeyGen(1^κ), every possible message m, and any possible $\sigma \leftarrow\!\!\$ $ Σ.Sign(m, sk), it holds that Σ.Verify(m, σ, pk) = true. In terms of security, there are multiple definitions, and we present the ones relevant for our context below.

The security of digital signatures is often defined through a security game where an adversary tries to forge a valid signature while interacting with a challenger who holds the secret key. For the scope of our paper, we only consider classical challengers (i.e., the signing oracle runs on a classical computer). We will use the notation C-adversary to refer to a classical adversary, and Q-adversary to refer to a quantum adversary with classical access to the signing oracle.

Security guarantees for digital signatures are often defined through the goals and constraints of the adversary. We only work with two security definitions, presented below: EUF-CMA (Existential Unforgeability under Chosen Message Attacks) and SUF-CMA (Strong Unforgeability under Chosen Message Attacks).

Definition 2 *(EUF-CMA security). We consider the EUF-CMA security game for a signature scheme Σ, where the adversary $\mathcal{A}$ interacts with a challenger $\mathcal{C}$ as follows:*

1. *The challenger $\mathcal{C}$ obtains a pair of keys from the key generation algorithm* (sk, pk) $\leftarrow\!\!\$ $ Σ.KeyGen(1^κ) *and sends* pk *to $\mathcal{A}$.*
2. *$\mathcal{A}$ may adaptively send a polynomial (in κ, the security parameter) number of queries m_i to the challenger $\mathcal{C}$. For each such query, $\mathcal{C}$ obtains $\sigma_i = \Sigma$.Sign(m, sk) and sends σ_i to the adversary. Note that $\mathcal{A}$ may send query m_{i+1} after receiving σ_i.*
3. *$\mathcal{A}$ may send a message-signature pair (m^*, σ^*). $\mathcal{A}$ wins the EUF-CMA security game if $m^* \notin \{m_i$ queried by the adversary$\}$ and Σ.Verify(m^*, σ^*, pk) holds.*

We say that Σ is C-EUF-CMA secure if any classical $\mathcal{A}$ wins the EUF-CMA security game with negligible probability (negl(κ)). Similarly, Σ is Q-EUF-CMA secure if any (possibly quantum) $\mathcal{A}$ that interacts with the signing oracle classically wins the EUF-CMA security game with negligible probability (negl(κ)).

Definition 3 *(SUF-CMA security). Similar to Definition 2, but replace EUF with SUF and step 3 with:*

3. *$\mathcal{A}$ may send a message-signature pair (m^*, σ^*). $\mathcal{A}$ wins the SUF-CMA security game if $(m^*, \sigma^*) \notin \{(m_i, \sigma_i) \mid m_i$ queried$\}$ and $\Sigma.\mathtt{Verify}(m^*, \sigma^*, \mathtt{pk})$ holds.*

Achieving SUF-CMA security implies achieving EUF-CMA security, and achieving the quantum variant of a definition implies achieving the classical variant.

We recall the security guarantees of the concrete digital signature schemes that we use:

- ECDSA achieves C-EUF-CMA security in the random bijection model [14].
- Dilithium achieves Q-SUF-CMA security in the quantum random oracle model [19] (which implies all the weaker security definitions introduced above).

2.2 Post-quantum Cryptography

Dilithium is a signature scheme without known weaknesses to quantum computers. Different parameter sets of Dilithium are called modes and correspond to estimated security levels. The cryptographic strengths of Dilithium are shown in Table 1. The hardness is quantified with respect to the underlying mathematical problems Learning With Errors (LWE) and Short Integer Solution (SIS). The LWE and SIS problems are conjunctured to be hard to solve. NIST made an attempt to translate these hardness levels to classical cryptography [29]. While classical and quantum security levels are hard to directly compare, we add these estimates to the table as an approximation.

Table 1. Cryptographic strength of Dilithium modes, as of NIST standardization round 3 (see [10], Table 1). The classical equivalent refers to NIST's estimation.

Mode	LWE	SIS (for SUF-CMA)	Classical equivalent
Dilithium2	112	112 (110)	SHA256 collision
Dilithium3	165	169 (159)	AES-192 key search
Dilithium5	229	241 (230)	AES-256 key search

2.3   Security Keys

Security keys allow user authentication through digital signatures. They are often implemented on embedded hardware to protect secret key material from extraction.

FIDO. Fast IDentity Online (*FIDO*, see [15]) is a set of standards to allow online authentication through asymmetric cryptography. This exchange of messages involves two protocols: the Client to Authenticator Protocol (*CTAP*, see [11]), which enables the communication between the user's *Authenticator* and their *Client* (such as their browser, or their computer), and WebAuthn, which ensures the communication between the client and the server (*Relying Party*). Security keys act as authenticators and therefore implement CTAP.

CTAP. As part of a CTAP registration, the user generates a key pair, and sends the public key to the server. For a CTAP authentication, the user then proves possession of the private key (*Credential*) being stored on an authenticator. A credential can be stored in one of two ways: Either it is encrypted and sent to the relying party for storage, or it is stored locally in flash. We call these cases server-side key and resident key, respectively.

We describe the cryptographic commands in CTAP below (see Fig. 2). The CTAP protocol started with U2F [22], and since then evolved to its current version 2.1. The most important commands are Make Credential for registration and Get Assertion for authentication. Depending on usage of server-side or resident credentials, these commands use the following cryptographic operations:

R1) During registration, the security key generates a key pair.
R2) Registration returns the public key of the credential, and may return the encrypted private key (server-side key).
R3) Registration returns the public key of the credential, and may store the private key on flash (resident key).
A1) Authentication returns a signature over a response derived from the Relying Party's message.
A2) Authentication returns a signature, and may return an encrypted private key (server-side vs resident key).

3   Attacker Model

Security keys' main goal is to defend against remote attackers and phishing. Defense against local attackers with physical possession of the device are an explicit non-goal. Adversaries can attack the protocol on different levels: cryptographically, on CTAP level, or against the hardware device. In our cryptography analysis in Sect. 4, we consider different extended capabilities for attackers:

- Possession of a Cryptographically-Relevant Quantum Computer;
- Knowledge of a Dilithium weakness.

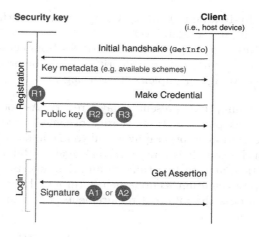

Fig. 2. Cryptographic operations in the CTAP protocol.

We acknowledge that FIDO's protocols mitigate downgrading the protocol already. They transmit the used algorithm over a channel that is considered secure in their attacker model.

Cryptographic Strength. We want our implementation to support all modes of Dilithium, to allow applications with strong security requirements. In particular, security keys are an important line of defense against account hijacking.

Non-goals. Local attacks against the hardware itself or faulty implementations are out of scope for this work. That includes local side-channel attacks. Indeed, Dilithium has been successfully attacked locally on e.g., the power side-channel [26]. We follow FIDO's security assumptions, listed in their Security Reference [16]. The two most important for our threat model are the following:

SA-3 Applications on the user device are able to establish secure channels that provide trustworthy server authentication, and confidentiality and integrity for messages (e.g., through TLS).

SA-4 The computing environment on the FIDO user device and the applications involved in a FIDO operation act as trustworthy agents of the user.

4 Hybrid Signatures

A hybrid signature scheme combines a classical signature algorithm with a post-quantum secure signature algorithm (in a construction commonly known as a *combiner*). Before discussing the design of our hybrid scheme, we explain why such an approach is relevant instead of simply replacing classically secure schemes with post-quantum secure schemes. We present the assumptions below:

1. Cryptographically-Relevant Quantum Computers (i.e., with enough qubits to break ECDSA) are not available yet.
2. Classical signature algorithms withstand attacks from classical computers.
3. The post-quantum secure signature algorithm might be breakable by classical computers due to design or implementation bugs.

The first two assumptions present today's reality. As soon as one of these two assumptions fails, post-quantum security becomes a requirement. On the other hand, post-quantum cryptography is still young, and attacks are still being discovered. One such example is a recent attack against Rainbow [4], one of the NIST standardization finalists. Our third assumption reflects this, and motivates the transition to post-quantum secure schemes through hybrid schemes.

We can now discuss the informal requirements a hybrid scheme H should satisfy:

1. If a quantum computer becomes available, and hence H's underlying classical scheme is broken, H should maintain the security of its underlying post-quantum scheme.
2. If a classical attack for H's underlying post-quantum secure scheme is discovered, H should maintain the security of its underlying classical scheme.

There are multiple natural options for designing a hybrid scheme that satisfies such guarantees. An example is obtaining a hybrid signature by concatenating a classical signature with a post-quantum secure signature. Although simple, this approach indeed maintains the existential unforgeability of the underlying schemes [6].

On the other hand, for our concrete instantiation, Dilithium is strongly unforgeable, while ECDSA is existentially but not strongly unforgeable [14]. Concatenation unfortunately would not maintain Dilithium's strong unforgeability: one could simply replace the ECDSA part of the hybrid signature with another valid ECDSA signature.

Intuitively, this issue can be solved by first signing a given message m with the X-EUF-CMA secure scheme, obtaining σ_1, and afterwards obtaining σ_2 by signing (m, σ_1) with the X-SUF-CMA secure scheme. The hybrid signature for the message m is $\sigma = (\sigma_1, \sigma_2)$. This approach is called *Strong Nesting* [6] and is the basis of our hybrid scheme.

Replacing ECDSA with Ed25519 is another possible fix, as the latter is strongly unforgeable [8]. However, as all security keys already implement ECDSA, a hybrid protocol that uses ECDSA benefits from code reuse.

We make use of the suggestion of Bindel et al. [6] of prepending a constant label to the message to be signed. As an alternative construction with the same properties, one could choose a random label during key generation and store it in both the secret and public key. We decided to use the constant label approach because it leads to smaller key size. This label essentially encodes an algorithm identifier bound to the scheme, and restricts an adversary from trivially deriving partial signatures for messages not having the chosen label as a prefix (if the underlying schemes are secure). We exclude this label from the theoretical analysis and consider it part of the message for the rest of this chapter.

We now formally present our hybrid signature scheme. Given two signature schemes Σ_1 and Σ_2, we define the secret and public keys as pairs of their counterparts in the given underlying schemes. Below we present the pseudocode of the KeyGen() function.

$$\mathcal{H}(\Sigma_1, \Sigma_2).\text{KeyGen}(1^\kappa)$$

$\text{sk}_1, \text{pk}_1 \leftarrow\!\!{\scriptstyle\$}\; \Sigma_1.\text{KeyGen}(1^\kappa)$

$\text{sk}_2, \text{pk}_2 \leftarrow\!\!{\scriptstyle\$}\; \Sigma_2.\text{KeyGen}(1^\kappa)$

$\textbf{return } \text{sk} = (\text{sk}_1, \text{sk}_2), \text{pk} = (\text{pk}_1, \text{pk}_2)$

When signing a message m, the signer obtains a Σ_1-signature for m, followed by a Σ_2-signature for (m, σ_1). The hybrid signature is then the pair (σ_1, σ_2). In practice, these pairs can be implemented as a simple concatenation if σ_1 has predictable length, or a concatenation with a separator. The pseudocode of the signing and verifying functions is presented below.

$$\mathcal{H}(\Sigma_1, \Sigma_2).\text{Sign}(m, \text{sk} = (\text{sk}_1, \text{sk}_2))$$

$\sigma_1 \leftarrow \Sigma_1.\text{Sign}(m, \text{sk}_1)$

$\sigma_2 \leftarrow \Sigma_2.\text{Sign}((m, \sigma_1), \text{sk}_2)$

$\textbf{return } \sigma = (\sigma_1, \sigma_2)$

$$\mathcal{H}(\Sigma_1, \Sigma_2).\text{Verify}(m, \sigma, \text{pk})$$

$(\sigma_1, \sigma_2) = \sigma$ and $(\text{pk}_1, \text{pk}_2) = \text{pk}$

$\textbf{return } (\Sigma_1.\text{Verify}(m, \sigma_1, \text{pk}_1) \wedge$

$\Sigma_2.\text{Verify}((m, \sigma_1), \sigma_2, \text{pk}_2))$

We include the result below, which can be proven immediately using the fact that the underlying schemes are correct.

Lemma 1. *If Σ_1 and Σ_2 are correct, then $\mathcal{H}(\Sigma_1, \Sigma_2)$ is also correct.*

Security Analysis. We now show that our hybrid scheme $\mathcal{H}(\Sigma_1, \Sigma_2)$ maintains the security guarantees of its underlying components. In the statements, we use $X \in \{C, Q\}$ to specify whether we consider classical or post-quantum security.

The following Lemma 2 can be derived from the work of Bindel et al. [6] (Theorem 7).

Lemma 2. *If Σ_1 is X-EUF-CMA secure, then $\mathcal{H}(\Sigma_1, \Sigma_2)$ is X-EUF-CMA secure as well.*

We add the result below, stating that $\mathcal{H}(\Sigma_1, \Sigma_2)$ does not only maintain EUF-CMA security, but also maintains Σ_2's SUF-CMA security guarantees. We include the proof in the appendix.

Lemma 3. *If Σ_2 is X-EUF-CMA secure (resp. X-SUF-CMA) secure, it follows that $\mathcal{H}(\Sigma_1, \Sigma_2)$ is X-EUF-CMA secure (resp. X-SUF-CMA) as well.*

We recall that ECDSA achieves C-EUF-CMA security in the random bijection model, while Dilithium achieves Q-SUF-CMA security in the quantum random oracle model, and we note that our hybrid scheme and proofs use the underlying components as black-boxes. Then, the above shows that our scheme $\mathcal{H}(\text{ECDSA}, \text{Dilithium})$ at least maintains the security guarantees of ECDSA and Dilithium (in their corresponding models).

5 A SK-Friendly Implementation

Security keys often run on embedded hardware devices with tight performance constraints. Our work is based on the open source security key *OpenSK* [31]. OpenSK is a firmware that implements CTAP 2.1. It works as an application on top of the embedded operating system TockOS [23]. For this work, we run OpenSK on a Nordic nRF52840 development kit [30] with a 64 MHz ARM Cortex-M4F MCU. The nRF52840 comes with a TRNG for randomness, and we run all CTAP communication over USB.

To support different hardware targets, we want our firmware including Dilithium, namely the key generation and signing algorithm, to fit 64 kB of RAM. For embedded hardware, we discuss various trade-offs between speed, memory usage and key sizes. We describe our changes to Dilithium compared to the reference implementation. We focus on obtaining a hardware security key-friendly Dilithium implementation for all Dilithium modes.

5.1 CTAP Requirements

Time to login affects usability. In addition, there are some limits for FIDO operations in the specification:

– User presence and user verification tokens usually timeout after 30 s (i.e., see 5. in [11]), but are guaranteed to be valid for at least 10 s. We therefore aim for commands to finish within 10 s.
– The size of a CTAP message over USB cannot exceed 7609 B (see 11.2.4. Message and packet structure in [11]).

Following the command naming from Sect. 2.3, this yields the following priorities:

R1 ⇒ Key generation must finish in less than 10 s.
R2 ⇒ Key pairs must be smaller than 7 kB.
R3 ⇒ The private key should be small to allow storing additional credentials.
A1 ⇒ The login operation is more frequent than registration. Signing should be as fast as possible.
A2 ⇒ A private key and signature together must be smaller than 7 kB.

The Dilithium modes 3 and 5 achieve the desired security requirements. However, for the reference implementation, they fail some requirements due to the large sizes of the key pair and signature. Namely, both miss requirements R3 and A2, and Dilithium5 misses requirement R2.

In the following sections, we describe how we achieve these requirements within the memory limits of embedded hardware. Our main focus consists of reducing the private key size and the memory footprint significantly. The experiments for speed benchmarks can be found in Sect. 6.

5.2 Dilithium Optimizations

Our implementation offers two modes: first, a high speed mode, which follows the original implementation with the exception that we reduce the key size. Second, a low memory footprint mode. To reduce Dilithium's memory footprint, we used known optimization tricks, similarly to [7]. We recompute some intermediate values and effectively trade additional computations (performance) to reduce memory usage.

Both the key generation and the signing algorithm of Dilithium require computations on vectors and matrices of polynomials stored on the stack memory, together with intermediate results. The signing algorithm of the reference implementation of Dilithium [32] keeps on stack 49 such polynomials for Dilithium2, 76 for Dilithium3, and 118 for Dilithium5. Each such polynomial requires 1 kB. The secret key and the array of bytes used to compute the signature are stored on the stack at the same time, which leads to a stack usage of at least 53 kB for Dilithium2, 83 kB for Dilithium3, and 127 kB for Dilithium5. This makes the reference implementation of Dilithium infeasible for our RAM target, especially since we aim for the security levels of Dilithium3 and Dilithium5.

As a first measure, we take into account the life cycle of variables and we arrange the code into multiple blocks, such that the polynomials are only stored on the stack when needed, and afterwards the memory can be recycled. This is still not enough to meet our requirements.

Fortunately, the computations on polynomials are done sequentially (polynomial by polynomial), and OpenSK does not have parallel execution. This enables us to only store a few polynomials at a time, instead of a significant number of large structures. While using this approach reduces the stack usage, it requires some of the intermediate results to be recomputed, and hence it increases the runtime significantly.

Discarding Information from the Secret Key. Dilithium's secret key is an array of bytes comprising the encoding of an array of polynomials, t_0, and the information necessary for computing the array t_0. At a high level, from the secret key, one can derive a matrix of polynomials, A, and two vectors of polynomials, s_1 and s_2. The array t_0 is obtained by reducing each coefficient of $t = A \cdot s_1 + s_2$ modulo 2^d, where d is a parameter. Then, storing the encodings of t_0 is not necessary. To further decrease Dilithium's memory footprint, we can simply recompute these polynomials when signing instead.

Encoding a single polynomial of t_0 into the secret key takes 416 B. In the case of Dilithium2, the encoding of t_0 requires 1664 B. For Dilithium3 and Dilithium5, the encoding requires 2496 B and 3328 B respectively. Then, the size of the secret key gets reduced significantly: from 2528 B to 864 B in the case of Dilithium2, from 4000 B to 1504 B in Dilithium3, and from 4864 B to 1536 B in the case of Dilithium5.

Recomputing t_0 every time we sign helps us decrease Dilithium's memory footprint even more, with a caveat in terms of runtime since this recomputation needs to be done whenever we sign a message. Indeed, this change negatively affects the performance of Dilithium, but it remains reasonable (see experiments in Sect. 6).

Only Storing a 32 B Seed. Dilithium's key generation uses a 32 B seed as source of randomness, which is then expanded to compute the components of the secret and public keys. We can store only this seed and recompute the secret key deterministically based on the stored seed whenever we sign. This adds a small runtime overhead, while saving a significant amount of storage space. For Dilithium5, we reduce the private key size from 4864 kB to 32 kB. From our benchmarks in Sect. 6.2, we can see that the speed overhead is 8.2%.

We want to note that discarding information from the secret key during computation is still useful: recomputing the polynomials in the vector t_0 when needed requires less stack memory than storing its encoding.

5.3 CTAP Implementation

To indicate support for $\mathcal{H}(\text{ECDSA}, \text{Dilithium})$, we added a new algorithm identifier *Hybrid*. When a relying party requests a Hybrid credential, we follow the CTAP procedure as usual. For simplicity, the only change of the encoding of public keys compared to that in ECDSA is the addition of an extra field with the bytes of the Dilithium public key. For registration of server-side credentials, we only add a 32 B seed of the Dilithium private key that is part of the Hybrid credential. All data is encoded as a CBOR map.

During authentication, the signature is computed with $\mathcal{H}(\text{ECDSA}, \text{Dilithium})$. The partial ECDSA signature is ASN.1 DER encoded like standard ECDSA signatures in CTAP.

5.4 Side-Channel Resilience

As per our attacker model, local attackers are out of scope, and we consider time-based remote side-channels only. Our Dilithium implementation should not leak information about its secret key through the computation time as measurable from outside the device.

The paper introducing Dilithium (Section 5.4 in [13]) explains that their implementation does not leak information about the secret key. Indeed, as Dilithium's signing algorithm may attempt to generate multiple signatures until one that satisfies a set of conditions is found, an adversary can gain information about the number of attempts, or about the conditions previous attempts did not meet. The reasons why a signature attempt is rejected do not depend on the secret key, instead they are based on pseudorandom information. Hence determining which conditions where the reason why a signature attempt was rejected does not help the adversary derive information about the secret key.

Our modifications to Dilithium indeed change the computation compared to the reference implementation. However, our implementation still does not branch depending on the secret data, and hence we maintain the same guarantees.

6 Experiments

We benchmark Dilithium on different target architectures, compare the 3 modes, and evaluate the speed difference of the stack optimized version.

6.1 Dilithium Reference Implementation

Achieving higher security levels demands a higher run time and space usage. Table 2 states the average speed of the Dilithium key generation and signing algorithms over 1000 executions on an x86-64 architecture[1], and the size of the keys and the signature.

Table 2. Average run times on an x86-64 architecture and the key and signature sizes of the reference implementation of Dilithium.

Scheme	Runtime (ms) of		Key size (bytes) of		
	KeyGen	Sign	Private	Public	Sign.
Dilithium2	0.08	0.31	2528	1312	2420
Dilithium3	0.15	0.53	4000	1952	3293
Dilithium5	0.22	0.61	4864	2592	4595

6.2 Dilithium Embedded

The changes from Sect. 5.2 enabled us to execute Dilithium in all modes on the Nordic nRF52840 development kit [30]. The performance was measured on the device and the elapsed time printed out via the debugging interface. Table 3 shows the performance we have obtained. In what we call speed mode, we selectively apply some stack optimizations to be able to sign messages with Dilithium2 on embedded hardware. This allows evaluating the impact of the recomputations only applied to stack mode. To measure the computational cost of our hybrid scheme, we ran the equivalent experiment to the Dilithium benchmarks, but we use the full hybrid scheme.

If not stated otherwise, all binaries are compiler-optimized for size. To compare our runtime to other benchmarks, we also show results compiled for speed in Table 4. Note that the code runs as an application on top of an operating system. Therefore, performance benchmarks don't directly compare to other implementations, as some time is spent inside i.e., syscalls. For an estimate of our relative performance when compiled for speed, we convert the measured time to clock cycles by multiplying with the processor speed of 32768 kHz. Those numbers are reported with their relative performance compared to Bos et al. [7].

The binary size of an application running Dilithium on TockOS is 9.3 kB with compiler optimization level -Oz. This size increases to 26.8 kB using -O3.

---

[1] We have used a MacBook Pro (13-inch, 2020), with processor 2.3 GHz Quad-Core Intel Core i7, and memory 16 GB 3733 MHz LPDDR4X.

Table 3. We show the performance obtained by our Optimized Stack mode implementation of Dilithium on the Nordic nRF52840 development kit [30]. The runtime in milliseconds is averaged over 1000 executions, and the stack usage is measured with stack painting. We added runtime speed for ECDSA as a baseline, and to explain the difference between pure Dilithium and Hybrid measurements. Signing with Dilithium2 speed mode exceeds our target memory usage.

Key generation	Stack (in kB)	Runtime (ms)		Signing	Stack (in kB)	Runtime (ms)	
		Pure	Hybrid			Pure	Hybrid
ECDSA	0.3	115.7		ECDSA	3.0	188.0	
Dilithium2 (speed mode)	41.6	70.3	192.0	Dilithium2 (speed mode)	77.1	420.4	687.8
Dilithium2	14.4	82.3	207.5	Dilithium2	17.0	1053.1	1417.5
Dilithium3	19.4	142.4	258.5	Dilithium3	17.9	2077.3	2420.7
Dilithium5	21.4	271.4	393.1	Dilithium5	19.2	3305.1	3378.5

Table 4. We repeated the Dilithium benchmarks from Table 3 with the compiler optimizing for speed rather than binary size (-O3 instead of -Oz) to compare them. We also compare the speed to Bos et al. [7]. Since they report clock cycles, we estimate ours by multiplying our runtimes with our clock frequency.

Key generation	Runtime -O3 (ms)	Relative to		Signing	Runtime -O3 (ms)	Relative to	
		-Oz	Bos			-Oz	Bos
ECDSA	51.9	45%		ECDSA	73.3	39%	
Dilithium2 (speed mode)	63.2	90%	71%	Dilithium2 (speed mode)	363.0	86%	64%
Dilithium2	72.3	88%	81%	Dilithium2	956.1	91%	170%
Dilithium3	129.5	91%	83%	Dilithium3	1955.0	94%	176%
Dilithium5	223.6	82%	85%	Dilithium5	2723.8	82%	201%

We highlight that our Dilithium implementation runs solely on the stack; no heap is required. This benefits embedded devices that don't support heap allocation. The memory footprint was measured with stack painting: Before entering the function that we want to measure, we write a fixed byte pattern into the unused stack. After the function returns, we read back the stack to see where the byte pattern was overwritten.

With this method, we can measure the actual stack usage of each function. Therefore, our reported numbers represent our implementation and depend e.g., on the compiler version used. This explains why our numbers are higher than reported theoretical optima (see [7]). The stack usage is deterministic and does not depend on the inputs' concrete values. Our measurement method also implies that input messages for signing and the RNG are not counted for its memory usage, but outputs are.

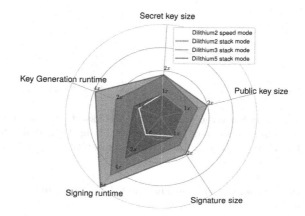

Fig. 3. Comparison of sizes and speeds of Dilithium modes on embedded hardware. The reference in white is Dilithium2 without recomputating parts of the key to save memory. To set the computation speed into perspective, we compare the scaling with the key and signatures sizes. Note that the shown key sizes are after restoring from the 32 byte seed.

Figure 3 summarizes how Dilithium modes scale, and how our stack optimizations impact the speed of operations.

Since Dilithium's signing has a retry loop, its signing speed has a long tail. The distribution of measurements for our Dilithium5 signing benchmark is shown in Fig. 4. To not cause timeouts, CTAP operations should be faster than 10 s. Signing with Dilithium5 achieves that in 97% of the operations. Key generation is faster and more predictable, taking 271 ms on average, with 1 ms standard deviation.

6.3   Register and Authenticate Speed

Different from pure cryptography measurements above, the performance measurements for the CTAP commands MakeCredential and GetAssertion were measured on the USB host, and include a full message exchange. All measurements use server-side keys (see Sect. 5.1). MakeCredential takes 792 ms with 2 ms standard deviation. GetAssertion has the same long-tail timing distribution as signing (see Fig. 4).

We simulated 2000 calls to the security key to register and login. MakeCredential calls took between 786 and 797 milliseconds, whereas GetAssertion has much more variance, due to its signing retry logic described above (see Fig. 4). The time distribution shows that 20% of all calls finish within 2 s. On average, a command takes 3.9 s to complete. 97% of all authentication attempts finished within the CTAP timeout of 10 s, as stated in our requirements in Sect. 5.1.

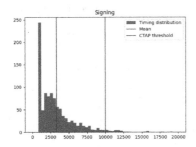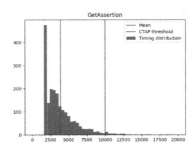

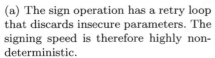

(a) The sign operation has a retry loop that discards insecure parameters. The signing speed is therefore highly non-deterministic.

(b) GetAssertion commands have a similar long tail, depending on the number of retries when signing with Dilithium.

Fig. 4. Timing distributions of signing and the CTAP command GetAssertion, using the Dilithium5 mode.

7 Conclusion

In this paper, we proposed a practical way to upgrade security-key authentication via FIDO's CTAP to PQC. To do so, we have designed and evaluated a hybrid digital-signature scheme that combines a classical scheme, ECDSA, with a PQC one, Dilithium. This hybrid scheme ensures that the security guarantees of each underlying scheme are maintained even when one of the scheme becomes insecure

To demonstrate the practicality of this scheme, we have implemented it in the open-source security-key firmware OpenSK, benchmarked its performance, and released our contribution as open-source software with an Apache2 license. This way, we encourage other researchers to reproduce our results on a nRF52840 chip.

Our implementation is designed to overcome the intrinsic resource limitations of current security key hardware platforms while maintaining reasonable runtimes. Our evaluation of this implementation has demonstrated its feasibility even when using Dilithium's highest security mode, which comes with the highest resource requirements.

A   Appendix

We include the formal proof that was omitted in the main body of the paper.

Lemma 3. *If Σ_2 is X-EUF-CMA secure (resp. X-SUF-CMA) secure, it follows that $\mathcal{H}(\Sigma_1, \Sigma_2)$ is X-EUF-CMA secure (resp. X-SUF-CMA) as well.*

Proof. We show that, for every X-adversary $\mathcal{A}$ that wins the X-EUF-CMA (resp. X-SUF-CMA) security game for $\mathcal{H}(\Sigma_1, \Sigma_2)$ with probability $p_\mathcal{A}$, there is an adversary $\mathcal{B}$ that wins Σ_2's X-EUF-CMA (resp. X-SUF-CMA) security game with probability $p_\mathcal{B} \geq p_\mathcal{A}$.

The adversary $\mathcal{B}$ can be constructed as follows:

- $\mathcal{B}$ receives the Σ_2 public key pk_2 from the challenger $\mathcal{C}_{\Sigma_2}$.
  Since $\mathcal{A}$ expects a hybrid public key, $\mathcal{B}$ generates its own pair of Σ_1 keys $(\mathsf{sk}_1, \mathsf{pk}_1) \leftarrow\!\!{}^{\$} \Sigma_1.\mathsf{KeyGen}(1^\kappa)$, and then sends $\mathsf{pk} = (\mathsf{pk}_1, \mathsf{pk}_2)$ to $\mathcal{A}$.
  Note that the keys received by $\mathcal{A}$ are generated from the same probability distribution as in $\mathcal{H}(\Sigma_1, \Sigma_2)$'s security game.
- When receiving a message query m_i from $\mathcal{A}$, $\mathcal{B}$ uses its own secret key sk_1 to compute the first part of the hybrid signature: $\sigma_{1,i} \leftarrow\!\!{}^{\$} \Sigma_1.\mathsf{Sign}(m_i, \mathsf{sk}_1)$.
  Afterwards, to obtain the Σ_2-component of the hybrid signature, $\mathcal{B}$ sends $m'_i := (m_i, \sigma_1)$ as a signing query to the challenger $\mathcal{C}_{\Sigma_2}$ and obtains $\sigma_{2,i} = \Sigma_2.\mathsf{Sign}(m'_i, \mathsf{sk}_2)$.
  When receiving $\sigma_{2,i}$ from $\mathcal{C}_{\Sigma_2}$, $\mathcal{B}$ computes $\sigma_i := (\sigma_{1,i}, \sigma_{2,i})$ and sends it to $\mathcal{A}$. Note that σ_i is a valid hybrid signature:
  $$\mathcal{H}(\Sigma_1, \Sigma_2).\mathsf{Verify}(m_i, \sigma_i, \mathsf{pk}) = \mathsf{true}$$
- When receiving the forgery $(m^*, \sigma^* = (\sigma_1^*, \sigma_2^*))$ from the adversary $\mathcal{A}$, $\mathcal{B}$ obtains its own forgery $((m^*, \sigma_1^*), \sigma_2^*)$ and sends it to $\mathcal{C}_{\Sigma_2}$.

Since $\mathcal{B}$ simulates the X-EUF-CMA (resp. X-SUF-CMA) security game for $\mathcal{H}$ perfectly towards $\mathcal{A}$, $\mathcal{A}$ maintains its success probability $p_\mathcal{A}$.

We show that, whenever $\mathcal{A}$ wins the simulated game, $\mathcal{B}$ wins the X-EUF-CMA (resp. X-SUF-CMA) security game for Σ_2.

If $\mathcal{A}$ wins the simulated X-EUF-CMA security game, $m^* \notin \{\text{queries } m_i\}$. It immediately follows that $(m^*, \sigma_1^*) \notin \{\text{queries } m'_i\}$.

If $\mathcal{A}$ wins the simulated X-SUF-CMA security game, $(m^*, \sigma^*) \notin \{(m_i, \sigma_i) \mid m_i \text{ query}, \sigma_i \text{ response}\}$. If this is the case, we need to show that $\mathcal{B}$ has never received σ_2^* as a response from $\mathcal{C}_2$ to the signing query (m^*, σ_1^*). Assuming that $((m^*, \sigma_1^*), \sigma_2^*) = (m'_i, \sigma_{2,i})$ for some query-response pair $(m'_i, \sigma_{2,i})$ in $\mathcal{B}$'s interaction with $\mathcal{C}_2$, we obtain that $(m^*, \sigma^*) = (m_i, \sigma_i)$, which contradicts that $\mathcal{A}$'s forgery was successful.

Both in the X-EUF-CMA case and in the X-SUF-CMA case, if $\mathcal{A}$ has sent a successful forgery, then $\mathcal{H}(\Sigma_1, \Sigma_2).\mathsf{Verify}(m^*, \sigma^*, \mathsf{pk}) = \mathsf{true}$ holds, and hence $\Sigma_2.\mathsf{Verify}((m^*, \sigma_1^*), \sigma_2^*, \mathsf{pk}_2)$ holds as well.

It follows that $\mathcal{B}$ wins the X-EUF-CMA (resp. X-SUF-CMA) security game for Σ_2 with probability $p_\mathcal{B} \geq p_\mathcal{A}$.

Finally, as Σ_2 is X-EUF-CMA (resp. X-SUF-CMA) secure, $p_\mathcal{B} \in \mathsf{negl}(\kappa)$, and therefore $p_\mathcal{A} \in \mathsf{negl}(\kappa)$.

Since $\mathcal{A}$ was chosen arbitrarily, we obtain that every X-adversary has negligible probability in winning $\mathcal{H}(\Sigma_1, \Sigma_2)$'s X-EUF-CMA (resp. X-SUF-CMA) security game. $\qquad\square$

References

1. Abdulrahman, A., Hwang, V., Kannwischer, M.J., Sprenkels, D.: Faster kyber and dilithium on the cortex-M4. In: Ateniese, G., Venturi, D. (eds.) ACNS 2022. LNCS, vol. 13269, pp. 853–871. Springer, Cham (2022). https://doi.org/10.1007/978-3-031-09234-3_42

2. Azarderakhsh, R., Elkhatib, R., Koziel, B., Langenberg, B.: Hardware deployment of hybrid PQC: SIKE+ECDH. In: Garcia-Alfaro, J., Li, S., Poovendran, R., Debar, H., Yung, M. (eds.) SecureComm 2021. LNICST, vol. 399, pp. 475–491. Springer, Cham (2021). https://doi.org/10.1007/978-3-030-90022-9_26

3. Bernstein, D.J., Hülsing, A., Kölbl, S., Niederhagen, R., Rijneveld, J., Schwabe, P.: Leveraging secondary storage to simulate deep 54-qubit sycamore circuits. In: Proceedings of the 2019 ACM SIGSAC Conference on Computer and Communications Security, pp. 2129–2146 (2019)

4. Beullens, W.: Improved cryptanalysis of UOV and rainbow. In: Canteaut, A., Standaert, F.-X. (eds.) EUROCRYPT 2021, Part I. LNCS, vol. 12696, pp. 348–373. Springer, Cham (2021). https://doi.org/10.1007/978-3-030-77870-5_13

5. Bindel, N., Cremers, C., Zhao, M.: FIDO2, CTAP 2.1, and WebAuthn 2: provable security and post-quantum instantiation. In: 2023 IEEE Symposium on Security and Privacy (SP), Los Alamitos, CA, USA, pp. 674–693. IEEE Computer Society (2023). https://doi.org/10.1109/SP46215.2023.00039

6. Bindel, N., Herath, U., McKague, M., Stebila, D.: Transitioning to a quantum-resistant public key infrastructure. In: Lange, T., Takagi, T. (eds.) PQCrypto 2017. LNCS, vol. 10346, pp. 384–405. Springer, Cham (2017). https://doi.org/10.1007/978-3-319-59879-6_22

7. Bos, J.W., Renes, J., Sprenkels, A.: Dilithium for memory constrained devices. In: Batina, L., Daemen, J. (eds.) AFRICACRYPT 2022. LNCS, vol. 13503, pp. 217–235. Springer, Cham (2022). https://doi.org/10.1007/978-3-031-17433-9_10

8. Brendel, J., Cremers, C., Jackson, D., Zhao, M.: The provable security of Ed25519: theory and practice. Cryptology ePrint Archive, Paper 2020/823 (2020). https://eprint.iacr.org/2020/823

9. Castryck, W., Decru, T.: An efficient key recovery attack on SIDH. In: Hazay, C., Stam, M. (eds.) EUROCRYPT 2023. LNCS, vol. 14008, pp. 423–447. Springer, Cham (2023). https://doi.org/10.1007/978-3-031-30589-4_15

10. CRYSTALS-Dilithium Algorithm Specifications and Supporting Documentation. https://pq-crystals.org/dilithium/data/dilithium-specification-round3-20210208.pdf. Accessed 08 Feb 2023

11. Client to Authenticator Protocol (CTAP). https://fidoalliance.org/specs/fido-v2.1-ps-20210615/fido-client-to-authenticator-protocol-v2.1-ps-errata-20220621.html. Accessed 05 Feb 2023

12. Dowling, B., Hansen, T.B., Paterson, K.G.: Many a mickle makes a muckle: a framework for provably quantum-secure hybrid key exchange. In: Ding, J., Tillich, J.-P. (eds.) PQCrypto 2020. LNCS, vol. 12100, pp. 483–502. Springer, Cham (2020). https://doi.org/10.1007/978-3-030-44223-1_26

13. Ducas, L., et al.: CRYSTALS-dilithium: a lattice-based digital signature scheme. IACR Trans. Cryptogr. Hardw. Embed. Syst. **2018**(1), 238–268 (2018). https://doi.org/10.13154/tches.v2018.i1.238-268. https://tches.iacr.org/index.php/TCHES/article/view/839

14. Fersch, M., Kiltz, E., Poettering, B.: On the provable security of (EC)DSA signatures. In: Proceedings of the 2016 ACM SIGSAC Conference on Computer and Communications Security, CCS 2016, pp. 1651–1662. Association for Computing Machinery, New York (2016). https://doi.org/10.1145/2976749.2978413

15. FIDO Alliance. https://fidoalliance.org/. Accessed 05 Feb 2023

16. FIDO Alliance security reference. https://fidoalliance.org/specs/fido-v2.0-id-20180227/fido-security-ref-v2.0-id-20180227.html. Accessed 05 Feb 2023

17. Greconici, D.O.C., Kannwischer, M.J., Sprenkels, D.: Compact dilithium implementations on Cortex-M3 and Cortex-M4. IACR Trans. Cryptogr. Hardw. Embed. Syst. **2021**(1), 1–24 (2020). https://doi.org/10.46586/tches.v2021.i1.1-24
18. Kannwischer, M.J., Rijneveld, J., Schwabe, P., Stoffelen, K.: pqm4: testing and benchmarking NIST PQC on ARM Cortex-M4. Cryptology ePrint Archive, Paper 2019/844 (2019). https://eprint.iacr.org/2019/844
19. Kiltz, E., Lyubashevsky, V., Schaffner, C.: A concrete treatment of Fiat-Shamir signatures in the quantum random-oracle model. In: Nielsen, J.B., Rijmen, V. (eds.) EUROCRYPT 2018. LNCS, vol. 10822, pp. 552–586. Springer, Cham (2018). https://doi.org/10.1007/978-3-319-78372-7_18
20. Koblitz, N.: Elliptic curve cryptosystems. Math. Comput. **48**, 203–209 (1987)
21. Information Technology Laboratory: Digital Signature Standard (DSS). Technical report, National Institute of Standards and Technology (2013). https://doi.org/10.6028/nist.fips.186-4
22. Lang, J., Czeskis, A., Balfanz, D., Schilder, M., Srinivas, S.: Security keys: practical cryptographic second factors for the modern web. In: Grossklags, J., Preneel, B. (eds.) FC 2016. LNCS, vol. 9603, pp. 422–440. Springer, Heidelberg (2017). https://doi.org/10.1007/978-3-662-54970-4_25
23. Levy, A., et al.: Multiprogramming a 64kB computer safely and efficiently. In: Proceedings of the 26th Symposium on Operating Systems Principles, SOSP 2017, pp. 234–251. ACM, New York (2017). https://doi.org/10.1145/3132747.3132786
24. Li, S., et al.: FALCON: a Fourier transform based approach for fast and secure convolutional neural network predictions. CoRR abs/1811.08257 (2018). http://arxiv.org/abs/1811.08257
25. Lipp, B.: An analysis of hybrid public key encryption. Cryptology ePrint Archive, Paper 2020/243 (2020). https://eprint.iacr.org/2020/243
26. Marzougui, S., Ulitzsch, V., Tibouchi, M., Seifert, J.P.: Profiling side-channel attacks on dilithium: a small bit-fiddling leak breaks it all. Cryptology ePrint Archive, Paper 2022/106 (2022). https://eprint.iacr.org/2022/106
27. Migliore, V., Gérard, B., Tibouchi, M., Fouque, P.-A.: Masking dilithium. In: Deng, R.H., Gauthier-Umaña, V., Ochoa, M., Yung, M. (eds.) ACNS 2019. LNCS, vol. 11464, pp. 344–362. Springer, Cham (2019). https://doi.org/10.1007/978-3-030-21568-2_17
28. NIST Announces First Four Quantum-Resistant Cryptographic Algorithms. https://www.nist.gov/news-events/news/2022/07/nist-announces-first-four-quantum-resistant-cryptographic-algorithms. Accessed 07 Feb 2023
29. NIST Post-Quantum Cryptography FAQs. https://csrc.nist.gov/Projects/post-quantum-cryptography/faqs. Accessed 13 Feb 2023
30. Nordic nrf52840. https://www.nordicsemi.com/Products/Development-hardware/nrf52840-dk. Accessed 05 Feb 2023
31. OpenSK. https://github.com/google/OpenSK. Accessed 05 Feb 2023
32. PQCrystals: Dilithium. https://github.com/pq-crystals/dilithium. Accessed 10 Feb 2023
33. Raavi, M., Wuthier, S., Chandramouli, P., Balytskyi, Y., Zhou, X., Chang, S.-Y.: Security comparisons and performance analyses of post-quantum signature algorithms. In: Sako, K., Tippenhauer, N.O. (eds.) ACNS 2021. LNCS, vol. 12727, pp. 424–447. Springer, Cham (2021). https://doi.org/10.1007/978-3-030-78375-4_17
34. Rivest, R.L., Shamir, A., Adleman, L.M.: A method for obtaining digital signatures and public key cryptosystems. Commun. ACM **21**(2), 120–126 (1978). https://doi.org/10.1145/359340.359342

Multi-armed SPHINCS+

Gustavo Banegas and Florian Caullery[✉]

Qualcomm France S.A.R.L, Valbonne, France
fcauller@qti.qualcomm.com

Abstract. Hash-based signatures are a type of Digital Signature Algorithms that are positioned as one of the most solid quantum-resistant constructions. As an example SPHINCS+, has been selected as a standard during the NIST Post-Quantum Cryptography competition. However, hash-based signatures suffer from two main drawbacks: signature size and slow signing process. In this work, we give a solution to the latter when it is used in a mobile device. We take advantage of the fact that hash-based signatures are highly parallelizable. More precisely, we provide an implementation of SPHINCS+ on the Snapdragon™ 865 Mobile Platform taking advantage of its eight CPUs and their vector extensions. Our implementation shows that it is possible to have a speed-up of 15 times when compared to a purely sequential and non-vectorized implementation. Furthermore, we evaluate the performance impact of side-channel protection using vector extensions in the SPHINCS+ version based on SHAKE.

Keywords: SPHINCS+ · Post-Quantum Cryptography · Digital Signature Algorithms · Hash-based Signatures

1 Introduction

With the last development in the standardization of Post-Quantum Cryptography (PQC) schemes, the migration to these new algorithms has become more and more urgent. However, the constraints for this transition depend highly on the deployment environments and will dictate the choice of algorithms among the standardized options. It is thus important to know about the performance of every scheme on specific targets. Among the standardized algorithms, signatures schemes based on hash functions are standing out by their strong and well-studied security assumptions.

From an historical view, hash-based signatures started with the seminal work of Lamport on One Time Signature (OTS) [17]. Building on Lamport's OTS scheme, Winternitz [14] and Merkle [20] proposed schemes that could sign more than one bit efficiently. Being built on symmetric primitives (hash functions) these schemes are inherently resistant to quantum attacks as long as the underlying primitive is also secure. Some of the most recent hash-based signatures are eXtended Merkle Signature Scheme (XMSS) [9] and its Multi-Trees variant XMSS^{MT} [15], as well as Leighton-Micali Signature (LMS) [19]. These three

J. Zhou et al. (Eds.): ACNS 2023 Workshops, LNCS 13907, pp. 500–514, 2023.
https://doi.org/10.1007/978-3-031-41181-6_27

schemes are now part of the RFC 8708 [11], and the NIST SP 800-208 [22]. At a high level, LMS and XMSS are built over One Time Signatures and therefore suffer from a security loss if they sign two different messages with the same key material. Hence, one needs to keep track of the signatures already issued making these schemes *stateful*.

Unfortunately, this approach might not be realistic for several use-cases. On top of that, the NIST Post-Quantum Cryptography standardization process [21] did not allow for stateful candidates. To overcome these problems, Bernstein et al. proposed a tweak on XMSS in [5], and developed a scheme called SPHINCS relying on Few Times Signature (FTS) instead of OTS schemes and some amount of randomization to make it *stateless*. Its variant SPHINCS$^+$ [5,7] has been chosen to be a standard in the NIST process. We remark that despite some small degradation in its security claim [23], SPHINCS$^+$ continues to be secure.

When one makes a comparison of the finalists in the NIST process, SPHINCS$^+$ presents the longest signatures of the three standardized schemes, the two others being Falcon [12] and Dilithium [3]. Also, the latency for a signature generation is considerably higher. To illustrate the difference, we can use the data from SUPERCOP[1]. On an Intel® i5, SPHINCS$^+$ signature is 11 times slower than Falcon and 60 times slower than Dilithium. It thus becomes important to tackle the performance issue and implement SPHINCS$^+$ taking advantage of modern environments.

Contributions. We concern ourselves with the scenario of implementing SPHINCS$^+$ on mobile phones with high-performance System on Chips (SoC). These devices can be tasked with signing a message with stringent time constraints. On the other hand, they often have multiple cores available for parallelism. More specifically, we are exploring strategies to accelerate SPHINCS$^+$ on a Snapdragon® 865 that supports four ARM® Cortex-A77 and four Cortex-A55. Our implementation techniques allow us to speed-up the optimized implementation based on SHA-256 proposed in the SPHINCS$^+$ submission package by a factor of 15. We chose to illustrate our approach SPHINCS$^+$ since it uses XMSS^{MT} as a basic structure and our results could easily be extended to the original XMSS^{MT}. Moreover, we present details when one uses a side-channel protected version of SHAKE in SPHINCS$^+$. Note that we only discuss the signature procedure in our paper as the verification procedures is a simple hash chain and is on par with other algorithms performance-wise.

Organization of Paper. In Sect. 2 we succinctly introduce SPHINCS$^+$. Section 3 presents our test platform. We then describe the optimization that we apply using Single Instruction Multiple Data (SIMD) in Sect. 4 and those using multithreading strategies in Sect. 5.

---

[1] https://bench.cr.yp.to/results-sign.html.

2   SPHINCS$^+$

SPHINCS$^+$ was announced to be standardized in the ongoing process from NIST on Post-Quantum Cryptography. As mentioned earlier, its security relies on the symmetric primitive that it uses, in this case, a hash function, meaning that, as long as this hash function is quantum-safe, SPHINCS$^+$ is safe too. Its construction depends on three main blocks:

- A FTS scheme called Forest Of Random Subset (FORS),
- A OTS scheme named Winternitz One time Signature + (WOTS+),
- A variant of the Merkle tree Signature scheme eXtended Merkle Signature Scheme (XMSS) called XMSS^{MT} (MT stands for Multi-Tree).

Note that those subcomponents only support one or a limited number of signatures. This is circumvented by the instantiation parameters that allow virtually an infinite number of signatures. On top of that, the signature material that will be used is selected by deriving a pseudo-random index from a public seed, and the message. This makes unlikely the reuse an OTS. We now give a short description of the subcomponents.

2.1   FORS

The FORS is a FTS scheme, and in the words of [5]: "an improvement of HORST [6] which in turn is a variant of HORS [24]". FORS starts by selecting a hash-function that outputs a n-bytes hash, a parameter value $t > 1$ that is a power of 2, and a parameter k. The secret key is composed of kt random strings of n bytes each. A FORS tree is a Merkle tree whose t leaves are secret key values. The roots of all the k trees are then hashed all together to compose the public key of FORS. To sign the message M, the signature process is the following:

1. Hash m, and the hash is split into k parts;
2. each part is interpreted as an integer in $0, \ldots, t-1$;
3. use each of those integers gives to get the index of the leaf to use in the corresponding FORS tree;
4. the leaf and the nodes of the tree are necessary to rebuild the tree root (i.e. the *authentication path*), and it is used as the signature of the corresponding part;
5. the full signature is the concatenation of all the signatures of the different parts.

Figure 1 illustrates a FORS structure. The verification process is simply the hash sequence necessary to obtain the top root, and the comparison with the public key.

2.2 Winternitz One Time Signature+

The other subcomponent used by SPHINCS+ is the OTS introduced by Hülsing in [14] called Winternitz One Time Signature (WOTS+). WOTS+ starts by selecting a hash-function that outputs a n-bytes hash, a parameter value $w > 1$ that is a power of 2 and an extra parameter l_2 that represents the checksum length. The private key is composed of $l_1(:= 8 * n / \log_2(w)) + l_2$ blocks of n-bytes. The public key is composed of all the private key blocks hashed w times. After hashing the message M, a WOTS+ signature is obtained as follow:

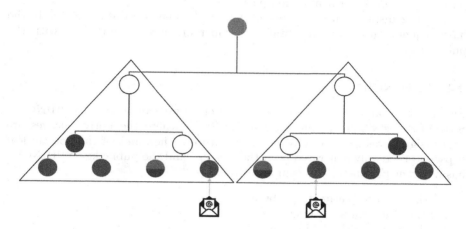

Fig. 1. FORS signature explained. The red nodes are the secret key parts, the green node is the public key, the blue nodes are the part of the signature. The blue nodes written *ots* are part of the One Time Signature while others are part of the Authentication path. Blue and red nodes are part of both the signature and the private key, the empty nodes are being reconstructed during the verification. (Color figure online)

1. It splits the hash into l_1 parts;
2. each part is interpreted as an integer b_i in $0, \ldots, w - 1$;
3. hash the i-th private key block b_i times;
4. compute a checksum with as the sum of all the $w - b_i$ and express that number in l_2 integers in $0, \ldots, w - 1$;
5. hash the l_2 remaining private key a number of times given by the checksum integers;
6. the signature consists of all the obtained hashes.

The verification procedure is simply the completion of the hash chains and comparisons with the public key blocks.

2.3 XMSS^{MT}

The last building block is a hyper tree scheme called XMSS^{MT}. To understand the scheme, one needs to notice that it is possible to use an unbalanced Merkle tree to hash the public key of WOTS+ into a single block. Then, by placing 2^a WOTS+ public keys as the leaves of the Merkle tree, one can compress those 2^a keys into one, that describes XMSS. XMSS^{MT} is built over XMSS by placing an XMSS tree over 2^a XMSS trees, so that each leaf of the top tree will sign the public key of the tree below. One can repeat this process iteratively to obtain d layers of trees. This allows for a faster public key generation when compared to a XMSS tree of height da, as only the public key of the top tree has to be computed. The signature of XMSS^{MT} is the concatenation of the WOTS+ signatures of the XMSS trees root, and the nodes necessary to reconstruct the public key (i.e. the authentication path).

Figure 2 displays the structure of XMSS^{MT}. The verification is simply the hash sequence necessary to obtain the top root, and a comparison with the public key.

2.4 SPHINCS$^+$

Finally, after all the previous subcomponents, we can describe SPHINCS$^+$. SPHINCS$^+$ is simply an instance of XMSS^{MT} where the bottom leaves are FORS signatures instead of WOTS+ signatures. The index of the bottom leaf is pseudo-randomly generated from the message and the public key. SPHINCS$^+$ has different parameters, we simplify them as:

- n : the security parameter in bytes.
- w : the Winternitz parameter.
- a : the height of the XMSS trees.
- d : the number of layers in the hypertree.
- h : the height of the hypertree being equal to da.
- k : the number of trees in FORS.
- t : the number of leaves of a FORS tree.

Table 1 gives the concrete parameters, we acquire them from the reference documentation [5].

Table 1. Parameters of SPHINCS$^+$.

Parameters	n	h	d	$\log(t)$	k	w	bit security	NIST sec. lvl	signature (B)
SPHINCS$^+$-128 s	16	63	7	12	14	16	133	1	7,856
SPHINCS$^+$-128f	16	66	22	6	33	16	128	1	17,088
SPHINCS$^+$-192 s	24	63	7	14	17	16	193	3	16,224
SPHINCS$^+$-192f	24	66	22	8	33	16	194	3	35,664
SPHINCS$^+$-256 s	32	64	8	14	22	16	255	5	29,792
SPHINCS$^+$-256f	32	68	17	9	35	16	255	5	49,856

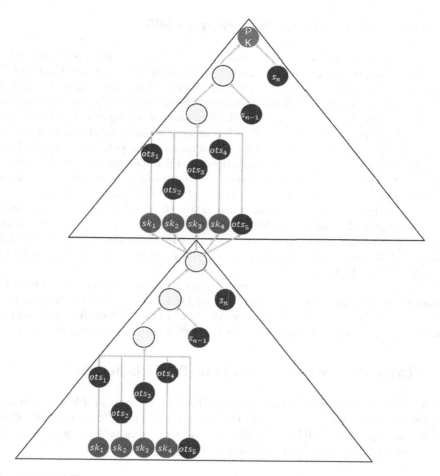

Fig. 2. XMSS^{MT} signature explained. The red nodes are the secret key parts, the green node is the public key, the blue nodes are the part of the signature, the empty nodes are being reconstructed during the verification. (Color figure online)

Note that the security claims of the authors of SPHINCS+ and do not integrate the latest cryptanalysis results of [23]. The parameters will certainly evolve according to these attacks, and we will update our implementations when an official change will be made.

3   Our Test Platform: Snapdragon 865

In our tests, we use a Snapdragon® 865. The 865 is an octa core processor, and in its composition it has four ARM® processors Cortex-A77, and four Cortex-A55. Qualcomm® uses different speeds in the processors. Also, they define one Cortex-A77 as Gold tier running at 2.8GHz, three at Silver tier running at 2.4GHz, and the four Cortex-A55 running at 1.8GHz with the DynamIQ ARM® technology.

In our setup, the Snapdragon® 865 is embedded in a smart phone Samsung S20 FE 5G running Android 11. The architecture of the processors is ARM-v8a and all of them have NEON vector coprocessors that operates on 128 bits vectors. The NEON coprocessors have dedicated cryptographic instructions which can accelerate symmetric primitives like AES and SHA-256 but not SHA3.

To compile our code, we are using Clang 14.0.6 with "-Ofast" flag that auto-vectorizes the code and our multithreading is done via posic thread (`pthread`). We are running our compiled code directly on the target via the Android Debug Bridge (ADB) tool, and without an intermediate application. All our results are averaged over 1,000 runs.

We make sure that our code is running on a certain core via the C function `sched_setaffinity`. Note that the Android OS allows to use the three Cortex-A77 at Silver tier, and the four Cortex-A55 but not the Cortex-A77 at Gold tier. This means that we can effectively use 7 out of 8 cores in our experiments.

4   SIMD Improvements on Our Test Platforms

Prior to any optimization work, the first thing to do is to profile the reference implementation. Our analysis shows that the hash computation represents 99.6% of the time spent in SPHINCS+. The natural step from this analysis is to find strategies to accelerate the underlying hash functions.

4.1   Using SIMD to Speed-Up SPHINCS+

The reference implementation of SPHINCS+ uses the tree hash algorithm given by [10]. The algorithm in [10] is the most optimal currently available in the literature. For the optimized implementations, two strategies are given; The first one applies to the SPHINCS+ variant using Haraka, and it uses the AES-New Instructions (AES-NI) available on both modern Intel processors and ARM-Neon to speed-up single node computations. The speed-up obtained is directly depending on the ratio between the AES-NI and the pure software AES. The second strategy uses the fact that vector instructions can be used to compute independent hashes in parallel. For example, on ARM-Neon, as Keccak operates on lanes of 64 bits and each vector of ARM-Neon is 128 bits, one can store two independent Keccak states on 25 vectors, and then compute the result of the permutation over the two states at once. When one uses this strategy, it results in a speed-up of *roughly* a factor of 2. The only drawback is that one hash computation is wasted during the computation of the tree root but that is marginal. The AVX2 optimized implementation of SPHINCS⁺ with SHA-256 uses the second strategy. However, it computes 8 independent hashes in parallel since AVX2 vectors can go up to 256 bits, and SHA-256 operates on 32 bits words. These strategies were first mentioned in [16].

Contrary to Intel AVX2, ARM-Neon offers native instructions to speed-up the computation of SHA-256. One natural question is which strategy is better? Should we use native instructions or take advantage of vectorization to compute several (4 in that case) instances of SHA-256 in parallel. To answer this question, we implement both options and compare them. Our benchmark shows that the throughput of the SHA-256 instructions is around 5 times higher on Cortex-A77 and Cortex-A55 than computing 4 SHA-256 in parallel with Neon instructions. The results are given in Table 2. Hence, we use the native SHA-256 instructions instead of the 4 parallel computations. This fact was already pointed out in [16] for Cortex-A72 and Cortex-A5 and we confirm that those results extrapolate to more recent ARM processors. We also added the comparison with Haraka which is an AES-based hash function specific to SPHINCS⁺. We implemented it in the way advised in the ARM Software Optimization Guides for Cortex A77 and A55 [1,2] to take advantage of the pipelining and the instruction fusion. However, Haraka remains slower than SHA-256 on Neon.

Table 3 shows the comparison between our implementation using Neon instructions and the other strategies. For simplicity, we use SPHINCS⁺ with different primitives but all are the implementations uses security parameter 128f. To differentiate our implementations from the reference package, we present them in italic. It is clear that the SHA-256 variant based on our implementation of SHA-256 with Neon intrinsics is the fastest on our test platform. In the rest of the work, we will use this implementation as a benchmark as any speed-up on it can only translate to equivalent or more important speed-up on slower parameters. We show also for the sake of comparison the performance of Dilithium-90 s version (e.g. replacing calls to SHA3 by AES) for a security level 2. We use the implementation of [4] using the AES Neon instructions.

Table 2. Performance comparison on a single core in op/s (higher operations per second is better).

Primitive	Cortex-A55	Cortex-A77
SHA-256-Neon (ours)	$3,955,226$	$9,486,676$
SHA-256 × 4	$688,912$	$2,145,526$
Haraka Neon	$2,589,348$	$9,047,010$

Table 3. Performance comparison on a single core in op/s (higher operations per second is better). The parameters set chosen is SPHINCS$^+$-128f.

Primitive	Cortex-A55	Cortex-A77
SPHINCS$^+$ SHA-256 Neon sign (ours)	19	42
SPHINCS$^+$ Haraka Neon sign	12	35
SPHINCS$^+$ SHAKE256 Neon sign	3	8.6
Dilithium2-90 s sign	2,548	4,624

4.2 Using SIMD to Mitigate Side-Channel Attacks

Some use-cases might require protection against side-channel attacks. Recent works show that vector cryptographic instruction might not offer a satisfying level of protection, see for example [13,18]. Hence, we propose to target SHAKE and implement the software countermeasures described in [8] to raise the level of protection against side-channel attacks.

We recall that Keccak, the underlying permutation of SHAKE, is defined by two operations repeated for 24 rounds over a state of 1600 bits: λ and χ, λ being a purely linear layer and χ being the non-linear part. The countermeasure proposed in [8] is using two or three shares, that is, every value x of the state is decomposed into two or three values a and b, possibly c, such that $x = a \oplus b$ or $x = a \oplus b \oplus c$. The linear layer λ is kept and applied on the two shares of each value as it is linear (i.e. we have $\lambda(x) = \lambda(a) \oplus \lambda(b)(\oplus \lambda(c))$). The non-linear layer χ requires more work. The operation χ is defined by $x_i \leftarrow x_i \oplus ((x_{i+1} + 1).x_{i+2})$ where the indexes are computed in a specific way. Keccak is usually implemented in a bitsliced manner, meaning that χ will be actually performed with operands of 64 bits (we refer the reader to [8] for a full description of Keccak and its implementation). The two-shared computation of χ is done using the following formula:

$$a_i \leftarrow a_i \oplus ((a_{i+1} + 1).a_{i+2}) + a_{i+1}b_{i+2}$$

$$b_i \leftarrow b_i \oplus ((b_{i+1} + 1).b_{i+2}) + b_{i+1}a_{i+2}.$$

The authors of this countermeasure then remark that the formulas can be simplified by

$$a_i \leftarrow a_i \oplus ((a_{i+1} + 1).a_{i+2}) + a_{i+1}b_{i+2} \oplus (\bar{b}_{i+1}.b_{i+2}) + b_{i+1}a_{i+2}$$

$$b_i \leftarrow b_i,$$

and that we can pre-compute a fixed mask b such that $b \oplus \lambda(b)$ has a minimal Hamming weight. We argue that such optimization defeats the purpose of masking as a fixed mask satisfying this condition has a vast majority of its bits fixed to 0 and we would be back to perform the operations on an unmasked value. For this reason, we implement the countermeasure without the simplification.

To use make the most out of vector instructions, we put a masked 64bits value into the first part of a Neon vector and its mask in the second part. That is done as presented in Listing 1.1 for a value x.

Listing 1.1. masking in Neon intrinsic

```
uint64_t x;
uint64_t b = rand_64();
uint64x2_t masked_vector = {x ^ b, b};
```

Performing the χ operation is then a simple matter of programming with Neon intrinsics and can be done, for example, as presented in Listing 1.2.

Listing 1.2. χ in Neon intrinsic

```
uint64x2_t v0 = {a0, b0};
uint64x2_t v1 = {a1, b1};
uint64x2_t v2 = {a2, b2};

uint64x2_t result = vnegq_s32(v1);
//Negates v1

result = vandq_u64(result, v2);
//result = result AND v2
// result = {(a1 + 1).a2, (b1 + 1).b2}

v2 = vextq_u64(v2, v2, 1);
// swap v2 -> v2 = {b2, a2}

v2 = vandq_u64(v2, v1);
// v2 = {a1.b2, b1.a2}

result = veor3q_u64(result, v2, v0);
//XOR 3 ways

return result;
```

We implemented the whole Keccak permutation using this technique and measured the impact on the performance. The results are presented in Table 4. Note that we are comparing to the reference implementation in the SPHINCS+ package that performs 2 Keccak permutation in parallel. Our result shows that the permutation itself suffers a slow-down of around 60% without including the random generation of the mask. If we include the generation of the mask, we are observing that the permutation is now more than 10 times slower. This would translate into a signature time 10 times slower as well. Considering that SPHINCS+ with SHAKE is already performing less than 10 signatures per second, we deem this countermeasure as not realistic in an real-world context, unless paired with the multithreading strategy depicted in Sect. 5.

Table 4. Performance comparison on a single core in op/s (higher operations per second is better). The parameter for SPHINCS$^+$ is 128f.

Primitive	Cortex-A55	Cortex-A77
SHAKEx2 (ref. impl.)	$377,786$	$1,060,445$
Masked SHAKE w/o random mask generation	$117,233$	$391,236$
Masked SHAKE with random mask generation	$22,099$	$82,911$

5   Parallelization Strategies

On a mobile platform, some applications can consider more important to sign a single message than have a higher throughput. In this context, we present a trade-off between fast signing a message and throughput. To speed-up signing in mobile devices, we propose to use multithreading on SPHINCS$^+$. It is important to remark that SPHINCS$^+$ is highly parallelizable. This is possible because the secret key used in the subtrees are solely depending on the master secret key seed and the indexes that are derived from the message. This remark is also valid for FORS and XMSS^{MT}.

5.1   When Multithreading Goes Wrong

One of the ways to parallelize computations in SPHINCS$^+$ is to parallelize a single tree hash. For this, one assigns the computation of the nodes to different threads and wait to join the results in a top thread that would compute the root. This strategy might be valid in other contexts, but the subtrees height we are dealing with is at maximum 14 for FORS, and 8 for XMSS^{MT}. Creating a thread to perform at best 2^{13} hash operations is not a positive trade-off as we show in Table 5. The timing for creating an empty thread is already longer than performing a single tree hash on both Cortex-A55 and Cortex-A77.

Table 5. Thread creation versus SHA-256 in op/s.

	Cortex-A55	Cortex-A77
SHA-256-Neon	$3,955,226$	$9,486,676$
Thread creation	$3,803$	$6,730$

5.2   Multithreading on FORS

FORS is based on the computation of multiple independent subtrees root, and a final hash of all these roots concatenated. We assign a certain number of trees to each of the threads. As expected, we found out that the speed-up is directly linked to the number of cores that can be mobilized. The first conclusion here is that the time used to create the threads is low enough when compared to the tree hashing operations in each thread. To measure this difference, we pushed the number of threads to the number of FORS trees (we assigned one thread per tree hash). We illustrate our results for the fastest variant 128f-simple with SHA-256 intrinsics in Fig. 3[2]. The second conclusion is that FORS on four Cortex-A55 is as fast as on a single Cortex-A77, this makes one Cortex-A77 a more attractive choice than a distribution of computations on the smaller cores.

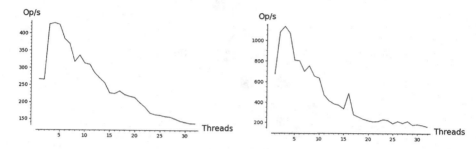

Fig. 3. Performance of multithreaded FORS 128f-simple with SHA-256 intrinsics. The abscissa is the number of threads an the ordinate is the number of FORS signatures generated per second. The right graphic is for Cortex-A77 and the left one for Cortex-A55.

5.3   Multithreading on XMSS^{MT}

Multithreading for XMSS^{MT} requires a bit more care than FORS as each roots of a subtree needs to be signed by the tree above. That means that, naively, a thread should wait for the computation of the top root of another thread to be able to start, rendering multithreading effectively useless. However, to compute the authentication path in an XMSS tree, we do not necessarily need to know the message to sign but only its leaf index, we hence use that fact to compute the different parts of the signature in parallel while delegating the signature of the top root of each thread to that same thread (except for the one computing the top tree root). This results into slightly unbalanced thread as earlier thread will often compute one WOTS+ signature more than the last one as shown in Fig. 4. What is lost with that strategy is that the WOTS+ signature is normally computed during the computation of the leaf value. This is impossible while we do not know the value of the root to sign, effectively leading to computing this particular WOTS+ twice. Our results show that it only has a marginal effect, and the speed-up is up equivalent to the number of cores available as can be seen for the variant 128f-simple with SHA-256 intrinsics in Fig. 5.

---

[2] We are only showing our improvements on the fastest parameter sets as the ratio thread creation time over thread execution time is the least favorable for our experiment. The improvements for slower parameter set will only be better.

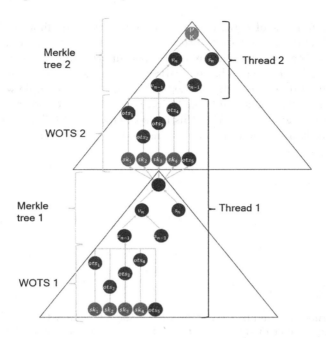

Fig. 4. Graphical description of our multithreading strategy

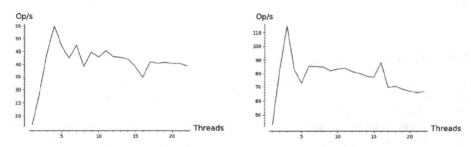

Fig. 5. Performance of multithreaded XMSS^{MT} 128f-simple with SHA-256 intrinsics. The abscissa is the number of threads an the ordinate is the number of XMSS^{MT} signature generated per second. The right graphic is for Cortex-A77 and the left one for Cortex-A55.

5.4   Merging in Best Case Scenarios

As one can notice, the FORS computation on 4 Cortex-A55 takes roughly the same time than the computation of the XMSS^{MT} part of the signature on the three available Cortex-A77. Hence, by simply waiting for the computation of FORS to be done on the Cortex-A55 and computing its WOTS+ signature on one of the Cortex-A77, we can parallelize efficiently the full SPHINCS$^+$ signature. We measured the performance in this optimal scenario and found out that we can reach 114 signature per second compared to the 40 from the single thread implementation and 8 of the reference implementation. That means an improvement by a factor of roughly 3 when compared to the best implementation and 15 to the reference.

6   Conclusion

We have shown that SPHINCS$^+$ can greatly beneficiate from a rather simple parallelization strategy on a mobile platform and can come closer to the performance of lattice-based cryptography but are still an order of magnitude slower even while using a lot more resources. We also showed that it is more efficient for hash-based signatures to use SIMD instructions to speed-up a single symmetric primitive computation than using SIMD to compute several primitives in parallel.

Open Problems. One future work would be to see if that remark still stands for ARM architecture equipped with Scalable Vector Extensions and SHA3 optimizations. Also, we have seen that software-based side-channel protections are too expansive for realistic deployment. One solution for this problem could be to get the randomness from an efficient hardware Random Number Generator. However, not every microprocessor has such capability and speeding up the random generation in pure software is still an open problem.

References

1. ARM. Arm cortex-a55 core software optimization guide. https://developer.arm.com/documentation/EPM128372/0300/?lang=en
2. ARM. Arm cortex-a77 core software optimization guide. https://developer.arm.com/documentation/swog011050/c/
3. Bai, S., et al.: CRYSTALS-Dilithium: Algorithm specifications and supporting documentation (2021). Specification v3
4. Becker, H., Hwang, V., Kannwischer, M.J., Yang, B.-Y., Yang, S.-Y.: Neon NTT: faster Dilithium, Kyber, and saber on cortex-a72 and apple m1. IACR Trans. Cryptographic Hardw. Embed. Syst. **2022**(1), 221–244 (2021)
5. Bernstein, D.J., et al.: SPHINCS$^+$, 2017. NIST Submission. https://sphincs.org/resources.html
6. Bernstein, D.J., et al.: SPHINCS: practical stateless hash-based signatures. In: Oswald, E., Fischlin, M. (eds.) EUROCRYPT 2015. LNCS, vol. 9056, pp. 368–397. Springer, Heidelberg (2015). https://doi.org/10.1007/978-3-662-46800-5_15
7. Bernstein, D.J., Hülsing, A., Kölbl, S., Niederhagen, R., Rijneveld, J., Schwabe, P.: The SPHINCS$^+$ signature framework. In: Cavallaro, L., Kinder, J., Wang, X., Katz, J. (eds.) Proceedings of the 2019 ACM SIGSAC Conference on Computer and Communications Security, CCS 2019, London, UK, 11–15 November 2019, pp. 2129–2146. ACM (2019)
8. Bertoni, G., Daemen, J., Peeters, M., Van Assche, G., Van Keer, R.: Keccak implementation overview. https://keccak.team/files/Keccak-implementation-3.2.pdf

9. Buchmann, J., Dahmen, E., Hülsing, A.: XMSS - a practical forward secure signature scheme based on minimal security assumptions. In: Yang, B.-Y. (ed.) PQCrypto 2011. LNCS, vol. 7071, pp. 117–129. Springer, Heidelberg (2011). https://doi.org/10.1007/978-3-642-25405-5_8

10. Buchmann, J., Dahmen, E., Schneider, M.: Merkle tree traversal revisited. In: Buchmann, J., Ding, J. (eds.) PQCrypto 2008. LNCS, vol. 5299, pp. 63–78. Springer, Heidelberg (2008). https://doi.org/10.1007/978-3-540-88403-3_5

11. Internet Engineering Task Force. Use of the HSS/LMS Hash-Based Signature Algorithm in the Cryptographic Message Syntax. Internet-Draft RFC 8708, Internet Engineering Task Force (2020)

12. Fouque, P.A., et al.: Falcon: Fast-fourier lattice-based compact signatures over NTRU (2020). Specification v1.2

13. Haas, G., Aysu, A.: Apple vs. EMA: electromagnetic side channel attacks on apple CoreCrypto. In: Proceedings of the 59th ACM/IEEE Design Automation Conference, DAC 2022, pp. 247–252, New York, NY, USA (2022). Association for Computing Machinery

14. Hülsing, A.: W-OTS+ – shorter signatures for hash-based signature schemes. In: Youssef, A., Nitaj, A., Hassanien, A.E. (eds.) AFRICACRYPT 2013. LNCS, vol. 7918, pp. 173–188. Springer, Heidelberg (2013). https://doi.org/10.1007/978-3-642-38553-7_10

15. Hülsing, A., Rausch, L., Buchmann, J.: Optimal parameters for XMSS^{MT}. In: Cuzzocrea, A., Kittl, C., Simos, D.E., Weippl, E., Xu, L. (eds.) CD-ARES 2013. LNCS, vol. 8128, pp. 194–208. Springer, Heidelberg (2013). https://doi.org/10.1007/978-3-642-40588-4_14

16. Kölbl, S.: Putting wings on SPHINCS. In: Lange, T., Steinwandt, R. (eds.) PQCrypto 2018. LNCS, vol. 10786, pp. 205–226. Springer, Cham (2018). https://doi.org/10.1007/978-3-319-79063-3_10

17. Lamport, L.: Constructing digital signatures from a one-way function. Technical report, Technical Report CSL-98, SRI International Palo Alto (1979)

18. Liardet, P.Y.: A potholing tour in a SoC. https://eshard.com/posts/sca-attacks-on-armv8

19. McGrew, D., Curcio, M., Fluhrer, S.: Leighton-micali hash-based signatures. Internet-Draft draft-mcgrew-hash-sigs-11, Internet Engineering Task Force (2019)

20. Merkle, Ralph C..: A certified digital signature. In: Brassard, Gilles (ed.) CRYPTO 1989. LNCS, vol. 435, pp. 218–238. Springer, New York (1990). https://doi.org/10.1007/0-387-34805-0_21

21. NIST. Post-Quantum Cryptography Call for Proposals (2018). https://csrc.nist.gov/Projects/Post-Quantum-Cryptography/Post-Quantum-Cryptography-Standardization/Call-for-Proposals Accessed 01 Jan 2020

22. National Institute of Standards and Technology: Recommendation for stateful hash-based signature schemes. U.S. Department of Commerce, Washington, D.C, Technical report (2020)

23. Perlner, R.A., Kelsey, J., Cooper, D.: Breaking category five SPHINCS+ with SHA-256. In: Cheon, J.H., Johansson, T. (eds.) PQCrypto 2022. Lecture Notes in Computer Science, vol. 13512, pp. 501–522. Springer, Cham (2022). https://doi.org/10.1007/978-3-031-17234-2_23

24. Reyzin, L., Reyzin, N.: Better than BiBa: short one-time signatures with fast signing and verifying. In: Batten, L., Seberry, J. (eds.) ACISP 2002. LNCS, vol. 2384, pp. 144–153. Springer, Heidelberg (2002). https://doi.org/10.1007/3-540-45450-0_11

SPANL: Creating Algorithms for Automatic API Misuse Detection with Program Analysis Compositions

Sazzadur Rahaman[1(✉)], Miles Frantz[2], Barton Miller[3], and Danfeng (Daphne) Yao[2]

[1] University of Arizona, Tucson, USA
`sazz@cs.arizona.edu`
[2] Virginia Tech, Blacksburg, USA
[3] University of Wisconsin-Madison, Madison, USA

Abstract. High-level language platforms provide APIs to aid developers in easily integrating security-relevant features in their code. Prior research shows that improper use of these APIs is a major source of insecurity in various application domains. Automatic code screening holds lots of potential to enable secure coding. However, building domain-specific security analysis tools requires both application domain and program analysis expertise. Interestingly, most of the prior works in developing domain-specific security analysis tools leverage some form of data flow analysis in the core. We leverage this insight to build a specification language named SPANL[1] for domain-specific security screening. The expressiveness analysis shows that a rule requiring any composition of dataflow analysis can be modeled in our language. Our evaluation on four cryptographic API misuse problems shows that our prototype implementation of SPANL does not introduce any imprecision due to the expressiveness of the language([1]SPANL stands for Security sPecificAtioN Language.).

Keywords: Program Analysis · Specification Language · API Misuse

1 Introduction

Platform API misuses [6,7,18,21,22] are a common source of software vulnerability in high-level language platforms such as Java and Android. For example, Java cryptography libraries (such as JCA, JCE, and JSSE[1]) [6,15,22], Spring security framework [21], Android system APIs [12,13] are widely misused by the developers. There are some other non-system APIs misuses that have serious security consequences in the Android ecosystem. For example, non-system APIs [23] to access sensitive information (location, IMEI, passwords, etc.), cloud service APIs

---

[1] JCA, JCE, and JSSE stand for Java Cryptography Architecture, Java Cryptography Extension, and Java Secure Socket Extension, respectively.

© The Author(s), under exclusive license to Springer Nature Switzerland AG 2023
J. Zhou et al. (Eds.): ACNS 2023 Workshops, LNCS 13907, pp. 515–529, 2023.
https://doi.org/10.1007/978-3-031-41181-6_28

for information storage [28], etc. Prior research revealed a multitude of causes behind this API misuse problem. The lack of cybersecurity training [21], insecure and misleading suggestions in StackOverflow [7,21], lack of understanding of the underlying APIs [6,22], are some of them. It is speculated that large language model-based automatic code generation tools will add fuel to the fire. Thus, development-time security screening has become a vital need.

There has been an extensive body of research on building static analysis tools for development-time security screening for Java and Android platforms [8,12,15,19,23,26]. Most of these efforts focused on either improving the detection capability [26] or detecting a new class of misuses [12]. However, the detection rules and types of vulnerabilities are immutable in most of the frameworks. This implies that extending existing frameworks for i) detecting new classes of vulnerabilities or ii) domain-specific security screening is largely hindered by the necessity of in-depth program analysis expertise. To address this challenge, Kruger et al. [19] designed a specification language (named CrySL [19]) to model cryptographic API misuses. However, CrySL's specification language is tightly coupled with its underlying detection mechanism (i.e., typestate analyses). Given a data object, typestate analyses define a valid sequence of operations that are allowed on the object. In CrySL, it is unclear how to express compound rules involving constants that are not known beforehand (i.e., return true if, all constant values to reach program point x, are not in the set of all constant values to reach program point y). In this paper, we tackle the following research question. *Is it possible to develop a universal specification language to express a wide variety of program properties (which we call, modeling for analysis) that can be used for domain-centric security and correctness checking?*

Existing work on finding API misuse vulnerabilities (e.g., improper use of cryptographic APIs [26], Android's fingerprint APIs [12], third-party cloud APIs [28], payment application APIs [20], etc.) suggests that most of the application-level API misuse problems can be modeled with dataflow-based program properties. Inspired by these works, we propose a new specification language that can be used to model any security rule that can be expressed in any arbitrary composition of various dataflow analysis algorithms. Next, we build a system named SPANL that takes rule specification written in our language and Java code as input and outputs the analysis result. Specifically, our main technical innovation is to allow compositions of basic dataflow analyses to model program properties.

The contribution of this paper is summarized as follows.

- We design a universal specification language named SPANL, to model meta-level program properties that can be detected by using a composition of various forms of data-flow analyses. We theoretically prove the expressiveness of the language.

– To further demonstrate the expressiveness, we model 4 composite security rules from [26] in SPANL language. Our experimental evaluation on CryptoApi-Bench [8] shows that SPANL's performance is similar to CryptoGuard [26].

SPANL decouples application domain expertise from program analysis expertise and enables quick adoption of data flow analyses-based security screening to any application domain.

2 Need for Domain-Specific Security Screening

There is an emerging need for scientific methods to enable domain-specific security checking. Existing work in this space mostly targets individual domains e.g., improper use of cryptographic APIs [26], Android's fingerprint APIs [12], third-party cloud APIs [28], payment application-specific APIs [20], etc. However, the approach of building a new tool to i) either improve coverage in an existing domain, or ii) enable security screening in a new domain significantly hinders its potential.

Additionally, software targeted for the payment card industry [5], IoT industry [14,16,24,27], health care industry [10], etc., needs to follow certain security guidelines dictated by a governing body [5] or law [10]. These guidelines are created to protect the stakeholders by ensuring industry-wide baseline security. For example, the payment card industry (PCI) data security standard (DSS), prescribes that *"Render all passwords unreadable during storage and transmission for all system components"* [25]. This implies that passwords should be either encrypted or hashed before transmitting or storing. One can assume that a composition of data flow analysis can be leveraged to implement this rule. However, modeling this rule in a generalized fashion is challenging. Firstly, identifying a data element to be a password is non-trivial. Secondly, APIs for communication and storage is vastly dependent on the usage of underlying frameworks. For example, communication APIs in the Spring framework [18] are significantly different than Apache Struts [2]. Database APIs for MyBatis framework [4] are significantly different than Hybernate [3]. This implies that modeling *one program-property* to implement this rule for different software or domains is infeasible. However, a specification language to model security properties for automatic screening address this issue by *i)* decoupling domain expertise from program analysis algorithms, *ii)* enabling easy framework/domain/application-specific customization.

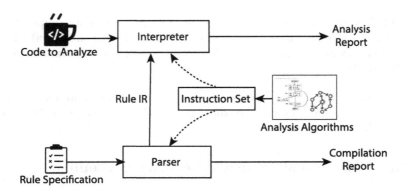

Fig. 1. System components of SPANL.

3   System Design

In this paper, we present SPANL (Fig. 1). SPANL defines a well-structured specification language to enable domain-specific security validation. Next, we provide a brief overview of our system.

3.1   Overview

The specification language in SPANL is guided by an extended Backus-Naur form (EBNF) grammar. EBNF is a collection of extensions to the Backus-Naur form (BNF) [11] to design modern compilers. We call each rule modeled in SPANL's specification language as *rule specification*. Given a rule specification, Parser parses the rule and creates a representation for execution. Then, the interpreter runs instructions from the rule specification and produces the analysis results (Interpreter in Fig. 1). The instruction set of the language is dictated by the various forms of data flow algorithms, which we discuss next.

$$\text{SPANL} ::= \textbf{APIs: } a \textbf{ Operations: } o \textbf{ Emits: } \epsilon \textbf{ Constraints: } c \textbf{ Exec: } s$$

$$v, \; a_{id}, \; o_{id}, \; \epsilon_{id}, \; c_{id} ::= \gamma$$

$$\textit{Values} \quad x ::= n \mid s$$

Type Enviornment $\Gamma ::= \; . \mid \Gamma$

γ : identifiers

n : Int

s : String

τ : Set of program-points

$\bar{\tau}$: A homogeneous array of τ or $\bar{\tau}$

Fig. 2. Overall structure of the SPANL specification language

3.2   Algorithms in SpanL

Data flow analyses enable a wide range of security applications in Java and Android platforms. Given a starting point, data flow analysis is a technique used to prove facts about a program. Given a set of definitions (starting point), forward dataflow analysis (aka reaching definition analysis) calculates if the definitions *reach* a given program point. Given a program point (starting point), backward dataflow analysis (aka liveness analysis) calculates a set of variables that are *live* at the program point. These algorithms are found to be used for cryptographic code screening [15,22,26], network [17,26], Android API misuses [13], payment application security validation, etc. Therefore, the current version of SpanL, offers security screening with inter- and intra-procedural forward and backward dataflow analysis with the support of various types of starting point definitions.

3.3   Components of SpanL Language

In Fig. 2, we present the overall structure of the SpanL specification language with various identifiers, values, and the type environment of the language. Code written in SpanL language contains 5 code sections, which we discuss next.

API Section. API section (Fig. 3) contains various API definitions, that can be referred from other sections of the SpanL code. These API definitions are reusable across various rules. Each API section has unique identifiers (a_{id}). The method signature of an API requires name and type pairs for both method arguments and the return variable, which is used to define the starting points in our dataflow analysis.

$$
\begin{aligned}
\textbf{API Group } a &::= a_{id} : a'\, a \mid a_{id} : a' \\
\textbf{API } a' &::= methodSig\ a' \mid methodSig \\
methodSig &::= ret\ className\text{: methodName}(args) \\
ret &::= <name : Type> \mid <\textbf{void}> \\
args &::= args,\ <name : Type> \mid\ <name : Type> \\
methodName, name &::= v \\
Type &::= basicTypes \mid basicTypes[] \mid className \mid className[] \\
className &::= className.v \mid v \\
basicTypes &::= \textbf{int} \mid \textbf{char} \mid \textbf{byte} \mid \textbf{boolean}
\end{aligned}
$$

Fig. 3. Grammar for parsing the API section

Operation Section. Operation section defines various static analysis operations that are needed to be performed in order to validate the rule. These operations are referred to from various instructions in the execution section. SpanL supports 5 types of operations (Fig. 4), i.e., inter-, intra-procedural forward and backward dataflow analysis and iteration. An operation produces a set of program points (τ) after its execution. These operations are referred from the execution section by using their identifiers (o_{id}).

$$
\begin{aligned}
\textbf{Operation } o &::= o \mid o_{id} \; : \; o_1 \mid o_{id} \; : \; o_2 \\
o_1 &::= \textit{inter byApi} \mid \textit{inter byRegex} \mid \textit{intra on byApi} \mid \textit{intra on byRegex} \\
\textit{inter} &::= \textbf{inter-backward} \mid \textbf{inter-forward} \\
\textit{intra} &::= \textbf{intra-backward} \mid \textbf{intra-forward} \\
\textit{byApi} &::= \textbf{with } a_{id} \textbf{ and } v \\
\textit{byRegex} &::= \textbf{with } x \\
o_2 &::= \textbf{iterate } \textit{on} \\
\textit{on} &::= a_{id} \mid \bar{\tau}
\end{aligned}
$$

Fig. 4. Grammar for parsing the Operation section

Emit Section. Emit sets contain the guidelines for collecting information from each of the operations defined in the operation sections. SPANL supports two types of *emit sets*, i) explicit and implicit. Emit sets that are explicitly defined in the emit set section are explicit emit sets. These emit sets can be used in various constraints in the constraint section or printed in the execution section. There are two types of implicit emit sets. i) simple, and i) compound. If an operation defined in the operation section doesn't have an explicitly defined emit set, then an implicit emit set is attached to it. These are called simple emit set, which collects all the program points after the execution of the corresponding operation. Compound emit sets are created as a result of compound operations. Explicit emit sets are of three types, i.e., constants, instruction, and API invocation based emit sets (Fig. 5). The inclusion criteria for constants can be specified by types or regular expressions. All the program points containing a value of the specified type or matching the regular expression will be added to the emit set. In an instruction-based emit set, all the program points matching the regular expression are collected. Invocation-based emit sets are used to collect program points containing the specified API invocations, which are identified by a_{id}.

$$
\begin{aligned}
\textbf{Emitsets } \epsilon &::= \epsilon \mid \epsilon_{id} \; : \; \epsilon' \\
\epsilon' &::= \textit{constants} \mid \textit{instructions} \mid \textit{invocations} \\
\textit{constants} &::= \textbf{constants of-type } \textit{Types} \mid \textbf{constants matches } x \\
\textit{Types} &::= \textit{Types, Type} \mid \textit{Type} \\
\textit{instructions} &::= \textbf{instructions matches } x \\
\textit{invocations} &::= \textbf{invocations matches } a_{id}
\end{aligned}
$$

Fig. 5. Grammar for parsing the Emit section

Constraint Section. This section defines various constraints that are used in the conditional instructions in the execution section. These constraints are defined by using emit sets, constant values, and API references. A single constraint in SPANL involves one emit set. Constraints support two sets of conditioning on emit sets, i.e., *in* and *empty* (Fig. 6). *in* can be used to check whether a set of values exists in the emit set or not. *empty* constraints can be used to check whether an emit set is empty or not.

$$
\begin{aligned}
\textbf{Constraints } c &::= c \mid c_{id} \ : \ c' \\
c' &::= in \mid empty \\
in &::= \{vals\} \ \textbf{in} \ \{\epsilon_{id}\} \mid \{vals\} \ \textbf{not in} \ \{\epsilon_{id}\} \\
empty &::= \{\epsilon_{id}\} \ \textbf{empty} \mid \{\epsilon_{id}\} \ \textbf{not empty} \\
vals &::= vals, \ x \mid x
\end{aligned}
$$

Fig. 6. Grammar for parsing the Constraint section

Execution Section. Execution section contains specific instructions required to be executed to validate a rule. SPANL supports three types of instructions, i.e., operation, conditional and print instructions. Operation instructions are used to execute the operations defined in the operation section. Additionally, it supports some compound operations in the form of set union, subtraction, and join based on the results of other operations. The *join* of two operations indicates that the trailing operation is executed by using the output of the leading operation as its starting point. Conditional and print instructions are used to support conditional branching and print various types of messages to the standard output, respectively.

$$
\begin{aligned}
\textit{Stmt} \qquad s &::= v := o \mid o \mid \textbf{print}(x) \mid \textbf{if } \delta \textbf{ then } s_1 \textbf{ else } s_2 \mid \textbf{for } v \textbf{ do } s \mid s \mid \\
&\quad\ v := \textbf{array}(i) \mid v' := v.get(i) \mid v.set(i, o) \\
\textit{Operation} \qquad o &::= (o) \mid o_1 + o_2 \mid o_1 - o_2 \mid o_1 \oplus o_2 \mid v \mid o_{id} \\
\textit{Conditional Expression} \qquad \delta &::= \delta_1 \textbf{ and } \delta_2 \mid \delta_1 \textbf{ or } \delta_2 \mid (\delta) \mid \textbf{not } \delta \mid c_{id}
\end{aligned}
$$

Fig. 7. Grammar for parsing the execution section

Figure 7 shows that SPANL's execution supports various types of instructions including, *if, for, add, sub, join, assign* and *print*. Here, the type of *array(i)* is $\bar{\tau}$. $\bar{\tau}$ has two built-in functions *get(i)* and *set(i, o)*. As the name implies *get* is used to access an element of the array and the *set* is used to set an element in the array. Assign statements offer the functionality of assigning the output of an operation (a set of program points) to a variable. In addition to the basic operations (invoked by o_{id}), SPANL also supports some compound instructions i.e., set addition and subtraction and join operations. The join of $o_1 \oplus o_2$ indicates the execution o_1 by using the output program points of o_2 as the starting point. We present the judgments of the type system for the execution section in Fig. 8.

$$\frac{\Gamma \vdash \delta : \text{boolean} \quad \Gamma \vdash s_1 : \tau \quad \Gamma \vdash s_2 : \tau}{\Gamma \vdash (\text{if } \delta \text{ then } s_1 \text{ else } s_2) : \tau}\text{IF-OP} \qquad \frac{\Gamma \vdash v : \tau \quad \Gamma \vdash s : \tau}{\Gamma \vdash (\text{for } v \text{ do } s) : \tau}\text{FOR-OP}$$

$$\frac{\Gamma \vdash o_1 : \tau \quad \Gamma \vdash o_2 : \tau}{\Gamma \vdash (o_1 + o_2) : \tau}\text{ADD-OP} \qquad \frac{\Gamma \vdash o_1 : \tau \quad \Gamma \vdash o_2 : \tau}{\Gamma \vdash (o_1 - o_2) : \tau}\text{SUB-OP}$$

$$\frac{\Gamma \vdash o_2 : \tau \quad \Gamma \vdash o_1 : \tau}{\Gamma \vdash (o_1 \oplus o_2) : \tau}\text{JOIN-OP} \qquad \frac{\Gamma \vdash x : \text{Int, String}}{\Gamma \vdash (\text{print}(x)) : \text{boolean}}\text{PRINT-OP}$$

$$\frac{\Gamma \vdash o : \tau}{\Gamma \vdash (v := o) : \tau}\text{ASSIGN-OP} \qquad \frac{\Gamma \vdash i : \text{Int}}{\Gamma \vdash (v := \text{array}(i)) : \bar{\tau}}\text{ARRAY-CREATION-OP}$$

$$\frac{\Gamma \vdash v : \bar{\tau} \quad \Gamma \vdash i : \text{Int}}{\Gamma \vdash (v' := v.get(i)) : \tau}\text{GET-OP} \qquad \frac{\Gamma \vdash v : \bar{\tau} \quad \Gamma \vdash i : \text{Int} \quad \Gamma \vdash o : \tau}{\Gamma \vdash (v.set(i,o)) : \text{boolean}}\text{SET-OP}$$

Fig. 8. Type judgements for execution section.

4   Expressiveness of the Language

In this section, we analyze the expressiveness of SPANL specification language. First, we discuss expressiveness theoretically and then we show several case studies by modeling various security rules.

4.1   Expressiveness Analysis

Corollary 1. *If the allowed analysis mechanisms are of forward (f) and backward (b) dataflow analysis, then from a program point $p : x = \$r.func(a_1, a_2, \cdots, a_k)$, one can start $2k+3$ numbers of analysis, including $k+1$ backward data flow analysis by using \$r and $a_i \; \forall i \in [1, k]$ as starting criteria, $k + 2$ forward data flow analysis by using x, \$r and $a_i \; \forall i \in [1, k]$ as starting criteria. So if the number of possible analyses can be run from a program point p is $O = \{o_i\}, \forall i \in [1, |O|]$, then $|O| \leq 2k + 3$.*

Definition 1. *Super-analysis set. If P_{o_i} represents the set of all the reachable program points after running an analysis o_i from a program point p, then P_{o_i} can be expressed as $p \xrightarrow{o_i} P_{o_i}$. Let O is the set of a maximum number of data flow analysis that can be run from p. Running O analysis from p can be expressed as $p \xrightarrow{O} P_O$, where $P_O = \cup\{P_{o_i}\}, \forall i \in [1, |O|]$ and $|O| \leq 2k + 3$. Here, we define P_O as the super-analysis set for p. This means, P_O can not be further extended by running new analyses from p.*

Definition 2. *Super-analysis join sets. If ρ_i is the set of all program points returned after starting the super-analysis from program point p_i and then recursively continue super-analysis by using the results and starting criteria until no new program points are reached. Then ρ_i can be expressed as follows.*

$$\rho_i = p_i \overset{O_1}{\leadsto} \cdots \{P_o\}_j \overset{O_j}{\leadsto} \cdots \{P_o\}_n$$

Definition 3. *Mutually exclusive super analysis join sets. Let the super-analysis sets, starting from program point $1, 2, \cdots, n$ are $\rho_1, \rho_2, \cdots, \rho_n$. We call two super-analysis sets ρ_i, ρ_j mutually exclusive if $\rho_i \subsetneq \rho_j, \forall i, j \in [1, n]$.*

If ρ_i and ρ_j are mutually exclusive super-analysis join sets, then combining both of them would increase more coverage of the analysis.

Definition 4. *Simple rule. A rule is simple if the expressiveness of its security property is bounded by a super-analysis join set.*

Definition 5. *Compound rule. A rule is compound if it requires at least two mutually exclusive super analysis join sets to model the security property of the rule.*

Theorem 1. *The expressiveness of a security property that can be detected by using a composition of various data flow analyses, is bounded by the compound rule with all mutually exclusive super analysis join sets.*

Proof. A compound rule that would need all the *mutually exclusive super-analysis join sets* combinely represents the set of all possible compositions of dataflow analysis that can be run on a program. That means if a security property can be expressed by a composition of data flow analysis, it must be bounded by the compound rule with all mutually exclusive super analysis join sets.

SPANL supports joining (JOIN-OP), and combining multiple analysis sets (ADD-OP, SUB-OP). This means SPANL language contains all the properties of expressing a compound rule. Thus, SPANL can be used to define all possible combinations of data flow analysis possible on a given program.

Listing 1.1. Rule to detect insecure RSA keys

```
APIs:
kpg_apis:
 <kpg: KeyPair> KeyPairGenerator: getInstance(<algo: String>)
 <kpg: KeyPair> KeyPairGenerator: getInstance(<p: Provider>,
                                               <algo: String>)

kpg_init:
  void KeyPairGenerator: initialize(<size: int>)

Operations:
```

```
o1: inter-backward with kpg_apis and algo
o2: intra-forward with kpg_apis and kpg
o3: inter-backward with kpg_init and size

Emits:
  {kpg}: *
  {algo}: constant of-type java.lang.String
  {size}: constant of-type int, java.lang.Integer

Constraints:
    c1: kpg_init in {kpg}
    c2: {"RSA"} in {algo}
    c3: {2048, 4096} not in {size}

Exec:
    o1, o1 ⊕ o2
    if c2 and (not c1):
        print ("Must invoke initialize for RSA")
    if c1:
        o3 ⊕ o2
        if c2 and c3:
            print ("Key size must be {2048, 4096}")
```

4.2 Case Studies

In this section, we present 4 case studies of cryptographic API misuse in SPANL language, i.e., i) insecure use of RSA, ii) insecure hostname verifier, iii) insecure symmetric crypto, and iv) insecure symmetric keys usage. These case studies are commonly found in existing literature [22,26].

In Listing 1.1, we show the code written in SPANL language to detect insecure RSA key uses. Note that, this is one of the most complex security rules that involves multiple rounds of analysis. The default use of the RSA key pair generator uses 1024 bit key size. Thus, one requires to invoke the initialize method with proper key size i.e., 2048, 4096 to generate secure RSA keys. Here, we first define two API groups for getInstance and initialize APIs. Next, we define the set of operations to be performed with these APIs. $o1$ is used to determine if the key pair is of RSA. Then $o2$ is used to find if initialize method was invoked on the generated key pair instance. Finally, $o3$ is used to find the value of the key size parameter of the initialize method invocation. The emit set defines what values should be collected in each operation. The left-hand side indicates the set and the right-hand side contains the criteria. For example, $\{kpg\} : *$ indicates to store all the program points reached after running $o2$. Next, the constraints and Execution section defines the corresponding constraints and the sequence of instructions to run, respectively. In the execution section, $o1, o2$ join with $o1$ indicates running operation $o2$ by using the outputs of $o1$ as starting points.

The code for other case studies is presented in the appendix. Note that, while modeling these rules we followed the mapping between the program property and the rule outlined in CryptoGuard [26].

5 Experimental Evaluation

In this section, we present the evaluation results of our SpanL system.

Implementation. We implemented SpanL in Java. We used ANTLR [1] for parsing and validating the rule specification code written in SpanL language. Our current implementation supports both backward and forward intraprocedural data flow analysis. To support inter-procedural backward data flow analysis, we leveraged the version implemented in CryptoGuard [26], which is path insensitive. Our current prototype does not support inter-procedural forward data flow analysis, which can be easily added in the future.

Experiment Design for Evaluating Expressiveness. There can be two sources of imprecision in SpanL, i) imprecision due to imprecise modeling of a security rule, ii) imprecision induced by the underlying analysis algorithm. Since the main contribution of SpanL is the specification language, thus we only focus on the expressiveness in our evaluation. Specifically, we ask the following research question: *Is there any imprecision due to modeling a security property in SpanL?*

To answer this question, we designed the following experiment. We modeled 4 cryptographic API misuse rules (Sect. 4.2) from CryptoGuard in SpanL. Since our implementation reuses CryptoGuard's algorithms, any deviation in our result from CryptoGuard would indicate imprecision in the model. To test this, we run CryptoGuard and SpanL in CryptoApi-Bench [9]. CryptoApi-Bench is a benchmark containing various cryptographic API misuse vulnerabilities.

Table 1. Expressiveness evaluation results on CryptoApi-Bench. It indicates that SpanL does not introduce new imprecision than its underlying algorithms (which were reused from CryptoGuard).

Detection Goals	CryptoGuard			SpanL		
	TP	FP	FN	TP	FP	FN
Insecure RSA keys	4	1	1	4	1	1
Insecure hostname verifier	1	0	0	1	0	0
Insecure symmetric crypto	30	5	0	30	5	0
Insecure symmetric keys	5	1	2	5	1	2

Experimental Result. In CryptoApi-Bench, there is a total of 6 cases (5 true positives (TP) and 1 true negative cases (TN)) of insecure RSA key usage.

It has 1 instance of insecure hostname verification, 36 instances (30 TP, 6 TN) of insecure symmetric ciphers, and 9 (7 TP, 2 TN). In Table 1, we show the evaluation results of both SPANL and CRYPTOGUARD. It shows that modeling the security rules in SPANL did not incur new imprecision, indicating the expressiveness

6   Conclusion

Enabling domain-specific security screening is important to ensure baseline security in various application domains. Prior research [13,17,18,25] showed that various domain-specific security rules can be modeled as API-centric data flow problems. In this paper, we designed a specification language to model such problems that can be automatically checked. Then we built a system named SPANL, to run codes written in our specification language for automatic code screening. The expressiveness analysis shows that a rule requiring any composition of dataflow analysis can be modeled in our language. Our evaluation on four cryptographic API misuse problems shows that our prototype implementation of SPANL does not introduce any imprecision due to the expressiveness of the language.

Acknowledgements. This work has been supported in part by the National Science Foundation under Grant No. CNS-1929701.

Appendix

Listing 1.2. Rule to detect insecure hostname verifier

```
APIs:
host_name_apis:
 boolean HostnameVerifier: verify(<name: String>,
                                   <session: SSLSession>)

Operations:
    o1: intra-backward host_name_apis with "return"

Emits:
  {o1_out}: *

CONSTRAINTS:
    c1: "@parameter1: javax.net.ssl.SSLSession" not in {o1_out}

Exec:
  o1
  if c1:
      print("verify method is not properly implemented!")
```

Listing 1.3. Rule to detect insecure symmetric ciphers

```
APIs:
crypto_apis:
  Cipher Cipher: getInstance(<name: String>)
  Cipher Cipher: getInstance(<name: String>, <p: Provider>)

Operations:
    o1:  inter-backward with crypto_apis  and name

Emits:
{name}: constants of-type java.lang.String

Constraints:
  c1: {"AES/ECB", "DES", "RC4", "IDEA"} in {name}

Exec:
o1
if c1:
    print("Found broken crypto instances")
```

Listing 1.4. Rule to detect insecure symmetric keys

```
APIs:
sk_apis:
  void SecretKeySpec: SecretKeySpec(<keyBytes: byte[]>)
  void SecretKeySpec: SecretKeySpec(<keyBytes: byte[]>,
                                    <p: Provider>)


Operations:
    o1: inter-backward with sk_apis and keyBytes

Emits:
  {keyBytes}: constant of-type java.lang.String, byte[]

Constraints:
  c1: {keyBytes} not empty

Exec:
  o1
  if c1:
      print("Keys must not be derived from constants")
```

References

1. Antlr: Quick start. https://www.antlr.org/. Accessed 20 Feb 2023
2. Apache struts. https://struts.apache.org/. Accessed 20 Feb 2023
3. Hybernate: Everything data. https://hibernate.org/. Accessed 20 Feb 2023
4. Mybatis 3: Introduction. https://mybatis.org/mybatis-3/. Accessed 20 Feb 2023
5. Payment Card Industry (PCI) Data Security Standard: Requirements and security assessment procedures. https://www.pcisecuritystandards.org/documents/PCI_DSS_v3-2-1.pdf (2018) (2018)
6. Acar, Y., et al.: Comparing the usability of cryptographic APIs. In: IEEE S&P 2017, pp. 154–171 (2017)
7. Acar, Y., Backes, M., Fahl, S., Kim, D., Mazurek, M.L., Stransky, C.: You get where you're looking for: the impact of information sources on code security. In: IEEE S&P 2016, pp. 289–305 (2016)
8. Afrose, S., Rahaman, S., Yao, D.: CryptoAPI-Bench: a comprehensive benchmark on java cryptographic API misuses. In: 2019 IEEE Cybersecurity Development, SecDev 2019, Tysons Corner, VA, USA, 23–25 September 2019, pp. 49–61 (2019)
9. Afrose, S., Xiao, Y., Rahaman, S., Miller, B.P., Yao, D.: Evaluation of static vulnerability detection tools with java cryptographic API benchmarks. IEEE Trans. Softw. Eng. **49**(2), 485–497 (2023)
10. Annas, G.J.: HIPAA regulations: a new era of medical-record privacy? N. Engl. J. Med. **348**, 1486 (2003)
11. Backus, J.W.: The syntax and semantics of the proposed international algebraic language of the zurich ACM-GAMM conference. In: Information Processing, Proceedings of the 1st International Conference on Information Processing, UNESCO, Paris 15–20 June 1959, pp. 125–131 (1959)
12. Bianchi, A., et al.: Broken fingers: on the usage of the fingerprint API in android. In: 25th Annual Network and Distributed System Security Symposium, NDSS 2018, San Diego, California, USA, 18–21 February 2018 (2018)
13. Bosu, A., Liu, F., Yao, D.D., Wang, G.: Collusive data leak and more: large-scale threat analysis of inter-app communications. In: AsiaCCS 2017, pp. 71–85 (2017)
14. Department of Justice: Securing your "internet of things" devices (2017). https://www.justice.gov/criminal-ccips/page/file/984001/download
15. Egele, M., Brumley, D., Fratantonio, Y., Kruegel, C.: An empirical study of cryptographic misuse in Android applications. In: ACM CCS 2013, pp. 73–84 (2013)
16. European Union Agency for Network and Information Security: Baseline security recommendations for IoT in the context of critical information infrastructures (2017). https://www.enisa.europa.eu/publications/baseline-security-recommendations-for-iot/@@download/fullReport
17. Fahl, S., Harbach, M., Muders, T., Smith, M., Baumgärtner, L., Freisleben, B.: Why eve and mallory love android: an analysis of android SSL (in) security. In: ACM CCS 2012, pp. 50–61 (2012)
18. Islam, M., Rahaman, S., Meng, N., Hassanshahi, B., Krishnan, P., Yao, D.D.: Coding practices and recommendations of spring security for enterprise applications. In: 2020 IEEE Cybersecurity Development, SecDev 2020 (2020). (to appear)
19. Krüger, S., Späth, J., Ali, K., Bodden, E., Mezini, M.: CrySL: an extensible approach to validating the correct usage of cryptographic APIs. In: 32nd European Conference on Object-Oriented Programming, ECOOP 2018, 16–21 July 2018, Amsterdam, The Netherlands, pp. 10:1–10:27 (2018)

20. Mahmud, S.Y., Acharya, A., Andow, B., Enck, W., Reaves, B.: Cardpliance: PCI DSS compliance of android applications. In: Capkun, S., Roesner, F. (eds.) 29th USENIX Security Symposium, USENIX Security 2020, 12–14 August 2020, pp. 1517–1533. USENIX Association (2020)

21. Meng, N., Nagy, S., Yao, D., Zhuang, W., Argoty, G.A.: Secure coding practices in java: challenges and vulnerabilities. In: ACM ICSE 2018. Gothenburg, Sweden (2018)

22. Nadi, S., Krüger, S., Mezini, M., Bodden, E.: Jumping through hoops: why do java developers struggle with cryptography APIs? In: ICSE 2016, pp. 935–946 (2016)

23. Nan, Y., Yang, Z., Wang, X., Zhang, Y., Zhu, D., Yang, M.: Finding clues for your secrets: semantics-driven, learning-based privacy discovery in mobile apps. In: 25th Annual Network and Distributed System Security Symposium, NDSS 2018, San Diego, California, USA, 18–21 February 2018 (2018)

24. National Institute of Standards and Technology: IoT device cybersecurity guidance for the federal government: Establishing IoT device cybersecurity requirements (2021). https://nvlpubs.nist.gov/nistpubs/SpecialPublications/NIST.SP.800-213.pdf

25. Rahaman, S., Wang, G., Yao, D.D.: Security certification in payment card industry: testbeds, measurements, and recommendations. In: Cavallaro, L., Kinder, J., Wang, X., Katz, J. (eds.) Proceedings of the 2019 ACM SIGSAC Conference on Computer and Communications Security, CCS 2019, London, UK, 11–15 November 2019, pp. 481–498. ACM (2019)

26. Rahaman, S., et al.: Cryptoguard: High precision detection of cryptographic vulnerabilities in massive-sized java projects. In: Proceedings of the 2019 ACM SIGSAC Conference on Computer and Communications Security, CCS 2019, London, UK, 11–15 November 2019, pp. 2455–2472 (2019)

27. US Chamber of Commerce: The IoT revolution and our digital security: principles for IoT security (2017). https://scglegal.com/wp-content/uploads/2018/02/2017-Denver-TR-1550-PP-The.IoT_.Revolution..Our_.Digital.Security.Final-002-WILEY-REIN.pdf

28. Zuo, C., Lin, Z., Zhang, Y.: Why does your data leak? Uncovering the data leakage in cloud from mobile apps. In: IEEE S&P 2016 (2019)

ZKBdf: A ZKBoo-Based Quantum-Secure Verifiable Delay Function with Prover-Secret

Teik Guan Tan[1]([✉]), Vishal Sharma[3], Zeng Peng Li[4], Pawel Szalachowski[2], and Jianying Zhou[2]

[1] pQCee Pte Ltd, Singapore, Singapore
tanteikg@gmail.com
[2] Singapore University of Technology and Design, Singapore, Singapore
jianying_zhou@sutd.edu.sg
[3] Queen's University Belfast, Belfast, UK
v.sharma@qub.ac.uk
[4] School of Cyber Science and Technology, Shandong University, Jinan, China
zengpeng@email.sdu.edu.cn

Abstract. Since the formalization of Verifiable Delay Functions (VDF) by Boneh et al. in 2018, VDFs have been adopted for use in blockchain consensus protocols and random beacon implementations. However, the impending threat to VDF-based applications comes in the form of Shor's algorithm running on quantum computers in the future which can break the discrete logarithm and integer factorization problems that existing VDFs are based on. Clearly, there is a need for quantum-secure VDFs. In this paper, we propose ZKBdf, which makes use of ZKBoo, a zero-knowledge proof system for verifiable computation, as the basis for realizing a quantum-secure VDF. We describe the algorithm, provide the security proofs, implement the scheme and measure the execution and size requirements. In addition, as ZKBdf extends the standard VDF with an extra "Prover-secret" feature, new VDF use-cases are also explored.

Keywords: Verifiable Delay Function · Zero-Knowledge Proof · Post-Quantum Cryptography

1 Introduction

The notion of delay may initially come across as a paradox. In the world of computing where systems are constantly tuned for higher processing throughput and more efficient communications while users demand shorter response time and immediate gratification, the need for delays seems counter-intuitive.

Yet, there are valid use-cases where delays are relevant. In 1996, Rivest et al. [46] introduced the concept of time-lock puzzles where a published secret is locked, and can only be opened after a specified period of time. Time-lock puzzles require the use of a computer to execute a sequence of commands, thus

J. Zhou et al. (Eds.): ACNS 2023 Workshops, LNCS 13907, pp. 530–550, 2023.
https://doi.org/10.1007/978-3-031-41181-6_29

consuming a certain amount of time, before the secret is revealed. They can be applied in the case of auction bids where a bidder submits a sealed auction bid which requires a duration longer than the auction window for it to be opened. The time-lock puzzle here prevents even the auctioneer from knowing the bid until after the close of the auction. Delays can also be used to regulate the number of requests received. Later constructions of delay functions include proof-of-sequential work (PoSW) by Mahmoody et al. [36] using sequential hash functions and Cohen et al. [15] which uses a hash-graph structure to optimize the verification efficiency of a hash-chain. On a different use-case, Dwork and Noar [19] proposed imposing a computational overhead for every email received in order to reduce the amount of SPAM mail in 1993. This concept was formalized as proof-of-work (PoW) by Jacobsson and Juels [29] and made famous when Nakamoto's Bitcoin [41] used PoW as the blockchain consensus mechanism for miners to propose blocks approximately every 10 min. Delays are also used to ensure fairness for leader elections. Snow White's sleepy consensus by Pass and Shi [43] relies on delay functions to account for all possible network latency when receiving inputs from active nodes to compute an unbiased leader, while not waiting in vain for nodes that are inactive.

Boneh et al. [7] provided the formal definition of a Verifiable Delay function (VDF) in 2018. VDFs differ from time-lock puzzles in their unique properties of not requiring a trapdoor operation while computing a deterministic and unpredictable output. For VDFs, the delay is on the side of the sender (or Prover) who has to prove to the receiver (or Verifier) that a T amount of time has elapsed. Informally, we view the time-lock puzzle as a fast-encrypt-slow-decrypt confidentiality analogy and VDF as a slow-generate-fast-verify integrity analogy for delay functions. This begs the question why isn't VDFs used more widely beyond consensus protocols and time-stamp / random beacons. In our research, we discover the inclusion of a prover-secret as part of the VDF protocol can open up more use-cases.

In this paper, we provide the realization of a quantum-secure VDF using ZKBoo by Giacomelli et al. [24] to implement a HMAC-SHA256 circuit. While using verifiable computing primitives to construct a VDF is proposed before [7,10,50], we include a security reduction of our implementation to ZKBoo with the Fiat-Shamir heuristic [22,53] to make our implementation quantum-secure without trusted setup. Other contributions include proposing a modified existential unforgeability under chosen-message attacks (EUF-CMA) [26] experiment for VDFs and extending the ZKBoo SHA256 implementation to HMAC-SHA256 [31]. The ZKBoo HMAC-SHA256 zero-knowledge proof of knowledge of the MACing key gives an additional "Prover-secret" feature to ZKBdf.

The organization of the paper is as follows. Section 2 introduces the background and related work. Section 3 provides the design of a quantum-secure VDF and security proofs. Section 4 describes the implementation of the proposed VDF with execution results. Section 5 concludes the paper. New VDF use-cases which make use of ZKBdf's Prover-secret feature are explored in the Appendix.

2 Background

2.1 Hash-Chain

The hash-chain consists of a sequence of One-Way Functions (OWF) H where the output of the previous OWF operation is treated as the input to the next OWF operation. For a delay parameter T, the hash-chain $Eval$ function is:

$$H^T(x) = \begin{cases} H(H^{T-1}(x)) & T > 1 \\ H(x) & T = 1 \end{cases} \tag{1}$$

Execution of the hash-chain requires the Prover to invoke H sequentially for T times. Assuming that the OWF function H is collision-resistant, a polynomial-bounded adversary will not be able to perform any meaningful pre-computation or shorten the process since the probability of guessing $H^{i+1}(x)$ when only $H^i(x)$ $\forall i < T$ is computed is negligible.

The verification of $H^T(x)$ is a matter of a time-space tradeoff. If only $[x, H^T(x)]$ is provided as the proof, then the Verifier will have to perform the same sequence of hashes as the Prover to verify $H^T(x)$. If the intermediate hash values $H^i(x)$ are also provided as part of the proof, then the Verifier can parallelize the verification process across multiple processing units, and shorten the verification time. Since execution complexity of the verification remains at $O(T)$ and can only be sped up through process parallelism, delay functions such as $Sloth$ [35] which use hash-chains are not VDFs but termed as a $pseudo-$VDF [7].

2.2 Verifiable Delay Function

Definition 1. *We define* $VDF = (Setup, Eval, Verify)$ *as triple of algorithms with the following syntax*

$Setup(\lambda) \rightarrow (e_k, v_k)$ takes in a security parameter λ, and outputs the evaluation key e_k, and verification key v_k.

$Eval(e_k, Cha, T) \rightarrow (Res, \pi)$ takes in the evaluation key e_k, a one-time challenge Cha along with the time delay T and outputs the response to the challenge Res and the corresponding proof π. $Eval$ must require at least T units of time to execute even on a parallel computer.

$Verify(v_k, Res, \pi, Cha, T) \rightarrow (result \in \{accept, reject\})$ takes in the verification key v_k, the response Res, proof π, challenge Cha, and time delay T and outputs $accept$ if and only if Res is the correct response to Cha and π is evaluated correctly. $Verify$ must be able to run at significantly less than T units of time.

The *Correctness* property of a VDF is defined such that the *Verify* function will accept the output generated by the *Eval* function while the *Soundness* property of a VDF states that the probability of

$accept \xleftarrow{R} Verify(v_k, Cha, Res', \pi', T)$ where $Res' \neq Res$ and $(Res, \pi) \xleftarrow{R}$ $Eval(e_k, Cha, T)$ is negligible. In addition, Boneh et al. [7] have listed three properties that embodies what a VDF has to exhibit:

- *Sequentiality.* Sequentiality is defined strictly with respect to the computation time of Res given (e_k, Cha) which cannot be less than T. The time required to generate proof π is excluded from the definition. However, we argue that the time needed to compute the proof π can also be taken into account. Hence, we re-define sequentiality as $Verify(v_k, Cha, Res, \pi, T) \rightarrow reject$ if time taken to compute (Res, π) from (e_k, Cha, T) is less than T when provided with polynomial-bounded computational power.
- *Efficient verifiability.* The $Verify$ is a public function that is expected to execute more efficiently as compared to $Eval$. It is required to complete in the order of $O(polylog(T))$ execution time.
- *Uniqueness.* For every input challenge Cha provided to $Eval$, there is a deterministic and unpredictable response Res. And it is computationally hard to find Cha when given only Res. This property makes VDFs applicable for use in random beacons and leader elections for distributed systems.

These three properties rule out time-lock puzzles, PoW, and PoSW as VDFs since time-lock puzzles do not have a publicly efficient verifiable operation, while the proofs generated by PoW and PoSW are not unique [15,29,36].

Constructing a VDF typically involves iterating a non-"parallelizable" (or serialized) process as many times as necessary to account for the T delay, while having an efficient mechanism to verify the process. In the VDF survey [8], the two VDFs by Pietrzak [44] and Wesolowski [54] respectively use a common serialized process:

$$f(x) = H(x)^{2^T} \text{ over an abelian group } \mathbb{G}, \tag{2}$$

where $H(x)$ is repeatedly squared T times. This has been recognized as insecure [8] against a quantum-capable adversary who can compute the order of $\mathbb{G}$ using Shor's algorithm [48] in polynomial time.

Quantum-Secure VDF. To construct a quantum-secure VDF, a logical hypothesis would therefore be: *Can a quantum computer running a randomness service function as a VDF?* Mahmoody et al [37] has shown this hypothesis to be flawed by proving the in-feasibility of a black-box random oracle functioning as a VDF. De Foe et al. [16] constructs a VDF using elliptic curve isogenies which is "quantum-annoying" but not quantum-secure. Chavez-Saab et al. [13] proposes the use of isogenies embedded as an arithmetic structure within a succinct non-interactive argument (SNARG) [23] to be quantum-secure, but recent discoveries on the weakness of supersingular isogenies [11] casts doubts on the claims. The VDF implementation that comes closest to being quantum-secure is Buterin's VDF [10], but (to our best knowledge) lacks formal quantum-security proofs. It makes use of an iterated block cipher with Minimal Multiplicative Complexity (MiMC) [1] that is run sequentially, and then builds a SNARG to prove that the computation was performed correctly.

2.3   ZKBoo

ZKBoo [24] is a zero-knowledge proof system for verifiable computation. When ZKBoo is used by a Prover to prove the hash result of computing an OWF, the Verifier has the assurance that the Prover knows the pre-image of the hash, without gaining any additional knowledge of the pre-image.

To generate the proof, ZKBoo uses Ishai et al.'s [28] secure multiparty computation MPC-in-the-head to create an AND-NOT-XOR-ADD boolean circuit sequence of three branches. Unlike subsequent MPC-in-the-head proof constructions such as KKW [30], preprocessing and other process optimizations for ZKBoo is limited which lends itself well as a VDF. At the beginning of the proof generation during the preprocessing stage, the secret is randomly split into three shares and a deterministic random sequence $R_i[]$ is generated. During the circuit computation stage which makes up the bulk of the computation, the three shares then step through the circuit along the three branches respectively. At each of the AND and ADD gates, the three branches are pair-wise intertwined $(1 \leftrightarrow 2, 2 \leftrightarrow 3, 3 \leftrightarrow 1)$ in a sequential manner and XOR with the deterministic sequence $R_i[]$ to ensure no steps are skipped. The final result of the computation is committed in the proof but only two of the three views will be revealed to the Verifier for verification. The choice of which two views is determined at the proof extraction stage using the Fiat-Shamir heuristic [22] to make the proof non-interactive. To increase the cryptographic strength (or assurance) of the zero-knowledge proof, the same boolean circuit is re-run using different shares which are randomly generated. Since each stage prepares the necessary information for the next stage, each stage must wait for the previous stage to complete before commencing. During verification, the Verifier takes in the generated proof, and walks through the two of three views and has $\geq 50\%$ assurance, but no additional knowledge, that the Prover knows the secret value used to create the three shares. Both proof and verify processes execute in $O(N)$ complexity and all runs are parallelizable.

The strengths of ZKBoo are that it does not require any trusted setup, has efficient circuits for small computations and each round in the proof generation and verification are parallelizable. ZKBoo, however, has a large proof size. Chase et al. [12] improves on ZKBoo by proposing ZKB++ which, in addition to reducing the proof size by almost half, introduces the use of the Unruh transformation [51] to arrive at security proofs in the Quantum Random Oracle Model [9].

2.4   Computationally Sound Probabilistic Checkable Proof (PCP)

PCP by Arora and Safra [2] is a system of proof that can efficiently reduce the verification time complexity of proofs by an order of $O(logN)$. It achieves this by first encoding the original proof into a local-testable format [4], then applying an oracle to select proof samples to be verified. The outcome is that the PCP verification process will yield errors for incorrect proofs with a high probability on low-degree testing, although proof generation time complexity and proof size remain asymmetrically larger. Separately, Kilian [33] introduces a zero-knowledge protocol where it is possible to use a subset of commitments to achieve concise arguments for a corresponding proof.

Micali's computationally sound proof [40] realizes a construction of Kilian's protocol and PCP using Merkle trees [39]. Computationally sound proofs build on PCPs by reducing the size of proof needed to be sent to the Verifier, thus optimizing both space and time complexity in the verification process. Briefly, Micali's construction works as follows during proof generation to extract k proof elements out of the complete set of proofs for verification:

1. Compute the full set of PCP proofs π.
2. Build a Merkle-tree with each of the proof elements in π placed as a leaf node using an oracle.
3. With the root node of the Merkle tree as the seed, use a sampling oracle to select k leaf nodes.
4. Package these k proof elements along with the branches of the Merkle tree that traverse up to the root node as the PCP proof to be transmitted to the Verifier.

During verification, the following happens:

1. Verify that the branches of the Merkle tree lead up to the root node.
2. With the root node as the seed, use the same sampling oracle to select the expected k leaf nodes.
3. Verify the proof of each of the leaf nodes. An honest Prover is expected to have minimally transmitted these k proof elements.

3   A Quantum-Secure VDF

Definition 2. *We define ZKBdf = (Setup,Eval,Verify) is a triple of algorithms as follows:*

ZKBdf.Setup() $\rightarrow (e_k, H(e_k))$ is run by the Prover. It generates a Prover-secret $e_k \in \mathbb{Z}^+$ and public commitment $H(e_k)$ which is published.

ZKBdf.Eval(e_k, Cha, T) $\rightarrow (Res, \pi)_T$ is run by the Prover. It takes in the previously generated Prover-secret e_k, the random challenge Cha from the Verifier, and the required delay parameter T. It returns $Res = HMAC(Cha, e_k)$ and zero-knowledge computational proof $\pi = \{v_k = H(e_k)\}$.

ZKBdf.Verify$(H(e_k), Res, \pi, Cha, T)$ $\rightarrow (result \in \{1, 0\})$ is run by the Verifier. It takes in the previously-generated challenge Cha, the response Res and proof π from the Prover, the required delay parameter T and the previously-published commitment $H(e_k)$. It returns 1 if and only if $Res = HMAC(Cha, e_k)$ and π is computationally verified correct.

The design intuition behind our proposed VDF, named ZKBdf (ZKBoo delay function) is to substitute the "hash" in the hash-chain with a serialized ZKBoo zero-knowledge proof of the pre-image of the hash, include an additional serialized ZKBoo circuit for HMAC to generate the unique return value, and then use PCP with Micali's Merkle Tree construction to reduce the size and time complexity of the verification. Such a design preserves the non-algebraic nature of the construction and adds a feature of "Prover-secret" into the VDF. We briefly describe how each property is designed into ZKBdf before describing the construction:

- **Execution asymmetry.** We introduce execution asymmetry between the the ZKBoo proof circuit and verify circuit in order to meet the VDF *Sequentiality* and *Efficient verifiability* properties.
    - *Sequentiality.* In Sect. 2.2, our re-definition of *Sequentiality* includes the time taken to compute the proof. Since ZKBoo [24] is not based on any algebraic primitives, we construct a serialized version of the ZKBoo proof generation in Sect. 3.2 by using the Fiat-Shamir heuristic [22] to make the random sequence $R_i[]$ for each subsequent round's proof circuit be dependent on the previous round. This dependency adds an additional verification step to the ZKBoo verify operation but does not affect the verification process which remains parallelizable for each round.
    - *Efficient verifiability.* We make use of computationally sound PCP [2,40] to reduce the computational complexity of $ZKBdf.Verify$ to $O(\text{polylog}(N))$, thus achieving the *efficiently verifiable* requirement. In addition, the Verifier can utilize a polynomial number of (up to $\log^k T$) parallel-processing resources to obtain execution speed-up of $ZKBdf.Verify$ as compared to $ZKBdf.Eval$ which can only run sequentially.
- **Uniqueness.** To ensure the VDF response by the Prover is deterministic and unpredictable, the $ZKBdf.Eval$ function will incorporate a Pseudo-random function (PRF) [25] to compute Res.
- **Quantum-secure.** We have to prove our modified version of ZKBoo+PCP proofs is quantum-secure. Informally, ZKBoo is an MPC-based zero-knowledge proof system that is proven secure in the random oracle model [28]. Next, the OWF boolean circuit used in our proposed VDF is a collapsing hash function and hence is quantum-resistant [52]. Finally, we retain the use of the size-efficient Fiat-Shamir heuristic [22] and rely on [14,17,53] to arrive at quantum-security proofs.

3.1   Prover-Secret Feature

As defined in Definition 2, the Prover-secret e_k is a value known only by the Prover and this knowledge can be publicly verified by calling the $Verify$ function without the need for trusted-setup. This feature can be used for use-cases where it is disadvantageous to all participants except for an honest Prover to run the $ZKBdf.Eval$ function. We discuss some of the use-cases in Appendix.

3.2   Serializing ZKBoo

Since both proof generation and verification of ZKBoo are parallelizable, we need to modify ZKBoo such that proof generation is serialized while proof verification

---

Algorithm 1: Modified $ZKBoo.Prove$ algorithm to be serialized.

```
 1 begin
 2 │   r ← seed; e_k ← secret;
   │   // Preprocessing Stage
 3 │   for i from 1 to T do
 4 │   │   {s_i^1, s_i^2} ← random;
 5 │   │   s_i^3 = e_k ⊕ s_i^1 ⊕ s_i^2;
 6 │   end
   │   // can't be run in parallel
 7 │   for i from 1 to T do
   │   │   // Circuit Computation Stage
 8 │   │   if i == 1 then
 9 │   │   │   R_i[] ← PRF(r)
10 │   │   else
11 │   │   │   R_i[] ← PRF(H(w_{i-1}))
12 │   │   end
13 │   │   while circuit is not complete do
14 │   │   │   if AND or ADD gate then
15 │   │   │   │   {w_i^1, w_i^2, w_i^3} ← gate operation using {s_i^1, s_i^2, s_i^3}, R_i[]
16 │   │   │   else
   │   │   │   │   // NOT or XOR gate
17 │   │   │   │   {w_i^1, w_i^2, w_i^3} ← gate operation using {s_i^1, s_i^2, s_i^3}
18 │   │   │   end
19 │   │   end
20 │   │   c_i ←result from {w_i^1, w_i^2, w_i^3}; // c_i is the commitment for round i
   │   │   // Proof Extraction Stage
21 │   │   Compute h = Hash(c_i);
22 │   │   b ← next 2 bits from h;
23 │   │   switch b do
   │   │   │   // w_i is the 2-of-3 view for round i
24 │   │   │   case 00
25 │   │   │   │   w_i ← w_i^1, w_i^2
26 │   │   │   endsw
27 │   │   │   case 01
28 │   │   │   │   w_i ← w_i^2, w_i^3
29 │   │   │   endsw
30 │   │   │   case 10
31 │   │   │   │   w_i ← w_i^3, w_i^1
32 │   │   │   endsw
33 │   │   endsw
34 │   │   otherwise
35 │   │   │   retry b with next 2 bits from h
36 │   │   endsw
37 │   end
38 │   w ← {w_1, ..., w_T};
39 │   c ← {c_1, ..., c_T};
40 │   return z = {c, w}
41 end
```

remains parallelizable. The trick we use is to change the way the deterministic sequence of random $R_i[]$ are generated. Instead of using the same seed to generate all the sequences, we use the Fiat-Shamir heuristic [22] to require the generation of $R_{i+1}[]$ be dependent on views w_{i-1} from the previous ZKBoo iteration:

$$R_i[] = \begin{cases} PRF(seed) & i = 1 \\ PRF(H(w_{i-1})) & otherwise \end{cases} \quad (3)$$

We therefore modify *ZKBoo Prove* to a serialized form in Algorithm 1 with changes marked in red. The main changes happen in lines 9 to 11 where instead of using a fixed seed to generate the sequences $R[]$ in all T iterations, we use the Fiat-Shamir heuristic [22] to require the generation of $R_{i+1}[]$ be dependent on the view w_{i-1} from the previous ZKBoo iteration. To prevent a grinding attack discovered by researchers from geometry.xyz, the hash operation in line 21 only hashes commitments that can be verified.

To accommodate this change, the generation of $R_i[]$ is moved out of the preprocessing stage to between lines 9 and 10 of the circuit computation stage with the logic updated to reflect Equation (3). Also, line 19 is changed from Compute $h \leftarrow Hash(c)$ to Compute $h \leftarrow Hash(c_i)$ so that both the circuit computation and proof extraction stages become serialized. Verification remains parallelizable since the values needed to compute $R_i[]$ are already known.

3.3   ZKBdf Construction

ZKBdf is described in Fig. 1. There are two parties in the protocol, namely the Prover, who needs to prove that the time delay T has taken place, and the Verifier, who wants the Prover to delay for T duration. The protocol flows can be separated into three stages: *i) Setup:* which needs to be done once; *ii) Challenge-Response:* where the Verifier will issue an unpredictable challenge and the Prover has to respond with the proof that T time has passed; and *iii) Verify:* where the Verifier will verify the Prover's proof.

Structurally, the Prover computes what looks like a two-dimensional ZKBoo-chain with a Merkle tree on top (see Fig. 2), before extracting the PCP [2, 40] proofs to be sent to the Verifier. Functionally, ZKBdf is superior to hash-chains and its derivatives due to the added "Prover-secret" feature from the HMAC proof. A Prover using ZKBdf can proof knowledge of the Prover-secret e_k to the public Verifier without revealing e_k. On the other hand, ZKBdf's proof size and bit-strength increase with the delay parameter T since ZKBoo's iterative proof generation is the primary driver of the delay. This is in contrast with Buterin's VDF [10] whose MiMC delay circuit is separate from the argument proof.

The proposed ZKBdf also incorporates some of the properties related to continuous VDF [21]. Proof-generation is not an all-or-nothing process. A Prover can hand over a partial proof to another Prover to complete in a sequential manner, provided the Prover-secret e_k is shared. Similarly, a Verifier can verify part of the proof, or concurrently send partial proofs to other Verifiers.

Assumption. There is an underlying assumption in our design intuition that there exists a common OWF that i) can be mapped into a ZKBoo boolean circuit; ii) can function as an OWF in the Fiat-Shamir heuristic; and iii) can be used as part of the PRF for generating the VDF response. In our construction, we have chosen this function to be SHA-family [20] of algorithms. In Sect. 4, our proposed VDF will be using SHA-256 as it has well-studied implementations with a realized ZKBoo boolean circuit [24], is already widely used as a OWF [41], is a collapsing hash function [52], and is standardized for use as a PRF [31].

The rest of this section covers the formal proofs for ZKBdf's completeness and soundness, execution asymmetry, uniqueness, and quantum security.

- *Setup.*
  1. Both Prover and Verifier agree on a OWF $H()$ and delay T.
  2. Prover calls $ZKBdf.Setup$ to generate Prover-secret $e_k \in \mathbb{Z}^+$ and $commit = H(e_k)$ as the commitment.
- *Challenge-Response*
  1. Verifier generates random $Cha \in \mathbb{Z}^+$ and sends to Prover.
  2. Prover calls $ZKBdf.Eval$ to perform the following:
     (a) Compute $Res = HMAC(Cha, e_k) = H(e_k \oplus o_{pad}||H(e_k \oplus i_{pad}||Cha))$ [31,6] and perform T iterations of the serialized ZKBoo proof (Algorithm 1) to obtain $z = \{z_1, z_2, ..., z_T\}$ where $z_i = \{c_i = \{v_k = H(e_k), Res = HMAC(Cha, e_k)\}, w_i\}$
     (b) Build a Merkle tree [39] using all the elements of z as the leaf nodes.
     (c) Use Micali's construction [40] to select the index of leaf nodes $\{j_1, j_2, ..., j_{polylog(T)}\}$ to form the set of PCPs [2] $\pi = \{\pi_1, \pi_2, ...\pi_{polylog(T)}\}$
     (d) Each π_i consists of a branch of the Merkle tree from the root node leading to and including the leaf nodes z_{j_i-1} and z_{j_i}.
  3. Prover sends Res and π to the Verifier.
- *Verify*
  1. Verifier calls $ZKBdf.Verify$ which forks parallel processes for each $\pi_i \in \pi$ and checks that:
     (a) The Cha used by the Prover is correct.
     (b) Root node is the same for all π_i.
     (c) π_i is correctly selected based on Micali's construction. [40].
     (d) Merkle tree branch leading to z_{j-1} and z_j is verified correctly.
     (e) Verify $v_k == commit$.
     (f) Extract w_{j-1} from z_{j-1} and compute $R_j[] = PRF(H(w_{j-1}))$.
     (g) Verify ZKBoo proofs z_{j-1} and z_j for $\{v_k = H(e_k)\}$ and $\{Res = HMAC(Cha, e_k)\}$.
  2. Verifier accepts Res is pseudo-random and computed from $HMAC(Cha, e_k)$ without knowing the value of e_k.

Fig. 1. ZKBdf - ZKBoo delay function

3.4   Completeness and Soundness

Claim 1. *ZKBdf (Definition 2) satisfies the VDF conditions of completeness and soundness.*

Proof. Based on Definition 2, we arrive at:

$$Pr\left[\begin{array}{l} ZKBdf.Verify(H(e_k), \\ res, \pi, Cha, T) == 1 \end{array} \middle| \begin{array}{l} (e_k, H(e_k)) \xleftarrow{R} ZKBdf.Setup() \\ (res, \pi) \xleftarrow{R} ZKBdf.Eval(e_k, Cha, T) \end{array}\right] = 1 \quad (4)$$

Equation (4) satisfies the VDF correctness definition 2 in Boneh et al. [7].

In ZKBdf, the time delay parameter T defines the number of rounds ZKBoo is run. For every increment of T, ZKBdf linearly increases the time delay and exponentially increases (doubling) the security bit-strength of the proof. The existence of an algorithm O(poly(T)) $\mathcal{A}$ is

$$Pr\left[\begin{array}{l} ZKBdf.Verify(H(e_k), Res', \pi', Cha, T) \\ == 1 \\ (res', \bullet) \neq ZKBdf.Eval(e_k, Cha, T) \end{array} \middle| \begin{array}{l} (e_k, H(e_k)) \xleftarrow{R} ZKBdf.Setup() \\ (res', \pi') \xleftarrow{R} \mathcal{A}(e_k, Cha, T) \end{array}\right]$$
$$= \frac{1}{2^T} \leq negli(T) \quad (5)$$

Equation (5) satisfies the VDF soundness definition 3 in Boneh et al. [7].   □

3.5   Execution Asymmetry

Lemma 2 (Sequentiality). *If there exists an algorithm $\mathcal{A}$ where an adversary with polynomial-bounded computing resources can take $< T$ time-units to compute $(Res, \pi) \xleftarrow{R} \mathcal{A}(e_k, Cha, T)$, then*

$$Pr\left[ZKBdf.Verify(H(e_k), Res, \pi, Cha, T) == 1\right] < negli(T). \quad (6)$$

Proof. We have established that the modified *ZKBoo.Prove* algorithm (see Algorithm 1) has limited preprocessing steps and is non-parallelizable. Next, we take the assumption that the fastest time needed to complete 1 cycle of the ZKBoo HMAC-SHA-256 boolean circuit, z_i, is 1 time-unit.

- If $T == 1$, then by Claim 1 (*Soundness*) of ZKBdf, the fastest time possible to compute $(Res, \pi) \xleftarrow{R} ZKBdf.Eval(e_k, Cha, T) \geq$ time taken to compute $z_i = 1$ time-unit.
- If $T > 1$, then the computation of z_T can only start after $R_{T-1}[]$ is available. Since it is computationally infeasible to find $R_{T-1}[]$ (Equation (3)) without z_{T-1} and the probability of guessing $R_{T-1}[]$ is negligible, time taken to compute $(Res, \pi) \xleftarrow{R} ZKBdf.Eval(e_k, Cha, T) \geq$ time taken for z_{T-1} to be generated + time taken to compute $z_T = (T-1) + 1 = T$.

Since time taken for $(Res, \pi) \xleftarrow{R} \mathcal{A}(e_k, Cha, T) < T$, then $(Res, \bullet) \nleftarrow ZKBdf.Eval(e_k, Cha, T)$ and by Equation (5), Lemma 2 is true.   □

Lemma 3 (Efficient verifiability). *A Verifier requires $O(polylog(T))$ to complete the execution of $ZKBdf.Verify$ such that $ZKBdf$ remains computationally sound [40].*

Proof. Arora and Safra [2] has shown that to create sound PCPs, the probability that the verifier accepts each randomly-selected proof, given that the proof is incorrect, must be $< \frac{1}{2}$. Following from Claim 1 (*Soundness*) of ZKBdf, Micali's construction [40] is used in a Merkle tree (see Fig. 2) to reduce the size and execution complexity of the original set of ZKBoo proofs $z = \{z_1, z_2, ..., z_T\}$ into $\pi = \{\pi_1, \pi_2, ..., \pi_{polylog(T)}\}$.

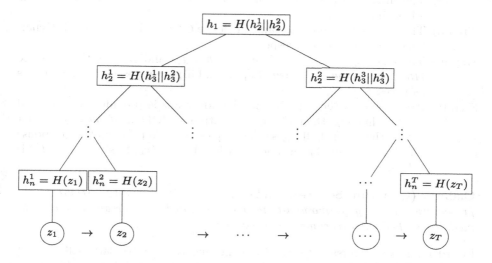

Fig. 2. Merkle tree of ZKBoo proofs to extract computational sound proofs

Each proof, $\pi_i = \{h_1, h_2, ..., h_n^{j_i-1}, h_n^{j_i}, z_{j_i-1}, z_{j_i}\}$ where j_i is the index randomly selected by the Fiat-Shamir heuristic, contains the branch of the Merkle tree from the root node leading to 2 leaf nodes z_{j_i-1} and z_{j_i}. Since both z_{j_i-1} and z_{j_i} are to be verified,

$$Pr\left[\pi_i \text{ is verified correct} \,|\, \pi_i \text{ is incorrect}\right] \leq \frac{2}{3} * \frac{2}{3} = \frac{4}{9} < \frac{1}{2} \qquad (7)$$

Equation (7) shows that the probability of a false negative verification of π_i is $\leq \frac{4}{9}$ which is $< \frac{1}{2}$ required for creating PCPs [2]. Since $|\pi| = polylog(T)$, $ZKBdf.Verify$ runs at $O(polylog(T))$. □

3.6 Uniqueness

Lemma 4 (Uniqueness). *The Res returned from ZKBdf.Eval is deterministic and in-distinguishable from random, unless the proof π is provided.*

Proof. In Challenge-Response step 2a of Fig. 1, we use the HMAC primitive [31] where $Res = HMAC(Cha, e_k)$. Since HMAC is a quantum-secure PRF [5,6,49] when using SHA-256 as the underlying hash function, Lemma 4 is proven.   □

3.7   Quantum-Secure

Definition 3. *We design a modified security experiment on the basis of EUF-CMA [26] for VDFs as a series of exchanges between a challenger and an adversary.*

Step i) The challenger performs *Setup* and sends the verification key v_k to the adversary.

Step ii) The adversary can choose any challenge Cha_i and time T_i ask the challenger to compute the response.

Step iii) The challenger performs $Eval(e_k, Cha_i, T_i)$ and returns the response (Res_i, π_i) to the adversary. Step ii) and iii) are repeated as many times as necessary.

Step iv) At the end of the experiment, the adversary is provided with e_k and T', and has less than T' time to output a challenge Cha' that is not within the set of challenges Cha_i requested in Step ii)., and the response (Res', π') that will return accept when $Verify(v_k, Res', \pi', Cha', T')$ is called.

Claim 5 (Quantum-Secure). *ZKBdf is EUF-CMA quantum-secure if the probability, that any polynomial-time quantum-capable adversary can win the modified EUF-CMA experiment, is negligible.*

In order for any adversary to win the experiment, the adversary will need at least one of the following 5 cases to happen with non-negligible probability:

Case a) Obtain the evaluation key e_k before Step iv); or

Case b) Obtain the challenge-response pair Cha', Res' before Step iv).; or

Case c) Start the generation of any ZKBoo-proofs z_i prior to having e_k; or

Case d) Generate the set of ZKBoo-proofs $z = \{z_1, ...z_T\}$ non-sequentially; or

Case e) Creating the proof $\pi = \{\pi_1, .., \pi_{polylog(T)}\}$ without needing to completely generate the set of ZKBoo-proofs z.

In ZKBdf, $v_k = H(e_k)$ where SHA-256 is used as the OWF $H()$. The collision-resistance of SHA-256 has been extensively studied [27,32,38] in both classical and quantum settings. Unruh [52] then showed that SHA-256 is a collapsing function which is "analogous to collision-resistance in the post-quantum setting". Hence, it is unlikely that Case a) happens.

Without knowledge of e_k, the adversary will have to guess the value of response $Res' = HMAC(Cha', \cdot)$ where $Cha' \notin \{Cha_1, ..., Cha_i\}$ previously done in Step ii). Since the response is proven unique in Lemma 4, it is unlikely that Case b) happens.

Each ZKBoo-proof z_i contains the zero-knowledge proof of $v_k = H(e_k)$ and $Res' = HMAC(Cha', e_k)$. Since the adversary does not have knowledge of e_k or Res' prior to Step iv), it is unlikely that Case c) happens.

Lemma 2 has shown ZKBdf to satisfy the sequentiality property in the classical setting. To prove sequentiality in the quantum setting, we have to show that the Fiat-Shamir heuristic [22] used to serialize (see Equation (3)) remains secure. This has been proven by Don et al. [17] on the basis that the hash is collapsing (which SHA-256 is) and thus implies that Case d) is unlikely to happen.

Finally, Chiesa et al. [14] has proven that Kilian's protocol [33] (which Micali's construction [40] is based on) is a collapsing protocol and can be used to securely construct a post-quantum argument of knowledge. This implies that Case e) is unlikely to happen and completes the proof of Claim 5.

4   Implementation

To realize the design, we implemented[1] $zkbdf.Eval$ and $zkbdf.Verify$ to observe the proof performance and proof size. As a benchmark, we also included a pseudo-VDF version of $zkbdf.Verify$, called $zkbdf.VerifyPseudo$[2], which performs the verification on the entire zkboo-proof, without the optimized PCP-proofs. This would allow us to understand the extent of execution and size optimization that computationally sound PCP provides. All executions were performed on an Intel I5-8250U 8th Gen machine with 8 CPU cores and 8GB RAM, running 64-bit Windows 10. No operating system level CPU scheduling or adjustments were done.

4.1   Execution

We want to observe how the value of delay T is translated into actual execution. Since the soundness property of ZKBdf is dependent on T, it is not meaningful if T is too small (i.e. < 50). We varied the time delay parameter T from 50 up to 350 in steps of 50 and captured the average execution times and proof sizes generated. Figure 3 plots the execution times of the 3 modules against delay T.

The execution times of $zkbdf.Eval$ can be observed to linearly increase with T while the execution times of $zkbdf.Verify$ increases less significantly since it executes in $O(polylog(T))$. Due to the parallel-CPU utilization during execution, $zkbdf.VerifyPseudo$ executes faster than $zkbdf.Eval$, but also increases linearly.

When comparing the ratio of verification time versus evaluation time (see Fig. 4), $zkbdf.Verify$ execution time drops below 10% of $zkbdf.Eval$ execution

---

[1] Source codes at https://github.com/tanteikg/zkbdf.

[2] We define $ZKBdf.VerifyPseudo(H(e_k), Res, z, Cha, T) \rightarrow (result \in \{1, 0\})$ as a function run by the Verifier. The difference with $zkbdf.Verify$ is that the input proof is the entire set of zkboo proofs z instead of the PCP proofs π. As a reference, $zkbdf.VerifyPseudo$ achieves the same completeness, soundness, sequentiality, uniqueness, and quantum-secure properties. It only does not achieve the efficient-verifiability property to make it a VDF.

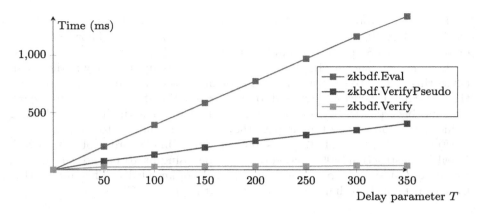

Fig. 3. Execution time against delay parameter T

time for $T > 100$ and continues to decrease to almost 2.5% when $T = 350$. *zkbdf.VerifyPseudo* execution time continues to hover at around 30% of *zkbdf.Eval* execution time even for increasing T.

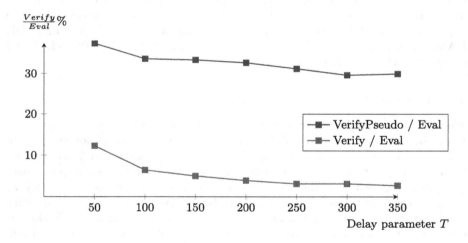

Fig. 4. Percentage of $\frac{Verify}{Eval}$ against delay parameter T

4.2 Proof Size

To understand the optimization in proof size due to Micali's construction [40], we list sizes of proofs against delay parameter T in Table 1.

Table 1. Size of proof (in bytes) against delay parameter T

Size	Complexity	T=50	T=100	T=150	T=200	T=250	T=300	T=350
z Proof	$O(T)$	1485200	2970400	4455600	5940800	7426000	8911200	10396400
π Proof	$O(polylog(T))$	360384	422224	484192	485792	487392	549488	551088

In comparison[3] with Pietrzak's [44] and Wesolowski's [54] VDFs, both their proof sizes grow at O(logT) complexity and remain below 200KB [55] even for large T values. While proof sizes of ZKBdf can be halved through ZKB++ optimizations [12], they are unlikely to approach the sizes below 200KB for large T values.

5   Conclusion

In this paper, we introduced ZKBdf, a provably quantum-secure VDF built on a ZKBoo [24] zero-knowledge proof of knowledge of a HMAC-SHA256 [31] secret key. In order to achieve the VDF property of sequentiality, the generation of each subsequent iterative ZKBoo proof is modified to include a Fiat-Shamir transform [22] of the previous view. The verification process of the set of ZKBoo proofs is then optimized using Micali's construction [40] to perform computationally sound PCP proof-verification [2] thereby achieving O(polylog(T)) in both execution and proof size. ZKBdf includes an added feature of "Prover-secret" on top of standard VDFs and new use-cases can be identified. Future work includes optimizing the ZKBdf proof sizes and exploring the use of ZKBdf in post-quantum authentication.

Acknowledgement. Jianying Zhou is supported by A*STAR under its RIE2020 Advanced Manufacturing and Engineering (AME) Industry Alignment Fund - Pre Positioning (IAF-PP) Award A19D6a0053. Any opinions, findings and conclusions or recommendations expressed in this material are those of the author(s) and do not reflect the views of A*STAR. Zengpeng Li is supported by the Natural Science Foundation of Shandong Province, China. (grant No. ZR2023MF045) and the Natural Science Foundation of Qingdao, China (grant No. 23-2-1-152-zyyd-jch)

Appendix - ZKBdf Application Areas

At present, we see the use of VDFs in consensus protocols for blockchains such as Ethereum (ethereum.org), Tezos (tezos.foundation) and Chia (chia.net) as well as in constructing time-stamping services and random beacons [21,34,50]. However, we believe that there is a wider use-case for VDFs if the functionality of a Prover-secret is included. In this appendix, we take an exploratory approach to identify other possible use-cases where applications can use ZKBdf to improve outcomes. These are described below.

---

[3] The quantum-secure VDF by Chavez-Saab et al. [13] lacks published implementation details for comparison.

A.1 Limiting Authentication Retries

We find a use-case where a delay function is needed during the authentication process to limit a brute-force attack against a backend authentication service. Broken Authentication is amongst the top 10 security risks highlighted by OWASP (Open Web Application Security Project) [42] where one of the ways to address such risks is to introduce an increasing delay for repeated failed authentication attempts. Such a setup, however, requires the backend authentication service to maintain failed authentication states for every user which inadvertently adds resource overheads and complexity especially in distributed systems. There are also many protocols such as Bitcoin [41], Transport Layer Security [45] and Wi-FI Protected Access (IEEE 802.11-2020) which do not require tracking of failed authentication attempts. A stateless delay mechanism using client-side puzzles is presented by Aura et al [3] where every authentication is preceded with a PoW challenge which the authentication client needs to solve, before the server verifies the solution. Similar mechanisms are also used to prevent brute-force denial-of-service network attacks and limiting peer-to-peer sybil attacks [18].

The advantage of using ZKBdf instead of a client-side PoW puzzle is that the number of authentication retries that a hacker can make is deterministic and no longer dependent on the amount of resources available to the hacker. Increasing the amount of CPU/memory resources at the hacker's end does not increase the number of authentication retries, and this will serve to deter hackers while not increasing the carbon footprint caused by ever-more complex puzzles.

A.2 Improving Auction Liveliness

In a classical English auction, an item is put on offer for participants to bid in an open outcry manner. The auctioneer asks for participants to place bids higher than the previous bid, and when an elapsed period has occurred without any participants placing any higher bids, the auction is closed with the winner being the participant who submitted the latest (and highest) bid. Online auctions that happen on the Internet, on the other hand, mostly do not have a concept of an elapsed time since the last bid. Instead, there is auction end-time whereby the highest bid received before the end-time is the winning bid. This has given rise to situations where participants are passive throughout most of the auction period and are only active at the closing moments of the auction where bid sniping [47] occurs.

The ZKBdf protocol could be used to allow honest participants to determine the end of the auction prior to the end-time. When a participant submits a valid highest bid, the participant is issued with a VDF challenge which effectively starts the elapsed time computation. If no higher bid is received prior to the participant completing the VDF challenge and submitting the response, then the participant would have won the auction, thus ending the auction. The advantage of using the VDF here is that we expect participants will no longer wait till the closing moments before bidding. Another possible positive outcome would be the detection of shill bidding (an agent working for a corrupt seller to bid up the price without any intention to buy) since the seller's agent is unlikely to submit the VDF response to close the auction.

References

1. Albrecht, M., Grassi, L., Rechberger, C., Roy, A., Tiessen, T.: MiMC: efficient encryption and cryptographic hashing with minimal multiplicative complexity. In: Cheon, J.H., Takagi, T. (eds.) ASIACRYPT 2016. LNCS, vol. 10031, pp. 191–219. Springer, Heidelberg (2016). https://doi.org/10.1007/978-3-662-53887-6_7
2. Arora, S., Safra, S.: Probabilistic checking of proofs: a new characterization of NP. J. ACM (JACM) **45**(1), 70–122 (1998)
3. Aura, T., Nikander, P., Leiwo, J.: DOS-resistant authentication with client puzzles. In: Christianson, B., Malcolm, J.A., Crispo, B., Roe, M. (eds.) Security Protocols 2000. LNCS, vol. 2133, pp. 170–177. Springer, Heidelberg (2001). https://doi.org/10.1007/3-540-44810-1_22
4. Babai, L., Fortnow, L., Levin, L.A., Szegedy, M.: Checking computations in polylogarithmic time. In: Proceedings of the Twenty-Third Annual ACM Symposium on Theory of Computing, pp. 21–32 (1991)
5. Bellare, M.: New proofs for NMAC and HMAC: security without collision-resistance. In: Dwork, C. (ed.) CRYPTO 2006. LNCS, vol. 4117, pp. 602–619. Springer, Heidelberg (2006). https://doi.org/10.1007/11818175_36
6. Bellare, M., Canetti, R., Krawczyk, H.: Keying hash functions for message authentication. In: Koblitz, N. (ed.) CRYPTO 1996. LNCS, vol. 1109, pp. 1–15. Springer, Heidelberg (1996). https://doi.org/10.1007/3-540-68697-5_1
7. Boneh, D., Bonneau, J., Bünz, B., Fisch, B.: Verifiable delay functions. In: Shacham, H., Boldyreva, A. (eds.) CRYPTO 2018. LNCS, vol. 10991, pp. 757–788. Springer, Cham (2018). https://doi.org/10.1007/978-3-319-96884-1_25
8. Boneh, D., Bünz, B., Fisch, B.: A survey of two verifiable delay functions. IACR Cryptol. ePrint Arch. **2018**, 712 (2018)
9. Boneh, D., Dagdelen, Ö., Fischlin, M., Lehmann, A., Schaffner, C., Zhandry, M.: Random oracles in a quantum world. In: Lee, D.H., Wang, X. (eds.) ASIACRYPT 2011. LNCS, vol. 7073, pp. 41–69. Springer, Heidelberg (2011). https://doi.org/10.1007/978-3-642-25385-0_3
10. Buterin, V.: STARKs, Part 3: Into the Weeds (2018). https://vitalik.ca/general/2018/07/21/starks_part_3.html. Accessed Apr 2023
11. Castryck, W., Decru, T.: An efficient key recovery attack on SIDH (preliminary version). Cryptology ePrint Archive (2022)
12. Chase, M., et al.: Post-quantum zero-knowledge and signatures from symmetric-key primitives. In: Proceedings of the 2017 ACM SIGSAC Conference on Computer and Communications Security, pp. 1825–1842 (2017)
13. Chavez-Saab, J., Henríquez, F.R., Tibouchi, M.: Verifiable isogeny walks: towards an isogeny-based postquantum VDF. Cryptology ePrint Archive (2021)
14. Chiesa, A., Ma, F., Spooner, N., Zhandry, M.: Post quantum succinct arguments. Electronic Colloquium on Computational Complexity, (38) (2021). https://eccc.weizmann.ac.il//eccc-reports/2021/TR21-038/index.html
15. Cohen, B., Pietrzak, K.: Simple proofs of sequential work. In: Nielsen, J.B., Rijmen, V. (eds.) EUROCRYPT 2018. LNCS, vol. 10821, pp. 451–467. Springer, Cham (2018). https://doi.org/10.1007/978-3-319-78375-8_15

16. De Feo, L., Masson, S., Petit, C., Sanso, A.: Verifiable delay functions from super-singular isogenies and pairings. In: Galbraith, S.D., Moriai, S. (eds.) ASIACRYPT 2019. LNCS, vol. 11921, pp. 248–277. Springer, Cham (2019). https://doi.org/10.1007/978-3-030-34578-5_10

17. Don, J., Fehr, S., Majenz, C., Schaffner, C.: Security of the fiat-Shamir transformation in the quantum random-oracle model. In: Boldyreva, A., Micciancio, D. (eds.) CRYPTO 2019. LNCS, vol. 11693, pp. 356–383. Springer, Cham (2019). https://doi.org/10.1007/978-3-030-26951-7_13

18. Douceur, J.R.: The Sybil attack. In: Druschel, P., Kaashoek, F., Rowstron, A. (eds.) IPTPS 2002. LNCS, vol. 2429, pp. 251–260. Springer, Heidelberg (2002). https://doi.org/10.1007/3-540-45748-8_24

19. Dwork, C., Naor, M.: Pricing via processing or combatting junk mail. In: Brickell, E.F. (ed.) CRYPTO 1992. LNCS, vol. 740, pp. 139–147. Springer, Heidelberg (1993). https://doi.org/10.1007/3-540-48071-4_10

20. Eastlake 3rd, D., Hansen, T.: US Secure Hash Algorithms (SHA and SHA-based HMAC and HKDF) (2011), https://tools.ietf.org/html/rfc6234. Accessed Apr 2023

21. Ephraim, N., Freitag, C., Komargodski, I., Pass, R.: Continuous verifiable delay functions. In: Canteaut, A., Ishai, Y. (eds.) EUROCRYPT 2020. LNCS, vol. 12107, pp. 125–154. Springer, Cham (2020). https://doi.org/10.1007/978-3-030-45727-3_5

22. Fiat, A., Shamir, A.: How to prove yourself: practical solutions to identification and signature problems. In: Odlyzko, A.M. (ed.) CRYPTO 1986. LNCS, vol. 263, pp. 186–194. Springer, Heidelberg (1987). https://doi.org/10.1007/3-540-47721-7_12

23. Gentry, C., Wichs, D.: Separating succinct non-interactive arguments from all falsifiable assumptions. In: Proceedings of the Forty-Third Annual ACM Symposium on Theory of Computing, pp. 99–108 (2011)

24. Giacomelli, I., Madsen, J., Orlandi, C.: ZKBoo: faster zero-knowledge for Boolean circuits. In: 25th {usenix} Security Symposium ({usenix} Security 16), pp. 1069–1083 (2016)

25. Goldreich, O., Goldwasser, S., Micali, S.: How to construct random functions. J. ACM (JACM) **33**(4), 792–807 (1986)

26. Goldwasser, S., Micali, S., Rivest, R.L.: A digital signature scheme secure against adaptive chosen-message attacks. SIAM J. Comput. **17**(2), 281–308 (1988)

27. Hosoyamada, A., Sasaki, Y.: Quantum collision attacks on reduced SHA-256 and SHA-512. Cryptology ePrint Archive, Report 2021/292 (2021). https://eprint.iacr.org/2021/292

28. Ishai, Y., Kushilevitz, E., Ostrovsky, R., Sahai, A.: Zero-knowledge from secure multiparty computation. In: Proceedings of the Thirty-Ninth Annual ACM Symposium on Theory of Computing, pp. 21–30 (2007)

29. Jakobsson, M., Juels, A.: Proofs of work and bread pudding protocols (extended abstract). In: Preneel, B. (ed.) Secure Information Networks. ITIFIP, vol. 23, pp. 258–272. Springer, Boston, MA (1999). https://doi.org/10.1007/978-0-387-35568-9_18

30. Katz, J., Kolesnikov, V., Wang, X.: Improved non-interactive zero knowledge with applications to post-quantum signatures. In: Proceedings of the 2018 ACM SIGSAC Conference on Computer and Communications Security, pp. 525–537 (2018)

31. Kelly, S., Frankel, S.: Using HMAC-SHA-256, HMAC-SHA-384, and HMAC-SHA-512 with IPsec (2007). https://www.ietf.org/rfc/rfc4868.txt. Accessed Apr 2023

32. Khovratovich, D., Rechberger, C., Savelieva, A.: Bicliques for preimages: attacks on skein-512 and the SHA-2 family. In: Canteaut, A. (ed.) FSE 2012. LNCS, vol.

7549, pp. 244–263. Springer, Heidelberg (2012). https://doi.org/10.1007/978-3-642-34047-5_15

33. Kilian, J.: A note on efficient zero-knowledge proofs and arguments. In: Proceedings of the Twenty-Fourth Annual ACM Symposium on Theory of Computing, pp. 723–732 (1992)

34. Landerreche, E., Stevens, M., Schaffner, C.: Non-interactive cryptographic times-tamping based on verifiable delay functions. In: Bonneau, J., Heninger, N. (eds.) FC 2020. LNCS, vol. 12059, pp. 541–558. Springer, Cham (2020). https://doi.org/10.1007/978-3-030-51280-4_29

35. Lenstra, A.K., Wesolowski, B.: A random zoo: sloth, unicorn, and trx. IACR Cryptol. ePrint Arch. **2015**, 366 (2015)

36. Mahmoody, M., Moran, T., Vadhan, S.: Publicly verifiable proofs of sequential work. In: Proceedings of the 4th Conference on Innovations in Theoretical Computer Science, pp. 373–388 (2013)

37. Mahmoody, M., Smith, C., Wu, D.J.: Can verifiable delay functions be based on random oracles? ICALP (2020)

38. Mendel, F., Nad, T., Schläffer, M.: Improving local collisions: new attacks on reduced SHA-256. In: Johansson, T., Nguyen, P.Q. (eds.) EUROCRYPT 2013. LNCS, vol. 7881, pp. 262–278. Springer, Heidelberg (2013). https://doi.org/10.1007/978-3-642-38348-9_16

39. Merkle, R.C.: One way hash functions and DES. In: Brassard, G. (ed.) CRYPTO 1989. LNCS, vol. 435, pp. 428–446. Springer, New York (1990). https://doi.org/10.1007/0-387-34805-0_40

40. Micali, S.: Computationally sound proofs. SIAM J. Comput. **30**(4), 1253–1298 (2000)

41. Nakamoto, S.: Bitcoin: A peer-to-peer electronic cash system (2008). https://bitcoin.org/bitcoin.pdf. Accessed Apr 2023

42. OWASP: OWASP Top Ten 2017: A2:2017-Broken Authentication (2017). https://owasp.org/www-project-top-ten/2017/A2_2017-Broken_Authentication. Accessed Apr 2023

43. Pass, R., Shi, E.: The sleepy model of consensus. In: Takagi, T., Peyrin, T. (eds.) ASIACRYPT 2017. LNCS, vol. 10625, pp. 380–409. Springer, Cham (2017). https://doi.org/10.1007/978-3-319-70697-9_14

44. Pietrzak, K.: Simple verifiable delay functions. In: 10th Innovations in Theoretical Computer Science Conference (ITCS 2019). Schloss Dagstuhl-Leibniz-Zentrum fuer Informatik (2018)

45. Rescorla, E.: The transport layer security (TLS) protocol version 1.3 (2018). https://tools.ietf.org/html/rfc8446. Accessed Apr 2023

46. Rivest, R.L., Shamir, A., Wagner, D.A.: Time-lock puzzles and timed-release crypto (1996)

47. Roth, A.E., Ockenfels, A.: Last-minute bidding and the rules for ending second-price auctions: evidence from eBay and Amazon auctions on the internet. Am. Econ. Rev. **92**(4), 1093–1103 (2002)

48. Shor, P.W.: Polynomial-time algorithms for prime factorization and discrete logarithms on a quantum computer. SIAM Rev. **41**(2), 303–332 (1999)

49. Song, F., Yun, A.: Quantum security of NMAC and related constructions. In: Katz, J., Shacham, H. (eds.) CRYPTO 2017. LNCS, vol. 10402, pp. 283–309. Springer, Cham (2017). https://doi.org/10.1007/978-3-319-63715-0_10

50. Starkware: Presenting: VeeDo a STARK-based VDF Service (2020). https://medium.com/starkware/presenting-veedo-e4bbff77c7ae. Accessed Apr 2023

51. Unruh, D.: Non-interactive zero-knowledge proofs in the quantum random oracle model. In: Oswald, E., Fischlin, M. (eds.) EUROCRYPT 2015. LNCS, vol. 9057, pp. 755–784. Springer, Heidelberg (2015). https://doi.org/10.1007/978-3-662-46803-6_25
52. Unruh, D.: Collapse-binding quantum commitments without random oracles. In: Cheon, J.H., Takagi, T. (eds.) ASIACRYPT 2016. LNCS, vol. 10032, pp. 166–195. Springer, Heidelberg (2016). https://doi.org/10.1007/978-3-662-53890-6_6
53. Unruh, D.: Post-quantum security of Fiat-Shamir. In: Takagi, T., Peyrin, T. (eds.) ASIACRYPT 2017. LNCS, vol. 10624, pp. 65–95. Springer, Cham (2017). https://doi.org/10.1007/978-3-319-70694-8_3
54. Wesolowski, B.: Efficient verifiable delay functions. In: Ishai, Y., Rijmen, V. (eds.) EUROCRYPT 2019. LNCS, vol. 11478, pp. 379–407. Springer, Cham (2019). https://doi.org/10.1007/978-3-030-17659-4_13
55. Yang, Z., Qin, B., Wu, Q., Shi, W., Liang, B.: Experimental comparisons of verifiable delay functions. In: Meng, W., Gollmann, D., Jensen, C.D., Zhou, J. (eds.) ICICS 2020. LNCS, vol. 12282, pp. 510–527. Springer, Cham (2020). https://doi.org/10.1007/978-3-030-61078-4_29

SecMT – Security in Mobile Technologies

SecMT 2023

Fourth Workshop on Security in Mobile Technologies

20 June 2023

Program Chairs

Eleonora Losiouk — University of Padua, Italy
Yury Zhauniarovich — Delft University of Technology, The Netherlands

Web Chair

Eleonora Losiouk — University of Padua, Italy

Program Committee

Marco Casagrande — EURECOM, France
Tooska Dargahi — Manchester Metropolitan University, UK
Olga Gadyatskaya — Leiden University, The Netherlands
Mohammad Ashiqur Rahman — Florida International University, USA
Antonio Ruggia — University of Genoa, Italy
Nikita Samarin — University of California at Berkeley, USA
Giorgos Vasiliadis — Hellenic Mediterranean University & FORTH-ICS, Greece

If You're Scanning This, It's Too Late! A QR Code-Based Fuzzing Methodology to Identify Input Vulnerabilities in Mobile Apps

Federico Carboni⬥, Mauro Conti⬥, Denis Donadel(✉)⬥, and Mariano Sciacco⬥

Department of Mathematics, University of Padua, Padua, Italy
{federico.carboni,mariano.sciacco}@studenti.unipd.it,
mauro.conti@unipd.it, denis.donadel@phd.unipd.it

Abstract. In recent years, QR (Quick Response) codes have gained popularity in facilitating information sharing with camera-equipped devices like smartphones and tablets. This technology is suitable for multiple applications, such as verification of COVID-19 vaccination, multi-factor authentication, or ease URL and contact sharing. Despite its huge adoption, security researchers have mainly focused on using QR codes as a vector for phishing attacks, exploiting the simplicity of hiding malicious URLs in a not human-readable format. However, this is just the tip of the iceberg of the potential QR codes have in being a suitable vector for cyberattacks.

In this paper, we design a fuzzing-based methodology to discover bugs and vulnerabilities in mobile applications receiving inputs from QR codes. Our framework is suitable for many different application categories, and it is highly flexible in handling various behavior of the apps before and after the scan takes place. We implemented our methodology in a toolkit, *QRFuzz*, which enables testing multiple codes in an automated way, looking for crashes, errors, and abnormal behaviors in applications. In our first experiment, we tested 20 popular Android apps with a dictionary of strings containing symbols, weird ASCII characters, and known malicious payloads. Our tests on about two thousand payloads showed that our tool correctly scanned almost all the given codes. During our first testing, we found a crash on a popular social application with over 1 billion downloads and on the official Italian COVID-19 vaccination verification app. To the best of our knowledge, this is the first framework enabling the fuzzing of applications via QR codes. We open-sourced *QRFuzz*[1] so that other researchers can tackle the issue and developers can independently identify bugs.

Keywords: QR Code · Android · Fuzzing · Mobile applications

In the last decades, one-dimensional barcodes have been one of the most used solutions for saving small pieces of information in a machine-readable format.

© The Author(s), under exclusive license to Springer Nature Switzerland AG 2023
J. Zhou et al. (Eds.): ACNS 2023 Workshops, LNCS 13907, pp. 553–570, 2023.
https://doi.org/10.1007/978-3-031-41181-6_30

They are easy to scan and employ in a vast number of applications. The primary use of one-dimensional barcodes is found in shop articles, where there is the need to store small information such as an identification number, thus helping to match an item with a record in a database. Nevertheless, the amount of information one can save might not be enough, especially if someone wants to store lots of data without having a strong dependency on a centralized database. These needs lead the way for the development of two-dimensional barcodes, also known as QR (Quick Response) codes, that are a simple solution to fit data in small 2D-representation of symbols and shapes. QR codes guarantee a reliable way to store data in a machine-readable format and a quick approach for the end user to read this kind of information with a smartphone or a dedicated scanner.

In recent times, QR codes gained huge popularity for payment purposes reaching over 2.4$ trillion of global spending in 2022 [13]. Besides payments, QR codes have also been employed for mobile marketing communication [25]. For example, a consumer can scan a QR code to access a retailer's website for product information or a restaurant's menu. Furthermore, many mobile apps, such as bike-sharing, social media, and shopping apps, come with a built-in QR code scanner. This brought a huge difference in the market field, especially in the customer experience [9].

Like every other computer science technology, QR codes have also been interested in cyberattacks. Since the content is encoded in a not human-readable format, they have been intensely employed to conduct fraud and to launch phishing attacks [15,31]. Furthermore, based on the expected scanner, QR codes can be a vector for more technical well-known attack techniques, such as command, HTML, or SQL injections [12].

Based on these premises, in this work, we designed a methodology to assess the robustness of QR code-based input fields using fuzzing. Moreover, we developed an open-source tool, and we performed several experiments to prove the efficiency of the methodology. To sum up, the main contributions of this paper are the following:

- We designed an automated methodology to identify QR code input bugs and vulnerabilities through a fuzzing-based approach.
- We developed *QRFuzz*, a tool implementing our methodology that can be employed as an autonomous testbed to scan multiple QR codes and gather in-depth logs from the applications.
- We performed several tests on 20 of the most downloaded applications in the US and Italy, assessing the tool's reliability, which was able to correctly scan the 93% of the codes in an average of 5.3s each.
- We identified bugs in a popular social network app with more than 1 billion downloads and on the official Italian COVID-19 pass verification app. Due to the bugs, the applications crash when exposed to maliciously crafted QR codes.
- We open-sourced *QRFuzz*[1], allowing other researchers to use it and extend its capabilities.

---

[1] Github repository: https://github.com/spritz-group/QRFuzz

The paper is organized as follows. Firstly, we introduce some background knowledge to understand the QR code technology in Sect. 1, providing insights into related works. Then, we present the methodology and *QRFuzz*, our tool to automate the QR code fuzzing of Android applications in Sect. 2. In Sect. 3, we introduce the experiment we performed to validate the methodology, while Sect. 4 illustrates the results we obtained, focusing on the applications where we found several crashes. Finally, we conclude the paper and describe some future works in Sect. 5.

1 Background

In this section, we introduce the QR code technology in Sect. 1.1, we describe the fuzzing technique in Sect. 1.2, and we present related works in Sect. 1.3.

1.1 QR Code Technology

The QR code is a bi-dimensional barcode that can be easily read by mobile and electronic devices. It stores information as a series of pixels in a square-shaped grid. Since many smartphones and tablets are natively equipped with QR reader apps, they are often used in advertising and marketing campaigns to make complex URLs easily shareable. In recent years, the usage of QR codes has started to rise as a tool to simplify specific application functions. They have been employed to facilitate login verification, such as connecting a messaging application to a browser or logging in to streaming services on smart TVs without typing the password. Another popular application is contact sharing, where a user can create a QR code containing its contact details, thus simplifying the distribution to other users. Videogames also use QR codes to transfer items between users and share direct access to unique content with the community [21].

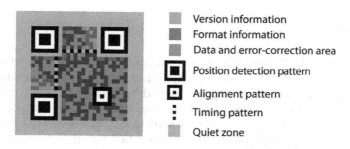

Fig. 1. QR Code structure (Version 2) [8]

Even if many different versions of QR codes are available, the de-facto standard is presented in Fig. 1. It has three positioning markings and a variable number of alignment markings to adjust the orientation. The area surrounding the markings is reserved for the format and version info. The code contains an L-shaped sequence of 0 s and 1 s in the upper-left part of the QR that the reader utilizes to identify each pixel's size. It also requires a white "quiet zone" all around the square. This type of QR code can store up to 4296 alphanumeric characters (in a square of 177×177 modules). If fewer data are needed, Micro QR codes can store only 35 characters but require only one position detection square. On the contrary, iQR codes are rectangular codes able to store up to 40,000 numeric characters with an error correction up to 50%. Finally, Atzec code contains data encoded in concentric square rings with a bulls-eye detection pattern at its center. It does not need a quiet zone and can contain 3067 characters.

1.2   Fuzzing

In recent years, the number of research on fuzzing has been increasing. Fuzzing is a technique used to discover a variety of bugs automatically by sending numerous malformed payloads to a target [16]. It has been shown to be effective in identifying bugs that are difficult, if not impossible, to discover by manual code review. A recent example is CVE-2020-9385, a null pointer dereference in Zint, a barcode encoding library supporting over 50 symbologies [11]. The main idea behind fuzzing is that a piece of software might react in a bizarre way if solicited with a particular input value. Since there are almost infinite possible inputs, advanced fuzzing techniques can dynamically generate payloads based on feedback from previous inputs, trying to reach all the code available in the software. Even if the main bugs discoverable by fuzzing are memory corruption bugs, if correctly instrumented, fuzzing techniques can uncover other bugs, such as race conditions and deadlocks. Many tools are available to instrument applications and perform fuzzing. American Fuzzy Lop (AFL) [10] and AFL++ [5] are two widely used tools for fuzzing binary applications, while software like ffuf [7] are used to fuzz web applications.

1.3   Related Works

Security and QR Codes. QR codes are a double-edged sword when discussing security. On one side, QR codes are helpful in improving some security aspects, such as secure authentication achieved using data-hiding algorithms with embedded code [26]. They can be applied, for instance, to online banking, healthcare, or to improve the security of blockchain wallets [14]. Moreover, QR codes can be combined with steganography and data encryption to enhance secret communications [22]. On the other side, QR codes can represent a threat to users. One problem with these codes is that, as with other encoding mechanisms such as RFID [24], the user cannot easily distinguish between a benign and a malicious QR code only by looking at it. This fact is often exploited to commit fraud and phishing attacks [31]. Kieseberg et al. [15] show how an attacker can insert a custom URL inside a QR code to trick the user with a cloned website using a phishing approach. In the same way, the attacker can create a QR code for payment, redirecting to a different bank account, thus committing fraud. These are attacks on the application's logic; therefore, the app scanning the QR code should work without problems. Alternatively, attacks might aim at breaking the app's normal behavior. For example, an aggressor can create a QR code that performs classic attacks on applications such as SQL injection, command injection, or buffer overflow once the app reads it, thus using the code as the attack vector. To prevent these attacks, the developer can validate the input [3,28]. Input validation is a well-known technique countermeasure to these attacks, but in large software with many different I/O functionalities, it might be hard to implement it properly. Furthermore, since QR codes are generally not created by the final user, developers can wrongly think validation is unnecessary. Our tool is mainly focused on finding these cases where there is no proper input validation: the goal is to generate malicious QR codes that cause unexpected behaviors in the mobile application under test.

Testing of Mobile Apps. Testing mobile applications is a crucial step to ensure the release of a reliable and safe product. The oldest way to test apps is through the so-called monkey testing. It exploits pseudo-random streams of user events, such as touches, clicks, or gestures, together with system-level events. Many tools are available to provide these functionalities [1,4], but they are limited and cannot test all the possible features of an application. Some fuzzers have been proposed in the mobile ecosystem to overcome this lack. DroidFuzzer [30] is a tool targeting activities that accept outside MIME data in the Android system. Caiipa [17] is a cloud service to test apps in different contexts, such as with device heterogeneity, variable wireless network speeds, locations, and unpredictable sensor inputs. The authors claim that the tool can find almost ten times more bugs with respect to monkey testing. Another example of the application of fuzzing in mobile apps is proposed in [27], where authors apply fuzzing to test the security of bank applications.

QR Code Testing on Mobile Apps. While some efforts have interested fuzzing in mobile applications, only a few projects considered the QR codes as vectors for attacks. Small research has been conducted by Averin and Zyulyarkina [2], who tested a few malicious QR codes on Android and iOS readers. However, the authors do not discuss how the codes have been provided to the applications and do not offer an open-source tool to automatize this time-consuming phase, thus preventing other users from expanding the work. Furthermore, they considered only four general-purpose readers without looking at applications that contain sensitive data while using QR codes to offer specific functionalities to the user. Some examples of malicious QR codes are offered in [29], but they are too few to be employed for fuzzing. Furthermore, no automated methodology is designed. Finally, Homan and Breese [12] obtained good results by testing Android general purpose QR code scanners looking for SQL, HTML, and JavaScript injections. Their results are promising, but the research does not consider applications that use codes for specific purposes, and the scanning parts have been done manually without an automated tool. Though, to the best of our knowledge, no works are approaching the testing of mobile apps with an automated fuzzing-based methodology specific for applications using QR code in their logic.

2   A Fuzzing-Based Methodology with *QRFuzz*

In this section, we present the methodology behind *QRFuzz* in Sect. 2.1. Then, we describe the current design and implementation of the toolkit, its components, and its capabilities in Sect. 2.2.

2.1   Methodology Design

Input validation can be cumbersome. To help researchers verify the correctness of the validation process of input collected via QR codes, we developed a methodology to automate the testing through fuzzing. We defined a framework suitable for different use cases, based on each app's behavior. The objectives that we want to achieve through this methodology are the following:

- The fuzzing process shall be divided in repeatable and recoverable **phases**.
- The fuzzing process shall be **automated** and **unsupervised**, meaning that the process does not require human supervision once started.
- The results of the fuzzing process shall report an **in-depth analysis** of the app's behavior, both from the business logic and the UI/UX.

We started by analyzing different mobile applications with QR code scanning capability. The goal of this analysis aimed to identify recurrent patterns to divide the fuzzing process into phases. By induction, we identified 4 repeatable phases, as shown in Fig. 2:

1. **Go To Scan** phase. It requires the fuzzing process to open the app and proceed to the scanning page. During this phase, the fuzzing process must prepare and load the QR code for the next phases (e.g., using queues or just-in-time QR code generation).
2. **Scan QR Code** phase. It requires the mobile app to use the camera and scan the QR code. During this phase, the log collection must occur to monitor the app's behavior before and after the scan.
3. **Anomaly Detection** phase. It requires the fuzzing process to check whether the mobile app behaved as expected (e.g., an element appears as expected under normal circumstances). During this phase, the fuzzing process must save visual logs (e.g., screenshots) and technical logs (e.g., app events, debug output). Lastly, the fuzzing process must continue with the next QR code.
4. **Back to Scan** phase. It requires the mobile app to proceed to the scanning page and repeat the *Scan QR Code* phase until no other codes are available for scanning. This phase should be able to recover from errors and anomalies that happened in previous phases, even completely reopening the application if it crashes.

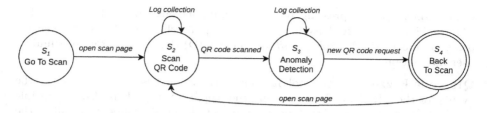

Fig. 2. Finite State Machine of the fuzzing process.

After identifying these phases, we defined the malicious payload composition process. This process comprises two possible kinds of payloads, according to our analysis:

- **Standard**. The payload is made of any kind of strings, regardless of any app-specific format. Examples include common command or SQL injection payloads, not printable characters, or weird encoding. This approach shows whether a basic QR code sanity check has been implemented in the app.
- **Ad-hoc**. The payload must reflect the app-specific QR code format. It could be a prefix or suffix that must be included in the code or require an advanced payload generation process containing encoding or encryption. This approach goes beyond basic QR code sanity checks and could improve the coverage of the application's code reached by the scanner.

The fuzzing process shall consider both approaches to cover multiple scenarios whenever possible, namely when an ad-hoc payload exists and it is possible to identify and reverse engineer its format. If an app reacts by providing feedback only when triggered with an ad-hoc QR code, it may indicate that the app is configured to respond only to specific ones. However, bugs could be discovered even during this phase since QR codes are still decoded to allow the app to decide what action to take. In other words, with different versions of QR codes, it is possible to reach different states of the application execution. Regarding the payload itself, the QR code generation process could use malicious words taken from dictionaries of different categories, which could be augmented using permutations on the original dataset, possibly using machine learning techniques.

2.2 *QRFuzz* Implementation

To demonstrate the feasibility of our methodology, we developed *QRFuzz*, a toolkit implementing the key concepts of our approach. Figure 3 schematizes the architecture of our tool. The main components of *QRFuzz* are the QR Code Fuzzer and the QR Code Generator, which interact with the smartphone through *Appium* [6]. It is a tool capable of interacting with the Android operating system (as well as iOS with minor changes) to navigate throughout the application. It comprises an Appium Server, which connects the computer and the smartphone. Based on a driver script (the Appium Client), it can perform actions on the smartphone, such as pressing buttons, taking screenshots, and reading ADB (Android Debug Bridge) logs. In detail, the Appium client identifies a UI element using an anchor (in Android, *xpath* or element ID) that is employed to simulate user interaction.

QR Code Fuzzer. It is the toolkit's core part that orchestrates and triggers the events for the QR Code Generator and the Appium Server. It is also responsible for the testing life cycle of each payload. In detail, this component initializes the Appium Server to prepare the app, executes the steps in the app to reach the QR code scanning page, and starts each scanning iteration. On each iteration, the QR Code Fuzzer checks if the code alters the normal execution of the app or not (i.e., search for an anchor that should appear if the QR code has no anomalous effect).

An app inspector is required to instruct Appium into invoking the correct steps for each application. The app inspector is a class made for each mobile app under testing that requires three methods:

- goToScan. This method executes the initial part of the test, where the app starts and the driver navigates to the QR code scanning page. It is also in charge of recovering the app if a crash occurs.
- getResultView. This method checks if the code has been scanned successfully and if the app behaves as expected.
- goBackToScan. Finally, this method is used after the code scan event to return in the scan section of the app and iterate with the following code.

This approach expands the implementation of fuzzing tests to all kinds of applications. Moreover, at any point during the iteration, the QR Code Fuzzer could stop the execution and recover the previous session whenever a failure is encountered. For example, if the app crashes, the script can restart the app and restore the testing session. Furthermore, the QR Code Fuzzer saves the ADB logs by filtering for the process ID of the app to collect only the relevant logs. In addition to this, the QR Code Fuzzer saves each visual result for every malicious payload tested by taking a screenshot. If the app under test shows an anomaly (e.g., app crash) or not (i.e., the app behaves as expected), the component saves an entry in a report file. In this report, there is also a reference to the employed payload to trace back the vulnerabilities in case of anomaly.

QR Code Generator. The other fundamental building block of *QRFuzz* is the QR Code Generator, which is in charge of generating codes at runtime based on a dictionary and then visualizing them on the screen. It can generate standard general-purpose and ad-hoc codes from an app-specific template.

The QR Code Generator iterates through the dictionary and, for each word, generates a bitmap image of the requested code and notifies the QR Code Fuzzer that the code is ready. The following payload is processed upon receiving the request from the QR Code Fuzzer. This approach is entirely event-based and fail-proof. For instance, suppose the QR Code Fuzzer stops the iteration due to a crash of the application. In that case, the QR Code Generator will wait for the QR Code Fuzzer to be ready before proceeding with the next code. This coordination is made up by employing a JSON file that handles the states of the two components and may also be used to restart a previously interrupted analysis.

Fuzzing Process Execution. Figure 3 summarizes the main steps of *QRFuzz*. The smartphone scans a code (1), then the Appium Server detects the completed scan and reports the results to the QR Code Fuzzer (2). This latter requests a change of the visualized code (3) that the QR Code Generator handles by updating the code (4) and sends a notification of completion to the QR Code Fuzzer (5). Finally, the smartphone is instructed to scan the new code (6).

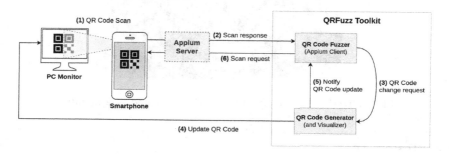

Fig. 3. Overview of the *QRFuzz* components.

3   Experiments

In this section, we will introduce the experimental setup we built to test *QRFuzz*. The hardware setup we employed is described in Sect. 3.1, while Sect. 3.2 describes the applications we tested. Finally, in Sect. 3.3, we introduce the dataset of malicious payloads we employed.

3.1   Experiment Setup

The hardware setup to use *QRFuzz* is minimal, as illustrated in Fig. 4. We employed the following components:

- A Raspberry Pi connected to a PC monitor running *QRFuzz*.
- A One Plus 3 smartphone, updated to Android 11.0 and connected via USB to the Raspberry Pi with ADB enabled.
- A tripod to adjust the phone height to face the PC monitor directly.

The first step is to attach the smartphone to the computer and start the Appium Server in the host computer to accept the client included in the QR Code Fuzzer component. Then, the QR Code Generator can be started as well. This component will show a sample code that will be substituted after each iteration by the loaded words from the dictionaries. Finally, the QR Code Fuzzer can be launched to start the fuzzing process.

Fig. 4. Testbed setup with a smartphone pointed at a monitor.

3.2   Tested Apps

We tested some of the most popular applications on the Play Store, where vulnerabilities may have a higher impact because of the large number of active users. We manually analyzed the 25 most downloaded applications in the US and Italian download ranks to verify if QR codes have been used. Some applications, such as *Spotify* or *Snapchat*, use proprietary codes, similar to barcodes or QR codes. Since the specification of these codes is not publicly available, we decided to remove them from our pool of applications to test. However, it may be possible to reverse engineer some of these codes and to adapt the code generator to work also with proprietary codes [20]. Ultimately, we decided to test 20 applications (plus a second version of *Instagram*, as detailed in Sect. 4.2), which are depicted in Table 1. We selected a pool of apps from various categories, from payments to social networks. For each app, we tested the complete dictionary in both the standard and ad-hoc format. However, there were some exceptions. Some applications have no ad-hoc version of the codes: they are general-purpose scanners (*QR & Barcode Reader*) or search engines (*Google Lens, UC Browser*). *WhatsApp Messenger* employs codes to connect a smartphone with the web interface, but since the payload of the code is encrypted, we decided to test the standard version only. *Wallapop - Buy & Sell Nearby* employs ad-hoc code that we could not obtain and analyze. Similarly, the structure of the ad-hoc payload for *IO, l'app dei servizi pubblici* (the Italian's public administration app) and *Broadlink* were too general to be meaningful: therefore, we decided to use the standard codes only.

Table 1. Percentages of correctly scanned codes in each application. Results in parenthesis show manually computed scores, while ad-hoc results for *Instagram* are discussed in Sect. 4.2.

Application	Version	Type	ad-hoc %	standard %
Banco Posta	23.09.06	Payments	93,2	99,8
Broadlink	1.7.14	IoT	X	95,4
Discord	167.21.00	Messaging	99,9	97,6
Ebay	6.63.1.3	Shopping	(98,3)	(97,3)
Facebook	391.1.0.37.104	Social	100	98,1
Google Lens	1.14.220323019	Scanner	(99,4)	
Instagram (v223)	223.1.0.14.103	Social	98,7	*50,1*
Instagram (v269)	269.0.0.18.75	Social	98,1	*51,1*
IO, l'app dei servizi pubblici	2.11.0.5	Public	X	96,1
Line	13.02.02	Messaging	97,4	96,1
PayPal - Send, Shop, Manage	8.18.1	Payments	(75,4)	(56,4)
Postepay	15.21.05	Payments	99,5	99,9
QR & Barcode Reader	2.08.05	Scanner	99,3	
Satispay	3.26.1	Payments	99,4	95,7
Telegram	8.8.0	Messaging	99,5	99,6
TikTok	28.04.05	Social	94,9	82,6
Twitter	9.46.00	Social	98,7	99,7
UC Browser	13.4.0.1306	Browser	98,1	
Verifica C19	1.2.4	Public	99,6	99,2
Wallapop - Buy & Sell Nearby	1.150.4	Shopping	X	(100)
WhatsApp Messenger	2.23.3.79	Messaging	X	99,8

3.3 Malicious Dictionaries

In order to obtain meaningful results, we collected fuzzing strings to be inserted into the payload data field. Each payload can be used as it is for a standard code or employed to generate an ad-hoc payload, de facto duplicating the size of the dataset. For our experiments, we built the following dictionaries for a total of about 950 possibly malicious strings, covering a wide area of languages, charsets, and known vulnerabilities:

- **cmdinj**. It contains common command injection payloads.
- **formatstr**. It contains payloads employed in format string vulnerabilities testing, with different lengths.
- **json**. It contains possible JSON injection strings that might cause issues during parsing.
- **lfi**. It contains local file inclusions payloads.
- **metachars**. It contains chars encoded with different techniques.
- **naughty-strings**. It contains a wide collection of strings composed of chars from esoteric encoding (i.e., emoji, Chinese characters).
- **special-chars**: It contains special characters such as question marks, apex, and different quotation marks.

- **sqli**. It contains typical SQL injection payloads for different databases.
- **ssi**. It contains payloads used to trigger SSI (Server-Side Includes) injection vulnerabilities.
- **xss**. It contains classic payloads to trigger XSS (Cross-Site Scripting) vulnerabilities.
- **xxe**. It contains typical XXE (XML External Entity) injection payloads.

4   Results

In this section, we present the results we obtained from our experiments. In Sect. 4.1, we analyze the reliability of our tool, describing possible issues *QRFuzz* may encounter. Instead, in Sect. 4.2 and Sect. 4.3, we discuss and analyze bugs we found in a popular social network application and in the official Italian COVID-19 vaccination checker app, respectively.

4.1   Reliability Results

We performed our experiments with different kinds of dictionaries to execute fuzz testing with multiple symbols and strings. Table 1 illustrates the successful scan rate for each application tested, which are near 100% for most applications, with an overall mean of 93.6%. Most apps obtained similar results in ad-hoc and standard tests because, in both cases, the applications under test showed the UI element expected by the QR Code Fuzzer. The *Paypal* application was abnormally slow in decoding certain QR codes, and it caused it to miss some scans, thus decreasing the performance on the table. An app showing weird behavior was *Wallapop - Buy & Sell Nearby*, which seems to scan all the code we provided but displays an error on new activities only on the biggest ones. Finally, the *Instagram* standard case is instead discussed in Sect. 4.2.

Since the applications considered cover a wide range of domains, the scanner's behavior differs significantly between applications and, furthermore, between QR code types. Many applications, such as *Line* or *TikTok*, always return some kind of response in a way Appium can detect, like a snackbar (Fig. 5a) or a new activity (Fig. 5b). Unfortunately, with other apps, the situation is more complex. As an example, *Satispay* shows an overlay not detectable by the Appium framework, as presented in Fig. 5c. Therefore, in these cases, our tool is slower because it has to wait a sufficient amount of time to make sure the application has successfully decoded the code before collecting a screenshot and pass to the following code. Eventually, other applications, such as *Instagram*, behave in different ways based on the content of the QR code scanned, as we will discuss in Sect. 4.2. Independently of these notification strategies, *QRFuzz* can handle all the different situations if a suitable inspector is defined. The absence of detectable notifications may corrupt results on the log file. In these cases, we must fall back to screenshots to detect successfully scanned codes. By checking image differences between screenshots, we can estimate the rate of correctly scanned codes. In Table 1, we highlighted these cases using parenthesis.

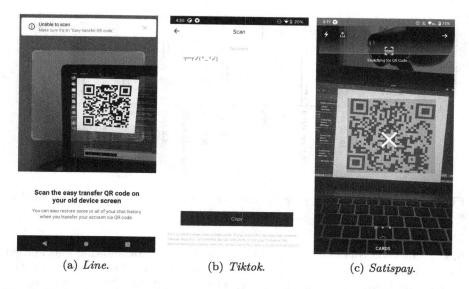

(a) *Line.*   (b) *Tiktok.*   (c) *Satispay.*

Fig. 5. Each app returns a different error when scanning an unexpected kind of code: (a) and (b) are detectable by Appium, while (c) is not.

Another critical insight we can get from our experiments is related to scan timings. In Fig. 6, we reported the mean scan time for each application, divided between ad-hoc and standard codes. The overall average scan time is 5.3s, but it is interesting to notice that each application has its own architecture: for instance, the path and the number of buttons to be pressed to reach the QR code scanner section are always different, which justifies high differences between scan times. The errors in Fig. 6 provide another piece of information. High errors could mean that some of the codes took a lot of time to be scanned and be a hint that a crash may have happened. The rationale behind it is that, after a crash or freezing, the app must be restarted, and this will take more time than closing an error activity or pressing back to return to the scan section. Furthermore, we encounter some errors while performing the scan of several codes in a row, probably caused by Appium itself or by the rise of temperature on the smartphone's camera.

4.2 Instagram Case

Instagram is a popular social network developed by Meta with over 1 billion downloads on the Play Store [18]. Although it is accessible from the browser, the app is required to use its full functionality. A novel feature provides a comfortable way to exchange contacts and posts by creating and scanning QR codes linked to the desired content. By reverse engineering some of the codes, we find out the application is expecting a QR code containing a link starting with the `instagram.com` domain, followed by the path of the profile or posts we want to

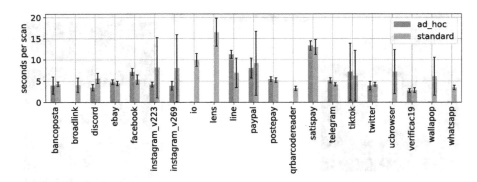

Fig. 6. Mean scan time and error for the 99 percentile of each application related to ad-hoc and standard codes.

link. If the code contains a valid link to a profile, a dialog showing information about the account is shown (Fig. 7a shows what happens when scanning the QR code of the Meta profile on *Instagram*). Otherwise, if the URL has the correct domain but a wrong path, a dialog appears showing the URL to the user and asking for confirmation before opening it, as shown in Fig. 7b. Finally, if the correct domain is not provided in the code, a generic error appears in a toast, which is not detectable by Appium (Fig. 7c). It is crucial to notice that, even in this latter case, the QR is still scanned and decoded by the application to decide on what notifications to raise. *QRFuzz* is able to manage each of these alerts and process them accordingly.

While using our framework with *Instagram*, we encountered several crashes. A clue of a possible problem is visible from the graph in Fig. 6 because of the huge error in the scan times of the *Instagram* app. While using the first version we tested (`223.1.0.14.103`), the app crashes using the JSON dictionary. By manual testing, we discovered a bug that makes the application crash while passing a QR code containing a colon. A similar issue was found with a novel version (`269.0.0.18.75`) that crashes with the same payloads.

To be more precise, several different payloads make the application close unexpectedly:

– Just one single colon inside the payload (i.e., `:`);
– A colon enclosed by two symbols (e.g., `":"` or `{:}`);
– A colon as the start or end of a string (e.g., `:whatever` or `whatever:`).

We investigated the crash employing the ADB logs collected by *QRFuzz*. In both *Instagram* app versions, the crash was caused by a fatal exception in the `ArLinkScanController.FrameHandlerThread` class. In detail, the app crashes because of a `SecurityException` related to the URL parsing. During the investigation, we found out that the problem was probably tackled by the security team at Meta between the two versions because, in the oldest version, the exception was caused by an expected scheme name, while in the updated version, the

(a) Correct link to the Meta profile.   (b) Correct domain but a wrong path.   (c) Wrong domain.

Fig. 7. Different behaviors of the *Instagram* app exposed to QR codes with encoded data with various formats.

error was related to sanitization that was added during the development of the novel version.

During our research, we encountered another crash with payloads such as https://www.instagram.com/, where the colon has been URL-encoded. In this case, the crash was caused by a comparison between Java URI and Android URI of the payload, probably applied as a security measure. However, the two URI are different since Java URI decodes URL-encoded characters, while Android URI does not.

We disclosed the vulnerability to the team at Meta that acknowledged our finding, even if they did not find a security impact on the bug. However, this example aims to illustrate our tool's potential and why it should be adopted to test QR code-enabled applications.

4.3 VerificaC19 Case

VerificaC19 is the official Italian application to enable operators to verify the validity and authenticity of Green Passes [19]. Green Passes are personal certifications issued individually by the health authority in the form of QR upon COVID-19 vaccination, recovery, or negative test. They may be requested to access public places such as restaurants, stores, hospitals, and public transportation, based on the spread of the virus and on the laws in force. In order to test the application using the ad-hoc approach, we reverse-engineered the specific Green Pass encoding. During the validation of the QR code, indeed, the application returns from the checking function with a negative result as soon as one of the multiple decoding steps fails. In particular, the *VerificaC19* decoder performs the following operations:

1. Checks and remove the prefix *"HC1:"*.
2. Decodes the string from the *Base45* format.
3. Decompresses using *Zlib*.
4. Decodes the bytes according to the *COSE* specification (CBOR Object Signing and Encryption).
5. Verifies that the packet contains the *kid* field.
6. Validates the JSON content.
7. Decodes the *CBOR* object.
8. Obtains the certificate from the repository using the *kid*.
9. Checks the certificate with a custom validation function.

During our tests using the *QRFuzz* tool to scan the ad-hoc variants of the QR codes, we discovered that *VerificaC19* crashes when presented with the encoding of an empty JSON file instead of the one representing user data. We analyzed the ADB logs provided by our tool and discovered that this vulnerability occurs during the parsing of the payload, making the validation function return in a `NullPointerException`. The aforementioned crash of the application may be exploited for malicious purposes, such as health fraud, preventing the relevant authorities from correctly verifying people's health status. We discovered the vulnerability in the app version `1.2.4`, but it was fixed in the upcoming releases.

5   Conclusions and Future Works

In this paper, we presented the first automated methodology to validate QR code-based input in mobile applications using fuzzing. To prove the efficiency of the method, we developed *QRFuzz*, an open-source tool that can be used to discover bugs in applications supporting QR codes. By using *QRFuzz*, we found bugs in *Instangram*, a popular social network application with more than 1 billion downloads, and on *Verifica C19*, the official Italian COVID-19 vaccination verification app, which makes the apps crash just by scanning a QR code.

However, being this framework the first one, several improvements could be possible. Firstly, a software-only approach is under development. It should increase the scalability of *QRFuzz* and avoid accidental crashes happening for hardware-related problems, such as the camera's heat after several hours of testing. Moreover, this approach could be achieved using Android emulators or even cloud services to automate and parallelize the execution of the toolkit. For example, an Android emulator running on a virtual machine could use a virtual video device that shows the QR code as a simulated camera. Moreover, it would be possible for each experiment to spawn different virtual machines, depending on the app under test, so as to parallelize the workflow. Secondly, an automated dictionary-free generation of payloads should be added to the tool, possibly considering more interaction with the application using tools such as Frida [23] to enable coverage-based fuzzing. Thirdly, low-level attacks could be employed as a third type of QR codes in our methodology during QR code generation. Each code may contain visual errors requiring error correction that could generate different behaviors in different applications, depending on the libraries employed. Lastly, it would be interesting to fully support iOS applications' tests to replicate the same attacks of the Android counterpart. It would also be interesting to highlight the differences in terms of scanning performance, crash detection, and app behaviors.

Acknowledgements. We would like to thank Omitech S.r.l. for supporting Denis Donadel.

References

1. Android Developers: UI/Application Exerciser Monkey. https://developer.android.com/studio/test/other-testing-tools/monkey
2. Averin, A., Zyulyarkina, N.: Malicious QR-Code threats and vulnerability of blockchain. In: 2020 Global Smart Industry Conference (GloSIC), pp. 82–86 (2020). https://doi.org/10.1109/GloSIC50886.2020.9267840
3. Cao, C., Gao, N., Liu, P., Xiang, J.: Towards analyzing the input validation vulnerabilities associated with android system services. In: Proceedings of the 31st Annual Computer Security Applications Conference, pp. 361–370 (2015)
4. DroidPilot Team: DroidPilot. https://droidpilot.wordpress.com/
5. Fioraldi, A., Maier, D., Eißfeldt, H., Heuse, M.: AFL++: combining incremental steps of fuzzing research. In: 14th USENIX Workshop on Offensive Technologies (WOOT 20) (2020)
6. Foundation, J.: Appium.io (2022). https://appium.io/
7. fuff: Fuzz Faster U Fool (2023). https://github.com/ffuf/ffuf
8. Gao, Z., Zhai, G., Hu, C.: QR-Code structure image. In: The Invisible QR Code (2015). https://doi.org/10.1145/2733373.2806398
9. Garg, G.: QR Code Statistics 2023: Up-To-Date Numbers On Global QR Code Usage. https://scanova.io/blog/qr-code-statistics/
10. Google: American fuzzy lop (2023). https://github.com/google/AFL, original-date: 2019-07-25T16:50:06Z
11. Hartlage, C.: CVE Hunting: Fuzzing ZINT. https://www.code-intelligence.com/blog/cve-hunting-with-fuzzing
12. Homan, J., Breese, J.: QR Code hacking - detecting multiple vulnerabilities in android scanning software. Inf. Syst. (2022). https://proc.conisar.org/2022/pdf/5756.pdf
13. Juniper Research: QR Code Payments: market forecasts, key opportunities and competitor leaderboard 2022–2026. https://www.juniperresearch.com/researchstore/fintech-payments/qr-code-payments-research-report
14. Khan, A.G., Zahid, A.H., Hussain, M., Riaz, U.: Security of cryptocurrency using hardware wallet and QR code. In: 2019 International Conference on Innovative Computing (ICIC), pp. 1–10 (2019). https://doi.org/10.1109/ICIC48496.2019.8966739
15. Kieseberg, P., et al.: Malicious pixels using QR codes as attack vector, pp. 21–38. Springer, Cham (2012). https://doi.org/10.2991/978-94-91216-71-8_2
16. Li, J., Zhao, B., Zhang, C.: Fuzzing: a survey. Cybersecurity $1(1)$, 1–13 (2018). https://doi.org/10.1186/s42400-018-0002-y

17. Liang, C.J.M., et al.: Caiipa: automated large-scale mobile app testing through contextual fuzzing. In: Proceedings of the 20th Annual International Conference on Mobile Computing and Networking, pp. 519–530 (2014)
18. Meta: Instagram: a photo and video sharing social networking service owned by American company meta platforms. https://play.google.com/store/apps/details?id=com.instagram.android
19. Ministero della Salute: VerificaC19 App Source Code on Github (2021). https://github.com/ministero-salute/it-dgc-verificaC19-android
20. Pushkov, A.: Cracking Spotify Codes and making a quest out of it (2020). https://dev.to/ale/cracking-spotify-codes-and-making-a-quest-out-of-it-3jdn
21. QR Code Tiger: QR Code in Video Games: Providing immersive gaming experience. https://www.qrcode-tiger.com/qr-codes-video-games
22. Rani, M.M.S., Euphrasia, K.R.: Data security through QR code encryption and steganography. Adv. Comput. Int. J. (ACIJ) **7**(1/2), 1–7 (2016)
23. Ravnås, O.A.V.: Frida: A world-class dynamic instrumentation toolkit for android (2023). https://frida.re/docs/android/
24. Rieback, M.R., Crispo, B., Tanenbaum, A.S.: Is your cat infected with a computer virus? In: Fourth Annual IEEE International Conference on Pervasive Computing and Communications (PERCOM 2006), pp. 10-pp. IEEE (2006)
25. Sang Ryu, J., Murdock, K.: Consumer acceptance of mobile marketing communications using the QR code. J. Direct Data Digit. Mark. Pract. **15**(2), 111–124 (2013). https://doi.org/10.1057/dddmp.2013.53
26. Saranya, K., Reminaa, R., Subhitsha, S.: Modern applications of QR-Code for security. In: 2016 IEEE International Conference on Engineering and Technology (ICETECH), pp. 173–177. IEEE (2016)
27. Schneider, M.A., Wendland, M.F., Akin, A., Sentürk, S.: Fuzzing of mobile application in the banking domain: a case study. In: 2020 IEEE 20th International Conference on Software Quality, Reliability and Security Companion (QRS-C), pp. 485–491 (2020). https://doi.org/10.1109/QRS-C51114.2020.00087
28. Scholte, T., Robertson, W., Balzarotti, D., Kirda, E.: Preventing input validation vulnerabilities in web applications through automated type analysis. In: 2012 IEEE 36th Annual Computer Software and Applications Conference, pp. 233–243. IEEE (2012)
29. Shielder: MalQR: a collection of malicious QR codes & barcodes you can use to test the security of your scanners (2022). http://malqr.shielder.com/
30. Ye, H., Cheng, S., Zhang, L., Jiang, F.: Droidfuzzer: fuzzing the android apps with intent-filter tag. In: Proceedings of International Conference on Advances in Mobile Computing and Multimedia, pp. 68–74. MoMM 2013, Association for Computing Machinery, New York, NY, USA (2013). https://doi.org/10.1145/2536853.2536881
31. Yong, K.S., Chiew, K.L., Tan, C.L.: A survey of the QR code phishing: the current attacks and countermeasures. In: 2019 7th International Conference on Smart Computing & Communications (ICSCC), pp. 1–5. IEEE (2019)

Enabling Lightweight Privilege Separation in Applications with MicroGuards

Zahra Tarkhani[1] and Anil Madhavapeddy[2(✉)]

[1] Microsoft Research Cambridge, Cambridge, UK
[2] University of Cambridge, Cambridge, UK
ztarkhani@microsoft.com

Abstract. Application compartmentalization and privilege separation are our primary weapons against ever-increasing security threats and privacy concerns on connected devices. Despite significant progress, it is still challenging to privilege separate inside an application address space and in multithreaded environments, particularly on resource-constrained and mobile devices. We propose MicroGuards, a lightweight kernel modification and set of security primitives and APIs aimed at flexible and fine-grained in-process memory protection and privilege separation in multi-threaded applications. MicroGuards take advantage of hardware support in modern CPUs and are high-level enough to be adaptable to various architectures. This paper focuses on enabling MicroGuards on embedded and mobile devices running Linux kernel and utilizes tagged memory support to achieve good performance. Our evaluation show that Micro-Guards add small runtime overhead (less than 3.5%), minimal memory footprint, and are practical to get integrated with existing applications to enable fine-grained privilege separation.

1 Introduction

More than ever, we depend on highly connected computing systems in today's world, where over 6.3 Billion people use smartphones, and 35.82 billion IoT (Internet of Things) devices are installed worldwide [49]. Our growing reliance on edge-cloud services in recent years has been constantly and increasingly threatened by a wide range of security and privacy breaches at scales never seen before [4,5,41,53]. The attack surface of modern applications includes a mixture of traditional attack vectors with new threats within/across various dependencies and system abstractions.

Many software attacks target sensitive content in an application's address space, usually through remote exploits, malicious third-party libraries, or unsafe language vulnerabilities. Processing highly sensitive data in a single large compartment (e.g., process or enclave) leads to real threats that require effective

---

This paper will appear at the ACNS-SecMT2023 (Security in Mobile Technologies).
Z. Tarkhani—This work was done when the author was affiliated with the University of Cambridge.

J. Zhou et al. (Eds.): ACNS 2023 Workshops, LNCS 13907, pp. 571–598, 2023.
https://doi.org/10.1007/978-3-031-41181-6_31

protection against: *(i)* attackers can exploit vulnerabilities in less secure parts of the code to leak information, escalate privileges, or take control of the application or even the host. *(ii)* an application's secret data (e.g., private keys or user passwords) can be leaked in the presence of untrusted code parts or compromised third-party libraries like OpenSSL [23]; *(iii)* privileged functions or modules can be misused to access private content [22]; *(iv)* applications written in memory-safe languages such as Rust or OCaml are vulnerable via unsafe external libraries that jeopardize all other safety guarantees [6,35]; and *(v)* in multithreaded use cases, attackers can exploit vulnerabilities (e.g., TOCTOU or buffer overflows) so the compromised thread can access sensitive data owned by other threads [1]. This whole class of attacks could be avoided by providing a practical way to enforce the least privilege within a shared address space. Table 1 summarizes some of these real threats that intra-process protection is effective against.

Hence, the importance of in-address space security threats results in significant improvement in hardware support for efficient memory isolation [9,11, 31,58]. However, existing simple APIs for utilizing such hardware features are not effective due to the complexity of attacks as well as various hardware limitations [20,43,55] in security and performance particularly for resource constrained devices. These systems mainly require specific programming languages or rely on x86 features which are not practical for wide range of IoT and mobile devices.

Table 1. A representative selection of vulnerabilities that cause sensitive content leakage. The attacks with a tick can be mitigated by using **MicroGuards** protection.

	example CVE	Description	MicroGuards
In-Process threats	CVE-2021-3450	Improper access control in shared library	✓
	CVE-2021-29922	unsafe language binding	✓
	CVE-2021-31162	Rust runtime memory corruption	✓
	CVE-2019-9345	Shared mapping bug	✓
	CVE-2021-45046	thread-based privilege escalation	✓
	CVE-2019-9423	missing bounds check	✓
	CVE-2019-15295	unsafe third party library	✓
	CVE-2019-1278	unsafe third party library	✓
	CVE-2018-0487	unsafe third party library	✓
	CVE-2017-1000376	unsafe native bindings	✓
	CVE-2014-0160	Heartbleed bug	✓
	CVE-2021-3177	Python ctypes memory leak	✓
	CVE-2021-28363	Python ctypes memory leak	✓
Other	CVE-2018-0497	SW side-channels	
	CVE-2017-5754	HW side-channels	

Many security-sensitive applications such as OpenSSH [44] rely on process-based isolation to separate their components into different privileged processes. However, this usually requires redesigning an application from scratch using a multiprocess architecture (e.g., Chrome) and is difficult for many multithreaded applications such as web servers. Previous work such as Privtrans [18] and Wedge [16] provide automatic process-based isolation of applications with a huge overhead ($\approx 80\% - 40x$ slowdown).

Conventional process abstractions such as `fork` introduce security and efficiency issues [13], and alternatives such as `clone` are not fine-grained enough to switch between data sharing and copying between process address spaces for security-critical resources. This lack of flexibility in the underlying interfaces means developers cannot easily prevent in-process attacks, and so multithreaded applications are difficult to privilege separate. This class of attacks could be avoided by providing a practical way to protect memory within an address space.

In this paper, we present MicroGuards, a new OS abstraction for enforcing least privilege on slabs of memory within the same address space. It takes advantage of modern hardware features to provide a flexible and efficient way to define trust boundaries to isolate sensitive data while supporting familiar APIs for secure multithreading and memory management. We provide a virtual memory tagging and access control abstraction within the kernel, then extend the kernel to support mapping MicroGuards to threads; hence, any thread can selectively protect or share its memory compartments from untrusted code within itself or from any untrusted thread (see Fig. 1).

Hence, we designed a new memory compartmentalisation abstraction to overcome this limitation efficiently. MicroGuards virtual memory tagging layer bypasses most of the kernel's paging abstraction to enable isolated blocks of tagged memory which could be mapped to the undelying hardware features such as ARM MD (memory domains) or MTE (memory tagged extension) for stronger isolation enforcement and performance optimization. Moreover, these hardware features are difficult to use securely (require a strong access control mechanism) and portably due to differing semantics across the Linux Kernel virtual memory abstraction and hardware provided features (Sect. 2). Note that MicroGuards virtual memory layer can also be enabled with available simple address space translation mechanism and without hardware-based memory tagging capabilities. However, it is specifically designed for properly utilizing such beneficial hardware security features. Hence, MicroGuards is a high-level OS abstraction that aims to:

- develop a new kernel-assisted mechanism based on mutual-distrust for intra-process privilege separation that supports isolating private contents, a secure multithreading model, and secure communication within a shared address space.
- explain how to utilize modern CPU facilities for efficient memory tagging to avoid the overhead of existing solutions (due to TLB flushes, per-thread page tables, or nested page table management).
- show that the implementation is sufficiently lightweight ($\approx 5K$ LoC) to be practical for IoT and mobile devices with a minimal memory footprint.

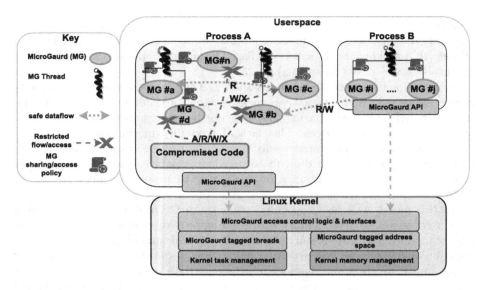

Fig. 1. High-level architecture of MicroGuards: it provides in-process isolation as well as thread-granularity privilege separation so each MicroGuard thread can tag itself, its address space, and define its own trust boundaries.

- evaluate our implementation using real-world software such as Apache HTTP server, OpenSSL, and Google's LevelDB, which shows MicroGuards add negligible runtime overhead for lightly modified applications.

The remainder of this paper elaborates on the CPU hardware features we use (Sect. 2), describes the architecture (Sect. 3) and implementation of Micro-Guards (Sect. 4), presents an evaluation (Sect. 5) and the tradeoffs of our approach (Sect. 6).

2 Background

2.1 ARM VMSA

ARM virtual memory system architecture (VMSA) is tightly integrated with the security extensions, the multiprocessing extensions, the Large Physical Address Extension (LPAE), and the virtualization extensions. VMSA provides MMUs that control address translation, access permissions, and memory attribute determination and checking for memory accesses. The extended VMSAv7/v8 provides multiple stages of memory system control; for operation in Secure state (e.g., EL1&0 stage 1 MMU) and for operation in Non-secure state (e.g., EL2 stage 1 MMU, EL1&0 stage 1 MMU, and EL1&0 stage 2 MMU). VMSAv8.5 adds more MMUs for additional isolation in the secure world. Each MMU uses a set of address translations and associated memory properties held in TLBs. If an implementation does not include the security extensions, it has only a single security state, with a single MMU with controls equivalent to the Secure state MMU controls. A similar argument is valid for when am implementation does not include the virtualization extensions.

System Control coprocessor (CP15) registers control the VMSA, including defining the location of the translation tables. They include registers that contain memory fault status and address information. The MMU supports memory accesses based on memory sections or pages, supersections consist of 16MB blocks of memory, sections consist of 1MB blocks of memory or 64 KB blocks of memory, and pages consist of 4 KB blocks of memory. Operation of MMUs can be split between two sets of translation tables, defined by the Secure and Non-secure copies of TTBR0 and TTBR1, and controlled by TTBCR. For hyp mode stage 1, The HTTBR defines the translation table for EL2 MMU, controlled by HTCR. For stage 2 translation, The VTTBR defines the translation table, controlled by VTCR. Access to a memory region is controlled by the access permission bits and the domain field in the TLB entry.

ARM Memory Domains (MDs). A domain is a collection of contiguous memory regions. The ARM VMSAv7 architecture supports 16 domains, and each VMSA memory region is assigned to a domain. First-level translation table entries for page tables and sections include a domain field. Translation table entries for super-sections do not include a domain field (super-sections are defined as being in domain 0). Second-level translation table entries inherit a domain setting from the parent first-level page table entry. Each TLB entry includes a domain field. A domain field specifies which domain the entry is in, and a two-bit field controls access to each domain in the Domain Access Control Register (DACR). Each field enables access to an entire domain to be enabled and disabled very quickly without TLB flushes so that whole memory areas can be swapped in and out of virtual memory very efficiently. Hence DACR controls the behavior of each domain and is not guarded by the access permissions for TLB entries in that domain. Also, DACR defines the access permission for each of the sixteen isolation domains. The DACR is a 32-bit read/write register and is accessible only in privileged modes. When the security extensions are implemented DACR is a banked register, and write access to the secure copy of the register is disabled when the CP15SDISABLE signal is asserted high. To access the DACR you read or write the CP15 registers. For example: 'MRC $p15, 0, <Rt>, c3, c0, 0$' for reading from DACR and 'MCR $p15, 0, <Rt>, c3, c0, 0$' for writing to DACR. Data Fault Status Register (DFSR) holds status information about the last data fault in MDs. It is a 32-bit read/write register, accessible only in privileged modes. These registers are banked when security extensions are enabled, so we could have separate 16 domains inside TrustZone secure world as well as the normal world.

Table 2. ARM memory domains access permissions

Mode	Bits	Description
No Access	00	Any access causes a domain fault
Manager	11	Full accesses with no permissions check
Client	01	Accesses are checked against the page tables
Reserved	10	Unknown behaviour

The four possible access rights for a domain are No Access, Manager, Client, and Reserved (see Table 2). Those fields let the processor *(i)* prohibit access to the domain mapped memory–No Access; *(ii)* allow unlimited access to the memory despite permission bits in the page table– Manager; or *(iii)* let the access right be the same as the page table permissions–Client. Any access violation causes a domain fault, and changes to the DACR are low cost and activated without affecting the TLB.

ARM MDs look like a good building block for in-process memory protection. Changing domain permissions does not require TLB flushes, and they do not require extensive modifications to the kernel memory management structures that might otherwise introduce security holes due to inevitable TLB and memory management bugs [61].

Though ARM MDs are a useful isolation primitive in concept, the current hardware implementation and OS support suffer from significant problems that have prevented their broader adoption:

Scalability: ARM relies on a 32-bit DACR register and so supports only up to 16 domains. Allocating a larger register (e.g., 512 bits) would mean larger page table entries or additional storage for domain IDs.

Flexibility: Unlike Intel MPK, ARM-MDs only apply to first-level entries; the second-level entries inherit the same permissions. This prevents arbitrary granularity of memory protections to small page boundaries and reduces the performance of some applications [21]. Also, the DACR access control options do not directly mark a domain as read-only, write-only, or exec-only. So the higher-level VM abstraction should resolve these issues.

Performance: Changing the DACR is a fast but privileged operation, so any change of domain access permissions from userspace require a system call. This is unlike Intel MPK that makes its Protection Key Rights Register (PKRU) accessible directly from userspace.

Userspace: There is no Linux userspace interface for using ARM-MD; it is only used within the kernel to map the kernel and userspace into separate domains. In contrast, Linux already provides some basic support for utilizing Intel MPK from userspace.

Security: Though the DACR is only accessible in privileged mode, any syscall that changes this register is a potential breach that could cause the attacker to gain full control of the host kernel (e.g., through the misuse of the put_user/get_user kernel API in CVE-2013-6282). Also, since only 16 domains are supported, guessing other domains' identifiers is trivial, making it essential not to expose these directly to application code.

Address Space Identifier. The VMSA permits TLBs to hold any translation table entry that does not directly cause a translation fault or an access flag fault. To reduce the software overhead of TLB maintenance, the VMSA differentiates between *global pages* and *process-specific pages* through the Address Space Identifier (ASID). A global virtual memory page is available for all processes on the system, and a single cache entry can exist for this page translation in the TLB. A non-global virtual memory page is process-specific, associated with a specific ASID. The ASID identifies pages associated with a specific process and provides a mechanism for changing process-specific tables without maintaining the TLB structures. Hence, multiple TLB entries can exist for the same page translation, but only TLB entries that are associated with the current ASID are available to the CPU (x86 supports a similar mechanism, called PCID). On ARMv7, the current ASID is defined by the Context ID Register (CONTEXTIDR), and on ARMv8, the ASID is defined by the translation table base registers that causes better performance compare to ARMv7. Each TTBR contains an ASID field, and the TTBCR.A1 field selects which ASID to use. If the implementation supports 16 bits of ASID, then the upper 8 bits of the ASID must be written to 0 by software when the context being affected only uses 8 bits. ASIDs/PCIDs are useful for relatively faster context switching [38] and more efficient page table isolation as shown in design of kernel page-table isolation (KPTI or PTI, previously called KAISER [27]) for mitigating Meltdown vulnerability [37].

MTE and PAC. Memory Tagging Extension (MTE), also called memory coloring, is introduced in Armv8.5-A. Memory locations are tagged by adding four bits of metadata to each 16 bytes of physical memory (this is the Tag Granule). Tagging memory implements the lock. Hence, pointers and virtual addresses are modified to contain the key. In order to implement the key bits without requiring larger pointers, MTE uses the TBI (top byte ignore) feature of the Armv8-A Architecture. When TBI is enabled, the top byte of a virtual address is ignored when using it as an input for address translation similar to PAC (Pointer Authentication Code) design. This allows the top byte to store metadata. Memory tagging and pointer authentication both use the upper bits of an address to store additional information about the pointer: a tag for memory tagging, and a PAC for pointer authentication. Both technologies can be enabled at the same time. The size of the PAC is variable, depending on the size of the virtual address space. When memory tagging is enabled at the same time, there are fewer bits available for the PAC.

MTE adds a new memory type, Normal Tagged Memory, to the Arm Architecture. A mismatch between the tag in the address and the tag in memory can be configured to cause a synchronous exception or to be asynchronously reported. When the asynchronous mode is enabled, upon fault, the PE updates the TFSR_EL1 register. Then the kernel detects the change during context switching, return to EL0, kernel entry from EL1, or kernel exit to EL1. MTE is currently supported by LLVM, and when it is enabled, a call to malloc() will allocate the memory and assign a tag for the buffer. The returned pointer will include the allocated tag. If software using the pointer goes beyond the limits of the buffer, the tag comparison check will fail. This failure will allow us to detect the overrun. Similarly, for use-after-free, on the call to malloc() the buffer gets allocated in memory and assigned a tag value. The pointer that is returned by malloc() includes this tag. The C library might change the tag when the memory is released. If the software continues to use the old pointer, it will have the old tag value, and the tag-checking process will catch it.

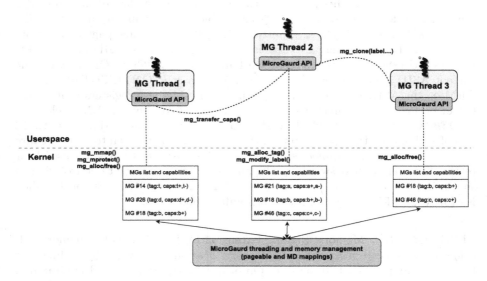

Fig. 2. Simple MicroGuards simple threading example: each MicroGuard thread is a security principal, it can define security policies for controlling its own MicroGuards collection, and pass its capabilities to other threads for secure sharing. The kernel then enforces MicroGuard security policies and handles its virtual memory management.

3   MicroGuards

We now describe the implementation of MicroGuards, which is an abstraction over the underlying kernel and hardware memory management for efficient intra-process isolation. MicroGuards abstraction has an emphasis on security, performance, and extensibility to support various hardware memory tagging primitives through a higher-level interface that hides the hardware limitations (Sect. 2.1).

3.1   Design Principles

The MicroGuards interface aims to enforce least privilege principle for memory accesses via the following guidelines:

Fine-Grained Strong Isolation: All threads of execution should be able to define their security policies and trust models to selectively protect their sensitive resources. Current OS security models of sharing ("everything-or-nothing") are not flexible enough for defining fine-grained trust boundaries within processes or threads (lightweight processes).

Performance: Launching MicroGuards, changing their access permissions, sharing across processes, and communications through capability passing should have minimal overhead. Moreover, untrusted (i.e., MicroGuards-independent) parts of applications should not suffer any overhead.

Efficiency: MicroGuards should be lightweight enough even for mobile and IoT devices running on a few megabytes of memory and slow ARM CPUs.

Compatibility: It is difficult to provide strong security guarantees with no code modifications, and MicroGuards is no exception. We move most of these modifications into the Linux kernel (increasingly popular for embedded deployments [2]) and provide simple userspace interfaces. MicroGuards should be implemented without extensive changes to the Linux and not depend on a specific programming language, so existing applications can be ported easily.

To achieve fine-grained isolation with mutual-distrust, we need a security model that lets each thread protect its own MicroGuards from untrusted parts of the same thread as well as other threads and processes. Simply providing POSIX memory management (e.g. `malloc` or `mprotect`) is inadequate. As a simple example, attackers can misuse the API for changing the memory layout of other threads MicroGuards or unauthorized memory allocation. The Micro-Guards interface needs to *(i)* provide isolation within a single thread; *(ii)* be flexible for sharing and using MicroGuards between threads, and *(iii)* provides the capability to restrict unauthorized permission changes or memory mappings modification of allocated MicroGuards. Previous work such as ERIM [55] or libMPK [43] does not offer such security guarantees since their focus is more on performance and domain virtualization.

We derive inspiration from Decentralized Information Flow Control (DIFC) [34] but with a more constrained interface – by not supporting information flow within a program, we avoid the complexities and performance overheads that typically involves. Existing DIFC kernels such as HiStar [59] achieve our isolation goals, but requires a non-POSIX-based OS that opposes our compatibility goal. To have a practical and lightweight solution, we therefore built Micro-Guards over a modified Linux kernel, and internally utilizing modern hardware facilities such as ARM MDs for good performance.

3.2   Threat Model and Assumptions

This paper focuses on two types of threats. First, memory-corruption based threats inside a shared address space that lead to sensitive information leakage; these threats can be caused by bugs or malicious third-party libraries (see Table 1). Second, attacks from threads that could get compromised by exploiting logical bugs or vulnerabilities (e.g., buffer overflow attacks, code injection, or ROP attacks). We assume the attacker can control a thread in a vulnerable multithreaded application, allocate memory, and fork more threads up to resource limits by the OS and hardware. The attacker will try to escalate privileges through the attacker-controlled threads or gain control of another thread, e.g., by manipulating another thread's data or via code injection. The adversary may also bypass protection regions by exploiting race conditions between threads or by leveraging confused-deputy attacks.

MicroGuards thus provides isolation in two stages: firstly within a single thread (through mg_lock/unlock calls), and then across threads in the same process. We consider threads to be security principals that can define their security policies based on mutual-distrust within the shared address space. We protect each thread's MicroGuards against unauthorized, accidental, and malicious access or disclosure. Therefore, the TCB consists of the OS kernel, which performs this enforcement. It also assumes developers correctly specify their policies through the userspace interface for allocating MicroGuards and transferring capabilities.

MicroGuards are not protected against covert channels based on shared hardware resources (e.g., a cache). Systems such as Nickel [47] or hardware-assisted platforms such as Hyperflow [25] could be a helpful future addition for side-channel protection on MicroGuards.

3.3   MicroGuards Access Control Mechanism

Each MicroGuard is a contiguous allocation of memory that (by default) only its owner thread can access, add/remove pages to/from it, and change its access permission. Our modified Linux kernel enforces the access control via a dynamic security policy based on DIFC [59] and a simpler version of the Flume [34] labeling model.

Each MicroGuard thread t has one label L_t that is the set of its unique tags. Privileges are represented in forms of two capabilities θ^+ and θ^- per tag θ for adding or removing tags to/from labels. These capabilities are stored in a capability list C_p per thread p. To improve its performance, MicroGuards have only one unique secrecy tag assigned internally by the kernel when created by mg_create. For improving security, none of MicroGuards API propagates tags in the userspace; all APIs access control is done internally within the kernel. The kernel allows information flow from α to β only if $L_\alpha \subseteq L_\beta$. Every thread p may change its label from L_i to L_j if it has the capability to add tags present in L_j but not in L_i, and can drop the tags that are in L_i but not in L_j. This is formally declared as $(L_j - L_i \subseteq C_p^+) \wedge (L_i - L_j \subseteq C_p^-)$.

Table 3. MicroGuards access control system calls. Pi represents principal i, L as a label that is a list of tags ($t*$) and their capabilities ($c*$).

syscalls	Description
mg_alloc_tag()$\rightarrow t$	allocate a unique tag
mg_modify_label(L)	modify a thread's label/tag
mg_transfer_caps($L \rightarrow c*, p$)	passing capabilities to thread p
mg_declassify($L \rightarrow t*$)	thread declassification or endorsement
mg_grant($L \rightarrow t*, p1, p2$)	adds an acts-for or a delegation link
mg_revoke_grant($L \rightarrow t*, p1, p2$)	removes an acts-for or a delegation link
mg_lock ($L \rightarrow t*$)	disables access to an object
mg_unlock ($L \rightarrow t*$)	enables access to a locked object
mg_clone ($L, int(*fn)(void*)...$) $\rightarrow p$	creates a thread

When a thread has θ^+ capability for MicroGuard θ, it gains the privilege to only access MicroGuard θ with the permission set by its owner (read/write/execute). The access privileges to each MicroGuard can be different; hence, two threads can share a MicroGuard, but the access privileges can differ.

Having a θ^- capability lets it declassify MicroGuard θ. This allows the thread to modify the MicroGuard memory layout by add/remove pages to it, change permissions, or copy the content to untrusted sources. Unsafe operations like declassification require the thread to be an owner or an authority (**acts-for** relationship) then via **mg_grant** and **mg_revoke** calls (see Table 3).

3.4   MicroGuards Threads

Each MicroGuard thread may have multiple MicroGuards attached to it. There is no concept of inheriting capabilities by default (e.g., in the style of **fork**) as this makes reasoning about security difficult [13]. Here, a tagged thread can create a child by calling **mg_clone**; the child thread does not inherit any of its parent's capabilities. However, the parent can create a child with a list of its MicroGuards and selected capabilities as an argument of **mg_clone**. For instance, in Fig. 2, thread 3 is a child of MicroGuard thread 2, which only gets "plus" capabilities for both shared MicroGuards 18 and 46 via **mg_clone** with a specific Label passed by its parent thread.

For a MicroGuard to propagate, it must be through transferring capabilities; this can be done directly by calling **mg_transfer_caps** for "plus" capabilities and **mg_grant** for declassification. Both these operations are also possible via specific arguments of **mg_clone** syscall when creating a child thread. Figure 2 shows how each thread can use the MicroGuards API for creating tags, changing labels, and passing capabilities to other threads. For instance, thread 1 gains access to MicroGuard 18 by directly getting the b^+ capability from thread 2. Since it does not have the b^- capability, it cannot change MicroGuard 18 permissions or its memory mappings.

Table 4. Some of userspace MicroGuards memory management API. Each MicroGuard has an *id* and is a tagged kernel object internally. MicroGuards access control is checked within the kernel.

Name	Description
mg_create → id	Create a new MicroGuard
mg_kill(*id*)	Destroy a MicroGuard
mg_malloc(*id, size*) → void*	Allocate memory within a MicroGuard
mg_free(*id, void∗*)	free memory from a MicroGuard
mg_mprotect(*id, ...*)	change an MicroGuard's pages permission
mg_mmap(*id, ...*)→ void*	Map a page group to a MicroGuard
mg_munmap(*id, ...*)	Unmap all pages of a MicroGuard
mg_get(*id*)→ *perms*	Get a MicroGuard permission

Table 3 describes the userspace MicroGuard API. A thread can create a tag by calling `mg_alloc_tag`, and the kernel will create and return a fresh unique tag. The thread that allocates a tag becomes its owner and can give the capabilities for the new tag to other threads. Each thread specifies its security policies by mutating its labels via `mg_modify_label`, and can declassify its own MicroGuards via `mg_declassify`.

Threads can lock access or permission changes of their MicroGuards via `mg_lock`, which temporarily change MicroGuard tag to restrict any modifications of MicroGuards state. A locked MicroGuard can only be accessed by calling `mg_unlock`.

MicroGuards Memory Management. To provide in-process isolation with good performance (Sect. 3.1) we provide a virtual memory management abstraction within the kernel for MicroGuards-aware memory tagging, mappings, protection, page faults handling, and least privilege enforcement. This abstraction bypasses most of the kernel paging abstraction that improves its performance. Furthermore, it hides the intricacies of hardware domains. Then we provide a userspace library on top of our modified kernel, using our MicroGuards-specific system calls, for managing MicroGuards memory. An application creates a new MicroGuard by calling `mg_create`; the kernel creates a unique tag with both capabilities (since it is the owner) and adds it to the thread's label and capability lists, and returns a unique ID. A MicroGuard can be kernel-backed (just depending on commodity pagetable for isolation) or hardware-backed which maps a MicroGuard to finer-grained memory safety/tagging features. We extend the kernel VM layer to support MicroGuards and maintain a private per-MicroGuard virtual page table (`pgd_t`) that is loaded into the TTBR register when the thread needs to do memory operations inside an MicroGuard during a lightweight context switch. An internal MicroGuard data structure maintains its address space range and permissions as shown in the following codelisting 1.1.

```
struct mg_struct {
    //operation bitmaps: set to 1 if mg[i] is allowed to do this operation, 0 OW
    DECLARE_BITMAP(mg_Read, MG_MAX);
    DECLARE_BITMAP(mg_Write, MG_MAX);
    DECLARE_BITMAP(mg_Execute, MG_MAX);
    DECLARE_BITMAP(mg_Allocate, MG_MAX);
    int mg_id;
    struct mutex mg_mutex;
    struct mem_segment *mg_range;
};
```

Listing 1.1. Internal MicroGuard data structure

Threads (or Linux tasks) in a process share the same mm_struct that describes the process address space. Having separate mm_struct for threads would significantly impact system performance, as all the memory operations related to page tables should maintain strict consistency [29]. Instead, we extend mm_struct to embed MicroGuard metadata within it as lightweight protected regions in the same address space as shown in Listing 1.2. It stores a per-MicroGuard pgd_t for threads and other metadata for memory management, fault handling, and synchronization.

The standard Linux kernel avoids reloading·page tables during a context switch if two tasks belong to the same process. We modified check_and_switch_context to reload MicroGuard page tables and flush related TLB entries if one of the switching threads owns an MicroGuard. We further mitigate the flushing overhead using ASID tagged TLB feature and ARM MDs. We modify mmap.c to keep track of MicroGuard-mapped memory ranges and add mg_mmap/mumap operations.

The kernel handle_mm_fault handler is also extended to specially manage page faults in MicroGuard regions, so an MicroGuard privilege violation results in the handler killing the violating thread.

```
struct mm_struct {
...
#ifdef CONFIG_MG
    struct mg_struct *mg_metadata[MG_MAX];
    atomic_t num_mg;      /* number of mgs */
    pgd_t *mg_pgd_list[MG_MAX]; /*mg Page tables per threads.*/
    int curr_using_mg;
    spinlock_t sl_mg[MG_MAX];
    struct mutex mg_metadata_mut;
    DECLARE_BITMAP(mg_InUse, MG_MAX);
#endif
... };
```

Listing 1.2. Extending the Linux kernel mm_struct with MicroGuards metadata.

Example code 1.3 shows a basic way of using MicroGuards to protect sensitive content in a single thread. Then the owner thread maps pages to its MicroGuard by calling mg_mmap that updates the MicroGuard's metadata with its address space ranges. The kernel allows mappings based on the thread's labels and free hardware domains. If there is a free hardware domain, it maps pages to that domain and places it to MicroGuards cache. When the MicroGuards already exists in the cache, further access to it is fast. When there is no free hardware domain, we have to evict one of the MicroGuards from the cache and map the new MicroGuard metadata to the freed hardware domain; this requires storing all the necessary information for restoring the evicted MicroGuard, such as its permission, address space range, and tag. The caching process can be optimized by tuning the eviction rate and suitable caching policies similar to libMPK [43].

The application uses mg_malloc and the MicroGuard ID to allocate memory within the MicroGuard boundaries (mg_malloc), and mg_free to deallocate memory or mg_mprotect to change its permissions (see Table 4). The owner thread can use mg_lock to restrict unauthorized access to it by accident or other malicious code; this is helpful for mitigating attacks inside a single thread. Then application developer can allow only his trusted functions or necessary parts of the code to gain access by calling mg_unlock (e.g., our single-threaded OpenSSL use case in Sect. 5.2).

```
/* create a microgaurd (i.e., mg_id) */
int mg_id = mg_create();

/* map a memory region to the mg */
memblock = (char*) mg_mmap(mg_id, addr, len, prot , 0, 0); //

// set permissions by mg_mprotect

/* allocate memory from mg */
private_blk = (char*) mg_malloc(mg_id, priv_len);

/* make mg inaccessible */
lock_mg(mg_id);

//... untrusted computations ....//

/* make mg accessible */
unlock_mg(mg_id);

//... trusted computations ....//

/* cleanup mg */
mg_free(private_blk);
mg_munmap(mg_id, memblock,len);
```

Listing 1.3. Basic MicroGuards usage

Our current implementation of MicroGuards utilizes ARM-MDs for efficient in-process virtual memory tagging; as a result, only code running in supervisor mode can change a domain's access control via the DACR register (Sect. 2.1) or remap private addresses to another domain through the TTBR domain bits. However, note that MicroGuards abstraction is designed to support similar hardware memory tagging features such as MTE and PAC with straightforward changes; mostly by replacing the backed for MicroGuards memory management API (mg_malloc layer) since the threading and other kernel changes are architecture-agnostic. Our API and mappings prevent unauthorized permission changes for MicroGuards, and we also do not provide a userspace API for direct modification of the DACR. Threads security policy enforcement is done by adding custom security hooks in the kernel's virtual memory management and task handling layers. It checks access based on the correct flow of threads labels (Sect. 3.4). We extend the kernel page fault handler for MicroGuards-specific cases. Illegal access to MicroGuards causes domain faults which our handler logs (e.g., violating thread information) and terminates it with a signal.

4 Implementation

MicroGuards Kernel: The MicroGuards core access control enforcement and the security model is implemented in the form of a new Linux Security Module (LSM) [42] with only four custom hooks. The LSM initializes the required data structures, such as the label registry and includes the implementation of all access control system calls (Table 3) for enforcing least privilege. This includes locking MicroGuards, changing labels, transferring capabilities, authority operations, and declassification based on the labeling mechanism (Sect. 3.4).

We modify the Linux task structure to store the metadata required to distinguish MicroGuards tasks from regular ones. Specifically, we add fields for storing MicroGuards metadata, label/ownership as an array data structure holding its tags (each tag is a 32-bit identification whose upper 2 bits stores plus and minus capabilities), a capability list; all included as task credential data structure. We implemented a hash table-based registry to make operations (e.g., store, set, get, remove) on these data structures more efficient.

The LSM also provides custom security hooks for parsing userspace labels to the kernel (copy_user_label), labeling a task (set_task_label), checking whether the task is labeled (is_task_labeled), and checking if the information flow between two tasks is allowed (check_labels_allowed). These security hooks are added in various places within the kernel to MicroGuards are guarded against unauthorized access or permission change by either the POSIX API (e.g., mmap, mprotect, fork) or the MicroGuards API. For example, forking a labeled task should not copy its labels and capability lists, and this is enforced using the MicroGuards LSM hooks. As another example, to avoid a task performing unauthorized memory allocation into a random MicroGuard or mapping pages to it, the security hooks are in the kernel's virtual memory management layer where the MicroGuards memory management engine (Table 4) can enforce correct access.

The MicroGuards virtual memory abstraction is implemented as a set of kernel functions similar to their Linux equivalents (e.g., do_mmap, do_munmap and do_mprotect) with similar semantics but with additional arguments that are required for enforcing the least privilege on MicroGuards. When an application creates a MicroGuard by calling mg_create (or mg_mmap for the first time), a MicroGuard ID passed as an argument that is associated with in-kernel metadata, together with the MicroGuard tag, and its capabilities that would be added to the task credentials.

When MicroGuards are mapped to hardware domains, the exact physical domain number is hidden from the userspace code to avoid possible misuse of the API. The mappings between MicroGuards and hardware domains are maintained through a cache-like structure similar to libmpk [43]. A MicroGuard is inside the cache if it is already associated with a hardware domain; otherwise, it evicts another MicroGuards based on the least recently used (LRU) caching policy while saving all require metadata for restoring the MicroGuard mapping and permission flags.

Users can get their MicroGuards permissions by calling mg_get, and quickly change its permission through mg_mprotect if the requested permission change matches one of the domain's supported options (Table 2) or undergo the small overhead of a dynamic security check otherwise. Any violation of MicroGuards permissions causes a MicroGuards fault that leads to the violating thread being terminated. To protect MicroGuards against API attacks, all memory management system calls check whether the caller thread has the appropriate capabilities using the security hooks.

Creating a MicroGuard adds a new tag and owner capabilities to the task credential, and the userspace library also provides a management API for modifying labels and capabilities. Each thread can use mg_transfer_caps for passing the plus capabilities to other threads, mg_grant_revoke for handling authorities, mg_lock to prohibit access to a MicroGuard, and mg_unlock to restore access. The mg_lock/unlock operations are helpful in limiting in-process buggy code from accessing MicroGuards content.

Userspace: To reduce the size of the TCB, we did not modify existing system libraries and instead provided a userspace library to invoke MicroGuards system calls. This library supports a familiar API for memory management within a MicroGuard, including mg_malloc and mg_free for memory management. We provide a custom memory allocator similar to HeapLayer [15] that allocates memory from an already mapped MicroGuard. For each MicroGuard, there is a memory domain metadata structure that keeps essential information such as the MicroGuard address space range (base and length) and the two lists of free blocks from the head and tails of the MicroGuard region that is used when searching for free memory.

5   Evaluation

We evaluated our implementation of MicroGuards on a Raspberry Pi 3 Model B [3] that uses a Broadcom BCM2837 SoC with a 1.2 GHz 64-bit quad-core ARM Cortex-A53 processor with 32 KB L1 and 512 KB L2 cache memory, running a 32-bit unmodified Linux kernel version 4.19.42 and glibc version 2.28 as the baseline. We use microbenchmarks and modified applications to evaluate Micro-Guards in terms of security, performance, and usability (Sect. 3.1 and Sect. 2.1) by answering the following questions:

– What is the initialization and runtime overhead of MicroGuards? How does using hardware domains impact performance?

- Are MicroGuards practical and adaptable for real-world applications? How much application change and programming effort is required? What is the performance impact? How does it perform in a multi-threaded environment?
- What is the memory footprint of MicroGuards? How much memory does it add (statically and dynamically) to both the kernel and userspace?

5.1 Microbenchmarks

Creating MicroGuards: Table 5 tests the cost of creating and mapping pages to MicroGuards using mg_mmap when MicroGuards are directly mapped to hardware domains, 1MB aligned memory regions with only 16 MicroGuards support, as compared to virtualized MicroGuards when there is no free hardware domain and requires evicting MicroGuards from the cache. The results show that the direct use of hardware domains improves MicroGuards performance by 4.9% compare to the virtualized one. Note that creating MicroGuards is usually a one-time operation at the initial phase of an application.

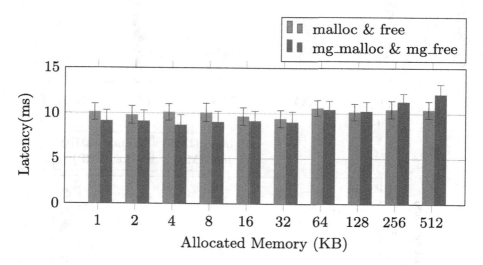

Fig. 3. Cost of MicroGuards memory allocation (malloc & free). On average mg_malloc outperforms malloc by a small rate (0.03%).

Table 5. Cost of creating MicroGuards when directly mapped to hardware domains vs virualised mapping that requires MicroGuards caching. The results are average of 10000 runs.

Operation	Overhead	stddev
Direct mg_mmap/munmap	4.8%	±0.17%
Virtualised mg_mmap/munmap	10.01%	±0.15%

Memory Protection and Allocation

We measure the cost of memory protection for baseline Linux where protection is per-process, and on MicroGuard threads where protection is per-thread and either implemented in software or hardware.

Table 5 shows the average results of 10000 runs of our microbenchmark comparing the cost of mg_mprotect with mprotect on baseline kernel. The results show mg_mprotect is 1.12x slower than mprotect, but the MD-backed mg_mprotect is 1.14x faster than baseline for some permissions (none and r/w) that supported by DACR register and do not need a TLB flush. Note that since hardware memory domains do not have flexible access control options, we cannot benefit from a control switch of domains using the DACR register for all possible permission flags such as the RO, WO, and EO variants.

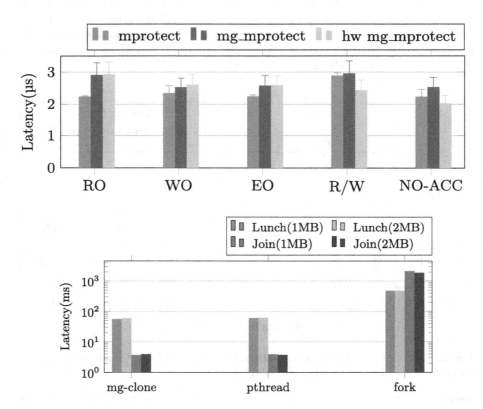

Fig. 4. Overhead of creating MicroGuard-enabled threads: the results are the average of 100000 runs with 1MB and 2MB heap sizes. On average, mg_clone latency is 5.39% lower than of pthread_create.

Table 6. Memory overhead of MicroGuards in Linux Kernel and userspace

Overhead	Linux Kernel	Userspace
Added LoC	3023	2405
Static Memory footprint	static(7 KB) slab(204 KB)	Static(10 KB)

Allocating memory using `mg_malloc` is on average 1.08x faster than glibc `malloc` for blocks ≤ 64 KB and introduces a small overhead (8.3%) for blocks greater than 64 KB (see Fig. 3). This cost can be optimised by using high-performance memory allocators. The results are average of running microbenchmarks 20000 times, and shows using MicroGuards provides reasonable overhead for memory allocation and permission changes.

Threading: We tested the cost of MicroGuard threading operations (creating and joining) through `mg_clone` that creates MicroGuard-aware threads. The test uses the `clone` syscall with minor modifications to restrict any credential sharing with the child by default (instead it provides additional clone options for passing parent's capabilities to its child). We implemented `mg_join` using `waitpid`. Figure 4 shows `mg_clone` outperforms `pthread_create` by 0.56% and `fork` by 83.01%. This gain is attributed to the MicroGuard operations simply doing less work for initializing new threads.

Codebase Overhead: Another factor towards the usability of MicroGuards is the size of the codebase, which is important both from a security perspective and the resource limitations of small devices. We implemented MicroGuards as a Linux kernel patch with no dependency on any userspace libraries. As Table 6 shows it adds less than $5.5K$ LoC in total to both the kernel ($\approx 3K$ LoC) and userspace ($2.5K$ LoC). It adds 7 KB to the kernel image size and adds 204 KB for kernel slabs at runtime. The userspace library only needs ≈ 10 KB of memory. These results show the MicroGuards memory footprint is small and suitable for many resource-constrained uses.

5.2 OpenSSL

Cryptographic libraries are responsible for securing all connected devices and network communication, yet have been a source or victim of severe vulnerabilities. Given these libraries' critical role, a single vulnerability can have a tremendous security impact. The well-known OpenSSL's Heartbleed vulnerability [23], for example, enabled attackers to access many servers' private data (up to 66% of all websites were vulnerable). More recently, GnuTLS suffered a significant vulnerability allowing anyone to passively decrypt traffic (CVE-2020-13777). Lazar et al. [36] studied 269 cryptographic vulnerabilities, finding that only 17% of the vulnerabilities they studied originated inside the cryptographic libraries, with the majority coming from improper uses of the libraries or interactions with other codebases. However, recent studies show that about 27% of vulnerabilities in cryptographic software are cryptographic issues, and the rest are system-level issues, including memory corruption and interactions with the host or other applications/libraries [17].

Hence, we modified OpenSSL to utilize MicroGuards for protecting private keys from potential information leakage by storing the keys in protected memory pages inside a single MicroGuard or multiple MicroGuards assigned per private key. Using multiple MicroGuards provides stronger security while adding more overhead due to the cost of caching MicroGuards.

To enable MicroGuards inside OpenSSL, all the data structures that store private keys such as EVP_PKEY needed protected heap memory allocation. This meant replacing OpenSSL_malloc wit mg_malloc and using mg_mmap at the initialization phase for creating one or multiple (per session) MicroGuards to store private keys. After storing the keys, access to MicroGuards is disabled by calling mg_lock. Only trusted functions that require access to private keys (e.g., EVP_EncryptUpdate or pkey_rsa_encrypt/decrypt) can access MicroGuards by calling mg_unlock. Modifying OpenSSL required fairly small code changes, and added 281 lines-of-code.

We measured the performance overhead of MicroGuards-enabled OpenSSL by evaluating it on the Apache HTTP server (httpd) that uses OpenSSL to implement HTTPS. Figure 5 shows the overhead of ApacheBench httpd with both the original OpenSSL library and the secured one with MicroGuards. ApacheBench is launched 100 times with various request parameters. We choose the TLS1.2 DHE-RSA-AES256-GCM-SHA384 algorithm with 2048-bit keys as a cipher suite in the evaluation.

The results show that on average MicroGuards introduces 0.47% performance overhead in terms of latency when using a single MicroGuard for protecting all keys, and 3.67% overhead when using a separate MicroGuard per session key. In the single MicroGuard case, the negligible overhead is mainly caused by in-kernel data structure maintenance for enforcing privilege separation and handling MicroGuards metadata. In the multiple-MicroGuards case, since httpd utilizes more than 16 MicroGuards (allocates a new MicroGuard per session), it causes higher overhead due to the caching costs within the kernel.

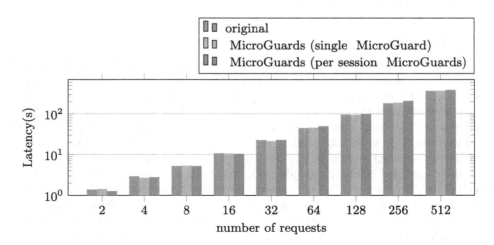

Fig. 5. Overhead of httpd on unmodified OpenSSL vs MicroGuards-enabled one.

5.3 LevelDB

Google's LevelDB is a fast key-value store and storage engine used by many applications as a backend database. It supports multithreading for both concurrent writers to safely insert data into the database as well as concurrent read to improve its performance. However, there is no privilege separation between threads, so each could have its private content isolated from other threads. We modified LevelDB to evaluate performance overhead of using the MicroGuards threading model when each thread has its own private storage that cannot be accessed by other threads.

We replaced the LevelDB threading backend (`env_posix`) that uses pthreads with MicroGuards-aware threading, where each thread creates an isolated Micro-Guard as its private storage and computation. We used the LevelDB `db_bench` tool (without modification) for measuring the performance overhead of Micro-Guards.

We generate a database with 400K records with 16-byte keys and 100-byte values (a raw size of 44.3MB). The number of reader threads is set to 1, 2, 4, 8, 16, and 32 threads for each successive run. The threads operate on randomly selected records in the database. The results in Figs. 6 and 7 show how multithreading can improve the performance of LevelDB, and utilising MicroGuards adds a small overhead on write (5%) and read (1.98%) throughput. As with OpenSSL previously, modifying LevelDB required only adding 157 lines-of-code around the codebase.

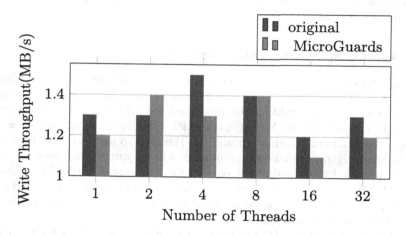

Fig. 6. LevelDB: performance overhead ofMicroGuards-based multithreading compare to pthread-based in terms of write throughput (5%).

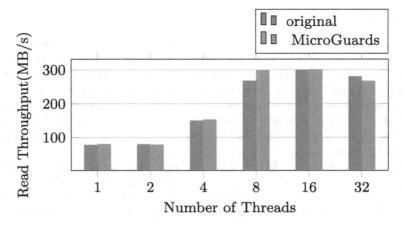

Fig. 7. LevelDB: performance overhead ofMicroGuards-based multithreading compare to pthread-based in terms of read throughput (1.98%).

6   Discussion and Conclusion

We have shown that MicroGuards provides a practical and efficient mechanism for intra-process isolation and inter-thread privilege separation on data objects. It adds small performance overhead and minimal memory footprint, which in essential for mobile and resource-constrained devices. However, the mechanism can still be taken further.

6.1   Address Space Protection Limitations

For single-threaded scenarios (e.g., event-driven servers), although MicroGuards can protect sensitive content from unsafe libraries or untrusted parts of the applications, it can be vulnerable if the untrusted modules are also MicroGuards-aware and already use the MicroGuards APIs. The application can use mg_get to query MicroGuard information and use the API to access them. This is not an issue when the untrusted code is running in a separate thread since the kernel does not provide it the capabilities required for accessing the other MicroGuards. It should be possible to modify popular event-driven libraries (e.g., libuv) to use threads purely to separate sensitive information such as key material, but we have not yet implemented this.

Various covert attacks [47] and side-channel attacks such as Meltdown [37] and Spectre [32] demonstrate how hardware and kernel isolation can be bypassed [30]. MicroGuards are currently vulnerable to these class of attacks, although the existing countermeasures within the Linux kernel are sufficient protection. We believe these types of attacks are important security threats, and hardening MicroGuards against them could be significant future work.

6.2   Compatibility Limitations

Providing a solution that is compatible with various operating systems and heterogeneous hardware is challenging. Though we picked our base kernel on Linux and built the abstraction with minimal dependencies, some application modification is still required. We believe that building more compatibility layers into our existing userspace implementation is possible and are open-sourcing our code to gather further feedback and patches from the relevant upstream projects we have modified.

Although Linux is the most widespread general-purpose kernel for embedded devices, as well as being the base for Android, still many even smaller devices depend on operating systems such as FreeRTOS. These often use ARM Cortex-M based hardware features for isolation (such as memory protection units (MPUs) [8,54]), or more modern CPUs with memory tagging extension [11]. We plan to explore the implementation of the MicroGuards kernel memory management on these single-address space operating systems, as well as broadening the port to Intel and PowerPC architectures on Linux (where the memory domains support is generally simpler to use than on ARM).

7   Related Work

There are many software or hardware-based techniques for providing process and in-process memory protection.

OS/Hypervisor-Based Solutions: Hardware virtualization features are used for in-process data encapsulation by Dune [14] by using the Intel VT-x virtualization extensions to isolate compartments within user processes. However, overall, the overheads of such virtualization-based encapsulation are more heavy-weight than MicroGuards. ERIM [55], light-weight contexts (lwCs) [38] and secure memory views (SMVs) [29] all provide in-process memory isolation and have reduced the overhead of sensitive data encapsulation on x86 platforms. The MicroGuards provides stronger security guarantees and privilege separation, allows more flexible ways of defining security policies for legacy code – e.g., without the use of threads as in our OpenSSL example, its small memory footprint makes it suitable for smaller devices, and it takes advantage of efficient virtual memory tagging by using hardware domains to reduce overhead. Burow et al. [19] leverage the Intel MPK and memory protection extensions (MPX) to efficiently isolate the shadow stack. Our efforts to provide an OS abstraction for in-process memory protection is orthogonal to these studies, which all have potential use cases for MicroGuards. Our focus has also been on lowering the resource cost to work well on embedded and IoT devices, while these projects are also currently x86-only. HiStar [59] is a DIFC-based OS that supports fine-grained in-process address space isolation, which influenced our work, but we focused on providing a more general-purpose solution for small devices by basing our work on the Linux kernel instead of a custom operating system. Flume [34] proposed process-level DIFC as a minimal extension to the Linux kernel, making DIFC work with the languages, tools, and OS abstractions already familiar to programmers. It also introduced a cleaner label system (which HiStar have later adopted). Likewise, other DIFC-based systems only support per-process protection. They also add large overhead [34,57] or need specific programming language support [45]. MicroGuards, however, do no aim to enforce dataflow protection on all system objects, but only focuses on threads and address space objects to enable very lightweight privilege separation.

Compiler and Language Runtime: Various compiler techniques introduce memory isolation as part of a memory-safe programming language. These approaches are fine-grained and efficient if the checks can be done statically [24]. However, such isolation is language-specific, relies on the compiler and runtime, and not effective when applications are co-linked with libraries written in unsafe languages. MicroGuards abstractions are fine-grained enough to be useful to these tools, for example, to isolate unsafe bindings. Software fault isolation (SFI) [46,56] uses runtime memory access checks inserted by the compiler or by rewriting binaries to provide memory isolation in unsafe languages with substantial overhead. Bounds checks impose overhead on the execution of all components (even untrusted ones), and additional overhead is required to prevent control-flow hijacks, which could bypass the bounds checks [33]. ARMLock [62] is an SFI-based solution that offers lower overhead utilizing ARM MDs. Similarly, Shreds [20] provides new programming primitives for in-process private memory support. MicroGuards also uses ARM MDs for improving the performance of intra-process memory protection, but is a more flexible solution for intra-process privilege separation; it provides a new threading model for dynamic fine-grained access control over the address space with no dependency on a binary rewriter, specific compiler or programming language.

Hardware-Enforced Techniques: A wide range of systems use hardware enclaves/TEEs such as Intel's SGX [7] or ARM's TrustZone [10] to provide a trusted execution environment for applications that against malicious kernel or hypervisor [12,26,28,40,52]. The trust model exposed by these hardware features is very fixed, and usually results in porting monolithic codebases to execute within the enclaves. Hence, there are wide ranges of attack vectors, which many are memory vulnerabilities inside enclaves or their untrusted interface, in such systems [48,50]. EnclaveDom [39] utilizes Intel MPK to provide in-enclave privilege separation. MicroGuards provide better performance and more general solutions with no dependency on these hardware features; hence it can be used for in-enclave isolation and secure multi-threading to improves both security and performance of enclave-assisted applications [51]. Ultimately, dedicated hardware support for tagged memory and capabilities would be the ideal platform to run MicroGuards on [60]. We are planning on supporting more of these hardware features as future work, with a view to analyzing if the overall increase in hardware complexity offsets the resource usage in software for embedded systems.

References

1. Format string vulnerability in the Cherokee. https://www.cvedetails.com/cve/CVE-2004-1097/. Accessed 5 Jan 2020
2. IoT developer survey 2019. https://iot.eclipse.org/resources/iot-developer-survey/iot-developer-survey-2019.pdf
3. Raspberry Pi 3 Model B. https://www.raspberrypi.org/products/raspberry-pi-3-model-b
4. Cyber security breaches survey 2018 (2018). https://www.gov.uk/government/statistics/cyber-security-breaches-survey-2018
5. List of data breaches (2018). https://en.wikipedia.org/wiki/List_of_data_breaches
6. Almohri, H.M., Evans, D.: Fidelius charm: isolating unsafe rust code. In: Proceedings of the Eighth ACM Conference on Data and Application Security and Privacy, pp. 248–255. ACM (2018)
7. Anati, I., Gueron, S., Johnson, S., Scarlata, V.: Innovative technology for CPU based attestation and sealing. In: Proceedings of the 2nd International Workshop on Hardware and Architectural Support for Security and Privacy, vol. 13. ACM New York (2013)
8. ARM: CMSIS-Zone. https://arm-software.github.io/CMSIS_5/Zone/html/index.html
9. ARM: Architecture reference manual; ARMv7-A and ARMv7-R edition (2012). https://static.docs.arm.com/ddi0406/c/DDI0406C_C_arm_architecture_reference_manual.pdf. Accessed 26 May 2020
10. ARM: ARM®v8-M Security Extensions: requirements on development tools (2015)
11. ARM: ARM architecture reference manual ARMv8, for ARMv8-A architecture profile documentation (2018). https://developer.arm.com/docs/ddi0487/latest. Accessed 26 May 2020
12. Arnautov, S., et al.: SCONE: secure Linux containers with Intel SGX. In: OSDI, vol. 16, pp. 689–703 (2016)
13. Baumann, A., Appavoo, J., Krieger, O., Roscoe, T.: A fork () in the road. In: Proceedings of the Workshop on Hot Topics in Operating Systems, pp. 14–22. ACM (2019)
14. Belay, A., Bittau, A., Mashtizadeh, A., Terei, D., Mazières, D., Kozyrakis, C.: Dune: safe user-level access to privileged CPU features. In: Presented as part of the 10th USENIX Symposium on Operating Systems Design and Implementation (OSDI 2012), pp. 335–348 (2012)
15. Berger, E.D., Zorn, B.G., McKinley, K.S.: Composing high-performance memory allocators (2001)
16. Bittau, A., Marchenko, P., Handley, M., Karp, B.: Wedge: splitting applications into reduced-privilege compartments. In: USENIX Association (2008)
17. Blessing, J., Specter, M.A., Weitzner, D.J.: You really shouldn't roll your own crypto: an empirical study of vulnerabilities in cryptographic libraries. arXiv preprint arXiv:2107.04940 (2021)
18. Brumley, D., Song, D.: Privtrans: automatically partitioning programs for privilege separation. In: USENIX Security Symposium, pp. 57–72 (2004)
19. Burow, N., Zhang, X., Payer, M.: SoK: shining light on shadow stacks. In: 2019 IEEE Symposium on Security and Privacy (SP), pp. 985–999. IEEE (2019)
20. Chen, Y., Reymondjohnson, S., Sun, Z., Lu, L.: Shreds: fine-grained execution units with private memory. In: 2016 IEEE Symposium on Security and Privacy (SP), pp. 56–71. IEEE (2016)

21. Cox, G., Bhattacharjee, A.: Efficient address translation for architectures with multiple page sizes. ACM SIGOPS Operating Syst. Rev. **51**(2), 435–448 (2017)
22. Deng, Z., Saltaformaggio, B., Zhang, X., Xu, D.: iRiS: vetting private API abuse in iOS applications. In: Proceedings of the 22nd ACM SIGSAC Conference on Computer and Communications Security, pp. 44–56. ACM (2015)
23. Durumeric, Z., et al.: The matter of heartbleed. In: Proceedings of the 2014 Conference on Internet Measurement Conference, pp. 475–488. ACM (2014)
24. Elliott, A.S., Ruef, A., Hicks, M., Tarditi, D.: Checked C: making C safe by extension. In: 2018 IEEE Cybersecurity Development (SecDev), pp. 53–60. IEEE (2018)
25. Ferraiuolo, A., Zhao, M., Myers, A.C., Suh, G.E.: HyperFlow: a processor architecture for nonmalleable, timing-safe information flow security. In: Proceedings of the 2018 ACM SIGSAC Conference on Computer and Communications Security, pp. 1583–1600. ACM (2018)
26. Frassetto, T., Gens, D., Liebchen, C., Sadeghi, A.R.: JITGuard: hardening just-in-time compilers with SGX. In: Proceedings of the 2017 ACM SIGSAC Conference on Computer and Communications Security, pp. 2405–2419. ACM (2017)
27. Gruss, D., Lipp, M., Schwarz, M., Fellner, R., Maurice, C., Mangard, S.: KASLR is dead: long live KASLR. In: Bodden, E., Payer, M., Athanasopoulos, E. (eds.) ESSoS 2017. LNCS, vol. 10379, pp. 161–176. Springer, Cham (2017). https://doi.org/10.1007/978-3-319-62105-0_11
28. Guan, L., et al.: TrustShadow: secure execution of unmodified applications with ARM TrustZone. In: Proceedings of the 15th Annual International Conference on Mobile Systems, Applications, and Services, pp. 488–501. ACM (2017)
29. Hsu, T.C.H., Hoffman, K., Eugster, P., Payer, M.: Enforcing least privilege memory views for multithreaded applications. In: Proceedings of the 2016 ACM SIGSAC Conference on Computer and Communications Security, pp. 393–405. ACM (2016)
30. Hunt, T., Jia, Z., Miller, V., Rossbach, C.J., Witchel, E.: Isolation and beyond: challenges for system security. In: Proceedings of the Workshop on Hot Topics in Operating Systems, pp. 96–104. ACM (2019)
31. Intel: Intel® 64 and IA-32 architectures software developer's manual (2019). https://software.intel.com/sites/default/files/managed/39/c5/325462-sdm-vol-1-2abcd-3abcd.pdf
32. Kocher, P., et al.: Spectre attacks: exploiting speculative execution. arXiv preprint arXiv:1801.01203 (2018)
33. Koning, K., Chen, X., Bos, H., Giuffrida, C., Athanasopoulos, E.: No need to hide: protecting safe regions on commodity hardware. In: Proceedings of the Twelfth European Conference on Computer Systems, pp. 437–452. ACM (2017)
34. Krohn, M., et al.: Information flow control for standard OS abstractions. In: ACM SIGOPS Operating Systems Review, vol. 41, pp. 321–334. ACM (2007)
35. Lamowski, B., Weinhold, C., Lackorzynski, A., Härtig, H.: Sandcrust: automatic sandboxing of unsafe components in Rust. In: Proceedings of the 9th Workshop on Programming Languages and Operating Systems, pp. 51–57. ACM (2017)
36. Lazar, D., Chen, H., Wang, X., Zeldovich, N.: Why does cryptographic software fail? A case study and open problems. In: Proceedings of 5th Asia-Pacific Workshop on Systems, pp. 1–7 (2014)
37. Lipp, M., et al.: Meltdown. arXiv preprint arXiv:1801.01207 (2018)
38. Litton, J., Vahldiek-Oberwagner, A., Elnikety, E., Garg, D., Bhattacharjee, B., Druschel, P.: Light-weight contexts: an OS abstraction for safety and performance. In: 12th USENIX Symposium on Operating Systems Design and Implementation (OSDI 2016), pp. 49–64 (2016)

39. Melara, M.S., Freedman, M.J., Bowman, M.: EnclaveDom: privilege separation for large-TCB applications in trusted execution environments. arXiv preprint arXiv:1907.13245 (2019)

40. Mo, F., Tarkhani, Z., Haddadi, H.: SoK: machine learning with confidential computing. arXiv preprint arXiv:2208.10134 (2022)

41. Morgan, L.: List of data breaches and cyber attacks in October 2017 – 55 million records leaked (2017). https://www.itgovernance.co.uk/blog/list-of-data-breaches-and-cyber-attacks-in-october-2017-55-million-records-leaked/

42. Morris, J., Smalley, S., Kroah-Hartman, G.: Linux security modules: general security support for the Linux kernel. In: USENIX Security Symposium, Berkeley, CA, pp. 17–31. ACM (2002)

43. Park, S., Lee, S., Xu, W., Moon, H., Kim, T.: Libmpk: software abstraction for Intel memory protection keys. arXiv preprint arXiv:1811.07276 (2018)

44. Provos, N., Friedl, M., Honeyman, P.: Preventing privilege escalation. In: USENIX Security Symposium (2003)

45. Roy, I., Porter, D.E., Bond, M.D., McKinley, K.S., Witchel, E.: Laminar: practical fine-grained decentralized information flow control, vol. 44. ACM (2009)

46. Sehr, D., et al.: Adapting software fault isolation to contemporary CPU architectures (2010)

47. Sigurbjarnarson, H., Nelson, L., Castro-Karney, B., Bornholt, J., Torlak, E., Wang, X.: Nickel: a framework for design and verification of information flow control systems. In: 13th USENIX Symposium on Operating Systems Design and Implementation (OSDI 2018), pp. 287–305 (2018)

48. Singh, J., Cobbe, J., Quoc, D.L., Tarkhani, Z.: Enclaves in the clouds: legal considerations and broader implications. Commun. ACM **64**(5), 42–51 (2021)

49. StewardJack, J.: The ultimate list of internet of things statistics for 2022 (2021). https://findstack.com/internet-of-things-statistics/

50. Tarkhani, Z.: Secure programming with dispersed compartments. Ph.D. thesis, University of Cambridge (2022)

51. Tarkhani, Z., Madhavapeddy, A.: Enclave-aware compartmentalization and secure sharing with Sirius. arXiv preprint arXiv:2009.01869 (2020)

52. Tarkhani, Z., Madhavapeddy, A., Mortier, R.: Snape: the dark art of handling heterogeneous enclaves. In: Proceedings of the 2nd International Workshop on Edge Systems, Analytics and Networking, pp. 48–53 (2019)

53. Tarkhani, Z., Qendro, L., Brown, M.O., Hill, O., Mascolo, C., Madhavapeddy, A.: Enhancing the security & privacy of wearable brain-computer interfaces. arXiv preprint arXiv:2201.07711 (2022)

54. Tock: Finer grained memory protection on Cortex-M3 MPUs. https://github.com/tock/tock/issues/1532

55. Vahldiek-Oberwagner, A., Elnikety, E., Duarte, N.O., Sammler, M., Druschel, P., Garg, D.: ERIM: secure, efficient in-process isolation with protection keys (MPK). In: 28th USENIX Security Symposium (USENIX Security 2019), pp. 1221–1238 (2019)

56. Wahbe, R., Lucco, S., Anderson, T.E., Graham, S.L.: Efficient software-based fault isolation. In: ACM SIGOPS Operating Systems Review, vol. 27, pp. 203–216. ACM (1994)

57. Wang, J., Xiong, X., Liu, P.: Between mutual trust and mutual distrust: practical fine-grained privilege separation in multithreaded applications. In: 2015 USENIX Annual Technical Conference (USENIX ATC 2015), pp. 361–373 (2015)

58. Watson, R.N., et al.: Cheri: a hybrid capability-system architecture for scalable software compartmentalization. In: 2015 IEEE Symposium on Security and Privacy (SP), pp. 20–37. IEEE (2015)
59. Zeldovich, N., Boyd-Wickizer, S., Kohler, E., Mazières, D.: Making information flow explicit in HiStar. In: Proceedings of the 7th Symposium on Operating Systems Design and Implementation, pp. 263–278. USENIX Association (2006)
60. Zeldovich, N., Kannan, H., Dalton, M., Kozyrakis, C.: Hardware enforcement of application security policies using tagged memory. In: OSDI, vol. 8, pp. 225–240 (2008)
61. Zero, P.: Introduction: Bugs in memory management code (2019). https://googleprojectzero.blogspot.com/2019/01/taking-page-from-kernels-book-tlb-issue.html
62. Zhou, Y., Wang, X., Chen, Y., Wang, Z.: ARMlock: hardware-based fault isolation for ARM. In: Proceedings of the 2014 ACM SIGSAC Conference on Computer and Communications Security, pp. 558–569. ACM (2014)

SiMLA – Security in Machine Learning and its Applications

SiMLA 2023

Fifth Workshop on Security in Machine Learning and its Applications

19 June 2023

Program Chair

Ezekiel Soremekun   Royal Holloway, University of London, UK

Web Chair

Salah Ghamizi   University of Luxembourg, Luxembourg

Publicity Chair

Badr Souani   University of Luxembourg, Luxembourg

Program Committee

Alexander Bartel	Umeå University, Sweden
Apratim Bhattacharyya	Qualcomm AI Research, USA
Sudipta Chattopadhyay	Singapore University of Technology and Design, Singapore
Maxime Cordy	University of Luxembourg, Luxembourg
Salah Ghamizi	University of Luxembourg, Luxembourg
Martin Gubri	University of Luxembourg, Luxembourg
Sakshi Udeshi	Lumeros AI, Singapore
Jingyi Wang	Zhejiang University, China

Eliminating Adversarial Perturbations Using Image-to-Image Translation Method

Haibo Zhang[1]([✉]) [iD], Zhihua Yao[2] [iD], and Kouichi Sakurai[3] [iD]

[1] Department of Information Science and Technology, Graduate School of Information Science and Electrical Engineering, Kyushu University, Fukuoka, Japan
zhang.haibo.892@s.kyushu-u.ac.jp
[2] Faculty of Economics and Business Administration, The University of Kitakyushu, Kitakyushu, Japan
zhihuayao@alumni.usc.edu
[3] Department of Information Science and Technology, Faculty of Information Science and Electrical Engineering, Kyushu University, Fukuoka, Japan
sakurai@inf.kyushu-u.ac.jp

Abstract. Convolutional neural networks are widely used for image recognition tasks, but they are vulnerable to adversarial attacks that can cause the model to misclassify an image. Such attacks pose a significant security risk in safety-critical applications like facial recognition and autonomous driving. Researchers have made progress in defending against adversarial attacks through two approaches: enhancing the neural networks themselves to be more robust and removing the perturbation added to the image through pre-processing. This paper is based upon a recent defense model that belongs to the latter approach, which utilizes image-to-image translation to regenerate images perturbed by adversarial attacks. We optimized the training process of their model and tested the model performance against more recent and strong attacks. The results show that the model is able to regenerate images attacked by the state-of-the-art attack, the AutoAttack, and restores the classification accuracy to a level over 83% to that of the original images.

Keywords: Adversarial attack · Defense method · Image-to-image translation

1 Introduction

Convolutional neural networks (CNNs) have been widely used in image recognition tasks, such as object detection, facial recognition, and autonomous driving. However, it has been shown that these models are vulnerable to adversarial attacks, which are intentional modifications made to an image that is imperceptible to human eyes but can cause the model to misclassify the image [1].

Adversarial attacks pose a significant security risk in applications such as facial recognition, where an attacker could use an adversarial example to bypass the system and gain unauthorized access. In autonomous driving, an attacker

J. Zhou et al. (Eds.): ACNS 2023 Workshops, LNCS 13907, pp. 601–620, 2023.
https://doi.org/10.1007/978-3-031-41181-6_32

could use an adversarial example to cause a self-driving car to misclassify a stop sign or traffic light, leading to potentially dangerous situations. Therefore, developing robust defenses against adversarial attacks is critical for the deployment of machine learning systems in safety-critical applications [2].

Adversarial attacks can be classified into two categories: white-box and black-box attacks. In a white-box attack, the attacker has complete access to the model's architecture, parameters, and training data. This means that the attacker knows exactly how the model works and can use this knowledge to generate adversarial examples that are specifically designed to fool the model. In contrast, in a black-box attack, the attacker has limited access to the model and does not have access to its internal workings or parameters. The attacker may only have access to the input and output of the model. Black-box attacks are more challenging to carry out than white-box attacks because the attacker must infer the model's parameters and vulnerabilities through trial and error. White-box attacks are typically more powerful and effective than black-box attacks because the attacker has full knowledge of the model's vulnerabilities. Representative white-box attacks including but not limited to limited-memory BFGS attack (L-BFGS) [3], fast gradient sign method (FGSM) [1], basic iterative method (BIM) [4], projected gradient descent (PGD) [5], DeepFool [6], Jacobian-based saliency map attack (JSMA) [7], One-Pixel attack [8], and AutoAttack [9].

Opposite to generating adversarial examples, researchers also made much progress in defending against adversarial attacks. These approaches can be broadly divided into two categories. In the first category, the neural networks themselves are enhanced to be more robust. Adversarial training is a prominent example, as it involves incorporating adversarial examples into the training data set to retrain the network. However, it can be computationally expensive [10]. The second category aims to remove the perturbation added to the image by pre-processing. Defense methods fall in this category including but not limited to high-level representation guided denoiser (HGD) [11], Pixel Defend [12], Mag-Net [13], Pixel deflection [14], ComDefend [10], Defense-Gan [15], and Feature Pyramid Decoder (FPD) [16].

However, all of the proposed pre-processing methods try to remove the perturbations from the original image, which is similar to wiping the dirt from a picture. This approach does make most of the dirt gone, but there will be traces. A new way of thinking is to print a brand new picture using the same data, surly without any dirt. This approach is proposed by Zhang et al. [17] in 2021, which utilizes image-to-image translation (Pix2pix [18]) to regenerate images that are perturbed by adversarial attacks. However, their model is only evaluated against FGSM attack and PGD attack. There are much stronger attacks such as the C&W attack [19] and AutoAttack [9]. Also, they arbitrarily decided the number of training epochs, which is time consuming and may cause overfitting problem. This paper aims to optimize the training process and evaluate the model performance against state-of-the-art attacks.

The contribution of this paper is 1) We use a validation set in the training process to determine the best number of training epochs. Zhang et al. [17] only used a training set in the training process, and they arbitrarily choose the number of epoch to be 300. We use a validation set to determine the best number of training epochs, thus shortening the time required for training and preventing the model from over-fitting. 2) Zhang et al. [17] use a randomly selected training set, which also contains images that are misclassified by the classifier in the first place. A concurrent work with theirs [20] suggests that doing so is meaningless and will interfere with the training process. Therefore, we use a training set that only includes randomly selected images that can be correctly classified before any attacks. 3) We showed that the model performs well even against the strongest adversarial attack, which is the AutoAttack [9], and restored the classification accuracy to a level close to the original images (Over 83%). When regenerating images attacked by the C&W attack [19], the classification accuracy is improved from 0% to over 86%.

Our paper has the following limitations. 1) All experiments are done in a white-box setting, that is we utilize knowledge of attacks and train attack-specified defense models. However, this is often not the case in real life situation. In future work, we consider training a defense model that is universally applicable to all kinds of adversarial attacks and test its performance in a black-box setting, which is a situation closer to reality. 2) Lacking of ablation tests. We propose optimizations that is theoretically correct, but we did not provide ablation tests to prove there are actually improvements from the original model. In future work, we will provide the results of ablation tests. 3) No comparison with related works. Since the data sets used in this study and related works are different, the reported results are not directly comparable. In future works, we will use the same data sets to evaluate the performance of our model and models from related works against various attacks. 4) Lack of evaluation against adaptive attacks [21,22]. Our study does not include an evaluation of our defense model against adaptive attacks, which are attacks designed specifically to bypass the defenses. Adaptive attacks can pose a significant challenge to the defense mechanisms, as they are tailored to exploit weaknesses in the model's architecture or training process. In future work, we will assess the robustness of our defense model against such adaptive attacks to provide a more comprehensive understanding of its effectiveness in practical scenarios.

The remainder of the paper is organized as follows. Section 2 reviews related works on both attack and defense methods. Section 3 illustrates the theoretical basis of our proposed method and describes the experimental procedures. Section 4 presents and evaluates the experimental results. Finally, Sect. 5 concludes the paper.

2   Related Work

Image recognition, also known as computer vision, is the ability of a computer system to identify and interpret objects, patterns, or features in visual images. It involves analyzing and processing digital images to recognize and categorize objects, people, or scenes. Image recognition systems use machine learning algorithms and deep neural networks to extract features from images and match them to known patterns or objects in a database. Image recognition has various applications, such as identifying faces in images, detecting objects in autonomous vehicles, and analyzing medical images.

While image recognition technology has advanced significantly in recent years, it is not without vulnerabilities. One of the vulnerabilities of image recognition is that the system can be easily fooled by small changes in an image that are imperceptible to the human eye but can significantly impact the image recognition algorithm's output, which is called adversarial attacks. For example, an attacker can add small perturbations to an image that can cause the system to misclassify the image, such as identifying a picture of a panda as a gibbon [1].

In the next subsection, we introduce three mainstream adversarial attack methods.

2.1   Adversarial Attacks on Image Recognition

Fast Gradient Sign Method. In 2014, Goodfellow et al. [1] proposed the fast gradient sign method (FGSM) for generating adversarial examples, which is often used as a baseline attack to evaluate the robustness of a model against adversarial attacks. The FGSM attack is a simple and effective attack that can be applied to a wide range of machine learning models. Despite its simplicity, the FGSM attack can cause significant damage to machine learning models, including image recognition systems.

The attack starts by calculating the gradient of the loss function with respect to the input image. The loss function represents the error between the predicted output of the model and the true output. By taking the gradient of the loss function with respect to the input image, the attacker can determine the direction of the gradient ascent that will cause the output of the model to change the most. Once the gradient is calculated, the attacker scales it by a small value called the epsilon value. The epsilon value determines the magnitude of the perturbations that will be added to the input image. The attacker then adds the scaled gradient to the input image to create a new image that is slightly different from the original image but still visually similar, which can be formulated as

$$x_{adv} = x + \epsilon sign(\nabla_x \mathcal{L}(\theta, x, y))$$

where x_{adv} is the adversarial image, x is the original input image, y is the ture lable of x, ϵ is a multiplier to ensure the perturbations are small, $\mathcal{L}$ is the loss function, and θ is the parameters of the model.

The resulting perturbed image is then fed into the image recognition system, which misclassifies it due to the added perturbations. The attack is successful if the misclassification occurs, as the attacker can use this vulnerability to deceive the model into making incorrect predictions. As FGSM only requires one back-propagation step, it is fast at generating adversarial examples. Therefore, FGSM provides a solution to tasks that require a large number of adversarial examples to be generated.

Projected Gradient Descent. Three years later after Goodfellow et al., [1], Madry et al. [5] proposed the Projected Gradient Descent (PGD) attack, which is an iterative version of the FGSM attack. The PGD attack works by iteratively calculating the gradient of the loss function and making small perturbations to the input image until the model is misclassified.

The attack starts with an initial image that is fed into the model to obtain its output. The attacker then calculates the gradient of the loss function with respect to the input image and makes small perturbations to the image in the direction of the gradient ascent. After each iteration, the perturbed image is projected onto a certain range of values to ensure that the image remains visually similar to the original image. This range is often defined as the Lp ball, where p is a positive integer that determines the size of the range. The projection ensures that the perturbations are not too large, and the resulting image is still recognizable. The PGD attack is repeated for a certain number of iterations, or until the model is misclassified. The number of iterations and the size of the perturbations are two hyperparameters that can be adjusted to optimize the attack. The PGD attack can be formulated as:

$$x^{t+1} = Clip_{x,\epsilon}(x^t + \alpha sign(\nabla_x \mathcal{L}(\theta, x, y))$$

where $Clip$ denotes the projection on to the surface of x's ϵ-neighbor ball, and α represents the step size. The PGD attack is a more powerful and robust version of the FGSM attack, as it allows the attacker to make multiple small perturbations to the input image until the model is misclassified. The attack is particularly effective against models that have been trained with adversarial examples.

The Carlini & Wagner Attack. In the same year as Madry et al. [5], Carlini & Wagner [19] developed a stronger attack method. The C&W (Carlini and Wagner) attack is a type of optimization-based adversarial attack, and it is considered one of the most potent attacks against state-of-the-art image recognition models.

The C&W attack works by solving a constrained optimization problem, where the objective function is the difference between the original image and the perturbed image, and the constraints are the conditions that the perturbed image must satisfy, such as remaining visually similar to the original image and being misclassified by the model. In order to find adversarial perturbations, they introduce auxiliary variables with a pixel value constraint. The pixel intensity must fall within the range (0,255), which naturally fits into the loss function and facilitates optimization. The C&W is capable of producing samples correctly classified by human eyes, but incorrectly classified by the well-trained classifier.

The C&W attack is more sophisticated than other adversarial attacks, such as FGSM and PGD attacks, as it uses a more complex objective function that allows the attacker to make more targeted and powerful perturbations to the input image. The attack is particularly effective against models that have been trained to be robust against other types of adversarial attacks.

AutoAttack. In 2020, Crose and Hein proposed the AutoAttack [9], which consists of an ensemble of four diverse, parameter-free adversarial attacks. The four attacks are: 1) Auto-PGD (Projected Gradient Descent): An adaptive version of the popular PGD attack that automatically adjusts its hyperparameters during the optimization process to find the best adversarial examples. 2) APGD-DLR (Auto-PGD with DLR loss): A variant of Auto-PGD that employs the difference of logits ratio (DLR) as the loss function, making it more effective against models with non-standard output layers. 3) FAB (Fast Adaptive Boundary): An attack based on a different optimization algorithm that is faster and often more effective in finding adversarial examples compared to PGD-based attacks. 4) Square Attack: A black-box attack that only relies on the model's output and does not require access to the gradients. It generates adversarial examples by iteratively perturbing the input within a small l infinity ball around the original image.

AutoAttack provides a more reliable evaluation of a model's adversarial robustness by combining these four attacks. If a model is resistant to all of them, it indicates a higher level of robustness against adversarial examples. AutoAttack has been widely adopted in the research community to compare the performance of different adversarial defense methods.

2.2 Defense Approaches to Adversarial Attacks

Various defense methods have been developed against adversarial attacks, and they can be divided into two main categories. One approach is enhancing the robustness of the classifier by training it using attacked image samples, which is also called adversarial training. Representative adversarial training approaches are Kurakin et al. [23], Tramèr et al. [24], Kannan et al. [25], Xie et al. [26], Shafahi et al. [27]. Another approach is detecting perturbations added to the input image and eliminating them as much as possible to ensure the classifier's accuracy [28]. Some representative defense methods are high-level representation guided denoiser (HGD) [11], Pixel Defend [12], MagNet [13], Pixel deflection [14], ComDefend [10], Defense-Gan [15], and Feature Pyramid Decoder (FPD) [16]. Our approach belongs to the latter category, and we will introduce two related works that are most comparable to our proposed methods.

Image Reconstruction. Zhang et al. [20] use an image reconstruction network consisting of 16 residual blocks [29] to reconstruct perturbed images, each block consists of two convolutional layers followed by a batch normalization layer [30], and a parametric rectified linear unit (PReLU) activation function [31] after the first batch normalization layer. Then, they use a feature extraction network that is pre-trained for image classification to estimate the perceptual loss function based on the differences between input and output images in terms of features. They also added a random resizing layer and a random padding layer to the end of their model, which is another method that aims to mitigate adversarial effects proposed by [32].

Zhang et al. [20] use a training set that only contains images that can be correctly classified by the classifier. They consider that the model will gain better performance than a model trained by a randomly selected training set. They use two test sets to evaluate the model performance. One is a test set that only includes images that can be correctly classified before the attack (test set 1), and the other includes images that are randomly selected (test set 2). When using Inception_v3 as the target classifier, their model can improve the classification accuracy of FGSM, PGD and C&W-perturbed images from 26.48%, 0.03%, 1.06% to 74.66%, 71.6% and 75%, respectively (test set 2). For their test set 2, the classification accuracy of original clean images is 76.7%, and the improvement from perturbed images to reconstructed images is from 26.48%, 0.03%, 1.06% to 74.66%, 71.6% and 75%, respectively.

Image-to-Image Translation. A concurrent work with Zhang et al. [20] is Zhang et al. [17], which uses a variation of conditional generative adversarial nets (Pix2pix) proposed by [18] to generate images that are very close to the cleanliness of target images from perturbed inputs. They also improve the original Pix2pix algorithm by adding the perceptual loss and achieved more preferable results.

These two works are similar in terms of pre-processing images without altering the classifier, and the use of perceptual loss. However, many differences exist between the two works. For instance, they are different in the network structure, how the model is optimized, and how the image is generated. Our work is based on Zhang et al.'s [17] model, so we leave the detailed explanation to the next section.

Zhang et al. [17] only use a randomly selected test set to evaluate their model. They test the model performance against FGSM attack and PGD attack on MobileNet_v2, Inception_v3 and ResNet_101. Although the result is not directly comparable, they obtain similar but less satisfactory results with Zhang et al. [20].

3   Method Proposed by This Study

The adversarial attack defense method proposed in this study is based on the implementation of image-to-image translation techniques. Common image translation techniques include Pix2pix [18], CycleGAN [33], StarGAN [34], UNIT [35] and so on. The image-to-image translation technique can be traced back to the earliest proposal of Generative Adversarial Networks (GAN) [36].

GAN is a deep learning model for generating new data, such as images, videos, audio, etc. GAN consists of two neural networks: a generator and a discriminator. The role of the generator is to generate new data, it receives a random noise vector as input and tries to transform it into an output similar to the training data. The role of the discriminator is to evaluate the similarity between the data generated by the generator and the training data. The discriminator gradually improves the accuracy of its evaluation during the training process to distinguish as much as possible between real and generated data.

Conditional Generative Adversarial Network (CGAN) [37] is a variant of GAN that controls the generation process by introducing conditional information between the generator and discriminator. CGAN can make the generated samples have more specified features and attributes by introducing conditional information in the input. Image-to-image translation can be seen as a special case of CGAN. In CGAN, the input noise vector is conditioned to generate a specific class of images. The image-to-image translation task, on the other hand, generates the corresponding output image conditional on the input image.

In this study, the proposed defensive model used the Pix2pix algorithm, which uses the framework of CGAN to learn the mapping relationship between the input image and the output. In terms of image denoising, Pix2pix can achieve image noise reduction by taking noisy images as input and noiseless images as output and learning the mapping relationship between them. However, we prefer to understand this process as image re-generation.

3.1 An Improved Pix2pix Method

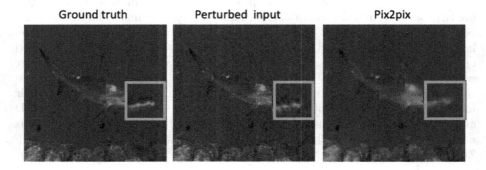

Fig. 1. The images recovered by Pix2pix method.

It is proved through experiments that the original Pix2pix method can reduce the interference of adversarial samples to image recognition models to a certain extent, as Fig. 1 shows. However, the images reconstructed by the Pix2pix method still retain a part of the noise visible to human eyes, which motivates us to propose an improved Pix2pix method to solve this problem.

First, we retain the overall framework of the Pix2pix approach, i.e., the U-Net model for the generator and the Patch-GAN for the discriminator.

– **U-Net** is a deep learning model for image segmentation tasks [38]. The U-Net structure consists of an encoder and a decoder. The encoder extracts features by gradually reducing the spatial size of the image through convolution and pooling operations while increasing the number of channels. The decoder then maps these features back to the spatial size of the original image and reconstructs the image by deconvolution and upsampling operations. To maintain the semantic information of the features, U-Net adds a **skip connection** between the encoder and the decoder, combining the feature map of the encoder with the corresponding feature map of the decoder.

The skip connection is a crucial component of the U-Net architecture, which enables the simultaneous utilization of both shallow and deep feature information to obtain more accurate and complete segmentation results. This design also helps to prevent gradient-vanishing or exploding. Therefore, we believe that the U-Net structure is highly applicable to image re-generation. As shown in Fig. 2's part (a), after perturbed image input, the predicted image (generated output) is generated by an encoder (consisting of 8 blocks, each containing a convolutional layer, a batch normalization layer and the activation function $LeakyReLU$) and a decoder(consisting of 7 blocks, each containing a deconvolutional layer, a batch normalization layer and the activation function $ReLU$), and a final deconvolutional layer.

– **PatchGAN** is a type of discriminator used in GANs. It was first proposed in the paper "Image-to-Image Translation with Conditional Adversarial Networks" by Isola et al. in 2017 [18]. The PatchGAN architecture is designed to classify image patches as either real or fake. Instead of outputting a single scalar value indicating the probability that the entire input image is real or fake, PatchGAN divides the image into small patches and outputs a two-dimensional array of values, where each value represents the probability that the corresponding patch is real or fake, as shown in Fig. 2's part (b).

The advantage of using PatchGAN is that it provides more fine-grained feedback to the generator about which parts of the image need improvement, rather than just providing a binary classification of the entire image. This helps the generator to produce more realistic images with more detail and texture.

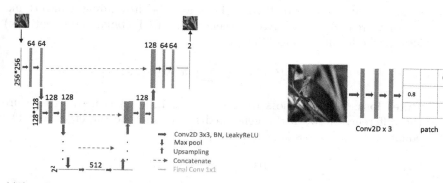

(a) The architecture of U-Net was used in this study.

(b) The architecture of Patch-GAN consists of 3 layers of Conv2D.

Fig. 2. The architecture of U-Net and Patch-GAN were used in this study.

In this study, in addition to keeping the original GAN loss (discriminator GAN loss and generator GAN loss) of CGAN architecture, and the pixel loss of the Pix2pix method. We also add perceptual loss as one of the important components of our proposed method.

1. Discriminator Loss:
   - The discriminator loss of CGAN is typically defined as a binary cross-entropy loss, given by the following equation:

   $$\mathcal{L}_{cGAN}(D) = -\frac{1}{N} \sum [(log(D(x,y))) + (log(1 - D(G(x,z),y)))]$$

   where:
   - N is the number of samples in the batch
   - $\sum$ denotes summation over all samples in the batch
   - x is an input image
   - z is a random noise vector or a conditional label
   - y is a target output image
   - G is the generator function that takes x and z as input and generates fake samples $G(x,z)$
   - D is the discriminator function that takes real and fake samples and z as input and outputs a probability score for each sample

   The first term represents the discriminator's loss when trying to correctly classify the real data samples. The second term represents the discriminator's loss when trying to correctly classify the generated data samples.

2. Generator Loss:
   - **CGAN loss** for generator: The generator's loss is typically defined as the difference between the discriminator's prediction on the generator's output and the target label, which is usually 1 (indicating that the output is a real image). The generator tries to minimize this loss by generating samples that are more realistic and can fool the discriminator into thinking they are real. In a CGAN, the generator's BCE (binary cross-entropy) loss can be formulated as follows::

   $$\mathcal{L}_{cGAN}(G) = -\frac{1}{N} \sum [log(D(G(x,z)))]$$

   - **Pixel loss**: The pixel loss (also known as L1 loss) is used to measure the difference between the generated image and the target image. The equation for pixel loss is as follows:

   $$\mathcal{L}_{L1}(G) = ||y - G(x,z)||_1$$

   where G(x, z) is the generated image from random noise x and a conditional variable z, y is the target image, and $||.||_1$ denotes the $L1$ norm.
   In other words, pixel loss is the sum of the absolute differences between each pixel in the generated image and the corresponding pixel in the

target image. The goal of training the Pix2Pix model is to minimize this pixel loss during the training process, which encourages the model to generate images that are as close as possible to the target images.

- **Perceptual loss**: Perceptual loss is a type of loss function used in deep learning for image and video processing tasks [39]. It is a way to measure the difference between two images or videos based on their perceptual similarity rather than just their pixel-wise differences. The advantage of using perceptual loss over traditional pixel-wise loss functions, such as mean squared error, is that it takes into account the high-level features and semantics of the image or video, rather than just the low-level pixel values. We simultaneously extract features from each layer of both the generated image and the target image, then calculate the perceptual loss for all layers except for the top layer by using the pre-trained VGG19 model [40] to achieve the feature extraction.

$$\mathcal{L}_{perceptual}(G) = \sum_{k} a_k ||V_k(y) - V_k(G(x,z))||_1$$

where:

- V denotes the pre-trained model VGG19
- k is the kth layer in both generated image $G(x,z)$ and target image y
- ak refers to taking the mean of the differences between the features extracted from the target image and the generated image

- **Objective function**: The objective function of our proposed method is to learn a mapping function from an input image to an output image using the pix2pix algorithm. The final objective function is a weighted sum of three losses:

$$G^* = \min_{G} \max_{D} \mathcal{L}_{cGAN}(G, D) + \lambda_1 \mathcal{L}_{L1}(G) + \lambda_2 \mathcal{L}_{perceptual}(G)$$

Here, λ is a hyperparameter that controls the trade-off between pixel loss and perceptual loss. By adjusting the value of λ, we can control the quality and the sharpness of the generated images. In specific experiments, we found that the recovery of images is better when the value of λ_1 is 100, and the value of λ_2 is 1.

3.2 Training Progress

Training Environment. This experiment was done on the NVIDIA GeForce RTX 3060 Ti. The programming language used is python and the deep learning framework is tensorflow_2.

Data Preparation. We randomly selected 8 images that can be correctly classified by the Inception_V3 [41] model from each category of the ILSVRC2012 ImageNet [42] data set. Since there are 1,000 categories in the ImageNet data set, the total number of images in our data set is 8,000. From each category, we randomly choose 5 images for training, 1 image for validation and 2 images for testing (testset_1). We implement four types of attacks on each image, therefore, the total size of our training set, validation set and test set are 20,000 images, 4,000 images and 8,000 images, respectively. All images are resized to 256 * 256, which is the input image size of our model.

For the three attacks implemented, i.e., FGSM, PGD, and C&W, we used the attack function of Cleverhans [43]. For the AutoAttack, we used the attack function of Adversarial Robustness Toolbox v1.2.0 (ART) [44]. Through experiments, we find that the higher the attack degree of the training dataset, the better the trained generative model will be. Therefore, we increase ϵ to 0.1 for FGSM, PGD and AutoAttack, as a way to improve the image generation ability of the generative model. Additionally, we set the norm value to np.inf, signifying an adversarial attack based on the $L\infty$-norm constraint. In this scenario, the attacker can manipulate one or multiple pixel values in the input data without exceeding the given norm limitation, ultimately leading to erroneous predictions by the machine learning model. In the PGD attack, a total of 40 iterations are performed (nb_iter = 40). During each iteration, the perturbation is updated along the gradient direction of the loss function, with a step size (stride) of 0.01 (eps_iter = 0.01). For the C&W attack, the authors demonstrated in their paper [19], through empirical evidence, that compared to other attack methods (such as the FGSM), the C&W attack can identify smaller perturbations under the $L2$-norm constraint, thereby rendering the attack more effective. Consequently, we have employed the C&W attack under the $L2$-norm constraint as one of the attack models in our study.

It is worth mentioning that in the official AutoAttack source code provided by ART, the default value for epsilon is set to 0.3. However, an excessively high epsilon value, although resulting in more pronounced attack effects, may also lead to the loss of image information, rendering the recovery model incapable of extracting useful information to restore the attacked image. Therefore, in our study, we set the epsilon value in AutoAttack to 0.1, enabling strong attacks while minimizing the loss of image information.

Network Architecture. Figure 3 explains the model architecture of our proposed method for perturbed image re-generation. This method uses a CGAN architecture, which consists of a generator network (*Generator*) and a discriminator network (*Discriminator*). The *Generator* takes a perturbed image x as input and generates a corresponding output image $G(x)$. The *Discriminator* tries to distinguish between target image y and fake output images. At this

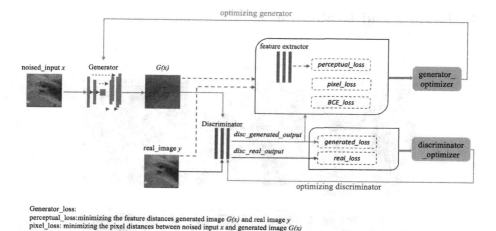

Fig. 3. The training progress of our proposed method.

point, the loss values generated by the *Generator* and the *Discriminator* need to be calculated simultaneously. As Sect. 3.2 illustrated, the *Generator* calculates losses values including cGAN_loss, pixel_loss and perceptual_loss. We refer to these loss values as generator_loss. The *Discriminator* calculates the discriminator_loss mentioned in Sect. 3.2, which includes two parts, the generated_loss between discriminated generated output $G(x)$ and fake labels, as well as the real_loss between discriminated target image y and true labels. The next step is to optimize the *Generator* and *Discriminator* by using gradient optimization.

Training. During training, the generator network is trained to generate output images that are realistic and match the corresponding input images. The discriminator network is trained to correctly classify the generated output images as real or fake. The training process involves minimizing the generator's loss and maximizing the discriminator's loss. In this experiment, we separately trained three models for FGSM-attacked images (with $\epsilon = 0.05$), PGD-attacked images (with $\epsilon = 0.05$) and C&W-attacked images. The total epoch of each model training is set to 200, and it is divided into two parts. The first part is 150 epochs and the learning rate is set to 0.0002. This is to enable the model to reach the convergence state more quickly. The second part is 50 epochs, and the learning rate is set to 0.000002 to fine-tune the model.

4   Results and Evaluation

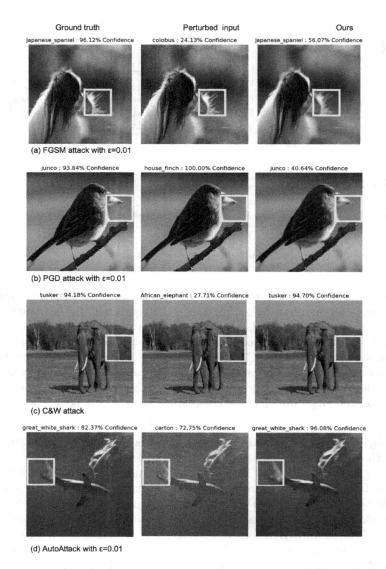

Fig. 4. The examples after adversarial attacks and after recovering them by our model. FGSM, PGD and AutoAttack are implemented with $\epsilon = 0.01$.

4.1   Experiment Results

Figure 4 reflects the examples after adversarial attacks and after recovering them by our model. Based on experimental evidence, it has been demonstrated that adversarial attacks can cause errors in the classification results of images. For instance, the confidence level of the original classification result may decrease, or the image may be classified into an incorrect category. However, after applying our model recovery approach, the image can be successfully classified into its original correct category. Alternatively, if it cannot be classified into the correct category, our approach can increase the proportion of the confidence interval for that category.

4.2   Accuracy

To evaluate the performance of our model, we first calculate the classification accuracy of the original image, attacked image and generated image for three attack methods. Table 1 shows that the classification accuracy decreases significantly after all three types of attacks, and increases largely after we regenerate the image. To compare the result with related works, we also use a second test set that contains 2,000 randomly selected images (testset_2). As a result, we successfully improved the classification accuracy to an extent near the original picture, the relative accuracy ratio of the generated image to the original image is 84%, 85%, and 91% for FGSM attack ($\epsilon = 0.01$), PGD attack ($\epsilon = 0.01$) and C&W attack, respectively. Although the result is not directly comparable, we obtained similar results with Zhang et al. [17] when against FGSM attack and PGD attack. We also proved that the model is also useful to defend the C&W attack, the strongest adversarial attack to date, and achieved the best defensive performance among all three attacks.

Table 1. The classification accuracy of original images, attacked images and generated images by our proposed model. Testset_1 consists only of images that can be correctly classified before attacks, and testset_2 consists of randomly selected images.

Attacks		Ground truth	Attacked images	Generated images
FGSM	testset_1	100%	25.85%	76.75%
	testset_2	77.85%	29.1%	65.45%
PGD	testset_1	100%	2.4%	77.45%
	testset_2	77.85%	5.7%	70.75%
C&W	testset_1	100%	0.0%	86.4%
	testset_2	77.95%	7.34%	71%
AutoAttack	testset_1	100%	0.5%	83.57%
	testset_2	77.85%	0.3%	67.23%

4.3   Peak Signal-to-Noise Ratio

Peak Signal-to-Noise Ratio (PSNR) is a commonly used metric to evaluate the quality of image reconstruction or restoration. It measures the ratio between the maximum possible value of a signal and the power of the noise that affects the fidelity of its representation [45,46]. In general, a higher value of PSNR indicates a better quality reconstruction or compression of an image or video. In the context of image-to-image translation, PSNR can be used to evaluate the quality of the generated images compared to the ground truth images.

Figure 5 depicts the change in the PSNR values of the recovered output images relative to the original images (clean images) during the training process of the recovery models for the four types of attacks. As can be observed from Fig. 5, the PSNR values for both the attacked images (at epoch = 0) and the recovered images (at epoch = 199) for AutoAttack are significantly lower compared to the other three attacks (FGSM, PGD, and C&W). This further demonstrates the potency of AutoAttack.

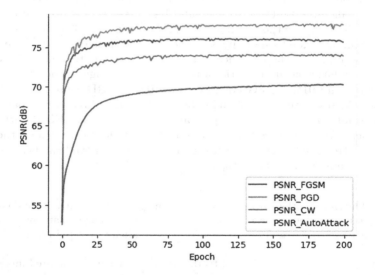

Fig. 5. The change in PSNR values during the training of the image generation model for the four attacks.

4.4   Time Consumption

In the approach proposed in this study, an image-cleansing layer is added prior to the classification neural network, which inevitably results in increased time consumption. We have experimentally determined that our model incurs an average additional time cost of 0.02 s for one image. This inclusion of the image purification layer does not significantly impact the overall efficiency of the image classification process.

Another time-consuming issue related to the method introduced in this paper is that pre-processing all input images unavoidably leads to extra time consumption that could have been avoided. In cases where an attacker launches a large-scale adversarial attack on a specific input image dataset, our model is capable of effectively purifying these contaminated images. However, if the attacker only targets a small number of images or doesn't conduct any adversarial attacks, our model may result in a substantial amount of unnecessary time usage. In the absence of attacks, the image remains unchanged after being processed by the filtering layer and merely contributes to excessive time consumption. Consequently, the next step for this model is to implement essential adversarial attack detection before the purification layer. Effective adversarial attack detection can significantly enhance the speed of image pre-processing.

5   Conclusion and Future Directions

In this paper, we optimized the model which defends classifiers from adversarial attacks using image-to-image translation method. We showed that it can regenerate images attacked by the state-of-the-art adversarial attack (AutoAttack) and restore the classification accuracy from 0% to a level over 83% to that of the original images. However, in unreported experiments, we find the model does not perform well on small images (images from MINST and CIFAR10). Fortunately, our method is a pre-processing model that does not alter the classifier. Therefore, this shortage can be covered by combining it with other defense models that are specialized in small images, which we will leave for future studies.

In conclusion, our study has identified several limitations, including the white-box experimental setting, lack of ablation tests, absence of direct comparison with related works, and no evaluation against adaptive attacks. Moving forward, we aim to address these limitations by developing a more universally applicable defense model, providing ablation test results, employing the same datasets for comparison against related works, and assessing our model's robustness against adaptive attacks. By addressing these concerns, we hope to offer a more rigorous evaluation of our defense model, ultimately enhancing its effectiveness and applicability in real-world adversarial scenarios.

Acknowledgement. This work is partially supported by JSPS international scientific exchanges between Japan and India (Bilateral Program DTS-JSPS) (2022–2024). We thank four anonymous referees for their valuable comments that improved the quality of the manuscript.

References

1. Goodfellow, I.J., Shlens, J., Szegedy, C.: Explaining and harnessing adversarial examples. arXiv preprint arXiv:1412.6572 (2014)
2. Xu, H., et al.: Adversarial attacks and defenses in images, graphs and text: a review. Int. J. Autom. Comput. **17**, 151–178 (2020)

3. Szegedy, C., et al.: Intriguing properties of neural networks. arXiv preprint arXiv:1312.6199 (2013)
4. Kurakin, A., Goodfellow, I.J., Bengio, S.: Adversarial examples in the physical world. In: Artificial Intelligence Safety and Security, pp. 99–112. Chapman and Hall/CRC (2018)
5. Madry, A., Makelov, A., Schmidt, L., Tsipras, D., Vladu, A.: Towards deep learning models resistant to adversarial attacks. arXiv preprint arXiv:1706.06083 (2017)
6. Moosavi-Dezfooli, S.-M., Fawzi, A., Frossard, P.: DeepFool: a simple and accurate method to fool deep neural networks. In: Proceedings of the IEEE Conference on Computer Vision and Pattern Recognition, pp. 2574–2582 (2016)
7. Papernot, N., McDaniel, P., Jha, S., Fredrikson, M., Celik, Z.B., Swami, A.: The limitations of deep learning in adversarial settings. In: IEEE European Symposium on Security and Privacy (EuroS&P), pp. 372–387. IEEE (2016)
8. Su, J., Vargas, D.V., Sakurai, K.: One pixel attack for fooling deep neural networks. IEEE Trans. Evol. Comput. **23**(5), 828–841 (2019)
9. Croce, F., Hein, M.: Reliable evaluation of adversarial robustness with an ensemble of diverse parameter-free attacks. In: International Conference on Machine Learning, pp. 2206–2216. PMLR (2020)
10. Jia, X., Wei, X., Cao, X., Foroosh, H.: ComDefend: an efficient image compression model to defend adversarial examples. In: Proceedings of the IEEE/CVF Conference on Computer Vision and Pattern Recognition, pp. 6084–6092 (2019)
11. Liao, F., Liang, M., Dong, Y., Pang, T., Hu, X., Zhu, J.: Defense against adversarial attacks using high-level representation guided denoiser. In: Proceedings of the IEEE Conference on Computer Vision and Pattern Recognition, pp. 1778–1787 (2018)
12. Song, Y., Kim, T., Nowozin, S., Ermon, S., Kushman, N.: PixelDefend: leveraging generative models to understand and defend against adversarial examples. arXiv preprint arXiv:1710.10766 (2017)
13. Meng, D., Chen, H.: MagNet: a two-pronged defense against adversarial examples. In: Proceedings of the 2017 ACM SIGSAC Conference on Computer and Communications Security, pp. 135–147 (2017)
14. Prakash, A., Moran, N., Garber, S., DiLillo, A., Storer, J.: Deflecting adversarial attacks with pixel deflection. In: Proceedings of the IEEE Conference on Computer Vision and Pattern Recognition, pp. 8571–8580 (2018)
15. Samangouei, P., Kabkab, M., Chellappa, R.: Defense-GAN: protecting classifiers against adversarial attacks using generative models. arXiv preprint arXiv:1805.06605 (2018)
16. Li, G., Ding, S., Luo, J., Liu, C.: Enhancing intrinsic adversarial robustness via feature pyramid decoder. In: Proceedings of the IEEE/CVF Conference on Computer Vision and Pattern Recognition, pp. 800–808 (2020)
17. Zhang, H., Sakurai, K.: Conditional generative adversarial network-based image denoising for defending against adversarial attack. IEEE Access **9**, 169 031–169 043 (2021)
18. Isola, P., Zhu, J.-Y., Zhou, T., Efros, A.A.: Image-to-image translation with conditional adversarial networks. In: Proceedings of the IEEE Conference on Computer Vision and Pattern Recognition, pp. 1125–1134 (2017)
19. Carlini, N., Wagner, D.: Towards evaluating the robustness of neural networks. In: 2017 IEEE Symposium on Security and Privacy (SP), pp. 39–57. IEEE (2017)
20. Zhang, S., Gao, H., Rao, Q.: Defense against adversarial attacks by reconstructing images. IEEE Trans. Image Process. **30**, 6117–6129 (2021)

21. Carlini, N., et al.: On evaluating adversarial robustness. arXiv preprint arXiv:1902.06705 (2019)
22. Tramer, F., Carlini, N., Brendel, W., Madry, A.: On adaptive attacks to adversarial example defenses. In: Advances in Neural Information Processing Systems, vol. 33, pp. 1633–1645 (2020)
23. Kurakin, A., Goodfellow, I., Bengio, S.: Adversarial machine learning at scale. arXiv preprint arXiv:1611.01236 (2016)
24. Tramèr, F., Kurakin, A., Papernot, N., Goodfellow, I., Boneh, D., McDaniel, P.: Ensemble adversarial training: attacks and defenses. arXiv preprint arXiv:1705.07204 (2017)
25. Kannan, H., Kurakin, A., Goodfellow, I.: Adversarial logit pairing. arXiv preprint arXiv:1803.06373 (2018)
26. Xie, C., Wu, Y., van der Maaten, L., Yuille, A.L., He, K.: Feature denoising for improving adversarial robustness. In: Proceedings of the IEEE/CVF Conference on Computer Vision and Pattern Recognition, pp. 501–509 (2019)
27. Shafahi, A., et al.: Adversarial training for free!. In: Advances in Neural Information Processing Systems, vol. 32 (2019)
28. Chakraborty, A., Alam, M., Dey, V., Chattopadhyay, A., Mukhopadhyay, D.: Adversarial attacks and defences: a survey. arXiv preprint arXiv:1810.00069 (2018)
29. Gross, S., Wilber, M.: Training and investigating residual nets (2016). http://torch. ch/blog/2016/02/04/resnets.html
30. Ioffe, S., Szegedy, C.: Batch normalization: accelerating deep network training by reducing internal covariate shift. In: International Conference on Machine Learning, pp. 448–456. PMLR (2015)
31. He, K., Zhang, X., Ren, S., Sun, J.: Delving deep into rectifiers: surpassing human-level performance on imagenet classification. In: Proceedings of the IEEE International Conference on Computer Vision, pp. 1026–1034 (2015)
32. Xie, C., Wang, J., Zhang, Z., Ren, Z., Yuille, A.: Mitigating adversarial effects through randomization. arXiv preprint arXiv:1711.01991 (2017)
33. Zhu, J.-Y., Park, T., Isola, P., Efros, A.A.: Unpaired image-to-image translation using cycle-consistent adversarial networks. In: Proceedings of the IEEE International Conference on Computer Vision, pp. 2223–2232 (2017)
34. Choi, Y., Choi, M., Kim, M., Ha, J.-W., Kim, S., Choo, J.: StarGAN: unified generative adversarial networks for multi-domain image-to-image translation. In: Proceedings of the IEEE Conference on Computer Vision and Pattern Recognition, pp. 8789–8797 (2018)
35. Liu, M.-Y., Breuel, T., Kautz, J.: Unsupervised image-to-image translation networks. In: Advances in Neural Information Processing Systems, vol. 30 (2017)
36. Goodfellow, I., et al.: Generative adversarial networks. Commun. ACM **63**(11), 139–144 (2020)
37. Mirza, M., Osindero, S.: Conditional generative adversarial nets. arXiv preprint arXiv:1411.1784 (2014)
38. Ronneberger, O., Fischer, P., Brox, T.: U-Net: convolutional networks for biomedical image segmentation. In: Navab, N., Hornegger, J., Wells, W.M., Frangi, A.F. (eds.) MICCAI 2015. LNCS, vol. 9351, pp. 234–241. Springer, Cham (2015). https://doi.org/10.1007/978-3-319-24574-4_28
39. Johnson, J., Alahi, A., Fei-Fei, L.: Perceptual losses for real-time style transfer and super-resolution. In: Leibe, B., Matas, J., Sebe, N., Welling, M. (eds.) ECCV 2016. LNCS, vol. 9906, pp. 694–711. Springer, Cham (2016). https://doi.org/10.1007/978-3-319-46475-6_43

40. Simonyan, K., Zisserman, A.: Very deep convolutional networks for large-scale image recognition. arXiv preprint arXiv:1409.1556 (2014)
41. Szegedy, C., Vanhoucke, V., Ioffe, S., Shlens, J., Wojna, Z.: Rethinking the inception architecture for computer vision. In: Proceedings of the IEEE Conference on Computer Vision and Pattern Recognition, pp. 2818–2826 (2016)
42. Russakovsky, O., et al.: ImageNet large scale visual recognition challenge. Int. J. Comput. Vis. **115**(3), 211–252 (2015). https://doi.org/10.1007/s11263-015-0816-y
43. Papernot, N., et al.: Technical report on the CleverHans v2.1.0 adversarial examples library. arXiv preprint arXiv:1610.00768 (2018)
44. Nicolae, M.-I., et al.: Adversarial robustness toolbox v1.2.0. CoRR, vol. 1807.01069 (2018). https://arxiv.org/pdf/1807.01069
45. Chikkerur, S., Sundaram, V., Reisslein, M., Karam, L.J.: Objective video quality assessment methods: a classification, review, and performance comparison. IEEE Trans. Broadcast. **57**(2), 165–182 (2011)
46. Wang, Z., Bovik, A.C., Sheikh, H.R., Simoncelli, E.P.: Image quality assessment: from error visibility to structural similarity. IEEE Trans. Image Process. **13**(4), 600–612 (2004)

Federated Learning Approach
for Distributed Ransomware Analysis

Aldin Vehabovic[1]([✉]), Hadi Zanddizari[1], Farook Shaikh[1], Nasir Ghani[1],
Morteza Safaei Pour[2], Elias Bou-Harb[3], and Jorge Crichigno[4]

[1] University of South Florida, Tampa, FL 33620, USA
{vehabovica,hadiz,nghani}@usf.edu
[2] San Diego State University, San Diego, CA 92182, USA
msafaeipour@sdsu.edu
[3] University of Texas San Antonio, San Antonio, TX 78249, USA
elias.bouharb@utsa.edu
[4] University of South Carolina, Columbia, SC 29208, USA
jcrichigno@cec.sc.edu

Abstract. Ransomware is a form of malware that uses encryption methods to prevent legitimate users from accessing their data files. To date, many ransomware families have been released, causing immense damage and financial losses for private users, corporations, and governments. As a result, researchers have proposed a range of ransomware detection schemes using various *machine learning* (ML) methods to analyze binary files and action sequences. However as this threat continues to proliferate, it is becoming increasingly difficult to collect and analyze massive amounts of ransomware executables and trace data at a common site (due to data privacy and scalability concerns). Hence this paper presents a novel *distributed ransomware analysis* (DRA) solution for detection and attribution using the decentralized *federated learning* (FL) framework. Detailed performance evaluation is then conducted for the case of static analysis with rapid/lightweight feature extraction using an up-to-date ransomware repository. Overall results confirm the effectiveness the FL-based solution.

Keywords: Ransomware · malware detection · federated learning

1 Introduction

Ransomware has evolved rapidly over the last decade and is now one of the most serious cyberthreats facing users and organizations today. This malware executes a multi-stage kill-chain to find and infect victim hosts, encrypt their data files, and extract ransom payments. Expectedly, ransomware represents one of the most lucrative revenue stream for cybercriminals today, many of who now offer *ransomware-as-a-service* (RaaS) [1] as well. Furthermore, many attackers are also targeting large organizations due to the potential of sizeable

J. Zhou et al. (Eds.): ACNS 2023 Workshops, LNCS 13907, pp. 621–641, 2023.
https://doi.org/10.1007/978-3-031-41181-6_33

payouts. Overall, many different ransomware "families" have been developed and weaponized, with most focusing on Windows users as this is still the most widely-used *operating systems* (OS) type in the enterprise today.

Given these challenges, researchers have been actively studying ransomware analysis schemes in recent years. The main objective in many of these efforts is to identify ransomware programs based on their static or dynamic characteristics and prevent harmful activities. For example, *static analysis* schemes [2] analyze the artifacts of malicious binary files. Hence these methods can be integrated into network-based defenses to analyze incoming files or attachments and detect ransomware earlier in the transmission stage of the kill-chain [1]. Meanwhile, *dynamic analysis* methods [2] track host system and/or network communication activities to detect ransomware after infection. These schemes can also be integrated into host/network-based defenses, but focus on later stages in the kill-chain (post-infection). Overall, many static and dynamic analysis designs also use *machine learning* (ML) algorithms to process large amounts of ransomware data and extract generalized behaviors, see surveys in [1–3].

Nevertheless, as ransomware threats continue to proliferate and diversify, users are being impacted across many domains and sectors. Therefore it is becoming increasingly difficult to collect and analyze massive amounts of ransomware executables and user/system/network trace data at a common (centralized) site. Clearly, this approach poses major privacy and scalability concerns. Foremost, off-site transmission and sharing of sensitive end-host data and network logs is problematic for many users and organizations [2]. Data pre-processing and ML training at a single location also imposes high computational burdens and bandwidth transfer overheads depending upon the type of data being shared (static, dynamic). Inevitably, these limitations complicate the real-world application of many ransomware solutions that use centralized ML training. In addition, most studies have used datasets containing a mixture of older ransomware families targeting Windows 7/8 systems (from mid-2010s time frame) [2].

In light of the above, there is a pressing need to develop new ransomware analysis schemes to detect *and* attribute the latest threats with improved scalability and privacy. Of key concern are threats targeting Windows 10/11, the most prevalent OS in enterprise environments. Hence this paper presents a novel ransomware solution which leverages *federated learning* (FL), a decentralized and collaborative ML framework designed to address scalability and privacy concerns [4,5]. Indeed, FL has already been applied to range of problems in image/voice recognition, keystroke prediction, smart grids, fraud detection, etc. [5,6]. Recent studies have also proposed some FL-based cybersecurity schemes, e.g., for *Internet of Things* (IoT) intrusion detection, network anomaly detection, and traffic recognition [7–10]. However the further application of this distributed ML paradigm for ransomware analysis (particularly detection and attribution) has not yet been considered. Hence this topic forms the key motivation for the work herein, and several key contributions are made:

1. Novel *distributed ransomware analysis* (DRA) architecture for ransomware detection and attribution based upon the FL framework. This solution

embodies a generic approach which can implement a wide range of static and dynamic ransomware analysis schemes.
2. Use of a new ransomware dataset repository with some of the latest families targeting Windows 10/11, i.e., including Babuk/Babyk, BlackCat, Chaos, DJVu/STOP, Hive, LockBit, Netwalker, Sodinokibi/REvil, and WannaCry. Since new malware can have much fewer available samples, this repository is limited to under 1,500 binary executables to model realistic scenarios.
3. Detailed evaluation of the DRA framework for the case of static ransomware analysis. Specifically, rapid/lightweight feature extraction is done using Windows *portable executable* (PE) files, and FL performance is then tested using decentralized *neural-network* (NN) based classifiers.

To the best of the authors' knowledge, this is the first known study on FL for ransomware detection and attribution. This paper is organized as follows. Section 2 presents a review of ransomware detection schemes as well as recent FL-based cybersecurity schemes. Subsequently, Sect. 3 details the new DRA architecture and its distributed FL algorithm. The ransomware dataset repository is then detailed in Sect. 4, including sample collection and feature selection/extraction. Detailed performance results are then presented in Sect. 5 for the case of static analysis, followed by conclusions and future work directions in Sect. 6.

2   Literature Review

Ransomware follows a well-established kill-chain sequence comprised of several key stages, i.e., reconnaissance, distribution/delivery, installation/infection, communication, encryption, and extortion/payment [2]. As a result, researchers have proposed a range of schemes for ransomware detection and mitigation targeting different stages in this sequence. A brief taxonomy and overview of some of these methods is presented along with recent FL-based security solutions.

2.1   Ransomware Detection

Ransomware analysis has received much attention in the past decade. Various survey articles have also appeared in this domain, detailing different (sometimes overlapping) taxonomies to classify the proposed solutions, e.g., including static or dynamic analysis schemes, network-based or host-based methods, forensic analysis techniques, etc. [1–3]. Consider some details.

Static analysis methods analyze binary malware executables to detect artifacts of malicious behaviors [1]. Common techniques here include code analysis for malware author attribution, code/segment de-anonymization, reverse engineering, ransomware server address and domain prediction, etc. [2]. For example, [11] specifies a multi-level framework to classify ransomware. This scheme analyzes raw binary files, assembly code, and libraries using Linux object-code dumps and portable executable parsers. ML classifiers are then trained using the extracted data, yielding detection rates around 90%. Meanwhile, [12] presents a scheme to analyze operational code sequences. These sequences are transformed into N-grams, and *term frequency-inverse document frequencies* (TF-IDF) features are generated to train classifiers (decision tree, RF, etc.). Results show detection rates around 90%. However, code-based analysis is a slow and labor-intensive approach [13] which is better suited for post-infection forensic analysis.

Recent efforts have also generated other features for static analysis. For example, [14] presents a unique ransomware classification scheme which uses image processing for feature extraction. Namely, ransomware binary files are first converted to grayscale images, and texture analysis is then used to compute features. Results for several classifiers show good accuracy (97%) for a small dataset containing a mix of older and newer ransomwares (379 samples). However, this scheme imposes higher computational burdens for large datasets and does not consider benign applications. Meanwhile, [15] details another static ransomware analysis scheme which computes/extracts entropy and image-based features from binary files and uses them to train a Siamese NN classifier. Tests for a small dataset with about 1,000 samples and 10 ransomware families show accuracy values in the mid-90% range but notably lower precision and recall rates (upper 70% range). Also, most of the ransomware families used here are older (from mid-2010s time frame) and benign applications are not considered.

Researchers have also used Windows PE format files for static malware analysis. These files contain metadata and other information for binary executables and enable very fast/lightweight feature extraction, i.e., versus more compute-intensive image or entropy-based methods above. However, most studies using PE files have focused on the generic malware detection problem (and not ransomware classification). For example, a 2016 study [16] uses malware samples from VX Heaven (now inactive) to train several ML-based detection classifiers using about 10 PE file features. Results show detection rates over 90%. Meanwhile, [17] extracts PE file features from a dataset with 5,500 malware and 1,200 benign samples (from the early 2010s) and uses customized rules to achieve 95% detection rates. Also, [18] extracts a small set of PE file features from a dataset with 1,200 malicious and benign samples. Several classifiers are then trained, yielding over 95% detection accuracy. However, these studies use malware datasets which are almost a decade old and provide few details on composition. To address this concern, [19] presents an updated study on ransomware detection *and* attribution using static PE file analysis. A new repository is curated comprising of 9 of the latest ransomware families (about 1,200 samples) and benign applications (2,000 samples). Results for several ML classifiers show impressive detection and attribution percentages in the mid-90% range with up to 15 features.

Meanwhile dynamic analysis examines run-time actions and events at the network and/or host levels. Namely, dynamic network-based schemes analyze packet traces for ransomware activity, e.g., server communications, *domain name service* (DNS) queries, networked storage access, etc. For example, [20] presents a detection scheme for the Locky ransomware (2016) which collects behavioral/non-behavioral traffic features in a testbed and then trains several classifiers. Results show a mean detection rate of 97%. Meanwhile, [21] presents a ransomware detection scheme using advanced *neural network* (NN) classifiers which yields over 97% detection rates for older ransomware threats such as CryptoWall, TorrentLocker, and Sage. The NetConverse scheme [22] also uses ML methods to analyze Windows host traffic for several families from the 2010s time frame. Results show high detection rates, over 95%. Finally, [23] presents a deep learning approach to detect and classify abnormal traffic from Windows 7 hosts, and results show high detection rates for several families.

Dynamic host-based schemes monitor local system activities to detect ransomware operations and possibly recover encryption keys. These methods are more latent as they use virtual run-time environments to execute binary files and capture traces, i.e., *virtual machines* (VM) or sandboxes. A range of actions can be tracked here, including *application programmer interface* (API) calls, *dynamic link library* (DLL) calls, and memory and file operations. For example, [24] monitors for file encryption/deletion, persistent desktop messages, etc. Results show successful detection of about 96% of older ransomware. Meanwhile, [25] presents a scheme to monitor/store encryption keys and facilitate ransomware detection and recovery. This solution can mitigate about 12 out of the 20 families tested. Recent efforts have also targeted ransomware "paranoia" activities, i.e., pre-attack actions to detect environments and avoid fingerprinting. For example, [26] monitors pre-attack API calls and uses *natural language processing* (NLP) to extract features. Findings confirm that many ransomware families generate distinguishable API fingerprints. Also, [27] presents a host-based framework for API call monitoring. Some older ransomware families (such as Reveton, Locky, Teslacrypt, etc.) are fingerprinted to extract features and build frequency pattern trees for real-time detection of API sequences.

Although the above works provide some key contributions, notable concerns still remain. Foremost, the majority of studies have focused on older ransomware families targeting dated Windows 7/8 systems (mid-2010s). Given the persistent nature of this malware, it is imperative to focus on newer threats to Windows 10/11 OS users. Furthermore, new releases will likely have fewer samples to analyze, posing added challenges. Hence "data-centric" ML solutions must achieve effective performance with constrained datasets. Finally, ransomware detection/attribution schemes must have amenable run-time complexity and ideally tackle threats in the earlier distribution/delivery stages to minimize damage [2]. It is here that static analysis is more expedient for examining suspicious executable payloads/downloads. By contrast, dynamic analysis requires more latent tracking and analysis of network or host activities and is better suited for latter stages in the kill-chain. Finally, it is important to consider attribution, i.e., ransomware classification, as this represents a logical next step after detection.

2.2   Federated Learning (FL) in Cybersecurity

FL is a decentralized learning framework developed by Google in 2016. This solution uses multiple end-point clients to train ML models under the coordination of a central server [4]. Namely, "global" learning is done over multiple (synchronous or asynchronous) communication rounds. In each round, the server selects a subset of clients and sends them its latest global ML model parameters. Clients then perform "local" training with their own data and only send back model parameter updates. The central server uses these updates to revise its global ML model parameters and then repeats the process.

Overall, FL provides some key benefits for large ML problems. Foremost, user privacy is greatly improved as sensitive data stays at local hosts. Computational scalability is also much better since many systems are involved in the distributed learning process. Finally, bandwidth scalability (efficiency) also increases since raw datasets do not need to be transferred to a central server. As a result, FL has seen strong traction in a diverse range of areas, e.g., image/voice recognition, keystroke prediction, smart grid operation, fraud detection etc. [5,6]. Many further variants of this approach have also been proposed, as surveyed in [28]. Although a detailed review of these works is out of scope herein, some key contributions include revised training and averaging methods for unbalanced datasets, compression/quantization methods to reduce FL communication overheads, client failure recovery techniques, detection and mitigation of malicious clients (adversarial FL), and fully distributed "peer-to-peer" FL schemes.

Now researchers have also applied FL to the security domain. For example, [7] presents a FL framework to train *deep NN* (DNN) models for multiple tasks such as anomaly detection, traffic recognition, and classification. Tests with older traffic profiles (2016) show good detection accuracies for various anomalous events, on par with centralized schemes. Meanwhile, [8] details a FL-based DeepFeed solution for intrusion detection in cyberphysical systems using *convolutional NN* (CNN) models. Results with real-world industrial network data show good detection accuracy, exceeding some centralized schemes. Meanwhile, [9] presents a FL scheme for anomaly detection of compromised IoT devices. Here, local access gateways monitor traffic and map packet streams to symbols. Language processing methods are then used in conjunction with *recurrent NN* (RNN) algorithms. Results for the Mirai malware show very good attack detection (over 95%) and low run-time complexity. Finally, [10] presents another FL approach for IoT malware detection using supervised and unsupervised ML algorithms for anomaly detection (with packet data). Again, FL gives very good performance, closely matching centralized classifiers. The authors also test several adversarial FL setups with model poisoning attacks. Results show a notable decline in accuracy when over 25% of clients are compromised. However, as noted earlier, the further application of FL for ransomware analysis has not been considered.

3 Distributed Ransomware Analysis (DRA)

The continued growth of ransomware is posing many operational challenges for threat detection and mitigation. Most notably, it is increasingly difficult (infeasible) to collect large amounts of raw data from massive user bases and transfer it to a common site for analysis. Indeed, privacy concerns will prevent many users and organizations from sharing their sensitive file/trace logs in the first place.

Additionally, bandwidth transfer overheads can be very high, and a single centralized computing facility may not be able to process extreme amounts of data and train large models. Inevitably, these constraints will limit the effectiveness of ML-based solutions. Hence there is a pressing need to develop new ransomware analysis frameworks which address these critical concerns.

Now scalability and privacy demands in large ML problems are not new, and researchers have proposed various solutions such as privacy preserving computation and *federated learning* (FL) [4] (Sect. 2.2). Of these, the latter is the most scalable as it distributes and decentralizes training over multiple computational nodes. Hence a novel *distributed ransomware analysis* (DRA) solution is developed using the FL framework. This setup is shown in Fig. 1 and comprises of several *client sites* communicating with a *central server*. This architecture features a generic design that can be tailored for a full range of ransomware analysis schemes, both static and dynamic (Sect. 2.1). Furthermore, it is assumed that the whole setup operates in a trusted manner, i.e., careful vetting/pre-selection of client sites, authenticated and encrypted communications, encryption of training data, etc. The DRA architecture and its associated FL algorithm are now presented, followed by a detailed performance evaluation study in Sect. 5.

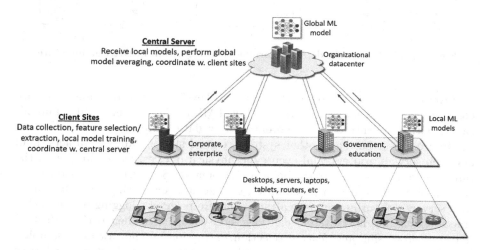

Fig. 1. Distributed ransomware analysis (DRA) framework using federated learning

3.1   Client Sites

Client sites in the DRA architecture mirror the roles of client nodes in the FL architecture [4]. These entities are located at carefully-selected, trusted organizations with large user bases, e.g., such as corporate campuses, government facilities, academic institutions, and even network service provider *points of presence* (PoP). Note that it is not feasible for individual systems (such as servers, laptops, etc.) to act as FL clients. The main reason here is that individual devices will not be able to collect a sufficient number of ransomware samples for effective ML training (data scarcity). Hence DRA client roles are placed at vetted institutional sites which have access to much larger volumes of raw data from many users and systems. As there are generally fewer client sites involved here, i.e., tens-hundreds, this approach embodies a cross-silo FL approach [10].

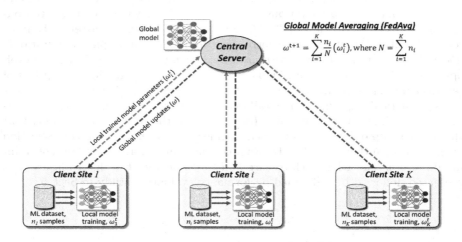

Fig. 2. Logical view of federated learning (FL) algorithm in DRA architecture

Overall, DRA client sites perform several key functions, including raw data collection, feature selection/extraction, local ML model training, and communication with the central server. Foremost, raw data samples are collected from the internal user base and other systems, e.g., desktops, laptops, tablets, mail and web servers, routers, and even cyberphysical devices. Depending upon the ransomware analysis approach being implemented (Sect. 2.1), data acquisition can entail a wide range of possibilities, e.g., such as extracting email files from mail servers, capturing webpage attachments from servers, logging router packet traces, extracting host/system call logs, etc. Client sites then perform further data pre-processing and feature selection/extraction on the raw data samples. Namely, feature selection identifies a subset of parameters of interest, whereas feature extraction selects parameters to generate ML insights. The extracted features are then collected to build a local ML training/testing dataset, Fig. 1.

Now client sites must also communicate with the central server to participate in the distributed FL training process. A logical overview of this strategy is shown in Fig. 2, along with sample client site psuedocode in Fig. 3. Namely, the training process is jumpstarted when a client site receives parameters for the initial global ML model from the central server, i.e., denoted by ω. Since NN-based algorithms are most amenable to FL implementation [5], these parameters will typically correspond to weight vectors for *feedforward NN* (FNN), *deep NN* (DNN), *convolutional NN* (CNN), or *long short-term memory* (LSTM) networks

#

Input: Receive global ML model parameters from central server, ω

Partition local ML dataset (n_i samples) into B batches

/* *Train local ML model over given epochs and batches* */

for j=1 to E **do**

   for k=1 to B **do**

      Train local model over k-th batch of data

      Update local ML model parameters $\omega \rightarrow \omega_i^t$

Output: Send updated ML model parameters, ω_i^t, to central server

Fig. 3. Centralized FL local training algorithm at client site i

[29]. Client sites then train the received model using their local data. In particular, it is assumed that client site i has a local ML dataset with n_i samples, and this is further split into B batches for training over E epochs, see Fig. 3. Finally, the updated local model parameters at each round t, ω_i^t, are sent back to the central server for further processing and updating. Overall, localized model training allows client sites to retain their sensitive data.

3.2 Central Server

The central server in the DRA architecture manages the distributed, decentralized ML training process for ransomware analysis. Akin to its namesake in the FL setup [4], this entity communicates with the client sites to update the global ML model parameters. Sample psuedocode for the central server algorithm is also presented in Fig. 4 based upon the FedAvg algorithm [4]. Namely, training is done over T communication rounds with the client sites. In each round, the central server selects a subset of K client sites to participate in the training and sends them its latest global model parameters, ω. It then waits for the local client training sessions to complete and receives/processes parameter updates, i.e., where ω_i^t denotes the updated ML model parameters from client site i in round t (Figs. 3, 4). Note that Fig. 4 shows a synchronous FL training approach where all clients respond in each iteration. However, this detail is not specific to the DRA architecture and can be easily modified for asynchronous operation, e.g., by specifying client site selection and update processing [4,5].

Finally, client site updates are appropriately averaged to revise the global ML model parameters, ω. Although a wide range of options are possible here, without loss of generality, the FedAvg [4,5] approach is used in Figs. 2 and 4. Namely, model averaging is done in a weighted manner based upon the size of each client site's dataset, i.e., proportional to $\frac{n_i}{N}$, where $N = \sum_i n_i$ is the aggregate amount of training data across all K client sites chosen. Overall, this method is well-suited for *independent identically distributed* (IID) datasets. However, researchers have also proposed modified FL server averaging schemes for

---

Input: Initial global ML model parameters, ω_0

/* Iterative FL training process over T rounds */
for $t = 1$ to T **do**

Select K client sites

for $i = 1$ to K **do**
Send latest global ML model ω to i-th client site

Wait to receive local updates from all K client sites, ω_i^t

Average to update global ML model parameters: $\omega \leftarrow \omega^{t+1} = \sum_{i=1}^{K} \frac{n_i}{N} \omega_i^t$

Output: Final global ML model parameters, ω

Fig. 4. Centralized FL averaging algorithm at central server

heterogeneous (non-IID) local data [5], and these techniques can be further integrated into the central server algorithm (left for future study).

4 Ransomware Dataset Repository

Realistic datasets are critical for effective ML solutions. However, as noted in Sect. 2, most ransomware detection studies have at least in part, used older datasets with Windows 7 malwares. Indeed, many old ransomware control servers are no longer active as malactors have shifted to other families. In light of this, the new ransomware dataset repository curated in [19] is used. This dataset contains binary executables of some of the most prevalent ransomware threats today, as per the IBM X-Force Threat Intelligence Index, i.e., Babuk/Babyk, BlackCat, Chaos, DJVu/STOP, Hive, LockBit, Netwalker, Sodinokibi/REvil, and WannaCry (Table 1). Namely, 9 families are chosen, and a number of Windows application executables are also collected to build a benign class and improve classifier performance. As per Fig. 5, repository design involves two key steps, empirical data collection and feature extraction/selection, detailed next.

4.1 Empirical Data Collection

The work in [19] collects a realistic set of raw binary files, with the goal of mirroring data collection at client sites (Sect. 3.1). Now the size and diversity of input data will impact ML classifier performance. For example, most algorithms yield better generalization (class separation) with larger datasets and equal representation across classes. However, given the rapidly-changing nature of ransomware, it can be difficult to obtain a sufficient number of samples for each family under consideration. Hence effective solutions must achieve good detection and attribution performance with more constrained "minimalist" datasets, i.e., only hundreds of samples per ransomware family. Note that other recent studies have also used smaller datasets with under 2,000 samples [14,15]. This requirement is well-aligned with broader trends in *artificial intelligence* (AI) to develop more "data-centric" solutions for specialized problems [30]. Consider some further details.

Malware samples are extracted from various online sites to capture some of the latest ransomware threats. Now many portals allow users to upload/download malware executables, e.g., `MalwareBazar`, `Triage`, `VirusShare`, and `VirusTotal`, etc. However, these repositories provide varying access and usability. For example, `VirusTotal` and `VirusShare` require user registration to access private repositories. Detailed cross-checking and analysis of samples also reveals notable duplication across portals. For example, many Sodinokibi samples on `MalwareBazar` match those on `Triage`. There is also notable discrepancy between the number of samples for each family. For example DJVu is relatively abundant whereas Babuk/Babyk is more scarce and harder to find. Finally, repositories (such as `VirusShare`) do not label their raw data, further complicating collection. Hence samples from these large unlabeled data dumps have to be analyzed individually using hashing programs and then cross-checked with other labelled samples (a tedious and time-consuming process). While other repositories like `VirusTotal` may have labelled samples, they do not allow researchers to download them freely. Given these realities, there is potential for a lack of diversity (even scarcity) of unique samples for new ransomware families.

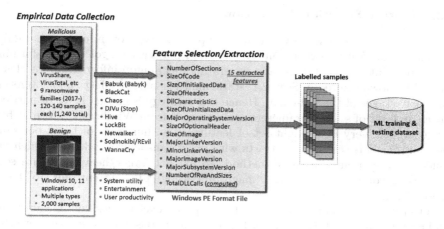

Fig. 5. Ransomware repository design and static PE file features (as per [19])

In light of the above, a "minimalist" raw dataset is collected for the 9 ransomware families [19]. Specifically, only 140 executable samples are gathered for each family, yielding a total of 1,260 malicious samples (under 1,500 samples). However, unlike some recent studies in ransomware classification [14,15], a large number of Windows 10/11 applications are also downloaded to build a benign

Table 1. Empirical ransomware dataset (as per [19])

Family	Samples	Avg. Size	Avg. PE File
Babuk (Babyk)	140	0.19 MB	32.68 KB
BlackCat	140	3.91 MB	1,147 KB
Chaos	140	0.49 MB	35.2 KB
DJVu (STOP)	140	0.71 MB	66.2 KB
Hive	140	3.51 MB	403.9 KB
LockBit	140	1.30 MB	171.5 KB
Netwalker	140	0.26 MB	35.72 KB
Sodinokibi	140	0.30 MB	50.89 KB
WannaCry	140	7.62 MB	21.83 KB
Benign	2,000	26.86 MB	155.88 KB

class (2,000 in total). These programs are collected from a range of websites and include system utility, entertainment, and productivity tools (Fig. 5). Overall, the addition of a benign class is crucial for ML purposes as it can help establish a more clear delineation between malicious programs and reduce classification errors. Further details on the collected samples are also presented in Table 1.

4.2   Feature Selection/Extraction

ML performance is also very dependent upon the type of input training data. It is here that feature extraction (engineering) plays a vital role in transforming raw sample files (executables) and generating meaningful information for classifiers [29]. Now as noted in Sect. 2.1, static analysis is more effective for targeting the early stages of the kill-chain. Hence this strategy is chosen here. In particular a small set of static parameters are extracted from Windows PE format files to generate a very lightweight set of features (i.e., hundreds of bytes per sample, Fig. 5). This selection contrasts with other ransomware schemes which use much more compute-intensive methods to extract larger/heavier feature sets, e.g., using code extraction [12], image processing [14], and entropy [15] based methods.

Overall, PE format files are used to support executables running in 32-bit and 64-bit Windows OS settings [31] (and similar constructs also exist for other OS types). This file uses the *common object file format* (COFF) and contains key information for the OS loader to run wrapped executable code. Namely, a PE file specifies memory mapping and permissions and is comprised of initial lead-in headers and multiple sections. Each section contains actual file contents (such as code or data) and has its own header [31]. Overall, PE files contain a wealth of static information, and different executables can have unique non-overlapping parameters as per functionality. As a result, it is important to extract a proper subset of parameters here, i.e., feature vectors. Foremost, a chosen feature should exist in the PE format files for all executables in the repository. Additionally, selected parameter ranges should exhibit sufficient variability across classes.

In light of the above, PE files are generated for all raw executable files. Careful experimentation is then done to select a total of 15 PE file parameters and construct labelled feature vectors to build the aggregate ML training/testing dataset, Fig. 5 (i.e., 1,260 ransomware vectors and 2,000 benign vectors). Only entries from the *Image_File_Header*, *Image_Optional_Header*, and *Image_Section_Header* sections are chosen here, along the lines of earlier studies in [16–18]. Some selected PE parameters include *NumberOfSections*, *SizeOfCode*, *SizeOfHeaders*, etc. Note that PE format files also contain information on *dynamic-link library* (DLL) calls, and this can shed light on program functionality. For example, most ransomware programs use encryption, socket-based communication, and registry-modification functions. Hence the total number of DLL calls is also added to the feature vector, i.e., *TotalDLLCalls* (Fig. 5). Note that this is a *computed* feature and not a parameter read in from the PE file.

5   Performance Evaluation

As detailed in Sect. 3, the DRA architecture represents a generic approach which can implement a wide range of (NN-based) ransomware analysis schemes. Hence this framework is evaluated for the case of static analysis using the ML training/testing dataset curated in Sect. 4. All model development and testing is done using the Keras and TensorFlow libraries, along with other Python-based toolkits such as Pandas, Numpy, and Sklearn. Complete details on the testing setup and results from the performance evaluation study are now presented.

Table 2. Aggregate dataset partitioning (1,260 ransomware and 2,000 benign samples)

Clients	Ransomware					Benign		Malware %
	Training		Testing			Training	Testing	
	Per Family	Total	Per Family	Total				
$K = 1$	120	1,080	20	180		1,700	300	38%
$K = 2$	60	540	20	180		1,700	300	24%
$K = 3$	40	360	20	180		1,700	300	17%
$K = 4$	30	270	20	180		1,700	300	14%

FL performance is tested for a varying number of client sites ($K = 2, 3, 4$) by partitioning the ML training/testing dataset, see Table 2. Recall that this aggregate dataset contains feature vectors (samples) for each raw binary file (where each feature vector contains 15 extracted PE file parameters, Fig. 5). Now there are 140 samples per family and 2,000 benign applications, i.e., total of 10 classes. Hence 120 samples from each ransomware family are randomly selected for training (1,080 total) and the remaining 20 are used for testing (180 total). This partitioning represents a 85/15% split between training and testing data. Next, the 120 ransomware samples (per class) are further partitioned between the client sites, yielding several local ML training datasets, i.e., full 120 samples per class for $K = 1$ (centralized ML), 60 samples per class for $K = 2$ client sites (540 total), 40 samples per class for $K = 3$ client sites (360 total), and 30 samples per class for $K = 4$ client sites (270 total), see Table 2. Meanwhile the benign dataset is not partitioned between the client sites, thereby yielding a higher percentage of non-malicious training data. This choice mirrors realistic settings where regular applications downloads will exceed ransomware downloads. Moreover, there may be high commonality between application downloads across organizations, and hence it is plausible to use the same set of benign samples across client sites. Accordingly, the benign samples are split in a 85/15% manner, with 1,700 samples randomly selected for training and the remaining 300 for testing (per client site). Overall, the proportion of ransomware training data declines with the number of client sites, i.e., malware percentage, Table 2. For example, with 4 client sites there is more than 6 times less training data (i.e., 270 vs 1,700 samples). Carefully note that in practice, different regions (client sites) will experience varying types of ransomware attacks. These differences will yield unbalanced datasets with possibly different underlying distributions, and are left for future study.

Ransomware analysis is conducted using a range of supervised ML classifiers. These algorithms are trained and tested for the classification/attribution problem with 10 classes, i.e., 9 ransomware, 1 benign (Sect. 4). Foremost, the FL approach uses the supervised FNN algorithm (with gradient descent) to train local ML models at client sites. This network has 2 hidden layers and 32 nodes per layer, yielding a relatively small set of parameter weights (i.e., ω, Sect. 3). As noted earlier, FL can be used with many NN variants, but the FNN algorithm is chosen here given the smaller dataset sizes and feature vectors involved. Client sites train their local models over E epochs and send model parameter updates to the central server. Meanwhile, global training is done over T rounds. Several centralized ML algorithms are also used for comparison purposes, including centralized FNN ($K = 1$), *support vector machines* (SVM), and *random forest* (RF) [29]. These classifiers are evaluated using the complete dataset with a 85/15% partitioning between training/testing samples. All results (FL, centralized) are averaged over 50 independent trails, with each using different randomized selections of the requisite dataset partitions. The control parameters for different ML algorithms are also fine-tuned to achieve the best classification rates.

Several metrics are used to gauge the ML classifiers, including accuracy, precision, recall, and F1 score. For example, precision is a measure of correctness whereas recall is a measure of relevance [29]. Two additional metrics are also defined to capture the *binary* detection capabilities of multi-class classifiers, i.e., selection between ransomware and benign. Consider mis-classification in more detail. Here, incorrectly classifying ransomware as benign is much more problematic than mis-classifying it as another family (as it may bypass network or host defenses). To quantify this, a *ransomware detection rate* (RDR) is defined:

$$RDR = \frac{T_{rs}}{T_{rs} + F_{rs}} \tag{1}$$

where T_{rs} is the total number of ransomware testing samples across all families that are classified as (any family of) ransomware, and F_{rs} is the total number of ransomware testing samples across all families that are mis-classified as benign, i.e., total number of ransomware testing samples is $(T_{rs} + F_{rs})$. This metric is similar to recall and treats all ransomware families as a single malicious class, i.e., tracks false negatives. Similarly, a *benign detection rate* (BDR) is also defined:

$$BDR = \frac{T_{bn}}{T_{bn} + F_{bn}} \tag{2}$$

where T_{bn} is the total number of benign testing samples classified as benign, and F_{bn} is the total number of benign testing samples mis-classified as ransomware, i.e., total number of benign testing samples is $(T_{bn} + F_{bn})$. Note that the false negative classification of benign applications is generally less of a security threat than false negative classification of ransomware programs.

Table 3. Results for FL with varying client sites, K (FedAvg)

2 Client Sites	Accuracy	Precision	Recall	F1 Score
Global Avg. Model	**91.87%**	**86.01%**	**86.67%**	**91.82%**
Client site 1	86.52%	78.57%	79.37%	86.30%
Client site 2	88.34%	78.59%	79.22%	87.34%
3 Client Sites	Accuracy	Precision	Recall	F1 Score
Global Avg. Model	**92.11%**	**87.40%**	**86.57%**	**91.90%**
Client site 1	86.02%	77.86%	75.64%	85.33%
Client site 2	82.90%	73.89%	74.56%	82.13%
Client site 3	81.47%	73.55%	75.95%	81.49%
4 Client Sites	Accuracy	Precision	Recall	F1 Score
Global Avg. Model	**92.46%**	**87.69%**	**86.40%**	**92.43%**
Client site 1	79.93%	72.22%	72.61%	79.53%
Client site 2	83.70%	73.29%	74.41%	83.48%
Client site 3	85.48%	71.91%	71.73%	83.76%
Client site 4	85.49%	72.23%	71.41%	80.20%

Detailed results for the FL scheme are first presented in Table 3 for varying numbers of client sites (K values). In each case, the table lists the accuracy, precision, recall, and F1 scores for the global averaged FNN model (in bold) followed by the individual local client site models. These findings show vastly improved model generalization with FL, with the global models exceeding the individual client models by sizeable margins for all metrics. For example, average accuracy is 3–12% higher, precision is 7–15% higher, recall is 7–15% higher, and F1 scores are 4–13% higher. These are very impressive results and indicate that organizations can greatly improve their ransomware defenses by participating in FL-based schemes, i.e., while retaining data privacy and maintaining smaller datasets. Furthermore, FL accuracy is also very high. For example, the accuracy (and F1 score) with 4 client sites is close to 92.5%, i.e., correct attribution of over 18 out of 20 samples. These results also closely match some centralized ransomware classification schemes (Sect. 2.1) many of which implement heavier feature extraction and ML computation algorithms, e.g., image and entropy-based features, deep NN designs, etc. [14,15]. By contrast, the FL setup herein uses very small feature vectors (15 parameters) and basic FNN models.

Table 4. Results for ML models (averaged over 50 independent runs)

| Distd. FL | Accuracy | Precision | Recall | F1 Score | Binary | |
					RDR	BDR
2 clients (FNN)	91.87%	86.01%	86.67%	91.82%	94.92%	94.99%
3 clients (FNN)	92.11%	87.40%	86.57%	91.90%	93.04%	95.86%
4 clients (FNN)	92.46%	87.69%	86.40%	92.43%	93.27%	96.43%
Centralized	Accuracy	Precision	Recall	F1 Score	Binary	
					RDR	BDR
FNN	91.48%	86.84%	84.68%	91.27%	92.06%	96.69%
SVM	90.44%	91.16%	75.60%	89.86%	80.39%	97.85%
RF	96.02%	94.41%	92.07%	95.98%	95.72%	99.05%

Next, the performance of all ML classifiers is presented in Table 4. Here the respective FL percentages are the same as the global model averages from Table 3. First consider multi-class attribution, as measured by the accuracy, precision, recall, and F1 scores. Foremost, the FL approach outperforms its centralized FNN counterpart for varying numbers of client sites. In particular with $K = 4$ client sites the accuracy and F1 scores are 1% higher. These gains come despite using much smaller training datasets at the client sites, e.g., only 270 ransomware samples for $K = 4$, Table 2. Again, this is another key result as it demonstrates the ability of decentralized FL setups (with smaller client sites) to achieve similar or better ransomware attribution compared to less practical centralized setups (requiring much more training data). Furthermore, the FL approach also outperforms the SVM algorithm by over 2% in terms of accuracy. However, the centralized RF scheme (trained with global data) gives the best results, with accuracy and F1 scores averaging about 3.5% higher than FL.

Also, Table 4 presents *binary* detection results, as measured by the RDR and BDR metrics (Eqs. 1, 2). The former is deemed more important as it captures the mis-classification rate of ransomware. Overall, FL gives very good RDR values, up to 94.92%, and within 1% of the RF scheme which has the best

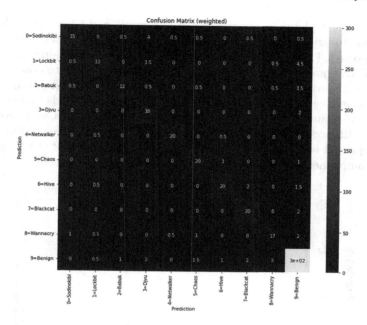

Fig. 6. Sample multi-class confusion matrix for FL ($K = 4$ client sites, $E = 1$ epoch)

binary results. Namely, this scheme yields a false negative rate of about 1 in 20 malicious samples. These results are impressive and match those from earlier studies on binary detection of older ransomware threats, Sect. 2. Also, the BDR values are higher than the RDR values since training datasets have a larger proportion of benign data as per real-world settings (Table 2). Note that the FNN-based schemes (including distributed FL) give slightly lower BDR values than the other ML algorithms, i.e., by about 1–2.5%. Nevertheless, the related BDR percentages are still close to 97%, i.e., 1 error in about 33 benign samples.

To investigate detailed per-class behaviors, Fig. 6 shows a sample averaged confusion matrix for FL with 4 client sites (rows 0–9 represent ransomware families and row 10 represents benign applications). Note that the numbers in row 10 are larger as there are more benign testing samples, Table 2. Here, the majority of ransomware and benign application samples are correctly classified, i.e., diagonal entries dominate. Furthermore, most mis-attributed ransomware samples are still classified as some form of ransomware, although LockBit and Babuk show higher averages, i.e., 4.5 (22.5%) and 3.5 (17.5%) out of 20, respectively. Hence the potential damage from false negatives is relatively small for most ransomware cases. Meanwhile, Fig. 7 plots the average accuracy and F1 scores for the global FL model with $K = 4$ client sites and varying epoch counts (E). These results shed light on the local FL training process and indicate better performance with $E = 4$ epochs (also observed for several other K values).

Finally, Fig. 8 plots the accuracy, precision, recall, and F1 scores at the end of each communication round for the global FL model with $K = 4$ client sites (and $E = 4$ epochs). For reference sake, corresponding accuracy values for the centralized FNN classifier are also plotted. The objective here is to observe the FL training process over multiple rounds. These plots show very rapid progression, with performance improving rapidly within the first 10 rounds and stabilizing by about 15 rounds. By contrast, the centralized FNN tales more rounds to improve, with accuracy picking up after 9 rounds. Overall, these results demonstrate improved responsiveness and learning with the distributed FL approach, further complementing its inherent privacy and scalability benefits.

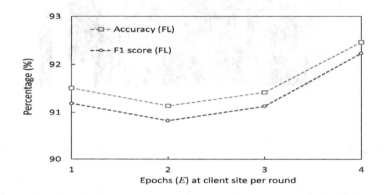

Fig. 7. Accuracy and F1 score results for $K = 4$ client sites (averaged over 50 trials)

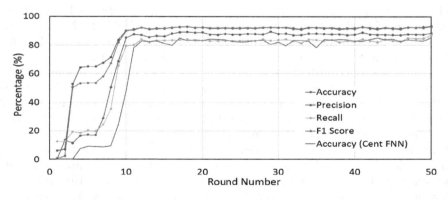

Fig. 8. Sample progression of FL training (`FedAvg`, $K = 4$ client sites, $E = 4$ epochs)

6   Conclusions and Future Work

Ransomware presents a persistent threat to users and organizations. Researchers have developed various solutions to detect and classify this malware using *machine learning* (ML) schemes to analyze binary files and system/network activities. However, growing scalability and privacy concerns make it difficult to collect and analyze massive amounts of data at a centralized site. Hence this study presents a novel *distributed ransomware analysis* (DRA) framework for detection and attribution using *federated learning* (FL). This architecture embodies a generic approach which can implement both static and dynamic analysis schemes. A realistic dataset repository comprising of some of the latest ransomware threats is used to conduct a detailed performance evaluation study for the case of static analysis with rapid/lightweight feature extraction from Windows *portable executable* (PE) format files. Overall findings confirm superior performance for the FL-based approach, with global ML model performance notably exceeding locally trained models. The FL approach also closely matches or outperforms some centralized ML algorithms in terms of attribution accuracy and binary detection.

Overall, this effort presents one of the first studies on ransomware detection and attribution using the decentralized FL framework and provides a strong basis for further study. Foremost, a broader set of static and dynamic features can be used to improve local model training (leveraging existing work on ransomware detection). Further efforts can also address FL bias and variability concerns.

Acknowledgements. This work has been supported in part by Cyber Florida. The authors are very grateful for this support.

References

1. Moussaileb, R., Cuppens, N., Lanet, J.-L.: Bouder: a survey on windows-based ransomware taxonomy and detection mechanisms: case closed? ACM Comput. Surv. **54**(6), 1–36 (2022)
2. Vehabovic, A., Ghani, N., Bou-Harb, E., Crichigno, J., Yayimli, A.: Ransomware detection and classification strategies. In: IEEE Black Sea Communications Conference 2022, Sofia, Bulgaria (2022)
3. Berrueta, E., Morato, D., Magaña, E., Izal, M.: A survey on detection techniques for cryptographic ransomware. IEEE Access **7**, 144 925–144 944 (2019)
4. McMahan, H.: Communication-efficient learning of deep learning from decentralized data. In: AISTATS 2017. Ft. Lauderdale, FL (2017)
5. Li, Q., et al.: A survey on federated learning systems: vision, hype and reality for data privacy and protection. arXiv:1907.09693 (2021)
6. Hudson, N., Hossain, M., Hosseinzadeh, M. Khamfroush, H., Naeini, M., Ghani, N.: A framework for edge intelligent smart distribution grids via federated learning. In: IEEE ICCCN 2021 (2021)
7. Zhao, Y., Chen, J., Wu, D., Teng, J., Yu, S.: Multitask network anomaly detection using federated learning. In: 10th International Symposium on Information and Communication Technology (SoICT 2019), Ha Long Bay, Vietnam (2019)
8. Li, B., Wu, Y., Song, J., Lu, R., Li, T., Zhao, L.: DeepFed: federated deep learning for intrusion detection in industrial cyberphysical systems. IEEE Trans. Ind. Inf. **17**(8), 5615–5624 (2021)

9. Nguyen, T., Marchal, S., Miettinen, M., Fereidooni, H., Asokan, N., Sadeghi, A.: Dïot: a federated selflearning anomaly detection system for IoT. In: IEEE International Conference on Distributed Computing Systems (ICDCS), Dallas, TX (2019)

10. Rey, V., Sanchez, P., Celdran, A., Bovet, G., Jaggi, M.: Federated learning for malware detection in IoT devices. arXiv:2104.09994 (2021)

11. Poudyal, S., Subedi, K.P., Dasgupta, D.: A framework for analyzing ransomware using machine learning. In: IEEE 2018 SSCI (2018)

12. Zhang, H., Xiao, X., Mercaldo, F., Ni, S., Martinelli, F., Sangaiah, A.: Classification of ransomware families with machine learning based on N-gram of opcodes. Futur. Gener. Comput. Syst. **90**, 211–221 (2019)

13. Mulders, D.: Network based ransomware detection on the samba protocol. MS thesis, Department of Mathematics, TU Eindhoven (2017)

14. Wang, B., Liu, H., Han, X., Xuan, D.: Image-based ransomware classification with classifier combination. In: ACM Advanced Information Science and System (ACM AISS), Sanya, China (2021)

15. Zhu, J., Jang-Jaccard, J., Singh, A., Welch, I., Harith, A.S., Camtepe, S.: A few-shot meta-learning based Siamese neural network using entropy features for ransomware classification. Comput. Secur. **117**, 1–11 (2022)

16. Kim, D., Woo, S., Lee, D., Chung, T.: Static detection of malware and benign executable using machine learning. In: 8th International Conference on Evolving Internet, Barcelona, Spain (2016)

17. Liao, Y.: PE-header-based malware study and detection. Semantic Scholar (2021)

18. Rezaei, T., Hamze, A.: An efficient approach for malware detection using PE header specifications. In: 6th International Conference on Web Research (ICWR), Tehran, Iran (2020)

19. Vehabovic, A., et al.: Data-centric machine learning approach for early ransomware detection and attribution. In: 8th IEEE/IFIP NOMS Workshop on Analytics for Network and Service Management (AnNet 2023), Florida, Miami (2023)

20. Almashhadani, A., Kaiiali, M., Sezer, S., O'Kane, P.: A multi-classifier network-based crypto ransomware detection system: a case study of Locky ransomware. IEEE Access **7**(1), 47 053–47 067 (2019)

21. Homayoun, S., Dehghantanha, A., Ahmadzadeh, M., Hashemi, S.: DRTHIS: deep ransomware threat hunting and intelligence system at the fog layer. Future Gener. Comput. Syst. **90**, 94–104 (2019)

22. Alhawi, O.M.K., Baldwin, J., Dehghantanha, A.: Leveraging machine learning techniques for windows ransomware network traffic detection. In: Dehghantanha, A., Conti, M., Dargahi, T. (eds.) Cyber Threat Intelligence. AIS, vol. 70, pp. 93–106. Springer, Cham (2018). https://doi.org/10.1007/978-3-319-73951-9_5

23. Roy, K.C., Chen, Q.: DeepRan: attention-based BiLSTM and CRF for ransomware early detection and classification. Inf. Syst. Front. **23**(2), 299–315 (2020). https://doi.org/10.1007/s10796-020-10017-4

24. Kharaz, A., Arshad, S., Mulliner, C., Robertson, W., Kirda, E.: UNVEIL: a large-scale, automated approach to detecting ransomware. In: USENIX Security 2016, Austin, TX (2016)

25. Kolodenker, E., Koch, W., Stringhini, G., Egele, M.: PayBreak: defense against cryptographic ransomware. In: Asia CCS 2017, Abu Dhabi, UAE (2017)

26. Molina, R.M.A., Torabi, S., Sarieddine, K., Bou-Harb, E., Bouguila, N., Assi, C.: On ransomware family attribution using pre-attack paranoia activities. IEEE Trans. Netw. Serv. Manag. **19**(1), 19–36 (2022)

27. Molina, R.M.A.: RPM: ransomware prevention and mitigation using operating systems sensing tactics (2022, submitted)

28. Kairouz, P.: Advances and open problems in federated learning. arXiv:1912.04977 (2021)
29. Geron, A.: Hands-On Machine Learning with Scikit-Learn, Keras, and TensorFlow, 2nd edn. O'Reily Media (2022)
30. Ng, A.: Ai minimalist. IEEE Spectr. **59**(4), 23–25 (2022)
31. Li, Q.: Definitive Guide to Windows PE Large Systems Security Technology. Machinery Industry Press (2000)

Forensic Identification of Android Trojans Using Stacked Ensemble of Deep Neural Networks

Mohammed M. Alani[1,2(✉)] (ID), Atefeh Mashatan[1] (ID), and Ali Miri[1] (ID)

[1] Toronto Metropolitan University, Toronto, Canada
m@alani.me, {amashatan,ali.miri}@torontomu.ca
[2] Seneca College of applied Arts and Technology, Toronto, Canada

Abstract. As the user base of Android operating system grows steadily, the ecosystem became a growing target for malicious actors. With Trojans representing over 93% of all Android malware, this type of malicious code becomes a serious threat to Android users. In this paper, we present a forensic identification system to identify Android trojan families based on dynamic features extracted from malicious applications. Our proposed system is based on a stacked ensemble of deep neural networks. The proposed system was tested using CIC-AndMal-2020 dataset, and have shown accuracy and F_1 score exceeding 0.98 in identifying trojan families effectively.

Keywords: android · trojan · malware · classification

1 Introduction

Android operating system (OS) has established its place at the top of the mobile operating systems around the world with steady growth since its start in 2008. Android OS represents 71.8% of all mobile devices globally as at the end of 2022 [24]. In addition to mobile devices, Android has also been ported to operate on tablet computers, Internet-of-Things (IoT) devices in multiple contexts, in addition to its use in automotive, media devices, among other applications. This significant user base has made Android an interesting target for malicious actors.

Android OS was targeted by a rapidly growing types of malware for many years. Threat actors created complex mechanisms to hide and distribute infected applications to a large number of users, and utilized legitimate-looking applications to deliver dangerous malicious code. Throughout the years, malicious applications were downloaded by users from legitimate and non-legitimate marketplaces, in addition to sideloading. Threat actors were successful in obfuscating their malware in different ways to bypass screening performed by Google before offering their applications in the Google Play Store, the major source of downloading applications by Android users. Many incidents through the years showed that this screening process was not capable of pre-emptively identifying malware before it is downloaded by a large number of users (sometimes exceeding two million users [25]).

J. Zhou et al. (Eds.): ACNS 2023 Workshops, LNCS 13907, pp. 642–656, 2023.
https://doi.org/10.1007/978-3-031-41181-6_34

Different types of malware were designed by threat actors to perform different tasks. Trojans comprise 93.93% of all Android malware [23]. *Trojans* are a specific type of malicious software that is disguised as a benign program. The malicious actor creates it usually by injecting malicious code or files within a legitimate program and shares it with the target, mostly though social engineering. Trojans can be used to achieve different targets. For example, banking trojans are used to capture online banking credentials, or perform hidden transactions. In addition to conducting their own malicious activity, trojans can be used to deliver sophisticated payloads such as spyware, ransomware, along with other types of malware. In general, trojans can be divided into the following categories based on the malicious activity they perform:

1. Downloader trojan: A trojan designed to deploy other malicious code such as key-loggers, rootkits, and ransomware [14].
2. Spyware: A trojan designed to observe and collect sensitive user information such as banking information, credentials, and Personally Identifiable Information (PII) [14].
3. Backdoor trojan: A trojan designed to create a passage for the attacker to access resources on the target machine. This trojan can deliberately create a vulnerable environment to enable the attacker's access [14].
4. Rootkit trojan: A trojan designed to hide its existence by performing multiple elusive actions. It has the capability to hide its files and/or code from the memory of a device to avoid detection [14].
5. Infostealer trojan: A trojan designed to steal sensitive information, such as saved credentials of any kind such as banking information, email credentials, etc.

While Android malware and trojan detection has been a subject of many research studies [15,19], forensic analysis and malware and trojan family identification did not receive as much attention. Forensic identification of specific trojan families can help in achieving several goals such as identifying the creator of the trojan (attribution). It could also help in improving the detection process, and elimination methodologies by identifying similarities between different trojan types. It could also improve incident response to trojan incidents by identifying similar behaviors, and associating them with similar response techniques. This identification of the trojan family, if performed at an early stage in the infection, could lead to identifying the next move of the trojan, and how to prevent it from succeeding.

In this paper, we present a forensic identification system to identify trojan families. The proposed system is based on a stacked deep neural network (DNN) ensemble to improve the performance of the DNN classifiers. This stacked-ensemble technique has not been previously used (to the best of our knowledge) in identifying Android trojan families. The proposed system relies on features extracted from dynamic analysis of trojan-infected applications within the Android environment. The proposed system architecture has proved to outperform individual DNN-based solutions in terms of accuracy and F_1 score. The proposed system performance was optimized to achieve significant improvements in performance metrics. Such classification system can have a significant impact on incident response, trojan attribution, and malware eradication.

The next section will present review of previous research works, while Sect. 3 presents an overview of the proposed system. Section 4 presents the experimental setup, dataset information, and experiment methodology, and the results are presented in Sect. 5. The results discussion and comparative analysis is presented in Sect. 6, and the last section presents the conclusions and direction of future work.

2   Related Works

As mentioned in Sect. 1, malware detection within the Android environment has been the subject of many studies during the past few years. However, we will keep the focus on Android trojan detection and classification.

Analysis of malware is considered a cornerstone in developing detection and categorization systems, and hence, the detection and categorization of trojans. Static analysis of malware is based on analysing the malicious code without running it. This includes techniques of examining information within the manifest file, and the application code itself, if possible [5].

Dynamic analysis of malware is based on running the malicious code and observing its behavior. This includes examining certain indicators in memory and storage, and how they are impacted by the malware actions. It also focuses on observing the communications that the malicious code performs with other processes and on the network [18].

Many detection and categorization related works rely on feature that are either extracted from static analysis, or dynamic analysis. Other papers combine the use of static and dynamic features extracted from applications to help in the detection and classification process, usually referred to as hybrid detection [17].

In 2019, Aminuddin and Abdullah proposed a machine learning based Android trojan detection system [6]. The proposed system is based on two stages; in the first stage, information gain algorithms is used to identify the most significant system calls, and in the second stage, a random forest classifier would perform the prediction. When tested, the proposed system showed an accuracy of 81.2%.

Cai et al. presented, in 2019, an Android malware detection and categorization system based on app-level profiling, named DroidCat [9]. The proposed system builds an application profile based on inter-component communications, and method calls to help in identifying malware. The proposed system utilized four datasets representing applications collected between 2009 and 2017 from VirusShare and AndroZoo. In categorizing malware families, DroidCat was able to deliver F_1 score of 0.9706.

Dehkordy et al. presented, in 2020, a machine learning-based trojan family classification system based on kNN Classifier Based on Manhattan Distance Metric [11]. The proposed system relied on static features extracted from Android applications request permissions, and application intents. The proposed system was trained and tested using a subset of Drebin and AMD datasets with about 4,500 samples only. Testing showed that the classifier worked with accuracy of 97.83%.

Keyes et al. introduced, in 2021, an entropy-based malware analyzer based on dynamic features [13]. While the work is relevant to general malware classification, it utilizes the same dataset used by our proposed system; CIC-AndMal-2020, which include trojans in addition to other types of malware. The proposed system analyses dynamic features to classify malware samples into different categories. In addition, other classifiers were created to classify each category to different families with varying accuracies. In overall category classification, decision tree classifier produced an accuracy of 98.4%.

Bai et al. presented, in 2021, predictive behavioral analysis of Android banking trojans [8]. This study, although focused on categorizing five different banking trojan families, presented interesting results. The study built its own dataset with samples extracted from VirusTotal 2016–2017 trojan and benign applications that included 10,642 samples. The proposed system, namely DBank, presented an F_1 score of 0.941.

Ullah et al. presented, in 2022, another machine learning based trojan detector that utilises SVM classifier [26]. The proposed system combines the use of static and dynamic features in a multi-layer approach to improve detection accuracy. The proposed system, namely TrojanDetector, was tested using CIC-AndMal-2020, Cantagio-Mobile, and VirusShare datasets using multiple classical machine learning classifiers. SVM outperformed RF, LR, and DT in its detection accuracy with an accuracy of 96.64%.

Seraj et al. presented, in 2022, an Android trojan discovery system based on convolutional neural networks [22]. The proposed system relies on static features extracted from application permissions. The dataset created and used included 11 trojan families with 2,593 samples only. The proposed system presented an accuracy of 98.06%.

3   Proposed System

The proposed system is focuses on identifying the trojan family of a sample application. As the system relies on dynamic features extracted by observing the behavior of the application within a sandbox. An overview of the proposed system operation is shown in Fig. 1.

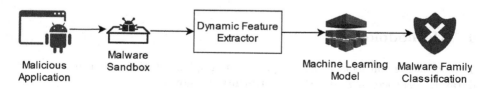

Fig. 1. An overview of the proposed system operation

As shown in Fig. 1, once the application is running inside the sandbox, the features are extracted using a tool named AndroidAppLyzer [4]. The extracted features are then passed as input to the previously-trained machine learning model that would perform the prediction. The produced prediction resembles the specific trojan family of the trojan implanted within the application.

The machine learning model chosen for the proposed system is a stacked ensemble of five neural networks as shown in Fig. 2. The stacked ensemble is composed of two levels of classifiers; base classifiers that would be trained to make the multi-class classification independently, and the meta classifier taking the different classification results of all base classifiers and learning how to use them to produce better predictions. The final output of the ensemble classifier is the output of the meta classifier. In our proposed system, all of the five base classifiers are deep neural networks, while the meta classifier is a decision tree classifier, as shown in the figure. The stacked ensemble model was chosen because of its capability of improving the prediction accuracy. Stacking ensembles are suitable for heterogeneous weak learners by learning them in parallel, and combining them by training meta-learner to output a prediction based on the different weak learner's predictions rather than the actual input data [16]. The base classifiers were chosen to be based on neural networks because of their higher ability to handle highly-dimensional data when compared to classical machine learning [21].

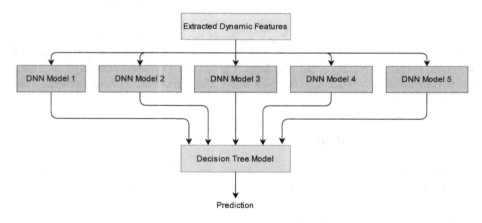

Fig. 2. Proposed stacked ensemble model

4   Methodology

The following subsection will explain the implementation environment, the dataset, preprocessing, and the experimental design.

4.1   Implementation Environment

All preprocessing, training, and testing was performed in the following environment:

- Operating system: Windows 10 Professional
- CPU: AMD Ryzen 5 3600, 4.2 GHz
- GPU: Nvidia RTX3060Ti 8 GB RAM + RTX3060 12 GB RAM
- RAM: 128 GB
- Python v3.10.8 [3]
- Tensorflow v2.10.0 [2]
- SciKit Learn v1.1.3 [1]
- Talos v1.4 [7]

4.2   The Dataset

The dataset used in our experiment was CCCS-CIC-AndMal-2020, which was introduced in 2020 by [20]. This dataset was built by performing dynamic analysis of 200,000 Android malware applications which were labelled and categorized by family with the help of VirusTotal website. In addition, the dataset included 200,000 benign samples. The malware samples collected were categorized into adware, backdoor, file infector, no category, Potentially Unwanted Apps (PUA), ransomware, riskware, scareware, trojan, trojan-banker, trojan-dropper, trojan-sms, trojan-spy and zero-day. As our research is specifically focused on Android trojans, we picked all the samples within the categories trojan, trojan-banker, trojan-dropper, trojan-SMS, and trojan-spy. In total, these samples were 15,027 distributed over 76 different trojan families.

Each sample in the dataset includes 142 dynamic features that were extracted from these samples, such as memory heaps allocated, free memory heaps, number of bytes received from a network, and number of open files. A complete list of these features can be found in [20]. Each sample, includes two labels; one identifying the category, and another identifying the family. Upon detailed analysis of the dataset, we were able to make the following observations:

1. There is significant imbalance between different trojan families. Some families included as little as one sample only, while others included over 1,900 samples.
2. One of the features was the SHA-256 hash generated from the application.
3. There were no missing data within the dataset.

4.3   Preprocessing

Based on the observations mentioned earlier, we performed the following preprocessing steps:

1. The category label was removed as all of the included samples were different types of trojans.

2. The SHA-256 hash feature was removed as different obfuscation techniques used by malicious actors, even the simple ones, would result in a significant change in the hash. Hence, it is not a meaningful feature for our purpose.
3. For balancing purposes, we removed samples from families that have under 100 samples. This decision was made to provide higher accuracy in the multi-class classifier being built as these samples are significantly underrepresented. This resulted in leaving 21 trojan families.
4. To improve balancing among the remaining 21 trojan families, we performed random over-sampling based on the highest number of samples, which was 1,940 samples from the "mytrackp" trojan family.
5. As the proposed system utilizes DNNs to build the ensemble, we re-scaled all data using MinMax scaler.

These preprocessing steps resulted in a dataset of 40,740 samples, equally distributed over 21 trojan families. Each sample holds 141 dynamic features.

4.4   Experimental Design

The experiments performed in the research were performed based on the following steps:

1. The dataset was split into 75% training subset, and 25% testing subset using stratified random split.
2. A group of five deep learning models were created to form the ensemble.
3. The created DNNs were optimized to deliver optimum performance using a package named Talos.
4. A stacking ensemble was built using the trained five DNN classifiers.
5. Performance metrics were measured for the ensemble model.
6. To ensure its generalization, the proposed model was subjected to 10-fold cross-validation.

5   Results

5.1   Performance Metrics

Using the basic four performance measures of True Positive(TP), True Negative (TN), False Positive (FP), and False Negative (FN) we calculate the following performance metrics in our experiments:

1. Accuracy

$$Accuracy = \frac{TP + TN}{TP + TN + FP + FN} \tag{1}$$

2. Precision

$$Precision = \frac{TP}{TP + FP} \qquad (2)$$

3. Recall

$$Recall = \frac{TP}{TP + FN} \qquad (3)$$

4. F_1 score

$$F_1 score = 2 * \frac{\frac{TP}{TP+FN} * \frac{TP}{TP+FP}}{\frac{TP}{TP+FN} + \frac{TP}{TP+FP}} \qquad (4)$$

In our experiments, we have not measured timing parameters in our experiments as forensic experiments are conducted in an "offline" manner without the use of real-time processing. Hence, the timing parameters has very limited impact on the forensic investigation process.

5.2   Testing Results

The neural networks we built in multi-layer perceptron architecture, and then optimized to maximize their performance. The DNN optimization steps in our experiments resulted in selecting the following hyperparameters as the best performing combination:

- The network architecture chosen was 141-256-1024-256-21, where there 141-neuron input layer, 256-neuron hidden layer 1, 1024-neuron hidden layer 2, 256-neuron hidden layer 3, and a 21-neuron output layer.
- The activation function was ReLU for all hidden layers, and Sigmoid for the output layer.
- The initializer was He Normal [10].
- The Optimizer was Nadam with a learning rate of 0.001 [21].
- The loss function was categorical cross-entropy.
- Batch size of 512 was chosen with 20 epochs.

The five DNNs were trained using 75% of the data samples, that were chosen based on stratified random split. Testing was performed using the remaining 25% of the data samples. After training, these models were saved to be used later in constructing the ensemble model. These five models delivered an average accuracy of 0.92 during the testing phase.

The ensemble was then created as a stacked ensemble. In a stacked ensemble, a single model is trained to learn how to best combine the predictions of the contributing models. In our proposed system, the five DNN classifiers are considered base models (Level-0), while we create a Decision Tree classifier to act as the meta model (Level-1) model to learn how to combined the predictions of all Level-0 models to produce a better overall prediction. The DT classifier is known for its ability to use different feature subsets and decision rules at different stages of classification [12]. The hyperparameters of the DT classifier were as follows:

- criterion: gini
- splitter: best
- max_depth: none
- min_samples_split: 2
- min_samples_leaf: 1
- min_weight_fraction_leaf: 0.0
- max_features: 141

This method produced higher accuracy when compared to the performance of the DNNs alone, as shown in Fig. 3.

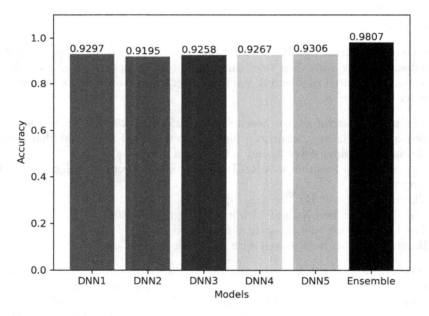

Fig. 3. Comparing ensemble model's accuracy to individual DNN models

Figure 3 shows that the stacked ensemble delivered an accuracy of 0.9807, while the highest DNN accuracy was 0.9306. The minor differences in the DNN networks performance are cause by different initializations of the weights based on He Normal Initializer. As accuracy alone might not necessarily reflect the model's performance, we measured other performance metrics, as shown in Table 1.

As shown Table 1, the multi-class classifier performed with a micro-average F_1 score of 0.9806, and a macro-average F_1 score of 0.9805. The table also shows that the classifier performed very well in detecting most families of trojans. The main classes that the classifier performed with less accuracy in detecting were "fakeinst", "smfrow", "sstheif", and "styricka". All other trojan families were detected with a minimum F_1 score of 0.96 and a maximum of 1.00. The classifier's confusion matrix plot is shown in Fig. 4.

Figure 4 shows that most trojan families were detected with very high accuracy, and low false-positives, and false-negatives.

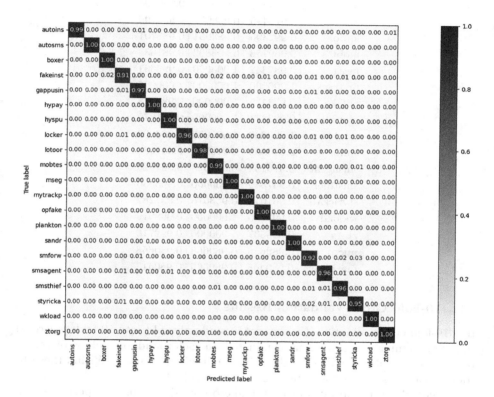

Fig. 4. Confusion matrix plot for the stacked ensemble classifier

Table 1. Stacked Ensemble Classification Report

Class	Precision	Recall	F_1 Score
autoins	0.989940	0.985972	0.987952
autosms	1.000000	1.000000	1.000000
boxer	0.983299	1.000000	0.991579
fakeinst	0.955947	0.907950	0.931330
gappusin	0.975709	0.965932	0.970796
hypay	0.998084	1.000000	0.999041
hyspu	0.993827	1.000000	0.996904
locker	0.976496	0.958071	0.967196
lotoor	0.992395	0.983051	0.987701
mobtes	0.969758	0.993802	0.981633
mseg	0.987342	1.000000	0.993631
mytrackp	1.000000	1.000000	1.000000
opfake	0.973415	1.000000	0.986528
plankton	0.983871	1.000000	0.991870
sandr	1.000000	1.000000	1.000000
smforw	0.943355	0.919321	0.931183
smsagent	0.973154	0.964523	0.968820
smsthief	0.947589	0.959660	0.953586
styricka	0.961014	0.953578	0.957282
wkload	0.997840	1.000000	0.998919
ztorg	0.985537	1.000000	0.992716
micro avg	0.980658	0.980658	0.980658
macro avg	0.980408	0.980565	0.980413

5.3   10-Fold Cross-Validation Results

In a 10-fold cross-validation, the dataset is randomly split into 10 folds where 10 round of training and testing are conducted. In each round, one fold is picked to be the testing subset while the other nine are used for training. Within these 10 rounds, each fold is used as a testing subset once [21].

Table 2 shows the results of the 10-fold cross-validation process performed on our proposed system.

As shown in Table 2, the mean values of the performance metrics are slightly higher than our previously obtained results. In addition, the standard deviation for all performance metrics is very low. This indicates that our proposed system can generalize well beyond its training dataset.

6   Discussions

As we examine the results presented in Sect. 5, we find that the proposed system has achieved its design goal of classifying trojan samples and identifying their families with high accuracy.

Table 2. Results of 10-fold Cross-Validation

Fold	Accuracy	Precision	Recall	F_1 score
1	0.986991	0.986807	0.987221	0.986919
2	0.984782	0.984851	0.984361	0.984515
3	0.984291	0.984101	0.983981	0.983980
4	0.988709	0.988960	0.988949	0.988936
5	0.988463	0.988235	0.988155	0.988146
6	0.989445	0.989563	0.989700	0.989590
7	0.988709	0.988664	0.988808	0.988691
8	0.988709	0.988526	0.988481	0.988477
9	0.983309	0.983494	0.983780	0.983551
10	0.988954	0.988690	0.988643	0.988593
Mean	0.987236	0.987189	0.987208	0.987140
St Dev	0.002145	0.002119	0.002160	0.002153

Table 3. Comparing proposed system performance to previous works

Paper	Technique	Classifier	Detection	Classification	Dataset	Samples	Families	Features	Accuracy	F_1 score
[6]	Dynamic	RF	✓		Drebin	6,160	–	61	81.2%	–
[26]	Hybrid	SVM	✓		CIC-AndMal-2020	–	–	141	96.64%	–
[13]	Dynamic	DT		✓ (Malware)	CIC-AndMal-2020	195,624	148	141	98.4%	–
[11]	Static	kNN		✓	Drebin and AMD			61	97.82%	–
[22]	Static	CNN		✓	[22]	2,539	11	449	98.06%	0.98
[8]	Static	RF	✓		[8]	10,624	–	110	–	0.941
Proposed	Dynamic	Ensemble-DNN		✓	CIC-AndMal-2020	40,740	21	141	98.07%	0.9806

Table 3 shows a comparison of our proposed system's performance with previous works. As our work is focused specifically on Android malware, we included only papers that target trojans, and not malware in general.

In Table 3, the columns "Detection" indicates whether the mentioned paper is targeting detection of trojans vs. benign applications. These papers usually use binary classifiers that would indicate either "trojan", or "benign". The next column, "Classification", indicates whether the paper is targeting the identification of the specific trojan family, not just identifying samples as trojans or benign.

While many research paper presented reasonable results, a few were relying on outdated datasets such as Drebin and AMD, in [6,11]. These outdated datasets were collected from malware samples between 2010 and 2012. With the evolving landscape of malware, and the new techniques malicious actors are using, there are no guarantees that such systems would perform well with newer samples.

As we compare our work with [8,26], it is obvious that both of these works were focused on trojan detection rather than classification, which leaves it out of the scope of comparison. The detection process studies distinctive features that differentiates trojan samples from benign samples, while our forensic identification process relies on differentiating between different trojan families.

The only comparable works were presented in [13,22], where the focus is on trojan or malware family classification rather than detection. The work presented in [22] utilizes 449 static features extracted from each sample. However, this work's dataset included 11 trojan families with 2,593 samples only, and no validation steps of any form were presented. This means that the results presented by [22] need to be further validated with a larger dataset to ensure generalization. The lack of validation when a small dataset is used is considered a significant issue, because there is no way of ensuring the robustness of the provided classifier. With such a small dataset, the testing was done using around 500 samples only. Hence, further validation is considered vital. The work presented in [13] is focused on identifying the malware family, rather than trojans. The work was based on creating individual classifiers for each category of malware. This resulted in splitting trojans into multiple categories (Trojan, Trojan_Dropper, Trojan_Banker, Trojan_SMS, and Trojan_Spy). The specific performance metrics of these classifiers were not presented in the paper. An overall accuracy of 98.4% was produced, but there are no indicators of how this was calculated. Hence, a clear comparison was not possible.

7 Conclusions and Future Work

In this paper, we presented a forensic classification system for Android trojans. The proposed system is designed to identify the trojan family with high accuracy. We used five DNN classifiers to construct the base classifiers for the stacked ensemble, along with a DT-based classifier as the meta-classifier.

The proposed system was trained and tested using CIC-AndMal-2020 dataset, and delivered an accuracy of 98.07%, with F_1 score of 0.9806. When compared to previous works, our proposed system proved to deliver better performance with a more recent dataset. Our test results were further validated by performing 10-fold cross-validation to ensure that our proposed model can generalize well beyond its training dataset.

Possible future direction in our research include the expansion to other types of malware, rather than trojans alone. Another research direction would be exploring the combination of static and dynamic features to improve the classification accuracy. Possible extensions also include validating the results with a second dataset, and utilizing time-based splits in training and testing to study the impact of the evolution of the trojan families on the accuracy of the system. Our future works also include analyzing the specific trojan families where the classifier performs less than perfect to have a better understanding of the differentiating behaviours between them, to improve the classifier's performance.

References

1. Scikit-learn: machine learning in Python—scikit-learn 1.2.1 documentation (2023). https://scikit-learn.org/stable. Accessed 1 Mar 2023
2. TensorFlow (2023). https://www.tensorflow.org. Accessed 1 Mar 2023
3. Welcome to Python.org (2023). https://www.python.org. Accessed 1 Mar 2023
4. Ahlashkari: AndroidAppLyzer (2023). https://github.com/ahlashkari/AndroidAppLyzer. Accessed 28 Feb 2023
5. Alani, M.M., Awad, A.I.: Paired: an explainable lightweight Android malware detection system. IEEE Access **10**, 73214–73228 (2022)
6. Aminuddin, N.I., Abdullah, Z.: Android trojan detection based on dynamic analysis. Adv. Comput. Intell. Syst. **1**(1) (2019)
7. Autonomio: talos (2023). https://github.com/autonomio/talos. Accessed 1 Mar 2023
8. Bai, C., Han, Q., Mezzour, G., Pierazzi, F., Subrahmanian, V.: DBank: predictive behavioral analysis of recent Android banking trojans. IEEE Trans. Dependable Secure Comput. **18**(3), 1378–1393 (2019)
9. Cai, H., Meng, N., Ryder, B., Yao, D.: DroidCat: effective Android malware detection and categorization via app-level profiling. IEEE Trans. Inf. Forensics Secur. **14**(6), 1455–1470 (2018)
10. Datta, L.: A survey on activation functions and their relation with Xavier and He normal initialization. arXiv preprint arXiv:2004.06632 (2020)
11. Dehkordy, D.T., Rasoolzadegan, A.: DroidTKM: detection of trojan families using the KNN classifier based on Manhattan distance metric. In: 2020 10th International Conference on Computer and Knowledge Engineering (ICCKE), pp. 136–141. IEEE (2020)
12. Han, J., Kamber, M., Pei, J.: 9 - classification: advanced methods. In: Han, J., Kamber, M., Pei, J. (eds.) Data Mining. The Morgan Kaufmann Series in Data Management Systems, 3rd edn., pp. 393–442. Morgan Kaufmann, Boston (2012). https://doi.org/10.1016/B978-0-12-381479-1.00009-5. https://www.sciencedirect.com/science/article/pii/B9780123814791000095
13. Keyes, D.S., Li, B., Kaur, G., Lashkari, A.H., Gagnon, F., Massicotte, F.: Entroplyzer: Android malware classification and characterization using entropy analysis of dynamic characteristics. In: 2021 Reconciling Data Analytics, Automation, Privacy, and Security: A Big Data Challenge (RDAAPS), pp. 1–12. IEEE (2021)
14. Kleymenov, A., Thabet, A.: Mastering Malware Analysis: The Complete Malware Analyst's Guide to Combating Malicious Software, APT, Cybercrime, and IoT Attacks. Packt Publishing Ltd. (2019)
15. Kouliaridis, V., Kambourakis, G.: A comprehensive survey on machine learning techniques for Android malware detection. Information **12**(5), 185 (2021)
16. Kyriakides, G., Margaritis, K.G.: Hands-On Ensemble Learning with Python: Build Highly Optimized Ensemble Machine Learning Models Using Scikit-Learn and Keras. Packt Publishing Ltd. (2019)
17. Odusami, M., Abayomi-Alli, O., Misra, S., Shobayo, O., Damasevicius, R., Maskeliunas, R.: Android malware detection: a survey. In: Florez, H., Diaz, C., Chavarriaga, J. (eds.) ICAI 2018. CCIS, vol. 942, pp. 255–266. Springer, Cham (2018). https://doi.org/10.1007/978-3-030-01535-0_19
18. Or-Meir, O., Nissim, N., Elovici, Y., Rokach, L.: Dynamic malware analysis in the modern era-a state of the art survey. ACM Comput. Surv. (CSUR) **52**(5), 1–48 (2019)

19. Qiu, J., Zhang, J., Luo, W., Pan, L., Nepal, S., Xiang, Y.: A survey of Android malware detection with deep neural models. ACM Comput. Surv. (CSUR) **53**(6), 1–36 (2020)
20. Rahali, A., Lashkari, A.H., Kaur, G., Taheri, L., Gagnon, F., Massicotte, F.: DIDroid: Android malware classification and characterization using deep image learning. In: 2020 The 10th International Conference on Communication and Network Security, pp. 70–82 (2020)
21. Raschka, S., Liu, Y.H., Mirjalili, V., Dzhulgakov, D.: Machine Learning with PyTorch and Scikit-Learn: Develop Machine Learning and Deep Learning Models with Python. Packt Publishing Ltd. (2022)
22. Seraj, S., Pavlidis, M., Polatidis, N.: TrojanDroid: Android malware detection for trojan discovery using convolutional neural networks. In: Iliadis, L., Jayne, C., Tefas, A., Pimenidis, E. (eds.) EANN 2022. CCIS, vol. 1600, pp. 203–212. Springer, Cham (2022). https://doi.org/10.1007/978-3-031-08223-8_17
23. Statista: Distribution of Android malware 2019 | Statista (2023). https://www.statista.com/statistics/681006/share-of-android-types-of-malware. Accessed 28 Feb 2023
24. Statista: Global mobile OS market share 2022 | Statista (2023). https://www.statista.com/statistics/272698/global-market-share-held-by-mobile-operating-systems-since-2009. Accessed 28 Feb 2023
25. Toulas, B.: Android malware apps with 2 million installs spotted on Google Play. BleepingComputer (2022). https://www.bleepingcomputer.com/news/security/android-malware-apps-with-2-million-installs-spotted-on-google-play
26. Ullah, S., Ahmad, T., Buriro, A., Zara, N., Saha, S.: TrojanDetector: a multi-layer hybrid approach for trojan detection in Android applications. Appl. Sci. **12**(21), 10755 (2022)

Posters

POSTER: Ransomware Detection Mechanism – Project Status at the Beginning of 2023

Michał Glet[✉] and Kamil Kaczyński

Military University of Technology, Warsaw, Poland
michal.glet@wat.edu.pl

Abstract. Ransomware must be treated as one of the most critical security threats. Ransomware attacks can cause permanent data damage which can be devastating to governments, enterprises, and ordinary users. We noticed that there is a big gap in the security solutions available on the market and that there is no good solution to prevent attacks using new versions of ransomware. Therefore, we launched a project in 2021 to fill this gap. In this article, we present the status of the ongoing project at the beginning of 2023.

Keywords: ransomware · cryptovirus · detection

1 Introduction

The project is addressing the topic of the early detection of the activity of ransomware software. It is being led by the Military University of Technology in Warsaw and TiMSI Sp. z o.o. Some of the results of the project will be published in the public domain and will be available free of charge for every Polish citizen. The project will end with specifications and a working Proof-of-Concept of the ransomware detection system. This mechanism would be able to detect ransomware activity at the very beginning stage and thus minimize the possible losses that this attack could have caused.

The first results of the project have been presented during ACNS2022 [1]. One year after, in this paper, we are presenting the next, most important, results.

2 Current State

The project started in the summer of 2021. During ACNS 2022 conference, we presented the status of the work at that time [1]. Since then, we have done a lot of research, design, development, mind-storming, engineering work and testing. The most important results are:

- Implementation of the detection primitives.
- Process monitoring and termination mechanisms.
- Self-protection mechanisms.

J. Zhou et al. (Eds.): ACNS 2023 Workshops, LNCS 13907, pp. 659–663, 2023.
https://doi.org/10.1007/978-3-031-41181-6_35

- Custom communication mechanism.
- Design of the detection system.
- Test environment and procedures.
- Early test results.
- Improvements and changes in the core detection ideas.

2.1 Implementation of the Detection Primitives

Detection primitives such as indicators, filter drivers, honeypots, etc. are an essential part of the whole detection system. The final effectiveness in ransomware activity detection relies on those primitives. That is why the implementation process has started with implementing the detection primitives. Because of the fact, that some primitives work as filter drivers [2], most of the implementations have been done in the C programming language. We have implemented all previously [1] described detection primitives.

2.2 Process Monitoring and Termination Mechanisms

The crucial part of the developed system is an effective mechanism for monitoring and keeping track of the process tree running in the operating system. There are some versions of ransomware that, for example, aggressively spawn new child processes and terminate themselves. By using standard process monitoring tools in such a situation, the child-parent relationship is lost because the parent is dead. Furthermore, there may be an active process in the system that is the parent of a dead parent and can, for example, monitor the activity of the spawned children and create new processes when the death of a spawned child is detected. As a result, we have developed a custom monitoring mechanism that keeps track and relations between all created and terminated processes in the operating system. Having an effective monitoring tool, that can create a process tree even when there are some dead process leaves, allow us to create a very effective process termination mechanism. We are sure that its power lies in its simplicity:

1. Detect ransomware process.
2. Find a complete process tree (all ancestors, all siblings, all preceding).
3. Deactivate processes recovery (recreation) mechanisms.
4. SIGKILL all processes from the tree.

The test results confirm that our approach is effective even for the most aggressively spawning ransomware software – after detection, we can successfully stop ongoing ransomware attacks.

2.3 Self-Protection Mechanisms

Even the most effective ransomware detection mechanism can fail if its functions are disabled by the ransomware. A common behaviour of most ransomware is to terminate selected processes before encrypting data. If such ransomware terminated processes from our detection mechanism, we would not be able to detect the attack. That is why we have developed self-protection mechanisms that try to prevent unwanted process terminations and, if they occur, attempt to restore the resources that were interrupted. Among other things, this mechanism is based on the idea of crowd computing [3] and the scheme that everyone knows everything about every other process from the detection system. We have also implemented techniques that tell us which process tried to terminate or terminated one of our processes. After such detection, we try to recover the aborted process and terminate the attacking process as potentially malicious.

2.4 Custom Communication Mechanism

Due to the fact that the detection system will consist of many running processes, we had to develop a secure, reliable and effective communication mechanism. During the research phase, we have analyzed many IPC solutions, including e.g. Component Object Model, data copy, dynamic data exchange (DDE), file mappings, mailslots, pipes, remote procedure calls (RPC), Windows sockets, asynchronous local inter-process communication (ALPC), communication ports. As a result, we have selected two of them which suit best our needs.

A developed custom communication mechanism is a very important part of the detection system. This is the only way that components running in the kernel mode communicate with the components running in the user mode and this is the only way the processes communicate which each other to exchange status messages, detection results and self-protection data.

2.5 Design of the Detection System

Developed and implemented detection primitives must work in conjunction and must be managed by other parts (processes) of the system. What is more, the detection results must be displayed (communicated) to the end user. That is why it was necessary to design the architecture of the whole detection system. The designed detection system consists of:

- Management module:

  - communication with the end user,
  - management of the detection module,
  - management of the attack and defence module,
  - management of the signals sent by detection primitives.

- Detection module:

  - honeypots,
  - data processing,
  - randomness checks,
  - privileges checks,
  - API calls check.

- Attack and defence module:

- custom communication mechanism,
- process monitoring,
- process termination,
- self-protection.

2.6 Test Environment and Procedures

Our project is coming to an end so we had to prepare a test environment which is as close as possible to the common user workstation. This environment will be used many times in many tests. It is crucial to test the detection effectiveness of the different ransomware in the same, production-like systems. Only because of this, we will be able to collect reliable and reproducible test results. What is more, we have prepared test scenarios and test procedures to ensure the high quality of the testing process.

2.7 Early Test Results

After the implementation of the detection primitives, we conducted tests that confirmed or denied the desired detection ratio. These tests were the first basis for modifications, improvements, and changes in core detection ideas. During the test, we were using a lot of different versions of the ransomware software, e.g.: LockerGoga, KeyPass, PartyTicket, Akagi, BlackMatter, LokiLocker, WhiteRabbit, AvosLocker, Cuba, Dharma, DoejoCrypt, Epsilon, HDLocker, Jormungan, MalwareDeveloper, Maoloa.

The final test results showed that in cooperative work the developed primitives can detect the activity of all the ransomware used during the tests.

2.8 Improvements and Changes in the Core Detection Ideas

The early test results lead us to introduce changes and improvements in the detection primitives. The most important changes are:

- Cryptography API usage indicator – the tests showed that this is an almost useless indicator. With a high probability, we will not use it in the final solution.
- File API usage – the test showed that this is one of the most useful indicators. Because of this we have introduced some performance changes and expanded the list of monitored API functions.
- Process/thread API usage – the test showed that this is a useful indicator. Because of this we have introduced some performance changes and expanded the list of monitored API functions.
- Network API usage – we have added a new indicator that monitors network API functions usage. The indicator monitor functions that ransomware often uses to find mapped network resources.
- Overall performance and resource utilization improvements.

3 Upcoming Challenges

The main result of this project will be a working Proof-of-Concept of the ransomware detection system. Below we have described the main challenges we will deal with in the nearest future:

- Implementation of the detection system – we have created a design and architecture of the system. Now we must implement it.
- Testing and improvements – we have created a test environment and selected a large set of ransomware software that was not used during previous test phases. We will use them to verify detection system effectiveness in a production-like test environment. The test results will be analyzed, and necessary improvements will be implemented.

Acknowledgement. This work is partially funded by The National Centre for Research and Development, Poland. The project number is CYBERSECIDENT/490737/IV/NCBR/2021. The project will last till the end of the year 2023.

References

1. Glet, M., Kaczyński, K.: POSTER: ransomware detection mechanism – current state of the project. In: Zhou, J., et al. (eds.) Applied Cryptography and Network Security Workshops. ACNS 2022. Lecture Notes in Computer Science, vol. 13285, 616–620. Springer, Cham (2022). https://doi.org/10.1007/978-3-031-16815-4_36
2. Windows client documentation, Filter Drivers, Microsoft, https://learn.microsoft.com/en-us/windows-hardware/drivers/kernel/filter-drivers. Accessed 04 2023
3. Crowd computing, Wikipedia, https://en.wikipedia.org/wiki/Crowd_computing. Accessed 04 2023

POSTER: AuthZit: Multi-modal Authentication with Visual-Spatial and Text Secrets

Joon Kuy Han[1], Dennis Wong[2(✉)], and Byungkon Kang[1]

[1] SUNY Korea, Incheon, South Korea
[2] Macao Polytechnic University, Macao, China
dennis.wong@sunykorea.ac.kr

Abstract. Designing a fallback authentication mechanism that is both memorable and strong is a challenging problem because of the trade-off between usability and security. This challenge is particularly pronounced for accounts that require infrequent authentication, where the authentication secrets must remain secure and easy to recall without frequent reinforcement. Inspired by people's strong visual-spatial memory and memory via association, we introduce a novel system AuthZit to help address this problem. AuthZit encodes authentication secrets as paths through a 3D map of places in real life navigated in the first person and birds-eye perspective, along with a textual secret tagged with this path. We evaluated the usability and security of our design in two dimensions: memorability after one month and speed through a user study with 20 participants. Our results suggest that (1) user authentication secrets in AuthZit are memorable, and (2) authentication using AuthZit was not significantly slower to enter.

Keywords: Human computer interaction · Fallback authentication · Visual-spatial · Usable security

1 Introduction

The increasing number of passwords that users have to remember and their complicated password composition policies make it challenging for people to remember their passwords [10]. A recent study [5] demonstrated that 45% of participants experienced at least one account lockout in a year. When users are unable to recall their passwords, fallback authentication schemes are required for users to regain control of their accounts. Communication-based password resets and security questions are the most common approaches for fallback authentication. Communication-based password resets such as by email or mobile phone work well, but they may not be appropriate in certain situations [7] (e.g., when users lost the password for the email service itself). Hence, security questions have been popularly used as an alternative that takes advantage of users' personal information, but they are not easy to achieve both in terms of both security

J. Zhou et al. (Eds.): ACNS 2023 Workshops, LNCS 13907, pp. 664–668, 2023.
https://doi.org/10.1007/978-3-031-41181-6_36

and usability [6,9]. Several approaches have been proposed using geographical and spatial medium for fallback and infrequent authentication [3,7].

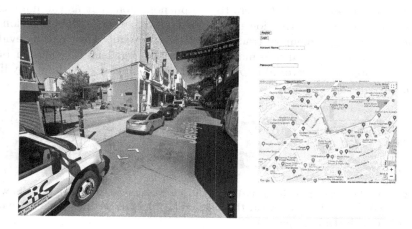

Fig. 1. With AuthZit, users navigate through a user-created path in first person-perspective with textual tags as authentication secrets.

Inspired by Azit a Korean slang that is based on the Russian word 'agit-punkt' which refers to a special and secret place where one often goes to or where close friends meet, we propose a novel fallback authentication method called AuthZit (see Fig. 1) based on *method of loci*[1] [4] and *levels-of-processing effect*[2] [2].

In this paper, we propose AuthZit, and our work can be summarized as follows:

1. We design, implement, and evaluate AuthZit, a proof-of-concept visual-spatial authentication system combined with textual inputs.
2. We conducted a user study to evaluate the usability and effectiveness of AuthZit and found that users were able to successfully authenticate using AuthZit.

2   System Design

Cognitive Effects on Authentication: *Spatial learning* strategies were found in cognitive psychology that people have exceptionally strong visual-spatial memories [4]. One notable thing among these strategies is the "method of loci",

---

[1] Items to be remembered are cognitively imprinted at different points in a familiar space.

[2] More deeply encoded information becomes accessible to more cues at the time of recall.

where items to be remembered are cognitively imprinted at different points in a familiar space [1]. The method of loci has its origins to ancient Greek and Roman orators, who used the technique to memorize speeches.

Levels-of-processing effect refers to the phenomenon that as the number of connections between information increases, it produces more elaborate, longer-lasting, and stronger memory traces. *Levels-of-processing effect* can be evident by observing how textual information is easier to recall for the human brain when associated with pictorial information than recalling text without any illustration [8].

Fig. 2. With AuthZit, users finds and designates a location as their secret (A) in which then they create a path to arrive at the location (B). Lastly, users assign a textual tag to associate with the location (C).

AuthZit consists of the following three steps: 1) Location designation, 2) path routing, and 3) AuthZit text tagging. Figure 2 shows a high-level description of how AuthZit works.

Step 1. Location Designation: In the first step, a user enters a location name or address he/she would like to designate as their AuthZit, that would be easily memorable and recognizable to the user, but would be difficult for others to guess. An example AuthZit might be one's favorite childhood arcade. The user is specifically informed that the location will be used as a password so it must not be easily guessable by others (e.g., home, landmarks).

Step 2. Path Routing: Next, the user moves away from the designated location using the first person perspective as shown in Fig. 1 to create a path. We specifically informed the user that the path cannot be a straight line and required at least three turns in the path. The end of this path would be the starting point at which user would be when the authentication begins. During authentication, the user will be asked to navigate back to his/her AuthZit.

Step 3. Textual Tagging: Finally, the user enters his/her textual password consisting of at least two words for the location. The user was additionally advised to create the corresponding textual password associated with the location. However, the user was reminded that the provided texts would also be used for his/her password to discourage the user from choosing a text that could be easily guessable due to the location.

3   User Study

Our initial motivation for designing AuthZit was to create a memorable and secure fallback authentication scheme. For our initial user study, we experimentally evaluated AuthZit for two key performance measures: 1) long-term memorability with infrequent authentication, and 2) authentication speed. Long-term memorability after extended disuse was our key measure of interest, because AuthZit is designed for fallback authentication, where secrets should be easily memorable for long-term without a lot of repetitions. Next, we measured authentication speed because of its importance in usability and deployability.

First Session: To test AuthZit, we ran a user study with 20 participants in an online setting. Participants were compensated $10 for participating in the 20 min user study with their personal computer. Participants were informed of the purpose of the study and were given a few attempts of using AuthZit to get familiarized with AuthZit before the experiment began. Once familiarized, participants were instructed to create an authentication secret using AuthZit and verify that they remember it by authenticating right after creation.

Second and Third Session: One week after the first session, we invited users back to perform another memorability test. Users were placed in the initial path and were asked to navigate to their AuthZit location and input the correct textual password. Another memorability test was conducted in a third session that took place three weeks after the second one (i.e. one month after the first session). Users were instructed to perform the same tasks as they had done for the second session.

For statistical testing we performed the pairwise Fisher's Exact Test (FET), which yields more accurate confidence for relatively smaller sample size and the t-test for creation and authentication time.

The results of our experiments are summarized in Table 1.

Table 1. Average, median, and std. of registration and completion time in secs and average auth. success rate per trial.

Attempt	Time (sec) Avg./Med./Std.	Auth Succ. Rate
Registration	144.3/149.1/25.6	–
Auth. Initial Authentication	44.7/46.3/9.7	100%
Auth. After One Week	46.8/48.6/10.2	90.0%
Auth. Trial One Month	46.7/44.0/9.5	90.0%
Average Auth.	46.3/47.9/9.9	93.3%

4 Conclusion and Future Work

In this paper, we designed and evaluated AuthZit, a fallback authentication system that encodes authentication secrets as visual-spatial paths along with associated text. Our user study results demonstrate that AuthZit users had a high success rate of authentication with little reinforcement. While it may take more time for users to register and log-in using AuthZit, we believe the benefits of AuthZit outweigh the costs. In future work, we plan to increase explore methods to increase the security of AuthZit by studying path comparisons. We also plan to conduct large-scale user studies to evaluate AuthZit for longer periods of disuse, and compare it with conventional existing fallback authentication systems in terms of security and memorability. Furthermore, we plan to conduct user studies with close adversaries and test our system's resilience towards shoulder-surfing attacks.

Acknowledgements. This work was supported by the National Research Foundation of Korea (NRF) grant funded by the Korea Government (MIST) (No. RS-2022-00165660) and the Macao Polytechnic University research grant (Project code: RP/FCA-05/2023).

References

1. Bower, G.H.: Analysis of a mnemonic device: modern psychology uncovers the powerful components of an ancient system for improving memory. Am. Sci. **58**(5), 496–510 (1970)
2. Craik, F.I., Lockhart, R.S.: Levels of processing: a framework for memory research. J. Verbal Learn. Verbal Behav. **11**(6), 671–684 (1972)
3. Das, S., Lu, D., Lee, T., Lo, J., Hong, J.I.: The memory palace: exploring visual-spatial paths for strong, memorable, infrequent authentication. In: Proceedings of the 32nd Annual ACM Symposium on User Interface Software and Technology, pp. 1109–1121 (2019)
4. Foer, J.: Moonwalking with Einstein: The Art and Science of Remembering Everything. Penguin (2012)
5. Habib, H., et al.: User behaviors and attitudes under password expiration policies. In: Fourteenth Symposium on Usable Privacy and Security (SOUPS 2018), pp. 13–30. USENIX Association, Baltimore (2018). https://www.usenix.org/conference/soups2018/presentation/habib-password
6. Han, J.K., Kang, B., Wong, D.: HWAuth: handwriting-based socially-inclusive authentication. In: SIGGRAPH Asia 2021 Posters, pp. 1–2 (2021)
7. Hang, A., De Luca, A., Smith, M., Richter, M., Hussmann, H.: Where have you been? Using {Location-Based} security questions for fallback authentication. In: Eleventh Symposium on Usable Privacy and Security (SOUPS 2015), pp. 169–183 (2015)
8. Peeck, J.: Retention of pictorial and verbal content of a text with illustrations. J. Educ. Psychol. **66**(6), 880 (1974)
9. Rabkin, A.: Personal knowledge questions for fallback authentication: security questions in the era of Facebook. In: Proceedings of the 4th Symposium on Usable Privacy and Security, pp. 13–23 (2008)
10. Shay, R., et al.: Encountering stronger password requirements: user attitudes and behaviors. In: Proceedings of the Sixth Symposium on Usable Privacy and Security, p. 2. ACM (2010)

POSTER: Integration of End-to-End Security and Lightweight-SSL for Enhancing Security and Efficiency of MQTT

Hung-Yu Chien[✉] [iD]

National Chi-Nan University, Nantou County, Taiwan, Republic of China
hychien@mail.ncnu.edu.tw

Abstract. Message Queue Telemetry Transport (MQTT) is one of the most popular Internet of Things (IoT) communication protocols. The MQTT standards suggest the adoption of TLS/SSL in the underlying layer to facilitate the authentication and protect the transmissions. A MQTT system consists brokers, publishers, and subscribers. However, a TLS/SSL-enabled MQTT system still cannot protect the privacy against a curious broker.

The End-to-End (E2E) MQTT security is one such mechanism to ensure the security between a publisher and a subscriber, and to protect the privacy against a curious broker. Here, we notice one weakness of such E2E-MQTT solutions. The layering of the TLS/SSL channels and the E2E channel incurs the extra overhead that a message is encrypted and decrypted triple times, and it increases the broker's unnecessary loading.

In this study, we leverage the benefits of adopting both TLS/SSL and the E2E channel, while enhancing the efficiency. We keep the authentication mechanism and the integrity function of TLS/SSL, but eliminate its encryption. Some preliminary designs and evaluations verify the merits of the integrated approach.

1 Introduction

MQTT is a message-oriented protocol and is based on the publish-subscribe interaction pattern. A MQTT system consists of a set of clients (publishers and subscribers) and a broker who acts as an intermediary among the clients. A publisher publishes its messages with a specified topic to a broker which forwards the messages to those subscribers which have subscribed the same topic.

Conventional MQTT standards [1] (MQTT 3.1 and its precedent versions) support the account-password authentication and they do not support the encryption by themselves. The standards assume the system adopt TLS/SSL in the underlying layer to protect the privacy of the transmissions. In the rest of this paper, we use the term SSL to refer to both SSL and TLS. To enhance the security support of MQTT systems, many works (like [2–7]) have been proposed and evaluated.

Among those MQTT-security-enhancements, some researchers concern the E2E security of the publisher-subscriber channel. In a paired publisher-subscriber interaction of an SSL-enabled MQTT model (Fig. 1), there are two separate SSL channels: one

© The Author(s), under exclusive license to Springer Nature Switzerland AG 2023
J. Zhou et al. (Eds.): ACNS 2023 Workshops, LNCS 13907, pp. 669–674, 2023.
https://doi.org/10.1007/978-3-031-41181-6_37

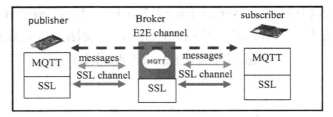

Fig. 1. The MQTT-SSL architecture

is the publisher-broker channel and the other is the broker-subscriber channel; we call them the outer channels. The E2E channel concerns the security and the privacy of the publisher-subscriber interactions. Mektoubi et al. [8] adopt the asymmetric-key-based approach to achieve the E2E security; however, the scheme adopts the costly public-key-based encryption to encrypt the messages, and each potential subscriber should manage to get the corresponding private key; it is too costly. The MQTLS scheme [9] distributes an E2E key by a publisher; it is required that all the subscribers should issue their CON-NECT requests before the publisher's CONNECT request; otherwise, the publisher fails to issue the E2E key for that client; this requirement limits the practical application of the scheme. SEEMQTT [11] also concerns the E2E security where a publisher delegates its decryption authority to a pool of the key stores, via the secret sharing mechanism; those designated subscribers should contact the pool of key stores, get verifications from them to recover the decryption key; this arrangement aims at those scenarios where it is difficult for the publishers to directly verify their subscribers and to protect the privacy against a curious broker. Chien [10] designs an E2E channel model (as shown in Fig. 1), using MQTT 5.0; in this model, each message sent from a publisher to a subscriber would be encrypted triply and decrypted triply. We can see that the existent MQTT E2E channel schemes all suffer from different degree of extra computational overhead, and we find that some of the extra overhead could be reduced significantly.

Therefore, we aim at designing an integrated MQTT-SSL-E2E scheme which leverage the benefits of both the existent TLS/SSL authentication and the E2E channel, while eliminating those unnecessary extra overhead.

2   Preliminaries

Before introducing our proposal in Sect. 3, we first review some key operations of TLS/SSL protocol and discuss the overhead of them.

An TLS/SSL-Enabled MQTT Model

A MQTT system can be configured to facilitate the broker-client mutual authentication using TLS/SSL. The protocol stack of an SSL-enabled MQTT system is shown in Fig. 2, where the SSL protocol stack consists of four sub-protocols.

Here, we assume the clients and the broker perform the SSL mutual authentication. In such a setting, the two entities mutually authenticate each other and establish an SSL-channel session key, via the SSL handshake protocol. When the client and the broker finish the handshake protocol, the SSL-channel session key is then passed to the SSL record protocol. After that, the MQTT client and the broker would pass their messages to their SSL record protocol, where the SSL record protocol encrypts/decrypts the messages, using the SSL-channel session key.

The Operation of SSL Record Protocol

The operation of SSL record protocol is shown in Fig. 3. When an application (for example, MQTT) passes its messages to the SSL record protocol, it first fragments the messages into several chunks and then compresses all the chunks; each compressed chunk is then appended with its chunk digest (MAC- message authentication code); finally, the aggregated chunk-MAC is encrypted, and is added with the SSL record protocol header.

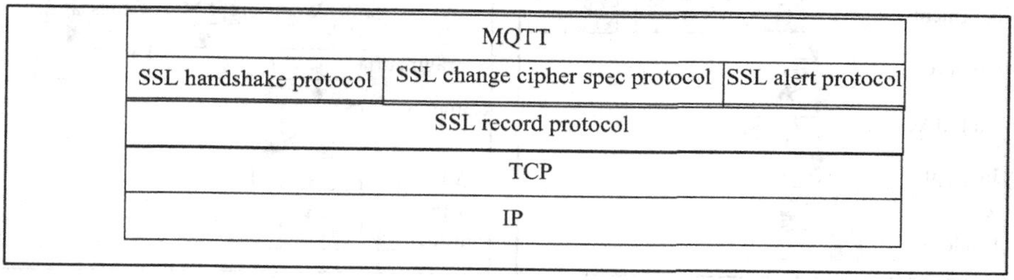

MQTT		
SSL handshake protocol	SSL change cipher spec protocol	SSL alert protocol
SSL record protocol		
TCP		
IP		

Fig. 2. Protocol stack of an SSL-enabled MQTT system

The Transmission Pattern of an SSL-Enabled MQTT System

From Figs. 1 and 2, we can see that it takes two pairs of (encryption, decryption) for a message transmitted from a publisher to a subscriber. One pair is done on the publisher-broker channel, and the other is required on the broker-subscriber channel. We note that the broker can peek at the content of the messages, as it can decrypt the encrypted messages.

For an application which concerns the privacy against the broker, one can build an E2E channel between a publisher and a subscriber, in addition to the SSL channels. In such a setting, each publisher-broker-subscriber transmission involves three encryptions and three decryptions; two (encryption, decryption) pairs result from the two SSL channel, and one pair from the E2E channel.

3 New Approach of Integrating E2E-MQTT and the Lightweight TLS/SSL

We notice that the combination of the existent E2E MQTT schemes (like []) with the existent client-broker authenticated key agreement schemes (like SSL and any secure authentication schemes) would involve their pairs of (encryption, decryption). As the E2E publisher-subscriber channel has provided the necessary confidentiality and integrity protection, the confidentiality provided by the outer channels (like SSL) is redundant.

We should note that the integrity provided by the outer channels is still necessary, as the broker still needs to verify the integrity of the received messages, and only forwards those valid encrypted messages.

3.1   The Lightweight TLS/SSL Record Protocol

Based on the above observations, we design a lightweight-SSL record operation as shown in Fig. 4. Here, we preserve the mutual authentication and the integrity check of the SSL protocol, but eliminate the confidentiality function of the SSL record protocol (the E2E channel has already provided the function).

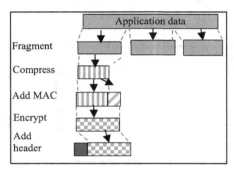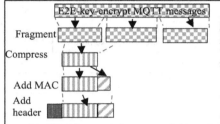

Fig. 3. Operation of SSL record protocol

Fig. 4. Operation of our lightweight-SSL record protocol

3.2   The Publisher-Subscriber E2E Channel

The publisher-subscriber E2E channel can be built as follows. Each pair of (publisher, subscriber) exchange their certificates, verify the certificates, and build a common Diffie-Hellman (DH) secret, based on the (public key, private key) pairs. This DH secret can be used to derive the E2E session key, or it can be used to deliver a E2E session key. Due to the space limit, we skip the details. Interested readers are referred to [10] for the details.

4   Preliminary Security Analysis and Performance Evaluation

Now we have designed the model of an integrated E2E-MQTT with the lightweight SSL. We have detailed an E2E-MQTT design using MQTT 5.0. Some preliminary security analyses are given as follows. The lightweight SSL protocol provides the mutual authentication between a client with its broker, and the integrity protection of the SSL-channel transmissions. The publisher-subscriber E2E channel ensures the security and the privacy, against any outsiders and the curious broker. Table 1 summarizes some features comparison.

Based on the comparison, we can see that the integrated lightweight-SSLE2E MQTT can ensure the security and the privacy against a curious broker while it demanding only one pair of (encryption, decryption).

Table 1. Comparison of the related models

	Naïve MQTT	SSL MQTT	SSL-E2E MQTT	Lightweight SSL-E2E MQTT
Privacy against outsiders	No	Yes	Yes	Yes
Privacy against broker	No	No	Yes	Yes
Number of (encryption, decryption) per publisher-broker-subscriber message	0	2	3	1
Mutual authentication	Client-broker[1]	Client-broker	Client-broker, publisher-subscriber	Client-broker, publisher-subscriber

5   Conclusions and Future Work

Up to now, we have designed an integrated E2E MQTT with the lightweight SSL. Now we are working on the detailed designs using MQTT APIs, and have been working on the implementations. In the future, we will have a complete evaluation of the related models, and plan to validate the performance in some real application scenarios.

Acknowledgements. This research was funded by the Ministry of Science and Technology, Taiwan, R.O.C. grant number MOST 111–2221-E-260–009-MY3.

References

1. ISO/IEC 20922:2016, Information technology -- Message Queuing Telemetry Transport (MQTT) v3.1.1. https://www.iso.org/standard/69466.html. Accessed 25 Mar 2022
2. OASIS, MQTT Version 5.0, 07 March 2019. https://docs.oasis-open.org/mqtt/mqtt/v5.0/mqtt-v5.0.html. Accessed 01 Apr 2022
3. Chien, H.Y., Wang, N.Z.: A novel MQTT 5.0-Based over-the-air updating architecture facilitating stronger security. MPDI Electron. **11**(23), 3899 (2022). https://www.mdpi.com/2079-9292/11/23/3899
4. Firdous, S.N., Baig, Z., Valli, C., Ibrahim, A.: Modelling and evaluation of malicious attacks against the IoT MQTT protocol. In: 2017 IEEE International Conference on Internet of Things (iThings) and IEEE Green Computing and Communications (GreenCom) and IEEE Cyber, Physical and Social Computing (CPSCom) and IEEE Smart Data (SmartData), pp. 748–755 (2017)
5. Chien, H.Y., et al.: A MQTT-API-compatible IoT security-enhanced platform. Int. J. Sens. Netw. **32**(1), 54–68 (2020)
6. Chien, H.-Y., Lin, P.C., Chiang, M.L.: Efficient MQTT platform facilitating secure group communication. J. Int. Technol. **21**(7), 1929–1940 (2020)
7. Chien, H.Y., Qiu, G.H., Hung, R.W., Shih, A.T., Su, C.H.: Hierarchical MQTT with edge computation. In: The 10th International Conference on Awareness Science and Technology (iCAST 2019), Morioka, Japan, pp. 1–5 (2019)
8. Mektoubi, A., Hassani, H.L., Belhadaoui, H., Rifi, M., Zakari, A.: New approach for securing communication over MQTT protocol a comparison between RSA and elliptic curve. In: 2016 Third International Conference on Systems of Collaboration (SysCo), Casablanca, Morocco

9. Lee, H., Lim, J., Kwon T.: MQTLS: toward secure MQTT communication with an untrusted broker. In: 2019 International Conference on Information and Communication Technology Convergence (ICTC), pp. 53–58 (2019)

10. Chien, H.-Y.: Design of end-to-end security for MQTT 5.0. In: The 4th International Conference on Science of Cyber Security - SciSec 2022, Matsue city, Shimane, Japan 10–12 August 2022

11. Hamad, M., Finkenzeller, A., Liu, H., Lauinger, J., Prevelakis, V., Steinhorst, S.: SEEMQTT: secure end-to-end MQTT-based communication for mobileIoT systems using secret sharing and trust delegation. IEEE Internet Things J. **10**(4), 3384–3406 (2023)

POSTER: Stopping Run-Time Countermeasures in Cryptographic Primitives

Myung-Hyun Kim, Taek-Young Youn, and Seungkwang Lee(✉)

Dankook University, Yongin-si, Gyeonggi-do, Republic of Korea
{taekyoung,sk.cryptographic}@dankook.ac.kr

Abstract. White-box cryptographic implementations with masking and shuffling have been proposed to protect against key extraction attacks. However, higher-order Differential Computation Analysis (HO-DCA) and its variants have been developed to break these countermeasures without having to perform reverse engineering. These non-invasive attacks are, however, costly to perform and can also be prevented by adapting novel constructions of masking and shuffling methods. This poster presents a simple binary injection attack on state-of-the-art masking and shuffling countermeasures. By injecting just a few lines of assembly code, the attacker can nullify run-time random sources, rendering randomness ineffective in hiding key-sensitive intermediate values. Our proposed attack mainly consists of hijacking the GOT entries and function calls to overcome run-time countermeasures protecting white-box cryptographic implementations.

Keywords: White-box cryptography · Masking · Shuffling · Binary injection attack

1 Introduction

The primary objective of white-box cryptography is to protect secret keys against invasive attacks, even in hostile environments, where an adversary has full control over the software implementation. Chow *et al.* proposed white-box implementations of AES and DES in 2002 by obfuscating full-round operations into key-instantiated lookup tables using linear and nonlinear transformations [4,5]. However, these implementations were found to be vulnerable to cryptanalysis attacks by Billet *et al.* Differential Computation Analysis (DCA) [3] is, on the other hand, a non-invasive attack used to break white-box cryptographic implementations. DCA is based on statistical analysis of computational traces and can recover the key without the need for reverse engineering. Unlike power traces used in Correlation Power Analysis (CPA), computational traces are noise-free and provide more accurate results.

© The Author(s), under exclusive license to Springer Nature Switzerland AG 2023
J. Zhou et al. (Eds.): ACNS 2023 Workshops, LNCS 13907, pp. 675–679, 2023.
https://doi.org/10.1007/978-3-031-41181-6_38

To protect against DCA, countermeasures such as rum-time masking and shuffling techniques from the gray-box model have been widely adopted. Generally speaking, masking divides sensitive variables into multiple shares and process them securely to prevent information leakage [6]. Shuffling, on the other hand, randomizes the order of independent operations to disturb the alignment of computational traces. In addition, dummy shuffling adds dummy operations to hide the real computation sensitive function among redundant computations [1]. These obfuscation methods, however, have been shown to be vulnerable to higher-order DCA (HO-DCA) and higher-degree HO-DCA (HDHO-DCA) attacks [2,7]. Unfortunately, the time complexity of higher-order attacks steeply increases as the dimension of the computational traces increases, and the new masked and shuffled implementation is likely to overcome this type of non-invasive attacks.

Here we focus on the fact that these countermeasures heavily depend on run-time random sources like random number generators and deterministic cryptographic algorithms, making them susceptible to invasive attacks. To achieve the objective of white-box cryptography, it must withstand white-box attacks. Additionally, key protection should be assessed using this invasive attack model in hostile environments. With this perspective in mind, this poster presents simple binary injection attacks on existing countermeasures that rely on run-time number sources, demonstrating their vulnerabilities in the presence of white-box attackers. To the best of our knowledge, this is the first demonstration of the white-box attack on masked and shuffled implementations.

2   Current Work

2.1   Key Idea Behind

To defeat countermeasures that rely on randomness, run-time random sources must be disabled so that key-dependant intermediate values are exposed. Generally speaking, a random number generator can be implemented by using either shared libraries or user-defined functions. In this section, we introduce simple binary injection attacks, enforcing the random number generator to always output a fixed value.

One of the easy ways to produce a sequence of random numbers is to call rand() provided in shared libraries. Lazy binding in Linux ELF binaries resolves unknown references to functions located in shared libraries, using the *Procedure Linkage Table* (.plt) and the *Global Offset Table* (.got) sections. In other words, the address of rand() can be found in its GOT entry once it is called. The steps ❶-❻ shown in Fig. 1 present the overall procedure of lazy binding to call rand() for the first time. By replacing the GOT entry with the address of the injected code, the attacker is enable to manipulate the behavior of rand(). If the injected code always returns zero, the sensitive variable is then no longer protected.

Using user-defined functions to generate random numbers, on the other hand, does not depend on the GOT entry, so hijacking a GOT entry has no effect. In this case, the attacker must locate the calls and overwrite them to replace with the manipulated calls to the injected code. It is important to notice that many of well-known countermeasures take advantage of cryptographic functions to generate a sequence of random numbers which is uniformly distributed; standard block ciphers are often adopted to guarantee high entropy of the outcome.

Assume that a cryptographic function F is used as a random number generator, and its prototype is F(arg1, arg2, arg3, arg4, $\cdots$). Following the System V calling convention for x64, the first six arguments are passed to the registers RDI, RSI, RDX, RCX, R8, and R9 in that order. If the attacker intends to disable the randomness provided by F, the injected code must correctly identify the register where F's output will be stored and implement measures to ensure that it generates a sequence of fixed constants. If arg2 is the ciphertext of F, the injected code inserts 16 zeros into the memory space pointed to by RSI. In the case that F returns its outcome with an n-th argument, the injected code must use the corresponding register as defined by the calling convention.

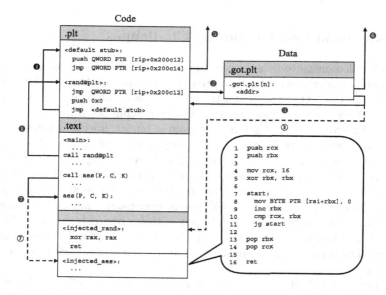

Fig. 1. Proposed attack. Solid line: benign function calls, Dashed line: hijacked function calls.

2.2   Disabling Random Sources with Injected Code

Our injected code nullifies countermeasures such as masking and shuffling by hijacking the calls to functions used as random sources. The steps ③ and ⑦ shown in Fig. 1 illustrate the hijacking of the GOT entry of rand() and the calls to aes(P, C, K), respectively.

First, rand() is manipulated to always return zero. The function prototype for rand() is defined as int rand(void), which returns an integer value between 0 and `RAND_MAX`. The return value is conventionally stored in RAX. The code label `<injected_rand>` in Fig. 1 shows how to fix the return value of `rand()` to zero using just two lines of assembly code.

In addition to returning a random number, a cryptographic function can provide one of its arguments as a source of randomness. As mentioned earlier, the first six arguments are conventionally passed to general-purpose registers, meaning that the target register is dependent on the position of the random source among the arguments. The solid line ❼ in Fig. 1 is the call to a user-defined cryptographic function `aes(P, C, K)`, where P, C, and K represent the plaintext, the ciphertext, and the secret key, respectively. Suppose that each byte of the ciphertext is used as a random number to hide a sensitive value. To clear the 16 bytes of the ciphertext, the injected code inserts 16 zeros into the memory space pointed to by RSI. However, if the user-defined function returns the random number in the fourth argument, then RCX at Lines 4 and 10 must be replaced with another register, such as R10, to prevent overwriting the base address of the output array at Line 8 with the counter at Line 4.

3   Conclusion and Upcoming Challenges

This poster demonstrated the binary injection attack, capable of defeating the cryptographic countermeasures that are dependent on run-time random sources. We redirected the GOT entries and the calls to shared libraries and user-defined functions to our injected code, consistently producing zeros instead of random numbers. To protect the target binary from a binary injection attack, various binary anti-tampering techniques can be employed. First, code obfuscation can make the code more difficult to understand and reverse engineer. Next, integrity checks are another technique used in binary anti-tampering. These checks are designed to detect modifications to the binary code. There are several types of integrity checks, including hash-based checks, checksums, and digital signatures. Encryption is also commonly used in binary anti-tampering techniques. The code is decrypted at runtime using a key that is kept secret. Overall, these techniques can be used in combination to provide a multi-layered approach to binary anti-tampering.

Our upcoming challenges are as follows. First, we will collect publicly available white-box cryptographic implementations protected by state-of-the-art masking and shuffling countermeasures. With these samples, we will provide the performance comparison between HO-DCA and HDHO-DCA using compiled binaries and DCA using manipulated binaries with our injected code. To be specific, the number of computational traces required to recover a subkey and the elapsed time will be evaluated. In addition, we will demonstrate the hijacking of calls to functions in static libraries. The target functions to be hijacked include not only `rand()` but also various cryptographic primitives with different prototypes. For each different prototype, different code might be injected to disable target random sources. Last but not least, we will develop an automation tool that detects all random sources in binaries and injects the code based on the characteristics of the random source. For instance, if the randomness is required to generate random numbers for masking and dummy operations, it will inject zero-returning code. Alternatively, if the target function is expected to generate a random permutation of consecutive numbers, the injected code generates a fixed sequence, making it ineffective.

Acknowledgement. This work was supported by Electronics and Telecommunications Research Institute (ETRI) grant funded by the Korean government [20ZR1300, Core Technology Research on Trust Data Connectome, 50%], and by Institute of Information & communications Technology Planning & Evaluation(IITP) grant funded by the Korea government (MIST) (No. 2022-0-01022, Development of Collection and Integrated Analysis Methods of Automotive Inter/Intra System Artifacts through Construction of Event-based experimental system, 50%).

References

1. Biryukov, A., Udovenko, A.: Dummy shuffling against algebraic attacks in white-box implementations. In: Canteaut, A., Standaert, F.-X. (eds.) EUROCRYPT 2021, Part II. LNCS, vol. 12697, pp. 219–248. Springer, Cham (2021). https://doi.org/10.1007/978-3-030-77886-6_8
2. Bogdanov, A., Rivain, M., Vejre, P.S., Wang, J.: Higher-order DCA against standard side-channel countermeasures. In: Polian, I., Stöttinger, M. (eds.) COSADE 2019. LNCS, vol. 11421, pp. 118–141. Springer, Cham (2019). https://doi.org/10.1007/978-3-030-16350-1_8
3. Bos, J.W., Hubain, C., Michiels, W., Teuwen, P.: Differential computation analysis: hiding your white-box designs is not enough. In: Gierlichs, B., Poschmann, A.Y. (eds.) CHES 2016. LNCS, vol. 9813, pp. 215–236. Springer, Heidelberg (2016). https://doi.org/10.1007/978-3-662-53140-2_11
4. Chow, S., Eisen, P., Johnson, H., van Oorschot, P.C.: A white-box DES implementation for DRM applications. In: Feigenbaum, J. (ed.) DRM 2002. LNCS, vol. 2696, pp. 1–15. Springer, Heidelberg (2003). https://doi.org/10.1007/978-3-540-44993-5_1
5. Chow, S., Eisen, P., Johnson, H., Van Oorschot, P.C.: White-box cryptography and an AES implementation. In: Nyberg, K., Heys, H. (eds.) SAC 2002. LNCS, vol. 2595, pp. 250–270. Springer, Heidelberg (2003). https://doi.org/10.1007/3-540-36492-7_17
6. Seker, O., Eisenbarth, T., Liskiewicz, M.: A white-box masking scheme resisting computational and algebraic attacks. IACR Trans. Cryptogr. Hardw. Embed. Syst. **2021**(2), 61–105 (2021)
7. Tang, Y., Gong, Z., Chen, J., Xie, N.: Higher-order DCA attacks on white-box implementations with masking and shuffling countermeasures. IACR Trans. Cryptogr. Hardw. Embed. Syst. **2023**(1), 369–400 (2022)

POSTER: Swarm-Based IoT Network Penetration Testing by IoT Devices

Thomas Schiller[1]([✉]) and Sean Mondesire[2]

[1] School of Modeling Simulation and Training, University of Central Florida,
Orlando, USA
schiller@knights.ucf.edu
[2] Institute of Simulation and Training, University of Central Florida, Orlando, USA
sean.mondesire@ucf.edu

Abstract. Internet-of-Things (IoT) networks are of raising significance. IoT devices are prone to attacks, but computational powerful at the same time. This work proposes IoT penetration testing (pen-testing) by IoT devices to produce IoT networks that are less prone to vulnerabilities. A network simulator uses three different algorithms to show that swarm-based algorithms could be used for multi-agent network pen-testing. The results so far show the superiority of the swarm-based algorithm over the single-agent linear approach. Interesting dynamics can be seen when the algorithms are applied on a larger scale with more devices (computer agents).

Keywords: Penetration Testing · IoT · Cybersecurity · Simulation · Swarm

1 Extensions to Prior Work

Parts of this work have been submitted to the 2023 Annual Modeling and Simulation Conference (ANNSIM 2023) by the same authors and will be presented at that conference in May this year. However, this contribution to the ACNS 2023 extends this work. It will provide a description of the algorithms used for the experiments. It will further provide results from experiments on a smart home level and the larger scale of a smart building level. These results have not been published before and provide a view into the dynamics when applied on different scales.

To deliver an introduction to the topic and idea of swarm-based IoT pen-testing by IoT devices, the introduction section includes parts from the ANNSIM 2023 submission. However, the methodology and the results are the focus of this poster submission.

2 Introduction

In today's world, digital services and technology play a crucial role in private and business networks. The Internet of Things (IoT) device network has

J. Zhou et al. (Eds.): ACNS 2023 Workshops, LNCS 13907, pp. 680–684, 2023.
https://doi.org/10.1007/978-3-031-41181-6_39

emerged as a notable example, experiencing rapid growth in recent years. By 2030, an individual's smart home network will be predicted to contain over 30 devices [1]. However, IoT devices are vulnerable to cyber-attacks, posing security risks; penetration testing (pen-testing) can help identify and mitigate these risks (e.g., [3,5]) [6].

Many IoT devices, like smart TVs and refrigerators, have substantial computational power and can run sophisticated network services, making them potential targets for attacks and valuable pen-testing tools at the same time. Because smart home IoT devices often have spare capacity, using them for pen-testing seems feasible [6].

Traditional pen-testing is a highly structured, human-centric process [7]. Although some aspects can be automated, human-in-the-loop and human-on-the-loop remain standard practices. Autonomous pen-testing is still in its early stages; there are research gaps in multi-agent swarm-based pen-testing and IoT pen-testing by Iot devices (e.g., [2,8]). This research aims to explore the feasibility and performance of IoT swarm-based pen-testing and pen-testing of IoT devices by IoT devices [6].

3   Methodology

To conduct the research, a network simulator has been developed called Cyber-SimSwarmIoT. This network simulator is based on CyberSim [4] but extended with further functionality. CyberSimSwarmIoT is a constructive and agent-based simulator to simulate networks in the IP4 range. It is highly adjustable. Different scenarios can easily be developed. In the simulation, every agent has a simplified pen-testing action range, e.g., *nmap*, *netstat*, or *SQL injection*. Agent actions are stored on a blackboard that each agent can access. However, each agent has its own blackboard and can only see actions done by itself or on itself. There is no global knowledge or central control.

CyberSimSwarmIoT is capable of running multiple simulations in parallel at the same time to utilize multiple CPU cores for Monte Carlo simulations. All results are stored automatically and can be accessed in human-readable format with built-in analysis tools. After the final publication of this research, Cyber-SimSwarmIoT will be published under the MIT license to provide future research opportunities and replicability.

Three algorithms are developed to test the IoT pen-testing by IoT devices scenario. The first algorithm is a single agent for linear pen-testing. It mimics human pen-testing behavior. The second algorithm is a swarm algorithm based on queues. The agents can communicate and store network discoveries from other agents in queues. The queues are then processed in stack order. The third algorithm is based on Particle Swarm Optimization (PSO). PSO is an established and well-discovered nature-based swarm algorithm mimicking the behavior of bird flocks. In research, it is often used for comparison to newer and more advanced nature-based algorithms. In CyberSimSwarmIoT, the queue-based and the PSO-based algorithm can be adjusted with the communication level between the agents. The PSO can further be tweaked with the inertia weight.

All three algorithms are utilized with two different pre-defined networks. The first network represents a smart home network with 30 devices in a /24 subnet. The second network represents a smart home building with 512 devices in a larger subnet. The smart home network has four vulnerabilities that the algorithms should detect. The larger network contains twelve vulnerabilities.

4   Preliminary Results

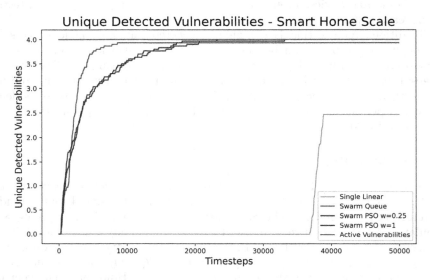

Fig. 1. This graph shows unique detected vulnerabilities for the smart home environment (30 devices). The swarm algorithms are superior to the single linear agent algorithm. The queue-based algorithm detects vulnerabilities faster than the PSO. The graph shows the aggregation of 30 simulation runs of each algorithm.

The results, so far, show the superiority of both swarm algorithms (queue and PSO) to the single linear agent for the smart home and the smart building - which was expected. In comparison to the PSO algorithm, the queue algorithm detects vulnerabilities faster. Figure 1 shows the results for the smart home.

When comparing the smart home with the smart building, it can be seen that the smart building has a higher rate of all detected vulnerabilities. Figure 2 shows the rate of all detected vulnerabilities for the smart home. Figure 3 shows the same for the smart building. This is due to the higher number of agents. This also results in a higher detection rate of vulnerabilities with a lower probability of success. Further, was the smart building experiment run with a lower communication and inertia weight resulting in less communication yet a high detection rate. This leads to the conclusion, that the communication and inertia weights needs to be adjusted according to the size of the network to work efficiently.

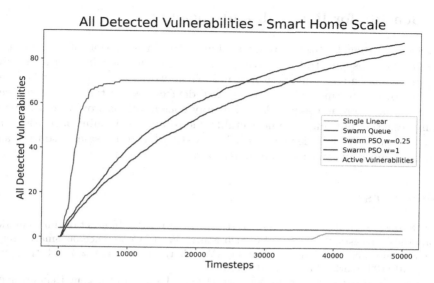

Fig. 2. This graph shows all detected vulnerabilities for the smart home environment (30 devices). Both swarm algorithms detect vulnerabilities multiple times. This provides better results in detecting all active vulnerabilities since some attacks for vulnerabilities have a low probability of success. The graph shows the aggregation of 30 simulation runs of each algorithm.

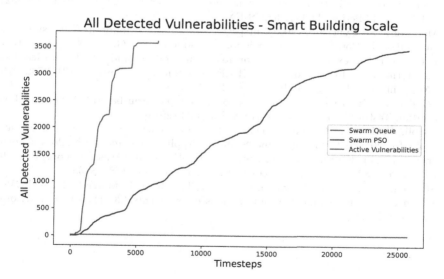

Fig. 3. This graph shows all detected vulnerabilities for the smart building environment (512 devices). A higher number of agents leads to a higher repeated detection of vulnerabilities, although the communication level and inertia weight was lower than with smart home environment (Fig. 2). The graph shows one simulation run.

5   Benefits for Research and Society

Research can benefit from this work, due to the introduction of swarm-based and autonomous penetration testing. The society can benefit long-term with safer networks (smart home networks and IoT networks in general). Further does the idea of pen-testing IoT devices by IoT devices need little added resources. No extra hardware is needed. Added energy consumptions would be a topic of future research, but might be neglectable due to increasing minituarization and increased power of IoT devices. Utilizing existing hardware safes resources and leads to a more efficient use of resources already gathered.

References

1. Al-Sarawi, S., Anbar, M., Abdullah, R., Al Hawari, A.B.: Internet of things market analysis forecasts, 2020–2030. In: 2020 Fourth World Conference on Smart Trends in Systems, Security and Sustainability (WorldS4), pp. 449–453 (2020). https://doi.org/10.1109/WorldS450073.2020.9210375
2. Campbell, R.G.: Autonomous Network Defence Using Multi-Agent Reinforcement Learning and Self-Play. Master of Science, San Jose State University, San Jose, CA, USA (2022). https://doi.org/10.31979/etd.8pey-takb. https://scholarworks.sjsu.edu/etd_theses/5253
3. Florez Cardenas, M., Acar, G.: Ethical Hacking of a Smart Fridge: Evaluating the cybersecurity of an IoT device through gray box hacking (2021). Backup Publisher: KTH, School of Electrical Engineering and Computer Science (EECS) Issue: 2021: 451 Pages: 46 Series: TRITA-EECS-EX
4. Mondesire, S.: CyberSim (2023). https://github.com/DrMondesire/cybersim
5. Neshenko, N., Bou-Harb, E., Crichigno, J., Kaddoum, G., Ghani, N.: Demystifying IoT security: an exhaustive survey on IoT vulnerabilities and a first empirical look on internet-scale IoT exploitations. IEEE Commun. Surv. Tutor. **21**(3), 2702–2733 (2019). https://doi.org/10.1109/COMST.2019.2910750
6. Schiller, T., Mondesire, S.: Human-out-of-the-Loop Swarm-based IoT Network Penetration Testing by IoT Devices. ANNSIM 2023 (2023)
7. Shebli, H.M.Z.A., Beheshti, B.D.: A study on penetration testing process and tools. In: 2018 IEEE Long Island Systems, Applications and Technology Conference (LISAT), Farmingdale, NY, pp. 1–7. IEEE (2018). https://doi.org/10.1109/LISAT.2018.8378035. https://ieeexplore.ieee.org/document/8378035/
8. Standen, M., Lucas, M., Bowman, D., Richer, T.J., Kim, J., Marriott, D.: CybORG: a gym for the development of autonomous cyber agents (2021). http://arxiv.org/abs/2108.09118 [cs]

POSTER: Advancing Federated Edge Computing with Continual Learning for Secure and Efficient Performance

Chunlu Chen[1]([✉]), Kevin I-Kai Wang[2], Peng Li[3], and Kouichi Sakurai[1]

[1] Kyushu University, Fukuoka, Japan
chen.chunlu.270@s.kyushu-u.ac.jp, sakurai@inf.kyushu-u.ac.jp
[2] The University of Auckland, Auckland, New Zealand
[3] The University of Aizu, Aizuwakamatsu, Japan

Abstract. Federated Learning (FL) and the Internet of Things (IoT) have transformed data processing and analysis, overcoming traditional cloud computing limitations. However, challenges such as catastrophic forgetting in continuous training scenarios arise. To address these, we propose an FL framework that supports continual learning while enhancing system security. We preserve critical knowledge through the incorporation of Knowledge Distillation (KD), addressing the issue of catastrophic forgetting. In addition, we have integrated encryption techniques to secure the updated parameters of clients from potential threats posed by attackers.

Keywords: Federated Learning · Continual Learning · Security

1 Introduction

With the rapid development of the Internet of Things (IoT) and the proliferation in mobile devices, edge computing has emerged as a promising paradigm for addressing challenges in data processing and analysis at the network edge. Edge computing refers to the practice of performing computation and data processing closer to the source of data generation, which can be at the network edge or within the terminal devices themselves [1,2]. This approach has the potential to overcome limitations of traditional cloud computing, such as high latency and bandwidth constraints. However, it also introduces potential risks and challenges, such as security and privacy concerns for data within edge devices. In addition, in edge computing, training data is frequently dispersed and subject to dynamic changes over time, which poses challenges to the training process [3]. If traditional machine learning approaches are employed, model retraining becomes necessary whenever new datasets are added, resulting in increased computational costs and reduced efficiency due to the need for data integration and model retraining [4]. It has been well recognized that retraining may also lead to catastrophic forgetting, a phenomenon in which a model might forget or lose its

J. Zhou et al. (Eds.): ACNS 2023 Workshops, LNCS 13907, pp. 685–689, 2023.
https://doi.org/10.1007/978-3-031-41181-6_40

understanding of previous tasks as it learns a new task, resulting in decreased performance on prior tasks [5,6]. Catastrophic forgetting poses challenges for the application of continuous and incremental learning, such as autonomous driving, smart assistants, facial recognition, and others, where models must constantly adapt to new tasks and data while maintaining good performance on previous tasks.

Continual learning (also known as Lifelong learning), proposed as a solution to the catastrophic forgetting issues, refers to machine learning models that continuously adapt to new data and learn new tasks during training while retaining knowledge from previous tasks [7,8]. Continual learning is characterized by sequential nature of the learning process, concretely by sequences of tasks [4]. Each task, denoted as t, consists of a set of classes that are mutually exclusive with the classes in other tasks, whether they are previous or future tasks, with t representing the task-ID [9]. Continual learning on edge devices enables better adaptation to dynamic environments, as models can continuously learn and improve based on real-time data collected by devices. Moreover, continual learning can effectively handle Non-Independent and Identically Distributed (Non-IID) data with significant variations [10], which is common in edge computing environments due to the substantial differences in data collected by various devices. However, in continual learning, models consistently adapt to new data and learn new tasks during training, providing potential attackers with opportunities to compromise model performance or leak sensitive information. For example, attackers may exploit model parameters or outputs to infer sensitive information about training data, or they could sabotage the model's performance on other tasks by providing erroneous data.

To address these security and privacy issues, we seek to develop a training framework that supports continual learning while enhancing system security. To achieve this goal, we establish a Federated Learning (FL) framework for continual learning. FL trains on local devices, eliminating the need to store and process sensitive data on a central server, thereby reducing the risk of privacy leakage [11,12]. Additionally, implementing continual learning in a FL environment allows distributed devices to better adapt to dynamic environments and address catastrophic forgetting issues [3], as models on each local device update using local data without affecting models on other devices. By performing incremental learning on local devices, models can retain knowledge from previous tasks while learning new ones, thus avoiding catastrophic forgetting [13,14]. Furthermore, this collaboration improves model adaptability, reduces latency, and enhances data security and privacy protection, opening up new opportunities for a wide range of applications.

2   Methodology

2.1   Our Framework

As illustrated in Fig. 1, we consider FL system comprising a server and N edge devices, along with two training tasks. We assume that the server is consid-

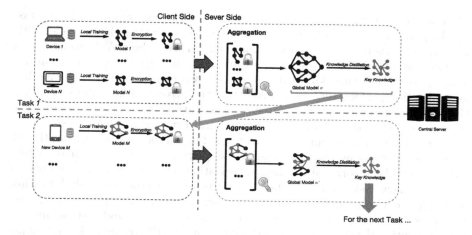

Fig. 1. The training process of Continual Learning-based Federated Learning

erably more powerful than the devices. The data is distributed across multiple devices, which can be locally exploited for the FL training process without being transferred. We assume that, in a continuous time horizon requiring sequential training of multiple tasks, each client n can access only their private dataset for each task. The server disseminates the initialized model to the clients participating in Task 1, who subsequently train it using their respective local private data. Following training, clients employ encryption algorithms to secure the local model (or parameters) before transmitting them to the server. Upon receipt, the server decrypts the aggregated local models (or parameters) and updates the global model w. Subsequently, the server extracts key knowledge from the updated global model through the application of Knowledge Distillation (KD) techniques and retains this information on the server. During Task 2, the server distributes both the global model w, which was trained on Task 1, and the key knowledge to clients engaged in Task 2. These clients then train the model using their local private data. After completing the training, clients encrypt the local model (or parameters) and forward them to the server. The server decrypts the collected local models (or parameters), aggregates them, and updates the global model to w'. Finally, the server extracts key knowledge from w' and retains it for utilization in subsequent tasks.

2.2 Knowledge Preservation and Security

In our proposed approach, we prevent catastrophic forgetting by maintaining key knowledge from previous tasks using the Elastic Weight Consolidation (EWC) method [15]. EWC is a regularization-based method designed to prevent forgetting of old knowledge by incorporating a regularization loss term when learning new data (tasks). This technique helps to constrain the model's parameters during the learning process, preserving essential information from previous tasks while adapting to new data [16]. In addition, during the training of each task in FL, participants are allowed to collaboratively train the global model without exposing their local data. By combining FL with the EWC algorithm, we enable continuous learning across multiple tasks in edge computing scenarios. This approach leverages knowledge from previous tasks to enhance the model's generalization performance while protecting the privacy of local data. Our continual learning approach allows the model to continuously update and evolve as it receives new tasks and data, maintaining its accuracy and robustness.

In terms of security, our approach stores data on local clients within the FL framework, mitigating the risk of centralizing sensitive data on a single server. Additionally, by incorporating the regularization term, we constrain the weight updates of new tasks, reducing the risk of overfitting to the new task data while retaining knowledge from previous tasks. Furthermore, in our proposed scheme, we introduce encryption techniques to safeguard clients' updated parameters from potential threats posed by attackers. In the FL framework, commonly used encryption algorithms include Homomorphic Encryption (HE), Differential Privacy (DP), and Secure Multi-Party Computation (MPC). These algorithms ensure the security of the system while protecting data privacy. However, these encryption algorithms may have an impact on computational efficiency and model accuracy. Thus, constructing lightweight encryption algorithms remains an important direction of our research.

3   Conclusion

FL allows edge devices to train models locally, avoiding the need to transmit raw data to central servers and thus protecting user privacy. It also enables continual learning and model updates based on local data changes and real-time requirements, ensuring adaptability to environmental changes and achieving real-time optimization and improvement of models at the edge. In this paper, we propose a training framework that supports continual learning while enhancing system security. We preserve critical knowledge through the incorporation of KD, addressing the issue of catastrophic forgetting. Additionally, we introduce encryption techniques to safeguard clients' updated parameters from potential threats posed by attackers.

Acknowledgement. This work is partially supported by JSPS international scientific exchanges between Japan and India (Bilateral Program DTS-JSPS) (2022–2024). The research of the first author is partially supported by the Japan Science and Technology Agency, Support for Pioneering Research Initiated by the Next Generation (JST SPRING) under Grant JPMJSP2136. The research of the second author is partially supported by the International Exchange, Foreign Researcher Invitation Program of National Institute of Information and Communications Technology (NICT), Japan.

References

1. Nguyen, D.C., et al.: Federated learning meets blockchain in edge computing: opportunities and challenges. IEEE Internet Things J. **8**(16), 12806–12825 (2021)
2. Mao, Y., You, C., Zhang, J., Huang, K., Letaief, K.B.: A survey on mobile edge computing: the communication perspective. IEEE Commun. Surv. Tutor. **19**(4), 2322–2358 (2017)
3. Park, T.J., Kumatani, K., Dimitriadis, D.: Tackling dynamics in federated incremental learning with variational embedding rehearsal. arXiv preprint arXiv:2110.09695 (2021)
4. Usmanova, A., Portet, F., Lalanda, P., Vega, G.: A distillation-based approach integrating continual learning and federated learning for pervasive services. arXiv preprint arXiv:2109.04197 (2021)
5. Mitchell, T., et al.: Never-ending learning. Commun. ACM **61**(5), 103–115 (2018)
6. Van de Ven, G.M., Siegelmann, H.T., Tolias, A.S.: Brain-inspired replay for continual learning with artificial neural networks. Nat. Commun. **11**(1), 4069 (2020)
7. Hadsell, R., Rao, D., Rusu, A.A., Pascanu, R.: Embracing change: continual learning in deep neural networks. Trends Cogn. Sci. **24**(12), 1028–1040 (2020)
8. Parisi, G.I., Kemker, R., Part, J.L., Kanan, C., Wermter, S.: Continual lifelong learning with neural networks: a review. Neural Netw. **113**, 54–71 (2019)
9. Masana, M., Liu, X., Twardowski, B., Menta, M., Bagdanov, A.D., van de Weijer, J.: Class-incremental learning: survey and performance evaluation on image classification. IEEE Trans. Pattern Anal. Mach. Intell. **45**, 5513–5533 (2022)
10. Criado, M.F., Casado, F.E., Iglesias, R., Regueiro, C.V., Barro, S.: Non-IID data and continual learning processes in federated learning: a long road ahead. Inf. Fusion **88**, 263–280 (2022)
11. McMahan, B., Moore, E., Ramage, D., Hampson, S., Arcas, B.A.: Communication-efficient learning of deep networks from decentralized data. In: Artificial Intelligence and Statistics, pp. 1273–1282. PMLR (2017)
12. Mothukuri, V., Parizi, R.M., Pouriyeh, S., Huang, Y., Dehghantanha, A., Srivastava, G.: A survey on security and privacy of federated learning. Future Gener. Comput. Syst. **115**, 619–640 (2021)
13. Schwarz, J., et al.: Progress & compress: a scalable framework for continual learning. In: International Conference on Machine Learning, pp. 4528–4537. PMLR (2018)
14. Zhu, K., Zhai, W., Cao, Y., Luo, J., Zha, Z.J.: Self-sustaining representation expansion for non-exemplar class-incremental learning. In: Proceedings of the IEEE/CVF Conference on Computer Vision and Pattern Recognition, pp. 9296–9305 (2022)
15. Kirkpatrick, J., et al.: Overcoming catastrophic forgetting in neural networks. Proc. Natl. Acad. Sci. **114**(13), 3521–3526 (2017)
16. van de Ven, G.M., Tuytelaars, T., Tolias, A.S.: Three types of incremental learning. Nat. Mach. Intell. **4**, 1185–1197 (2022). https://doi.org/10.1038/s42256-022-00568-3

POSTER: A Fine-Grained Metric for Evaluating the Performance of Adversarial Attacks and Defenses

Haibo Zhang[1]([✉]) [iD], Zhihua Yao[2] [iD], and Kouichi Sakurai[3] [iD]

[1] Department of Information Science and Technology, Graduate School of Information Science and Electrical Engineering, Kyushu University, Fukuoka, Japan
zhang.haibo.892@s.kyushu-u.ac.jp
[2] Faculty of Economics and Business Administration, The University of Kitakyushu, Kitakyushu, Japan
zhihuayao@alumni.usc.edu
[3] Department of Information Science and Technology, Faculty of Information Science and Electrical Engineering, Kyushu University, Fukuoka, Japan
sakurai@inf.kyushu-u.ac.jp

Abstract. Over the past decade, the development of both adversarial attack methods and defense strategies has accelerated rapidly. Classification accuracy has been predominantly used as the sole metric for assessing model performance. However, when the reported accuracy rates of two models are identical or very similar, it becomes challenging to determine which model is superior. To address this issue and offer more insights into model performance, this study introduces a novel classification performance metric: the confidence gap. This metric is defined as the difference in confidence level between the true label and either the top 1 prediction or the second-best prediction, depending on the accuracy of the image classification. The confidence level, as indicated by its sign, reflects the correctness of the classification and provides more detailed information on the robustness of the classification result. Recognizing that evaluation results may be inconsistent when employing different criteria, we recommend that future research in this field should report the confidence gap alongside accuracy rates.

1 Introduction

Adversarial attacks present significant security challenges within the domain of image recognition. Attackers can create adversarial examples by introducing subtle, imperceptible perturbations to the input, leading to incorrect classifications by the model [1]. Since the introduction of adversarial examples, researchers have been investigating various techniques for generating such samples and devising methods to defend against these attacks. However, the primary focus of the research community has been on the development of algorithms, while the establishment of metrics to evaluate the performance of these models has received comparatively less attention.

© The Author(s), under exclusive license to Springer Nature Switzerland AG 2023
J. Zhou et al. (Eds.): ACNS 2023 Workshops, LNCS 13907, pp. 690–694, 2023.
https://doi.org/10.1007/978-3-031-41181-6_41

1.1   Accuracy Rate

The simplest performance metric is the accuracy rate. Given a test set with n images, the accuracy rate is defined as the average of the correctly classified images. Mathematically, let t_i be equal to 1 if the ith image is classified correctly and 0 if it is classified incorrectly. Then, the accuracy rate can be expressed as:

$$Accuracy\ rate = \frac{1}{n}\sum_{i=1}^{n} t_i$$

The accuracy rate is a fundamental and widely used metric for evaluating model performance, primarily due to its simplicity and ease of implementation. As a result, researchers often employ the accuracy rate as the sole metric for assessing their models. Prominent works on adversarial attacks that report accuracy rates include, but are not limited to, the Carlini-Wagner (C&W) attack [2], the Projected Gradient Descent (PGD) attack [3], and AutoAttack [4]. Similarly, most representative works on defense models report accuracy rates as the performance metric for their methodologies.

Despite its prevalent use, the accuracy rate is not an ideal metric. As we will demonstrate in the results section, the accuracy rate does not provide any information about the model's robustness. Although some researchers present the standard deviation of the accuracy rate, we argue that this measure is not meaningful because the accuracy rate is the average of 0 s and 1 s. The standard deviation of such data reaches its maximum value when the number of 1 s and 0 s is equal and converges to 0 when one value increases in number while the other decreases. Consequently, when the accuracy rate is extremely high or low, the standard deviation will also be small, potentially misleading us into believing that the model's accuracy will remain stable in future tests.

1.2   Confidence Gap

To address this issue, we propose confidence gap as an alternative performance metric , which is defined as the difference in confidence levels between the true label and either the top prediction or the second-best prediction, contingent upon whether the image is classified correctly. Specifically, the confidence gap equals the difference between the confidence level of the true label and that of the top prediction when the image is misclassified, and the difference between the confidence level of the true label and that of the second-best prediction when the image is correctly classified.

Let C_{tl} denote the confidence level of the true label, C_1 be the confidence level of the top 1 prediction, and C_2 be the confidence level of the second-best prediction. Then, the confidence gap can be mathematically expressed as:

$$Confidence\ Gap = \begin{cases} C_{tl} - C_1, & if \quad C_{tl} \neq C_1 \\ C_{tl} - C_2, & if \quad C_{tl} = C_1 \end{cases}$$

By definition, the confidence gap ranges between -1 and 1. A positive confidence gap indicates correct classification. A larger confidence gap implies that the true label has a substantially higher confidence level than the second-best classification, suggesting that the model exhibits high confidence in its top classification (i.e., the true label), with the second-best classification being a relatively distant alternative. This implies that the model is likely performing well and can accurately distinguish the true class from other potential classes.

Conversely, a positive confidence gap close to zero signifies that the true label has only a marginally higher confidence level than the second-best classification, indicating that the model has low confidence in its top classification, and other possible classes are relatively close in terms of probability. This suggests that the model may not perform as well and could be more prone to errors or misclassifications.

If the value of the confidence gap is negative, it indicates that the true label is not the top 1 prediction, and therefore, the image is misclassified. If an attack can generate adversarial examples that cause the classifier to misclassify images with a high absolute value of the confidence gap, it suggests that the attack is potent and might successfully deceive various classifiers or penetrate different defense models. Conversely, a negative confidence gap near 0 implies that the model introduces minimal distortion to the image to alter its classification. In such cases, an adversarial sample generated for one specific classifier may not be effective in fooling other classifiers or defense methods.

2   Methodology and Results

2.1   Experimental Design

We evaluate four renowned adversarial attacks: FGSM [1], PGD, C&W, and AutoAttack. For FGSM, PGD, and C&W, we employed the attack function from Cleverhans [5], as referenced in the literature. Meanwhile, for AutoAttack, we used the attack function from the Adversarial Robustness Toolbox v1.2.0 (ART) [6].

Algorithm 1. Calculate Confidence Gap

1: **procedure** CONFIDENCE_GAP(probs[top1, top2, ..., end], true_label)
2:     **if** probs[top1] = true_label **then**
3:         **return** probs[top1].confi - probs[top2].confi
4:     **else**
5:         **for** $i \leftarrow 1$ **to** len(confi_list) - 1 **do**
6:             **if** probs[i] = true_label **then**
7:                 **return** probs[i].confi - probs[top1].confi
8:         **return** probs[end].confi - probs[top1].confi

We randomly selected six images that can be correctly classified by the Inception_V3 model [7] from each category of the ILSVRC2012 ImageNet dataset [8] to form our test set. As there are 1,000 categories in the ImageNet dataset, the total number of images in our test set amounts to 6,000. We divided the test set into six subsets, with each subset containing 1,000 images, representing one image from each of the 1,000 categories. We report the accuracy rate, standard deviation of accuracy, and the average confidence gap for each of the four models using the first subset (Test_1) in Table 1.

2.2   Results

As shown in Table 1, the accuracy rate for the C&W attack is 0%, and for the AutoAttack, it is 1.37%. If we were to evaluate the two attack models solely based on accuracy rates, the conclusion would be that the C&W attack is stronger than the AutoAttack. When considering the standard deviation as a metric for robustness, the C&W attack has the lowest standard deviation, suggesting that the C&W attack would consistently achieve a 100% success rate. However, if we evaluate the two models using the confidence gap, the C&W attack has a low absolute value of the confidence gap at 8.9%, while the AutoAttack has a high absolute value of the confidence gap at 89%. This implies that there is likely to be more variability in the future performance of the C&W attack than in the AutoAttack.

Table 1. The Comparison of Different Performance Metrics Using Test_1 Subset

Attacks	Accuracy(%)	Standard Deviation(%)	Confidence Gap(%)
Clean image	100	0	74.77
FGSM	28.09	44.98	−9.24
PGD	6.59	24.83	−81.09
C&W	0	0	−8.91
AutoAttack	1.37	11.6	−89.08

Table 2. Additional Results on Accuracy and Confidence Gaps from Other Test Sets

%	Test_2		Test_3		Test_4		Test_5		Test_6	
	Acc	CG	Acc	CG	Acc	CG	Acc	CG	Acc	CG
C&W	1.95	−7.57	2.44	−6.63	0.98	−9.34	1.46	−7.52	1.95	−7.55
AutoAttack	1.28	−88.07	1.34	−89.04	1.41	−88.91	1.31	−87.67	1.40	−88.08

Due to inconsistencies between the conclusions drawn from accuracy rates and confidence gaps for the two attacks, and considering that both attacks are highly representative and claim to be the strongest attacks, we conducted five additional tests using other subsets on these two attacks. The results are presented in Table 2. It can be observed that the performance of AutoAttack is relatively stable, while that of the C&W attack fluctuates. In the five test runs,

C&W outperforms AutoAttack only in Test_4, with AutoAttack outperforms in the other tests. Based on the results in Table 2, it can be concluded that AutoAttack is stronger and more reliable than the C&W attack, which contradicts the conclusions drawn from accuracy rates alone.

3   Conclusion

In summary, the confidence gap encompasses all information pertaining to accuracy while also serving as an indicator of robustness. In instances where there is an inconsistency in evaluation results between the accuracy rate and confidence gap, we demonstrate that the confidence gap is a more reliable metric, as it effectively predicts the stability of model performance in subsequent tests.

Acknowledgement. This work is partially supported by JSPS international scientific exchanges between Japan and India (Bilateral Program DTS-JSPS) (2022-2024). We thank Prof. Hideki Murahara for his helpful comments, which greatly improved the quality of this manuscript.

References

1. Goodfellow, I.J., Shlens, J., Szegedy, C.: Explaining and harnessing adversarial examples, arXiv preprint arXiv:1412.6572 (2014)
2. Carlini, N., Wagner, D., "Towards evaluating the robustness of neural networks." In: IEEE Symposium on Security and Privacy (SP), vol. 2017, pp. 39–57. IEEE (2017)
3. Madry, A., Makelov, A., Schmidt, L., Tsipras, D., Vladu, A.: Towards deep learning models resistant to adversarial attacks. arXiv preprint arXiv:1706.06083 (2017)
4. Croce, F., Hein, M.: Reliable evaluation of adversarial robustness with an ensemble of diverse parameter-free attacks. in International Conference on Machine Learning, pp. 2206–2216. PMLR (2020)
5. Papernot, N., et al.: Technical report on the cleverhans v2.1.0 adversarial examples library. arXiv preprint arXiv:1610.00768 (2018)
6. Nicolae, M.-I., et al.: Adversarial robustness toolbox v1.2.0. CoRR, vol. 1807.01069 (2018).https://arxiv.org/pdf/1807.01069
7. Szegedy, C., Vanhoucke, V., Ioffe, S., Shlens, J., Wojna, Z.: Rethinking the inception architecture for computer vision. In: Proceedings of the IEEE Conference on Computer Vision and Pattern Recognition, pp. 2818–2826 (2016)
8. Russakovsky, O., et al.: ImageNet large scale visual recognition challenge. Int. J. Comput. Vis. (IJCV) **115**(3), 211–252 (2015)

POSTER: Integrating Quantum Key Distribution into Hybrid Quantum-Classical Networks

Juris Viksna$^{(\boxtimes)}$, Sergejs Kozlovics, and Edgars Rencis

Institute of Mathematics and Computer Science, University of Latvia, Raiņa bulv. 29,
Riga, Latvia
`juris.viksna@lumii.lv`

Abstract. In this work, we outline our recent developments of building experimental Quantum Key Distribution (QKD) network. The main focus is on the integration of QKD technologies into classical communication networks and assessing and exploiting the possibilities of how quantum technologies can complement existing cryptographic solutions. In particular: 1) we outline the conceptual architecture of the hybrid network developed by gradually adding individual QKD links to it; 2) describe a new protocol for delivering QKD-generated keys as a service; 3) describe the requirements for key management and user authentication in such hybrid networks and how these can be solved with the available technologies.

The developed protocol establishing QKD-keyed TLS connection uses Post Quantum Cryptography (PQC) algorithms for the secure delivery of QKD keys. It demonstrates how the strengths of QKD and PQC technologies can complement one another.

Keywords: Quantum Key Distribution · QKD as a Service · hybrid quantum-classical networks · post-quantum cryptography

1 Motivation and Conceptual Network Structure

Quantum Key Distribution (QKD) is a mechanism for agreeing on encryption keys that relies on the properties of quantum mechanics to ensure that keys have not been eavesdropped or modified by a third party. Commercial devices providing QKD links are becoming increasingly widespread, and in recent years there has been intense and growing activity on research and development focused on building experimental and commercial QKD networks and assessing their suitability and advantages for various use cases [10], a particularly wide range of such projects have been linked to OpenQKD initiative. One of the driving factors behind this is the perceived urgency to develop cryptographic solutions that

The work has been supported by the European Regional Development Fund project No. 1.1.1.1/20/A/106.

J. Zhou et al. (Eds.): ACNS 2023 Workshops, LNCS 13907, pp. 695–699, 2023.
https://doi.org/10.1007/978-3-031-41181-6_42

are secure against attacks by quantum computers, with QKD being regarded as such. Nevertheless, there are problems (notably user authentication) that QKD does not solve, and there is also uncertainty about the exact level of security that currently available physical QKD devices can provide [5]. The benefits of using QKD in the approbated use cases have not always been clearly explained, particularly regarding integration with the existing supporting classical cryptosystems. As a step towards the widely anticipated 'Post-Quantum Era,' QKD can be regarded as a technological solution that is partially competing with quantum-safe asymmetric algorithms (PQC), and there are several good reasons to prefer the latter [8]. At the same time, the security of PQC algorithms still has to withstand the test of time. In this context, the history of their development has not been spectacularly convincing (with yet another PQC candidate very recently being broken [3]). In our work, we try to understand and address these shortcomings/ambiguities by profiling a bottom-up approach for developing QKD infrastructure and assessing the benefits that communication networks can gain from gradually introducing quantum communication links into them.

In most of the described use cases, QKD networks have been designed with the top-down approach by building a top-layer backbone network for processing highly secure data transmissions and all other communication services placed in less-secured subordinate levels below it. In our proposition, we consider hybrid quantum-classical communication networks being built by gradually introducing point-to-point QKD links within the network. With the network growth, they can become interconnected and lead to the appearance of interconnected subnetworks. Each subnetwork S is then regarded as a potential source of QKD resources, from which the users with access to S via classical communication channels can benefit. Each direct QKD link between A and B we treat as *perfectly secure* in the sense that it generates at both nodes A and B identical keystreams that are completely inaccessible by malicious attackers (although practically available QKD devices might not entirely match such assumption). We consider the nodes in each subnetwork S as *trusted nodes*, meaning there is a secure key management and authentication mechanism within the whole component S. Notably, such a mechanism must be software-defined and independent of manufacturers of QKD devices, their supported APIs, etc. In broader terms, the whole network thus partitions into three layers: the QKD Layer (consisting of linked pairs of quantum devices and with assumed perfect security), the Control and Key Management Layer (software-based, solely for QKD device management), and the Service Layer (software-based, for access of users to QKD resources via classical communication channels).

2   Quantum Keys as a Service

With the list of successful use cases demonstrating the benefits of quantum cryptography and QKD expanding rapidly [9,10], it is natural that there is increasing interest in taking advantage of the availability of QKD-generated keys for communications between devices that are not directly connected with quantum links. At the conceptual level, there are several proposals describing 'software-defined' quantum key distribution networks [1]. However, such proposals are mostly limited to sketches of the overall network architecture or recommendations [6], without providing explicit implementation details.

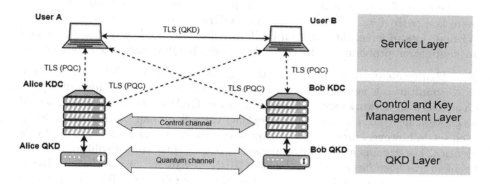

Fig. 1. Butterfly protocol for establishing a QKD-keyed TLS session

A characteristic feature of these proposals, however, is the reliance of each of the users on a single geographically closest QKD node (*Alice* or *Bob*) with which the particular user communicates. Since this communication is over a classical encryption channel (such as a TLS link), the overall security does not exceed the security of the used classical encryption scheme. Still, it can be debated that longer communication links need a higher level of security, and the use of QKD-generated keys for long-range connections in combination with less secure connections for acquiring these keys locally still provides an overall security improvement, e.g., in the context of cloud-based environments [2].

We have attempted to overcome such 'weakest link' vulnerability by proposing the so-called 'butterfly protocol' (Fig. 1). For two users A, B wishing to communicate it requires connecting independently to two Key Distribution Centres (KDC), linked, correspondingly, to *Alice* and *Bob* from paired QKD devices. The protocol establishes a QKD-keyed TLS session between users A and B with encryption keys delivered as a service by the contacted KDCs. The connections to KDCs can be made using classical TLS (v1.3) communication channels; in our implementation, however, we have strengthened these by use of PQC algorithms (SPHINCS+ for certificate signatures and FrodoKEM for key exchange). Only part of QKD session keys are relayed by each of the two involved KDCs, and the added security of the butterfly protocol is based on (the currently unproved) assumption that a successful man-in-the-middle attack will require compromising two independent TLS communication links.

The protocol has been developed in detail [7] (submitted for review). Currently, we have finalized its implementation and have started testing using real QKD devices. The current implementation assumes the availability of a single pair of linked QKD devices. However, the adaptation for larger networks generating synchronized QKD keystreams is straightforward.

3   Key Management and Authentication

By its design the proposed quantum-classical communication framework assumes the presence of subsets S of nodes such that for every pair of nodes $A, B \in S$, there is a path $A = N_1, \ldots, N_r = B$ with QKD secured links from N_i to N_{i+1}. Without loss of generality, we can limit the discussion of key management and authentication problems to the nodes from a single QKD-connected component.

Key Management. A given pair $(Alice, Bob)$ of coupled QKD devices provides simultaneous generation at both nodes of synchronized key-identifier pairs (K_{idx}, idx). In networks with a larger number of QKD-connected nodes, it would be convenient to have access to identical key value/identifier pairs at all nodes in each set S, however, for communication purposes, it suffices on request to obtain identical keystreams at two given nodes $A, B \in S$. The known solution for this problem has been described in [4] as the 'BBN Key Relay' protocol and is based on the use of some of QKD keystream material as OTP keys for encryption of others. Given a path of linked nodes $A = N_1, \ldots, N_r$, let K_i be a key shared by N_i and N_{i+1}. $K_1 = K_{AB}$ then can be chosen as QKD-generated key for the pair A, B, transmitted via intermediate nodes as $K_{out} = K_{in} \oplus K_i$ ($K_{in} = K_1$ at N_2), and recovered as $K_{AB} = K_{in} \oplus K_{r-1}$ at the node B. An additional layer of symmetric encryption is used to ensure the integrity of the transmitted keys.

The scheme requires the use of r QKD keys for establishing a single shared secret K_{AB}, and that can become too resource-demanding in larger networks. However, at this stage, for prototype development, we focus on networks with QKD-connected components containing no more than a few tens of nodes and with only a few interconnecting links between each pair of nodes. Thus the requirement for extra QKD keys is not considered a significant constraint.

Authentication. Quantum cryptography alone does not provide a solution to user authentication, and reliance on classical cryptography methods for solving this problem is needed. In classical communication networks, authentication is usually based on digital certificates. The overall security, however, will not exceed the security of the used key exchange and digital signature schemes.

For QKD networks, authentication based on PQC algorithms has been proposed [11]. It might be de-facto secure; however, for such a scheme, it remains unclear what added level of security QKD-generated keystreams could provide to that given by the used PQC algorithms.

The absence of a convenient and scalable authentication mechanism for QKD devices is likely one of the reasons manufacturers tend not to be too informative about particular solutions adopted for their products. However, the specifications suggest that a query and signed response mechanism based on secret symmetric key K_{AB} pre-assigned to specific pair devices is generally used for this purpose. It involves random challenges $rand_A$ and $rand_B$ generated correspondingly by *Alice* and *Bob* and sent to the coupled devices, which sign them accordingly as $resp_A = H(K_{AB}, req_A)$ and $resp_B = H(K_{AB}, req_B)$.

Commercially available QKD devices are pre-coupled by their manufacturers and do not provide access to the secret keys. Without feasible alternatives for node authentication apart from reliance on pre-shared secret symmetric keys, thus a similar additional external authentication layer needs to be added for manufacturer-independent QKD authentication. At the current stage, we plan to supply individual secret symmetric keys K_{AB} for each pair A, B of network devices and, for authentication, use the challenge-response mechanism outlined above. For hierarchical networks, there is a good potential to develop a key propagation protocol by using QKD-generated keys and OTP encryptions to transmit authentication keys (as well as the routing information) from the known parent node about its newly added child. For this, however, more detailed knowledge about the 'typical use cases' is needed.

4   Conclusion

The described conceptual structure of hybrid quantum-classical networks is primarily based on the needs of currently ongoing experimental development and testing of QKD devices in our institution, which likely can be matched by the needs and experience of other academic environments. Due to the very high costs of physical QKD devices, we plan to build a simulated environment that will include both physical and virtual quantum devices and allow to test performance of networks including several tens of QKD links. The functionality of the underlying Control and Management Layer is still in the planning stage but sufficiently advanced to start development gradually. As a concrete use case for Service Layer, QKD as a Service protocol has been implemented and is currently being tested. The software is available at https://qkd.lumii.lv.

References

1. Aguado, A., et al.: The engineering of software-defined quantum key distribution networks. IEEE Commun. Mag. **57**(7), 20–26 (2019)
2. Cao, Y., et al.: The evolution of quantum key distribution networks: on the road to the qinternet. IEEE Commun. Surv. Tutor. **24**(2), 839–894 (2022)
3. Castryck, W., Decru, T.: An efficient key recovery attack on SIDH. Technical report. Paper 2022/975, Cryptology ePrint Archive (2022)
4. Elliott, C., Yeh, H.: DARPA quantum network testbed. Technical report. AFRL-IF-RS-TR-2007-180, BBN Technologies Cambridge (2007)
5. Gonzalez-Payo, J., et al.: Upper security bounds for coherent-one-way quantum key distribution. Phys. Rev. Lett. **125**(26:260510), 1–15 (2020)
6. ITU-T: Overview on networks supporting quantum key distribution. Technical report. Y.3800, International Telecommunication Union (2019)
7. Kozlovics, S., et al.: Quantum key distribution as a service and its injection into TLS (2023). In: 18th International Conference on Information Security Practice and Experience, ISPEC 2023, LNCS, 19 p. Springer (2023)
8. Mattsson, J., et al.: Quantum technology and its impact on security in mobile network. Technical report 12, Ericsson Technology Review (2021)
9. Mehic, M., Niemec, M., et al.: Quantum key distribution: a networking perspective. ACM Comput. Surv. **53**(5:96), 1–41 (2020)
10. Stanley, M., et al.: Recent progress in quantum key distribution network deployments and standards. J. Phys. Conf. Ser. **2416**(012001), 1–13 (2022)
11. Wang, L., et al.: Experimental authentication of quantum key distribution with post-quantum cryptography. NPJ Quantum Inf. **7**(67), 1–7 (2021)

POSTER: Adaptive Moving Target Defense: Enhancing Dynamic Perturbation Through Voltage Sensitivity Analysis in Power Systems

Muhammad Nouman Nafees, Neetesh Saxena[✉], and Pete Burnap

School of Computer Science and Informatics, Cardiff University, Cardiff, UK
{nafeesm,saxenan4,burnapp}@cardiff.ac.uk

Abstract. Moving target defense (MTD) strategies significantly protect power systems against stealthy false data injection attacks. However, traditional MTD approaches in power systems predominantly focus on single-parameter perturbation, leaving gaps in addressing the complexity and unpredictability of attack surfaces. In this work, we present a novel MTD strategy that departs from the traditional approach and utilizes multiple parameter perturbations to enhance the resilience of power systems against cyber threats while ensuring system stability. Our contributions include investigating the impact of individual and combined parameter perturbations on power system stability and performance, utilizing voltage sensitivity analysis to identify critical parameters, and considering the trade-offs between system security and operational constraints. The proposed algorithm dynamically perturbs the selected parameters, incorporating insights from the power flow Jacobian matrix analysis, and continuously adapts the MTD strategy based on the obtained results.

Keywords: Moving target defense · Dynamic perturbation · Voltage sensitivity analysis

1 Introduction

The perturbation technique in Moving Target Defense (MTD) is crucial in safeguarding power systems from stealthy False Data Injection (FDI) attacks. By dynamically modifying system parameters and configurations, MTD increases the attack surface's intricacy and unpredictability, posing considerable challenges for adversaries attempting to comprehend and exploit the system.

Previous research in this area has primarily focused on perturbing single parameters [1,3]; however, this study investigates the impact of combined parameter perturbations on system performance and stability. The advantage of considering multiple parameters lies in a more comprehensive and robust MTD strategy. Nonetheless, it necessitates rigorous analysis of power system stability when perturbing multiple parameters, and a clear limit of perturbation should be thoroughly investigated. This approach ensures that the MTD strategy does

J. Zhou et al. (Eds.): ACNS 2023 Workshops, LNCS 13907, pp. 700–704, 2023.
https://doi.org/10.1007/978-3-031-41181-6_43

not compromise the power system's stability and performance while enhancing its resilience against cyber threats. In this context, voltage sensitivity analysis in power systems plays a crucial role in identifying the critical parameters that significantly influence system stability and performance, ultimately enabling more effective defense strategies.

1.1 Contributions

In this work, we contribute to the field of MTD research by exploring the feasibility and effectiveness of adaptive perturbation strategies in power systems. We investigate the impact of individual and combined parameter perturbations on the power system's stability and performance, employing voltage sensitivity analysis to identify critical parameters.

To implement the adaptive MTD strategy, we propose an algorithm that dynamically perturbs the selected parameters, incorporating insights from the power flow Jacobian matrix analysis [2]. The algorithm determines and applies parameter perturbations within their defined ranges while considering system constraints and operational requirements. By iteratively exploring different combinations of parameter perturbations and continuously adapting the MTD strategy based on the obtained results, our algorithm significantly contributes to the novelty and advancement of MTD research in power systems.

2   Methodology

In this section, we outline the steps to investigate the impact of dynamic perturbation strategies for MTD on power system performance. The methodology includes simulating parameter perturbations and conducting voltage sensitivity analysis.

2.1 Sensitivity Analysis Approach

We thoroughly investigate the effectiveness of adaptive MTD perturbation strategies by incorporating additional power systems components such as Distributed Flexible AC Transmission System (D-FACTS) devices, load profiles, generator settings and voltage set-points, and transmission line parameters using PowerWorld Simulator. This expanded analysis allows us to investigate the interactions and impact of these components on the power system's resilience to FDI attacks, ultimately enhancing power system security.

We conduct a sensitivity analysis to pinpoint the most critical parameters and determine their optimal combinations. Then, we perturb individual parameters within their operating limits, observing the impact on system performance and stability. We calculate the sensitivity indices for each parameter, representing the relative change in bus voltages per unit change in the parameter. The sensitivity indices enable us to quantify the impact of each parameter on the system's voltage profile, allowing for a more targeted and efficient approach when designing adaptive MTD strategies. We rank the parameters based on their sensitivity indices, identifying those with the most significant impact on the system, and use the ranked parameters to explore different combinations to maximize the MTD benefits while maintaining system stability and performance.

2.2 Algorithm for Dynamic Parameter Perturbations

The power flow Jacobian matrix is crucial to numerous optimization, security, operation, and planning applications in power systems. To this end, it contains the partial derivatives of the active and reactive power flow mismatch equations concerning voltage magnitudes and phase angles, and it is typically very sparse. To implement the adaptive MTD strategy, we develop an algorithm that dynamically perturbs the selected parameters, incorporating the insights from the power flow Jacobian matrix analysis.

Algorithm 1. Dynamic Parameter Perturbations

1: Initialize the IEEE 9-Bus System with PowerWorld Simulator and SimAuto interface.
2: Define perturbation ranges and limits for each parameter, considering system constraints and operational requirements:
   - Voltage magnitudes: $V_{min} \leq V \leq V_{max}$
   - Transmission line limits: $|S| \leq S_{max}$
   - Generator real/reactive power limits: $P_{min} \leq P \leq P_{max}$, $Q_{min} \leq Q \leq Q_{max}$
3: Use a random number generator to select perturbation values for chosen parameters within their defined ranges.
4: Apply the perturbations to the IEEE 9-Bus System through the SimAuto interface.
5: Monitor the system's performance and stability, recording the relevant data.
6: Evaluate the effectiveness of the MTD strategy based on observed changes in system performance and stability.
7: Iterate the process, exploring different combinations of parameter perturbations, and continuously adapting the MTD strategy based on the obtained results.

---

3 Simulation and Results

In this section, we discuss the simulation setup and results of our investigation on the impact of dynamic perturbations strategies for MTD on power system performance. We perform individual and combined parameter perturbations and analyze their effects on system stability and analyze its efficacy. Stability refers to the ability of the power system to maintain a stable voltage profile and frequency response, while efficacy refers to the efficiency and reliability of the system in maintaining its process with perturbations.

3.1 Simulation Setup

To investigate the impact of adaptive MTD strategies on power system performance, we conduct simulations using the PowerWorld Simulator. The IEEE

Table 1. Results of Individual and Combined Parameter Perturbations

Perturbation Type	Parameter	Impact on Stability	Efficacy
Individual	Generator active power	Moderate	Moderate
Individual	Generator voltage setpoints	High	Moderate
Individual	Load profiles	Moderate	Low
Individual	D-FACTS devices (affecting line reactance)	High	Moderate
Combined	Generator active power and D-FACTS devices	High	Moderate
Combined	Load profiles, tap settings, and D-FACTS devices	Moderate	High

9-Bus System, with three generators and base kV levels of 13.8 kV, 16.5 kV, 18 kV, and 230 kV, is used as the test case. This system is relatively easy to control due to its limited number of voltage control devices and complex lines of powers of hundreds of MVA each. We consider a range of power system components for perturbation, including generator settings, voltage set-points, load profiles, and D-FACTS devices (affecting the reactances of the transmission lines).

3.2   Individual and Combined Parameter Perturbations

We perform both individual and combined parameter perturbations within their respective operating limits. The perturbations are applied to the 9-Bus System using the SimAuto interface. Based on our proposed algorithm, we can dynamically search for the best parameters to perturb for implementing MTD in power systems. This adaptive approach allows us to select optimal combinations of parameters that maximize the security benefits while minimizing the impact on system stability and performance. The results of these perturbations are presented in Table 1.

3.3   Impact of Perturbations on Power System Stability and Performance

We conduct a sensitivity analysis to identify the most critical parameters significantly affecting the system's stability and performance. The sensitivity indices for each parameter are calculated, representing the relative change in bus voltages per unit change in the parameter. Based on the sensitivity analysis, we identify the most critical parameters, such as load profiles, tap settings and D-FACTS devices (affecting transmission line reactance), and their combinations that can be used to implement an effective MTD strategy while maintaining the system's stability and performance. The findings help develop a more robust and adaptive cybersecurity approach for power systems, considering the trade-offs between security and operational constraints.

4   Discussion and Conclusion

We summarize the key findings of our study on the adaptive MTD strategy for power systems, focusing on the insights from sensitivity analysis and dynamic parameter perturbations. Lastly, we present the conclusion.

4.1   Discussion

Our study presents a MTD strategy that leverages the insights gained from voltage sensitivity analysis and dynamic parameter perturbations. The proposed approach introduces unpredictability and complexity to power systems, making it more challenging for adversaries to plan and execute cyber-attacks. In this direction, the critical parameters and their combinations identified through simulations and sensitivity analysis play a vital role in implementing this defense strategy.

The trade-offs between system security and operational constraints must be carefully managed. While increasing the number of perturbed parameters can improve defense effectiveness, it may introduce additional operational complexities and costs. For instance, deploying D-FACTS devices can enhance system security but requires investment and ongoing maintenance expenses.

4.2   Conclusion

In conclusion, based on voltage sensitivity analysis and dynamic parameter perturbations, the MTD strategy provides a robust and adaptive cybersecurity approach for power systems. By balancing system security and operational constraints, we enhance power system resilience against cyber-attacks and other threats. Future work will evaluate the proposed MTD strategy's effectiveness against stealthy FDI attacks and assess its ability to reveal such attacks by combining them with anomaly detection techniques and Kalman filter-based detection methods. These enhancements will further bolster the defense capabilities of power systems, ensuring their security and reliability amid evolving cyber threats.

References

1. Lakshminarayana, S., Belmega, E.V., Poor, H.V.: Moving-target defense for detecting coordinated cyber-physical attacks in power grids. In: 2019 IEEE International Conference on Communications, Control, and Computing Technologies for Smart Grids (SmartGridComm), pp. 1–7. IEEE (2019)
2. Talkington, S., Turizo, D., Grijalva, S., Fernandez, J., Molzahn, D.K.: Conditions for estimation of sensitivities of voltage magnitudes to complex power injections. IEEE Trans. Power Syst. (2023)
3. Zhang, M., Fan, X., Lu, R., Shen, C., Guan, X.: Extended moving target defense for ac state estimation in smart grids. IEEE Trans. Smart Grid **14**, 2313–2325 (2022)

POSTER: PriAuct: Privacy Preserving Auction Mechanism

Neha Joshi[1,2]($\boxtimes$), Abhishek Thakur[2], and A. Antony Franklin[1]

[1] Indian Institute of Technology, Hyderabad, India
cs19resch11005@iith.ac.in, antony.franklin@cse.iith.ac.in
[2] Institute for Development and Research in Banking Technology, Hyderabad, India
AbhishekT@idrbt.ac.in

Abstract. Most of the emerging services and workflows use infrastructure across multiple organizations. This work proposes a privacy-preserving auction mechanism to facilitate cost efficiencies while minimizing the exposure of operational aspects like QoS parameters. It leverages homomorphic encryption using bilinear pairing, to improve bids privacy. Only the winning bid is publicly disclosed. The mechanism provides public auditability and collusion resistance. Measurements of performance overheads, through simulation in various scenarios, are discussed. Basic security proof is also provided.

Keywords: Privacy · Homomorphic Encryption · Bilinear Pairing · Auction · Resources · Services

1 Introduction

Telecom industries and cloud operators (referred as sellers in this work), provide on-demand connectivity and delivery of edge computing resources. This entails offering resources as a service to end users (referred as buyer in this work). To facilitate such trades, double auction mechanisms allowing both buyers and sellers to continuously submit their prices until they converge have been extensively researched [1]. As the network expands, a third party that acts as a middleman (referred as auctioneer) between the sellers and buyers is required. The auctioneer's primary responsibility is identifying the best seller to meet the buyer's requirements. While the auctioneer plays an important role in the auction process, it may introduce various challenges in the resource selection mechanism. It interacts with the sellers and buyers to obtain information such as available resources, cost, QoS metrics, etc. However, there is a lot of exposure of private information to the auctioneer.

Motivation: Sellers and buyers are reluctant to share their information with the other participants including auctioneer [2]. Details of the network, including their identity, cost trends, and resource specifications, can aid in predicting the participants business strategy, application logic and usage patterns. Further in

J. Zhou et al. (Eds.): ACNS 2023 Workshops, LNCS 13907, pp. 705–709, 2023.
https://doi.org/10.1007/978-3-031-41181-6_44

realm of networks and compute, disclosing such private information can compromise network security. The risk of collusion between participants is an additional threat.

The key contributions of PriAuct are:

1. a novel cryptography auction mechanism without revealing the specification, including type, cost, and QoS parameters.
2. achieves collusion resistance, by preventing two or more entities from cooperating and gaining unauthorized access to each other's resource information.
3. evaluate performance of the proposed system.
4. feature comparison with the existing system.

2   PriAuct Overview

The PriAuct model comprises three main entities: buyers, sellers, and auctioneer. In context of telecom and cloud services, Buyers are users who want to purchase resources from network domains, while sellers are network domains that offer their resources, such as connectivity, firewalls and virus scanners. The auctioneer is responsible for conducting and managing the auction process.

System Goals: The security and privacy guarantees provided by the PriAuct system are as follows: a) *Correctness:* The system accurately identifies the buyers with the winning bid. b) *Privacy:* The bids of all buyers except for the winner remain confidential. Further, the information exchange between buyers and sellers should be concealed from auctioneer. c) *Collusion-Resistance:* Even if two parties come together they cannot learn about other bid information. At best they can uncover the range for bids where they have participated.

2.1   Preliminaries

PriAuct system relies on bilinear maps [3] and the BGN homomorphic cryptosystem [4] for constructing the auction mechanism.

1. *Bilinear maps:* The bilinear map e is a function, $e : G \times G \to G_1$ and g is the generator of group G such that,
   - It follows the bilinear property. $\forall(g,g) \in G, \forall(a,b) \in \mathbb{Z}, e(g^a, g^b) = e(g,g)^{ab}$.
   - It is Non-degenerate. $\exists(g,g) \in G$ such that $e(g,g) \neq 1$, where 1 is the identity of G_1.
2. *Homomorphic encryption:* The Boneh-Goh-Nissim (BGN) cryptosystem is a public-key encryption system that provides both confidentiality and homomorphic properties. This scheme allows for one level of multiplication and multiple levels of addition.

3 Privacy-Preserving Auction Mechanism

For users $U_1 \dots U_N$ with bids $b_1, \dots, b_N$ and an real adversary $\mathcal{A}$, the protocol *Pri-AUC* implementation includes following functions:

- **Setup** $\mathcal{S}(k)$: Given a security parameter $k \in Z^+$, generate bilinear pairing parameters by using algorithm $\mathcal{G}(k)$ is $(e, q_1, q_2, g, u, G, G_1)$. Let $n = q_1 \cdot q_2$ where q_1, q_2 are two k-bit primes and $g \xleftarrow{R} G$ is a random generator. Compute $u = g^z$ where $z \in Z^+$. The public key pk$= (n, G, G_1, e, g, h = u^{q_2})$ and secret key sk$= q_1$.
- **Bid-Generate** $\mathcal{BG}(b, \text{pk}, r_{1A}, r_{2A}, r)$: To generate the encrypted bid from plaintext bid $b \in Z^+$, do the following:
  1. Return $\tau = (a = g^b h^r, c = g^{r_{1A}} h^r, d = g^{r_{2A}} h^r)$.
- **Bid-Randomization** $\mathcal{R}(\tau, \text{pk}, r_{1B}, r_{2B}, \overline{r})$: To add randomization to the bid τ, do the following:
  1. Compute $\overline{c}(= c \cdot g^{r_{1B}} h^{\overline{r}} = g^{r_{1A} + zrq_2 + r_{1B} + z\overline{r}q_2}), f(= g^{r_{2B}} h^{\overline{r}})$.
  2. Compute $\overline{\tau}(= e(a, \overline{c}) \cdot e(d, f) = e(g, g)^{(b+zrq_2)x} \cdot e(g, g)^y)$ where $x = r_{1A} + zrq_2 + r_{1B} + z\overline{r}q_2$ and $y = (r_{2A} + zrq_2) \cdot (r_{2B} + z\overline{r}q_2)$.
  3. Return $\overline{\tau}$.
- **Bid-Computation** $\mathcal{C}(\overline{\tau}, \text{sk})$: To recover $(b(r_{1A} + r_{1B}) + r_{2A} \cdot r_{2B})$ from bid $\overline{\tau} \in G_1$, do the following:

$$(\overline{\tau})^{q_1} = (g_1^{(b+zrq_2)x+y})^{q_1} = g_1^{bxq_1 + r_{2A} \cdot r_{2B} q_1} \in G_1$$

Let $\overline{g} = g^{q_1}$. To recover $b(r_{1A} + r_{1B}) + r_{2A} \cdot r_{2B}$, it suffices to compute the discrete log of $(\overline{\tau})^{q_1}$ base$\overline{g}$.

Above functions are used by *Pri-AUC* as follows:

1. Users $U_i, \forall i \in (1, N)$ executes algorithm Setup $\mathcal{S}(k)$ to obtain the public keys pk$_i = (n_i, G_i, G_{1i}, e_i, g_i, h_i = u_i^{q2i})$ and secret keys sk$_i = q_{1i}$.
2. For $i \in (1, N - 1)$,
   (a) U_i selects random $r_{1i}, r_{2i}, r_i \in [0, x - 1]$ and executes algorithm Bid-Generate $\mathcal{BG}(m_i, \text{pk}_i, r_{1i}, r_{2i}, r_i)$ to obtain τ_i. U_i shares τ_i to the user U_{i+1}.
   (b) U_{i+1} selects random $r_{1i+1}, r_{2i+1}, r_{i+1} \in [0, x - 1]$ and executes algorithm Bid-Generate $\mathcal{BG}(m_{i+1}, \text{pk}_{i+1}, r_{1i+1}, r_{2i+1}, r_{i+1})$ to obtain τ_{i+1}. U_{i+1} shares τ_{i+1} to the user U_i.
   (c) U_i executes the algorithm Bid-Computation $\mathcal{C}(\overline{\tau}_i, \text{sk}_i)$ to obtain $m_i(r_{1i} + r_{1i+1}) + r_{2i} \cdot r_{2i+1}$.
   (d) U_{i+1} executes similar to steps c and obtains $m_{i+1}(r_{1i} + r_{1i+1}) + r_{2i} \cdot r_{2i+1}$.
   (e) Steps c,d are logged with auctioneer to ensure truthfulness of encrypted bid.

Audit of winning bid: In case of dispute by other bidders, it may be necessary to verify that the winning bid is not altered. Let $y = x(r_{a1} + r_{b1}) + (r_{a2} \cdot r_{b2})$ be the winning bid. To verify the correctness, both parties reveal their randomization i.e., (r_{a1}, r_{a2}) and (r_{b1}, r_{b2}). Logs from auctioneer is used for verification.

Security Proof:

Line equation assumption [5]: Given a point on an X-Y plane, for euclidean geometry, infinite lines pass through it. *Hard Problem:* The equation of a line can not be computed if only a single point lying on that line is given.

If an adversary $\mathcal{A}$ can break the privacy of the bid with non-negligible advantage, then there exists an algorithm $\mathcal{B}$ that can solve the line equation problem with an equivalent advantage. Hence assuming that solving the line problem is hard, one can prove that *Pri-AUC* is secure.

Given an adversary $\mathcal{A}$ that breaks the privacy of the bid in *Pri-AUC* with non-negligible advantage $\varepsilon(\tau)$ construction of algorithm $\mathcal{B}$ that can solve the line equation is as follows.

1. $\mathcal{B}$ receives a challenge instance (y_2, x_2) where $(y_2 = x_2 \cdot m + c)$. Here, m and c are unknown, and the challenge is to retrieve (y_1, x_1) such that $y_1 = m \cdot x_1 + c$.
2. $\mathcal{B}$ selects a random vertical plane $y_{\mathcal{A}'}$ and invokes adversary $\mathcal{A}$ with input $(y_2, x_2, y_{\mathcal{A}'})$. Here, x_2 is the plaintext bid of the adversary and y_2 is the encrypted bid. y_A is the encrypted bid of algorithm $\mathcal{B}$. The adversary $\mathcal{A}$ computes the bid x_A with advantage tau..
3. $\mathcal{B}$ can compute the line equation given that it now has computed the two points (y_2, x_2, y_A, x_A).

Since $\mathcal{A}$ breaks the privacy of the bid with non-negligible advantage, it follows that $\mathcal{B}$ can solve the assumption with non-negligible advantage. Therefore, we have shown that if *Pri-AUC* is not secure, then the assumption is not hard. This proves that the proposed auction protocol *Pri-AUC* is secure, assuming the given assumption is hard. Furthermore, m and c include randomization values known only the the bidder. Hence the system is resistant to collusion since no party can obtain the real bid details without knowledge of the other party's randomization.

Table 1. Comparison between various privacy preserving auction mechanism

System	Bid privacy	Bidders privacy	Distributed party	Non-trusted hardware	Public auditability	Collusion resistant
[6]	✓	✗	✓	✓	✗	✗
[7]	✓	✗	✗	✓	✗	✗
[8]	✓	✗	✓	✓	✗	✗
[9]	✓	✗	✗	✗	✗	✗
PriAuct	✓	✗	✗	✓	✓	✓

Comparison and Experimental Result: Table 1 compares PriAuct with existing work. Figure 1a shows the PriAuct system performance using GOLANG (Ubuntu 20.04, Intel Core i5 1.6 GHZ, and 16 GB RAM). The processing time

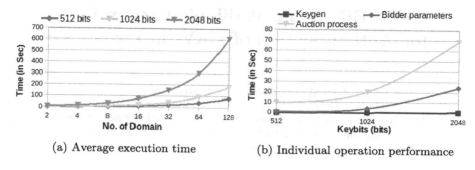

(a) Average execution time   (b) Individual operation performance

Fig. 1. PriAuct system performance

increases uniformly as the domain numbers increase. Figure 1b shows the average processing time of each individual operation for varying keybit size.

Conclusion and Future Work: The paper presents PriAuct, a privacy-preserving auction mechanism with bid hiding and collusion prevention. However, it reveals Bidder's identity, which is an ongoing research by authors. Exploration of distributed ledgers and smart contracts for implementing the auctioneer is another future work.

References

1. Zou, S., et al.: Resource allocation game under double-sided auction mechanism: Efficiency and convergence. IEEE Trans. Autom. Control **63**(5), 1273–1287 (2017)
2. Chen, C., et al.: Distributed federated service chaining: a scalable and cost-aware approach for multi-domain networks. Comput. Netw. **212**, 109044 (2022)
3. Groth, J., Sahai, A.: Efficient non-interactive proof systems for bilinear groups. In: Smart, N. (ed.) EUROCRYPT 2008. LNCS, vol. 4965, pp. 415–432. Springer, Heidelberg (2008). https://doi.org/10.1007/978-3-540-78967-3_24
4. Boneh, D., Goh, E.-J., Nissim, K.: Evaluating 2-DNF formulas on ciphertexts. In: Kilian, J. (ed.) TCC 2005. LNCS, vol. 3378, pp. 325–341. Springer, Heidelberg (2005). https://doi.org/10.1007/978-3-540-30576-7_18
5. Faber, R.L.: Foundations of Euclidean and Non-Euclidean Geometry. Dekker, New York (1983)
6. Gao, W., et al.: Privacy-preserving auction for big data trading using homomorphic encryption. IEEE Trans. Netw. Sci. Eng. **7**(2), 776–791 (2018)
7. Liu, B., et al.: PANDA: privacy-aware double auction for divisible resources without a mediator. In: Proceedings of the 19th International Conference on Autonomous Agents and MultiAgent Systems (2020)
8. Cheng, K., et al.: Towards efficient privacy-preserving auction mechanism for two-sided cloud markets. In: ICC 2019–2019 IEEE International Conference on Communications (ICC). IEEE (2019)
9. Chen, Guoxing, et al. "SgxPectre: stealing intel secrets from SGX enclaves via speculative execution. In: 2019 IEEE European Symposium on Security and Privacy (EuroS&P). IEEE (2019)

POSTER: Using Verifiable Credentials for Authentication of UAVs in Logistics

Ken Watanabe[(⊠)] and Kazue Sako

Department of Computer Science and Communication Engineering,
Waseda University, 3-4-1 Okubo, Shinjuku-ku, Tokyo, Japan
kenwaz113@ruri.waseda.jp

Abstract. Verifiable Credentials (VCs) have been widely adopted as a format for asserting information through use of digital signature technique, and offer versatile usages. The World Wide Web Consortium (W3C) has standardized the data model for VCs [1], and the motivation for this study is to verify the applicability of its data model through a concrete, realistic scenario. For verification, we have chosen a scenario where Unmanned Aerial Vehicles (UAVs) collaborate to deliver packages. As a contribution of this study, we demonstrate how we can selectively disclose attributes of UAVs yet ensure its mission under an authorized contract. Furthermore, we propose a method for issuing receipts through use of VCs and Verifiable Presentations (VPs) that guarantees completion of delivery while UAVs remain anonymous. For this function, we developed a new format for VP, namely 'VP with Message.' These features have been implemented through a demo application.

Keywords: Verifiable Credential · Selective Disclosure · Authentication Protocol · UAV

1 Introduction

A Verifiable Credential (VC), whose data model has been standardized at the World Wide Web Consortium (W3C) [1], is a credential that certifies a holder's set of attributes by the issuer's signature. The credential contains information about a holder's attributes such as names and identifiers. The holder can selectively disclose the attributes to the verifier without revealing unnecessary or sensitive data as a Verifiable Presentation (VP). The data model for VCs is used in many cases, such as COVID-19 vaccination certificates [2].

The motivation for our research is to verify the applicability of its data model in a concrete, realistic scenario that goes beyond just showing and checking a document like a vaccine certificate, and also involves mutual authentication. For verification we have chosen a scenario where Unmanned Aerial Vehicles (UAVs) collaborate to deliver packages.

These research results were obtained from the commissioned research (No. 03901) by National Institute of Information and Communications Technology (NICT), Japan.

J. Zhou et al. (Eds.): ACNS 2023 Workshops, LNCS 13907, pp. 710–715, 2023.
https://doi.org/10.1007/978-3-031-41181-6_45

In this study, we make several contributions. We demonstrate how to perform selective disclosure for privacy enhancement using VCs and VPs in this scenario. Furthermore, we propose a method for issuing receipts through use of VCs and VPs that guarantees completion of delivery while UAVs remain anonymous. Also, we found signed documents such as contracts can be expressed as a VC and serve as a source for mutual authentication. These features we propose have been implemented through a demo application.

2   A Scenario for Confirming the Applicability of VC

In this section, we present a scenario of UAV collaboratively delivering packages to check applicability of VCs. We describe players and basic procedures.

2.1   Players and Purpose

There are 5 types of players: *Sender* (S), *PrimeContractor* (PC), *Subcontractor* (SC), *UAV* (U) and *Recipient* (R). *Sender* asks *PrimeContractor* to deliver packages to *Recipient*. The *PrimeContractor* requests $Subcontractor_1$ and $Subcontractor_2$ to collaboratively deliver the packages. Each *Subcontractor* assigns the task to their respective UAVs. When relaying the packages, both players need to authenticate that they are working under same *PrimeContractor*. Also, a player that handed over the packages need a receipt from a *UAV* to confirm successful relaying. Each player has a unique identifier and a key pair.

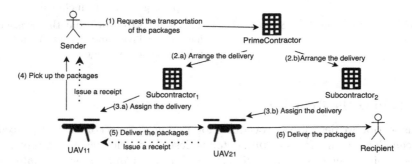

Fig. 1. Overall delivery scenario

2.2   Procedures in the Scenario

Procedures in the scenario are depicted in Fig. 1.

(1) *Sender* requests package delivery to *PrimeContractor*. (2.a, 2.b) *PrimeContractor* subcontracts the package delivery to $Subcontractor_1$ and $Subcontractor_2$. (3.a, 3.b) Each *Subcontractor* assigns the package delivery task to their respective UAVs, UAV_{11} and UAV_{21}. (4) UAV_{11} proceeds to pick up the packages from *Sender* and (5) delivers it to the location of UAV_{21}. (6) Finally, UAV_{21} delivers the packages to *Recipient*. When relaying packages, the player who receive the packages issues a receipt.

3   Our System

In our system, we represent contracts as VCs. There are 4 types of contracts as detailed in Sect. 3.1. How to mutually issue VCs is explained in Sect. 3.2. The existence of contracts are proved through VP in selective-disclosure manner as described in Sect. 3.3.

3.1   Types of Verifiable Credential

Contracts using VC are utilized between the *Sender* and *PrimeContractor*, *PrimeContractor* and *Subcontractor*, and *Subcontractor* and *UAV*. The types of VC are shown in Table 1.

Table 1. 4 types of VC

VC	(Issuer, Holder)	Description
TransportContract	(S, PC), (PC, S)	TransportContractID, the *PrimeContractor* identifier and packages info are included
DeliveryContract	(PC, SC_1), (SC_1, PC), (PC, SC_2), (SC_2, PC)	TransportContractID, DeliveryContractID, the *Subcontractor* identifier, packages info, are included
DeliverDriver	(SC_1, U_{11}), (SC_2, U_{21})	DeliveryContractID, the UAV identifier and packages info are included
PackageReceipt	(U_{11}, S), (U_{21}, U_{11})	This is used to prove that the packages has been relayed and it contains info related to the packages

3.2   Issuing the Contract

In this section we describe a procedures for issuing VC as a contract. A procedure between *Sender* and *PrimeContractor* is described below as an example.

As depicted in Fig. 2, both *Sender* and *PrimeContractor* mutually issue TransportContractVC to each other. This process ensures that both players can prove that a contract has been issued between them. Additionally, a unique identifier, TransportContractID, is included in both contracts. Similar procedure for issuing VCs are carried between *PrimeContractor* and *Subcontractor*.

3.3   Relaying the Packages

In this section we describe a procedures for relaying the packages using VCs. A procedure between *Sender* and UAV_{11} is described below as an example. There are two features involved in relaying the packages. The first feature is mutual authentication before relaying packages. The second feature is to issue the receipt. In Fig. 3, the flow diagram summarizing the two features is depicted.

Mutual Authentication. For mutual authentication, both *Sender* and UAV_{11} create Verifiable Presentations (VPs) from their VCs. Both players create VPs to provide a minimum set of attributes for authentication. (1) UAV_{11} creates a VP from two VCs, namely the DeliveryContract VC issued by *PrimeContractor* and the DeliveryDriver VC issued by *Subcontractor$_1$*. (3) The *Sender* creates a VP from the TransportContract VC issued by *PrimeContractor*.

Both players confirm that they are collaborating under same *PrimeContractor*. *Sender* verifies a UAV by the chain of VCs in a VP. *Sender* confirms that the UAV is owned by *Subcontractor*, who has a contract with *PrimeContractor*, who has a contract with *Sender*. By using selective disclosure technique with zero-knowledge proofs and linking properties of Linked Data format, mutual authentication can be performed without showing other information, such as UAV identifiers.

Issuing a Receipt. *Sender* receives a receipt that can prove the package was accepted by UAV_{11}. The receipt is expressed as a PackageReceipt VC. (R.a) To ensure that *Sender* cannot determine which UAV is authenticating, UAV_{11} creates a fresh key pair for the PackageReceipt VC on each authentication. The new public key generated by UAV_{11} is conveyed to the *Sender* within a 'VP with Message' (1), which is a new data format we developed. The details will be described in the next paragraph. (R.b) UAV_{11} creates the PackageReceipt VC. (R.c) *Sender* verifies the PackageReceipt VC using the received public key to ensure it was created correctly.

We now describe our new data format for VP, called 'VP with Message', which is used in (1) in Fig. 3. This data format allows Holder of VC to embed arbitrary messages in VP, which results in adding signature of knowledge to the message. Using this approach, we can embed new public key as the message in VP. This key will be used to verify the signature on PackageReceipt VC. This allows *Sender* to confirm that the receipt was created by the authenticated UAV.

3.4   Implementation

We created a demo application based on the proposed procedures. We adopt BBS+ signatures [3] to perform unlinkable authentication, and use Linked-Data based VC to execute zero-knowledge proofs necessary for selective disclosure [4]. For enhancing BBS+ signature, we extended from zkp-ld libraries [5] such as a VP with Message.

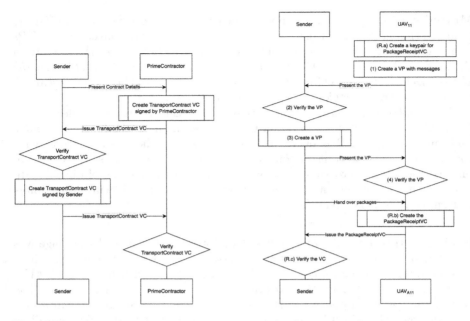

Fig. 2. Procedure of issuing a contract   **Fig. 3.** Procedure of relaying packages

4   Conclusion

This study explores the applicability of VCs and VPs in a scenario where UAVs autonomously deliver packages. In the scenario, we have shown that VCs can be utilized for package delivery contracts, authentication between UAVs, and issuing receipts between UAVs. We proposed a new data format for VP to enable issuing receipts by anonymous UAVs. Additionally, we have shown that the selective disclosure feature of VPs enables anonymous authentication. By implementing these features in a demo application, we have showed the feasibility and effectiveness of using VCs and VPs in UAV delivery systems. One challenge that arises is the inability to hide which *Subcontractor* the UAV belongs to. This is because the issuer of VCs cannot be hidden. This research highlights the potential for these technologies to enhance privacy in authentication.

References

1. Verifiable Credentials Data Model v1.1 W3C Recommendation (2022). https://www.w3.org/TR/vc-data-model/
2. European Union, Eu digital Covid certificate. https://commission.europa.eu/live-work-travel-eu/coronavirus-response/safe-covid-19-vaccines-europeans/eu-digital-covid-certificate

3. Au, M.H., Susilo, W., Mu, Y.: Constant-size dynamic k-TAA. In: De Prisco, R., Yung, M. (eds.) SCN 2006. LNCS, vol. 4116, pp. 111–125. Springer, Heidelberg (2006). https://doi.org/10.1007/11832072_8
4. Yamamoto, D., Suga, Y., Sako, K.: Formalising linked-data based verifiable credentials for selective disclosure. In: 2022 IEEE European Symposium on Security and Privacy, Workshops (EuroS&PW), pp. 52–65 (2022)
5. Yamamoto, D.: ZKP-LD. GitHub Organization. https://github.com/zkp-ld

POSTER: A Card-Based Protocol that Lets You Know How Close Two Parties are in their Opinions (agree/disagree) by Using a Four-Point Likert Scale

Yuji Suga[(✉)] [iD]

Internet Initiative Japan Inc., Iidabashi Grand Bloom,
2-10-2 Fujimi, Chiyoda-ku 102-0071, Japan
suga@iij.ad.jp

Abstract. Card-based protocols are commonly used for scenarios where two parties need to perform an AND operation. These protocols are known for providing a non-embarrassing way to confess love, as the other party cannot determine whether the input is 0 or 1.

This paper proposes a new card-based protocol that involves four cards distributed between two parties, and is based on the assumption that all four values are accepted. The protocol asks both parties to indicate how close their opinions are on a four-point scale ($0 =$ not at all disagree, $1 =$ somewhat disagree, $2 =$ somewhat agree, and $3 =$ strongly agree), which is commonly used in surveys. The protocol consists of three patterns: complete agreement, approximate agreement (cases with inputs $\{0,1\}$ or $\{2,3\}$), and disagreement. The results are only known to the parties, and the inputs are kept secret from the third party. It should be noted that our Likert scale excludes the neutral response "undecided". Furthermore, the case of our proposal has the algebraic structure as one of the association schemes with 4 points.

Keywords: Card-based protocols · Non-committed protocols · Five card trick · Top-to-Bottom swapping · Likert scale

1 Backgrounds and Contributions

A computation in which only the output is obtained while keeping the input values secret is called multi-party computation, and applications based on this technique have recently come into use in practice. There are card-based protocols that realize confidential computation using physical cards such as Trump cards, the most common of which are two-color cards, which use cards with only two different suits written on them. The basic elements of the two-party protocol, such as AND and XOR operations, have been proposed, and more advanced computations are possible through the building up of the basic protocols.

J. Zhou et al. (Eds.): ACNS 2023 Workshops, LNCS 13907, pp. 716–721, 2023.
https://doi.org/10.1007/978-3-031-41181-6_46

This paper focuses on non-committed card-based protocols that involve using two cards of two different types with backside indistinguishability. In committed card-based protocols, the output follows a format based on the encoding rules of the input (for example, a one-bit input by the user is the following general encoding rules: $\boxed{\clubsuit}\boxed{\heartsuit} = 0$, $\boxed{\heartsuit}\boxed{\clubsuit} = 1$). On the other hand, in non-committed protocols, the results are obtained by disclosing all the cards used at the time of the protocol outage.

One limitation of this paper is that it only considers using cards with precisely the same pattern on both the front and back sides (e.g., business cards or Mahjong tiles), instead of cards with suits as typically used in card protocols. In this case, $\boxed{\downarrow}$ can be equated with $\boxed{\clubsuit}$ and $\boxed{\uparrow}$ with $\boxed{\heartsuit}$. Using the same pattern cards increases the number of variations that can be entered from the cards distributed to each player.

For example, in the Five-Card Trick and the extended Five-Card Trick with three-valued input, two cards are distributed to each player. While this provides a great advantage, it has been pointed out that input that deviates from the encoding rules is possible, and additional measures are needed to control such inputs, such as limiting them to three variations from the four candidates.

1.1 Contributions of This Paper

The authors focused on the feasibility of the proposals in card-based protocols, and although using two-color cards has been the main research approach, we focused on the up-down cards (a set of cards that allows two types of input: $\boxed{\uparrow}$ or $\boxed{\downarrow}$) as a realistic solution, as it is a bundle of cards that can be obtained at any time. The methods using up-down cards have not been sufficiently studied, and there is room for further research on their feasibility and whether protocols can be constructed in practical and simpler ways. This paper has the following advantages:

- Indicating that the use of up-down cards is a realistic solution.
- Achieving 4-valued input protocols instead of 2-valued input (using 2 color cards).
- Providing an application that has never been done before, our protocol is designed to allow users to input values on a Likert scale and output only the proximity of their opinions.

2 Previous Non-committed Card Protocols

The output of the protocol is committed, meaning that the result obtained when the protocol stops is in a format based on the encoding rules of the input. On the other hand, non-committed protocols obtain results by disclosing all the cards that were used when the protocol was finished.

2.1   Original Five-Card Trick with 2-Color Cards

The Five-Card Trick is a two-user non-committed protocol that uses two types of cards: hearts and clubs. The protocol involves an AND operation between two users.

When the two inputs are a and b, where $a, b \in 0, 1$:

$$\boxed{?}\boxed{?}(= \overline{a})\;\boxed{\heartsuit}\qquad\boxed{?}\boxed{?}(= b).$$

The five cards are arranged in a row with the center card facing down, and then cut randomly using circular substitution. The circular substitution selects one of the following five operations with equal probability: the identity operation (id), or the five operations c_5, c_5^2, c_5^3, c_5^4 (where the circular substitution is c_5) that permute the cards in the bundle. Here, $\boxed{?}$ denotes the backside-up position.

Before the random cut, the center card $\boxed{\heartsuit}$ should be turned over to the backside-up position, and all five cards are shuffled face-down. The initial state of the five cards is shown in Table 1. Since the cards are shuffled using cyclic substitution, $a \wedge b = 1$ only when three $\boxed{\heartsuit}$ cards appear in a row out of five cards. In addition, all three cases where $a \wedge b = 0$ are considered identical, so the input values of a and b cannot be determined from the output alone, this feature is a crucial aspect of the protocol.

Table 1. Initial input state of the Five-Card Trick

(a,b)	sequence				
(0,0)	♡	♣	♡	♣	♡
(0,1)	♡	♣	♡	♡	♣
(1,0)	♣	♡	♡	♣	♡
(1,1)	♣	♡	♡	♡	♣

2.2   Three Card Trick with Same Pattern Cards

For example, if the encoding rule is $\boxed{\downarrow} = 0$ and $\boxed{\uparrow} = 1$, Table 2 is initially obtained when the user inputs the same as the Five-Card trick, i.e., the extra card in the middle is $\boxed{\uparrow}$ and each user inputs one backside card a and b from each side [2]. Let us call this the Three-Card Trick.

Table 2. Initial states of the Three-Card Trick

(a, b)	sequence
(0,0)	↓ ↑ ↓
(0,1)	↓ ↑ ↑
(1,0)	↑ ↑ ↓
(1,1)	↑ ↑ ↑

As in the Five Card Trick, three cards are randomly cut to disturb the input, but only when $a \wedge b = 1$ are three cards lined up in a row, including the extra card, at the output. On the other hand, in the Five Card Trick, the three cases where $a \wedge b = 0$ are all identical, but as shown in Table 2, they are not identical because the number of cards that become ↑ is different, and the input a, b cannot be kept secret.

Therefore, the following technique is used. The idea is similar to the method used to implement the random bisection cut [3] in an intuitive way, and it involves randomly swapping the upper and lower cards (this operation is called up-and-down shuffling [4]). One possible method is to use an extra card to hide the face of the first of the three cards in the random-cut card stack, and then remove the extra card after switching the top-bottom relationship by tossing it or by other means. In any case, shuffling up and down means that ↓ and ↑ are swapped, and the initial input state changes as follows in the Three Card Trick.

Table 3. Initial position after Top-to-Bottom swapping on the Three-Card Trick

(a, b)	sequence
(0,0)	↑ ↓ ↑
(0,1)	↑ ↓ ↓
(1,0)	↓ ↓ ↑
(1,1)	↓ ↓ ↓

The Three Card Trick also shows that it is an optimal AND operation protocol for the number of input cards.

When comparing the states in Table 2 and Table 3, it is observed that after both of the random cut and top-bottom shuffle, there can be 0, 1, 2, or 3 cards that are ↑, and when $a \wedge b = 1$, there are either 0 or 3 cards that are ↑.

Moreover, when $a \wedge b = 0$, the output can be obtained with 1 or 2 $\boxed{\uparrow}$ card(s), while the inputs a, b remain confidential.

Therefore, all six possible patterns, namely $\boxed{\downarrow\,\downarrow\,\uparrow}$, $\boxed{\downarrow\,\uparrow\,\downarrow}$, $\boxed{\uparrow\,\downarrow\,\downarrow}$, $\boxed{\downarrow\,\uparrow\,\uparrow}$, $\boxed{\uparrow\,\downarrow\,\uparrow}$, and $\boxed{\uparrow\,\uparrow\,\downarrow}$ are considered identical, indicating that the protocol is secure with respect to input confidentiality.

3   A Proposal Method

Two users each input a and b using two up-down cards. The encoding rules are shown in Table 4. The following is a discussion of the "Type" (maximum number of consecutive cards facing the same direction) when the initial state about a concatenation of input a and b.

If Type-1 and Type-4 are identical, then the following 3-pattern classification on a 4-step Likert scale is consistent with the 4-step Likert classification scheme that we are designing here. Additionally, if we consider the adjacency matrix of a 4×4 matrix, it is consistent with the association scheme with rank 4 presented in Table 5.

In order to identify Type-1 and Type-4, the following operations are performed: The first and third cards are each divided into two parts, and the second and fourth cards are each divided into two parts, and then each part is shuffled up and down. This operation is similar to the random bisection cut, but note that each card is shuffled up and down instead of being shuffled into a bundle.

Table 4. Initial state about a concatenation of input a and b

$a\backslash b$	$\boxed{\uparrow\,\downarrow}$	$\boxed{\downarrow\,\uparrow}$	$\boxed{\uparrow\,\uparrow}$	$\boxed{\downarrow\,\downarrow}$
strongly disagree(0) $\boxed{\uparrow\,\downarrow}$	Type-1	Type-2	Type-3	Type-3
somewhat disagree(1) $\boxed{\downarrow\,\uparrow}$	Type-2	Type-1	Type-3	Type-3
somewhat agree(2) $\boxed{\uparrow\,\uparrow}$	Type-3	Type-3	Type-4	Type-2
strongly agree(3) $\boxed{\downarrow\,\downarrow}$	Type-3	Type-3	Type-2	Type-4

Table 5. An adjacency matrix of Table 4

$a\backslash b$	0	1	2	3
strongly disagree(0)	[0]	[1]	[2]	[2]
somewhat disagree(1)	[1]	[0]	[2]	[2]
somewhat agree(2)	[2]	[2]	[0]	[1]
strongly agree(3)	[2]	[2]	[1]	[0]

The shuffled cards can be classified into the following two types τ_0 or τ_1 (Table 6).

Table 6. State of a deck of the two-card after Top-to-Bottom swapping

	Identical deck
τ_0	↑ ↑ , ↓ ↓
τ_1	↑ ↓ , ↓ ↑

If τ_0 is found for both card bundles, then it indicates that the first and third cards and the second and fourth cards are Type-1 or Type-4, respectively, as shown in the following table. Similarly, if the two-card bundle is split into τ_0 and τ_1, then only Type-2 is possible, and only Type-3 is possible if both two-card bundles are τ_1.

References

1. Boer, B.: More efficient match-making and satisfiability the five card trick. In: Quisquater, J.-J., Vandewalle, J. (eds.) EUROCRYPT 1989. LNCS, vol. 434, pp. 208–217. Springer, Heidelberg (1990). https://doi.org/10.1007/3-540-46885-4_23
2. Marcedone, A., Wen, Z., Shi, E.: Secure Dating with Four or Fewer Cards, Cryptology ePrint Archive, Paper 2015/1031
3. Ueda, I., Miyahara, D., Nishimura, A., Hayashi, Y., Mizuki, T., Sone, H.: Secure implementations of a random bisection cut. Int. J. Inf. Secur. **19**(4), 445–452. Springer (2020)
4. Shinagawa, K.: Card-based cryptography with dihedral symmetry. N. Gener. Comput. **39**, 41–71 (2021)
5. Suga, Y.: How to implement non-committed card protocols to realize AND operations satisfying the three-valued logics. In: 2022 Tenth International Symposium on Computing and Networking Workshops (CANDARW) (2022)

POSTER: Collaborative Authority-Based Searchable Encryption Using Access Control Encryption

Dequan Xu[1], Changgen Peng[1(✉)], Youliang Tian[1], Hai Liu[1], Ziyue Wang[2],
and Weizheng Wang[3]

[1] Key Laboratory of Public Big Data, College of Computer Science and Technology,
Guizhou University, Guiyang 550025, China
{gs.dqxu20,cgpeng,yltian,hailiu}@gzu.edu.cn
[2] Graduate School of Natural Science and Technology, Kanazawa University,
Kanazawa 920-1192, Japan
icnlwzy19960122@stu.kanazawa-u.ac.jp
[3] Department of Computer Science, City University of Hong Kong,
Hong Kong SAR, China
weizheng.wang@ieee.org

Abstract. In this poster, we propose a novel searchable encryption (SE) scheme that leverages access control encryption to enhance the security and flexibility of search operations. Our approach requires collaborative authority users to authorize data users for SE requests, ensuring that only authorized users can access the encrypted data. The proposed scheme utilizes keyword and collaborative authority user IDs as attributes in the access control encryption, allowing for the design of different search permissions tailored to specific use cases. We conduct a thorough correctness analysis to demonstrate the robustness of our approach.

Keywords: Searchable encryption · Access control encryption · Collaborative authority · Data privacy

1 Introduction

Searchable encryption (SE) is a cryptographic technique that allows secure searches over encrypted data stored on remote servers [3]. In some applications, it is crucial to have collaborative authority users to authorize data users in SE.

Existing SE schemes [1,2,4,5] do not adequately address this requirement. Therefore, we propose a new type of SE that incorporates access control encryption. Our scheme uses keywords and collaborative authority user IDs as attributes in the access control encryption to design various search permissions. Our proposed scheme consists of several algorithms: Setup, CKeyGen, UKeyGen, Encrypt, CTrapdoor, UTrapdoor, and Search. The Setup algorithm initializes the system, choosing two multiplicative cyclic groups and defining a bilinear

J. Zhou et al. (Eds.): ACNS 2023 Workshops, LNCS 13907, pp. 722–726, 2023.
https://doi.org/10.1007/978-3-031-41181-6_47

map. The CKeyGen and UKeyGen algorithms generate secret keys for the collaborative authority user and data user, respectively. Encrypt is responsible for creating an encrypted index using the public parameter, access policy, and keywords associated with the encrypted data. CTrapdoor and UTrapdoor generate the collaborative search trapdoor and user trapdoor, respectively. Finally, the Search algorithm tests whether the data user's attribute set and the collaborative authority user's identifying information meet the access policy, returning search results or an empty result accordingly.

In conclusion, we present a novel searchable encryption scheme that enables collaborative authority users to authorize data users by employing access control encryption. By leveraging keyword and collaborative authority user ID attributes, our scheme offers a flexible and secure solution to address the need for collaborative authorization in searchable encryption applications.

2   Problem Statement

2.1   System Model

The system model comprises four entities: Trust Authority (TA), Data Owners (DO), Data Users (DU), Collaborative Users (CU), and Cloud Server (CS). This scheme can be used in various settings (e.g., health, finance, and government), so we present a general model to illustrate this system.

TA is responsible for generating the public parameters of the system and the secret keys for CUs and DUs. Then, TA distributes the secret keys to the relevant participates in a secure channel and publishes public parameters. **DO** encrypts the plaintext and generates the encrypted indexes with a self-defined access policy associated with the DU and CU. Then, DO uploads the ciphertext and indexes to the cloud server for sharing. **DU** generates a trapdoor using the keywords of it interested. **CU** generates the collaboration trapdoor. **CS** is responsible for storing and retrieving the encrypted data. It stores the encrypted data and encrypted indexes from DO. Upon receiving the query trapdoor and attribute set from the DU, CS executes the match protocol on behalf of the authorized user to output the data of the user interested. In the process, if the attributes of DU and CU satisfy the access policy of the indexes, the corresponding encrypted data can be retrieved.

2.2   The Detailed Construction

Setup(1^λ): Given the security parameter λ, TA chooses $\mathbb{G}_1$ and $\mathbb{G}_2$ as two multiplicative cyclic groups. The order of both $\mathbb{G}_1$ and $\mathbb{G}_2$ are the prime p, and the bilinear map $e : \mathbb{G}_1 \times \mathbb{G}_1 \rightarrow \mathbb{G}_2$ holds. At the same time, TA selects hash function $H_1 : \{0,1\}^\star \rightarrow \mathbb{G}_1$ as a random oracle and $H_2 : \{0,1\}^\star \rightarrow \mathbb{Z}_p$ as a one-way hash function. Then, TA selects random elements a, b, c, $\beta \in_R \mathbb{Z}_p$ as the system master secret key $MSK = (a, b, c, \beta)$ and an element $g \in_R \mathbb{G}_1$ as the generator and outputs the public parameter as

$$PK = (e, \mathbb{G}_1, \mathbb{G}_2, p, H_1, H_2, g, g^a, g^b, g^c, g^\beta, g^{1/b}). \tag{1}$$

CKeyGen(MSK, ID_{CU}): Given the master secret key MSK of the system and the identity information ID_{CU} of the CU, TA selects the permitted keyword $\hat{w}_i \in \hat{W}$ for the collaborative authority user and a random element $r_{ID} \in_R \mathbb{Z}_p$ and computes the secret key of CU as

$$SK_{ID_{CU}} = (ID_{CU}, C = g^{\frac{(ac-\beta)}{b}}, C_{ID} = g^\beta H_1(ID_{CU})^{r_{ID}}, C'_{ID} = g^{r_{ID}}, \hat{w}_i). \quad (2)$$

UKeyGen(MSK, S): Given the master secret key MSK of the system and an attribute set S of DU, TA picks the random element $r_j \in_R \mathbb{Z}_p$ for each attribute $j \in S$ and computes the secret key of DU as

$$USK_S = (S, D = g^{\frac{(ac-\beta)}{b}}, \{D_j = g^\beta H_1(j)^{r_j}, D'_j = g^{r_j}\}_{j \in S}). \quad (3)$$

The secret key is sent to the relevant entity securely.

Encrypt$(PK, \mathcal{T}, W_i)$: Given the public parameter PK, the access policy $\mathcal{T}$, and a set $W_i = \{w_1, \ldots, w_n\} \bigcup \hat{w}'_i$ of keywords associated with the encrypted data, DO chooses a polynomial q_x for each node x in the $\mathcal{T}$ from root to leaf and assigns its degree as d_x. For the root node R of $\mathcal{T}$, DO selects the random element $r_{i,1} \in_R \mathbb{Z}_p$ and sets $q_R(0) = r_{i,1}$, where $r_{i,1}$ is shared by each leaf node of $\mathcal{T}$. Then, DO randomly assigns d_R to define node R completely. For any other node x of $\mathcal{T}$, DO selects the polynomial $q_x(0) = q_{parent(x)}(index(x))$ and randomly assigns d_x to define node x completely. Let $Y = Y' \bigcup Y_{ID_{CU}}$ represent all the leaf nodes in the $\mathcal{T}$, and $y = y' \bigcup y_{ID_{CU}}$ represent each leaf node of the $\mathcal{T}$. Then, DO selects $r_{i,2} \in_R \mathbb{Z}_p$ for each keyword $w_i \in W_i$ and the permitted keyword $\hat{w}'_i \in W_i$ and calculates the index ciphertext $CT_{\mathcal{T},W_i} = (\mathcal{T}, C', \{C_{y'}, C'_{y'}\}_{y \in Y}, C_{y_{ID_{CU}}}, C'_{y_{ID_{CU}}}, \{C_{w_i}, C'_{w_i}\}_{w_i \in W_i}, C'_{\hat{w}'_i})$ as

$$C' = g^{br_{i,1}};$$
$$\forall y' \in Y' : C_{y'} = g^{q_{y'}(0)}, C'_{y'} = H_1(Atts(y'))^{q_{y'}(0)};$$
$$C_{y_{ID_{CU}}} = g^{q_{y_{ID_{CU}}}(0)}, C'_{y_{ID_{CU}}} = H_1(Atts(y_{ID_{CU}}))^{q_{y_{ID_{CU}}}(0)};$$
$$\forall w_i \in W_i : C_{w_i} = g^{cr_{i,2}}, C'_{w_i} = g^{a(r_{i,1}+r_{i,2})} g^{bH_2(w_i)r_{i,2}};$$
$$C'_{\hat{w}'_i} = g^{a(r_{i,1}+r_{i,2})} g^{bH_2(\hat{w}'_i)r_{i,2}}. \quad (4)$$

DO sends the encrypted index $CT_{\mathcal{T},W_i}$ to the CS.

CTrapdoor$(PK, SK_{ID_{CU}})$: Given the public parameter PK and secret key $SK_{ID_{CU}}$, CU picks $q_1 \in_R \mathbb{Z}_p$ and generates the collaborative search trapdoor as

$$ctk_{\hat{w}_i} = (ctok_1 = (g^a g^{bH_2(\hat{w}_i)})^{q_1}, ctok_2 = g^{cq_1}, ctok_3 = C^{q_1} = g^{(acq_1 - \beta q_1)/b},$$
$$ctok_4 = C_{ID}^{q_1} = g^{\beta q_1} H_1(ID_{CU})^{r_{ID}q_1}, ctok_5 = C'^{q_1}_{ID} = g^{r_{ID}q_1}, q_1). \quad (5)$$

CU sends the collaborative search trapdoor $ctk_{\hat{w}_i}$ to the DU.

UTrapdoor(PK, USK_S, W'_i): Given the public parameter PK, the secret key USK_S of the DU, and the keyword set W'_i of DU interested, DU selects a polynomial $\hat{q}_{\hat{x}}$ for each query keyword $w'_i \in W'_i$ as the leaf node $\hat{x}$ to construct a query access structure $\mathcal{T}'$ similar to the way in the Encrypt process. Let $\hat{Y}$ represent all the leaf nodes in the $\mathcal{T}'$. DU assigns $\hat{q}_{\hat{R}}(0) = q_1$ as the root node of the $\mathcal{T}'$ and continue to computes the query trapdoor as

$$utkw_i' = (\forall j \in S : \{utok_3 = D_j^{q_1} = g^{\beta q_1} H_1(j)^{r_j q_1}, utok_4 = D_j'^{q_1} = g^{r_j q_1}\};$$

$$\forall w_i' \in W_i' : \{utok_1 = (g^a g^{bH_2(w_i')})^{\hat{q}_{\hat{x}}(0)}, utok_2 = g^{c \cdot \hat{q}_{\hat{x}}(0)}\};$$

$$utok_5 = D^{q_1} = g^{(ac-\beta)q_1/b}. \tag{6}$$

DU sends the trapdoor $TK_q = (ctk_{\hat{w}_i}, utkw_i')$ to the CS.

Search$(CT_{\mathcal{T},W_i}, TK_q)$: Given the encrypted index $CT_{\mathcal{T},W_i}$ from DO and the trapdoor TK_q from the DU, CS first tests whether the DU's attribute set S and the CU's identifying information meet the access policy $\mathcal{T}$. If meeting, CS continues to run the search algorithms and responds to the search result to the DU; otherwise, the CS will return $\perp$.

Step 1: if node $y_{ID_{CU}}$ is a leaf node of the access policy $\mathcal{T}$ in the encrypted index and there is $ID_{CU} = Atts(y_{ID_{CU}})$, then CS computes

$$E_{y_{ID_{CU}}} = \frac{e(ctok_4, C_{y_{ID_{CU}}})}{e(ctok_3, C'_{y_{ID_{CU}}})} = e(g,g)^{\beta q_1 q_{y_{ID_{CU}}}(0)}. \tag{7}$$

If node y' is a leaf node of the access policy $\mathcal{T}$ in the encrypted index and there is $j = Atts(y')$, for each attribute $\forall j \in S$, CS computes

$$E_{y'} = \frac{e(utok_3, C'_y)}{e(utok_4, C'_{y'}))} = e(g,g)^{\beta q_1 q_{y'}(0)}. \tag{8}$$

Note that Eq. (7) and Eq. (8) get the same results (i.e., $E_y = E_{y_{ID_{CU}}} = e(g,g)^{\beta q_1 q_{y_{ID_{CU}}}(0)} = E_{y'} = e(g,g)^{\beta q_1 q_{y'}(0)} = e(g,g)^{\beta q_1 q_y(0)}$) when considering the identifying information of the CU as an attribute of the DU. Thus, to simplify, we consider the CU as an attribute of the DU. When the $H_1(ID_{CU}) \neq H_1(Atts(y_{ID_{CU}}))$ or attribute $j \notin S$, set $E_y = \perp$.

Let node y be a non-leaf node in the $\mathcal{T}$. Considering the recursive compute case, suppose x be all children nodes of y, and k_y be a threshold k_y-sized set of x, there is each children node x of y such that $E_x \neq \perp$. Then, CS computes

$$E_y = \prod_{x \in k_y} E_x^{\Delta_{i,k_y'}(0)}, (i = index(x), k_y' = \{index(x) : x \in k_y\})$$

$$= \prod_{x \in k_y} (e(g,g)^{\beta q_1 q_x(0)})^{\Delta_{i,k_y'}(0)}$$

$$= \prod_{x \in k_y} (e(g,g)^{\beta q_1 q_{parent(x)}(index(x))})^{\Delta_{i,k_y'}(0)}$$

$$= \prod_{x \in k_y} e(g,g)^{\beta q_1 q_y(i) \cdot \Delta_{i,k_y'}(0)}$$

$$= e(g,g)^{\beta q_1 q_y(0)}. \tag{9}$$

Then, the value E_R is computed by CS in a bottom-up fashion as

$$E_R = e(g,g)^{\beta q_1 q_R(0)} = e(g,g)^{\beta q_1 r_{i,1}}. \tag{10}$$

Step 2: the secret value $E_{\hat{R}}$ can be used to check whether the query keywords W_i' and the permitted keyword $\hat{w}_i$ of TK_q are matched with the CT_{T,W_i}. Let node $\hat{x}$ be a leaf node in the query access structure T'. For the $\hat{w}_i$, CS computes

$$E_{\hat{w}_i} = \frac{e(C'_{\hat{w}_i'}, ctok_2)}{e(C_{w_i}, ctok_1)} = e(g,g)^{acr_{i,1}q_1}. \tag{11}$$

For each keyword $w_i' \in W_i'$, CS computes

$$E_{w_i'} = \frac{e(C'_{w_i}, utok_2)}{e(C_{w_i}, utok_1)} = e(g,g)^{acr_{i,1}\hat{q}_{\hat{x}}(0)}. \tag{12}$$

Let node $\hat{x}$ be a non-leaf node in the T'. Considering the recursive compute case, suppose x be all children nodes of $\hat{x}$, and $k_{\hat{x}}$ be a threshold $k_{\hat{x}}$−sized set of x, there is each children node x of $\hat{x}$ such that $E_x \neq \bot$. Then, CS gets

$$E_{\hat{x}} = e(g,g)^{acr_{i,1}\hat{q}_{\hat{x}}(0)}. \tag{13}$$

Then, the value $E_{\hat{R}}$ is computed by CS in a bottom-up fashion as

$$E_{\hat{R}} = e(g,g)^{acr_{i,1}q_1}. \tag{14}$$

At last, CS checks whether Eq. (15) holds.

$$E_{\hat{w}_i} = E_{\hat{R}} = e(utok_5, C') \cdot E_R. \tag{15}$$

If not, output "No"; otherwise, output "Yes" and respond to the matching results to DU.

Acknowledgement. This work was supported by the National Natural Science Foundation of China under Grants 62272124.

References

1. Chaudhari, P., Das, M.L.: Privacy preserving searchable encryption with fine-grained access control. IEEE Trans. Cloud Comput. **9**(2), 753–762 (2019)
2. Chaudhari, P., Das, M.L.: KeySea: keyword-based search with receiver anonymity in attribute-based searchable encryption. IEEE Trans. Serv. Comput. **15**(2), 1036–1044 (2020)
3. Hahn, F., Kerschbaum, F.: Searchable encryption with secure and efficient updates. In: Proceedings of the 2014 ACM SIGSAC Conference on Computer and Communications Security, pp. 310–320 (2014)
4. Michalas, A.: The lord of the shares: combining attribute-based encryption and searchable encryption for flexible data sharing. In: Proceedings of the 34th ACM/SIGAPP Symposium on Applied Computing, pp. 146–155 (2019)
5. Yu, Y., Shi, J., Li, H., Li, Y., Du, X., Guizani, M.: Key-policy attribute-based encryption with keyword search in virtualized environments. IEEE J. Sel. Areas Commun. **38**(6), 1242–1251 (2020)

Author Index

Printed in the United States
by Baker & Taylor Publisher

Printed in the United States
by Baker & Taylor Publisher Services